ALSO BY DAVID HACKETT FISCHER

Fairness and Freedom

Champlain's Dream

Liberty and Freedom

Washington's Crossing

Bound Away

The Great Wave

Paul Revere's Ride

Albion's Seed

Growing Old in America

Historians' Fallacies

The Revolution of American Conservatism

AFRICAN FOUNDERS

How Enslaved People Expanded American Ideals

David Hackett Fischer

Simon & Schuster

NEW YORK LONDON TORONTO SYDNEY NEW DELHI

Simon & Schuster
1230 Avenue of the Americas
New York, NY 10020

Copyright © 2022 by David Hackett Fischer

All rights reserved, including the right to reproduce this book or portions thereof in any form whatsoever. For information, address Simon & Schuster Subsidiary Rights Department, 1230 Avenue of the Americas, New York, NY 10020.

First Simon & Schuster hardcover edition May 2022

SIMON & SCHUSTER and colophon are registered trademarks of Simon & Schuster, Inc.

For information about special discounts for bulk purchases, please contact Simon & Schuster Special Sales at 1-866-506-1949 or business@simonandschuster.com.

The Simon & Schuster Speakers Bureau can bring authors to your live event. For more information or to book an event, contact the Simon & Schuster Speakers Bureau at 1-866-248-3049 or visit our website at www.simonspeakers.com.

Interior design by Paul Dippolito

Manufactured in the United States of America

10 9 8 7 6 5 4 3 2 1

Library of Congress Cataloging-in-Publication Data is available.

ISBN 978-1-9821-4509-5
ISBN 978-1-9821-4511-8 (ebook)

For Suzy, Annie, and Judy, with love

CONTENTS

TABLES

Credit information for the tables can be found on pages 901–905.

AFRICAN FOUNDERS

INTRODUCTION

Slavery time was tough, it like looking back into de dark, like looking into de night.

—Amy Chavis Perry, former slave in Charleston, S.C.[1]

The slave is in chains—but how is one to eradicate his love of liberty? . . . How is one to blot out his intelligence, which he might possibly use to break his bonds?

—Gustave de Beaumont, 1835[2]

O N MAY 11, 1831, two lively young aristocrats strolled down the gangway of the steamship *President* into the swirling chaos of lower Manhattan. Officially, Alexis de Tocqueville and Gustave de Beaumont had come to study American prison systems. Unofficially, another purpose was to keep out of a French prison themselves, after the Revolution of 1830.

For nine months, these French visitors made an intellectual tour of the American republic. Doors flew open to them everywhere. They visited most regions in the country, talked with many people, and wrote very different books on what they learned in the New World. Tocqueville published his great and hopeful treatise on democracy in America, and its future in Europe. Beaumont brought out a tragic novel on the persistence of slavery in the United States, the progress of racism in America, and its growth in the modern world.[3]

Both men were amazed by the contradictions they observed in the same society, and even in the same scenes. In the United States, they found that the rule of law coexisted with savage violence. They discovered throughout America a broad equality of manners and deep inequality of wealth. Most of all, they were astonished by the coexistence of freedom with slavery, and equality with racism. "Surely it is a strange fact," Beaumont wrote, "that there is so much bondage amid so much liberty."[4]

That paradox has long been near the center of American history, and it has been studied in different ways. From the early nineteenth to the mid-twentieth century, six generations of American scholars were mostly Whig historians of their nation. Their work tended to center on ideas of liberty and freedom, equal rights and republican self-government. Major themes were the triumph of those ideas and institutions over tyranny and slavery.

In the United States, these Whig historians celebrated the prohibition of the foreign slave trade by Congress, which took effect on January 1, 1808, the first day when it could be forbidden under the federal Constitution. They praised Abraham Lincoln's Emancipation Proclamation on September 22, 1862, five days after the Union victory at Antietam.

Whig historians also honored the abolition of slavery by the Thirteenth Amendment in 1865. They acclaimed the prohibition of racial injustice by the Fourteenth Amendment in 1868, which made citizens of all persons born or naturalized in the United States and entitled them to "equal protection of the laws" with no distinctions of race. And they praised the Fifteenth Amendment in 1869–70, which prohibited the denial or abridgment of the right to vote in the United States "on account of race, color, or previous condition of servitude."

Major questions for Whig historians were about sources of strength in American values and institutions, and how they might be made stronger. Failures were closely studied, and limits were fully discussed, but the prevailing mood of America's leading scholars tended to be optimistic from the nineteenth to the mid-twentieth century, with exceptions such as Henry Adams, Brooks Adams, and the later work of Charles Beard.[5]

Then, in the late twentieth and early twenty-first centuries, the purposes of American historians began to change. New generations of scholars continued to study the same subjects, but in a very different spirit. Their work tended to center less on American liberty, freedom, equality, and democracy. It gave more attention to American slavery, racism, inequality, injustice, and corruption. Major questions in academic discourse were increasingly about the roots of racial oppression, the corruption of capitalism, the decay of political institutions, the failure of reform movements, and the decline of American leadership. With many important exceptions, the tone of much American historical writing turned deeply negative during the early twenty-first century. It remained so as these words were written, in 2021.[6]

ANOTHER FRAME OF HISTORICAL THINKING: NEW USES FOR AN OLD IDEA OF HERODOTUS

This project takes yet another approach. It returns to the history of what is now the United States, but does not begin with predominantly positive or negative judgments about the main lines of American history. Instead, it starts with a different set of ethical assumptions. One is that slavery, racism, and racial oppression in many forms have long been great and persistent evils in America and the world. Another is that vibrant traditions of freedom and liberty and the rule of law have long continued to be sources of enduring strength, especially in the United States, most of all in our own time.

In that spirit, this book is an inquiry into what happened when Africans and Europeans came to North America, and the growth of race slavery collided with expansive ideas of freedom and liberty and rule of law in the European and mostly English-speaking colonies that became the United States.

The operative word is inquiry. This open-ended method has deep roots in historical scholarship, and it has been radically renewed in our time. Early practitioners were Greek historians of the oldest school on record, the school of Herodotus. He gave us a new idea of history in the fifth century before the Christian era. It appeared in the title of the book he called *The Histories of Herodotus*, which in his old Greek meant literally "The Inquiries of Herodotus." Modern editions are still in print, and widely read in many languages after 2,600 years.[7]

In the school of Herodotus, history was not primarily a story, or an argument, or a thesis, or a polemic. In actual practice it sometimes became any or all of those things. But it tended to begin in another way, as an inquiry with a genuinely open end. It started not with answers but questions, about events that actually happened.

Herodotus tells us that he searched for "true wonders" in the world. He was well aware that such a search could miscarry in two ways at once. Some of his findings were more wonderful than true. And others were more true than wonderful. But he and his followers kept at it, and they did so by a method that the Greeks were among the first to call empirical.

From its ancient Greek root, "empirical" meant a form of open inquiry, and also a pursuit of truth that seeks to derive knowledge from the evidence of experience. In our own twenty-first century, these ancient ideas of open inquiry and empirical truth have gained a new importance, in part because of hostile assaults upon them from many directions.

We find this hostility even in our schools and universities, where strident demands for "political correctness" are frequently heard from faculty, students, and administrators. In public discourse during the twenty-first century, we have seen a growing disregard for truth, and a cultivated carelessness of fact and evidence. More extreme when these words were written in the years 2020 and 2021 are deliberate falsehoods, actively concocted and widely deployed in new forms of rhetoric and communication. And this is only one trend among many others, of willful contempt for truth and even for ideals of truthfulness in our world.

But at the same time, diametrically opposite trends also have been growing in the twentieth and twenty-first centuries. Old ideas of genuinely open truth-seeking by empirical inquiry have greatly expanded in recent years, often with the progress of new digital forms of knowledge, despite counter-movements in the corruption of public media, and in the decay of public discourse.

As these words are written, some scholars are also learning to combine new digital methods of truth-seeking, with old-fashioned *Sitzfleisch* in a library chair, surrounded by stacks of books and heaps of manuscripts. In historical writing, history teaching, and many other disciplines, some of these old and new methods of open inquiry have been most effective when used together.

TOWARD AN EMPIRICAL HISTORY OF AFRICANS IN EARLY AMERICA: THE RAPID GROWTH OF HISTORICAL DATABASES IN RECENT YEARS

In historical scholarship during the early twenty-first century, some of these new methods and tools of truth-seeking have been put to work on a large scale in the history of slavery and race in America. Among the most important and useful of these tools are the careful construction of empirical databases. Increasingly, this work has been done by teams of scholars, who combine traditional sources with digital methods on a new scale.

For the history of African slavery in America, the leading example is the Trans-Atlantic Slave Trade Database, a major project of quantitative research, with free and open digital access to all who wish to use it. Its leaders are David Eltis and David Richardson. They organized and led international teams of scholars who worked together on this project for many years. By 2008, they gathered data on nearly 35,000 transatlantic slave voyages from 1501 to 1867. For each voyage they sought to establish dates, owners, vessels, captains, African visits, American destinations, numbers of slaves embarked, and numbers landed. They have been able to find much of this material for an estimated 80 percent of the entire transatlantic African slave trade.[8]

This online database continues to receive additions and corrections, but its creators believe that these changes are "never likely to be major." So far that has proven to be the case. The database is now widely used around the world. It has been very helpful in this inquiry, and many others.

With corrections for missing voyages, Eltis and Richardson have estimated the entire size of the transatlantic slave trade with more comprehension, precision, and accuracy than before. They reckon that in 366 years, slaving vessels embarked about 12.5 million captives in Africa, and landed 10.7 million in the New World. A horrific discovery is a careful estimate that the Middle Passage took a toll on more than 1.8 million African lives. In this quantitative database, the numbers are people. The global scale of human suffering has become in some ways more easy to measure, but more difficult to comprehend.[9]

Many answers have flowed from this database, and some have become questions in their turn. For example, its data show that of approximately 10.7 million Africans who survived the Middle Passage in the Atlantic slave trade, about 4.8 million went to South America, 4.7 million to the Caribbean islands, 800,000 to Central America, and only about 400,000 to North America within the present boundaries of the United States. These differences of scale pose large questions about the diversity of slavery in different parts of the New World, and its variations in space and time.[10]

The success of this database has inspired other empirical projects on slavery. American historian Gregory O'Malley created another Intra-American Slave Trade Database, for voyages between American colonies, mostly from the British West Indies to other American destinations from 1619 to 1807. O'Malley found data for more than 7,600 intercolonial American voyages, which had been excluded by definition from the transatlantic database. They carried about 300,000 slaves, of which approximately 200,000 went from the British West Indies to ports outside the British empire. Another 70,000 went to mainland British colonies, and 30,000 to other British possessions.[11]

O'Malley's findings have changed our understanding of early American slavery in an important way. Some American historians have long believed that many or even most slaves who came to the mainland colonies in North America had been "seasoned" in the Caribbean, or born and raised there, or were "Atlantic Creoles" who had been raised there and in other Atlantic places. There was some truth in these beliefs, during early years of the slave trade to North America. But overall, O'Malley found them to be very much mistaken. In his database of slaves shipped from the West Indies to North America, 92 percent were "new negroes" from Africa, who were quickly trans-shipped through West Indian ports to mainland colonies. Only about 8 percent were "seasoned" or "Creole" West Indian slaves.[12]

Similar findings have emerged from yet another set of three important databases, constructed by Gwendolyn Hall. Two of these databases include records of individual slaves and free people of color in Louisiana. This material shows that few "Creole" or "seasoned" slaves came to Louisiana from the West Indies, again with some important exceptions such as the large West Indian migration to Louisiana in 1809.[13]

Gwendolyn Hall also constructed a third database, smaller but more detailed, for slaves in Louisiana's Pointe Coupée Parish. Some of them arrived by way of West Indian and mainland North American ports, but her sources made clear that "almost all slaves brought in by traders from St. Domingue, Jamaica, the United States, and Cuba came directly from Africa."[14]

Yet another set of databases has been constructed for slavery and the slave trade to Virginia and Maryland. A recent leader is Lorena Walsh, building on earlier work by colleagues called the Chesapeake Group, including Allan Kulikoff, Lois Green Carr, Russell Menard, and many others. Major comparative studies of high importance also have been done by Philip Morgan and other scholars, who identified places of origin for Virginia and Maryland slaves, and compared them with other regions.[15]

By careful and comprehensive quantitative research, Lorena Walsh found that the great majority of slaves arriving by sea in the Chesapeake colonies had been born and raised in Africa. Here again, she also observed that only a small minority came from the West Indies, and they were mostly African-born slaves who had been transshipped to the mainland.

Lorena Walsh and Douglas Chambers also found evidence that within this large flow, smaller clusters of African slaves shared origins and cultures, and bonded together in the Chesapeake. Gwendolyn Hall had earlier made similar findings of African clusters in databases for Africans in Louisiana. William Piersen also found different sorts of more diverse African clusters in New England. In the works of many other scholars and also in our own inquiries, we have found other African clusters in the Hudson Valley, the Delaware Valley, coastal Carolina, lowcountry Georgia, the western frontier, southern borderlands, and maritime regions.[16]

Taken together, these various databases tell us that about 458,000 slaves came by sea to mainland British North American colonies, mainly from African and West Indian ports. Of that total, more than 95 percent had been born in Africa.[17]

Also important for the history of African slave trade to North America were earlier data sets of a different kind, which consist mainly of documentary collections published in book form. Most comprehensive is still Elizabeth Donnan's *Documents Illustrative of the History of the Slave Trade to America*, published from 1930 to 1935 in four thick quarto volumes. They are still very useful, and have been put to work in this inquiry.[18]

Other small and more specialized data sets have also been compiled and published by scholars. An inventive example is a creative compilation by Linda Heywood and John Thornton of "names borne by the earliest African inhabitants of English and Dutch colonies in the Americas," 1616 to 1674. Names sometimes help to identify ethnic, regional, and religious origins of Africans in North America. This is merely one of many studies by Thornton and Heywood, centering on the history of West Central Africa with much attention to American linkages.[19]

Yet another recent compilation of major importance is a massive project by Paul Heinegg, a genealogist who has gathered and published records for the ancestry of many thousands of free African American nuclear families, in 893 nominal lines of descent for Virginia, Maryland, Delaware, and North Carolina, from their founding to "about 1820." Most of these lineages descended from unions of male African slaves with female servants of British, Irish, and European origin who were formally free. By law in many English colonies, the condition of their children followed the status of their mother and the children became free in early America, though their fathers had been African slaves. Heinegg added detailed evidence of migration, settlement, occupation, and more. His work has transformed our knowledge of slaves and free people of African ancestry in early America.[20]

THE SCALE OF THE AFRICAN SLAVE TRADE

How many slaves were sent abroad from Africa? Historians have offered many answers to this question, which included much larger numbers than the Atlantic slave trade. A careful estimate, in the middle range of the best research, is that at least 26 million men, women, and children were carried as slaves out of tropical Africa, by land and by sea, in a period of 1,300 years from 600 AD to 1900. Some scholars reckon that the true total was as high as 30 million. This great traffic flowed in three directions: north across the great African deserts; east over the Indian Ocean and Red Sea; and west beyond the Atlantic Ocean to America.

The Atlantic slave trade, large as it was, included less than half of the entire foreign slave trade from Africa. Another 14 to 16 million slaves were taken north across the Sahara, and east to the Indian Ocean and the Red Sea. Even these estimates are thought by some scholars to understate the magnitude of the entire African slave trade. Parts of it were much older than the Atlantic slave trade. For at least five thousand years, captives were carried from tropical Africa to Mediterranean and Mesopotamian regions. This commerce was suppressed in the nineteenth and twentieth centuries, but some of it revived in the late twentieth and early twenty-first centuries.

Some of this traffic continues today, in variant forms. Judy and I witnessed it on dusty roads in the Sahel. There we saw battered open-stake trucks, packed with young African males and females, all being driven east. We were told that they were bound for distant markets, and some of them would be put to work in conditions close to slavery.

This quasi–slave traffic in our own time is not unique to Africa. It also flows from South Asia, East Asia, South America, and Eastern Europe and is truly global in its extent. Much of it goes to the Middle East, some of it to Western Europe and sweatshops in Los Angeles, New York, and other American cities. Such is the strength and scale of demand for these workers in the twenty-first century, that many governments including the United States have been unable to suppress this latter-day global slave trade in our contemporary world.[21] Some of these masters of mistreatment of contemporary people in bondage are themselves illegal immigrants who live outside the law.

THE IMPORTANCE OF GOING THERE

As empirical evidence of African origins in early America has expanded, historians in the United States have grown more interested in West and Central African cultures, societies, economies, polities, historical processes, and geographic places from whence slaves came to North America.

The American historian Francis Parkman strongly advised scholars and literati to respect three rules of historical research and writing on any given subject. His first rule was "Go There!" The second was "Do It!" And Parkman's

third rule was "Write It!" He urged the importance of free travel, careful observation, close attention to fact, a large frame of thought, and presentation
of empirical findings, in an engaging style that people might genuinely wish
to read. To those ends, Parkman insisted that "going there" was a vital component of historical research and writing.[22]

On that advice, my wife, Judy, and I agreed that an American historian
with a growing interest in Africans who came to the United States might
begin by going to Africa. On that assumption, we went there together, on a
journey of about a month, in January 1997, between our teaching terms. It
was a brief visit, by any measure. But it made a profound difference in our
thinking about Africa.

Our purpose was to begin to learn about Africa at first hand, and to visit
at least some of the many African regions and cultures from which slaves had
come to America. We had done the same thing before, when writing *Albion's
Seed*, about British regional origins of British colonists in North America. We
did it again for a book on New Zealand, and once more for a book on Samuel
Champlain and New France, when we tried to go everywhere that Champlain
went in Europe and America.

In all these projects, we found that Francis Parkman was right. Going there
always makes a difference, and it does so in many ways for the framing and execution of a historical inquiry. It also makes a major difference in the teaching
and learning of history. I can often identify students who at an impressionable
age had been taken by their families to historical places. The difference is evident in the exercise of historical imagination, and an understanding of history
as something that actually happened, and also an awareness that it is relevant
to us in another historical moment.

Our travels in Africa also had other purposes. They were shaped in part
by Judy's interests as a biologist and botanist. We organized our travel with
advice from many experts, and then set off on our own, traveling not only
to large cities, but to rural areas and small villages in Senegal, Mali, Ghana,
and Côte d'Ivoire. Other places were on our agenda, but were on the State
Department watch lists, or otherwise difficult to access.

Always, we were accompanied by young African drivers, guides, soldiers, and
translators whom we hired with the aid of American Express. They helped us
with African languages in which we had a particular interest, so that we could
talk directly with Bamana and Asante soldiers, Fulani herders, Mande farmers,
Fante boatbuilders, Wolof traders, Malian musicians, village elders, and griots
who were custodians of memory in different ways.

And we remember the support of African "Big Men" and "Mercedes Mamas." One Mercedes Mama rescued us single-handed from a sticky situation with a street gang in the Côte d'Ivoire. And we especially recall conversations with bright and lively African children, and spirited teenagers who shared the creativity of their music and speech.

We went there in the late 1990s, a time of comparative peace in many parts of West Africa. In 1997 we could travel freely through many parts of the African countryside. We were welcomed almost everywhere.

To travel in Africa is to discover again and yet again the enormous scale and unimaginable beauty of this great continent. It is also to observe its vast abundance, teeming diversity, deep dynamics, and inexhaustible creativity. Individual Africans came to America from many small parts of their continent in West and Central Africa, and yet the entire area was larger than the continental United States.

As a measure of its scale, my student, teacher, and friend Richard Rath suggests that one might take a world map and extend a line from the top of Senegal south to the bottom of Angola. Then if one turns that same line 180 degrees, and runs it north from Senegal, it reaches Norway.

As an example of Africa's abundance of life, we had an experience in northern Senegal, where we visited eighteenth-century centers of the slave trade in Dakar, and then traveled overland to the small seaport of Saint-Louis, still flourishing at the mouth of the Senegal River, on the border between Senegal and Mauritania. After we visited the coastal region, we rented a boat and explored the valley of the Senegal River, which was an important slave route to America, especially for the early Louisiana slave trade. Today a large part of the river is preserved as a national park.

The month was January when we were on the river, and the storks had returned to Africa from their rooftop nests in Europe. Unimaginable numbers of storks covered the trees for many miles along the banks of the Senegal River. It was an indelible image of indescribable beauty, and also of life's vast abundance on this great continent.

We were surprised and instructed many times by the scale of Africa, by the complexity of its history, and by the diversity of its environments, peoples, cultures, and languages. We were also struck over and over by its intricate historical connections with other parts of the world, and most of all by the haunting beauty of this vast continent.

In the course of our travels, we also learned in a new way about large numbers of African slaves who had been taken not only west across the Atlantic Ocean, but also north across the Sahel and the Sahara to the Mediterranean, and east to the Red Sea, the Indian Ocean, and the Middle East and South Asia. Scholars in Africa, Europe, and North America have made many recent attempts to estimate the magnitude of these many trading patterns, summarized in Table 1.1.

AFRICAN ORIGINS OF SLAVES IN NORTH AMERICA: DIVERSITY AND TIGHT CLUSTERS FROM EVERY REGION

In early North America, every major colonial region imported African slaves. No two regional patterns were quite alike, and each region was unique in its timing, rhythm, size, scale, and mix of African origins. But even as these American regional patterns were never the same, they tended to be similar in several ways that are fundamental to this inquiry.

First, each American region, without exception, tended to draw slaves out of most major African regions in the Atlantic slave trade, from northern Senegal to southern Angola. In our inquiries, slaves came from Senegal and Gambia, Upper Guinea, Futa Jallon, the Windward Coast, Sierra Leone, the Gold Coast and Slave Coast, the upper Niger Valley, Benin, and Biafra to nearly every coastal North American region from New England and New Netherland to the Hudson and Delaware Valleys, the Chesapeake Bay, coastal Carolina, Florida, the Gulf Coast, and Louisiana.

Other slaves from West Central Africa also came to every American region, in much the same way. They were called by different names. They tended to be collectively called Congo in French Louisiana, Angolan in South Carolina, and were known by both names in Dutch New Netherland. All of these Central African groups were present in every slave-importing American region, with heavy concentrations in the early seventeenth century, and again in the early nineteenth century, with smaller numbers in between.

Most major American slaving regions received slaves from English trading posts in Gambia. French Louisiana drew more heavily from Senegal and Mali. Many came to every North American colony from Guinea, the Gold Coast, the Bight of Benin, and the Niger Valley.

A striking example of this diversity in most American colonies were small numbers of slaves who came to British America from East Africa and

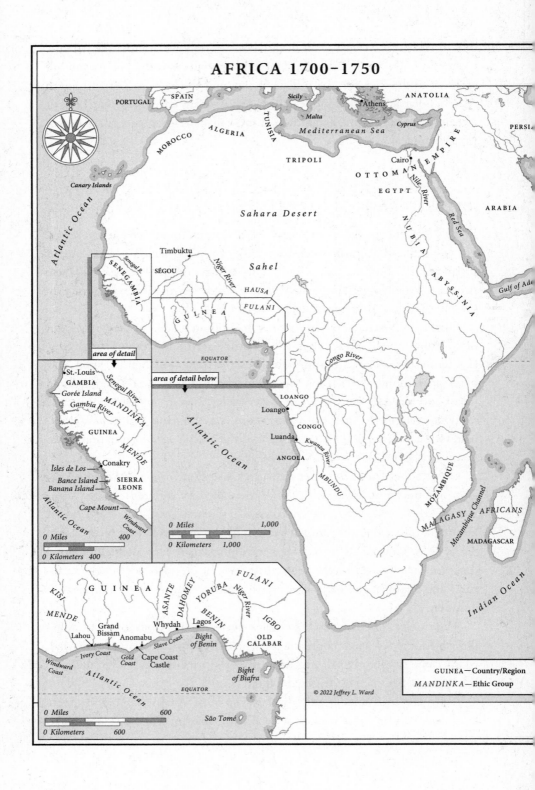

AFRICA 1700–1750

PORTUGAL
SPAIN
Sicily
Athens
ANATOLIA
PERSI

MOROCCO
ALGERIA
TUNISIA
Malta
Mediterranean Sea
Cyprus

TRIPOLI
Cairo
OTTOMAN EMPIRE

Canary Islands
EGYPT
Nile River
ARABIA

Atlantic Ocean
Sahara Desert
NUBIA
Red Sea

Timbuktu
SENEGAL R.
SENEGAMBIA
SÉGOU
Niger River
Sahel
ABYSSINIA
Gulf of Ade

HAUSA
FULANI
GUINEA

EQUATOR
Congo River

area of detail
area of detail below
LOANGO
Loango
CONGO

St.-Louis
GAMBIA
Senegal River
Gorée Island
MANDINKA
Gambia River
Luanda
Kwanza River
ANGOLA

GUINEA
MENDE
MBUNDU

Îsles de Los
Conakry
SIERRA
LEONE
Bance Island
Banana Island

Cape Mount
Windward
Coast

Atlantic Ocean

0 Miles   400
0 Kilometers 400

Atlantic Ocean

0 Miles   1,000
0 Kilometers 1,000

MOZAMBIQUE
Mozambique Channel
MALAGASY AFRICANS
Indian Ocean
MADAGASCAR

KISI
GUINEA
ASANTE
DAHOMEY
YORUBA
FULANI
Niger River
MENDE
BENIN
IGBO
Lahou
Grand
Bissam
Anomabu
Whydah
Lagos
OLD
CALABAR
Ivory Coast
Slave Coast
Bight
of Benin
Windward
Coast
Gold
Coast
Cape Coast
Castle
Bight
of Biafra
Atlantic Ocean
EQUATOR

© 2022 Jeffrey L. Ward

0 Miles   600
0 Kilometers 600
São Tomé

GUINEA—Country/Region
MANDINKA—Ethic Group

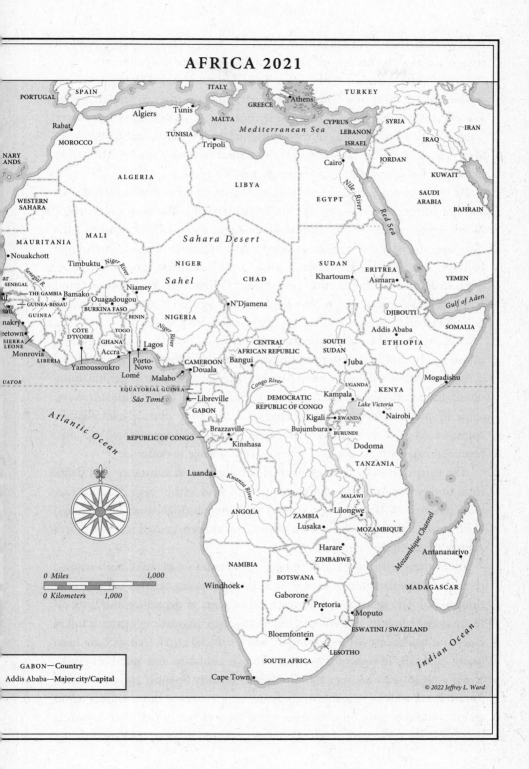

AFRICA 2021

PORTUGAL
SPAIN
ITALY
GREECE
Athens
TURKEY

NARY
ANDS

Algiers
Tunis
MALTA
Mediterranean Sea
CYPRUS
LEBANON
SYRIA
IRAN

Rabat
TUNISIA
Tripoli
ISRAEL
IRAQ

MOROCCO
Cairo
JORDAN
KUWAIT

WESTERN
SAHARA
ALGERIA
LIBYA
EGYPT
SAUDI
ARABIA
BAHRAIN

MAURITANIA
Nouakchott
Sahara Desert
Nile River
Red Sea
YEMEN

ar
Senegal R.
SENEGAL
Timbuktu
Niger River
NIGER
CHAD
SUDAN
Khartoum
ERITREA
Asmara
Gulf of Aden

au
GUINEA-BISSAU
THE GAMBIA
Bamako
Sahel
Niamey
Ouagadougou
N'Djamena
DJIBOUTI
SOMALIA

nakry
GUINEA
BURKINA FASO
BENIN
NIGERIA
Oue R.
Addis Ababa
ETHIOPIA

eetown
CÔTE
D'IVOIRE
TOGO
Niger River
CENTRAL
AFRICAN REPUBLIC
SOUTH
SUDAN

SIERRA
LEONE
GHANA
Lagos
Bangui
Juba

Monrovia
LIBERIA
Accra
Porto-
Novo
CAMEROON
UGANDA
KENYA

Yamoussoukro
Lomé
Malabo
Douala
Congo River
Kampala
Mogadishu

UATOR
EQUATORIAL GUINEA
São Tomé
Libreville
GABON
DEMOCRATIC
REPUBLIC OF CONGO
Kigali
RWANDA
Lake Victoria
Nairobi

Atlantic Ocean
REPUBLIC OF CONGO
Brazzaville
Kinshasa
Bujumbura
BURUNDI
Dodoma

Luanda
Kwanza River
TANZANIA

ANGOLA
ZAMBIA
Lusaka
MALAWI
Lilongwe
MOZAMBIQUE
Mozambique Channel

0 Miles 1,000
0 Kilometers 1,000
NAMIBIA
ZIMBABWE
Harare
Antananarivo

BOTSWANA
MADAGASCAR

Windhoek
Gaborone
Pretoria
Moputo

Bloemfontein
ESWATINI / SWAZILAND

GABON—Country
Addis Ababa—Major city/Capital
SOUTH AFRICA
LESOTHO
Indian Ocean

Cape Town

© 2022 Jeffrey L. Ward

Madagascar. They were sometimes called Malagasy Africans and were often recognized as a distinct group. These East Africans were not numerous in any American colony, but some of them appeared in every major North American region without exception. This common pattern of diversity in African origins was of critical importance in every American region. Its primary effect was to create a mixture of African cultures, skills, material systems, and religious beliefs. A leading result was a stimulus to cultural creativity among Africans in many parts of North America and every major region.

At the same time, that general rule of African diversity also coexisted with another important tendency. Within broad overall patterns in every major North American region, we also found evidence about small groups of Africans who shared similar regional, ethnic, and linguistic origins. Gwendolyn Hall was one of the first American historians to call these groups "clusters," often with distinct African ethnic identities. William Piersen also wrote about "clusters" of African slaves in New England, but he used it in another sense to describe smaller and more mixed groups in northern colonies.

A cluster is something more than a plurality of people. In both of those meanings, it implies connections or associations of different kinds. Regional clusters of African slaves in early America were occasionally large, but more often very small. They tended to be internally connected in different ways: some by places of origin, and by languages that were mutually intelligible, common religious beliefs, cultural values, shared skills, spatial connections, historical experiences, and also by places of residence in America.

The distribution of these African clusters varied in substance and detail from one North American region to another. And within each American region, patterns of African origin tended to change through time. They tended to be stronger in some places than others. But clusters existed in most North American slaveholding regions.

All of these patterns of African origin, large and small, have been studied recently by scholars from a variety of sources. Shipping records tell us something about African regions and much about ports of departure, but little directly about ethnicity and culture. Onomastic and linguistic evidence is full of clues and has been used in systematic ways. Official entry records have been useful especially in eighteenth-century French Louisiana and Spanish Florida. It was a pleasure to use very full nineteenth-century Spanish entry records in Puerto Rico, which I was able to study in San Juan. All of those sources tell us about cultural origins. So also does onomastic evidence of names and naming processes. The testimony of traders and owners, and in some cases the writings and oral memories of slaves themselves, also help on questions of ethnicity, religion, and cultural origins.

Genomic evidence for African origins is also beginning to become available. At the date of this writing in 2020–21, it is still relatively sparse for Africa, by comparison with more abundant materials for Western Europe and North America. But it is rapidly increasing everywhere. Geneticists and genealogists have been working together on these sources, and they report that preliminary African genomic results appear to be broadly consistent with other historical sources on the Atlantic slave trade. But patterns are still very tentative, and we have made no use of African genomic evidence for this inquiry. Hopefully it will add to our knowledge in important ways.

EUROPEAN ORIGINS OF SLAVE OWNERS IN NORTH AMERICA

In the New World of North America, African slaves had to deal with a great variety of slaveholders. Within what is now the United States, European and British origins of slave owners also combined broad diversity with concentrations and clusters in major regional cultures of the United States. Those patterns are also an important part of this inquiry, which is about the interplay of European and African cultures in North America.[23]

Some of the most enduring cultural differences in major regions of the United States developed during the early colonial era. From 1629 to 1775, the great majority of immigrants were broadly British, but they came from different regions, held different religious beliefs, and had different purposes in mind. Most of them spoke English, but in different regional dialects. Many were Protestant, but of different denominations. They shared British traditions of liberty and freedom but understood that common heritage in profoundly different ways.

A large part of that subject was explored in *Albion's Seed*, a companion volume to *African Founders*. New England's Great Migration of twenty thousand Puritans and others (1629–40) introduced distinctive ideas of ordered freedom, mainly as rights of belonging to communities of free people.

Virginia's great migrations came in the mid-seventeenth century (ca. 1640–76). They were more than double the size of New England's Great Migration, and very different in social composition. The flow to Virginia and southern Maryland brought a small elite of high-born gentry, a minority of yeoman farmers, and many unfree servants. More than 75 percent of British migrants

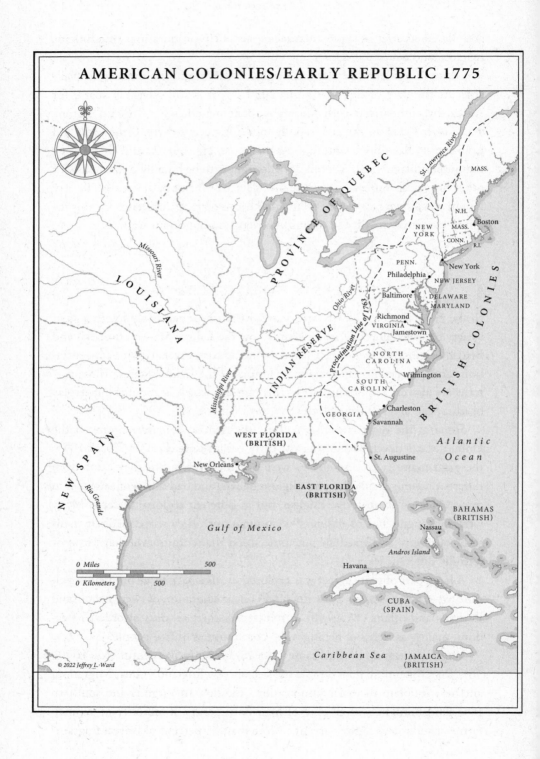

AMERICAN COLONIES/EARLY REPUBLIC 1775

PROVINCE OF QUÉBEC

St. Lawrence River

MASS.

N.H.

MASS.

Boston

CONN.

R.I.

NEW YORK

PENN.

New York

Philadelphia

NEW JERSEY

Baltimore

DELAWARE

MARYLAND

Richmond

VIRGINIA

Jamestown

Missouri River

L O U I S I A N A

Ohio River

Proclamation Line of 1763

INDIAN RESERVE

NORTH CAROLINA

SOUTH CAROLINA

Wilmington

Mississippi River

GEORGIA

Charleston

Savannah

B R I T I S H   C O L O N I E S

WEST FLORIDA
(BRITISH)

Atlantic
Ocean

NEW SPAIN

Rio Grande

New Orleans

EAST FLORIDA
(BRITISH)

St. Augustine

BAHAMAS
(BRITISH)

Nassau

Andros Island

Gulf of Mexico

0 Miles   500

0 Kilometers   500

Havana

CUBA
(SPAIN)

Caribbean Sea

JAMAICA
(BRITISH)

© 2022 Jeffrey L. Ward

to colonial Virginia came to America as bound servants, compared with less than 25 percent to New England. Virginia's leaders shared ideas of hegemonic liberty as an idea of rank, which gave many rights to planters, some rights to yeomen, a few rights to servants, and nearly no rights to slaves.

Pennsylvania's great Quaker migration (1675–1715) was yet another story. It brought a unique idea of reciprocal liberty and freedom, derived from Quaker preaching, founded on the Four Gospels and the Golden Rule, and inspired by the teaching of Jesus, that "what you do for the least of my brethren you do for me."

The last, longest, and largest British colonial migration (1715–75) came mainly from the borderlands of northern England, the lowlands of Scotland, the marches of Wales, the north of Ireland, and other Irish counties. Some of them are called Scots-Irish. Throughout those contested regions, rival rulers had inflicted misery and violence on the inhabitants for a thousand years. After the Act of Union in 1707, the English Parliament increased its hegemony. Many emigrants responded by moving to the American backcountry, where they introduced a distinctive idea of natural liberty as the right to be left alone, with as little government as possible, which still prevails in some interior parts of the United States.

These British migrations founded distinct regional cultures in the New World. And in each of these English-speaking American regions, a deep diversity of British origins was further compounded by Spanish, French, and Dutch colonies in North America, and deepened by different clusters of African slaves.

Persistent evidence of the cultural consequences appeared in the mid-twentieth century, when historical linguists led by Hans Kurath carefully identified different regional dialects of American English in the United States. Cultural historians led by Henry Glassie and others also found similar regional differences in empirical patterns of material culture and vernacular architecture through the eastern United States.

Early colonial founders of these regions and their descendants also controlled patterns of immigration for many years. They shaped the flow of other immigrants in long-settled regions for as many as eight generations before a national system of immigration emerged in the United States during the nineteenth century.

These regional patterns are still evident today. In 2017, they were put to a genomic test in a large study by geneticists and genealogists on the present population of North America. They did a "fine-scale cluster analysis" of 770,000 genomes among individual American families of European origin who had at least three generations of ancestors in what is now the United States. The linkages in this inquiry comprised 500 million genetic connections, in the estimates of its authors. The results yielded a pattern of five major genomic clusters in the United States. They also observed that these clusters correlate with the four major colonial migrations as reported from historical sources in *Albion's Seed*. A fifth major cluster was in coastal Carolina, which was not part of *Albion's Seed* because a large majority of its population was African in origin.

Regional cluster patterns did not derive entirely from a common genetic origin in small groups of colonial founders from particular parts of England. Rather, the colonial founders established effective control of large processes of regional migration, from as early as 1607 to the gradual establishment of an effective immigration policy by a functioning federal government, mostly in the nineteenth century. Distinctively different genomic clusters in each American region descended more broadly, from regional migration processes that were created and partly controlled by founding populations, rather than solely from the founders themselves.[24]

Yet another dimension of regional diversity appeared in variant proportions of Africans in different parts of North America. In some northern parts of New England, African Americans were less than one percent of the population.[25] In the Deep South, on Butler's Island in coastal Georgia, African Americans were 99 percent of the inhabitants in the early nineteenth century, and 99.7 percent in the census of 1870. The range of regional and local ratios between African Americans and European Americans was as broad as the limits of possibility, and never twice the same.[26]

OTHER PRIMARY SOURCES FOR AFRICAN SLAVERY IN NORTH AMERICA: EMPIRICAL EVIDENCE FROM SURVIVING PLANTATION RECORDS

Another vast trove of primary sources appears in the "Records of Antebellum Southern Plantations," as the largest collection of them is called. These materials began to be gathered by labor historian Ulrich Phillips, in the nineteenth and early twentieth centuries, and were deposited in state archives and research libraries throughout the South. The major collections have continued to grow. Many of these plantation records have been microfilmed and made available in a vast collection on more than 1,200 reels of manuscript material at last count. Sets have been acquired by major university libraries. We have used the microfilms in the Brandeis University Library.

Most of these manuscripts came from larger plantations, mainly during the last six and a half decades of slavery, from 1800 to 1865, but some were earlier. They variously included plantation accounts, lists of slaves, data on births and deaths, records of slave rations, partial descriptions of clothing, blankets, housing and punishments, crop records, harvest returns, and personal journals and diaries of plantation owners. Very often, plantation wives kept the books, wrote the journals, and managed the complex accounts of large plantations. Their records often include primary sources for other questions about the experience of bondage in America, by women both slave and free. Increasing use has also been made of unwritten sources for the study of slavery in America. The study of North American slavery through the study of vernacular archaeology and material culture greatly expanded in the late twentieth century. So also did special fields of research on music, dance, visual arts, material culture, and surviving vernacular architecture.

PRIMARY EVIDENCE FROM THE TESTIMONY OF SLAVES: PERSONAL ACCOUNTS OF INDIVIDUAL EXPERIENCES, ACTS, AND CHOICES

Scholars have also used other sources to learn about acts and thoughts among individual Americans of African descent. This evidence exists in large numbers and great variety. It allows us to study not merely broad behavioral patterns, but also the acts and thoughts of individual slaves, as people who made choices, and choices that made a difference in the world.

Of great value are oral slave narratives. Many were collected as a New Deal project during the mid-1930s, from conversations with elderly former slaves about the experience of bondage in their youth, and their lives after slavery. The Library of Congress holds about 2,300 interviews of former slaves, mostly in typescript. Nearly all have been published and are also available online for research and teaching. Less often used are more than five hundred surviving photographs of ex-slaves who were interviewed in this very large project.

Hundreds of other slave narratives from the 1930s are not in the Library of Congress. They survive in other archives, mostly of southern states. Of special value are slave narratives for Louisiana in Baton Rouge, and for Virginia in the Virginia State Library at Richmond.

The quality of these interviews is uneven. Historians led by Paul Escott have carefully assessed patterns of strength and weakness in these sources. Other historians have also learned how to use them with great care and success, as Charles Joyner creatively used the excellent interviews by Genevieve Willcox Chandler in the Waccamaw Valley of coastal South Carolina. He did so with great care and accuracy.[27]

Very different sets of slave narratives also survive as recordings of oral interviews. Some of them are in the American Folklore Collection at the Library of Congress. They were recorded on aluminum discs in the 1930s and 1940s, later remastered by expert technicians at the Smithsonian Institution, and made available in digital form by teams of linguists. Oral interviews in English have been edited by Ira Berlin, Marc Favreau, and Steven Miller, and issued on tape and compact disc.[28]

Even more valuable, but less frequently used, are other interviews of elderly slaves in Louisiana, recorded on early wax cylinders in French Creole dialects collectively called Gombo. These Creole recordings are of excellent quality and extraordinary importance. We listened to them in the American Folklore Collection, both as a record of experience in bondage, and as an expression of a unique Afro-French language in the lower Mississippi Valley, which differed both from Afro-English speech in Louisiana, and from Afro-French in the Caribbean, Africa, and the island of Mauritius in the Indian Ocean.

These oral recordings of former Louisiana slaves are important in more ways than one. Some historians have expressed skepticism about the authenticity of written transcripts. Recorded oral interviews are different that way. They have an immediacy and authenticity that is beyond cavil. For fair-minded listeners, hearing is believing. And they are consistent with written records.

Yet another important genre of individuated primary sources are hundreds of written slave narratives that have been published in large numbers and various forms. Most of these many published narratives from former slaves were collected and printed in the nineteenth century as part of the antislavery movement. Nobody has made a definitive count of them. One volume alone, Benjamin Drew's *North-Side View of Slavery* (Boston, 1856), includes 113 individual narratives by slaves who escaped from the United States and reached Canada.

These many printed narratives of former slaves are of high importance, and some of them are major contributions to American literature. Frederick Douglass published three autobiographies, all centered on his experience of slavery in Maryland, each with unique strengths. A narrative by Solomon

Northup of slavery in Louisiana, *Twelve Years a Slave*, is of especially high importance. It was published in 1853, not primarily as part of the antislavery movement (though it is profoundly hostile to slavery), but as a major American literary work. In 1968, Northup's entire narrative was carefully researched by historians Sue Eakin and Joseph Logsdon for a scholar's edition, with many annotations and citations. By almost every test its careful accuracy was confirmed in substance and detail.

Other written slave accounts were printed as confessional narratives as early as the seventeenth and eighteenth centuries. Different narratives of much value also appear in records of religious conversion, and as confessional narratives by convicts, and also in military pension narratives by former slaves from the War of Independence to the Civil War. Still more appear in family histories. Altogether, by a conservative estimate, these various narratives, interviews, and memoirs survive for more than five thousand slaves in what is now the United States.

Yet more materials have been found in testimony by slaves that have been preserved in records of court cases. Philip Schwarz has set a new standard for the use of legal sources in the study of slaves and slavery in Virginia, and elsewhere.[29]

EMPIRICAL EVIDENCE OF EXTREME CRUELTY AND PHYSICAL ABUSE OF SLAVES IN NORTH AMERICA

Empirical methods have recently been put to work in new ways for another fundamental source of slavery's history in North America. Some of it has come from new and carefully controlled inquiries into the physiological impact of North American bondage on its victims. The largest project began in 1982 when excavations for a new office building in lower Manhattan unearthed an important and largely forgotten African Burial Ground in New Netherland and New York. After much debate, a team was organized and led by African Americans to study what had been found. They directed the exhumation and careful examination of remains by forensic pathologists, and reburial with care and respect.

Before these results became available, many historians (including myself) thought that we knew about the cruelty of slavery in early America. But much careful empirical inquiries yielded evidence that human bondage was worse than we had known, and in an unexpected way. Forensic pathologists found repeated evidence of the relentless destruction of human bodies by forced labor in slavery. Bodies of slaves were bent and broken in ways that would have caused constant pain and suffering. Many slaves in early America, and even in northern towns and cities, were literally worked to death. Evidence survives in the bodies of male and female slaves, old and young, both house servants and field workers, from the seventeenth to eighteenth centuries.

This New York project was the largest and most detailed of its kind in the United States. It inspired empirical inquiries in other colonies and states, with smaller numbers but similar results. In Connecticut, a family of physicians used the skeleton of a long-serving slave to teach anatomy for many generations. Pathologists studied these remains and once again found evidence of severe physical damage by overwork. Other exhumations came from small burial grounds in the Carolinas, Georgia, and Louisiana. All showed evidence of physical damage caused mainly by overwork. This fundamental fact of human bondage appeared wherever it was studied by empirical methods.[30]

Another empirical inquiry also found evidence of physiological damage of a different kind, deliberately inflicted in beatings and unimaginable tortures of slaves by masters and overseers. A team of my very able Brandeis students made a quantitative study of advertisements for runaway slaves in newspapers of Virginia and South Carolina, from the mid-eighteenth to mid-nineteenth century. They quantified evidence of scars, wounds, and deliberate destruction of body parts, all from descriptions written by slave owners themselves. Frequencies of extreme abuse varied by time and place, but they existed throughout the history of slavery in North America. The more we learn about the abuse of slaves in North America, the worse it appears. Horrific evidence from physical remains and other sources has been found in every North American region without exception, from New York and New England to Maryland and Virginia, lowcountry Carolina, Georgia, Louisiana, the western frontier, and even Quaker Pennsylvania.[31]

A contributing cause may have been the impact on slavery of libertarian masters in the United States. Some, not all or even most, but many members of slaveholding elites in a republic founded on liberty and freedom, claimed a sovereign right to practice slavery without interference, however they pleased. It might be understood as a libertarian form of *laissez-faire*, which became *laissez-asservir*, a master's liberty to enslave. Most colonial and state governments enacted restraining laws, but some masters clearly believed they possessed a higher law to treat their slaves as severely as they pleased.

FREQUENT ACTS OF RESISTANCE BY AFRICAN SLAVES, MOSTLY IN NONVIOLENT FORMS

If we ask how many African slaves resisted their bondage, the same answer emerges from many sources. In short, approximately all slaves resisted slavery in one way or another. Their resistance took many forms, and it varied in space and time, from one American region to another.

The form of resistance was highly variable. A large proportion of violent resistance tended to recur in a small number of places: notably parts of lower New York, Southside Virginia, coastal Carolina, certain parts of Louisiana, and Maryland's lower Eastern Shore south of the Choptank River, which H. L. Mencken called Trans-Choptankia. Violent slave resistance occurred less frequently in New England, northern Maryland, eastern Pennsylvania, and parts of North Carolina, but it occurred everywhere.

Widely distributed but comparatively rare were individual acts of violence or even homicide against masters and mistresses by poisoning, arson, and other methods. More nearly universal were acts of theft, damage, disorder, disruption, sabotage, delay, and escape.

By far the most frequent and most successful forms of resistance took an entirely different form. These were constructive and often creative efforts of slaves in every region to build complex cultures and associations among themselves by collective efforts from which the master classes were largely excluded. These actions were sometimes small but they had large consequences. They helped to create a broad array of Afro-European cultures which in turn shaped North American cultures.

In that process, they also made a difference in the values and institutions of America itself, and very much for the better. The creativity of African slaves in some ways diminished their suffering and improved the conditions of their lives. They also helped to make North American colonies more open, more creative, and more free than most British and European founders had intended them to be.

DYNAMICS OF AFRICAN CULTURES IN EARLY AMERICA: CONTINUING CREATIVITY AND ITS CONSEQUENCES

What appears in these materials are not simple patterns of replication of African or European cultures in America, but more complex and inventive processes that became a key to creativity in an open society. Much detailed work

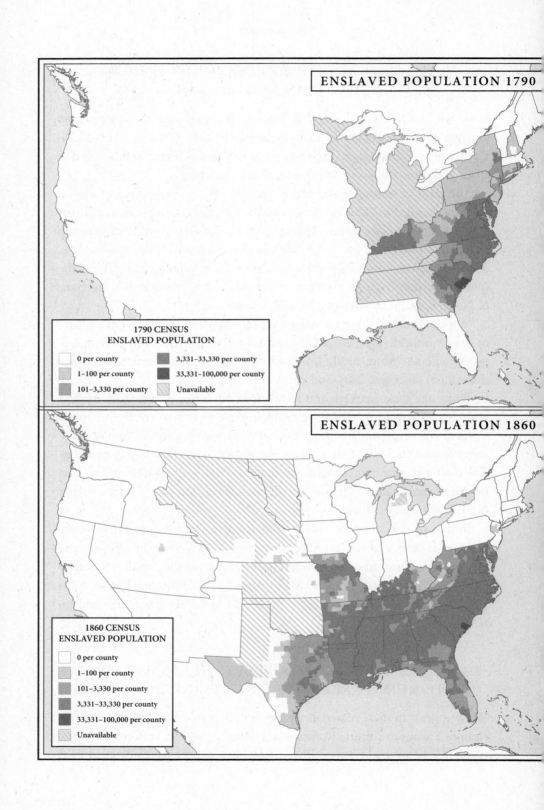

ENSLAVED POPULATION 1790

1790 CENSUS
ENSLAVED POPULATION

0 per county
1–100 per county
101–3,330 per county
3,331–33,330 per county
33,331–100,000 per county
Unavailable

ENSLAVED POPULATION 1860

1860 CENSUS
ENSLAVED POPULATION

0 per county
1–100 per county
101–3,330 per county
3,331–33,330 per county
33,331–100,000 per county
Unavailable

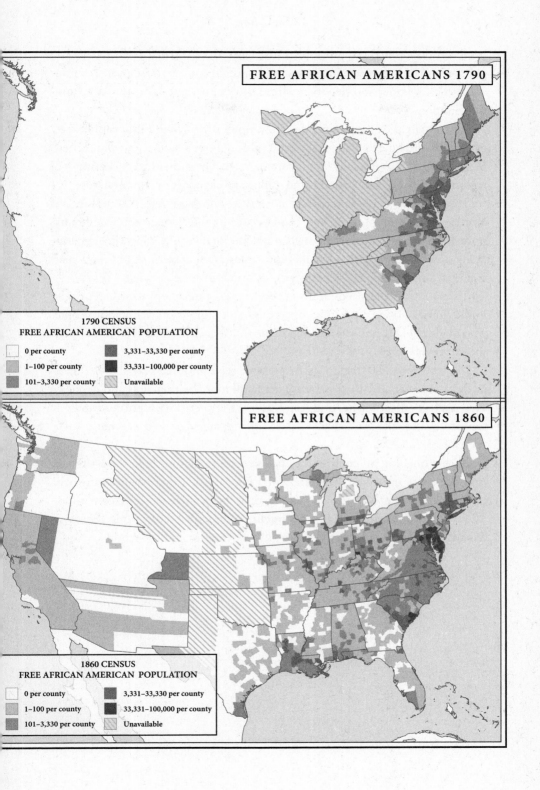

FREE AFRICAN AMERICANS 1790

1790 CENSUS
FREE AFRICAN AMERICAN POPULATION

0 per county		3,331–33,330 per county
1–100 per county		33,331–100,000 per county
101–3,330 per county		Unavailable

FREE AFRICAN AMERICANS 1860

1860 CENSUS
FREE AFRICAN AMERICAN POPULATION

0 per county		3,331–33,330 per county
1–100 per county		33,331–100,000 per county
101–3,330 per county		Unavailable

has been done on these processes of invention that flowed from particular parts of African cultures: language and speech, music and dance, religion and ethics, folklore and material culture, agriculture and industrial arts, and much more.

Individuals and groups tended to draw upon African and European sources to create something new in local cultures throughout what became the United States. They did so in many ways. Patterns varied by individual and from one region to the next, but shared some important elements in common.

The chapters that follow study nine Afro-European regional cultures in North America. All of them were founded during the colonial era by migrants from Europe and Africa. Each was creative in its diversity, which operated in many ways to distinguish one American region from another. All of them had an impact on the culture, values, and institutions of America itself.

This is a history that flowed from the acts and choices of individual people in the midst of others. It was an open process, a story of stories, about people who made choices, and choices that made a difference in their world, for open societies everywhere.

In every American region, Africans both slave and free played a vital role in these processes. By their presence, and still more by their acts and choices, they made a difference in American history. They acted with purpose and resolve to change the ways that free and open systems worked in what is now the United States.

In that ongoing process, African people who came mostly in slavery made America more open and more free, in a long process that began with their earliest arrivals, and continues among their descendants in our own time. These many acts and consequences might be understood as among the most dynamic and most enduring African gifts to America and the world.

TABLE 1.1 Estimates of Total Foreign Slave Trade Out of Africa,
650–1900 (Total Slaves Transported from Africa)

PERIOD	SAHARA, SAVANNA & HORN OF AFRICA	RED SEA & EAST AFRICA	ATLANTIC TRADE	TOTAL
Source:	Austen	Austen, Lovejoy	Lovejoy; Eltis @ Richardson	
650–800	150,000			
801–900	300,000			
901–1100	1,740,000			
1101–1400	1,650,000			
1401–1500	430,000			
1501–1600	550,000			
650–1600		2,400,000		
1450–1500			81,000	
1501–1600			338,000	
1601–1700	700,000	200,000	1,876,000	
1701–1800	700,000	600,000	6,495,000	
1801–1900	1,506,250	1,925,000	4,027,000	
Totals	7,906,250	5,125,000	12,817,000	25,648,250

TABLE 1.2 Estimates of the Foreign Slave Trade from Africa

Trans-Sahara Slave Trade

Mauny	1400–1900	10,000,000
Austen (1)	650–1900	9,387,000
Austen (2)	650–1400	4,800,000
	1400–1900	4,512,500
Total		**9,312,500**
Inikori	900–1500	4,813,000
	1500–1880	3,986,000
Total		**8,799,000**

Red Sea, East African Coast, and Indian Ocean

Austen	800–1800	3,100,000
	1801–1900	1,925,000
Total		**5,025,000**
Lovejoy	800–1600	2,400,000
	1600–1700	200,000
	1700–1800	600,000
	1800–1900	1,487,000
Total		**4,787,000**
Inikori	800–1500	2,100,000
	1500–1900	2,900,000
Total		**5,000,000**

Total Slave Trade from Sub-Saharan Africa

Inikori	650–1900	29,787,000
	1500–1890	22,256,000

PART ONE

NORTHERN REGIONS

Chapter 1

NEW ENGLAND

Puritan Purposes, Akan Ethics, American Values

New-England is originally a plantation of Religion, not a plantation of Trade.

—John Higginson, *The Cause of God and His People in New-England*, 1663[1]

Akan ethics and theology can stand as equals with any equivalent conceptions in European culture.

—C. A. Ackah, *Akan Ethics*, 1988[2]

IN THE YEAR 1717 or thereabout, a child was born on the Gold Coast of Africa. His parents called him Kofi, an Akan day name that commemorated the day on which he was born. English speakers translated it as Friday's Child.[3] Kofi was an Asante slave. At the age of ten he was sold at least three times, first to a Fante trader, then to an agent of the British Royal African Company, and once more to a Yankee captain who carried him across the sea to Newport in Rhode Island.[4]

In New England, Kofi became the property of Ebenezer Slocum, perhaps as part of a wedding dowry. In 1742, Ebenezer sold him yet again for 150 pounds to his nephew John Slocum, a Quaker who had scruples about slavery and allowed Kofi to buy his liberty. The young freedman took the name of his benefactor and called himself Coffe Slocum. He married Ruth Moses, a Wampanoag Indian, and learned to read and write alongside their children. Slowly he made his way as a farmer and carpenter on the southern coast of Massachusetts.

It was a hard struggle. For many years he toiled on desolate Cuttyhunk Island, twelve miles at sea. Then he moved his family to Chilmark on Martha's Vineyard, perhaps to be near Ruth's Indian kin. They moved again to the mainland town of Dartmouth with its large Quaker community. There he flourished in whaling and trade and became a man of property. In 1766, he

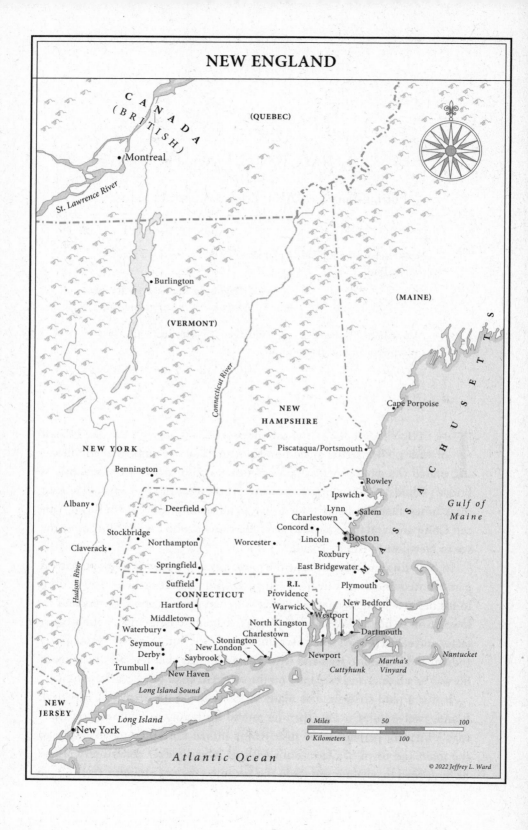

NEW ENGLAND

C A N A D A (BRITISH)

(QUEBEC)

•Montreal

St. Lawrence River

•Burlington

(VERMONT)

(MAINE)

Connecticut River

NEW
HAMPSHIRE

Cape Porpoise

NEW YORK

Piscataqua/Portsmouth

•Bennington

Rowley

Ipswich•

*Gulf of
Maine*

Albany•

Deerfield•

Lynn• •Salem

Charlestown

Concord•

•Stockbridge

Northampton•

Worcester•

Lincoln•   Boston

Claverack•

•Springfield

Roxbury

East Bridgewater

Hudson River

Suffield•

R.I.

Plymouth•

CONNECTICUT

Providence•

•Hartford

Warwick•

New Bedford•

Middletown•

North Kingston

•Westport

Waterbury•

•Dartmouth

Seymour•

Charlestown

Stonington•

Derby•

New London•

•Trumbull

Saybrook•

Newport•

Cuttyhunk

*Martha's
Vinyard*

Nantucket

•New Haven

Long Island Sound

NEW
JERSEY

Long Island

•New York

Atlantic Ocean

M A S S A C H U S E T T S

0 Miles   50   100

0 Kilometers   100

bought a handsome farm of 116 acres and paid for it with 650 Spanish silver dollars. Yankee neighbors called him Mister Coffe Slocum. The title pleased him and he used it with pride, as he also did his Akan day name.[5]

We can follow the progress of Coffe Slocum in his own words because he kept a journal and saved his exercise books. They survive in manuscript at the New Bedford Library, and are truly a national treasure. Coffe Slocum's writings are striking for their consciousness of right and wrong. He lived by a complex ethic of getting and keeping, of giving to others, and "doing good to all." That combination ran through many passages in his writing: "Daarmouth, Chechiemark, Cullhonk, Nossnour, and Romykes and Care Dare Ere Fear Give We Heare are . . . good Do good all Do good to all . . . Give Give Give . . . Good Do Good at all times I lern read AbcdABBBDDJAATM Coffe Slocum Mister."[6]

To study these passages is to discover that Coffe Slocum brought together several moral traditions in his thinking. Some of them derived from Puritan and Quaker beliefs that Max Weber collectively called the Protestant ethic. These were ethics of serving God in one's calling by getting and keeping, and doing well in the world. Another part of Puritan and Quaker ethics (which Weber largely missed) was about giving to others, and "doing good to all." Coffe Slocum engaged all of these ideas in his thinking.[7]

At the same time, he also engaged Fante and Asante ethics of right conduct that he had learned as an African child. Today, in Ghana's modern universities, a large literature has developed on "Akan Ethics," which have deep roots in West Africa and are increasingly studied by moral philosophers through the world.[8]

Protestant and Akan ethical and religious beliefs differed in important ways. In revealed religions such as Christianity, Judaism, and Islam, ethical systems are perceived as a product of divine revelation, in the form of sacred texts. Akan moral beliefs had another foundation. They centered on an idea of ethics as derived from the needs and customs of a people and were reinforced by the gods rather than dictated by them. Kwame Gyekye observes that "rather than regarding African ethics as religious, it would be more correct to regard African religions as ethical."[9]

In some ways, Puritan-Quaker and Fante-Asante ethics were similar. Both centered on the importance of ethical action in the world. Some of Coffe Slocum's phrases are similar to an Akan "country prayer" recorded by Anglican missionary Thomas Thompson at Cape Coast, circa 1750: "Yancumpong m'iphih meh, mah men yeh bribbe ummouh. May the Creator preserve me and grant I may do no evil."[10]

In both cultures, these ethical imperatives were a philosophy of doing, and they applied to individual and collective acts. An Akan proverb taught that "when virtue founds a town, the town thrives and abides." Three Akan proverbs were: "to possess virtue is better than gold," and "virtue comes from character," and "character comes from actions."[11]

These ideas sought to link ethics of being and doing within individual lives, and to apply them in active engagement with others in the world. They were designed for use. Both sets of ethical traditions, Fante-Asante and Puritan-Quaker, centered on a moral and material integration of "doing well" and "doing good."

The moral passages in Coffe Slocum's journals were not examples of static African "survivals," or of rote borrowing from Puritan and Quaker beliefs. They were something new in the world—another ethic that emerged when African and European traditions met in the mind of a very bright and able Akan-speaking freedman in eighteenth-century New England.

Coffe Slocum himself lived these ethical ideas. He put them to work in his own life, taught them to his many children, and passed them on to some of his twenty-two grandchildren. His descendants were taught to do well and do good in the same acts. They also learned a dual ethic of getting and keeping, and giving to others.

In the process, Coffe Slocum's descendants enlarged the ethical traditions of their African heritage. They also expanded Puritan and Quaker beliefs by combining them, and by putting them to work for people of different origins in New England. They took pride in their African roots, New England associations, and also their American Indian ancestry. All those connections broadened the reach of their ethical beliefs.

The result was a mixed identity that inspired Coffe Slocum's children and grandchildren to invent another naming tradition. His sons converted their father's Akan day name into their family surname. Coffe Slocum's sons called themselves John Cuffe and Paul Cuffe. Other children and grandchildren did the same thing in New England.[12]

As Coffe Slocum's family grew into an extended Cuffe clan, they followed his example in other ways. Together they constructed an interlocking network of thriving enterprises in southeastern Massachusetts. Several sons acquired large farms in Dartmouth and neighboring towns. His daughter Ruth Cuffe and granddaughter Naomi Cuffe and their husbands ran a successful store in New Bedford. His son Paul owned a flourishing shipyard in Westport, building coastal sloops and schooners, a full-rigged ship of 268 tons, and the beautiful brig *Traveller*, which was his pride and joy. Paul Cuffe sailed them himself, and he began to build a fortune from trading ventures, in partnership with his brothers and sisters and

Captain Paul Cuffe and his beloved brig *Traveller*, 1812

leading Quaker and Puritan merchants. They tended to capitalize voyages separately to spread the risk, and traded actively along the coast of the United States.

In 1811, Paul Cuffe's brig *Traveller* carried a cargo to Britain and caused a sensation. The London *Times* ran a piece on her arrival, and observed that she was "perhaps the first vessel that ever reached Europe, entirely owned and navigated by negroes." Similar reports appeared in the gazettes of Dublin and Edinburgh.[13]

None of this came easily. Several of Paul Cuffe's early vessels were plundered by pirates and seized by "refugees" on the south coast of New England. In one encounter, he was lucky to escape with his life. During the War of Independence he was captured at sea by the Royal Navy and barely survived his stay in a British prison. In southern Maryland, after the war, slaveholders were shocked when Paul Cuffe's trading vessel arrived with an African American owner, captain, and crew—a dangerous moment they all survived.

Other troubles followed in New England. The Cuffe family was helped by many upright Puritans and well-meaning Quakers, but hindered by Yankee racists who resented their success. The Cuffes responded by working for the rights of Africans and others in New England. Paul Cuffe himself has been called a "one-man civil rights movement" in the new American republic.[14]

At the same time, he also became a world figure, a leader in an international movement to end the Atlantic slave trade, and a founder of the new African nations of Sierra Leone and Liberia as part of an effort to end slavery through the world. He actively supported the colonization movement, the antislavery struggle, and the rights of free African Americans in the United States, all at the same time, with no sense of conflict or contradiction.[15]

In the nineteenth, twentieth, and twenty-first centuries, American descendants of Kofi Slocum multiplied throughout the United States. The twelfth generation runs a family website and organizes family reunions. They continue to enlarge an African, Indian, Puritan, and Quaker heritage into a broad American ethos, which they also helped to create and expand.[16]

AFRICAN SLAVES AND THE NEW ENGLAND WAY

Even as Cuffe Slocum's extended family cherished their African roots, they also worked within an Anglo-American regional tradition. It was called the New England Way as early as the seventeenth century. In our time it still preserves a strong regional identity and a creative presence in the American republic.

The New England Way is a dynamic tradition—always in motion, never at rest. It grew in large measure from the interplay of many population movements. Most important was the Puritan Great Migration of about twenty thousand people who founded the Massachusetts Bay Colony (1629–40). The dynamics that scientists in several fields variously call the founder effect were strong in New England.

Another immigrant group were the *Mayflower* Pilgrims who arrived in 1620. Their progeny founded Plymouth and its surrounding towns, which are still perceived as a special place called the Old Colony in Massachusetts. Other groups of radical Puritans, Seekers, Quakers, Separatists, and free spirits settled in southern Massachusetts, Rhode Island, and the Providence Plantations. More conservative Puritans founded the colonies of Hartford, New Haven, New London, and Saybrook in Connecticut. Others, both Puritans and refugees from Puritanism, moved northeast to New Hampshire, Maine, Nova Scotia, and northwest to Vermont.

After 1789, control of American immigration gradually passed from state and local leaders to the federal government, and an increasing diversity of other ethnic groups settled in New England. Four francophone flows came from the north: Quebeçois habitants, Acadien farmers, Breton fishermen, and roaming *coureurs de bois* (bush rangers). Each of these groups spoke its own patois, and preserved distant roots in different regions of Canada and France.[17]

New England later attracted large numbers of Catholic Irish, Italians, Jews, Armenians, and others. Each of these many ethnic groups cherished its own heritage. At the same time, they also became New Englanders. They lived in Yankee houses, grew accustomed to town meetings, began to talk like Yankees, and learned to play by Yankee rules.

After English Puritans and American Indians, the first of these many ethnic groups to increase and multiply in New England were African slaves. On the expanding periphery of the western world, an abundance of what Frederick Jackson Turner loosely called free land led to an insatiable demand for unfree labor. The results included servitude in Western Europe, serfdom in Eastern Europe, *encomienda* in New Spain, as well as African slavery in every American colony without exception. Some New Englanders tried to enslave American Indians with little success, brought servants from home, and then began to buy African slaves. Several studies have found more Africans in New England than in Virginia by 1640.[18]

By 1790, the first federal census found about sixteen thousand people of African descent in New England—a small number by comparison with later plantation colonies to the south. But through many generations, these Afro-Yankees had an importance beyond their numbers. By their presence, and still more by their thoughts and acts, they made a difference not only in New England, but throughout much of the United States.

Most of all, these African New Englanders began to enlarge the principles and purposes of the Puritan founders, and to extend the organizing principles of New England. The result was a constellation of expanding ideas that became fundamental to an open society in North America. Once started, these expansive ideas kept growing in ways that continue to make a profound difference in our world. That is a central theme of this book.

AFRICANS IN NEW ENGLAND BEFORE PURITANS: SLAVERY IN A STATE OF NATURE

In 1629, when the Puritans began their Great Migration to Massachusetts Bay, they discovered that a few European settlers had preceded them. Most lived outside the law, and some kept African slaves in conditions that were cruel and brutal beyond imagining.

In early America, a condition worse than slavery in an organized society was slavery in a state of nature, beyond the reach of law and government. An example was Samuel Maverick, a lawless adventurer and slaver who built his own private fort on Massachusetts Bay in 1623, before the Puritans arrived. It stood apart on Noddle's Island, now part of Boston's Logan Airport. Maverick held at least three African slaves, and severely abused them. An English visitor named John Josselyn observed their suffering at first hand, and tried to intervene:

The second of October, about 9 of the Clock in the morning, Mr. Maverick's Negro woman came to my chamber window, and in her own Country language and tune sang very loud and shrill. Going out to her, she used a great deal of respect toward me, and willingly would have expressed her grief in English, but I apprehended it by her countenance and deportment, whereupon I repaired to my host, to learn of him the cause, and resolved to entreat him in her behalf, for that I had understood before, that she had been a Queen in her own Country, and observed a very humble and dutifull garb used toward her by another Negro who was her maid. Mr. Maverick was desirous to have a breed of Negroes, and therefore seeing she would not yield by perswasions to company with a Negro young man he had in his house; he commanded him, will'd she nill'd she, to go to bed to her, which was no sooner done but she kickt him out again. This she took in high disdain beyond her slavery, and this was the cause of her grief.[19]

That early account of African slavery in Massachusetts Bay before the Puritan Great Migration described a lawless system of extreme inhumanity. A cruel master bred his slaves as if they were animals, and did so by violence, assault, and rape that violated many canons of Christian ethics.

The Puritans judged Samuel Maverick to be "an enemy to the Reformation at hand," and encouraged him to depart. Several of his descendants moved south and west and found a home in Texas. There another Samuel Maverick (1803–70) became infamous for grazing his cattle on the open range and refusing to brand them according to the custom. Unmarked cattle began to be called mavericks. The family name became a synonym for Americans who went their own way, in defiance of custom, law, and right conduct. For some Americans, it became a praise word.[20]

In New England before the Puritans, other acts of inhumanity toward Africans occurred, and some were worse than Samuel Maverick's. At an early fishing station in Maine, John Josselyn recorded a horrific story about a "waggish lad at *Cape-Porpus*, who baited his hooks with the drown'd *Negro's* buttocks, so for Pork and Beef." The story was told as a joke, but it was not a joke.[21]

THE GROWTH OF A SLAVE TRADE FROM AFRICA TO NEW ENGLAND, 1700–1775

During the Puritan Great Migration, as early as 1638 and probably earlier, African slaves began to multiply within the "Bible Commonwealth," slowly at first, but steadily. Governors of three Puritan colonies testified that with a few exceptions the first of these African slaves came by way of Barbados. As late as 1708, Rhode Island's governor Samuel Cranston informed the British Board of Trade that "the whole and only supply of Negros to this colony is from the island of Barbados from whence is imported one year with another, betwixt twenty and thirty."[22]

It was much the same in Connecticut, where Governor William Leete wrote in 1680, "As for Blacks, there comes sometimes three or four in a year from Barbados."[23] As late as 1709, he reported that "no voyages had come directly from Africa, and but few from any other place."[24]

In Massachusetts Bay, Governor Simon Bradstreet reported in 1680 that "there hath been no company of blacks or slaves brought into the country for the space of fifty years," except one vessel from Madagascar in 1678. "Now and then," he wrote, "two or three Negroes are brought hither from Barbadoes, and the total are about 100 or 120." Several historians believe that their numbers were larger, and their origins were more diverse. Some were "new Africans" who were transshipped from Barbados to Boston. But a scattering of advertisements also tell us that some of these Africans had been in the West Indies long enough to "speak pretty good English."[25]

After 1700 that pattern changed. The flow of slaves to New England increased, and it came more directly from Africa.[26] Boston newspapers routinely advertised the sale of slaves, both individuals and small "parcels."

November 10, 1712

A Young negro girl born in Barbados that speaks good English, to be sold by Mr. Grove Hirst, merchant, and to be seen at his house in Tremont Street, Boston.

August 3, 1713

Three Negro men and two Women to be Sold and seen at the House of Mr. Josiah Franklin at the sign of the Blue Ball in Union-Street Boston.

September 13, 1714

To be disposed of by Mr. Samuel Sewall Merchant, at his Warehouse near the Swing-Bridge in Merchant's Row Boston, several Irish Maid Servants . . . also Four or Five likely Negro boys.

November 17, 1726

Several choice Gold Coast Negroes lately arrived. To be sold at Mr. Bulfinch's, near the Town Dock, Boston.

July 19, 1739

To be sold by John Vryling, living in Beacon Street, Two very likely young Negro Girls, and a Negro Boy, just imported from Mounserrat, and can understand and speak pretty good English, and are already very handy in a Family.

October 7, 1740

Just imported from the Coast of Africa, and to be Sold by Mr. John Jones, on board the brigantine *Poultney*, now lying at Clark's Wharff, A Parcel of likely Young Negroes, Men and Women, Boys and Girls; to be seen on Board said Vessel.

November 4, 1762

Just imported from Africa. And to be Sold Cheap . . . a few prime Men and Boy Slaves from the Gold Coast.[27]

These brief notices reveal many things about New England's slave trade. They tell us that Boston's most eminent families engaged in it. Grove Hirst, the merchant who advertised a young girl for sale in 1712, was the son-in-law of Samuel Sewall, the leading Puritan magistrate in Massachusetts. Josiah Franklin, who sold slaves at Boston's Blue Ball tavern, was a stepbrother of Benjamin Franklin. John Jones, who offered a "parcel" of Africans at Clark's Wharf, was the brother-in-law of Peter Faneuil, Boston's leading merchant.

Slave buyers were heavily concentrated in large and prosperous towns of New England. Among them were ministers, magistrates, merchants, and affluent families. Children of these elites tended to be raised at an impressionable age by African slaves.

AFRICAN REGIONAL ORIGINS IN NEW ENGLAND: THE RANGE OF DIVERSITY

New England's African slave trade reached its peak from about 1715 to 1775. In that period of sixty years, shipping records tell us that slaves arrived from many African regions. Boston gazettes advertised new Africans for sale from Senegal and Gambia, the Grain Coast and Windward Coast, Benin and Biafra, West Central Africa, and a few from East Africa and Madagascar. The range of origins was almost as broad as Africa's Atlantic coast, from Saint-Louis in northern Senegal to Luanda in southern Angola. Its effect was to enrich the diversity of African cultures in New England, as it did in every early American coastal region.[28]

The poet Phillis Wheatley wrote with pride that her African homeland was Gambia. Others said that she came to Boston from Senegal, and she bore the name of the ship *Charming Phillis* that brought her. Both statements may have been correct.[29]

In North Kingston, Rhode Island, a legendary slave named Senegambia spoke and sang of his origins in the griot tradition that is still strong in his African region. He enriched the African folkways in Rhode Island's South County.[30]

Other West Africans came to New England from Dahomey, between Togo and Nigeria. In the eighteenth century they were called Paw Paw slaves, after the principal port of Popo, and they contributed elements of their culture to the mix. When New England slaves came together, they played a game of chance by throwing down four cowrie shells, and betting on the number that landed with their open side up. The name of the game was Paw Paw.[31]

Other New England slaves in the seventeenth and eighteenth centuries came from Central Africa. In one Massachusetts list of African slaves at least five bore Bantu names, and other slaves were said to be from Congo and Angola.[32]

Other "Malagasy slaves," as they were called, came to New England

from Madagascar and East Africa, as they did to New York and the Chesapeake. One early runaway notice in Boston (1704) sought the return of Penelope, "about 35 years old." Her owner described her as a "well set middle
sized Maddagascar Negro Woman" who "speaks English well," and carried
"several Sorts of Apparel; one whereof is a flowered damask Gown." She
had come from what is now the Malagasy Republic in the Indian Ocean,
by way of East African seaports near the Mozambique Channel, which became part of the Atlantic slave trade near the end of the seventeenth century.[33]

Within that broad range of diversity of African origins, several sets of New
England records also show strong patterns of concentration in time and place.
In the peak period from 1710 to 1775, a majority of New England's slaves
came from one African region, and many of them passed through a single
African seaport.

An early set of data was compiled by Elizabeth Donnan, a pioneer in this
effort. She found that most of New England's slaves came from the Gold
Coast, in the modern nation of Ghana. Further, Donnan's research found that
of eighty slave voyages from Africa to New England, fifty-five (69 percent)
found their primary source of slaves at the Gold Coast port of Anomabu.
Other New England slaves were also purchased at nearby Cape Coast Castle,
Mouree, Great Koromantine, Little Koromantine, and Elmina, all within ten
miles of Anomabu.[34]

The larger and more comprehensive Trans-Atlantic Slave Trade Database
yielded similar evidence that about ten thousand arriving slaves were carried
directly to New England from Africa. Of that number, it found that about
6,600 came from the Gold Coast—a pattern similar to Donnan's findings
and ours. It also identified Anomabu as the leading African port in the New
England traffic, followed by Cape Coast Castle. The port of Elmina also had
a sizable trade, and some of it went to New England, but most were sent in
Dutch ships to Dutch Guinea and Brazil.[35]

Evidence for this pattern of African origin appears not only in shipping
records, but also in other sources. Three sets of onomastic data on African
naming patterns (discussed below) confirm the importance of the Gold
Coast in New England's slave trade from 1710 to 1775. They also indicate
that this geographic concentration was also an ethnic pattern of origins from
Akan-speaking cultures, mostly Fante and Asante.[36]

English castle at Anomabu

Other slaves came to New England not directly from Africa itself, but by way of the British West Indies. Many were "new Africans," who were trans-shipped to the North American mainland. In the mid-eighteenth century, these slaves also came in large proportions from the Gold Coast and Anomabu.[37]

In 1997, Judy and I went to Anomabu, seventy miles west of Ghana's capital city of Accra. It was easily reached on excellent coastal roads, but our very able Asante and Fante driver and translators did not want to take us there, and for a very good reason. In that year, Anomabu's massive eighteenth-century British slaving castle of Fort William was serving as Ghana's high-security prison. The castle itself had a dark and sinister air. Our guides kept their distance, and urged us to do the same. We followed their advice, but explored the upper and lower town of Anomabu, the adjacent coast, and inland regions.[38]

The Anomabu prison was closed in 2001. An effort began to preserve the castle as a historic site, with a cultural center and a library. Architectural historians also sought to restore handsome eighteenth-century buildings in the lower town of Anomabu. The coastline itself is becoming a tourist destination with attractive beaches, palm groves, and seaside resorts that attract Ghanaian families from Accra and visitors from Europe. Anomabu itself is also part of an expanding coastal economy, long known for its boatbuilders and fishermen. It has been chosen as the home of a new Ghana College of Fisheries, which admitted its first students in the fall of 2016.[39]

In the mid-eighteenth century, Anomabu became for a time the most active port for the slave trade on the Gold Coast. The Dutch had planted trading "factories" there by 1640. They were followed by Swedes and Danes, and later by the British, who dominated the trade in the eighteenth century, and opened it to New England captains.[40] Altogether, the magnitude of Anomabu's Atlantic slave trade from 1652 to the nineteenth century has been reckoned at 466,000 slaves from this one port alone, based on sources and estimates in the Trans-Atlantic Slave Trade Database.[41]

The period of its greatest prosperity ended abruptly in 1806, when a major war began between the powerful Asante empire to the north and prosperous Fante states on the coast. On June 15–16, 1806, an Asante army attacked Anomabu and killed an estimated ten thousand of its fifteen thousand African inhabitants. Soon afterward, in 1807, the United States Congress and Britain's Parliament abolished the Atlantic slave trade, to take effect in 1808. Asante leaders wanted to keep the trade going with other nations. It revived at Anomabu, but much reduced from its earlier scale.[42]

At its eighteenth-century peak, English-speaking traders dominated Anomabu's slave trade. Most of it went to the British West Indies, especially Jamaica and the Leeward Islands. Other traffic flowed to Britain's North American colonies. On the American mainland, the largest numbers went to South Carolina, and but greatest proportions of this regional trade were in New England.[43]

New England's slave trade was shaped in no small part by the complex structure of these African markets. From Boston, Newport, Providence, Portsmouth, and Piscataqua, Yankee slavers generally cleared not for a specific African port but for "the African coast" or "the Guinea Coast" in its broad meaning. Often they called first at the Cape Verde Islands off northwest Africa to replenish water and supplies. Then they ran south along Africa's Windward Coast, trading American rum, lumber, and foodstuffs for African palm oil, ivory, ebony, gold dust, and some slaves. But the bulk of the slave buying on these voyages was done farther south and east, at a cluster of trading castles on Africa's Gold Coast, with Anomabu near its center.[44]

New England's share of the Anomabu trade expanded rapidly in the mid-eighteenth century. In 1760, the Rhode Island ship *Fox* took aboard a large cargo of "choice Gold Coast slaves" at "Annamaboe Castle." Her captain found four other New England ships riding at anchor under the guns of the new British fort.[45] In 1762, another Yankee trader went to Anomabu and found six slavers from Rhode Island alone.[46] In 1765, a Newport trader counted nine North American slave ships there. Five of them came from his home port, and eight from New England.[47]

Yankee captains also visited the large British center at Cape Coast Castle ten miles west of Anomabu, and the factories at Koromantine three miles to the east, and sometimes the old Portuguese and Dutch castles at Elmina, five miles west of Cape Coast. Elmina (Portuguese for "the mine") had also been a traditional center of the gold trade, which gave the African Gold Coast its name.[48]

But the center of New England's slave buying was Anomabu. Traders from Rhode Island and Massachusetts established close relations there with an integrated elite of African and English merchants. Their leader was Eno Baisee Kurentsie or John Corrantee to anglophones, an African trader who became the virtual ruler of Anomabu. On the coast he was renowned for his daily routine. In the morning he governed the town in palavers with Akan captains, Fante *caboceers*, Asante leaders, and other *Abirempongi* or Big Men in this region. In the afternoon he received European and American traders while seated in his bathing tub, sipping Rhode Island rum, and smoking American tobacco through "a long pipe that rested on the ground." He made a special effort to welcome New Englanders.[49]

John Corrantee had a son, William Ansah Sessarakoo, "Prince of Anomabu," who had been sent to England in the care of a slave trader who died

Portrait of William Ansah Sessarakoo, son of Eno Baisee Kurentsie (John Corrantee) of Anomabu

at sea. By mistake, the prince was taken to Barbados and sold as a slave. His powerful father learned what had happened, quickly obtained his freedom, and sent him to London. There he was celebrated as "The Royal African," and received by the royal family. His story was written in various forms by Blake, Burns, Coleridge, and Wordsworth. Something similar happened to other highborn Africans. Together they gave rise to a large, and largely forgotten English and American literature, where rank and class became more powerful than race.[50]

As we shall see below, several sons of African leaders were also sent to eighteenth-century New England for their education. After 1746, at least two others were said to have attended Princeton, a rare and important instance of continuing cultural exchange between North America and West Africa in the eighteenth century.

NORTH AMERICAN CONNECTIONS: CAPTAIN WANTON'S TANGLED WEB

In the spring of 1758, an odd-looking vessel called the *King of Prussia* sailed from Newport, Rhode Island, for the coast of Africa and the port of Anomabu. She was of a mixed rig called a snow, with big square yards on two masts and long fore-and-aft booms on her mizzen for sailing close to the wind, somewhat like the mixed rig later called a bark.

Her master, Captain Joseph Wanton, was something of a mixed rig himself. He was a Quaker, so "conscientiously scrupulous" in his faith that he refused to swear an oath even when his life depended on it. Always he "affirmed" his Quaker truths. But like many another Rhode Island Friend he was also a professional slave trader.

In Newport, Captain Wanton belonged to the Fellowship Club, a fraternity of pious captains and merchants, some of them Quakers. They were forbidden to swear, and solemnly "affirmed" never to engage in gaming, quarreling, heavy drinking, and warfare. And yet they saw no contradiction between Quaker beliefs and their highly profitable career, bartering quantities of New England rum for African slaves who had been seized by violence and held by force.

On Africa's Leeward Coast, Captain Wanton built a career by sailing against the wind in more ways than one. In April of 1758, he headed for Africa with a full cargo of rum in 144 barrels and hogsheads. It was a dan-

gerous time to be at sea. Britain and France were then at war, and Captain
Wanton hurried across the ocean, keeping outside the shipping lanes. He
made a landfall on May 20 at Cape Mount (near Robertsport in Liberia)
and ran down the coast, trading as he went, until he reached his destination
at Anomabu. There, by the end of July, Wanton traded most of his Yankee
rum for fifty-four slaves and twenty ounces of gold dust—a profitable exchange.

His business was nearly completed when a big Bordeaux privateer swooped
down on his little ship at Anomabu. The French corsair had sixty guns and
a crew of six hundred. Wanton had eleven men, and as a Quaker he did not
believe in fighting. The French captured them all, along with two other Newport slavers, and set their crews ashore. Anomabu's ruler, John Corrantee,
protected the Americans, bought one of their ships from the French corsairs,
and helped the Rhode Island slave traders get home.

Captain Wanton quickly returned to sea. After the Peace of 1763 he traded
profitably with the French who had seized his ship. The Wanton family continued slave trading with John Corrantee in Anomabu until the American
Revolution. In many ways the story of Captain Wanton personified New
England's slave trade at its pinnacle of prosperity in the mid-eighteenth century.[51]

ANOMABU'S INTERIOR SLAVE TRADE: THE
LONG MARCH OF BROTEER FURRO

In Anomabu, Captain Wanton dealt with African merchants who bought
captives from many sources. Some arrived by sea in a coastal commerce.[52]
Most came from a large hinterland that stretched hundreds of miles into the
interior of West Africa. Parts of this vast region near the coast were densely
forested. Some of this woodland and its great trees survive today in Ghana's
Kakum National Park, a place of incredible beauty, which we visited. It gave
us a sense of the country through which many slaves were carried to the
coast.[53]

Running inland through this wooded coastal region in the eighteenth century was a network of paths. They connected farming villages and small industrial hamlets where potters, metalsmiths, and weavers achieved levels of
technical refinement that were in some ways superior to European artisans
before the industrial revolution.

They are still working there today. On our travels we were fascinated by the weavers and were invited to visit their workplaces. Most were men who worked alone, weaving long strips of bright and handsome kente cloth on long narrow looms.

In this African region, many paths ran between the coast and the inland city of Kumasi, capital of the expanding Asante empire, and a major trading center through many centuries, as it is today. We went there and were amazed by the scale of Kumasi's vast open-air market, where many things were for sale, and the traders were often highly skilled.

In the eighteenth century, a vast web of West African paths carried many slaves southward to the busy port of Anomabu. A firsthand account of this overland traffic appears in the narrative of a slave called Broteer Furro in Africa, and later known as Venture Smith in New England. He tells us that he was born about 1727, the son of a prince in a place he called "Dukandarra in Guinea." One day, his father took a new bride without the consent of his first wife, which was "contrary to the custom." She left him with her three children, and gave Broteer, then aged five, to a master who lived about 140 miles from Dukandarra, near a great river that flowed in a westerly direction.[54]

Broteer was recovered by his father, who brought him and his mother back home. When Broteer was about ten or twelve, Dukandarra was attacked by a large force of raiders "from a nation not far distant," armed with European muskets and "instigated by some white nation." Broteer remembered that "the very first salute I had from them was a violent blow on the head with the fore-part of a gun."

He was made to watch as his father was tortured to death, in a vain attempt to find his hidden wealth. Then the invaders put a rope around Broteer's neck, tied him to a coffle of other prisoners, and marched him south "about four hundred miles." They attacked more villages, captured other Africans, and came at last to a place "contiguous to the sea, called in African Anamaboo."

Here a larger force of Africans attacked Broteer's captors. "I was then taken a second time," he remembered. "All of us were then put into the castle and kept for a market." One day Broteer was put in a canoe and delivered to the Rhode Island ship *Charming Susan.* He was bought by a Yankee crewman as a private venture, a common practice on the coast. The price was four gallons of rum and a piece of calico. After that transaction, Broteer Furro was renamed Venture Smith and carried to New England, where he later wrote one of the most important Afro–New England slave memoirs. We shall meet him again.[55]

New England captains came to Anomabu for many reasons, but one reason most of all. Their Yankee customers much preferred the slaves who were sold there. In the English jargon of the eighteenth-century slave trade, African captives on that part of the coast were called Coromantees. It was a geographic expression, related to the early coastal towns of Little and Great Kormantine (today Kormantse), three miles from Anomabu.[56]

Many Coromantees came to New England from what was then called Fanteland in Ghana, which included many small Fante states on the Gold Coast. Other Coromantees were from the expanding Asante empire in the interior.[57] Both spoke Akan languages, in a variety of Fante and Asante dialects that were (and are) mutually intelligible.[58]

Many English slave traders believed that Coromantees were "the best negroes on that whole coast" and valued them highly in several ways at once.[59] They were widely perceived to be physically the strongest people in West Africa. When male and female slaves of many ethnic origins were measured for height in Jamaica during the eighteenth century, "Coromantees" were the tallest of the major African groups.[60]

Yankee slavers also believed that Coromantees were better able to survive New England winters, often a severe test for people from tropical climates. One writer observed that "Gold Coast and Whidah Negroes . . . live hardily."[61]

New Englanders also respected Coromantees in another way as "the most sensible negroes on the coast."[62] One described them as "the best, being cleanest limbed and more docile" slaves.[63] Another writer thought them to be the "most hardy, serviceable, docile and useful."[64] In early American usage, docile meant teachable and quick to learn, after the Latin verb *doceo*, to teach. Coromantee slaves were thought to be docile in that sense.

They were far from docile in the twenty-first-century meaning of being easily controlled. Europeans on the coast often observed that Akan-speaking people shared a strong warrior ethic. Males in Fanteland were organized into military companies called *asafo*, and trained for war with elaborate regalia, rituals, dances, and huge cloth flags that were symbols of their culture and history.[65]

A very strong warrior tradition existed also among Asante to the north. The scale and violence of warfare increased in the eighteenth century, when a great king, Osei Tutu, founded the Asante empire. Here as elsewhere in other

African regions, periods of dynastic warfare increased the flow of captives to slave markets.[66]

These Fante and Asante military traditions were brought to the New World. On West Indian islands where slaves were severely abused, Coromantees earned a reputation as among the most militant and violent of Africans. They led the great Jamaica slave revolt in 1690, founded major Jamaican communities of maroons or escaped slaves by 1739, and organized the Antigua independence movement of 1736. They were at the center of Tacky's War in Jamaica, the Berbice slave war in Guyana in 1763, and Demerara's great slave rebellion of 1823. These events were among the largest and most successful slave risings in the history of the British West Indies.

Coromantee leaders were highly respected for their honor, courage, and endurance, especially by British soldiers who fought them in repeated "Ashantee wars." In the Leeward Islands, Governor Christopher Codrington wrote of Coromantees, "There was never a rascal or coward of that Nation. Not a man of them but will stand to be cut to pieces without a sigh or a groan."[67]

Some West Indian planters felt differently. A leading slave owner, Edward Long of Jamaica, disliked and feared Coromantee slaves. He introduced a special bill to prohibit their import.[68] Others who knew Coromantee slaves testified that they were formidable enemies, but responded differently to kindness, honesty, and humanity. They were said to be "ferocious if angered, unmindful of danger, unwilling to forgive a wrong, but loyal if their devotion could be captured."[69]

What proportion of New England's African slaves came from Akan-speaking Fante and Asante ethnic cultures? Shipping records from the African slave trade tell us much about the geography of African origins, but less about ethnicity. Not all captives for sale at Anomabu came from Fante and Asante ethnic groups. Ghana historian Kwasi Konadu described a "common practice of sending small vessels from Anomabu to procure captives from Benin and Lagos, and then selling them as Gold Coast captives." But as he observed, the same reports also noted that these efforts at ethnic misrepresentation were often in vain, as "the slaves of the Gold Coast are easily distinguished."[70]

For transatlantic historians, the question of ethnic origin remains difficult but not impossible. Onomastic evidence of naming patterns helps with this problem. Akan-speaking cultures in what is now western Ghana shared many distinctive naming customs that included male and female day names, birth order names, delivery names (circumstances of childbirth), twin names, and family names. Day names in particular were (and are) widely used in both Asante and Fante cultures.

At least three different onomastic data sets survive for African naming patterns in New England. Several lists supply the names of Africans who were elected "Negro governors" in Massachusetts, Connecticut, New Hampshire, and Rhode Island, from 1740 to 1845. Most had British, biblical, or classical names. Of thirty identifiable Negro governors in New England, ten had African names, of which seven were Akan, and came from Fante and Asante cultures.[71]

Another onomastic source in New England are military muster rolls. They include hundreds of African Americans in New England who took up arms against British forces in 1775. Here again, the names of most slaves were British, biblical, or classical. But in one set of lists, twenty militiamen "of color" on Massachusetts muster rolls had African names, of which twelve (60 percent) were Akan names, both Fante and Asante. The other names were scattered through African regions. Another sixteen militiamen were American Indians, mostly Algonkian and Iroquoian.[72]

The largest source of African names in New England is advertisements for runaway slaves, which yielded similar results. Once again most African names were of Akan origin.

These onomastic tests of African ethnic origin yielded very small samples, but all three found that a majority of 60 to 70 percent of African names in eighteenth-century New England came from Akan-speaking Fante and Asante cultures.[73] These results are consistent with evidence of geographic ports of departure in shipping records, both in data gathered by Elizabeth Donnan, and also in the Trans-Atlantic Slave Database. They also match the testimony of traders, owners, and colonial officials.[74]

Taken together, this material supports three conclusions on African origins of New England slaves. First, they came from a very broad range of African regions and cultures along much of the Atlantic coast from Senegal in the north to Angola in the south, and also a few from Madagascar by way of East African ports. Second, within that very broad range, a majority of African slaves in eighteenth-century New England came from what is now Ghana, mainly from Anomabu (much the largest) with a secondary linkage to Cape Coast Castle, and other places nearby. Third, onomastic evidence finds that as many as two thirds of African slaves in eighteenth-century New England came from Fante or Asante cultures, spoke Akan languages, were given Akan day names, and shared common ethnic, cultural, and linguistic origins.

In its totality, this pattern of African regional and ethnic origins in New England differed from other major regions on the mainland of colonial

North America. But it was similar in some ways to Jamaica and several of
the British Leeward Islands, where the slave trade tended to have similar
timing.

A PURITAN MIDDLE WAY FOR SLAVERY IN NEW ENGLAND

In New England, the institution of slavery differed in form and substance
from other North American colonial regions. It was deliberately designed by
Puritan masters and mistresses who shared a sense of conscience and distinctive ways of thinking about human bondage.

On slavery as a moral question, English Puritans in Britain and North
America responded in different ways. Some opposed it entirely, as did Richard Baxter (1615–91), an outspoken English theologian and moralist, often
imprisoned for writings that combined Puritan passion with Shakespearean
prose. He became a major figure in the English Civil War, an advisor to leaders of the Commonwealth and Protectorate, and later an architect of the Stuart Restoration without diminishing his Puritan principles.

Baxter never came to New England, but his writings were said to have been
read more widely there than the work of any other Puritan author. In 1673,
he published a short but powerful polemic against human bondage. In a summary sentence, he asserted "the inconsistence of slavery with every right of
mankind, with every feeling of humanity, and every precept of Christianity."
His indictment of slavery was one of the most comprehensive on record. And
it was delivered with a fury that has few equals in antislavery literature—both
in its horror of human bondage, and its empathy for the enslaved.[75]

Another Puritan was one of the first active abolitionists in the English-
speaking world. Samuel Rishworth lived on Providence Island, a short-lived
English colony off Nicaragua's Mosquito Coast. It had the same founding
dates as New England's Great Migration, but it was a distant and very different
place. Rishworth became the secretary of Providence Island. He was said to be a
"godly man," of "much esteem" for "piety and judgment," and was described as
"a gentleman of means and learning." Historians later described him as a "Puritan of the true New England type." Like the founders of the Massachusetts Bay
Colony, he also believed that "God's people stand on a hill." Rishworth was a
man of conscience who spoke in support of "poor men" and English servants.
He strongly opposed the keeping of African slaves, with no success. Providence
Island was rapidly becoming a plantation colony when Spain seized it.[76]

In New England, other leaders were also hostile to slavery from the start. In 1642, the deputy governor of Maine, Thomas Gorges, insisted that the use of slaves in place of servants would be totally "unlawful."[77] In 1652, Roger Williams's colony of Rhode Island and Providence Plantations enacted a law that forbade servitude for life, and prohibited "black mankind or white" to serve by "covenant bond or otherwise" for more than ten years, unless under the age of fourteen, in which case they must be freed at the age of twenty-four. That prohibition was repeated in 1675 and also extended to Indian slavery, but both Rhode Island laws were dead letters by 1708.[78]

The best remembered voice against slavery in New England was that of Puritan magistrate Samuel Sewall. In 1700, his pamphlet *The Selling of Joseph* was the first abolitionist tract published in North America. Sewall's antislavery argument had deep roots in his Puritan faith.[79] He reasoned from scripture that "all Men, as they are sons of Adam, are Coheirs, and have equal Right to Liberty." Further, he insisted that the selling of Joseph as a slave to the Ishmaelites was against God's law. He wrote that "Joseph was rightfully no more a Slave to his Brethren, than they were to him," and "there is no proportion between Twenty Pieces of Silver, and LIBERTY."[80]

Samuel Sewall

Sewall insisted that all slave trading was "manstealing" and that the rule of scripture in Exodus 21:16 was very clear: "He that stealeth a man and selleth him, or if he be found in his hand, he shall surely be put to Death."

This strong Puritan moralist also condemned what we would call racism, a double anachronism in his time, which had nothing quite like our modern ideas of "race" or our many ideological "isms." Samuel Sewall wrote that "black as they are, seeing they are the Sons and Daughters of the First Adam . . . they ought to be treated with a Respect agreeable." He also condemned laws that forbade sexual relations and prohibited intermarriage between Africans and Europeans.

Sewall was not alone in his stand against slavery and racism. Prominent leaders in New England congratulated him on *The Selling of Joseph*. In 1701, the selectmen of Boston asked the Massachusetts General Court "to put a period to negroes being Slaves." Through the years that followed, Boston's elected leaders several times instructed their representatives in the General Court to work "for the total abolishing of slavery among us." [81]

Other New Englanders went in the opposite direction, and one of them in particular became an ardent defender of slavery. John Saffin was another Boston judge, a wealthy merchant, an active slave trader, a slave owner himself, and a Puritan who "kept the Covenant," all at the same time. He was also a literary figure, an essayist, and a poet. In the Puritan way, John Saffin thought much about slavery, wrote at length about it, and published New England's first sustained defense of slavery as an answer to Samuel Sewall's attack. Many scholars are familiar with that exchange. Less well known is Saffin's poetry on what we would call race and racism. One poem was called "The Negroe's Character."

Cowardly and cruel are those *Blacks* Innate,
Prone to Revenge. Imp of inveterate hate,
He who exasperates them soon espies,
Mischief and murder in their very eyes.
Libidinous, Deceitful, False, and Rude
The spume Issue of Ingratitude.
The Premises consider'd, all may tell
How near good Joseph they are parallel.

Here was one of the first sustained American defenses of race and racism as a rationale for slavery, and also one of the first written expressions of extreme race-hatred. It surfaced in Boston as early as 1701, and appeared full blown in John Saffin's writings. He also gave this racist idea a peculiar Puritan twist by blaming the victim—not for inferiority but for depravity, another neo-Calvinist touch.[82]

Ironically, Saffin himself also became one of the most depraved early masters of African slaves on record in New England. An example was Saffin's treatment of his slave Adam, whom he had pledged to emancipate on the biblical model after seven years of faithful service.

When the time came, Saffin broke his solemn promise and refused to set Adam free. In this instance, New England ethics were stronger in the slave than in his master, and Adam sued for his freedom. Saffin outdid himself in infamy. He appointed himself the presiding judge, sat in judgment on his own case, packed the jury, and delivered angry instructions in his own favor.

Adam appealed, with success. The Massachusetts House of Representatives was appalled by Saffin's gross miscarriage of justice. It ordered a new trial before another judge. In a landmark case, Adam was released from bondage, and became a free man.[83]

A MIDDLE WAY IN PURITAN LAW: SLAVES AS BIBLICAL BONDSERVANTS

Many Puritans did not go the way of either John Saffin or Samuel Sewall. Here, as elsewhere, they followed the middle way, which they applied to many subjects in sermons, customs, and laws.

A leader was William Ames, an English Puritan theologian who never came to America, but was a leading architect of the covenant theology that had a major impact in New England. Ames wrote that "Liberty is in real value next unto life." He did not forbid slavery but argued that any master who exercised absolute power over a slave violated the teachings of Christ. Ames sought an ethical middle ground, not as a compromise, but a strong position in its own right.[84]

To that end, Puritan leaders in New England colonies enacted the first systems of slave law in English-speaking America. The primary model was always the Bible: not the New Testament and four Gospels of Matthew, Mark, Luke and John, but the Old Testament's law books of Exodus, Deuteronomy, and Leviticus. They became the source for several slave codes in the New England colonies.

The first system of laws was written by John Cotton and called *Moses His Judicials*. On the subject of slavery, an early draft had only one brief passage in seven words, but it went straight to the point. It read in its entirety, "Man-stealing, to be punished by death." Cotton, like Sewall, drew it from Exodus and Deuteronomy. As we have seen, he added an explanatory note: "He that stealeth a man and selleth him, or if he be found in his hand, he shall surely be put to death." In that sweeping phrase, he prohibited the capture, sale, and keeping of slaves. The mandatory penalty was death. In 1639, New Haven Colony adopted *Moses His Judicials* as its legal code.[85]

The Massachusetts Bay Colony went another way. Its *Body of Liberties* (1641) and *Lawes and Liberties of Massachusetts* (1648) forbade "bond slaverie, villeinage or captivities in the colony" for all people except "lawful captives taken in just wars, and such strangers as willfully sell themselves or are sold to us." It condemned slave raiding for profit, and made it a capital crime called "man-stealing." But it allowed "bond slaverie" of "lawfull Captives," and required that "these shall have all the liberties and Christian usages which the law of God established in Israel concerning such persons."[86]

These double-acting rules were not mere Calvinist casuistry. They were strictly enforced in the case of *Smith v. Keyser* (1646). Two New Englanders had joined a British raiding party which attacked an African village, killed many people, seized several captives, and brought two of them to Massachusetts. Here they fell out over the spoils and went to law. The General Court ruled that the captives had been taken unjustly, and ordered that they be returned to Africa "by the first opportunity (at the charge of the Country for the present)." It was done. The two Africans were freed and returned to their homeland. Smith and Keyser appear not to have been punished in any other way. The verdict in this case, like the law itself, was not a judgment against slavery, but against unjust enslavement by "man-stealing."[87]

The Massachusetts *Body of Liberties* recognized lawful forms of slavery, and justified their existence by reference to the Old Testament. At the same time, it limited the power and authority of masters on the model of Exodus, Deuteronomy, and Leviticus. Many Puritans believed that slavery in Massachusetts should not be for life, but for a term of years. African slaves throughout New England were often given their freedom after a period which variously appeared in the Bible as five or six or seven or ten years. Practices varied from one Puritan master to another. In general, the biblical rule was not meant to free a master from the support of aged slaves. Its purpose was

to free slaves in the prime of life, and to establish a system of humane slavery, which New England Puritans tried to require in many ways at once, with
mixed results.[88]

Humane slavery is a contradiction in terms. But that impossible idea
had real consequences for the enslaved. Through much of the seventeenth
century, slavery in Puritan Massachusetts was not entirely race-bound. An
example in 1638 was a white English servant named William Andros, who
assaulted his master and conspired to kill him. Andros was ordered to be
"delivered up as a slave" for an indeterminate period. Later he was returned
from slavery to servitude "for the rest of his time." Another white man
named Marmaduke Barton was "condemned to slavery and to be branded,
and to remain in slavery till the Court take further orders about him." Several runaway advertisements in New England explicitly referred to slaves as
"indented servants." But increasingly most African slaves served for life in
New England, and the condition became hereditary, unlike the servitude of
most English workers.[89]

But at the same time, the Puritan law codes in New England also acknowledged the humanity of African slaves in other ways that differed from
bondage in the Chesapeake, the Carolinas, and the Caribbean. Through the
seventeenth century, the laws and courts of Massachusetts (and of most Puritan colonies) recognized that slaves possessed many human rights. Slaves
could acquire property, and could also transfer it freely, and they did so
in Massachusetts. Some became landowners while remaining slaves themselves.

In the seventeenth century, African slaves in Massachusetts were allowed to
intermarry with Europeans and American Indians, and they did so. Statutes
forbidding intermarriage were enacted in the eighteenth century, but intermarriage continued. Slaves were permitted to enter into marriage covenants,
which in some towns were encouraged, and even required.

Slaves had full access to courts of law in New England. They could sue
their masters, and more than a few did so. In civil and criminal trials they had
rights of due process, and also a right to trial by jury. They could challenge individual jurors, but they did not have the right to trial by their peers, as slaves
were normally forbidden to sit on juries in New England.

Puritan laws required masters to treat slaves humanely and to respect their
rights. Ministers preached frequently on that theme. A leading example was
Cotton Mather. Like most New England clergy, Cotton Mather accepted the
existence of slavery, but severely condemned abuses of a master's power. Cen-

tral to his way of thinking was the state of a slave's soul. He urged masters to allow religious instruction, encouraged the presence of slaves at meetings, and supported prayer meetings conducted by slaves.[90]

With him were many Puritan divines. The Reverend John Ballantine wrote, "Masters of Negroes ought to be men of great humanity. They have arbitrary power, may correct them at pleasure, may separate them from their children, may send them out of the country."[91]

A prominent example was Jonathan Edwards (1703–58), the leading Puritan theologian of his generation, and also a slave owner. He had lived with slaves in his early life, bought a slave in 1731, and continued to own them until his death in 1758. Edwards studied the ethics of slavery, looked for guidance in scripture, found a passage in Job 31:13, and copied it almost word for word: "If I despise the cause of my man or maidservant when they plead with me, and when they stand before me to be judged by me, what then shall I do when I come to stand before God to be judged by him. . . . I am God's servant as they are mine, and much more inferior to God than my servant is to me." Here was another Puritan rule from scripture: judge not, lest ye be judged.[92]

Edwards went farther in his own thinking on the subject of race, as well as slavery. He wrote, "We are made of the same human race, and [God] has given us the same nature. . . . In these two things are contained the most forceable reasons against the master's abuse of his servant." Edwards believed that African slaves and New England masters were of the same race, a common belief in the seventeenth and early eighteenth centuries. In his thinking, that idea became an argument against the abuse of slaves, but not against slavery itself. Here was yet another example of the Puritan middle way, in its attachment to slavery, its intimations of humanity, and its ethical instability.[93]

SLAVE RESISTANCE AND NEW ENGLAND LAW

Wherever slavery existed, acts of extreme violence were committed by masters against slaves, and by slaves against masters. New England's laws imposed severe punishments for both. Where no statute existed, New England courts applied biblical law. When all else failed they invoked the scripture rule of an eye for an eye.

A horrific case occurred in Middletown, Connecticut. Barney, the slave of Jonathan Allyn, castrated his master's son. Barney was indicted and pleaded guilty before the Superior Court at Hartford, but the court reported that it was unable to sentence him, because Connecticut had no law explicitly against such an act.

The Superior Court referred the case to the legislature. It was unwilling to act, because Puritan colonies in general, and Connecticut in particular, strictly forbade the use of statutes that were ex post facto. The legislature instructed the court to "proceed and cause such punishment . . . according to their best skill and judgment." The court searched scripture for a rule, and found it in Exodus 21:24: "An eye for an eye, tooth for tooth, hand for hand, foot for foot." For the crime of castrating his master's son, Barney was ordered to be castrated. Samuel Peters wrote that the sentence was carried out.[94]

In 1681 an African slave named Marja was indicted for burning down a building in Roxbury. She was burned at the stake. In 1755, Phillis, slave of John Codman, poisoned her master and was burned alive. Male accomplices in both cases were hanged. The women received the severe English punishment for "petty treason," a crime not merely against a master, but against a master's authority.[95]

In general, slave revolts were less common in Massachusetts than in other colonies. This was so despite the fact that Akan-speaking slaves led many of the most violent rebellions in the Caribbean. New England's Akan slaves actively resisted their bondage, but they did so in other ways with more success.

Altogether, New England Puritans created the first system of slave law in English-speaking America, and one of the most distinctive. It was designed to give strong support to slavery, but also to respect the humanity of the enslaved. In that combination, the Puritan founders of Massachusetts created a very peculiar institution of human bondage, in their own inimitable middle way.

THE BRUTALITY OF SLAVERY IN NEW ENGLAND, AND ITS HUMAN TOLL

Historians who have studied the material condition of African slaves in early New England conclude that "a common status did not exist." Account books and court records describe the lives of slaves who were able to move toward freedom by their own efforts. But they were a very small minority. Less than 5 percent of New England slaves became free before 1760.[96]

The material condition of Africans in New England was diverse and dynamic. It began that way, and grew more so through time, unlike other large plantation systems which in some cases tended to harden into orthodoxy.

Small-unit slavery in New England came down to individual masters and slaves, in conditions that varied through the full range of possibility.

As always, slavery took a terrible human toll. New England had its full share of cruel, predatory, and tyrannical masters. Many slaves, probably most, suffered from hard and heavy labor. Some were literally worked to death. Clear evidence has emerged for a slave called Fortune, who belonged to Dr. Preserved Porter in Waterbury. Connecticut. Fortune died in 1798, and his remains were preserved by several generations of physicians in the Porter family. His skeleton was used for instruction at their "School of Anatomy" for many years.

In the late twentieth century, Dr. Sally Porter Law McGlannan donated the skeleton to the Mattatuck Museum, which authorized its examination by forensic pathologists. They found evidence of "multiple enthesopathies," and of ligaments and muscles that had been torn from bones by heavy weights and burdens. Their conclusion was that Fortune had been "worked to death when enslaved by the Porter family."

Fortune's remains were withdrawn from public display, and he was finally laid to rest in Waterbury's Riverside Cemetery in our century. In 2004, Connecticut's poet laureate Marilyn Nelson wrote a cantata called "Fortune's Bones: The Manumission Requiem." Fortune's remains in Connecticut told yet another story about the brutality of human bondage, much as did forensic studies in New York City's African Burial Ground. Empirical evidence of permanent physical damage caused by extreme cruelty and relentless exploitation of slave labor has turned up in every early American region.[97]

SPATIAL DISTRIBUTION OF NEW ENGLAND SLAVES: CLUSTER PATTERNS

At the start of the eighteenth century, African Americans were about one percent of New England's population, rising to 2.4 percent (about sixteen thousand), by 1774–75. In this region, as elsewhere in North America, Africans were not distributed evenly across the countryside. We find strong patterns of clustering in many forms. The largest clusters formed in seaport towns. By 1775, Afro–New Englanders were 5 percent of the population in Portsmouth, 9 percent in New London, 10 percent in Boston, and 20 percent in Newport. In 1752, the largest cluster was in Boston, with 1,514 Afro-Americans in that small town of about fifteen thousand souls.[98] Clusters of another kind appeared in Rhode Island's Narragansett country, with its large plantations, good soil, a mild climate by New England norms, and lower mortality for people of African descent. An example was rural Charlestown, Rhode Island, where Afro-Americans were 30 percent of the population.

Yet another sort of clustering was the town of Dartmouth in southeastern Massachusetts. It had at one time the largest Quaker population in the state, and a strong maritime economy with job opportunities for slaves and free Blacks. These small clusters were large enough to sustain community and comity among some Africans in New England.[99]

In New England generally, historian Joanne Melish found in her research that "many male slaves" had a "relatively free and independent work life," while remaining in bondage. Joshua Hempstead had a slave named Adam who managed a farm of two hundred acres in Stonington, Connecticut, while his master lived in New London, ten miles away.[100] Newport Greene was sent to sea, with instructions to find his own employment and earn money for his master, Dr. Amos Throop of Providence in Rhode Island, a common pattern.[101]

Yet another example was Venture Smith, a legendary character of extraordinary physical strength and high moral courage whom we have already met. He has been called an African Paul Bunyan in New England's folk history. As a slave he was able to work both for his master and himself, acquired his own land, and operated it as a farm. Later he made enough money to buy his freedom.[102]

All of this evidence is important to an understanding of slavery in New England. Human bondage was a brutal business everywhere. But the human spirit of individual slaves survived and even flourished, especially when they were able to form families, and where clusters of Africans came together.

In actual practice, New England slaves were allowed more freedom of movement than slaves elsewhere. Patterns varied, with specific restraints in some towns, and general restrictions on "nightwalking" after the nine o'clock curfew, which applied to everyone in Massachusetts, but with different penalties.

Masters permitted slaves to own firearms outright, and in the seventeenth century slaves served in the "train bands," which were New England's town militia. Restrictions of various kinds were later imposed, but slaves continued to serve with their masters in New England's many military campaigns, and they frequently carried arms.

SURVIVAL OF AFRICAN CUSTOMS IN NEW ENGLAND

In 1777, German Baroness von Riedesel was traveling through western New England with prisoners taken at the Battle of Saratoga. She was surprised to observe "many families of free blacks who occupy good houses, and have means, and live entirely in the style of the other inhabitants."[103]

The buildings looked that way from the outside. Some survive today, and still have that appearance. But inside, something else was evident. Interesting things happened in these homes when African and English cultures met and mixed.[104]

In Connecticut's Fairfield County, much recent research has been done on an old house that still stands in Newtown. It was the home of a former African slave named Cato, who was freed by his mistress sometime between 1776 and 1783. He bought a half-acre lot in 1784 and built a house which is still occupied and lovingly preserved by the owners, who call it Cato's House.

It combines elements of two building traditions. The post-and-beam construction follows English and Anglo-American customs in many ways. But its dimensions and the placement of posts are more African. The plan is square, rather than the conventional rectangular proportions of most early Anglo-American buildings.

Interesting details survive in the stone-built basement. One stone is marked with a large chiseled X at eye level, and the upper left line is twice the length of others. Another chisel line was carved perpendicular to that line, with a circle. These elements were called spirit marks and appear on African artifacts. Some historians believe them to be African images of the cosmos, and of cosmic harmony among its elements.

At the same time that African traditions were preserved by the makers of these marks, other English elements were adopted in a creative Afro-Anglo culture among African slaves in New England. An example was another feature of Cato's House, found in a crawl space under a kitchen lean-to. A shoe was carefully concealed beneath the kitchen floor, in a tight place that is difficult to access. The shoe was a crude and battered male brogan of a sort often worn by New England slaves. On its top side were African spirit marks similar to those on the basement stones. But the placement of the hidden shoe itself was an old English folk custom that survived from the thirteenth to the twentieth centuries. Here again, as so often in early America, African and English elements were combined.[105]

Many New England slaves kept these and other African customs. Material evidence has turned up in the form of carved stone gods and artifacts of many kinds—pottery, textiles, pipes, walking sticks, necklaces, bracelets, and more, often in combination with British, European, and American Indian elements. African customs also appeared in forms of worship, combined with Christian marks and symbols. Titus Kent, a slave of Reverend Ebenezer Gay of Suffield, Connecticut, was a go-to-meeting Christian. At the same time it was said that "He always carried a frog's foot in his pocket to keep off the colic demon, for he thought there was a special imp for each disease. Around his neck he carried four rattle-snake's buttons suspended as to hang over his lungs." [106]

THE PERSISTENCE OF AFRICAN SPIRIT LIFE OF NEW ENGLAND SLAVES: CASEY'S SOUL VISITS HOME

In the town of Concord, Casey, born in Africa, was captured by raiders when he was twenty, taken from his wife and child, and held as a slave in Concord, Massachusetts. Thoreau and his Transcendentalist friends were deeply interested in Casey, and knew him well. They remembered that he "used to say he went home to Africa in the night and came back in the morning."

Thoreau thought he was talking about a recurrent dream. But ethnographer William Piersen observes that "for Casey these night visits were more than dreams. Many West Africans believed the soul wandered from the body at night and returned to the slumberer in the morning. For them, Casey's dreams were truly 'soul visits' home." [107]

AFRICAN SPIRITUAL BELIEFS AND PRAYER MEETINGS IN NEW ENGLAND

Throughout New England, slaves were often required to attend church, and frequently did so, sitting apart in special seats. Sometimes they were encouraged to join in Christian prayer meetings. One such group was meeting regularly in Boston as early as 1693. It was called a "Society of Negroes," and gathered on Sabbath evenings with much encouragement from Cotton Mather and other ministers. [108]

Part of the religious life in this region was the spiritual stirrings that swept through New England from the first "Awakenings" that John Cotton inspired in 1633. They continued in the spiritual movements led by Solomon Stoddard in the late seventeenth century, in the Great Awakenings of Jonathan Edwards and James Davenport in the early eighteenth, the Second Great Awakenings in the new republic, and systemic revivalism and other movements in the nineteenth and twentieth centuries. All these movements reached African slaves, and they in turn had an impact on new forms of expressive worship. African women were much involved. At Newport in 1765, Susanna Anthony and Sarah Osborn led prayer meetings for large numbers of slaves, as many as three hundred in 1766, five hundred in 1767.[109]

At the same time, African slaves were preaching and leading prayer meetings in New England. One leader (among many) was John Quamino, who had been born in Anomabu about 1754 or 1755. His father, an African man of wealth, sent him to Rhode Island "for learning," in the care of Captain David Lindsay, who treacherously sold him as a slave to Captain Benjamin Church.[110]

In Newport, John Quamino attended Sarah Osborn's prayer meetings, and she helped him learn to read and write English in the 1760s. In 1773, he won a lottery prize, and used it to buy his freedom. He married a woman called Duchess, a prominent Newport slave who became a major figure in her own right.[111]

John Quamino led prayer meetings and preached to slaves in his native Fante and English, with much encouragement from Ezra Stiles and Samuel Hopkins, two eminent clergymen who became his mentors. With the help of Stiles, Quamino also became a full member of Newport's Congregational Church. Quamino was sent to study at Princeton, in preparation for a missionary career in Africa. Before he could take up his African mission, he died at sea in 1779.[112]

The Afro-English missionary Philip Quaque knew John Quamino. While living in New England, Quamino managed to maintain family ties in Anomabu, a rare occurrence in eighteenth-century America, but not unique. Other Africans in New England were able to do the same thing. One of them was Bristol Yamma, an Asante freedman in Rhode Island who also was sent by Samuel Hopkins to Princeton in preparation for a missionary career. The saga of these men brings out a little known part of African slavery in New England.[113]

ASSOCIATION AMONG NEW ENGLAND SLAVES

African slaves in New England, living in the households of their masters, rapidly developed a distinctive pattern of association that set them apart from slaves in other cultural regions. In brief, the associational lives of Afro-Americans were individually rich but collectively impoverished.

Many sources tell us that African slaves rapidly became part of the families that owned them—not equal by any means, but closely integrated in the do-mestic lives of their owners. On weekdays, slaves worked alongside their mas-ters and mistresses. Morning, noon, and night they ate the same food, often at the same table. They were catechized with the children of the household, an old New England custom by which children and servants were taught together.

At the same time, collective association with other Afro-Americans happened less frequently than in other regions, and on a smaller scale. This was partly the inexorable result of demographic patterns, and partly also the result of policy. In most early New England colonies the authorities actively discouraged gath-erings of African slaves. But they never succeeded in stopping them altogether. Scattered evidence survives of secret meetings of slaves, often purely for pleasure. In Deerfield, a slave named Cato, while supposedly riding his master's horse to a drinking pond, met secretly with other slaves, also mounted on their owners' animals. They organized their own impromptu races. Cato was caught, and in-sisted that the horse had run away with him to the race grounds.[114]

New England slaves also met more openly together on militia training days, and holidays. Many observers also remarked on the enthusiasm with which they observed Guy Fawkes Day. They were also in trouble for making merry on the Puritan Sabbath. At every opportunity, slaves seized opportu-nities to come together, drink a little, tell stories, and play African gambling games with sea shells.[115]

In 1817, a Black ship's steward named William Read was confined on board the ship *Canton Packet* in Boston Harbor, on a day when other Afro-Americans gathered in town. Young Read was so angry that he ignited two barrels of gunpowder and blew the stern off the ship.[116]

In most systems of slavery, the master class sought to maintain its hege-mony by the discipline of time. In consequence, slaves in many places con-tested that practice, and found ways to pry open possibilities for control of their lives.

This happened everywhere slavery existed, but it had a special edge in New England. Puritans and Quakers gave particular attention to the discipline of time, and addressed that problem in fundamental ways that could be rec-onciled with African ethics. Puritan masters often allowed limited temporal liberties. Slaves responded by improvising their own temporal events and ex-tending their boundaries.

A remarkable example occurred in the towns around Lynn, Massachusetts, in the mid-eighteenth century. In Lynn itself, Thomas Mansfield owned a fa-mous slave called King Pompey, who was said to have been a prince among his African people. Late in his advancing years, Pompey was given his freedom, and he moved into a wooded tract on the east side of the Saugus River.

Every year, according to several accounts, "he was host, guest of honor, and master of ceremonies" for slaves in "all the neighboring towns" to celebrate their African origins. Masters gave their slaves the day off, and sometimes added spending money. On May 27, 1741, Benjamin Lynde did that for two of his slaves, Scipio and William. We know of it from a note in the master's diary: "Scip 5s and Wm 2s 6d for a negro's hallowday."[117]

Something similar happened in Rhode Island, where the Reverend James MacSparran was a master we know well from his journals, letter books, and abstracts. MacSparran owned a prominent slave named Stepney, whom he valued and respected. Stepney became a moral leader of African Americans through much of Rhode Island and New England.

The reach of his reputation appeared after his sudden death on May 2, 1745. Stepney drowned when his boat sank in a small pond. The news spread swiftly and a funeral followed two days later. Many slaves and some free people of color in Rhode Island were able to attend. They came in large numbers from North and South Kingston, and other towns across the state. Several children of slaves born soon after the accident were named Stepney. James MacSparran himself preached a funeral sermon at King's Chapel in Boston, before what was described as "a great assembly of negroes," with a eulogy of Stepney as his "first, best, and most principal servant." Many New England slaves traveled long distances on short notice, with permission of their masters, to gather together in mourning. These events demonstrated the extent to which New England slaves were able to gain some control over their time and movements within that cultural frame.[118]

AFRICAN SLAVES AND NEW ENGLAND HOLIDAYS

By the mid-eighteenth century, these gatherings of slaves became regular events in New England. Something similar happened in many slave systems throughout the New World, but they took different forms from one region to another. In Catholic colonies, African slaves were able to stop work and celebrate holy days at Easter and Christmas, and a great secular holiday before the beginning of Lent. Some French Catholic colonies, like France itself, had more saints than days in the year, not counting Sundays. Some of these many saint's days created opportunities for slaves to interrupt the temporal tyranny of bondage.

Puritan New England posed a special challenge that way. Most Christian holidays, even joyous festivals of Easter and Christmas, were condemned as popish abominations, especially in Massachusetts Bay. Exceptions were towns in parts of southern Rhode Island, and eastern and western Connecticut, where Anglicans settled in larger numbers. Christmas and Easter were celebrated there by masters and slaves in traditional Christian ways, but not in the Puritan heartland of Massachusetts.

In much of Puritan New England, worldly activities were also strictly forbidden on the Sabbath. Even cooking was prohibited on the extended Puritan Sabbath which ran from sundown Saturday to sunup Monday—hence Boston's cold baked beans. Most travel was forbidden for masters, mistresses, and slaves alike, and Sabbath breaking was punished severely.

But what the Puritans prohibited in one way they permitted in another. New England customs presented other opportunities for time off from hard labor, and African slaves were quick to seize them. In Puritan towns, Thursday was Lecture Day. It was the time when wedding banns were announced, evildoers were punished, and special thanksgiving feasts and fasts were called. All that brought a break in the labor of bondage when slaves had some time of their own.

Similar days of freedom in New England were linked to annual events such as Militia Training Days, when each town's "train band" mustered for drill on "training fields" that still bear that name. Much of the town took the day off and came to watch. A happy time was had on Training Days by men and women, elders and children, servants and especially by slaves.[119]

NEW ENGLAND'S "NEGRO ELECTION DAYS": THE GROWTH OF AN ANNUAL AFRO-PURITAN FESTIVAL

Before the end of the seventeenth century, the Puritans replaced the old Christian holy days with a new set of unique regional holidays—Thanksgiving Days and Training Days, as just mentioned, and most of all, Election Days.

On Election Days, Puritan colonies installed their governors, deputy governors, and assistants. By the mid-eighteenth century, African slaves in New England created their own version of that event, with the encouragement of their masters. After a colony celebrated its election, African slaves and freedmen held their own "Negro Election Day," as it was called, to select officers called "Negro governors" in corporate Connecticut and Rhode Island, and "Negro kings" in the royal colonies of Massachusetts and New Hampshire. It was an annual custom, observed for more than a century from the mid-eighteenth to the mid-nineteenth century. Each New England colony and state chose its own dates, usually in May or June, and kept them every year.[120]

Celebrations continued for many days around the event—often for a week or more. The day itself began with a beating of drums. The slaves dressed elaborately for the occasion in fantastic colorful costumes. Often they were allowed to borrow the finery of their masters and mistresses. At the Negro Election Day in Derby, Connecticut, the governor-elect was described as "caparisoned with gay feathers, flowers and ribbons of red, white, and blue."

Negro Election Days commonly began with a procession in which the assembled crowd marched behind the incumbent Negro governor to the polling place, usually beneath a great tree in an open field. There were speeches, and then the vote was taken, sometimes by ballot, sometimes by outcry or a standing count.

"An Election Parade of a Negro Governor"

The results were followed by an inaugural military parade. Some slaves were allowed to carry their masters' firearms and edged weapons on Election Days, and to make a *feu de joie* at its climax. Masters also allowed their slaves to use horses. In southern Rhode Island, slaves were "mounted on the best Narragansett pacers, sometimes with their master's swords, with their ladies on pillions."

Then came games that included old British folk sports, African stick fighting, and African wrestling. Dancing followed with music that combined elements of European, Amerindian, and African traditions.

And there was often a feast. Slaves would arrive to find chairs and tables arranged and decorated with garlands and spring flowers. Food was abundant, but drinking was strictly limited.[121]

Music was part of the festivities, and much of what Congregational clergyman William Bentley called "the most fatiguing dances."

Negro Election Days were widely held, not only in provincial capitals, but also in shire towns (county seats), half-shire towns (where courts also met), major seaports, centers of inland commerce, and other communities.[122]

In some towns, special sites were reserved for the occasion. "Negroes in Boston were allowed to have unmolested use of the Boston Common, with an equality of rights and privileges with the white people" on Negro Election Days. Salem's site was "the Plain." In Hartford they gathered on "the Neck, near North Burial Ground."[123]

These Negro Election Days sometimes went on for several days. William Pynchon's slave took three days off for "the Negro Election." In Lynn, Massachusetts, they continued through four days. Attitudes varied among New England owners, but as time passed some of them allowed their slaves to take off as much as a week's work or more. In Warwick, Rhode Island, a frustrated master noted "8 days lost at negro election."

Similar customs also developed on holidays in colonies throughout the West Indies, and North and South America. They often combined elements of a traditional Roman Saturnalia, when roles of masters and servants reversed for a day. There were many other parallels, but New England Election Days were unique in their totality. This was the only American region where some English colonists elected their governors before the Revolution. In New England, celebrations marked not the election itself but the report of its result—a political annunciation day.[124]

For African slaves and freedmen in New England, these events also had an important function. African slaves and freedmen elected one of their own men, as the ceremonial head of a celebration, and as an active leader of their community for an annual term. A formal process of nomination was followed by a contested election in which all African men could participate. They did so by voting out loud (viva voce), which had long been customary in New England elections. Similar events occurred in Massachusetts, New Hampshire, Connecticut, and Rhode Island.

In Connecticut alone, twenty-eight elected Negro governors have been identified, and many more served in that office. Of that number, about a third were described as "Africans of rank and their descendants," or by a similar phrase. Some were slaves who were thought to have descended from families of high rank in Africa, or were recognized as having African titles. Among them were King Pompey in Lynn, Massachusetts; Prince Robinson in South Kingston, Rhode Island; Tobias Pero and his son Eben Tobias in Derby, Connecticut; and the family lineage of Jubal Weston, Nelson Weston, and Wilson Weston in Seymour, Connecticut. Those who had African names were nearly all speakers of Akan languages, either Fante or Asante.[125]

These governors (or kings as they were sometimes called in royal colonies) were often described as physically big men. An example was Quash Freeman in Derby, Connecticut, described as "a giant six-footer," and "a man of Herculean strength." It was said that "he could take a bull by the horns and by the nose and at once prostrate him on the ground. No one ever dared to molest or tried to make him afraid, and when he was approaching from a distance he awakened the sense of a coming thunder cloud." Another example was Eben Tobias, who was remembered as "of the very finest physical mold, being over six feet tall and admirably proportioned."

Others were described as outstanding in character. It was said of Roswell Freeman that no one had "a higher standard of right, better principles, kinder instincts as a friend and neighbor, was more respected in his position, or more worthy of the good esteem of his contemporaries."[126]

Occasionally an elected Negro governor proved to be unfit for service in various ways: a pathological liar or deeply dishonest; an outright thief and corrupt; a narcissist, entirely absorbed in self; a boor without manners or respect for others; a demagogue who turned people against one another; a cruel sadist who found pleasure in inflicting pain on others. When that happened, New England slaves themselves sometimes took action. Failed Negro governors were removed from office by a process similar to impeachment. The memory of their infamy was preserved in oral culture as an emblem of disgrace and an example to others.

New England's Negro governors were given real power and responsibility through their year in office. They were expected to settle disputes among slaves, to punish crimes against other slaves, and to try cases of theft, assault, and marital infidelity. Governors organized court sessions, conducted trials, and authorized punishments such as fines, whippings, or the "bastinado, with a 'cobbing board,'" which was administered by an elected slave sheriff or constable.[127]

African New Englanders themselves controlled these events. They did so mostly as slaves before 1780, and later as freedman into the 1850s. Something quite extraordinary was happening here. New England masters were sharing a measure of legitimate power and authority with African slaves, in a way that went beyond ceremonial practices in other parts of the New World.

Many other colonial cultures included festivals and holidays in which slaves were chosen to lead processions or preside over events. New England's Negro governors were different. Many of them actually governed. They were chosen in Negro elections that gave power to slaves and granted a measure of control over the conditions of their life in slavery. This power-sharing also served the interest of New England masters in ways that were alien to systems of more arbitrary bondage.

The inaugural ceremonies for Negro governors included African rituals of purification, with roles for women, as in Odwira rituals in West Africa, which were symbolic of the life-force in the community. Historians have found evidence of other African customs in these New England events.[128]

GENDER AND RANK AMONG AFRICAN WOMEN IN NEW ENGLAND: QUAMINO OF NEWPORT

African women in New England also achieved less formal positions of substantive rank, power, and wealth. In that process, they also found ways to make this exceptionally open and permeable system of slavery yet more open and free. Often they did it by individual effort. Some became market women, as in many African cultures and most American regions. Others succeeded in excelling at different economic roles.

An example was Quamino, a Coromantee woman who worked as a kitchen slave for several families in southern New England. She gained a reputation as the "most celebrated cake baker in Rhode Island" and built a catering business in Newport. She and her husband were able to buy their freedom, acquired their own house, and every year they put on a dinner party for the three families who had owned Quamino.

She was a woman of presence and dignity, and was said to be the daughter of an African prince. The people of Rhode Island called Quamino the "Duchess of Newport"; Duchess also became a term of address. It was a testament to her manner, grace, and bearing, and described the respect that was shown to her by people of every condition in the town.[129]

Other slave women achieved high standing in surprising ways. In the town of Providence, Rhode Island, Mary Bernoon was a slave who flourished as an eighteenth-century smuggler—an honorable profession in old New England, if done in an appropriately civic spirit. She and her husband, Emanuel Bernoon, gained their freedom in the 1730s. In 1736, they opened a catering business, and followed it with a highly successful oyster house. By her husband's death in 1769, the value of their estate was reckoned at 2,000 Spanish silver dollars.[130]

Slave women were also honored in other roles. Among them was Chloe Spear, born a slave in Africa about 1750, and brought to Boston. Even after many years in America she spoke what some heard as "broken English," and others as an African power of spiritual expression. It was written that "white New Englanders recalled Chloe Spear precisely for her own inventive skill in conveying her ideas in metaphors that originated in her own mind."[131]

Chloe remembered the agony of her early years in Boston, when she felt so alone and heartsick that she "wished for death." In the sky over Boston, she would watch the waning of a winter moon, the coming of darkness, and then the first sliver of new moon. She dreamed of the African idea that as "a young moon would appear after the old one was gone away," so also the first child born after the death of another would be the same spirit. And she would be carried away, and born again in her distant home.[132]

Others listened and learned from her. They marveled at her "gift of invention," her "power of expression," and her ability to convey spiritual ideas in metaphors that originated in her own mind. Chloe Spear joined African and biblical and New England images and ideas in a new genre of spiritual expression. Its creativity flowed from the fusion of languages and cultures, African and European, in early New England.[133]

Stories multiplied about other women like Chloe Spear. They were African slaves who became seers, and spoke to the condition of many people, women for the most part, and many others. They were everywhere in America, but something special happened in New England, where children of the Puritans had been taught to listen and learn with an intensity of mind and spirit that was unique to this region. The founders of this very special culture had been inspired by English Puritans and independents such as Oliver Cromwell, who was one of them in many ways, and almost joined them in America. He also shared with them his passionate conviction that "a seeker was the next best to a finder." [134]

Many generations of Puritan preachers had taught the people of New England to be seekers in that spirit. They sought what Calvinists called signs, or clues to divine intentions wherever the evidence appeared in the world. African seers such as Chloe Spear spoke to the condition of these Puritan seekers. She added to spiritual seeking—another dimension of spiritual finding. [135]

AFRICAN MEN AS SPIRITUAL STRIVERS

John Jack had been born in Africa around the year 1713, and bred in old New England. He lived in Concord, Massachusetts, and learned a trade as a skilled shoemaker, but remained in bondage most of his life. In 1754, he appeared in Concord's probate records, not as a man but human livestock, appraised in his owner's estate as if he were an animal. But this did not discourage him. John Jack was a striver. In 1761, he was able to buy his freedom at about the age of forty-eight, acquired eight acres of arable field and meadowland, with a home of his own. He was known to drink more than a little too much, but he earned the esteem of his fellow townsmen in Concord.

Even with his drinking problem, there was something special about the character of John Jack. New Englanders were quick to notice and respond. On his passing in 1773, his friend, lawyer, executor, and town Tory Daniel Bliss celebrated his character in a poem that survives today because it was carved into his Concord tombstone. It preserved the memory of a man who was a "slave to vice" and yet became a free man of virtue. Some people in Concord still remember him that way.

> God wills us free, man wills us slaves
> I will as God wills, God's will be done
> Here lies the body of JOHN JACK
> A native of Africa who died
> March 1773 aged about 60 years
> Tho' born in a land of slavery,
> He was born free
> Tho' he lived in a land of liberty,
> He lived a slave.

Till by honest, tho' stolen labors toil
He acquired the source of slavery
Which gave him his freedom
Though not long before
Death the grand tyrant
Gave him his final emancipation
And set him on a footing with kings
Tho' a slave of vice
He practiced those virtues
Without which kings are but slaves.[136]

GROWING PATTERNS OF RESISTANCE
BY NEW ENGLAND SLAVES

In every system of human bondage, resistance was nearly universal, and took many forms. Men and women, young and old, house slaves and field slaves, all studied their opportunities and made the most of them.

In what is now the United States, important differences developed from one region to another, both in patterns of resistance and also in responses from the master class. African cultures also made a difference, and so did regional conditions of American bondage. In England's Caribbean colonies Akan-speaking Coromantee slaves from Fante and Asante cultures of what is now western Ghana won a reputation for organizing large armed rebellions, and also for escaping from bondage, and founding maroon communities that preserved their independence for many generations. These Coromantee leaders were held in high respect by disciplined British Regulars who were sent against them. Something similar happened in West Africa, where the British Army fought many "Ashantee wars," and suffered major defeats.[137]

Altogether, Herbert Aptheker's massive research found evidence by his own count of "approximately 250 revolts and conspiracies" by slaves in what is now the United States. Later inquiries have found many more. But there was one regional exception. By Atheker's definition of a slave revolt as an actual armed rising of at least ten slaves with freedom as their object, he found no slave revolts in the New England colonies that became six American states, the only region in the United States where that was the case. It was not a function of numbers of slaves. Many slave revolts occurred in New York and New Jersey where numbers were not very different from New England.[138]

In New England, slaves actively resisted their bondage, but they chose other means. A few attempted to murder their master or mistress. In 1681, Maria the slave of Joshua Lamb in Roxbury, Massachusetts, was found guilty of setting fire to her master's house. She was burned alive. That same year, Jack, a slave of Samuel Woolcot or Wolcott, attempted to set fire to a home in Northampton. Jack was hanged and his body was "burned to ashes" much as Maria had died—"a burning for a burning," Cotton Mather later observed.[139]

In 1755, John Codman of Charlestown in Massachusetts was murdered by two of his slaves, Mark and Phillis. Mark had a family of his own across the river in Boston. He asked his master for more time to earn money for their support and was refused. Phillis had formed a relationship with a man named Quacko in Boston. They wanted to live together, and she offered to pay her master 40 pounds for permission to do so. John Codman refused yet again. Mark and Phillis joined together and killed him.

Both confessed to his murder, and testified that their goal was not freedom, but more autonomy within slavery. They had hoped to replace a hard master with one who was more accommodating. Mark acquired a deadly poison from the slave of a Boston apothecary, and Phillis served it to her master with his morning porridge. In 1755, she was burned alive for murder. Mark was hanged as her accomplice, and his body was ordered to be displayed in an iron cage on a main road to Charlestown. His remains were still there twenty years later, when Paul Revere passed them on his midnight ride in 1775 and mentioned it as a familiar landmark in his accounts. But these homicides by slaves were rare in New England.[140]

SLAVES WHO FREED THEMSELVES
IN EARLY NEW ENGLAND

More New England slaves resisted their bondage in other ways. The courts were open to them, and they frequently sought freedom by lawful means. They also seized economic opportunities that came their way. Altogether, between 5 and 10 percent of African slaves in Massachusetts gained their freedom before 1775, in many cases by their own efforts.

An early example was Peter Swinck, the first African settler in the western town of Springfield, Massachusetts. His Dutch name suggests that he ran away from New Netherland to New England as early as 1650—a perilous trip. New Englanders took him in, to the fury of former Dutch masters. Peter Swinck was protected and welcomed by the people of Springfield, and became a servant for a fixed term of John Pynchon, the founder and leader of the town. Swinck received land on condition that he work there "till his time expired." The town gave him a seat in the meetinghouse, and sometime before 1660 he took a wife named Mariah. They survived the destruction of King Philip's War in 1675, and helped to rebuild their ruined town. By 1685, Peter Swinck was a freeholder with fifty-five acres of land, including a two-acre house lot and three tracts of arable farmland. Their children were given Old Testament names much favored in Puritan New England: Abraham, Susannah, and Miriam.[141]

Another Springfield story was the saga of Roco, a slave who was brought into the town by John Pynchon, and put to work making turpentine and tar. He got into trouble with a woman named Margaret Riley, probably an Irish servant. Roco admitted that "he had upon Riley's tempting him the carnal knowledge of her body." The result was not the hysteria and brutal violence that often happened in other places and later periods. Roco received a fair hearing, pleaded guilty, and got the usual Puritan punishment for fornication, which was much the same for racially mixed couples as for others. Roco was offered a choice of fifteen lashes or a fine of three pounds.

He took the lashes and saved his hard-won capital. In the years from 1685 to 1695 Roco rapidly improved his material condition. He was able to work both for his master and for himself in making naval stores. Another laborer testified in 1693 that the "burning of Pine Trees" was "such sore worke he would not doe that for 3 shillings a day." Roco kept at it. He acquired sixty acres, leased a sawmill, and ran it while still a slave, with free men working for him. He married another Pynchon slave named Sue, and in 1695 bought the freedom of himself and his wife for "Twenty-Five barrels of good cleane pure Turpentine" and "Twenty one barrels of Good merchantable Tarr." The purchase price required huge and heavy labor. The Pynchons drove a hard bargain, but kept their word. Roco and Sue both gained their freedom.[142]

THE SELF-EMANCIPATION OF JENNY SLEW, SPINSTER OF IPSWICH, AND THE AWAKENING OF JOHN ADAMS, 1765

A large number of slave women in New England played prominent roles as strivers for their own liberty. Among them was Jenny Slew of Ipswich, Massachusetts. In 1765, she went to court, and presented herself in the eyes of the law as "Jenny Slew, Spinster." She filed an action against her master, "John Whipple, Junior, of said Ipswich, gentleman." She accused her owner of "unlawfully taking her with force and arms," and "holding her captive for three years against her will," and committing "other injuries against the peace and to her person." She demanded her freedom, with civil damages of twenty-five pounds plus costs.

In court John Whipple made a joke of Jenny Slew. He argued that there was "no such person in nature as Jenny Slew of Ipswich, aforesaid, Spinster." One might imagine Whipple's friends laughing in the courtroom as a gentleman of Ipswich made a mockery of Jenny Slew as a spinster and a slave. After several delays, a conservative jury found for Whipple. The judge ordered that Jenny Slew should be "remanded back into slavery," and required to pay costs.

But Slew was just getting started. In 1766, she engaged Benjamin Kent, one of the Bay Colony's leading barristers, who later became attorney general of Massachusetts. He carried her case on appeal to the Massachusetts Superior Court, at a session in Salem. It ordered a new trial before a jury of Salem people, who had small respect for John Whipple of Ipswich, and were not amused by his cruel attempts at humor. The Salem jury brought in a verdict for Jenny Slew, and the high court ordered her to be set free. It also required her former master to pay damages of 9 pounds, and costs of 4 pounds.

Sitting in the courtroom and paying close attention was another rising barrister, John Adams. The case was a revelation to him, and he made a special record of it in his diary. Adams wrote that he "heard the Tryall of an Action for Trespass brought by a Molatto Woman, for Damages, for restraining her of her Liberty." He added, "This is called suing for Liberty; the first action that I ever knew, of the sort, tho' there have been many."

This important trial in Salem preceded other cases in London (1772), and its judgment was more sweeping. It also quickened the conscience of John Adams. Eight years later, he would be in a unique position to do something fundamental about slavery in Massachusetts.[143]

AFRICAN FREEDOM PETITIONS, 1773–74

As the imperial quarrel grew into a conflict between British leaders and New England colonists, African slaves joined in. They began to demand their own rights of liberty and freedom. In 1773, as the imperial conflict approached the breaking point, a group came together in Massachusetts and described themselves as "many slaves living in the Town of Boston, and other Towns in the Province." They sent petitions to Lieutenant Governor Thomas Hutchinson, the Council, and the General Court of Massachusetts. They claimed to speak for all slaves, protested against the condition of their bondage, and demanded full rights of liberty and freedom. This was not a single act, but a sustained campaign that went on for many months, with repeated petitions, pamphlets, broadsides, and articles in newspapers.[144]

In May 25, 1774, another "Grate Number of Blackes of the Province," sent another petition to Royal Governor Thomas Gage. They wrote that "we have in common with all other men a naturel right to our freedoms," and demanded "that we may obtain our natural right, our freedoms, and our children be set at liberty at the yeare of twenty-one." General Gage, himself with large slaveholdings in the West Indies, appears to have made no reply, at least none that we have found.

But these slave petitions reached other people. They inspired Abigail Adams to think about them—and then to think again. On September 22, 1774, she sent an account of the petition campaign to husband John, who was at the Continental Congress in Philadelphia. Abigail's first thought had a hostile edge. She called it "a conspiracy of the negroes." But then she thought again, and wrote to her husband, "I wish most sincerely there was not a slave in the province; it always appeared the most iniquitous scheme to me to fight ourselves for what we are daily robbing and plundering from those who have as good a right to freedom as we have. You know my mind upon this Subject."[145]

SLAVES IN MILITARY SERVICE DURING THE REVOLUTIONARY WAR

In 1775, more than 80 percent of Africans in Massachusetts were slaves, and probably close to 95 percent throughout British colonies in North America. When the Revolution began, and fighting spread through the thirteen colonies, slaves had hard choices to make. They went different ways, mainly by region, but always seeking their freedom.

In southern states from Maryland to Georgia, many slaves left their American Whig masters, and sought freedom by joining the British side. When British armies marched through the Carolinas and Virginia, they were followed by large numbers of fugitive slaves, who left their owners in scenes similar to what would happen with Union armies in the South during the Civil War.

In the middle states from New York to Pennsylvania, slaves went three ways. Some supported the American cause, and others turned to the British. More than a few did something else. They followed men such as the legendary Colonel Tye, an escaped New Jersey slave who organized a third force of African slaves and British servants, and led them in a struggle for their own cause.

Yet another pattern appeared in New England. In the old Puritan colonies, a large majority of African slaves supported the American Revolution. Many took up arms to fight for American independence and for their own.

In all of these ways, slaves in every region made choices which they believed most likely to lead to their own emancipation. In New England, slaves studied the question with care, and made formal inquiries of Whig leaders. During the spring of 1775, "Negroes in the counties of Bristol and Worcester" petitioned the "Committees of Correspondence convened in Worcester, to assist them in obtaining their freedom." The slaves demanded a straight answer, and got what they asked. On June 14, 1775, the Massachusetts Revolutionary Convention in Worcester passed a resolution "that we abhor the enslaving of any of the human race, and particularly of the NEGROES in this country. And that whenever there shall be a door opened or opportunity present for anything to be done toward the emancipating the NEGROES, we shall use our Influence and Endeavour that such a thing may be effected. Attest. William Henshaw clerk." [146]

Even earlier, when the fighting began at Lexington and Concord on April 19, 1775, at least forty men of color from eleven Massachusetts towns, most of them slaves, joined their masters and went to war against British Regulars at Lexington and Concord. Their names appear on surviving muster lists for that day. Actual numbers were larger, and they grew. At Bunker Hill on June 17, 1775, at least 150 slaves mustered from more than fifty New England towns and fought for the American cause, which they believed to be their cause as well, and the cause of freedom for the enslaved. At Saratoga, the numbers of African Americans in New England regiments rose to four hundred on October 17, 1777. They were more than eight hundred at the Battle of Monmouth on June 28, 1778. Many others served at sea aboard New England privateers, which promised freedom and fortune, and often delivered both.[147]

Subsequent research on individual New England towns has found evidence of many more slaves who fought in the American Revolution. A meticulous project for the small town of Lincoln, Massachusetts, identified fourteen Afro-Yankee "patriots in arms," a majority of slaves in that little community. Many demanded freedom for their service, and most of them received it.[148]

When George Washington took command of the Continental Army in Massachusetts on July 3, 1775, he was a great Virginia planter, who had long been comfortable with race slavery. He was shocked to discover that New England units had enlisted many African American soldiers in their ranks. Washington took a southern slaveholder's approach to the question, and issued General Orders to all his officers that "you are not to enlist any deserter . . . stroller, negro, or vagabond, or person suspected of being an enemy to the liberty of America, nor any under eighteen." He further ordered that slaves and freedmen should be discharged from the army forthwith.[149]

New England military leaders refused outright, and Washington tried compromise. He obtained authorization from the Congress that "the free negroes who have served faithfully in the army at Cambridge may be re-enlisted therein, but no others."[150]

New Englanders refused again. Washington issued new General Orders: "As the General is informed, that Numbers of Free Negroes are desirous of enlisting, he gives leave to recruiting Officers, to entertain them." The enlistments continued. On Christmas night in 1776, when Washington crossed the Delaware, more than 60 percent of his small army were New Englanders, and their units included many former slaves, serving as free men.[151]

By 1777, the Baroness von Riedesel observed in western Massachusetts that "the negro can take the field in place of his master, and so you do not see a regiment in which there is not a large number of blacks."[152] In 1778, after the Battle of Monmouth, the adjutant general of the Continental Army made a survey of "black troops in the army," and counted 586 on active duty in fourteen Continental regiments. The leading units were New England regiments.

Later in the war, the First Rhode Island Regiment enlisted entire companies of African Americans, which were observed by New Englanders to be among the best units in the Continental Army, for discipline, stamina, and courage.

With these events, and much encouragement from his friend the Marquis de Lafayette, Washington's thinking on race and slavery changed during the war. And after the war, he corresponded with antislavery leaders in Britain and Europe, received their writings and read them. He stopped the use of whipping at Mount Vernon, ceased selling slaves on principle, and ordered that all his slaves be freed at his death. Of ten slaveholding presidents, Washington was the only one to do so. His widow, Martha, tried to carry out his wishes in some ways.

The history of George Washington in the Revolution might be studied in conjunction with the revolution in George Washington on slavery and race. Both were linked to military events in the War of Independence, to his experience with New Englanders in the army, and especially to Afro-Yankees in arms during the most difficult moments of the war. Here again, Washington increasingly linked the conduct of the War of Independence to the expanding principles of the American Revolution. Agents of that expansion were often American soldiers of African ancestry.[153]

THE SELF-EMANCIPATION OF WALTHAM'S PRIVATE FELIX CUFF, 1780

The spirit of these Afro–New England men-at-arms appeared in the career of Private Felix Cuff, of Waltham, Massachusetts. After his military service, he fought his own private war of independence, as did many others.

In the American Revolution, military service of individual New England slaves was often followed by their emancipation, commonly with the master's consent. But sometimes it happened in other ways. In the town of Waltham, Felix or Phelix Cuff was a slave who enlisted as a private in the regiment of Colonel Cyprian Howe. When his term of service ended in 1780, Private Cuff came home to Waltham. His master, Edward Gearfield, tried to reclaim him as a slave, seized his arms and "accoutrements," and even tried to take Cuff's clothing as the master's property.

Cuff would have none of it, and insisted that he was free. With "two negro friends" he retreated to a cave on a hill called Snake Rock in Waltham, and prepared to defend his freedom. Gearfield appealed for military assistance to General William Heath, who took the master's side. The army sent Lieutenant Eliphalet Hastings to make an arrest, and a fight followed. By all accounts, Hastings and his party met "a warm reception" and "came back empty handed."

All the parties—Felix Cuff, his embattled friends, his former master, and the army—carried the case to the elected selectmen of Waltham. The selectmen agreed unanimously that slaveholder Gearfield had grossly falsified the material facts of the case and had "no demand in justice on the said Phelix as a slave." Further, the selectmen reported that Felix's arms and accoutrements belonged not to the master but to the town, and that Cuff himself had bought his clothing and possessions with his own money. His former master had falsified those facts as well.

The judgment of Waltham's selectmen was supported by three leading citizens who comprised the town's military committee. The town meeting also appears to have added its support. In 1780, with strong backing from many of his fellow townsmen, Private Felix Cuff became his own master. Ten years later the first manuscript U.S. Census of 1790 reported that "Felix Cuffer" was a free man who lived in his own Waltham home, with his wife and a family of three.[154]

SLAVERY'S END IN MASSACHUSETTS: JOHN ADAMS'S CONSTITUTION OF 1780 AS A SPUR TO SELF-EMANCIPATION

As the War of Independence approached its climax, the old Puritan Commonwealth of Massachusetts became one of the first American states to put an end to slavery within its borders. It did so not by a single decisive act, but in an extended process that was rooted in its laws and customs, and in the actions of slaves themselves.

As we have seen, from the early seventeenth century slaves in Massachusetts had full access to the courts. They could sue their masters for freedom and often did so, sometimes with success. In 1780–81, these court cases suddenly began to multiply in Massachusetts. Individual slaves went to law, seeking freedom for themselves and their families.

Slavery ended in Massachusetts through a period of ten years, from 1780 to 1790. It happened in a web of individual acts and choices. The prime movers were individual slaves themselves, male and female, young and old, acting separately or in small groups.

One such case was brought by a slave called Quaco, the Akan day name for Wednesday's child. By the year 1781 he had become Quock Walker, a grown man about twenty-seven years of age. With his brother he was held in slavery by Nathaniel Jennison in Barre, Worcester County, Massachusetts.

Walker insisted that he was a free man, that he had been promised his freedom by a former master, and he demanded his rights. Jennison and several men seized him, beat him cruelly, and held him against his will. With help from friends, Quock Walker went to law, and sued Jennison for assault and battery in the Worcester County Court.

The jury delivered a verdict for Walker, found Jennison guilty of assault, and required him to pay damages of fifty pounds. The master appealed and more trials followed—six in all. Finally, in 1783, the case reached the new Supreme Judicial Court of Massachusetts, which had been created by John Adams in the Massachusetts constitution of 1780.

Chief Justice William Cushing heard Quock Walker's case, and delivered the charge to the jury. He told them that something was new in the Massachusetts law of slavery. John Adams had drafted Article I of the Massachusetts constitution with one very long sentence: "All men are born free and equal, and have certain natural, essential, and unalienable rights; among which may be reckoned the right of enjoying and defending their lives and liberties; that of acquiring, possessing, and protecting property; in fine, that of seeking and obtaining their safety and happiness."

Cushing summarized the operative words in his charge to the jury: in the Commonwealth of Massachusetts, "all men are born free and equal and that every subject is entitled to liberty, and to have it guarded by the laws as well as his life and property." On that basis, Cushing instructed the jurors that "the court are therefore fully of the opinion that perpetual servitude can no longer be tolerated in our government." [155]

The jury agreed, and Walker went free. Dubious historians have debated the importance of his case as a precedent for the abolition of slavery in Massachusetts. But the man who lost the case was clear on what had just happened. Slaveholder Nathaniel Jennison left the courtroom, took his remaining slaves to Connecticut where slavery was still in force, and sold them. Among the victims was Quock Walker's brother. [156]

THE SELF-LIBERATION OF ELIZABETH "MUMBETT" FREEMAN

In western Massachusetts, a female slave took a leading role in this process. Elizabeth "Mumbett" Freeman was born around 1742 to African parents in the Dutch town of Claverack, New York. When she was six months old, her Dutch master sold her to Colonel John Ashley of Sheffield, Massachusetts. According to a local legend she arrived in winter at "the bottom of a sleigh, covered with straw." [157]

Mumbett and other slaves in the household were much abused by Colonel Ashley's wife, Hannah. In 1781, Hannah Ashley took a hot fireplace shovel and was about to strike Mumbett's younger sister. Mumbett interceded and took the blow herself. It fell with such force that Mumbett carried the scar

Elizabeth "Mumbett" Freeman

for the rest of her life. She left the house, went to Theodore Sedgwick, a lead-ing lawyer in Stockbridge, and asked if she could "claim her liberty under the law."

He asked what could have put such an idea into her head? She explained that she had heard men around the table talking about the Massachusetts constitution, and "the Bill o' Rights said that all were born free and equal, and that, as she was not a dumb beast, she was certainly one of the nation." Mumbett added that "In all they said she never heard but that all people were born free and equal, and she thought about it, and resolved that she would try whether she did not come in among them." [158]

Sedgwick took her case to the Berkshire County Court in 1781. Mum-bett won her freedom and became a living legend in western Massachusetts. Her story was told by Harriet Martineau, by Catharine Maria Sedgwick, and many others. She went to work as a free woman in Theodore Sedgwick's household in Stockbridge, and the Sedgwicks thought of her as a member of their family. They had the curious custom of burying each other in a great circle called the Sedgwick Family Pye. Mumbett was buried with them, next to Theodore Sedgwick.

Mumbett also had another family of her own. Her great-grandson was W. E. B. Du Bois. In his writings, he remembered her with pride, as an inspiration for his stellar career in American and world history.[159]

THE CENSUS OF 1790 AND SLAVERY'S "SINGULAR" END IN MASSACHUSETTS

The first United States Census of 1790 endeavored to count slaves throughout the new republic. In Massachusetts, census takers reported that no slaves remained within its boundaries—the first and only American state without slaves in that year.

Jeremy Belknap later explained how it happened: "The following anecdote . . . has never been made public," he wrote.

> In 1790, a census was ordered by the General Government then newly established, and the Marshal of Massachusetts District had the care of making the survey. When inquired for *slaves*, most people answered none,— if anyone said he had one, the Marshal would ask whether he meant to be singular, and would tell him that no other person had given in any. The answer then was, "If none are given in, I will not be singular," and thus the list was completed without any number in the column for slaves.[160]

Robert Romer searched the evidence in Massachusetts and wrote that "if any Blacks (or Indians) were held as slaves after about 1800, the practice was not overt." His latest examples of bondage were Phillis and Sabina, slaves of James Chandler, minister in Rowley. Both were freed by 1789. A few slaves remained in bondage, and kidnappings by criminals with sales to southern states continued in the nineteenth century. But I can find no evidence of any slave who was held openly in Massachusetts after 1790. None were found by any census taker from 1800 to 1860.[161]

THE RAPID DECLINE OF SLAVERY IN NEW ENGLAND, 1774–1800

Every New England state ended slavery in its own way, but all were variations on a theme unique to this region. Some historians prefer to tell a tangled story of a protracted "gradual emancipation." But they do it mainly by centering on the texts of "gradual emancipation laws," or on the continuing process of binding out pauper children by Massachusetts towns, a practice different from slavery in that state. They do not as a rule try to count actual numbers of slaves in New England.

As late as 1774, a controlled quantitative test by historian Jackson Turner Main found that about 80 percent of African Americans in New England were slaves, perhaps more. By 1800, less than 5 percent remained slaves throughout the entire region—a sweeping revolution in status within the span of one generation. It was achieved not by gradual emancipation acts, but by the acts and choices of individual slaves and masters, on a very broad scale. And the slaves often took the initiative.[162]

We have seen the pace of transformation in Massachusetts. In the largest New England state, probably 80 percent of Blacks were slaves on the eve of the Revolution; by 1790 the first federal census identified 5,463 African Americans in the state and reported that they were all "free persons."

The District of Maine was part of Massachusetts until the Missouri Compromise in 1820. Here again, in 1790, census takers in Maine's five counties of York, Cumberland, Lincoln, Hancock, and Washington found 520 African Americans, and reported that all were free. It was the same again in every subsequent census. Probably a few may have remained in bondage, but Maine's African Americans had moved decisively beyond slavery by 1790.

New Hampshire was broadly similar to Massachusetts. Its constitution declared in 1783 that "all men are born equal and independent," with natural rights to "life and liberty." Some thought it ended slavery; others disagreed. While the debates went on, most New Hampshire slaves found ways to free themselves, many by military service. In 1773, a colonial census had reported 674 slaves in New Hampshire. By 1790, the census found 158. Their numbers fell to eight in 1800, three in 1830, and one in 1840. The state did not formally abolish slavery until 1857, but slavery in New Hampshire had effectively ended fifty years earlier, once again by the individual acts of masters and slaves.[163]

Vermont's first constitution in 1777 forbade any male to be held as a "servant, slave, or apprentice after he arrives at the age of twenty one years, nor any female after she arrives to the age of eighteen, unless they are bound by their own consent."[164] Vermonters remember this provision (which was reenacted in 1791 when Vermont joined the Union), as the first formal prohibition of slavery by any American state. So it was, but it allowed masters to keep young slaves, and permitted bondage by "consent," which happened rarely.[165] In 1790, the *Vermont Gazette* reported that the census in Bennington found twenty-one negro males and fifteen females and "to the honor of humanity, NO SLAVES."[166]

Some Vermonters continued to own slaves.[167] Ethan Allen kept several African "servants," and his daughter Lucy Allen Hitchcock brought two slaves from Alabama to Vermont as late as 1835.[168] A small illicit slave trade existed with New York and Canada, but it had been forbidden by law as early as 1786, and again in 1791. Slavery was not formally abolished until Vermont ratified the Thirteenth Amendment in 1865. But the great majority of African American slaves had lived free in Vermont since 1800.

Rhode Island and Connecticut were slower to end slavery, but the regional rule operated even there. The number of Rhode Island's slaves fell from 3,761 in 1774 to 954 in 1790, and 384 in 1800, when more than 90 percent of African Americans were free. By 1840, the federal census found five slaves in Rhode Island.

In Connecticut, the Trumbull Census in 1774 reported 6,464 Blacks, more than in any other New England colony.[169] Jackson Turner Main estimated from probate records and census data that 80 percent, 5,172, were slaves in that year.[170] Then came the Revolution. In Connecticut the proportion of African Americans in slavery fell to 2,764 (49 percent) in 1790, 16 percent by 1800, and less than one percent by 1830.[171] Rhode Island and Connecticut enacted many "gradual emancipation laws," which have dominated some of the scholarship. But slavery itself ended in another way.

RISING RACISM IN NEW ENGLAND: FREE AFRICAN AMERICANS FIGHT BACK

A universal law has often operated through much of American history. When race slavery, or other systems of racial inequality declined, racism tended to increase, and new forms of racial violence were quick to follow. It happened in the southern states after the Civil War, again in the United States after the successes of the civil rights movement in the mid-twentieth century, and also in New England after the American Revolution.

Massachusetts was a case in point. Nearly all of its slaves were free by 1790, and some of them met a rising intensity of racism in the early republic.[172]

Much of the most violent racism in that era occurred in Boston. Gangs of young hoodlums drove African Americans off the Common, and chased them through the streets. In 1797, Afro-leader Prince Hall described "the daily insults you meet with in the streets of Boston, much more on public days of recreation." Individual people of color, men and women, and even children and the elderly, were assaulted by gangs of young thugs, "twenty or thirty at a time."

Prince Hall observed that this violence was not done by most Bostonians, and "not by the men born and bred in Boston, for they are better bred, but by a mob or horde of shameless, low-lived, envious spiteful persons." This was the rage of an oppressed white underclass, themselves trapped by poverty and ignorance in the new republic, and very different from the anti-abolition "broadcloth" mobs that multiplied in the 1830s. Broadcloth was a fabric worn by men of means in that era.[173]

After the Revolution, African Americans in New England did not turn the other cheek. One of their leaders in Boston was Colonel George Middleton (1735–1815). He made a good living from his skill with horses as a hostler, coach driver, stablekeeper, breeder, and breaker of spirited mounts. His rank had been earned by military service in the Revolutionary War, by combat at Groton Heights, and service in other campaigns on the coast of New England.

Flag of Afro–New England soldiers in the Revolution

At the end of the war Middleton commanded a unit of former slaves who called themselves "The Bucks of America," and served with strong support from Whig leaders. An account set down in 1855 noted that

> at the close of the Revolutionary War, John Hancock presented the colored company, called the "Bucks of America," with an appropriate banner, bearing his initials, as a tribute to their courage and devotion throughout the struggle. The "Bucks" under the command of Colonel Middleton, were invited to a collation in a neighboring town, and *en route* were requested to halt in front of the Hancock mansion, in Beacon Street, where the Governor and his son united in the above presentation.[174]

In 1787, George Middleton built a house at 5 Pinckney Street. It still stands there today, and is said to be the oldest surviving residence on Beacon Hill.[175] After the war, he also became a leader (one of many) in Boston's African American community. Journalist Lydia Maria Child knew him and wrote a short sketch. Middleton was a man of the Enlightenment, with many talents and skills. He was known equally for his expertise as a horse breaker, and for his virtuosity with a violin. Most of all, those who knew him spoke of his extraordinary courage.

Mrs. Child remembered an occasion when the African community in Boston held their annual celebration of freedom on the anniversary of the end of the slave trade. She watched as they were attacked by "hundreds" of young white hoodlums, and driven off the Common. As the mob crossed the crest of Beacon Hill, they suddenly met Colonel Middleton, who came out of his house with a loaded musket. He presented it at the mob, "and in a loud voice shrieked death to the first white who should approach." He stood bravely against this howling mob of white rioters, while "clubs and brickbats were flying in all directions." Other African Americans were quick to join Colonel Middleton. Together they faced down the mob and dispersed it.[176]

But the majority rallied to urban reformers, mostly conservative Federalist leaders such as Josiah Quincy Jr. and John Phillips, who had good relations with African American Bostonians. In 1822, Boston changed from a town meeting system to a city government with health regulations, professional firemen, and a police force that slowly began to enforce order. But the riots grew worse during the 1830s in Boston and many American cities. Race violence continued, but the trend was toward urban order.

Another danger in the nineteenth century was the rise of Irish militia companies who sometimes attacked African Americans in New England. The result was the organization of freedmen's self-protection societies. An example was Springfield, where freedmen formed their own militia company by 1820. In 1850, one African American group called the United States League of Gileadites founded self-protection societies in Springfield and other towns, to keep racist mobs and slave catchers at bay. A sympathetic observer, William Wells Brown, in 1854 described "ten or fifteen" Blacks in Springfield, "all armed to the teeth," who opposed the Irish militia and were accepted by Congregational neighbors.[177]

FIGHTING CRIMINAL KIDNAPPERS OF
AFRICAN AMERICANS IN NEW ENGLAND

Worse than the hoodlums and street thugs were hardened criminals who preyed upon free African Americans in the North. They were professional kidnappers, funded by southern slave traders and aided by corrupt northern officials. Their business was to seize free people of color, carry them south by sea, and sell them into slavery for a large profit. Much at risk were African Americans in seaport cities such as Boston, where kidnapped men, women, and children could be spirited away in small coastal vessels.

In February 1787, three free Afro-Bostonians named Cato, Luck, and Wendham were offered jobs as stevedores aboard the sloop *Ruby* (Captain Solomon Babson). While they worked in the hold, the sloop suddenly sailed, and they were made prisoners. The vessel headed north to Salem, and the same thing happened. More freed men were kidnapped, and the sloop disappeared over the horizon.

One of the victims in Boston was a Freemason. Prince Hall and twenty-two members of the African lodge learned what had happened and went into action. They brought the established Boston clergy into it, and Reverend Jeremy Belknap submitted a strong petition to the Massachusetts General Court. On March 26, 1787, it passed a law "to prevent the Slave Trade, and for granting relief to the Families of such unhappy persons as may be kidnapped or decoyed away from this Commonwealth." The Masons also asked Governor John Hancock to intervene. Hancock and the French consul in Boston sent letters to governors of many West Indian islands.

A reply came from the governor of the French island of Saint-Barthélemy. The kidnapped Bostonian Freemason had been offered for sale to a merchant who was also of that fraternity. Perhaps they recognized each other by exchanging secret Masonic signs and passwords. The merchant went directly to the governor, the victims were released, and their kidnappers went to prison. Cato, Luck, and Wendham returned to New England in triumph and freedom, and Boston leaders joined the celebration.[178]

That episode in 1787 marked the beginning of a long struggle for the rights of free African Americans against southern kidnappers until the Civil War. Actively involved were voluntary associations in Boston such as the African Masonic Lodge and the Africa Society. African churches and ministers in Boston took leading roles. And white leaders also joined in.

They also became more active in helping escaped slaves who fled to New England. In these cases, southern owners and slave hunters had federal law on their side, in the Fugitive Slave Act of 1793, the later Fugitive Slave Act of 1850, and the U.S. Constitution. But many people in Puritan New England had always believed in a higher law. And most of the African community pitched in.

A dramatic example was the rescue of two female fugitive slaves, Eliza Small and Polly Ann Bates, who escaped in Maryland and reached Boston on July 30, 1836. The flight of two women from slavery was comparatively rare, and the news spread swiftly. Professional slave hunters tracked them down, seized them, and brought them into federal court, demanding their return under the Fugitive Slave Law of 1793.

Afro-Bostonian women turned out in large numbers, and the kidnappers lost control of events. When the case went to trial, a dramatic scene ensued. Women filled the courtroom. Suddenly a command was given. An "old black cleaning woman 'of great size' wrapped her arms around the chief officer of the court" and immobilized him. Other women carried the runaway slaves out of the court to a waiting coach, and the fugitives vanished.[179]

The rescue of Eliza Small and Polly Ann Bates was done by the African American women of Boston, much as the African American Freemasons had acted to liberate Cato and Luck and Wendham, with help from white leaders, and broad support in the town.

FORMING FREE AFRICAN COMMUNITIES
IN NEW ENGLAND STATES

By 1790, the great majority of slaves throughout New England were free, and many were quick to gather in small communities. In northern Vermont, freed slaves began to settle in the town of Hinesburg east of Lake Cham-

plain, and just south of the busy town of Burlington. There they founded
a new settlement called "the Hill." An excellent book by Elise Guyette tells
their story.[180]

First to arrive were Shubael and Violet Clark and two small children.
He was a revolutionary veteran from New Milford, Connecticut; she may
have been from Massachusetts. In 1795, they came to Hinesburg and were
able to buy one hundred virgin acres for ninety pounds. They chose well.
The land was on a hill that averaged four hours more sun than the valleys.
They built a log cabin and cleared a farm that in 1818 was taxed for sixteen
improved acres and two oxen. They also raised cattle and pigs on their own
woodlands.[181]

Other freed slaves settled nearby; by 1810, they formed a community and
were living in Hinesburg. They came from Connecticut and Massachusetts,
and some had major trouble on the way. The Brace and Prince families suffered much from hostile whites "pulling down their fences, destroying their
crops, burning their hayricks, killing their animals, and spreading slanderous
lies."[182]

The Hill was different. The former slaves built a Baptist church where
Blacks and whites worshipped together. There was also a busy schoolhouse at
the bottom of the hill, attended by children who came from "families repre-
senting the entire social spectrum." The schoolhouse still stands. It has been
restored and is maintained as a testament to the New England idea of a common school.[183]

Small communities of African Americans multiplied throughout New England after 1790. Some were urban neighborhoods in large towns. Examples
in Connecticut were New Guinea and New Liberia in New Haven, Hog River
in Hartford, and "The Triangle" of about ten houses in Middletown. Some of
these little communities such as Scott Swamp in Farmington were desperately
poor. Others were more affluent, such as Bean Hill on the outskirts of Norwich. Several Negro governors lived in Bean Hill.[184]

Some of these settlements were segregated by race. Others were integrated for many generations. An example of the latter was Deep River, a
neighborhood of Saybrook in Connecticut. Its very able historian, Katherine Harris, writes that they worshipped together in the Deep River Baptist
Church, went to grammar schools and later high schools together, played
on the same baseball and track teams, and worked side by side at Pratt,
Read & Company, a factory that made piano keys and actions. Race con-

flicts were frequent in other Connecticut towns such as Hartford and New Haven, but not in Deep River. The story of race relations in New England was very mixed.[185]

THE GROWTH OF AFRICAN VOLUNTARY SOCIETIES

Something else happened in the cities of New England. Before the Revolution, urban slaves lived with their owners in every American city and were most numerous in the most affluent neighborhoods. Below the Mason-Dixon line, slaves often dwelled in their own small buildings on alleys behind their masters' homes. The result in Baltimore, Richmond, and later Washington was the growth of alley communities and a web of activity that was called alley life in these cities.

Boston was different. This crowded and close-built city had less room for alleys, and cellars were another problem with the city's water table. Slaves often lived above their owners in attics or garrets. When an earthquake struck Boston in 1727, Cotton Mather felt his house shake. His first thought was that his servants were acting up, over his head.

After the Revolution and the end of slavery in Massachusetts, residence patterns changed. From 1790 to 1860, Census returns found that Afro-Bostonians were concentrated in one part of the city. By 1860, about three quarters (1,672 of 2,261) lived on the north side of Beacon Hill and in adjacent parts of West Boston. In residence patterns, Boston was one of the most racially segregated cities in the United States.[186]

The north side of Beacon Hill rapidly acquired the institutions of a New England community—a sturdy brick-built African meetinghouse and African school on Smith Court, which still stand today on the Black Heritage Freedom Trail.

Even earlier, in the late eighteenth century, Black Bostonians had begun to construct something else—a set of institutions that were less a community than a society of plural groups. Among them were a great number of new voluntary associations.

A leader in Boston was Prince Hall (1735–1807), an African American slave of William Hall, perhaps manumitted in 1770. His master wrote that he was "no longer reckoned a slave, but [has] been always accounted as a free man by us."[187]

He had access to books and learning at an early age, became highly literate, and was articulate in speech and writing. By occupation Prince Hall was a successful "leather dresser" who built a business in Boston, doing much specialized and highly skilled work. One document survives for the supply of leather drumheads to Massachusetts regiments in the Revolutionary War. He also ran another business as a caterer and cook, known by Bostonians as their "outstanding expert" on turtle feasts, which were much in demand in eighteenth-century America. The Reverend Jeremy Belknap knew him well, and described him as a "tall, lean Negro of great dignity," who "always carried himself with the air of one who ruled many," a classic example of an African Big Man in America.[188]

Prince Hall was also what Americans call a joiner. He became a member of a Congregational church in 1772. Soon afterward he and fourteen friends founded a Masonic Lodge in Boston. They were not at first welcomed by established American lodges, but British regiments stationed in Boston had their own "travelling lodges." One of them, in the 38th Foot, strongly supported the African lodge, which was recognized by the London Grand Lodge after the war. Other African lodges appeared in Rhode Island and Pennsylvania in 1787. They also were not accepted by American Freemasons, but were recognized in London.

In 1791, Boston's African American Freemasons also organized the Prince Hall Grand Lodge, which rapidly recognized other table lodges throughout the United States, in the face of strong racist opposition especially in the South. The founder, leader, and namesake of this movement was Prince Hall himself, working with an original group of African Masons in Boston. The movement kept growing, to a peak in the twentieth century. At its height, circa 1955–60, African lodges of "Prince Hall Freemasonry" had 300,000 members, a large part of middle-class African Americans in the United States. Many African American women also belonged to the Masonic Order of the Eastern Star.[189]

Prince Hall believed deeply in the American republic, even as he spoke strongly against its racist flaws. To his friend and colleague Jeremy Belknap, he wrote in 1795, "Harmony in general prevails between us as citizens, for the good law of the land does oblige everyone to live peaceably with all his fellow citizens. . . . There is a great number of worthy good men and good citizens, that are not ashamed to take an African by the hand; but yet there are to be seen the weeds of pride, envy, tyranny, and scorn, in this garden of peace, liberty and equality."[190]

Other African voluntary associations multiplied rapidly in New England

after the Revolution. In 1789, they were invited to use Fanueil Hall for religious services on Tuesday and Friday afternoons. Soon they founded their
own churches, which by 1860 comprised six denominations. Other institutions, such as the Free Church and Tremont Temple, were integrated in Boston from the start.[191]

AFRICAN AMERICANS AND THE RIGHT TO VOTE IN NEW ENGLAND

Another challenge arose in 1780, when the new Massachusetts constitution
took effect. The rights of citizenship that it extended to the people of the
"commonwealth" were not as broad as the promise of the American Revolution or the rights in the U.S. Constitution. Here again, New Englanders of
African descent took the lead in expanding another fundamental principle of
the American republic.

We have met two of the drivers, who were sons of African slave Coffe Slocum: Paul and John Cuffe, whose long campaign for suffrage we have noted.
They recruited supporters in other towns, approached legislators one by one,
and suffered many defeats through three years of effort. Finally, in 1783, the
Massachusetts legislature enacted a new statute "rendering all free persons of
color liable to taxation, according to the established ratio for white men, and
granting them all the privileges, belonging to the other citizens," including
the right to vote.[192]

The Cuffe family and many African Americans worked within the system to change it. Others remembered the passage of the new law as "a day
equally honorable to the petitioners and the legislature—a day which ought
to be gratefully remembered by every person of color, within the boundaries
of Massachusetts." [193]

Their success was larger even than that. The sons of an African slave
persuaded the citizens of Massachusetts to enlarge one of the founding
principles of a free republic in the United States. They also persuaded the
Massachusetts General Court to grant voting rights to all free male citizens
without restriction of race. It was a major step forward, not only for African Americans, but for the American republic itself, for democracy, and the
rights of all humanity.

Suffrage reform also became an instrument of other reforms. Paul Cuffe
became active in the politics of the new nation and gave his support to the

Federalist Party, as did their children, and most politically active African Americans. Others later became Whigs and Republicans, strongly supported the Union cause in the Civil War, and worked for the enactment of the Thirteenth, Fourteenth, and Fifteenth Amendments.

Maine, Vermont, and New Hampshire also enfranchised adult males without restrictions of race. Connecticut allowed African Americans to vote in the early republic. These voters also tended to support Federalist-Republicans and strongly opposed the Democratic-Republican Party of Jefferson, Madison, and Monroe. In the elections of 1818, Democrats gained control of the state, gave Connecticut a new constitution, and disfranchised African Americans.

For many years Rhode Island also denied the vote to most African Americans and to poor people of all ethnic groups. Its charter of 1663 enfranchised only freeholders and eldest sons. For many years it excluded more than half of adult males in the colony, including African Americans, until after the Dorr Rebellion in 1842, when they finally gained the vote.

From the start, schooling was a compulsory part of the New England Way. As early as 1642, the Massachusetts General Court required every family to educate its children. By 1647, every town was ordered to maintain common schools for that purpose. By the early nineteenth century, free children in Connecticut attended common schools for ten years on average—the highest in the world.

But New England's common schools were not at first open to the children of African slaves. More than a few Massachusetts masters punished slaves who tried to learn how to read and write. In Boston, Chloe Spear's master put her "under penalty of being suspended by two thumbs, and severely whipped. He said it made negroes saucy to know how to read." [194]

But other New England masters went a different way. Some encouraged their slaves to read and study the Bible for the sake of their souls. At the same time, literacy increased a slave's value in the region, as did a basic command of arithmetic.

Slaves who learned to read and write and cipher were often self-taught. An example was Prince Richards, of East Bridgewater, Massachusetts, who "learned to write by using a charred stick." Many slaves learned to read and write in childhood by asking free children to teach them. [195]

By the early eighteenth century, private schools for African slaves were beginning to appear in New England. In 1718, Cotton Mather founded a "night charity school" in Boston for African and Indian children. It has received much attention. Historian Alice Earle also found evidence of a "Negro Day School" in Boston by 1728.[196]

Some teaching occurred in families and churches, with Congregational clergy in the lead. Minister Benjamin Colman kept note of the "many hours he spent teaching the African slaves." Reverend William Bentley used the catechism as a way of teaching African children to read and write, as did others.[197]

By the late eighteenth century, a few African American children were able to attend New England town schools. In Rhode Island, William Brown remembered that his grandfather was "an uneducated teamster," but his four children all went to winter schools in Providence.[198]

Jeremy Belknap wrote that by 1788 African children were permitted to attend town schools in Boston, but he knew of none who did so. He testified that many were literate, and they had learned to write and read at home, or in private schools.[199]

In other parts of Massachusetts, when district schools began to be required in the 1790s, town school committees excluded children of color. That happened in the town of Westport. There, as we have seen, descendants of Coffe Slocum, led by his son Paul, responded by building a handsome school of their own. They called it Cuff's School, made it one of the best schoolhouses around, and offered it to the town on the condition that all children could attend together, without restriction by color. The town agreed. Cuff's School has been called the first fully integrated town school in New England. Certainly it was one of the first.[200]

The establishing of Cuff's School was not the end, but the beginning of a long struggle for equality of educational opportunity in Massachusetts that continues to our time. It was fought town by town in the Commonwealth, and many of these battles were won by African Americans. By 1845, large towns such as Salem, Lowell, Worcester, and New Bedford admitted children to public schools without restriction of race.[201]

The major test was Boston. African American leader William C. Nell was raised on the back side of Beacon Hill, and followed his father as a founder and leader of movements against slavery and for equal rights. Nell was a student in a segregated school. His record as a superb student entitled him to the Franklin Medal, but the honor was denied because of his race.

Later William Nell led a campaign for the integration of town schools in Boston, with annual appeals to the School Committee, year after year, with no success. Later they went to law and carried the case to the Supreme Judicial

Court of Massachusetts. The deeply conservative Justice Lemuel Shaw heard the case, and supported segregation. To that end he espoused and may have invented the bizarre doctrine of "separate but equal." In 1855, William Nell and other African American leaders lobbied the Massachusetts state legislature, and won a great victory: the legislature enacted a law integrating public schools throughout Massachusetts.

CAMPAIGN AGAINST SLAVERY AND RACISM: INSPIRED BY AFRICAN NEW ENGLANDERS

Through the long struggle against slavery and racism, New Englanders supplied most of the leaders in the American antislavery movement. James McPherson studied the regional origins of major antislavery leaders during the critical period from 1830 to 1860. He was able to identify the roots of 567 antislavery leaders throughout the United States, and found that 63 percent were New England born.[202]

Quakers had taken the lead in the antislavery movement from 1750 to 1830 through much of the United States and Britain. But from 1830 to 1860 that pattern changed. In terms of religious affiliation, McPherson also discovered that 47 percent were Congregationalists or Unitarians, and 20 percent were Quakers. The rest belonged to a variety of denominations.[203]

After 1830, the national center of the American movement against race slavery and racism migrated to New England. How did it happen? For many antislavery leaders in New England, a major reason was personal. They turned against slavery in part because their lives and thoughts and feelings had been touched directly by people of African descent.

An example was the New England abolitionist leader Henry B. Stanton. He wrote, "In my childhood we had a negro slave whose voice was attuned to the sweetest cadence. Many a time did she lull me to slumber by singing this touching lament. It sank deep into my breast, and moulded my advancing years. Before I reached manhood I resolved that I would become the champion of the oppressed colored races of my country." [204]

Harriet Beecher Stowe also "grew up under the tutelage of old black slaves." She testified in her preface to *Uncle Tom's Cabin* that much of this great antislavery work flowed from "personal knowledge" of African Americans in her life.[205] Catharine Maria Sedgwick wrote a piece about Mumbett, who looked after her as a child and inspired her support of the antislavery movement.[206]

James McPherson also made another discovery about these antislavery New Englanders. Contrary to some iconoclastic writing about abolitionists, he found strong evidence that most of them also worked actively against racism, as well as against race slavery. They were often inspired by African slaves they had known.[207]

PHILLIS WHEATLEY AND EXPANDING
IDEAS OF HUMANITY

The presence in New England of African slaves and their descendants changed the culture and values of others in this region, in ways that were more consequential than their numbers might suggest.

In the New World African Americans built on some of the ways of English Puritans and American Yankees but did not merely copy them. The descendants of Africans transformed those regional traditions in many of their major parts. Most of all, they enlarged their ethical values and purposes.

A leading example was a young African child, about seven or eight years old, who was brought to Boston aboard the slave brig *Phillis* on July 11, 1761. Phillis Wheatley later wrote of her New England mistress, "I was a poor little outcast & a stranger when she took me in; not only into her house but I presently became a sharer in her most tender affections. I was treated by her more like her child than her servant; no opportunity was left unimprov'd." [208]

Her mistress, Susannah Wheatley, taught young Phillis to read. John Wheatley remembered that "she in sixteen months time from her arrival attained the English language . . . to such a degree as to read any, the most difficult parts of the Sacred Writings, to the great astonishment of all who heard her." She also taught herself to write with pieces of chalk and charcoal on the walls of the house.[209]

Her early learning centered on religion. Her owners belonged to the New South Church. But they baptized her in 1771 at the Old South Church.[210] It was more open, more evangelical, and more supportive of the great transatlantic evangelist George Whitefield, who preached there three times. Phillis Wheatley may have heard him, and she rejoiced in the reach of his ecumenical message. In one of her best poems, "On The death of the Rev. Mr. George Whitefield," she rejoiced in "the music of thy tongue," and celebrated his universal message for all humanity:

Phillis Wheatley

Take him my dear *Americans*, he said
Be your complaints on his kind bosom laid:
Take him ye *Africans*, he longs for you,
Impartial Saviour is his title due.[211]

With this message in mind, Wheatley turned to literature, and found her
inspiration in the English poets of the Augustan school. Alexander Pope was
a model for poetic language in its form, structure, and elaborate construction
of rhyme and meter. She mastered it with incredible speed, and composed a
stunning virtuoso piece, addressed to the undergraduates of Harvard College
as early as 1767, six years after she had arrived in a slave ship. She was about
fourteen.[212]

After Pope, her most important poetry model was Thomas Gray, best
known for "Elegy Written in a Country Churchyard." It was an inspiration,
not in form but substance. It was at once an elegy, literally, a lament for
death, loss, and suffering of individual people everywhere, and at the same
time a celebration of their human spirit and humanity itself. More than half
of Wheatley's poems were elegies, often explicitly so. They embraced the Africans, Americans, British, and classical figures she admired.

Her elegies were strengthened by the suffering that she had known: separation by brute force from her African family, and the mortality of the Middle Passage, which was far worse on her voyage than most slave ships. At the age of seven or eight she witnessed the deaths of many slaves, and saw the dead and even the dying thrown overboard to the sharks that followed slave ships. In America she witnessed more loss and suffering by people she loved, and who loved her. And she wrote about it in a poem on "fair freedom" in another key:

> Should you, my lord, while you peruse my song,
> Wonder from whence my love of *Freedom* sprung,
> Whence flow these wishes for the common good,
> By feeling hearts alone best understood.
> I, young in life, by seeming cruel fate
> Was snatch'd from *Afric's* fancy'd happy seat;
> What pangs excruciating must molest,
> What sorrows labour in my parent's breast?
> Steel'd was that soul and by no misery mov'd
> That from a father seiz'd his babe belov'd:
> Such, such my case. And can I then but pray
> Others may never feel tyrannic sway?[213]

Readers were astonished by her command of language. And many more were inspired by the meaning of her poetry, which spoke more to their condition than to ours.

Most of all, her verse was a large-spirited celebration of a common spirit in all people everywhere. Here was a vision that reached far beyond the Puritan idea of a small elect. A leading example was "An Hymn to Humanity," a vision of Christ's universal mission:

> Each human heart inspire
> To act in bounties unconfin'd,
> Enlarge the close contracted mind,
> And fill it with thy fire.[214]

Phillis Wheatley was widely read and celebrated in New England. In 1773, her poems were sent to London for publication in a single volume. With it went an "attestation, addressed to the Publick" that "the poems were (as we verily believe) written by PHILLIS, a young Negro Girl, who was but a few years since, brought an uncultivated Barbarian from Africa, and has ever since been, and now is, under the Disadvantage of serving as a Slave in a Family in this Town. She has been examined by some of the best Judges, and is thought qualified to write them.

It was signed by eighteen eminent men in Boston: Governor Thomas Hutchinson and Lieutenant Governor Andrew Oliver, John Hancock and James Bowdoin, six wealthy merchants, and seven senior ministers. They were New England men of different politics and many Christian beliefs. Phillis Wheatley's work reached a large public in Britain and Europe: members of the aristocracy and the royal family, and leaders of the Enlightenment such as Voltaire and Franklin, and many more.

In 1776, when Thomas Jefferson wrote his ringing declaration of human equality, a German scholar also published the first elaborate argument for racial inequality, Johann Friedrich Blumenbach's doctoral dissertation, *On the Natural Variety of Humanity*. He argued at length that humanity is divided into five races, and was the first to name them Caucasian, Mongolian, Malayan, African, and American. He asserted as empirical fact that these races could be distinguished by skin color and skull size, which correlated with differences in intelligence and moral judgment.[215]

Among the first Americans to adopt this theory of racial inequality was Thomas Jefferson, in his only full-length book, *Notes on the State of Virginia*, written in 1781, and published anonymously in 1785. In a discussion of race slavery in Virginia he asserted that Blacks are "in reason much inferior" and "in imagination dull, tasteless and anomalous." This was offered as a judgment on all Africans he had known, with no exceptions. "Never yet could I find that a black had uttered a thought above the level of plain narration."

Jefferson's leading example was the highly praised poetry of Phillis Wheatley. He asserted that "the compositions published under her name are below the dignity of criticism," which relieved him of the burden of a critical test. To his disgrace, Jefferson added the deceitful insinuation that her poems were not only flawed but fraudulent. Jefferson also did the same thing when he similarly attacked the Black mathematician Benjamin Banneker.[216]

Very different was the response of George Washington. In 1775, during the siege of Boston, Wheatley was a refugee in Providence. Washington had recently taken command of the Continental Army. She wrote a long poem of praise, celebrating his many merits, and most of all the moral strength of his leadership:

> Fam'd for thy valour, for thy virtues more
> Hear every tongue thy guardian aid implore!

Busy running the Boston campaign, Washington was slow to respond, but when he did, it was with grace, generosity, kindness, and praise for Wheatley's talent. He wrote, "I thank you most sincerely for your polite notice of me, in the elegant lines you enclosed, and however undeserving I may be of such encomium and panegyrick, the style and manner exhibit a striking proof of your great poetical Talents."

Washington invited her to visit his headquarters and added, "I shall be happy to see a person so favoured by the Muses, and to whom nature has been so liberal and beneficent in her dispensations." In his letter Washington made no reference to race, but only to her "great poetical talents." Probably they met at Cambridge, in March of 1776.[217]

Wheatley's other admirers included General James Wolfe, who took Quebec from the French, and American naval hero John Paul Jones, who called Wheatley "the Celebrated Phillis, the African Favorite of the Nine [Muses] and of Apollo." Before Jones joined the U.S. Navy, he had been a mate aboard slave ships in African trade. He had come a long way.[218]

Wheatley even seems to have influenced German scientist Johann Friedrich Blumenbach. He began to have second thoughts about his work on race. In 1806, he modified his racist model from fixed law to a statistical tendency, changed it yet again and began to argue for the unity of all humanity. In support he offered evidence of Blacks who excelled at poetry, "above all those of Phillis Wheatley of Boston who is justly famous."[219]

Racist attacks and arguments over Phillis Wheatley continued with attacks by Black nationalists who hated and despised her. They were offended by one short poem, "On being Brought from Africa to America."

> 'TWAS mercy brought me from my *Pagan* land,
> Taught my benighted soul to understand
> That there's a God, that there's a *Saviour* too:
> Once I redemption neither sought nor knew.
> Some view our sable race with scornful eye,
> "Their colour is a diabolic die,"

Remember, *Christians*: *Negros*, black as *Cain*,
May be refin'd and join th' angelic train.[220]

A common complaint was that Wheatley's poetry was "too white," and the poet herself had a "white mind." These Black nationalist critics accused her of "the Uncle Tom syndrome," and called her "early Boston Aunt Jemima," and much more.[221] Other Black nationalists asserted that she never wrote against slavery or the slave trade or racism, which is false—she wrote often and eloquently against them. Ironically these Black nationalist attacks were disturbingly close to those of racist Thomas Jefferson.

Historian and literary critic Henry Louis Gates Jr. studied the many assaults on her from the late nineteenth century to the late twentieth century and offered another perspective. On her poetry, Gates observes that "our task, as readers" is "to learn to read Wheatley anew unblinkered by the anxieties of her time and ours. . . . The challenge isn't to read white or read black; it is to read. If Wheatley stood for anything it was the creed that culture was, could be, the equal possession of all humanity. It was a lesson she was swift to teach, and that we have been slow to learn. But the learning has begun."[222]

But on the subject of race Wheatley also rose to a refinement of thought that reached far beyond her critics. Her purpose was not to elevate one race above another, but to aim higher, and to frame an idea of humanity that embraced all people equally. Phillis Wheatley did not work alone toward that goal. It was an idea and a purpose that came to many Africans who arrived as slaves in New England.

These Africans in New England sought their own freedom and something more. Many of them in different ways joined actively in an effort to enact a larger idea of a free and open society than would have existed without them. They also joined elements of their own African cultures to the purposes and goals that Europeans had brought to New England and America. In that process they played a major role in creating something new in the world—an expansive idea of freedom and justice, truly for all humanity to share.

Chapter 2

HUDSON VALLEY

Dutch Capitalists, Angolan Entrepreneurs, American Strivers

Our national character is well known. We delight in commerce. It is apparent in our habits.

—Adriaen van der Donck on the Dutch people of Old and New Netherland, 1655[1]

The market [was] the cornerstone of the socioeconomic edifice in the Kongo . . . internal trade was open to everyone without exception.

—Georges Balandier, quoting travelers on the people of Congo and Angola, 1595–1676[2]

IN THE SPRING OF 1613, the Dutch ship *Jonge Tobias* anchored in the lower Hudson River. Captain Thijs Mossel was having trouble with an enterprising "black Mulatto" named Juan Rodriguez, who liked the look of Manhattan Island and asked permission to leave the ship. The captain refused, and Rodriguez threatened to "jump overboard" if "not allowed to depart."

The two men struck a bargain. Rodriguez renounced all claims on his Dutch employers, and the captain gave him "80 hatchets and some knives" for trade goods, with weapons for his own defense. Juan Rodriguez went ashore alone, and this "black Mulatto" became the first documented non-native settler on record to seek his fortune in what is now the city of New York.[3]

A few months later, the Dutch trading ship *Fortuyn* arrived. Her captain, Hendrick Christiaensen, met Rodriguez, and together they went into the fur business.[4] The two of them were doing well when Captain Mossel returned with a sinister Dutch official named Hans Hontom. They were not pleased to find a former associate making money with a rival, and told him that he was "bound" to their service.[5] Rodriguez insisted that he was "a free man." They called him a "black rascal" and tried to enslave him.[6]

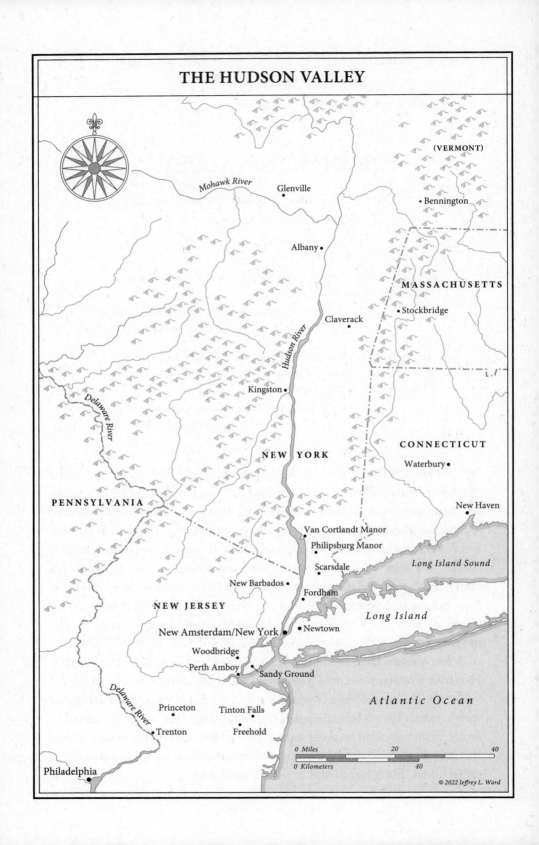

THE HUDSON VALLEY

Mohawk River

Glenville

(VERMONT)

Bennington

Albany

MASSACHUSETTS

Claverack

Stockbridge

Hudson River

Kingston

CONNECTICUT

Waterbury

NEW YORK

Delaware River

New Haven

PENNSYLVANIA

Van Cortlandt Manor

Philipsburg Manor

Long Island Sound

Scarsdale

New Barbados

Fordham

Long Island

NEW JERSEY

New Amsterdam/New York

Newtown

Woodbridge

Perth Amboy

Sandy Ground

Delaware River

Princeton

Tinton Falls

Atlantic Ocean

Trenton

Freehold

Philadelphia

0 Miles   20   40

0 Kilometers   40

© 2022 Jeffrey L. Ward

Rodriguez fought for his freedom, suffered a serious wound, and was rescued by Manhattan Indians. They drove off his attackers, and helped him recover.[7] He remained on the island, married an Indian wife, fathered a family, and built a successful business in bearskins and beaver pelts.[8] Several scholars have called him "Manhattan's first merchant."[9]

Rodriguez also succeeded in another way, as an intermediary between American Indians and European traders in the Hudson Valley. Many had failed in that role. Early contacts were often unimaginably brutal, and the worst violence came from the Europeans. Earlier in 1609, Henry Hudson's Anglo-Dutch crew had anchored in the river that bears his name. They began to fight the Indians on their first day of contact.[10]

Later, Rodriguez's mortal enemy Hans Hontom made major trouble with the Mohawks near Albany. He seized a Mohawk chief on the river and held him for ransom. Even after the ransom was paid, Hontom attacked his victim with insane violence, and "cut off the male organs of the chief, causing his death."[11] The infuriated Mohawks tracked Hontom to Albany, attacked the Dutch post, destroyed a ship in the river, killed cattle in the fields, and threatened the ruin of the colony.[12]

Other conflicts between the Dutch and Indians grew even more violent. In 1640, Dutch director-general Willem Kieft demanded that the Indians along the river must pay Dutch taxes. When they refused, Kieft started a major war and caused many atrocities.[13]

Between those violent events, Manhattan Island enjoyed a brief interval of peace that coincided with Rodriguez's time there. It allowed the Dutch to plant the small town of New Amsterdam in 1624. One of the first female Dutch colonists, Catelyn Trico, remembered that founding moment as a happy time when "Indians made covenants of friendship" and "were all as quiet as Lambs, and came and traded with all the freedom imaginable."[14]

Juan Rodriguez is thought to have had a hand in helping to build good relations. Today, New York's large Dominican community happily remembers him as a founder of their adopted city. In 2012, they led a campaign to name a street in his honor. From 159th to 218th Streets, upper Broadway is now Juan Rodriguez Way.[15]

Rodriguez's American career was not unique. Many Africans worked as intermediaries between Indians and Europeans in early years of contact.[16] These African "go-betweens" had a flair for languages and a gift for dealing with strangers whose cultures were unlike their own. In many parts of Africa, young people became polylingual by necessity and multicultural by choice.

Arab sources tell us that they had been doing so long before the first Europeans appeared on the Atlantic coast.

In the New World, Africans continued those roles from the sixteenth to the eighteenth century. Their talents as linguists and intermediaries were among the first of Africa's many gifts to the New World. That same flair for languages has continued to flourish in the linguistic creativity of rap and hip hop to our time.[17]

NEW NETHERLAND

On Manhattan, Juan Rodriguez also played another role. As a trader who got on with Indians and some Europeans, he helped to open the way for the founding of New Netherland.

This Dutch colony lasted barely four decades, from 1624 to 1664. But in that short span, Europeans and Africans invented new ways of coexisting in America, much to their mutual gain. At the same time, they also invented a creative calculus of plural ethnicity in an important region that is now a major part of the United States. Elements of ethnic diversity and creativity persisted

"Nieu Amsterdam," Dutch image, ca. 1624–99, with an affluent woman of mixed origins, a Dutch trader with a weapon in reach, and a very small cross buried in his trade goods. Near their feet, four African slaves bear the burden of the Dutch enterprise.

for many generations in the Hudson Valley. As we shall see, that legacy survives in the distinctive regional culture of metropolitan New York, and it has become fundamental to American culture in our time.

More than most North American colonies, New Netherland began with one central purpose in mind. It was wholly owned by a profit-seeking Dutch business corporation and dedicated entirely to the pursuit of wealth through capital investment and colonial trade. The result was an intensity of material striving that was widely shared among rich and poor alike, and also evident in entrepreneurial rivalry among different ethnic groups. Something of that spirit also appeared in American regions such as New England, but it was tempered by other purposes. Dutch founders of New Netherland were quick to notice the difference. One of them wrote that New Englanders "call themselves Puritans because they seek after purity in the Orthodox Religion. They wished not to live in England, desiring not wealth, but merely necessaries and a moderate condition." [18]

New Netherland's founders from top to bottom shared an exceptionally strong passion for the pursuit of wealth. Dutch historian Johan Huizinga observed similar attitudes in European Netherlands through many centuries and most ranks. He wrote that "whether we fly high or low, we Dutchmen are all bourgeois—lawyer and poet, baron and labourer alike." [19]

In America, this Dutch pursuit of material gain took a variety of forms. Prince Maurice of Nassau and his ministers promoted American colonies as a source of global wealth for the Dutch Republic and the ruling House of Orange.[20] Another material purpose appeared among Dutch investors in the West India Company, the corporate monopoly that owned and ran New Netherland.[21] Their inspiration was the Dutch East India Company, which in 1609 declared a dividend of 329 percent, a capitalist's dream. In 1628, the West India Company's Vice Admiral Piet Heyn captured a Spanish silver fleet and the directors paid a dividend of 50 percent.[22]

Other material motives were strong among individual migrants who came to New Netherland. Many of them arrived with no capital and few possessions. They staked their lives on the pursuit of personal wealth in a dangerous new world. These adventurers were very mixed in their origins. The first colonists spoke the dialects of every Dutch province.[23] Others were Belgian Flemings and Walloons, French Huguenots and German Lutherans, English Puritans, Scottish Presbyterians, Swiss Calvinists, Welsh Quakers, Irish Catholics, and Iberian Jews.[24]

In 1642, Director-General Willem Kieft told a visiting Jesuit that "four or five hundred men" in New Netherland spoke "eighteen different languages." [25]

Anyone was welcome in the colony who could boost the profits of the West India Company. The Dutch directors were happy to receive Augustine Herrman, a Bohemian entrepreneur who joined the Council and acquired baronial estates in America. They tolerated Anthony van Salee, variously called "Salee the Turk" and the "Black Mohammedan." An Islamic son of an African mother and a Dutch pirate, he acquired a large estate near Coney Island.[26]

Other colonies in North America were also diverse, but New Netherland was unique in the character of its diversity. Dutch corporate leaders followed the example of the Netherlands itself. The company issued an "Order of Government" (1629), which placed the colony and New Amsterdam firmly in the hands of a company director and council of Dutch businessmen. They rejected elections and assemblies, but allowed individuals and groups to make frequent use of petitions.

This customary Dutch right of petition became important to the colony, and also to our story. In the words of one historian, it became "a most effective form of popular influence," and not only by European colonists. Clusters of African slaves were quick to make the most of it, as we shall see.[27]

This Dutch governing system also allowed self-rule in small settlements, subject to oversight by the Council and director-general. By 1664, New Netherland had eighteen towns and villages, plus many trading posts on the Delaware River in the south, the Connecticut River to the east, and the Hudson and Mohawk Rivers in the north.[28]

On the Dutch model, the company guaranteed "freedom of conscience" to its colonists. But on orders from home it allowed only the Calvinist "Reformed Religion" to be practiced openly. This limited form of toleration was granted freely to anyone who increased the prosperity of the colony. It was good for business and promoted a dynamic culture of high creativity. But it did little for harmony and peace.[29]

From the start, visitors observed that New Netherland was "unruly" from top to bottom. In 1633, a visiting English sea captain was invited to dine with the Dutchmen who ran the colony. He wrote that even these men at the top "became intoxicated and got into such words that [he] could not understand how . . . there should be such unruliness among the officers of the Company, and that a governor should have no more control over them." He added that he was not accustomed to it among his own countrymen.[30]

The material-minded Dutch colony was also "unruly" in other ways. Its entrepreneurial culture made officers, colonists, servants, and even slaves into business rivals. In 1638, the company's directors in Europe complained that "many self-seeking persons" have "spoiled the commerce of the Company" by "buying more cheaply, and selling for less" in "clandestine trade" to "the great and immense damage and loss of the Company." Directors enacted strict "ordinances against clandestine trade," with small success.[31]

Yet another sort of unruliness grew from collisions among ethnic groups, which was a problem from the start. It reached a climax under Peter Stuyvesant, the last Dutch director-general. His angry clashes with Jewish colonists are well remembered. Less familiar were his conflicts with Lutherans, Calvinists, Anabaptists, Mennonites, Quakers, Puritans, and Anglicans. This strife has been blamed on Stuyvesant himself, but it began before his time and continued after New Amsterdam became New York City, even to our time.

And yet always, amid much ethnic conflict there were surprising exceptions. Governing directors Willem Kieft and Peter Stuyvesant quarreled with many groups, but they got on with Africans, slave and free. More to the point of this inquiry, Africans invented ingenious ways of getting on with them, and thereby hangs a tale.

NEW NETHERLAND'S AFRICAN SLAVES: THE ANGOLA-CONGO WAVE OF 1626–54

After the Dutch, the second-largest ethnic group in early New Netherland were African slaves. Their numbers were small at the start, but the West India Company was desperately short of labor, and African slavery rapidly increased.[32]

In 1625, the Dutch Republic was at war with Spain and Portugal, and the West India Company did not have reliable access to the African coast. It dealt with the problem by ordering captains to attack Portuguese and Spanish slave ships on the high seas, and seize their human cargo as a spoil of war, and bring them to New Netherland.

It was a dirty business, even by the abysmal standards of the Atlantic slave trade. In 1628, a Dutch squadron tried to seize an Iberian slaver in the Caribbean, and "accidentally sank it with all its cargo." Its cargo were living slaves. One cannot even imagine the concentrated cruelty, violence, and horror of that scene.[33]

As early as 1625 or 1626, a Dutch private armed vessel brought a dozen captured Africans to New Netherland.[34] Other slaves followed in growing numbers. In 1628, the privateer *Bruin Visch* took two dozen Angolan slaves out of a Portuguese vessel and carried them to New Amsterdam. Two years later *Bruin Visch* stopped another Portuguese ship from Angola and seized

fifty slaves. About thirty were female, and New Netherland's African population began to grow by natural increase. Most of these early slaves had been African born. A few came by way of Caribbean and South American colonies.[35]

A question of growing interest to historians is about the African origins of
these slaves. Two different answers have been suggested, and both are correct.
Many historians have stressed a diversity of African origins. That judgment
is accurate in substance and detail for the entire span of slave trading in the
Hudson Valley and North America.[36]

Within that larger frame, historians have also found other patterns. The
flow of slaves across the Atlantic tended to move in strong wavelike movements. Individual waves were often highly concentrated in time and place of
African origin. Even mixed shiploads often included smaller clusters of African slaves who shared languages, cultures, skills, and experiences.

It was that way in New Netherland from 1626 to 1655, a pivotal period
for the peopling of this colony. African scholars have described that era as
the time of a large "Angolan Wave" in the entire Atlantic slave trade. John
Thornton and Linda Heywood observe from deep research and long experience that it was a moment when "the vast majority of Africans crossing
to the Americas . . . came from West Central Africa." Other inquiries have
confirmed their judgment.[37] From 1620 to 1650, Africans from Angola and
Congo were estimated to be 90 percent of the entire Portuguese slave trade
to America.[38]

It was much the same among Dutch traders. As early as 1644, the West
India Company's own historian, Johannes de Laet, compiled data from captains' records for sixteen company slave ships. From 1624 to 1636, they delivered 2,356 slaves to Dutch colonies in America. Six of these ships left no
record of African origins. Of the rest, nine out of ten acquired their slaves in
"Angola." Heywood and Thornton found that "the same 90 percent ratio" also
appeared in Spanish documents for those years. Similar patterns are evident
in the Trans-Atlantic Slave Trade Database.[39]

So dominant was the Angolan wave in this period that similar patterns
of origin appeared among slaves who were bought in Africa, or captured at
sea, or purchased by interlopers, or shipped from one American colony to
another.[40]

In New Netherland itself, evidence of West Central African origins comes
not only from shipping records but also from naming patterns. Slaves in this
colony were given forenames of Christian saints, and surnames that often
identified a place of origin. A striking example was the first recorded marriage

of Africans in New Amsterdam's Dutch Reformed Church, on May 5, 1641. It joined "Anthony van Angola, widower of Catalina van Angola, to Lucie d'Angola, widow of Laurens van Angola."[41]

Heywood and Thornton searched New Amsterdam's surviving records from 1626 to 1664, and found a total of 172 recorded names in a slave population that numbered about 375 at the end of that period. Overall, "approximately 70 percent" of these names referred to Angola or Congo or Loango in West Central Africa. Heywood and Thornton ran similar tests for other colonies. They observed that this Angolan wave was evident in most colonies during that same period in the mid-seventeenth century, but they also concluded that "in no English or Dutch American colony does the central African origin of naming show up more than in New Netherland."[42]

Among all of New Netherland's slaves on record from 1626 to 1664, only five African place names did *not* refer to Angola, Congo, or Loango. Two were from the Cape Verde Islands, and three from the Isle of São Tomé ("Santomee"). Both were Portuguese possessions at that time, closely linked to the Atlantic trade with West Central Africa.

Other slaves bore surnames such as "Portugee," "Negro," "Negritto," "Negrinne," or variants on "Creole," such as "Crioel" or "Hilary Criolyo," which suggested American birth. But some of these other names were combined with African places. Anna Negrinne was also called Anna van Angola. Francisco Bastien Negro was also recorded as Bastien van Angola Negro. Altogether, the evidence of names in New Netherland before 1650 shows that the great majority of slaves had homelands in West Central Africa. Most came from Angola, many from Congo, and a few from Loango.[43]

SEVENTEENTH-CENTURY ANGOLA AND CONGO: AFRICAN PLACES IN TIME

West Central Africa is a large equatorial region, with an Atlantic coast of seven hundred nautical miles, from Pointe-Noire near the equator to Benguela at 12 degrees south latitude. In American equivalents, the length of its coastline equals the distance between New England and Florida. But it is only 20 percent of Africa's entire Atlantic slave coast.[44]

Writers in seventeenth-century Europe sometimes used "Angola" or "Kongo" for all of West Central Africa. Dutch leaders in New Netherland tended to refer to the entire region as Angola. French leaders in Louisiana called all of it Congo or Kongo. But people who lived there tended to give these place names more specific meanings. Loango referred to a northern kingdom and its coastal region of open bays.[45] The mid-coast was called Kongo, which was also the name of the great river (which is now the Zaire), and of a densely settled region, much of which is today's Republic of the Congo.[46] Farther south was Angola, a third area included the Kwanza Valley, and also an area ruled by kings with the title of Ngola, and inhabited by the people called Mbundu.

The Kwanza River and two other streams meet the sea near the Bay of Luanda, which became a major center for the Atlantic slave trade. Luanda (not to be confused with Loango five hundred miles to the north) is now the name of a great metropolis of five million people, the capital of modern Angola.[47]

All these Central African regions of Angola, Congo, and Loango were very large. Each had its own mix of cultures and history, but they also shared important elements. In all of them, most people spoke one of two large families of western Bantu languages: Ki-kongo to the North, and Ki-mbundu in the Angolan South. These speechways were closely related. Europeans observed that native speakers of one tongue could quickly pick up another without instruction—which meant that many slaves from these regions were able to talk to each other. This African pattern had important American consequences, especially in New Netherland.[48]

The people of Loango, Congo, and Angola also shared similar religious beliefs. Throughout those great regions, religions flourished in great variety, but many possessed a common core. They tended to be deeply spiritual faiths. Like other world religions, but more than most, they shared a belief in the profound importance of spirits, and the reality of the spirit world. People in Central Africa believed in a multitude of nature spirits, water spirits, and earth spirits. They also believed in spiritual souls—invisible, animate, powerful, and often immortal entities that inhabited the bodies of people, animals, and objects. Many (not all) Central Africans also believed in transmigration of souls from one body to another. They venerated the souls of ancestors through shrines and rituals which had powers of their own. And they worshipped many gods, which they understood not in anthropomorphic terms but as spirits called *nzambi*. These divine spirits were often led by the spirit of the one great god, Nzambi Mpungu, who was thought to be the Creator of the Universe.[49]

The history of these African religions was long, varied, and ever-changing. After 1490, they began to change in a new way. At about that date, Roman Catholic missionaries came to West Central Africa, and were welcomed by rulers who were among their first converts. In the sixteenth and early seventeenth centuries, many Central Africans adopted Christianity.[50]

The evidence of names and baptisms shows that slaves who came to New Netherland from this region were often Christians before they crossed the Atlantic. They had tended to become Christian without giving up indigenous African faiths. Physical evidence of burials, artifacts, emblems, and signs all show that African religious beliefs were brought to New Netherland, and combined with Christianity for many generations. These religious traditions interacted to create new Afro-European cultures in America. They have had a continuing impact in our time, in religious beliefs and secular applications.[51]

Another common element in West Central Africa was the material culture of this region. It was highly developed before the first Portuguese ships arrived, and expanded rapidly in the sixteenth century. Agricultural output was revolutionized by the global flow of new crops in this era, on a scale much larger than a transatlantic "Columbian exchange." By the early sixteenth century, bananas, yams, and taro were introduced to Africa from India and Malaysia. Productive varieties of beans and cowpeas and other crops arrived from other parts of Africa. Maize, sweet potatoes, and ground nuts were carried from America to Congo between 1548 and 1583. Manioc was brought from the New World to Luanda by 1600. These crops spread rapidly through Central Africa. Agricultural productivity rapidly increased and rates of population growth rose in West Central Africa—even after the expansion of warfare and the slave trade took a heavy toll.[52]

Industrial production also developed in this region before European contact. Skilled African ironworkers met a large domestic demand for products that matched European iron in quality. Small superheated African blast furnaces made steel that was thought superior to most European technologies before the seventeenth century.[53] Textiles throughout West Central Africa were distinguished by variety of fibers, quality of weaving, beauty of fabrics, quantity of production, and extent of markets. In 1611, Congo weavers exported more than sixty-five thousand feet of cloth to Angola, and other woven goods were sent to Europe.[54]

The economies of West Central Africa were remarkable for the range and density of their markets before European contact. Historian Jan Vansina has creatively used archaeological evidence to reconstruct trade routes in early Central Africa. He did it by mapping the distribution of complex African manufactures such as flange-welded clapperless bells, and exquisitely balanced throwing knives.[55]

Central African monetary systems supported exchange networks over long distances. Shell coins and fabric currency were widely used on the Atlantic coast and in the interior of Central Africa. European visitors in the sixteenth and seventeenth centuries were surprised by the size of commercial cities, and amazed by dense networks of trading villages. People of many ranks and conditions participated actively in African markets. Women often played leading roles—then and now. In the late twentieth century, Judy and I met them throughout West Africa, where they were called Mercedes Mamas. Angolan, Congolese, and Luandan slaves brought to America this African experience of market relations. They also brought an entrepreneurial spirit that flourished in New Netherland during the seventeenth century.[56]

Political cultures and social systems also were highly developed in West Central Africa. The kingdoms of Congo, Loango, and Ngola were strong independent states in the sixteenth and seventeenth centuries. They were divided into districts, and districts into villages, and villages into large households of ten to forty people, each collectively called "the House." A House was commonly led by its "Big Man," who was expected to command respect and obedience not only by power and wealth, but also by wisdom and justice, by dignity and gravitas, and by a largeness of spirit.[57] These extended Houses also had Big Mamas, senior women whose pathways to power and leadership flowed through the household, family, and commerce. When Africans were brought as slaves to New Netherland, Big Men and Big Mamas emerged among them. Europeans learned to treat them with respect.[58]

People who lived in Angola, Congo, and Loango early in the seventeenth century shared a dynamic heritage of language and religion, politics and economics, comity and society. They carried much of it to America, where it became even more dynamic. In New Netherland from 1625 to 1650, a large majority of African slaves had roots in Bantu-speaking regions of Angola and Congo. They could communicate with each other in related African languages. And they also had much experience in Africa of complex market economies, highly developed African communities, and extended households.

These were small beginnings, and patterns in the slave trade with the Hudson Valley would change in later generations. But as we often find, small beginnings made a large difference in the history of great nations.

The people of West Central Africa also shared something else: a dynamic history of violent conflict and rapid change. The kingdoms of this region were often at war with each other. That continuing strife was compounded by other conflicts that grew more violent and destructive in the sixteenth and seventeenth centuries. A leading cause was a double invasion of Central Africa. Portuguese seamen were trading along the coast of Congo and Angola as early as 1480, before Columbus came to America. By 1516 the king of Ndongo sent ambassadors to the Portuguese court, and affluent Angolan and Congolese families sent their sons to school at Lisbon. Catholic missionaries were invited into Central Africa, and they converted Central Africans to Christianity in the late sixteenth and early seventeenth centuries. Even in the interior of Congo and Angola, many native people met Europeans from the early sixteenth century on.[59]

By 1575 Portuguese soldiers had begun to conquer parts of Angola. Their leader was Banha Cardoso, a malign figure, cruelly maimed in imperial warfare. He became the Portuguese governor of Angola, and sent wealth home to Lisbon from the mines of Africa, and from a large expansion of the slave trade.

He was able to do so in part because the heartlands of Angola and Congo also suffered another invasion from the highlands of Central Africa, by aggressive groups sometimes known as Imbangala and Jaga. Firsthand accounts survive from Andrew Battell, an English seaman who soldiered with Portuguese forces through eighteen years of warfare in Angola and Congo.[60] His account of horrors he had seen as a captive of the Imbangala would scarcely be credible if they were not confirmed by another Portuguese eyewitness, Duarte Lopes, and other primary sources.[61]

The Imbangala, as we shall call them, appear in this hostile evidence as a predatory people who worshipped dark spirits, engaged in sorcery, practiced cannibalism, and made a virtue of violence. They moved into a country of sedentary villages, lived apart in stone forts perched high on rocky hills, and attacked peaceable people who were unable to resist them. The Imbangala raided villages, hunted people with man-killing animals, murdered infant children, enslaved young adults, and wrecked fields and forests.[62] In 1611, Portuguese governor Banha Cardoso made an alliance with the Imbangala and they went into the slave trade together. From 1611 to 1641, the Imbangala captured slaves on a large scale and sold them to the Portuguese, who carried them to America. The captives were Angolan and Congolese farmers, artisans, and villagers. The victims were often prosperous, industrious, entrepreneurial people, with strong families and communities. Many had been converted to Christianity, and were hated for their faith by the Imbangala, who killed and captured them in large numbers.

That pattern differed from the African slave trade in other times and places. Throughout a long history, African slavers bought many people who were already captives, prisoners, or slaves. The Imbangala reversed that usual pattern. Historian Jan Vansina observes that the Imbangala enslaved their social betters and sold them to the Portuguese, "a revolt of the have-nots against the haves."[63] The Imbangala were also said to have had a particular hostility to Christian converts. Many thousands of these Angolan and Congolese captives were shipped to the New World. Most went to South America and the Caribbean. Others were carried as slaves to New Netherland.

DUTCH SLAVERY IN NEW NETHERLAND

As Africans began to multiply in New Netherland, Dutch leaders at home were troubled by slavery. Among them was Hugo Grotius, a major founder of modern international law and leading advocate of "natural law" in world affairs. In 1625, he wrote that "slavery is against nature. Mankind by nature is free." But then he thought again, and came to the conclusion that slavery was lawful where captives would otherwise be executed in a "just war," and also where slaves were treated humanely. On those grounds, Grotius wrote a qualified defense of slavery and the slave trade. Leaders of the Dutch West India Company were quick to follow his judgment. Willem Usselincx argued in 1627 that it was "better to enslave captives than to kill them," if the slaves were treated justly.[64]

Dutch theologians debated slavery in another way. Their Synod of Dort in 1619 approved the taking of slaves in just wars, but forbade the enslavement of Christians. Other clergy urged that slavery should be limited to a fixed number of years, on biblical models in Deuteronomy and Leviticus. A few affirmed that slaves were "fellow human beings," and invented a new application of the Golden Rule—that slaves should not be given tasks which masters would reject for themselves, on the grounds that they are "fellow human beings." These moral scruples did not end Dutch slavery, but changed the way it worked in some cases.[65]

In New Netherland, Africans were called *slaven* from the start, unlike as in some early English colonies. In 1628, first minister Jonas Michaelius referred collectively to all Africans in New Netherland as "Angoolischen slavinnen," Angolan slaves.[66]

Further, the word *slaven* (slaves) was used interchangeably with *swarten* (Blacks)—a proto-racial idea from the start. Dutch courts and councils in New Netherland acted on the assumption that *swarten* were *slaven* unless proof positive existed to the contrary.[67] In 1642, for example, the French privateer *La*

Garce arrived at New Amsterdam with Africans who had been taken out of a Spanish ship.[68] The Africans insisted they had been free, but Dutch authorities in New Netherland decreed that "negroes" were presumed to be slaves by reason of their negritude, unless they had proof of their freedom.[69]

Also in Dutch New Netherland slavery was a hereditary status from the start. Every slave was assumed to be in bondage until explicitly released by masters or company officers. Slaves were required to do the will of their owners. In all these ways, Dutch bondage was like many systems of slavery.[70]

But in other ways, slavery in New Netherland was sui generis. In the beginning it was primarily a system of corporate bondage. Most slaves were owned by the West India Company, and they were forced to work on company projects.[71] Others were leased to high company officials such as Director-General Wouter van Twiller, who operated a tobacco farm with six slaves. The last director-general, Peter Stuyvesant, used his office to acquire more than forty slaves for his own use, the largest individual holding in the colony.[72]

Margaretha van Raephorst, wife of Cornelius Tromp, with slave child

On orders from home, company officers began to sell slaves to individual purchasers, often at a discount to encourage the market, and to attract Dutch settlers. Slaves were offered as an inducement for investment to landed patroons in the Hudson Valley, ironmakers in East Jersey, and fur traders on the Delaware and Connecticut Rivers. Like retailers in our time, the Dutch West India Company sold slaves with something like a money-back guarantee. It allowed buyers to return slaves who were unsatisfactory, or to exchange them.[73] But in New Netherland the West India Company itself remained the largest slave owner.[74]

THE DARK REALITY OF DUTCH SLAVERY: HEAVY LABOR AND HARD TREATMENT

Historians have written that bondage in New Netherland was "mild" by comparison with other colonies. Not so. Here as elsewhere slavery was a hereditary status of forced labor for the material gain of masters. "Force" and "labor" and "material gain" were fundamental. Dutch slavery in the Hudson Valley was a cruel and brutal business, as bondage was in most times and places. The more we learn empirically about slavery everywhere, the worse it appears. Dutch slavery was no exception to this rule.[75]

In 1639, for example, Jacob Stoffelsen was "overseer over the negroes belonging to the Company" at New Amsterdam. He wrote proudly of the forced labor that he had extracted from "the said negroes." By his own account, he drove the company slaves relentlessly in "building Fort Amsterdam, which was completed in the year 1635, and also in cutting building-timber and firewood for the Large House as well as the Guardhouse, splitting palisades, clearing land, burning lime, and helping to bring in the grain in harvest time, together with many other labors, which we have done with the negroes."[76]

That long list was not the half of it, and "we" was hardly the word. Company slaves also dredged docks and built wharfs in New Amsterdam, working in foul tidal waters, day after day. They graded roads on rocky ground, cleaned filthy streets, built windmills, and carried heavy timbers on their backs. They maintained the Dutch church building, kept the fort in repair, and raised food for the garrison. They did the same thing at Fort Orange near Albany, and Oyster Bay on Long Island, and other Dutch settlements.

In early years these African men and boys lived in barracks and some of them appear to have labored in chains with European convicts chained beside them. The Provincial Council tried a white felon who had wounded two of the "company's negroes" and sentenced him to "take their place in chains." Dutch slaves also suffered heavy corporal punishment. Some were severely flogged and maimed by ear cropping.[77]

The worst of slavery was incessant labor, which took a heavy toll. Hard evidence has emerged from three primary sources: accounts by Dutch overseers, testimony from slaves of Dutch masters, and physical evidence from the African Burial Ground where slaves were buried in lower Manhattan from as early as 1632 to the late 1780s.[78]

In the twentieth century, a new building was constructed on part of that old cemetery, near the present intersection of Broadway and Chambers Street. Skeletal remains of many African slaves were found there. Some were exhumed with great respect and much controversy. The empirical results revealed the heavy cost of human bondage in the Hudson Valley.[79]

In a careful study of individual African slaves by the methods of forensic pathology, scholars and scientists reported that "many appear to have been literally 'worked to death.'" Their bodies were severely deformed by hard labor. Men, women, and even children showed evidence of deep skeletal damage, and lesions where muscles had been ripped away from bones by the stress of heavy toil. Mature male slaves had hypertrophy of major bones, extreme osteoarthritis, and major skeletal destruction. The cause was clear to pathologists who did the analysis. Spines, joints, and bones of slave men bore many scars of extreme stress, caused by prolonged lifting, hauling, and overwork. Slave women died with "ring fractures" around the base of their skulls, where heavy burdens on their heads had literally broken their necks. The vertebrae of one slave woman had been "thrust into the base of her skull by the weight of the loads on her head." Even slave children had severe neck and back injuries, caused by burdens too heavy for small bodies to bear. This was the worst of slavery—not the beatings and whippings alone, cruel and violent as they were, but incessant overwork.[80]

Physical evidence from Manhattan's African Burial Ground also confirms that slaves in New Netherland and early New York suffered not merely from corporal punishment, but also from deliberate acts of extreme violence. One grave held "a young woman's broken body—facial bones shattered by many blows, wrists broken, arms fractured, and her rib cage penetrated by a lead musket ball that was still embedded in her chest." She had been

killed by repeated acts of savagery. Physical evidence of forensic pathology
tells us that this violence against slaves occurred frequently in the Hudson
Valley, as it also did in other systems of forced labor. In combination with
other evidence, it tells us that it happened in Dutch, English, French, and
American slavery.[81]

Other supporting evidence for the brutality of slavery under Dutch masters from the early seventeenth to the late eighteenth century came directly
from slaves themselves. One of the most explicit documents was the narrative
of John Jea, an "African preacher" highly respected for his integrity. He was
born in Africa at "Old Calabar" in 1773, brought as a slave to New York with
his parents, circa 1775, and bought by the Dutch family of Albert and Anetje
Trihuen (or Terhune) in Flatbush, Kings County, now Brooklyn. It was an
area settled by Dutch farmers, most of whom owned slaves.

John Jea remembered that his Dutch master forced slaves on his farm to
work in winter "from four in the morning till ten at night," an eighteen-
hour workday. In the summer, he remembered that the workday was longer. It ran from "from about two o'clock in the morning to ten or eleven at
night." Jea recalled that "the horses usually rested about five hours in the
day while we were at work, thus did beasts enjoy greater privileges than
we did."

These Dutch slaves lived on corn mush and sour milk, with three ounces of
dark bread a day, "greased over with hog's lard." At work they were routinely
"corrected with a weapon an inch and a half thick and that without mercy,
striking us in the most tender parts." If they complained, they were lashed to
four poles in the ground and flogged "in a manner too dreadful to behold."
Slaves who dared to "lift up our hand or foot against our master or mistress"
were summarily killed by "shooting them with a gun, or beating their brains
out with some weapon in order to appease their wrath." His master "told us
that when we died, we should be like the beasts that perish," with no hope of
eternal life.

John Jea recalled that his master was "very cruel . . . and yet we esteemed
ourselves better used than many of our neighbors," who were also Dutch.
Clearly, there were better masters and worse ones in the Hudson Valley. But
the testimony of company overseers, the horrific evidence of forensic pathology, and the memory of slaves themselves all confirm that Dutch slavery in
New Netherland was not "mild," and that masters were sometimes violent
and cruelly exploitative.[82]

SOLIDARITY AMONG NEW NETHERLAND'S
ANGOLAN AND CONGO SLAVES

Violence also occurred between slaves. In 1641, a fight broke out among Africans in the woods near their quarters. A slave named Jan Premero was killed for reasons unknown, and eight slaves were charged with his murder. The Dutch Council recorded that all of them "confessed that they did it jointly [*gecompaereert*]." The Dutch demanded to know who struck the fatal blow, and got the same answer from every slave: "They themselves did not know, for they had done it together."[83]

In this case the death penalty created a dilemma for New Amsterdam's Dutch businessmen. A loss of eight prime slaves at 300 guilders each threatened their profits. On reflection, the Council ruled that only one of the eight slaves needed to be executed—a saving of 2,100 guilders. The defendants were ordered to draw lots, and the loser was Manuel Gerrit de Reus, a big and heavy man.

He was led through a large crowd and placed on a ladder with two stout nooses around his neck. As he was about to be turned off, the ladder broke and both ropes snapped. Manuel de Reus crashed to the ground, "stunned but alive."

Dutch Calvinists, like English Puritans, did not believe in accidents. They regarded Manuel's survival as a divine sign and demanded that his life be spared. He was reprieved, and permitted to marry, raised a family, and became a leader of other slaves.[84]

Angolan and Congolese slaves acted together in another brutal case. In 1646–47, they seized a slave named Jan Creole, and accused him of sodomy with a ten-year-old boy named Manuel Congo. Dutch Protestants were horrified by that crime, as also were English Puritans, French Catholics, and African slaves. Jan Creole was tried, found guilty of sodomy, and sentenced to be "choked to death" until the life ebbed out of him. His body was ordered to be burned to ashes in a blazing fire.[85]

In such cases, old European customs also required the death of the victim. The Dutch ordered that the small Congolese child "on whom the abominable crime was committed" should be taken to the place of Jan Creole's execution, tied to a stake, and surrounded with a pile of kindling. All that was done, but the fire was not lit. Young Manuel Congo was flogged severely and released—an act of mercy in old New Netherland. One wonders if the slaves had objected strongly to the death of Manuel Congo. He was one of their own.[86]

"HALVE VRYDOM," OR HALF-FREEDOM, INVENTED ON THE INITIATIVE OF ANGOLAN SLAVES WITH THE AGREEMENT OF DUTCH CAPITALISTS

While slavery in New Netherland was cruel and brutal, in some ways it became more flexible than bondage in other colonies. Dutch businessmen were less interested in maintaining absolute dominion over their slaves than in extracting the largest return on their capital investment. To that end, everything was negotiable among these early American capitalists—everything except capitalism itself.

The absence of a formal slave code and the presence of an entrepreneurial spirit among both Dutch masters and African slaves combined to create a more fluid system of bondage than in some other systems.

That fluidity was compounded by the collective efforts of a small group of Angolan and Congo slaves. They shared an instrumental and entrepreneurial spirit that had been strong in their African homelands. In New Netherland, they used it to improve their condition.

Slavery in New Amsterdam rapidly became a complex system of bargaining. Dutch masters and Angolan slaves together redefined conditions of bondage for their mutual gain. Something similar happened in other slave systems, but in New Netherland this process had a special intensity and a unique result. A materialist and market-centered Dutch culture made slavery itself into a commodity, which was redefined by a marketlike process of bargaining for material gain. This became an opportunity for slaves, and a source of profit for their masters.

Part of the opportunity came from Dutch masters who were quick to discover that money might be made by combining bondage with special privileges and obligations. Another part of it came from company directors who offered specific liberties in return for special military service, which lowered the overhead costs of colonial defense. The most important initiatives came from African slaves. They sought to transform bondage for their own advantage and were quick to seize opportunities that came their way.

To study evidence of this bargaining in New Netherland is to discover that the initiative came directly from the slaves themselves. At an early date, African slaves in New Netherland began to win privileges for themselves. Some were allowed to join a church. Others were permitted to marry, to baptize their children, and raise a family. Many were able to master a skill, from which both masters and slaves had something to gain. Canny Dutch masters were quick to learn that sometimes it was in their material interest to engage the self-interest of their slaves, who in turn used that possibility to transform their bondage.

Slaves in New Netherland were also quick to discover the customary Dutch right of petition. They claimed it for themselves and established its legitimacy by repeated use. Petitioning was a key that unlocked many possibilities.

As early as 1634, slaves in New Amsterdam petitioned for a right to be paid for their labor. Their request did not at first succeed, but in 1635 five African slaves may have found a way to travel from Manhattan to the Netherlands, perhaps as seamen aboard a Dutch ship in the company's service. They took their petition to higher authority in Europe, and asked to be paid for work on public projects in New Netherland.[87]

Incredibly, Dutch leaders agreed. By 1639, African slaves who were building the fort at New Amsterdam received eight guilders a month for their labor—the same rate that was paid to European laborers.[88]

Slaves also claimed access to the courts when payments were in dispute, and they got that too. In 1639 two slaves, Pedro Negretto and once again Manuel de Reus, sued for wages that had been promised but not paid. They won their case.[89]

That was only the beginning. In 1644, eleven slaves joined together and petitioned for freedom outright. They claimed to have been in New Netherland for "eighteen or nineteen years." Once again places of African origin appeared in some of their names: Paulo Angola, Simon Congo, Peter Santome [São Tomé], Anthony Portuguis, Jan Fort Orange. Some of these men belonged to the same close-knit group of slaves who had acted together to expand their rights and privileges.[90]

Dutch director-general Willem Kieft and his Council agreed to their major demand. He acknowledged they had indeed served the company for "18 or 19 years" and added that they had "long since been promised their freedom." On his recommendation, the Council ruled that these men "and wives" were released from slavery "for the term of their natural lives, hereby setting them free and at liberty on the same footing as other free people here in New Netherland."[91]

That agreement flowed not from altruism but interest. Profit-seeking Dutch masters were quick to see an opportunity for material gain in several ways. Slaves won a precious gift of freedom, and masters gained a labor system that was more flexible and also more profitable. Owners got the benefit of a slave's labor in the prime of his productive years. Thereafter slaves were required to support themselves in declining years, which saved owners that expense.

The canny businessmen of the West India Company also insisted on adding other terms that guaranteed a steady annual return on their investment. Each year every freedman with a farm was required to pay the company "thirty skepels" (roughly two bushels) of maize or wheat or peas or beans, plus a fat hog valued at 20 guilders. Freedmen in trade were required to make an equivalent payment in furs or wampum. The company also reserved the right to conscript a freed slave's labor whenever needed, in return for payment of "fair wages." Failure of former slaves to meet any of these obligations was cause for re-enslavement.[92]

Kieft called this condition "vrydom," freedom outright. Others both Dutch and African described it more accurately at the time as "halve vrydom," half-freedom.[93] After 1644, it was granted with increasing frequency, usually by petition, and in variant forms. An elderly African woman named Mayken van Angola asked for her freedom after "having served as a slave since

Peter Stuyvesant

1628." She got it. In 1662, three slave women petitioned for half-freedom. Director-General Peter Stuyvesant was happy to agree, on one condition, that at least one woman would do his housework. The deal was done.[94]

To repeat, the initiative came from a small tight-knit cluster of African slaves, mostly Congolese and Angolan in origin and culture. Their chosen instrument was the Dutch system of petitioning.

To most of these petitions, the hard-driving directors of the Dutch West India Company added yet another "express condition," which was the cruelest and most profitable of all—that "their children, at present born and yet to be born, shall remain bound and obligated to serve the Honorable West India Company as slaves."

Many slaves later petitioned for an end to that cruelty. Company directors were willing to agree, but only if parents paid a sum equal to the market price of each child, or supplied another slave of equivalent value. Here again, everything was negotiable in the commercial world of old New Amsterdam.[95]

MANHATTAN'S "LAND OF THE BLACKS"

After Kieft's war with the Indians broke out, the Dutch Company and the director himself offered half-free slaves yet another inducement, in return for a new obligation. At least thirty-five former slaves were given land of their own, in exchange for military service. Angolan and Congo slaves were quick to seize that opportunity—perhaps while entering into secret negotiations with the Indians.

The land they were offered lay about a mile north of New Amsterdam's palisade. It may have been Manhattan's worst land, with steep hills, deep swamps, and rough terrain strewn with granite boulders. But it was their land, and Dutch leaders began to call it the "Land of the Blacks." It was formally granted by the director-general of New Netherland, with the Council's approval. Once again, initial grants went mainly to that same small circle of African slaves who came mostly from Angola and Congo and had been early petitioners for rights and privileges.[96]

Most of these land grants also went to Africans who had married and formed families. Serious bargaining took place on questions of inheritance. By 1662, at least three landowners in the Land of the Blacks were African widows from Angola. Other lands passed to children. By those agreements a large minority of African slaves in New Amsterdam gained a customary right to own land on terms similar in some ways to freeholds in English law. Their possessions were more free than they were.[97]

These lands were granted to half-free Africans north of the town, and east of Broadway. Some African slaves had long lived apart from others in New Netherland. As early as 1639, company slaves lived in work camps. One was called the "quartier van de Swarten," on the edge of the East River near today's Roosevelt Island.[98] Later rulers of the colony also encouraged other settlements of half-free slaves. During the 1650s and 1660s other grants were made in what is still called the Bowery, between Prince Street and Astor Place, close to Peter Stuyvesant's estate. Other grants followed in Brooklyn.[99]

HALF-FREEDOM AND AFRICAN LEADERS: MANUEL TROMPETTER, "CAPTAIN OF THE BLACKS"

African slaves in New Netherland also found other ways to improve their condition, and to help others in bondage. A leading example (of many) was a slave who arrived perhaps in 1625. He had a skill that was useful to his Dutch masters, and they named him for it: Manuel Trompetter. Part of his function was to serve the colony's military commanders with his trumpet, which led to another opportunity. In 1642–43, after Kieft's War, the Dutch found themselves severely overmatched by infuriated Indian neighbors. Director Kieft hired mercenary soldiers from other Dutch colonies and New England. He also enlisted "the strongest and most active of the negroes" in a "black militia." Each was equipped with "a small ax and half pike" and later more lethal weapons.[100]

Manuel Trompetter was made a "Captain of the Blacks," as were other African leaders who followed. In that role he appears to have won the respect of the Dutch and the affection of his fellow Africans, who went out of their way to help his family. In 1663, after Trompetter and his wife, Anthonia, had passed away, their surviving daughter, Christina, was eighteen years old. By the rules of half-freedom she remained a slave of the West India Company. The survivors of Manuel Trompetter's militia company rallied to Christina's support. A new "captain of the blacks," Domingo Angola, bargained with Dutch company officers for her freedom. They were willing to agree, if the company was given another slave of equivalent value, or hard cash equal to Christina's market price (and then some) of 300 guilders. As always in New Netherland, almost everything was for sale—if the price was right.

After hard bargaining by both sides, the deal was done on September 16,

1664. A prosperous private Dutch trader, Govert Loockermans, paid the West India Company 300 guilders for Christina's emancipation, and got something in return. Before the year was out, Christina became the wife of Swan van Loango, an unmarried slave of Loockermans. The daughter of Trompetter became a free married woman, and her children would be free as well—thanks to the intervention of her father's comrades, as he had intervened for them. Once again, these formidable Africans, mostly of Angolan and Congolese origin, looked after each other. They functioned as a band of brothers, and worked their will on the Dutch leaders of the colony—often at a negotiated price. With individual enterprise and collective effort these slaves found ways of turning the Dutch capitalist institutions of New Netherland to their own purposes.[101]

Manuel Trompetter was not unique in his leadership. Other Big Men also emerged among Africans in New Netherland. One of the first on record was Bastiaen or Sebatiaen, also called Captain of the Blacks. His namesake, the original Saint Sebastian, had been a soldier who made many Christian converts in the Roman empire, and was executed by Diocletian when he refused to stop. He became a role model for some Portuguese warriors in Angola.

Bastiaen was one of a few free Blacks in early New Netherland, a mariner who came by way of Paraíba in Brazil, and became a valued employee of the West India Company for a salary of eight florins a month. Bastiaen appears to have been regarded with respect and genuine affection by slaves. They named their children after him and asked him to be a witness to marriages and baptisms.[102]

The variable size of grants in the Land of the Blacks identifies other leaders among African slaves. The largest grant on record (eighteen acres) went to Manuel Trompetter. Five other half-free slaves received grants of ten to twelve acres: Domingo Angola, who succeeded him as Captain of the Blacks, Gracia d'Angola, Cleyn [Little] Manuel, Groot [Big] Manuel, and Manuel Gerrit de Reus. They had been among the first slave-petitioners for freedom.[103] Thirty others also received lesser grants, and improved them. These landowning, half-free Africans were not a small part of New Amsterdam's African population. Most of the first thirty-six grants went to men with families, who were described in a Dutch document as having wives and "many children." On a conservative assumption that mean family size averaged between two and three children, these half-free African families who lived on their own farms in the Land of the Blacks would have been between a quarter and a third of the 375 Africans in New Amsterdam, circa 1664. Later, other company slaves acquired similar half-free status in New Amsterdam and other parts of New Netherland during the last years of the Dutch colony.[104]

At the same time, a few privately owned slaves won freedom in other ways. On Long Island, several did so by their own initiative after long service, hard labor, and persistent effort. At Gravesend, Long Island, for example, the slave Anthony and Maria his wife were manumitted by the Dutch Council after they presented evidence that they had been promised freedom by their owner. Also freed, or half-freed, were "Francisco of Bushwick," "Black Hans" of Brooklyn, and "Peeter the Negro" of Southampton. These and other Africans formed a community of freed slaves on Long Island.[105]

Within the walls of New Amsterdam, other private slaves of individual masters were able to buy their freedom. Some continued to live with families of former owners, or resided near them in the town. Freedom did not come easily, and Dutch masters drove hard bargains. Historian Graham Hodges writes, "For all emancipated blacks . . . freedom would be hard earned and only after many years of service."[106]

ANOTHER PATH TO FREEDOM: THE AFRO-DUTCH FAMILY OF JAN DE VRIES AND SWARTINNE DE VRIES

Other Africans in the Hudson Valley were able to live outside of slavery in a different way. People in New Netherland were more open to race mixing than their English neighbors, though less so than in French Louisiana, Spanish Florida, or Portuguese Brazil. In New Amsterdam, some of these mixed marriages were supported by Dutch clergy and company officers.

A case in point was the family of Swartinne and Jan de Vries. His roots were in Friesland, across the Zuider Zee in the northern Netherlands. He followed the profession of arms, and soldiered with honor in the expanding Dutch empire—possibly in Africa, probably in Brazil, certainly in the Caribbean.[107]

In 1644, he was ordered to command a detachment of Dutch troops in New Netherland, and was given a seat on the Council. This tough, plain-talking, hard-bitten captain despised the businessmen who were running the colony. He had a violent falling-out with Director-General Kieft, "calling the director a liar and attempting to strike him, and assaulting another councillor," according to the Council Minutes.[108]

Captain de Vries was removed from command, and ordered home to stand trial. Superiors in the Netherlands heard his case, cleared his name, and sent him back to the colony. He lived openly with a slave woman named

Swartinne, long remembered as Black Beauty for her appearance and grace. Captain de Vries and Swartinne appear to have married before 1647. He emancipated her. Their son was accepted as legitimate and baptized Jan de Vries II in New Amsterdam's Dutch Reformed Church. Soon afterward, his father was lost at sea. Before his death he chose as the child's guardians two literate former slaves named Paolo de Angola and Clara Criole. They had been trusted friends of Captain de Vries and became the executors of his estate.[109]

Jan de Vries II later married, and his descendants settled near Groote Kill with the families of Augustine van Donck and Claes Emanuel. Their ancestry was also a mix of Europeans, Africans, American Indians, and other strains. They accumulated money, land, and property. But their historian writes that "culturally they were Dutch. They had Dutch names, spoke the Dutch language, lived in Dutch colonial farm houses, and were members of the Dutch Reformed Church."[110]

The de Vries, van Donck, and Emanuel families were not happy when Dutch New Netherland became English New York in 1664. They moved west, and joined others to buy a large tract called the Tappan Patent, beyond the Hudson River near the boundary between New York and New Jersey. They increased and multiplied for many generations. Later census records and other documents listed some as white, and others as free people of color. They had land of their own, and in the census of 1790 several owned slaves. They were a proud and sturdy people, and became an important presence in the hinterlands of the Hudson Valley. We shall meet them again.[111]

A THIRD PATH TO FREEDOM: SALEE THE TURK, GRIETSE REYNIERS, AND NEW AMSTERDAM'S AFRO-DUTCH UNDERWORLD

New Amsterdam was a rough, rollicking seaport town. Other colonial settlements were more than a little that way, but New Amsterdam went farther. It capitalized vice, converted it into an industry, and made it pay. New Amsterdam rapidly developed a highly profitable underworld on the model of Old Amsterdam, but with stronger Afro-European connections, and memorable characters.

Prominent among them was Grietse Reyniers, a German woman who came to New Amsterdam in 1633. She became the mistress of Director Wouter van Twiller, then left him to make a business of prostitution, in the entrepreneurial spirit of the Dutch colony.

Reyniers brought many gifts to her business, including a genius for advertising. According to sworn testimony she announced, "I have long been the
whore of the nobility. From now on I shall be the whore of the rabble." In
one riotous tavern scene that might have been painted by Pieter Brueghel or
Jan Steen, she used a broomstick to measure the "male members" of her customers and charged accordingly—all this from recorded testimony before the
Dutch Council.[112]

After a few years, Grietse Reyniers startled the town yet again by marrying
the "Black Mohammedan," Anthony Jansen van Salee, the affluent Islamic
son of an African woman and a highly successful Dutch pirate. In New Amsterdam, "Salee the Turk" and Grietse his wife had busy careers on both sides
of the law.[113]

In 1638–39, they were defendants in 16 percent of all criminal cases that
came before the Dutch Council.[114] The authorities could not decide what to
do with them. As problems multiplied, the Council ordered Salee to be banished from the colony. But his wealth was increasing, and the Council reconsidered. They revoked his exile from New Netherland, and merely banished
him to Brooklyn. There he acquired two hundred acres and continued to be
an active investor in the colonial economy.[115]

Reyniers and Van Salee raised at least four daughters. When one of them
was born, Grietse asked the midwife about the baby's color, and was told that
it was "about the same" as Salee the Turk, much to her relief.[116] Their daughters were very attractive, and as lively as their parents. They married into many
families of wealth and prominence. Among their descendants were a progeny
of Vanderbilts, Whitneys, Frelinghuysens, two Dukes of Marlborough, President Warren Harding, Humphrey Bogart, and Jacqueline Bouvier Kennedy.
Mrs. Kennedy told New York genealogists that she had known about a line of
descent from Anthony van Salee, but had been informed that he was a Jewish
gentleman. The genealogists did not pursue the subject.[117]

In early New Netherland, the many surviving court cases involving Reyniers and Van Salee are windows into an Afro-Dutch underworld of money,
sex, power, and opportunity. As early as 1638, this underworld was highly developed in New Amsterdam on the model of Old Amsterdam, where Simon
Schama wrote that "the city's sexual entrepôt in some ways was a distorted
mirror image of its more licit commerce." In America it offered a path beyond
half-freedom, to freedom and a half. That pattern has persisted in the Hudson
Valley through four centuries, from Dutch New Amsterdam to English New
York, and the American metropolis that we know today.[118]

FORMATION OF AFRO-DUTCH FAMILIES

There was yet another side to Afro-European culture in the Hudson Valley. Its very able historian, Joyce Goodfriend, observed from long study that Africans in New Amsterdam had "more success in building stable family life" than did slaves in other regions of North America. Several scholars have been skeptical, but surviving evidence supports her judgment. Even more interesting is evidence of the many ways in which they did it. Some of these families were nuclear on the west European model; others were similar to extended African families. Many managed to combine both elements.[119]

African slaves actively bargained with their Dutch masters such as Van Rensselaers and Stuyvesants to form families and to hold them together. Some Dutch clergy (not all of them) supported the formation of families by conducting marriage and baptismal ceremonies for slaves—more so than in other North American slave systems. Goodfriend believes that other slaves married in traditional African ceremonies, and some did both. These slave families took many forms—single-headed and double-headed, nuclear and extended, monagamous and polygamous, slave and free.[120]

When slave unions were disrupted by death, Dutch church records provide striking evidence of rapid remarriage and active support of children. Here was evidence of a depth of purpose among both Dutch masters and African slaves in maintaining strong families. An example from the Dutch Reformed Church in New Amsterdam was the christening of a slave child named Anthony in August 1643. Dorothy Angola, widow of Paolo d'Angola, stood as a witness, in a role that was comparable to a godparent in other Christian denominations. Later the child Anthony became an orphan. His witness Dorothy Angola and her husband adopted him. Church records hold other instances of what has been called the "reabsorption" of orphans, widows, and widowers in slave families. In New Netherland, slave witnesses played a constructive role.[121]

Further evidence of family strength appeared in the descent of names. Baptized children of Dutch slaves "often carried the names of older men and women in the community." Historians have reconstructed this process in the family of the slave Claes Emanuel. After the first generation, baptized children continued to receive European forenames of Christian saints, often inherited from parents and grandparents: Jan, Domingo, Pieter. Further, scholars have observed that in New Amsterdam the offspring of slaves "often maintained African surnames even in freedom." These sustained efforts supported slave families, and restored them after they were broken. They succeeded through the combined intervention of African slaves and Dutch masters—engaging both cultures to mutual gain.[122]

In the African Burial Ground, physical evidence survives of strong bonds of affection between husbands and wives, parents and children of slave families in New Netherland. One man was interred in a plain coffin; "someone had painstakingly fashioned a heart-shaped object on its lid with brass tacks." It combined African motifs with western emblems of love in an Afro-European design.

Another very young child was buried with a silver earring hanging from a pendant around its neck. Other emblems included African beadwork, bracelets, necklaces, girdles, waistbands, and small troves of cowrie shells, or bits of stone and shell, or pieces of silver in a pouch tied with a leather thong. Slaves who had been victims of appalling cruelty were laid to rest with emblems of enduring love from families, friends, and relations. These tokens combined African artifacts with European symbols in creative combinations. Here again, the strongest pattern was not merely the preservation of African or European artifacts, but a third pattern that drew upon both. Elements of traditional cultures were combined to create something new in the world.[123]

AFRO-EUROPEAN RELIGION

Also striking among these African families was the strength of religious belief. Many Angolan and Congo slaves had been converted to Christianity before they came to America. At the same time these Christians also shared indigenous African religions. In New Netherland as in other American places, they created a faith of deeper meaning to themselves by combining elements of different religions. Evidence appeared in burial practices and mortuary customs, "in many instances blending Christian rituals with traditional African customs." This pattern appeared in West Central Africa and also in New Netherland.[124]

New Amsterdam's Calvinist minister Everardus Bogardus welcomed slaves to his Dutch Reformed Church. It is interesting to discover that he had also worked for the West India Company in Africa. From 1641 he performed church weddings among slaves in America, and baptized their children as well. That process promoted the formation of nuclear families, and also encouraged the growth of extended kin networks. It also reinforced ties of community.[125]

As time passed, other Dutch Reformed ministers in New Netherland grew hostile to African conversions and refused to perform baptisms and marriages of slaves. The apparent cause was a concern that Christianity could undercut slavery itself. But as the clergy withdrew from this work, Dutch laymen became more active in their place. Peter Stuyvesant supported a chapel for slaves near his home. His wife sponsored a school for the spiritual instruction of children of African slaves and European tenants, who attended class together. Later, when Dutch clergy refused to baptize the children of slaves, a friend wrote that "with great forethought on the part of Madame Stuyvesant, your honor's spouse, they were presented at the baptismal font." Other Dutch laymen such as Cornelius van Borsum set aside land for slave burial grounds. These efforts persisted in the Hudson Valley for many generations, longer than in New Netherland itself.[126]

African and Dutch culture also mixed together on religious holidays, especially Christmas, and most of all Pentecost, the seventh Sunday after Easter, known as Whitsuntide to the English, and Pinkster to the Dutch. It celebrated the descent of the Holy Spirit to the apostles of Jesus Christ, and was a day of triumph and celebration. For slaves and servants in New Netherland it became a day of high carnival which combined African and Dutch customs.[127]

DYNAMICS OF AFRO-DUTCH SLAVERY:
PATTERNS OF CHANGE AND PERSISTENCE

In the 1640s, numbers of African slaves in New Netherland began to grow more rapidly. A major factor was the cost of free labor. The expense of keeping a European servant for one year was greater than the purchase of an African slave for life.[128] Demand for slaves surged. A measure was the price of prime hands, which in New Amsterdam rose from 300 guilders in 1646, to 450 in 1660, and 600 in 1664. Even so, slaves were cheaper than free workers.[129]

Altogether, incomplete records show that at least 467 slaves were brought to New Netherland from 1626 to 1664.[130] At the same time, Africans in the entire colony grew to about eight hundred, out of about eight thousand inhabitants—10 percent of the population.[131] The capital of New Amsterdam in 1664 included about 375 Africans in a total population of 1875—20 percent.[132] Approximately 75 to 100 Africans in New Amsterdam were free, or half-free, or some of their slave children were raised as free.[133]

After 1650, the pattern of African origins in New Netherland became more diverse, as Dutch slaving voyages multiplied along the Atlantic coast of Africa. The Dutch West India Company had strong regional preferences in slaves. Johannes Postma observed from long study that "Dutch merchants and masters knew clearly who they did not want." They shared a general European prejudice against Ibo slaves from the Bight of Biafra, whom they called "Calabaries" after the ports of Old and New Calabar. Dutch purchasers complained that Africans from this region took badly to bondage, and described them as "lazy," "crazy," and "retarded," which was grossly inaccurate, but a persistent belief. The Dutch West India Company forbade slave trading in the Bight of Biafra, on pain of the loss of the ship and goods. Merchants protested that these instructions were too restrictive, but the orders were often repeated. In the late seventeenth century, Biafrans were 0.1 percent of Dutch slaves, in sharp contrast with some English colonies.[134]

In West Africa the company had a preference for slaves from the Bight of Benin, which briefly became a leading source of slaves carried to all parts of America by the Dutch West India Company: 66 percent at mid-century; 89 percent at the century's end.[135]

A pivotal moment was the arrival of the ship *Wittepart* in 1655, with three hundred slaves (160 men, 140 women) from the Bight of Benin. The company also licensed the ship *St. John*, circa 1652, to obtain slaves for New Netherland on the Guinea Coast.[136] In 1656, the ship *Bontekoe* arrived from upper West Africa. A third of its captives were to be taken to Curaçao; the rest went to New Amsterdam.[137] These arrivals increased the diversity of African origins in New Netherland, but the older trade from West Central Africa also continued.

Altogether, Manhattan Island in its Dutch period became a powerful magnet for adventurers and entrepreneurs of many nations, creeds, and colors. Of importance were the origins and purposes of Dutch founders. Also important were the origins, acts, and choices of African slaves who shared an entrepreneurial spirit that had roots in their African homelands. They played the capitalist game of getting and keeping with remarkable success. As this unique colony grew more diverse, its core character survived and flourished.

In the midst of that diversity, a major factor was the early predominance of Angolan and Congolese origins for more than thirty years. That fundamental fact promoted comity and solidarity among slaves. They were able to form families, and acquire property. Most important, they looked after one another. By striving together and sharing initiatives, many became at least half-free. They developed a distinctive Afro-European culture of their own.

As we shall see, these small beginnings would have a long reach in the Hudson Valley. They did so after Dutch New Netherland became the English colony of New York, and later an American state. As New York became the great metropolis of the American republic, it developed distinctive patterns of society, ethnicity, and culture.

THE "LIVING LEGACY" OF AFRO-DUTCH WAYS IN THE HUDSON VALLEY

In the Anglo-Dutch hostilities of 1664, a squadron of British warships arrived at New Amsterdam. Both Dutch and African people in the colony knew what was coming. Eight African slaves had suddenly been made half-free in December 1663. They appear to have known that half-freedom was not recognized in English law, and they feared the worst for themselves and their families. These half-free slaves went to the Dutch Council "with folded hands and bended knees," and petitioned that they be "released from their slavery and be granted freedom" full and complete, before the British took over the colony. Director-General Peter Stuyvesant and the Council agreed. As one of their last acts, they prepared certificates of manumission for half-free company slaves. They also confirmed new land grants of houses and lots near Stuyvesant's farm, and urged the freed slaves to "move into a village" on their own land.[138]

Private Dutch slaves remained in bondage, but the new British rulers were quick to note something special in their culture and character. An English captain who had been held prisoner in New Amsterdam observed that "their blacks were very free and familiar; sometimes sauntering about among the whites at meal times, with hat on head, and freely joining occasionally in conversation as if they were one and all of the same household."[139]

Joyce Goodfriend writes that African slaves in early New Netherland were "far from being inert victims of their condition, and urban blacks were alert, inventive, risk-taking people." She observed: "Supported by a reservoir of spiritual beliefs they struggled to affirm their separate and distinct identity while combatting the assaults of bondage." She added, "The legacy of New Amsterdam's strong black community, with its nucleus of free blacks—in part, a living legacy—gave newly arrived slaves a vital model for group life."[140]

Building on their African heritage, Angolan, Congolese, and Luangan slaves developed a strong sense of solidarity among themselves. They engaged their own entrepreneurial traditions with those of Dutch masters, expanded their own rights and privileges, invented unique Afro-European customs in America, and enlarged their own agency in the process.

At the same time, they also helped to shape a distinctive pattern of cultural pluralism in the Hudson Valley, which combined strong conflict among ethnic groups and complex concord within them. That cultural dynamic had enduring consequences for the future of its region. Elements of its seventeenth-century origins survived when New Netherland became the British colony of New York, and yet again when the British colony was transformed into an American state. Angolan and Congo slaves and profit-seeking Dutch businessmen had active roles from the start.

ENGLISH NEW YORK: PERSISTENCE AND CHANGE

In 1664, the English conquered New Netherland. The Dutch briefly recovered their old colony in the Third Anglo-Dutch War of 1673, but were forced to surrender it once more, this time for good.

England's Stuart King Charles II gave the colony to his brother James, Duke of York, as a proprietary grant. New Netherland became New York, and it was ruled from the top down in the Stuart way. In 1685, the duke became England's King James II, and his deputies became absolutist governors over much of North America. Together they provoked the Glorious Revolution of 1688–89 in both England and five American colonies, and they were removed from office. The result was a remarkably stable revolutionary settlement in England, and a deeply unstable outcome in the American colonies.

What followed in New York was a century of rapid growth and increasing conflict, which overflowed into violence. From 1673 to 1775, the Hudson Valley suffered large tenant rebellions, bloody slave revolts, and even more bloody repressions. All of these were violent collisions between a narrow English elite, increasingly assertive of arbitrary powers, and an expanding population of ethnic diversity, increasingly conscious of their individual and collective rights.

Africans were at the center of these events. British conquerors of New Netherland were surprised to find former slaves living in various degrees of freedom. They were amazed to discover a Land of the Blacks north of New Amsterdam, and demanded an explanation. Were land grants to former slaves lawful? In 1665, the much maligned Dutch director-general Peter Stuyvesant answered to his credit that "all of these parcels of land were given to the aforesaid Negroes in true and free ownership, with such privileges as all tracts of land are bestowed on the inhabitants of [this] province." Further, Stuyvesant added that the land was theirs by right and justice, as they had "cleared and cultivated" it with their own labor, and it had been "owned and possessed unmolested for many years."[141]

The new British rulers were bound by treaty to respect existing rights of property, and generally they did so. But they also acted quickly to reverse the direction of change. In 1665, British officials carefully limited indentured servitude to Europeans who "willingly sell themselves into bondage" for specific terms. In 1679, Governor Edmund Andros also prohibited slavery of American Indians, and the Council ordered the release of Christian Indians from bondage.[142]

At the same time the new British regime strongly supported African slavery, and increasingly defined it in explicitly racial terms. Repeated laws confirmed the right to keep slaves. In the 1670s and 1680s, colonial leaders attracted wealthy immigrants with the award of large "manors" such as Fordham, Morrisania, Pelham, and Scarsdale, to be developed with tenants, servants, and slaves.

English rulers also encouraged the immigration of wealthy Barbadians such as Lewis and Richard Morris. They joined the ruling elite, and were among the largest slave owners in New York and East Jersey. Other Barbadians bought fifteen thousand acres in Bergen County and named it New Barbados. They brought their slaves, and introduced the harsh practices of West Indian slavery.[143]

In the city of New York, the number of slaves doubled from 375 in 1664 to 700 in 1698.[144] In part these numbers grew by natural increase, a rare event in slave populations, where deaths have tended to be more common than births, from systems of ancient slavery to twentieth-century slavery in barbaric Nazi and Japanese camps, and Stalinist gulags. But New York was different. A census for the entire colony, circa 1724, by customs officer Francis Harrison counted 1,087 "blacks" under the age of eight in a total population of 6,171 "blacks young and old." The proportion of children was smaller than among whites, but larger than most slave regimes.[145]

Mortality rates of African Americans were high in New York, mainly during winter months, mostly from pulmonary diseases that took a heavy toll on immigrants from equatorial Africa. In 1702, an epidemic in New York City reduced the population of slaves and free Blacks by 10 percent in one deadly season. After 1703 numbers began to rise more rapidly in New York

City: 970 in 1712, 1362 in 1723, 1577 in 1731, 3,137 in 1771, roughly a threefold increase. In the entire colony as a whole, the African population increased even more rapidly, from 2,170 in 1698 to 19,883 in 1771—nearly a tenfold growth.[146]

Most of this increase came from the expanding Atlantic slave trade. The most comprehensive data have been gathered by David Eltis, David Richardson, and their many colleagues for the Trans-Atlantic Slave Trade Database. They found evidence that approximately 9,000 slaves disembarked at New York and Perth Amboy in East Jersey from 1655 to 1775. They also estimated an undercount of 41 percent, which would yield a corrected estimate of approximately 15,300 slaves who arrived in New York and East Jersey from 1655 to 1775.[147]

One consequence was an increasing diversity of African origins. Slaves were brought to New York from many parts of Africa and the New World—a trend of much importance in our story. Many African ethnic groups, each with its own mix of languages and cultures, began to form in English New York and East Jersey.

ARRIVALS FROM WEST AFRICA

One of the most visible African groups were slaves from the Gold Coast in what is now Ghana. Many were carried to America by ships trading with the British Royal African Company. Founded in 1664, it claimed a monopoly of the slave trade from West Africa to British colonies in the West Indies and North America. A controlling interest in the company was held by England's royal family including the Duke of York, together with some of his associates who governed New York.

The Royal African Company acquired many of its slaves from English trading castles in West Africa, shipped most of them to the West Indies, and carried others to New York. The trade was actively promoted by royal officials in the service of the Duke of York, men such as Francis Harrison, a former officer in the company's West African trading forts who became a customs official in New York.[148]

These slaves have been known by many names. Academic writers in the twenty-first century call them Akan, after a family of languages in West Africa. British traders in the eighteenth century knew them as Coromantee, after the port of Kormantine on the coast of Ghana. In the early eighteenth century, British factors bought these slaves from Fante traders, who had captured many of them in wars with Asante rivals. These Akan-speaking Asante slaves were a small minority in New York, but they had a prominence out of proportion of their numbers. Others from Benin were called Paw Paw or Popo. A few from the Bight of Biafra were called Calabar Negroes. In ethnicity many of them tended to be Ibo or Ibibio.[149]

"MALAGASY NEGROES"

Yet another part of New York's slave trade came from Madagascar, off the coast of East Africa. Parliament gave the British East India Company a monopoly of commerce in the Indian Ocean and East Africa, but forbade it to trade directly with the American colonies. Merchants in New York, especially Frederick Philipse, Jacobus van Cortlandt, and John Cruger were quick to seize an opportunity.[150] They organized an illicit and highly profitable commerce with Arab slavers, African chiefs, and American pirates such as Captain Kidd. Cargoes of liquor, gunpowder, and weapons were bartered for slaves on the island of Madagascar. Shiploads of slaves arrived in New York from Madagascar as early as 1698, in numbers large enough to glut the New York market. Many of these slaves called themselves Malagasy, as Madagascar is now called the Malagasy Republic. The flow continued as late as 1721 when a ship brought "Malagasy Negroes" to New York.[151]

Glimpses of this illegal trade survive in scattered records. A clue to its scale also appears in advertisements for runaway slaves in New York newspapers. They made frequent reference to Madagascar and Malagasy Negroes, and described them as a distinct ethnic group, with a different appearance from West African and Central African slaves. The evidence of the Trans-Atlantic Slave Database confirms the importance of the Madagascar slave trade in this period, and the depth of corruption in New York.[152]

SPANISH NEGROES IN ENGLISH NEW YORK

Yet another New York slave trade developed on the high seas. During colonial wars, British and Dutch privateers made a profitable business of preying upon Spanish and Portuguese vessels in American waters. Captives were taken to New York, where its corrupt Vice Admiralty Court condemned passengers to slavery "by reason of their color which is swarthy," unless they could submit proof they were free. Many dark-complected seamen and passengers were sent to the auction block on Manhattan, protesting their freedom in vain.

In 1740, during the War of Jenkins' Ear, an English privateer captain named John Lush seized a Spanish merchant ship, captured nineteen "negroes and mulattoes," and carried them to New York. They were hard-bitten Spanish seamen, armed with seamen's clasp knives. All spoke Spanish, and some could speak English as well, and appear to have been men of strength and character, and they protested they were free.

Some appear to have been treated well by their purchasers, who testified to their "good character" and said they "never had a more faithful servant" than these men, and so allowed them many liberties in New York City, including freedom of movement after their work was done. But the seamen hated their captor, Captain John Lush, whom they despised as a liar and cheat. They also loathed New York's judges and town officials, who regarded their complexions as proof of slavery and sold them into bondage.[153]

Their mistreatment went on for years, until the Spanish governor of Hispaniola learned of their fate, and sent an officer to warn that if the "Spanish Negroes" were not released, English prisoners from New York would be treated as slaves. Some of these Spanish Negroes were eventually set free. But in the meantime, they became yet another ethnic group of Africans in New York.[154]

WEST INDIAN SLAVES: THE DEFIANCE OF WARD'S WILL

Other clusters of slaves from the Caribbean islands became a large part of New York's imports in the early eighteenth century. By two official counts from 1715 to 1741, 66 percent of slaves arriving in New York came from the West Indies. Most of them arrived from the three British islands of Jamaica, Barbados, and Antigua.[155]

Buyers in New York complained that West Indian owners sent "refuse slaves" who were ill or aged. Others were thought to be "troublesome" and regarded with suspicion in New York by magistrates and masters alike.

A leading example in every sense was a slave named Ward's Will. On "credible information," a New York court found that Will had been involved in "two conspiracies in the West Indies," the first at St. Johns in the Danish Virgin Islands, the last on Antigua in 1736. While drinking with other slaves at a New York tavern "in Easter holidays," Will was heard to say that a master "would not allow him to come to his wife, but before it was long he would shew him a trick, and that the negroes here [in New York] were cowards; for that they had no hearts as those at Antigua." Will was tried, found guilty of "conspiracy," and sentenced to be burned alive, not for an overt act, but for his attitude. He remained defiant to the end. Judge Daniel Horsmanden wrote that "The pile being kindled, this wretch set his back to the stake, and raising up one of his legs, laid it on the fire." The memory of his spirit survives to our time.[156]

Royal officials in New York tried to deal with these problems by levying higher taxes on slaves imported from the West Indies. The predictable result was more smuggling, less control over the trade, and more West Indian rebels who contributed their defiance to the culture of New York. New York captains landed them illegally on Long Island, western Connecticut, and East Jersey. These "West Indian Negroes" continued to form distinct ethnic groups on Manhattan, with their own dialects and culture.[157]

At the same time, Dutch merchants and patroons used long-established linkages to continue the older flow of African slaves through the Dutch port of Curaçao in the Caribbean, and directly from Angola and Congo. They also traded with Dutch stations in what are now Benin and Togo, on the "Slave Coast," east of the Gold Coast.[158]

An example was the Philipse family. Its founder, Frederick Philipse (1626–1702), came to New Netherland as a carpenter. He married Margaret Hardenbroek, and together they built one of the largest fortunes in the Hudson Valley.

The family's seat was Philipsburg Manor, which spanned two hundred square miles along the Hudson River, from Spuyten Duyvil to Ossining. It included industrial villages called Upper Mills near Sleepy Hollow, and Lower Mills at what would later become the factory city of Yonkers. This family also owned much real estate in New York City and New Jersey. These holdings remained in the family through four generations, to great-grandson Frederick Philipse III (1720–1785).[159]

The Philipse family were among New York's largest slave owners. In 1700, Philipse's will listed by name twenty-one slaves in his upriver estate, and another six in his New York City residence. By 1750, the number of slaves had grown to seventy-six in Philipsburg alone.[160]

The Philipses were also very active slave traders in Africa. In 1685, Philipse's ship *Charles* sailed to Soyo just south of the Congo River, took aboard a full cargo of slaves, sold some of them in Barbados, and brought the rest to Philipsburg's Upper Mills. Historian Dennis Maika writes that "this small, ethnically coherent group of Congolese became the core of the Upper Mills slave community." Later it included other slaves from West Africa and Madagascar.[161]

Many Philipse slaves at the Upper Mills community also worked in the slave trade. Nicholas Cartagena was skilled at languages and he served aboard the Philipse slave ship *Charles* as a "linguistor" on African voyages. Even as a slave himself, he was also able to trade in slaves on his own account, and later bought his own freedom with profits from the trade. Others included an African woman named Marramita who worked as a cook aboard Philipse slave ships. A slave cooper named Frank was sent to sea on slave ships, making wooden tubs for use in the Middle Passage.[162]

THE "REAFRICANIZATION" OF SLAVES
IN ENGLISH NEW YORK

This expansive slave trade caused a surge in New York's African population, and a shift in its culture. Several historians have called this process a "reafricanization" of New York in the eighteenth century.[163]

African customs and rituals appeared in many ways. New Yorkers complained of what Anglican military chaplain John Sharpe called "heathenish rites" in the African Burial Ground, and of "feverish drumming and chanting" in the night. These African sounds after dark disturbed the sleep of Manhattan's master class and filled them with alarm. New York's Common Council banned night burials and limited mourners to twelve people at each African funeral. But the slave trade kept growing, and "feverish drumming and chanting" continued in the night.[164]

The spread of African customs also appeared in other forms during this period. New York's clergy in the eighteenth century complained that slaves were practicing polygamy on an African model. The Reverend John Sharpe also testified to the prevalence of polygamous marriages. So did the French Huguenot missionary Elias Neau. "I thunder against polygamy," Neau wrote in 1718, but by his own estimate he had little effect.[165]

Language changed too. New York's slaves were increasingly polylingual in European, Amerindian, and African languages. The linguistic skills of Africans were much in evidence. Many quickly learned Dutch and English. Others spoke Spanish, Portuguese, French, and two were described as speaking even Welsh and Irish Gaelic. Their mastery of American Indian languages multiplied as traders reached farther into the interior of the continent.

Many African languages were spoken in eighteenth-century English New York. The Bantu languages of West Central Africa persisted, and were reinforced by a continued flow from other regions. Akan languages were spoken by slave leaders in New York City. Malagasy speakers arrived from Madagascar. These speechways compounded the diversity of New York and East Jersey, and contributed to the continuing complexity of pluralist culture of this region.[166]

GROWTH OF MULTIPLE CREOLE CULTURES AND SPEECHWAYS AMONG NEW YORK SLAVES

Another dimension of diversity appeared in new "Creole" (native) cultures and languages. They developed among slaves who had been born and raised in Dutch New Netherland and English New York. Their primary languages became Dutch and English, but at the same time they were still African. Language was a clue to their complex identities.

In 1744, for example, an Annapolis physician named Alexander Hamilton was traveling in New York with his Maryland slave Dromo. Near Coney Island, Dromo asked directions from a woman on the road. She answered in a dialect called Black Dutch. It was incomprehensible to Dromo's Black English. Doctor Hamilton had an interest in languages and recorded their exchange:

"Dis de way to York?" says Dromo.
"Yaw, dat is Yarikee," said the wench, pointing to the steeples.
"What devil you say?" replys Dromo.
"Yaw, mynheer," said the wench.
"Damme you, what you say?" said Dromo again.
"Yaw, Yaw," said the girl.
"You a damn black bitch," said Dromo, and so rode on.[167]

Black Dutch speechways developed in a diversity of different forms throughout New York and East Jersey. They continued to be spoken and studied into the early twentieth century. Professor John Dyneley Prince reported, circa 1910, "A small colony of old negroes living on the mountain back of Suffern, New York who still use their own dialect of Jersey Dutch, but they are very difficult of access, owing to their shyness of strangers."[168]

Other Afro-English dialects developed among native-born "York Negroes" as they called themselves. These modal groups took their identity not from an African ethnic group or region, but from their place of residence in the New World, and from Creole patterns of mixed language and ethnic cultures unique to this region.[169]

"CUSTOMS OF THE COUNTRY": DYNAMICS OF CHANGE IN ENGLISH NEW YORK

In 1703, nearly forty years after New Netherland became New York, a census was taken in New York City. It found that the Dutch were still a majority in the town's free population at 52 percent. Many of these Dutch families owned African slaves, as did members of every large ethnic group, including free Africans. But the Dutch were still the largest group of masters, and their customs persisted for many years.[170]

Through much of the eighteenth century, slaves were most heavily concentrated in counties, towns, and neighborhoods that had been predominantly Dutch. At mid-century, a census in 1749 found that "blacks" in the entire colony of New York were 16.8 percent of the population. After East and West Jersey combined to form New Jersey they were 10.8 percent in 1745. In Dutch areas such as New York's Kings County (Brooklyn), "blacks" were 34 percent of the population. They were 20 percent in Bergen County, New Jersey. The city of New York in 1749 had a third of the colony's population (13,294 of 36,474) and 17.8 percent were African: the highest level of urbanization in any North American region.[171]

Overall, the entire region of New York and New Jersey had about ten thousand slaves in 1745–49, and their numbers were growing rapidly, doubling to twenty thousand in 1775. In North America, this was much the largest concentration above the Mason-Dixon line.

Some Dutch masters, as we have seen, worked their slaves very hard. But they also used incentives and bargaining to extract more profit at less cost from slave labor. This traditional pattern of Afro-Dutch slavery persisted in the English colonies of New York and New Jersey. More than fifty years after the end of Dutch rule, the English slave owner Cadwallader Colden called it "the Custome of the Country." Colden was rich and powerful, a holder of high offices, owner of an estate of three thousand acres and a mansion in New York City. But for all his wealth and power, he had trouble controlling a female slave, and complained of "her abusive tongue" and "sullenness." In 1717, he wrote to a West Indian merchant of "the Custome of the Country that will not allow us to use our Negroes as you do in Barbados when they Displease you."[172]

Two different truths have been told about the dynamics of this system in the Hudson Valley. English officials complained that slaves in New York were treated too leniently. Supreme Court justice Daniel Horsmanden frequently criticized New York masters for allowing their slaves an "excess of liberty" in an increasingly open process. The royal governor, Lord Cornbury, was specially outraged by what he called the "great insolency" of slaves in New York City.

A countervailing truth has been told by historians of slavery. They reported evidence that in New York's English period from 1664 to 1775, Africans both free and slave were caught in a "closing vise" of increasing repression. By contrast with the Dutch period, these scholars also observed that in English New York, "slaves found avenues to freedom closed," and "free blacks found their rights being eroded." [173]

Which of these views are correct? The short answer is both. Two trends coexisted in the Hudson Valley, and we may observe their interplay in many events. In 1696, New York City's mayor William Merritt commanded an "illegal assembly" of slaves to disperse. A slave named Prince came forward, and with his bare hand struck the mayor full in the face. Prince was seized and sentenced to be "stripped naked from the middle upwards . . . tyed to the tail of a cart . . . drawn round the City," and "at every corner of every street to receive eleven lashes on his Body." In 1696, New York City had above one hundred street intersections. Prince's penalty, if fully executed, would have been more than a thousand lashes—enough to shred his bodily flesh and kill even a strong man. [174]

This sentence of whipping through the streets of English New York was very similar to "flogging through the fleet," which was the penalty for striking a ship's officer in the Royal Navy. The combination of "great insolency" in Prince and extreme severity of his punishment was fundamental to the dynamics of slavery in English New York. Growing "liberties" by "insolent slaves" led to greater repression by angry masters and city officials, which in turn caused more "liberties" by infuriated slaves. That pattern shaped the history of slavery in New York through its English period.

GROWING ETHNIC PLURALISM AMONG SLAVE ASSOCIATIONS IN ENGLISH NEW YORK

This double dynamic of liberty and repression was most visible in the city of New York during the early and middle years of the eighteenth century. About a third of the colony's slaves lived in the city, and perhaps another third came and went on errands for their masters or their own business. [175]

New York's census of 1737 found that African slaves resided in every ward, in proportions of between 11 and 25 percent. Most slaves lived with their owners, and slept in attics, cellars, outbuildings, or "negro kitchens." But their activities were not confined.[176] Household and artisanal slaves were often the earliest to rise in the morning, and the last to sleep at night. Every morning and evening, one of their first and last tasks was to fetch water from town pumps, which they did without direct supervision. These and other errands gave them much freedom of movement. The rhythm of their lives allowed slaves to meet others in complex webs of association.[177]

The associations took many forms. Some of the larger groups were what we would call gangs, each with its own turf. Before 1740, two major gangs of African slaves divided much of New York City into territories of their own invention. One gang was called the Fly Boys, after the Fly Market where Maiden Lane met the East River. Another gang was called the Long Bridge Boys, near a wood-built ferry landing on the west side. According to one contemporary account, these gangs were subdivided into "companies," with "captains" and "headfellows." [178]

More numerous, but smaller in size than the territorial gangs, were tavern groups of slaves who had money enough to buy drink, and especially food. New York slaves often complained that meager rations from miserly masters were not enough to live on. Hungry bondsmen gathered together in cellars and back rooms of taverns, early in the morning and late at night. While the master class was abed and the City Watch was sleeping, slaves ate and drank together, and "played cards and dice." So lucrative was their business that one tavern keeper held regular cockfights for their amusement. Another sponsored a dance every other night, with African drummers and slave fiddlers.[179]

Other associations were criminal rings of varying size and strength. Slaves who were themselves a species of property tended to think of larceny from the master class as a form of liberation. One of these rings called itself the Black Guard. Another was led by Caesar and Prince, both prominent slave leaders and Big Men in the town. In 1735 or 1736, they broke into the cellar of Richard Baker's tavern and stole several barrels of gin, then called Geneva. They were caught, carted through the town, and whipped five lashes at "every street corner." Thereafter they defiantly called themselves the Geneva Club and ran another crime ring in the city for at least five years.[180]

Larger criminal combinations in New York included slaves, free Blacks, and whites. Some operated on a surprising scale. One group of slaves broke into a storehouse and stole "fifty or sixty" firkins of butter—more than a ton and a half of butter! They delivered it to tavern keeper John Romme, who trafficked in stolen goods and was able to find a buyer for that very large supply of a perishable commodity.[181]

Yet another category of slave associations were ethnic groups. Leading examples were New York's "Spanish Negroes," a formidable group, as we have seen, mostly seamen captured at sea and sold as slaves. In New York, they clubbed together after dark. Three other ethnic groups were Akan-speaking slaves, and "Malagasy men," and "West Indian Negroes."[182]

Some of these ethnic associations of slaves in New York were modeled on secret societies in Central and West Africa, with clandestine rituals and coded passwords. Irish soldier William Kane observed one such secret society of slaves in a New York tavern. Its members drew a black ring on the floor, and every member put his left foot inside the ring. The rituals included bloodletting, blood mixing, and sacred blood oaths.[183]

Yet other secretive slave associations borrowed freely from European fraternal orders. One group called itself Freemasons and formed a Black lodge that was not recognized by white Masons, but organized itself on a Masonic model. A few groups in eighteenth-century New York went a third way. They were pluralist associations of slaves and freedmen, Africans and Indians, European soldiers and seamen. Their variety reflected the growing diversity of English New York.[184]

These many different groups were similar in one respect. Most were described as for men only. No evidence of associations among slave women has turned up in English New York, but probably they existed, as they had in Africa.

In New York, these associations were most active on holidays, especially Christmas and Pentecost. It became a time of High Carnival for slaves in New York, with the knowledge and permission of their masters—a custom that was kept in other ways among many systems of slavery throughout America.[185]

In the early and mid-eighteenth century, evidence for many varieties of slave associations appeared in court testimony. The authorities were troubled by their very existence, and more so by their activities, which were fundamentally hostile to the official culture of New York. Some were known to support crime, and to encourage armed resistance. But the authorities were unable to suppress them, and many of these groups operated with impunity in English New York City.[186]

Other African associations formed throughout the colony. A surprising example in Queens County on Long Island was "a group of enslaved and independent Africans" who "formed themselves into a military company for recreation and entertainment." After 1741 they were "ordered to disband." [187] But these groups continued to exist. Their combined effect was a transformation of Afro-European cultures into a more pluralist system. Once again, slave leaders played instrumental roles in its development.

CAPTAIN JACK, "A SLAVE WHO LOOKED LIKE A GENTLEMAN"

In English New York, some African American slaves rapidly acquired power and authority over others in bondage. More than a few achieved a high degree of independence from their owners, and lived complex lives with multiple roles. In working hours these slave leaders tended to be master craftsmen, or majordomos, or foremen over other slaves. [188]

After dark, some of them became leaders of another kind, in a shadow world that awakened when masters and rulers slept. A leading example was an African slave known to New Yorkers by several names. The master class called him "Comfort's Jack" after his prosperous Dutch owner, Gerardus Comfort, a master cooper who lived in a fashionable house on New Street near the town center. He owned a thriving cooperage on the west edge of town, with its own shops, barn, stable, a pier on the Hudson River, and another house where some of his slaves lived together. They included male artisans and laborers and a slave cook named Jenny. Comfort's Jack was firmly in charge.

Sometimes Jack worked with two of his owner's sons-in-law, but more often he had no supervision. It was said that "his master was frequently absent from home for days and weeks together, which left him too much at liberty." Others observed that Jack "looked upon the [west end] house as his own, and himself as his own master." [189]

Comfort's cooperage also had a special asset. The Comfort slaves dug a well in the yard, and tapped into an abundant underground stream which came to be known as having some of the "sweetest water in New York." Families throughout the city were allowed to use it. "Every day, morning and afternoon," slaves were sent with wooden kegs "to fetch tea-water" from Comfort's Well as it was called. These slaves were a large part of the city's population. They came to know Comfort's Jack, and called him Captain Jack for his manner, bearing, and leadership. One court document described Jack as a slave who "looked like a gentleman." [190]

Other slaves in town came to know Jack in yet a third way, and called him Uncle Jack, Cousin Jack, or Brother Jack in the African sense of "a brother by another mother." Some of these slaves also called him their countryman, for he appears to have belonged to a larger group of New York's Akan-speaking Coromantee slaves. [191]

Jack's first language appears to have been an Akan dialect. A New York judge with a tin ear wrote that "his dialect was so perfectly negro and unintelligible it was thought that it would be impossible to make anything of him without the help of an interpreter." But it appears to have been unintelligible only when Jack wished to make it so. Jack also spoke a broken but forceful English that most other people could understand. It included Afro-English expressions that suggested a former connection to Jamaica, and linked him to expanding circles of West Indian slaves in New York City. [192]

Captain Jack also moved in yet another orbit. Next door to Comfort's Cooperage was Hughson's Tavern, the most notorious "disorderly house" in New York City. It was run by John Hughson and his wife and daughter, both named Sarah. At the same time it was also an active brothel, with a busy Irish prostitute named Peggy Kerry who was famous for her bright red hair and lively manner. She was known through the city as the "Newfoundland Irish beauty," and was said to serve all comers, including African slaves. She lived in a boardinghouse run by a free Negro named Frank, and had a lover and protector pimp who was another slave leader named Varick's Caesar after his owner, baker John Varick. [193]

John Hughson's busy tavern was another center of yet another business. The owner himself fenced stolen goods and operated a smuggling ring. Probably he used Comfort's Pier on the Hudson River without interference by customs officers who were bribed to look the other way.

Hughson's tavern also became a favorite gathering place for African associations. One Sunday a slave came to visit Captain Jack. He was taken next door to Hughson's "where there were about twenty negroes," and Jack "gave him drink." On holidays there were special feasts for slaves at Hughson's Tavern, and dances with African drummers and fiddlers. [194]

Many of New York City's slave leaders met together at Hughson's. Among them was Irish Peggy's protector, Varick's Caesar, and also Auboyneau's Prince, slave of merchant John Auboyneau; and Philipse's Cuffe, slave of

Adolph Philipse, a wealthy merchant, successful manufacturer, and great landowner. All were American variants of African Big Men. We shall meet them again.[195]

AFRICAN BIG MEN IN THE RURAL HUDSON VALLEY: PHILIPSBURG'S CAESAR

Similar patterns developed throughout the Hudson Valley. Other slave leaders in rural New York were selected by their masters to serve in roles of responsibility. One example was a highly skilled African slave-artisan named Caesar (no kin to Varick's Caesar). He was Congolese in origin, as were many slaves who worked with him. They were owned by the Dutch Philipse family, and lived on the huge manor of Philipsburg along the Hudson River north of Manhattan.[196] Caesar became responsible for managing a large industrial complex at the Philipse manor called the Upper Mills. At the same time he was also the leader of a community of Angolan and Congo slaves who worked there.[197]

By all accounts Caesar was a man of extraordinary competence, strength,

"Caesar: A Slave," daguerreotype, 1851

dignity, and moral authority. The tone of his leadership was reminiscent of African Big Men who led villages and extended families and Houses in West Central Africa. In Philipsburg he was held in respect and esteem by masters and slaves alike. After his death, later generations both African and European tended his grave. The tombstone survived to the twentieth century, in an African burying ground where many Philipse slaves were interred near the legendary village of Sleepy Hollow.[198]

THE MANY ROLES OF PETER THE DOCTOR

A key to the condition of slavery in this colony was a small number of free Negroes in New York. Their numbers had multiplied in New Netherland from 1643 to 1664. English rulers began by accepting rights of personal freedom and property holding that Dutch slaves had gained in the past, but they placed narrow limits on emancipation in the future. New laws raised the cost of emancipation by requiring masters to post a bond of 200 pounds in cash—for many people a prohibitive sum. Manumissions were actively discouraged in other ways, but they continued.[199]

Individual free Blacks in New York learned to defeat the law of bondage by using English courts, the English tradition of the rule of law, the English common law of property, and the ancient Anglo-Saxon folkright that a man's home was his castle. More than a few of these free Blacks owned nominal slaves who were often their wives, children, or blood relations.

In 1720, for example, Peter Porter was a free Negro who made an agreement for manumission of his slave Nanny, but only after his death. They lived together as husband and wife in the sanctity of their home as if she were free, and they insisted that the arrangement was nobody's business but their own. In effect, Porter seized upon English law to protect the de facto freedom of his common-law wife in America.[200]

Yet other free Negroes were protected by affluent masters of African origin, who emancipated their own slave consorts and mulatto children at heavy expense, no matter what the price. An example was John Fortune, a free Negro cooper, who owned a slave woman named Maryta. In 1724, he manumitted her, married her, and also freed their son, Robin. He paid the manumission fee, and nobody could stop him.[201]

Free Blacks were a small minority in English New York. Their numbers grew slowly, but they kept growing. So also did their liberty and freedom. A vital core of free or half-free Africans persisted after the conquest of New

Netherland. In 1679, Jasper Danckaerts observed that along the country road called Broadway, beyond the walls of the town, on "both sides of this way were many habitations of negroes, mulattos and whites. These negroes were formerly the proper slaves of the [West India] Company. They have ground enough to live on with their families," and they were living in freedom, fifteen years after the Dutch lost the colony.[202]

They were still there in 1692, when the New York Common Council complained of "frequent randivozing [rendezvousing] of Negro slaves at the houses of free negroes without the gates." And they were there again in 1737 when other visitors described their continuing presence north of the city. Through the eighteenth century, neighborhoods of "free Negroes" persisted in northern "out wards," living on their own land beyond the gates of New York City. They preserved a Dutch "custom of the country" for more than a century.[203]

Other free African Americans also continued to live inside the palisade of New York City, and a frustrated English Common Council found itself unable to control them. One of these "free negroes" was an extraordinary character who was known by several names. The Court of General Sessions referred to him as the "Negro Man called Peter of the City of New York, Labourer, otherwise commonly called Peter the Doctor." In the daytime he appears to have worked for white employers as "Peter the Labourer."

After dark, this extraordinary man had another business as Peter the Doctor, an African conjuror who did a flourishing practice among slaves and free people. His conjure arts were also in demand among white folk and even some of the town fathers. In 1712, Peter got into serious trouble. He was reported to have given rebel slaves a white powder that was promised to protect them from the weapons of the master class. He was arrested, tried, and sentenced to death, but pardoned by the governor. In 1715, Peter the Doctor was living free at his own home in New York's East Ward, the most affluent neighborhood in the city. He was presented before the Court of General Sessions for "entertaining" slaves in his house. A new law was passed to "revoke property rights" of free Negroes within the City. But Peter defied the law, kept his house, preserved both of his identities, and continued to serve slaves and free people from his home in the East Ward.[204]

Even as these free Afro–New Yorkers were small in number, their social roles grew larger, to judge by a swelling volume and variety of complaints. Reports survive of "free negroes" who "entertained" slaves and European servants. Others operated nocturnal markets involving slaves, free Blacks, and white purchasers.

They were prominent in what was called a "convivial interracial world" that came alive after dark in New York's cellars and sheds. The music and merriment of these gatherings attracted seamen, soldiers, prostitutes, wayward sons of the town fathers, and probably at least a few of the fathers themselves. New York's free Blacks were sometimes the organizers and go-betweens at these events. Even as courts and legislatures tried to restrain them and reduce their numbers, New York's few free Blacks became more active than ever.[205]

REPRESSION OF AFRICAN SLAVES

In the early eighteenth century, New York's master class was growing more fearful of the slaves in their midst. Increasing clusters of slaves from the West Indies were a cause of special concern. White masters and magistrates were also frustrated by a spirit of autonomy in slave associations, and by increasing numbers of New York City slaves who refused to behave slavishly.

Masters tried to restrict their slaves in various ways. Legislators in New Jersey and New York enacted slave codes of increasing severity. Judges and juries went beyond the law, and were allowed to invent horrific punishments. But these deliberate efforts to create fear among the enslaved, paradoxically created more fear among the master class.

This climate of fear generated sudden storms of panic, rage, hysteria, and unimaginable cruelty. An example was a horrific event in the Long Island village of Newtown, settled by New Englanders. An African slave woman was denied permission for "going abroad on the sabbath," which was customary in the colony. She persuaded the family's Indian slave Sam to murder their English master William Hallet, his wife, and five children, which he did with an axe as they lay sleeping, on the night of February 10, 1708. The two slaves were arrested, tried "under special commission," found guilty, and executed. The African woman was burned alive. A special horror was invented for the Indian slave, who struck the fatal blows with an axe. He was placed alive in a gibbet or iron cage, and mounted astride a "piece of iron," with an edge sharpened like that of an axe, and set in such a way that it continued to cut deep into his crotch. It was said that "he lived some time in a state of delirium, while the blood, oozing from his lacerated flesh, streamed from his feet to the ground."[206]

Black codes and punishments also grew more extreme. In 1709, New Jersey's assembly passed a law that required castration of slaves for rape, and also for any act of willing "fornication" with white females. In London, Queen Anne was appalled. She commanded her Privy Council to disallow the law, as it "never was allowed by, or known in the Laws of this Kingdom." [207]

In New York, repeated laws forbade slaves to gather even in small groups without the permission of owners. A statute in 1682 prohibited more than four slaves to meet together. The penalty was whipping. Its failure appeared in another law that reduced the number of slaves who could gather together from four to three, and ordered every town in the colony to maintain a "Negro Whipper" at its own expense. This also did not succeed. New ordinances forbade slaves over the age of fourteen to be abroad after sunset, unless with their master's consent. Repeated laws in 1702, 1708, and 1712 excluded slaves from taverns or sports without a written pass. Later laws testified to the failure of these measures in preambles complaining that "slaves were gathering in great numbers," for "rude and unlawful" activities.[208]

Travel by slaves without permission of masters was subject to severe penalties. In 1705, the New York legislature ordered that any slave caught more then forty miles north of Albany must be put to death.[209] Trading by slaves without permission from masters was prohibited by repeated regulations. Free white people who did business illegally with slaves were guilty of a felony; those who merely failed to report knowledge of illegal trading by others could be convicted for a misdemeanor. Free Negroes who traded with slaves could be sentenced to reenslavement. All of these laws failed, and illegal trade between white and Black, slave and free, continued to expand in New York.[210]

Free Negroes in particular were subject to many restrictions. At the demand of white cartmen, all "men of African descent" were forbidden to drive a cart in the city of New York. The law was violated with impunity by masters, slaves, and freedmen alike. Another city ordinance required all free Negroes in New York City to indenture themselves to masters. It was not enforced.[211]

GROWING RESISTANCE

A parallel trend to growing repression by the master class was increasing resistance among slaves. These tendencies interacted through the entire history of English New York from 1664 to 1776. Resistance took many forms. Even the most severe masters were defeated by it, but at heavy cost to the enslaved.

One such case happened at New York City in 1677. An English-speaking blacksmith named John Cooley bought "a Negroe slave, who as it appeared since was very sick, indisposed and defective; And withall soe stubborne, sullen, and Lazy, that he would do neither the least chore . . . nor use the Least motion for his Bodely health." The master consulted physicians, who told him that "if he did not constreine or force his said Negro speedily to use or fall to some bodily exercise, he would immediately and of necessity dye." Cooley "inflicted mortal wounds on his slave" and "the said negro dyed the 9th day of his chastisement." [212]

A MURDERED MASTER: LEWIS MORRIS IN EAST JERSEY, 1691

In East Jersey's Monmouth County, the number of African slaves increased at twice the rate of European settlers. One of the largest holdings belonged to Lewis Morris of Passage Point, who owned forty slaves in 1677, and sixty-seven in 1691. He employed them in his iron mines, forges, and mills at Tinton Falls. His African slaves created families on African models—extended and consanguine, with many children. Only a small minority (as few as 10 percent) were nuclear families. The families in turn formed a cohesive community. In company with many slaves in this region, they shared association as a habit, and agency as a tradition.

Very different were the attitudes of their master. In company with other slave owners, Lewis Morris had come to East Jersey from Barbados, and managed his plantations on the Caribbean model, with absolute dominion and great severity.

In 1691, his slaves accused him of murdering a woman in bondage. They assumed on the basis of Dutch precedents that colonial leaders would hear their grievances, and took their case by petition to higher executive authority, as slaves had often done in New Netherland. But East Jersey was now an English colony and they had no success. Then they tried to bring a charge of murder against their master. Again, the English court did nothing.

When all else failed, the outraged slaves of Lewis Morris rose together and murdered their master. At last the authorities acted. They tried seven slaves for homicide, acquitted five, and convicted two. The judicial penalty of this English court was typically more savage than the act it sought to punish. Each of the two convicted slaves had a hand cut off and burned before their eyes.

Then they were strangled slowly, until they were "dead, dead, dead," in the language of the court. The penalty was designed to inflict extreme pain, not merely as an instrument of control but also as an expression of fury and fear among the master class.[213]

GANGS OF RESIDENT AFRICAN RUNAWAYS:
HARLEM MAROONS, 1690

As the slave trade grew larger, small groups of newly arrived African slaves increasingly decided that the most effective form of resistance was to run from their masters. Some disappeared into the American forest and were never seen again. Others joined the Indians. More than a few fled into the night, and kept close to outlying European settlements.

In 1690, a group of fugitive slaves, variously described as "African-born," and "maroons" were reported to be living on northern Manhattan, in wooded land near the small country village of Harlem. They survived on what they stole from masters, or were given by slaves. One surviving account reported that Harlem maroons "terrorized Dutch farmers." We have found no evidence that they attacked others, or committed acts of violence, or were ever caught.[214]

Other maroons lived in the region for many years. In 1702, Governor Cornbury was told that "fugitive Africans had established camps on Long Island," and "lived by pilferage and raiding." He ordered them to be killed "if they cannot otherwise be taken." They were still there in 1708, and again in 1712, and once more in 1740.[215]

AN AFRICAN EXPLOSION:
NEW YORK'S SLAVE REVOLT OF 1712

In New York City, other slaves responded by armed revolution, the first full-fledged North American slave revolt on record.[216] It happened in the Hudson Valley on April 6, 1712. It grew from one of the many circles of association among slaves in New York City. Primary evidence survives from John Sharpe, an Anglican army chaplain stationed at Fort George near what is now the Battery. He talked with some of the rebels, and recorded their remarks. They told him they were "Negro Slaves here of ye Nations of Coromantee & Papa [sic]." Their purpose was "to destroy all the Whites in order to obtain their freedom," a revolution by any standard. In Sharpe's words the leaders "kept their Conspiracy secret that there was not the least suspicion . . . till it came of execution."[217]

The slaves he called "Coromantee" were a warrior people in what is now Ghana, who had been captured and sold by their Fante rivals. The "Papa" came from Little and Great Popo, near what is now Ouidah on the coast of Benin. "Papa" and "Coromantee" were of different nations, but they appear to have been able to communicate.[218]

They complained of "hard usage," by which they appear to have meant brutal beatings by sadistic masters, and short rations by miserly masters which were often reported in English New York. And that was not the worst of it.

Akan-speaking Asante and Fante slaves were people of pride and dignity, but in New York (unlike New England) they were treated without respect. They had known slavery in Africa, but slaves there were often members of a larger community. In New York, they were aliens, and their only ties were to each other.

These Asante were trained to a warrior ethic of courage and honor, but that too was denied to them. Of all the many forms of abuse which slaves suffered, it was perhaps this "hard usage" that was most oppressive for some of them. Worse, these Africans regarded their captors as a "people without honor."[219]

At the end of a long winter, these slaves met together on the holiday of March 25, 1712, New Year's Day in the old Julian calendar, which was still kept in the British empire. Some slaves had the day off. They organized themselves into a secret brotherhood, "the conspirators tying themselves to secrecy by sucking ye blood of each others hands."[220]

Together they made plans to rise against their oppressors. One of them said that their purpose was to "destroy the city, and murder every white person." Clearly their intent was to lead a general rising of Africans in New York, but their ultimate goal was not clear. They might have intended to move into the interior of the continent and found their own African settlement, or they may have planned to seize ships and sail away. Their acts and choices revealed they expected to survive. "To make them invulnerable as they believed, a free Negro who pretends sorcery gave them a powder to rub on their cloth which made them so confident." This was Peter the Doctor.[221]

They actively recruited "Spanish Negroes," perhaps for their knowledge of ships and the sea. Other Africans of different origins also joined in—a danger to any conspiracy, but the secret was kept. The leaders were careful to move quickly, before rumors could spread. Judging by their acts, some of these Akan-speaking leaders knew what they were about, and planned their rising as a military operation. They were able to collect weapons in great variety, and carefully hid them in an orchard. At midnight on April 6, 1712, they mustered among the trees behind a house in the city's East Ward. Between twenty-five and fifty slaves, men and women, turned out. Again, most were said to be "Coromantee." They armed themselves with muskets, pistols, axes, swords, knives, and daggers.

At about two o'clock in the morning, they carefully prepared an ambush and set a building ablaze. Inhabitants of these early wood-built American towns responded urgently to a fire alarm, and came running headlong toward the blaze. The slaves "stood in the streets and shot down and stabbed as many as they could." About eight people were killed and twelve wounded.[222]

Colonial leaders acted quickly. New York's royal governor Robert Hunter was a long-serving British soldier, colonel of the Royal Scots Dragoons, and a brigadier in the British Army. He had much experience of wars in Europe and domestic insurrections in Scotland, Ireland, England, and Jamaica. In New York, he had recently suppressed a rising of angry German Palatine tenants on a Hudson River manor. In a world without professional police, British Regulars were the order keepers of the Empire, with long service in that role.[223]

Hunter fired the colony's alarm cannon, and ordered a detachment of Regulars under "a proper officer" to run to the scene of the revolt. They drove the slaves north, out of the city. The next morning Hunter called out the militia of New York. Their orders were to form a cordon and "drive the Island."[224]

Altogether they captured about seventy slaves and a few freedmen. Six slave leaders killed themselves rather than surrender. Special courts were organized, and jury trials continued through April and May. Altogether, twenty-seven captives were released and forty-three were tried by jury, of whom another eighteen were acquitted or discharged. About twenty-five were convicted, and most were sentenced to death.

Under the laws of New York, the form of execution was left to judges and civil leaders. These Anglo "friends of order" were more violent and brutal than the African rebels. A great wave of fear, panic, hysteria, and rage had followed the revolt. Jurists and jailers in English New York inflicted as much pain as they could devise. Three slaves were burned alive at the stake. One was roasted over a slow fire, and took eight hours to die. Another was broken slowly on a wheel, and one more was "hung alive in chains" until he died of privation in a public place for everyone to witness. A pregnant slave woman named Abigail was sentenced to death, but allowed to live until her child was born. Then she too was executed. Her treatment was so unspeakably cruel that it was said she suffered more than any of the others.[225]

Royal governor Hunter was appalled by this savagery. He intervened to urge clemency for five men, much to the fury of many New Yorkers. The attorney general of the colony defied the governor, and tried to have him removed. But in London, the Privy Council supported Hunter, and issued full pardons for three defendants. Among them was Peter the Doctor, and his career continued.

In 1713, the New York Assembly passed a severe "Negro Act." It forbade any Free "Negro, Indian or Mulatto to hold real estate in New York," and sought to destroy the entire class of free people of color in the colony. The law was opposed by royal officials, and did not entirely succeed, but it reduced landholding by some freed slaves within the town.[226]

For many years after the Slave Revolt of 1712, acts of brutal repression continued to spread through New York and eastern New Jersey, and reached a peak in the 1730s. In 1734, thirty slaves in New Jersey were tried for conspiracy and rebellion. On very little evidence, one slave was hanged, several were maimed, and many were whipped. That same year, a slave in New York City was convicted of rape of a girl aged fourteen or fifteen. Investigation found that there had been no rape, but only an allegation of a possible attempt. Even so, the slave was found guilty and burned at the stake before a large crowd, while many slaves were compelled to watch. In 1738, two slaves in Trenton were executed for attempting to poison their master and his family. Other slaves were punished for "conspiracy," or for "attempts" of various kinds, and in a few cases for actual violence. In 1739, a slave in New Jersey's Somerset County was infuriated by his treatment at the hands of an overseer. He attempted to kill the overseer's wife, murdered a small child, set fire to a barn, and destroyed a thousand bushels of grain. He was caught and burned alive.[227]

These events were not unique to New York and New Jersey. In the 1730s, a great wave of slave revolts and conspiracies spread through Virginia (1730), Louisiana (1730–32), the Virgin Islands (1733), Jamaica (1734), Antigua (1736), Pennsylvania (1738), Maryland (1738), and South Carolina (1734–39). But New York had more than most.[228]

THE GREAT SLAVE INSURGENCY OF 1741 AND ITS LEGACY

Soon afterward, another crisis of order suddenly erupted in New York City. Judge Daniel Horsmanden called it the "New York Conspiracy." Historians have understood it in different ways. Some scholars believe that there was no conspiracy, but only a great wave of panic and hysteria, comparable to the Salem witch trials. Others are convinced that it was an actual slave revolt.

Marxist historians think of it as a revolution of New York's underclass, Black and white, slave and free together. Other writers interpret its repression as an outbreak of anti-Catholic hysteria. More recently, historians have argued that it was neither a revolution nor a revolt, but a set of multiple "plots" which gave rise to violent repression. All of these many interpretations accurately describe some part of what happened, but none encompasses the entire event.

A more accurate understanding is to think of it not as a single conspiracy or revolt, but as a broad insurgency that continued for nearly a month in the early spring of 1741. It was not as tightly organized as revolutions seek to be, but it grew from a multitude of groups who had different purposes in mind. No single group or individual controlled it, but many were involved. The diversity of slave associations in eighteenth-century New York shaped the structure of this event.[229]

It started on Wednesday, March 18, 1741, the day after St. Patrick's Day, which was a holiday for some servants and slaves in New York. At about noon, a fire broke out at the Governor's House inside Fort George on the southwestern tip of Manhattan. The March wind was high, and flames spread quickly. In two hours, most of the major buildings in the fort were aflame, and many were destroyed. As munitions began to explode, the fire leaped the walls of the fort and reached the rooftops of the town. Then suddenly the wind changed, and a heavy rainstorm extinguished the flames. The city itself was saved, but its seat of imperial power at Fort George was reduced to ruin.[230]

The fire might have been an accident. It could have been caused by roofers who were working with heated soldering irons on a windy day. But other fires followed, and some were deliberately set. Exactly one week later, on Wednesday, March 25, a great fire damaged the mansion of Captain Peter Warren, kinsman of Chief Justice James DeLancey. And precisely a week after that, Wednesday April 1, All Fools' Day, a massive fire destroyed a warehouse on the East River. Three days later, on Saturday, April 4, multiple fires broke out in a cow barn, a private home, a coach house, and a stable. On Monday, April 6, four more fires broke out. Evidence of arson was found in nests of hay and live coals. The slave leader Cuff Philips was observed running from one blaze. Several people reported snatches of conversation among slaves. One was heard to have said "Fire, Fire, Scorch, Scorch, A LITTLE, damn it, By-and-By."[231]

Altogether, this slave insurgency continued for more than three weeks—one of the longest events of its kind in American history. It was followed by an even longer counterinsurgency that went on for the better part of a year.

Mobs of angry whites began to roam the streets of New York. They seized slaves, and threatened to take over the city. The authorities moved quickly. New York's Supreme Court empaneled a grand jury of merchants and slave owners. Two justices became prosecutors, assisted by the entire bar. All the lawyers in town agreed to participate. Hundreds of slaves were arrested, jailed, and examined. Indictments were returned, and tried before juries. Witnesses were paid for their testimony. Some of the most graphic accounts came from prostitutes and tavern maids.[232]

Many different people were linked to these events. An impoverished teacher was accused of being a Catholic priest in disguise, because he had some knowledge of Latin and Greek. He was tried separately as the arch-conspirator in a "popish plot." Servants, prostitutes, and tavern keepers were also implicated. But the great majority of the accused were slaves of African or West Indian origin. Many had been engaged in organized crime against the master class, in the form of theft, burglary, and smuggling. Others had a different goal, which was to escape from bondage, and some did so. More than a few struck directly at centers of power in the colony, and much testimony strongly suggests that some of them attempted to lead a full-scale revolt.

Multiple groups of slaves were actively involved. Several historians have made a strong case for the leadership of Akan-speaking slaves. By one count, 38 percent of those burned at the stake in 1741 had Akan names, the largest single group. But most leaders were of various other backgrounds. West Indian slaves were thought to be much involved, as were some of the "Spanish Negroes."[233]

As always after slave risings, actual punishments were more violent than alleged crimes. Altogether, more than two hundred slaves were taken into custody in 1741—roughly one third of New York City's 674 male slaves over the age of ten in the census of 1737.[234] In those arrests, 208 were identified by name. At least another eight got away and were never found. Also arrested were a few freedmen, and as many as thirty whites. John Romme, the white tavern keeper and dealer in stolen goods was implicated, but vanished without a trace.[235]

Together, of all those many suspects, a total of 152 "Blacks" and twenty "Whites" were formally charged and brought to trial. About 126 were found guilty and thirty-five were executed. Fourteen slaves were burned alive before large crowds, who never seemed to tire of this savagery. Another twenty-one were hanged, of whom four were white. Among them was Peggy Kerry, the

"Newfoundland Irish Beauty" with her bright red hair, and John Hughson the tavern keeper. After the hangings, the bodies of at least three dead slaves were displayed in iron gibbets until they rotted away.

A larger number of slaves "confessed" and were expelled from the colony: seven free whites were "deported" and eighty-four slaves were "transported," on pain of death if they returned. Among them was Captain Jack, probably sold to the West Indies.[236]

Within New York City, the total number of slaves and free Blacks fell by about 10 percent, and then began to revive. By 1771, the number of slaves had increased by 40 percent.[237] The slave trade changed in ways that reflected growing concern about Caribbean slaves. Before the Great Slave Insurgency about 70 percent of New York's slaves came from the West Indies in the English period. Afterward, 70 percent came from Africa.[238]

After the trials ended, rumors of conspiracy and reports of arson continued to increase. In February 1742, a house caught fire in New York City near the Old Dutch church. A slave named Tom confessed, and was hanged.[239] Justice Horsmanden empaneled a grand jury to search for evidence of a conspiracy, but the jurors refused to return indictments. Conservative New York officials wrote in despair that "the insolence of the negroes is as great, if not greater than ever."[240]

Owners lived in mortal fear of poisoning by slaves in their own households. There was much talk of secret spells and potions by slave-sorcerers.[241] Cases of alleged poisoning of masters and mistresses by slaves continued for many years.

A measure of fear was the violence inflicted on slaves. One example was the case of Phyllis, a young slave of childbearing age. Her master, a tailor named Lowder, accused her of attempting to poison him. She was arrested and sent to the city's jail. After five weeks in prison she was released "due to severe illness," and returned to the custody of her master. He confined her in a small closet, chained her to a wall, and gave her inedible food, crawling with worms. Neighbors heard her cries. One of them, Susannah Romme, took Phyllis some tea. Master Lowder was reported to be "greatly angered," and responded by denying Phyllis water. It was said that "neighbors could hear Phyllis call for water day and night." The coroner found that "Phyllis died of starvation while delivering a bastard child," and that she had been "confined in a small cell with a chain around her neck."[242]

In the mid-eighteenth century, slavery in the Hudson Valley became more cruel and punitive. In runaway notices, masters themselves documented the

severity of punishments they inflicted on their slaves. In 1756, the slave Caesar ran away twice in Woodbridge, New Jersey. The second time, he managed
to escape while wearing "a pair of Iron Pot-Hooks around his neck with a
chain fastened to it that reached his feet," according to his master.

The slave Scipio escaped in August of 1757, with "hands pinioned behind
him . . . a large Bump over one of his Eyes; his Buttocks pretty well marked
with the Lash." At about the same time, the fugitive Jacob was described as
having "a Scar in the right side of his forehead, one on his left temple . . . and
another on the Crown of his Head . . . a lump on each shoulder by being
flogg'd." In 1761, another fugitive slave named Quaco was reported by his
master as wearing an "iron Collar with two Hooks to it round his neck, a pair
of Hand-cuffs with a chain to them, six feet long." [243]

Punishments and slave crimes escalated in a cycle of increasing savagery. A
slave in New Jersey's Somerset County burned his master's barn and killed the
master's child with an axe. The slave was captured, and burned alive. Another
slave in New York City was accused of attempted rape. He also was burned
alive before a great crowd. Many slaves were compelled to watch.[244]

THE AWAKENING OF ANTISLAVERY
IN THE HUDSON VALLEY

The horror of these events caused some people of conscience to turn against
slavery. By and large, New Yorkers and New Jerseyites lagged behind Pennsylvania Quakers and New England Puritans. But as early as 1715, one brave
soul was writing at length against slavery in the Hudson Valley. John Hepburn
knew about unfree labor from his own experience. In 1685, he migrated from
his native England as an indentured servant, and lived in Freehold, East Jersey,
a few miles south of the slave port at Perth Amboy. He made many Quaker
friends and shared some of their beliefs.

Hepburn became so troubled by slavery that he wrote a book against it,
called *The American Defence of the Christian Golden Rule, or an Essay to Prove
the Unlawfulness of Making Slaves of Men.* It was printed in New York City
in 1715—an octavo of ninety-four pages. In North America it had been preceded by antislavery works of Quaker George Keith in 1693, and Puritan
Samuel Sewall in 1700. Hepburn combined their very different biblical beliefs and argued that slavery violated both the Mosaic commandments in the
Old Testament and the Gospels of Christ in the New Testament.[245]

Other voices began to be raised in the Hudson Valley. Anglican leaders of New York's Trinity Church spoke and wrote against slavery as early as 1730. They followed the Bishop of London, who urged clergy to think of Africans in bondage as "not upon the same level with laboring beasts, but as Men-Slaves and Women-slaves." Anglican lay leaders in New York such as Governor Robert Hunter and Justice Daniel Horsmanden also spoke against slavery.[246]

Others spoke not against slavery itself, but its cruelty and corruption. Their leader was George Whitefield, the itinerant Anglican evangelist. He did not oppose slavery, and owned slaves to the end of his life. But he strongly condemned the brutality of slave owners and spoke frequently against it.

In 1740, Whitefield preached in New York to an audience estimated at five or six thousand people, including many slaves, and he issued a warning to cruel masters. "Considering what usage they commonly meet with, I have wondered that . . . [slaves] have not more frequently rose up in Arms against their Owners." In Philadelphia, Whitefield published that message from the press of Benjamin Franklin. In New York, infuriated masters accused White-field of inciting slaves to violence in the Insurgency of 1741. He reached a very broad public.[247]

Leaders of the new Methodist movement also became strongly antislavery. Francis Asbury, an Anglican clergyman who was a founder of Methodism in New York, preached against slavery at New York City in 1771 and on Long Island and East Jersey in 1772. Other Christian groups also took collective action against slavery. In 1774, Quakers in New York's Yearly Meeting condemned the buying and selling of slaves by members of the Society of Friends. German Lutherans were the unsung heroes of the Christian antislavery movement. They actively supported Arie van Guinee, a native of West Africa who came from Surinam to New York in 1705, joined the Lutheran church, moved to East Jersey where he built a Lutheran congregation of free Blacks.[248]

African slaves themselves began to preach the Christian gospel against human bondage. As early as 1740, a master in New Jersey's Middlesex County described one of them, his runaway slave Simon, aged about forty, "a well set fellow, bred and born in this country, talks good English, can read and write, is very slow in his Speech, can bleed and draw Teeth, pretending to be a great Doctor, and very religious, and says he is a Churchman; Had a dark gray Broadcloth Coat, with other good Apparel, and peak'd toe'd shoes." He rode "a black Horse," with "a black hunting saddle."[249]

In January 1775, another master in East Jersey's Bergen County advertised for the return of a "Negro man and his Wife." The man was described as "serious, civil, slow of speech, low in stature, reads well, is a Negro Preacher, about 40 years of age." With him was his wife, Jenny, who was "smart, active and handy," and "likely to look upon." [250]

NEW YORK SLAVES TURN TO OTHER METHODS OF NONVIOLENT RESISTANCE: LITIGATION

After the defeat of armed revolt and the failure of violent insurgency in 1712 and 1741, slaves in New York continued to strive for freedom. Some of them worked within the legal institutions of Britain's imperial system, and did so with growing success.

Britain's old colonial system in the eighteenth century, for all its cruelty and corruption, was grounded in the rule of law. Here again, African slaves were quick to recognize an opportunity, and they seized it. In New York from 1745 to 1758, more than fifty "Spanish Negroes" won their freedom from American masters in a British Vice Admiralty Court. They acted with the legal assistance of New York's attorney general, and added diplomacy to law with help from Spanish officials. After they won their case, some of their masters sought compensation from the Crown, without success. Others tried to kidnap their former slaves, which fared no better. When slaves began to work successfully within the law, some of their masters increasingly worked outside it—a double shift of growing importance in American history.[251]

The successful litigation of Spanish Negroes inspired others. Juan da Costa filed a petition in New York, claiming to be a free mulatto and a subject of the king of Portugal and sought his freedom. The case record survives, with no evidence of its result.[252]

A Carib Indian named Cumana also made a formal complaint to New York's attorney general, declaring that he was a free man, kidnapped at sea while fishing near his Caribbean home, taken as captive to New York, and sold to a master named Abraham Pawling in Tappan, New Jersey. The outcome of this case is unknown, but a record survives with similar documents from other slaves, in the manuscripts of Attorney General John Tabor Kempe.[253]

RUNAWAYS

From 1742 to 1775, no major slave rebellions ocurred in New York and New Jersey, but resistance increased in other forms. The most common act was to run away. By the measure of notices in local newspapers, advertisements for runaways in New York and East Jersey increased from fifteen in the period 1716–39, to sixty-four in the 1740s, 123 in the 1750s, and 141 in 1760s.[254]

In these notices, 86 percent of fugitives were young males. Most ran from small farms in rural parts of the colony. A common purpose was to "put as much distance as possible between themselves and their masters." They went in every direction. Some ran into the woods to the west and north, and hoped to join the Indians, or escape to New France. A few went south toward towns and cities where they hoped to disappear in a population of strangers, sometimes with complex disguises. One master advertised for a small male slave named Polly who will "endeavour to pass for a woman."[255]

Others headed east to New England, which was thought to offer fugitives more opportunities to be accepted as a freedman. An example was a "likely negro man named Cuff" who "speaks English pretty well for a Guinea negro and very flippant . . . a plausible smooth Tongue Fellow." He ran from his master in Dutchess County, and was believed to be "making toward the Eastward," where he had been in Norwalk, Connecticut, and "passed there for a free negro." At least six runaway notices survive for Hudson Valley slaves who sought refuge in New England.[256]

The largest number of fugitives in the Hudson Valley ran toward saltwater, most commonly in New York City. A primary purpose was to find a short-handed ship, and a desperate captain who asked no questions.

LITERACY AS A TOOL OF RESISTANCE

Even as slavery grew more repressive in the Hudson Valley, it also continued to become more open in other ways during the eighteenth century. The literacy of slaves slowly increased. Much to the fury of some masters, the Church of England and its Society for the Propagation of the Gospel in Foreign Parts sponsored a school for slaves (1705–23?) in New York. The teacher, Elias Neau, was a French Huguenot who had taught prisoners and galley slaves in France. Slaves in New York responded warmly to him. In 1707, he reported that "above 100" were in classes on reading, catechism, and music. Neau wrote, "I observe with pleasure that they strive who shall sing best." He wrote that "the oldest negroes and negresses" attended "most constantly."[257]

Some Anglicans in New York's Trinity Church were also active in teaching and baptizing slaves. From 1733 to 1747 Richard Charleton offered instruction in reading and religion to as many as seventy students in a school at Trinity. Joseph Hildreth and the Reverend Samuel Auchmuty continued that effort for many years. In 1761, Auchmuty wrote, "For some years past I have not baptized less than 80 or 90 Negro children and often upwards of 100, besides, several adults."[258]

Runaway slave advertisements showed a slow but steady increase in literacy among slaves: four notices before 1750, six from 1751 to 1760, and eleven from 1761 to 1775. Individual examples appeared throughout the region. In Somerset County, New Jersey, a slave named Arch was described as able to "read the Bible very well," and write his own pass. Another slave called Ned from Suffolk County, on the eastern end of Long Island, "can both read and write and probably wrote himself a Pass." Another measure of literacy was the increasing mention of forged masters' passes, from two in the 1740s, to thirteen in the 1750s, and thirty-six in the 1760s.[259]

EXPANDING SKILLS

Another measure of this opening process appeared in the rapid growth of marketable skills among slaves. Once more, a leading source is the evidence of advertisements for runaways in the Hudson Valley. From 1716 to 1783, a total of 123 slave notices identified 177 occupations and skills. Nearly half of these fugitives had multiple occupations. Overall, the most striking pattern was not merely the range of skills, but their rapid growth. Before 1740, the number of listed skills and occupations had been small, and their variety was smaller still. During the troubled decade of the 1740s, the numbers fell to even lower levels. Then, after 1750, the trend suddenly reversed. Skills and occupations among fugitive slaves began to grow at a great rate, multiplying fourfold from 1751 to 1759, and kept on growing through the century.[260]

Also striking was the increasing specialization of skills among slaves in the Hudson Valley. Throughout the entire period, only a small minority of runaways were described as domestic servants (29) and farm workers (12). In a group of 177 runaways, 123 were identified as having specific skills and "trades," and in great variety before 1775. Many had maritime trades and occupations. Some were "seamen" or "privateersmen"; others were slave "shipwrights," "mastmakers," "sailmakers," and "caulkers"; and some worked on the waterfront as "longshoremen."

Many others were skilled craftsmen or worked in industrial occupations as carpenters, metalsmiths, coopers, masons, weavers, watchmakers, grist millers, potash makers, butchers, bakers, tailors, weavers, and masons. Some were described as having what would later be called professions: the Hudson Valley before 1775 had runaway slave doctors, a slave dentist, many slave preachers, a "cunning person," and even a "mathematician."

The most frequently mentioned skill among runaways was musician: no fewer than 51 musicians were mentioned among 127 fugitives. They included 44 fiddlers, three drummers, two singers or songsters, two fifers, and one player of the French horn. Why so many musicians in general and fiddlers in particular? We might also ask where fugitives could hope to find a place of refuge. One answer would be that they could hide in plain sight at a tavern, where people would be accustomed to the presence of strangers. An occupation often welcome in a taproom with no questions asked was that of a fiddler.

Runaway slaves also found other places of refuge and employment. Maritime trades offered many opportunities. And the iron mines, furnaces, and foundries of New Jersey were always short of labor. The Schuyler mine alone employed two hundred African Americans. Forges and furnaces needed woodcutters and teamsters. The iron industry also offered training in skilled jobs. Graham Hodges also found that "Blacks fled to the mines and forges because of better wages and greater freedom.[261]

SLAVES WITH GROWING POWERS OF CHOICE IN THE HUDSON VALLEY

Historians of bondage in eighteenth-century New York and New Jersey have observed that individual slaves had increasing opportunities for choice in the conditions of their lives. Some parts of this expanding process of opening possibilities appear to have been stronger for slaves in the Hudson Valley than anywhere else in North America.

Historian Shane White writes, "A practice that appears to have been associated particularly with slavery in New York and New Jersey differentiated the institution there from that in the South. . . . Material on slavery around New York does contain a surprising number of references to slaves voicing opinions about their future, bargaining with their masters over the conditions of their enslavement, and even negotiating with third parties to buy them from their owners. . . . Such modifications had allowed some slaves a greater measure of control over their lives, and helped, if only marginally, to ameliorate the rigors of slavery."[262]

Throughout the Hudson Valley, in the eighteenth century, slaves were also gaining greater powers of choice in the selection of masters, places of residence, type of work, and terms of employment. This practice became a regional custom. In particular, slaves were also allowed to go abroad by themselves, and find a new master, with much freedom of choice in that respect. Sometimes they were looking for a hiring arrangement. In other cases they searched for someone to buy them. In both cases, masters hoped for more money in their pocket, while slaves hungered for more freedom and better quality of life.[263]

Shane White found many striking examples in public advertisements and private correspondence. In 1750, for example, a slave owner in New York City advertised for "a Negro wench named Phoebe aged about 45 years." She "had a note with her to look for a master, but has not returned."[264]

In other instances, a "likely young negro fellow" was "sold for no fault, but as he inclines to live in the city, as he was brought up in one." A female slave was put up for sale, "not chusing to go into the country" with her owner. Another slave was advertised for sale, having "an aversion to living in the country." Yet a third was sold because "he will not live in the country." Peter Gansevoort's slave Gustavus was allowed "to change his situation on account of his dislike of doing housework."[265] Esther Burr, the mother of Aaron Burr, wrote that she was "exceedingly busy, expect company, and our Negroes are gone to seek a master. Really my dear I shall be thankful if I can get rid of them."[266]

Even as laws of slavery in this British colony became more repressive, some customs shifted in the opposite direction. In short, slaves in colonial New York were increasingly acting like New Yorkers.

PAN-AFRICAN CULTURE

Slaves in English New York, for all their diversity, also created among themselves some elements of a culture they shared in common. A leading example was Pinkster, a Christian holy day on Pentecost Sunday or Whitsunday, the seventh Sunday after Easter, the day of the descent of the Holy Spirit on the Apostles. Pinkster was a special day in New Netherland as early as 1628.[267]

It became important in new ways in colonial New York. African slaves were given a holiday, and they observed it in different ways. Throughout the Hudson Valley, many celebrated it as a secular event. An eyewitness account in 1737 described a great gathering of "Negroes divided into Companies, I suppose according to their different nations." They came together on "a Plain partly covered with Booths and well crowded with whites." Slaves were allowed to celebrate their holiday with music, dancing, singing, food, drink, and merriment, sometimes in the presence of their masters.[268]

For other slaves, Pinkster was a deeply religious event. It was a celebration of Christ's resurrection, when the Holy Ghost appeared as a "Holy Wind." Slaves gathered together around preachers and shared the occasion as a spiritual event. One after another became a "mouthpiece of God." A great wave of ecstasy spread through the group in spoken dreams, trances, visions, and speaking in tongues. Shane White wrote of Pinkster as "one of the most important and revealing cultural phenomena in the history of the Black experience in America."[269]

GROWTH, CHANGE, AND CONTINUITY IN THE HUDSON VALLEY

From 1700 to 1775, slavery in British New York and East Jersey changed in many ways at once. Numbers of slaves increased rapidly throughout the Hudson Valley—more rapidly than free whites. In census records for the colony of New York, the number of "blacks" (slave and free) increased from 1,692 in 1703 (13.2 percent of the population), to 4,794 in 1737 (15.6 percent), and 10,559 in 1771 (17.3 percent) The proportion of people identified as "Blacks" in New York's population by 1771 was much larger than that of all African Americans in the United States, circa 2015 (about 13 percent).[270]

People identified as "blacks" in these colonial census records were mostly slaves. Very few people of African descent were free before 1775. Scattered data suggest that free people of color actually declined in number and proportion throughout the Hudson Valley. Manumission and emancipation were increasingly restricted by law.

At the same time, the system of bondage was becoming more open. Slaves, often by their own initiative, were increasingly able to read and write. By a "Custome of the country" that was uniquely strong in the Hudson Valley, slaves also gained more opportunities to choose their masters and mistresses, to select places of residence, to learn skilled trades, to pursue specialized occupations, and to bargain for wages. Slaves continued to construct their own complex circles of association, especially in the city of New York. They created their own customs and speechways, from a mix of African and European cultures. Visiting Europeans commented on the spirit of slaves in the Hudson Valley. Masters complained of insolence in slaves who refused to behave slavishly.

This system of slavery itself was also changing in another way. More people began to raise their voices against human bondage in the Hudson Valley during the eighteenth century. These dissenters were Black and white, slave and free, male and female, young and old, Quaker and Methodist, Old Light and New Light. In 1775, hereditary bondage was stronger than ever in the Hudson Valley, when measured by numbers of slaves. But at the same time, slavery was slowly losing legitimacy—an unstable combination.

THE AMERICAN REVOLUTION AND
SLAVES IN THE HUDSON VALLEY

Then came the American War of Independence. Thousands of African Americans, slave and free, joined actively in that great event on both sides. They did so in many different ways, but almost always in pursuit of their own liberty and freedom.

In New England, most slaves of military age fought for American independence, with promises of emancipation that were often but not always made good. In southern colonies below the Potomac, slaves in large numbers joined the British Army against their Whig masters.

In New York and New Jersey, slaves were more divided. Some fought against the Revolution with British and Loyalist forces. Others enlisted in the Continental Army, or signed aboard Patriot privateers. More than a few slaves went a third way and took up arms as independent partisans for their own rights. Whichever path they took, the acts and choices of slaves helped to transform the Revolution. They broadened its ideals and extended its reach through the world. Some slaves had a major impact, as a few leading examples might make clear.

AFRO-LOYALIST: SERGEANT THOMAS PETERS,
"THE GEORGE WASHINGTON OF SIERRA LEONE"

After Washington's army was severely defeated at New York in 1776, British forces occupied the city and the surrounding countryside, and held it through the war. Many slaves seized the opportunity to free themselves. They left their masters by the thousands and escaped to British lines.

An example was Thomas Peters, born to high rank in West Africa, kidnapped and carried to French Louisiana, and sold to a hard master named William Campbell in Wilmington, North Carolina. Peters escaped three times. He was cruelly whipped and branded, but never broken. In 1776, he escaped again and joined the British Army in New York. With many other fugitive slaves he was enrolled in a Pioneer Company and quartered in "negro barracks" that multiplied in the city. Living conditions were miserable, but they were formally free, and many fought against their American masters.

Thomas Peters rose to the rank of sergeant and served with British forces throughout the war. Pioneer companies built and manned a ring of small strongpoints around the city, near road junctions and ferry crossings. Examples were the fort at Bergen Neck in New Jersey, Colonel Cuff's blockhouse at Dobbs Ferry in New York, the "Negro Fort" at Kingsbridge crossing from Manhattan to the mainland, Fort DeLancey at New Barbados Neck, and Tom Ward's Fort at Bull's Ferry, both in New Jersey.

These Black pioneers were not merely labor battalions. They fought as special forces against American Whigs. In 1780, Anthony Wayne's Continental infantry struck back at Tom Ward's fort at Bull's Ferry in hard fighting with heavy casualties. The Continentals were defeated by Black Loyalists fighting for their own freedom from Whig masters. Peters was twice wounded, and served with honor through the war.[271]

When the war ended, George Washington demanded that Peters and thousands like him be returned to their American masters, or compensation should be paid. Sir Guy Carleton, the last British commander in New York City, refused. He sympathized with escaped slaves and allowed them to emigrate to other parts of the British Empire where they could live free.

Thomas Peters and many veterans with their wives went to Nova Scotia with a promise of freedom and a farm. The promises were not kept.[272] Peters sailed to England and met top British antislavery leaders. Granville Sharp, William Wilberforce, and Thomas Clarkson were much impressed by his bearing and presence, and still more by his "eloquence, passion and spirit." With their support he led 1,190 former slaves to Sierra Leone. Thomas Peters is remembered today as a founder of that nation. He has been called "the George Washington of Sierra Leone."[273]

AN AFRO-WHIG: "RIFLE JACK" PETERSON, 2ND NEW YORK CONTINENTALS

Other African Americans in the Hudson Valley took up arms for the Patriot cause. From 1776 to 1783, they served in New York's Continental regiments. Among them was John Peterson, a "mulatto" slave, raised "in the family" of Isaac Sherwood on Van Cortlandt Manor. After the war began, Colonel Philip van Cortlandt raised the Second Continental Regiment of New York Infantry. Isaac Sherwood joined as lieutenant, and John Peterson enlisted as a private. He could not hope for a commission, but became a leader in another way. Peterson was known as a crack shot. He owned his own hunting rifle and brought it with him. The men in his regiment called him "Rifleman Jack" with high respect. He helped organize an elite unit of marksmen in that regiment and saw heavy fighting in the Hudson Valley. Rifle Jack is remembered for his service at Saratoga, where American rifles made a difference in critical moments. He was said to have also played a role in the West Point campaign, the repulse of HMS *Vulture* on the Hudson River, the capture of Major John André, and the defeat of the traitor Benedict Arnold.[274]

Much evidence is emerging about other African Americans who fought for American independence, first in New England's militia, then in the Continental Army. By the war's end they soldiered in their own units, called the Bucks of America in Massachusetts, and the Negro Battalion in Rhode Island. The extent of their service appeared in the summer of 1778, when Adjutant General Alexander Scammell compiled a "return of negroes" in the army under George Washington in New Jersey and New York. Scammell identified 755 "Negroes" in fourteen Continental brigades and Continental regiments that were raised from New England to North Carolina. Of that number, 586 "Negro" Continental soldiers (78 percent) were recorded as "present and fit for duty, and on duty," a higher proportion than among white soldiers.[275] Overall that report found that at least 4 percent of Continental infantry were Afro-Americans in 1778, and a larger proportion by 1781.[276]

Another very large number of African Americans, slave and free, enlisted in the Continental Navy and in various state navies. In 1777 and 1778, Connecticut's largest man-of-war, *Oliver Cromwell*, had five "negro marines" aboard.[277] Many more served in privateers, "private armed vessels" that sailed under "letters of marque and reprisal," which authorized them to attack British ships. Privateer captains hired large numbers of Africans. Their pay tended to be the same as that of white shipmates of similar skills. Some served in menial roles as landsmen and servants. Many others were able seamen on blue-water voyages, skilled pilots on coastal service, carpenters, sailmakers, helmsmen, marines, and master gunners. Most of these men had been slaves before the Revolution. Many were freed for their service.[278]

AFRO-PARTISANS: EAST JERSEY'S COLONEL TYE AND HIS THIRD FORCE

Others went yet another way. Among them was a gifted Afro-American leader called Colonel Tye. Before the war he had been a slave named Titus, the property of John Corlis, a Quaker master in Monmouth County, New Jersey. In 1775, Quaker meetings urged Corlis to emancipate his slave. Corlis refused, and Titus ran away. His master advertised for his return in the *Pennsylvania Gazette*, and described Titus as "about 22 years of age, not very black, near 6 feet high; had on a grey homespun coat, brown breeches."[279]

He went to Virginia and is thought to have joined the Loyalist Ethiopian Regiment, recruited by British royal governor Lord Dunmore, with a promise of emancipation for those who served. After Dunmore's defeat, Titus returned to New Jersey and led a "motley band" of former slaves and white servants. They allied themselves with British forces some of the time, but mainly they were independent fighters in pursuit of their own rights. As the group grew larger, Titus began to be called Colonel Tye. He earned the respect of allies and enemies alike for his courage and skill in small actions. And he also gained a reputation for treating noncombatants with humanity, and opponents with honor. In one of the cruelest theaters of the war, Colonel Tye became a model of principled leadership that drew others to his cause. He soldiered through five years of war until he suffered a minor wound and died of tetanus in 1780.[280]

His band kept fighting to the war's end, under another partisan leader, Colonel Stephen Bleuke, a "free Black" from Barbados.[281] Yet another partisan was Major Tom Ward, who led a force of foragers and woodcutters in Bergen County, and worked from the fort at Bull's Ferry on the Hudson. Ward and his men defeated an attack by the Continental Army in July 1780.[282]

RACHEL'S REVOLUTION: THE CUMULATIVE
POWER OF INDIVIDUAL ACTS

As the long War of American Independence approached its end in Dutchess County, New York, a slave named Rachel resolved to free herself from bondage. In 1781, she ran away from her master. He accused her of stealing his property by taking the clothing on her back. Rachel was outraged by the charge of theft. They were her clothes. Probably she had made them. A week later she came back, set fire to her master's house, and escaped to British lines in New York City. Then she disapeared and probably took a new identity.[283]

Rachel was not alone. Many slaves acted independently to free themselves from slavery in the Hudson Valley. In 1783, British leaders in New York City compiled a book-length list of 3,000 former slaves who were given freedom and passage from New York: 1,336 men, 914 women, and 750 children. That "Book of Negroes" includes a former slave named Rachel, from "Sussex County in Maryland." There was (and is) no Sussex County in Maryland.[284]

AFTER THE REVOLUTION: THE REVIVAL
OF SLAVERY IN NEW YORK

For many other people of color in the Hudson Valley, the end of the War of Independence brought no immediate change in their condition. After a great revolution for human rights, race slavery began to grow rapidly again in the Hudson Valley—much to the surprise of this Whig historian. The federal census of 1790 found 25,798 people of color living in New York State, and of that number 21,324 (82 percent) were slaves, more than before the Revolution. It was much the same in New Jersey.[285]

In that respect New York and East Jersey were very different from New England and Pennsylvania, where slavery ended more quickly. Foreign travelers were quick to observe the contrast, and also to explain it. Brissot de Warville wrote that in the Hudson Valley "the base of the population is made up of Dutch . . . a people less willing than others to part with property."[286]

The census of 1790 confirmed his impression. In the United States as a whole, four fifths of all American families with Dutch surnames lived in the Hudson Valley. Within that region, Dutch families were more likely than other ethnic groups to keep slaves. The proportion of slaveholding Dutch families was 28 percent; Scottish families, 16 percent; Irish, 15 percent; English and Welsh, 11 percent.[287]

Larger slaveholdings were even more concentrated. In New York County on Manhattan Island, of all families with ten or more slaves, 80 percent had Dutch surnames. Local concentrations of slaveholding were highest in Dutch areas such as Kings County (Brooklyn) where 39.5 percent of white households owned slaves in 1790, more than in any county above the Mason-Dixon line except possibly Bergen County, New Jersey. It was also a larger proportion of slaveholding in that year than among free families in Maryland (36.5 percent), South Carolina (34.0 percent), and North Carolina (30.7 percent). In Albany, with its very large Dutch population, 80 percent of free family heads owned slaves.[288]

The persistent strength of the Dutch population in this region, and of slaveholding among the Dutch, explained the slow progress of abolition in the Hudson Valley. When the New York legislature debated the question, Federalist antislavery leader Erastus Root observed that most opponents of abolition were "slaveholders . . . chiefly Dutch. They raved and swore by Dunder and Blixen that we were robbing them of their property. We told them they had none, and could hold none, in human flesh." [289]

But support for slavery was not primarily about race. A close student of these debates, Arthur Zilversmit, found that in New York "ultimately, all pro-slavery arguments turned on the question of property rights." [290] One pro-slavery writer in New York spoke for many slave owners when he said that emancipation and civil rights for freed slaves would be "the total subversion of OUR liberties." But that was only part of the problem.[291]

ATTEMPTED ABOLITION BY STATUTE: A
FIFTY-YEAR FAILURE, 1776–1827

In the new republic most free people in the Hudson Valley were against slavery, and many passionately opposed it. Prominent among them were Quakers, Congregationalists, Methodists, German Lutherans, French Huguenots, and New Englanders of all persuasions. In the politics of the new republic, the slavery question cut obliquely across emerging party lines. The strongest support for abolition, and for aid to freed slaves, came from a large number of moderate Whigs in the American Revolution. Many later became Federalist leaders. Gouverneur Morris, John Jay, and Alexander Hamilton strongly supported emancipation and civil rights for freed slaves. They were joined by many centrist Democratic-Republicans such as George Clinton and Daniel Tompkins.

But this movement for abolition of slavery failed in New York and New Jersey even as the majority of free families owned no slaves, and wanted no part of human bondage. Here was one of the great recurrent failures of American political institutions—not only in regard to slavery itself, and not merely in the early republic. In every American generation, small minorities with strong material interests have often succeeded in stopping urgent reforms, against the will of the majority. They do so by exploiting the complexity of our constitutional systems. Checks and balances designed to prevent tyranny and to protect property are often used to promote it. This was the legislative history of slavery in the Hudson Valley for many years.

As early as 1777, Gouverneur Morris tried to include an antislavery clause in New York's constitution. It passed by a large majority on the first vote, but was defeated by parliamentary tactics. In 1785, Quaker Edmond Prior filed a petition against slavery which led to the first legislative debate, and a bill for gradual emancipation of all slaves born after the fourth of July in that year. It also failed. A false friend amended an antislavery bill to make it so radical that it lost its majority. He was young Aaron Burr, "already adept at muddying political waters" in the words of one who knew him.[292]

Aaron Burr

Annual efforts finally succeeded in passing a bill for the very gradual emancipation of slave children born after July 4, 1799. Masters were allowed to
hold them as servants to the age of twenty-eight if male or twenty-five for
females, and were required to educate them. But slave owners were given the
option of abandoning them to the state. The human consequences were sometimes more cruel and destructive than slavery itself.

At last in 1817, a major breakthrough in New York was made by Daniel
Tompkins, a reform-minded Democratic-Republican, soon to be vice president of the United States under James Monroe. Tompkins succeeded in en-
acting a law that emancipated all slaves in New York on July 4, 1827. Some
masters defied the law, and a few slaves remained in bondage as late as 1848.
But African Americans celebrated July 5, 1827, as New York's Emancipation
Day. It had been delayed for half a century by political obstruction, against
the will of the majority.

In New Jersey, the process of emancipation was even slower. The census
of 1790 found more than eleven thousand slaves (more than 80 percent of
all African Americans in the state). Slavery was most deeply entrenched in
Dutch areas such as Bergen County. Repeated attempts to abolish slavery
failed in the state assembly, mainly by minority obstruction that persisted
for ninety years. Though most people in the state were against slavery, the
census of 1830 reported that 2,254 slaves were still living in New Jersey.
By 1840, their numbers were reduced to 419, of which 224 were living in
Bergen County. The census of 1860 found that 18 slaves were still living in
New Jersey. But even then, abolition and emancipation could not pass the
assembly. The New Jersey legislature also rejected the Thirteenth Amendment to the federal Constitution. Slavery in New Jersey ended at last when
other states ratified the Thirteenth Amendment on December 18, 1865, and
New Jersey grudgingly acquiesced, nearly a century after the Declaration of
Independence.[293]

FREEDOM BY SELF-LIBERATION: SUCCESS
BY INDIVIDUAL ACTION OF SLAVES

While assemblies debated and occasionally resolved, slaves in New York and
East Jersey did not wait to be freed by others. After the American Revolution they began to free themselves by self-liberation—and in large numbers.
This great process is a forgotten story in the American history of liberty and
freedom.

Self-liberation happened in many ways. The most direct method was to walk away. After 1783, running was increasingly unnecessary in an era when more people were turning against bondage. Slave advertisements provide a rough, incomplete measure of numbers, trends, and timing. Graham Hodges and Alan Brown collected notices for fugitives in New Jersey and New York before 1776. They found 54 runaways in the period from 1716 to 1750 (thirty-five years), and 237 from 1751 to 1776 (twenty-five years). Then came a great surge. Another study by Shane White found 1,232 advertised runaways from 1771 to 1805 (thirty-five years).[294]

The increase came in two periods. The first happened during the War of Independence, from 1775 to 1783. After the peace, runaway notices dropped nearly to zero from 1783 to 1785. Then they began to rise again, and this second surge was much the largest and longest in the state. It began in 1785, peaked from 1794 to 1799, and continued into the early nineteenth century. Most fugitives acted alone, or in very small groups. Their leading destination was New York City. Census returns found that numbers of "free people not white" within the city trebled from 1,036 in 1790 to 3,332 in 1800. Much of that increase consisted of slaves who had freed themselves.[295]

At the same time, even more slaves gained freedom by obtaining a formal deed of manumission from their masters, duly registered in county offices. Manumissions were often granted by masters at the request of slaves, in a process of bargaining and negotiation. From 1783 to 1810, clerks in New York County (Manhattan) recorded 301 manumissions, and 35 more in probate records. These numbers were for one county out of fifteen in 1790.[296] Another study of New York's six southern counties found 2,045 manumissions. These numbers were actually greater than runaways, and their timing was different. In New York County, 86 percent of manumissions came in the decade from 1801 to 1810—a surge that followed the passage of the Gradual Manumission Act of 1799.[297]

A third method of self-liberation was by contractual agreement between a slave and a master, somewhat comparable to indentured servitude. These contracts commonly specified the conversion of bondage for life into a fixed term of service, often six years, with freedom to follow. An example was a contract made by the slave Yat with his owners, John Glen and daughter Sarah Glen of Glenville, New York. They agreed that Yat would become free after six years, if he met many conditions that were laid out in excruciating detail. They included a final payment of $90.[298]

Another example centered on a broken contract between David Cowell, a physician in New Jersey, and his slave Adam. We know about it because the master placed an advertisement in the *New-Jersey Gazette* for the sale of Adam. In the next issue, Adam placed his own advertisement warning the public that Dr. Cowell had "no legal right" to sell him, because the master had drawn up and signed a freedom contract for a "consideration that had alrady been paid," and proof of payment existed. Dr. Cowell brought suit in the New Jersey Supreme Court, and won a judgment that Adam was his lawful property. But Adam disappeared, and could not be found. Later that year, the *Gazette* reported the death of Dr. Cowell. Adam appears to have made good his freedom.[299]

Yet another form of self-liberation was simple and straightforward act of purchase, by slaves themselves. Some had been able to work for themselves and save the money. Others had a friend or family member who pitched in. This method of self-liberation was frequently used by freed slaves who bought wives, children, parents, and relatives and set them free.

One more form of liberation during the last years of the Revolution was freedom in return for military service. This happened often in New England during the war, but it was less common in New York. In 1781, when New England states were enlisting slaves in return for emancipation, New York recruited slaves for military service, not by offering their freedom, but by paying masters a bounty.[300]

In short, thousands of slaves in the Hudson Valley found many ways to free themselves by individual acts of self-liberation, long before New York's General Emancipation Act of 1827. Two leading historians agree that the great majority actually did so. David Gellman studied census returns for southern New York and found that "by 1810, three quarters of the African Americans living in Suffolk and Queens Counties were counted as free. By 1820, over 80 percent of Blacks in Suffolk, Queens and Westchester Counties were nominally free, and over 95 percent in New York City."[301]

Shane White concluded from other evidence that most masters and slaves had "come to some sort of arrangement . . . well before this date [of 1827]." He found that it often happened on the initiative of slaves themselves, and that "New York Blacks had established a tradition of opposition to slavery that few, if any, states could equal."[302] One might add that slaves in the Hudson Valley built upon a history of agency that had taken many forms, and persisted for more than seven generations in New Netherland, British New York, and the American republic.

NEW YORK CITY AS A MAGNET OF
MATERIAL OPPORTUNITY

What did these thousands of self-liberated slaves in the Hudson Valley do with their liberty? Most of them moved to the city, where free people "not white" increased sixteen-fold in fifty years from 1790 to 1840, mostly by migration. The rate of growth was greatest in the years between 1790 and 1820.[303]

New York was the most dynamic city in the new American republic. In 1774, it had been a smaller town than Boston and Philadelphia. By 1820, it was much the largest city in the United States, twice the next two cities combined. Its growth was self-sustaining. By 1860, New York City with its suburbs became the first American metropolis with more than a million inhabitants. Its wealth increased even more rapidly than its population—profoundly unequal in its distribution, but growing at a great rate.[304]

The engine of New York's growth in the early republic was its seaport. A vast expansion of foreign and coastal trade created many opportunities for freed slaves. Shorthanded ships in its crowded harbor offered entry-level jobs in abundance. Even unskilled freedmen from inland farms could sign on as "landsmen" and "green hands." After a voyage or two, they could qualify as "able seamen," who were much in demand. The evidence of seamen's protection certificates showed that about 20 percent of seamen in northern ports were freed slaves.[305]

At sea they met less race prejudice in a ship's foc'sle than in many other workplaces.[306] And in northern ports, a seaman's pay tended to be much the same for Blacks and whites of similar skills.[307] And an able seaman's pay was large enough to transform many lives. An example appears in the autobiography of Moses Grandy, a slave who freed himself from his master in Virginia. He came north and found a berth as able seaman aboard the *James Murray*, earning $12 to $18 a month. After one long voyage to the East Indies and shorter ones to the Mediterranean, he had saved $300 and "bought the freedom of his wife."[308]

Freedmen and fugitive slaves in New York also found work along the waterfront as stevedores, longshoremen, and day laborers, with few questions asked. These jobs offered less pay, more prejudice, and much violence from poor whites who were rivals for the same work. But many a former slave got started that way, and some were able to move up. Other freedmen and runaways found brighter opportunities by mastering skills in shipyards, sail lofts, and ropewalks. They worked as caulkers, sawyers, painters, riggers, and sail-makers. The stories of many a middle-class Afro-American family began that way in northern seaports, especially New York.

Historian Shane White made a careful study of residence and employment among "freed Blacks" in New York City, from census records, directories, and other sources. For 1790 he found that about a third (34 percent) of "free black" men and women lived in affluent white households and worked as servants—much as slaves had done before, but they were free. The other two thirds (65 percent) lived in Black households and boardinghouses. The remainder (1 percent) were in the city's almshouse, hospital, and prisons.

From 1790 to 1810, these proportions remained roughly the same, even as the free Black population grew rapidly. Shane White was able to identify the occupations of 406 male heads of free Black families in census records of 1800 and 1810. He found that 41 percent were mariners or unskilled laborers or servants, 33 percent were artisans in great variety, and 22 percent were shopkeepers and sellers of food, drink, and services. About one percent were in professions, medicine, and the ministry.

White noted that his sample undercounted laborers and servants and did not include the unemployed. But he concluded that the range of occupations was "more open than historians have assumed." In a comparison with other studies for Philadelphia and Boston, he found that "New York offered recently freed Blacks more opportunities than did other American cities."[309]

Free Black women outnumbered freedmen in New York, and many had paying jobs. Most were in domestic service, or took in washing. Surprising numbers ran their own businesses as washerwomen, bakers, caterers, seamstresses, and market women. Many free Black women in growing numbers became keepers or owners of boardinghouses.[310] Other freed slaves met with less success, and some could not make a go of it. The early seaport cities were hard, cruel places, and New York City has been called the most heartless of all. City officials took some Africans into the almshouse and hospitals. Other freedmen turned to crime—stealing to survive, in desperate crimes of poverty.

NEW YORK'S AFRICAN AMERICAN OYSTERMEN

Most African freedmen found work in New York, and some created their own opportunities for moving up. A leading example was the oyster industry. At its peak in the nineteenth century, an estimated 765 million oysters were harvested every year from coastal waters around New York.[311]

It was dangerous work in harsh conditions. From the late eighteenth to the mid-nineteenth century, a large part of this industry passed into the hands of independent and highly skilled African America oystermen. They were not a proletariat, by Marx's definition. Many oystermen owned their own tools and worked for themselves. By hard labor they acquired the small boats and long tongs of their specialized trade. And they became expert at their challenging job.

By the mid-nineteenth century, they exhausted some of the local oyster banks in the waters around New York. With their jobs at stake, they replanted the banks with breeding stock imported from the Chesapeake Bay.

Later in the mid-nineteenth century, this highly profitable industry was reorganized by larger firms, but they continued to do business with individual African American oystermen, who had settled with their families near the water.

An example was the village of Sandy Ground, on the south side of Staten Island. In the census of 1850, a third of Sandy Ground's inhabitants were families of oystermen. They founded an African American community, built their own church, and got on with their neighbors of other ethnic groups. Some descendants still live there. They have established the Sandy Ground Historical Society and remember their history with great pride.[312]

Other African American oystermen moved to Manhattan and operated oyster wagons, oyster shops, oyster bars, and oyster restaurants throughout the city. Some of the best restaurants were owned by African Americans and catered to an upmarket clientele. A leading example was Thomas's Oyster Bar, run by Thomas Downing and his son George on Broadway. Another was Cato's Tavern north of the city. Both attracted a clientele from the city's white elites, but sadly they could do so only by excluding African American diners. Even so, the Downings offered employment opportunities to people of color, and were highly respected throughout the city. In the great New York riots of 1834, racist mobs were allowed to destroy the homes of abolitionists, but when the rioters threatened to wreck Thomas's Oyster Bar, they were instantly stopped.[313]

MARRIAGE AND FAMILY

Urban life in New York also attracted young African Americans by offering something better than a job—an opportunity to marry, form families, and live in a home of their own. A major change occurred in the condition of their lives. They were able to form households and live together in families, which too often had been difficult or impossible for slaves.

After the Revolution, and through the early republic, free African American families were more likely to have both the father and mother present, and households were better able to remain intact through childbearing years, more so than in other regions. A remarkable study by Gary Nash from manuscript census schedules in 1820 identified 527 African American children in New York City. Of that number, 505 (95.8 percent) lived in households with two parents present. The oft-repeated image of broken, unstable, single-headed African American families was not correct for New York City in the early republic.[314]

Another study of New York City found that 96 percent of Black children under the age of fourteen lived in households with both parents present. A state law in 1809 legalized marriages of Black men and women, and established the legitimacy of all children born within them. The law caused many legal complications, but it also "prompted widespread marriages between slaves and freed blacks."[315]

AFRICAN AMERICAN NEIGHBORHOODS, 1783–1830

After the Revolution, African American neighborhoods began to multiply in New York City. They were not racial ghettos. In 1790, most slaves tended to live downtown with their owners in Dock and East Wards, the most affluent in the city. Free African Americans lived uptown in northern wards. The 1790 census found that nearly half lived in a one ward (Montgomerie), and a third on one street (Fair Street).[316]

By 1810, slaves were rapidly disappearing, and free African Americans had expanded through three wards in a belt across the north side of the city. A leading example was the Sixth Ward, on either side of the Collect Pond and the African Burial Ground, which had long been near the center of the "first free Black settlements" in English New York.

Another central neighborhood was the notorious Five Points where families of all races lived together in a system of vertical stratification. African Americans dwelled in cellars and attics, European Americans on the floors in between. In the nineteenth century this neighborhood attracted many visitors, notably including Charles Dickens, who wrote one of the most graphic descriptions of the Five Points on record. He was appalled by its material poverty, misery, crime, prostitution, but fascinated by its cultural life, invigorated by African American music and dancing.

Middle-class African American neighborhoods began to multiply through the city and its outskirts, and we can identify their founders. One of them

"Five Points, New York City," 1827, by George Catlin

formed on Bayard Street in the early republic and attracted a colony of emigrants from Haiti. Some were the ancestors of African American historian Carla Peterson. She has written their history, centering on her great-great-grandfather Peter Guignon, born at 1814 Bayard Street, to Haitian parents.[317]

Other small African American neighborhoods formed in Manhattan during the early and middle decades of the nineteenth century, and some survived for generations. James Weldon Johnson, a leader of the Harlem Renaissance in the twentieth century, became their historian. He wrote that "the major portion of the negro population of the city lived in Sullivan, Bleecker, Thompson and Grove Streets, Minetta Lane and adjacent streets." In the late 1920s he added, "Some of these nests still persist. Scattered through Greenwich Village and Little Italy, small groups of Negroes may be found who never lived in any other part of the city."[318]

One of the most interesting African American communities was Seneca Village, which developed on open farmland north of the city between the lines of Seventh and Eighth Avenues, from 83rd to 88th Streets, north and south. In 1825, the owner decided to sell the land in fifty small tracts. Two African American leaders saw an opportunity. Andrew Williams, a highly successful bootblack, bought three tracts, and Epiphany Davis, a feed dealer, acquired twelve more. Both were members of the African Society for Mutual Relief. They did well in New York, but always remembered where they came

from, and how they arrived. Epiphany Davis hung in his home an engraving
of an African slave ship, so that his children would never forget.

Their primary purpose was to build an African American community.
With their help, other African families bought more than half the tracts by
1832. Together they built the community called Seneca Village, with more
than twenty-five African American families living there. It kept growing. An
entire community flourished there and was said to include "the largest groups
of black landownings in the city." It was also a strong community, with an
active church and one of the best schools for African American children in
the city. Sadly, it was destroyed by another altruism, when the entire area was
taken by eminent domain and made into Central Park.[319]

Many other African American village neighborhoods followed in Manhattan and especially in Brooklyn. After 1827, the Lefferts family sold small
tracts of their Brooklyn land to former slaves. By 1830, a village emerged as
the community of Weeksville. Some of its early buildings still survive, in parts
of what are now Bedford-Stuyvesant. And Weeksville itself still preserves its
identity. These and other neighborhoods and hamlets began to function as
African American communities.[320]

CREATING A NEW COMITY:
THE NEW-YORK AFRICAN SOCIETY

In 1784, a small gathering of slaves and freedmen founded a new institution
called the New-York African Society. Its purpose was described as spiritual
and benevolent: to spread the gospel of Christ among Africans in New York,
to promote a sense of common purpose, and to help Africans in need by mutual assistance.[321]

It was also something new in its design—a "voluntary association" as Tocque-
ville would later call it. That sort of organization had been uncommon in
America before 1776 (except for churches), though not unknown. After the
Revolution, voluntary associations began to multiply in the new republic.
They took many forms: business corporations, political parties, religious
school and library societies, military units, civic groups for the building of
roads and bridges, and much more. Tocqueville regarded them as distinctly
American in their structure and function.

African Americans were quick to use voluntary associations for ethnic purposes. The New-York African Society may have been the first. It appears to

have been founded in 1784, and publications began to appear by 1786, which make it the first of its kind that is firmly on record. Many other African American voluntary associations followed: the Philadelphia Free African Society in 1787, Boston's African Society in 1796, and Newport's African Union Society of uncertain date.[322]

Present at the creation at New York's Society was Jupiter Hammon. He was an extraordinary leader, born in 1711 and a slave all his days to the family of Henry Lloyd on Long Island. His master was a devout Christian who thought it his duty to prepare his slaves for a better life in this world and the next. To that end he founded a school for children of all races. Among them was Hammon, who learned to read and write on a high level of proficiency, read the Bible with his master, and became a slave preacher. At the same time, he also became the first published African American poet. Jupiter Hammon was also trained to high responsibility in commerce and managed his master's business with skill and success. He was given his own property, part of it an orchard that he managed for income. Very late in life, Hammon was offered his freedom. He refused on grounds of age, but strongly supported the liberty of all young people in bondage.[323]

At one of the first meetings of the New-York African Society Hammon was invited to deliver an address on these subjects. In a voice of quiet dignity, with much discussion of his faith, he urged that all Christians support a comprehensive program of gradual emancipation, until "all the young negroes were free." He recommended that the African Society seek to prepare slaves for freedom by instruction in religion, morality, and vocational skills, so that they could flourish in the American republic. The New-York African Society pursued all of these many purposes.[324]

CHURCHES: A SPIRITUAL FRAME FOR VOLUNTARY ASSOCIATIONS

In 1796, members of the New-York African Society also adopted another goal. They wanted to have their own place of worship, apart from white congregations where they never felt entirely welcome. The result was a small "African Chapel" that met in a cabinetmaker's shop. It grew rapidly into a church called African Zion or Mother Zion, with its own building by 1800. It allied itself with the Methodist Episcopal Church, but it remained a self-governing African American voluntary society. Nine founders were its first trustees. Four of the nine could not write, but they knew what they were about. The trustees issued subscription books, raised money for land and a building in 1800, and paid their debts on time. The church opened in 1806, and soon was filled to overflowing.[325]

Mother Zion became a major presence in New York, and a model for other African churches. Close behind were African Baptists, who founded the Abyssinian Baptist Church in 1808. At first they could only recruit an itinerant minister, but the congregation framed its own written constitution, drafted by-laws, established rules of discipline, and drew up articles of faith. All the officers were men, but 75 percent of 245 members were women. More than a few were formidable Big Mamas, who did not suffer disorder in their Baptist fellowship.[326]

Other groups were quick to follow these examples. Many obstacles lay in their path. Existing congregations and ministers had been unhappy with African Americans in their churches, but became even more unhappy when they formed churches of their own. More trouble came on Sunday mornings, when menacing crowds of violent young white hoodlums disrupted services. The founders of Mother Zion asked the New York Common Council for police protection, and got it. A special New York police "watch station" was built outside the church and manned on Sundays.[327]

Peter Williams, founder of the African Methodist Episcopal Zion Church in New York City

Sojourner Truth, born into slavery, went on as an abolitionist and women's rights advocate

THE NEW-YORK MANUMISSION SOCIETY, 1785: AN ALLIANCE ACROSS CLASS, RACE, AND RELIGION IN THE NEW REPUBLIC

At the same time that the New-York African Society was getting started, another voluntary association appeared in the city. On January 25, 1785, nineteen self-described "free citizens and Christians" founded the "New-York Society for Promoting the Manumission of Slaves, and Protecting Such of Them as Have Been, or May Be Liberated."

The two societies were similar in their stated goals, but different in other ways. The African Society consisted entirely of Afro-American members, who had comparatively few material resources. The Manumission Society was primarily white. Its members were among the richest and most powerful men in New York City. Their numbers rapidly increased to 120 by 1790, and their efforts continued to 1849.[328]

The society's moving spirit and first president was John Jay, a wealthy lawyer and landowner, draftsman of New York's first constitution, governor and chief justice of the state, coauthor of the Federalist Papers with Hamilton and Madison, leading architect of American foreign policy, and chief justice of the U.S. Supreme Court. He was deeply religious, strongly hostile to slavery, and genuinely devoted to the cause of helping freed slaves succeed as citizens in a free republic even as he continued to own slaves himself.[329]

Other members of the Manumission Society included Federalist leaders Alexander Hamilton and Robert Troup, the moderate Antifederalist Melancton Smith, New York's mayor James Duane, U.S. senator Rufus King, merchant-banker Alexander McDougall, head of the Bank of New York, and William Woolsey, head of New York's Chamber of Commerce. A third of the society were affluent Quaker leaders such as John Murray Jr. and Willet Seamen. Many New England Congregationalists such as Noah Webster later joined.[330]

Many of these founders had owned slaves in 1785, but by 1790 only 22 percent did so. They were genuinely devoted to the entire abolition of slavery in New York, by a program of gradual emancipation. The Manumission Society was not a debating club. It was organized for action, with many standing committees that had specific functions.

Its first purpose was abolish the slave trade in New York, which largely succeeded. The second was to enact gradual emancipation, which failed in the state legislature, despite a massive campaign. A third purpose was to promote manumission by many methods, and to simplify the process.

Yet a fourth purpose of the Manumission Society was to protect freedmen from kidnapping and false arrest, a major problem in northern cities. From 1792 to 1814 it freed 429 African Americans who had been unjustly enslaved, and it intervened to stop illegal purchase and sale of free Africans in at least forty-four cases. It ended the practice by city officers of arresting runaways and punishing slaves at the request of owners. And it also rescued fugitive slaves in direct violation of the first federal Fugitive Slave Act of 1793.

A large part of the moneyed men in New York City supported the Manumission Society. It succeeded in getting a law through the legislature that prohibited the sale of "negroes imported into the state of New York." The society also worked to improve quality of life for individual slaves and freedmen. It acted against masters who refused to educate their slaves, and helped to provide schooling for many young African American children.[331]

WORKING ACROSS THE COLOR LINE:
AFRICAN FREE SCHOOLS, 1787

One of most important functions of the Manumission Society was to work closely with African leaders, in combined efforts that crossed lines of class, ethnicity, religion, and race. In New York City, immediately after the Revolution, leaders of both races and many ethnic groups learned to work together, uneasily but effectively.

Part of it was an application of customary New York attitudes: that no one is entirely to be trusted or distrusted, and also that one should extend one hand to help those in need, but keep the other hand on your pocketbook. Through the early republic, small numbers of New Yorkers from both races worked together on large causes in this wary way. The leaders of the Manumission Society and the African Society were in the vanguard.

In 1787, these groups tackled a major problem for the children of freed slaves. They founded the first African Free School, with a grand total of twelve students. The next year it had sixty students. In 1789, they began to admit children of slaves with permission of masters. In 1793 a second African Free School opened for girls. The system kept growing. By 1834, it had constructed seven school buildings for about 1,400 students.[332]

Engraving from *The History of the New-York African Free-Schools*

Another goal was the training of students for skilled trades and the learned professions. And a special purpose was to support a school for girls. It started with a white headmaster, Cornelius Davis, and his wife. Many of their students became prominent in the next generation of African American leaders in New York.

CHILDREN IN NEED: THE AFRICAN DORCAS ASSOCIATIONS, 1828

As schools began to open, a major problem began to recur. Poor students were slow to join them. On investigation it was found that at least part of the cause could be remedied. Poor children lacked clothes to wear in school, or shoes for walking. Women of color went to work on these problems. They organized the African Dorcas Association, and many other voluntary associations.

One group was called the Daughters of Israel. Its mission was "to afford assistance to the sick and distressed—to feed the hungry and clothe the naked." The method of organization was interesting. It was thought to have been a "secret society" on the African model, with "initiation procedures," and solemn pledges. The Daughters of Israel were secretive in some ways, but not shy. They marched in parades, wearing white dresses, caps, and ribbons. They defied the racist thugs, who kept their distance. These formidable ladies reclaimed the streets of Manhattan for peaceful purposes.[333]

ETHNIC FESTIVALS AND CELEBRATIONS

As Pinkster faded away in the early nineteenth century, other customs took its place. Annual African celebrations increased and multiplied. Among them were anniversaries of emancipation in the British West Indies, and celebrations of Haitian independence. Both were observed by parades, assemblies, speeches, music, songs, and dances.

Routine gathering places for African Americans were New York's public markets. These were large covered market buildings that combined many small stalls for vendors of food and drink, with open spaces for gatherings and events. The Catherine Market, opened in 1786, became a favorite place for "public negro dancing," as it was called. Here, skilled dancers met in competition. The dance forms preserved African practices. An example was the dance called "patting Juba," or "Juba dancing." Historians have traced a line

"Dancing for Eels at Catharine Market, N.Y."

of descent from African *djouba*. Other dances were done with the tapping of toes and heels on wooden boards in competitive dance contests. This "public negro dancing" developed at the Catherine Market, where butchers, fishermen, and other vendors had stalls.

Another "unique dancing style" was introduced by Black vendors from Long Island and New Jersey. Early accounts described it as a "break down" or "shake down," performed on a board five to six feet long, while "others tapped out the music by beating their hands on the sides of their legs in complex rhythms with the tapping of heels." This was one of many beginnings for American tap dancing.[334]

Later came the dance halls. Edward Judson described the many steps of a "juba dancer" in "Pete's New York Dance Hall." The movements had many African elements, but the central idea was a creative fusion of multiple traditions—Irish jigs, German jogs, Scottish flings, Virginia reels, seamen's hornpipes, double shuffles, pigeon wings, toe tappers, and heelcrackers. African American dancers excelled in this fusion of forms, but everyone was welcome to try, and all were invited to contribute something new. It happened in every American region, but the dancing was said to be especially creative in New York, at least by New Yorkers.[335]

Much of it was marked by complex musical structures with an interplay of melodic lines and complicated interplay of multiple rhythms, each moving against the others. Some visitors were appalled and others heard nothing but cacophony. To alien ears it did not sound like music at all. Strangers complained about sounds of "frightful dissonance," but others came back for more.[336]

Some of the most vivid descriptions were recorded by travelers, both domestic and foreign, Charles Dickens chief among them. These observers were amazed by the diversity of street life in New York. A major part of it was an African American urban vernacular culture that combined African dress, music, and dance with many other American ethnic traditions, in a microcosm of the city itself.[337]

A TIME OF TROUBLES: A SURGE OF RACISM IN THE NINETEENTH CENTURY

Then, after fifty years of progress, things began to go wrong for African Americans in New York in the middle decades of the nineteenth century. Part of the problem was the growth of racism in New York and elsewhere.

In American history, racism has not been a constant but a variable which came, went and came again. It was not quintessentially American, though some would have it so. Always racism was a countermovement to the great and central themes of democracy, freedom, liberty, and what historian J. R. Pole called the American ideal of "equality of esteem."

It was also not rooted in the founding of America, as some mistakenly believe. Perceptions of race are very old, but ideologies of racism are errors of modernity. The defining model appeared ironically in 1776, when Johann Friedrich Blumenbach published his dissertation at Göttingen, *On the Natural Variety of Humanity.*[338]

In the nineteenth century, Blumenbach's idea of race hardened into an ideology of racism. To that end, a definitive work was Joseph Arthur comte de Gobineau's *Essay on the Inequality of the Human Races* (Paris, 1853), an argument for absolute white supremacy and all-out war on race mixing in every sense.

Troubles for African Americans began to grow in New York and every other American region with a surge of racism, and explosions of race violence. In most American places, its drivers were mobs of enraged young white males who saw the progress of Black freedmen as deeply threatening to their jobs and wages, and whose greatest pride was in their idea of belonging to a master race.

Other New Yorkers became deeply hostile to the free Africans and the anti-slavery cause for different reasons. The city's trade with the slaveholding South grew rapidly in the nineteenth century. Some of the race mobs were led by cotton traders in lower Manhattan. But at the same time, other New Yorkers of European origin strongly supported people of color.

TIMES OF TROUBLE: BLACKBIRDERS AND OTHER KIDNAP RINGS IN NEW YORK

As early as 1784, criminals in the new republic increasingly operated as racial kidnap rings. They roamed the streets of northern cities, seized free people, and sold them into southern slavery. New York became a major center for this activity, though it was not unique.

In the 1820s, a criminal gang called the Blackbirders became active in the slums of lower Manhattan. They made a flourishing business of kidnapping both free Blacks and fugitives. Commonly they preyed not upon the weak, but upon African Americans who were young, strong, and fit, and would bring high prices as premium field hands in the South. Street gangs worked closely with even more sinister rings of corrupt New York officials such as Richard Riker, the city's recorder from 1815 to 1838, and constable Tobias Boudinot.

In 1826, a white kidnapper in New York seized an entire family of escaped slaves. A large crowd of Blacks gathered at City Hall and attempted to recover their freedom. But prominent lawyers for the kidnappers dominated the judicial processes with strong support from city officials. The crowds drew larger, and this family of escaped slaves was rescued by brute force, but many were not so fortunate. A new Fugitive Slave Law in 1850 was often supported by northern officials in New York especially.[339]

As organized African American institutions grew stronger, they began to take a hand in other ways, seeking to rescue slaves within the law, by raising money to buy their freedom from owners in the South.

Some historians think that kidnapping declined in New York City during the early nineteenth century. But a federal Fugitive Slave Act in 1850 gave it a new lease on life. The law was strongly supported by northern politicians called doughfaces ("northerners with southern principles"), and it was quickly put to work in New York and other free states.

On September 26, 1850, a fugitive slave named James Hamlet was arrested in New York City. A gang of private slave catchers seized him by brute force. He was taken to U.S. commissioner Alexander Gardiner, who ordered Hamlet to be put on board a steamship and returned to slavery in Maryland. The family that owned him announced they would sell Hamlet to northerners for $800. In New York City, two thousand African Americans met at the African Methodist Zion church and raised the money to make Hamlet a free man.

The Fugitive Slave Act was still a factor in New York City on November 1860, when the fugitive slave John Thomas was seized by a kidnap gang in broad daylight, sent south to Richmond, and sold for $700 in the month of Abraham Lincoln's election.[340]

EXPLOSIONS OF RACIAL VIOLENCE IN NEW YORK AND MANY NORTHERN CITIES

In nineteenth century, racial violence broke out in most northern cities, but it varied from one place to another. Cincinnati's race riots in the 1820s had one central purpose, which was to drive Blacks from the city. More than two thousand African Americans were forced to leave.

New York City went its own way. The race riots were larger than in other cities, more frequent, and more violent. African American New Yorkers were not passive victims. When white racists took to the streets in New York City, African Americans fought back, more than elsewhere. Black mobs sometimes started the riots, and attacked white racists.

In August 1801, for example, a mob of 250 Afro-Americans tried to free twenty slaves who had been held by Madame Jeanne Mathusine Droibillan Volunbrun. Fifty police turned out and suppressed the riot, but only after a fight.

In New York City's theater riots of August 1822, a white mob invaded the African Grove Tea Garden and Theatre on Park Street and assaulted actors and actresses. Historian Shane White writes that the racial violence had been "unusual at the turn of the century, but by the 1820s and 1830s it had become common."[341]

Even New York's large anti-Black draft riots in the summer of 1863 were met by strong resistance from Afro-American New Yorkers. A mob of Draft Act rioters invaded the Five Points. The inhabitants both Black and white made common cause against the rioters, poured cauldrons of boiling water on them from the upper floors of tenements, and sent the scalded mob fleeing for their lives.

AFRICAN AMERICANS IN A CITY OF STRIVERS

New York in our time is the largest metropolitan region in the United States. Its area is small by the measure of other cultural regions, but metropolitan New York is home to more than 10 percent of people in the United States. It also has its own distinct character, culture, and urban folkways. It is a city of strivers, a word that came into English from the Dutch *strijven*, always with a double meaning, "to make great effort," and "to be in conflict or contention."

At present, metropolitan New York is home to the largest urban African American population in the United States. They are more than three million strong, and are 16 percent of the metropolitan region, about the same proportion as in the eighteenth century.

At the time of this writing, within the city of New York the largest concentration is in Brooklyn, where 900,000 African Americans live in an area of four square miles. Another diverse concentration lives in Harlem, with areas of deep poverty, but also a growing Afro-American middle class. And it is the home of a Black upper class, some of it in the area of four blocks collectively called Striver's Row.

African American New Yorkers are diverse, and ever changing in their diversity. Today, immigrants from every nation in Africa are joining others from the Caribbean, Central America, South America, and many regions within the United States. More than a few African Americans are old-stock New Yorkers, who remember their heritage with great pride. They maintain many active historical societies throughout the city, from the Weeksville Heritage Society on Hunterfly Road in Brooklyn, to the Sandy Ground Historical Society on Staten Island.

These New Yorkers have inherited a dynamic Afro-European culture. It has been continuously reinvented by their own efforts and initiative in five different eras, each with its own dynamics. First came the Afro-Dutch era of half-freedom in the mid-seventeenth century; and then the diversity of Afro-English slave culture from 1664 to 1783; following that, an Afro-American metropolitan culture of free people in the early American republic from 1783 to the mid-nineteenth century, and then the cosmopolitan Afro-American culture in the world capital of the twentieth century. Along the way were periods of great stress and difficulty in the heavy labor of Dutch slavery, the harsh repression of British slavery, the intense racism and race violence in the mid-nineteenth century, and cultural conflicts in the twentieth century.

INVENTING THE IDEA OF AFRICAN
AMERICANISM, A NEW CONCEPTION OF
HYPHENATED ETHNICITY, CIRCA 1782

Through it all, in New York and other cities during the early republic, freed slaves invented new ideas of themselves, and in that process they also created a new American ethnicity which spread rapidly to other groups. Before 1775, other identities were more prominent. Slaves were commonly called Blacks in New Netherland, Negroes in English New York, and "Coloreds" in my native Maryland.[342]

From the late seventeenth to the mid-eighteenth century, many groups and individuals were also identified by specific African origins as the slave trade became more diverse. In the Hudson Valley they were called "Coromantee" or "Coromantine negroes" if they came from Ghana; "Popaw," or "Pappa" or "Pawpaw negroes" from Benin; "Calabar negroes" from the Bight of Biafra; "Angola" and "Kongo negroes" from Central Africa, and "Malagasco" negroes from Madagascar.[343] Others were called "Spanish Negroes," "West Indian Negroes," and more.[344]

In the era of the American Revolution, these many groups in the Hudson Valley and other cities began to speak of themselves as "African." Why? Historian Craig Wilder answers, "It subordinated cultural divisions between black people," and became "a leveler between black and white New Yorkers." It also elevated place above race, and it became an instrument of agency and autonomy. "Negro" and "Black" were names that others had given them. "African" was a name they gave themselves.[345]

The word entered common usage very quickly, and rapidly became the universal term of choice in the new republic. As former slaves became free, "African" was used not merely to describe themselves, but also their families, churches, schools, societies, meetings, movements, books, and causes. It became an instrument of collective effort and ethnic belonging. Its many applications described a new sort of comity.

At the same time, freed slaves in North America also coined another phrase for themselves. As early as 1782, they also began to call themselves "African American." The first published use on record appeared in Philadelphia's *Pennsylvania Journal*, on May 15, 1782. A bookseller advertised two sermons by an anonymous author described as "African American."[346]

The timing was not an accident. This new phrase began to be heard in the late eighteenth century, while the American Revolution was still in progress.

In its original context this early example had a special meaning. It referred to an African author who celebrated the American and French victory at Yorktown, and "the capture of Cornwallis." In that instance, "African-American" meant a person of African origin who supported the American War of Independence. In the new republic the expression quickly acquired the broad meaning that it has possessed ever since, and it inspired a family of related words: "Africo-American" by 1788, "Black American" by 1818, "Afro-American" by 1830.[347] In 1831, "Afric-American" was used in meetings that opposed the colonization movement.[348]

Lexicographers report evidence that "African-American" appears to have been older than other "hyphenated American" ethnic terms. Something earlier may turn up, but in Mitford Mathews's *Dictionary of Americanisms*, the first recorded use of "German-American" dated from 1824; and the earliest uses of "Irish-American" from 1832 and 1836. Many hyphenated identities followed in the next two centuries. "African American" was not invented by Jesse Jackson and his contemporaries in the 1980s and 1990s, though they gave it wings. This new ethnic word had appeared two centuries earlier, and instantly was put to work.

Yet another set of phrases came a little later. In 1837, Samuel Cornish became the editor of the New York *Weekly Advocate* and changed its name to the New York *Colored American.* He wrote often about "people of color." Some scholars think that this phrase derived from the French *gens de couleur*, but that phrase had referred to people of mixed ancestry, and was used to distinguish brown from Black. Samuel Cornish's purpose was to bring brown and Black "people of color together in a common cause," to distinguish "colored Americans" from Africans, and to celebrate the belonging of all people in a common humanity and nationality. Each of these successive phrases described a larger vision.

This new invention of hyphenated ethnicity became a fundamental American idea of profound importance in the United States. It first appeared in the most ethnically diverse cities, New York and Philadelphia, spread rapidly to Boston and Baltimore and other urban places, and then reached through the country at large. In its many applications, this idea of hyphenated ethnicity greatly enlarged the idea of America itself, and something similar was put to work in many other nations of increasing diversity. Here is yet another African gift to America and the world.

Chapter 3

DELAWARE VALLEY

Quaker Founders, Guinea Achievers,
American Reformers

He cautioned me against conversing or stopping with any man on
the road unless he wore a plain, straight collar on a round coat,
and said "thee" and "thou." By following his instructions I arrived
safely in Philadelphia.

—James Williams on his escape from southern slavery[1]

IN THE CITY OF Philadelphia, on August 10, 1768, Ann Elizabeth Fortune sat down to write her last will and testament. She began by describing herself as a "free Negroewoman born in His Majesty's Dominions," single and never married. With no husband or children of her own, she left a large estate to her niece Abigail Forten, aged five, daughter of her brother Thomas Forten, who also lived in Philadelphia.

There was much for Abigail to inherit. Her aunt owned a handsomely furnished house on Chestnut Street near the center of Philadelphia. The will mentioned a feather bed, walnut furniture, looking glasses, paintings, fine china, silverware, jewelry, a wardrobe of "silk and dimity gowns," a bolt of "green satin" cloth, and more.

All these cherished possessions were to be preserved for Abigail and given to her when she came of age. The house itself was ordered to be sold, and the proceeds invested with great care, for Abigail's use when she turned twenty-one. Detailed instructions made clear that this "free Negroewoman" knew much about managing money in early Philadelphia.[2]

Historians have been curious to know more about Ann Elizabeth Fortune and the source of her wealth. One clue appears in her will. This "free Negroewoman" owned an African slave named Jane, whom she ordered to be emancipated. Another clue was a notice that had appeared twenty-seven years earlier, in the *Pennsylvania Gazette* on October 3, 1751: "To be sold, a Parcel of likely

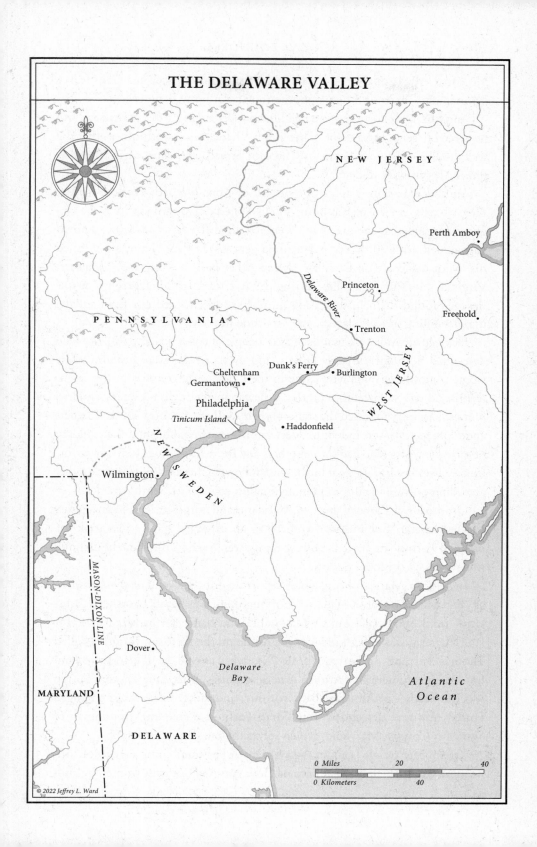

THE DELAWARE VALLEY

NEW JERSEY

Perth Amboy

Delaware River

Princeton

PENNSYLVANIA

Trenton

Freehold

Dunk's Ferry

Cheltenham
Germantown

Burlington

WEST JERSEY

Philadelphia

Tinicum Island

Haddonfield

NEW SWEDEN

Wilmington

MASON-DIXON LINE

Dover

Delaware
Bay

Atlantic
Ocean

MARYLAND

DELAWARE

| 0 Miles | 20 | 40 |
| 0 Kilometers | 40 | |

© 2022 Jeffrey L. Ward

Negroes, very reasonable. . . . N.B. Said Negroes may be seen at a Free Negroe Woman's in Chestnut Street, opposite to Mr. Anthony Benezet's."[3]

Ann Elizabeth Fortune was a neighbor and friend of Anthony Benezet, and he agreed to serve as executor of her estate. That connection confirms that she was the "Free Negroewoman in Chestnut Street" who worked in Philadelphia's African slave trade.[4]

Another question is about the origins of Ann Elizabeth Fortune herself. Her will tells us that she was born "in His Majesty's Dominions," and the language suggests that she may have been born free. This was where our knowledge ended until 2005, when the gifted genealogist Paul Heinegg published his major databases on freeborn African Americans in Maryland, Delaware, Virginia, and North Carolina during the seventeenth and eighteenth centuries. He found them in surprising numbers, and changed our fundamental understanding of race, slavery, and servitude in early America.[5]

Heinegg identified thousands of free "people of color" in early America who descended from African slave fathers, and mothers who were freeborn white women, mostly servants who came to the Chesapeake colonies in the seventeenth and early eighteenth centuries. By law in many English colonies, children of mixed ancestry followed the status of their mothers. Infants with slave fathers and mothers who were indentured servants became free at birth. Other children of mixed ancestry who had slave mothers and free white fathers were not so fortunate. They became slaves at birth, again following the condition of the mother according to law and custom in many English colonies in North America.

On the lower Eastern Shore of Maryland and Virginia, Paul Heinegg discovered several "free mulatto women" in an extended family that took the name of Fortune or Forten. Both spellings were used in the same household, sometimes by the same person.

In 1743, a Maryland constable's report described several of these women as "full as dark as most Mallatos." Among them was Sarah Fortune, a "Mulatto" from Somerset County, Maryland, who had been baptized in 1715. Paul Heinegg was able to identify her as the mother of a son variously called Thomas Fortune or Forten (1740–73), who moved to Philadelphia and founded an eminent free African American family. This same Thomas Forten was the brother of Ann Elizabeth Fortune, and father of her heiress Abigail Forten. All were descended from Sarah Fortune, a free mulatto woman of Somerset County, Maryland, which solves the puzzle of ancestry.[6]

Yet another puzzle is about Ann Elizabeth Fortune's complex web of connections in Philadelphia. She formed close personal ties with women in Philadelphia's most prominent Quaker families. A witness to her will was Hannah Cadwalader, mother of Lambert Cadwalader and matriarch in one of Philadelphia's most eminent Quaker clans. Another witness was Margaret Stevenson, a niece of Hannah Cadwalader.

Ann Elizabeth Fortune was actively involved in the African slave trade and a slave owner herself. At the same time, her close friend and neighbor Anthony Benezet was an early leader of Philadelphia's antislavery movement, a founder of African schools in the region, and Philadelphia's most prominent advocate of human rights for African Americans in the mid-eighteenth century.

Anthony Benezet is less familiar to us today than other antislavery Quakers such as John Woolman, whose intense and intimate personal writings are still widely read. But in the judgment of French and British reformers, Anthony Benezet was the most influential antislavery writer in the western world.[7]

At the same time, he also became the executor of Ann Elizabeth Fortune's estate, and the appraiser of her property was Joseph Marriott, a Quaker relative of Anthony Benezet. This tangle of relationships differed from common understandings of race and slavery in early America. It also takes us to the heart of another unique system of bondage and freedom in early North America.

Three English colonies of West Jersey, northern Delaware, and eastern Pennsylvania comprised a distinct region in the Delaware Valley. It was prosperous, and its thriving settlement of Philadelphia rapidly became the largest city in eighteenth-century North America above the Rio Grande.

The Delaware Valley and its metropolis were unique in their mix of cultures. This was a region where Quakers and Africans, prosperous slave traders and impassioned antislavery leaders, English and Scots-Irish, African slaves, flourishing "free Negroewomen," and many others lived complex and closely connected lives. It was also a region that led the early American republic in formally opposing human bondage, and supporting many reform movements, with Africans and Quakers and many others working together as leaders in those causes.

EARLY AFRICANS ON THE DELAWARE

Africans found their way into the Delaware Valley at an early date, more than a century before the first Quaker colonists arrived. Early in the seventeenth century, small European settlements in great variety began to multiply along the Delaware River. Individual Africans were present from the start. Some of their descendants still live there and became leaders through many generations.

Dutch traders from New Netherland erected a chain of fortified fur-trading

posts on the river from 1624 to 1664. Much of the hard labor and heavy lifting was done by Dutch-speaking African slaves. Among them was an African
slave with the Dutch name Van Dyne or Van Duyen. In the mid-seventeenth
century, he married a Lenni Lenape Indian woman, settled in the Delaware
Valley, and together they produced a large family. For many generations, descendants named Vandine became families of free African American leaders in
Philadelphia and Bucks County. We shall meet several of them.[8]

Other Africans arrived in 1639 with founders of New Sweden in the lower
Delaware Valley. One of them was an African called Antoni Swartz, or Black
Anthony. Probably he had been taken from an Iberian vessel by the Swedish
warship *Fogel Grip* around that year. His name appears on three lists of settlers
in New Sweden from 1644 to 1655, each time with a different spelling. Swedish documents uncertainly described him as a "Morian" or "Angoler," either a
Moor from North Africa or an Angolan from West Central Africa.

Like many other Africans in America, Antoni Swartz had a gift of tongues. Perhaps in his childhood he had lived in the midst of many African speechways. On
the Delaware River, he quickly learned Swedish, Dutch, and Indian languages—
enough to use them and to get ahead in this valley of opportunity. Soon he was
described as a free man, working as a servant for Johan Printz, governor of New
Sweden. At one point he was sailing the governor's "little sloop" on the river.

Swedish colonists built at least nineteen settlements in the Delaware Valley, and once again Africans did much of the work. Black Anthony probably
visited those places in the governor's sloop, and may have made himself useful
as a go-between. In 1648, and again in 1654, he was living on Tinicum Island
in the Delaware River, near what is now the Philadelphia airport. In our time
it is a good place for travelers to remember this well-traveled African who preceded them, four centuries ago.[9]

The Delaware Swedes also actively recruited Finnish colonists called "Forest Finns," who were highly skilled at constructing log buildings. They are
thought to have been the first to introduce that quintessential American artifact, the log cabin, to the New World. And here again, some of the hardest
labor of logging was done by Finnish-speaking African slaves. Probably Black
Anthony picked up some Finnish to go with his Swedish, and he may have
worked with them as well.[10]

Other Africans came to the Delaware Valley in another way. Some of them
were brought in by Augustine Herrman (ca. 1621–86), a fabulous character
from Eastern Europe. He and his family had been banished from his native Bohemia (now part of the Czech Republic) for their Hussite faith. He was raised in

the Netherlands, migrated to New Amsterdam, and he explored the Delaware Valley, following Indian paths on the back of a great white horse that became a legend in this American region. Herrman acquired a large Dutch land grant that stretched from the Delaware Valley to the Chesapeake Bay. He named it Bohemia Manor after his homeland, and settled it with the help of Czech-speaking African slaves. His two wives, many children, and grandchildren produced a large progeny, as also did his slaves. Today a diversity of families in Maryland, northern Delaware, and southern Pennsylvania trace their descent from Augustine Herrman of Bohemia Manor and his African slaves.[11]

THE FRIENDS' MIGRATION

In 1675, the scale of settlement along the Delaware River suddenly changed, when English Quakers began to arrive in large numbers. A large group about 1,400 strong came ashore that year on the east bank of the Delaware. Some of them came from Bridlington in south Yorkshire, and founded the town that is now Burlington, New Jersey. From 1682 to 1685, another and much larger Quaker migration brought about 7,200 souls in ninety ships. They landed on the west bank of the Delaware, founded the colony of Pennsylvania, and built the city of Philadelphia.[12]

This "Friends' Migration" was yet another seminal event in American history. In a half-century from 1675 to 1725, roughly 23,000 immigrants followed. They transformed the Delaware Valley, and created a distinctive American region in eastern Pennsylvania, western New Jersey, northern Delaware, and northeastern Maryland.

The Friends' Migration to the Delaware Valley was roughly the same size as the Puritan Great Migration to Massachusetts Bay. It had been set in motion by another spiritual movement in England, during a turbulent era of civil wars and religious strife between Anglican Cavaliers and Puritan Roundheads (1640–60), with a third to follow in the Glorious Revolution of 1688.

In the course of that conflict many distinctive religious groups emerged. One group were called Quakers from their intense physical expressions of a soaring spiritual faith. They were Christians who worshipped what they called "a God of Love and Light." Quakers also believed that an "Inner Light" existed within the individual souls of all humanity and needed only to be ignited. Many rejected the Puritan idea that salvation came only to an exclusive elite of God's Elect. In early years, English Quakers were an active evangelical movement, deeply engaged in converting others to their faith. Some of them shared a strong sense of spiritual equality unlike both the theology of Puritan Calvinism and the ecclesiology of the Anglican Church.

Quakers had no need of Puritan pulpits, Anglican altars, or Catholic hierarchy. In the spirit of their faith, they sought to live earthly lives of cultivated simplicity. Quakers did away with titles and addressed everyone as "Friend." They replaced elaborate manners of bowing and scraping, and English expressions of social subordination, by "knuckling the forehead," and "tugging the forelock." In that era, Quakers replaced these elaborate forms of social deference with a simple shaking of hands, an egalitarian custom that much of the world has adopted from them.

They also thought of themselves not as a church or a sect, but as a "Society of Friends" in their phrase. In the daily business of life, Quakers cultivated the plain style, and stripped away all things they called "needless," which became a favorite Quaker pejorative.

Like English Puritans, Quakers were also a People of the Book, but not the same book. Both of those groups followed the guidance of the Bible, but in profoundly different ways. Puritans closely studied the five "Books of Moses," which are also the leading books of law in the Old Testament: Genesis, Exodus, Leviticus, Numbers, and Deuteronomy.

Quakers went another way. In Robert Barclay's *Apology* (1675), a classic Quaker work, 80 percent of biblical citations were to the New Testament; in his *Catechism*, 93 percent.[13] And within the New Testament, Quakers closely studied the Four Gospels, of Matthew, Mark, Luke, and John, which are the leading sources for the words of Jesus in the Protestant Bible, printed in red ink in the author's Confirmation Bible. Most of all they harkened to the Golden Rule, and also to Christ's words, "What you do for the least of our brethren, you do for me."[14]

In another way, Quakers were similar to Puritans. Both believed in serving God by doing well in one's calling, and by practicing an austere lifestyle that Max Weber called worldly asceticism. This was not primarily an ethic of work, as Weber mistakenly believed, but an ethic of striving, which was at once broader and deeper. Quakers were relentless strivers, and many of them gained much material success in the New World. Weber believed that this ethic was strong among Christians, stronger among Protestants, and strongest among Puritans and Quakers.[15]

In early years some Quakers actively tried to convert others to their faith. They not only opposed other forms of worship, but sometimes actively disrupted them. People in authority regarded them as troublemakers, profoundly subversive of established social relations. Bad things began to happen to Quakers in seventeenth-century England, and again in Puritan Massachusetts, and once more in Sir William Berkeley's Virginia. In all these places, Quakers were whipped, chained, jailed, tortured, and hanged—which helped to give them a stronger fellow-feeling for the suffering of English prisoners and African slaves.

After much cruel persecution of Quakers in England by both Puritans and Cavaliers, the founder of the Society of Friends, George Fox, visited the New World in search of a Quaker homeland that might become a sanctuary for their faith. Fox studied many American sites, and in 1672 he was much drawn to the Delaware Valley for its mild climate, majestic river, fertile farmland, and rich environment. He also got on well with the Lenni Lenape people (today's Delaware Indians), and described them as "very loving." Quaker choices of settlement on the Delaware were highly purposeful and carefully planned, in part because of George Fox's experiences with Indians in the region.[16]

WILLIAM PENN: QUAKER COLONIZER
AND SLAVE OWNER

George Fox's very able follower William Penn became the leading Quaker colonizer. In 1675, he helped sponsor the large migration to West Jersey, and later led the much larger movement to Philadelphia across the Delaware River in 1681.

Many Americans recognize the name and the familiar oatmeal image of William Penn, but few remember what he thought and did. In both his acts and words he was a great transcendent figure in the history of Christianity. At the same time, he was also a very engaging man, much liked at Court by people who were far from his beliefs. England's King Charles II became his friend, and gave him a vast tract of the American forest, nearly as large as England itself. The king himself named it Penn's Wood, or Pennsylvania, in honor of his friend. William Penn himself meant it to be a Quaker utopia, dedicated to a spiritual idea of religious liberty, and soul freedom in the special Quaker sense.[17]

Penn came from a family of wealth, rank, and reputation. He was often reprimanded by other English gentlemen for mixing with Quakers. In 1671, Sir John Robinson told him: "I vow Mr. Penn I am sorry for you. You are an ingenious gentleman, all the world must . . . allow you that, and you have a plentiful estate. Why should you render yourself unhappy by associating with such a simple people?" To this rude remark, Penn answered that he preferred the "honestly simple" above the "ingeniously wicked." In the Friends' Migration, he found the company he preferred to keep.[18]

William Penn in early life as a soldier

William Penn as founder of Pennsylvania and settlements
in New Jersey and Delaware

Quakers had high hopes for their new home. Pennsylvania and its neighboring provinces were intended to be nothing less than a "Colony of Heaven" for "Children of Light." William Penn did not think of Pennsylvania as a retreat from the world, but as a model for emulation in Britain and Europe. Like Massachusetts Puritans, Maryland Catholics, and even some Virginia Cavaliers, Penn intended his American colonies in the New World to be an example for root-and-branch reform of the Old World.

PENNSYLVANIA'S FOUNDING VISION: QUAKER IDEAS OF RECIPROCAL LIBERTY

In the first generation of settlement, a small elite emerged in William Penn's Pennsylvania. Its core was a group of Quaker families whom Deborah Norris, a spirited Quaker in Philadelphia, later called "Our Mob."[19] This Quaker "connexion" was very tight. Of all the men who became members of Philadelphia's Corporation (an oligarchy who ran the town) at least 85 percent were Quakers, and they were increasingly related to each other.[20]

William Penn recruited large numbers of like-minded British colonists from the Midlands and North of England and also from the hill country of Wales where Quakers made many converts. He traveled to Europe in search of other kindred spirits and found them in the Rhine Valley among German-speaking Protestants of many denominations: Lutherans in large number, Calvinist reformers, German Pietists in great variety. From various parts of Europe, he recruited evangelical groups such as Moravians, and closed sects of Mennonites, Amish, Schwenkfelders, who shared some beliefs in common with Quakers. Penn also attracted settlers who did not join these groups but were sympathetic to their values.

In early years, the largest group were Quakers themselves, who were not a small sect in Britain's mainland American colonies. A survey by Edwin Gaustad of churches and meetings in all thirteen colonies, circa 1750, found that the Society of Friends were the third largest Christian denomination, after Congregationalists and Anglicans.[21]

With broad support, Quakers in the Delaware Valley invented unique systems of local government, and also created an open society of their own design. It was founded not on expedient ideas of religious toleration as in New Netherland, but on deep principles of religious freedom. Another fundamental idea was the Golden Rule. More than any group of American colonizers, Quakers extended to other people the rights they claimed for themselves.

In the Delaware Valley, the result was a system of reciprocal liberty that was unique in the early modern world.

Quaker Pennsylvania's idea of reciprocal liberty differed profoundly from the ordered liberty of Puritan New England, and also from the hegemonic liberty of Anglican Virginia. Among Friends, the leading symbol of reciprocal liberty was the "Great Quaker Bell," commissioned in 1751 by the Pennsylvania Assembly for the fiftieth anniversary of William Penn's Charter of Rights. The Great Quaker Bell is now called the Liberty Bell, by Americans who have forgotten the very special idea of liberty that inspired it. On the crown of the bell, the Assembly ordered a motto from the book of Leviticus: "Proclaim liberty throughout the land unto all the inhabitants thereof." Among the many ideas of liberty and freedom that migrated from Britain to what is now the United States, the Quakers were unique in the extent to which they granted to others the rights they demanded for themselves.[22]

A leading student of this subject summarizes the vital principle of Quaker liberty in a sentence: "Men will reciprocate if treated kindly and justly." This, he writes, was "the basis of Quaker dealings with other men."[23]

That idea of reciprocal liberty has continued to expand among many people in the United States, as an alternative to other models of freedom and liberty. It has changed in some ways. Today, reciprocal liberty has become less substantive and more procedural in its conception. It has been appropriated by those who believe that a free republic should not associate itself with any creed or doctrine other than that of secular freedom itself.

This way of thinking is profoundly different from other American ideas of a free society. In modern secular forms, the idea of a free society as a web of reciprocal rights and obligations still exists in competition with other principles of freedom and liberty in America. It is an idea that can reconcile many ideas of liberty and freedom to one another, as it actually attempted to do in the Delaware Valley.

GROWING DIVERSITY ON THE DELAWARE: FRIENDS, FRIENDLIES, AND OTHERS

With support from many like-minded people who were drawn to their example, Quakers dominated the institutional life of Pennsylvania, northern Delaware, and much of West Jersey for a century from 1675 to 1775. In the Pennsylvania assembly, Quakers were 75 percent of voting members until 1755, and more than 50 percent until 1774.[24]

As late as 1795, Joshua Evans also observed that in West Jersey "many of the people here abouts have had an education among Friends and are Friendly." The same was true in Pennsylvania.[25] Together these two groups of Friends and Friendlies, Quakers and non-Quaker sympathizers, became a majority of English-speaking settlers in the Delaware Valley by the end of the seventeenth century.

In 1702, James Logan reckoned that half the people of Pennsylvania were Quakers, and the rest divided among many smaller groups. We do not know for sure because Quakers forbade census taking in Pennsylvania, fearful of what happened in the Bible when King David tried to "number the people."[26]

But we do know that their numbers grew rapidly, doubling every twenty-eight years on the average. By 1766, Benjamin Franklin reckoned that between sixty and seventy thousand Quakers lived in Pennsylvania alone. Many others had spread through neighboring parts of New Jersey, northern Delaware, and northeastern Maryland. Throughout the Delaware Valley, the dominion of Friends continued to imprint a large part of their culture and institutions on the folkways of this region.[27]

Later, other groups began to multiply even more rapidly in this fertile land. By 1770, English Quakers were a minority in the colonies they had founded, and the Delaware Valley had become a mosaic of high complexity. But some of these other groups shared much in common with Quaker culture. Many had been recruited by William Penn because of that affinity, and they remained in the Delaware Valley because the Quaker colonies were congenial to their ways.[28]

There was comparatively little conflict between some German groups and English Quakers. Benjamin Franklin's slur upon the Germans as a race of "Palatine Boors" was the attitude of an arrogant New Englander—not a member of the Society of Friends. Quakers by and large welcomed German settlers, and lived comfortably beside them. German-speaking elites, for their part, rapidly assimilated English culture. Daniel Pastorius wrote to his sons, "Dear Children, John, Samuel, and Henry . . . though you are of high Dutch [German] Parents, yet remember that your father was naturalized, and you were born in an English Colony, consequently each of you [is] *anglus natus*, an Englishman by Birth."

Many Pennsylvania Germans anglicized their names. In Germantown, the family of Zimmermann became Carpenter, Rittinghuysen became Rittenhouse, and Schumacher became Shoemaker. Intermarriage was frequent among children of different national origins who shared the same religious faith. English, Irish, Welsh, and German Quakers rapidly became an extended cousinage.[29]

Germans of other Christian denominations did not intermarry with Quakers so often, but they came to terms with the Quaker establishment in other ways. In general, Germans did not run for the Pennsylvania General Assembly; they cast their votes for Quaker candidates and supported the "Quaker Party." German Protestants and English Quakers tended to stand together in the politics of Pennsylvania. This cultural alliance dominated the Delaware Valley for many years.[30]

It also supported the dominion of an English-speaking Quaker elite, which firmly maintained its cultural hegemony in the Delaware Valley for ninety-eight years. Of the first generation, Rufus Jones wrote that "we hear nothing of any men of prominence in these early days except Friends."[31]

From 1675 to 1745, the dominion of the Quaker elite tended to grow stronger rather than weaker. An indicator was the composition of the Pennsylvania General Assembly. In the year 1730, British Quakers made up 60 percent of that body. That proportion rose to 83 percent in 1745. Then it began to fall but was still 75 percent as late as 1755, when many Quakers withdrew from politics. Even after that event, the proportion of Quakers in the Pennsylvania Assembly was as high as 50 percent until 1773.[32]

Some people who settled in the Delaware Valley were distinctly "un-Friendly," and showed little sympathy for Quaker beliefs and customs. This category included a large part of the population in urban Philadelphia, which attracted its full share of the human flotsam and jetsam who washed ashore in every Atlantic seaport during the eighteenth century.

Another large group of decidedly "un-Friendly" immigrants appeared in growing numbers after 1716. They migrated from the borderlands of North Britain and Northern Ireland, and moved quickly to western Pennsylvania and northwestern New Jersey.

In the late eighteenth century, the meetinghouses of the Society of Friends became less numerous than the churches of other denominations in other parts of Pennsylvania and New Jersey. But in the Delaware Valley, the dominion of Friends and Friendlies continued long enough to imprint a distinctive culture upon this region.

It is easy to misunderstand the culture and society that the Quakers created in the Delaware Valley. Alan Tully warns us that "because of the dynamic nature of Pennsylvania society, observers have mistakenly described the social organization of the colony as fragmentary and weak. In fact Pennsylvania possessed a strong, coherent and flexible community structure. . . . Because different individuals identified with, and felt they belonged to, the local community as they perceived it, Pennsylvania society had a cohesiveness that appearances belied." [33]

Tully's judgment was accurate and important. The Delaware Valley and the middle colonies in general have sometimes been misunderstood as an amorphous melting pot that came about more or less by accident. Not so. Its Quaker founders deliberately created a coherent cultural framework, which allowed a special sort of open society to flourish there. They did it in a highly principled way. Some of its organizing principles survived in this region long after the Quakers themselves dwindled to a small minority—even to our time.

QUAKERS AND SLAVERY

In early settlements throughout the Delaware Valley, the Quaker idea of reciprocal liberty had one great and glaring exception: the growth of African slavery.

Here a moral rule met a material imperative in a new settlement where opportunities were abundant, and labor was in short supply. In Pennsylvania, Cadwalader Morgan summarized the problem in half a sentence, as "the scarcity of hands here, and how difficult they are to be had." [34]

So desperate was this shortage of labor that Pennsylvania Quakers began to keep slaves within two years of settlement. In November 1684, the Bristol slave ship *Isabella* brought 150 African captives to Philadelphia, then a town of about two thousand inhabitants. It was reported that all of these slaves were bought "in a matter of days." The purchasers were mostly Quakers. They were so desperate for labor that they nearly exhausted their cash reserves to buy these slaves and disrupted the colony's money supply. [35]

THE DELAWARE VALLEY AND ITS UNIQUE EXPERIENCE OF SLAVERY

Historian Frederick Tolles has written that "the Delaware River united West Jersey, Pennsylvania and Delaware into a single economic province, and linked it with the rest of the Atlantic community. It also unified the valley into a single culture area." [36]

The colonizers of this cultural region created one of North America's smaller slave regimes, and one that was unlike any other in the world. This system of slavery was founded, directed, and then later destroyed by Quakers, the first to do so.

To paraphrase Edmund Burke on another subject, English Quakers were the unfittest people on earth to hold another people in bondage. For a century, many English Friends became slaveholders in the Delaware Valley, but they remained deeply conflicted about human bondage. African slaves were quick to discover an opportunity, and made the most of it. Together Quakers and African slaves both became agents of events that followed.

The result was a very peculiar institution of human bondage. Despite its small size, it had large consequences and a long reach. In the century from 1684 to 1783, this system of slavery in the Delaware Valley became one of the most important cradles of antislavery thought and action in the world. Quaker owners and African slaves worked together in that cause, and Quakers became the first people in America to abolish slavery within their own society.

They also took up many related reforms, among them a movement for the rights of free people of color, and another for the rights of women such as Ann Elizabeth Fortune. Some Quakers became deeply concerned about the welfare of slaves and servants, paupers and prisoners, orphans and widows, invalids, the insane, and others in need. In their expanding concern for humanity, animals, plants, and all living things, many Quakers also worked together to develop a new reform tradition, which is today an enduring part of many open systems in America and the world.

At the same time, other Quakers were appalled by human bondage, and spoke strongly against it. They were among the first people in the world to do so in a sustained and organized way. As early as 1688, in the small settlement of Germantown, Pennsylvania, four men came together and bore witness against slavery. They were a mix of German, Dutch and English, Mennonite and Quaker origins—a cross section of the Friends' Migration. All were members of the Monthly Meeting in Germantown.[37]

With one voice, they condemned the "traffick of mens-body," and they did so explicitly on the grounds of the Golden Rule: "Now tho' they are Black, we cannot conceive, there is more Liberty to have them slaves, as it is to have other white ones. There is a saying that we shall do to all men like as we will be done our selves, making no difference of what generation, descent or Colour they are."[38]

Here was a ringing condemnation of race slavery, not merely in Pennsylvania, but throughout the world. These men were acting locally but thinking globally—a Quaker habit of thought, and for good and personal reasons. At the time that they were writing, other Quakers were held prisoners in England, and as slaves in North Africa. The captain of the ship that had brought Daniel Pastorius to America had been enslaved by pirates in Morocco.[39]

This written rejection of slavery was the first on record in the colony. It reverberated through many Quaker meetings. Other Quaker voices were raised against slavery. In 1693, another group gathered around George Keith, a Scottish Quaker in Philadelphia, and published a pamphlet against slavery. They repeated the Germantown arguments in stronger language, attacked wealthy Quakers who bought and sold slaves, and organized a movement that divided the Philadelphia meeting.[40]

In the Merion Friends Meeting, a third group led by Welsh Quaker Cadwalader Morgan spoke strongly against slavery as early as 1696, but on other grounds. What, he asked himself, "if I should have a bad one of Them . . . or when I went from home, & leave him with a woman or maid, and he should desire or seek to commit wickedness, if such a thing happened that it would be more Loss and Trouble to me, than any outward gain could countervail." Cadwalader Morgan's hostility to slavery differed from that of other Quakers. It centered on fears of violence, sexual aggression, material loss, and it also referred to African slaves as "Them."[41]

WILLIAM PENN'S UNSTABLE COMPROMISE ON SLAVERY

Many Quakers were divided in their hearts on these questions. Some accepted slavery, practiced it, and sought to ameliorate it. An example was set by the founder of their faith, English Quaker George Fox himself. He observed slavery at first hand in Barbados and was shocked by its inhumanity. As early as 1657, he sent a "Christian epistle" to "Friends beyond the sea, that have Blacks and Indian slaves." George Fox insisted that God "hath made all Nations of one Blood," and the Golden Rule extended to "all humanity of every color and condition." He did not oppose slavery outright, but in 1671 the founder of Pennsylvania urged masters to "deal mildly and gently with them and not use cruelty towards them, as the manner of some hath been, and is." The foundation of Fox's thinking was the Golden Rule: masters should "treat slaves as they would wish to be treated, and free them after long service." Further, in his *Gospel Family-Order*, Fox insisted that a plantation was a family, and that African slaves were kindred people.[42]

Even so, slavery rapidly took root in the Quaker colonies. William Penn himself became a slaveholder. In 1685, he advised his steward to "train up two, a man and a boy. . . . It were better they were blacks, for then a man has them always while they live." Penn favored the purchase of slaves because they could be owned for life. He acquired at least twelve Africans on his estate, which made him one of the larger slaveholders in the colony.[43]

At the same time when many Quaker leaders began to buy slaves, others started to sell them. Among early slave traders was William Frampton, a Quaker entrepreneur who moved from New York City to Philadelphia, where he ran a "brew house" and a "bake house." He also became an agent for Bristol slave merchants in the 1680s, and he owned at least seven slaves in his private accounts.

Another slave keeper was Samuel Carpenter, treasurer of the province. At his death he owned seven slaves: an elderly man called "Malagascar Jack," his wife, Sarah, a small girl, an old woman Hagar who was "past labour," two men named Mingo and Stepney, and a slave boy called Ishmael.[44]

A few Pennsylvania masters kept slaves on a larger scale. One of the largest holdings belonged to Jonathan Dickinson, owner of twenty-one slaves in Pennsylvania at the time of his death in 1722. He also owned two plantations in Jamaica and was active in the slave trade.[45]

With these prominent leaders, slaveholding became widespread in Quaker Pennsylvania during its early years. One survey of leading Friends in the Philadelphia Yearly Meeting found that 70 percent owned slaves in the years from 1681 to 1705.[46]

But other Quakers never accepted slavery. Cadwalader Morgan and Robert Piles agonized over their own decisions to buy slaves. They were divided not only by a collision of spiritual ideals and material realities, but also by conflicted values and competing interests.

The more that slavery was practiced by some Quakers, the more it was to be opposed by others. From the start, strident attacks from fellow Friends accused slaveholders of being accessories to war-making, kidnapping, "man stealing," false imprisonment, torture, rape, murder, adultery, and continuing violence. These relentless critics argued that forced bondage robbed slaves of the fruits of their own labor, stole their children, destroyed their families, broke many of the Ten Commandments in a single act, violated the Golden Rule, rejected the teachings of Christ, and defied explicit passages in the Bible that forbade slaves to be held for life.

All of these objections were firmly founded in fact, but slavery was profitable in the Delaware Valley, as it always had been and forever would be, from human bondage in the ancient world to persistent human trafficking in our time.

By 1700, William Penn himself was increasingly troubled by the growth of slavery in his Quaker utopia. He asked the Philadelphia Monthly Meeting to study the question, which "had lain upon his mind for some time." Penn urged Quakers to think about the enslaved and to "be very careful in discharging a Good Conscience toward them in all respects, but more especially for the good of their Souls." [47]

Quakers debated these questions in their meetings. For many years they urged caution and restraint, but did not require the prohibition of the slave trade, or the emancipation of slaves, or the abolition of slavery. In 1712, the Pennsylvania General Assembly, of which three quarters were Quakers, imposed an import tax on slaves, which was meant to be prohibitive. But imperial authorities in London intervened to keep the tax below that level. On the question of full emancipation of slaves, Quaker majorities in the assembly agreed that "it is neither just nor convenient to set them at liberty." [48]

AFRICAN ORIGINS OF SLAVES IN THE DELAWARE VALLEY

Who were these African slaves of Quaker masters? Where in Africa did they come from? How did they reach the Delaware Valley? What do we know of their lives? The first wave of African slave trading in this region began by 1684 or before. Slaves in this early period tended to come by way of the West Indies, but most were African born. Only a few had been "seasoned" in the Indies, and even fewer were Creoles born in America. [49]

Advertisements for sales and runaways in Pennsylvania described a broad diversity of West Indian islands from which Africans were transshipped to Philadelphia: Barbados, Jamaica, Bermuda, Montserrat, Guadeloupe, Dominica, and more. In the Delaware Valley, numbers of arriving slaves were small by comparison with other colonies, but surprisingly large in absolute terms. By 1710, African slaves were as much as 17 percent of Philadelphia's population. [50]

The first wave of arriving slaves reached a peak around 1712. Thereafter, the slave trade declined for a time in the Delaware Valley. Part of the cause was a great and growing fear of slave revolts, which spread through the colonies after the New York revolt in 1712. Another factor was an expanding flow of servants and free workers from Britain, Ireland, and Germany. A third was

European warfare, which interrupted the flow of North Atlantic migration. But each decline was followed by another surge.

After a long period of fluctuations, the largest wave of African slave trading in the Delaware Valley reached its peak in the years from 1759 to 1765, when the flow of European and British and Irish immigrants was reduced by war. Its leading historian, Darold Wax, found that "fully three-quarters" of arriving slaves in Pennsylvania's history came directly from Africa in those years.[51]

As the port of Philadelphia grew in size and complexity, the slave trade came to be dominated by a few mercantile houses: Garrett Meade and George Meade, Thomas Willing and Robert Morris, and Thomas Riche, who is least remembered but became the largest operator.

These dealers combined a transatlantic African trade with a coastal commerce in sloops and schooners. Much of their coastal slave trade centered on Philadelphia, and reached into northern Delaware and West Jersey, sometimes in surprising numbers. In 1762, the firm of Willing and Morris advertised that 175 newly arrived Gold Coast slaves would be sold in Wilmington. Many years later, Delawareans vividly remembered that event when "a vessel with two masts anchored in Christiana Creek with the deck full of Negro slaves from Africa."[52]

As the market expanded, more Quakers became slave traders. Some Philadelphia merchants "expressed discontent about being involved in the trade, but their complaints seem to have resulted more from the unhealthiness of the people they received than from any moral abhorrence of the slave trade."[53]

So wrote Jonathan Dickinson to his brother in the British West Indies. Historians Gary Nash and Jean Soderlund observe that Dickinson "acknowledged the existence of antipathy towards the trade among some Pennsylvania Quakers, but nevertheless he requested that more slaves be sent, as long as they were young and healthy."[54]

An increase in the supply of slaves caused prices to fall. Artisans and owners of small farms could afford to buy them. The result was an expansion of a secondary market in rural counties and small towns throughout the region.

Another factor, small at first, was what scholars call internal migration to the Delaware Valley from other American regions, and the Chesapeake region in particular. More than a few African Americans made their way from Maryland and Virginia to Pennsylvania. Some were freeborn. Cases in point were the stories of Ann Elizabeth Fortune and Thomas Forten, who came in freedom from the Eastern Shore of Maryland and Virginia. Others were fugitive slaves who fled across the Mason-Dixon line.

Larger numbers were brought by masters who were themselves in motion, such as John Beale Bordley of Maryland, who moved to Philadelphia, or George Washington when he briefly lived there. A few were sold by owners or heirs into the Philadelphia market. Others ran away and vanished into the alley life of Philadelphia, as did several slaves of George and Martha Washington, who lost their favorite cook that way, much to the fury of the first president. Later in life he turned strongly against slavery, emancipated his many slaves in his will, and persuaded Martha to do the same. George Washington was the only early American president to do that. His stay in Philadelphia may have been a factor.[55]

Another secondary migration of slaves came from other North American colonies, and increased the diversity of African origins in Pennsylvania, Delaware, West Jersey, and Philadelphia in particular. In the eighteenth century, circa 1767, an eyewitness observed that as many as a thousand Blacks came together in the city of Philadelphia on fair days, and "divided into numerous little squads, dancing, and singing, each in their own tongue, after the customs of their several nations in Africa."[56]

Altogether, the African American population in Pennsylvania doubled from 1740 to 1760, redoubled from 1760 to 1780, doubled yet again from 1780 to 1800, and doubled once more from 1800 to 1820. Total numbers remained small by comparison with some other colonies, but rates of growth were large. Overall the population of African descent in Philadelphia had a doubling time of about twenty years for nearly a century. Quantitative sources of total population are scarce for early Pennsylvania, partly because of Quaker scruples against "numbering the people." But the main lines of growth and change are clear.[57]

AFRICAN REGIONS OF ORIGIN: "NORTH GUINEA," GAMBIA, AND THE GOLD COAST

In the Delaware Valley, as in every other North American region, a diversity of African origins coexisted with patterns of concentration within that extended range. Historians have tended to stress one or the other of those two tendencies, but a combination of diversity and concentration was almost universally the case.

Philadelphia's slave buyers expressed strong preferences in their choice of Africans, and favored two broad areas in West Africa. William Cox, an active Pennsylvania slave trader, wrote in 1762, "It is generally allowed that the

Gambia slaves are much more robust and tractable than any other slaves from the Coast of Guinea, and more Capable of undergoing the Severity of the Winter Seasons in the North-American colonies, which occasions their being vastly more esteemed and coveted in this Province and those to the North-ward, than any other slaves whatsoever." [58]

Others wrote that Africans from Gambia were much valued in "northern provinces where the labour is not so hard as in Sugar-Plantations." Gambi-ans were reputed to be "of a mild sociable, and obliging disposition. . . . The women are good-natured, sprightly, and agreeable." This perception included more than the present nation of Gambia. It extended from Senegal to Guinea near the present city of Conakry. Important trading places were coastal islands such as Îles de Los. [59]

A second prominent region of African origins was the Gold Coast. The Philadelphia slave trading firm of Willing and Morris reported that Gold Coast slaves were preferred over most other Africans "on account of their nat-ural good dispositions and being better capable of hard labor." [60] Many buy-ers in Pennsylvania's small African trade thought that the Gold Coast was the source of "the stoutest and most sensible negroes on the coast." [61]

These attitudes, along with established English trading patterns in Gam-bia, Guinea, and the Gold Coast, shaped the African slave trade in the Del-aware Valley. Altogether, evidence survives for twenty-five voyages of record from Africa to the Delaware colonies. On average, they landed 116 slaves each, or about 2,900 slaves altogether. Twelve of the twenty-five voyages were recorded as coming from Africa in general. Thirteen were identified as coming from particular parts of Africa: five from the Gold Coast, and four from Gambia. Another four came from the "Guinea Coast" or "Guinea," a term used in different ways, sometimes loosely as a synonym for Africa it-self, but more often for a large African coastal region between Gambia and the Gold Coast. Upper Guinea or North Guinea referred to the coast from Senegal south to Liberia. It centered on the nation called Guinea today and the offshore Îles de Los. Lower Guinea ran from the Côte d'Ivoire through the Gold Coast. [62]

Slave ships in the Delaware Valley trade tended to call at several ports on the North Guinea coast until they filled their holds. There was a pattern to that process. These slave captains tended to start at Gambia and moved south and east, stopping at trading places on the Îles de Los, or near the present metropolis of Conakry in Guinea, or at Bance Island, today's Bunce Island in what is now Sierra Leone. [63]

ANTHONY BENEZET AND THE MANDINKA PEOPLE

In Philadelphia the great Quaker abolitionist leader Anthony Benezet (1713–84) took a deep and serious interest in African cultures and studied them with special care in Gambia and "North Guinea."[64] He read widely on the culture of West Africa, and devoured serious works of travel and description, especially by Michel Adanson, who lived there and learned African languages, and André Brue, and in particular Francis Moore, a factor for the Royal African Company in Gambia and North Guinea who was said to be a Quaker.[65]

Benezet took particular interest in Mandinka people, whom he called Mandingo or Malinke. Then, as now, they were the largest ethnic group in today's nation-states of Gambia and Guinea. In the twenty-first century, 99 percent of Mandinka are Islamic, and they were strongly so by the mid-eighteenth century. Benezet found many accounts that described Mandingo and Malinke people as self-governing in villages and small kingdoms, highly skilled and industrious, avoiding strong drink, actively engaged in educating their children, and attentive to teaching young students to read and write in Arabic. Many

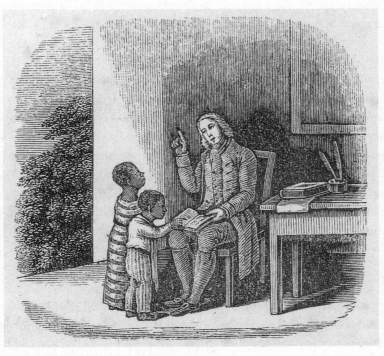

Anthony Benezet teaching African children

English and French traders and travelers lived among them in the eighteenth century, and described them as tolerant of others, and sharing a spirit of "great humanity and sociableness." In Philadelphia, Benezet knew many of them. His biographer Maurice Jackson writes, "He came to believe that the Malinkes of Senegambia and other Africans shared similar beliefs with Quakers on child rearing, drink, morality, and greed." He came to admire many Africans, Mandinka people most of all, and he celebrated their culture in his books.[66]

No other African trading places were as prominent in the slave trade to the Delaware Valley as were those of the North Guinea coast, followed by Gambia and the Gold Coast. Not many Pennsylvania slaves appear to have come from the Bight of Biafra. Comparatively few were from Congo or Angola (a factor of timing in the slave trade), and fewer came from East Africa, except occasional Madagascar slaves. Altogether, buyers in Philadelphia favored Gambian, Gold Coast, and Guinea slaves. Quakers such as Anthony Benezet went further in that direction. He spoke highly of "Malinke" or "Mandingo" slaves from this region of Africa and recognized a spiritual kinship with them.[67]

Quakers also had a great and growing preference for very young slaves. In a system of small-scale domestic slavery, where slaves lived in close proximity to their owners, young slaves were less threatening and more easily taught. As early as 1715, slave trader John Dickinson wrote, "Our people don't care to buy, except Boys and Girls."[68] From 1730 to 1765, out of a group of 465 slaves imported to Philadelphia, 263 were young boys and girls.[69]

Quakers also preferred to buy female slaves in larger than usual numbers. Pennsylvania's Atlantic slave trade in general was marked by an unusually high proportion of females. Nash and Soderlund write that "the greatly skewed sex ratios denoting high importation of men into the plantation areas of the West Indies, Carolinas and Chesapeake did not exist in the Quaker City." After the American Revolution, Philadelphia's African population had more females than males, a pattern similar to other northern cities, but stronger than most. In rural counties of Pennsylvania, that pattern was reversed.[70]

LAWS OF SLAVERY AND RACE IN QUAKER PENNSYLVANIA

During Pennsylvania's earliest years, from 1681 to 1700, European servants and African slaves had much the same rights. Both were regulated by statutes for the management of servants in general, passed in 1683 and 1693. They could marry, hold property, sue their masters, and testify in court. Edward

Turner, a leading student of slave law in the Delaware region, wrote from a legal perspective that "during the earliest years, slavery in Pennsylvania differed from servitude in but little, save that servitude was for a term of years and slavery was for life." It would be more nearly correct to say that Pennsylvania slaves were servants in perpetuity. Their condition was inherited by their children.[71]

Turner observed that "aside from this one fundamental difference [in length of bondage] . . . the incidence of each status were nearly the same. The negro held for life was subject to the same restrictions, tried in the same courts, and punished with the same punishments as the white servant." This was true in the early years.[72] Servants and slaves were forbidden to "hold commerce" in their masters' property. Both were required to carry passes when they traveled. Both could be punished at the discretion of the court for acts of violence.

But after 1700, the condition of slaves changed in the Delaware Valley, in large part because of growing fear of slave revolts throughout the American colonies. Pennsylvania did not have a slave code as such, but it did enact a Black code in 1726, which increasingly showed a highly developed sense of race.

Nash and Soderlund found the Black code of 1726 to be "most notable in the restrictions that it placed on free blacks." It limited freedom of movement by all Negroes, slave and free. It forbade marriage between any Black person and any white. Slaves were forbidden to carry arms without permission of their masters. Strict orders were given to constables for dispersing meetings of "negroes" that were thought to be loud and boistrous. New "Negro Courts" were created for Blacks, both free and slave. They were tried not by a jury of their peers, as were whites, but by two justices of the peace and "six of the most substantial freeholders of the neighborhood."[73] Penalties on Negroes became increasingly severe by reason of their negritude. A free Negro who married a white was ordered to be returned to slavery; no penalty attached to whites. Children of free Blacks were required by law to be taken from their parents without consent in all cases, even if the families were not poor. All Black children without exception were bound out to the age of twenty-one for females and twenty-four for males.

The law also imposed death penalties on Blacks convicted of burglary, murder, homosexual acts, and rape of a white woman (but not of a Black woman). The penalty for a Black man who tried to rape a white woman was castration, which horrified British officials and was disallowed in London.

For any attempt at robbery, theft, or fraud above 5 pounds, slaves were to be whipped, branded on the forehead, and transported from the province. Masters could decide whether to whip their slaves themselves, or have them whipped at the public whipping post.

Appeals from Negro Courts went to the Governor's Provincial Council. That body tended to be sympathetic to requests from masters for the security of their property, and sometimes very hard on slaves. An example was a case of Toney and Quashy, who had been convicted of burglary, and were sentenced to death by a Negro Court in 1707. Their masters asked the Council to allow them to sell the slaves out of the province, and "to have liberty to inflict on them such corporal punishment as may be requisite for a terror to others of their color."

The Provincial Council agreed, but increased the severity of corporal punishments "to make the Slaves Examples of Terror to Others of Their Complexion." The Council ordered Toney and Quashy to be led through the town "with their arms extended and tied to a Pole across their Necks" and "severely whipped all the way as they pass, upon the bare back and shoulders; this punishment shall be repeated for 3 market days successively; in the meantime they shall lie in irons in the prison, at the owners Charge," and "then transported out of the colony." That was the verdict of Pennsylvania's provincial councilors, who were themselves Quakers and slaveholders.[74]

Some small vestiges of humanity survived in other parts of Pennsylvania's Black code. The Pennsylvania legislature never defined slaves as chattels, though they were taxed as property, and continued to recognize their existence as human beings. Masters were forbidden to torture their slaves, or starve them, or overwork them. Masters who killed their slaves were prosecuted for murder as if they had killed free whites, and that law was enforced in Pennsylvania. In 1742, William Bullock of Philadelphia was sentenced to hang for having murdered his own slave.[75]

THE BRUTALITY OF HUMAN BONDAGE
IN THE DELAWARE VALLEY

Patterns of slave employment in this region were very different from those of the plantation colonies. Comparatively few Pennsylvania slaves worked in large gangs at field labor. Nash and Soderlund did a survey of employment in urban and rural Pennsylvania, and found that male slaves did many kinds of work. They were employed by ironmakers, millers, tanners, distillers, and many others.[76]

Most slaves in this region began by toiling at menial tasks, but runaway advertisements and masters' records reveal that slaves in the Delaware colonies advanced rapidly from laborers and apprentices to skilled workers. In the iron industry they became expert colliers, hammermen, forgemen, and blacksmiths. Other slaves mastered a broad range of skills as tinsmiths, masons, coopers, sugar makers, and charcoal workers. Their knowledge and experience created opportunities for them to bargain with owners over terms of employment.

Slave women worked in the house and on the farm, and also acquired special skills in great variety. One woman was advertised as "able to do town and country work, but most suitable for the country as she was brought up there, and is very handy and active in tending cattle and horses."[77]

Other advertisements for runaway slaves remarked on their qualities of intelligence and intellect. One notice described a slave woman named Esther as having "a cunning turn of wit," and did so in language which implied that her infuriated master had often been outwitted.[78]

In Pennsylvania, as everywhere else, slavery was a system of forced labor, and a brutal business. Evidence of cruelty was abundant in eighteenth-century sources. Some of it came from masters themselves in their advertisements for runaway slaves in Philadelphia gazettes. Fugitives were variously described as wearing handcuffs, leg-irons, chains, and "iron collars with hackles."

Philip Syng, a Philadelphia silversmith, published a runaway advertisement for his slave Cato, "a well-set fellow, and speaks good English. . . . When he went away he had irons on his legs and about his neck, but probably has cut them off, as he has done several times before on the like occasion." A Philadelphia brickmaker, John Coats, forced all of his slaves to wear iron collars with hackles. In other runaway notices, Pennsylvania masters described their own slaves as severely whip-scarred, and as bearing wounds caused by brutal beatings. Fugitives in the Delaware Valley were marked by repeated evidence of heavy labor and hard treatment: "lame," "thighbone broke." Slave women and girls were described as having been branded on their faces.[79]

Near Philadelphia in 1806, traveler Robert Sutcliffe saw a twelve-year-old slave boy wearing a locked iron collar and "from each side of it an iron bow passed over his head." In mid-January he observed that the child had no shoes, no stockings, no hat, and no gloves. He wore "a light linsey jacket and trowsers," made of a rough mix of wool and flax. Some runaway slaves bore the results of severe and even crippling injury from frostbite.[80]

DEATH AND LIFE ON THE DELAWARE: PATTERNS OF SLAVE DEMOGRAPHY

Bondage in Philadelphia was hard for many African slaves in another way, with high rates of morbidity and mortality, and low fertility. In the city's bills of mortality and newspaper accounts, historian Susan Klepp found much quantitative evidence for the reconstruction of mortality patterns. She estimated that crude death rates in Philadelphia averaged 67 per 1,000 per year for Africans compared with 46 per 1,000 for Europeans through the better part of a century. Comparable rates for both were about 10 per 1,000 in the late twentieth century.[81]

The cause was complex, but deficiencies in nutrition and housing were the major factors. Epidemics were very dangerous. Leading causes of death were smallpox, measles, pleurisy, tuberculosis, and many "febrile diseases." Infant mortality for people of color in Philadelphia was above 250 per 1,000 in the first year. Childhood mortality was over 500 per 1,000 in the first fifteen years of life.[82]

Even at these high rates, scholars have found evidence that bills of mortality underreported deaths of infants and children in Philadelphia during the eighteenth century. Archaeologists have discovered remains of small infants and "developed fetuses" in excavations of early privies of Philadelphia.[83]

URBAN LIFE OF AFRICANS IN PHILADELPHIA, CIRCA 1767

The majority of Pennsylvanians, both white and Black, lived in the country. But enslaved Africans were more urban than free Europeans: 35 to 40 percent lived in Philadelphia and suburbs called "Liberties," compared with 11 to 20 percent of free European colonists.[84]

Absolute numbers of slaves in early Philadelphia reached their highest peak in 1767 at about 1,500, or 9 percent of the city's total population. They lived within an area of about twenty-two city blocks, a spatial concentration that may have been without equal in other parts of British America.[85]

In that year, many Pennsylvania slaves, perhaps most of them, were African born. More than a thousand "new Negroes" had recently arrived from Africa in the six years from 1759 to 1766. That large wave has been called "the greatest infusion of African culture in Philadelphia's history." It was certainly so in its early history.[86]

African ways were much in evidence, especially in the city. Most striking was a custom of "tumultuous gatherings" by Africans on holidays, a custom that developed in most regions. A historian wrote that at the end of the colonial period, "more than a thousand slaves gathered for festivals in Washington Square," which would have been a large majority of slaves in the city at that time.[87]

These joyous crowds of city slaves were joined by others from the surrounding countryside. By comparison with other colonies, slaves and free Negroes were allowed much freedom of movement in the Delaware Valley. Slaves from Newcastle County in northern Delaware were given passes to visit Philadelphia on Sundays and holidays.[88]

Philadelphia's African slaves also gathered on more solemn occasions to mourn the passing of friends and relations. Part of the Strangers Burial Ground was reserved for slaves. Eyewitness accounts survive of "slaves from Guinea" who were observed "going to the graves of their friends early in the morning, and there leaving them victuals and rum." These assemblies allowed Africans, slave and free, to preserve a collective cultural identity in a strange new world.[89]

At the same time, African slaves also picked up the language and customs of Europeans in the Delaware Valley. As everywhere else in North America, African slaves in the Delaware Valley were quick to learn multiple languages. In 1762, Thomas Bartholomew advertised in Philadelphia for a fugitive named Joe, "alias Joseph Boudron," about twenty-three years of age, who "speaks good English, French, Spanish, and Portuguese." Pennsylvania runaway notices from 1728 to 1790 described at least fifteen slaves as fluent in three or more languages.[90]

In 1763, Henry Melchior Muhlenberg met a Gambian slave near Philadelphia who had been "taken from Africa to the French West Indies in 1761, captured by the English, and carried to Philadelphia, where he was purchased by a German innkeeper." Muhlenberg conversed with the slave at length and was astonished by his linguistic skills. This slave could speak "his Gambian native tongue, French, Danish, and English," and probably German as well.[91]

In the Delaware Valley during the mid-eighteenth century, slaves often possessed language skills and cultural knowledge that reached beyond the experience of their masters, as evidenced in the runaway notices.[92]

These advertisements also described a spirit of strength and autonomy in fugitive slaves. Thomas Graeme posted a notice for "a Molatto slave, named Will, about 29 years of age . . . an open bold countenance, somewhat pitted with the small-pox, speaks both English and Dutch, and is a very cunning, sensible fellow." [93]

Thomas Lawson wrote of a "coloured Mulattoe man named Billey" as "a very likely young fellow, about 20 years old . . . stout and strong made, has a remarkable swing in his walk, but is much more so by a knack he has of gaining the good graces of almost every body, who will listen to his bewitching and deceitful tongue . . . from his ingenuity he is capable of doing any kind of business." [94]

All this put a growing strain on the practice of slavery in the Delaware Valley—one of many strains that began to increase more rapidly than slavery itself in this region, during the eighteenth century. As these tensions increased, we can observe the gradual fraying of race slavery through much of this region in the mid-eighteenth century. Some of these stresses and strains grew from values and beliefs that prevailed among Quakers, which were increasingly at odds with human bondage.

THE FRAYING OF SLAVERY IN THE DELAWARE VALLEY

Something else began to happen in daily relations through the Quaker colonies and was observed by a thoughtful French traveler, Michel Guillaume Jean de Crèvecoeur. He made a point of visiting John Bartram, a gentle farmer and self-taught botanist who made a garden that Washington and Franklin loved to visit. Bartram invited his French visitor to share a meal with his Quaker family. Crèvecoeur was amazed to find that the master, his wife, their family, English servants, and African slaves all sat down to dinner together and shared the same food: "There was a long table full of victuals: at the lowest part sat his negroes, his hired men were next, then the family, and myself, and at the head the venerable father and his wife presided. Each reclined his head and said his prayers." [95]

Urban life in Philadelphia also increased opportunities for slaves to marry and form families, which was more difficult in the countryside where slaveholdings were small and scattered. But even in the cities family life among slaves was difficult to sustain in other ways. One study found that in a sample of twenty-nine slave families, twenty-three were "broad marriages" in which the parents had different owners and lived apart.

In early Philadelphia, urban slaves rarely lived together in their own family groups. A study of probate and marriage records in Philadelphia from 1682 to 1780 by Jean Soderlund found that less than a quarter of slave husbands and wives lived in the same houses. The rest had "broad marriages," with different owners. A more startling practice in Philadelphia was that "urban owners sold black children to other families" at an early age, or gave them to relatives. This pattern recurred with surprising frequency.[96]

One consequence was that married adult slaves sometimes lived alone, slept apart, and ate by themselves in the kitchen. But even so, this evidence also shows that slave families continued to form, even as they struggled against heavy odds. The old idea that slavery destroyed Black families is mistaken in this region. Wives and husbands, parents and children preserved connections even when they lived apart.[97]

Another pattern was that free and slave children in Pennsylvania households also found ways to bond together. They played together, and sometimes studied the free children's schoolbooks together, without the knowledge of elders. This was a normative experience in the Delaware Valley. Adult women, slave and free, also worked closely together in households. And in affluent slaveholding families, gentlemen bonded with their African manservants. A Quaker woman, Fanny Saltar, remembered hearing her grandfather say about 1750 that "he knew not only every gentleman in town, but every gentleman's black servant and dog."[98]

Fanny Saltar also recalled with great pleasure that in her childhood she bonded closely with a house slave she called Daddy Caesar. She wrote, "I liked to hear his talk as he sat in the old-fashioned chimney corner" and told African stories "in his dialect that was as much African as English." She also fondly recalled a slave cook called Mammy Katy, and remembered that "I loved to sit in her lap as she ate her breakfast."[99]

This was intimacy without equality or liberty for the enslaved. But it created close personal relations that were deep, genuine, long-lasting, and corrosive of slavery and racism in many ways.

In Pennsylvania there was also much evidence of race mixing, and it increased through time. The largest proportions were recorded in rural Pennsylvania. In Chester County, of all slaves registered by law in 1780, 16 percent were listed as "mulatto." Of slaves manumitted in four of Chester County's Quaker meetings, 30 percent were identified in the same way. Smaller proportions were registered in the city of Philadelphia, but this may have been a difference in record keeping. Other evidence has suggested that race mixing tended to be more common in the cities.[100]

Most mixed couples were unions of white males and Black women. But in eighteenth-century Pennsylvania, as in Maryland and Virginia, we also find evidence of mixing between white women with men of color. In 1764, for example, George Hays, a master in Berks County, Pennsylvania, advertised for the return of a "Mulattoe Servant Man, who passes for a Portugee, named James Johnson, about 35 Years of Age" in a "snuff coloured coat, red Jacket, and Leather Breeches, a Beaver Hat and some other Cloathing . . . he can play on the violin." The master added, "N. B. There is a White Woman that keeps with the Said Servant and passes for his Wife, of the name of Catherine, about 40 years of age." [101]

Mixed unions often appeared among runaway advertisements in the *Pennsylvania Gazette* during the mid-eighteenth century: two white convict servants were living with a "negro woman named Jenny" in a ménage à trois (1742). Other couples included a "mulatto servant man" with "an English servant woman named Anne Greene (1749). A "servant woman named Margaret Sliter . . . born in England" lived with "a Negro Man named Charles, a lusty able Fellow . . . pretends to be married to the aforesaid Margaret Slitter" (1761). And "a servant man named John Grocett an Englishman" lived with "a negro woman called Betty" (1762). [102]

Some of these fugitives had fled north from Maryland and Virginia; others had come south from New York and New England to the Delaware Valley. In runaway notices their masters thought them to be heading for Philadelphia, which by the mid-eighteenth century was widely believed to be more tolerant and free because of its Quaker origins. Early in the eighteenth century, more voices were raised against slavery and for the Golden Rule in the Delaware Valley than in any other American region. [103]

SCHOOLS AND THE FRAYING OF SLAVERY:
QUAKER TEACHING AND AFRICAN LEARNING

Even as George Fox and William Penn allowed slavery to continue, they both insisted that Friends must educate their slaves. Quaker owners divided on that question. Some were strongly opposed, but others concurred. Educational reform had long been of interest to Quakers. Penn himself wrote often on the subject. [104]

Pennsylvania's Frame of Government empowered the governor and the Colonial Council to "erect and order all public schools" in the province. An act of 1683 required that all children must be taught to read and write by the age of twelve, and also trained in a useful trade or skill, no matter whether their families were rich or poor. Heavy fines were threatened for noncompliance. A Friends Public School was founded and made open to poor children without fee. It still exists today as the very distinguished Penn Charter School.

Other Quakers wanted to go much farther. In West Jersey, Thomas Budd in 1698 proposed a system of Quaker schools for Pennsylvania and New Jersey, with a requirement that all children attend every day (half-session on Sunday), for seven years. Budd also urged that girls and boys be educated in separate classes, and that the schools offer training "in all the most useful arts and sciences." Boys were to be "instructed in some mystery or trade, as the making of mathematical instruments, joinery, turnery, the making of clocks and watches, weaving, shoemaking or any other useful trade." Girls were to learn "spinning of flax and wool, and knitting of gloves and stockings, sewing, and making of all sorts of useful needlework, and the making of straw work, as hats, baskets, etc."

Modern writers have misunderstood this idea of education as "vocational." It was something more and other than that—an idea of education for life in many roles. Thomas Budd also believed deeply in educational equality. "To the end that the children of the poor people, and the children of Indians, may have good learning with the children of the rich people," he wrote, "let them be maintained free of charge to their parents." [105]

This compulsory plan failed to find broad support in the Quaker colonies. On the subject of education, no public laws of any importance were passed in Pennsylvania from 1700 to 1776. John Woolman observed, "Meditating on the situation of schools in our provinces, my mind hath at times been affected with sorrow." But the remedy that he recommended of private charity in place of public support compounded the problem. [106]

Quakers founded many schools for their own children. In 1750, the Philadelphia Yearly Meeting supervised a network of fifty weekly meetings in the Delaware Valley. Of that number about forty maintained meeting schools for Quaker children. They expected other denominations to do the same, and many did so. [107]

We have no evidence that African American children attended Quaker meeting schools, but also no proof that they were excluded. This historian believes on the basis of individual cases that a few slave children attended meeting schools, but most did not. By the mid-eighteenth century, the presence of unschooled African American children in the Delaware became a challenge to Quakers of conscience, and also to others of many Christian denominations.

As early as the 1720s, some individuals took it upon themselves to open schools for slaves in Philadelphia. Among the first was Samuel Keimer, a bearded English mystic who came to Philadelphia in 1722, and opened a school with the avowed purpose of teaching slaves to read the Bible. He appears to have met much opposition, perhaps less for his school than his eccentric ways.[108]

During the Great Awakening, evangelists of many denominations visited the Delaware Valley and some spoke out on the subject of education of African children. When popular preacher George Whitefield came to Philadelphia he took a keen interest in the schooling of slaves. During the summer and fall of 1740 other evangelical ministers, including Gilbert Tennent, William Tennent, Samuel Blair, James Davenport, and John Rowland, urged the education of slaves. These divines were of many denominations—Anglican, Presbyterian, Congregationalist.

Missionaries were sent by the Anglican Society for the Propagation of the Gospel in Foreign Parts. In 1747, it hired William Sturgeon, a Yale graduate, to teach slaves and free Blacks in Pennsylvania. By 1749, Sturgeon was teaching, catechizing, and baptizing about fifty Blacks in Philadelphia.[109]

The most successful leader in the schooling of slaves in Pennsylvania was Anthony Benezet, a French Huguenot turned Quaker. His family had fled Catholic persecution from France to London. There they sent him to Quaker schools. In 1731, they moved again to Philadelphia, joined a Quaker meeting, and cultivated a habit of extreme "worldly asceticism."

The family was wealthy, and bought a thousand acres of land near Philadelphia. Benezet could have flourished in many callings or none of all. But after the death of his two children, he chose to become a teacher for the rest of his days. In Philadelphia he started with boys at the Penn English School, then opened his own school for Quaker girls. By 1750, he was also running day classes for free African children, and teaching children of slaves at night in his own home. In 1770, Benezet opened a school for African children, slave and free. With the encouragement of the Philadelphia Monthly Meeting, he built an African schoolhouse at his own expense in Willing's Alley, and kept it going to his death in 1784.[110]

Benezet also spoke and wrote actively in support of universal schooling for all children, especially children of slaves. He testified from his long experience of teaching that between Black and white children there was no difference in aptitude for learning, or in powers of reasoning and moral judgment. Many of his students became leaders in Philadelphia's African American community.

In Benezet's later years, he was described as a small wizened Quaker with a kindly manner and engaging ways. He was devoted to the welfare of slaves and free African children, and much beloved in the city. After his death in 1784, more than four hundred African Americans walked in his funeral, along with many Quakers and Anglo-Americans.[111]

The result of Quaker and African attitudes and acts was a large profusion of little schools, each supported by the efforts of individuals and by many ethnic and religious denominations. Quaker education developed through the initiative of individual meetings. Historians of education have found evidence of about sixty regular schools that were run by Quaker meetings by 1776. An equal number of neighborhood schools were also supported by Quakers.[112]

As other ethnic and religious groups settled in the Delaware Valley, they were encouraged to found their own church-related educational institutions. The results were less comprehensive than New England's system of town schools, but more so than Virginia's hierarchical system which created strong schools for a small elite, weak ones for the children of yeoman farmers, and no schools at all for children of white servants and Black slaves.

HOW AFRICAN SCHOOL CHILDREN IN PHILADELPHIA TAUGHT BENJAMIN FRANKLIN A LESSON ABOUT RACE

The success of these schools also had an important impact on white racists, and it converted one incipient racist in particular. Benjamin Franklin and his wife, Deborah, owned at least five slaves: Peter and Jemima, who were a couple, and three male slaves, named King, Othello, and George, and possibly several others.

In 1757, Franklin took Peter and King to England, while Jemima remained with Deborah. Franklin complained that his slaves did not work very hard for their master's profit, and often "pilfered" from him in acts of petty larceny. The thought that he had stolen their entire lives in at least five acts of grand larceny seems not to have occurred to this highly intelligent man—a clue to the segmented racial thinking that prevailed among even the most thoughtful masters.[113]

Franklin's early published thoughts on slavery were strongly racist. In 1751, those prejudices appeared in his essay called "Observations Concerning the Increase of Mankind." Franklin complained that "the Number of purely white People in the World is proportionately very small." In his thinking, "black" and "tawney" and "swarthy" included all the people of Africa and Asia, and many from Europe as well. Franklin perceived that "Spaniards,

Italians, French, Russians, and Swedes are generally of what we call swarthy Complexion, as are Germans also, Saxons only excepted, who with the English make the principal Body of White People on the Face of the Earth."[114]

Franklin posed a question: "Why increase the Sons of Africa, by Planting them in America, where we have so fair an Opportunity, by excluding all Blacks and Tawneys, of increasing the lovely White and Red? But perhaps I am partial to the Complexion of my Country, for such kind of Partiality is natural to Mankind."[115]

Soon afterward, he began to think differently. By his own account, the pivotal event was a visit to William Sturgeon's Philadelphia "Negro School" in 1763. Franklin was amazed at what he discovered there. He wrote, "I was on the whole much pleas'd, and from what I then saw, have conceiv'd a higher Opinion of the natural Capacities of the black Race, than I had ever before entertained. Their apprehension seems as quick, their memory as strong, and their Docility ["ability to learn," from the Latin *docere*] in every respect equal to that of white Children."[116]

By 1772, Franklin was writing actively against slavery, even as he continued to practice it. In 1785, he became president of the Pennsylvania Abolition Society, signed the society's sweeping antislavery petition, and presented it to Congress. In his last years, Franklin appears to have owned no slaves himself.

Here was a great awakening in a mind of extraordinary power. And the moment came in 1763 when Benjamin Franklin met a lively class of bright African American children in a Philadelphia Negro School. By his own account, it was the children who put him right. Franklin, raised to racism in Boston, had the intellectual integrity to correct an error in his thinking by the evidence of his senses. Would it always be so!

"IN SOULS THERE IS NO SEX": QUAKER IDEAS OF GENDER AND THE STATUS OF "NEGROE WOMEN" IN THE DELAWARE VALLEY

Among many sects and denominations of English-speaking people in the seventeenth century, Quakers moved farthest toward an idea of equality between the sexes. George Fox set the tone, writing in his journal as early as the year 1647: "I met with a sort of people that held women have no souls, adding in a light manner, no more than a goose. I reproved them, and told them that was not right, for Mary said, 'My soul doth magnify the Lord.'"[117] The bizarre idea that "women have no souls" was widely shared among English-speaking males in colonial America. In 1773, New Jersey tutor Philip Fithian was shocked to hear a party of Virginia gentlemen debate the question of whether "women had souls." [118]

To him it was obvious they did. George Fox and Philip Fithian shared a different way of thinking about gender. It took root among Quakers in the Delaware Valley at an early date, and had an impact on the condition of African women, as multiple examples suggest.

Many women of color were able to take advantage of opportunities that came to them in the Quaker colonies, where women were regarded as spiritual equals of men. Before the American Revolution, at least three African American women were able to leave wills that survive in Philadelphia's probate records. Among them was Jane Row, a "negro woman" who appears to have had three husbands, four sons, and owned real estate on Fourth Street. By every indication she was a formidable person. In the words of one historian, she "appears to have lived with a forceful independence." In her will she also left a large feather bed to her surviving husband, Henry Hainy, as a token of her "love and esteem." [119]

The achievements and autonomy of free "negroewomen" such as Jane Row and Ann Elizabeth Fortune appeared at an early date before 1770, and rested on a broad base. The laws of Quaker Pennsylvania allowed slaves to own property, and also extended that same right to women who were married and single, bound and free.

Quaker Pennsylvania was special that way, if not unique. Many Quakers (not all) shared the doctrine that "in souls there is no sex." [120] This idea held that differences of gender were merely carnal, that men and women were equal in the spirit, and that "spiritual power was one in the male and in the female, one spirit, one light, one life, one power, which brings forth the same witness." [121] That way of thinking was strong and sustained among Quakers and it spread to others in the Delaware Valley. It had consequences for many women of African origin, as a few stories might suggest.

BLACK ALICE OF DUNK'S FERRY:
PHILADELPHIA'S FAVORITE FEMALE GRIOT

More than in most American colonial towns, some African women achieved independence, affluence, and eminence in Philadelphia. A leading example, in every sense, was a slave woman personally known to four generations of Philadelphians as Black Alice, and renowned for her spirit, strength, and longevity.

Black Alice of Dunk's Ferry

The facts of Alice's improbable life were gathered by a prominent Pennsylvanian who knew her well. Doctor Samuel Coates, head of the Philadelphia Hospital, was a leading citizen in the town. With his encouragement, a biography was written of Alice while she was still alive, and published by Isaiah Thomas in 1804 with a portrait from life.[122]

Alice believed that she had been born at Philadelphia in 1686. She died in 1802, at the dubious age of 116. Her birth date is less than certain, but she had a very long life. Alice firmly believed that her parents were African slaves who may have arrived by way of Barbados, as part of Philadelphia's first large shipment in 1684.

She lived in Philadelphia as a child to the age of ten, when her master took her to Dunk's Ferry, about six miles north of the town. There Alice lived for much of her long life, and helped to run an active ferry service across the Delaware River. It was said that "her honesty also was unimpeached, for such was her master's confidence in it that she was trusted at all times to receive the ferriage money, for upwards of forty years."[123]

Strong and fit, Alice rode horseback from Dunk's Ferry to Philadelphia on Sundays, where she went to a church of her choice. It amused her to cover the ground at "full gallop" until she was ninety-five, when she was observed to slow down a little. Like other Philadelphia slaves, she had many Quaker friends and companions, but Alice preferred to worship as an Episcopalian and member of Christ Church. There she attended services with George Washington and other leaders of both the town and the American republic. They honored Alice with rituals of deference to her age and eminence.

Later in life she often stayed on Sunday nights with friends in Philadelphia. It is still remembered that "respectable citizens" of the town came to call on her. As Philadelphians of every condition gathered around, she told them stories of their forebears. Her mind and memory were said to be keen to the end of her long life.

Early in the nineteenth century, Alice fascinated her listeners with first-hand stories of Philadelphia's founders. She claimed to remember as a child "often lighting the proprietor's pipe" for William Penn himself. Alice knew the eminent leader George Logan and many other founders, and she fascinated others in the town with stories of their forebears.

In Philadelphia, Alice gained a growing reputation as a storyteller, and what we would call an oral historian. She did it in a way that drew upon African and Afro-American folkways. The recitations of Black Alice were a link in a living tradition. It ran from African griots who recited the oral history of West African villages, to African American storytellers in early America, and onward to rap artists in our time. In her later years Alice was more than an honored citizen. She became a living institution in the city of Philadelphia.

AFRICAN AMERICAN WOMEN AS FAMILY HEADS: A TALE OF TWO CREMONAS

Just northwest of Philadelphia, in the Edgehill section of Montgomery County's Cheltenham Township, a large symmetric stone-built house still stands on the Limekiln Pike just below the Waverly Road. For many years there was a small burial ground nearby. It held the remains of an early eighteenth-century Afro-American community, called Guineatown by some of its neighbors.

It was founded by two women, a mother and daughter, both named Cremona, with much support from leading Quaker men, not always in a spiritual way. The older Cremona was said to be a woman of surpassing beauty, grace, and intellect, and she was also an African slave.[124] Her owner was Humphrey Morrey (1650–1716), Philadelphia's first mayor in 1691–92, and one of Pennsylvania's founding generation of Quaker slave owners. He was also a man of landed wealth and a first purchaser in Cheltenham township.[125]

We know little of Cremona's early years. She was acquired by Morrey near the start of Pennsylvania's slave trade, received her freedom in the eighteenth century, and became one of "the earliest practicing black Quakers" with full membership in the Society of Friends.

This first Cremona also became the mistress of her owner's son and heir, Richard Morrey (1675–1753), who himself owned a large estate of about a thousand acres in Cheltenham, northwest of Philadelphia. Richard Morrey lived with Cremona as his consort, and in ten years they had five children: Robert, born about 1735; Caesar in 1737; Elizabeth in 1739; Rachel in 1742; and a daughter also named Cremona, born about 1745.

After this last birth, Richard Morrey emancipated his consort and their children. On January 22, 1746, he made an extraordinary written agreement with the elder Cremona. He agreed to "bargain and sell for consideration of one peppercorn . . . a total of 198 acres on his land in Cheltenham." The land (one fifth of his real estate in that township) was to be held by Cremona and her heirs for five hundred years.

Soon afterward, Richard Morrey died and the elder Cremona married a "free black African" named John Frey. Together they ran a large and flourishing farm on Cremona's 198 acres and also built the large stone house that still stands on the Limekiln Pike.

Cremona Frey allowed twenty-nine African Americans (and probably more) to settle on her land. Together they formed a community that neighbors called Guineatown, "after an area in Africa where the slaves originally came from," according to local lore.[126]

The younger Cremona also lived there, and in 1766 she married a free Black farmer named John Montier. They had four sons: Joseph in 1768, Solomon in 1770, Robert in 1775, and Hiram in 1780.[127]

In 1770 the elder Cremona died suddenly without a will. Her husband claimed the farm, and after his death the children agreed to divide the land equitably among themselves. The families of both Cremonas flourished there. Joseph Montier became a farmer "like his Dad," married his first cousin, stayed on the farm, and looked after his parents.

After their deaths in the early nineteenth century, Joseph Montier saw the estate through probate. Children, grandchildren, and cousins moved to Philadelphia where opportunities were more abundant, and they intermarried with Black middle-class and upper-class families. Robert Montier (1775–1815) became highly successful as a founder of a beer bottling business. His children also did well. Solomon Montier married Susanna Highgate, daughter of miller Moses Highgate, and they moved to Philadelphia with six children. He and four of his sons (Joseph, Richard, William, and Hiram Montier) went into the shoe business.[128]

Hiram Montier's daughter Jane became a dressmaker, and owner of family property in Cheltenham and Germantown. She died on November 30, 1888, at the age of sixty-eight, and the house passed out of the family. Later the burial ground was moved to make way for road improvements.

During the late nineteenth and twentieth centuries, other descendants of the two Cremonas succeeded in many lines of endeavor. Some became prominent in national and international affairs. A great-great-grandson of the elder Cremona's daughter Elizabeth was the singer and radical leader Paul Robeson. Another descendant, David Bustill Bowser, became an artist in Philadelphia. William Pickens, a descendant of both Cremonas, lectured at Beaver College (now Arcadia University) and gathered some of the family documents including original real estate and cemetery deeds.

Others followed military and naval careers. William Pickens's father-in-law, Wesley A. Brown, became the first African American to graduate from the United States Naval Academy. Lieutenant Harriet Pickens also was the first female African American to be commissioned as a WAVE officer in the navy during World War II. The abiding spirit of the two Cremonas is still strong in their posterity, women and men alike.[129]

QUAKER LEADERS TURN AGAINST SLAVERY: BENJAMIN LAY, JOHN WOOLMAN, AND APPEALS TO CONSCIENCE

The same spirit that appeared in attitudes of Quakers toward sex and gender was also evident in thoughts on slavery and race. The first generation of Quakers in Pennsylvania had divided over slavery. The problem was compounded by the fact that slavery worked well as an economic institution in the Delaware Valley, and many Quakers bought slaves.[130]

But within the first decade of settlement an antislavery movement began to develop in the Delaware Valley. As early as 1688, Quakers and kindred spirits in Germantown issued a testimony against slavery on the grounds that it violated the Golden Rule.[131] In 1696, two leading Quakers, Cadwalader Morgan and William Southeby, urged the Philadelphia Yearly Meeting to forbid slavery and slave trading outright. It refused, but in search of a compromise it agreed to advise Quakers "not to encourage the bringing in of any more Negroes, & that such that have Negroes be careful of them," which must have pleased nobody.[132]

The antislavery impulse grew steadily against strong resistance. A few Quakers invented many arguments against slavery, at first in attempts to persuade other Quakers. Most effective was an appeal to the Golden Rule to "do unto others as you would have them do unto you." The hard part was to persuade Quaker masters and mistresses that slaves were significant others.

It is interesting to observe the many ways in which Quakers went about that task of persuasion. Most spectacular was Benjamin Lay (1682–1759), a small man of strange appearance, not much above four feet, with a large torso, and arms nearly as long as his legs.

He was raised a Quaker in the east of England, had a turbulent and combative character, quarreled much with other Quakers, and was disowned by the London meeting. He left England for Barbados, and became a slave holder until he was overcome by horror at the brutality of West Indian bondage and consumed with guilt and rage, not least against himself for what he had done.[133] In 1731, Lay moved to Philadelphia with his long-suffering wife,

Benjamin Lay

Sarah, and devoted himself to the task of persuading Quakers to reject slavery and all its works. In meetings he urged others not to use sugar, and shattered their teacups to make his point.[134]

Lay disrupted Quaker meetings and invaded churches through the Delaware Valley, raging against human bondage. He began to use violent acts to oppose the greater violence of slavery. He dramatized the Golden Rule by kidnapping the child of a slaveholding Quaker family, and then lectured the frantic parents for having caused the same pain they experienced, by buying slaves who had been stolen from their African families. In 1737, he wrote a book called *All Slave-keepers, That Keep the Innocent in Bondage, Apostates*, a furious attack on slavery in general, and on individual Quaker slaveholders.[135]

In the following year Benjamin Lay appeared at a Quaker meeting dressed in a long coat. He said, "All you Negro masters who are contentedly holding your fellow creatures in a state of slavery . . . you might as well throw off the plain coat as I do." He threw open his coat and was dressed as a soldier, with a long sword. He brought out what appeared to be a Bible, and drove the sword through the book, which had been hollowed out. It held a bladder filled with blood-red pokeberry juice, which sprayed the members of the Quaker meeting. As women fainted, Lay collapsed. The Quakers thought he was dead. They carried his body outside the door, and fled from the meeting, stepping over his body.[136] Lay was disowned, and his writings disavowed. He moved into a cave and dressed in strange garments of his own making, so that nothing in his life would be contaminated by slavery. Historians have written that Lay's dramatics turned Quakers against his cause. But more recently Brycchan Carey studied the evidence again. He writes that Benjamin Lay's "stunts" marked a pivotal moment, when Quakers were turning against slavery and "Lay's message was getting through." His militant attack on slavery did not appeal to leading Quakers in 1739, but he was remembered by younger Quakers as an example of militant antislavery for generations that followed.[137]

A striking contrast with Benjamin Lay was John Woolman (1720–1772), often described by Quakers as a "Christlike" leader with a "beautiful soul." Born near Burlington in West Jersey, to a large family of prosperous and very pious Quaker farmers, he was raised to a religion of love.[138] A central theme was that "God loves all people universally," and our duty was "goodness toward every living creature."

Woolman found his calling when he was asked by an employer to draw up a bill of sale for a slave. He did it, but vowed that for rest of his days he would

John Woolman

bear witness against slavery. Always he spoke with a gentle voice and a spirit of moderation, working with others, never against them. His writings were effective that way, especially *Some Considerations on the Keeping of Negroes for Christians of Every Denomination* (1754). Through the years his published *Journal* reached readers of many faiths with its spirit. It also become a classic of American literature.[139]

A QUAKER AGAINST SLAVERY AND RACISM: ANTHONY BENEZET AND APPEALS TO CONSCIENCE, EVIDENCE, AND REASON

Important as John Woolman became in awakening the conscience of his readers against slavery, another Quaker had an even broader reach. We have already met Anthony Benezet as a devoted and much loved teacher of children, free and slave, white and Black. He also taught many adults that prevailing prejudices about Africa and Africans were grossly mistaken.

At the same time, Anthony Benezet was also a serious scholar and writer on race and slavery. He assembled a large library on many subjects, "more than a hundred books on science and medicine," and kept up with medical journals. Citations in his own writings also indicate a large collection in history and geography. He read widely on Africa, the slave trade, and slavery in the New World. Benezet wrote abundantly on these subjects and published eight pamphlets and books over a period of thirty years from 1754 to 1783.[140]

Always he wrote for a double purpose: to persuade others to act against slavery and racial prejudice. The central problems and themes remained the same, but his intended public grew steadily larger. Benezet first wrote and published for leaders of the Philadelphia Yearly Meeting. Then he began to address Quaker slave owners throughout the Delaware Valley. His pamphlets grew to the size of small books. Their subjects expanded from slavery to race, and from race to the cultures of Africa.

Benezet believed that race slavery in America did severe damage to African bodies and European minds. Unlike Benjamin Lay and John Woolman, he made his argument primarily by the relentless use of reason and empirical evidence. Some of his most powerful passages centered on the treatment of African slaves in the British West Indies, especially Jamaica. He searched for careful testimony from English scientists and scholars—men such as Hans Sloane, founder and developer of the British Museum.

Sloane described the seasoning process in West Indian slavery and its destruction of human life on an incredible scale. Masters told him that if six of ten of their new African slaves died in the seasoning, it was still "a gaining purchase." And if the survivors were able to cling to life for eight or nine years, their owners boasted that they made money, in this incredibly brutal business.[141]

Benezet also gathered careful eyewitness accounts by scientific observers of unimaginable punishments that were inflicted on African slaves in the British West Indies. Hans Sloane reported that in Jamaica "for rebellion the punishment is burning them by nailing them down to the ground with crooked sticks on every limb, and then applying the fire, by degrees, from the feet and hands, burning them gradually up to the head, whereby *their pains are extravagant*" (italics original).[142]

Sloane described the sadistic savagery of executions by other means: "Of some they break their bones whilst still alive on a wheel; others they burn or rather roast to death; others they starve to death, with a loaf hanging before their mouths." Benezet commented, "Thus they are brought to expire, with frightful agonies in the most horrid tortures." Sloane was struck by the sadistic savagery that slavery awakened in the minds of their masters and mistresses, and Englishmen who worked for them. Human bondage was horrific not only for the uses it would make of slaves, but also for the depraved masters that it made. And slaves themselves testified that mistresses were often more cruel.[143]

Benezet also reproduced Sloane's testimony that the punishment "for crimes of a less nature" was "gelding [castration] or chopping off half the foot with an axe." And merely "for negligence they are usually whipped by the overseers with lance-wood switches . . . after they are whipped till they are raw, some put on their skins pepper and salt, to make them smart; at other times, their masters will drop melted wax on their skins, and use several very exquisite torments." Further, travelers often observed these African slaves were dressed in rags and tatters. They were barefoot, severely malnourished, and with "bodies all whaled and scarred" from frequent whipping.[144]

English observers were doubly shocked and appalled that this "extreme oppression and inhumanity" was committed by Englishmen on Caribbean islands such as Jamaica that had long been under English control. One wrote that "it is a matter of astonishment how a people who as a nation are looked upon as generous and humane could engage" in "the practice of such extreme oppression and inhumanity" and do it "without remorse."[145]

Anthony Benezet also described the horrors of the slave trade in Africa. He did so again in a quiet voice, and added the testimony of very careful and accurate scientific observers. Benezet let the evidence speak for itself. And in the process, he systematically stripped away the arguments for slavery. He compared John Locke's argument that African "slaves are taken in a just war," with detailed primary accounts of how Africans were actually captured, how families and villages were shattered, and how extreme violence became a policy of slavers from many nations.[146]

In his writings Benezet also documented the horror of the shipborne Atlantic slave trade. He found examples of sadistic captains and crew who were sometimes in such a state of insane rage that they deliberately destroyed the lives of slaves aboard their ships and committed acts of inconceivable barbarity that diminished their own profits. After summarizing much of this evidence, Benezet added, "There cannot be in nature, there is not in all history an instance in which every right of man is more flagrantly violated."[147]

Benezet also exploded the myth of bondage as a school of civilization for primitive Africans, and did it in three ways at once. Benezet read very widely on African societies and cultures, in a literature that was growing rapidly in the eighteenth century. He gathered evidence that African economies were highly developed in commerce, industry, and agriculture. He was interested in African religious systems, the complexity of African ethical beliefs, the diversity of African cultures, and the strength of family life in many of them. At the same time, Benezet relentlessly demolished the fiction of racial inferiority, always in a quiet voice, but with clarity and strength.

In America he was supported by Quaker leaders in the Philadelphia Yearly Meeting and Pennsylvania's General Assembly. Many were persuaded not merely to agree, but to act. Benezet's works reached several expanding circles in North America. He made his major case against slavery by sustained arguments from empirical evidence, and by strong appeals to reason. That combination made his many publications useful to antislavery leaders in Britain and France, who were trying to persuade leaders in high places to act against the Atlantic slave trade.

Among his closest and most attentive readers in England was Granville Sharp, then an obscure clerk in the Ordnance Office, who discovered Benezet's writings in 1772 and later described how they changed his life. Something similar happened with Thomas Clarkson, John Wesley, and William Wilberforce. These men became the antislavery leaders in England, and later led the campaign to abolish the slave trade in 1807. Maurice Jackson writes that all of these leaders frequently cited Benezet, and called him "the father of their movement."[148]

By 1784, Benezet's work spread to France. It was discussed at the first meeting of the Societé des Amis des Noirs in Paris, the most important antislavery and antiracist association in Europe. Jacques-Pierre de Warville Brissot spoke at length about Benezet's writings and described "the immortal Benezet" as "founder" of the antislavery movement throughout the Atlantic world in America, Britain, and Europe.[149]

Benezet was also widely read by African writers. In three major publications he presented evidence that the idea of primitive African societies was a European myth, that Africans and Europeans, Black and white, were equal in powers of intelligence and judgment, that their children performed on the same level, and that apparent evidence to the contrary was the result of race slavery. In different ways his work was used extensively by an important generation of African writers: Olaudah Equiano, Charles Ignatius Sancho, Quobna Ottobah Cugoano, James Ukawsaw Gronniosaw, Lemuel Haynes, Richard Allen, and Absalom Jones.[150]

Benezet's biographer Maurice Jackson writes that after the death of John Woolman in 1772, Benezet became not only "the leading Quaker voice against slavery," but also "the leading crusader and theorist" of the expanding antislavery movement "in the western world." [151]

He reached a large public by telling stories of individual African slaves he had known and their suffering in bondage. In his last published work he wrote,

> A striking instance of this kind appeared in the case of a negro resid-
> ing near Philadelphia. From his first arrival [from Africa] he appeared
> thoughtful and dejected, frequently dropping tears when fondling his
> master's children; the cause of which was not known till he was able
> to be understood, when he gave the following account: that he had a
> wife and children in his own country; that some of these being sick, he
> went in the night time to fetch water at a spring, where he was violently
> seized and carried away by persons who lay in wait to catch men; from
> whence he was transported to America; that the remembrance of his
> family and friends whom he never expected to see any more were the
> principal cause of his dejection and grief. [152]

Benezet used these stories frequently to make a major point, that African slaves were not captured in a just war; that they were kidnapped by brute force; and their shattered families suffered the same agony of loss as did others in the world.

A FIRST DECISIVE VICTORY FOR THE ABOLITION OF AMERICAN SLAVERY: THE PHILADELPHIA YEARLY QUAKER MEETING, 1758

In 1712, a Quaker majority in the Pennsylvania General Assembly acted against the slave trade. It levied a prohibitive duty on the importation of slaves. The tax and others were disallowed in London by officers of the Crown, which had a stake in the African slave trade, as did many merchants and investors throughout the Atlantic basin, including Pennsylvania and other colonies.

In 1730 the Philadelphia Yearly Meeting cautioned its members against importing slaves, but Friends still continued to buy them. Quaker antislavery petitions and papers followed in growing numbers. Jean Soderlund, a leading scholar on the subject, finds that Quaker "antislavery reformers never contended that slavery was economically unsound." They insisted that it was morally corrupt, and at war with the deepest values of Christianity. [153]

As antislavery feeling expanded among Friends, slave owning steadily declined. Among leaders who gathered in the Philadelphia Yearly Meeting, the proportion who owned slaves fell from 70 percent before 1705, to 59 percent from 1706 to 1730, 34 percent from 1730 to 1754, and 10 percent after 1754—a sweeping transformation.[154]

The evidence of private journals and public testimony shows that many Quaker slaveholders were deeply troubled by the question of human bondage. Other Friends such as John Woolman were haunted by slavery even in their dreams. The question was discussed in many meetings, but unanimity was needed for agreement, and for many years it could not be obtained.

A turning point came in 1752, when Anthony Benezet became a member of the Overseers of the Press for the Philadelphia Yearly Meeting. This small body was responsible for approving publications by members of Quaker meetings throughout Pennsylvania, West Jersey, and Delaware. Those who defied its judgments could be disowned. As late as 1746, even John Woolman's very restrained *Considerations on Keeping of Negroes* was thought to be divisive and unfit to print.

After Benezet became an overseer of the press, the policy changed. Woolman's pamphlet was published with the approval of the overseers in 1754. That year Benezet and Woolman brought out *An Epistle of Caution and Advice, Concerning the Buying and Keeping of Slaves*. It was drafted by Benezet but was close to the teachings of Woolman, and very much a collaboration. Together they expressed concern for the increase of slavery in the colony, opposed the slave trade and the keeping of slaves, and urged owners to educate their slaves and prepare them for freedom.[155]

The appeals by these two Quakers were effective, but strongly resisted. Woolman and Benezet's objective was to win not merely a majority of the Philadelphia Yearly Meeting, but a consensus of all its members, and some continued to hold back. In 1758, the Yearly Meeting debated yet again the question of slavery and the slave trade. Once again consensus eluded them. Then, Benezet rose and spoke not about slavery, but about the children of Africa as children of God. Others remembered that "the spirit of the 'Christlike Woolman' was much in evidence." Working as brethren in their common cause, these two great spiritual leaders won not merely a majority but unanimity, an extraordinary achievement.

In that moment, the most eminent leaders of the Society of Friends throughout the Delaware Valley came together and agreed to a "unanimous concern" against "the practice of importing, buying, selling, *or keeping* slaves for term of life." Italics are added here. This was not merely a judgment against the slave trade, as is sometimes asserted, but against the practice of slavery.[156]

Gary Nash writes of that event as "the epic Yearly Meeting of 1758."[157] Maurice Jackson adds, "If there was a single moment when the beginning of a new period in the fight against slavery was catalyzed, it would be the 1758 Philadelphia Yearly Meeting."[158] Brycchan Carey agreed: "The Yearly Meeting of 1758 would prove to be historic. . . . The Yearly Meeting had at last invoked the Golden Rule a proof of the moral obligation all Quakers were under to immediately emancipate their slaves. . . . This, then, was the ruling that antislavery friends had sought for decades."[159]

The Yearly Meeting had broad influence on Monthly Meetings in Pennsylvania, Delaware, and West Jersey. Its judgment carried great weight among members of the Society of Friends throughout this region. This was the first decisive victory for the abolition of slavery anywhere in the western world. "The history of the early abolitionist movement," writes historian Arthur Zilversmit, "is essentially the record of Quaker antislavery activities."[160]

The number of slaves in Philadelphia began to fall very rapidly, even as the general population increased. In 1767, 590 slave owners held 1,400 slaves in a total population of 18,600. By 1775, 376 owners held 728 slaves in a population of 25,000. During the decade before the American Revolution, slavery in Philadelphia lost half its strength. After the Revolution, the number of slaves in Philadelphia fell even more rapidly, to 273 in 1790, 55 in 1800, and three in 1810.[161]

Historians continue to debate the cause of this decline. Materialists have argued that the prime mover was a change in the relative cost of free and slave labor. There is some truth in this judgment. But slavery among Quakers fell most rapidly in the mid-eighteenth century when the supply of free workers was interrupted by major European wars.

A sad truth about human bondage is that it has always been profitable for some individuals and nations that practiced it. A happy truth is that the antislavery movement was always driven by large-minded moral imperatives, among small groups of highly principled people.

Antislavery ideas of the Quakers were also held by others throughout the Delaware Valley. The attitudes of some German sects were similar to those of English Friends. Quaker abolitionists such as John Woolman and Anthony Benezet carried the cause to many people in the Delaware Valley.

In West Jersey one of the most effective appeals came from John Woolman's brother Abner, in a gentle manner and a quiet voice. Sometime before his death in 1772, he wrote to "his dear friends" in the Burlington Monthly Meeting, urging them to think about their slaves, and to ask themselves how they would feel if a slave's sufferings were visited upon themselves: "What would it be like, to be condemned to perpetual slavery for "no crime we had committed, or agreement made by us?" What if that condition were "entailed on our offspring?" What if we "had not been permitted to live with our wives and children, and were not able to relieve them? What if we were forbidden to provide for our old age, and sickness?"

He asked them to make this "sorrowful Exercise" and think again about the suffering that slavery inflicted on others. Its deepest wounds were not the heavy labor, nor the other cruel punishments, but the spiritual affliction of slavery.[162]

Quakers also took an active interest in the welfare of former slaves. Many masters helped to support their slaves after manumitting them. Others compensated them for their labor during slavery. When Abner Woolman in 1767 freed two slaves his wife had inherited, he decided to pay them a sum equal to the amount that the estate had been increased by their labor, and asked the Haddonfield (New Jersey) Monthly Meeting to help him compute a just sum.[163]

THE END OF SLAVERY IN PENNSYLVANIA

The Pennsylvania Assembly moved slowly against slavery, but move it did. Quakers frequently began by looking for limited reforms that could be broadly supported—a method often used in Quaker meetings which tried to act by universal agreement. They tried to do that in the Pennsylvania Assembly. In 1773, non-Quakers joined Friends within the Pennsylvania legislature in trying to stop the trade in human flesh by imposing a prohibitive duty on slaves. The measure passed with very strong support, but once again was disallowed by British imperial authorities. In January 1775, one of the first acts of Pennsylvania's Provincial Convention was to reject British oversight, and prohibit the importation of slaves.

Another method of prohibiting slavery that gained broad support was to act against attempts at reenslavement of freed people of color, which was happening in the Delaware Valley before the American Revolution. On April 14, 1775, Benezet called a meeting of ten men at Philadelphia's Rising Sun Tavern. They were brought together by the sad story of a woman, part African and part Indian, who was born free, but she and her three children were seized as slaves, and were about to sold to a southern colony.

Several Quakers went to her aid and bought her freedom. Two men at the meeting, Quaker merchant Israel Pemberton and merchant-tailor Thomas Harrison, helped several other people of color in similar circumstances. But there were many such stories, and their numbers were growing. The meeting agreed to found the Society for the Relief of Free Negroes Unlawfully Held in Bondage. They met four times in 1775, but then the war intervened, and they were unable to continue.[164]

But the American Revolution and its values began to have an impact on people not Quakers. Gary Nash writes that "other Philadelphians, not associated with the Society of Friends, took up the cause of abolition. . . . These men had been influenced by the Quaker appeals to conscience, by the natural rights ideology of the Revolution, and by their own quasi-enslavement when the British occupied Philadelphia." He observes that in the summer of 1778, two months after the British Army retreated from Philadelphia, a bill for the abolition of slavery was submitted in the Pennsylvania Assembly. It took two years, and many concessions to slave owners, for the Gradual Abolition Act to be passed in 1780.[165]

Pennsylvania's Gradual Abolition Act was very gradual indeed. By its terms, every person held in slavery before March 1, 1780, remained a slave for life. Children born after that date became free, but only after twenty-eight years in bondage. Even so, the passage of this abolition act was no small feat. In the state elections of 1780, many legislators who supported it were voted out of office.

But in other ways, the Abolition Act struck a fatal blow against slavery in Pennsylvania. In 1767, for example, 1,538 people of color had lived in Philadelphia, and 96 percent were slaves. The census of 1790 found 2,150 people of color in Philadelphia, and 14 percent were slaves, a major transformation in twenty-three years. About half of it occurred before the Abolition Act, often by the initiative of Quakers and slaves themselves. The other half came after the Abolition Act, partly because of it.[166]

But slavery persisted after 1780, and in at least one way the problem got worse. Money could be made by criminal gangs who kidnapped free people of color in Pennsylvania, carried them south across the Mason-Dixon line, and sold them to corrupt dealers in the southern states. Anthony Benezet reported, shortly before his death in 1784, that freed slaves were coming to him "almost daily and sometimes more," seeking to avoid reenslavement. Suicides by kidnapped freedmen increased a sense of urgency. The Society for the Relief of Free Negroes Unlawfully Held in Bondage was revived. In 1784 alone it dealt with twenty-two cases of unlawful enslavement. By 1787 it had "restored to liberty . . . upwards of one hundred persons." [167]

In the spring of 1787, this group decided to change its name, expand its numbers, and enlarge its mission. It became the Pennsylvania Society for Promoting the Abolition of Slavery and the Relief of Free Negroes Unlawfully Held in Bondage. The goal of some members was to put an end to slavery, not only in Pennsylvania, but throughout the world.

Another purpose was to support former slaves and help them succeed in freedom. In 1776, the new Pennsylvania constitution gave "every freeman at 21" the right to vote. It was the same again in the more conservative constitution of 1790. A particular challenge was to promote opportunities for freed people of color who swarmed into Philadelphia. In the new republic their numbers in the city and county multiplied fourfold from 2,489 in 1790 to 10,552 in 1820.

Opportunities were bright during the 1790s. African American business owners rapidly increased. Gary Nash made a count in Philadelphia city directories and found that Black "shopkeepers and proprietors of various kinds" increased from 15 in 1795 (out of 544 listed adult Black males); to 81 in 1811 (of 1,412 adult Black males); and 180 in 1816 (of 1,547). He also found that listed African American female proprietors increased from seven to nine to fifteen in the same period.[168]

In Philadelphia the majority of freed African Americans lived in poverty, with unsteady employment and improvised housing. The Pennsylvania Abolition Society created a committee on employment, which watched carefully and found that after 1806 unemployment and poverty began to grow.

But two major studies, by W. E. B. Du Bois in 1899 and Gary Nash in 1988, found many striking surprises. In the early republic, more free people of color in Philadelphia were able to form stable families. Their children increasingly went to school and became literate. These families went to church, belonged to benevolent societies, and saved small sums. Du Bois and Nash also discovered that, well into the nineteenth century, African Americans had much lower crime rates and incarceration rates than did Irish immigrants or native whites. They were less likely to be in city almshouses than were other ethnic groups. In the early American republic, free African Americans were beginning to get ahead. They did it with great difficulty in the face of many obstacles, and they also helped their children to get farther ahead.[169]

THE RISE OF AFRICAN CHURCHES

Of major importance was the growth of Black churches. Through much of the eighteenth century, Africans throughout the Delaware Valley continued to invent their own forms of Christianity. Ministers emerged spontaneously and led other slaves in new expressions of spiritual faith and expressive worship.

One of these religious leaders appeared in a fugitive slave notice for a man "commonly called Preaching Dick," who ran away from his master, Robert Grace, in August of 1746. He was described as a formidable figure in a bearskin jacket, brown linen trousers, and new shoes.[170]

These African Christians were not comfortable in austere Quaker meetings. Some felt more at home in Anglican churches. Others began to create new denominations of African Presbyterians, African Baptists, and first off the mark, African Methodists. A great center for this activity was Philadelphia, which in the late eighteenth century had the largest urban African American community in the United States.

Richard Allen

A leader was Richard Allen (1760–1831). He was born a slave to Benjamin Chew in Philadelphia and sold with his family to a farmer named Stokely Sturgis near Dover in Delaware. Both the master and the slave were converted by Methodist itinerant preachers who roamed the Eastern Shore, possibly by the great Freeborn Garrettson himself, who was said to have convinced Sturgis that his slaves would be counted against him at the last trump. Allen remembered that Sturgis was "more like a father to his slaves than anything else, a tender, humane man" who invited his slaves into his parlor for prayers, and encouraged them to read and write. When "he could not be satisfied to hold slaves," he invited Allen and his brother to buy their time for 60 pounds in gold and silver, or $2,000 in Continentals. They freed themselves by 1780.

Richard Allen worked as a free laborer, wood cutter, bricklayer, teamster, and he also became a Methodist exhorter. Methodist bishop Francis Asbury invited him to travel together, and Allen began to preach throughout Maryland and Pennsylvania. He was present with Asbury at the Christmas Conference in Baltimore in 1784, where the Methodist Episcopal Church was born. By 1786, he was living in Philadelphia and made it his home.[171]

Absalom Jones

There he worked with another great spiritual leader. Absalom Jones was born a slave in Delaware in 1746 and sold to a shopkeeper named Wynkoop in Philadelphia in 1760. In 1770, he married Mary King, a slave who lived next door. With the support of both masters, Absalom Jones was able to buy his family's freedom: first for his wife in 1778, which was important for the freedom of their children. Seven years later he also purchased his own freedom as well.[172]

With "coloured brethren," Absalom Jones and others worshipped at St. George's Church. As their numbers increased, they were asked to sit around the walls, or upstairs in the gallery. They refused, took their usual seats, fell on their knees, and began to pray. Jones later remembered, "we were dragged off our knees in St. Georges's Church." They walked out and never returned. In 1799 and 1800, Jones led other Africans in petitions to the legislature for immediate abolition of slavery, and to Congress for repeal of the first federal Fugitive Slave Law.[173]

VOLUNTARY ASSOCIATIONS

With astonishing speed, former slaves in Philadelphia also began to organize their own voluntary associations. This was urgent business, vital to their survival. In an unstable American economy, their primary purpose was to help each other through times of need. In an economy without a safety net, freed slaves had to provide for themselves.

A pivotal moment was the founding of the Free African Society in Philadelphia in 1787. Du Bois wrote, "How great a step this was, we of to-day scarcely realize . . . the first wavering step of a people toward an organized social life."[174]

Its leaders were Absalom Jones and Richard Allen. On April 12, 1787, they met in a private home and organized a voluntary benevolent society for the mutual assistance of its members. It was also intended to be an engine of social reform by collective action.[175]

W. E. B. Du Bois closely studied this new association. He observed that the "first leaders were Methodists," but "for a time they leaned toward Quakerism" as a model. Their meetings began with fifteen minutes of silent prayer, followed by simple Quaker ceremonies. They agreed to appoint monitors on Quaker models to give strong support to marriage and family life.

Many similar groups were quick to follow this example. By 1813, eleven

African benevolent societies were functioning in Philadelphia. By 1847, their numbers had increased to 106. They commonly required payment of one silver shilling each month. Funds were invested in the Bank of North America, and paid in a dole to families in need, and support for widows and orphans.

Du Bois found that in the late nineteenth century, in the city's Seventh Ward, 9,675 Philadelphians of color lived in 2,441 families, with 1,941 lodgers. About 17 percent belonged to benevolent societies, and 42 percent to insurance societies which were centered on that function. This was no small achievement. In a city without much of a safety net, a majority of African Americans, mostly former slaves, were able to achieve a measure of mutual protection by individual and collective effort.[176]

THE EMERGENCE OF SECULAR AFRICAN AMERICAN LEADERS

People of color in Pennsylvania also succeeded as leaders in other ways. Most prominent among them was James Forten (1766–1842). He had been born free in Philadelphia, and wrote with pride that his father, Thomas Forten, also "never wore the yoke." [177] He was the nephew of Ann Elizabeth Fortune, who with her brother Thomas had been free born in Maryland.

They moved to Philadelphia, and Thomas Forten became an apprentice sailmaker, working beside a white apprentice named Robert Bridges who became a close friend. Bridges inherited money enough to start his own sailmaking business. He hired Forten, and they continued to work together.

Thomas Forten married a free Black woman named Margaret Waymouth, who was born about 1722 and died 1806 at the age of eighty-four.[178] According to family tradition her father or grandfather had been born a slave and gained his freedom.[179]

Thomas and Margaret Forten lived in Philadelphia at Third and Walnut Streets, and belonged to an Anglican church, probably St. Paul's, which was near their home. At the age of forty-one Margaret gave birth to her daughter Abigail in 1763, and at forty-four to her son James on September 2, 1766.[180]

When very young James Forten learned to read, write, and cipher. He was also taught Quaker ethics of humanity, right conduct, hard work, and serious striving. One of his teachers was Anthony Benezet, a family friend. In 1773, Forten's father died suddenly, and James went to work at the age of six. Benezet found him a job in a grocery store.

James Forten

James Forten vividly remembered hearing the Declaration of Independence read at the Pennsylvania State House. He was nine years old, and strong for the American cause. He also remembered seeing George Washington's Continental Army march through Philadelphia. New England regiments made a strong impression, with "several Companies of Colored People, as brave Men as ever fought." They were an inspiration to him.[181]

In 1781, aged fourteen, Forten went to war himself as a ship's boy and "powder monkey" aboard Stephen Decatur's privateer *Royal Louis*. He came home from the first cruise with money in his pocket. The second cruise ended badly in a bloody battle with a British warship. Young Forten was the sole survivor of his gun crew and taken prisoner. The British captain was impressed by Forten's character and offered him freedom in England if he would work as a servant to his son. Forten refused, and he was sent to the dreaded prison hulk *Jersey* in New York Harbor, with a letter urging easy treatment and early release. Forten nearly perished, but other American prisoners helped him survive. After seven months he was released. Ill and emaciated, barefoot and in rags, he walked ninety miles home to his Philadelphia family, who had thought he was dead.

His mother nursed Forten back to health, and Robert Bridges gave him a job as an apprentice sailmaker, much like his father. He was soon promoted to journeyman, then foreman, supervisor, and manager of the business. It flourished in his hands.

In 1798, Bridges retired and offered to sell the business to Forten. With the help of Thomas Willing, one of Philadelphia's leading financiers, Forten acquired the firm, and made a great success of it. By 1807, he employed thirty workers of many ethnic groups. The firm was renowned for the quality of its products, and moderate prices. It rapidly gained a large part of the market.

Forten invested his profits in urban real estate, banking, and later railroads. He gained a sterling reputation for ability and integrity, and remained active in a brilliantly successful business career until the year of his death in 1842. He was also widely liked and respected through the city. Forten was described as "a gentleman by nature, easy in manner and able in intercourse, popular as a man of trade or gentleman of the pave, and well received by the gentry of lighter shade."[182]

Even as he continued in business, Forten also became prominent as a civic leader in many organizations. Among his favorites was the Philadelphia Humane Society, founded to aid people in distress, and in particular to rescue people from drowning in the Delaware River. Forten was not merely a supporter but an active rescuer, which he hugely enjoyed, probably to the horror of his family. He personally rescued twelve people from drowning, some of them in winter when Forten saved them at risk of his own life. In 1821, he received a special certificate from the Humane Society for heroism and devotion to others. He later said that it was among his most cherished possessions.[183]

Forten also took a leading role in Philadelphia, at what could have been a critical moment in the War of 1812. In 1814, British forces took their revenge for the American Revolution by burning the capital buildings in Washington. In a dangerous moment, Philadelphians rallied to the defense of their city. Forten was asked to muster African Americans as volunteers, first in building fortifications along the Delaware River, and then by forming themselves into military units. On September 21, 1814, Forten led thousands of volunteers, who were said to include three quarters of African Americans in the city. They went to work on the fortifications, side by side with Irish, German, and Anglo Philadelphians. Forten led them with a shovel in hand and labored beside them through the day. Afterward those African Americans organized as a fighting force, with Forten as one of their commanders. The war ended before they were engaged.[184]

Forten gave much of his time to his family. His second wife, Charlotte Vandine Forten (1785–1885), was descended from some of the earliest Africans in the Delaware Valley. When they married in 1804, leading merchants of many ethnic groups came to call, and drank punch at their wedding reception, a rare event. Together they had eight children. Most became active community leaders.

James Forten always worked to enlarge opportunities for African Americans, and at the same time to promote ethnic peace and harmony in Philadelphia. He was quick to speak against racism, strongly replied to newspapers that mocked people of color, and intervened against racist acts which were occurring with increasing frequency in nineteenth-century American cities.[185]

GROWING ETHNIC AND RACIAL TENSIONS

Through much of early American history, and for many years on the moving frontier, labor scarcity was a common problem in the New World, and on the expanding periphery of Europe. But in longer-settled regions, job scarcity became a growing problem in the nineteenth century, from the era of the new republic to our own time. Employment opportunities were especially scarce for newly freed American slaves, and also for European immigrants. The two groups were often rivals for entry-level jobs.

In Philadelphia after the American Revolution and the rapid growth of new waves of immigration, a fierce competition developed for jobs in the city, especially in unskilled and semiskilled jobs. A result was the rise of violent hostility by race, ethnicity, and religion. Most of these conflicts in American cities were driven by competition for work—often in short supply. Philadelphia had more than its share of this strife.

W. E. B. Du Bois studied this subject in Philadelphia, and published the results of his inquiry in his landmark book, *The Philadelphia Negro* (1899). He found evidence of a striking "change of public opinion in Philadelphia between 1790 and 1837." Du Bois wrote that "it arose from a combination of circumstances . . . peace and quiet and abundant work" in 1790, and then "a mass of poverty-stricken ignorant fugitives and ill-trained freedmen had rushed to the city," and "swarmed in the vile slums which the rapidly growing city furnished." They met intense competition from "equally ignorant" foreigners, who "outbid them in work, beat them on the streets," and "were enabled to do this by the prejudice which negro crime and the anti-slavery sentiment aroused in the city."[186]

"Black Sawyers Working in Front of the Bank of Pennsylvania, Philadelphia"

These conflicts were made worse by a major economic downturn in the early nineteenth century, one of the most severe in American history. The British Essex Decision in 1805 ended one of the strongest booms in American history and began to diminish opportunities for American commerce. With other events, the American economy declined for twenty years, and full recovery did not come until the mid-1820s. The people of Philadelphia suffered through the worst depression in the city's history. Unemployment rose as high as one third of the city's workers in the period from 1814 to the 1820s, worse than the Depression of 1929–40. The results were severe among Philadelphia's free Black population, who suffered from growing poverty and a rapid rise in mortality. In the difficult years from 1815 to 1819, sixty-two shiploads of desperately poor Irish immigrants suddenly arrived in Philadelphia. Even larger waves of immigration followed in the next three decades.[187]

BACKLASH: EXPLOSIONS OF RACIAL
VIOLENCE IN PHILADELPHIA, 1805–44

One of the cruelest patterns in American history is a recurrent rhythm in race relations from the late eighteenth century to our own time. Whenever progress was made in race relations, regression was sure to follow. It happened when slavery ended, state by state from 1780 in Massachusetts to 1867 in Texas. It also happened again with the success of the civil rights movement in the late twentieth century, and once more when an African American president was elected in 2008. In each of these eras, racists throughout the American republic were consumed with rage. Violent conflicts followed, along with periodic declines in the quality of American leadership.

In the city of Philadelphia something similar happened during the early

"Nightlife in Philadelphia—An Oyster Barrow in Front of Chestnut Street Theater"

years of the republic. Gary Nash writes that "by the turn of the century, black bondage was virtually extinct" in Philadelphia. The census of 1810 found only 10 slaves in Philadelphia.[188]

From 1789 to 1805, there were jobs for all. African Americans made rapid progress in employment, education, housing, and also in engagement in the civic life of Philadelphia. Then came a backlash. The American economy entered a period of long decline from 1804 to 1825. A pivotal moment was July 4, 1805. For many years since 1776, the people of Philadelphia, Black and white together, had gathered at Independence Hall to celebrate the day. They did it again in 1805, but this time it was different. An angry mob of violent young hooligans appeared. They attacked African American families and tried to drive them away. There was no effective city police to stop them, and the hooligans had their way. For many years thereafter, people of color were excluded from Independence Day celebrations in Philadelphia. Something similar happened on Boston Common, in lower Manhattan, and throughout many other American cities.

The violence was not entirely caused by whites. In 1804, the year before the Independence Day incident, angry young Black males had marched in the Philadelphia suburb of Southwark, "damning the whites and saying they would shew them Santo Domingo."[189]

These surges of racial anger and violence took many forms and fed upon themselves. The result in Philadelphia was an escalating series of increasingly violent racial and ethnic and religious riots—often white against Black, but also Protestant against Catholic, and native-born against immigrant.

Many American cities suffered in similar ways because of a large flow of immigration. At the same time, most American cities had grown faster than their local governments. Philadelphia County had twenty-nine separate urban jurisdictions. Order keeping was still in the hands of constables and watchmen who were overwhelmed by the growth of urban disorder.

In 1829, a major race riot broke out in Philadelphia. Among the triggers were Sunday services in African churches with new forms of expressive worship. On November 29, 1829, after a "loud and emotional service at an African Church," a riot broke out with violent attacks by white mobs on Black worshipers.[190]

Similar scenes happened on a larger scale in the Flying Horse Riot of August 11, 1834. Here Blacks and whites collided over access to a popular merry-go-round, and festive summer crowds suddenly turned into angry mobs. Several white gangs marched on Black neighborhoods in Moyamensing, an impoverished suburb west of the central city. They attacked Black males, killed at least one, and demolished shops, stores, and Black homes.

A larger purpose of white working-class mobs was to drive working-class Blacks out of Philadelphia. Other particular targets were African American churches as symbols of community. Two were destroyed. The mayor recruited a posse of three hundred citizens. They stopped some of the violence, but it broke out again and continued for two days. Similar race riots happened in New York, Boston, and other American cities in the summer of 1834.[191]

A very different event was Philadelphia's Abolition Riot of 1838. This was a response to the construction of one of the city's newest, largest, and most handsome public buildings. It had been designed to solve a civic problem. Mobs in Philadelphia had grown so violent that theaters refused any event which was even remotely controversial. A voluntary society called the Pennsylvania Hall Association was founded. The Pennsylvania Anti-Slavery Society took the lead, with many groups and civic leaders. More than two thousand people bought $20 shares, raised a capital of $40,000, and others contributed in different ways. A leading architect designed a handsome Greek Revival building, with fashionable shops on the first floor and a huge auditorium above. Over the stage was a large proscenium arch with the motto "Virtue, Liberty, and Independence." The building was dedicated on May 14, 1838. The next day an "Anti-Slavery Convention" of American women met there, and in the evening three thousand people attended another antislavery meeting.

Pennsylvania Hall, the new building of the Abolition Society, ca. May 14, 1838

Destruction of Pennsylvania Hall, May 17, 1838

A mob gathered outside. When the meeting ended, people left the building in a shower of missiles. Another reform meeting for men and women, both Black and white, was scheduled for the following day, which caused a further uproar. The mayor asked that there be no mixing of race and gender and was refused. He demanded the keys and closed the building. On May 17, 1838, a large mob set fire to the empty building and burned it in a huge conflagration.

This mob action differed from the race riots that preceded it. Pennsylvania Hall was destroyed by a classic "broadcloth mob," which drew its support not from an urban proletariat but from people of property in the city. A lithograph shows a mob of men in top hats and cravats, white broadcloth shirts and fashionable dark suits. The constables turned out and "kept order" by stopping attempts to save the building. Fire companies arrived and allowed the hall to burn to a shell, while carefully protecting nearby buildings. It was one of the most violent and destructive events in the city's history.

At the same time, it was also one of the most carefully controlled uses of urban disorder in nineteenth-century America. The mayor and other officeholders were complicit and the identity of the arsonists was carefully protected. It was known that many were merchants who did business with the southern states, an important part of Philadelphia's economy. Also involved were conservative political leaders in both parties, who regarded a temple of reform as a major threat. They were especially hostile to abolition, but also to reform movements in general.[192]

While this was happening, other mobs seized the moment to attack African churches. They even destroyed the Shelter for Colored Orphans, maintained by the Society of Friends, "while city officials stood by."[193]

RECLAIMING THE CITY

African Americans in Philadelphia did not give way before this surge of violence. In the summer of 1842, more than a thousand members of the Black Young Men's Vigilant Association organized a march on Lombard Street, to celebrate the anniversary of slavery's abolition in the British Caribbean. They were attacked by a large Irish Catholic mob of young racist hooligans who once again burned churches and houses. They attacked fire companies and constables until persuaded to stop by a courageous Catholic priest. Mayor John Morin Scott and Philadelphia constables responded mainly by arresting some of the African American victims.[194]

A turning point came with the riots of 1844, Philadelphia's worst outbreak of urban violence, by the measure of mortality. African Americans were not centrally involved. This was a clash between white Protestants and white Catholics. The trouble started when a Catholic bishop complained that a Protestant Bible was used in public schools. He asked that Catholic students be allowed to use the Church's Douay Bible. On May 7 and 8, 1844, Catholics and Protestants fought in the streets. Large white nativist mobs burned Catholic churches, sacked a seminary, and stoned the mayor. Fourteen people were killed, and many more were injured. Two months later, on July 6 and 7, 1844, violence erupted again. Thousands of Protestant nativists attacked Catholics. This was not a mob but an insurrection. It was met by five thousand Pennsylvania militia. Both sides fought each other with artillery and infantry volley firing.[195]

This collapse of urban order brought a change of policy from governments in the city of Philadelphia and the state of Pennsylvania. When the street violence in Philadelphia pitted whites against whites, and the scale of conflict approached the proportions of war, the authorities at last intervened. The Pennsylvania legislature ordered the city to combine its many ineffective governing institutions into a single consolidated municipal system. It also required the city to maintain a professional city police force that could keep at least a semblance of order.

Conservative leaders in Pennsylvania also intervened in another way. Here again they blamed the victims. In 1838, they added one word to a new requirement for manhood suffrage. "Whites" only would be allowed to vote. Free African American males in the state were required to pay taxes, but they lost the right of suffrage, which they had possessed since 1776. They did not regain it until the state ratified the Fifteenth Amendment to the Constitution in 1870.[196]

Philadelphia's violent race riots had other consequences. They changed the relative proportions of the Black population in city. It had risen sharply in the early republic, doubling from about 4.57 percent in 1790 to 9.45 percent in 1810. Then it began to fall slowly to 8.8 percent in 1820, and very rapidly thereafter to 3.28 percent in 1870. Strife and violence had taken a heavy toll.[197]

The race riots also changed the residential distribution of the city's Black population. By 1850, 90 percent lived in the tenements, shanties, and alleys of Moyamensing, which had the worst slums in the city. The other 10 percent were mainly in the old suburbs of Southwark and the Northern Liberties.[198]

A corrupt system of municipal magistrate courts added another burden to residents of these districts. Defendants were sent to prison for minor misdeeds, unless they paid a fee to the magistrate. Race prejudice was not the prime mover. Philadelphia's grossly corrupt municipal magistrates were lining their pockets at the expense of all the people. But impoverished people of color in Moyamensing and Southwark were more likely than others to land in jail.[199]

TAKING BACK THE STREETS: VIGILANT SOCIETIES AND BLACK ODD FELLOWS

Through all of these miseries, Philadelphia's African Americans kept striving for their rights. They worked hard to educate their children, and Du Bois found stunning evidence of a rapid rise in schooling and literacy rates among children of color, even through the difficult and violent years of the mid-nineteenth century.[200]

Parents struggled to hold their families together and they succeeded in most cases. Black churches increased in number and size. Benevolent associations and insurance societies multiplied to more than three hundred at century's end.

Black men and women with great courage defied the mobs and reclaimed

African Episcopal Church of St. Thomas in Philadelphia

the streets of the city for all citizens. One example, of many, was a fraternal organization called the Black Odd Fellows. These groups had first appeared as fraternal associations for white men only, and were similar in some ways to Freemasons, but more independent in spirit. They began to call themselves the Independent Order of Odd Fellows. In New York City, a group of African Americans proposed to organize their own lodge, but white American groups spurned them. They met a Black seaman named Peter Ogden, who belonged to a British lodge in Liverpool. He suggested that his Liverpool mates might be happy to sponsor a Black lodge in New York. In 1843, it was done. The result was a lodge of Black Odd Fellows who called themselves the Philomathean Lodge 646. The movement spread rapidly, and in 1844 Unity Lodge 711 was founded in Philadelphia.[201]

Many more groups of Black Odd Fellows followed. By 1851, twenty-five Black lodges formed throughout the northern states, with 1,500 members. The lodges of Black Odd Fellows had many functions and played an important social and economic role. To those ends, they created welfare funds and helped members and their families deal with loss of jobs, financial troubles, illness, and death.

At the same time, they were also moral societies that encouraged upright behavior. The lodges discouraged heavy drinking, gambling, criminal acts, violence, and sexual promiscuity that threatened family life. The Odd Fellows were strongly supported by their wives, who on their own initiative created women's auxiliaries called the Household of Ruth which became very active. Groups of men and women actively supported each other.

And in Philadelphia they did something more. A Black Odd Fellow named Amos Webber kept a wonderful set of "memory books" which survive today. They describe the fraternal activities of his Odd Fellows lodge in great detail.

Philadelphia's Odd Fellows made a special point of encouraging Black pride in a way that got everybody's attention. On Lodge Days they made a ritual of marching in regalia through the streets of Philadelphia and defied the fury of the enraged white mobs. The Odd Fellows debated among themselves how far they should march, and "how far it is prudent," given the violence that so many had seen and suffered. At first, they marched short distances from their lodge to an African church. Then they began to reach out. By the early 1850s, they were marching through much the city. Philadelphia's new municipal government supported them. The professionalized Philadelphia police turned out and marched with them. White hooligan mobs looked on but kept their distance. Then the white Odd Fellows turned out and marched with the Black Odd Fellows, and even the Freemasons joined in.

Before anyone realized what had happened, civilization returned to the streets of Philadelphia. In 1854, the battered city of Philadelphia was a long way from William Penn's Green Country Town, but something important had survived in the dynamics of its culture.[202]

THE LEGACY OF QUAKERS AND SLAVES IN PENNSYLVANIA: AN AMERICAN POLITICAL TRADITION OF PERMANENT REFORM

In the summer of 1681, William Penn and his fellow founder Thomas Rudyard had been hard at work in England, designing the Fundamental Constitutions and the Frame of Government for the new colony of Pennsylvania. A major purpose was to attempt a sweeping "reformation in government," not only for its own sake, but so that "an example may be Sett up to the nations." These English Quakers had suffered much from tyranny in the

Old World. Their purpose was to create something better in the New. Penn wrote, "There may be room there, tho' not here, for such an holy experiment."[203]

In America, Penn moved quickly to enact his "holy experiment." He erected the new Frame of Government by 1682. But no sooner had he done so than his Quaker colonists proposed sweeping reforms to his great reformation. The result was a new Frame of Government in 1683. Historians Richard and Mary Dunn wrote that the Pennsylvania colonists continued to ask for changes, and "over the next twenty years, they extensively rewrote William Penn's Constitution."[204]

William Penn succeeded far beyond the purposes of his own "holy experiment." He started the people of Pennsylvania and the Delaware Valley on a process of continuing reform that still goes on today. More than that, he started an American reform tradition, which has had a continuing (though not constant) presence in the great republic that became the United States of America.

The reform tradition that began with William Penn is one of the oldest in America, with deep roots. It is stronger than ever today, and still embodies the purposes and values of Quaker immigrants in the seventeenth century. A central purpose was to enact a set of radical Christian reforms that centered on liberty of conscience—not as a secular end in itself, but an instrument of salvation and Christian harmony.

Another fundamental purpose was to pursue this goal by peaceful means and to renounce violence and the use of force as a way of resolving differences. Yet a third goal was to follow the Golden Rule, and to treat others as one would wish to be treated. Implicit in that idea was the Quaker belief that all people are equally God's creatures.

In the Delaware Valley these Quaker beliefs became contested in major conflicts, not least among Quakers themselves. Some of the most profound conflicts developed between Quaker principles and the practice of African bondage, after many Quakers themselves became slaveholders.

The rapid growth of African slavery in early Pennsylvania, West Jersey, and Delaware had profound consequences on the people of this region, and in many ways at once. It caused some Quakers to compromise their most cherished principles but led others to enlarge those beliefs.

In that enlargement they awakened the first sustained antislavery movement in the modern world. Its founders and leaders were Quakers in England

and America: the Germantown "Quakers" George Keith and his Philadelphia Friends, Benjamin Lay in his Abington cave, John Woolman in West Jersey, and many more. At the same time, Anthony Benezet led an effort against the expanding ideas that we know as racism. Benezet was recognized by Clarkson and Wilberforce in Britain and by the Amis des Noirs in France as the most eminent leader of the international antislavery movement throughout the Atlantic world.

Gary Nash writes, "It is well known that Quakers led the way in this process."[205] Jean Soderlund adds also that "Delaware Valley Quakers were the first unified group to oppose black slavery—and in fact their movement became the primary wellspring of American social reform." The only other groups who came close in this time were Quaker meetings in southern New England and New York. The London Yearly Meeting also moved quickly but was a step behind the Philadelphia Yearly Meeting.[206]

All of this activity awakened a conservative countermovement that ironically was stronger among Quakers than in any other group in the early and mid-eighteenth century. Impassioned antislavery Quakers such as Benjamin Lay were disowned by their meetings for their attacks on Quaker slave owners.[207]

This epic struggle over slavery among Quakers spread quickly to other religious groups in the Delaware Valley. A quantitative study by Gary Nash found that Swedish Lutherans and Anglicans began to free slaves in their wills, and did so in numbers that approached that of the Quakers.[208]

This expanding movement created opportunities for African slaves in the Delaware Valley. They became active in their own striving against slavery in the Quaker colonies. They did it in ways that were different from prevailing patterns of resistance in the West Indies, or the mainland plantation colonies of the Chesapeake and Carolinas, or in Dutch New Netherland, French Louisiana, and Spanish Florida.

Slaves in the Delaware Valley (and also in New England, but not New York) rarely chose armed revolt or insurrection. They fought for their freedom in other ways, working mainly within the system, sometimes with Quakers who opposed slavery and supported equal rights. Others operated on the edges of the system, from a surprisingly early date. In 1726, from Philadelphia, there were "frequent complaints . . . that Negroes and other Blacks, either free or under pretence of Freedom, have resorted to and settled in the city," By one estimate in the mid-century, as many as two hundred or three hundred people of color were living in the city without masters, either free or "pretending to be free." This was one of many underworlds or outerworlds in early America.[209]

During the era of the Revolution, people of color and others in the Delaware Valley began to oppose slavery and racism in this new way, not as rebels or revolutionaries but as root-and-branch reformers within an established republican order. They were most strongly engaged in opposing slavery and promoting rights of freed people of color. These purposes were increasingly linked to a broad range of reforms, and to an expanding idea of reform in general.

We have already met the leading exemplar: James Forten, and have followed his rise to wealth and prominence in Philadelphia. We might add here evidence of his astonishing career as a reformer.

While continuing in business, building a fortune, and supporting a large and active family, Forten also became a leader of the antislavery movement, not only in Philadelphia or the Delaware Valley but through the United States and the world. He helped to lend money to William Garrison for the founding of *The Liberator*, and became a leading abolitionist in a way that won the sympathy of many whites.

Forten also worked tirelessly for the rights of free African Americans, in the face of a strong countermovement that sought to disfranchise all "people of color." Forten fought in court. He sued many times for the extension of suffrage rights of all Black males and was defeated again and again. Then he funded a political campaign to persuade voters and failed.

He redoubled his reform efforts. He supported African American newspapers throughout the country, such as Samuel Cornish's pioneering New York *Rights of All*, which did not succeed. But other newspapers began to flourish.[210] Forten took up a broad range of interlocking reforms: the abolition of slavery, the rights of freed people of color, aid to the poor, school reform, women's rights, the movement for world peace that flourished after 1815, the temperance movement, humane societies to help people in danger, prison reform, urban reform, rural reform, political reform, municipal reform, reform of institutions for the insane, and much more.

James Forten also supported the cause of reform in general. In 1834, he led a group of African Americans in founding the American Moral Reform Society. In Forten's large family, many children and grandchildren also became reformers, and did much to keep reform movements growing through the nineteenth century.

Robert Purvis

AFRICAN REFORM LEADERS: ROBERT PURVIS
AND HARRIET FORTEN PURVIS

Most active in the Forten family was Robert Purvis (1810–98), who married James Forten's daughter Harriet. His father was a Scottish immigrant who made a fortune as a cotton broker in South Carolina. His mother, Harriet Judah, was of mixed ancestry. Her parents were a Jewish businessman and a Morocco mother who was kidnapped and sold as a slave to South Carolina. By the American "one drop rule," that complex heritage made Robert Purvis a "person of color," which he embraced with pride and a sense of mission.[211]

His father moved the family to Philadelphia, schooled his sons at Philadelphia's Clarkson School and Amherst College, raised them as gentlemen. He died suddenly in 1826, and left them great wealth and a sense of mission in the world.

When Robert Purvis married Harriet Forten, they put their considerable wealth to work in a sustained effort to build an American reform tradition. They built on an extension of Quaker and African American reform efforts, and reached far beyond them. Primarily they worked against slavery and rac-

Harriet Forten Purvis

Executive Committee of the Pennsylvania Anti-Slavery Society

ism, and were deeply interested in the abolition movement. Purvis was a founder of the American Anti-Slavery Society. He embraced the cause of radical abolition, became a Radical Republican.

Purvis also helped to support Garrison's activities and supported the American Anti-Slavery Society in Philadelphia. Purvis and Forten built their houses with hidden rooms for runaway slaves. He became the head of the General Vigilance Committee, which helped slaves to escape in defiance of the Fugitive Slave Act. Overall, Purvis calculated that from 1831 to 1861, he helped an average of one slave to escape bondage every day for thirty years, which would total more than ten thousand slaves.

At the same time, Purvis strongly supported African American community life in Philadelphia. He funded a Library Company of Colored People, and supported the Equal Rights League for suffrage reform and full rights of citizenship for freed slaves.

Purvis also broadened his reform efforts to include the temperance movement. He became active in agricultural reform on his farm outside Philadelphia, served as a leader in the movement for women's rights throughout the

Charlotte L. Forten Grimké

United States, and became a founder of groups such as the Philadelphia Committee of One Hundred in 1884, which fought gross political corruption in Pennsylvania and throughout the U.S.[212]

Other members of the Forten family, male and female, young and elderly, also became active in these and other causes. They personified a movement that brought many African Americans to the support of reform in general. Charlotte Forten Grimké (1837–1914), grandchild of James Forten, and daughter of Robert Bridges Forten, was raised in the Purvis family after the death of her mother. She joined Gideon's Band assisting former slaves during the Civil War, and helped Sea Island slaves in South Carolina and Georgia build free communities that have survived for many generations even to our time.

In Pennsylvania, this was the legacy of Quakers and African Americans, working together through many generations. They helped to construct an American tradition of continuing reform which has become an enduring part of American culture, and an important presence in American public life.

TABLE 3.1 The African Slave Trade in the Delaware Valley, 1684–1766

1684 Ship *Isabella* of Bristol, Charles Jones, 150 slaves from Africa to Philadelphia, by way of Barbados

1747 June 25, brig *George* Charles Willing, "several Negro men and boys" from Guinea to Philadelphia via Barbados West Indies

1757 *William*, Capt. David Griffith, Gambia to New Jersey

1757 *Sally*, Capt. Thos Farmer, Africa to New Jersey

1759 May 24, June 21, unnamed vessel, James Simmon, "parcel," est. 50 slave, Africa to Philadelphia and West Indies

1760 August 14, schooner *Penelope* Carpenter, 95 slaves, parcel boys & girls, Gold Coast to Philadelphia and West Indies

1761 August 6 schooner *Hannah*, Thos Riche & David Franks, 100 slaves, "coast of Guinea" to Philadelphia, New Jersey, West Indies

1761 October 1, sloop *Company*, McCall & Wallace, 80 slaves, Gold Coast to Philadelphia/West Indies

1762 May 5, unnamed vessel, Wm. Rodman, "190 or 200 negroes," "Africa" to Philadelphia and West Indies

1762 May 6, brig *Nancy* Willing & Morris, 170 slaves, Gold Coast slaves to Philadelphia & Wilmington

1762 May 27, schooner *Sally*, Coxe & Oldman, 75 slaves, Gambia to Philadelphia and West Indies

1762 August 16, unnamed sloop, Wm. Plumsted & David Franks, 100 slaves, Guinea to Philadelphia and West Indies

1762 Unnamed vessel, Capt. Moore [Africa], to Philadelphia

1762 schooner *Sally*, Capt. Badger, 149/128 slaves, Gambia to New Jersey

1762 sloop *Three Friends*, Capt. Jas. Carpenter, 73 slaves [Africa], to Philadelphia

1762 vessel *Africa*, Capt. James Searing, Stephen Hammond, Africa to New Jersey

1763 October 8, schooner *Africa*, Thomas Riche, 80 or 100 slaves, Africa to Philadelphia, and New Jersey, and West Indies

1763 *Sally*, Capt. Thos. Farmer, 124 slaves, Africa to New Jersey

1764 June 21, sloop *Nancy*, Garrett & Geo. Meade, "parcel New Negroe Boys & Girls," to Philadelphia and West Indies

1764 July 19, sloop *Jenny*, "parcel Young Gold Coast Slaves" to Philadelphia and West Indies

1764 August 7, unnamed vessel, Thomas Riche, 160 or 165 or 170 slaves, to Philadelphia and West Indies

1764 September 20, brig *Africa*, Thomas Riche, 100 slaves, Coast of Guinea, to Philadelphia and West Indies

1764 unnamed vessel, Capt. Murdoch, 165 slaves [Africa] to Philadelphia

1765 July 25, ship *Granby*, 70 Negroes, Gold Coast to Philadelphia and West Indies

1766 August 21, sloop *Ranger*, James & Harvey, Capt. Wm. Harris, Gambia to Philadelphia

Total: 25 African Voyages of Record, Known Origins: Gambia 4, Gold Coast 5, Guinea Coast, 4

Number of slaves arriving in 14 voyages: total 1,632, average 116

TABLE 3.2 Slaves in Pennsylvania by County and Region, 1765–1810
Total Numbers and Percent of Population

SOURCE DATE	NASH & SODERLUND		U.S.CENSUS 1790	U.S.CENSUS 1810
	1765–70	1780–82		
Old Quaker Areas				
Philadelphia	1481	539	301 (0.7%)	2
Philadelphia County & Montgomery	412	c.400	196 (0.6%)	9
Bucks	n.a.	520	261 (1.0%)	11
Berks	n.a.	290	65 (0.2%)	4
Chester & Delaware	552	493	194 (0.5%)	7
Strongly German Areas				
Lancaster & Dauphin	106	838	586 (1.1%)	70
York & Adams	n.a.	793	499 (1.3%)	93
North British Areas				
Cumberland, Perry, & Franklin	n.a.	1149	553 (1.6%)	394
Westmoreland, Washington, Allegheny, & Fayette	n.a.	1140	834 (1.3%)	159
OTHER	**n.a.**	693	271 (0.4%)	
TOTAL SLAVES	5561	6855	3760	795

TABLE 3.3 Slaves in Mid-Atlantic Colonies and States, 1750–1800
Total Numbers and Percent of Total Population

	NEW YORK	NEW JERSEY	DELAWARE	PENNSYLVANIA
1750	11,014 (14.4%)	5,354 (7.5%)	5,740 (20.0%)	2,822 (2.4%)
1760	16,340 (13.9%)	6,567 (7.0%)	6,650 (20.0%)	4,309 (2.3%)
1770	19,062 (11.2%)	8,220 (7.0%)	7,050 (20.0%)	5,561 (2.3%)
1780	20,954 (10.0%)	10,060 (7.2%)	8,477 (19.0%)	6,855 (2.1%)
1790	21,193 (6.2%)	11,423 (6.2%)	8,887 (15.0%)	3,760 (0.9%)
1800	20,903 (3.5%)	12,442 (5.9%)	6,153 (9.6%)	1,706 (0.3%)

TABLE 3.4 Religious Affiliation of the
Pennsylvania Assembly, 1729–55

DENOMINATION	1729–30	1739–40	1745–46	1749–50	1754–55
Quaker	18	24	25	24	27
Anglican	3	5	2	1	1
Presbyterian	3	1	2	3	2
Baptist	2				
Dutch Reformed	1			1	1
Moravian					1
Deist				1	
NonQuaker				2	3
Unknown	3		1	1	
Total	30	30	30	32	36
% Quaker (Tully)	60%	80%	83%	75%	75%
% Quaker (Ryerson)	63%	90%	87%	75%	75%

TABLE 3.5 Ethnicity of Pennsylvania's
European Population, 1726–90

YEAR	ENGLISH-WELSH	SCOTS-IRISH	GERMAN	OTHER	TOTAL
1726	60%	12%	23%	5%	100%
1755	28%	28%	42%	2%	100%
1790a	35%	23%	33%	9%	100%
1790b	29%	30%	38%	3%	100%

PART TWO

SOUTHERN REGIONS

Chapter 4

CHESAPEAKE VIRGINIA AND MARYLAND

English Founders, West African Strivers, Afro-American Leaders

I am an Eastern Shoreman with all that name implies. . . . I love Maryland and the Eastern Shore.

—Frederick Douglass, born a slave, ca. 1818, Talbot County, Maryland[1]

I have always been proud that I am a Virginian.

—Booker T. Washington, born a slave, 1856, Franklin County, Virginia[2]

I have nothing more to offer than what General Washington would have had to offer had he been taken by the British and put to trial. I have adventured my life in endeavoring to obtain the liberty of my countrymen and am a willing sacrifice to their cause.

—A leader of Gabriel's Revolt on trial in Virginia, 1802[3]

I N 1790, the first federal census of the United States found that a majority of all African Americans in the country (55 percent) lived in the two Chesapeake states of Virginia and Maryland. That concentration appeared by the mid-eighteenth century, and persisted for many years. The last federal census of slaves in 1860 found that Virginia had more people in bondage than any other state, and Maryland had by far the most free people of African origin. Altogether, the combined African American population of these two states was much the largest concentration in the country.[4]

The character of slavery in Maryland and Virginia has been described as "mild" by comparison with what Chesapeake people call the lower South. Slaves such as Charles Ball testified that it was so. He had been enslaved in both regions, wrote at length about that experience, and his judgment should be received with respect.[5]

But quantitative tests for the present inquiry found repeated evidence that

CHESAPEAKE VIRGINIA AND MARYLAND

PENNSYLVANIA

MASON-DIXON LINE

Susquehanna R.

Wilmington

NEW JERSEY

• Frederick

Baltimore Canton

Doughoregan Manor •

Patuxent River

Delaware River

Dover

Potomac River

• Rockville

Delaware Bay

Bladensburg
• Georgetown

Annapolis •

Kent Island

MASON-DIXON LINE

DELAWARE

Alexandria •
Mt. Vernon •

Poplar Island

Oxford •

Choptank R.

Port Tobacco •

MARYLAND

Sotterley •

St. Clement's Island •

Potomac River

VIRGINIA

Sabine Hall •

Northern Neck

Rappahannock River

Pamunkey River

Mattaponi River

Chickahominy River

Richmond •
• Midlothian

York River

Chesapeake Bay

Williamsburg •

Merchant's Hundred/
Carter's Grove

Petersburg •

Jamestown

Blackwater River

James River

Carrollton •

Cape Charles

Norfolk

Cape Henry

Atlantic Ocean

0 Miles   20   40

0 Kilometers   40

© 2022 Jeffrey L. Ward

physical punishments of slaves were more frequent and more severe in Virginia than in South Carolina or Georgia.

Another comparative test was made by Daniel Flanagan from criminal trials of slaves before the Civil War. He found that in the United States during the mid-nineteenth century, the most severe state penal system for slaves was in Virginia, both in statute law and courtroom consequences.[6]

Worse, Chesapeake slave owners were more likely than masters and mistresses in other regions to break up families in bondage and sell them apart. Slaves often remembered the agony of forced separation as the cruelest of their many afflictions. All these comparisons tell us that the worst cruelties of slavery were more widespread and more harsh in the Chesapeake than in any other North American region. By many empirical tests, the burden of bondage in the Chesapeake states tended to be more heavy than in any comparable region.

And yet even as Chesapeake slaves suffered much, many were proud to be Virginians and Marylanders. A familiar example was Frederick Douglass, born of African ancestors on his mother's side and European forebears in his father's family. At the same time, Douglass wrote that he was doubly proud to be a native Marylander and an Eastern Shoreman.

Booker T. Washington shared similar feelings of pride about his birth and upbringing in Virginia. Harriet Tubman always remembered her Maryland "cabin quarter" as home. She cherished a deep affection for fellow slaves in southern Maryland, and for some free white women on the Eastern Shore, mostly antislavery Quakers and Methodists who helped her escape from bondage. She felt no affection for most slaveholders in Maryland and Virginia, to say the least. But through many travels in her long life, Harriet Tubman remembered the Eastern Shore of Maryland as her native place.

Douglass, Tubman, and Booker T. Washington had been born in slavery, and suffered much from violence and oppression. All rose to national leadership in the long struggle against slavery and racism. Their strength and effectiveness as American leaders derived in part from African American roots and Chesapeake experiences.

Slaves in other American regions also became successful leaders, but Chesapeake slaves tended to be more prominent in leading roles, partly because there were so many of them. But also important was the example of a strong regional tradition of leadership among slaveholding elites.

Chesapeake slaves were close and keen observers of Virginia and Maryland masters who excelled as American leaders in the early republic. Slaveholders from this region included the primary author of the Declaration of Independence in

1776, the commander in chief of the Continental Army from 1775 to 1783, the first president under the Articles of Confederation, the authors of the two leading drafts for the United States Constitution in 1787, the leading compositor of the Bill of Rights in the first federal Congress from 1789 to 1791, four of the first five presidents of the United States from 1789 to 1825, major legislative leaders in the United States Senate and House of Representatives from 1789 to 1815, and the chief justice of the United States Supreme Court for thirty-five of its first forty-six years. In the early republic, nearly all of these Chesapeake leaders owned slaves.

Later in the nineteenth century, as that founding generation faded away, some of their former slaves began to emerge as national leaders in American politics. Most could not vote or hold office, but many had a major impact on pivotal events in national politics. Some did so repeatedly, with major consequences for the course of American history.

These former Chesapeake slaves built on a regional tradition of leadership, and reached beyond it in creative ways. They learned from its strengths, corrected its weaknesses, and invented other new ways of leading from their own heritage and experience.

In that process, Chesapeake slaves who later became national leaders also reinvented American leadership itself, in fundamental and highly specific ways. In their hands, leadership in the United States became more expansive in its spirit, more inventive in its methods, more broad in its goals, and more humane in its results.

Through a pivotal period, their thoughts and acts helped to change the course of American history. At the same time, they also enlarged America's founding ideas and institutions in fundamental ways.

The creativity of their leadership might also be instructive for Americans of later generations, especially in the early twenty-first century, when we have been struggling with the failures of many national leaders in our time. We today have much to learn from men and women who had been born slaves in Maryland and Virginia and later became leaders of the American republic. They have had a long reach in the nineteenth, twentieth, and twenty-first centuries.

VIRGINIA'S FOUNDING VISIONS

This story of Africans in Chesapeake America had multiple beginnings. One began with small groups of English-speaking people who founded the Chesapeake colonies in the early seventeenth century, and gave this region a distinct character.

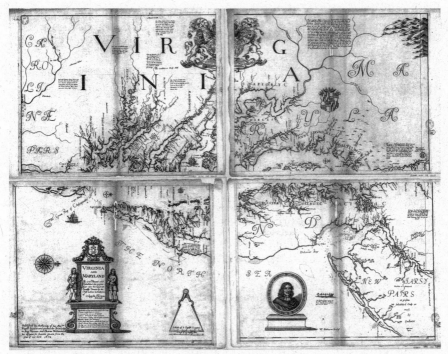

"Virginia and Maryland as it is planted and inhabited this present year, 1670"

As early as 1656, English writer John Hammond published a lively little pamphlet called *Leah and Rachel; or, The Two Fruitfull Sisters, Virginia and Maryland.*[7] He observed that these colonies shared a kinship, a culture, an economy, a region, and a troubled history that was riven by internal conflict.

Some of these conflicts rose from differences of religion, politics, and economic purposes. Others derived from collisions between dynamic ideas and institutions of liberty and freedom on the one hand, and entrenched systems of hereditary slavery on the other.

From the start, the founders of Virginia and Maryland had been inspired by noble purposes and large ideas. It is often forgotten by more secular American generations that their founding values were rooted in deep and abiding Christian faith. England's poet-preacher John Donne sent them on their way to America with a sermon: "Your principal end is not gain, nor glory, but to gain souls to the glory of God." When they reached Virginia in 1607, one of their first acts was to erect a great cross at the entrance to the Chesapeake Bay.

The same thing happened when the founders of Maryland arrived in 1634. At their landing place on St. Clement's Island, they also raised another massive cross. It is still there, rebuilt in gleaming white marble, as an enduring symbol of their largest purpose.[8]

English founders of Virginia and Maryland also shared another important goal, which was to live under laws that "Gentleman-Freeholders" themselves had helped to make. On July 30, 1619, Virginians created a House of Burgesses, the first fully elective General Assembly in the New World, with "two Burgesses elected out of each Incorporation and Plantation." Its framers designed a government with many moving parts: an elected House of Burgesses, an appointed Council with executive, legislative, and judicial powers, a governor with a veto, and a written Charter of Fundamental Law.

The founders of Maryland started late in 1634, but acted even more quickly to create bicameral institutions of self-government and the rule of law. For better and for worse, a later generation of Marylanders also invented an electoral college in their constitution of 1776. Four centuries later, these elements still survive in the Constitution of the United States and in forty-nine of fifty state governments. A rare exception is unicameral Nebraska.[9]

From the start, some of these founding principles were severely limited. In Jamestown's turbulent early years, the rule of law meant martial law. Most men in Virginia were not freeholders and had no share in self-government. For many years, a majority were landless laborers, tenants, servants, English convicts, Scottish prisoners of war, and later African slaves. Even middling ranks were a minority in Virginia—a pattern much like England itself, but profoundly different from early Puritan and Quaker colonies which established American models of a middling majority. Even so, founding principles and institutions were planted firmly in Virginia and given room to grow.

THE "MARYLAND DESIGNE"

Maryland began with even larger purposes. Its founder, Sir George Calvert, had served England's King James I as principal secretary of state, and he later became a close advisor to Charles I. In childhood, Calvert had been catechized secretly as a Roman Catholic. Later in life he publicly avowed his Catholic faith for conscience's sake, at heavy cost. That act required his resignation from public office in Protestant England, but he retained the gratitude of two sovereigns. James I raised him to the Irish peerage as the first Lord Baltimore, and Charles I gave him a royal gift of ten thousand square miles in America, which are now the state of Maryland.

This colony began with a unique vision that Lord Baltimore's friend Captain Robert Wintour called the "Maryland Designe." One driving purpose was compulsory toleration of all Trinitarian Christians—a carefully limited idea in Maryland's Toleration Act of 1649, but a long step forward in an intolerant era.

Captain Wintour added that a second large goal was to create a society where "freemen" could continue to "live free," and be "subject to only such lawes as themselves should make."

And a third object, more serious than it sounds, was to enable Maryland gentlemen "to live like Princes," and "enjoy the pleasures of friendly neighborhood." Through almost four centuries, male Marylanders of many creeds and classes have grown specially fond of that one.[10]

These many purposes were not easily realized. Maryland's Toleration Act attracted religious groups who were deeply intolerant of others. The colony suffered its first civil war in 1655, between Protestants and Catholics.

The idea of "living free" was a problem in another way. It fully applied only to male freeholders, who were a minority of Marylanders. And most difficult was Captain Wintour's third idea of a country where gentlemen could "live like Princes," which in early years required others to live in a very different way. Even so, the "Maryland Designe" took root as an ideal, and it began to grow.[11]

Other troubles arose in the Chesapeake colonies from material conditions and high mortality. English settlers in Virginia suffered much from "Indian wars" (which Europeans started) and from starving times, deadly epidemics, economic collapse, political disorder, and personal violence.

The toll in human life was shattering. Of about eight thousand colonists who came to Virginia from 1607 to 1623, only about 15 percent survived at the end of that period. Maryland's founders did better that way, but both Chesapeake colonies suffered much from high mortality.[12]

EARLY CHESAPEAKE LEADERS: THE RISE OF RULING ELITES

In part because of those troubles, the founding corporation called the Virginia Company collapsed in 1624. Its settlements became a royal colony, and the disorders continued. In 1625, Governor John Harvey knocked out a councilor's teeth with a cudgel and was himself "thrust out" of Virginia. He returned with a royal warrant for the arrest of his enemies, and was driven out again by brute force. Other leaders followed, and failed.[13]

Vice Admiral Sir William Berkeley

Then came a pivotal moment in Virginia's turbulent history. In 1641, England's Charles I chose as governor Sir William Berkeley, a staunch royalist soldier who fought for his king in England's wars. He led Virginia off and on from 1641 to 1676, and transformed the colony from a shaky settlement of about five thousand in 1635 to a thriving province of forty thousand by 1676.[14]

Berkeley brought to Virginia a vision of what Karl Mannheim later called in another context a "conservative utopia."[15] It centered on the idea of a highly stratified society of social orders, which were more rigid than social classes. At the top, he envisioned a small hereditary elite of birth and breeding, honor and virtue, wealth and independence. He also sought to develop a material order with a mixed and balanced economy, and a moral order sustained by religious unity under the Church of England.

With those goals in mind, Berkeley actively recruited a small but strong elite "of as good families as any subjects in England," in his own words. Of 152 Virginians who held high office in the colony, 77 percent were younger

sons of "armigerous" families, so called from their coats of arms registered at
the College of Heralds in London. The Virginia origins of this ruling elite
did not begin at Jamestown in 1607, or in the chaos of its early years. The
great majority of these leaders arrived from about 1641 to 1676. Many were
recruited by Sir William Berkeley. They intermarried with his encouragement.[16]

This group of favored families controlled the Royal Council, which distributed land in Virginia, and took the lion's share of wealth and power.
Together they dominated Virginia for eight generations. They deeply believed in ancestral English ideas of liberty and freedom, but in a very special sense. Edmund Burke, who knew their families, wrote of Virginia
gentlemen that "freedom is to them not only an enjoyment, but a rank
and privilege." [17]

Virginia's ruling gentry possessed many liberties and freedoms. Yeomen
in middle ranks also had some liberties, but not so many. Servants had few
liberties; and slaves had nearly none. This hierarchical system of hegemonic
liberty and freedom coexisted comfortably with servitude and slavery, because
it rested on assumptions of profound inequality which few Americans would
share today.[18]

In 1685, Durand de Dauphiné, a French nobleman from Languedoc, visited Virginia and met many of its leaders. He observed that "the gentlemen
called cavaliers are greatly esteemed and respected, and very courteous and
honorable. They hold most of the offices in the country." [19]

Most of them rose to political power through an established process. A
first step was selection to self-perpetuating county courts and parish vestries,
which were leading institutions of local government. Another was election to
the House of Burgesses, the legislature that wrote the laws of Virginia. The
third was appointment to the Royal Council of Virginia. With county courts
and the House of Burgesses, the Council supervised the granting and patent-
ing of land, and shaped the material base of the colony.[20]

Through many colonial disorders, this structure of power endured. In
1775, every serving member of Virginia's governing Council was descended
from a councilor who had served in 1675. Elements of this system persisted
long after the Revolution to the American Civil War, and in some Virginia
counties even to our time.

Something similar happened in Maryland. The Lords Baltimore divided
much of Maryland's most valued land into "manors" which were sometimes as
large as a thousand acres or more. Larger manors went to the Calvert family,

2nd Lord Baltimore, Cecil Calvert, first Proprietor of the
Province of Maryland

and their friends and relations. By 1676, Maryland had more than sixty manors. Some had their own feudal courts. Many had stewards and bailiffs; and
most had quitrents and other material forms of manorial obligation. These
were not mere vestiges of medieval custom. Surviving rent rolls fill battered
folio ledger books in the Calvert Papers at the Maryland Historical Society.
One of my tasks as a stack boy, seventy years ago, was to look after them. In
spare moments I studied these tomes, and was fascinated by their records of a
functioning manorial system in an early American colony.

For some years after the founding of Maryland in 1634, two thirds of its
governing Council were Catholic gentry, often relatives and friends of the
proprietary Calvert family. After leaders of England's Protestant Revolution of
1688 forbade Roman Catholics to hold office under the Crown, Maryland's
system shifted to Anglican families, but a small landowning elite continued to

dominate Maryland for many years, much as in Virginia, with similar values and the same ethic of leadership.[21]

These ruling elites could be utterly ruthless in the possession of power. In Virginia, an ambitious immigrant named George Fisher was warned by John Randolph "against disobliging or offending any person of note in the colony." Randolph explained that "either by blood or marriage we are almost all related, and so connected in our interests, that whoever of a stranger presumes to offend any one of us will infallibly find an enemy of the whole. Nor, right or wrong, do we forsake him till by one means or other his ruin is accomplished."[22]

But at the same time, these Chesapeake "gentlemen called cavaliers" lived by a code of right conduct which was a complicated thing. In a world of violence, the idea of a gentleman combined a warrior's virtues of courage, audacity, endurance, fortitude, and resolve. In a world of politics and statecraft, it was an idea of honor and service. In every endeavor these leaders were taught to conduct themselves with the manners of a gentleman, which in a world of inequality meant deference to superiors, respect to equals, and "condescension" to inferiors, in the original meaning of condescension as kindness and concern for people of lesser rank.

In dealing with people of every rank, the manners of gentlemen and ladies were expected to combine easy grace, instinctive courtesy, quiet dignity, and generosity of spirit, but also with strength and resolve. Maryland's official motto, chosen by George Calvert, summarized much of it in four Italian words: *fatti maschii, parole femine*, "manly deeds, womanly words." After the gender revolutions in the twentieth and twenty-first centuries, it has been changed officially to "strong deeds, gentle words."[23]

Women were a vital presence in these Chesapeake elites, and could be as ruthless as males of the species, if not more so. One of them in Virginia called herself a spirited She-Briton. Others asserted their rights not on grounds of equality but superiority to most men in mental strength and moral worth.

A leading example was Maryland's Mistress Margaret Brent (ca. 1601–71), born to an eminent Anglo-Catholic family of "noble descent," and related to the Lords Baltimore. In 1638, she came to Maryland with her brothers, received large land grants in her own name, employed many male servants, and managed the family's litigation with such success that she was appointed executrix of Governor Leonard Calvert's estate. On one occasion which lingered long in Maryland folk memory, Mistress Brent met with the Assembly and Council and demanded not one vote but two: one on grounds of her own interest, and another for her status as the governor's attorney and representative. Later Margaret Brent moved to Virginia with her brother and a dozen male servants. She and her family held large estates in both colonies.[24]

Throughout the Chesapeake region, these codes of conduct varied in detail within its ruling elites. One version was an austere stoic creed of disciplined service in military and civil careers. Exemplars were George Washington, Robert E. Lee, and George Catlett Marshall, all descended from Berkeley's elite on Virginia's Northern Neck between the Potomac and Rappahannock Rivers. George Marshall was born in Pennsylvania, but he came of Virginia stock, went to the Virginia Military Institute (not West Point), later married a Virginian, retired to Virginia, and became the very model of a stoic Virginia gentleman.

Many members of this Chesapeake elite pursued other callings and lived by different creeds. From the start, some were skilled businessmen who excelled at building fortunes in commercial farming with slave labor. Among them were many generations of Carters and related families in the fertile lower James and York and Rappahannock Valleys, the most prosperous part of Tidewater Virginia.

In the heartland of central Virginia, and west into the Piedmont, a third group of Chesapeake gentlemen combined public service with deep learning in law. Among them were George Wythe, George Mason, John Marshall, and many others. The leading model for a fourth group of Virginia gentlemen was George Washington, who excelled in three careers: military, economic, and political.

Other Chesapeake leaders were more diverse in origin. Some derived from North British border families who came later and settled in the western Piedmont and the Valley of Virginia. They included low-church Anglicans and moderate Presbyterians: Henrys and Stuarts, Wilsons and the Valley Jacksons. In the far southwest of Virginia, one of the most interesting elites and among the last to emerge was the Abingdon Junto. Its seat was the graceful town near the Tennessee-Virginia line.

Maryland's elites were similar in origin. Most prominent was a founding group of English and Irish Catholic leaders who included a progeny of Calverts, Carrolls, and many related families.[25] An example was the family dynasty of Charles Carroll the founder, his son Charles Carroll of Annapolis, and grandson Charles Carroll of Carrollton. They succeeded as great planters and private bankers who increased their wealth by very careful moneylending. At the same time, they were slave owners, commodity traders, land dealers, investors in industrial enterprise, and promoters of internal improvements.[26]

The Catholic Carroll family took a deep interest in public affairs, but in the eighteenth century they were forbidden to vote and hold office because of their religion, and not allowed to practice their faith openly in Maryland on orders from London. Imperial authorities also forbade Maryland to honor its founding vision of religious tolerance. The Carrolls became leaders of the American Revolution and strong supporters of its founding ideas of liberty and freedom. Charles Carroll of Carrollton lived to be the last surviving signer of the Declaration of Independence, and a living symbol of its principles and ethics. At the same time, the Carrolls were among Maryland's largest slave-holders.

AFRICANS IN THE CHESAPEAKE: THE FIRST WAVE FROM ANGOLA AND CONGO

In Virginia, the first large group of African arrivals on record were the familiar "20 and odd Negroes" who arrived in 1619.[27] They had been captured at sea by the English privateer *White Lion* (Captain John Jope), operating under Dutch letters of marque in company with another English vessel hopefully called *Treasurer* (Captain Daniel Elfrith).[28]

In 1619, these English privateers seized the Iberian slaver *San Juan Bautista* with a cargo of Angolan slaves. Captain Jope landed some of them at Jamestown, and exchanged them for provisions. Four days later Captain Elfrith arrived in Virginia with another thirty Angolan slaves, but he was forbidden to sell them. His letter of marque was found to be invalid, and put him at risk of arrest for piracy. Elfrith departed for Bermuda, where he found more buyers and fewer questions.[29]

These much fabled African captives were probably not the first in Virginia. Others may have come earlier. A muster list in March of 1620 counted thirty-two Africans: seventeen women and fifteen men. They were described as "not Christians," which may have been an error. Some may have become Roman Catholic in Africa. Several census records suggest that mortality rates were high, and numbers actually declined in some early years at Jamestown, which was as unhealthy for Africans as for Europeans. By 1624, only twenty-two Africans were counted; in 1625, about twenty-three.[30]

Thereafter, Africans began to arrive at a more rapid rate. In 1628, the Massachusetts ship *Fortune* captured yet another slaver from Angola "with many Negroes." Her New England captain carried them to Virginia and swapped them for a shipload of tobacco. By 1648, three hundred Africans were living in Virginia. Their rate of increase was high, but total numbers remained far below thousands of English servants in Virginia through the seventeenth century.[31]

A puzzle in Virginia is that the first large group of arriving Africans came as late as 1619, twelve years after the founding of Jamestown. In most North American regions, Africans appeared before the founding of major colonies. In New England, slaves were held by solitary English settlers before the founding of the Bay Colony and its Great Migration. In the Hudson Valley, a "black" or "mulatto" from Africa by way of Santo Domingo ran a fur business on Manhattan Island from 1613, eleven years before the founding of New Netherland. Throughout the Delaware Valley, Africans were working in Dutch trading posts by 1624, and Swedish settlements before 1639.

In Maryland, Africans were present at the first founding of the colony. Among them was "Francisco, molato," who may have arrived in 1634 aboard the *Ark* or the *Dove*, which together were Maryland's *Mayflower*. He was the servant of Jesuit Father Andrew White, chaplain to the Calvert family.[32]

Most early Africans in Virginia and Maryland came directly or indirectly from the West Central Africa regions of Congo, Loango, and Angola. Evidence of their origin appears in voyage records, and individual surnames such as Congo (1640), Cossongo (1635), and Longo (1635). Another second-generation African named John Johnson gained his freedom, acquired a tract of land, and called it Angola. This evidence of early West Central African origins in Anglo-American colonies was highly consistent. It also matched other evidence.[33]

These first Africans in the Chesapeake were rarely called "slaves." Some were described as "servants." But from the start their condition differed from English servitude. Early documents make clear that most of them served for life. Their purchasers also became owners of any children of female slaves, which was not the case for English servants. In short, whatever they were called, most of them were hereditary slaves. Some became free, not so much by formal emancipation or manumission, but by asserting their freedom in various ways, or by finding protectors in high places, or by descent from a freeborn woman.[34]

GETTING AHEAD IN EARLY MARYLAND:
THE SAGA OF MATHIAS DE SOUSA

Others among these first Africans gained freedom by their mastery of valuable skills before they came to the Chesapeake. An example was Mathias de Sousa, of mixed African and Portuguese origins. He came to Maryland in 1634 as a servant to Jesuit chaplains and missionaries. His masters were quick to discover that de Sousa could sail a boat, and was skilled at trading, and had a gift for languages, as did many Africans in America.

His Jesuit masters made de Sousa "skipper" of a small sailing pinnace. They sent him on voyages up the Chesapeake Bay to trade with the "Sesquihannough" Indians. He was allowed to hire his own crew, and soon had free men, English servants, and African slaves working for him. Later he became captain of a larger trading ship that belonged to John Lewger, Maryland's proprietary secretary. In March 1641, de Sousa was elected to the Maryland Assembly, with full voting rights.

Later he fell on hard times and lost much of his wealth, which was the downside of freedom. But de Sousa had a remarkable career, as did others of African descent in early American settlements. Historian Ira Berlin has helped us to understand his career. To Berlin's findings, one might add the importance of skills and aptitudes acquired in Atlantic Africa and put to work in the New World.[35]

AFRICAN SLAVES AND ENGLISH SERVANTS

In 1671, royal governor William Berkeley reported that Virginia's population included "2,000 black slaves" and 6,000 "Christian servants for a short time." The Africans had increased rapidly, but were still heavily outnumbered by English laborers in other forms of bondage.[36]

These two groups lived and worked closely together, and were quick to turn their coexistence to mutual advantage. After long hours of heavy toil, the living conditions of both English servants and African slaves were in some ways remarkably open and free. In 1698, Maryland's governor Francis Nicholson wrote to the Board of Trade in London that Africans had much freedom of movement, and often traveled over long distances in both Maryland and Virginia. "In each province," Nicholson wrote, "it is the common practice for them early on Saturday nights and Sundays, and on two or three days at

Christmas, Easter and Whitsuntide, to go and see one another even at thirty or forty miles distance."

More than that, Governor Nicholson added, "I have several times, both here and in Virginia, met negroes both as single or six or seven together in the night time." He observed that much of this movement happened with the knowledge of their masters, and even on their orders. "They send negro men [and] boys about the country when they have business. . . . Negroes learn all the public and private roads of the country." [37]

Nicholson also observed in 1698 that Chesapeake masters required slaves to use English names, and he observed that "most Negroes speak English." [38] With a language in common, Africans and English servants had many opportunities to meet and mix. Historian Douglas Deal found that before 1700, "racial segregation was not much in evidence. . . . Men and women of both races drank, smoked, caroused, fought, and slept together." T. H. Breen and Stephen Innes constructed individual examples in abundant detail, from Virginia's two counties on the Eastern Shore of Chesapeake Bay. Similar practices appeared in early Maryland. [39]

A surprise in recent scholarship has been a new trove of evidence about the number and nature of unions between English servants and African slaves in the early Chesapeake. Genealogist Paul Heinegg, whom we have already met, revolutionized our knowledge of this subject by compiling vital records for many free African American families in the Chesapeake colonies from 1619 to 1820. He reconstructed 591 lineages in Virginia and neighboring parts of North Carolina, and another 312 in Maryland and nearby Delaware— altogether 903 free African American lineages, with many thousands of nuclear families through multiple generations.

Heinegg discovered that "most [free] families descended from white servant women who had children by slaves or free African Americans." Altogether, he found that 67 percent of 903 lineages of free Afro-Anglo-Americans began by the union of an English female servant with an African male. Only 17 percent derived entirely from African Americans. About 10 percent included at least one American Indian ancestor. And only one percent of these free lineages descended from white male slave owners who had children by their slaves. Other children were forcibly conceived by white masters on female slaves, but tended to remain in hereditary bondage, following their mother's status. [40]

Most unions between British female servants and African male slaves happened before 1720, when changes in the law of slavery made them more difficult. Heinegg learned from the evidence of wills and letters and probate records that these unions were not the products of fleeting sexual contacts. They tended to be enduring common-law marriages, sustained by bonds of mutual support.[41]

Heinegg also made another interesting discovery. He reported that many African American founders and leaders were descendants of these unions, and not only in the Chesapeake itself. Their progeny spread from Maryland and Virginia through other parts of the United States. But many remained in Virginia and especially in Maryland, with its large number of free people of color.[42]

SLAVES AS REAL ESTATE IN VIRGINIA

Virginia's early laws on slavery were unique among British colonies, and they made a difference in the size and structure of slaveholding. A primary purpose was to create stability in families and continuity in families and estates of slaveholding Chesapeake gentry, who ruled the region from its founding to the Civil War.

In the formative years of the colony, Virginia slaves were not in general chattels or personal property. They were declared to be real estate. For purposes of inheritance Virginia slaves were bound to the estate, which meant they descended to heirs under laws of primogeniture and entail. This policy was adopted in Virginia for intestate estates, when the owner died without a valid will. We have learned especially from the research of Lorena Walsh that before 1776 many Chesapeake slaveholders welcomed laws of primogeniture and entail, and used them in part as tools for creating and protecting a more cohesive workforce.[43]

They also had another function. No slave could be forfeited by a master unless his lands were declared forfeit as well. To this status a few exceptions were made. Slaves remained chattels and personal property while in the possession of slave traders who brought them into Virginia. In some special circumstances they could be declared to be chattels, but only for the purpose of settling debts. And they could also be sold as chattels to protect an orphan's estate. Otherwise, the law of colonial Virginia was very clear. Before 1776, slaves on Virginia plantations were not personal estate but real estate. And they were not chattels but "tenants in tail," thus:

All negro, mulatto and Indian slaves within this dominion shall be held to be real estate and not chattels and shall descend unto heirs and widows, according to the custom of land inheritance; and be held in fee simple. Provided that any merchant bringing slaves into this dominion shall hold such slaves whilst they remain unsold as personal estate. All such slaves may be taken on execution as other chattels; slaves shall not be escheatable.[44]

Further, it was lawful for masters to

annex to the same lands and tenements, all or any slave or slaves which such tenant in tail shall during such his estate, purchase, acquire or be possessed of; and to declare that such slave or slaves, and their increase, so long as any of them are living, shall descend, pass and go, in possession, reversion or remainder, as part of the freehold.[45]

Virginia's legislators actively encouraged this practice of "annexing" slaves to the land, and they gave elaborate instructions on how it should be done. Here was another way of protecting large estates, and preserving strong family lines among the landed gentry in the Chesapeake colony.

In a later and more libertarian age, slaves in Virginia would be redefined as personal chattels for all purposes. But the older and more organic idea persisted for many years. It was sustained by a social idea that was shared by Sir William Berkeley and his Cavalier elite. This "conservative utopia," in Karl Mannheim's phrase, was an idealized system of distinct social orders anchored firmly in place by law and custom. It was also a structure of material relationships in which lands and slaves were kept in the hands of a small elite of birth, breeding, and wealth, and passed from fathers to sons in an orderly way. The slave law of Virginia was conceived primarily as an instrument of this idea.

A closely related purpose of Virginia's slave law was to strengthen the authority of masters over their own estates. This was also a patriarchal idea. Control of slaves belonging to a wife was vested in the master, unlike other property that she brought to the marriage.

Slaves themselves had scarcely any rights independent of their master, not even a right to life. The killing of slaves "under correction" was not a felony or even a misdemeanor. Masters who murdered their slaves "by mistake" were "free and acquit of all punishment and accusation for the same, as if the accident never happened." To repeat: "As if the accident never happened."[46]

While slaves had few rights, masters were permitted to grant them many privileges. A master could allow his slaves to hold property on any terms he wished, but in the eyes of the law a slave's possessions were not property, but "peculum" that belonged to the slave but were owned by the master. They remained part of the master's estate.

A master in Virginia was permitted to allow his slaves to assemble and meet at any of his quarters, or at a public mill, as long as they did not meet at night. He could send his slaves to church if he wished, and if he did so nobody could keep them away or punish them for coming to worship.

Masters could put deadly weapons in the hands of a slave. Many masters did so for hunting, but woe unto a slave who carried arms without permission. All these privileges were understood as rights belonging to the master, not to slaves themselves.[47]

The laws of Virginia allowed masters more latitude in these ways than did slave codes of other colonies. The social vision behind Virginia's slave law was a hierarchical world ruled by a small elite of powerful patriarchs who kept their slaves in subjection, attended to their needs, and treated them decently. That was the ideal, but the reality was often very different.

AFRICAN ARRIVALS IN THE CHESAPEAKE: THE GREAT WAVE OF 1701–75

In both Maryland and Virginia, most Africans arrived in the eighteenth century. Their numbers were much larger than earlier movements to the Chesapeake, though small by comparison with the Caribbean slave trade.

Estimates by various methods have yielded similar results. Overall, the most comprehensive quantitative evidence for voyages from Africa has been gathered for the Trans-Atlantic Slave Trade Database, with added corrections for undercounts by David Eltis and David Richardson. They reckon that 128,000 slaves landed in the Chesapeake during the full span of the colonial slave trade from 1619 to 1775.

Of that entire flow, the great majority arrived from 1701 to 1775, when an estimated 115,000 African slaves (82 percent) entered Virginia and Maryland. The pattern of their arrival made a single great wavelike movement: a rising wave of about 30,000 slaves from 1701 to 1725; a peak period of roughly 54,000 slaves from about 1726 to 1750; and a falling wave of 31,000 from 1751 to 1775.

In 1775, this African slave trade to the Chesapeake ended abruptly. Eltis and Richardson found evidence of only about 500 African arrivals from 1776

to 1800, and 70 from 1801 to 1825, which is probably an undercount of illegal trade.

Similar results also appear in the very careful early work by Elizabeth Donnan; and in subsequent studies by Allan Kulikoff, Russell Menard, Lois Carr,
and Darrett and Anita Rutman of the early Chesapeake Group; and also in
more recent work by Lorena Walsh, Douglas Chambers, and others.[48]

The result was a revolution in the ethnic composition of the Chesapeake
colonies. In Virginia, people of African ancestry grew from about 2 percent of
the population in 1648, to 5 percent in 1671, 16 percent in 1690, 25 percent
in 1710, 28 percent in 1740, and 37 percent in the census of 1790.

Trends and levels were similar in Maryland. People of African origin in its
population rose from 14 percent in 1707 to 30 percent in 1755 and 35 percent in 1790. Maryland's most complete colonial census in 1755 found a total
of 153,564 people, of whom 98,357 (64 percent) were free whites and 46,356
(30 percent) were "negroes" and "mulattoes" By that same year (1755), only
7,952 white servants and convicts were counted in Maryland. Their numbers
had fallen to 5 percent of Maryland's population, and 14 percent of the "total
bound work force." [49]

Leading factors were a continued rise in fertility among all ethnic groups,
and also growing African arrivals. Lorena Walsh reckons that from 1680 to
1697, "roughly three thousand new Africans were brought into the [Chesa-
peake] region." That flow rose to "at least 4,600" from 1698 to 1703, 14,000
from 1704 to 1718, and 19,000 from 1719 to 1729, and a much larger but
inexact number thereafter.[50]

AFRICAN REGIONAL ORIGINS IN THE CHESAPEAKE

Overall, Walsh also found that "more than nine out of ten slaves brought into
the Chesapeake in the eighteenth century either arrived directly from Africa
or were transshipped from the West Indies," after a very brief stop in the Caribbean.[51]

Through the full span of the Atlantic trade, slaves were brought to the
Chesapeake from many parts of Africa. But within that large frame of diversity, smaller movements from particular African regions went to specific
parts of the Chesapeake colonies. These more complex patterns also varied by
time. The result was a web of small subregional concentrations of African origin within a larger pattern of diversity in the Chesapeake region as a whole.

In the early years of the African trade to the seventeenth-century Chesapeake, as we have seen, the first arrivals of slaves tended to be more concentrated in their regional origins. Most of these Africans had their roots in Angola and Congo. Here again, historians of this subject have a major debt to John Thornton and Linda Heywood for their findings in the Vatican archives, their scholarship on West Central Africa, and their studies of European and American sources.[52]

The second wave in the Chesapeake slave trade in the eighteenth century was longer, much larger, and more diverse in African origins and American destinations. Southern and central Virginia in the James, York, and Rappahannock estuaries drew heavily from the Bight of Biafra, in what is now southeastern Nigeria.[53] Different patterns appeared in the upper Chesapeake, from the Potomac Valley, north through much of Maryland. Lorena Walsh found that most slaves came out of a broad area in West Africa, from Senegal to Casamance to Cape Mount, the Côte d'Ivoire and the Gold Coast. A very few, called Malagasy slaves, came from East Africa, especially Mozambique and Madagascar.[54]

Did buyers of slaves in Virginia and Maryland care very much about specific places of African origin? The answer is unequivocally no and yes in highly specific ways. Throughout the Chesapeake colonies, planters showed comparatively little preference for particular ethnic groups or geographic regions in Africa. A Maryland buyer wrote, "If they are likely young negroes, it's not a farthing matter where they come from."[55]

But Chesapeake slave owners were closely attentive to African ethnicity in another way. David Eltis writes that "planters discovered that they could better maximize plantation output by buying people of similar backgrounds to work together." Lorena Walsh agrees that when Chesapeake planters were offered a choice, "regional origins of the captives may have played a role" in that particular way. She found evidence that masters tried to acquire slaves of a single region who could work and live together. One purpose was economic: to increase output and efficiency. Another was demographic: to encourage higher rates of marriage and reproduction.[56]

AFRICAN CLUSTERS IN CHESAPEAKE SUBREGIONS: IGBOS, IBOS, AND IBIBIOS FROM BIAFRA IN THE LOWER TIDEWATER AND EASTERN PIEDMONT

In Virginia, yet another pattern of African origin also appeared. Through the full run of the slave trade, about half of all arriving Africans in the Chesapeake came from what is now southeastern Nigeria, where the great Niger River meets the Atlantic Ocean. Seamen named this part of Africa's Atlantic coast the Bight of Biafra. Its leading slave ports were called Old and New Calabar. Slaves of many ethnic identities were brought there. Many who came to the Chesapeake in the eighteenth century were from a cluster of related groups variously called Igbo and Ibo. A distinct but related people were called Ibibio. In the eighteenth-century slave trade, they were also called Calabar Negroes. In the twentieth century, along with other ethnic groups in southeastern Nigeria, they have often been called Biafrans and that coastal region was known to seamen as the Bight of Biafra.

Among total estimates of 128,000 African slaves who were brought to the Chesapeake, David Eltis and David Richardson and their team reported evidence in the Trans-Atlantic Slave Trade Database that about 58,000 (44 percent) came from the Bight of Biafra. Eltis and Richardson also estimate that "over 95 percent of slaves who came to the Chesapeake Bay area directly from Africa arrived in ships outfitted in Bristol, London or Liverpool. The Bight of Biafra was the single most important African region of trade for these vessels."[57]

Similar patterns emerged from pathbreaking research by Allan Kulikoff, and further analysis by Lorena Walsh of colonial naval office records for Virginia and other sources. She finds that "more than half" of Africans brought to the Chesapeake between 1698 and 1729 came from the Bight of Biafra, and a "majority were probably Igbo." Yet another important study by Douglas Chambers yielded similar results. Igbos and Ibos appeared in every major American colony without exception. But among the major regional slave systems in North America, the predominance of Igbo people was very strong in the Chesapeake, though it had also appeared in Barbados and Jamaica.[58]

Within the Chesapeake region, the dominance of Igbo slaves was highest in the vital heart of Virginia's lower Tidewater area, and especially the estuaries of the York, James, and Rappahannock Rivers. During the early eighteenth century, when Virginia slavery was developing into a system, its center was a web of Tidewater plantations along those three great rivers. From 1718 to 1726, 60 percent of slaves arriving in the York River came from Biafra, and many of these Biafran captives were called Igbo or Ibo. Others were Ibibio and related groups.[59] By every measure, these slaves were the largest single group of Africans in southeastern Virginia and northeastern Carolina. Many Igbo slaves were also prominent in parts of Virginia's Piedmont region.

Altogether this pattern of African ethnic and regional origins in Virginia and Maryland differed from the slave trade to New England, the Hudson

Valley, the Delaware Valley, the Carolinas, Georgia, the Gulf Coast, Louisiana, and also Puerto Rico, which are evident in superb Spanish entry records which we studied in San Juan.[60]

IGBO WAYS IN AFRICA

In Africa, the cultural distinctiveness of the Igbo people was often noticed by slave traders in the seventeenth and eighteenth centuries, and also by travelers and ethnographers from the eighteenth century to our own time. In early years, Igbos were thought to be backward and primitive by the standards of other African cultures. Their social system was perceived to be fragmented, atomistic, and individuated. Igbo polities were open and less authoritarian.

Throughout much of today's Nigeria, Igbo, Ibo, and kindred cultures in the southeastern part of that nation have had a striking double reputation. In the seventeenth and eighteenth centuries they were thought to be more primitive than their neighbors—lacking large states, powerful kingdoms, and strong rulers. Their social and political units tended to be smaller than in other African societies. They also had a different way of thinking about power and authority. Small groups and individuals had a spirit of independence and individuality. Igbo people said proudly of themselves "Igbo enwegh eze, The Igbo have No King."[61] An Igbo proverb was "Ike di na awaja na awaja, Power flows in many channels."[62]

Another striking paradox also appeared in the construction of Igbo identity. British explorer W. B. Baikie observed in 1856, "In Igbo each person hails . . . from the particular district where he was born, but when away from home all are Igbos." In West Africa, Igbo lived in smaller units. Attachments were more local, and large political structures were weak by comparison with more imperial African systems. But cultural similarities among kindred people were strong.[63]

The structure of power was also different—less authoritarian in ways that appeared in the condition of Igbo women. The role of women in Igbo society was different in degree from other African cultures. Their status was higher, and their cultural roles stronger.

In the nineteenth and twentieth centuries, as the native people of West Africa began to assimilate western institutions and cultures, other differences appeared between Igbo and other West African cultures. And in the twentieth century, literacy rates were high among the Igbo people. They successfully mastered many aspects of modern society. They were quick to advance in skilled professions, showed individual initiative, and rose rapidly in private business and public service. Their success was admired by some, and resented by others. Igbos began to be called the "Jews of Africa." In the twentieth century, their achievements were a leading cause of a violent conflict known as the Biafran War, after the Nigerian region where Igbos lived. It arose from cultural differences between Igbo and other ethnic groups in different regions of Nigeria.

OTHER AFRICAN ETHNIC GROUPS: WEST AFRICANS IN MARYLAND AND THE UPPER CHESAPEAKE

In Maryland's slave trade from 1704 to 1773, detailed quantitative research by Lorena Walsh yielded a surprising discovery. Through that period, she found that three quarters of slaves with known African origins came from a broad area along the upper coast of West Africa, from Senegal to the Gold Coast in what is now Ghana. Within that vast region, as many as two thirds of slaves (64 percent) came from two African areas. One area centered on southern Senegal, Gambia, Guinea, and Sierra Leone. The other drew mainly from what is now Ghana.[64]

These patterns in Walsh's quantitative data interlock with evidence from local history, legal documents, family genealogies, slave narratives, and archaeology. Those sources also provide more granular evidence of African cultures and customs and values that formed within small local communities and extended families. Three sets of examples follow, drawn from a large diversity of small constituent units within much of Maryland, Virginia, and the Potomac Valley. They demonstrate that small units introduced elements of African culture that persisted in particular ways through many generations.

FROM THE GOLD COAST TO MARYLAND'S DORCHESTER COUNTY: ASANTE TRADITIONS THROUGH THREE GENERATIONS OF HARRIET TUBMAN'S FAMILY

On Maryland's lower Eastern Shore, five miles below the Choptank River, a slave child was born around 1820, and named Araminta Ross. We know her better by her married name, Harriet Tubman, and remember her as a legendary leader in the struggles for the freedom of her people. All her life she fought in many roles: a conductor on the Underground Railroad, an abolitionist leader, a Civil War nurse and soldier with musket in hand, guiding a Union regiment in the Civil War, and after emancipation a fighter for racial justice, even coming to blows with railroad and streetcar conductors over segregation in the northern states during the late nineteenth century.[65]

Harriet Tubman was taught as a child that she came from a long line of fighters. She herself believed that she learned her fighting spirit from her American-born mother, "Rit," who had been raised in that tradition. On one occasion Rit had even taken an axe against her master. It happened when the master appeared with a Georgia slave trader and tried to seize her youngest boy for sale to the South. Rit hid her son in the woods for more than a month. When the master and the Georgia trader came to her cabin, Rit picked up the axe and said, "You are after my son, but the first man that comes into my house, I will split his head open." They retreated, and she kept her son.[66]

Tubman believed that Rit learned her formidable fighting spirit from Harriet's maternal grandmother, "a slave imported from Africa." Harriet remembered her as a "Shantee," raised in the warrior tradition of the Asante people.[67] New York journalist Frank Drake interviewed Tubman on that subject in 1907. Drake was well connected within her intimate circle of friends and reformers. She was open with him, shared the memories of her Maryland childhood in slavery, and told him that "the old mammies to whom she told her dreams were wont to nod knowingly and say, 'I reckon youse one o' dem 'Shantees, chile,' for they knew the tradition of unconquerable Ashantee blood, which in a slave made him a thorn in the side of the planter."

She also described in detail the ways in which African traditions were transmitted from one generation to another in America. In her experience, much of this work was done by "the old mammies." Their oral memory of her Asante heritage had a long reach in American history.[68]

The results appear when we study the life and work of Harriet Tubman as a militant fighter for freedom and justice. She took special pride in her descent from an American-born mother and an African-born maternal grandmother. And she cherished an African American heritage that was Asante in origin. Much work has been done by scholars in Africa on the transmission of values through many generations among the Asante, a proud, strong, highly principled people with a warrior ethic among men and women alike.[69]

That transmission continued among their descendants in America. It was one of many ways that an African heritage persisted in a new world. In Tubman's formative years, elements of a large and complex Asante culture were transmitted through many generations within extended Chesapeake slave families. Harriet Tubman put that heritage to work with important consequences for American history.[70]

AN ISLAMIC SLAVE ON MARYLAND'S EASTERN SHORE: AYUBA SULEIMAN DIALLO

The great wave of slave trading in the eighteenth century brought other African ethnic and religious groups to the Chesapeake, and greatly enriched the cultural diversity of this region.

Leading examples were Islamic slaves. They were known by many names in that era: Turks, Moors, Mahometans, Muslims, and more. Allan Austin, one of their leading historians in the United States, reconstructed the life stories of seventy-five Islamic slaves in early America, and he identified many more. Altogether, some scholars conclude that Islamic captives may have totaled as many as 10 to 20 percent of African slaves in North America.[71]

When Islamic Africans met European Christians in America, attitudes and acts were complex and highly variable on both sides. In early Maryland Islamic slaves were objects of curiosity, but rarely of hostility. They were often treated with respect when they practiced their faith, and admired for their persistence in keeping Islamic names and customs. Some were literate in Arabic, and several astounded their Christian owners by reproducing the entire Quran from memory.[72]

As early as 1682, a Virginia statute briefly recognized Islamic Africans as a separate group, and briefly declared that all persons were "hereby adjudged to be slaves" whose "parentage and native country are not Christian at the time of their purchase," except "Turks and Moors in Amity with His Majesty." That law was soon forgotten, but individual Islamic slaves found other ways to achieve freedom, sometimes with help from sympathetic Christians.[73]

A leading example was an Islamic slave who came to Maryland in 1730. His full name was Ayuba Ben Suleiman Hibrahema Diallo, which was translated as Job, son of Solomon, grandson of Abraham of Jallo.

He was of the African people called Fulani or Fulbe or Fula by the English, or Pula by the French after their language called Pular. Ayuba came from the high country called Futa Jallon below the Gambia River in today's southern Senegal and Guinea. His home was a commercial center called Bonda, which

Ayuba Suleiman Diallo

had been founded by his grandfather and run by his father, a learned imam, a wealthy merchant, and a powerful figure in this African region which Europeans would sometimes call the Switzerland of Guinea. Young Job was raised in the faith of Islam. He became the companion of Samba Galedeo Diego, a future king of Futa, and learned what English-speaking people recognized as the manners of a gentleman.[74]

In 1730, Job's father sent him on a trip to the Gambia River, with orders to sell two slaves for a supply of English writing paper. He was captured by Mandingo raiders, sold into slavery for a few cows, and sent to Maryland. There he was put to work in a tobacco field on Kent Island (now part of Queen Anne County). He failed at that labor, and was put in charge of tending cattle. His master, a kindly man named Tolson, never whipped him, but Job was unable to speak with other slaves. Children threw mud in his face when he prayed in the woods. In complete misery, Job ran away, was caught and jailed.[75]

Then his luck changed. He met an enlightened Maryland gentleman named Thomas Bluett, who was at the same time a lawyer, judge, minister, and missionary. Bluett found a Wolof slave who could translate Job's story into English. With his Maryland owner's permission, Bluett took Job to Annapoli, where a small circle of lawyers, ministers, and merchants took an interest in this bright young African. They were fascinated to discover that Job had the mind of a scholar and the manners of a gentleman, and they wanted to learn more about his Islamic faith.[76]

In 1733, with encouragement from James Oglethorpe, a great humanist, founder of Georgia, and director of the Royal African Company, Bluett took Job to London. On the Atlantic crossing, Bluett and the ship's captain taught Job to speak English, and Oglethorpe helped to raise money for Job's freedom.

In London, Bluett published in 1734 a book about Job and his cultural migrations. It was a sensation, and became a model for a literary genre that centered on a sympathetic narrative of the adventures of high-born African slaves. In this literature, rank became more powerful than race. Job's intellect and manners were engaging to Anglo-American gentlemen. He was invited to lead British theologians in discussions of comparative religion, which he did with grace and refinement. He worked on Arabic documents with Hans Sloane, founder of the British Museum. Job also helped the religious scholar George Sale to do an early English translation of the Quran, which won high acclaim.

All of this became an important part of the Enlightenment discovery of global cultures throughout the world—a major event in modern intellectual history. Job was lionized in London society. He asked to meet Queen Caroline, and it was arranged. For the occasion he commissioned a spectacular robe from a London tailor, which caused another sensation. The royal family and aristocracy received him as their equal, and showered him with tokens of esteem.[77]

After many adventures, Job grew weary of the London whirl, and asked to return to his African homeland. It was done. He resumed his early life, but maintained ties with British scholars and clergy, and tried to encourage international relations that might restrain the slave trade. He also worked tirelessly to promote understanding among the people of three continents. Always he conducted himself with the impeccable manners of an Afro-Islamic-Anglo-Maryland gentleman, until his death in 1773.[78]

AN ISLAMIC COMMUNITY OF FUTA JALLON SLAVES IN MARYLAND: YARROW MAMOUT, HIS SISTER HANNAH, AND FRIENDS IN GEORGETOWN AND ROCKVILLE

Even where numbers of Islamic slaves were small and scattered, some of them were able to find each other. Two cases in point were a brother and sister from Futa Jallon. They constructed an extended family and a small community of

Yarrow Mamout

Islamic slaves in what is now Montgomery County, Maryland, and the District of Columbia.

Yarrow Mamout (1736?–1823) had been born in Futa Jallon, the high country in Guinea. He was taught to read and write Arabic, raised in Islam, and remained faithful to its teachings through a long life. He was devout in daily prayers, and true to the African customs and Islamic ethics.[79]

Yarrow and his sister Hannah were enslaved together, put aboard the ship *Elijah*, carried to Annapolis in 1752, and sold apart.[80] Hannah became the slave of Joseph Wilson, who owned six hundred acres, four farms, and two taverns in what was then Prince George's County, and later became Montgomery County. She worked at Hungerford's Tavern in Rockville. Near the end of his career Wilson owned thirty-six slaves. Several had Fulani and Islamic names (another Yarrow, an Issac/Issaka, and others). They were thought to have arrived together in the *Elijah*. Much evidence confirms the existence of what James Johnston describes as a small "Black Muslim community in Maryland at Rockville in the late eighteenth century, probably centered on Hungerford's Tavern." It also reached into other towns such as Georgetown and Bladensburg, which are now within the district of Washington.[81]

Yarrow Mamout was bought by another master, Colonel Samuel Beall Jr., a wealthy landowner and miller in Georgetown, Maryland. Yarrow kept his Islamic faith, learned many skills, became a brickmaker, and then a master bricklayer. His services were in demand in a red-brick region where even the colonial capitals and churches were made of clay. His master asked Yarrow to make all the bricks for his mansion and outbuildings, and offered him his freedom when done. Samuel Beall died in 1795, shortly after the work was finished. His widow kept his promise and Yarrow was set free.[82]

From making bricks, Yarrow turned to making money. He did it with some success, but had trouble investing his earnings. The first hundred dollars were entrusted to an elderly merchant of high integrity, who died shortly afterward, and the money was lost. The next hundred dollars was put in the hands of a young merchant who went bankrupt, and Yarrow lost his earnings again. He saved a third sum, of $200, in 1793. This time he became an early investor in the first Bank of Columbia, and he watched the bank carefully, with good reason. The bank fell on hard times, but shortly before it failed, Yarrow withdrew his money. Probably he had inside knowledge from some of its directors, who were the wealthiest men in Georgetown and his personal friends.[83]

Yarrow later delighted in reciting the saga of his savings. His friend, the scholar and diplomat David Bailie Warden, tried to record the phonetic sound of Yarrow's own voice—a rare opportunity to hear the speech of an African slave in early Maryland:

Olda massa been tink he got all de work out of a Yaro bone. He tell Yaro, go free Yaro; you been work nuff for me, go work for you now. Tankee, massa, Yaro say, Sure nuff; Yaro go to work for he now. Yaro work a soon—a late—a hot—a cold. Sometime he sweat—sometime he blow a finger. He get a fippenny bit—eighteen pennee—gib him to massa to put by—put by a dollar till come a heap. Oh! poor massa take sick, die. Yaro money gone. Oh, Yaro, go to work again. Get more dollars—work—hard more dollars. Gib him now to young massa, he young, he no die. Oh, young massa den broke—den go away. Oh, oh, oh! Yaro old for true now. Must work again—worky, worky, get more dollar. Gib him this time to all de massa—all de massa can't die, cant go away. Oh, yaro—dollar breed now—every spring—every fall, you get dollar—chichen now.[84]

As Yarrow established himself in Georgetown, an extended family began to form around him. He remained in close touch with his sister Hannah. After Yarrow acquired a home, she moved from Rockville to Georgetown, and lived nearby in her own house. Hannah had a daughter who went to court, won formal recognition of her status as Yarrow's niece, and inherited part of his property. Yarrow himself married and had a son named Aquilla Yarrow, who was born a slave and owned by the mistress of Yarrow's wife. When the boy was seven or eight, Yarrow bought Aquilla's freedom. Later Yarrow discovered a conditional clause in the deed of manumission, and got a second agreement that Aquilla could "exercise every right of a freeman." [85]

Aquilla married a woman who took the name of Mary Turner Yarrow, and may have been descended from yet another Islamic slave who had come to Maryland aboard the *Elijah*. The Turner line increased through many generations, with a long record of educational achievement in Maryland from the nineteenth to the twenty-first century.

For more than seventy years, Yarrow Mamout was a prominent citizen of Georgetown. His portrait was painted by Charles Willson Peale in 1819 when Yarrow was eighty-three, still fit and active. It was painted again by the artist Charles Simpson in 1822, when Yarrow was about eighty-seven and showing his age. Simpson did a brightly colored painting on a commission from the Beall family, who had owned and freed Yarrow, and thought of him as a member of their family.

Yarrow Mamout lived for many years in his Georgetown house. He was "known by most of the inhabitants," and cherished for "good humor" and "good spirits." Neighbors remembered that he prayed in his garden as often as five times a day, and was often heard "singing praises to God." While Peale was painting his portrait, Yarrow told him that "man is no good unless his religion comes from the heart." [86]

KING CARTER'S DEVELOPMENT OF A CHESAPEAKE PLANTATION SYSTEM

From the start, African slaves tended to be owned by men of wealth in larger concentrations than English servants, mainly because of higher capital costs. As early as 1625, fifteen of twenty-three Africans in Virginia belonged to two English owners. Governor George Yeardley, the most powerful man in Virginia, owned seven Africans. Abraham Peirsey, the wealthiest settler, had eight. By 1648, an estimated three hundred "Negroes" were living in Virginia. Captain Samuel Matthews alone employed forty. Matthews and several wealthy men accounted for more than half of Virginia's Africans on their plantations.[87]

In early years, "plantation" was a name for any new settlement in Virginia. By the third quarter of the seventeenth century, the word had acquired its modern meaning for a distinct unit of production that dominated the economy of this region, and others to the south and west.

One of the best early descriptions of a Virginia plantation was written by William Fitzhugh, an armigerous gentleman of an affluent English family. He migrated from Bedfordshire to Virginia around 1670, with wealth enough to acquire large tracts of land. Fitzhugh was instantly accepted into Virginia's ruling elite. By marriage and purchase he acquired 24,000 acres of undeveloped lands, and a working plantation of 1,000 acres, with cleared fields and a Virginia gentleman's handsome house of thirteen rooms. Later it was described as "well furnished" with "all necessary houses" on the grounds, and fencing "for comfortable and genteel living." Fitzhugh developed his estate between 1671 and 1685.

His planting grounds were divided into four "quarters," each with its own "choice crew of negroes." Altogether Fitzhugh owned twenty-nine slaves and their number grew rapidly by natural increase. By 1686, he wrote that "most of them [were] this country born." Holdings of this size multiplied rapidly in Virginia during the late seventeenth century.[88]

Leading models for Chesapeake planters were the holdings of the Carter family. Its founder was John Carter (1613?–69), who arrived in the 1640s. By 1669, he employed thirty-four English servants and forty-three African slaves. His son Robert "King" Carter (1663–1732) acquired vast grants of land from his office as land agent in Virginia's Northern Neck. To work the soil he bought slaves in large numbers. After his death in 1732, he left an estate of 333,000 acres and more than a thousand slaves.[89]

Virginians called him King Carter for his great wealth and "haughty" manner. He built a church very near his plantation, and traveled to it every Sunday in a massive coach pulled by six horses. The congregation waited outside until he arrived. After King Carter's last trip, their smoldering resentment surfaced in graffiti on his headstone: "Here lies Robin, but not Robin Hood."[90]

Carter was little loved but much respected by other planters for his methods of management. He divided his large holdings of land and slaves into smaller plantations, which in turn were subdivided into quarters. In Carter's

Robert "King" Carter

own meticulous lists, the size of his quarters averaged between nine and fifteen adult slave men and women. Carter employed them in regimented gang labor, often with African "foremen," as he called them.[91]

King Carter himself sired a large family, with two wives and fifteen children. Six died in infancy and childhood, a mortality of 40 percent. Nine reached adulthood and married into families of leading Virginia planters. King Carter kept a close eye on his children and grandchildren. He helped them to acquire marriage partners, lands, and slaves. Their estates tended to grow rapidly.

An example was his daughter Elizabeth. She married Nathaniel Burwell, and King Carter bought them a plantation called Merchant's Hundred, later renamed Carter's Grove. It descended to grandson Carter Burwell. Once again, King Carter looked after it, and helped to buy slaves, mostly Igbo and related groups. The plantation system of the Carter family rapidly became a model for others in the Chesapeake colonies.

A distinctive system of plantation organization and slave ownership appeared in the Chesapeake at an early date. Nearly all slaves in the Chesapeake colonies were owned by individual masters—unlike early New Netherland, French Louisiana, and the Spanish colonies. In Virginia and Maryland, nearly all of these individual holdings took the form of plantation slavery, unlike most Puritan, Quaker, and Dutch colonies in North America, with some exceptions such as Narragansett planters and Hudson Valley patroons.

The size of Virginia plantations and slaveholdings grew rapidly through the eighteenth century. In 1700–1710, 39 percent of slaves lived on plantations with five slaves or less; only 10 percent were in units of twenty-one or more. By 1760–70, those proportions had nearly reversed: 15 percent of Africans lived on plantations with five slaves or less, and 33 percent on estates with twenty-one or more. In southern Maryland at the same time, 44 percent of slaves lived on plantations with more than twenty slaves, and about 26 percent were in holdings of eleven to twenty. Only 10 percent of Africans were held in groups of seven or less. As Chesapeake plantations grew larger, so did the number of small slave quarters. The size of quarters remained about the same.[92]

But numbers of great planters with hundreds of slaves remained small. On the eve of the Revolution a majority of freeholders or householders in Maryland and Virginia owned only a few slaves. The median number of slaves was three, and the modal number was one.[93]

That pattern persisted in the southern states as long as slavery survived. At its heart was a striking paradox. A large part of the free population thought of themselves as slaveholders, but held only a few slaves.

Another paradox was geographic. The original area of Maryland and Virginia before 1860 was very large, more than 75,000 square miles together. But throughout the region as a whole, units of residence for slaves tended to be small. That pattern differed from slavery in the Carolinas and the Caribbean. Ethnic concentrations among African slaves in the Chesapeake were reinforced by this process.

Historian Lorena Walsh also found in her study of the Carter plantations that "initial concentrations of Africans of particular ethnicities were further unintentionally perpetuated on large central tidewater estates by the practice of entail." She also discovered that by the 1720s "many gentry planters began entailing slaves in their wills," not all slaves, but the majority, so that the bulk of the family's wealth might be "passed on largely intact in the male line." This custom continued to the American Revolution, when primogeniture and entail were abolished in Virginia law.[94] But even then it was reintroduced in Kentucky (1793) where propertied Virginians settled.

The results of these slaveholding patterns were important for Virginia slaves themselves. Walsh observed that "elite gentry inheritance strategies, especially common in the York and Rappahannock districts, afforded the largest and most ethnically concentrated enslaved communities, more settled places of residence, and more generational continuity than was the lot of most Chesapeake slaves." In the area along those two rivers, Igbo slaves increased and multiplied. Other concentrations developed to the west on the Piedmont plateau.[95] As a consequence, slaves developed different subregional Afro-Chesapeake cultures of their own, more so than in northern colonies where customs and cultures of slaves and masters moved closer to one another.

SLAVE QUARTERS AND AFRO-CHESAPEAKE CULTURE

For slaves on larger plantations in this Chesapeake region, the most important unit of belonging was a subdivision often called a quarter.

The meaning of the word "quarter" in this region changed through time. In the late seventeenth century it often referred to a rectangular building also called a barrack, sometimes of about sixteen by twenty feet and more, occasionally as large as twenty by fifty, enough to house all or most slaves on a big plantation. By the 1720s quarters had become groups of smaller buildings. In 1724, Hugh Jones described them as a cluster of "small cottages called quarters." William Hugh Grove on April 17, 1732, wrote that quarters on York River plantations appeared like "little villages" of "7 or 8 distinct tenements" with "little platts for Potatoes and Indian Peas [corn]."[96]

Quarters were much the same in southern and central Maryland. Leading examples in every sense were the large plantations of the Carroll family through three generations. The family founder, called Charles Carroll the Settler, left an estate of fifty-six slaves. By 1773, his son Charles Carroll of Annapolis and grandson Charles Carroll of Carrollton, together owned 386 slaves. Their largest plantation was Doughoregan Manor, with ten thousand acres and 330 slaves. About 130 lived in one large quarter near the main house. The rest were distributed through nine outlying quarters, averaging twenty-two slaves each.[97]

Nearly all of the 386 Carroll slaves in the Maryland census of 1773 were connected to fourteen matriarchal lines of descent which bore the names of "Old Grace, Old Fanny, Rachel, Goslin Kate, Battle Creek Nanny, Banks' Nanny, Old Moll, Suckey, Nan Cook, Old Peg, Old Nell, Sams Sue," and two other families that were not named in inventory records.[98]

Slaves in twelve of these fourteen lines lived at Doughoregan Manor. Another line was at Poplar Island Quarter, and one more at Annapolis House Quarter. Ronald Hoffman found that "one or two families formed the nucleus on most quarters, with more than two-thirds of the children living with their parents."

Charles Carroll of Annapolis cared deeply for the strength and cohesion of slave families. Hoffman concluded that this concern derived not from altruism but material interest, and added, "It never occurred to him to care what they thought of him." For the Carroll family and many Chesapeake masters, slaves were not only their labor force, but also a large part of their working capital. Strong cohesive slave families tended to have rates of population growth which directly increased the owner's capital stock, and rate of capital accumulation.

Further, slave families added to the wealth of the Carroll family in other ways. Valuable skills developed within slave families, when parents trained children through several generations. Carpenter Harry had two carpenter sons and two more who were skilled wheelwrights. Owners gained much from their expertise.[99]

Slave quarters and family composition tended to be similar on large and middling plantations throughout the Chesapeake colonies. Different patterns prevailed on small farms with only a few slaves. Here broad marriages were common, and extended kinship continued at a distance.

CHESAPEAKE SLAVE HOUSING:
A DYNAMIC TRADITION

As the slave trade expanded in the eighteenth century, masters on larger plantations ordered their slaves to build shelters for themselves. In early years some of these structures had a strong African flavor. At Keswick Plantation in Midlothian, Virginia, a curious building still stands today. It is a circular structure, with a single door and several windows, an open fireplace in its center, and a round chimney. The building was built of brick, which is why it has survived. The brickwork is laid in a conventional European bond, with moldings and window sashes typical of Virginia's colonial architecture. But the shape and proportions of this building are remarkably similar to circular houses that were to be found in some parts of Africa. This structure is a rare surviving example of early slave barracks.

By the mid-eighteenth century, slave barracks yielded to single-family cabins or duplex dwellings. An early traveler in Maryland observed that, as a rule, "a negro Quarter is a number of Huts or Hovels, built at the same distance from the mansion House, where the negroes reside with their Wives and Families, and cultivate at vacant times the little spots allowed to them."[100]

Early examples of these "huts" tended to be small, crude, and simple. Through time, they became "more private, substantial and orderly." Evidence of increasing size by the end of the eighteenth century appears in measurements for the federal direct tax assessments in 1798.[101]

Their design also developed in other interesting ways. Gradually a modal house–type emerged in slave quarters throughout large parts of the Chesapeake colonies. It has been called the "up-and-down house." Often it was a one-room cottage or cabin with a sleeping loft above, which gave the buildings their name. These up-and-down slave houses were large by comparison with slave cabins in other American regions. In Maryland's St. Mary's County, early surviving slave quarters tended to be square, about sixteen by sixteen feet. Others were rectangles, roughly thirteen by twenty feet. At Sotterley Plantation, slave houses were sixteen by eighteen feet. They tended to grow larger through time. On Charles Carroll's Doughoregan Manor, their mean size was fifteen by twenty feet.[102]

These Chesapeake up-and-down houses were made of various materials and constructed by various techniques. At Sotterley they were made of strong planks, neatly sawn on all four sides, laid horizontally on top of one another, notched at the ends, and carefully pinned or pegged together. At Bacorove in Prince George's County, Maryland, they were "nogged" with bricks to make them warmer in the winter and cooler in the Chesapeake summer. Later, at Jefferson's Bremo in Virginia, slave houses were made of rammed earth, an architectural fad that drew Jefferson's attention in the early nineteenth century but did not catch on.

In the late eighteenth and early nineteenth centuries, the dimensions of these houses grew a little larger, and something important happened in the use of internal space. As time passed, the lower room was divided by partitions. Overhead sleeping lofts also could be closed off. In these changes, we find growing attention to privacy between parents and children, and the separation of adult generations as well. Here is physical evidence of change over time in the dynamics of slave families and marriages.

CHESAPEAKE SLAVE MARRIAGE
CUSTOMS AND OTHER CUSTOMS

Marriages changed too. Slave unions in early years tended to be casual, informal, and regulated by the will of master. A Virginia slave recalled, "Ef mastah
seen two slaves together too much he would marry them. Hit didn't make no
difference ef yer won't but fourteen years old."[103]

Other masters became increasingly attentive to age, but nearly all encouraged early marriages and frequent childbearing. One former slave later remembered such a conversation:

"How ole is you, Becky," asked Marsa.
"Sixteen, Marsa," she tole him.
"How ole' is you, Charlie?"
"I'm sixteen too, Marsa."
"Dats all right den. Cain't have no chillun marryin on my place."[104]

Slaves preserved strong marriage customs from Africa. Unlike their European masters and mistresses, African slaves maintained a strict cultural prohibition of first-cousin marriages. Practices among the European planter class
were the opposite. First-cousin marriages among the Chesapeake slaveholding
elite were widely encouraged as a way of keeping land and wealth within the
family, and they helped to make the Chesapeake elite into an extended cousinage. African Americans in the Chesapeake went a different way. They preserved a taboo against cousin marriages that lasted for many generations—a
striking pattern of cultural persistence from Africa.[105]

In the nineteenth century, even as some of these customs persisted, the
lives of Chesapeake slaves were increasingly regulated by other rituals of modern life, in ways uniquely their own. Examples were wedding ceremonies.
Masters and slaves together invented customs and traditions of legitimacy in
ways that changed through time and varied in different cultural regions.

The timing and season of slave marriages differed from one part of the
South to another. Almost everywhere, slave marriages were uncommon in the
seasons of heaviest farm labor such as the plowing time, planting time, and
harvest time. The marrying seasons came between or after these busy periods.
In Tidewater Virginia and coastal South Carolina, slaves married in December, especially at Christmastime, as their English masters and mistresses had
done before slavery appeared.

On sugar plantations in Louisiana, a favorite time for marriage was in August and September, after the lay-by, when the busiest work of cultivation had come to an end, but the harvest had not begun. Upcountry cotton plantations tended to have two marriage periods, one during the lay-by, the other in the winter. About one third of slave marriages occurred in December and January, and nearly a quarter in July. This bimodal pattern was very common.

In Virginia, wedding rituals for field slaves developed in a distinctive way. One common set of ceremonies were called lamp marriages. They normally happened on Saturday night, so as not to interrupt the work routine of the plantation. Tom Epps, a slave in Prince George's County, Virginia, recalled that "all de courtin' an' marryin' was done at night . . . marsa would hol' a light, read a lil' bit, an' den tell 'em dey was married."[106] The use of lamps developed into a folk ritual that was unique to slave marriages in this region, as whites were mostly married in the light of day. The lamps themselves became part of the ceremony.[107]

In the upper South, the weddings of house servants were often performed in a manner similar to the marriages of whites. They had no status in law, but customs were powerful. Weddings brought the two castes together. Often masters and mistresses served as members of these slave weddings—standing beside the bride and groom as "waiters" and "maids of honor." A former house slave, Fannie Berry, lived on a plantation near Appomattox Court House, and remembered her wedding day with vivid clarity. It was also a lamp marriage, but with a difference:

Elder Williams married me in Miss Delia Mann's (white) parlor on de Crater Road. The house still stands. The house was full of colored people. Miss Sue Jones and Miss Molley Clark (white) waited on me. Dey took de lamps and we walked up to de preacher. One waiter joined my han' an' one my husband's han'. After marriage de white folks give me a [re]'ception an' honey, talkin' bout a table—hit was stretched clean 'cross de dining room. We had everything to eat you could call for. No, didn't have no common eats. We could sing in dar an' dance old squaer dance all us choosed, Lord, Lord, I can see dem gals now on dat flo' skippin an' a trottin.' An' honey, dar was no white folks to set down an' eat fo' you.[108]

SLAVE FAMILIES

Chesapeake slaves in Maryland and Virginia testified to the profound importance of the quarter in their identity and their sense of belonging. Here again a leading example was Harriet Tubman (1820?–1913). She was born in Maryland's Dorchester County on the lower Eastern Shore. Later when she escaped to the North and freedom, she said, "I was free; but there was no one to welcome me to the land of freedom. I was a stranger in a strange land, and my home after all was down in the old cabin quarter, with the old folks, and my brothers and sisters. But to this solemn resolution I came; I was free, and they should be free also." [109]

Most plantations had a surplus of males over females, which encouraged women to form early unions on the same plantation. Nucleated households were the rule. Masters often gave each couple incentives for forming a union, including a cabin of their own. [110]

In the mid-eighteenth century, numbers of African slaves in the Chesapeake began to multiply more rapidly by natural increase. Mortality remained high, but fertility rose higher. By the 1750s African women were giving birth more frequently than European women, with shorter birth intervals and higher rates of intramarital fertility.

The timing of slave births appeared in parish registers, which have survived in particular abundance for York and Gloucester counties. Seasonality of slave births differed from those in white families. Several studies have found that slave women "usually conceived . . . from midsummer through the fall. Few conceptions began during winter or early spring. . . . Consequently many of the women were in the final stages of their pregnancies during the months of heaviest field labor." Similar patterns appeared in other plantation colonies such as South Carolina. Several historians have concluded from quantitative evidence that slave women carefully timed their conception cycles to reduce field labor. [111]

AGE AND YOUTH IN CHESAPEAKE SLAVERY: ANOTHER PAN-AFRICAN TRADITION

In Chesapeake bondage, slaves themselves testified that much attention was given to modes of address within the quarters. Titles were of high importance. These rules were carefully observed by master and slave alike, and were still strong in the author's Chesapeake youth. A slave in Maryland recalled that from "the most oppressed slave to the most refined white family's children at the South," all "are taught to respect the old, black or white. Their children call old colored people aunt and uncle by way of respect. None use the word 'nigger' but the low and vulgar." [112]

Another remembered,

Southern children were taught to call the colored people "aunt" and "uncle" as titles of respect. They resented being called by their names without their title, and considered that it spoke ill for the manners of a child who would do so rude a thing. People of the same age called each other "brer" and "sis." This referred not to the natural relationship, but often to relationships within the church. On formal occasions they were "Mr." and "Mrs." Ignorance of this led me into sad disgrace one night with my usually indulgent Mammy Maria. She had taken me to see her brother married. I heard her address him as Mr. Ferguson, and at once asked, "Mammy, what makes you call Henry Mr. Ferguson?" "Do you think 'cause we are black that we can't have no names?" was Mammy's indignant reply. She could not be angry more than a minute with "her white chillun." [113]

In long-established parts of the Chesapeake South, respect for age became embedded in the plantation system. Through much of Maryland and Virginia, old slaves were addressed as "Auntie" and "Uncle." In African American speech, these English words became terms of deference. Frederick Douglass remembered that "Auntie" and "Uncle" were used

according to plantation etiquette, as a mark of respect, due from the younger to the older slave. Strange . . . it may seem, among a people so uncultivated, and with so many stern trials to look in the face, there is not to be found among any people, a more rigid enforcement of the law of respect to elders than is maintained among them. . . . A young slave must approach the company of the older with hat in hand, and woe betide him, if he fails to acknowledge a favor, of any sort, with the accustomed "tankee." [114]

Douglass's autobiography began by reciting the roll of uncles and aunts on the plantation where he grew up. The portraits were not always affectionate. Some uncles and aunties were remembered as cruel, selfish, and tyrannical. Others were gentle, wise, and loving. Many elders were figures of authority, even as higher authorities above them were cruelly constraining.

In long-settled Tidewater regions where slave communities became very strong, a custom of old-age support developed among African Americans. Much to the moral outrage of slaves, masters found that they could "retire" slaves to the woods, and build them a hut, and the other slaves would look after them. Many reports survive of older slaves supported by their own kin.

In Virginia, Moses Grandy remembered:

> When my mother became old, she was sent to live in a little lonely log-hut in the woods. Aged and worn-out slaves whether men or women are commonly so treated. No care is taken of them, except perhaps, that a little ground is cleared about the hut, on which the old slave, if able, is to raise a little corn. As far as the owner is concerned, they live or die, as it happens; it is just the same thing as turning out an old horse.

He continued,

> Their children, or other near relations, if living in the neighborhood, take it by turns to go out at night with a supply saved from their own scanty allowance of food, as well as to cut wood and fetch water for them; this is done entirely through the good feelings of the slaves; and not through the masters' taking care that it is done. On these night visits, the aged inmate of the hut is often found crying on account of sufferings from diseases or extreme weakness, or from want of food or water in the course of the day; many a time, when I have drawn near my mother's hut, I have heard her grieving and crying on these accounts; she was old and blind too, and so unable to help herself. She was not treated worse than others: it is the general practice. Some good masters do not treat their old slaves so: they employ them in doing light jobs about the house and garden.[115]

Douglass described the same customs in Maryland. His grandmother's owners "took her off to the woods, built her a little hut, put up a little mud chimney, and then made her welcome to the privilege of supporting herself there in perfect loneliness; thus virtually turning her out to die."[116]

Benedict tells another story of how "an old worn-out servant was left without support. He went to another plantation among his kin, but they treated him unkindly and he resolved to go out into the woods to die." He had been abandoned both by his master and his fellow slaves. A pious born-again Baptist slaveholder found him there, and took him in.[117]

A system of age relations developed in a slavery of small units that were more granular than in other slave cultures. It was also a society in which slave kinship was strong, and kin groups functioned as a system of mutual aid, supporting individuals in need.[118]

VERNACULAR SPEECH AMONG CHESAPEAKE SLAVES

When Olaudah Equiano was carried as a slave to Virginia, he found himself in a state of total linguistic isolation. "We saw few or none of our native Africans and not one soul who could talk to me," he wrote. ". . . I had no person to speak to that I could understand. In this state I was constantly grieving and pining, and wishing for death rather than anything else." His only choice was to learn to "smatter a little imperfect English," which he did very quickly.[119]

By that process, many plantations developed their own dialects. Frederick Douglass remembered that at remote Lloyd Plantation on Maryland's Eastern Shore the speech of slaves was

> a mixture of Guinea and everything else you please . . . there were slaves there who had been brought from the coast of Africa. They never used the "s" in indication of the possessive case: "Capn ant'ney Tom," "Lloyd Bill," "Aunt Rose Harry," means "Captain Anthony's Tom," "Lloyd's Bill," etc. *"Oo you dem long to?"* means "Whom do you belong to?" *"Oo dem got any peachy,"* means "Have you got any peaches?"

Douglass added, "I could scarcely understand them, so broken was their speech."[120]

By constant collision with the hegemonic English of plantation owners and overseers, the rougher edges of this pidgin speech were rubbed off in all but the most isolated places. In that manner was born yet another African American dialect in the Chesapeake region, which Frederick Douglass called Guinea Talk or Guinea speech.[121]

This was one of the most anglicized of all the many Afro-European slave dialects in North America—fundamentally English in grammar and syntax, and distantly related to the speechways of southern England in the seventeenth century. But it also included distinctive patterns of pronunciation and vocabulary which set it apart from the speech of Anglo Marylanders and Virginians.

Advertisements for runaway slaves described this speech in mediating

terms, as "speaks English though somewhat Negroish," or "speaks remarkably good English for a negro," or "speaks rather more proper than Negroes
in general." But many of these Chesapeake advertisements stated that slaves
spoke "good English or "proper English," which as linguist J. L. Dillard notes
in another context was "a term Europeans seemingly never apply to a pidgin
and almost never to a Creole." [122]

The distinctive pronunciation of this dialect converted *th* into d, as in *dis*
for this, and *dat* for that, *dey* for they, and *dem* for them; *de* for the and *wid*
for with. Hard consonants tended to disappear, as in *chillin* for children. Final
consonants also vanished, as in *tole* for told, *ole* for old, *worl* for world, *o* for
of, and *prayin* for praying.

Chesapeake vowel shifts were common, in *iggle* for eagle, *ketch* for catch,
and *git* for get. Initial vowels were omitted in *long* for along, and *nuff* for
enough. Consonants also shifted, making *v* of w, as in *vinter* for winter; *b* for
v as *ober* and *neber*; *gw* for a hard g as *gwine* for going, an added *r* in *marster*
for master or *Warshington* for Washington, and an added *me* as in *bimebye* for
by and by. [123]

Adjectives were used in adverbial forms, as in "He looked weakly." The opposite was also the case. A Virginia slave named Jacob in Gabriel's Revolt was
reported to have said, "I could kill a white man as free as eat." [124]

Verb forms also changed in interesting ways, particularly the verb to be,
as in "I is." [125] Typical of Virginia was the use of the verb *do* where Gullah
speakers used be. Union colonel Thomas Wentworth Higginson wrote "*done*
is a Virginia shibboleth, quite distinct from *been* which replaces it in South
Carolina. Yet one of their best [Virginia] choruses, without any fixed words,
was 'De bell done ringing' for which, in proper South Carolina dialect, would
have been substituted, 'De bell been a-ring.'" [126]

Plural markers were regulated by different rules, or no rules at all. Often
the plural *s* was added to nouns, as in *womans* for women and *mens* for men.
But sometimes it disappeared where frequent usage did not employ it as did
the slaves Douglass knew on the Eastern Shore. [127]

In these and other instances, the rules of grammar were subordinated to the
needs of rhetoric, rhythm, and cadence in this predominantly oral speechway.
Repetition and redundancy were used for emphasis, as in "great long pile." [128]
Other examples of Guinea speech were "mistis" for mistress, "cotched" for
catched, "smut" for soot, and "powerful mad" for very angry. [129]

In all of these ways, the speech of Virginia slaves seemed to be "somewhat
negroish" to white observers. Many of these characteristics also appeared in

other African American dialects. But the slave speech of the upper South, where the majority of the population was white, tended to be closer to a form of English which had been carried out of the south and west of England during the mid-seventeenth century, to which many African elements were added. In all of those various ways, local dialects of Chesapeake Guinea speech differed from Gullah speech in South Carolina, Geechee in coastal Georgia, and Gombo in Louisiana.

Guinea talk also spread westward from Virginia to parts of Kentucky. One observer noted that

> In Kentucky, "Marster" or "Massa" was usually pronounced with a broad Virginia *a*, as in ah [or "Mahsta."] Also "Mistress" was never pronounced "Missus," but "Mistus" or "Mistis"—generally the latter, and applied to the head of the house, as marster did to the whole plantation. It was not unusual to hear a slave speak of ole marster and ole mistis, or simply ole mars or ole miss, likewise of young marster, young mistis. The younger members of a planter's family however were usually addressed and spoken of as Mahs Toms and Miss Caroline.[130]

SPIRITUAL AWAKENINGS AMONG CHESAPEAKE SLAVES

In the midst of these developing cultural customs, a spiritual revolution took place among Chesapeake slaves, and also many of their owners in the course of the eighteenth century. It spread rapidly through the American colonies and was well advanced before the American Revolution.

In that era, Chesapeake slaves invented a new intensity of spiritual life for themselves. Much of it happened in slave quarters. Some of it occurred at clandestine meetings in deep secluded groves of old-growth trees, where slaves could not be seen or heard by others.

Here they gathered among spreading oaks (more than fifty varieties of oak in Maryland). Other favored places were beneath towering tulip trees. Only one variety, but it was *Liriodendron tulipifera*, marvelous to behold for its great height, straight trunk, brilliant, bright green tulip-like blossoms and tulip-shaped leaves. These sylvan giants were still common in the 1930s, 1940s, and 1950s. From my Chesapeake youth, I vividly remember the mystery and wonder that these great trees awakened in the mind of a Maryland child.

In plantation quarters and forest retreats, Chesapeake slaves invented a new spiritual faith for themselves. In the quiet moments of their own personal communion, slaves also created new systems of belief that combined at least three spiritual traditions. They brought together the intense spirituality of their African origins, the Christian faith of their Anglo-Chesapeake masters, and the spiritual beliefs of American Indians.

As early as 1680 in Virginia's York County, English clergyman Morgan Godwin observed that African slaves made much use of material objects that were believed to possess spiritual power. They were variously described as amulets, charms, and puppets. Godwin wrote that slaves "place confidence in certain figures and ugly Representations . . . to protect them." [131]

Archaeologists in the late twentieth century found many of these spiritual amulets and similar devices in excavations around rural slave quarters, urban cellars, and plantation outbuildings. These sacred objects also turned up in underground storage pits below slave quarters, and in graveyards and burial grounds. Some were marked with Christian symbols. Others were incised with African designs. Many came from American Indians. At Mount Vernon's slave quarters for the "Mansion Farm," archaeologist Dennis Pogue found among a trove of buried treasures a raccoon's baculum or penis bone with its distinctive curve, three to four inches in length. American Indians had used it as a fertility symbol, and African slaves borrowed it on George Washington's home farm at Mount Vernon. [132]

We know from Morgan Godwin's observations that spiritual movements were stirring among Chesapeake slaves at least as early as 1680, and probably earlier. Some sources document its growth in the late seventeenth century, and a surge in the mid-eighteenth.

From those sources, slaves created something new in the world—a spiritual movement of astonishing power. Even as they suffered from the incessant violence and oppression of forced labor, they found strength and solace in a new religion of soul freedom that was very much their invention.

On first impression, mid-eighteenth-century surges of spiritual religion appear to have coincided with the Great Awakenings in New England, the middle colonies, and much of Protestant Europe. But spiritual movements among African slaves in the Chesapeake region differed in their chronology. This was not part of a sequence of wavelike Awakenings that Richard Shiels has documented in quantitative records of conversions and church memberships among Congregationalists in New England. It was nothing quite like the First and Second Great Awakenings, allegedly punctuated among Yankees by a period of spiritual sleep. Another great awakening happened differently among Chesapeake slaves. Once started, it never stopped.

Evidence appears in the writings of many observers. A cause was growing competition among Christian denominations in the Chesapeake. Established Episcopal parish churches were most widespread but least active in recruiting new members. Very different were Presbyterian preachers such as Samuel Davies (1723–61). He was schooled in the "Log College" that later became Princeton, of which he was president. In 1743, he studied the sermons of George Whitefield. In 1747, Davies accepted a call from Hanover Parish in Virginia. There he preached in the style of Whitefield, and soon had hundreds of communicants. What amazed him was the "considerable number of negroes."[133]

He reached them not only through sermons and services but also the printed word. After one meeting he wrote that "about 70 Negroes" came to ask if they could learn letters and begin to spell. He wrote, "I have had more success than usual among the POOR Negroes. I have baptized 150 adults . . . and have made it a point of conscience to teach such of them to read." Davies was "amazed at the speed of learning. . . . Their natural genius is not at all discouraging and when they set about learning in earnest, it is astonishing what progress some of them make."[134]

In the 1770s and 1780s, Chesapeake slaves also adopted a new and very open expressive intensity of religious worship. Eyewitness accounts describe an abundance of revivals among both African slaves and free whites. One such event was a revival near Petersburg, Virginia, in February 1788, with intense waves of emotion, in which "some especially the blacks, lay struggling till they beat the earth with their hands, head and feet, while others kicked holes in the ground."[135]

In the 1780s Methodist missionaries became active in the Chesapeake. A peak moment (one of many) came in the summer of 1787. While the Constitutional Convention was meeting in Philadelphia, Methodist revivalists from Maryland's Eastern Shore converted hundreds of whites and "half as many slaves" in nearby gatherings of growing intensity. On the Eastern Shore especially, preachers also won many masters and mistresses to Methodism. Many of these converts turned away from slavery.[136]

Among slaves in that region, the soaring message of Christianity in the Gospels also gained power from its linkage to the spiritual strength of African religious traditions. In the possession of slaves these various beliefs enlarged each other and acquired deep meaning. And in former English colonies they also joined with expansive Anglo ideas of liberty and freedom, as we shall see.

QUARTERS AS SCHOOLS FOR SLAVE LEADERS

Through the eighteenth century, slave quarters on large plantations in the Chesapeake increasingly became small functioning communities. Most were built at a distance from the planter's great house. Many quarters had slave leaders, who sometimes resembled the Big Men and Big Mamas of African tradition. Chesapeake planters and overseers learned to treat these figures with respect and even deference, and gave them much responsibility.

In other southern regions, field leaders were called drivers, a word that implied subservience to a master's will; and a distance from other slaves. The word "driver" was rarely used in the early Chesapeake. Slave leaders in Virginia and Maryland were more commonly called "foremen."[137]

King Carter, Virginia's most successful planter, also knew his slave leaders by their African ethnic origins. Two of his foremen were called "Ebo George at Totusky" and "Ebo George at Head of River." These African Big Men led gangs in field work, with added authority in the quarters. That system spread widely through the Chesapeake. In northern Maryland, for example, Henry Ridgely had three "outlying quarters" run by Black foremen named Mingo, Dick, and Toby, apparently without daily white supervision.[138]

Within the slave quarters, yet another pattern appeared. Slave women became leaders in regulating domestic life. They were strong and even dominant figures, much as in African families. The quarters themselves and the families within them were matrilineal and matrifocal. On the Carroll estates in Maryland, the quarters took the names of senior slave women. It was much the same on the plantations of the Lloyd family. Vivid descriptions appear in later revisions of Frederick Douglass's slave narrative, and relevant material survives in the Lloyd Papers at the Maryland Historical Society.

Here again we find an echo of African cultures in the way these Chesapeake quarters worked. Women had been exceptionally strong in African families and groups. They also tended to be active traders in Igbo regions, and were treated with respect. Similar patterns appeared in many parts of Africa and in middle Maryland.[139]

A GROWING SPIRIT OF RESISTANCE

Historian Trevor Burnard found that treatment of Chesapeake slaves tended to grow worse in the years from 1700 to 1740, with extreme use of force and harsh treatment.[140] A leading cause was a surge in the African slave trade, and the growth of the slave population. In 1736, William Byrd II wrote to the Earl of Egmont, "Numbers make them insolent & then foul means must do, where fair will not." [141]

Acts of resistance by slaves in Virginia increased through the eighteenth century, and surges of capital punishment tended to follow. Hangings for illegal assembly, conspiracy, and insurrection took a sudden jump around 1730. In that year, six slaves were found guilty and hanged. [142]

Concern regarding "outliers" and runaways also increased. In 1729, a group of slaves left their plantations and headed west into Virginia's Blue Ridge Mountains. They took weapons, ammunition, and farming tools, and clearly meant to found a community beyond the frontier. Virginia leaders were surprised and concerned. A large force went after them, and the slaves were captured. Lieutenant Governor Sir William Gooch reported to the Board of Trade that militia units were being trained "for the future." [143]

In the early eighteenth century, Virginia's slave law had showed little of the obsessive fear of rebellion that marked the codes in South Carolina and West Indies, where Blacks outnumbered whites. But as the number of slaves increased in the Chesapeake region, a growing purpose of Virginia's slave law was to deal with bondsmen who refused to accept the station that had been assigned to them. Virginia legislators passed laws to deal with the possibility of slave insurrections, but masters worried more about acts of individual violence than collective rebellion. They were also concerned about depredations by runaways who tended to stay close to the plantations in the Chesapeake colonies. Laws of special ferocity dealt with these "outliers" who ran away, remained nearby, and returned in the night to steal supplies and tools. They were increasingly feared. After 1705, at any master's request, outlying slaves could be outlawed by the reading of a proclamation at church on Sunday, and "any person or persons whatsoever" could kill such an outlying slave on sight. If the outlying slave was caught alive, the same law authorized punishment by castration. [144]

Castration appears to have been less common in the early Chesapeake than in South Carolina, but in the period from 1710 to 1720, it was ordered by Virginia's Middlesex County Court for a broad range of offenses. Christopher Robinson's slave George was castrated for "running away, lying out, and destroying people's Stocks." So also was Peter, a slave of John Parke Custis. [145]

A partial revulsion followed. In 1769, castration was forbidden by Virginia law except for the rape of a white woman. But it was ordered with some frequency for that offense, not only for the act itself, but also the attempt or for suspicion of an attempt, and even for what appear to have been consensual acts between a Black man and a white woman. Four cases of castration appeared in Virginia court records as late as 1782, but Philip Schwarz, historian of law in Virginia, noted a decline in rates of conviction.[146]

Through much of the eighteenth century, slave laws grew more violent, and so also did actual punishments. In 1737 and 1746, Virginia slaves were burned alive for murdering a mistress or master, the old English penalty for "petty treason" against a master, as opposed to "grand treason" against the sovereign.[147]

County courts also permitted the killing of slaves by masters and overseers "during correction." In 1705, a new law required masters to ask the approval of county courts for "dismemberment" of habitual runaways, which could mean the hamstringing or cutting of tendons, or actual amputation of toes or a foot. These actions appear to have multiplied through time. King Carter wrote in his brutal way, "I have cured many a negro of running away by this means." [148] For acts of "insubordination" by slaves and servants, the laws of Virginia authorized a hierarchy of brutal punishments: whipping for a first offense, amputation of ears for a second offense, and death by hanging for

"An Overseer Doing His Duty Near Fredericksburg Virginia, 1798"

a third. The advertisements by owners for the return of runaways provide a quantifiable source for the growth of violence against slaves. Overall, this evidence shows that extreme violence against slaves was more common in the Chesapeake than in Carolina.

RESISTANCE AND PUNISHMENT IN EIGHTEENTH-CENTURY VIRGINIA SLAVERY: THE SAGA OF LANDON CARTER AND HIS SLAVE TONEY

Even in the face of frequent and brutal punishment, Chesapeake slaves invented elaborate rituals of nonviolent resistance that could drive a master wild with fury and frustration. A case in point was Landon Carter's plantation at Sabine Hall. In 1770, Carter was master of nearly fifty thousand acres and approximately five hundred slaves. He held many positions of honor and trust in Virginia.

One would think that this gentleman of Virginia would have been supreme in power and dominion over his own plantations. But Carter's diary is a running record of frustration with slaves whom he was unable to dominate. Sometimes frustration overflowed in wild acts of irrational aggression, which further diminished his power and authority.[149]

Carter frequently punished his slaves with severity, often by his own hand. But he confessed to his diary that their behavior was worse after "correction" than it had been before. From Carter's own records one finds that in repeated tests of will, it was often the angry master who was defeated. The slave was much battered and bloodied, but often got the better of the master in a prolonged struggle.

A case in point was the saga of Toney, a slave carpenter on Carter's home plantation at Sabine Hall. Toney often infuriated Carter by working slowly, going about his own jobs, talking back, drinking so heavily that he was too drunk to work efficiently, and sometimes refusing to work at all, on grounds of illness, indisposition, or injury at the hand of his frustrated master.

On March 14, 1770, Toney was ordered to build a picket fence around a garden at Sabine Hall. Carter gave him his instructions and returned two hours later to discover that nothing had been done. Toney on his own initiative had gone off to do another job. "I asked him why he served me so," Carter wrote. "He told me because it would not answer his design."[150]

The master was outraged by this answer and attacked Toney with a walking stick. "The villain had so constantly interrupted my orders that I had given him about every job this year that I struck him upon the shoulders with my stick." So heavy were the blows that a stout hickory walking stick was "shivered to pieces." The next day Toney refused to work at all, and "laid himself up with a pain in that shoulder." Carter vowed that "Mr. Toney shall as certainly receive ample correction for his behaviour to me as that he and I live. . . . I might as well give up every negroe if I submit to this impudence." [151]

Toney was whipped again for that offense. A few days later he was sent back to build a picket fence by the dairy and the hen house. He worked more slowly than ever. Carter warned him that "he would certainly have another whipping," and the slave began to work very rapidly. But he nailed the fence palings so unevenly that some were a foot higher than the others. Carter raged against him, ordered him to start over, and rode away. He returned to find that the fence was more even, but this time "the pales were all laid slanting." Once again the master gave Toney a beating, and "as his left shoulder was to me I gave him one small rap upon it." The slave promptly downed tools, got "compleatly drunk," and refused to work at all, "saying that his shoulder was so sore he could not drive a nail." For this offense, the slave was locked up "for Monday morning's chastisement." [152]

Toney was reduced in rank to a field slave and sent out with a tobacco gang. According to his owner, he infected the entire gang with what Carter called his "villainy." The master wrote: "Toney I see is the conductor of this idleness. He leads the gang and . . . not one goes a hill before him, which is a certain proof of villainous lazyness and all shall pay for it tomorrow." [153]

Toney's resistance was not a solitary act. Among other slaves he was a leader—even a principled leader. Carter himself attributed Toney's behavior to the effect of what he called New Light Christianity. "I believe it is from some inculcated doctrine of these rascals that the slaves of the colony are grown so much worse." This powerful master was reduced to paroxysms of impotent fury. Carter often inflicted pain on Toney, but never broke his will or spirit. [154]

The story of Toney was not unique. On January 5, 1770, Carter's hands were prizing tobacco, and Carter raged furiously against all his "lazy people." On January 18, Carter's diary was a litany of complaint against many of his slaves. Toney was still "creeping and whindling [sic] about pretending to be sick." Nassau was "constantly drunk." Others were "malingering," or working slowly. [155] On January 23, Jimmy was punished for "pretending to be ill and lame." Carter tried another punishment: "I have forbid him coming home to his wife at night." [156]

Another bondsman whom Carter called that "scoundrel Nat" was a constant thorn in his side. "There will come a warm day for the punishment of these things," the angry master wrote in the privacy of his journal.[157] On February 6, Carter complained that all his wood gangs were working too slowly to please him. "My greatest puzzle is now wood for my fires and the keeping my people to get it for me, who with no better authority than what I see . . . will do nothing."[158]

Carter complained that slave women were as difficult to control as the men.[159] On February 20, a sheep was missing and a slave named Lydia was suspected of having killed it for food. "I have ordered her correction," he noted.[160] Peg and his spinners "instead of their usual day's work spun but 2 ounces apiece," and Peg his "cook wench" committed some act of favoritism to her daughter, "for which that lady and three spinners are all whipt this morning."[161]

When a Chesapeake master started a cycle of "correction," he sometimes became more vulnerable to his slaves than they were to him. If he treated them severely they could revenge themselves against his property. Landon Carter's slaves frequently did so, sometimes in very costly ways. On February 9, some of his bondsmen drove an entire herd of his cattle into a muddy cornfield where "each mired and died," a heavy loss to their owner. Carter commented, "When people can do this notwithstanding they have a plain level road, to be sure correction can never be called severity." On March 14, a draft ox was released by the young slave Manuel and fell down a gully, breaking its neck. "My orders were to whip that boy severely," Carter wrote. "For these things no justice can be done without a most severe correction."[162]

Carter's slaves found many means of retribution, and used them frequently. At Sabine Hall, even the house slaves were out of control. In late February of 1770, Carter had no fire on a cold night because his house servant Nassau was "most excessively drunk." The master of Sabine Hall sat shivering in the splendor of his mansion, cursing his defiant servant. In the morning, Carter enforced his "resolution of correcting the drunkenness in my family by an example on Nassau." But "the scoundrel Nassau" continued to defy him by getting drunk again.

This account comes entirely from a master in the eighteenth-century. Narratives of Virginia slaves told the same story of defiant workers, frustrated masters, and frequent punishment, followed by more defiance.[163]

One of many consequences at Sabine Hall was increasing rigidity in plantation management. Carter turned away from innovation. He confided to his diary that "carts and plows only serve to make overseers and slaves extremely lazy."[164]

Yet another consequence on many plantations was a complex three-cornered conflict among masters, overseers, and slaves. Each of these three groups exploited conflicts between the other two, and created yet more dysfunction in systems of forced labor.

An illustration appears in the narrative of William Grimes, a slave on another Virginia plantation during the late eighteenth century. He had much trouble with an overseer called Thead [*sic*]. On one occasion he remembered that

> Thead came to me, threatening to whip me, and caught hold of me for that purpose. I clinched him and told him that if he struck me, I would inform my master about his riding a favorite horse without my master's consent; that my master had already enquired of me why the horse grew so poor, but I would not tell him. The fear of detection induced him to let me go, telling me to be a good boy, and he would not flog me.[165]

FREEDOM AS A SPIRITUAL MOVEMENT AMONG TIDEWATER SLAVES

During the middle years of the eighteenth century, a new spirit was stirring among Chesapeake slaves. In 1752, three Virginia slaves called Peter, James, and Harry Cain stood trial before the Court of Brunswick County in Virginia. They were charged with "insurrection and conspiracy to commit murder," a capital crime in the colony. Peter was thought to be the leader, and he was sentenced to death. The others were tried for another crime that was not in the statute books. They were accused of "being privy to an Opinion entertained among many Negroes of having a Right to their Freedom, and not making a discovery thereof [to their masters?]." They were found guilty of a misdemeanor and ordered to receive thirty-nine lashes.[166]

The trial record of this curious case inspired Philip Schwarz, a historian of law in Virginia, to ask how many other slaves in Virginia claimed "having freedom as a right," and when and where and why. From his unique command of Virginia's county court records, Schwarz turned up case after case from about that same period. In Surry County he found two slaves, Will and Abraham, who were punished for "rebellious talk" as a misdemeanor in 1752. At Williamsburg another slave named Tom was found guilty of "rebellious speech," and given twenty-five lashes in 1753. In Lancaster County several slaves gathered "in a body," openly welcomed the news of Braddock's defeat in 1755, and "imagine that the French, will give them their Freedom."[167] Lieutenant Governor Robert Dinwiddie ordered they be "taken up" and punished.[168]

This insurrectionary spirit kept growing among Virginia slaves through the 1760s. In 1767, the slave Jupiter (alias Gibb), six feet tall with his back scarred by severe whipping, was accused of "stirring up the Negroes." He ran away and disappeared. During the Christmas season of 1769, an overseer in Hanover County tried to "correct" a field hand, and the result was a "pitched battle of 40 to 50 slaves." These clashes multiplied in the 1770s. In that era when free Virginians were insisting on their rights from British officials, enslaved Afro-Virginians demanded their own rights from the free Anglo-Virginians. The spirit of liberty was contagious. And when we look closely at the timing in the mid-eighteenth century, it often appears to have started to grow first among slaves.[169]

FREEDOM BEYOND THE BLUE RIDGE: THE SAGA OF BLACK NED, 1752

Other slaves found opportunities in Virginia's backcountry, before it came to be called the western frontier. An example was a slave born about 1711, and "commonly known as Black Ned." He first appeared in the "iron country" of eighteenth-century Pennsylvania, forty miles west of Philadelphia between the falls of the Schuylkill River and the forks of Brandywine Creek. An early account described him as "middle-siz'd and well set," wearing "an old leather jacket and breeches." He was owned by at least three ironmasters and worked at many jobs in the iron industry as a laborer, woodcutter, and carter. Most of his work was done around forges and furnaces. It was hard, heavy, dangerous labor, much of it done by slaves. Ned mastered many skills, learned to "speak both English and German," and somehow became able to read and write and do arithmetic and bookkeeping.[170]

His masters allowed Black Ned to buy his freedom at 6 pounds a year, on an early installment plan. It took six years, and he paid every penny of their price. With a receipt in his pocket as proof of freedom, he headed not east and north but west and south, into the Valley of Virginia beyond the Blue Ridge Mountains. There he took a full name for himself, Edward Tarr, saved his money, and searched for land.

In 1752, he explored Virginia's western frontier in the upper James River Valley and decided to settle in Augusta County. Its Great Wagon Road had become the major migration route for thousands of North British borderers from Pennsylvania and the Chesapeake region moving through the Valley of Virginia to pockets of rich soil in the Southern Highlands.

Ned established a busy blacksmith shop where he repaired broken wagons, fixed weapons, and made new tools that were urgently needed on the frontier. Ned's free white neighbors valued his presence, and fully accepted him when he married a "Scotch" wife. Intermarriage was unlawful in Virginia, but Ned was highly skilled at his smithy, and his wife made herself useful by baking bread and cakes for neighbors and travelers.

There was trouble when Black Ned took in another white woman named Anne Montgomery. Others alleged that she was "a common disturber of the peace and a woman of evil fame and behavior." But the people of Augusta County tended to be tolerant of Black Ned. He acquired 270 acres on the Wagon Road and flourished there. A kinsman of his former master appeared and attempted to reenslave Ned with no success. Neighbors and the local court rallied to Black Ned's support, noted that he had been a valued freeholder for ten years, and protected him. The Valley of Virginia grew at least a little more open and free by Black Ned's continuing efforts and example.[171]

LEGAL REFORM AND STRUCTURAL CHANGE IN THE CHESAPEAKE SLAVE-OWNING CLASS DURING THE REVOLUTIONARY ERA

From 1760 to 1799, ethical attitudes toward slavery were changing in Virginia and Maryland. In 1769, Virginia's legislature forbade castration of slaves for running away and staying away, on grounds that the "punishment is disproportionate to the offence, and contrary to the principles of humanity."[172]

That "spirit of humanity" increased during the revolutionary era. Special courts were created in Virginia for slaves accused of committing crimes, with specific rules of due process. After 1772, no slave could be condemned to death except by unanimous vote of four judges. Conservative masters such as Landon Carter were appalled, and feared the worst. "By the new law," he wrote, "a Negro now cannot be hanged, for there must be four judges to condemn him, and such a court I am persuaded will never be got . . . public frugality occasioned this law that they might not have too many slaves to be paid for."[173]

Landon Carter was mistaken about that. In fact, many slaves were sent to the gallows by Virginia's courts. But repression and control of slaves was not the only purpose of these statutes. Virginia's slave code was also a cultural artifact, designed to preserve an idealized social order. But the ideals themselves were changing in many ways during the era of the Enlightenment, the American Revolution, and the new republic.

MANUMISSION IN LAW AND PRACTICE, 1780–1830: RICHARD AND JUDITH RANDOLPH FOUND A FREE COMMUNITY OF FORMER SLAVES, 1796

The largest single victory against slavery in eighteenth-century Virginia was the Manumission Law of 1782. Several leading Virginians also proposed general schemes for the end of slavery in their state. In 1796, St. George Tucker published a comprehensive plan for gradual emancipation and emigration. George Wythe also presented a general scheme for "simple abolition," grounded not in broad ideas of humanity and equality, but the very opposite. Wythe condemned African slaves in general as "drones" and "pests of society," and wished to see them all removed from the state. Both of these proposals for the general abolition of slavery in Virginia failed, as did similar efforts in Maryland.

But the manumission movement in Virginia gave rise to individual acts of emancipation, sometimes on a large scale. One of them was the work of Richard Randolph, a younger cousin of Thomas Jefferson, stepson of St. George Tucker, and a student of George Wythe. Richard Randolph respected the humanity of his slaves. One of his closest and most cherished friends was his slave Syphax, his "body servant" who had also served his father and stepfather. Richard Randolph was sent north to college, not to those nests of Puritans at Harvard or Yale, or even to Presbyterian Princeton, but to Episcopal King's College in New York, now Columbia University. Syphax went with him.

When Randolph returned to Virginia, he suffered a sharp and sudden decline in his health, which often happened in the Chesapeake region. Young Randolph deeply disliked slavery, but he also inherited more than a hundred slaves. When his health failed in the 1790s, he wrote a will that condemned slavery in strong terms and expressed a heartfelt desire for the emancipation of all his slaves. After his death in 1796, his wife, Judith, sought to carry out his wishes. She freed nearly one hundred slaves and gave them a tract of land that was called Israel on the Appomattox River. A major effort was made to distribute land to each family. Other slave owners were appalled and tried to block it. Friends of Randolph and his wife helped the freed slaves defend their freedom. To the surprise of many in Virginia, the county courts upheld the will, and supported the slaves in their claims to freedom and property.

Colonel James Madison (not the president but another), publisher Edmund Ruffin, and other pro-slavery Virginians relentlessly attacked the settlement. They insisted that Israel on the Appomattox proved Africans to be unfit for freedom. But local manufacturers employed the "Israelites," as they were called. Israel on the Appomattox struggled, but survived.[174]

The news spread swiftly among Chesapeake slaves. Many years later, former Virginia slave Fannie Berry dictated her memoir of bondage in Virginia, and remembered that "there was a settlement called Umbler [?] in Appomattox. This, honey, wuz a Negro settlement. Dem people wasn't never slaves. They would hire dem selves to work for white folks but dey always went to dere own homes at night time." She also remembered that Israel on the Appomattox was a standing reproach to racists, pro-slavery writers, and to slavery itself in antebellum Virginia.[175]

EMANCIPATION AND VIRGINIA'S WESTWARD MOVEMENT: EDWARD COLES FREES HIS SLAVES ON THE OHIO RIVER

Edward Coles (1786–1868) was another young Virginia gentleman with a conscience. As an undergraduate at William and Mary, he asked his teachers "how the owning of men could be justified," and got a straight answer from the president of the college, yet another James Madison, who became Episcopal bishop of Virginia.

Bishop Madison "frankly admitted it could not be rightfully done. . . . Slavery was a state of thing that could not be justified on principle and could only be tolerated in our Country by . . . the difficulty of getting rid of it."

In 1808, Coles inherited a plantation of 782 acres in Albemarle County. An interval of public service followed. On his return, he resolved to sell his Virginia lands, lead all of his slaves to the free state of Illinois, and give them their freedom without conditions. In 1819, Coles put his slaves on a flatboat, and as they floated down the Ohio River, he told them they were all free. They could go where they wished or come with him to Illinois. He promised to give each family 160 acres of land to help them get started in freedom, and settled in a town that he called Edwardsville, Illinois.

Later Coles was elected governor of Illinois. He played a pivotal role in keeping slavery out of the northwest territories, and was an important founder of antislavery politics in the North. This native Virginian also gave strong support to a young friend named Abraham Lincoln, and to the abolition of slavery throughout the United States.[176]

So common was this impulse that the census of 1850 found that the state with the largest emigration of African Americans from Virginia to any state was Ohio, where slavery had been forbidden and they lived in freedom.

JOHN RANDOLPH OF ROANOKE AND HIS STRUGGLES WITH EMANCIPATION

Many other Chesapeake owners liberated their slaves in the early republic. The radical Jeffersonian leader John Randolph of Roanoke joined the international movement against slavery. He began to call himself an "ami des noirs," after the French movement of that name. At the same time, he was also one of the largest slaveholders in Virginia. At his death in 1833, Randolph left a large estate with 383 slaves, and three different wills on their disposition. The first will emancipated them all. The second added the acquisition of land for them, and provided $38,000 for their passage to another state.

But the third will reversed the first and second documents and ordered that all the slaves should be sold to other owners. Virginia courts declared that this third will was invalid, as Randolph was judged to have become insane and an opium addict when he wrote it. On this ground the courts supported the emancipation of Randolph's slaves.

The slaves were taken to Mercer County, Kentucky, where white settlers drove them away by threat of force. Many moved north across the Ohio River. Some were able to acquire land near Rossville, Ohio. Their descendants still live near Rossville and continue to celebrate an annual Randolph Freedom Day.[177]

EXPERIMENTS IN GRADUAL EMANCIPATION: JOHN HARTWELL COCKE

Always, even in the last years of slavery, a few enlightened planters were swimming against the rising tide of slavery in many southern states, and parts of Virginia and southern Maryland.

An example was General John Hartwell Cocke (1780–1866), a Virginia gentleman and master of Bremo plantation. Cocke was a slave owner who hated slavery and judged it to be "the great cause of all the evils of our land." He strongly supported gradual emancipation with colonization, and prepared his own slaves for freedom by teaching them to read and write. Cocke organized schools on his plantation and his wife taught slave children.

For that sustained effort General Cocke and his wife were ostracized by some Virginians. When ostracism failed to stop them, General Cocke was assaulted and severely beaten by racist thugs in 1835. But he and his literate slaves survived and continued to oppose race slavery and racism in Virginia.

GRADUAL EMANCIPATION: MARYLAND'S JOHN MCDONOGH AND HIS SLAVES

A Maryland friend of John Hartwell Cocke was another exceptional master. John McDonogh was an affluent Baltimore merchant of Scots-Irish background, who moved to New Orleans and made a large fortune there. In Louisiana McDonogh acquired many slaves, and increasingly came to detest slavery. On his own, he worked out a scheme of gradual emancipation, in which his bondsmen worked half of every Saturday to buy their freedom. He also taught his slaves to read and write, and sent several of them to Lafayette College in Pennsylvania. For this sustained private effort to end slavery on his own property, he was reviled in Louisiana, ostracized by planters and merchants, and driven from that state. McDonogh returned to Maryland and continued his efforts to free his slaves.[178]

In Maryland, McDonogh was not alone. John Kelso of Baltimore was a butcher who purchased three slaves in their teens, held them for eight to ten years, encouraged them to save their money, and manumitted them. Many others acquired slaves, converted their lifetime bondage into term slavery, and helped them prepare for a life of freedom. Other Chesapeake masters also turned against slavery in similar ways. In Baltimore, more than 20 percent of all slaves sold were not enslaved for life.

CHANGES IN THE CULTURAL CONDITION OF SLAVES: LITERACY AND FREEDOM

Some southern pro-slavery scholars of an earlier generation liked to believe that "the plantation was a school for the education of African savages."[179] If so, the curriculum did not include reading and writing.

Masters had many reasons for wishing to keep slaves in a condition of ignorance and illiteracy. Some believed that "to teach a Negro to read . . . would spoil him."[180] Others thought in more practical terms. Often mentioned was the pass system, which restricted the movement of slaves beyond their plantations without written permission. These passes were rough informal notes on small scraps of paper, often crudely scribbled by semiliterate masters, and easily forged by semiliterate slaves.

In most slave states, the teaching of slaves to read and write was forbidden by law. But a different pattern appeared in the laws of four states. Virginia and Maryland, Kentucky and Tennessee all formally allowed slaves to learn reading and writing, but only until the end of the eighteenth century.

In most of the South, slaves were not allowed to learn these dangerous skills. The results appear in quantitative evidence of fugitives reported by advertisements by their masters. In the upper and lower South taken together, during the eighteenth and nineteenth centuries, only 2 to 3 percent of runaway slaves were described by their masters as able to read or write.[181] Scholars have observed that masters were sometimes the last to learn about the literacy of their slaves.[182] But for the slaveholding South as a whole, the quantitative evidence of fugitive slave notices was generally confirmed by other sources, such as slave narratives. Peter Randolph was the only one of eighty-two slaves on Carter Edloe's plantation who could read or write.[183] Lewis Clarke recalled that "I never saw more than three or four that could properly read at all. I never saw but one that could write."[184] Overall, levels of literacy were very low. In the South as a whole, many sources suggest that about 2 percent of slaves were able to read or write.

THE GROWTH OF LITERACY AMONG CHESAPEAKE SLAVES

Always the great majority of slaves were illiterate, but literacy varied by region. It is not a surprise to find that the highest proportion of literate slaves were to be found in Virginia, Maryland, Delaware, and Kentucky, with large numbers among hired slaves and freed men and women.

Incomplete evidence appears in fugitive slave advertisements. Masters in Virginia reported that as many as 7 percent of their runaways could read or write or both. Another study of slave advertisements in a smaller area of Kentucky found that of 350 runaways, 71 were thought by their masters to be able to read or write—20 percent.[185]

Literacy increased slowly among Virginia slaves through the eighteenth century, but after 1799 that trend suddenly reversed in every region where we were able to measure it. A growing fear of slave rebellion in general, and the example of Santo Domingo and Haiti in particular, were major factors. This new trend continued in the 1830s. St. George Tucker wrote with alarm, "Every year adds to the number of those who can read or write, and the increase of knowledge is the principal agent in evoking the spirit we have to fear."[186]

This attitude was much reinforced by a great fear that swept the South after Nat Turner's Revolt in 1831. One of its many consequences was a concerted effort to keep slaves in ignorance. But the repression that followed Turner's rebellion deepened a trend that was already under way.

As always, individual masters and mistresses went different ways, and for a broad variety of reasons. John Hunter, raised a slave in Maryland, remembered that he was sent to school with the white children "to keep me out of the way." His mistress did not know what else to do with him. A new master was quick to take him out of school at the age of ten, saying he "knew too much anyhow," and decided to sell him. Hunter ran away to Canada and used his literacy to write a memoir.[187]

Other masters found it convenient to have a few literate slaves. Emily Burke remembered a slave who

> could read, write, cipher and transact business so correctly that his master often committed important trusts to his care. . . . He read with great eagerness every northern paper that came within his reach, and had by this means gained a good knowledge of the political state of our country. At the time I was there [1840], he was deeply interested in the election of President Harrison, as were slaves generally in the Southern states, for they were all Harrison men, and they were bold enough to assert publicly that "when William Henry Harrison became president of the United States, they should have their freedom," and "believing as they did, who could not lament the death of the worthy President."[188]

Many young slaves were secretly taught to read by white children. Dan Lockhart, a slave in Frederick County, Virginia, wrote that "the children had taught me to read."[189] James Sumler, born circa 1829, in Lower Norfolk County, Virginia, remembered that he "got the younger white children to teach me," while they hid together in a hayloft on Sundays.[190]

John Thompson, a slave in Maryland, was taught to read and write at the age of eight by a white orphan who was living in his master's household. At eighteen he read a speech by John Quincy Adams where he learned "there was a place where the Negro was regarded as a man, and not as a brute." His master found out, whipped him severely, and threatened to sell him south; but his mistress intervened and won him a reprieve. A little later he was accused of forging passes for other slaves, and escaped to the North.[191]

William Anderson recalled that as a child in slavery he bought a book and, "though very young, say about eight or nine years old, I often carried my book in my hat or pocket, for fear of detection, or hid it in the leaves or earth for fear of the lash." With the help of white children he learned his letters and practiced in the sand. But his master caught him, and "he would tell me that I was studying philosophy, and that he would whip it out of me." Anderson kept at it. After he learned to read, he organized a clandestine Sunday School for other slaves, but again "the white people found it out, and gave us our orders never to meet for instructions any more, on peril of the lash; and our little school was broken up forever."[192]

Literacy was more accessible for city slaves. Frederick Douglass wrote that he learned to read in Baltimore from "little white boys whom I met in the street." His mistress also instructed him. Douglass was a slave in a prosperous household where he had plenty to eat, but poor white children in Baltimore were often desperately hungry. Douglass was quick to seize an opportunity, and swapped bread for knowledge.[193]

Another young slave named Robert did much the same thing in Virginia. He gave apples to white children who taught him to read.[194] Henry Morehead, a slave in Louisville, sneaked away from his home to attend a night school, but his master "found it out, and sent policemen to break the school up. This put an end to my schooling—was all the schooling I ever had." Morehead was told that "I could learn rascality enough without it" and "that *niggers* going to school would only teach them rascality." He added, "I always felt injured when a slave and when free, at the use of that word."[195]

Other slaves combined literacy with the special skills of an oral culture and its powers of memory. One account came from a Virginia slave girl:

Was serving gal fo' missus. Used to have to stan' behind her at de table an' reach her de salt an' syrup an' anything else she called fo'. Ole Marsa would spell out real fas' anything he don't want me to know 'bout. One

day Marsa was fit to be tied, he was in setch a bad mood. Was ravin'
'bout de crops, an' taxes, an' de triflin' niggers he got to feed. "Gonna
sell 'em, I swear fo' Christ, I'm gonna sell 'em," he says. Den ol' Missus
ask which ones he gonna sell and tell him quick to spell it. Den he spell
out G-A-B-E and R-U-F-U-S. 'Course I stood there without battin'
any eye an' makin' believe I didn't even hear him, but I was packin' dem
letters up in my haid all de time. An soon's I finished dishes I rushed
down to my father an' say 'em to him jus' like Marsa say 'em. Father
say quiet-like, "Gabe and Rufus," an' tol' me to go on back to de house
and say I ain't been out. The next day Gabe and Rufus was gone—dey
had run away. Marsa nearly died, got to cussin' and ravin' so he took
sick. Missus went to town an' tol' de sheriff, but dey never could fin'
dose two slaves.[196]

Masters who wished to keep their slaves in subjection were right to fear
literacy. Often the ability to read and write led directly to freedom. Lewis
Hughes remembered learning with another slave named Thomas, a coachman
on the plantation. The two taught themselves to read and write with the aid
of itinerant plasterers who came to their plantation. They practiced by scrawl-
ing letters on the side of the barn. Their master discovered their letters and
ordered his driver to watch them carefully. "You must watch those fellows,
Louis and Thomas, if you don't they will get spoilt—spoilt. They are pretty
close to town here." Tom and Louis became more careful about where they
wrote their letters, but they kept learning. Soon Tom could write letters to his
family in Virginia, and he sent them in the mails. The postmaster gave them
to his master, and Tom was severely whipped. After his whipping, he wrote
himself a pass, and escaped.

A planter named George Larrimore in Virginia had a slave who was
taught to read and write, and quickly mastered the art of imitating the
handwriting of masters in the neighborhood. The slave used his knowledge
to forge passes for slaves including himself. He escaped to Philadelphia,
and sent back "a saucy letter" to his former owner, thanking him for his
education.[197]

When illiterate slaves became free, one of their first acts was to learn how
to read. William Johnson, who escaped to Canada, wrote, "I have been trying to learn to read since I came here, and I know a great many fugitives
who are trying to learn." After emancipation, Booker T. Washington wrote

a vivid chapter on literacy in his classic autobiography, *Up from Slavery*. He remembered in Virginia that it was like "a whole race going to school." That story tells three truths: the extent of illiteracy in slavery, the hunger for learning after emancipation, and the speed with which it was acquired. Masters and slaves alike were keenly aware that reading was freedom, and writing was power.

RISING RESISTANCE AMONG SLAVES AND BRUTALITY AMONG MASTERS

There were many ironies of slavery in a free society. For one, when bondage grew more humane in some ways, it came to be more actively resisted. There was a saying in the Old South: slaves with bad masters dreamed of good masters; slaves with good masters dreamed of freedom.

The spirit of resistance had always existed within slavery. During the late eighteenth and early nineteenth centuries, it grew rapidly in the Chesapeake region. In the early republic, slaves increasingly fought back. For a valuable slave who struck a white man in the Chesapeake, the most common penalty was not capital, but it was very severe. As a child, Josiah Henson watched helplessly when it was inflicted on his own father. Henson had been born near Port Tobacco, Charles County, Maryland, in 1789. One day, a white overseer tried to rape Henson's mother. His father came to her rescue, knocked down the assailant and nearly killed him. The overseer begged for his life, and promised no retribution. But word reached the authorities and Henson's father was sentenced to stand in the public pillory, receive one hundred lashes, and have one ear nailed to the pillory, and severed from his body.

His son never forgot that scene, and many years later he vividly described it.

> The day for the execution of the penalty was appointed. The Negroes from the neighboring plantations were summoned for their moral improvement to witness the scene. A powerful blacksmith named Hewes laid on the stripes. Fifty were given, during which the cries of my father might be heard a mile, and then a pause ensued. True, he had struck a white man, but as valuable property he must not be damaged. Judicious men felt his pulse. Oh! he could stand the whole. Again and again the

thong fell on his lacerated back. His cries grew fainter and fainter, till a feeble groan was the only response to the final blows. His head was then thrust against the post, and his right ear fastened to it with a tack; a swift pass of a knife, and the bleeding member was left sticking to the place. Then came a hurra from the degraded crowd, and the exclamation, That's what he's got for striking a white man. A few said "It's a damned shame." [198]

EXPLOSIONS OF VIOLENT RESISTANCE: GABRIEL'S REVOLT IN VIRGINIA

The example of the American Revolution of 1775, and the success of the great slave risings on the Caribbean islands inspired many attempts at armed revolt by slaves in the United States. A leading example was the attempted rising in Virginia called Gabriel's Revolt in 1800. It was disrupted by a massive storm, and led to extreme measures of judicial repression.

One of the leaders, probably not Gabriel Prosser himself, was asked by the judge if he had anything to say in his own defense. According to an eyewitness who was also a lawyer, the defendant responded in "a manly tone of voice, 'I have nothing more to offer than what General Washington would have had to offer had he been taken by the British and put to trial. I have adventured my life in endeavouring to obtain the liberty of my countrymen, and am a willing sacrifice to their cause.'" [199]

The Virginia slaves who organized Gabriel's Conspiracy were explicit in their respect for George Washington and others as revolutionary leaders, even as they rejected them as masters. [200] Gabriel's conspiracy was followed by the Easter Plot of 1802, for which ten slaves were executed in Virginia, and 231 transported for conspiracy and insurrection. [201]

Movements by Gabriel Prosser succeeded in one major way. What did freedom mean to slaves in the Chesapeake? Was it different from freedom among the master class? Did it vary from one region to another? Did it change through time? The short answer was yes, and yes again, and yes twice more. To slaves who were most cruelly oppressed, freedom meant an end to whips and chains and brutal treatment. To others it meant the right to live free, to form a family, and possess the power to preserve it.

A keen observer of these events was St. George Tucker. He listened to the Virginia slaves who organized Gabriel's Revolt and compared them with slaves who had joined Lord Dunmore's revolt in 1775. Tucker invited Virginia's master class to consider

> the prodigious change which a few years has made among this class of men. . . . Compare the late conspiracy with the revolt under Lord Dunmore. In the one case, a few solitary individuals flocked to that standard, under which they were sure to find protection. In the other, they in a body, of their own accord, combined in a plan for asserting their claims and rest their safety on success alone.

He added,

> The difference is, that then they fought for freedom merely as a good; now they also claim it as a right.[202]

Other Virginia gentlemen were deeply moved by the conduct and demeanor of these slave leaders. John Randolph of Roanoke, who was in the courtroom, wrote to Joseph Hopper Nicholson that they showed pride and courage, a "sense of their natural rights," and "a contempt for danger." Earlier in life, Randolph had been a self-styled "ami des noirs, a friend of blacks." Later he emancipated his slaves.[203]

The example of Gabriel Prosser and others who stood with him reverberated through many generations of African folklore. Folk ballads called "Gabriel's Defeat" and a sea chantey called "Gin'ral Gabriel" were sung by American seamen, slave and free, Black and white, for many years.[204]

NAT TURNER'S REBELLION: VIOLENCE, FEAR, PANIC, AND REPRESSION

The secular trend of increase in active freedom-seeking by people in bondage continued to the end of slavery. It was, however, interrupted from time to time when waves of panic, fear, and repression of slaves swept the South. One of those Great Fears occurred after the Haitian Revolution, which greatly frightened slaveholders throughout the Western Hemisphere.

Another panic occurred in 1831, after Nat Turner's insurrection, when slaves remembered that the white population turned upon them with savage violence. In Richmond, Henry Brown recalled that immediately after Turner's

The Nat Turner Rebellion

rising, "great numbers of slaves were loaded with irons; some were half-hung as it was termed—that is they were suspended from some tree with a rope round their neck, so adjusted as not quite to strangle them—and then they were pelted by men and boys with rotten eggs." [205]

In Edenton, North Carolina, Harriet Jacobs remembered that the news of Nat Turner's Rebellion

> threw our town into great commotion . . . it was a grand oppor-
> tunity for the low whites, who had no Negroes of their own to
> scourge. . . . Those who had never witnessed such scenes can hardly
> believe what I know was inflicted at this time. . . . Everywhere men,
> women and children were whipped till the blood stood in puddles at
> their feet. Some received 500 lashes; others were tied hands and feet
> and tortured with a bucking paddle, which blisters the skin terribly.
> The dwellings of the colored people, unless they happened to be
> protected by some influential white person, who was nigh at hand,

were robbed of clothing and everything else the marauders thought worth carrying away . . . many women hid themselves in woods and swamps.[206]

MASTERS RESPOND: THE MODERNIZATION
OF VIOLENCE IN THE CHESAPEAKE

The gentlemen-planters of Virginia and Maryland prided themselves (far beyond the fact) on knowing how to "manage their people" without harsh methods. They could not be forever pummeling "their people" without destroying both their property and their reputation. A British traveler in 1816 observed that Virginia slaves "are subject to the lash—but it is seldom used. A master is thought badly of, who treats his slaves ill."[207]

A gentleman slave owner in Virginia or Maryland faced a difficult dilemma. Compulsory slave labor required the application of force in the Chesapeake region, as everywhere else. In candid moments, most masters agreed that slaves could not be kept at work without violent compulsion. The result was a continuing conflict between ethics and interest, conscience and circumstance, a gentleman's honor and a slave driver's necessity. Slaves responded accordingly, with a mix of deference and deep disdain. William Wells Brown recalled that when his master, who was also his father, fell ill, "I prayed fervently for him—not for his recovery, but his death."[208]

"Negroes can't be governed except with the whip," a planter told a traveler. "On my plantation," he continued, "there wasn't much whipping, say once a fortnight, but the Negroes knew they would be whipped if they didn't behave themselves, and the fear of the lash kept them in good order."[209]

That master understood a dark truth that is too often forgotten in memories of the Old South. Slavery was fundamentally a system of forced labor. Its organizing purpose was to make people work against their will. To that end, its continuance required the repeated application of violence. The logic of this peculiar institution was inexorable in that respect. Wherever bondage existed in America, physical violence against slaves was always threatened and often applied—sometimes with savagery beyond belief.

The important questions here are not about whether violence existed in slavery, for those two things were one. The more interesting problems are about the form and function of violence, its frequent variations, its regional differences, cultural consequences and its patterns of change through time.

In general, variance in the use of violence by masters against slaves did not appear as a change of frequency in violent physical punishment, but rather as a more complex transformation in form and circumstance. Major changes also occurred in the climate of opinion that discouraged masters from advertising their cruelties. Even in the eighteenth century, some masters had shown signs of embarrassment in advertising the scars inflicted on their slaves. One Georgia owner sought the return of a slave-cooper who was "covered from the waist downwards with the marks of a severe correction," and added in italics, "*given him in the West Indies.*"[210]

Criminal courts in most slave states sometimes looked into cases of extreme maltreatment. So also did the churches. In some religious denominations, trials were conducted of slave holders who were thought to have abused their slaves.[211] Physicians also increasingly took action against cruel masters who had severely injured their slaves. Lewis Hughes, a Virginia slave, remembered an instance when an overseer whipped a slave so severely with a bullwhip that Hughes was sent for a doctor.

> When Dr. Hemingford, the regular family physician, came, he said it was awful—such cruel treatment, and he complained about it. . . . When Boss came home he was called on by the town officials, for the case had been reported to them. Boss, however, got out of it by saying that he was not at home when the trouble occurred. The poor slave was sick from his ill-treatment some four or five months, and when he recovered there was a running sore left on his body from the deep cuts of the whip, which never healed. I cannot forget how he looked, the sore was a sickening sight; yet when he was able to walk he had to return to the field.[212]

Public opinion exercised its sway against cruel and unusual punishments.[213] In general, these pressures placed constraints on both sides of the question. If a master treated his slaves more cruelly than others, he suffered the opprobrium of neighbors who visited their own guilt upon him. If he was more kindly than most, then neighbors would complain that "his niggers spoil our niggers."[214]

The market itself also increasingly imposed another set of limits. "Scars upon a slave's back," wrote Solomon Northup, "were considered evidence of a rebellious or unruly spirit, and hurt his sale."[215] As the internal slave trade grew larger, this factor became more prominent. In an open economy where slaves were capital and their value was fixed by the free market, a master could not exercise ab-

Engraving of Solomon Northup, from Northup's memoir,
Twelve Years a Slave

solute and unlimited force over his slaves without diminishing his own capital. Brutal torture and maiming of slaves yielded to a new refinement of cruelty.[216]

Masters responded to these pressures not by ceasing to use violence (without which slavery would have collapsed) but by using it in new ways. During the nineteenth century, the technology of punishment changed, becoming more elaborately rationalized, in ways that served the masters' interests.

In a perverse application of human reason, the technology of corporal punishment was refined. The whip itself was improved by modern science in the nineteenth century. One version of this new progressive lash was made of cord or thin strips of hide, or plaited leather about four feet long. Another used a light buckskin "cracker" about twelves inches in length. Only the cracker was intended to touch the slave's back. When it did so, it made a horrific noise and caused a painful sting, but did not break the skin or scar the flesh as severely as an old-fashioned cowhide or bullwhip. Dr. J. W. Monette recommended this modern whip and noted that in the circle of his acquaintance "very few

planters would allow slaves to be whipped on the bare back with a rawhide
or cowskin."[217]

Other masters preferred to use paddles, which caused great pain, especially when bored with auger-holes, but did not break the skin. These
instruments bruised and blistered the skin without cutting or scarring it.
A refinement on this invention was reported from Stafford County, Virginia, during the 1850s: "A strip of board perforated with holes and rough-
ened with tar and sand. The air, drawn through the holes as the board
smote the skin, would raise blisters, while sand increased the smart without
deeply cutting up the flesh, and thereby diminishing the market value of
the slave."[218]

In the mid-nineteenth century, many masters abandoned both the whip
and the paddle for the strap—a flat piece of leather that raised a painful welt
but did not cut or scar the body. This was thought to be moderate correction. Masters and mistresses used a strap on their own children. Another
punishment that left no marks was the water pump, in which a slave's head
was placed beneath a pump, and water was poured over his head for a long
period—a terrifying torture that simulated drowning and left no physical
marks. It was an American ancestor of water boarding.[219]

Whipping continued unabated to the end of slavery as the primary instrument of control. Quantitative evidence appears in studies by Paul Escott
of 397 slave narratives for the nineteenth century. Everywhere in the South
a majority of slaves reported personal experience of whippings or beatings.

THE PROFESSIONALIZATION OF VIOLENCE IN NINETEENTH-CENTURY SLAVERY: SLAVE WHIPPERS, SLAVE BREAKERS, SLAVE HUNTERS, AND SLAVE JAILERS

In the nineteenth century, North American slavery became modernized in
ways. The control of slaves gave rise to specialized professions throughout the
southern states. Moses Grandy remembered that "in all slave states, men make
a trade of whipping negroes. They ride about inquiring of jobs of persons who
keep no overseer . . . his fee is half a dollar. Widows and other females, having
negroes, get them whipped in this way."[220]

For hard cases, another specialized occupation in the nineteenth century
was the professional slave breaker. The most widely known example appeared
in the autobiographies of Frederick Douglass. On Maryland's Eastern Shore,
his master sent Douglass for a year to a farmer named Edward Covey, who

served Maryland's more affluent gentleman-planters as a professional "nigger breaker," as they called him.

In Douglass's own account, Covey nearly succeeded in breaking him by constant surveillance, frequent beatings, and ingenious punishments. Covey observed that Douglass took pride in his work, as did many slaves, and gave him jobs that were almost impossible to do well. On one occasion, Douglass was ordered to plow a field with a team of green oxen which had not been broken to the yoke. The agony of that impossible job was intense.

After many weeks of defeat, frustration, unremitting cruelty, and humiliating failure, Douglass tells us that he came very near the breaking point. He escaped that fate only by a desperate act of will and courage. Douglass waited until the two men were alone. Then he turned on Covey, attacked him with great violence, beat him severely, and broke the slave breaker. They made a dangerous agreement. Both men agreed to silence: Covey to preserve his reputation as a slave breaker; Douglass to survive unscathed—an ending that rarely happened.[221]

Some of this professional slave breaking was done by men who also became professional slave jailers. In the mid-nineteenth century, private slave jails multiplied in Baltimore, Richmond, Alexandria, and other Chesapeake towns. Several slave jails operated openly in the city of Washington, near the White House and the Capitol. Their primary business was slave trading and slave shipping, with secondary specialties in slave punishment and slave breaking. Some slave jails also dealt in slave kidnapping. Much of that business happened after dark. Many people knew what went on in these places, and some tried to stop it. In Baltimore, Elisha Tyson, the wealthy Quaker enemy of slavery, did so repeatedly, and even raided establishments where it was known to happen. But many people below the Mason-Dixon line looked the other way.

Slaves later remembered that the use of violence varied widely among slave owners. Some masters actively protected their slaves from physical abuse. One slave remembered of his owner that "even de paterollers 'spected him." Others recalled slaves who refused to be beaten and could not be broken. For them, other methods were invented. The common solution, used by many masters including George Washington, was to sell them to the West Indies in the eighteenth century or to the Deep South in the nineteenth. Slave markets became active instruments of control in all of these ways.

But the worst cruelty of Chesapeake slavery was not endemic violence, common as it was. Far more cruel was the active encouragement of family formation and family growth, followed by deliberate family disruption. Family separation through sales was openly practiced by owners and itinerant slave buyers on a large scale in Virginia and Maryland, more so than anywhere else in the United States.

A CAPITALIST REVOLUTION IN LATE CHESAPEAKE SLAVERY: FREE MARKETS, ENTREPRENEURIAL MASTERS, AND MONETIZED SLAVES

Other trends transformed American slavery as an economic system, especially in its later years. In the nineteenth century, the American economy grew at a great but unstable rate. Real wealth per capita doubled every thirty years. But that upward trend was broken by major market panics, shattering crashes, and deep depressions that began circa 1785, 1819, 1837, and 1857. Debt-ridden masters were vulnerable in these sharp downturns, and slaves were even more at risk.

Chesapeake masters responded to credit crises by monetizing their slaves in various ways. The most common method was to sell some of them into a large and insatiable southern market, a brutal business. Sales shattered slave families and caused great suffering. Even so, that practice grew inexorably everywhere, and this native Marylander notes sadly that it was most widespread in the Chesapeake region.

Another way to monetize slaves was to hire them out in a growing rental market, which has been comparatively little studied. This method was much preferred by masters who wished to gain income while preserving capital. Slaves also favored hiring, as a way of gaining a measure of control over their lives, without totally disrupting their families.

In the Chesapeake region, slave hiring gave rise to annual events at Christmastime, when masters and slaves gathered at "hiring grounds," often near county seats. In this process, slaves themselves became active agents. Their own masters sometimes did not attend, but sent slaves with a written pass, plus a few coins for food and shelter. The slaves often met prospective employers and bargained over terms.[222]

For hired slaves, results were often mixed. Some "hirelings" were cruelly used by employers who had no stake in their long-term health or welfare. Others gained more than they lost. Some worked at several jobs and were able to buy the freedom of their families. Parties to these transactions had more to gain when hired slaves moved to a town or city. Urban life was difficult in some ways for hired slaves, but it offered more jobs, higher wages, and greater opportunities.

URBAN GROWTH AND CHESAPEAKE SLAVERY

For Chesapeake slaves, other opportunities expanded in the half-century after American independence, when the entire region experienced an urban revolution which had a major impact on human bondage.

Most visible in the Chesapeake region was the rapid growth of Baltimore City. Founded circa 1729, Baltimore was a small village as late as 1776–77, when the Continental Congress took refuge there, and its members complained about the absence of urban amenities.

Baltimore's population doubled from 1776 to 1790, and redoubled in every decade through the early nineteenth century. By 1830, Baltimore was the second-largest city in the United States, larger than Philadelphia and Boston, and smaller only than New York. In 1860, it was by far the biggest city in the slaveholding states.[223]

Baltimore grew mainly from foreign trade. One of its two hundred urban neighborhoods is still called Canton, and was named by a merchant in the China trade. The city also profited from its inland communications. Freight costs to Baltimore from the Ohio and Mississippi Valleys were lower than to other Atlantic seaports, by a factor that Baltimoreans called the Differential in reverent tones.

At the same time, Baltimore also became an industrial city—first with flour mills and breweries, then shipbuilding, heavy industry, food products, and consumer goods. All this activity attracted migrants from Europe, the Caribbean, Appalachia, and the South.

Baltimore grew as part of an entire Chesapeake urban system, with an expanding web of smaller cities such as Washington, Richmond, and Norfolk, and shire towns in the 170 counties of Maryland and Virginia. From 1790 to 1860 these urban places attracted increasing numbers of African American slaves, hirelings, fugitives, and free people of color.

Many African Americans left accounts of this urban migration. The most familiar example is that of Frederick Douglass. His owner on the Eastern Shore sent him to work for a relative in Baltimore. Douglass later wrote that "life in Baltimore, when most oppressive, was a paradise," compared with plantation toil. He added, "I had something of the feeling about that city, which is expressed in the saying, that being 'hanged in England is better than dying a natural death in Ireland.'"[224]

Baltimore offered African Americans entry-level jobs as unskilled laborers, draymen, porters, deckhands, and stevedores. Families in the city also

employed growing numbers of maids, cooks, and washerwomen. In consequence, a majority of African American migrants to Baltimore were girls and
women. Openings also existed for boys and men in semiskilled jobs as sailmakers and ship-caulkers (Douglass's job), and skilled employment as blacksmiths. Slave women also found highly skilled work. Expert seamstresses and
dressmakers were often African Americans in the southern states. As people
of color multiplied, middle-class opportunities opened for teachers, ministers, funeral directors, barbers, tavern keepers, grocers, liquor dealers, retailers, and service trades who served an expanding free African American urban
population.

Many African Americans in Baltimore began in deep poverty, but some
began to accumulate wealth. An example was George Hackett, who arrived
from rural Maryland. He took a job as an unskilled coal heaver, saved his pay,
and bought the coal yard. Thomas Green, an immigrant from Barbados about
1813, began as a barber and bought rental properties. These entrepreneurs
thrived in the face of angry violence by Baltimore's legendary white mobs,
who assaulted Black workers, looted Black businesses, and burned Black
homes while town leaders looked the other way.[225]

Despite growing violence in Baltimore, many of these African Americans slowly began to get ahead. In 1813, a grand total of 39 "Free Negroes"
owned taxable property, assessed at a total of $8,463, an average of $217
each. By 1832, their numbers increased to 207 owners, and their taxable
wealth had grown to $157,113, with an average holding of $759. In 1860,
348 "Free Negroes" were assessed for $449,138, with an average of $1,291
each.

Tax assessments were a small fraction of actual wealth-holding, but the
trends were representative of growth rates. In forty-seven years from 1813 to
1860, numbers of recorded African American property owners in Baltimore
City increased ninefold (900 percent). The average size of individual holdings
rose sixfold (624 percent), and total assessed wealth rose 5,200 percent.[226]

Residence patterns showed another dynamic trend. African Americans
lived in all of Baltimore's many wards. In the most affluent neighborhoods,
slaves resided in attics, cellars, and kitchens of their owners' homes. Other
slaves and free families of color had small homes of their own, often on
alleys between major streets, sometimes with poor white neighbors next
door. An example was Slemmer's Alley, east of Jones Falls, on the southern
edge of Baltimore's Old Town. In 1827, city directories listed residents of
Slemmer's Alley as eight households, five white, and three Black. By 1850,

it listed forty-four households: twenty-nine white, fifteen Black. Some alleys became small communities, racially mixed. Similar patterns of "alley life" also appeared in Richmond, Washington, and other cities from the late eighteenth to the early twentieth century, when Jim Crow and racial zoning became the rule.[227]

In Baltimore other free people of color lived in neighborhoods of their own. The largest was in South Baltimore's 17th Ward, on the peninsula behind Locust Point, Whetstone Point, and Fort McHenry. By 1817, Baltimore also had growing African American middle-class neighborhoods. One of them was on Gallows Hill near the north edge of Old Town.[228]

As these populations increased, African churches multiplied rapidly in Baltimore. In 1793, a group of Black Methodists leased a building on Sharp Street near the waterfront, and asked permission of Methodist leaders to found their own church without white stewards or trustees. Bishop Francis Asbury refused to agree, but they went ahead anyway. By 1802, they owned a lot and erected a handsome neoclassical meetinghouse. Their leaders were laymen such as Richard Russell, a prosperous blacksmith; and Jacob Gillard, a carpenter and housewright. Both were active in many forms of community building.[229]

Other African churches appeared from New England to Savannah. Martin Delany observed, "Among our people, generally, the Church is the Alpha and Omega of all things."[230] But Baltimore was distinctive in one important way. Historians have observed that it had "the greatest denominational variety of black churches." By 1850, it had sixteen denominations of Black Protestantism, with dozens of churches and chapels, and thousands of members. The proportion of church members was higher among Black Baltimoreans than their white neighbors.[231] These churches in turn founded libraries and schools—both Sunday schools and day schools. They also encouraged the formation of societies for mutual aid. All were voluntary associations, founded and supported by African Americans before the Civil War.

These urban institutions also served a regional population that was larger than communities of color in the city itself. Through the early republic and beyond, rural slaves moved in and out of urban centers, especially on Sundays to attend church, and to sell their produce in street markets. Masters sent other slaves into cities on errands, sometimes as a regular routine. Chesapeake plantations kept their own boats, which were built, manned, and captained by slaves, and frequently in motion. The institutional life of the urban Chesapeake had a broad reach through the region.[232]

EMERGENT AFRICAN AMERICAN URBAN
LEADERS: BALTIMORE'S DANIEL COKER

A consequence of this urban activity was the emergence of African American
leaders in the Chesapeake. One individual example might represent that trend.
Daniel Coker (1780–1846) was a Methodist churchman with many roles and a
large following. He was a native Marylander, born Isaac Wright in Frederick or
Baltimore County. His father was an African slave named Richard Wright, and
his mother was an English indentured servant called Susan Coker.

An old Maryland law of 1715 required "mulatto bastards" to remain in
bondage to the age of thirty-one.[233] But his servant mother urged her son to
strive for freedom, and his siblings pitched in. A white half-brother taught
him to read and took him to school, where he excelled. In his teens he ran
away to New York, changed his name to Daniel Coker, continued his studies,
and found a calling. Bishop Francis Asbury recognized his talent, ordained
him as a Methodist deacon, and licensed him to preach.[234]

Daniel Coker

In 1802, Coker returned to Maryland where he was still in bondage. white friends helped him buy his freedom. He became active in Baltimore's Sharp Street Methodist Church, which was controlled by its white members. Coker also became a leader in another group that founded a new Bethel African Methodist Episcopal Church, entirely run by African Americans. In two years, Bethel had six hundred members, and Coker became their minister. He was recognized as "the leading black church figure in Baltimore."[235]

At the same time, he also founded two of Baltimore's best and most long-lived African schools: the Sharp Street African School, and Bethel School. Many of his students, male and female, became African American leaders in their turn. In 1820, Coker's pupil and protegé William Watkins founded the Watkins Academy for Negro Youth, a free classical secondary school. Every year it took in fifty to seventy African youngsters, and prepared them for leadership in business and the professions.[236]

In Baltimore, Daniel Coker was primarily known as a spiritual leader of African Americans, but he also reached people of other ethnic groups through much of northern Maryland. He became a highly successful evangelist, preaching in Hagerstown, Frederick, and other towns, but he worked mostly in Baltimore and the surrounding countryside. He also organized Methodist camp meetings on the Liberty Road northwest of Baltimore, and attracted large biracial crowds. White clergy were alarmed. At least one white convert was formally censured by his church for attending Coker's camp meeting.[237]

Coker was extraordinary in his embrace of different causes. In Maryland, he strongly opposed slavery, and was outspoken in support of complete abolition. At the same time, he also reached out to slave owners in hope of uniting many Christians in a common cause.

He also supported the colonization movement in Africa—not as a unitary solution for all Africans, but as one choice among many, for those who might wish to go that way. At the same time, he also worked actively for the extension of civil rights in the United States to all freed slaves. In 1816, Coker gave strong support to the Protection Society of Maryland, a biracial association that promoted the individual rights of freed slaves, by intervening in particular cases, and also by seeking to enact general measures in Maryland's House of Delegates and Senate. The Protection Society also tried to protect individual African Americans from gangs of kidnappers and predators who roamed the city.

Most of all, Daniel Coker was an architect of strong African American communities in Baltimore. He was a tireless promoter of opportunity in jobs and housing, and a builder of strong institutions for young and old alike. In politics he was an advocate of political rights for all free men. That effort was much needed in Baltimore, after a Jeffersonian reform act in 1802 extended voting in Maryland to all white men, and disfranchised people of color in the same act. In Maryland, Jeffersonian democracy grew in part by supporting racism, as did Jefferson himself. Most free African Americans became supporters of the Federalist Party, which in Maryland tended to be conservative on many questions, but liberal on the rights of free African Americans.

More striking than the wide range of Daniel Coker's many causes was the large spirit with which he served them. Something of that spirit appears in a portrait engraved by John Sartain, circa 1820. It is the cultivated image of an African American leader of mixed ancestry, dressed in a black clerical suit of impeccable cut, with an immaculate white shirt and stock of the latest fashion. His posture is upright, and his firm features are set in a candid gaze. It is an image of intelligence, maturity, strength, and confidence, combined with a warmth that appears in the hint of a smile that animates his face. His hair proudly displays his African origin, in combination with the latest refinements of European fashion that prevailed among African American elites in the new republic. Altogether this refined engraving of Daniel Coker is the image of something new in the American world—a Chesapeake African American Gentleman of a New School, born in bondage, and raised in a regional tradition of leadership that combined a spirit that was both suaviter in modo, and fortiter in re.[238]

That same spirit appeared in Coker's writings, especially an antislavery pamphlet of forty-three pages that he wrote and published in Baltimore in 1810, "humbly dedicated to the People of Colour in the United States of America." It was radical in substance, moderate in tone, and sweeping in its argument for a total abolition of slavery, to be achieved gradually throughout the United States.

Coker called it *A Dialogue Between a Virginian and an African Minister*.[239] He invented a dialogue that took the form of an extended conversation between an Anglo-Chesapeake gentleman of the Old School, and an Afro-Chesapeake preacher of what Methodists called the New School. Both of Coker's characters, Afro and Anglo, kept the manners and codes of Chesapeake gentlemen. Elaborate courtesies are exchanged in a spirit of mutual respect. The two men listened intently to each other and they shared a passion for truth, individual rights, and the rule of reason. Both were believing Christians, and they made frequent reference to scripture in their conversations. Both cherished the values of the American Revolution, and shared a common respect for liberty, freedom, and human rights. One was thinking mainly about the right of slaves to freedom. The other was concerned about the right of masters to their liberty and property.

In Coker's pamphlet, through argument after argument, each exchange ended when the Anglo-Chesapeake gentleman yielded to reason, logic, and scriptural authority. After many rounds of discussion, he agreed in the abstract that "there should not be a slave in the United States. But how this could be brought about, I cannot see." [240]

The Afro-Chesapeake minister proposed a gradual process that led to total emancipation by a fixed date. He suggested that slaves should work for themselves one day a week, and when they earn a "stipulated sum" they would gain another day, until they succeeded in purchasing their "entire freedom." The master's rights of property were respected, and the slave's right to freedom was achieved. The Virginia gentleman at last agreed: "*That* might be done, and in my opinion, ought to be done." And they also agreed to unite in the publication of such a plan. [241]

Many (not all, or even most) of the slaveholding class respected Daniel Coker, in part because of the spirit of refinement that he brought to his many causes. Coker's pamphlets also offered evidence of "what God is doing for Ethiopia's sons in the United States." One pamphlet included lists of African ministers in holy orders in Philadelphia, New York City, Boston, and Baltimore. Others listed local African preachers of the author's acquaintance in Baltimore, and identified fifteen African churches with a membership count of 31,884. A third added a list of "descendants of the African race who have given proofs of talents," by their own published writings. [242] All this had an appeal to Maryland gentlemen in the nineteenth century.

RURAL AFRICAN AMERICAN LEADERS: UNCLE JACK IN SOUTHSIDE VIRGINIA, 1746–1843

In Virginia's Prince Edward County, another African American spiritual leader emerged during the late eighteenth century. People both slave and free called him Uncle Jack. He had been born in Africa around the year 1746, kidnapped as a child of seven, and carried as a slave to the lower James River in Virginia. There he was bought by a planter named Stewart, and put to work near Nottoway, which was then part of Prince Edward County, between the Appomattox and Roanoke Rivers.

Slavery had hard edges in Southside Virginia. In the mid-nineteenth century, an Anglo resident called it a place of "moral darkness." As late as the mid-twentieth century it was a fortress of Jim Crow, and the strongest bastion of resistance to civil rights in the Chesapeake region.

But Uncle Jack found a way to flourish there, as a moral leader who was held in high esteem by people of many ranks and creeds and ethnic origins. There was something about Jack that attracted people from the start. As a small boy he learned English on his own initiative, by persuading his master's children to teach him to read in return for gifts of nuts and fruits. Always he was described as having a "great acuteness of mind." He learned not only to read and write, but also taught himself "to speak English without an accent."

He was converted to evangelical Christianity by Anglo minister, John Blair Smith, later president of Hampton-Sydney College. Uncle Jack said to him, "He turned my heart inside out." Jack himself began preaching to slaves, and was licensed by Baptists to meet actively with their fellowships. Soon he was asked to speak before members of the master class, found himself welcomed to plantation houses on Virginia's Southside, and was "encouraged to mingle with the best society the country afforded." [243]

Jack traveled widely through rural neighborhoods and won the hearts of Black and white, slave and free, with his gospel message and Christian manner. Many people in the region began to call him Uncle Jack. He cultivated the humility and simplicity of Jesus, lived in a simple log cabin, and dressed in the plainest clothing. A great lady of the planting class presented him with a "well made black suit of the finest fabric." Jack wore it once, and returned it with thanks. He explained that "if I wear them I shall be obliged to think about them, even at meeting." [244]

Much of what we know about him comes from the writings of white fellow clergy in many denominations, who held him in high respect. The leading source is a book-length biography by William Spotswood White, a leading Presbyterian minister who knew him well, and was inspired to write his biography a few years after Jack's death.

Jack lived a long and active life for nearly a century. After his death in 1843, at the age of about ninety-seven, people mourned his passing as "one of the most gifted and honored sons of old Virginia." Jack was remembered in Southside Virginia as a spiritual leader who raised the tone of moral choices in a slave society that had much need of them. [245]

Uncle Jack gained a special place in the lives of many who knew him, but he was not unique. Other spiritual leaders flourished in Chesapeake slavery. In Maryland, Harry Hosier was renowned for the power of his preaching. In Virginia, Charles Grandy had a long reach from his home near Norfolk. Others were women such as Jarena Lee.

These Chesapeake preacher-leaders cultivated different voices for different groups. Like Uncle Jack, they could preach to masters in the speech of the master class. To slaves they spoke African English and preached in a different way, with emotional appeals that awakened a more emotional response. One Chesapeake slave said of a white clergyman, "We ain't kered a bit 'bout dat stuff he was telling us, cause we wanted to sing, pray, and serve God in our own way. You see, 'ligion needs a little motion specially if you gwine feel de spirit." [246]

CHESAPEAKE SLAVES WHO BECAME INSTRUMENTAL LEADERS IN NATIONAL POLITICS

By the mid-nineteenth century, some of these individual Chesapeake slaves began to have an impact on national affairs throughout the United States. As late as 1860, none could vote or hold office in Maryland or Virginia. Individual examples follow of Chesapeake slave leaders who gained instrumental roles in the coming of the American Civil War, and the expansion of American rights.

Many of these American actors were men and women who began their lives as slaves in Maryland and Virginia. They were heirs to a tradition of leadership among slave owners whom they observed in their native region. They learned from it, reached far beyond it, and became leaders themselves.

These Chesapeake slave leaders often began by seeking freedom for themselves, their families, and friends. That purpose grew into a larger goal of freedom and liberty for all people in bondage. Some of them reached beyond that effort to a larger goal of enlarging freedom and liberty, equity and justice throughout America and the world. The exemplars that follow are Chesapeake-born slaves who became leaders in pivotal events, and models of open, principled, and effective leadership in an opening society for generations to come.

Among hundreds of armed risings by slaves within the United States, one of the most important is little remembered today. As recently as 1999, some conservative writers were still condemning it as a crime of "mutiny" and "murder," which it was not. Progressive writers call it "the most successful slave revolt in American history."[247] It was that and something more: an event that created the example of a slave leader who inspired many African American leaders to follow.

MADISON WASHINGTON, 1841: A CHESAPEAKE LEADER OF THE MOST SUCCESSFUL SLAVE REVOLT IN AMERICAN HISTORY

On October 24, 1841, the slave brig *Creole* sailed from Richmond for New Orleans with a cargo of tobacco and slaves. For her crew of ten seamen and four slave traders it started as a routine voyage in Virginia's vast coastal slave trade to seaports in the Deep South. The captain brought along his wife and children.

According to formal manifests and sworn statements by her officers, the ship carried 139 slaves. Later inquiry found evidence of 186 slaves on board. Either way, she was severely overloaded. An act of Congress in 1819 forbade a ship of *Creole*'s 158 tons to carry more than sixty-three people. Her human freight was nearly three times that lawful limit.[248]

Creole departed from the inland port of Richmond at midnight on October 25, 1841, and sailed down the James River in darkness. The captain (a slave trader himself) stopped at remote landings along the river and bought yet more slaves who were not on the manifest. Another common practice in the coastal slave trade was to kidnap free people of color, break up their families, and sell them apart. It was a dirty business, corrupt to the core. Some of the coastal slave trade was on the edge of the law, and much was far beyond it.[249]

Creole's slaves were crowded in two cargo holds: males in one hold, females in another, living and sleeping among stacks of tobacco boxes. Six female slaves aged thirteen to thirty were forced to sleep in a deck cabin with mates, guards, and traders as "housekeepers," a common corruption on coastal slave voyages.[250]

A few male slaves were permitted to move freely through the ship. Among them was Madison Washington, a Virginia slave, twenty-two years old. Many accounts described him as a "big man," "very strong," a man of presence and spirit, with the bearing of a leader.[251] Two years before, Washington had escaped from bondage in Virginia, and reached the northern states and Canada.[252] He met leading abolitionists, who were much impressed and recruited him as a leader in the antislavery movement. He said no. Against their advice he decided to go back to Virginia, in a desperate effort to free his wife and family. He was captured, and sold to a Louisiana trader, a common fate of Virginia runaways.

On board the *Creole*, the ship's captain chose Washington as "chief cook" or "steward," and ordered him to select a team to distribute food for the slaves. That role allowed Washington to meet all the slaves on board. It also enabled him to form a larger group of slave leaders to help with cooking and serving. They talked about the cruelty and violence of the captain and slave traders, and were also quick to observe their careless incompetence. Washington's team was able to arm themselves with knives, clubs, and capstan bars. One of them stole a pistol and ammunition. With Madison Washington as their leader, they resolved to seize the ship.

An opportunity came on the night of November 7, 1841, off the coast of Florida. The captain turned the ship into the wind, heaved to, and retired for the night, as did all the crew and traders, except a mate and a trader who had the watch.

Washington laid a trap for the watch standers. They were told that a male slave was in the women's hold. When they went to remove him, they met Washington instead, who shouted to his companions and they swarmed on deck.

A violent struggle followed, both sides fighting for their lives. The captain rushed on deck with a Bowie knife and turned his dog on the slaves. The animal fought "ferociously," mauling several slaves, before being killed. The captain was severely wounded and climbed high in the upper rigging. The hated head trader on board drew his pistol and killed a slave. Washington and another slave attacked him with a knife and a capstan bar, and the trader fell dying. Several of the crew were wounded, all were made captive, and the slaves quickly gained possession of the ship.

The defeated crewmen and traders were confined in their cabins. Madison Washington took firm control, posted guards, and ordered a large breakfast for all hands. The former captives celebrated their freedom with a wild triumph. Some wanted to kill all the slave traders and ship's officers and throw them overboard. Madison Washington said something like, "No more blood!" By common consent he stopped the violence.

Then he led his comrades in binding the wounds of friends and enemies alike, with a humanity that slave traffickers had never shown to them. Even the hated captain was allowed to live, and was sent below with his wife and children to tend to his wounds.

Washington ordered the mate to navigate the vessel, and told him to plot a course for Liberia, but the ship lacked water for so long a voyage. A Virginia slave called Blacksmith Ben suggested a different plan. He knew that a year earlier the American slave schooner *Hermosa* had run aground in the Bahamas. The slaves had been set free by Bahamian officials under British laws that had abolished the slave trade and slavery.[253]

The mate was ordered to turn the *Creole* toward Nassau in the Bahamas, where they arrived two days later, on November 9, 1841. As the ship entered port, she was met by the harbor pilot and his crew. All were African Americans and many had themselves escaped from bondage. They informed the *Creole* rebels that under British law they would be free in the Bahamas. A roar of triumph rose from the former slaves.

A celebration followed among free African Americans who were a majority of Nassau's population. The slave ship was surrounded by a swarm of small Bahamian boats, manned by large numbers of African Americans. Many were escaped slaves, and they were strong in support of these former captives who had freed themselves.

On the other side, the pro-slavery United States consul in Nassau quietly recruited a party of American seamen in the town and organized a clandestine mission to seize the *Creole* by stealth. Their goal was to retake the ship, and capture or kill the freed slaves. They organized an assault, but were defeated by Washington and his comrades, with help from Bahamian allies.

British authorities intervened. On April 16, 1842, Madison Washington and eighteen surviving comrades were put on trial in the Bahamian Admiralty Court. British Admiralty judges ruled that these American slaves had every right under British law to fight for their freedom. They were found not guilty of piracy, and mutiny, and murder, and were set free.

Possibly a decisive factor was Washington's intervention to protect the lives of the captain, crew, and even the hated slave traders. Evidence in his support came in testimony from slave traders and seamen whose lives he had spared.

The former slaves aboard the *Creole* were given a choice. They could stay with the ship, continue to New Orleans, and return to bondage if that was their preference. Five of them made that choice, perhaps in the hope of being reunited with families. But most chose to remain in the Bahamas, and probably intermarried with some of its many African American inhabitants.[254]

Reports of this event spread swiftly in the United States. It also inspired the first published African American work of historical fiction, written by Maryland-born Frederick Douglass about the life and career of Madison Washington. It was the story of a Virginia slave who led America's most successful slave rebellion. Douglass also portrayed him as a model of humane and heroic leadership in the cause of liberty and freedom.

Douglass reached a large public with his writing. He urged readers to remember Madison Washington and to emulate his leadership, his courage, and also his humanity. Douglass himself was inspired to combine those qualities of leadership in his own career. He encouraged other Americans, slave and free, to do the same, in the era of the American Civil War.

A SLAVE LEADER BY EXAMPLE OF DRAMATIC ACTS: HENRY BOX BROWN, 1849–51

Another and very different Chesapeake model of African American leadership appeared in the career of Henry Box Brown (ca. 1815–97). He was born a plantation slave in Louisa County, near the center of Virginia. By his own account, his master treated him with humanity, and he was not beaten or abused. Brown arranged to be hired out as a factory worker in Richmond. He was able to marry a woman who was the slave of another master, and they began to raise a family in a rented home. Henry Brown made an agreement with his wife's owner to pay installments toward the price of their freedom.

But then her master broke his word and kept the money. It was a shattering blow, and a wrong without a remedy in Virginia's corrupt court system.[255] Brown resolved do something about it. First, he decided to escape to liberty in a free state. His second goal was to strike a blow against slavery. The only question was how to do it. Escape from bondage in central Virginia was difficult and dangerous.

At his job in Richmond he began to observe an opportunity in the rapid improvement of transportation. American interstate economic growth derived from an expanding national market for materials and products.

With two friends, Brown made a plan to ship himself in a freight box from Virginia to Pennsylvania. Discreet inquiries were made with abolitionists in Philadelphia. The freight business was studied with care. Brown and his friends built a wooden box two feet wide, three feet long, and two feet, eight inches high. The dimensions were carefully matched to a standard size in the shipping business. The box was made with air holes, lined with heavy woolen cloth and furnished with a bladder of water and a package of biscuits.

On March 23, 1849, Brown climbed into his box. Friends nailed it shut and took it to the Richmond office of the Adams Express Company. It was addressed to Passmore Williamson, a prominent Philadelphia merchant who received many such shipments, and was widely known in the freight business. Not so familiar in Virginia was his membership in the Pennsylvania Anti-Slavery Society.

Freight connections were complex between Richmond and Philadelphia but remarkably swift in 1849. Shipments went by wagon to a train and onto a steamboat, by wagon again, another train, steamboat, a wagon once more, a railroad, a ferryboat, a railroad yet again, and finally a delivery wagon in Philadelphia. The speed was incredible. In 1849, a freight box from Richmond could reach its Philadelphia destination in little more than a night and a day.

The crate was carefully marked "this side up," but carelessly turned upside down before it left the freight office. It was thrown right side up by workers who sat on it and ate their lunch. Many misadventures followed, but the shipping connections worked. After a passage of twenty-seven hours, the box was delivered to the office of Passmore Williamson in Philadelphia.

Several abolitionists opened the box, and to their amazement, out climbed Henry Brown. He greeted them in a mannered Chesapeake way, said "How do you do, Gentlemen," and fainted perhaps from the unaccustomed shock of being vertical again.

The news of this extraordinary escape from slavery began to travel faster and farther than the box itself. Pious antislavery preachers took Henry Brown's survival to be a sign of Divine Providence. In some accounts, the emergence of Brown from his box was described as a "resurrection."

Henry Brown also revealed an American genius for promoting himself

Henry Box Brown emerging from his box

and his cause. He adopted "Box" as his middle name. Henry Box Brown toured the northern states with the original shipping crate, and reenacted his escape to growing crowds. He also took a leading role in organizing public events, and delivered many antislavery speeches. Other fugitive slaves spoke on the antislavery circuit, often with great eloquence, and reached a large public. By reenacting the escape with his box, Brown reached a larger public.[256]

More than that, he also helped to stimulate a growing secessionist spirit in the slave states, by linking freedom of interstate communications to antislavery and individual human rights. The natural movement of ideas, writings, images, and even of a fugitive slave himself was perceived below the Potomac as profoundly threatening to what had now become the South's "peculiar institution."

Its defenders tried to shroud the entire South in what has been called a "cotton curtain." A spirit of paranoia spread through the slave states. Strict new laws were enacted and enforced to restrict communications between free and slave states. Henry Box Brown stimulated these efforts but weakened their effect by the ingenuity and impact of his dramatic act.[257]

After the passage of a new Fugitive Slave Act in 1850, Henry Box Brown moved to England in fear of arrest, which further enlarged his role. He became increasingly active in a global antislavery movement through much of the English-speaking world.

After the Civil War and emancipation Henry Brown reinvented himself as a stage magician.[258] But historians remember him for his escape from slavery. In the twenty-first century the reputation of Henry Box Brown is growing yet again. Drama historian Martha Cutter writes that his escape has been continuously recreated "on television, in performance pieces, musicals, operas, books for children, graphic narratives, and even a wax figure at Baltimore's National Great Blacks in Wax Museum." The creativity of this Afro-Chesapeake slave leader has become a continuing inspiration to young people everywhere. In my experience, the story of Henry Box Brown rarely fails to awaken even a soundly sleeping class.[259]

Continuing interest in Box Brown is also strongly evident today in the southern city of Richmond. For many years its most prominent monuments honored Robert E. Lee, Stonewall Jackson, and other Confederate and Revolutionary leaders. In the late twentieth century, new monuments began to be erected in Richmond to honor African American leaders such as Arthur Ashe. And on Richmond's attractive Canal Walk there is also an unusual monument in the form of a large empty bronze box with an open lid. It is an enduring tribute to the creative example of Henry Box Brown. Today he is honored for his acts by many people in his native state of Virginia.

ANTHONY BURNS AND THE FUGITIVE SLAVE ACT, 1854: A VIRGINIA LEADER IN SUSTAINED ACTS OF NONVIOLENT RESISTANCE TO SLAVERY

Anthony Burns, or Tony to those who knew him, was born a slave in Stafford County, Virginia, on May 31, 1834. His master was John Suttle, a quarry operator. Tony's elderly parents were both slave leaders—a common pattern in the Chesapeake. His mother was John Suttle's "head cook," which meant that she had many roles and much responsibility. His father was

Anthony Burns

"superviser" of other slaves in Suttle's quarry, which supplied stone for the White House and Capitol in nearby Washington. Tony was their thirteenth and final child.[260]

Stafford was an impoverished part of Virginia. Its once fertile fields had been ruined by incompetent farming. John and Catherine Suttle were deep in debt. After their deaths, the estate passed to their son Charles Francis Suttle, who ran a dry goods store in Falmouth, and became a state legislator, militia colonel, and sheriff of Stafford County. He also was heavily in debt, and mortgaged his slave Tony to a creditor named William Brent, who gained the use of Tony's time.

Tony persuaded his new employer to allow him to "hire his own time" in Richmond, a common arrangement that was lucrative both for masters and slaves. In that river city, Tony organized his own escape from bondage, with the help of Yankee seamen who smuggled him aboard a coastal vessel. He reached Boston in February or March of 1854, and took a job as a baker's assistant, but he could not make bread rise, and was fired. He found work in a clothing store with more success, and began to establish himself as a free man in a free state.

Then he made a major mistake. He wrote a letter to his literate brother, and had it mailed from Canada, but inside he identified his location in Boston. The postal service delivered it to Tony's master. Charles Suttle appears to have had a double interest in Tony. He wanted to recover the value of his property, but was also thinking of his reputation among Virginia planters, as a defender of slavery against meddling Yankees and hated abolitionists.

Suttle and his creditor William Brent went to Boston, hired professional slave hunters, and obtained Tony Burns's arrest under the Fugitive Slave Act of 1850. The event caused thousands of Bostonians to riot in support of Burns. But the president at the time, Franklin Pierce, was a "Doughface," or "a northern man with southern principles." He sent to Boston a massive force of Regular infantry, artillery, marines, and warships with orders to take Tony Burns back to the slaveholding South, which they did.

Northern opinion was outraged. Money was raised to buy Burns's freedom, more than his owner could resist. Burns was liberated and went to Oberlin College. He became a minister, an eloquent speaker against slavery, a living image of liberation, and a symbol of the growing depth of corruption in the slaveholding South. After 1854, northern opinion turned increasingly against slaveholding southerners as a mortal threat to a free republic, partly because of growing corruption in Washington, the violent pursuit of fugitive slaves, and President Franklin Pierce's mobilization of American military force in pursuit of Tony Burns in particular.

Surviving photographs and engravings of Anthony Burns reinforced his iconic role, and were reproduced with great frequency in the events that followed. He appears as a handsome, upright young African American, in the prime of early adulthood and dressed as a gentleman. His complexion is dark and his features reflect moral strength and intelligence. At a pivotal moment in American political history, Anthony Burns made himself a leading image of a large and noble cause of liberty and freedom from slavery in the northern United States.

VIRGINIA-BORN SLAVE LEADERS AGAINST SLAVERY: DRED SCOTT AND HARRIET ROBINSON SCOTT

Dred Scott (1799–1858) was born a slave in Southampton County, Virginia. By family tradition he was named Etheldred, perhaps after Ethelred the Unready, the troubled Saxon king. In 1818, Dred Scott's Virginia owner Peter Blow moved his family and slaves south to a plantation near Huntsville, Alabama, and then west to St. Louis, Missouri, in 1830.

There the Blow family sold Dred Scott to John Emerson, an army surgeon who took him to military posts in free states and the territories of Illinois, Wisconsin, Minnesota, and Iowa, where "involuntary servitude" and slavery had been prohibited by the Continental Congress in the Northwest Ordinance of 1787, and again by the Congress of the United States in the Missouri Compromise of 1820.

In 1837, Scott was living at Fort Snelling, then in free Wisconsin territory, near what is now Minneapolis, Minnesota. Scott met another Virginia slave, Harriet Robinson, and they decided to marry. Harriet's easygoing master, Lawrence Taliaferro, was also a justice of the peace. He joined them in a formal ceremony that was permitted only to free people, and sold her to Dr. Emerson so they could live together.

When Emerson was ordered to southern military posts, Dred and Harriet Scott remained in the North, and were leased as servants to other officers. They lived in virtual freedom, and the first of four children was born in free territory.

In 1837, the Scotts returned to Missouri, a slave state. Dred Scott was hired out to many people, but continued living in virtual freedom, and he saved money enough to buy the liberty of his entire family. But his new owner was now Eliza Irene Sanford, the widow of Dr. Emerson. She insisted on hiring out Dred Scott as a source of income for herself.

In St. Louis, Scott was able to get himself leased to the law firm of Ros-

Dred Scott and his wife, Harriet

well Field. He learned about the complex law of slavery and freedom in the West, and became aware of rulings by Missouri courts that slaves who lived in free territory became free themselves. Some cases proclaimed a judicial rule: "Once free, always free."

On that basis, Dred and Harriet Scott sued for their freedom, first in separate cases, then together. A search has found that their filing was the only joint freedom suit by a husband and wife in fifty years of Missouri court records.

In 1848, a Missouri court ruled against them. Dred and Harriet Scott petitioned for a new trial, and another appeal followed in 1850. They kept trying through twelve years, expanding their case to seek freedom not only for themselves but their children.

By 1852, they had earned the respect and support of many people who knew them in Missouri. Others were persuaded to help. Among them were members of the Blow family, who had first owned Dred Scott in three slave states. Later they had left the South, and some of them joined the antislavery movement. In 1854, a third trial followed, this time in a federal court at St. Louis, Judge Robert Wells presiding. He was a Virginia-born slaveholder. There was no testimony and no oral argument. The jury brought in a verdict that all the Scott family were slaves.

Dred and Harriet Scott appealed yet again. They were hard drivers, Harriet especially. More people helped with legal expenses. Scott's legal employer Roswell Field took the case pro bono, and carried it through many layers of appeal, ultimately to the United States Supreme Court.

There the case was inaccurately called *Scott v. Sandford*, and heard by Chief Justice Roger Brooke Taney, an odd character, a Maryland Federalist who had become a Jacksonian Democrat. He was also a Maryland planter who had freed his own slaves in early life, but became a strong defender of slavery as an institution. On March 6, 1857, in separate opinions, a majority of the court rejected Scott's suit.

Chief Justice Taney also went farther. He asserted that the Northwest Ordinance of 1787 could not extend freedom or citizenship to any person of color. And the court ruled that the Missouri Compromise, passed by Congress in 1820, was unconstitutional in excluding slavery, depriving masters of their property, and extending freedom and citizenship to people of African ancestry. This was only the second case in which the Supreme Court had declared an act of Congress unconstitutional.

Further, Taney and other justices added obiter dicta that went far beyond the case itself. They ruled that no slave or descendant of a slave could ever be free, or become a citizen, or bring a freedom suit in any court of the United States; that Congress could never abolish slavery anywhere; and that no federal or state court could deprive an owner of his property in a slave.

Southern defenders of slavery were jubilant. But the Dred Scott case became an epic disaster for their cause. Dred and Harriet Scott lost in the courtroom, yet won a resounding victory in the court of northern public opinion. By 1857, a growing majority of Americans lived in free states. Many people who had not turned against slavery themselves expressed outrage against the Dred Scott case. It had great impact on national elections that followed in 1858.

Southern slaveholders and their northern allies lost control of Congress in 1858, in large part because of the reaction to the Dred Scott case. Southerners also lost the presidency in 1860, and after four years of bloody struggle, they lost the Civil War. The Dred Scott decision was overturned by the Thirteenth, Fourteenth, and Fifteenth Amendments to the Constitution, which abolished slavery throughout the United States, and affirmed rights of citizenship without limits of race, ethnicity, or previous condition of bondage.

The Dred Scott case truly became a pivotal event in American history. Its drivers and leaders were two Virginia-born slaves, Etheldred and Harriet Scott. Even after they lost their appeal to the Supreme Court, they won their freedom and were manumitted by their owners. Scott died of tuberculosis in 1858; Harriet and their two children survived. The long struggle of these slaves for freedom through the federal courts continues to reverberate in our own time.[261]

LEADERSHIP BY MILITANT ACTION AGAINST
SLAVERY BY CHESAPEAKE WOMEN IN BONDAGE

On Chesapeake plantations, many slave leaders were women. Some of them also continued to lead free communities of color in the new republic. By the mid-nineteenth century, some of these African American women became national leaders, and made a major difference in the course of political events before they could vote or hold office.

Among the most successful female leaders was Harriet Ross Tubman Davis (1820/22?–1913), known to history as Harriet Tubman, and to her family and friends as Hatt. She was born a slave in Dorchester County on Maryland's

Harriet Tubman

Eastern Shore. Her parents, "Ben" Ross (1787–1871) and Harriet "Rit" Ross (ca. 1787–1880), were leaders in their own right and biographies have been written about both of them.[262]

As we have seen, Harriet Tubman also cherished the example of her African grandmother, who brought to America a militant Asante tradition that helped shape Tubman's life and work.

From her early years Tubman carried two sets of enduring memories. One centered on love and support within her family. The other was about monstrous violence, careless cruelty, and continuing acts of bad faith by masters, mistresses, and overseers.

As a child of five, young Harriet was hired to mind a small baby for a woman named Miss Susan. Whenever the baby cried, Harriet got a whipping; she remembered one day when she was whipped five times, and with such severity that she bore the scars for life. It grew worse in her teens. One fatal day an infuriated overseer hurled a heavy weight at another slave, and hit Harriet "by mistake." The blow fractured her skull, damaged her brain, and left a wound that never healed. Through most of her life Harriet Tubman suffered severe pain, sudden seizures, and intense visions with deep spiritual meaning.[263]

When her owner died, Harriet believed that she would be sold south. She ran north to freedom, with help from Quaker women on the Eastern Shore, probably Hannah Leverton and Hester Kelley, and was spirited from one safe house to another through Maryland and Delaware. Later she told her friend Sarah Hopkins Bradford of the moment when she reached the free state of Pennsylvania. "When I found I had crossed that line," she said, "I looked at my hands to see if I was the same person. There was such a glory over everything the sun came like gold though the trees, and over the fields, and I felt like I was in Heaven."[264]

In Philadelphia she worked as a maid, saved her wages, and found a calling.[265] She began to organize escapes from slavery, first for her own extended Maryland family. She started with a niece in 1850, then a brother and his friends, and a group of eleven friends and relations. At the same time, she worked with others to organize an expanding web of Quakers, antislavery Methodists, free people of color, fugitive slaves, and for a time with Frederick Douglass. The web reached from the Eastern Shore to Baltimore, Wilmington, Philadelphia, upstate New York, and lower Canada. One of her last missions was to take her elderly parents north to Canada and safety.

A biographer has found evidence that Harriet Tubman personally led to freedom at least seventy slaves in thirteen groups, and probably many more. She also helped to plan the escape of another fifty or sixty slaves. Altogether Tubman was believed to have helped more than three hundred Maryland and Virginia slaves to reach freedom. Rewards of $40,000 were posted for her arrest.[266]

At the same time, she worked with many others to construct an entire system of escape from slavery. By her own acts and thoughts, and collaboration with others, she also helped to build a tradition of principled leadership, courage, and resolve that had deep roots in her native place.

Like her Asante grandmother, she was a fighter, even a warrior, and she could be ruthless with others. She carried a pistol and did not hesitate to use it. On one occasion, several male fugitives in one of her groups "grew weary, foot-sore and bleeding," and dropped to the ground and said they would rather go back to slavery, threatening to compromise the entire party. An eyewitness remembered that Tubman drew her gun and pointed it at their heads. They struggled to their feet, and kept moving north to freedom.[267]

Those who knew Harriet Tubman testified that "there was a hardness about her character in the face of adversity that must have been hereditary."[268]

She also worked with John Brown, who called her General Tubman, but probably did not support the Harpers Ferry raid. When the Civil War began she went south to Hilton Head in South Carolina with a strong Union force that took possession of many Sea Islands. Tubman served as a nurse and also marched with Union troops, sometimes carrying a weapon in one hand, and bandages in the other. She worked to liberate many slaves in lowcountry South Carolina and Georgia. On one expedition alone, she helped to free 750 slaves and lead them back to Union lines.

After the war and the abolition of slavery, Tubman fought for civil rights and equality of all American people before the law. She strongly opposed Jim Crow in places of public accommodation. On trains she sat in seats that were reserved for whites. In October 1866 she was traveling aboard a Camden & South Amboy train from Philadelphia to New York on a government half-fare ticket. The conductor shouted, "Come! Hustle out of here. We don't carry niggers for half fare." She refused, and he tried to remove her by brute strength. She was stronger. He called for help and two men, some say three or four, pulled her out with such force that they wrenched and may have broken her arm, and threw her into the baggage car, and may also have cracked several ribs. She called him a copperhead scoundrel, and he nearly choked her. Many friends helped her recover, and she tried to sue the railroad without success.[269]

Two years later Tubman challenged Jim Crow again, when she defied segregation on a Washington street car, and once more she was removed by brute force. These were battles that she lost, but she fought them to the end.

In later years Harriet Tubman joined Susan B. Anthony and fought for a woman's right to vote. She lived frugally, and devoted her resources to helping others to the end of her life in 1913. After her death, Harriet Tubman's reputation continued to grow, both for her many militant causes that she led, and also for the moral character of her leadership. The Episcopal and Lutheran Churches both elevated her to sainthood.

Altogether, Harriet Tubman might be remembered as a warrior saint in the time-honored Christian tradition of Saint George, Saint Michael, and Joan of Arc. A modern monument in Ypsilanti, Michigan, represents her in that militant spirit, grasping a rifled musket with one hand, and leading a slave child to freedom with the other.[270]

A MARYLAND SLAVE WHO BECAME A WORLD LEADER AGAINST SLAVERY AND RACISM: FREDERICK DOUGLASS

The best known of these many Chesapeake slaves who became national and international leaders was Frederick Douglass. He was born on Maryland's Eastern Shore, around 1818, the son of an African American mother and an Anglo-American father, whose identity he never knew. His first full name was Frederick Augustus Washington Bailey. Always he identified with both sides of his ancestry. His first wife was African American and at the end of his life Douglass chose to be buried by her side in Rochester, New York. His second wife was white and he was devoted to her as well. His argument was not with white racism or Black racism but with race prejudice, and racial oppression in its many forms. Douglass had firsthand experience of the cruelty and suffering that race slavery inflicted on its victims.[271]

Always, even as he fought slavery and racism at every turn, Douglass also identified with other parts of the culture and values in his native slaveholding region. He wrote with respect about the founders of the American republic in Virginia and Maryland. He remarked that "the patriots of the American Revolution clearly saw and with all their inconsistency, they had the grace to confess the abhorrent character of slavery, and to hopefully predict its overthrow and complete extirpation." And he made clear that he was thinking specifically of Washington and Jefferson, Madison and Monroe, Luther Martin of Maryland, and also two Yankees, Benjamin Franklin and John Adams.[272]

Frederick Douglass

Douglass learned to lead in many ways at once, partly from the example of these leaders, all slaveholders except Adams. For many years his primary instruments were the pen and the printed word. At the same time, he was a founder of major movements and an organizer of new associations. He worked closely with presidents, served in diplomatic posts, and was the first African American to be nominated as vice president of the United States.

Like many revolutionary founders he was prepared to use many means in the cause of liberty and freedom. Douglass observed after the Civil War that "a Man's rights rest in three boxes: the ballot box, the jury box, and the cartridge box."[273]

But unlike many of those earlier founders Douglass believed deeply in full equality of rights for all people. He wrote, "I utterly deny that we are originally, or naturally, or practically, or in any way, or in any important sense inferior to anybody on this globe."

He expressed his contempt for inequality by making a joke of it and said:

"This charge of inferiority is an old dodge. . . . It is only about six centuries since the blue-eyed and fair-haired Anglo-Saxons were considered inferior by the haughty Normans."[274]

Douglass was a man of extraordinary strength and courage, one of the strongest and most effective leaders in the long struggle against slavery and racism in its many forms. He became a national leader of the American republic, and a world leader of many movements for human rights. With the passage of time his stature has only continued to grow.

MARYLAND AND VIRGINIA SLAVE LEADERS TRANSFORMED AMERICAN LEADERSHIP

In 1853, Frederick Douglass looked back over the history of Virginia, and wrote that this state was renowned as "the mother of statesmen" and a nursery of heroes in the great republic.

But he added that not all of her children had won the fame they deserved. Douglass believed that some of Virginia's greatest leaders, and the "truest, manliest, and bravest" of her children, had languished in "undeserved obscurity," and "hold no higher place in the memory of the grand old Commonwealth than is held by a horse or an ox."[275]

He was thinking of leaders who had been born slaves in Virginia, and Maryland. By any test, two of the Chesapeake region's greatest leaders were Douglass himself and Harriet Tubman, both native Marylanders who had been born in bondage.

Just when the Virginia dynasty of slaveholding Chesapeake presidents was beginning to run thin in the mid-nineteenth century, other leaders emerged from the anonymous ranks of their Chesapeake slaves. They were men and women, originally field hands and house slaves, who went on to become American leaders in many national roles. Some began to learn about leadership within slave quarters. Others did so in African American communities that formed throughout Chesapeake towns and cities. Their numbers and achievements increased rapidly in the nineteenth century. A surprising number went on to become leaders in national affairs. Many of them moved on a world stage.

What did these Chesapeake slave leaders share in common? And what might we learn from them? First we can study how attentive they were to learning from others—even from their oppressors. A great Roman statesman observed, "Fas est ab hoste doceri," "It is right to learn from our enemies." That is what these Maryland and Virginia slaves had the wisdom to do.

Many of these slaves became close observers of the old regime. They studied strengths of leadership in slaveholders such as Washington and Jefferson, learned from them, and then moved beyond them. They built on a great but deeply flawed Chesapeake tradition, and made it greater and less flawed. They broadened the tradition in many ways, preserved its virtues and corrected its vices. They preserved early American ideas of liberty and freedom, and enlarged them by stronger linkages to equality and broader ideas of humanity. They became believing Christians, but turned away from the moral corruption of many Christian clergy who supported slavery in the time of its greatest cruelty and oppression. They gave a new depth of meaning to the teaching of Jesus, that "what you do for the least of my brethren you do for me."

Many of these Chesapeake slave leaders of African origin also tended to be highly principled in their purposes and acts. They became moral leaders who were deeply conscious of an ethical dimension in their thoughts and acts—more so than were their owners and enemies.

They were also highly mannered leaders who understood the importance of treating people decently and with respect, from long experience of having been treated in other ways. They valued human dignity, respected the feelings of others, and understood the importance of doing the right thing in the right way.

They also became instrumental leaders who understood the urgency of effective action. Leadership was not a game for them. It was also not a goal in itself, but an instrument of other and much larger goals.

This invented tradition of African American leadership in Maryland and Virginia was complex in its character and origins. It developed from many precursors, but it also had a character and integrity uniquely its own. These Chesapeake leaders, free and slave, kept a code of honor and courage. They were not solitary people, but learned to work closely with others. They also had long memories of the past, and shared a special way of thinking historically about problems in the present and the future. They also added a distinctive style that was summarized in two regional mottos. In Maryland, it was *fatti maschi, parole femine*. Among Virginians it was *suaviter in modo, fortiter in re*. They learned these things from one another, not by precept but example.

Other different but equally important and instrumental patterns emerged in other African American regions by parallel processes, but never twice in the same way. A contrasting case in point is the regional culture of Gullah and Geechee slaves in coastal South Carolina and Georgia, our next order of business.

TABLE 4.1 Frequency of Violent Punishments Against Slaves, 1750–1839
Evidence from Slaveholders in Notices of Runaways

DECADE	PERCENT DESCRIBED AS BEARING PHYSICAL EVIDENCE OF:						
	WHIPPING	BRANDING	MAIMING	IRONS	GUNSHOT/ BAYONET	TOTAL %	NUMBER
Tidewater Virginia Runaway Slaves							
1750–59	7.3	3.6	5.4	3.6	0.0	19.9	55
1770–79	8.0	8.0	7.1	0.8	0.0	23.0	113
1790–99	9.9	8.4	4.2	0.0	1.4	23.9	71
1810–19	5.0	0.7	2.1	0.0	2.1	10.0	140
1830–39	1.9	0.0	2.9	0.0	1.9	5.8	103
Overall	5.4	3.7	3.9	0.6	0.8	15.0	482
Lowcountry South Carolina Runaway Slaves							
1750–59	5.7	7.9	2.3	1.1	0.0	21.6	88
1770–79	4.5	6.0	3.0	0.0	1.5	14.9	67
1790–99	2.9	5.9	4.4	0.0	1.5	14.7	68
1810–19	0.0	0.0	2.5	3.8	0.0	6.3	79
1830–39	0.0	0.0	3.9	0.0	0.0	3.9	76
Overall	2.6	4.0	3.2	1.6	0.5	12.4	378

Note: These numbers are computed as a proportion of all runaway slave notices that included physical descriptions in Virginia and South Carolina newspapers held by the American Antiquarian Society. The work was done by a team of three very able undergraduate researchers: Susan Irwin, Donna Bouvier, and Marc Orlofsky, who taught their teacher. The same researchers are responsible for Table 4.2.

TABLE 4.2 Literacy of Runaway Slaves as Reported by Masters,
1750–1839

PERIOD	PERCENT REPORTED BY MASTERS AS ABLE TO:					
	READ	WRITE	READ & WRITE	TOTAL	NUMBER OF SLAVES	PERCENT LITERATE
Virginia						
1750–59			1	1	135	0.7%
1770–79			4	4	253	1.6%
1790–99	5	4	5	14	189	7.4%
1810–19		1	6	7	349	2.0%
1830–39	6	1	5	12	255	4.7%
South Carolina						
1750–59	1			1	181	0.5%
1770–79	1		4	5	398	1.3%
1790–99	5	6	6	17	353	4.8%
1810–19		2	7	9	536	1.7%
1830–39	6	2	6	14	530	2.6%

TABLE 4.3 Frequency of Reports in Slave Narratives of Abuse by
Owners in the Upper and Lower South in the Nineteenth Century

	PERCENTAGE REPORTING ABUSE	
	UPPER SOUTH	LOWER SOUTH
Whipping	60.5	62.2
Sales	11.4	6.1
Murder	6.6	7.4
Forced Sex	5.4	4.3
Other cruelty	2.4	5.7
Asserts no cruelty	4.2	5.7
Punishment for cause only	0.6	2.6

Note: In this study by Paul Escott, the "Upper South" includes Maryland, Virginia, Kentucky and North Carolina. "Lower South" includes Alabama, Mississippi, Louisiana, and Texas. Paul D. Escott, *Slavery Remembered: A Period of Twentieth-Century Slave Narratives* (Chapel Hill, 1979), 58. Sample sizes are 230 for the upper South and 167 for the lower South.

Chapter 5

COASTAL CAROLINA, GEORGIA, AND FLORIDA

Barbadian Planters, Gullah Geechee Cultures, American Roots

An important message in this journey is that we are all linked . . . through our histories of growth and survival in this country.
—Michelle Obama, on her Gullah roots in South Carolina, 2008[1]

ON AUGUST 23, 1670, the English frigate *Carolina* anchored in the Ashley River, near the present site of Charleston. The ship's captain, Henry Brayne, was also a prosperous Barbadian slave owner. He liked the look of South Carolina, and sent five people ashore to start a plantation. They included an overseer, three "Christian servants," and "one lusty Negro man," the first person of African descent on record in this new colony.[2]

Others were quick to follow. In September of 1670, the Bermuda sloop *Three Brothers* delivered to Governor William Sayle three "Negro servants" called John Senior, Elizabeth, and John Junior. They were the first documented African family group on record in South Carolina, and also the first to appear by name.[3]

Governor Sayle died in 1671, and his successor, Sir John Yeamans, imported eight more African "servants" from Barbados. Within months, their numbers multiplied to "several dozen Negroes," who were also called servants. Some of them were sent to the interior, probably to raise livestock. They were given firearms, horses, and much autonomy.[4]

By 1672, about one third of South Carolina's population were of African descent. They began to be called slaves, and their numbers grew more rapidly than in any North American colony. In 1720 an early census from "exact lists as delivered by inquisitors" found 18,393 inhabitants, of whom 11,828 were

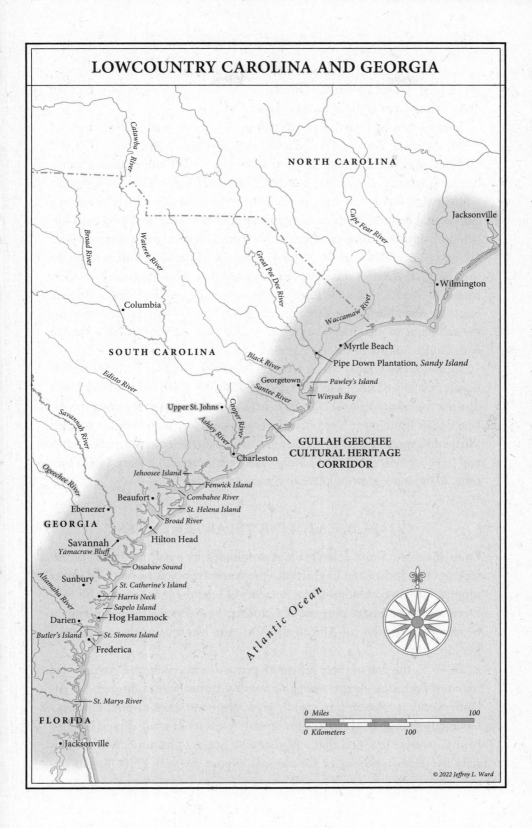

LOWCOUNTRY CAROLINA AND GEORGIA

NORTH CAROLINA

Jacksonville

Catawba River

Cape Fear River

Wilmington

Broad River

Wateree River

Great Pee Dee River

Waccamaw River

Columbia

SOUTH CAROLINA

Black River

Myrtle Beach

Pipe Down Plantation, *Sandy Island*

Edisto River

Georgetown

Pawley's Island

Santee River

Winyah Bay

Cooper River

Upper St. Johns

Savannah River

Ashley River

Charleston

GULLAH GEECHEE CULTURAL HERITAGE CORRIDOR

Ogeechee River

Jehoosee Island

Fenwick Island

Beaufort

Combahee River

Ebenezer

St. Helena Island

GEORGIA

Broad River

Hilton Head

Savannah

Yamacraw Bluff

Ossabaw Sound

Sunbury

St. Catherine's Island

Altamaha River

Harris Neck

Sapelo Island

Darien

Hog Hammock

Butler's Island

St. Simons Island

Frederica

Atlantic Ocean

St. Marys River

FLORIDA

Jacksonville

0 Miles   100

0 Kilometers   100

© 2022 Jeffrey L. Ward

African slaves, nearly two thirds of South Carolina's population. A Swiss visitor in 1737 wrote that South Carolina "looks more like a negro country than like a country settled by white people."[5]

That pattern continued through many years. In the first federal census of 1790, the three "Districts" of coastal South Carolina had a total of 28,862 "Whites" and 79,223 "Blacks." By that measure nearly three quarters of inhabitants in the Carolina lowcountry (73 percent) were of African descent.[6]

In coastal South Carolina, these African slaves rapidly created a regional culture of their own. By the mid-eighteenth century it began to be called Gullah, probably from Angola. A kindred culture later emerged in coastal Georgia, and was called Geechee, probably from the Muskogean Indian name for the Ogeechee River. A colleague has suggested that "Gullah" came from Gola people in West Africa, and "Geechee" from "Kissi" people of Upper Guinea, but these resemblances are very remote. Whatever its origin, Geechee became the call name of an African culture in coastal Georgia, which had a kinship with Gullah culture in coastal Carolina.[7]

In 2006, the United States Congress and the National Park Service officially recognized the "Gullah Geechee Cultural Heritage Corridor" as a distinct American regional culture. It runs three hundred miles along the Atlantic coast from lower North Carolina to upper Florida and reaches roughly thirty miles into the interior, farther inland along the major rivers. The Gullah and Geechee heritage has had a long presence in American history. In our own time, it also has a growing place in American culture.[8]

COASTAL CAROLINA'S PLANTER ELITES

From the start, South Carolina was dominated by small groups of profit-seeking West Indian and English entrepreneurs. There was no talk of Cavalier utopias, Puritan commonwealths, Societies of Friends, or Sanctuaries for Soul Freedom. The primary purpose of Carolina's founders was to make money, by using forced labor of African slaves to raise lucrative market crops for a world market.[9]

In 1672, the first of these early entrepreneurs came from the overcrowded island of Barbados. As the reports of South Carolina spread through the Atlantic world, its planter class rapidly grew larger and more diverse. Historian George Rogers studied the origins of early planters in what is now Georgetown County. He found that a planter elite began to form on Winyah Bay, sixty-five miles northeast of Charleston, around the year 1710. Rogers observed that "no *Mayflower* sailed into Winyah Bay. None of these settlers . . . came in groups; they came as individuals." [10]

They were of mixed origin, mostly English, Scots, and French, with a scattering of many others. But most of them came on the same errand. They built plantations on the dark rich soil around Winyah Bay, and along the Pee Dee River, the Black River, and the beautiful Waccamaw River. All of these rivers flow through the bay to the ocean. Together, they drain nearly half of coastal South Carolina.

Something similar happened along the Santee River, South Carolina's largest stream, which drains much of the upcountry. And it happened again on the Ashley and Cooper Rivers, shorter and smaller than the Santee, but they come together at Charleston "to form the Atlantic Ocean," as some Charlestonians like to say. Farther south, four fertile river valleys were also colonized: the Edisto, Combahee, Broad, and Savannah Rivers, and others in Georgia and North Florida. [11]

Of equal importance were the fabled Sea Islands along the Atlantic coast of South Carolina and Georgia—thousands of islands altogether, in many varieties. Most numerous are the more than 2,900 "marsh hummock" islands, some with hundreds of acres. Most prominent are the big barrier islands, with long strands of white sand facing the ocean, and deep deposits of alluvial soil behind. Rainfall is abundant in the Sea Islands, about fifty inches a year. The growing season approaches three hundred days, thirty days longer than the Carolina mainland, and twice that of New England. [12]

Coastal Carolina became highly productive but dangerously unhealthy, especially in its long growing season. A lethal combination of chronic illness and epidemic disease caused high mortality among both Europeans and Africans. Conditions grew worse with the arrival of new diseases from Europe (tuberculosis, pneumonia, and other respiratory illnesses) which took a heavy toll on Africans. Other diseases came from Africa (falciparum malaria, yaws, yellow fever, dengue fever) and were deadly to Europeans. During the most dangerous months, some wealthy planter families could move to comparative safety. The Rutledge family summered in eighteenth-century Rhode Island. But most Europeans and African slaves remained at risk through the sickly seasons, and both suffered much.

In this region, families of every rank experienced shattering losses. Wealthy planter families produced many children in the hope that a few might survive, and they intermarried through eight generations. The result was the rapid formation of what the English called "connexions" of interbred families.

There was much ethnic diversity in the origins of these intermingled plant-ing families, but most of them shared a single purpose. They sought to build family fortunes from plantation agriculture and African slavery, and many did so with high success. In the Continental Congress, representatives from other colonies were astounded by the opulence of members who came from coastal South Carolina. By 1774, comparatively small planter elites in coastal Caro-lina produced more large fortunes than other North American regions. And most of their wealth grew from the labor of many African slaves.

AFRICAN ORIGINS OF SLAVES IN COASTAL CAROLINA

South Carolina's great planters took an active interest in the origins of their slaves, and had strong opinions about which Africans were more useful to their purposes.[13] Unlike Virginians and Marylanders, Carolinians knew that they did not want "Ibos" from the port of Calabar on the Bight of Biafra, now southeastern Nigeria. These free-spirited African people were thought to prefer death to slavery, and were reputed to be frequently suicidal. Charleston slave trader Henry Laurens often instructed his suppliers not to send "Ibos" in particular, and "Calabar negroes" in general. "Calabar slaves won't go down when others can be had in plenty," Laurens wrote, in reference to the South Carolina market.[14]

Like many British slave owners, South Carolina planters strongly pre-ferred the Africans called Coromantees by English-speaking people in the eighteenth century. Many were Akan-speaking Asante and Fante people from the Gold Coast in what is now western Ghana. They were proud warrior peo-ple, highly respected by English purchasers. John Atkins, a ship's doctor in the slave trade, wrote that of all the Africans he had seen, "those from the Gold Coast are accounted best, being cleanest limbed and more docile." Here again he meant "docile" in the eighteenth-century sense of quick to learn, rather than the twentieth-century sense of "submissive and meek." Coromantees were anything but meek. They were known to be highly dangerous to masters who abused them, but loyal and faithful when treated well. A West Indian planter wrote that "no man deserved a Coromantee that did not treat him like a friend rather than a slave."[15]

The first African arrivals in South Carolina included a large proportion of these "Gold Coast Negroes." But the supply was unstable, and competition was intense. They brought high prices and were snapped up by New England traders and West Indian buyers, who often got first crack. Henry Laurens often complained about the small numbers and high prices of Gold Coast slaves, who were his first choice.

After these "Coromantees," Carolina planters in the early eighteenth century favored Angolan and Congo slaves from West Central Africa. During the seventeenth and early eighteenth centuries, they became available in greater numbers than other Africans. In that period, they rapidly became the largest regional group of African slaves in early South Carolina. Records of shipping lists, slave traders, and advertisements for runaway slaves showed similar patterns of African origin.

From 1700 to 1740, Angolan slaves predominated in the Carolina trade. Many studies have found that in the peak years of the 1730s, between 67 and 84 percent of slaves arriving in South Carolina came from Angola and the Congo Basin. By 1740, about forty thousand Africans and twenty thousand Europeans were living in coastal South Carolina. Taken together, a majority of the entire population in the Carolina lowcountry may have come from West Central Africa.[16]

That trend ended abruptly in 1740. A major factor was the Stono Rebellion in 1739, led by about twenty Angolan slaves, with many more involved in various ways. We shall meet these Stono rebels again in another part of this inquiry. Suffice to say that some of them were skilled soldiers who had been captured in African wars. They knew how to use firearms and edged weapons, fought with practiced skill, and lived by the discipline of a warrior ethic. Some of these Angolan slaves had become Christians in Africa. They had been converted by Roman Catholic missionaries, which gave them another reason to dislike their Protestant masters. A purpose of the Stono Rebellion was not to end slavery in South Carolina, but to escape from a Protestant English colony to Catholic Spanish Florida.[17]

The rebellion alarmed planters in South Carolina. Fear of further revolts, and the outbreak of war between England and Spain, caused South Carolinians to reduce their slave trade in the early 1740s, and to limit the flow from Angola.

A second wave of African slave trading began in the late 1740s and continued until the start of the American Revolution in 1775. In that span of about twenty-five years, at least fifty thousand Africans (probably more) were brought to South Carolina. After 1749, their regional origins shifted from Angola to West Africa. One relevant factor appeared in a Charleston advertisement, which announced the arrival of "a choice cargo of Windward and Gold Coast negroes, who have been accustomed to planting rice."[18]

Altogether, more than two thirds of African slaves imported to South

Carolina during the period from 1749 to 1775 came from Senegambia, the Windward Coast, and Gold Coast. Less than 15 percent were Angolans in this middle period of the Carolina slave trade.[19]

Then came the American War of Independence. The Continental Congress urged the closure of the African slave trade to North America. During the disorder of the war years, many slaves in South Carolina and Georgia seized the opportunity to escape from their masters and to flee the colonies. They regarded British troops as their liberators. Coastal South Carolina experienced a decline of its African population in that period.

After the War of Independence, Carolinians rapidly reopened the African slave trade in 1783–84. The result was South Carolina's third era of slave importation, the largest in its history. In data that survive from 1804 to 1807, slaves arrived in South Carolina at the rate of at least eight thousand a year, a flow four times greater than in earlier periods. It continued until Congress prohibited the Atlantic trade in 1807, to take effect on January 1, 1808, the earliest date when Congress could act under the constitutional compromise on slavery in 1787.

Thereafter, a clandestine slave trade of uncertain size persisted for many years. One very large shipment arrived as late as 1858, in open defiance of the federal government. But the magnitude of this forbidden trade appears to have been small by the measure of prior movements.[20]

That third major period of African migration from 1784 to 1807 once again drew heavily from Angola and Congo in West Central Africa. Overall, several historians have estimated that more slaves in lowcountry South Carolina descended from Bantu-speaking people in West Central Africa than from any other region. But the same evidence also shows a large minority from West Africa, and a broad diversity of other origins.[21]

FOUNDERS OF GEORGIA: JAMES OGLETHORPE AND HIS PHILANTHROPIC ELITE

South of the Savannah River, another story began to develop in the neighboring colony of Georgia. The coasts and islands of South Carolina and Georgia are often studied as a single unit, with good reason. From North Florida to the lower coast of North Carolina, this entire region is broadly similar in its ecology.[22] But its early history was more diverse. One major factor was a difference of founding purposes in South Carolina and Georgia. Another was a difference of timing. Georgia began in 1732 as a utopian experiment by En-

James Edward Oglethorpe

glish philanthropists. They denied to themselves any profit from the colony, and prohibited slavery outright until 1751.

The founding of Georgia was driven by an extraordinary leader, General James Edward Oglethorpe (1696–1785). He was a paradoxical man of many causes and multiple careers: a battle-scarred soldier with a social conscience, a practical parliamentary politician with a statesman's vision, a Latin poet at Eton and Oxford, and a philosopher of the Enlightenment. Through a long life, he was also a courtier who became highly skilled in the slippery arts of pleasing his political superiors. On active duty, this rugged Scottish soldier slept in the open, wrapped in his kilt and tartan. In London, he was a polished gentleman who moved easily through the genteel jungle of London drawing rooms. He was a man of honor who killed more than one person who insulted him. At the same time, he was a humanist who sympathized deeply with sufferings of others.

In London, James Oglethorpe was a man of many causes. He worked for the welfare of British seamen who had been the victims of brutal press gangs, sadistic captains, starvation rations, storms, shipwrecks, and bloody battles at sea. In Parliament, he led a campaign to protect convicts from corrupt jailers, and made a sustained effort to deliver debtors from imprisonment. He embraced the cause of "agrarian laws" to aid the rural poor who could find no work in England, and he came to the aid of urban children from broken families. In Parliament, he worked with members of the Gaols [Jails] Committee to create opportunities for ex-convicts upon release from horrific English prisons. Oglethorpe's brief experience as an officer in the Royal African Company also turned him against slavery at an early date. His wide philanthropic purposes embraced destitute families and many victims of inhumanity.[23]

To help serve these causes, Oglethorpe and his friends in Parliament proposed an experimental American colony. They called it Georgia after England's German King George II, who gave them strong support. Their primary object was to create a society where unfortunate people could enjoy the fruits of their own labor. Many founding Trustees of Georgia, as they called themselves, shared these high purposes. Altogether the founding of Georgia was yet another story of early American altruism which deserves to be better remembered, especially in eras of interest in modern American corruption. The large intentions of Oglethorpe and the Georgia Trustees were in some ways comparable to the purposes of John Winthrop and New England's Puritan leaders, the goals of William Penn and the founders of the Quaker Pennsylvania, and the vision of George Calvert for proprietary Maryland.

THE EARLY GROWTH OF SLAVERY IN GEORGIA: A CONFLICTED HISTORY

In his plans for Georgia, yet another of Oglethorpe's purposes became more important. He and other Trustees regarded slavery as profoundly subversive of their philanthropic purposes. In 1732, they prohibited slavery outright in Georgia.[24] Their decision was ratified by an Act of Parliament and supported by George II. Some officials in Georgia tried to enforce that rule for twenty years, but on a very small scale. In 1741, the Town Court of Frederica seized and sold one Negro slave, "pursuant to the law against Negroes."[25]

Oglethorpe encouraged a diversity of settlers in Georgia. Prominent among them were private adventurers who paid their way. Another small but important group were British borderers from the lowlands of Scotland and the North of England, led by Patrick Tailfer, David Douglass, Patrick Houstoun, and Andrew Grant. Some of them tended to support slavery and actively promoted it. Others were English and Welsh merchants such as Robert

Williams, who also wished to open a slave trade to Georgia. In 1738, Williams circulated a petition for the introduction of slavery and was joined by 117 signers. Half were independent colonists who lived mostly in Savannah. The other half were charity settlers who also hoped to acquire slaves.[26]

Other settlers in Georgia supported Oglethorpe and strongly opposed slavery. Among them were Highland Scots who planted a settlement at Darien and submitted a petition against slavery.[27] Also opposed were the Salzburgers, German-speaking Pietists who founded the settlement of Ebenezer, at the confluence of the Ebenezer and Savannah Rivers. They had come by way of Charleston and were appalled by the "cruel usage of negroes" which they had observed in South Carolina.[28] Yet other opponents of slavery were settlers that Oglethorpe had recruited for a fortified town of Frederica on St. Simons Island.[29]

In the midst of these many disputes, African slaves were smuggled into Georgia by individual planters. A few had been brought in before Oglethorpe arrived. Within the new colony, the shortage of labor was so severe that some strong opponents of forced bondage began to hire slaves from others. Even the antislavery Salzburgers rented slaves from Carolina when they built their settlement at Ebenezer. The founders of Savannah and individual planters also brought their own slaves, and numbers began to multiply, slowly at first but with growing momentum.

The debate over slavery in Georgia continued in Parliament. On one side were Oglethorpe, his Georgia Trustees, and their philanthropic friends. On the other were powerful parliamentary lobbies of absentee sugar planters, slave traders, and individual settlers. They found strong support in London from British writers on political economy, such as Malachy Postlethwayt, who believed that slavery was a key that unlocked colonial productivity and imperial prosperity.[30]

In 1750, the Trustees of Georgia abandoned their utopian experiment. Restrictions on landholding ended, and restraints on slavery were repealed. At the same time, Georgia also became a royal colony, and the granting of lands passed from Oglethorpe's philanthropists to a royal governor and Council. The first Tuesday of every month became "Land Day, or Land Tuesday." Governor James Wright, Lieutenant Governor John Graham, and members of Georgia's Royal Council awarded themselves large grants. Much of the best land went to a small circle of their friends and associates. Some of it was used to buy slaves.[31]

The result was a social and economic revolution in Georgia as sudden and sweeping as any in American history. Part of it was an extraordinary surge in levels of wealth concentration, greater even than in South Carolina. By 1771, the two wealthiest Georgians were Royal Governor James Wright with eleven plantations, 25,000 acres, and 523 slaves; and Lieutenant Governor John Graham with 26,000 acres and 277 slaves.

Other members of the Royal Council also did well, often rising from humble origins to great wealth. James Habersham had come to Georgia as a schoolteacher in 1738. He helped to manage the colony's public accounts and rose to the rank of acting governor in 1771–73. Noble Jones arrived in the first small group of immigrants and became surveyor of lands. He and Habersham managed business for the Trustees and acquired large plantations of their own.[32]

Altogether, several studies have found that by 1773, sixty planters in Georgia owned more than half the land in the entire colony. An even higher level of concentration developed among owners of slaves. By 1773, sixty Georgia planters (about 6 percent of all slave owners and 0.3 percent of all free inhabitants) owned about 75 percent of slaves in the core counties of coastal Georgia.[33]

Other entrepreneurs flourished on Georgia's western frontiers. One of their leaders was a woman, Mary Musgrove Matthews, daughter of an American Indian mother and a white father. She and her husband, John Musgrove, were living at Yamacraw Bluff when Georgia's first settlers came ashore, and supplied them with provisions. She was central to relations between colonists and Creek Indians, as an interpreter and frontier diplomat. Her second and third husbands pursued land claims that became bitterly contested. She was more successful, and in 1760 she received the biggest land grant ever made to a woman in the colony—6,200 acres on St. Catherines Island and the mainland.[34]

The result of all these events was a revolution in the peopling of Georgia. Numbers of African slaves grew slowly until the second half of the eighteenth century. Then, after 1750, growth rates of slavery began to surge, and kept on surging. Transatlantic shipping records alone yield an undercount of arriving slaves, as many slaves came overland. In the years 1752 and 1753 alone, entrepreneurs brought more than a thousand slaves into the colony from South Carolina.[35]

Most of Britain's North American colonies doubled their populations every generation (about twenty-five years), a very rapid rate of growth. By contrast, Georgia's population doubled or even trebled every decade.[36]

AFRICAN ORIGINS OF SLAVES IN COASTAL GEORGIA

Where did most of Georgia's slaves come from? As in every other North American region, that simple question has a complex answer. From 1755 to 1764, some slaves continued to come by land from South Carolina. Others arrived in coastal vessels from Charleston and the Sea Islands. A secondary flow came by way of the West Indies, mostly "new Africans" in small sloops that carried other commodities. More than half of these "new Africans" came to Georgia from traders in St. Kitts and Jamaica. Most had been born in Africa. That pattern persisted for ten years.[37]

As in most American colonies, an important fact about Georgia's African slave trade was its diversity of African origins. Here again, slaves were brought to Savannah from every major trading region along Africa's Atlantic coast from the Senegal River to Angola. A few arrived from more distant ports on the Indian Ocean in Madagascar and East Africa. As in every colonial region of North America, one finds in Georgia the same paradox of a broad diversity of African origins, combined with local concentrations from a few leading regions.

The patterns differed from those of South Carolina, largely because of timing. The major flow of African slaves into Georgia began eighty years after South Carolina. After 1765, the largest flow of slaves from Africa to Georgia came from what traders variously called Guinea, Upper Guinea, or North Guinea. That broad area extended from parts of the present African nations of Senegal and The Gambia at its north end, to Sierra Leone and Liberia in the south. Altogether, 61 percent of Georgia's slaves came from this region.[38]

African trading places of prominence were the Îles de Los, near the present African metropolis of Conakry, now the capital of modern Guinea. Another prominent port was Gorée Island, near the present capital of Dakar in Senegal. Also important in the slave trade to Georgia during this period were Bance Island and the Banana Islands in Sierra Leone.[39]

These forts and factories on the coast of Upper Guinea drew African captives from a large hinterland, with many dynamic African cultures and languages. From the mid-eighteenth to the mid-nineteenth century, linguists have identified about forty speechways within the great family of Mande languages. The *Mande-Tan* or northern Mande embraced Mandingo, Malinke, Dyula, Koranko, and others from Senegal and Gambia to the republic of Guinea. The *Mande-Fu* or southern Mande included Kpelle, Jallonke, Mende, Tomo, Shanga, Vai, and others from the present Republic of Guinea

south to Sierra Leone and Liberia. Together, Mande languages provided the
most common means of discourse in Upper Guinea.[40]

Guinean slaves who came to Georgia from Africa from the mid-eighteenth
to the early nineteenth century tended to share this family of related languages
and cultures, which embraced many African groups in Upper Guinea. For all
their diversity, many Mande-speaking slaves could communicate with one another, and bond among themselves. Some did so in Georgia.

Another important consequence of this trade was a flow of Islamic slaves
from Upper Guinea to coastal Georgia and South Carolina. Michael Gomez,
a leading authority on African Muslims in America, writes that "coastal islands such as Sapelo, St. Simons, St. Helena, and their environs, were also
the collective site of the largest gathering of African Muslims in early North
America, establishing a legacy that continues to the present day." Much evidence appeared in the early research of Lorenzo Dow Turner, who found
hundreds of Islamic names in Georgia and South Carolina. As we shall see,
Islamic slaves rapidly became leaders and managers on Sea Island plantations
in coastal Georgia and South Carolina.[41]

Yet a third consequence of this strong flow from Upper Guinea was a distinctive pattern of ethnic diversity throughout coastal Georgia, and other regions in the interior of that large state. Part of it grew from the diversity of
many cultures and languages that coexisted within a large and very mixed
African region of Upper Guinea. Another part developed from a larger diversity in the area between Upper Guinea and other African regions of the Gold
Coast, the Bight of Benin, the Bight of Biafra, and Central Africa.

Another pattern was a function of time. The slave trade came later to Georgia than to South Carolina, Virginia, Maryland, and Louisiana. It was also
more concentrated in time. The effect of that temporal pattern was to reinforce the exceptional strength and persistence of African cultures in coastal
Georgia.

Striking evidence of that persistence appears in *Drums and Shadows: Survival Studies Among the Georgia Coastal Negroes*, one of the most important
studies of any regional African culture in North America. It was yet another
creative product of the New Deal's Federal Writers' Project, written in the
1930s, published in 1940, reprinted in 1949 and 1986, and continuously rediscovered by writers and scholars. It is enriched by the photographs by Malcolm and Muriel Bell. The entire work is a sequence of chapters on twenty
small communities in coastal Georgia. These individual histories tend to center on themes of dynamic continuity, not in a scattering of African surviv-

als, but in an entire fabric of African American culture. One central theme is about cultural persistence, which remained very strong in 1940. Another is about the strength of community building among Geechee slaves in coastal Georgia, which continues to this day.[42]

Even as a majority of Africans in coastal Georgia came from Upper Guinea, about 40 percent came from other African regions. Evidence in the Trans-Atlantic Slave Trade Database through the full span of Georgia's recorded slave trade from 1750 to 1860 shows that about 23 percent were from Angola and Congo in West Central Africa, and 15 percent were from the Gold Coast.

The volume of Georgia's slave trade fluctuated with events. African imports to Georgia ended abruptly during the War of Independence, and many slaves left the state with Loyalist owners and the British Army. When peace returned in 1783, the Georgia slave trade revived. Upper Guinea retained its importance, and in the period from 1783 to 1808, important flows came from the Île de Los. Other sources were Gorée Island at Dakar in Senegal, British forts in Gambia, and Bance Island and Banana Island in Sierra Leone. A secondary trade came from the Gold Coast. Angola became more prominent after 1800, and a few slaves were identified as coming from Biafra. Among American regions, this pattern was unique to Georgia.

BONDAGE AND SLAVE LAW IN SOUTH CAROLINA

As early as 1690, South Carolina adopted a system of slave law. It had a different character from slave codes in other mainland colonies of North America. In its origins, it borrowed heavily from the West Indies, especially the island of Barbados. The first major Carolina slave laws in 1690 and 1696 copied Barbadian statutes word for word in some sections. The result was an exceptionally materialist and obsessively security-minded system of slave law. It differed in this and many other ways from Cavalier Virginia, Puritan New England, Catholic Maryland, Quaker Pennsylvania, Dutch New Netherland, and French dominions in North America.[43]

The first of these differences concerned the legal right of enslavement itself. Virginians and New Englanders made painstaking efforts to create a legal rationale for slavery in religious and ethical terms. Carolinians wasted no ink on such an effort. Preambles to their slave laws asserted that slavery existed in South Carolina because "the plantations and estates of this province cannot be well and sufficiently managed and brought into use, without the labor and services of negroes and other slaves." There were no legal niceties about the moral legitimacy of slavery and no pious discussions of Christian imperatives. The primacy of material motives was openly proclaimed in the South Carolina slave code itself. In all these ways, slavery in South Carolina was defined by custom and material interest, much as it had been in Barbados.

A second and closely related issue dealt with slavery as a legal condition. The statutes of South Carolina declared that "all negroes, mulatos, mustizos or indians, which heretofore have been sold, or hereafter shall be bought and sold for slaves, are hereby declared slaves; and they, and their children, are hereby made and declared slaves, to all intents and purposes" except those few who could prove they were free. Historian Eugene Sirmans wrote, "Custom, not law, defined the negro's status," an approach that allowed Barbados and South Carolina "to impose upon the negro the conditions of servitude desired by his master without English interference." In other words, a slave was a slave was a slave in South Carolina.[44]

A third major purpose of the slave laws was to define the status of slaves as property. South Carolina's leaders were very clear on that subject. Chancery Courts and probate laws in the colony defined slaves as chattels as early as 1693, and continued to do so until the end of slavery. In 1725, Acting Governor Arthur Middleton wrote that slaves "have always been and are always deemed as goods and chattels of their masters." In 1740, the Carolina slave code ratified this custom: "All negroes and indians" not free were declared to be "absolute slaves" and "chattels personal, in the hands of their owners and possessors, and their executors, administrators and assigns, to all intents, constructions and purposes whatsoever."[45]

These ideas of "absolute slaves" as "chattels personal" derived from the West Indies, and had a powerful resonance in South Carolina. The codes of this colony gave the master absolute dominion over his slaves—more so than in Virginia. They arose not only from Caribbean customs and economic interests, but also from a cultural imperative that was growing stronger in the English-speaking world. Strong Lockean conceptions of property rights entered directly into the founding of Carolina. John Locke himself drafted the Fundamental Constitutions of Carolina, which provided explicitly that "every freeman of Carolina" shall have "absolute power and authority over his negro slaves." This provision also followed West Indian precedents.[46]

Under the early slave laws of South Carolina, a master could treat his slaves with extreme severity. He held their lives in his hands. A master could put his slaves to death, or maim them, or punish his slaves as savagely as he thought necessary. The law held that "if any slave, by punishment from the owner for running away or other offense shall suffer in life or limb, no person shall be liable to the law for the same."

The Carolina code offered some protections to slaves. Whites were forbidden to kill negroes merely as an act of "wantoness, or only of bloody-mindedness, or cruel intention." But if they did so, the crime was not murder, and the penalty was not death but a fine of 50 pounds.[47] A system of due process was also established for slave trials and convictions. But its primary purpose was to protect the property rights of the master, not the human rights of the slave. Even the imperatives of Christianity were subordinated to the owner's authority. A statute in 1696 allowed any "negro or Indian slave" to "receive and profess the Christian faith," but only if the master wished it so.[48]

South Carolina's slave laws were written by a small lowcountry minority who were deeply conscious that they were surrounded by a large, dangerous, and hostile slave population. The preamble to the slave code proclaimed as a self-evident truth that "Negroes and other slaves . . . are of barbarous, wild, savage natures."[49]

This climate of fear in South Carolina gave rise to the only important constraints on masters' freedom of action. The Carolina slave code required owners and overseers to keep their slaves under constant surveillance—a requirement that did not exist in Virginia. Every "slave house" was to be searched at least once every fourteen days for "clubs, guns, swords and mischievous weapons." In 1722, that list was enlarged to include "cutlasses, lances, and other offensive weapons."

Every master was also required to "keep all his guns and other arms, when out of use, in the most private and least frequented room in the house."[50] In 1722, each master was further required to keep his weapons under lock and key. These statutes and others showed a depth of insecurity that did not exist in the Chesapeake colonies.[51]

Slave-owning South Carolinians worried that "negroes and other slaves" who kept horses would "convey intelligences from one part of the country to another and carry on their secret plots and contrivances for insurrections and rebellions." The revised law in 1722 forbade slaves and Negroes to keep horses, canoes, and boats for the same reason.[52]

Masters were commanded by law to keep their slaves busy so that they did not have time to make trouble. It was forbidden to "give or allow any Saturday, in the afternoon, to any negro or slave as hath been accustomed formerly, upon the penalty of seven shillings."[53]

The law expressed particular fear of field slaves. Any house slave or slave in livery could leave the plantation on Sundays and holidays. Other slaves could not do so. Sunday gatherings of slaves in Charleston were strictly prohibited.[54]

An elaborate system of written passes was constructed by law to control the movement of slaves. If any slave was found away from the plantation without written permission of the master, "it is hereby declared lawful for any white person to beat, maim or assault, and if such negro or slave cannot otherwise taken, to kill him."[55]

The economic independence of slaves was rigidly restricted by law in early South Carolina, far beyond other colonies. Masters could not allow a slave to work for himself even if he brought the money home, but he could be hired to another master.[56] Other early laws forbade South Carolina slaves "to plant for themselves any corn, peas or rice, or to keep for themselves any stock of hogs, cattle or horses."[57] In Virginia, they were commonly encouraged to raise their own food, which later happened in the Carolina lowcountry as well.

Penalties for resistance or disobedience by slaves were brutal in South Carolina, more so than in Virginia. For petty pilfering of goods worth as little as 12 pence, a South Carolina "slave or negro" was to be punished by forty lashes for the first offense, branding or loss of an ear for the second offense, slitting of the nose for the third, and death for the fourth.[58]

For running away, the first offense brought a heavy whipping; the second offense, branding with the letter R on the right cheek; for the third, loss of an ear; the fourth, castration for males (females were to be branded again and to lose the other ear); and for the fifth offense, "the cord of one of the slave's legs to be cut off above the heel," or else the death penalty, if the court preferred.[59] And death was also the penalty for even attempting to escape.

The Carolina slave code recognized few rights for slaves—not even a right to life. But it was careful to respect rights of property for owners. The Assembly recognized an inalienable right of masters to be compensated by the colony for the execution of their human property, and statute law required that it be done.[60]

In 1739, after the Stono Rebellion and the violent repression that followed, South Carolina's slave code was revised and even reformed in a few respects. An attempt was made to improve the material condition of slaves. New laws forbade slaves to be "beaten, bruised, maimed or disabled" without "sufficient cause or lawful authority." Slaves could not be made to work more than fifteen hours a day from March to September, or more than fourteen hours from September to March.[61] Masters were required to provide "sufficient cloathing, covering and food."[62] But people in bondage were forbidden to wear clothing "above the condition of slaves."[63]

In other ways, control of slaves became more rigid after the rebellion. Male slaves were forbidden to travel the highways in numbers larger than seven. Any assembly of slaves could be dispersed. No strong liquors could be sold to slaves. They could not be taught to write, though there was no law against reading. No slaves could be kept on a plantation in the colony without the presence of a white man.[64]

Special laws were passed to deal with the danger of poisoning, and went far beyond Virginia statutes in their rigor. Slaves were forbidden to work as apothecaries, or to practice medicine, or to deal in rice or corn. "Lunatic" slaves were ordered to be kept secure by each parish, if masters were unable to do so.[65]

After 1739, the slave law of South Carolina made the colony into an armed camp, constantly alert against the danger of slave revolt. All white males were ordered to carry arms to church on Sunday. The Charleston Watch was required to muster during divine services.[66] In the Christmas season, and most of all on Christmas Day, the colony went on high alert. Masters were required to carry a "gun or a pair of horse pistols" with at least six charges of powder and ball.[67]

Altogether, the slave code of South Carolina was designed for a society that was very different from the Chesapeake colonies. A major factor was the pattern of population growth. Coastal Carolina was a place where slaves greatly outnumbered free people and servants. Members of the master class lived with a deep sense of mortal danger. Through the long history of slavery in South Carolina, free women of the master class testified that they were always afraid.

SLAVE LAW IN GEORGIA: A CONTESTED TRADITION

In Georgia, the first major law about slavery was proposed by the Trustees, passed by the British Parliament in 1734, and approved by the Crown in 1735. It was called "An Act for Rendering the Colony of Georgia more Defencible by Prohibiting the Importation and Use of Black Slaves or Negroes into the same."[68]

Here was James Oglethorpe's founding vision of a colony without slavery altogether. Parliament justified it by appeals to security and prosperity, not humanity. But from the start, many Georgia planters insisted that slavery was necessary for the prosperity of the colony, and even for its survival. They argued at length that few free white workers could be recruited, and fewer could survive the climate of coastal Georgia.

James Oglethorpe and the Georgia Trustees had remained steadfast against slavery for near twenty years. But Oglethorpe himself undercut the argument to security by a dramatic military victory. In 1742, a large Spanish expedition attacked Georgia. Oglethorpe, with a much smaller force, defeated them at the Battle of Bloody Marsh. It was a "brilliant bit of soldiering," as British Regulars liked to say.[69]

Colonists instantly seized upon the event to increase their demand for slaves. In London, the Georgia Trustees at last gave way. They reluctantly agreed to permit slavery, starting in 1751, but allowed only a limited number and added strict rules to protect slaves from cruelty and abuse. Corporal punishment of slaves was permitted, but not to endanger life or limb. Masters were required to provide "instruction in the Christian religion," and a full day of rest on Sundays.[70]

As slavery multiplied rapidly in Georgia, owners of slaves gained increasing representation in the colonial legislature, and they proceeded to frame their own detailed slave code. It was enacted by the Georgia Assembly on February 5, 1755, and approved by the Georgia Council in nine days, with the approval of Georgia's governor, John Reynolds.

Georgia's first system of slave law applied broadly to "Negroes, Indians, Mulatos, and Mestizos." It was meant to mediate between the material demands of masters, and a continuing concern for humanity among the Trustees. It instructed Governor Reynolds to restrain "any inhuman Severity, which by ill Masters or Overseers may be used towards their Christian Servants & their Slaves."[71]

That element was combined with other purposes. The Georgia slave code of 1755 closely followed the laws of bondage in South Carolina and the British West Indies. It decreed that all slaves "shall be deemed in law to be Chattels personal in the Hands of their owners and possessors . . . to all intents and purposes whatsoever." Further, they were slaves for life, and that condition was hereditary. It applied to all "who now are or shall hereafter be in the province and all their Issue and offspring" and required that they were to "be and to remain forever hereafter absolute Slaves, and shall follow the condition of the mother."[72]

Georgia's first slave code had two major purposes. The first was to ensure that slaves would be "kept in due Subjection and Obedience." To that end, Georgia's leaders borrowed heavily from the brutal laws and customs of South Carolina and the West Indies.

One example was a provision that "slaves who shall attempt to raise an insurrection or to entice other slaves to run away and leave this Province to suffer death." Another was that slaves "absent from their place of abode without a ticket" were to be punished severely, and "slaves refusing to be examined by any White person . . . may be lawfully killed." Further, "not more than seven Men slaves" were allowed "to travel together on the high Roads without a white person with them." And "slaves [were] not to be taught to write and persons offending to forfeit £15."

The second purpose of the laws in 1755 was that owners of slaves should be "restrained from exercising too great Rigour and Cruelty over them," so that "the Public peace and order of this province may be preserved." But the penalties were much less severe than for similar acts of violence against free whites. Examples were provisions that "persons killing a slave in a sudden Heat of passion &c to forfeit £50," and "any persons exercising any cruelty towards them to forfeit £10," and "owners of Slaves refusing to provide them with sufficient Clothing and Food to forfeit not exceeding £3." Also "persons who shall put any Slave to Work on Sunday shall forfeit ten Shillings Sterling." In all of those ways, Georgia's slave code of 1755 preserved at least something of Georgia's founding purposes, and James Oglethorpe's guiding principles. But it was moving rapidly in another direction.

After 1755, Georgia's Assembly legislated frequently on slavery, sometimes in periodic panic attacks, triggered by reports of slave revolts through the next century. As a result, slave law in Georgia, as in South Carolina, became more harsh and cruel through time. Reports of alleged poisoning of masters and mistresses triggered epidemics of fear and legislation. The code of 1755 barely mentioned poisoning of masters in a long list of capital crimes. In 1761, a Charleston newspaper reported that slaves had "again begun the hellish practice of poisoning." Georgians responded with a new slave law in 1765 which added many paragraphs on the subject of poisoning by slaves.[73]

Slave revolts anywhere in North America tended to lead to increasing severity everywhere. After Gabriel's Revolt in Virginia (1800), where free Negroes were thought to be involved, Georgia banned manumission of slaves except by legislative act. Nat Turner's Rebellion by a literate slave leader was followed by many restrictions on reading and writing.

But from time to time, a more liberal spirit also stirred in the state of Georgia. In 1765, when the revolutionary movement was growing rapidly through the colonies, a new Georgia law granted free Blacks "all the rights, priviledges, powers, and immunities whatsoever which any Person born of British parents within this province may, can, might, could, or of right ought to have," with one exception. Free Blacks could not "vote or be Elected" to the Georgia Assembly. Later it was followed by more limits and qualifications.

And there were also occasional expressions of a more general spirit in different ways. In 1833, a fire broke out in the Georgia State House and the building was saved by Sam, "a negro slave" who "extinguished the blaze." Both houses of a grateful legislature voted to purchase Sam from his master and set him free.[74] In these occasional events something of the spirit of James Oglethorpe briefly revived in Georgia, but more as the exception than the rule.

RELATIONS BETWEEN MASTERS AND SLAVES IN THE LOWCOUNTRY

A curious paradox appeared in the culture of coastal Georgia and South Carolina. In a distant way, some Sea Island slaves identified strongly with the families that owned them. An example on St. Simons Island was an elderly female former slave who was addressed as Maum Rhina, a title of respect. She told an interlocutor, "I hol' my head jus as high as my Missus. I'se a Wylly nig'ah."

Wylly slaves despised Hazzard slaves who lived nearby. When one Wylly master was killed by Dr. Hazzard, his neighbor and physician, a feud began between the Wylly and Hazzard slaves, and continued for more than a century after slavery.[75]

Even as strong identities formed that way, many slaves had little personal contact with whites—not even with their own masters and mistresses. At the same time, most of the master class had close associations with house servants and other slave leaders. It is said that some masters and mistresses in Coastal Carolina had been tended in early childhood by slave wet nurses. More than a few learned a Gullah dialect as their first language, and English later.

But even as some strong identities were formed, many slaves on large lowcountry plantations had little personal contact with their own masters and mistresses. Ben Horry, a slave born on Brookgreen Plantation, remembered "everybody can't go to boss folks."[76] A St. Helena slave on one of the Fripp plantations recalled, "Missis don't hab nutting to do wid nigger."[77]

At the same time, many white workers of the master class had close associations with a few slaves—Black managers, field drivers, skilled artisans, and favored house servants. J. Motte Alston remembered that in his own family Mrs. Motte "had no guard save old Allard, a West Indian negro, who faithfully slept at the door of her bedroom. I remember Allard quite distinctly, with his bald head and French pronunciation. He had all the silverware in his charge at Fairfield. His whole occupation was to see that it was kept bright."[78]

Among masters, some of the deepest and most enduring connections with slaves were formed in childhood and even infancy, when children in the big house had slave wet nurses and slave playmates who were sometimes half brothers and half sisters. Visitors from Western Europe or North America were astonished to meet wealthy South Carolinians who combined the manners and dress of the European aristocracy with the Gullah speechways of their slaves. It was said of Benjamin Allston Sr., master of a great Waccamaw plantation, that "his language was like a negro's, not only in pronunciation but even in tone."[79]

The result was a very peculiar institution indeed—a system where white masters became partly African in their culture, and slaves carved out a cultural space for their African heritage, which was deeper and stronger in the lowcountry than in other regions of early North America.

THE EMERGENCE OF AFRICAN COMMUNITY LEADERS: BILALI MAHOMET, PLANTATION MANAGER

Another distinctive feature of lowcountry slavery was the exceptional importance of slave managers. These men were to be found in every region, but they were most prevalent in coastal Carolina, where they managed entire plantations, and were treated with respect and deference by masters, overseers, and slaves alike. In the dangerous summer months, slave managers were often left to run the entire estate.

In the early years of slavery, these managers were often African-born. An example was Bilali Mahomet, who became the sole manager of five hundred slaves on Thomas Spalding's Sapelo Island plantation, one of the largest estates in the Sea Islands during the early republic. Also remembered in slave narratives as Ben Ali, Bu Allah, and Belali Mahomet, he had been born to a family of great wealth and property in the Fulani culture of West Africa during the mid-eighteenth century. He was raised in or near Timbo, a major center of Afro-Islamic culture in the uplands of what is now Guinea-Conakry. In Africa he may have been a slave trader himself, and was carried captive to Georgia with all his family. He was described as tall, "coal black" with fine features, an arrogant manner, and a commanding presence. Bilali was a devout Muslim, literate in Arabic, and fluent also in his native Fulfulde, French, and English. In Georgia, he owned a Quran and kept Arabic manuscripts in his own hand; a fragment survives in manuscript of a treatise on Islamic law. All his life he wore a fez, carried a prayer rug, and carefully observed his religion. He took several wives and fathered many daughters, who were given African and Arabic names such as Medina, Yaruba, Fatima, Bentu, Hesta, Magret, and Challut. Their descendants are numerous in the United States today.

Bilali ran the Spalding estate on Sapelo without an overseer, and sometimes was left in sole command by his master. Several times he saved the plantation from catastrophe. During the War of 1812 he kept the slaves together and organized a defense against British raiding parties, writing to his master "I will answer for every negro of the true faith, but not for these Christian dogs of yours." Again in 1824 when a hurricane hit the island, Bilali got the slaves to safety and saved his master from ruin.

Bilali Mahomet became a famous figure in the Sea Islands. He was not unique. Another African manager was his close friend of similar name and doubtful relation, Salih Bilali, who ran the even larger plantations of the Couper family on St. Simons Island and the Altamaha River, with five hundred slaves under his orders. In African ethnicity Salih Bilali was a Fulbe, born in 1765 and raised in Kouna. He was literate in Arabic, owned a Quran, and was a devout Muslim. Those who knew him said that he was "tall, thin, but well made with small features." He too was trusted with great power, and sometimes had sole responsibility for hundreds of slaves. His master wrote, "I have several times left him for several months, in charge of the plantation, without an overseer; and on each occasion he has conducted the place to my entire satisfaction." [80]

AFRICAN "WATCHMEN" AS INTENDANTS AND STEWARDS

By the end of slavery, African leaders in the lowcountry were mostly native-born Americans who had assimilated much of European culture without abandoning that of Africa. Frederick Law Olmsted met one such a man when he visited a lowcountry plantation. He was called "the watchman" by his owner. But Olmsted noted that

> his duties, however, as they were described to me, were those of a steward, or intendant. He carried by a strap at his waist, a very large number of keys, and had charge of all the stores of provisions, tools and materials of the plantation, as well as their produce before it was shipped to market. He weighed and measured all the rations of the slaves and feed for the cattle, superintended the mechanics, and made and repaired, as was necessary, all the machinery, including the steam-engine. In all

these departments, his authority was superior to that of the overseer. The overseer received his private allowance of family provisions from him, as did the head-servant of the mansion, who was his brother.[81]

Olmsted became interested in this man and inquired about his origins. He had been the son of a house servant who was raised among the children of his master. He was made a "waiter," but at his own request was apprenticed to a blacksmith. His master paid $500 to have him trained as a machinist and an engineer. The master forced him to return to the plantation, and gradually gave him exceptional powers and privileges.

"The watchman was a fine-looking fellow," Olmsted noted. "As we were returning from church, on Sunday, he had passed us, well dressed and well mounted, and as he raised his hat, to salute us, there was nothing in his manner or appearance, except his colour, to distinguish him from a gentleman of good breeding and fortune." Everywhere in the slave states there were such men. But they were exceptionally numerous and powerful in the lowcountry of Carolina and Georgia.[82]

AFRICAN DRIVERS AS PLANTATION LEADERS: PHILIP WASHINGTON OF PIPE DOWN PLANTATION

In 1859, Mary Ann Petigru's husband died and she became the owner of Pipe Down Plantation on Sandy Island in the Waccamaw River. With all her other responsibilities, Pipe Down was more than she felt able to manage, and she resolved to sell it. Mary Ann Petigru asked her cousin Governor Robert F. W. Allston to buy the plantation with its slaves, as she felt "unequal to the management and care of them." Allston refused, and explained that "he had his hands full managing his own property," which included six plantations and many hundreds of slaves, not to mention the state of South Carolina.

The Pipe Down slaves were quick to learn of these discussions, and actively involved themselves. The slaves met together and sent to Governor Allston a delegation led by their head driver, Philip Washington. Allston's daughter Elizabeth Allston Pringle remembered Washington as a "very tall, very black man, a splendid specimen of the negro race." In 1859, he was fifty-three years old. Philip Washington went to the governor and delivered a request from the Pipe Down slaves to buy the plantation. Washington "pleaded the cause with much eloquence," and told the governor that the Pipe Down slaves "had fixed on him as the one owner they desired." Allston refused again.

Philip Washington persisted. A special appeal was made to Allston's "chivalry" and also to the "intense feeling of the negroes." Terms of purchase were adjusted to include only a token cash payment and a large mortgage. Governor Allston listened, and at last agreed. With Philip Washington's leadership the Pipe Down slaves succeeded in hiring their own master. In that process, they kept their families together, and preserved their community intact.[83]

All parties assumed that the question was settled, but the year was 1859. In December of 1860, South Carolina's slaveholders were so infuriated by the election of Abraham Lincoln that they became the first state to secede from the Union. The first shots of the Civil War were fired at Fort Sumter. Governor Allston died in 1864. His estate was bankrupt, and Pipe Down Plantation went on the market.

Its former slaves were now free. Many still lived on Sandy Island. Philip Washington continued to function as their community leader, in freedom as he had done in bondage. He went to the new Freedman's Bank in Charleston, and managed to raise money to buy 382 acres, not the whole of Sandy Island but enough for the former slaves of Pipe Down Plantation to acquire their own land.

Descendants still own that land today. They live in villages on Sandy Island, and fought successfully for many years to keep a bridge from being built to the mainland. The rest of the island is now owned by the Nature Conservancy and protected from development.

With our friend Charles Joyner we visited Sandy Island by boat, the only way there, and we were welcome. It is a place of extraordinary continuity, both in its ecology, and in the preservation of Gullah culture and community. The people of Sandy Island commute by boat to jobs and schools of their choice along Myrtle Beach and the "Grand Strand." They engage the twenty-first century on their own terms and preserve their own ways, thanks in no small part to their nineteenth-century head driver, plantation manager, and community leader, Philip Washington.[84]

DRIVERS AS "VILLAGE HEADMEN,"
"PLANTATION POLICE," AND "TASK BOSSES"

Most lowcountry plantations also had slave drivers. They were selected for size and strength, judgment and maturity. Their powers were greater than drivers in other parts of the South. In the Sea Islands they were also called headmen, with responsibilities that reached beyond supervision of labor. Throughout the Spalding plantation on Sapelo Island in Georgia, for example, the slaves were divided into small "villages," each with its own village headman. Philip Morgan has observed that "drivers in South Carolina were more often managers than mere gang leaders," and "were valued for their ability to take decisive and independent action."[85]

Frederick Law Olmsted observed the same pattern through much of coastal Carolina. "A good driver," he observed, "is very valuable and usually holds office for life. His authority is not limited to the direction of labour in the field, but extends to the general deportment of the Negroes. He is made to do the duties of policeman, and even of the police magistrate. It is his duty, for instance, on Mr. X's estate, to keep order in the settlement; and, if two persons, men or women, are fighting, it is his duty to immediately separate them, and then to whip them both."[86]

A lowcountry driver's responsibility in the rice fields differed from those of other regions in the South, partly because of the task system. They laid out the fields themselves and divided them in half-acre tasks for full hands. They also participated actively in fixing the tasks of individual slaves, which tended to vary by age, strength, and gender. Olmsted observed that "the advice of the drivers is commonly taken in nearly all the administration, and frequently they are, *de facto*, the managers. Orders on important points of the plantation economy, I have heard being given by the proprietor directly to them, without the overseer's being consulted or informed of them; and it is often left with them to decide how long to flow the rice-grounds—the proprietor and overseer deferring to their more experienced judgment."[87]

From a slave's perspective, much depended on the disposition of the driver. One freedman remembered, "Some of de people fare good in slavery time en some of dem fare rough. Dat been accordin to de kind of task boss dey come up." Many drivers looked after individual slaves, and protected them. A few went the other way. Former slaves also remembered angry drivers who gave individual slaves impossible tasks, which could lead to heavy punishments.[88]

Other important slave leaders in the lowcountry were boat captains, often called patroons in coastal Carolina. Philip Morgan observed in his comparative studies that they had "more autonomy" in South Carolina than in the Chesapeake. They tended to be watermen of long experience with knowledge of the coast, and also with many friends in coastal plantations and towns.[89]

Some field slaves became major leaders and powerful figures without having a formal title or rank. A case in point was the career of a renowned slave named Old John Drayton. He belonged to Major William Meggett Murray on Edisto Island, and became a living legend in the Sea Islands—a Gullah equivalent of Paul Bunyan. Former slave Ephraim Lawrence remembered some of his exploits, and told an interviewer about the relationship between Old John and his master. It is a long story, but special for its substance and vivid Gullah style, partly anglicized in the source, but preserving many layers of meaning:

Old John Drayton was de smaa'test of all de nigger de maussa place. He wuk so haa'd some time dat Maussa jest got to stop him, or he kill heself. I nebber see sech uh man fer wuk in all my life. Maussa t'ink uh lot ob um, 'cause he been uh good field hand, beside know lot 'bout cutting 'ood [wood] and building fence. What been more old John play fer all de dance on de plantation. He fair mek fiddle talk. When maussa gib uh dance he always call 'pon John.

Yas suh, dat man sure could play. W'en he saw down on de fiddle and pull out dat june [tune], "Oh, de Monkey marry to de Babboon Sister," he mek paa'son dance [a patricular parson, or any parson, or any person for that matter—all in one Gullah word].

One day more dan all, Maussa Murray send wud to John dat de cow der break out ob de pasture, and he got to mend de fence quick. But John done promise some nigger on Fenwick Island to play fer uh dance, and he steal paa't and go. ["steal path and go," a Gullah idiom that meant to leave by stealth]. Dat been Friday night and maussa say John got to finish de fence by sundown the next day.

W'en Old John ain't show up Saturday morning, Maussa ax eberybody where he been and de nigger all band togedder and tell Maussa dat dey see him leabe in uh boat to go fish and ain't seen since. Maussa been worry sure 'enough den cause he t'ink John might drown. He 'gage four men to shoot gun all ober creek to mek John body rise. Atter dat dey drag all 'bout in de gutter. Maussa gone bed wid heaby haa't [heavy heart] cause he been very fond ob old John.

John come back from Fenwick Island early Monday morning and 'fore day clean he in de 'odd [wood] der cut fence rail. Now one hundred rail been call uh good day wuk, but Old John decide he going to do better dan dat. He find fibe [five] tree grow close togedder, and he cut piece out ob every one. Den he chop at the biggest tree till he fall, and dat tree knock all de rest ober wid um.

W'en all dem tree fall togedder, it make sech uh noise, dat ole maussa hear um in he bed, and hasten to dress so he kin see w'at der go on in de woods. Maussa saddle de horse and ride 'till he git to de center ob de noise and dere he see Old John cutting 'way like he crazy. Maussa been mad sure 'nough, but den he glad to see John ain't drown. he staa't to say some t'ing but Old John interrupt, and sing out: "Go 'way Maussa, I ain't got time to talk wid you now."

Old John den gather up five ax, and go to de five tree laying down on de ground. He dribe uh axe in ebery tree and den grab uh heaby maul. W'en maussa look on, he tek de maul and run from one tree to torrer and quick as he hit de ax, de tree split wide open. Maussa staa't to say some t'ting 'gain but John ain't let him talk. He say: "Go on home to Missus, Maussa, I too shame, great God I too shame! Go on home."

Maussa tun 'round in he track and go home widout uh wud, 'cause he see de old nigger ain't going to gib him any satisfaction 'bout Saturday. W'en he go back in de wood dat evening he check up and find dat John done cut five hundred rail. Oh, dem been man in dose day, I tell you.[90]

AFRICAN BIG MAMAS: MARY CHESNUT'S MOLLY

Slave women also had leading roles, as drivers and fanners with other female field slaves, and also as head cooks who supervised the servants, and did not hesitate to shape up their mistress from time to time.

Mary Boykin Chesnut recorded a run-in with her head cook, Molly. One day Mrs. Chesnut had two surprise guests for supper. The word arrived just as she was sitting down to her midday dinner with a friend called Sally G:

We sent for Molly to order some cake. She came to the dining room door with a fiery face, which she wiped with her apron.

"Name o' God! Why don't dey ax you dere? It is cook, cook in dis house, from daylight to dark. Yo' time is come to be axed somewhere." She spoke at the top of her voice.

"Molly, you forget yourself," I said in a low tone. Sally G's little maid standing open-mouthed, all eye-balls and white teeth.

"Blige to talk dish here way. You'll soon have nothing left for yo'self to eat."

Mary Chesnut confided to her diary, "Molly's temper was always violent. And as Buck told her, she had no manners ever—but then she is the best cook, the best dairy maid, the best washerwoman, and the best chambermaid I know." And Molly was more than all that. She ran much of the big house, the dairy, and much more. Molly's temper appears to have been a carefully controlled instrument, and it was applied even to her mistress in ways that shifted the flow of power in the Big House.[91]

LOWCOUNTRY SLAVERY AS AN ECONOMIC SYSTEM

Many cash crops were tried in the Carolina lowcountry. For a brief period in the mid-eighteenth century, planters raised indigo, a plant that produced a deep rich blue dye that was much valued in the English textile industry. Parliament enacted a subsidy in 1749, and production surged from less than 100,000 pounds of indigo a year in 1747 to more than a million pounds in 1775. War and Independence ended the bounty. It revived briefly in the 1780s and 1790s, then faded.

South Carolinians had a saying that indigo was a slave-killing crop. The fields had to be clean of weeds and the plants had to be kept free of insects, which both required incessant labor. The worst of it came after the harvest when the indigo plants were fermented in large vats of lime water, with much stirring and beating. The rotting plants produced a foul stench.

In the nineteenth century many planters gave it up, but indigo was raised in Horry County to the end of slavery. Accounts appear in late slave narratives. William Oliver, "born in Horry, a boy in slavery time," remembered, "Indigo? Cut the bush down. Put it in sacks. Let it drip out. Call that indigo mud." [92]

The leading money crop was rice, a staple through much of Africa. Rice had been grown on a large scale in West Africa from Senegal south to the Ivory Coast, and it was also cultivated in West Central Africa, East Africa, and Madagascar.[93] Techniques varied from one region to another. In more arid African regions, various methods of dry cultivation were common. In what is now Guinea, a slave trader named Captain Gamble described in detail an African method of rice cultivation remarkably similar to what later developed in South Carolina:

The Bagos are very expert in Cultivating rice and in quite a Different manner to any of the Nations on the Windward Coast. The country they inhabit is chiefly loam and swampy. The rice they first sow on their dunghills and rising spots about their towns; when 8 or 10 inches high [they] transplant it into Lugars made for their purpose which are low flat swamps, at one side . . . they have a reservoir that they can let in what water they please, [on the] other side is a drain out so they can let off what they please. The instrument they use much resembles a turf spade with which they turn the grass under in ridges just above the water which by being confined stagnates and nourishes the root of the plant. Women & girls transplant the rice and are so dextrous as to plant fifty roots singly in one minute. When the rice is ready for cutting they turn the water off till their harvest is over then they let the water over it and lets it stand three or four seasons it being so impoverished. Their time of planting is September.[94]

Captain Gamble made a drawing of Baga rice fields with reservoirs and water flows. Other travelers noted similar methods on tidal rivers throughout Africa.[95]

One of the most highly developed Africa rice-growing regions was on the island of Madagascar. Probably in the period 1693–96, several private armed vessels called privateers by their friends and pirates by their victims, found their way to Charleston with loot gained in raiding the coast of East Africa. It is probable that they brought Madagascar rice seed to the lowcountry, with slaves who were skilled in growing it. Madagascar rice was well suited to the American environment and became widely used in Carolina and Georgia during the eighteenth century.[96]

South Carolina planters sought out slaves who were skilled in rice production. Methods of cultivation throughout the lowcountry followed African patterns in many details. Transplanting rice into the field was done by making a hole with the heel, inserting the seed, and scraping in dirt with the foot, just as in Africa. Cultivation was done with a hoe by long lines of slaves, singing African work songs. The rice was winnowed in "fanning baskets" of African origin. Rice was "cleaned" or "pounded" with wooden mortars and pestles of African design. All of these methods were used in coastal Carolina and Georgia.[97]

A distinctive labor system developed in coastal Carolina and Georgia— one of many labor systems in North American plantation slavery. On upland cotton farms and sugar plantations in the lower Mississippi Valley, gang systems were widely used. In some parts of Virginia, both for tobacco and wheat, another method developed that Lewis Cecil Gray described as a team system.

And on small farms with fewer than five slaves, individual work systems were the rule. All of these systems were also used in various combinations.

But in lowcountry Carolina and Georgia, task systems were highly developed, and they were used for Sea Island cotton as well as for rice. To center these different labor systems entirely on crop types is an error. Deeper roots were to be found in the entire web of regional cultures. Gullah and Geechee slaves were actively engaged in their development.

Every day, each slave was given a specific task of clearing, ground-breaking, trench-digging, and sowing. A daily task was commonly designed to be completed with less than a full day's labor. Tasks were also adjusted for the age and health and fitness of slaves, as half-hands or quarter-hands.[98] When slaves finished their daily tasks, the rest of the day was their own. They could use that time in their own family garden plots for consumption and sale, or in hunting or fishing, or craftwork.[99]

Tasking systems appeared in the eighteenth century, and early descriptions survive from visitors, masters, and slaves. For later periods, masters' accounts became more systemic, and more accounts of the task system came from slaves themselves, who described tasking in terms of their personal experience. They often commented on an interesting paradox. The system of individual tasks in the lowcountry allowed much cooperative effort among slaves, who helped each other. Surviving accounts describe slaves who had trouble completing their tasks. Other slaves helped them, and in the completion of individual tasks, they sometimes worked together. Within task systems, Charles Joyner found evidence of "cooperative work systems" that had been "widespread in West Africa. Stronger and faster slaves helped weaker and slower ones."[100]

The task system sometimes gave slaves considerable time for themselves. Tasks were often done by three in the afternoon. Slaves could do double tasks in one day, and have the next day off for fishing or hunting, which some masters encouraged.[101]

LOWCOUNTRY SLAVERY AS A DEMOGRAPHIC SYSTEM

North of Charleston, the tidal Waccamaw River flowed parallel to the Atlantic coast. It included some of the most fertile and productive rice lands in the country. But it also created an environment of mortal danger in the mosquito season, for Europeans especially, but also for Africans.

One of the most successful Waccamaw planters was Plowden C. J. Weston. He built a big barnlike structure on a long stretch of sand called Pawley's Island. It was a barrier island that separated the Waccamaw River Valley from the Atlantic. On it, Weston built an "ocean house," only a few miles from his rice plantation and big house on the river. But that short distance made a major difference for health and life chances.

When the weather grew warm and the mosquitoes began to multiply, Weston moved his family to the ocean house. They took with them a good many slaves, a reminder that malaria (especially the lethal falciparum malaria that may have been carried to America by slave ships) took a toll of both masters and slaves.

Plowden Weston's summer refuge still stands. We visited and stayed there with Charles Joyner and his family. It had been converted into a happy hostelry called the Pelican Inn, beautifully set with the ocean to the east, and views of sunsets across marshes to the west. On its open shady southern verandah there was an old joggling board—a long sagging plank supported at either end by two uprights on rockers. It was used by courting couples. Judy and I tried it, after fifty years of matrimony. We began by sitting apart at each end, and were joggled together in the middle.

Here again, some slaves went with the master's family to their summer house. A lowcountry house slave remembered, "I don't know nothin 'bout crops, cause we summered. Family went to Plantersville."[102]

In summertime the rice coast of Carolina and Georgia long remained one of the most dangerous regions in America, for the health of both Africans and Europeans. For many generations, death rates of Europeans were higher than those of Africans, but the climate of the rice coast was also mortal for slaves as well. In the early nineteenth century, slaves on the rice plantations of the Ball family had a life expectancy at birth of only 19.8 years for male slaves, and 20.5 for females.[103] The mortality of infants was very high.[104]

Other evidence of the conception cycle shows another striking pattern. Conceptions of slave women had a different timing from free women, Black and white, in southern parts of North America. The third trimester of slave pregnancies commonly coincided with the peak period of labor on South Carolina rice plantations, in August and September when the crop was harvested and threshed.[105]

In the coastal counties of Georgia, African slaves greatly outnumbered European populations. Chatham, Liberty, and Glynn Counties all had large Black majorities in 1790. By 1820, Black majorities also existed in much of upper Georgia as well—Burke, Richmond, Columbia, Wilkes, Oglethorpe, Greene, Hancock, and Baldwin Counties—the nucleus of a broad "plantation belt" that would overspread much of the state by 1860. Many demographic patterns in coastal Georgia spread upcountry, but without the coastal Geechee culture.[106]

LOWCOUNTRY SLAVERY AS A CULTURAL SYSTEM: REGIONAL SPEECH WAYS

In 1734, an angry planter advertised in Charleston's *South Carolina Gazette* for the return of "four young Negro men slaves and a girl who . . . speak very good (Black) English."[107] This is the earliest known reference to distinct "(Black)" speechways that developed among African slaves of European owners in North America.

On the much vexed question of its origins and character, scholars have long disagreed. One angry planter believed that his slaves were deliberately speaking a new dialect of "(Black) English" to deceive him. But others who spoke European languages found this speech of slaves to be nearly incomprehensible and believed that it was mainly African.

More recently, some linguists have come to regard that Black speech in America as a distinct language that began to develop among traders on the coast of Africa as a pidgin, which was nobody's native tongue. Pidgin was a simplified way of speaking that borrowed from several languages. These linguists believe that children of slaves in the New World adopted this pidgin as a native language, called Creole speech. This "Pidgin-Creole model" is useful and has dominated the field for a generation.[108]

But there are also other ways to think about this subject. To study it more broadly is to find that Africans in their native lands, and also in America, had a gift for speaking and thinking in more than one language at a time. They came from a vast area of West and Central Africa where as many as eight hundred native languages have been identified in the era of the Atlantic slave trade. They were as different from one another as were the languages of Europe.[109] At the same time these languages also shared many broad family resemblances. Among African slaves in the Atlantic trade, most languages have been classified by linguists as belonging to a single group called Congo-Kordofanian. It included five linguistic subfamilies called West Atlantic, Mande, Gur-Voltaic, Kwa, and Bantu-Congo. These very large groups include hundreds of languages.[110]

Africans commonly lived and worked among people who spoke different languages that were in some ways related. They developed skills for working in multiple languages. An important example of this linguistic dexterity (despite a recent attempt to call its authenticity into question) was an Igbo slave from Biafra, Olaudah Equiano, whom we have met earlier. He recalled after his capture in Africa that "from the time I left my own nation, I always found somebody to understand me till I came to the sea coast. The languages of the different nations did not totally differ, nor were they so copious as those of the Europeans, particularly the English. They were therefore easily learned, and, while I was journeying thus through Africa, I acquired two or three different tongues." [111]

This African gift of tongues had many uses in North America. It appeared among many people in the New World who picked up other African, European, and Native American languages. As early as the sixteenth century, Africans were working as translators. In North America there were instances of European immigrants who met native speakers of Iroquoian and Algonkian languages, and they were able to communicate through an African slave. We have found evidence of African translators working that way in the St. Lawrence Valley, New England, the Hudson Valley, Delaware Valley, and Chesapeake region in the seventeenth and eighteenth centuries.

Other Africans put their linguistic skills to work by developing multilingual dialects and speechways in great variety. In the Hudson Valley, Afro-Dutch speechways called Black Dutch emerged at an early date. Afro-French speechways called Gombo appeared in Louisiana. And other Afro-English ways of speaking developed in the Chesapeake, where Frederick Douglass called them Guinea speech. He summarized them in a sentence as "a mixture of Guinea and everything else." [112]

Some linguists and historians have come to agree that these regional speechways were truly new languages. Among the most interesting were Gullah in coastal Carolina, and Geechee in coastal Georgia. They developed from the interplay of multiple African languages with varieties of European speech, in rough proportion to the mixture of populations in each region.

In northern New England, where Africans were less than one percent of the population, they learned to speak mostly in English. In the Sea Islands of coastal Carolina and Georgia where in some cases Africans were 99 percent of the population, their speech remained more strongly African. But everywhere, Africans moved back and forth between languages, and combined different elements in dynamic mixtures more easily and more creatively than their European masters were able to match.

This extraordinary gift of tongues derived in part from a facility for linguistic invention that has persisted among Africans in the United States for many generations. Yet another result in the late twentieth century was the invention of rap and hip hop. Through it all, these Afro-European speechways in America created new possibilities for creative expression and understanding. In particular they were especially strong in their power to communicate spiritual ideas that African Americans called soul. On this subject the methods of linguistics and cultural history reinforce each other. Together they help us to understand the astonishing range of creative expression that has enriched both African and European languages in America and the world. Gullah and Geechee speech are leading cases in point.

The most distinctive and most carefully studied of these African American languages is Gullah, the language of coastal Carolina, its river valleys, and Sea Islands. Gullah is also one of the oldest African North American languages on record. It was called by that name as early as 1739. Examples of Gullah speech were recorded in the eighteenth century.[113]

Gullah may be the most African speechway in English-speaking North America—more so than Gombo, Guinea, Afro-French, or Black Dutch. It was very different from English in its many varieties, some of which are incomprehensible to non-Gullah speakers.

Early students of Gullah thought it was a dialect of English. Some called it "broken English," and one thought it "the worst English in the world."[114] More recently, linguists and historians have come to study it as a distinctive language in its own right.[115] Gullah has its own rules of grammar and syntax. Gender distinctions are expressed not by pronouns such as "he" and "her" but by prefixes or suffixes ("chillun-gal"). Elizabeth Botume wrote, "I never knew whether they were talking of boys and girls. They spoke of all as him."[116]

Many English markers do not appear in Gullah. Plural markers such as the final "s" are often missing, as in "three thing" for "three things." Possessive markers are also absent and replaced by pronouns as in "John he wife" for "John's wife." Third person singular present tense markers are missing, as in the Gullah proverb "what bark here bite yonder." The definite article is often absent. The verb "to be" as a copula is frequently missing ("I know my people poor").

Verbs are constructed differently from English. Gullah tends to have no passive voice. Present and past tenses are often the same, and temporal distinctions are expressed by an added verb or noun. Verb tenses place less importance on the time of an action (past, present, future). But Gullah verbs distinguish more carefully than English among modes of action. They indicate whether an action is habitual, or conditional, or obligatory, or completed, in ways that do not commonly occur in other languages. Gullah speech also adds many unique elements for emphasis, rhythm, and tone. It repeats words for those purposes. The subject or object of a sentence is first stated, then repeated by a pronoun: "Old rabbit, he jump." Double and even triple negatives are used for emphasis. ("I don't write nobody no letter.") Negative statements have inverted order ("Don't nobody know that"), for greater oral impact. Adjectives are attached to nouns as a suffix to increase impact ("sunhot").

Interrogative or declarative sentences are distinguished not by word order but by differences of tone. In all of these ways, the grammar and syntax of Gullah resembles African languages, even as vocabulary draws mainly from English.[117]

Carolina Gullah and Georgia Geechee speechways drew much from many African languages. This has occasioned an argument over the dominant African influences. Cornelia Bailey of Sapelo Island, a native Geechee speaker, visited Sierra Leone and testified to a strong connection between languages in Sierra Leone and Geechee speech in coastal Georgia. She later wrote, "Everywhere I went in Sierra Leone, I saw similarities to Sapelo. *Everywhere.*"

Her informed judgments are to be received with high respect. Some African linguists and historians agree: among them Ian Hancock, P. E. Hair, Walter Rodney, Littlefield, and many more arguments for the Windward Coast by Wood and Littlefield.[118] But there is also another expert judgment from Lorenzo Dow Turner, an African American linguistics scholar. He did extensive and meticulous field research in many parts of Africa and coastal Carolina and Georgia. He centered his thinking on Gullah but also studied Geechee. About 60 percent of his American informants were in South Carolina and 40 percent were in coastal Georgia.

Turner reported his findings in what is still the most important empirical study yet completed on this subject. He found many linkages between African languages and Gullah, and demonstrated beyond doubt that Gullah was not an English dialect but a language in its own right, with an elaborate structure, and a combination of both English and African elements.[119]

On the question of leading African linkages. Turner found from an empirical study of thousands of names and words that the largest African sources for Gullah were the Bantu languages of Angola and the Congo Basin. He also identified a second strong source from the languages of Upper Guinea, and estimated that as many as 20 percent of Gullah words came from Sierra Leone. Turner also discovered other words and names from languages in other parts of West Africa.[120]

Turner's findings are consistent with regional distributions in the Atlantic slave trade to South Carolina. Evidence from patterns in this trade would suggest a difference between Carolina Gullah and Georgia Geechee, with stronger links to Upper Guinea in the latter. But they would also suggest a breadth of borrowing from many African languages and cultures in both areas.

GEECHEE SPEECH AND VARIANTS IN COASTAL AND INTERIOR GEORGIA

These Gullah and Geechee cultures also spread into the interior. By the late twentieth century, as development surged along the coast, the density of South Carolina's African American population was greater in a second tier of inland counties than directly on the coast.[121] The same pattern appeared in Georgia's Cornelia Bailey, a Geechee leader and gifted writer.[122] In her writings, she noted a difference between the speech of the Sea Islands, spoken by "black people who lived about thirty miles inland." Bailey, a saltwater Geechee speaker, wrote that "we thought our speech was more musical than theirs because we laundered words" and "talked a little faster, with fewer rest stops between our words, so that everything we said ran together. We'd listen to them and say, 'Can't they talk any faster than that? People don't have all day.' Then we'd shake our heads and say, 'Ah those freshwater Geechee, what do they know?'"[123]

Bailey wrote that both Gullah and Geechee speakers could identify a speaker's island by his speech, and would say "Aah, he's from St. John's" or "She's from Ossabaw." But she also found that in general "Geechee and Gullah people sound pretty much alike."[124]

THE USES OF GULLAH AND GEECHEE LANGUAGES

Gullah and Geechee languages had many vital functions in coastal Carolina and Georgia. Each developed as a lingua franca among slaves who came from many parts of Africa, with different languages. Charles Joyner wrote, "On any given morning in a Georgia rice field, an enslaved African would meet more Africans from more ethnic groups than he or she would encounter in a lifetime in Africa." [125] These Gullah and Geechee languages were also instruments of comity and community building among slaves, and they were vital to those ends.

Gullah and Geechee were also vehicles of expression, with extraordinarily broad ranges of meaning and feeling. Much that has been written by linguists about the character of these languages has centered on their structure and grammar, which are helpful to our understanding in many ways. But these variant speechways also had different functions. One of the most important and enduring functions in African American cultures was to express spiritual meaning in many ways—the life of the spirit in its height and depth, and also its power to stir the soul.

Gullah and Geechee and Gombo and Guinea could all be called soul-languages. To hear these languages when they were deployed in the great spirituals and shouts, and also in plaintive work songs and grief songs, and yet again in songs of happiness and rejoicing, is to discover that these are great and powerful languages. English and French and Spanish are great languages too, but when it comes to the life of the spirit and the stirring of soul, English and French and Spanish can't come close to Gullah and Geechee, or Louisiana Gombo or Maryland Guinea talk for that matter. Have a listen at the Library of Congress, or wherever you can hear it for yourself. Hearing is believing.

LOWCOUNTRY BUILDING WAYS

From the start, Gullah and Geechee folkways were creative in many other ways. One of them appeared in material culture and building ways. On St. Simons Island in coastal Georgia, there was an old slave named Okra. He had been born in Africa, and as late as 1860 he kept alive the memory of his homeland. One younger American-born slave recalled many years later, "Now ole man Okra an ole man Gibson an ole Israel, dey's African. . . . Dey tell us how dey lib in Africa. Dey laks tuh talk. It funny talk an it ain't so easy tuh unnuhstan but yuh gits use tuh it. Dey say dey buil deah own camp deah an lib in it." [126]

Ole man Okra built an African house for himself on St. Simons Island. He made it with daub and wattle walls and a thatched roof of palmetto leaves. Another slave remembered, "Ole man Okra he say he wahn a place lak he hab in Africa so he buil im a hut. I membuh it well. It wuz bout twelve by foeteen feet an it hab dut flo [dirt floor] and he buil duh side lak basket weave wid clay plastuh on it. It hab a flat roof wut he make from bush and palmettuh, and it hab one doe an no winduhs." [127]

Okra's master, James Couper, was not happy to learn what Okra had done. In North America, some masters tried to separate slaves from their African origins. Couper ordered Okra to demolish the African house. Another slave remembered, "Massah make 'im pull it down. He say he ain wahn no African hut on he place." [128]

Cultural historians have gone looking for these "African huts," but only a few have been found in what is now the United States. The story of Okra helps to explain why. In the beginning, a great many traditional African houses were probably constructed in the New World. Wherever African-born slaves had an entirely free hand, they built African houses for themselves. The fugitive slaves called maroons constructed entire African villages deep in swamps and forests of America.

African slaves in coastal Carolina also began by building African houses for themselves. Most were temporary structures, and quickly disappeared. But one of them miraculously survived long enough to be photographed in

Romeo Thomas house, Edgefield District, 1908

Romeo Thomas house, side view

1907. It was built by a Bakongo slave named Tahro, one of the last slave immigrants, who was captured in Central Africa and carried after 1858 to Edgefield County, South Carolina. His new master named him Romeo, but Tahro held firmly to his ancestral ways, and built an African house for himself. It was a small building, about seven feet wide and ten feet deep, with a frame of wood and walls of lath, tied together by string. Sheaves of straw were hung inside to seal and insulate the walls. The roof was thatched with straw and held together with horizontal poles.[129]

Tahro told others that his hut was exactly like one he had built in Africa. Traditional Central African houses in Angola and the Congo had much the same appearance.[130]

HALL AND PARLOR COTTAGES IN LOWCOUNTRY CAROLINA

African houses such as Tahro's were rarely allowed to stand in coastal Carolina and Georgia. Masters intervened, and required their slaves to build cottages on western lines. Gradually a distinctive regional pattern developed, different from the up-and-down slave houses in the vernacular architecture of the Chesapeake colonies.

Carolina slave housing ran more to what has been called "hall and parlor cottages." These slave houses were so small that from the outside they appeared to have only a single room. But in fact they were elaborately subdivided. A center door opened into the "hall," with its European fireplace. To the side was a small space called the "parlor." And other smaller spaces were also partitioned off.

English actress Fanny Kemble described these hall and parlor cottages on Butler Island in 1838–39. They were duplex units for "two families sometimes eight or ten in number," with brick chimneys and fireplaces. She described them as very small: "One room, about twelve feet by fifteen, with a couple of closets, smaller and closer than the staterooms of a ship, divided off from the main room and each other by rough wooden partitions, in which the inhabitants sleep."

These hall and parlor cottages were built beside others. Behind the cottages was a canal open to the sea, which was used as a latrine, and flushed twice a day by the tide. Mrs. Kemble was appalled by the squalor of slave quarters on Butler Island—"filthy and wretched in the extreme." She may have been one of the few plantation mistresses to venture inside them.

These houses comprised a village; or several villages on large plantations. All the houses on a lowcountry plantation tended to be wide open—slave quarters and the big house too. Storerooms were kept under lock and key, but living spaces were open. Mrs. Kemble described her own bedroom that way. "The doors open by wooden latches, raised by means of small bits of packthread . . . how they shut I will not attempt to describe, as the shutting of a door is a process of extremely rare occurrence throughout the whole southern country."[131]

The houses were built of various materials—wood in the great majority of cases, and occasionally brick as at Boone Hall near Charleston in coastal Carolina where they still stand today. On Hermitage Plantation in Chatham County, Georgia, the slave quarters were hall and parlor houses, also built of brick with hipped roofs, porches, and solid brick fireplaces, and chimneys on one side.[132]

Some masters and slaves preferred to build in "tabby," a rough cement made of crushed oyster shells, and as durable as concrete in the difficult environment of the Sea Islands. Tabby buildings have survived for three centuries and more. Some historians believe that tabby was of African origin. Others think of it as Spanish. It was used in the early nineteenth century on Thomas Spalding's Ashantilly Plantation near Darien, Georgia.

Old Spalding estate on Sapelo Island, 1910

In the nineteenth century, the hall and parlor houses of Carolina and Georgia evolved into another common plan called the "tenement house." This was often a duplex with two family units under the same roof. Each had a "hall" or living room–kitchen, with doors at each outer end; a fireplace on a center wall; and two or three smaller "parlors" or "sleeping apartments" to the side. Tenement houses of this sort were used on the South Carolina rice plantation of James Sparkman as early as 1838. They were found in 1856 by traveler Frederick Law Olmsted on the rice coast of Georgia. He measured eighty-four double tenements on William Aiken's Jehossee Island Plantation. The parlor was twenty-one by ten feet, and the sleeping apartments ten feet square.[133]

These slave houses tended to be laid out in a regular pattern on both sides of a street. One slave remembered, "De slave lib on de Street, each cabin had two room. De master don't gib you nutting for yo' house—you hab to git dat de best way you can. In our house was bed, table and bench to sit on. My father mek dem. My mother had fourteen chillen—us sleep on floor."[134]

Large plantations had several villages. Butler Island had four slave villages, and several smaller hamlets. House servants lived apart, close to the master and mistress, and were allowed to use the yard. One recalled, "I don't know nothing about de street on de plantation, and what dey do dere, cause I ain't had no 'casion for go dere. I raise in de yard, I didn't wear de kind ob clothes de field hand chillen wear, and I get my dinner from de kitchen." [135]

"A NATION WITHIN A NATION": SLAVE VILLAGES, COMMUNITY, AND CULTURE

Alexander Garden wrote of lowcountry slaves, "They are as 'twere a Nation within a Nation, in all country settlements. They live in contiguous houses and often 2, 3 or 4 families of them, in one house slightly partitioned into so many apartments, they labour together converse almost wholly among themselves." [136]

On larger plantations, in early years when slaves were mostly male immigrants from Africa, masters ordered that barracks be constructed, often by the slaves themselves. A few of these early structures have survived. They show strong African influences.

As time passed, masters increasingly asserted their own architectural authority. Slaves continued to build their own houses, but not just as they pleased. African choices were constrained by European owners, and by a new American environment. Within those limits, African builders quickly mastered European styles and American materials. Nuclear one-family houses began to emerge. They grew gradually larger, more elaborate, and more complex.

Specific patterns and architectural forms varied broadly from one American region to another. But at the same time, underlying unities also appeared—similar to those in Africa, but not the same. From New England to the Caribbean, Afro-American houses tended to cluster together in various ways. Something of the spirit of African village architecture was cultivated wherever possible, in combination with western ideas of individuality. The process was not one of replication, but something more interesting—a creative synthesis of cultural and material elements from Africa, Europe, and America in a new vocabulary of vernacular architectural forms. [137]

GULLAH AND GEECHEE ARTS AND CRAFTS

An important part of Afro-American folkways were its arts and crafts, which developed very rapidly in the New World. These were often functional skills such as basketry, quilting, and woodworking. They tended to be part-time activities of the sort that could be pursued for a few hours at a time, put down, and taken up again. They were also easily accessible to slaves who had few tools and little capital to call their own.

Mostly they supplied the simple needs of a rural society, but there was nothing simple in their design or development. Afro-American craftways drew creatively upon the aesthetics of different folk traditions. They were neither a replication of African customs, nor an imitation of European and American practices. This was something new in the world, a highly creative union of folkways from three continents.

In Savannah's Old Fort section, or "neighborhood" to inquisitive Yankees, an interviewer in the 1930s found a craftsman who was highly conscious of the craft tradition in which he worked. "Near this section," the interviewer wrote, "lives a negro basket maker, who claims that he is carrying on the tradition of his ancestors. He stated that for generations the men of his family had engaged in wood carving, basket making, and various phases of weaving, and that the craft had been passed from father to son. He himself makes only baskets." [138]

In Yamacraw, Georgia, another old artisan named James Cooper said much

A Gullah woman makes a sweetgrass basket in Charleston's City Market

the same thing. It was said that he could fix most anything from a cracked pot to a roller skate, and also knew a few "sure cures" for many a lowcountry illness. But he was mainly known in the neighborhood as Stick Daddy, for the beautiful walking sticks that he carved. "I nevuh bin taught," he told his interviewer, "I took up cahvin as paht time jis fuh the fun of it. Muh gran-fathuh, Pharo Cooper, he used tuh make things from wood an straw, sech as baskets an cheahs an tables an othuh things fuh the home. I guess I sawt of inherited it from him." [129]

A continuity of that sort from Africa to early-twentieth-century America has been documented on St. Helena Island. In 1909, a local writer published a photograph of a former slave named Alfred Graham. He had been taught to make baskets by his great-uncle, a slave-immigrant who had learned the skill in Africa. Alfred Graham in turn taught George Holloway, who became a teacher of basketry at the Penn School on St. Helena Island, which survives today as Penn Center. It is a flourishing center of cultural preservation and creativity. [140]

Some things were brought from Africa. In Savannah, a boy found in a trash pile an old carved spoon that was probably the product of another continent.

It was made of teak, and, judging from the dark polished surface of the wood and its general appearance, it might well be more than a century old. The bowl is shallow, about two by three inches, and the whole length is about seven inches. The most unusual feature of the spoon is the carved figure of a disproportionate little man forming the handle. Of particular interest are the flat cranium, the exaggerated ears, the gash-like mouth, the queerly shaped nose, the long dangling arms, and the short tapering legs which appear to be far too small for the rest of the body. [141]

Elements of design were highly complex. A cane found in Savannah had "a man's head for a handle, but the stick proper is so covered with minute, unpatterned criss-crosses that the little figure of a man upside down, a horned head upside down, and an undetermined object which may be either man or animal, are noticed only when the cane is carefully studied." [142]

The dynamics of this Afro-European culture in America appear in Gullah and Geechee basketry, and quilts and coverlets. In lowcountry Carolina and Georgia, a distinctive style of sea grass basketry developed. Baskets made from coiled grasses had long been common throughout Africa and many other parts of the world. They were known in Europe, and also among American Indians. Sea Island slaves drew freely upon all of these various folk traditions to create a unique style of Afro-American basketry distinctive to the lowcountry of Carolina.

Lowcountry baskets were made from local materials that grew along the coast: sweet grass (*Muhlenbergia filipes*), which grows behind sand dunes along the ocean, and bulrush (*Juncus roemarianus*), which flourishes in tidal marshes. The grass coils are sewn together with pieces of palmetto in show baskets, and with splints of strong white oak for work baskets, and sometimes decorated with longleaf pine needles. This combination of materials is unique to the Carolina and Georgia lowcountry.

Each basket began with a special knot which often told where in the lowcountry the maker worked. Often an overhand knot was used; sometimes other knots. In many of the Sea Islands, one end of a grass bundle was coiled and sewn round the knot and the other cut flat on the inside of the bottom. On the mainland, both ends tended to be coiled around the knot. Sea Island baskets were sewn with palmetto; mainland basketmakers tended to use strips of oak.

These baskets began to appear in the Carolina lowcountry at an early date. Probably they were made by slaves in the late seventeenth century. Fragments have survived from the early eighteenth century. Broken bits of coiled grass baskets have been found in an eighteenth-century privy that served the Heyward-Washington house in Charleston. Specialized fanner baskets (for fanning rice kernels from the rice chaff) appeared in inventories of Carolina estates as early as 1730. They were thought to have been in use as early as the seventeenth century.[143]

Techniques of basket-making were remarkably stable, but not static. They preserved strong continuities for many generations, but with creative inventions. Patterns tended to vary in detail from place to place in coastal Carolina and Georgia. During the 1930s in Savannah, Georgia, and its vicinity, "white oak and bulrushes are selected as the material from which to make the baskets and they are stitched with scrub palmetto. Those made of bulrushes are of the coil type. A kind of thin rope is made from this grass which then twisted around and sewed tightly together. . . . The baskets made from white oak are plaited."[144]

Baskets were not made for show, and they were put to heavy use. Of vital importance in rice growing were lowcountry fanner baskets. After the grain was harvested in the rice fields, it was threshed to beat the heads off the grain, then winnowed by fanning in the wind with broad flat fanning baskets. Other baskets were used for storage, and for carrying goods to market. Well into the twentieth century on the streets of Charleston one found baskets which "vendors balance gracefully on their heads as they walk about the city, displaying a colorful array of merchandise." [145]

Traditional crafts changed in many ways. Early accounts referred mainly but not exclusively to male basketmakers. This was a period when women were absorbed in spinning and weaving. As textiles took less time, women increasingly became basketmakers. [146] Craft traditions formed in slavery continued to persist for many generations after emancipation, even to our own time.

Another art form is ornamental ironwork by Afro-American blacksmiths in lowcountry towns. Many Charleston houses have beautiful wrought iron gates and grilles which help to give this city its distinctive appearance. Much of this work was done by slaves. Today it is still a flourishing craft tradition, kept alive by Afro-American artisans who inherited skills from their ancestors.

At Charleston in 1980, one of the leading ornamental ironworkers was Philip Simmons. He had been born in 1912, and raised on Daniel Island, across the Cooper River from Charleston. In 1925 he became the apprentice to Peter Simmons (no kin), a Charleston blacksmith who had been born a slave in St. Stephens Parish in 1855. Peter Simmons's father, Guy Simmons, and his grandfather had also been ironworkers. They taught him what they knew, as they had been taught before by blacksmiths who had been born in the eighteenth century. It was a hard school. Peter Simmons's father used his sledgehammer to drive home a lesson—"used to turn the back of the hammer and hit on the head or shoulder," as a way of reinforcing a pedagogic point. A lesson once learned by that method was not soon forgotten. [147]

Philip Simmons in turn trained his own apprentices who have carried this craft tradition into the twenty-first century, in an unbroken line of Afro-American ironworkers that began in the eighteenth. Their work is to be seen in the streets of Charleston today—gates and grilles of astonishing beauty and creativity which bring together elements African, European, and American in a unique and harmonious whole. Patterns of persistence, change, and creativity in Gullah and Geechee basketry are evidence of these vibrant cultures as living traditions.

Angolan slaves brought a strong reputation as skilled artisans. The Charleston area became a leading center in North America for Afro-American artisanal skills and remains so to this day. Historian Daniel Littlefield found that Angolan slaves were "more prominent than any other African group among

Egret Gate, St. Michael's Alley,
Charleston, South Carolina

fugitives who were listed for trades," and "their skills were among the most useful or most called for." [148]

HOPPIN JOHN AND SHE-CRAB SOUP:
GULLAH CUISINE AS A COMMUNAL AFFAIR

Other creative and instrumental expressions of Gullah and Geechee cultures were the foodways of coastal Carolina and Georgia. Historian Charles Joyner, one of the pioneers in this field, writes that "slaves ate the grains, fruits, vegetables and meats of the New World environment, but to those foodstuffs slave cooks applied an African culinary grammar—methods of cooking and spicing, remembered recipes, ancestral tastes."[149]

The cuisine of the Sea Islands was very distinctive—perhaps a little less creative than Louisiana's Gombo cookery, but more varied than the corn diet of the upcountry. Rice, sweet potatoes, and black-eyed peas were the staples, and much use was made of fish and salt meat.

Rice was the favorite foodstuff, cooked with practiced skill by slaves so that each grain was firm. Also popular were sweet potatoes. White potatoes were rarely used because they did not keep in the climate. A standard weekly ration for a grown slave was one peck of milled rice, or two pecks of unhusked "paddy" rice which was thought to be equivalent.[150]

Beyond the grain ration, black-eyed peas were another staple of lowcountry cuisine. A great Gullah and Geechee favorite was Hoppin John, in which black-eyed peas were cooked with rice and bits of meat. One former slave on a Waccamaw Plantation remembered sitting "over his plate of hopping John . . . peas and rice, 'hopping John.' Someone says peas and hominy cooked together makes 'limping lizzie in the Low country.' But that is another story."[151]

These mixed rice, vegetable, and meat or fish dishes were an African tradition that was continuously reinvented in the lowcountry, with endless variations in pilaus of various kinds, and bits of salt meat, fish, or vegetables. In place of black-eyed peas, collard greens or cabbage were also used. One former slave remembered that her family "have own garden dat my mother en sister would work en my mother done all de cookin for de slaves cause our folks all eat out de same pot. Cook rice en fat meat en dese collard greens en corn bread en cabbage. Make plenty of de cabbage en eat heap of dem."[152]

In the Carolina lowcountry meat rations were smaller than in other southern regions. On four Edisto Island plantations meat averaged less than half the allowances in the upcountry. Fish were highly variable. One slave remembered that "we didn't get much fish in slabery 'cause we nebber hab boat. But sometime you kin t'row out net en ketch shrimp. You kin also ketch 'possum and raccoon wid your dawg." Many recent studies of trash pits in plantation quarters have found abundant evidence of hunting, trapping, and fishing by slaves after their daily tasks were done.[153]

The diversity of lowcountry diet appears in Carolina and Georgia garden plots. Slaves were often encouraged by masters to grow their own food. In South Carolina they raised the crops of three continents—okra, rice, and nuts from Africa; red peppers, sweet potatoes, corn, squash and beans, and tobacco from America; peas and cabbage from Europe.[154] Complex soups were widely used. Gullah cooks drew heavily upon the shellfish of the region, with results of their invention such as Carolina she-crab soup.

Slaves also ate on the job. One slave remembered, "You carry dinner to field in your can and leabe it at de heading [end of row]. W'en you feel hongry you eat.[155] But eating was also a communal affair. An ex-slave in South Carolina remembered that "there would be a large bowl and a large spoon for each group of larger children. There would be enough children in each group to get around the bowl comfortably. One would take a spoon of what was in the bowl and then pass the spoon to his neighbor." Fanny Kemble found her husband's Georgia slaves eating out of "small cedar tubs or an iron cookpot with iron spoons and pieces of wood until everyone would have a spoonful. Then they would begin again, and so on until the bowl was empty." A former slave recalled "There was one woman in there cooking that was called 'Mammy,' and she seed to all the chillen."[156]

In the West Indian plantations, slave rations were reputed to be much inferior in quantity and quality to those on the mainland. Slave heights were considerably smaller in the Caribbean islands. Slaves in North America also tended to grow taller through time. Much evidence and many descriptions yield similar results.

MARRIAGE CUSTOMS IN GULLAH AND GEECHEE CULTURE

Marriage ways were distinctive in coastal South Carolina and Georgia. It was observed in the Sea Islands, "although slavery made them in great measure regardless of the *ceremony* of marriage, it did not take away their birthright of modesty, or the idea of fidelity between man and wife."[157]

In the eighteenth and early nineteenth centuries, slaves in this region improvised their own wedding customs. One of these traditions was called the peanut marriage. An observer wrote, "During the early nineteenth century a rather curious ceremony was observed on the coast plantations. The man would go to the cabin of the woman whom he desired, would roast peanuts in the ashes, place them on a stool between her and himself, and while eating propose marriage. If the man was accepted, the couple repaired to his cabin immediately, and they were regarded as man and wife."[158]

Another ritual was called "marrying in blankets." A slave explained, "We comes together in the same cabin; and she brings her blanket and lay it down beside mine; and we gets married that a-way."[159] After the Civil War, a federal tax gatherer asked slaves in the Sea Islands about their marital status and was told, "Parson Blanket married us" or "we married ourselves." He reckoned that these answers came "seven times out of ten."[160] Customs of peanut marriages and blanket marriages were sometimes combined. Blankets were spread out and covered with small but cherished gifts, with food commonly among them. The exchange ratified both the proposal and its acceptance.[161]

Marriages were less frequently disrupted by sales in coastal South Carolina and Georgia than in Virginia and Maryland. A consequence and cause was that slave families in this region were stronger and more enduring than in other parts of the South. But in other ways, Sea Island slavery could be every bit as brutal in the lowcountry as in other regions in its impact on marriage. On a Florida plantation, slaves remembered that marrying couples were required to have sexual intercourse in the presence of the master or the overseer as a condition of matrimony. Owners wanted to be sure that the marriage could be consummated and would add to their wealth by producing more slaves. The idea that such a practice was a denial of decency and humanity to the enslaved never mattered to masters (and there were many) who thought of their slaves as livestock.[162]

For house servants, customs were apt to be very different, and on some plantations their marriages sometimes resembled weddings among the master class. In the mid-nineteenth century, weddings of house slaves normally took place in December, often in the Christmas season, when masters and mistresses were apt to be on the plantation. These Christmas weddings were communal events that sometimes caught up the entire plantation. The high point was the wedding feast, a hot supper with hams and turkeys and a vast display of food. Special wedding cakes were baked, and wine flowed abundantly—a custom uncommon in other regions.[163] These house slave wedding festivals were among the great events in this culture. The bride was decked in garlands and flowers that still bloomed in December, and sometimes with sweet-smelling orange blossoms. The wedding ceremony itself was often held at night, but in a manner different from Virginia lamp ceremonies. Jacob Frederick recalled the marriage of his slave nurse Charity to the slave Handy:

> On the evening of the marriage, the broad raised walk from their quarter to our dwelling was brilliantly lighted with piles of lightwood knots at frequent intervals on each side of the walk. The bridal couple was preceded by torch bearers whose long burning sticks dripped pitch. The couple was followed by all the [slave] quarter. . . . Father, from the back porch, impressively read the ritual that made them man and wife, and assigned them a cabin in which to begin a new home.[164]

Charles Joyner, from his study of rice plantations on the Waccamaw River, observed that "for reasons both sincerely altruistic and the same time self-serving, the rice planters of the Waccamaw actively promoted slave marriage." They did it in part because "with hundreds of slaves they regarded the family relationship as the key to a stable social order." Joyner also believed that the African heritage of strong families was another factor. He wrote that "the slaves' creative response to the masters' notions of family was mediated by the cultural grammar of African familial traditions."[165]

GULLAH AND GEECHEE NAMING CUSTOMS AND EXTENDED FAMILIES

Customs of child-naming among Gullah and Geechee slaves in this region were distinctive and complex. More than in most regions, there was a struggle between masters and slaves over the names of slave children. Charles Joyner finds much evidence that "slaves and masters vied with one another for the right to name the children." Each group had its own imperatives. Slaves inherited African traditions that "the power to name was perceived as the power to control, to order reality." Masters believed owners possessed a sovereign right to name their property as they pleased.[166]

A solution to this problem was the use of multiple forenames. Many slaves were given one name by their owners. Another or sometimes several others were widely used by the slaves themselves.

The choice of names by owners commonly favored prominent Carolina slaveholding families. One planter remembered, "A number bore well-known Carolina names . . . From Lord Anson probably came that name borne by no less than three negroes on the place—old Anson—young Anson—and little Anson. There was old Dorset once trunk-minder, Simmons the carpenter, Blake a plough-boy, Vincent and old Pinckney the cow-minder and others."

Even as late as the mid-nineteenth century, other lowcountry names continued to commemorate the Barbadian origins of South Carolina. The same planter recalled that "the poultry woman was called Willoughby, having probably derived her name from forefathers who came from Barbados, where they were owned by one or another of the great Willoughby family."[167]

Slaves had mixed feelings (to say the least) about the names their owners gave them, and the mixture was often a function of feelings about the masters themselves. Some hated their owner names and rejected them when they could. But others bore them with pride. An example was Liverpool, last surviving slave of Major Pierce Butler, who said that he was "Butler born," and "Butler I shall be until I die." [168]

At the same time Gullah and Geechee children received other forenames from slaves. They were called "basket names," because they tended to exist in multiples. One literate freedman tried to set down all the names of his own children in a family Bible. He was baffled by their number and variety. "So many people give them basket names," he wrote, "I ain't 'zactly know myself which de right one." [169]

Many of these basket names were African in origin. The extent of African naming was widespread in coastal Carolina and Georgia. Lorenzo Dow Turner collected them in his many years of field research throughout the low-country and in Africa. Turner identified more than a thousand basket names of African origin in lowcountry South Carolina and Georgia, and he was able to trace them to more than thirty African languages from Senegal to Angola. He also found that a person having multiple basket names was common in African cultures. [170]

These African names persisted for generations in the lowcountry. As late as 1860, many slaves still bore African names. John Inscoe found that the proportion who did so tended to be higher, and to persist for a longer period in the lowcountry than in other North American regions. [171]

Other basket names were English equivalents of African practices. Some were day names, which commemorated the day on which a child was born, or the circumstances of the birth. They had been widely used in Akan, Efik, and other African languages. In coastal Carolina and Georgia, most day names were African, but some were English. On one plantation list, basket names included Quaw, Quakoo, Quash, Cuffee, and Cudjo, but also Monday and Friday. [172]

In keeping with African practices, Carolina slaves also received basket names that came from weather, or harvest conditions at the time of birth. Examples found by John Inscoe in his study of slave names included children named Rainy, Freeze, Starry Night, Stormy, Earthy, and Eartha. An example was the great twentieth-century singer Eartha Kitt, who was born to Gullah parents in South Carolina, and named for "a good harvest at the time of her birth." [173]

Many lowcountry Gullah and Geechee people also received other nicknames which were distinct from basket names, because they came later in life. But they were unlike routine English nicknames in their creativity, humor, power of expression, and purpose. Gullah nicknames commemorated a turn of fate, sometimes in a whimsical way. One Gullah individual was nicknamed "Beep-Beep," for escaping injury from an automobile by the sudden sounding of a horn. Nicknames also described a line of descent. Another male was nicknamed Betsy Ben, as he was Ben the son of Betsy. A third was nicknamed Coodle because he liked to attend funerals. Coodle derived from the Ewe noun kudu for a "death announcement." [174]

Gullah slaves rarely had surnames until the end of slavery. One member of the master class asserted flatly that "the negroes had *no* surnames to the knowledge of their owners." [175] But Gullah slaves, especially house slaves, took "titles" that were given by other slaves. One was called "Peter Polite." A woman who was "Old Hagar" to her owners was known to slaves as "Miss Kittle" and she used that name herself. [176]

The descent of names in families of Carolina slaves had a distinctive character. It was different from family naming customs in European onomastics, and also from African American cultures in other regions. [177]

Striking examples are reported by Cheryll Ann Cody from the estate of Peter Gaillard, fifty miles from Charleston in Upper St. Johns Berkeley Parish. She followed the history of naming through four generations in one slave family from 1786 to 1833, and found a pattern of high complexity. A three-generation nuclear naming rhythm occurred, the names of grandparents repeated in grandchildren. But it was part of a much broader naming pattern which used the names of parents and grandparents in a complex combination with uncles, aunts, cousins, and especially siblings. In the fourth generation of the family of Nero and Binah, the children of young George and Nanny were named Moses, Essencia, Nero, Eurias, Jonas and Johnny. Many relatives were commemorated, but not in the manner of onomastic folkways in the master class. Especially striking in Gullah and Geechee naming was the repetition of names from uncles, aunts, and cousins. The result was a much broader network of naming, and a linkage of names through extended families of lowcountry slaves. [178]

GULLAH AND GEECHEE CHILDWAYS AND AGEWAYS

In the Sea Islands and the Carolina lowcountry, the distinctiveness of child rearing may be summarized in a sentence. Here children grew up in African households within an environing Gullah or Geechee population that was also predominantly African in ancestry. A close nurturing process was the rule here. Well into the nineteenth century, newborn slave infants were swaddled, swathed, and capped by their mothers, much to the horror of masters and mistresses, who had long since abandoned that practice. Fanny Kemble described how she struggled to suppress this custom, in vain.[179]

When mothers were toiling in the rice fields, small children would be sent to a special building called the "chillun house." Here they were looked after by elder women. Historian Charles Joyner writes, "This followed a common West African practice of utilizing the skills of the elderly."[180]

A woman who looked after the young was called "nuss" (nurse) in Gullah. One former slave remembered, "My Pa sister, Ritta One, had that job. Nuss the children. Chillun house. One woman nuss all the chillun while they ma in the field—rice field. All size chillun."[181] Here as elsewhere in slavery, early childhood was remembered as happy and carefree. "Slave chillen play mud-pie, mek house out ob sand, and secher t'ing."[182]

Old slaves remained part of the plantation community in the Sea Islands. Pierce Butler's inventory in 1815 found that of 525 Sea Island slaves on nine plantations, 78 (14.9 percent) were fifty or over—an exceptionally large proportion by comparison with slaveholding in other regions. Most of these older slaves were female on the Butler plantations; younger slaves were mostly male.[183]

Older slaves continued to do light work—if nothing else they were sent to keep the rice birds at bay. Those too old or ill to work were looked after in buildings called hospitals on Pierce Butler's plantations. In 1815, Butler maintained at least three hospitals on his plantations. One was an enormous building, 50 by 160 feet. Many large plantations in the Sea Islands maintained their own "hospitals"—these were often hospitals in the morbid eighteenth-century sense of places were people went to die.[184] One major factor here was the scale of plantation life. Another was the more communal quality of African American culture on the Sea Islands.

In these slave communities, attitudes of respect toward age were strong—as in most slave cultures—if anything even stronger and deeper than in the Chesapeake. But the attitudes and language of age relations were differently expressed among Gullah folk. Older slaves in coastal Carolina were as a rule not called "Uncle" and "Auntie" as in the Chesapeake, but "Daddy" and "Maumer"—a terminology that implied an even more direct sense of authority, obligation, and responsibility.[185]

This usage spread among the master class, and it persisted even into the twentieth century in lowcountry South Carolina. An interviewer in 1937 met an elderly slave named Adeline Johnson who was still living on a "plantation" in upcountry South Carolina. The interviewer noted, "Adeline fits into this picture as the old negro mauma of the plantation, respected by all white and black, and tenderly cared for. She has her clay pipe and stick, ever with and about her." [186]

GULLAH AND GEECHEE DEATHWAYS: "WE BEAT DUH DRUM TO LET EBRYBODY KNOW"

African customs were stronger in the Sea Islands than anywhere else in British America. But they were combined with the folk customs of other cultures to create a distinctive set of deathways that were part African, part Christian, and part European.

In the lowcountry, the death of a slave was an event of importance, observed with great ceremony. Charles Joyner writes, "For Blacks on the Waccamaw— as in Africa and elsewhere in the New World—funerals were the real climax of life, the time when one was reunited with one's ancestors." [187]

Here was a different way of thinking about death and life itself. Each individual life was seen as a link in a great chain. Sea Island slaves created their own deathways by freely appropriating African, European, and American customs in their own way. Christian elements were combined with those of other faiths. But all was done with a purpose—to express a single coherent idea of death and life that dominated this culture.

In Georgia, most memorable were the deep-throated African drums that sounded through the Sea Islands whenever a slave returned to his ancestors. The old customs were still alive as late as the 1930s when interviewers talked with Uncle Jack Tattnall and Uncle Robert Pinckney, two ancient river men of Wilmington Island.

"When a pusson die," Jack Tattnall said, "we beat duh drum tuh let ebrybody know bout duh det [death]. Den dey come to duh wake an sit up wid duh body."

Robert Pinckney added, "Wen a man's countryman die, he sit right wid um all night. . . . Attuh dey pray, dey come in an put deah han on duh frien an say goodbye. Den dey go home."

Uncle Jack went on, "We beat duh drum agen at duh fewnul. We call it duh dead mahch. Jis a long slow beat. Boom-boom-boom. Beat duh drum. Den stop. Den beat it agen." [188]

As late as 1937, Liza Basden of Harris Neck, forty miles south of Savannah, told an interviewer, "In the ole days they always use tuh beat the drum at the funeral an they still does it tuhday. As they take the body tuh the graveyard, they beat the drum as they move long. They put the body in the grave. Then they mahch roun an sing an beat the drum." [189]

Another important Sea Island custom was called the "settin-ups." This was very much like the folkways of Virginia and Maryland, but with a different purpose. A Black woman in Sudbury, Georgia, explained, "We all sit wit duh body an sing an pray and keep duh spirit company." The mourners touched the corpse to say farewell. "We sing an we puts our hands on duh corpse tuh say goodbye. It bad luck not to do dis." [190]

As the body went to rest, it was touched by all the other mourners. "Ebrybody put duh hands on duh body tuh say goodbye," said Rosa Sallins of Harris Neck. "Yuh speak to duh pusson too, an tell um a las message," said Anna Johnson. [191]

Always there were variations from one plantation to another, and one island to the next. Sam Mitchell, a slave at Woodlawn on Ladies Island, remembered that "W'en slave die, mauusa let me berry um in de daytime," but he recalled that "some Maussa mek dem wait 'till night time. Nigger preacher preach funeral." [192]

Lowcountry funerals were commonly held at night, with the mourners carrying pine knot torches in their upraised hands. Grief was openly displayed. At the climax, the somber mood of mourning yielded to an ecstasy of celebration. White planters, even those who thought they knew their slaves, did not really understand. One wrote, "When conducted by torchlight, the whole ceremony seems to be a mimicry of the savage war dance." He could not have been more mistaken. In fact it was something very different—a distinct expression of ways of thinking about death and life, and about belonging to a community and a culture. [193]

The grave itself was invested with importance. More than other places, lowcountry slaves were laid to rest among their own kin. An interviewer noted the strength of this custom throughout coastal Georgia, and was told by Elizabeth Roberts, "We nebuh bury strainjuh's wid our own folks. Ef a strainjuh die yuh, we bury em in duh straingjuh's lot." [194] She added, "Folks alluz hab two fewnuls. We hab one wen dey die an den once a yeah we hab a suhvivce fuh ebrybody wut died durin duh yeah. Duh preachuh say a prayuh fuhrum all." [195]

It was believed that "Duh spirit nebuh go in duh groun wid duh body," said Emma Stevens of Sudbury, "it jis wanduh roun."[196]

Graves were decorated in elaborate ways. "Yuh put dishes an bottles an all duh pretty pieces wut dey lak on duh grabe. Yuh allez break deze tings fo yuh put um down." An interviewer asked why, and was told, "Yuh break duh dishes so dat duh chain will be broke. Yuh see, duh one pusson is dead an ef yuh dohn break duh tings, den duh udduhs in duh fambly will die too. Dey will folluh right long."[197]

GULLAH AND GEECHEE COMITY AND COMMUNITY

Patterns of association among slaves in the Carolina and Georgia lowcountry were different from other regions. Whites were few and far between. Many Sea Islands were small and separate from one another. Associational networks tended to be less extensive than in Virginia, and not as elaborately organized as in the deep southern upland Black Belt plantations. Quiltings, shuckings, log-rollings, and work frolics were uncommon. "Slave don't do mucher frolic," one former bondsman said of St. Helena Island.[198]

But what the Sea Island comity lost in complexity, it gained in intensity. Altogether, associational networks were as intricate as in other regions—but in different ways. A case in point was the comity on Butler Island, Georgia, an irregular holding of about two square miles which Fanny Kemble described as "neither liquid nor solid but a kind of mud sponge floating on the bosom of the Altamaha."[199]

So insular were the lives of these slaves there that one who knew them wrote, "These Butler negroes were a race apart. They never, until years after the [Civil] war, mingled with other negroes. They had a particular lingo, which one had to be familiar with before one could understand it. An old Butler Island woman named Aunt Jerusalem used to sell me figs and blackberries, early English peas and chickens, the latter which she counted this way: Dish yuh one, dish yuh narra, dish yuh tray pun top uh tarra. Dish yuh make five wid he laig all tie togarra." These Gullah slaves had invented not only their words and language but their own arithmetic.[200]

A former slave who had lived on Butler Island before emancipation had the same memory of old field slaves who as late as the 1930s still occupied the old slave quarters. "Sebral uh dem hans wuz bery old people," said she. "Dey speak a funny language an none uh duh rest ub us coudn hardly unuhstan a

Thomas Chaplin's plantation, Tombee, on St. Helena Island

wud dey say. Dey hab special name fuh all kine uh ting, but duh only ting I membuh is dat dey call a watuh bucket a 'juba haltah.'"[201] Slaves on neighboring islands regarded the Butler slaves with fear and wonder. It was widely believed along the Altamaha that the Butler folk could fly, and that they flew back to Africa from time to time.[202]

Within the narrow limits of this special world, the associational lives of slaves were of high complexity. The primary relationships were family groups, both families of origin and families of marriage, all entangled in an extended cousinage as intricate as the Ptolemies. Each Butler slave lived in a hamlet, called a camp in the patois of the island. There were four camps altogether, of about ten to twenty houses each. Each functioned as another orbit of association. The slaves ate supper together in their hamlets, grits and rice served in cedar piggins. Every working slave also belonged to a gang or "troop," as Fanny Kemble called them. The task system was used on Butler's Island, as elsewhere in the lowcountry, but in 1838 the slaves did their daily field tasks in these troups under the eye of a driver.[203]

After field tasks were done, the Butler slaves gathered in age groups to do their other chores. Kemble observed the nubile young women together by the river's edge, drawing water.[204] The old women also met together. Small children ran together in packs.[205] And Kemble remembered that the "young people" all gathered at the river landing giving "shrieks and yells of joy." This pattern of age association had been a strong tradition in African cultures. It persisted powerfully in the Sea Islands, as did segregation by gender.

Every Saturday, the Butler slaves were allowed to go across the Altamaha River and visit the nearby town of Darien, which could be seen from the island. Kemble saw "parties of three or four rowing boats of their own building, laden with their purchases, singing, laughing, talking, and apparently enjoying their holiday to the utmost." [206]

By 1838, most Butler slaves were shouting Baptists. One Sunday a month they were permitted to attend church in Darien. Every other Sunday they had their own worship on the island, gathering at the home of London, a slave cooper who had taught himself to read, and preached from the Bible. [207]

On special occasions all the slaves on the island assembled together. For a funeral (there were many funerals on the Butler plantation) slaves all marched to the burying place, "many of the men carrying pinewood torches." All knelt together in the sand while London, a slave and "head cooper," read from the Book of Common Prayer. [208]

They also flocked together at the island landing, a small wharf, whenever the plantation's handsome little schooner tied up alongside, and its slave crew brought news of the larger world. When the schooner came in view, a great conch shell was sounded, and the slaves came together.

The result was a complicated system of association on Butler Island. Some slaves moved in only a few concentric circles. Others had broad associational lives. A leading example was London, who made the wooden barrels, casks, and buckets that were much used on the island. He became the island's "Methodist preacher," with the knowledge and support of master Pierce Butler. In 1839, Fanny Kemble, who had married the master's son, was present when London delivered a Gullah funeral sermon on Lazarus rising from the dead. He spoke in what Kemble described as a "peculiar sort of jargon which is habitual Negro speech." She was deeply moved by it, and greatly admired London's eloquence. [209]

COMMUNITY EVENTS: GULLAH CHRISTMAS, NORTH CAROLINA JONKONNU

In the Carolina lowcountry, the great festival came at Christmas. December was called Christmas Month. [210] It was a celebration very different from Anglo-Saxon culture in other American regions. A Sea Island slave recalled,

"Us nebber know nutting 'bout Santa Claus 'till Freedom. But on Christmas maussa gib you meat and syrup and maybe t'ree day widout wuk."[211]

The Christmas gatherings in the Carolina lowcountry were much more African than in other regions. One account describes African languages and African sports.[212] Christmas dances were held here, as in many other parts of the South. But the dancing itself was different. Two musciologists described a dance that they observed in the Sea Islands called "I'm going away to see Aunt Dinah," and in some ways superficially resembled a Virginia reel. The step was a skip, performed by women and men in two parallel lines. One observer wrote, "The couples skip, forward for four beats, swing each other for four and skip back to place for a final count of four. Experienced square dancers may find this 'move' of twelve counts against a melody of sixteen to be difficult or jarring. In practice it gives an unexpected syncopation to an otherwise routine figure."[213]

In North Carolina, from Cape Fear to Albemarle Sound, coastal slaves kept another Christmas folkway variously called Jonkonnu, Jukanoo, and John Canoe. Harriet Jacobs, born and raised a slave in Edenton, North Carolina, gave us the fullest description of this custom in the early nineteenth century. She remembered:

"Music and Dance in Beaufort County," ca. 1785

Every child rises early on Christmas morning to see the Johnkannaus. Without them, Christmas would be shorn of its greatest attraction. They consist of companies of slaves from the plantations, generally of the lower class. Two athletic men in calico wrappers have a net thrown over them, covered with all manner of bright-colored stripes. Cows' tails are fastened to their backs, and their heads are decorated with horns. A box, covered with sheepskin, is called the gumbo box. A dozen beat on this, while others strike triangles and jawbones, to which bands of dancers keep time. For a month previous they are composing songs, which are sung on this occasion. These companies of a hundred each turn out early in the morning, and are allowed to go round to twelve o'clock, begging for contributions. Not a door is left unvisited where there is the least chance of obtaining a penny or a glass of rum. They do not drink while they are out, but carry the rum home in jugs, to have a carousal. These Christmas donations frequently amount to twenty or thirty dollars. It is seldom that any white man or child refuses to give them a trifle. If he does, they regale his ears with the following song:

Poor massa, so dey say;
Down in de heel, so dey say;
Got no money, so dey say;
Not one shillin, so dey say;
God A'mighty bress you, so dey say.[214]

Masters welcomed and encouraged this Christmas custom, and may have helped to spread it. Harriet Jacobs's own master, James Norcom, wrote his daughter in 1838, "Had it not been for the John Koonahs that paraded through town in several successive gangs, Christmas day would have pass'd without the least manifestation of mirth, cheerful joy or hilarity."[215]

On other parts of the Carolina coast, the customs were a little different. It was called John Kunering, and the dancers were "kuners." They pranced through the streets of the town, singing:

Hah! Low! Here we go!
Hah! Low! Here we go!
Hah! Low! Here we go!
Kuners come from Denby![216]

Guion Johnson recalled,

> With the rattling of bones, the blowing of cows horns, and the tinkling
> of tamourines, the singing slaves . . . in their "Kuner" costumes, would
> halt wherever an appreciative crowd gathered. Strips of brightly colored
> cloth which had been sewn to their usual garments fluttered gayly as
> the kuners danced. They wore masks, some with horns, beards, staring
> eyes, enormous noses, and grinning mouths. All were men, but some
> were disguised as women. After a few songs, one of the dancers would
> approach the spectators with his hat extended and collect the pennies
> which were the kuners' reward. Shouting again another chant, they
> were off again in search of another crowd and more pennies.[217]

This custom is thought to have originated among Akan-speaking people in
Ghana. The meaning of its name is much debated, but may have derived from
a legendary leader in Axim. Virtually identical customs were kept in Jamaica,
Bahamas, Belize, and Honduras. A great variety of broadly similar folkways appeared throughout lowcountry Carolina, Georgia, the West Indies, and Africa.[218]

In Carolina, white masters claimed to have invented it, which they did not.
One wrote mistakenly in 1824,

> These festivities are not only tolerated by whites, but virtually created
> by them; for without the aid voluntarily contributed by their masters,
> their servants would be destitute of the means of making or enjoying
> them. . . . Although trifling evils sometimes result from these extraor-
> dinary indulgences, they continue to be tolerated and practiced. It is
> to be regretted that drunkenness is too common on these occasions;
> but this also is habitually overlooked and never punished, unless it
> becomes outrageous or grossly offensive.[219]

GULLAH COMMUNICATIONS:
DRUMS AND CONCH SHELLS

Throughout the Sea Islands, slaves communicated by drum and conch shell—
especially by drum. The drums announced every birth and death, and told
who it was and where and when. On other occasions, they warned of danger
and opportunity, when masters and overseers came and went.

White folk heard the throbbing drums with a mix of feelings—fear and fascination altogether. Sometimes masters endeavored to suppress them. But sooner or later every master disappeared and the drums went on for generations. This system of communication worked well for some sorts of news, and badly for others. Sea Island slaves learned instantly of insular events in their own neighborhood, but they were slow to hear of great happenings in the world at large. When a northern fleet appeared in Port Royal Sound early in the Civil War, and commenced firing on a Confederate fort at Hilton Head, a Sea Island slave was heard to say, "Heah come dem damn Britishers again."

GULLAH AND GEECHEE RELIGION: RING SHOUTS AS A VITAL TRADITION

The history of religion in coastal Carolina and Georgia is a subject of dispute among scholars. Some believe that African slaves were not converted to Christianity in early years. Others more recently discovered that in West Central Africa, many Angolan and Congo people were converted to Christianity in the sixteenth and seventeenth centuries, even before before they were enslaved and carried to America.[220]

The history of African American religion in coastal Carolina and Georgia spans the full range of Gullah and Geechee culture. It is a complicated story. From an early date, lowcountry slaves built their own plain wooden "praise houses," which belonged to them. One Sea Islander remembered, "Slave had dey own chu'ch on plantation wid nigger preacher, but on 'munion Sunday, you had to go to w'ite folks chu'ch in Beaufort and sit up stair."[221]

An important and distinctive form of worship in coastal Carolina and Georgia were ring shouts. They first appeared in this region, and were widespread by the early nineteenth century. Many visitors were fascinated by ring shouts and discussed them at great length. Among them was Sir Charles Lyell, a British scientist who studied them in coastal McIntosh County, Georgia, in 1845.

The ring shout tradition was also described in coastal Carolina and Georgia by Union soldiers such as Colonel Thomas Wentworth Higginson, and by northern reformers who worked with Gullah and Geechee slaves.[222]

Ring shouts were also a communal form of worship, deeply emotive.

Praise house at Sapelo, 1939

Gullah ring shouters

They were always performed by groups, not by individuals. Commonly they were done on wooden floors in praise houses. They were always sacred, never secular, and sometimes they inspired deep trancelike states. Shouts were commonly done on Sundays, and special long shouts were performed at Christmas and on New Year's Day. The ring shout was many things at once. It was often a pattern of physical movement that was something like a dance, but always regarded as profoundly different from secular dancing. It was musical, with strong rhythms, but was very different from secular music.

Ring shouters often carried broomsticks and beat them on the wooden floors of praise houses in complex rhythms. They moved their feet and hands in rhythmic ways, sometimes shuffling, sometimes stamping, sometimes tapping toes and heels. Hands were held together before the body, and clapped in rhythmic movements with multiple beats of more complexity. Bodies moved in many ways at once: knees bending, bodies dipping, and torsos rocking, again in multiple rhythms, and different beats at the same time. People commonly did ring shouts by moving in a circular counterclockwise direction, always counterclockwise, but the pace and patterns of movement were variable. One comparatively simple variant was called "walking around." Others grew more complex.

Yet another part of ring shouts was the singing. Shout songs were always sacred, and very different from field hollers and work songs. Shouts also differed from spirituals, though sometimes spirituals were adapted for the purpose of shouting. Shouts were a form of worship, intended to create deep spiritual emotions in the shouters. The verses were often repeated, and the repetition sometimes promoted a trancelike state.

Ring shouts later migrated to other parts of the South. William Wells Brown described them in Tennessee where he observed groups of women performing them in a Nashville church, circa 1880. John and Alan Lomax observed ring shouts in Louisiana in 1934.[223] Other Afro-American regions developed different religious traditions. Scholars have found that "The application of the word 'shout' varied in the southern regions. In Virginia and North Carolina, it referred to a peculiar motion of the body during a solo rather than a group performance."[224] Maryland, Virginia, and parts of North Carolina had a very different tradition of religious shouts that tended to be performed by individuals. The seat and center of collective spiritual ring shouts was coastal Carolina and Georgia. They were a vital part of this regional culture.

THE LEGACY OF GULLAH AND GEECHEE CULTURES

After slavery Gullah and Geechee families went different ways. Some gained land of their own in the lowcountry. St. Helena Island is a classic example. In the early twenty-first century Judy and I toured the island with some of its leaders, and saw large numbers of well-tended homes where African American families live and flourish on land of their own.

Throughout coastal Carolina and Georgia, some former slaves worked as tenants or laborers. Others moved inland and became sharecroppers. Many headed for the lowcountry cities of Savannah and Charleston. In the early twentieth century, others headed north, in chain migrations to New York, Chicago, Philadelphia, Boston. Studies of African American migration from the rural South to the cities gave much attention to "social problems" among African Americans in the North. The shift from rural to urban economies and social conditions was thought to have been very difficult. Material problems such as poverty and underemployment were believed to be compounded by violence, disorder, and prejudice. Migrants from the Sea Islands were thought by some academic sociologists to have an especially difficult time because of their isolation, primitive conditions, and differences of language. Gullah and Geechee speechways were thought to compound these problems.

In the 1920s, sociologist Clyde Kiser did a careful study of these urban migrants from the Carolina lowcountry. He centered an inquiry on Gullah people who had been born and raised on St. Helena Island. From 1900 to 1930, the island's African American population fell nearly 50 percent, mostly by migration to urban centers. Kiser followed three hundred St. Helena emigrants to five cities: Savannah, Charleston, Philadelphia, New York, and Boston.[225]

Kiser found that St. Helena islanders in general did better than other southern emigrants in northern cities. Important advantages derived from their schooling. The Penn Center, still operating, on St. Helena provided "perhaps the best Negro education in the South at that time."[226] Most St. Helena islanders had also been independent owners of small farms since the Civil War. But another factor was even more important in Kiser's judgment. Gullah people from St. Helena Island possessed what Kiser called "cultural integrity."[227]

In New York City, Kiser reported evidence that Sea Islanders formed strong families, and founded neighborhood groups in Harlem, Brooklyn, and

Queens.[228] They created religious institutions similar to those they had known at home. In the cities they reinvented in an urban setting the social cohesion of the Sea Islands. Many joined Baptist congregations, very strong institutions such as Abyssinian Baptist, Metropolitan Baptist, and Walker Memorial. One of the liveliest was Convent Avenue Baptist Church. Others were Methodist congregations, such as the Metropolitan African Methodist Episcopal Church. Many more were small improvised groups. Altogether a survey of 160 Black churches in Manhattan found that 122 met in "residences, basements, and store fronts."[229]

Many of these congregations in New York were Gullah or Geechee. They continued forms of worship that they had known on St. Helena Island, with ring shouts and group dancing, and a spontaneity of music and speech. Gullah and Geechee cultures continued their creativity in urban settings, from Charleston and Savannah to New York and Chicago. In Harlem, Gullah and Geechee ring shouts persisted in the 1950s, sometimes incorporating elements of jazz piano, and jazz drumming in place of the broomstick beats.[230]

Leading jazz musicians came to learn from the vernacular culture of these ring shouts and carried their spirit into new musical forms. Harlem jazz pianist Willie "the Lion" Smith was interviewed on that subject by jazz historians Rudi Blesh and Harriet Janis. Willie the Lion told them, "Shouts are stride piano—when James P. [Johnson] and Fats [Waller] and I would get a romp-down shout going, that was playing rocky, just like the Baptist people sing. You don't just play a chord to that—you move it, and the piano players do the same thing in the churches, and there's ragtime in the preaching. Want to see a ring-shout? Go to the Convent Avenue Baptist Church any Sunday."[231]

James P. Johnson composed a jazz piano piece called "Carolina Shout." It had a long reach on the music of Duke Ellington and many other American composers. And as it traveled it grew: Gullah and Geechee ways continued as a living tradition in America through the twentieth century, and even to our time.

Gullah and Geechee congregations in northern cities continued to function after the music stopped. When a service and a shout ended the people tended to "linger in the church and around the doors and steps, as they have been accustomed to do."[232]

They also did something else. Many kept connections with relatives and friends in St. Helena Island, from whence they came. They visited over long distances. Children were sent home for summer, to live with extended families, to help with family work on the land, and to stay in touch. In New York, Kiser found that "practically every islander in New York has close relatives in the city," and in time of need they helped each other.[233]

It happened differently in other cities. In Savannah, Gullah and Geechee people lived in two segregated neighborhoods called Yamacraw and the Fort. In Charleston, they tended to reside in small "nests" of alleys and courts. In northern cities, residential groups were more scattered. But they found each other, formed new families, and helped one another in time of need.

They also socialized together and maintained ties to coastal Carolina. In Savannah, a social club called the Emporia was joined by most St. Helena islanders. It supported round-trip return visits to the island.[234] In New York City, they founded voluntary associations such as the Penn School Club (1926) and the St. Helena League (1929).[235] They also married together. Kiser found that among sixty-one women of marriagable age who went from St. Helena to New York City, twenty-seven married men from the island, and most of the others married men from coastal Carolina and Georgia.[236]

In short, when St. Helena islanders moved from the lowcountry to cities north and south, Kiser found that they preserved a strong sense of mutual identity and individual self-respect and even increased it. They also developed a stronger race consciousness as people of African descent, and used it in a constructive way.[237]

A GULLAH HERITAGE IN THE WHITE HOUSE

In 2009, three generations of a family with Gullah roots moved into the White House. Michelle Robinson Obama descended in part from coastal Carolina ancestors. Some of her forebears had been Gullah slaves, perhaps on Friendfield Plantation, or Maryville Plantation, both of which were near Georgetown, the heart of the Carolina rice coast.[238]

Michelle Obama's forebears were extraordinary people, as many Gullah folk tended to be. Her great-grandfather, Fraser Robinson Sr., was the first in his line born free, in 1884. When ten years old, he lost his arm in an accident and grew up with a major handicap in a dangerous world of extreme violence and increasing racism. The odds were stacked against him, but others offered a helping hand. He learned to read and write, got a good job in the lumber business, worked for himself in other trades, became an elder in the Bethel Methodist Church, acquired some land of his own, and built a large four-bedroom house for his very able wife, Rosella, and their family in Georgetown. They also sent their son Fraser Robinson Jr. to the only Black high school in Georgetown County.

Fraser Robinson Jr. followed a Gullah friend to Chicago in the Great Depression. When the United States entered World War II, he joined the army, fought in Italy, rose to master sergeant, became highly skilled in electronics, and after the war got a steady civil service job in the Post Office. His son Fraser Robinson III provided a stable home for four gifted children, required them to work hard, and paid part of their way. All went to college, two to Princeton and Harvard. They also were taught at home to remember their African American origins with pride.

One of those gifted children was Michelle Robinson Obama. She had a complex heritage. All four of her grandparents had multiracial ancestors. But in her childhood special emphasis was put on Gullah roots. She was taught to remember them with pride and to experience them for herself. After Michelle was ten, her parents took her back to Georgetown in South Carolina for the summer. She lived among her Gullah relations, worked in family gardens, and went to church.[239]

When the Obamas moved into the White House, that heritage went with them. Quilts were made to tell the story of Michelle Obama's Gullah roots. They were displayed on a float in the inaugural parade, and exhibited in the Smithsonian. Michelle Obama's mother moved into the White House, and lived there through the presidency. A vegetable garden was planted on the White House grounds, with many purposes and layers of meaning. The Obama children worked in it as their forebears had done in coastal Carolina. One meaning among others was an echo of Gullah traditions. When Michelle Obama was asked about her ancestry, she said that in many ways life in America was a journey with others, and "an important message in this journey is that we are all linked . . . through our histories of growth and survival in this country."[240]

CORNELIA BAILEY'S GEECHEE ROOTS

Another memorable Geechee story played out on Sapelo Island in coastal Georgia, in the small Geechee village of Hog Hammock. This was the home of Cornelia Walker Bailey, direct descendant of Islamic slaves who came there three centuries ago.

When we met her, Cornelia Bailey had become a gifted writer and teacher, but most of all a storyteller. She wrote of herself as an "African Griot" who kept the oral history, and "was in charge of remembering." Her stories are about many things, but much of them are about the importance of community life that has been strong on Sapelo for many generations. It is an idea of community that links youth to age, in bonds of soul and spirit.[241]

In the small village at Hog Hammock, people come from a long distance to meet Cornelia Bailey, as we did, and met and talked in her kitchen. Like many others they came to learn from her experience. The heritage of her people is increasingly of interest to others. It is important not as a survival of a world we have lost, but as a clue to something of importance in the world of the living.

THE DISCOVERY OF GULLAH AND
GEECHEE CULTURE

People of other cultures in the United States have been discovering the Gullah and Geechee heritage as relevant to their own history. That process of discovery began among the "Gideonites" who moved from the North to coastal Carolina and Georgia during the Civil War. Their story is beautifully told by Willie Lee Rose in a classic and compulsively readable work of American history.[242]

The legacy of Gullah and Geechee culture expanded in the 1920s and 1930s, and gained new strength in the late-twentieth and twenty-first centuries. An excellent new history by Melissa Cooper follows it through time. Much of it is about the persistence of Gullah and Geechee culture, and its growing presence in the "American Imagination." This is not merely a memory. It is a living process of growth and creativity. Every historian who writes about Gullah and Geechee cultures, every linguist who studies the creativity of Gullah and Geechee speechways, every musician who picks up the complex cadences of a ring shout, and others in many disciplined inquiries, are building on that vibrant African and American tradition. Despite fears for its extinction, it is very much alive today.[243]

And all of this is also about something else—the importance of roots in Gullah and Geechee people. Some Americans imagine themselves to be a rootless people, but they are often mistaken. Nearly all of us have roots in one way or another, even when we don't consciously remember them. Gullah and Geechee cultures are a classic model of American roots. Their history has much to teach us about the strength of American roots, especially among people on the go.

Today Americans still tend to be a people in motion—less so than before by the measure of past migrations, but we are still a people on the move. Like Gullah and Geechee people who moved to New York and Chicago and the White House, Americans tend to be people with portable roots. We build our roots into our lives in various ways. Mostly we carry them in our heads and hearts, wherever we go. An interesting paradox is that American portable roots often grow stronger in that process. This is what Gullah and Geechee people did when they were moved from Africa to coastal Carolina and Georgia, and then again when they moved themselves to Chicago and New York. Here is a complex process of persistence and change, of cherished ways and fresh creativity, which are at the heart of the American condition.

TABLE 5.1 African Origins of Slaves Arriving in
South Carolina, 1716–1807

William Pollitzer's Studies of Shipping Lists

| | PERCENTAGE OF SLAVES IN EACH PERIOD | | | |
REGION	1716–44	1749–87	1804–07	TOTAL
Senegambia	7.4	25.2	1.7	19.7
Sierra Leone	0	6.6	4.7	6.0
Windward Coast	0.2	16.7	17.9	17.3
Gold Coast	2.8	13.1	11.4	13.4
Bight of Benin	0	2.2	0	1.5
Bight of Biafra	4.7	0.8	2.5	2.5
Angola and Congo	51.0	14.8	52.0	39.0
East Africa	0	0	1.6	0.5
Unspecified	33.9	20.7	8.2	15.7
Percent Africa	100.0	99.9	100.0	100.0
Total Africa	22,117	63,210	29,461	114,788
Total West Indies	1,155	5,491	30	6,676
Total Number	23,272	68,701	29,491	121,464

TABLE 5.2 African Origins of Slaves Arriving in South Carolina, 1701–1808

	Three Studies of Voyages and Naval Office Records			
	SHIP LISTS CURTIN	NAVAL OFFICE LITTLEFIELD	ELTIS & RICHARDSON	TRANSATLANTIC SLAVE TRADE
DATES	1733–1807	1717–67	1701–1808	
African Region				
Senegambia	19.5	19.9	19.5	44,000
Sierra Leone	6.8		14.2	32,000
Windward Coast	16.3		8.4	19,000
Gold Coast	13.3		12.4	28,000
Bight of Benin	1.6		1.9	4,400
Bight of Biafra	2.1	5.1	10.2	23,000
Angola and Congo	39.6	75.0	32.8	74,000
Madagascar and East Africa	0.7		0.7	1,500
Total	100.0	100.0	100.1	
Number embarked				225,900
Number landed				187,000
Deaths in Middle Passage				38,900

TABLE 5.3 African Origins of Fugitive Slaves in South Carolina, 1730–90

Two Studies from Runaway Notices		
REGION OF ORIGIN	RUNAWAYS FISCHER ET AL.	RUNAWAYS POLLITZER
DATES	(1730–89)	(1730–90)
Senegambia	18.9	12.7
Sierra Leone	2.2	6.0
Guinea, Windward Coast	3.3	30.4
Gold Coast	6.7	5.9
Bight of Benin	3.3	0.0
Bight of Biafra	15.6	13.3
Angola and Congo	50.0	31.7
Total	100.0	100.0
Number	364	480

TABLE 5.4 African Origins of Fugitive Slaves
in South Carolina, 1730–89

REGION	1730–39	1740–49	1750–59	1760–69	1770–79	1780–89	TOTAL
Senegambia							
Gambia	10	4	21	19	4		58
Mandingo, Malinke			1	6	5		12
Bambara, Bamana				4			4
Fullah, Fula				1	1		2
Sierra Leone							
Timine					1		1
Windward Coast				4			4
Kishee					8		8
Grain Coast				1	9	1	11

Leeward Coast

Gold Coast			2	2	7		11
Coromantee		1	2	9	3	1	16
Pawpaw, Papa		1	4	15	10		30

Bight of Biafra

Ibo, Ebo	3	6	10	14	8	3	44
Calabar	1	1	2	1	2		7
Moco					1		1

Congo and Angola

Angola	26	25	18	31	39	7	146
Congo				2	1	6	9

Total | | | | | | | **364**

TABLE 5.5 Population Growth in South Carolina, 1708–90

DATE	WHITES	FREE NEGROES	SLAVES	TOTAL	SOURCE
1708				5,500	
1720a	6,465		11,828	18,393	census
1720b	5,220		11,828	17,048	census
1747	25,000		40,000	65,000	estimate
1769	45,000		80,000	125,000	estimate
1775	70,000		104,000		estimate
1790	140,178	1,801	107,094	249,073	census

TABLE 5.6 African Origins of Slaves Arriving in Georgia, 1755–98

Karen Bell's Study of Shipping Records in the National Archives

AFRICAN CAPTIVES CARRIED INTO SAVANNAH BY ORIGIN, 1755–67

Place of Origin	Number
Upper Guinea	1,188
West Central Africa	90
Caribbean/West Indies	1,485
South Carolina	98
Other North America	4
Total	n.a.

AFRICAN CAPTIVES CARRIED INTO SAVANNAH BY ORIGIN, 1768–80

Place of Origin	Number	Percent (of all)	Percent (of Africa)
Upper Guinea	2,932	(68%)	(79%)
Gold Coast	287	(6%)	(8%)
West Central Africa	500	(12%)	(13%)
Caribbean	337	(8%)	
Origin Unknown	280	(6%)	
Subtotal Africans	3,719		(100%)
Total	4,336	(100%)	

AFRICAN CAPTIVES CARRIED INTO SAVANNAH BY ORIGIN, 1784–98

Place of Origin	Number	Percent (of all)	Percent (of Africa)
Upper Guinea	3,046	(49%)	(60%)
Gold Coast	1,518	(24%)	(30%)
Angola and West Central Africa	335	(5%)	(13%)
Caribbean	185	(6%)	(7%)
Origin Unknown	1,146	(18%)	
Subtotal			5,084 (100%)
Total	6,230	(100%)	

Note: Upper Guinea includes Senegambia, Sierra Leone, the Windward Coast, and the Ivory Coast.

TABLE 5.7 African Origins of Slaves Arriving in Georgia, 1766–58

Evidence from the Trans-Atlantic Slave Trade Database
Origins of Slaves carried dirctly from Africa to Georgia, 1766–1858

ORIGIN	NUMBER OF SLAVES	PERCENT
Upper Guinea	15,300	(61.4%)
Gold Coast	2,200	(15.3%)
West Central Africa	5,800	(23.3%)
Total	**24,900**	**(100.0%)**

Note: Approximately 80 percent of these estimates are from documented voyages; Eltis and Richardson added corrections of 20 percent as their estimate of missing voyages.

TABLE 5.8 African Origins of Fugitive Slaves in Georgia, 1760–99

Evidence from Advertisements in Savannah Newspapers

	1760–69	1770–79	1780–89	1790–99	TOTAL
Upper Guinea					
Gambia	3				3
Mandingo	1	2	1		4
Bamba, Bambara	2	5			7
Fullah, Fula, Fulbe			1	2	3
Guinea	26	28	11	2	67
Sierra Leone		2			2
Gola	1				1
Kishee	2				2
Gold Coast					
Coromantee	2	1	6		9
Bight of Biafra					
Ibo, Ebo, Eboe	2	4	7	1	14
Congo and Angola					
Angola	6	1	14	2	33
Congo, Conga	6		4	2	12

Unidentified

Suroga	1				1
Total	**61**	**45**	**43**	**7**	**156**
Total Upper Guinea	**35**	**37**	**13**	**4**	**89**

Percent from Upper Guinea (57%)

TABLE 5.9 Population Growth in Georgia, 1732–1860

Evidence of Census Data and Official Estimates

DATE	WHITE	BLACK	TOTAL	SOURCE
1733–34	437	12	449	Census
1751	1,900	420	2,320	Estimate (Trustees)
1753	2,381	1,066	3,447	Returns (Wright)
1760	6,000	3,578	9,578	Returns (Wright)
1766	9,900	7,800	17,700	Estimate (Wright)
1773	18,000	15,000	33,000	Estimate (Wright)
1790	52,886	29,662	82,548	U.S. Census
1800	102,000	60,000	163,000	U.S. Census
1810	145,000	107,000	252,000	U.S. Census
1820	190,000	151,000	341,000	U.S. Census
1830	297,000	220,000	517,000	U.S. Census
1840	408,000	284,000	691,000	U.S. Census
1850	522,000	385,000	906,000	U.S. Census
1860	592,000	466,000	1,057,000	U.S. Census

Chapter 6

LOUISIANA, LOWER MISSISSIPPI, AND THE GULF COAST

French, Spanish, and Anglo Rulers; Bamana, Benin, and
Congo Slaves; American Pluralism in the Mississippi Valley

French Louisiana was a chaotic world where cultural materials
brought by Africans often turned out to be the most adaptive.

—Gwendolyn Midlo Hall[1]

Greater flexibility and willingness to accept native culture on its
own terms . . . led to a far greater degree of interaction between the
cultures in New France than in England's colonies.

—Gary Nash[2]

THE HISTORY OF AFRICANS in Louisiana has many beginnings.
One of them starts in the village of Old Ségou, on the great Northern
Bend of the Niger River, in what is now the Republic of Mali. We
went there in 1997, Judy and I, traveling by Air Mali from Dakar to Bamako,
then by car on the ancient caravan road to Timbuktu.[3]

Some people of Old Ségou cultivate a distance from the modern world,
but they welcome visitors with an interest in history. Their village was the
home of Mamari Kulubali, a great leader who founded the West African empire of Ségou in the early eighteenth century. In that process he also played a
role in the peopling of Louisiana.[4]

Mamari's village is handsomely set on a hill overlooking the Niger River.
When we were there, herds were grazing on green banks, and farmers were
preparing their fields for crops. In 1997 the scene was prosperous, peaceful,
and even serene.

But three centuries earlier, there was no serenity in Ségou. Griots, who are
custodians of oral memory in Mali, still sing their sagas of what happened
there. They tell of a time before 1700, when a Bamana hunter followed his

LOUISIANA, GULF COAST, & LOWER MISSISSIPPI

NEBRASKA

ILLINOIS

INDIANA

Fort Orleans

Missouri River

St. Louis

MISSOURI

Fort de Chartres

Ste. Genevieve

Ohio River

KANSAS

KENTUCKY

Arkansas River

OKLAHOMA

ARKANSAS

TENNESSEE

Mississippi River

Memphis

MISSISSIPPI

Yazoo River

ALABAMA

Red River

LOUISIANA

Natchitoches

Los Adaes/Adayes

Natchez

TEXAS

Point Coupée

Mobile

Pensacola

Baton Rouge

Biloxi

Lafayette

New Orleans

English Turn

German Coast

Fort de la Boulaye

Tiger Island

Barataria Bay

Balize

Gulf of Mexico

0 Miles	100	200
0 Kilometers	200	

© 2022 Jeffrey L. Ward

Tomb of Biton Mamary Coulibaly (Mamari Kulubali) in old Ségou, Mali

quarry into the Niger Valley. He settled there, founded a family, and had a son named Mamari Kulubali, who was also trained to hunt. One morning, Mamari wounded a large animal. He tracked it to the Niger River, and killed it. According to one saga, he heard a vulture talking with a hyena. The animals agreed that a hunter as great as young Mamari was destined to be a king.[5]

Mamari returned to his Bamana village and met the bachelors of his age society, who were about to choose a leader. Some favored a nobleman's son, but Mamari was elected, though his family was of humble rank. The nobles said he could not serve, and a fight began. Mamari and his friends won. Other villages rallied to their cause. Strangers and outcasts placed themselves under Mamari's leadership. The fighting spread through other Bamana kingdoms and Mamari gained more victories.

By force of arms he founded a great empire, and ruled it until his death in 1755. He was succeeded as emperor by his brothers, and they were followed by their family slave, Ngolo Diarra. The rise of Ngolo Diarra from slave to emperor of Ségou is a clue to the complexity of human bondage in Africa.[6]

After each victory, Mamari Kulubali captured some of the men who fought

against him. Many were Bamana warriors like himself, and he did not wish
to kill them. Mamari ordered them to be enslaved and sold far away, beyond
the possibility of return.[7]

At that moment, French slave traders were founding a West African
empire of their own. They had moved from the Atlantic coast deep into
the interior of the continent, and built Fort St. Joseph as a major trading
base at Galam on the Senegal River, four hundred miles from the sea. They
bought some of Mamari Kulubali's captives and carried them downstream
to the Atlantic port of Saint-Louis, where French ships took them around
the world.[8]

Some of these warrior-slaves were sent east to the Mauritius Islands in the
Indian Ocean. Others went west to Louisiana. In the twentieth century, linguists discovered striking similarities between Afro-French speechways that
developed at the same time in Mauritius and Louisiana, on opposite sides of
the world.[9]

By 1731, as we shall see, Bamana warriors became the largest African ethnic group in Louisiana. They arrived with other Mande-speaking captives
whose languages were closely related to Bamana. In this first African migration to Louisiana, other slaves also came from Senegal seaports. Among
them were Wolof and Fulani people who spoke different languages but had
long lived near one another. An observer wrote that they "can ordinarily
understand each other, though their languages and cultures ('castas') are diverse."[10]

Altogether, these slaves from Senegal and Mali were between two thirds
and three quarters of all Africans who came to Louisiana in its French period
from 1699 to 1766. A smaller but important flow also came from another
West African region around Benin. And yet another single ship carried slaves
to Louisiana from Congo in Central Africa.[11]

WEST AFRICA AND LOUISIANA:
A KINSHIP OF CREATIVITY

In early Louisiana, most of these African slaves did not arrive as solitary
strangers who had been stripped of their cultural heritage—a common mis-
conception of the Middle Passage in American history. Here again, as in every
North American colony, some slaves came alone, but others came in clusters.
Various patterns of clustering among African slaves appeared in all North

American regions, from New England and New Netherland and the Delaware Valley in the north, to the Chesapeake, Carolinas, Georgia, and Louisiana in the south. Patterns and processes of clustering were never twice the same, but everywhere they made a difference in the history that followed.

In Louisiana this pattern of clustering among African slaves was noticed by Gwendolyn Midlo Hall.[12] The cultural consequences have been discussed by scholars from both sides of the Atlantic. In our time, the West African scholar Ibrahima Seck came to Louisiana, and observed many historical resemblances to his homeland. The drivers were clusters of West African slaves who carried their culture with them in the slave trade, and introduced elements of it to Louisiana, from 1718 to 1731.[13]

An example of material culture, broadly familiar to many historians, was the migration of rice, in the variety *Oryza glaberrima*. Probably it had been first domesticated in the middle Niger Valley. Scholars have learned precisely how rice came to Louisiana, when it arrived, who brought it, and how, and why. In 1719 and 1721, it arrived aboard two slave ships, *Aurore* and *Duc du Maine*. Each captain had been instructed by the French Company of the West to buy three or four barrels of rice for seed, and to purchase slaves who knew how cultivate it. It was done, and by 1720 African *Oryza glaberrima* was growing in Louisiana. In early years, this African staple, with African methods of raising and cooking it, helped to sustain a struggling American colony.[14]

Much else came to Louisiana in this African slave trade. Oral folktales about animal characters in eighteenth-century Senegal and Mali and other parts of West Africa are very much like stories that folklorist Alcée Fortier collected in nineteenth-century Louisiana. These are not vague and distant resemblances. On both sides of the Atlantic, favorite folktales are similar in themes, plots, characters, and even specific names, acts, and conversations.[15]

Other similarities appeared between African languages and Louisiana's regional Afro-French speechways that emerged by the mid-eighteenth century. In Louisiana they were collectively called Gombo by the nineteenth century, and Creole in our time. Surviving examples of spoken Gombo appear in recorded testimony of slaves before Louisiana's Superior Council as early as 1731. Other examples can be heard in conversations by elderly former slaves, recorded on wax cylinders in the early twentieth century, and preserved in the American Folklore Collection at the Library of Congress. These old voices still ring strong with pride and confidence. Their Afro-French speechways have power and spirit, and a range of expression that are clues to its persistence and creativity.

Today, the number of native Gombo speakers in Louisiana is small and shrinking. But younger people, both African and European in origin, are teaching themselves to speak and write and think in Gombo. Some are creating new poetry and prose in that old language, as instruments of their own identity in our time.[16]

These various cultural patterns should not be understood as African "survivals" in America. They were part of a more dynamic process. Elements of African and European and American Indian languages were combined to create something new in the world. When we hear Gombo spoken on old recordings and listen carefully, we discover that it became more expressive in some ways than the African and European languages from whence it grew. The same thing happened in cultural processes of storytelling, in material tasks of problem-solving, and in the social construction of comity in new forms.[17]

It also occurred in other genres of expression, such as music. Some of the most vibrant and creative linkages between West Africa and Louisiana are to be found in the music of both regions. Mali and Senegal have long been renowned for the creativity of their musical traditions, as have Louisiana in general and New Orleans in particular.

One morning in Mali's capital city of Bamako, two native Bamana speakers guided Judy and me through a collection of very old African musical instruments. They were similar in striking ways to instruments of slaves in early Louisiana, as sketched by Benjamin Latrobe on a visit to New Orleans in 1819.[18]

Our hosts in Bamako mentioned in passing, "We have a word for music we like. We call it Jassy. It means sweet." That usage was new to us. We wondered if it could be a clue to the much debated origins of "jazz," both in the word itself and the music it describes. It might be so, or maybe not. Jassy music and the word itself have traveled widely through the world, and in many directions. Inquiries continue.[19]

Other musical linkages of a different kind appeared in the ancient instruments that we saw in Bamako, and Latrobe sketched in New Orleans. It was the same again for the intricate rhythms of music in both places, and for the unequal notes and accented upbeats that Louisianians would later call swing, and also for the complex interplay of performers and auditors that Latrobe and many others observed.

These patterns indicate a kinship of creativity in the music of Mali and

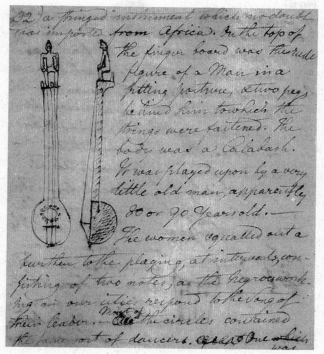

Benjamin Henry Latrobe's journal, showing a stringed instrument with body that was a calabash

Afro-French Louisiana. It was evident to observers in the eighteenth and early nineteenth centuries, and it is still developing in the dynamic music of these American and African regions in the twenty-first century. A question for historians is about their origins.[20]

OLD WAYS IN NEW SOCIETIES: FOUNDER EFFECTS IN LOUISIANA

Through twelve generations, many other groups of people came to Louisiana. They learned to draw on French and African cultures which were among the first to take root in Louisiana. And they introduced elements from many cultures around the world. From the start, Louisiana was a place of extraordinary diversity, and grew more so. That continuing process is stronger than ever today.

Many groups were prominent in its long history. But those who came from France and Africa before 1740 had many of the more consequential roles, because of their timing. They came at an early date, and had an impact comparable to what some biologists, geneticists, and linguists have called a "founder effect." In genetics this phenomenon has been understood as the creation of a new gene pool, with a loss of genetic variation that happens when a small population moves away from a larger one.[21]

Other founder effects worked differently in historical processes. In early American colonies, small groups often came together and formed new populations and cultures. By comparison with the larger groups from whence they came, each of these small units tended to be less diverse. But in a new colony they commonly mixed with other small groups and created a larger population that became more diverse. This happened not as a fixed determinism, but as an open process through the interplay of individual acts and choices. The earliest choices often had the longest reach, even to our time.

That is what happened in the founding of Louisiana. A diversity of American Indians were already on the scene. The first francophone settlers were themselves a mix of many groups. They ran the colony, but not just as they pleased.

The first African slaves cherished their own ways and were themselves also diverse. They quickly became a majority. By Louisiana's census of 1727, 51.7 percent of the population were of African origin. That proportion rose to 76.9 percent in the census of 1741, the highest African concentration on record in any mainland North American region.[22]

A complex culture of creative diversity developed rapidly among Louisiana's people. Much of it was an artifact of founding purposes. More of it grew from the interaction of founding groups. In that long process something new was created in America from a mix of older African, European, and American Indian materials. It included new ways in agriculture, foodways, folkways, music, and much more.

Much of this happened among African slaves within the experience of their bondage, which tended to be hard and cruel everywhere, especially in French Louisiana. Human bondage in the lower Mississippi Valley gained a grim reputation from the start, and in some ways it grew worse through time.

But something extraordinary happened in the responses of African slaves to their condition. Over an extended period, they created composite cultures among themselves, and also invented new systems of comity, association, interaction, identity, and belonging.

Comities develop in all functioning societies, and they are fundamental to free and open systems. These patterns emerged in every North American region at an early date. African slaves of European masters were important in the creation of new Afro-European comities in America. That complex process of cultural invention was especially visible in the colony of Louisiana, in large part because of its early diversity, which would later grow throughout American culture.

LOUISIANA'S SMALL BEGINNINGS, AND A LARGE IDEA FROM FRENCH CANADA

In North America, every new colony began with a founding idea. It was typical of French Louisiana that it started with many founding ideas, each with its own drivers.

The first francophone leaders of Louisiana did not come from France itself. They were French-speaking native sons of Canada, led by members of the prolific Le Moyne family. By 1698, eleven Le Moyne brothers had grown to maturity in Montreal when it was still a frontier settlement. They were raised among *coureurs de bois* (bush rangers) and American Indians, and trained as soldiers, seamen, and explorers. Two of these Le Moyne brothers led the founding of Louisiana. Together they deliberately increased its diversity, and also introduced new and enduring ways of thought.

Pierre Le Moyne, Sieur d'Iberville

Their first leader was Pierre Le Moyne (1661–1706), a French Canadian nobleman with the title of the Sieur d'Iberville. He commanded the first successful French colonizing voyages to the Gulf Coast in 1698–99, 1700, and 1701–02, and has been widely recognized as the "founder of Louisiana."[23]

Iberville, as he is remembered, built the first fortified settlements on the southeastern fringe of the French colony, near the present sites of Biloxi in Mississippi and Mobile in Alabama. In the first Louisiana census of 1699 the largest group of Iberville's settlers were French Canadian *seigneurs* and *coureurs de bois*. A second census in 1700 listed them by name, as more than half of Louisiana's population.[24]

Among them was Iberville's younger brother, Jean-Baptiste Le Moyne, Sieur de Bienville (1680–1767). He is remembered not as the founder but the "father of Louisiana." Bienville was ordered to sail up the Mississippi River and build a fort on the first piece of solid ground, which he did at Fort de la Boulaye, fifty miles upstream. Later, Bienville founded New Orleans in 1718,

Jean-Baptiste Le Moyne, Sieur de Bienville, founder of New Orleans

and served three separate terms as governor of Louisiana, from the death of his elder brother in 1706 to 1743. On retirement he moved to France, where he defended Louisiana against a host of critics, and died in harness at the age of eighty-seven.[25]

In Canada, France, and Louisiana, the brothers Iberville and Bienville have long been celebrated for their many achievements. More recently, some scholars have become more critical, and with good reason. Much evidence of corruption and profiteering survives from Louisiana's early years. Iberville and Bienville were involved in it. A lively book by anthropologist Shannon Lee Dawdy calls Louisiana the "Devil's Empire." She links its founders to "rogue colonialism," a double disgrace in academe, and judges the brothers Iberville and Bienville as "the most roguish of early colonials." [26]

That judgment contains important elements of truth, but much of it comes from testimony by enemies such as Antoine De La Mothe, Sieur de Cadillac. Other evidence shows a different side of these complex French Canadian founders and fathers of Louisiana. Iberville, Bienville, and others were carriers of a unique Canadian heritage that is still strong today. It centers on an idea of humanity, and it derived from the founders of New France: the large purposes of Henri IV, the principled leadership of Pierre Dugua, Sieur de Mons, and the acts and values of Samuel Champlain.

This spirit of humanity appeared in Canada at a very early date, and it continues to be a living Canadian tradition. At the date of this writing in the twenty-first century, Canada's outgoing governor General David Johnson and incoming prime minister Justin Trudeau both identified themselves with the humane spirit of Samuel Champlain.[27]

In Canada, from 1604 to 1635, Champlain was able to establish peaceful relations with many North American Indian nations. His mentor and model was Henri IV, first Bourbon king of France, who brought tolerance and peace to a divided nation until his assassination by a religious fanatic in 1610. In the same spirit, Champlain made peace with more than fifty American Indian nations and built relationships that endured for many generations. When several Iroquois nations continued to make war in the St. Lawrence Valley, Champlain defeated them in small punitive expeditions, and made a precarious peace even with the Mohawk that continued for nearly twenty years.[28]

Champlain also urged Indians and French alike to treat others humanely, *humainement* in his word. Important linguistic clues to the history of that idea have emerged from the new empirical tool of the Google Ngram Viewer, and in its application to a vast Google "corpus" of millions of printed French texts.

This source tells us that the adverb *humainement* first appeared in print during the era of Champlain, and the founding of New France in Canada. Its earliest known usage was by Champlain himself, among his Canadian colleagues. The use of that abstraction in its adverbial form tells us that they were actually trying to put ideas of humanity and humanism to work in the New World.[29]

To that end, Champlain recruited many bright young Frenchmen and sent them to live among American Indians, with orders to study their ways, learn their language, and improve understanding. And he called them *truchements*, go-betweens. At the same time, he invited young American Indians to live among the French, with permission from Indian leaders. He also encouraged intermarriage. In 1633, Champlain met Indians of the Montagnais nation and told them that he had a dream, that "our young men will marry your daughters, and henceforth we shall become one people."[30]

Many French *coureurs de bois* and American Indians shared Champlain's dream. *Métissage*, in its broadest meaning as the mixing of diverse people and their different ways, was perceived by Champlain as a positive good, and a policy of high importance for New France. It has had a long reach in the history of that great nation. Once, when I was speaking at Laval University, a colleague came up afterward. She said on the subject of *métissage*, "We have a saying in Canada: scratch a family and find feathers."[31]

Bienville and Iberville had been raised in that early Franco-Canadian tradition of *humanité*. Nearly a century after Champlain, they introduced that idea to Louisiana, much as Champlain and his *truchements* had done in Acadia, Quebec, Montreal, Huronia, northern New England, and the Pays d'en Haut around the Great Lakes.

In 1700, one of Iberville's first acts was to create his own Louisiana *truchements* in the lower Mississippi Valley. He sent "young cabin boys to live among the Chickasaw and learn their language," exactly as Champlain had done. Once again, it worked. Louisiana's first census of 1699 listed these individual cabin boys by name. In 1700, master carpenter and journalist André Pénicaut was with Iberville when they visited the Muskogean Bayagoula people, and "left with their chief a little French boy to be taught the sauvage language." Later they returned and "found the little French boy that M. d'Iberville had left there on the way upriver. He could already speak their language very well."[32]

Bienville established relations of mutual respect with many Indian nations in the lower Mississippi Valley. He fought some of them from time to time when necessary to keep a larger peace, as Champlain had done in the St. Lawrence. But he also worked at establishing good relations, and was held in high esteem by Indian leaders, again much like Champlain.

Iberville also actively encouraged intermarriage between the French and Indians. Bienville, at one point, preferred that French settlers should marry French wives for reasons of state. But in Louisiana's early years, that was not an option. No French women are known to have lived in the colony until 1704.

Even after the first shipload of twenty-three "marriageable girls" reached Biloxi that year, one of the leading Catholic clergy in the colony, Henri Roulleaux de la Vente, wrote to the French vicar general for Louisiana in 1704, "the blood of *les sauvages* does no harm to the blood of the French."[33]

With astonishing speed, small French parties of *coureurs de bois*, *habitants*, *sieurs*, and missionaries advanced thousands of miles into the heartland of North America. In Louisiana's founding year, French-speaking traders and settlers established a mission at Cahokia on the Mississippi River in what is now the state of Illinois. The "commandant for the Illinois Country" was Pierre Dugué de Boisbriand, a Canadian cousin of the Le Moyne family. In 1718, the Sieur de Boisbriand also built Fort de Chartres in Illinois. The next year he started a settlement at Kaskaskia sixteen miles away.[34]

These French Canadian community builders often married Indian women. Surviving French records for the Illinois country show that twenty-one children were baptized from 1701 to 1731. Seventeen (81 percent) had French fathers and Indian mothers.[35] Some officials from France were not pleased. Governor Étienne de Périer complained to the Comte de Maurepas that in the Illinois country, "the majority of habitants have married sauvagesses; they have themselves become sauvages, that is to say, very difficult to discipline."[36]

But other leaders in Louisiana actively supported Franco-Indian marriages. The Sieur de Cadillac observed that Frenchmen in Louisiana sought marriage with "Indian women whom they prefer to French women."[37] Indian and French marriages spread swiftly in the northern Mississippi Valley, which the French called Upper Louisiana. Mixed families called Métis dominated that central North American region for as many as six generations before the English moved in. Within a formal frame of official disapproval, a widespread popular tolerance of *métissage* between the French and Indians was a continuing theme, both in lower Louisiana and the Pays d'en Haut of the upper Mississippi Valley.[38]

A recent study by Claiborne Skinner found that in French settlements throughout the Mississippi Valley, "well into the 1720s, the majority of brides were Indian." He observed that intermarriage "had distinct limits: unions of

white women and Indian men did not happen." But Skinner also discovered
that "among Métis families, however, the children might marry either red
or white spouses" without limits of gender. Through the heartland of North
America, we find much evidence that Champlain's dream of humanity had a
broad reach among French Canadians and American Indians in the Mississippi Valley.[39]

Later, as we shall see, sexual relations also increased between French men
and African women, but this was a different story. Slavery was centrally
involved, and these relations were often brutally coerced. They developed
wherever race slavery existed, but in Louisiana something else happened.
Afro-European *métissage* became institutionalized in ways that had no equal
in most other regions of what is now the United States.[40]

Positive attitudes toward Afro-European *métissage* were not universally
shared in Louisiana, especially after Anglo-Americans arrived in large numbers. In the nineteenth century, an ideology of racism rapidly increased among
the French, Spanish, and Anglo-Americans. A language of racism appeared,
not only in colonial English, but also in colloquial Creole French with pejorative slang words such as *négraille*. It was more nearly the product of a period
than of a place and time.[41]

Even so, a culture of *métissage* would continue in Louisiana for more than
three centuries, even through the period of hyper-racism, in the nineteenth
and early twentieth centuries. Despite the spread of racism, a persistent theme
of race mixing runs deep and strong in the grain of this regional culture. So
also does an enduring idea of a common humanity. We have met it and cherish it among friends and historians such as Gwendolyn Midlo Hall, who is
an example to us all.

LOUISIANA'S FOUNDING *FLIBUSTIERS*

Another way of thinking about Louisiana appeared among the second-largest
group who were present at the creation of this complicated colony. In 1698,
Governor Iberville recruited fifty free spirits from the Caribbean isles. He
called them *flibustiers*, a word often translated into English as freebooters.[42]

Louisiana's first census in 1699 found thirteen of these people in residence. The census takers listed them by name and identified them as *flibustiers*. The others were presumably out *flibustiering* at the time. These men were
not universally admired, to say the least. Others called them rogues, thieves,
predators, murderers, rascals, poltroons, and pirates. Those words accurately

described many *flibustiers*, but not all of them. Some were men of honor who only preyed upon the king's enemies in time of war, and were more like privateers than pirates. Others were rogues and scoundrels from start to finish.[43]

Leaders such as Iberville made Louisiana a haven for these men, on condition of good behavior in the colony, and a share of the loot. French leaders actively encouraged them to attack English neighbors when the two empires were at war. Iberville himself led a force of *flibustiers* in an assault on the beautiful English West Indian island of Nevis, during the War of the Spanish Succession. They conquered the island, collected a ransom from the inhabitants, and returned to their base in Louisiana. Iberville was planning another assault on the English colony of South Carolina when he died suddenly in 1706 of yellow fever, already a scourge in Louisiana.[44]

Later, the leading activity of freebooters shifted from plunder, piracy, and privateering to smuggling—a growth industry in American colonies from New England to New Orleans. Louisiana's *flibustiers* flourished in this illicit commerce through much of the eighteenth century, often with active collaboration of people in high political office.[45] An exemplar during the eighteenth century was a Franco-Irish *flibustier*, variously called Michael Fitzgerald, Michael F. Gerald, and Gerard Fitzmaurice. In New Orleans he was a leading dealer in contraband goods for many years and had much use for multiple names.[46]

In the early nineteenth century, freebooters continued in business on Louisiana's Gulf Coast, but turned from smuggling to slaving. Familiar examples were the three Laffite or Lafitte brothers, who operated from Barataria Bay and New Orleans.[47] Others were the Bowie family, who moved from Maryland to Texas, and continued to be active in the international slave trade long after the United States and the United Kingdom both banned it in 1807–08.[48]

Descendants of these *flibustiers* operated from bases in Texas, Mexico, the coastal islands in the Gulf of Mexico, and southern Louisiana. At the same time, they maintained business ties in New Orleans for many years.[49] A notorious associate was Beverly Chew, who was collector of customs in American New Orleans, a leader in Louisiana's illegal slave trade, and something of a freebooter himself, all at the same time.[50]

Altogether, twelve generations of freebooters have flourished along Louisiana's Gulf Coast. They moved in and out of New Orleans and operated on both sides of the law. Some were men of violence who lived free and died hard. Others preferred more subtle methods. Many shared an idea of liberty that was far removed from that of Thomas Jefferson and the Marquis de Lafayette. Here was a hardy tradition that might be called Louisiana libertarian, a freebooting spirit that entered the fabric of life throughout this region as early as 1699. Some of it survives in the twenty-first century.[51]

Partly as a consequence, Louisiana has suffered much from crime, corruption, and violence through its long history, even to our time. By empirical measures of exposed corruption such as annual per capita convictions of public officeholders, Louisiana has continued to rank among the most corrupt of American states in the twenty-first century—which, given the condition of other states, is no small superlative.[52]

At the same time, Louisiana in the twenty-first century has also tended to have the highest murder rates in the United States. In 2016 it ranked first for murders among fifty American states, as it had done twenty-eight years in a row.[53] This tradition of corruption, crime, and violence has spanned three centuries in Louisiana, from its founding *flibustiers* in 1699 to its new-modeled freebooters in our time.

OTHER FOUNDING TRADITIONS FROM FRANCE: CATHOLICISM AND ABSOLUTISM

While Canadian *coureurs de bois* and Caribbean *flibustiers* established their very different traditions in Louisiana, other leaders arrived from France, and introduced additional sets of founding ideas. Some of them tended to think of Louisiana not as an American colony, but a province of France. They saw it as an integral part of a great nation-state that became Europe's strongest military power, largest economy, and most dynamic cultural center in the early eighteenth century.

Later rulers of France from Louis XIV to Louis XVI believed that the strength of their kingdom flowed from the breadth of a universal Catholic faith, and the concentrated power of an absolute monarchy. Both ideas were transplanted to Louisiana, and interesting things happened to them in the New World.

Most important to many French leaders was their Catholic faith, and their vision of strength and power through spiritual unity. This Catholic idea, in its literal meaning of a truly universal church, reached out to almost all humanity, even to slaves. At the same time, it excluded Jews and Protestants who willfully refused to abandon their faith and join the True Church. After thirty years of strife in France during its civil wars of religion (circa 1560–89), and an interval of tolerance under Henri IV (1589–1610) and his son Louis XIII (1610–43), Louis XIV launched the people of France on a sustained experiment in compulsory uniformity. All subjects were compelled to adopt a universal Catholic faith. The King's Dragoons were ordered to round up Protestants in dreaded *dragonnades* and drive them out of France. That dual idea of a universal church and exclusion of other faiths was transplanted from France to French Louisiana.

French rulers also imposed on Louisiana an idea of absolute monarchy, and a system of authority that has differed profoundly from British colonies in North America. French Louisiana had no popular elections, no representative assemblies, nothing comparable to the ancient *parlements* of France, such as the Parlement of Paris, which was still functioning fitfully in the reign of Louis XIV.

Louisiana also had nothing like the old French custom of *cahiers de doléance* or petitions of grievance, which Champlain had supported among French settlers in Québec a century earlier. And early French settlements along the lower Mississippi had nothing resembling the cooperative assemblies that French settlers in northern Acadia (now Nova Scotia) created among themselves to manage their complex systems of dikes called *aboiteaux.*[54]

France and its colonies also had nothing like England's growing tradition of the rule of law, which was above even the Crown. In the reign of Louis XIV, the highest law was the will of the king. Strictly speaking, an absolutist king was not above the law. He *was* the law. Below the monarch were many laws and lawyers in France, but no rule of law functioned above the Crown.

And unlike the English-speaking American republics after 1776, absolutist France and French Louisiana (like England itself) had no citizens—only subjects, from the Latin verb *subjacio*, "to throw down and keep in subjection." Even the most exalted nobles in France were subjects of an absolute monarch. No one was a *citoyen* of France until after the Revolution of 1789.

Absolutism in France was not a unitary system. It operated through a complex structure of ministers, councils, companies, and institutions. The government of France under Louis XIV had many moving parts in a complex interlocking system.

Within that system, some of the king's subjects were granted many liberties—not as rights, but privileges (from the Latin *privilegium*, literally a private law), to hold property, or to move from place to place, or to gain control over particular aspects of their lives. A right of privilege was a specific exemption from a condition of prior restraint. In French dominions, a few people had many privileges. Many people had a few privileges. Some had nearly none.

All French subjects existed in a condition of obligation to the king's will.

Their dearest privileges could be canceled by the stroke of a pen on a *lettre de cachet*, a special document with the king's private seal. A *lettre de cachet* could order an arrest without warrant, torture without cause, imprisonment without trial, and execution without due process of law.

Paris, the City of Light, had many dark prisons where many French men and women had a way of disappearing. The city also had weekly executions in its streets, deliberately staged in prolonged public rituals of unimaginable horror. Their purpose was to inspire terror and obedience to the will of an absolute monarch.

Under Louis XIV, liberty as a natural right was not recognized in France or its possessions. But at the same time, other ideas of existential liberty were stronger in France and Louisiana than in England or its colonies. Historian Jerah Johnson observes that "France offered far greater freedom for individuals to associate not only with members of their own corporate group, but more important, with members of other groups as well." Slaves, too, were able to do so in some limited ways, even as they were treated badly in others. All of these French traditions were brought to Louisiana.[55]

A NEW EUROPEAN IDEA: LOUISIANA AS A COLONY OF THE ENLIGHTENMENT

At the same time, yet another set of countervailing ideas came to Louisiana from Western Europe. Chief among them was an expanding vision of a soaring new spirit called *Aufklärung* in Germany, *Schiarimento* in Italy, *Iluminismo* in Spain, *Éclaircissement* in France, and *Enlightenment* in England. Early in the eighteenth century, this idea became a movement among *philosophes* and *lumières* throughout Europe.

The capital of this movement was Paris, and its seat was France, where influential people thought of Louisiana as a colony of the Enlightenment. A leader of that idea was François-Marie Arouet de Voltaire (1694–1778), who became the personification of the French Enlightenment in his own time. Voltaire wrote to a friend in 1760, "If I were young, and in good health, and had not built Ferney, I would go and establish myself in Louisiana."[56]

Enlightened ideas were transplanted to French Louisiana by officials such as Marc-Antoine Caillot, whose memoir appeared in 1730 as a *Relation du Voyage de la Louisanne ou Nouvelle France*. He thought of himself as a carrier of the Enlightenment.[57] Other examples included the forgotten *philosophes*

Voltaire

Jean-Baptiste Prévost and Pierre Le Blond de la Tour; the engineer Pierre Baron, who was a planner of New Orleans; the French cartographer Le Maire, whose exquisite maps were an enlightened vision of Louisiana.

At the same time, other French officers in Louisiana were the opposite of Enlightenment and the rule of reason. Some were dark spirits—tyrannical, cruel, stupid, incompetent, and wildly irrational. Among the worst was the reviled Sieur de Chépart, commandant of the French fort and settlement at Natchez in 1728–29. By epic depravity and supreme incompetence Chépart nearly destroyed the colony, as we shall see.[58]

Other French leaders in Louisiana were men of wisdom, learning, and large purposes. Among some of them, the level of integrity and creative thinking rose very high. Several of the greatest works of early American literature were written in French about Louisiana. They deserve to be better remembered in the United States.[59]

More than a few of these enlightened francophone leaders were more European than French. An example was Antoine-Simon Le Page du Pratz, a gifted soldier and scholar of Dutch origin who went to France for his education and early career. In Louisiana he became the director of the King's Plantation, the largest unit of slave labor in early Louisiana. He led i in an enlightened way and wrote at length on that subject. His acts and purposes marked a pivotal moment in Louisiana's history and we shall meet him again.

ENVIRONMENTAL FACTORS: ECOLOGY AND HISTORY IN FRENCH LOUISIANA

As this struggling French colony began to grow in the early eighteenth century, its call name in Paris slang was not "Louisiane" but "Mississippy." From the start, the great river was recognized as the key that unlocked the riches of its enormous valley and became the center of its history.

The physical environment of this vast river valley made a difference in the cultures that developed there. The Mississippi River itself was dynamic and ever-changing. Every year it deposited new riches of alluvial soil on some of the most productive farmland in the world. But what this restless river created it also destroyed, by flood and mud and sudden disruptive changes of the river's location, direction, and flow.[60]

The river also made large areas of lower Louisiana into a range of swamps, lakes, and bayous (from the Choctaw *bayuk*, small stream). For European settlers this great web of wetlands was alien to their experience, hostile to their purposes, and never firmly in their control. American Indians and runaway African slaves, and small groups such as Cane River's "Creoles of Color," were quick to find many opportunities. They made parts of this region into their own territory.[61]

In that process the environment of the lower Mississippi Valley made a difference in the structure of power, and in relations among cultures in early Louisiana. It promoted the coexistence of different ethnic groups, and in some ways protected their differences.[62]

The environment of the lower Mississippi Valley also had another effect. It created ecological concentrations of what economists call "positional goods." Some of the most valuable lands were special places along the Mississippi that combined fertility with elevation and were high enough to escape the river's annual floods.

Leading examples were the Natchez Bluffs and surrounding elevations. Natchez was a much valued site for settlement by both Indians and French, and it became a cause of major conflict between them.

Later, French and American families acquired good ground around Natchez and used it to generate great wealth. As we shall see, some of these favored places along the river also promoted the concentration of wealth. Throughout the United States, the highest measures of wealth inequality on record in the United States developed not in northern cities (which also became very unequal), but in parts of the lower Mississippi Valley and what is now East Texas.

Quantitative studies of wealth distribution find that levels of inequality in Louisiana have long been among the highest in the United States.

Both extremes have been approached in American history. Perfect equality appeared very briefly in the first land distribution by Roger Williams at the Providence Plantation in Rhode Island. Perfect inequality was approached in Adams County, around Natchez in southern Mississippi, one of French Louisiana's first and most important valley settlements. High levels of inequality persisted there for many generations. This concentration of wealth in Adams County was among the highest on record in the United States at that time.[63]

Similar levels and trends of high inequality have been measured by historian Michael Wayne in Louisiana's Concordia Parish, directly across the Mississippi River from Adams County, and Natchez in Mississippi.[64]

Slavery was a major instrument of inequality in this region, but not its first cause. Inequality of landed wealth preceded slavery in most of the American South. Slavery tended to reinforce inequality, which emerged earlier and persisted longer from another cause. After the abolition of slavery in 1865, inequality in the lower Mississippi Valley persisted at high levels.[65]

The physical environment of the lower Mississippi Valley had many consequences. While it promoted an inequality of material condition, it also supported a diversity of cultures. Again and again, the great river attracted a broad variety of groups who often fought for dominion of this region's resources, and sometimes found ways to coexist.

That process appears to have happened among early Mesoamerican cultures, and later among North American Indians. By the seventeenth century, more than thirty native American Indian nations were living in the lower Mississippi Valley. They collided over hunting grounds, trading networks, access to tracts of terra firma along the river, and other positional goods that were defined by the material environment. These conflicts developed in many other places but had a special intensity in this region.[66]

Something similar happened yet again when other European settlers arrived in the eighteenth century. Control of the lower Mississippi Valley was held by France from 1699, by Spain after 1763 (effectively from 1769), and by the United States from 1803. Each of those nations managed the region differently. Many European ethnic groups moved in and occupied their own environments. Teutonic settlers in the early eighteenth century settled along the river's "German Coast," thirty miles north of New Orleans near the Bonnet Carré Bend.[67] Acadians from what is now Nova Scotia occupied "Cajun Louisiana," as it was called after them, after the mid-eighteenth century. *Coureurs de bois* from the St. Lawrence Valley settled at Pointe Coupée, the "cutoff point" near Baton Rouge, and other places upriver, and introduced their own distinct culture at an early date.[68]

Other ethnic groups followed in later periods: migrations of Canary Islanders and Malagueños to Spanish Louisiana during the late eighteenth century; some of America's first Sicilian families and Mafiosi to New Orleans in the nineteenth; settlements of Vietnamese fishermen to the south coast in the late twentieth; and more.[69]

The environment of the Mississippi Valley made a difference in all those ways. The people of Louisiana through its French, Spanish, and American periods continuously reinvented cultures of creative diversity many times in three centuries. The dynamics of that process are stronger than ever in the twenty-first century. But it began with mixtures of multiple French and African cultures in the early eighteenth century, and even earlier among a diversity of Native American groups.

The French know it well and say it best: *plus la diversité, plus l'unité.* In the age of Enlightenment, David Hume and James Madison were both quick to understand the uses of that idea. They helped to invent a new science of politics, and inspired the design of the early American republic, which was grounded in the uses of diversity as keys to liberty and freedom. In a later era, some of us have forgotten what they had learned.

THE PEOPLING OF LOUISIANA: A FAILURE OF FRENCH MASS MIGRATION

Together with distinct founding purposes and a unique physical environment, another major factor in the history of Louisiana was a complex process of migration. In the early eighteenth century, a small elite in Paris hoped that large numbers of French peasants would come to Louisiana as volunteers, and cultivate the American earth, and create a genuinely New France in the Mississippi Valley.

In a word, that purpose failed. One factor, often observed but rarely studied, was the extreme reluctance of French peasants to move abroad in large numbers. Nothing in the modern history of France (except perhaps the forced exile of the Huguenots or later movements of *pieds-noirs* to Algeria and back again) came close to the many mass migrations across the Atlantic that flowed from East Anglia, southern England, the north Midlands of Britain, Wales, Scotland, Ireland, Germany, Scandinavia, the Low Countries, Poland, Italy, the Balkans, Greece, Ukraine, and Spain.

French peasants preferred to stay home. And if they thought about moving anywhere, the soggy earth and dangerous climate of southern Louisiana was among their least attractive options.[70]

The largest group of French emigrants in Louisiana were half-free *engagés*, similar to indentured servants in English colonies. They were bound by their own consent to compulsory service for fixed terms, which were short by comparison with other forms of bondage, but longer than the life expectancy of European immigrants in early Louisiana.

Other French migrants to Louisiana were soldiers, bound by terms of voluntary enlistment, and ordered to America with their regiments. They were compelled to serve in abysmal conditions sometimes worse than those of African slaves, barely surviving on miserable rations in horrific quarters, with high rates of mortality. For misconduct they were punished with extreme brutality. One French soldier was sentenced to execution by having his head gradually crushed between two massive stones, which was thought to encourage correct thinking in other brains. Another French soldier was ordered to be executed by being slowly sawn in two. Many French soldiers deserted to the Indians, or fled to other colonies, or escaped aboard visiting ships.[71]

In early years, only a few French immigrants remained alive in Louisiana long enough to marry and start families. A special effort was made to stimulate marriage by encouraging the migration of "jeunes filles de bonnes familles." These legendary figures inspired a large romantic literature but contributed little to the demography of Louisiana.[72]

The French population of Louisiana grew very slowly.[73] Many French colonists died of fever or fled at their first opportunity. Among Europeans, mortality rates in southern Louisiana were higher than anywhere else in North America. In the early nineteenth century, careful comparative regional evidence of morbidity and mortality became available throughout the United States. It appeared in data compiled by the War Department for military installations in most states and territories. Throughout North America, these data showed that highest rates of illness and death were in Louisiana, along the lower Mississippi. Magnitudes of difference were very large. In Louisiana garrisons of the U.S. Army, average annual mortality rates among previously healthy young males of military age were higher than for entire populations in unhealthy southern cities such as Savannah during major epidemic years. Good mortality data for Louisiana in the early eighteenth century are not known to this inquirer, but death rates are thought to have been higher than in the early nineteenth century because of problems of diet, sanitation, and the contagion of shipboard epidemics, not to mention violence, cruelty, and chaos. Heroic attempts to build a large French population in Louisiana by voluntary migration failed in many ways at once.[74]

FORCED FRENCH IMMIGRANTS: LOUISIANA'S FAILURE AS A PENAL COLONY

After the failure of large-scale voluntary French emigration to Louisiana, the absolutist rulers of France did not hesitate to order the use of force on their own subjects. Involuntary emigrants were called *forçats* or forced exiles. The Scottish entrepreneur John Law was entrusted with the task of peopling the colony, and he promised to recruit six thousand European colonists for Louisiana. Crown officers allowed him to use powers of the absolutist state for conscription.

John Law

The flow of forced French emigrants to Louisiana from 1717 to 1720 was larger than the African slave trade in the entire French period from 1699 to 1763.[75]

The *forçats* themselves were diverse. Some were troubled sons of the French nobility. They were arrested by the state on the authority of a *lettre de cachet*, often at the request of relatives, who regarded them as dangerous to the honor and fortune of their own families.[76]

These aristocratic *forçats* were transported to Louisiana in surprising numbers. In 1717, Lieutenant Jean Dumont was ordered by the Company of the Indies to oversee two shiploads of five hundred prisoners who had been exiled to Louisiana. Among them was a draft of two hundred "noble forçats," as Dumont called them. These "younger sons of good family" were seized in the name of the king and confined in a great tower that still stands on the waterfront of La Rochelle, until ships were available. At least six of these men hurled themselves into the harbor, rather than sail to Louisiana. The rest were driven aboard ships with arms strapped behind their backs and legs shackled in irons.[77]

Lieutenant Dumont was also responsible for another group of three hundred military deserters who had been given a choice of exile to Louisiana or execution in France. Some of these unhappy men preferred the quick *coup de grâce* of a bullet to the brain to the prolonged agony of emigration.[78]

Other forced migrants were thousands of convicts, sentenced to Louisiana for various crimes. Records survive for 1,700 convicts in a period of three years from 1717 to 1720.[79] They constituted a hierarchy of crime. At the top were *contrebandiers*, or smugglers, who were a criminal elite in France. Among them were *contrebandiers du sel* or *faux-sauniers*, professional salt smugglers. They helped their countrymen to evade the hated *gabelle* or salt tax, which became an important cause of the French Revolution in 1789, and they were regarded by many people as national heroes. Salt smugglers and tobacco smugglers were also valued in Louisiana for their skill with boats and pilotage. They were widely perceived as resourceful and colorful rogues who kept a code of their own as they moved back and forth across the line between crime and commerce.

Below these *contrebandiers* was a broad miscellany of convicts. Many were sentenced to forced transportation for petty crimes such as the theft of food or fuel or clothing, often to help their own suffering families. Thousands of these people, who cared more about others than themselves, were exiled to Louisiana, where they were cruelly treated. But one would like to think that some of them brought an abiding spirit of humanity in the spirit of Jean Valjean.

Yet another group of forced emigrants were young women and girls who had been convicted of various offenses, often sexual in nature. In the period from 1717 to 1720 they included a party of 160 *putains* (prostitutes) and 96 *débaucheés* (often troubled teens), conscripted from La Salpêtrière, a "house of correction" for "wayward women" in Paris. In Louisiana, some of these *putains* and *débaucheés* became more successful than the *jeunes filles des bonnes familles*. They did a flourishing trade in the cabarets of New Orleans, which multiplied within a few years of the town's founding. Others married affluent *seigneurs* and *concessionaires* and rose rapidly in respectability and rank.[80]

Below those convicts in a hierarchy of crime and punishment were *galériens* who had been sentenced to long terms of hard service in the dreaded French galleys. They had been routinely chained to their oars, with pear-shaped wooden gags stuffed into their mouths to stifle cries of pain when they were whipped to make them row faster. Some of these galley slaves were conscripted for Louisiana.

Others in this hierarchy of misery and degradation were lower even than galley slaves. Some of the most abused and miserable souls in absolutist France were called *les gens sans aveu* (the unrecognized people), or *les inconnus* (the unknowns). In an elaborately rank-bound world they were people who had no rank at all. Shannon Dawdy writes that "in the late 1710s and 1720s, police sweeps through France's major cities collected vagrants, beggars, orphans, single women, the handicapped, and the mentally ill." These were *les gens sans aveu*, and some were shipped to Louisiana.[81]

All of these many *forçats* were not enough to start a self-sustaining population in Louisiana. With the approval of the Crown, John Law also employed French commercial companies to send out press gangs called *les bandouliers du Mississippi*. They took their name from the bandoleers of shot and gunpowder that they wore across their shoulders. These men were what Americans call bounty hunters. They scoured France in search of *les gens sans aveu*, and were paid by the head. Unwary people of many ranks found themselves at risk. Raids, roundups, and forced marches of captives resulted in riots in Paris and other French cities from 1717 to 1720. Reports multiplied of kidnapped children who had been seized on the streets by *les bandouliers* and shipped to Louisiana. Spasms of fear spread through French families. The result was a great revulsion from Louisiana, and also from the Crown and its corrupt contractors all at once. The commercial companies were ordered to desist.[82]

This system of forced migration became profoundly disruptive in Louisiana. When the hardest cases arrived, some were exiled even from their place of exile, and banished "in perpetuity" to La Balize, a place "swamped by the sea" near the mouth of the Mississippi. There they lived in misery until fevers and floods swept them away.[83]

These various groups of *forçats* were sent in such numbers that for a brief period French Louisiana became a virtual penal colony. But in 1720 the entire system of forced migration by convicts to Louisiana was brought to a sudden end by a disaster in Paris. That year, 107 men and women were confined in the prison of Saint-Martin-des-Champs in Paris, awaiting passage to Louisiana in a convict ship. Half of them attacked their guards, broke free, and escaped into the city. Chaos followed in the capital, and on May 9, 1720, officers of the Crown ordered the end of forced exile to Louisiana.[84]

Altogether, records survive for 7,020 French emigrants, convict and free, who were sent to Louisiana from 1717 to 1720. At the end of that period, only 1,082 people (15 percent) remained alive in the colony. About 85 percent died, or found a way to escape soon after their arrival. Even as a penal colony, early French Louisiana was a miserable failure.[85]

THE GROWTH OF AFRICAN SLAVERY: LOUISIANA AND THE FRENCH SLAVE TRADE

Before 1706, no evidence survives of Africans in Louisiana. Four censuses from 1699 to 1708 found no Africans, free or slave, in the colony through its first decade.[86]

The first African slaves may have arrived in Mobile (then part of Louisiana) perhaps as early as 1706, as part of the booty from the *flibustiers'* attack on Nevis in that year.[87] At least one African was imported by Bienville for his own use in 1709. In the census of 1712, ten *noirs* were reported to be living in the colony. Then, as migration from France failed, numbers of African slaves began to surge. Another census, on November 24, 1721, found 680 *noirs*, mostly reported as living near New Orleans and Mobile. Bienville himself owned twenty-seven slaves.[88]

The number of African slaves began to increase much more rapidly than that of European immigrants. French census returns reported that people of African descent rose to 33.3 percent of Louisiana's population in 1721, 51.7 percent by 1727, 67.9 percent in 1731, and an astounding 76.9 percent in 1741. That year, Africans outnumbered Europeans in Louisiana by more than three to one. The proportion of African slaves in Louisiana's population had suddenly grown larger than in any other European colony or region throughout mainland North America, at any time.[89]

After 1743, the African slave trade ended in French Louisiana for a generation. The proportion of Africans declined, but they remained a majority of Louisiana's population at about 55 percent or higher through the entire period of French and Spanish control to 1803.[90]

By the mid-eighteenth century, the burgeoning French slave trade had become a global system. Most seaports in France participated: Le Havre, Brest, Lorient, Nantes, La Rochelle, Bordeaux, and Marseilles on a large scale, and even smaller ports such as Dunkerque, Honfleur, Saint-Malo, Vannes, and Bayonne.[91]

Traffic to Louisiana was dominated by the Company of the West, which later became the Company of the Indies. Its primary home port was Lorient on the Bay of Biscay. On the coast of Africa, its agents built bases in the Isles d'Arguin off the coast of Mauritania, and traded actively from the Senegal River to the Guinea coast, Sierra Leone, and beyond.[92]

It also established a fort on Gorée Island, now surrounded by Senegal's capital city of Dakar. In the eighteenth century, Gorée was visited by ships of many nations, but dominated by the French. Today Gorée Island is a major historic site. Its "door of no return" is deeply moving, especially to African American visitors whom we met there. Its African trade has been mocked by some historians as a myth, but the slave trade at Gorée Island was very real in the eighteenth-century world. We in academe should treat that memory with respect.

In the early eighteenth century, French slavers worked their way up the Senegal River into the interior of West Africa. They maintained a trading post, Fort St. Joseph, on an island in the middle of the river near Galam, four hundred miles from the Atlantic.[93] Elaborate eighteenth-century nautical charts dated 1747 survive for the upper Senegal River and the anchorage at Fort St. Joseph. They include detailed plans of the fort itself and testify to its importance.[94]

The slave ships were mostly French in this early wave from 1718 to 1743. Nearly all of Louisiana's slaves came directly from Africa in French shipping before 1743. Here again, as in other North American regions, very few slaves were "Atlantic Creoles" from the West Indies. We cannot repeat too often that with a few exceptions, the great majority of arriving slaves in North America were African-born and African-bred, with highly developed African lan-

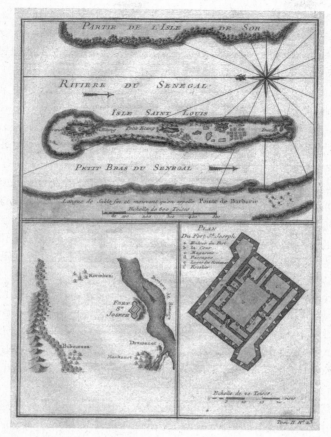

Fort St. Joseph, upper Senegal River

guages, African cultures, and African customs. But patterns of regional and ethnic origin in the African trade were in part a function of trading connections in Europe, which varied from one colony to another and tended to have linkages to different ports, rivers, and coastal regions.[95]

AFRICAN REGIONAL AND ETHNIC ORIGINS IN FRENCH LOUISIANA, 1718–31

Where in Africa did French Louisiana's slaves come from? The general patterns were similar in some ways to other slaveholding regions throughout North America.

First, slaves came to Louisiana from every part of Africa that was active in the Atlantic trade. That very large area reached from northern Senegal to southern Angola, and also included a few slaves from East Africa and Madagascar. The leading scholar on this subject is Gwendolyn Midlo Hall. Altogether, Gwendolyn Hall's Louisiana Slave Database from 1719 to 1820 and beyond included a total of 8,994 individual slaves were listed with some 217 African ethnic origins, of which she was able to identify 96. The result was a broad variety of African cultures, languages, skills, occupations, and experiences, which enriched the cultural life of Louisiana, as also it did in most slaveholding regions in North America.[96]

Second, that large pattern of broad diversity contained smaller concentrations of slaves who shared similar African languages, common cultures and strong identities. Hall describes this common tendency as a pattern of "clustering." It appears repeatedly in her empirical evidence on Louisiana. Something similar occurred in most North American regional systems with different distributions and intensities.[97]

As in most North American regions, those African slaves arrived in waves, and each wave had its own unique patterns of composition and concentration. For Louisiana's first (and smallest) wave during its French era, Hall estimated in her first major work (published in 1992) that about two thirds of Louisiana's slaves came from Senegambia: 4,204 slaves, 67.3 percent, of African slaves in the French period.[98]

After Gwendolyn Hall published her findings in 1992–93, several critics challenged her conclusion without citing primary evidence of their own.[99] More recent empirical studies have solidly confirmed the main lines of Hall's results, and even strengthened them. In 2010, David Eltis, David Richardson, and the team who constructed the Trans-Atlantic Slave Database reported an even stronger African regional concentration in Louisiana's slave trade during the French period—not Gwendolyn Hall's two thirds from Senegambia, but "nearly three-quarters" from that area.[100]

These later studies of Louisiana's first wave of slave trading also confirmed Hall's early findings that a smaller but important set of six slave voyages brought another 1,700 slaves to Louisiana from the vicinity of Benin (about 28 percent of the known African trade in the French period). In the mid-eighteenth century, they were mostly female, and their ethnic origins were identified as Fon, Aja, and Arada. These slaves are thought to have introduced important cultural and spiritual movements to Louisiana.

Also in the French period, at least one ship arrived from Cabinda in what is now Angola. It delivered 294 surviving slaves (4.7 percent of the whole), more than enough to introduce clusters of Bantu-speaking slaves, who were called Congo or Kongo people. Their linguistic and cultural impact was greater than the numbers would suggest. They are believed to have introduced Bantu words such as gumbo and gombo, and Congolese customs such as the dance called the Calinda, before 1732. This flow was reinforced by later and larger waves of "Congo" Africans.[101]

In summary, the first wave of Louisiana's African slave trade had three African regional components. The largest regional group (67 percent) came from Senegambia and Mali. It included ethnic clusters of Mande-speaking Bamana and Mandingo slaves, and also Wolof, Nat/Moor, and Fulani/Fulbe slaves. The second group (28 percent) came from Benin, with clusters of Aja/Fon/Arada slaves. A third group (about 5 percent) were "Congo slaves," as the French called them, who came mainly through the port of Cabinda. Each of these three African groups had an enduring impact on the cultural life of French Louisiana.[102]

It is also probable that French traders picked up at least a few slaves from the coast of Guinea near modern Conakry, and others from the Gold Coast in western Ghana, and probably some from Biafra, the home of Igbo and Ibibio slaves in southeastern Nigeria. In the Atlantic slave trade, these various groups had ways of turning up in many colonies. No hard evidence appears of their arrival in French Louisiana before 1763, but a few may have come there in that period.

All of this, to repeat, refers only to the first wave of African slaves who came to Louisiana, mostly from 1718 to 1731. After 1731, Louisiana's African slave trade nearly stopped for more than thirty years. The colony's African population continued to grow by natural increase from prior arrivals. Regional and ethnic origins in the French slave trade from 1719 to 1731 shaped the African population of Louisiana through its first seventy years. This first wave of African slaves played a seminal role in the formation of Afro-French cultures in Louisiana.

Thereafter, as we shall see, more diverse patterns of African and Afro-American arrivals appeared in a second wave of slave trading during Louisiana's Spanish period. And a third wave followed the American purchase of Louisiana in 1803. Things would grow more complex in these second and third waves, which were larger, more turbulent, and also more diverse in their cultural reach.

These patterns of African origin are increasingly clear in the empirical evidence of the Atlantic slave trade. A more difficult question is about the ethnic origins of African slaves, especially those who came from the coast of Senegal from 1718 to 1731. This African region was dynamic in its history, and complex in its ethnicity. That complexity is still evident today. We observed it at first hand in the small trading town of Saint-Louis, one hundred miles north of Dakar at the mouth of the Senegal River. Some of its architecture is remarkably similar to parts of the French Quarter in New Orleans.

Saint-Louis today is a busy center of coastal commerce. When we were there, its streets were crowded on trading days with entrepreneurs of striking diversity. We saw many Mauritanian merchants, dressed in traditional light blue robes, and busy on their cell phones. They were called Moors by eighteenth-century Europeans; and came to Saint-Louis from what is now Mauritania, just above the mouth of the Senegal River.

In Saint-Louis these Mauritanians traded with people of many other ethnic origins. One group were variously called Fulani, Fulbe, Fula, or Feulah. The French often called them Peulah. Later we met and talked with some of them in an inland village. They are a distinctive and deeply interesting people.

The Fulani, as we shall call them, have long been respected as highly skilled herders across much of the Sahel below the Sahara. An eighteenth-century traveler observed that the "industry of the Foulahs in pasturage and agriculture is everywhere remarkable. . . . In Bondou they are opulent in high degree. . . . They display great skill in the management of their cattle, making them extremely gentle by kindness and familiarity . . . besides the cattle . . . [they raise] excellent horses." Most were said to live "under the influence of the Mohammedan laws" but it was often reported that "religious persecution is not known among them." We also found a spirit of tolerance among them. And we shall meet them again in Carolina's cowpens and once more on the open range of Texas.[103]

Another African ethnic group on the coast of Senegal are called Wolof in academic writing. In our presence, they called themselves Djolauf or Jolauf. French scholars have also commonly referred to them as Senegals or Senegalese. Through many centuries they have been respected as highly skilled traders very active in commerce. The first recorded pidgin speech on West Africa's Atlantic coast in the mid-fifteenth century is thought to have been a mix of Wolof and Portuguese. Many Wolof people are distinctive in appearance: lean, tall, graceful, and handsome. Wolof women have become leading fashion models in Paris. And the men were still prominent in trade. When we returned to New York City, and talked with African sidewalk merchants on the streets of Manhattan, we found that some of them were Wolof.[104]

Most numerous in this region of Senegal and Senegambia were yet other ethnic groups who spoke a variety of Mande languages. This large linguistic family included Mandinka, Maninka, Malinke, Mandinga, Manya, Dyula, Duranko, Wangara, and Bamana—then as now one of the largest and most diverse linguistic and ethnic constellations in West Africa. Many of their Mande languages are mutually intelligible.

Closely related to this large Mande linguistic family were the people that the French call Bambara. In Mali, they are the largest ethnic group. We met many of them there and were told, over and over, politely but firmly, that the correct name of their people and their language and culture is not Bambara, but Bamana.

The Bamana language is part of a distinct culture with a strong tradition of oral history, still entrusted to griots or jeli who have long been hereditary bards of high rank. They draw upon a broad repertoire of legend, history, stories, songs, cosmology, and proverbs—many proverbs in a dense and very rich culture. One person observed that "a Bamana cannot speak two or three sentences without saying a proverb." [105]

The Bamana were a strong and formidable people, long known for military skill and martial spirit—so much so that in West Africa "Bamana" became a synonym for a good soldier with disciplined behavior and an austere style of life, much as did "Spartan" among the ancient Greeks. In Mali, Bamana people of our acquaintance tended to carry themselves with the pride and strength and the upright posture of a soldier. We also observed a strong sense of solidarity, and a spirit of mutual support. [106]

At the same time, they were and are a distinct ethnic and linguistic group, the largest in Mali at about 40 percent of the population. When we were there, nearly 80 percent of Mali's population were able to speak Bamana, which has become a lingua franca of that nation.

Most Mande-speaking people, including the Malinke, Mandingo, and Bamana, also shared similar religious beliefs in the eighteenth century. Three centuries ago, they were reported to be predominantly animist and spiritist. Today the great majority of Bamana in Mali are Islamic. With some exceptions (grossly overreported in mass media), most Islamic people we met in West Africa in the 1990s tended to practice their faith in a spirit that was tolerant and respectful of others. A minority of Bamana people, reckoned at about 20 percent, also cherish a syncretist faith which actively combines animist beliefs with Islam.

These various ethnic and linguistic groups together account for a large part of the population in the modern nation-states that include Senegal and Gambia in the west, Mali to the east, parts of Guinea, Burkina Faso, and the upper reaches of Ghana and Côte d'Ivoire to the south. Philip Curtin, a highly respected American historian of West Africa who knew this broad area well, wrote that it is "a region of homogeneous culture and a common style of history." Its languages are related in large linguistic families. People variously called Wolof, Sereer, and Senegalese are one family; Fulani and Fulbe and Peulah are another; and Mande, Mandinga, Malinke, and Bamana make a third.[107]

AFRICAN SLAVERY IN EIGHTEENTH-CENTURY SÉGOU: AN EYEWITNESS ACCOUNT

This broad region in West Africa, with its many ethnic groups, has had a continuing importance in African history. It gave rise to great empires in medieval and early modern Africa. Philip Curtin observed that the empires of Ghana, Mali, and Songhai all were founded in Senegambia. He wrote that even "the Islamic Almoravides empire . . . was founded on an island in the Senegal River." [108]

Later in the eighteenth century, this region also became the seat of the great empire of Ségou. In the process of its creation, the dynastic wars of Mamari Kulubali played a pivotal role in the expansion of the West African slave trade—a recurrent pattern in the relation between warfare and slavery throughout much of Africa's long history. The African slave trade to Louisiana did not rise primarily from European or American events, as much recent western historical writing tends to assume. Its origins flowed in large part from African events, often deep in the interior of this vast continent.

In the eighteenth century, the newly founded African Association in London decided to send an explorer into the interior of West Africa. His mission was to find the source of the Niger River, and to observe the country and its people. For that task these early British Africanists selected Mungo Park (1771–1806), a Scottish surgeon, scientist, and man of the Enlightenment. He became an African explorer of intelligence, courage, and resourcefulness. In the field, he was an accurate observer, a gifted writer, and he wrote a major work of travel and description, which is still in print and widely used.[109]

Mungo Park was one of the first Europeans on record to reach Mamari Kulubali's capital at Ségou, on July 21, 1796, spend some time there, and leave

Mungo Park

a written record. Park called it "Sego, the Capital of Bambarra." He described it as a constellation of many villages, and its size amazed him. He wrote, "The view of this extensive city—the numerous canoes upon the river—the crowded population, and the cultivated state of the surrounding country—formed a prospect of civilization and magnificence which I little expected to find in the bosom of Africa."[110]

Park was among the first to compare the Niger River in West Africa with the Nile in the east. He marveled at the fertility of this region, and its many market crops of rice, tobacco, indigo, and food stocks. He spent much of his time in the homeland of the Bamana people (and he also used the French error-term Bambara). Park observed that these people occupied a broad region from the Niger River west to the "upper reaches of the Senegal river, beyond Galam," which was the French trading fort in the African interior, four hundred miles from the sea.[111]

He left one of the earliest and most detailed accounts by a trained European scientist of culture and society in this interior part of West Africa. Park also studied the institution of African slavery throughout the region, and he estimated that slaves were "nearly in the proportion of three to one to the freemen. They claim no reward for their services except food and clothing, and are treated with kindness or severity, according to the good or bad disposition of their masters." Park observed that they entered bondage in different ways, but "the most numerous" were "slaves from their birth having been born of enslaved mothers."[112]

Park found that "custom . . . established certain rules with regard to the treatment of slaves." In particular, "domestic slaves, or such as are born in a man's own house, are treated with more lenity than those who are purchased with money. . . . The master cannot sell his domestic, without having first brought him to a public trial before the chief men of the place." He observed that "such of the domestic slaves as appear to be of a mild disposition, and particularly the young women are retained as his own slaves."[113]

Other slaves met a different fate. Park noted that "causes of slavery" included "famine, insolvency, commission of crime . . . adultery . . . [and] witchcraft." But by far the most common cause was defeat in war, for both "freemen or slaves as have taken an active part in the war." He also observed that most enslaved prisoners of war had been slaves before their capture. He wrote that "when Mansong, king of Bamberra, made war upon Kaarta . . . he took in one day 900 prisoners, of which number no more than seventy were freemen. . . . When a freeman is taken prisoner, his friends will sometimes ransom him by giving two slaves in exchange."

Park observed that "prisoners taken in war. . . . have no right of protection of the law, and may be treated with severity, or sold to a stranger . . . or put to death." When "the unsuccessful warrior begs for mercy beneath the uplifted spear of his opponent, he gives up at the same time his claim to liberty, and purchases his life at the expense of his freedom."[114]

He also noted that "others that display marks of discontent are disposed of in a distant country.[115] And he observed that some of these warrior-slaves "sustained the hardships of their situation with amazing fortitude." These were the slaves who were sent far away to places like Louisiana.[116]

Park met a group of thirteen "prime slaves" in Kamalia, "all of them prisoners of war, they had been taken by the Bambarra army in the kingdoms of Wassela and Kaarta, and carried to Segoo, where some of them remained three years in irons. From Sego, they were sent . . . up the Niger in two large canoes, and offered for sale at Yamina, Bammakoo and Kancaba at which places the greater number of the captives were bartered for gold dust." He noted that they were kept "constantly in irons," and "all of these fetters and bolts are made from native iron."[117]

Park observed that "the value of a slave, in the eye of an African purchaser, increases in proportion to his distance from his native kingdom; for when slaves are only a few days' journey from the place of their nativity they frequently effect their escape. . . . On this account the unhappy slave is frequently transferred from one dealer to another, until he has lost all hopes of returning to his native kingdom."[118]

He added that "slaves which are purchased by the Europeans on the coast are frequently of this description. . . . By far the greater number are brought down in large caravans from the inland countries of which many are unknown even by name to the Europeans." Many of these slaves from the interior of West Africa were bought by French traders in Fort St. Joseph at Galam and sold down the Senegal River to French captains at Saint-Louis on the coast.[119]

In the wars of Mamari Kulubali, many soldiers who had fought against him were enslaved in this way. It was the beginning of yet another global slave migration, which became the nucleus of a distinctive African American culture in Louisiana during the eighteenth century.

It made a difference in what followed, especially for Bamana warrior-slaves who were captured in war and deliberately sent to destinations such as Louisiana which were farthest from home. They were heavily male. The most common pattern of gender in the transatlantic African trade was two males to one female, but it was not universal. A study of gender among 8,442 African slaves in Louisiana from 1719 to 1820 found that 88.6 percent of Bamana slaves were male; only 11.4 percent were female.[120]

Many were slaves who had been taken captive in war. Bamana slaves were widely known for a warrior's pride, strength, dignity, and they expected to be treated with respect. When captured, they were sent far away because they were difficult to control. They also tended to be loyal to comrades, and they strongly supported each other. Many had been trained to seize the initiative, and they were quick to take leading roles.

Bamana slaves were not the only African warriors who came to North America. Fante and Asante slaves from the Gold Coast were also formidable soldiers. So also were some slaves from Angola and Congo. Later, in the nineteenth century, other soldiers would be enslaved in the West African Yoruba Wars, and sold to America—many to Puerto Rico where we found their records in the excellent archives of San Juan. A few also came to Louisiana. These warrior traditions became important in differentiating African cultures within American regions. Several had a major impact on American history.

CATHOLICISM, ABSOLUTISM, AND
AFRICAN SLAVERY IN LOUISIANA

In North America, other differences appeared between systems of slavery in French Louisiana, Dutch New Netherland, and British North America. Leading factors were religion and the role of the state, operating through variant systems of law.

A large part of Louisiana's economy was directed by the French state. For many years the largest owner of slaves in Louisiana was the King's Plantation, directly across the river from New Orleans. Its workers were called "the king's slaves."

Other owners and employers of slaves in French Louisiana were the Roman Catholic Church and its holy orders. Not a single Catholic cleric in the colony is known to have spoken out against slavery during the period of French dominion—a pattern different from that of English colonies with Puritan ministers and Quaker "missionaries." French Catholic Louisiana was also different from the colonies of Catholic New Spain. In New Orleans, novice Ursuline sister Marie-Madeleine Hachard wrote to her father in 1727, "We are taking a Moor to serve us." She explained, "As for us, my dear father, please do not be scandalized. It is the custom of the country." [121]

The Ursuline sisters did more than that. They operated their own plantation and increased their slaves from nineteen in 1732 to sixty-one in 1770.

Ursuline convent, New Orleans

Individual Catholic priests, Capuchin friars, and Ursuline sisters were closely attentive to the spiritual condition of their slaves. They actively sought to instruct them, and to administer the sacraments.[122]

But in other ways, slaves of the Catholic Church and its orders were sometimes treated worse than those owned by the state or private masters. Examples were two African women owned by the Ursulines. Both women were assaulted by a drunken soldier named Dochenet (or Pochinet), and severely wounded with a bayonet. Dochenet had earlier committed crimes against other slaves and robbed them at bayonet point. The Ursulines' Reverend Mothers Xavier and Magdalene refused to press charges against him, saying that "they would prefer to lose their negresses rather than do anything against charity toward their fellow men." Louisiana's Superior Council was less forgiving, and more protective of the slaves. It ordered Dochenet to be hanged.[123]

CONCESSIONAIRES: LOUISIANA'S LEADING PRIVATE SLAVEHOLDERS

Most slaves in French Louisiana were privately owned by "merchant-planters," also known as *concessionaires* after land grants called concessions that they received from the Crown. Among the most successful were former officers of the French army and navy, who combined technical training with experience of command, and obedience to the Crown. An example was Jean-Charles de Pradel, who came to Louisiana as a naval cadet and junior officer. He left the navy, acquired a concession, became a successful merchant-planter in New Orleans, and built a large fortune.[124]

Concessionaires such as Pradel played a vital role in the colony. Their numbers were small: altogether 119 concessionaires in 1719–21, rising to about three hundred by the end of the French era. Their "concessions" were grants of land in rectangular surveys along the Mississippi River, above and below New Orleans. This pattern of riparian land grants was widely used in French colonies. It can still be observed along the St. Lawrence River in Canada, and near Hulls Cove on land owned by French families along the coast of Mount Desert Island in Maine.[125]

Louisiana's concessionaires came from the lesser nobility or the upper bourgeoisie of France. In Louisiana, some bourgeois concessionaires invented their own quasi-titles which made up in creativity what they lacked in authentic quarterings of nobility. An example was Jean Dumont, the son of a Parisian middle-class family. In the New World, he converted his name into a title and

became "Jean-François-Benjamin Dumont de Montigny." Others mocked
him as "Dumont-*dit*-Montigny" (Dumont called Montigny). The editors of
his memoir observe that "self-ennobling was not uncommon in colonial Louisiana."[126] Other concessionaires came from Canada. The Le Moyne brothers
were joined by four Chauvin brothers, who also had been born in Montreal.
The Chauvins, like some of the Le Moynes, went first to France, obtained orders from the king to settle in Louisiana, and received formal concessions of
land in that way.

Some of the Chauvin brothers acquired one of the largest concessions in
Louisiana, near Tchoupitoulas, and made the most of it. Three Chauvins together developed their grant into one of "the finest and best cultivated concessions in the country." Charlevoix wrote that they had "brought nothing with
them to this country, but their industry." The three of them each adopted new
names with a *particule de noblesse*, and called themselves the Sieur de Beaulieu,
the Sieur de Léry, and the Sieur de la Frèniére. They also bought urban real
estate and owned one of the first cabarets in New Orleans, which appears to
have been profitable. The Sieur de Léry's sons rose to high office in Louisiana
and gained private wealth from public service. They were among the largest
slave owners in the colony.[127]

An even larger operator was their neighbor Joseph Dubreuil de Villars, a
French army officer who came to the West Indies as a bourgeois captain of
artillery. There was a limit to how high he could rise in the army, where top
commands were held by aristocrats, often in proportion to quarterings of
nobility on their family escutcheons. In 1719, Dubreuil left the army and
moved to Louisiana with his wife, two children, and an entourage of carpenters, joiners, tailor, shoemaker, and laborers. He acquired a concession of
prime river land at Tchoupitoulas and other estates. Three years later he was
listed in the census with forty-three African slaves, two Indian slaves, and two
French servants.[128]

Dubreuil also became a "Contractor of Public Works for the King." Many
of his slaves were employed on projects such as building levees. He was also
known as an improving farmer. Dubreuil raised cotton on his land and invented a cotton gin many years before Eli Whitney. He was said to be the first
in Louisiana to plant indigo, for which he was paid 1,311 livres by the Company of the Indies. Dubreuil experimented in sugarcane with less success. A
major problem was the difficulty of finding varieties of cane that could survive
even a mild Louisiana winter.

With a partner, he also invested in the slave trade and sent at least one ship to Africa. By 1746, Dubreuil owned five hundred slaves and was said to be the richest man in Louisiana. But his fortune came at a price that others were not willing to pay. Dubreuil gained a reputation for indifference to the condition of his human property, except in regard to the profit that he could extract from them.[129]

FRENCH ABSOLUTISM, LOUISIANA LEVEES, AND THE WITTFOGEL THESIS

Dubreuil also became a central figure in the construction of Louisiana's vital levee system. Its object was not to exclude water from arable fields along the river, but to control the flow with a system of dikes, drains, ditches, and later reservoirs. It started small. Dubreuil's first levees were two feet high. They were crudely made of earth and timber, and they leaked. The labor was enormous, and the work was hard and unhealthy for the slaves who were made to do it.[130]

And the neighbors complained. The Chauvin family next door protested that Dubreuil's levees flooded their land. The Superior Council of Louisiana intervened, and ordered the Chauvins to stop complaining and start constructing their own levees. All were to be built by drafts of 150 slaves from plantations along the river, working under the orders of a French army engineer.[131]

In 1727, officials further decreed that all landowners must build levees of the same size. By and large, these orders were obeyed. As early as 1732, levees ran along the Mississippi for about fifty miles along both sides of the river, and they were expanding at a great rate.[132]

Slavery became a vital part of this project. In 1731, Governor Étienne de Périer wrote at length on the subject. He observed,

> There are places such as the Natchez, Yazoos, and Arkansas where settlers can work with their families alone, but from sixty leagues (about 180 miles) above New Orleans to the lower part of the river, the lands can be drained and freed from water only by those who have negroes, since the work on levees and drainage is difficult and hard. Even though a man were not sick, no matter how good a settler he may be, in an entire year he would not put one arpent [about 83 to 88 percent of an acre] of land in condition to be planted [without slaves].[133]

The construction of levees along the Mississippi was done by a large system, which combined arbitrary government with absolute powers, concentration of wealth among concessionaires, forced labor by hundreds of slaves, and the command authority of military officers who were put in charge. All were conscripted on the orders of an absolute state.[134]

Private owners made their peace with this system of public enterprise, in part because it was vital to their wealth. The work of levee building could best be done by slaves in winter months when they were not heavily employed in the fields. Slaveholders profited in several ways at once, on the model of Joseph Dubreuil.

Planters were also required to make their slaves available for the construction of roads, bridges, fortifications, and urban improvements in New Orleans. This was Louisiana's version of the French *corvée*, an absolutist system of forced labor by French peasants, tenants, and laborers for public purposes. In France, the *corvée* was deeply hated, and it became a major cause of the revolution in 1789. In Louisiana, every newly acquired slave obliged an owner to provide another thirty days of *corvée* to the state each year—in effect, a labor tax of 10 percent on slave capital. In addition, slaves could also be conscripted whenever the authorities felt the need for their labor. At the same time, slave owners were constrained in other ways by the laws and edicts of the French colony, which sought to make slaves, masters, and soldiers all into instruments of an absolutist state.

THE FRENCH LAW OF SLAVERY IN LOUISIANA: THE *CODE NOIR* OF 1724

The legal status of slaves and masters in Louisiana was defined by a formal *Code Noir* or Black Code, uniquely designed for this colony, and issued in France. It followed an earlier code for the French West Indian islands in 1685, but with many changes.[135] These were complex documents. Louisiana's *Code Noir* had fifty-five articles. It differed fundamentally from other systems of slave law in North America—not least in the way it was made. In British colonies, slave laws were framed by elective colonial assemblies, subject to approval in London. Louisiana's Black Code was conceived in France. The first draft of the West Indian *Code Noir* had been written by the King's ministers in Paris under the direction of Jean-Baptiste Colbert (1619–83). It was proclaimed in Versailles after Colbert's death as an *edit du Roi*, on the orders of an absolute monarch. The people who lived in Louisiana were consulted only in a minimal way, and they were the last to get the word.[136]

The primary object of Louisiana's *Code Noir* was not to regulate African

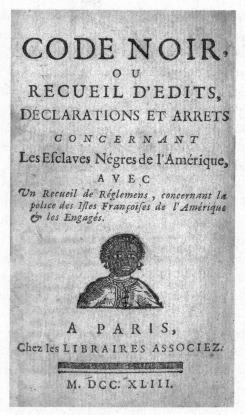

Le Code Noir, 1743 edition

slavery or race relations, but to stabilize an entire religious, social, and political system on a Roman Catholic and absolutist French model. Article I made no reference whatever to slaves or Africans or *nègres libres*. It was entirely about religious uniformity, ordered the immediate expulsion of all Jews from Louisiana, and imposed restraints on all other "declared enemies to the name of Christ."[137]

Special language was added in later articles to deal with Protestants in a more particular way. They were not expelled, but severely punished if they persisted in their faith. Repeat offenders against religious laws were declared "rebels" against the authority of an absolute monarch. The penalties explicitly included slow death by torture, such as breaking on the wheel followed by burning alive.[138]

Religious conformity was thought to be fundamental to social order in Louisiana. At the same time, the Roman Catholic Church was also required to embrace all of God's children, without exclusions by rank or race. Masters were ordered to have slaves baptized in the Catholic Church, instructed in Catholic doctrine, and married in a Catholic ceremony.[139]

Slaves were permitted to confess their sins and allowed to take Communion. All who did so were authorized to be buried in consecrated ground. Sundays and holy days were to be observed by slaveholders and slaves alike. Work was forbidden on holy days from midnight to midnight.[140]

In some ways Louisiana's *Code Noir* limited the power of masters even more than it restricted their slaves. An example was the power of punishment. The *Code Noir* allowed masters to administer "moderate punishment" by a whip or stick, or confinement in chains. Masters were not allowed to use more severe measures, and they were explicitly forbidden to torture or maim or mutilate their slaves.[141]

Torture was the prerogative of an absolute state. Slaves themselves were subject to very severe penalties for many crimes, but harsh punishments were to be administered only by a royal officer, who in Louisiana was usually the king's high executioner. Owners or overseers were explicitly forbidden to use torture themselves, on pain of severe penalties. When slaves were punished for major offenses, they were branded with a *fleur-de-lys*. That Bourbon emblem of royal authority was ordered to be burned into the flesh of every slave found guilty of a serious offense in Louisiana.[142]

But at the same time, another major purpose of the *Code Noir* was to recognize slaves as human beings. Here again we see the interplay of French absolutism with the Catholic ideal of a Universal Church for all humanity. The *Code Noir* compelled masters to treat slaves humanely, and it defined that obligation in detail. Masters were required to feed and clothe slaves adequately. The king's Superior Council in Louisiana was ordered to establish standards, rules, and specific obligations.[143]

Masters were ordered to protect the integrity of slave families in many ways. The same rules of marriage applied to slaves as to their owners, except the rule of parental consent. The *Code Noir* specifically prohibited the separation of slave husbands and wives, and of children under fourteen from their parents, either by private sale or public seizure. At the same time, it also prohibited all interracial marriages in Louisiana.[144]

The *Code Noir* also explicitly protected slave women from sexual abuse. Masters were forbidden to keep slaves as concubines. A master who made one of his slaves pregnant suffered the loss of ownership over the mother and child. Both were taken from him by the state. Masters were also required to maintain slaves who had been disabled by illness or age. If they failed to do so, public officers sent the slave to the nearest hospital, where delinquent masters were compelled to pay costs. If that provision was not honored, the state could take "a privilege over the plantation" and seize it in the king's name.[145]

Slaves were permitted to possess property with their master's permission, but were not allowed to own it, an idea taken from Roman slave law. Those possessions were at the same time the slave's "peculium" and the master's property. On this question and others, slaves were allowed to appear in court and testify against their masters.[146]

Historians have asked how much of the *Code Noir* was carried into practice and came to different conclusions. Clearly the code was not fully obeyed in a culture so diverse and complex, but most of it was observed in a general way. Catholicism was firmly established in French Louisiana, and it remains the leading faith in southern Louisiana to this day.[147] An important factor was the requirement of the *Code Noir* that slaves should be baptized in the Catholic faith, a practice widely but not universally observed.[148]

The prohibition of interracial Afro-European marriages was enforced in some cases, but *métissage* continued to grow, and race mixing occurred on a large scale, more so in Louisiana than in the French and British West Indies, largely as a function of demographic ratios. The best primary evidence for the extent of *mètissage* appears not in marriage records but baptismal registers, and was underreported even there.[149]

The *Code Noir* that came from France in 1724 had on its surface clear ideas of separation between *noir et blanc*, Black and white. But racist ways of thinking were not as strong as they would later become in the early nineteenth century, both in this colony and through the western world. Shannon Lee Dawdy, a history-minded anthropologist, writes of "Black" and "White," that "New Orleanians in the French period almost never used these terms in their censuses or legal documents." She links that fact to the "diversity of its founder population."[150]

Here was a curious paradox. Intellectual historians have found that vernacular ways of thinking about race and sex in French Louisiana tended to be more open, more complex, and more nuanced than in the *Code Noir*. And the human and Christian condition of slaves was elaborately protected by law. But social historians have also observed that actual treatment of individual slaves in French Louisiana was often cruel in the extreme.[151]

Legal historians have noted that Louisiana's *Code Noir* itself "constituted

the most racially exclusive colonial law of the French empire . . . even taking
the unprecedented step of banishing interracial marriages altogether." But
historians of gender have found that daily life in French Louisiana was very
different. It was marked from the start by a high frequency of interracial sexual relations among Europeans and American Indians. Illegal race mixing also
began to occur in different ways between French and Africans in Louisiana.

While Afro-European marriages were banned, sexual relations were common, and children of mixed ancestry were baptized in great and growing
numbers. In surviving records for 2,458 baptized slave children in New Orleans from 1744 to 1769, historian Cécile Vidal observed a striking trend. The
proportion identified as racially mixed rose from 4 percent in 1744 to 22 percent in 1759, and 31 percent in 1769. Further, among "baptized illegitimate
children of free women of color," 71 percent were racially mixed. Vidal compared those findings with other French colonies and found that rates of race
mixing rose much higher in Louisiana than in Martinique, Guadeloupe, and
Saint-Domingue, even as rates of interracial marriage remained low.[152]

Some mixed marriages were formally recognized in Louisiana, and even
confirmed by the Roman Catholic Church in New Orleans. A striking example occurred in 1725. A white woman, Marie Gaspart, native of Bruges,
married a free Black man, Jean Raphael of Martinique. A Catholic priest
performed the ceremony in the New Orleans church. The wife's family and
friends were present as witnesses, and the commandant general of Louisiana
gave his consent. Scholar Jennifer Spear wrote that "this marriage would have
been unusual anywhere in colonial North America." It was illegal in Louisiana, but it was done by special permission in this case, and carried out with
style and spirit. And it was not unique. Other mixed marriages were recorded
in 1723 and 1727.[153]

ENFORCING LOUISIANA'S *CODE NOIR*:
LOUIS CONGO, ROYAL EXECUTIONER

Overall, attitudes of French planters toward the *Code Noir*'s regulation of
slavery were mixed, to say the least. The code imposed many obligations and
constraints on masters.

To enforce its laws, the French colony employed royal officials called "high
executioners." Some were themselves African slaves, or former slaves. Three
appear in the records. One was called La Lanceur, "the Launcher," from the
speed of his hangings. He is believed to have performed the first public exe-

cution at the Place d'Armes in New Orleans. Another executioner was known by the name of Brutal.[154]

Much the best known was Louis Congo, a slave who came from Central Africa, probably on board the *Néréide* in 1721. Some years later he took the hated job of royal executioner, probably as a way of escaping bondage. Louis Congo boldly set his own conditions: freedom for himself and his wife, a plot of land, a supply of drinks, and a large fee for each punishment that he administered. Most of Louis Congo's requests were granted, except freedom for his wife. His fees were fixed by law, in a horrific table:

breaking on the wheel	40 livres
burning alive	40 livres
hanging	30 livres
flogging	10 livres
branding a *fleur-de-lys*, the lily of France	10 livres
affixing a *carcan* or iron collar	5 livres

The number of Louis Congo's victims is not known, but they were of every rank and condition. In 1728, he hanged an Indian slave named Bontemps for robbery and "aggravated desertion." A year later he executed a European merchant named Joseph Graff for killing a business associate. In 1731, as we shall see, he broke on the wheel eight Bamana slaves on charges of a conspiracy to seize the colony, kill all the French, enslave everyone else to Bamana masters, and make Louisiana a Bamana empire like Mamari's imperial Ségou.[155]

Louis Congo learned to read and write, kept his own accounts, prospered in his bloody trade, and acquired land on the outskirts of New Orleans, and some of it may have been near what would later be called Congo Square. At the same time, he was hated by Indians, Africans, and Europeans alike. In 1726 three Indian slaves tried to kill him, and nearly succeeded. Eleven years later he was assaulted by two African slaves and severely beaten. But Louis Congo had more lives than the proverbial Parisian cat.[156]

Some masters were happy to have their slaves punished by an officer of the Crown. They sent particular requests for penalties on repeat offenders. One planter asked that a slave named Guala be punished severely for having run away many times, but requested that he was not to be damaged as a worker. The royal executioner was careful to comply. He cut off the slave's ears and branded a fleur-de-lys on his shoulder.[157]

Other owners were reluctant to entrust their slaves to the state, or to Louis

Congo. The *Code Noir* of Louisiana prescribed some penalties that could not be applied to all slaves without destroying slavery itself. For example, the penalty for theft, even petty theft, was hanging, but Louisiana's Superior Council wrote, "If we hang all Blacks who steal, not one will be saved from the gallows, because they are all more or less thieves." And it added, who would not steal in their place. Here was a rare expression of humanity that may have been in the mind of at least one superior councilor.[158]

CODE NOIR'S CONSTRAINTS ON SLAVE OWNERS: INFURIATED MASTERS, IRRATIONAL CRUELTY, AND GROWING SLAVE RESISTANCE

Slavery, in many cultures, tended to become a lifelong system of forced labor for the gain of others. The primary instruments of force were various forms of physical violence, designed to combine maximal pain with minimal disruption of a slave's labor. The French legal system tried to regulate that process. The *Code Noir* imposed strict limits on the physical force that could be used on slaves, and it added many restraints and obligations on masters.

In a comparative study of slave punishments through French Louisiana, a curious double paradox presents itself. The laws of the French colony formally restricted the freedom of masters to punish their slaves. But in actual practice, extralegal punishments by angry planters sometimes became unimaginably severe.

The *Code Noir* and bylaws and interpretations in Louisiana forbade masters to administer more than twenty-five blows with a "soft whip." More severe punishments could be inflicted, but only by public institutions of justice and the royal executioner.[159] Even as private punishments inflicted by a master on a slave were restricted by law, public punishments of slaves were ferocious.[160]

Once those official processes were set in motion, the master had no control over the outcome. For acts of violent resistance to authority, the penalty in Louisiana, as in France itself, was to be broken on the wheel. It was a monstrous punishment of unimaginable cruelty. The victim was lashed to a large horizontal wagon wheel, and many bones in his body were systematically broken by separate blows, beginning with fingers and toes, then arms and legs and bones in the torso. To add to the torment, the horizontal wheel was turned so that the victim was always looking up into the sun until he died. All this was done by royal officials in the presence of large crowds in France and smaller ones in Louisiana.

Other Louisiana slaves were punished by being drawn and quartered or burned alive. Sometimes these horrific punishments were combined, and they were done in public spectacles of extreme cruelty in New Orleans, as in Paris. After the victims died, severed heads were placed on posts along roads and rivers, and left to rot for years, as warnings to others, a custom in other colonies.

This absolutist system was in some ways self-defeating. Frustrated masters who were forbidden to punish their slaves severely often resorted to illegal measures of extreme savagery. Surviving records of Louisiana's Superior Council provide examples of illegal punishments of unimaginable cruelty, forbidden by the *Code Noir*, but often inflicted by masters, managers, and *commandeurs* or slave drivers.

An example was the case of Jacques Charpentier, also called Le Roy, a monstrous sadist who in December 1727 became the manager of a Louisiana plantation. He had control over ten slaves belonging to Raymond Dauseville. In the period from 1727 to 1730, Charpentier used Dauseville's slaves to run his own private lumber business. He increased profits by underfeeding and overworking them. The slaves were not given Sundays off as the *Code Noir* required. Women with child were not allowed to stop two hours before sunset, as was the custom. Dauseville routinely raped his female slaves, and when they became pregnant, he beat them until they miscarried. At least four of his slaves aborted in that way. One did so three times. Male slaves were also brutally mistreated. One was found with an open wound the size of a large hand in his chest.[161]

Historians have written that this case was "one of the most shocking examples of systematic abuse of slaves ever encountered in surviving documents anywhere in the Americas." But it was far from unique. French Louisiana became a byword for brutality, even beyond cruel practices in Caribbean islands. The contradictions of an absolutist system of justice compounded the problem.[162]

A RISING SPIRIT OF RESISTANCE

As the slave trade increased in the late 1720s, Africans and American Indians responded with growing resistance. Increasing numbers ran away. Some disappeared into the swamps and bayous and were called maroons. The environment of Louisiana created many opportunities for *marronage*, as the French called it. Indian slaves were among the first maroons, and they were joined by Africans. For more than two centuries, to the outbreak of the American Civil

War in 1861, maroons lived in Louisiana wetlands very near the capital New Orleans. In 1726, the attorney general of Louisiana reported that "for a long time large bands of Indians and slaves have joined together and deserted and hang out around the city well armed." He reported that some of them survived mainly by preying on their former masters.

Other African runaways and maroons from Spanish colonies were also living in Louisiana even before the French arrived. American Indians told Governor Iberville that fugitive "cimarrones" had fled from Spanish masters in Mexico and founded a community in what is now western Louisiana, ten days' journey west of the Mississippi. The Indians reported that they were "numerous," and lived in families. Some of them spoke Spanish, but they refused to talk with Europeans and drove them away.[163]

With every surge of African arrivals, more slaves escaped into the swamps and woodlands. Some sought to live close to slaves in plantations in what the French called *petit marronage*. Others remained near New Orleans. In 1728, Governor Étienne de Périer reported that maroon groups were living near the capital, and some operated boldly inside the town. Something similar happened on the German Coast north of New Orleans, and in other parts of the colony.[164]

In a second pattern called *grand marronage* by the French, other maroons went deeper into the swamps, formed separate communities, and kept their distance. Some of these African maroons lived in peace near Indian groups. As early as 1727, an Indian captive described a maroon community called Natanapalle, where fifteen fugitive slaves, Indian and African, lived together. They were said to possess eleven muskets and a supply of ammunition.[165]

To African slaves in Louisiana, maroons became authentic American heroes. Many generations of slaves sang their praises in joyous folk ballads that were much like African sagas. One of them celebrated the exploits of Moluron, a fearless Black maroon who became an enduring Afro-Louisiana folk hero. In the sagas he ran many times from his master and was often caught, only to run again. The songs in Gombo celebrated his courage, autonomy, benevolent nature, indomitable spirit, and an inexhaustible good humor which were admired for many years:

Moluron! Hé! Moluron! Hé!
C'est pas 'jordi mo dans moune
Si yé fait ben avec moin, mo resté
Si yé fait mo mal, m'a-chap-pé!

Moluron! Hey! Moluron! Hey!
It's not today I'm in the world
If you treat me good, maybe I'll stay
If you treat me bad, I'm on my way![166]

THE NATCHEZ MASSACRE AND WARS OF 1729–30

Through the difficult decade of the 1720s, slave resistance rapidly increased in Louisiana. Acts of violence became more frequent, runaways multiplied in the struggling colony, and maroons such as Moluron found many places of refuge. Governor Périer expressed particular concern about growing numbers of defiant slaves who escaped to the swamps and bayous. Some lived beyond the reach of their masters, but very near New Orleans, they visited with impunity, some in the night, others even in daylight. The governor levied a heavy tax on slave owners, and used it to pay for patrols that pursued the runaways, with small success.

Périer increasingly came to regard slavery as a mortal danger to the colony. He specially feared alliances between African slaves and American Indians, and worried much about the Natchez nation to the north. The French had fought them in 1716 and 1724, built Fort Rosalie in their territory, and founded a flourishing settlement near what is now Natchez in Mississippi. By 1729 its French *habitants* included 200 men, 85 women, 150 children, and about 280 African slaves.

The Natchez Indians were increasingly unhappy, and a French commandant, the Sieur de Chépart, compounded the problem. Chépart personified the worst of French absolutism. In 1728, he was recalled to New Orleans on charges of tyranny, corruption, incompetence, and abuse of the Indians. Historians believe that Chépart was guilty of all those offenses and more, but he had powerful friends. Governor Périer returned him to his post in Natchez. In 1729, Chépart went farther. He seized much Indian land and made it his own private estate. Worse, some of the land was a sacred burial ground of the Natchez nation.[167]

The Indians decided to fight. They planned carefully, and made common cause with at least two African *commandeurs* or slave drivers. Then the Indians visited the homes of French settlers. With astonishing *panache*, they asked to borrow firearms for hunting, with the promise of game in return. On November 29, 1729, the Natchez suddenly attacked the French with their own weapons, destroyed the French settlement, and killed an estimated 229 French colonists: 138 men, 35 women, and 56 children. Another 50 French women, many children, and a few men were taken captive. When the attack began, African slaves divided three ways. Some joined the Natchez Indians. A few defended the French. Many tried to escape from both combatants, and fled into the wilderness.[168]

This fighting spread swiftly through the lower Mississippi Valley. French leaders exploited rivalries among Indian nations, and recruited warriors of the Choctaw nation. They attacked the Natchez, recaptured fifty to a hundred Blacks, and liberated all fifty French women. The Natchez retreated into the country of their Chickasaw allies, and the result was an expanding series of French and Indian wars. Altogether, the Natchez Massacre and its ensuing warfare killed 10 percent of Louisiana's French population. It destroyed outlying settlements, and spread panic through the colony.[169]

One of the worst acts of savagery was committed by the French on direct orders from Governor Périer. He deliberately tried to pit Africans against Indians in open warfare. To that end, he planned a mass killing of the Chaouacha, a small Indian nation south of New Orleans. Périer organized an attack and made it appear the work of Africans. He sent eighty armed Africans with French officer Louis Tixerant to attack a Chaouacha village, at a time when most of its men were hunting. Seven or eight men remained in the village, and all were murdered. Indian women were taken captive and carried to New Orleans. When Chaouacha hunters returned, they went directly to the governor and demanded their women and children. Périer freed them, but also wrote home to France, and made a boast of his brutality, much to the displeasure of his superiors. Some thought that he had offended the honor of France.[170]

SAMBA BAMBARA AND THE BAMANA
CONSPIRACY OF 1731

The Natchez Massacre and subsequent wars caused a crisis in Louisiana. Governor Périer wrote once again in 1731, "The greatest misfortune which could befall the colony, and which would inevitably lead to its total loss, would be a union between the Indian nations and the Black slaves. But happily there has always been a great aversion between them which has been much increased by the war, and we take great care to maintain it."[171]

By 1731, African leaders had emerged among Louisiana's slaves, and several were quick to start movements for freedom. One of them was known to the French as Samba Bambara. According to Le Page du Pratz, he was of the Bamana nation, and had a gift for languages and leadership. In West Africa he had worked as an interpreter for French slave traders at Fort St. Joseph, their interior post on the upper Senegal River. Samba Bambara did well for himself. He acquired a home in the seaport of Saint-Louis, lived there with his wife and family, and became a man of property.[172]

But in the mid-1720s, things had gone wrong for Samba Bambara in Africa. His marriage came apart, and according to Le Page du Pratz he was also thought to be involved in a rebellion that caused the loss of the French trading post Fort d'Arguin on an island off the coast of Mauritania. His former employers sold him into slavery, and he was sent to Louisiana in 1726. On board the slave ship *Annibal* he allegedly led a shipboard rebellion, and was clapped in irons.[173]

In Louisiana Samba Bambara's mastery of languages brought him to the attention of the colony's Superior Council. They employed him as an interpreter, and also as a driver of slaves on the King's Plantation, directly across the Mississippi from New Orleans.[174]

In June of 1731, French authorities in New Orleans began to hear rumors of a planned rising among slaves on the King's Plantation. Another clue emerged when an African woman was beaten by a French soldier in New Orleans. She shouted a threat that soon "the French would no longer insult negroes." The woman was brought before the governor, but nothing more could be learned from her.

A report was passed to Le Page du Pratz. Late one night he made his habitual rounds with an interpreter at his side and discovered a slave *cabane* with a light burning. Du Pratz went closer and recognized the voices of Samba Bambara, and another African *commandeur* on the plantation. Both were Bamana, and they were speaking in that language. With his interpreter, Le Page du Pratz could understand their conversation. It was about a revolt against the French. The plan was to rally hundreds of Bamana slaves, defeat French armed forces, and kill all French colonists along the Mississippi from the Gulf of Mexico to Pointe Coupée near Baton Rouge. Their object was to seize the entire colony, enslave other African ethnic groups, and found a Bamana empire in Louisiana.[175]

The revolt had been planned for June 24, 1731, and it was postponed to June 29. Le Page du Pratz learned about it in the intervening period. He summoned help from New Orleans. Samba Bambara and seven Bamana slaves were swiftly arrested. Under prolonged torture by "burning matches" they confessed. Eight Bamana captives were broken on the wheel, and the slave woman who had first revealed the plot was "hanged before their eyes." Probably the sentences were carried out by royal executioner Louis Congo.[176]

A few historians and at least one contemporary scholar have expressed skepticism about this event. It is true that for every actual slave rising, there were many rumors of revolts. But testimony of Le Page du Pratz makes clear that this was something more solid. Repeated evidence survives of a strong spirit of resistance especially among militant Bamana warrior-slaves in Louisiana during the mid-eighteenth century.

When slaves were accused of capital crimes in Louisiana, their fate was decided by interrogations before the colony's Superior Council. Records of its proceedings survive for thirty-one cases of major slave resistance from 1729 to 1752. The ethnic origins of accused slaves show a striking pattern. In four cases their ethnicity cannot be identified. Of the other twenty-seven, eighteen (67 percent) were explicitly described as Bambara/Bamana. Three others (11 percent) were called Samba (and appear to have come from Senegal), two were Wolof, and one each (3.7 percent) were Fulbe, Fon, and Sango. Throughout the French period, two thirds of all serious crimes before the Superior Council involved Bamana slaves. They were also identified as leaders of another major revolt, planned on December 15, 1731, to take place during midnight Mass on Christmas. It failed when French authorities learned about it.[177]

Yet another epic tale of Bamana resistance became a story of a rare success by Louisiana's slaves. It happened in the 1730s on the plantation of Joseph Chaperon, a French master who was infamous for many acts of unspeakable cruelty, which brought him frequently to the attention of Governor Bienville and Louisiana's Superior Council.

The French naval officer Jean-Bernard Bossu, "a very reliable witness," wrote that he actually saw Chaperon roast one of his slaves to death in a hot oven. Seeing that his victim's jawbones were drawn back in a rictus of death, Chaperon joked, "I think that he is still laughing," and picked up the poker and stirred the fire.[178]

Nobody interfered, and Chaperon was never prosecuted. He owned forty-one slaves in 1760, and they bore the marks of extreme maltreatment. Bossu wrote that this master became "the bugbear of the slaves." Other masters threatened disobedient slaves by telling them, "I am going to sell you to Chaperon."[179]

In the 1730s Chaperon had been abusing three slaves in particular. One of them was a Bamana warrior named Vulcain. He was hamstrung, probably for running away. Vulcain had a Bamana friend named Antoine, and Antoine had a Wolof wife called Fauchon. They met a mulatto seaman variously called Pierre, or Pedro de la Pie, who knew the waters of the Caribbean. Together they stole a boat from Pierre's master and sailed to Cuba. Later, other Louisiana slaves also escaped to Cuba. They reported that Chaperon's slaves had successfully reached Havana and were living free on that island. It was an amazing feat and became another part of the living legend of Bamana resistance.[180]

In Louisiana, these Bamana warrior-slaves gained an enduring reputation for courage, strength, dignity, presence, leadership and martial valor. Memories of them were strong in the late nineteenth century. One example appeared in the writings of George Washington Cable, born in 1844 to a wealthy slave-holding family in New Orleans. Like Louis Moreau Gottschalk, he was raised among African servants, became interested in African culture and music, and was knowledgeable about African ethnic groups in Louisiana. Cable also became a strong supporter for the rights of African Americans and the cause of racial justice—so much so that he was forced to leave the South and move to New England.

In 1886, Cable published in the *Century Magazine* a classic account of a Bamana warrior whom he may have seen dancing in New Orleans, possibly in Cable's childhood, perhaps not in Congo Square, but at another gather-

The bamboula, Congo Square

ing place, maybe in Dryades Street, or on the Levee. Cable vividly described a "glistening black Hercules, who plants one foot forward, lifts his head and bare, shining chest, and rolls out the song from a mouth and throat like a cavern . . . a *candio* or chief before he was overthrown in battle and dragged away. . . . He is of the Bambaras, as you may know by his solemn visage and the long tattoo streaks running down from the temples to the neck, broadest in the middle, like knife-gashes."

Cable described him as a leader and remembered seeing "his play of restrained enthusiasm catch from one bystander to another." Accounts of Bamana warriors and leaders among slaves were common in Louisiana from the early eighteenth century through much of the nineteenth century.[181]

THE CLOSURE OF LOUISIANA'S AFRICAN SLAVE TRADE

In 1731, French Louisiana's very active African slave trade came suddenly to an end. From that year to the end of the French dominion in 1763, only one African slave ship is known to have arrived in the colony, compared with twenty-four ships from 1718 to 1731. The trade was shut down for fear of revolt, and also of an alliance between multiple groups of African slaves and many nations of American Indians.

A brief attempt was made to revive the African trade in 1743. The leader was Joseph Dubreuil, the largest private slave owner in the colony. He raised trading capital in the form of a cargo of homegrown tobacco, bought the small ship *St. Ursin* (eighty tons), outfitted her at La Rochelle in France, and sent her to the African port of Saint-Louis on the Senegal River. There she found slaves in short supply, and sailed south to Gorée Island, where she had more trouble buying slaves. Finally she went to the Gambia River, and was able to complete a cargo of 220 slaves, "mostly women." One of the few men aboard was a slave named Joseph, "of the Bambara nation." When the ship reached Louisiana, only 190 slaves were still alive.[182]

With this venture, the African slave trade to Louisiana ended for twenty years. The cause was complex: conditions in West Africa, conflicts at sea between European powers, but most of all, strife in Louisiana where incompetent European leaders, Indian wars, and African revolts had become a major threat to the colony.

French Louisiana's slave trade from Africa had continued for only fourteen years. Even so, it had a long reach. Africans who came before 1732 became the nucleus of Louisiana's slave population through the French era. Patterns of African origin in range, region, culture, clusters, timing, and leadership had a major impact, as we shall see.[183]

MOVEMENTS FOR REFORM OF SLAVERY: LE PAGE DU PRATZ AND BIENVILLE

On January 23, 1731, authorities in France intervened to save Louisiana from imminent collapse. The ministers of Louis XV vacated the charter of the failed Company of the Indies and Louisiana became a royal colony. Governor Étienne Périer was removed. The former French Canadian governor, Jean-Baptiste Le Moyne, Sieur de Bienville, was recalled from retirement and ordered to replace him, with instructions to clean up the colony and reform the system. He would be followed by the Marquis de Vaudreuil, "le grand marquis."

Slowly the French colony began to grow again. In the aftermath of great crises, Louisiana's leaders began to think about systematic reform of slavery in the colony.

Among the leading reformers was Antoine-Simon Le Page du Pratz (ca. 1695–1775), director of the King's Plantation. He is thought to have been born in Holland and schooled in France. Le Page du Pratz became a soldier and served with Louis XIV's dreaded Dragoons through the cruel and bloody dynastic wars of the early eighteenth century. He knew at first hand the horrors that human beings are capable of inflicting on one another.

By profession, Le Page du Pratz became an engineer, an architect, and a public servant, formally trained in a *cours de mathématiques*. By inclination, he was a *philosophe*, a man of the Enlightenment, devoted to the rule of reason, knowledge, truth, and virtue in the world.

In 1718, Le Page du Pratz received several land grants in Louisiana and raised tobacco with a workforce of French *engagés* and African slaves. He took as his companion a beautiful and spirited young Chitimacha Indian woman in a Native American ceremony, with the approval of her family and nation.

A story of their life together tells us that she was fully his equal, and in some ways more than equal. One night a large alligator wandered into their camp. Le Page du Pratz ran for his gun and returned to find that his Indian companion had attacked the alligator with a billet of wood and beat it to death. She laughed merrily at his "timidity."

They lived happily together near Natchez, and he learned Native languages from his consort, as had many Canadian *coureurs de bois*, who described the learning process as "sleeping with a dictionary." Le Page du Pratz also explored the lower Mississippi Valley with American Indians as his guides, and he studied the country in scientific detail.

In 1728, he was offered a new job in Louisiana, and left Natchez shortly before the bloody war that followed. Le Page du Pratz was appointed director of the King's Plantation, at that time the largest in Louisiana, with a workforce that rose above five hundred slaves. He was also responsible for hundreds of other slaves who worked along the river, and for newly arrived African slaves who were brought to the King's Plantation for "seasoning" while they awaited a purchaser.

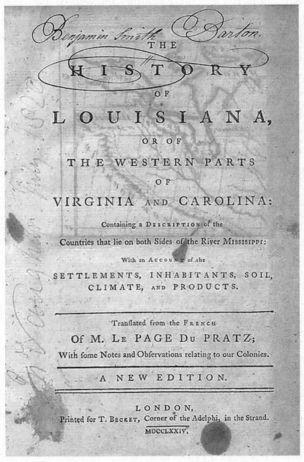

THE

HISTORY

OF

LOUISIANA,

OR OF

THE WESTERN PARTS

OF

VIRGINIA AND CAROLINA:

Containing a Description of the
Countries that lie on both Sides of the River Mississippi:

With an Account of the

SETTLEMENTS, INHABITANTS, SOIL,
CLIMATE, AND PRODUCTS.

Translated from the French

Of M. Le PAGE Du PRATZ;

With some Notes and Observations relating to our Colonies.

A NEW EDITION.

LONDON,
Printed for T. Becket, Corner of the Adelphi, in the Strand.
MDCCLXXIV.

The History of Louisiana, by Antoine Le Page du Pratz

Le Page du Pratz ran the Plantation for six years from 1728 to 1734. Then he returned to France and wrote at length about his experiences, first as a *Mémoir sur la Louisiane*, published in twelve parts by the *Journal Oeconomique* from 1751 to 1753, then as a single work in three volumes, called *Histoire de la Louisiane* (Paris, 1758). It is now available in other French and English editions, though not in a definitive scholar's edition. Altogether it is the most important eighteenth-century work on the history of Louisiana, and a major contribution to American literature.[184]

Le Page du Pratz wrote at length about Africans and slavery in Louisiana. He did so from long experience and with large purposes in mind, as a scientist and philosopher of the Enlightenment. The idea that slavery should, or could, be abolished outright seems not to have occurred to him, but he deeply believed that the condition of slaves might be reformed and improved by the application of reason, humanity, Christianity, and enlightened thinking.[185]

Le Page du Pratz's thinking was not racist. Racism as an ideology came after his time, as we shall see. He believed that African slaves were intelligent, and broadly knowledgeable, with highly articulated values and a wealth of cultural experience from which others had much to learn. As a long-serving director of the King's Plantation in Louisiana, he came to know many slaves well enough to form personal knowledge of Africans, not as a race but as diverse individuals who came from a variety of African ethnic and cultural groups, and also had a range of experience, in which he was much interested.

He deeply believed that Africans should be treated with respect, not least for the creative diversity of their own cultures, and also for what they had to teach others. He wrote, "Negroes must be governed differently from the Europeans, not because they are black, nor because they are slaves, but because they think differently from the white men." He did not approve of their beliefs in magic and superstition which were called "gris gris" in Louisiana as early as the 1730s, but he studied that too.[186]

Without opposing slavery, Le Page du Pratz and other enlightened leaders tried to build a stronger and more humane base for bondage in Louisiana, by organizing it on something more than violence. Brute physical force and other forms of coercion always remained vital parts of slavery wherever it existed. Human bondage, to repeat, was fundamentally a system of forced labor for the gain of others.

But a key part of the reforms of Le Page du Pratz was to link an idea of humanity and Christianity to human bondage. He wrote, "If they are slaves, it is also true that they are men, and capable of becoming Christians."[187]

For six years, Le Page du Pratz set an example with slaves on the King's
Plantation. He actively encouraged their catechism, urged masters to become
dutiful godparents of their slaves, and he actively assumed that serious role
himself on the King's Plantation. The functional role of godfather was important in the Roman Catholic Church. He wrote that "a Christian ought
to take care that the children be baptized and instructed, since they have an
immortal soul."[188]

Another leader in this effort was the Sieur de Bienville. In 1733, Bienville
returned to the colony to serve yet another term (his third) as governor. For
ten years, Bienville organized and led a concerted effort as governor, working
with the Superior Council, the Catholic Church, military commanders, and
leading planters.

Bienville's purposes, like those of Le Page du Pratz, incorporated some of
the ideas of humanity and Christianity that were written into parts of the
Code Noir of 1724, and reached beyond them. Bienville supported a sustained
campaign to encourage formal marriage and baptism of slaves. Another goal
flowed from a central irony of absolutism in France—that all subjects of the
king were his people and lived under his protection.

REFORM IDEAS IN FRENCH LOUISIANA: ORDER, REASON, HUMANITY, AND ENLIGHTENED SELF-INTEREST

Yet another major element in the thinking of Le Page du Pratz and Bienville
centered on Enlightenment ideas of reason and order. Le Page described in
detail his introduction of order in the King's Plantation. When he arrived,
in his own words, "the plantation looked like a forest half-cleared; the slaves'
cabins were scattered about here and there. These blacks had several little
pirogues that they used for crossing the river, to go and steal from the habitants on the other side, where the town is. Every Sunday, at least four hundred slaves could be found on the plantation, of whom two hundred and
fifty belonged there."

Le Page du Pratz went to work on "disorder" in many forms. He wrote,
"I ordered the land cleared and cultivated. I broke up the slaves' pirogues
and forbade them to ever have them again. I convened with the other settlers
about what we had to do to prevent slave gatherings, which could only lead
to trouble for the colony, and I succeeded in abolishing them." On that last
goal he appears to have had some limited success, for a brief moment. Even

to think about keeping hundreds of slaves on one side of the river when New Orleans beckoned from the other was beyond reason.[189]

His model of plantation management was presented as an appeal to a planter's enlightened self-interest. He explained, "If I advise the planters to take great care of their negroes, I at the same time show them that their interest is connected with their humanity."[190] He addressed himself to French slave owners in Louisiana, and argued that a policy of humanity had its practical uses and material rewards. "If it is your intention to draw advantage of them, is it not therefore wise to take all the care of them that you can?"[191]

Yet another organizing purpose of Le Page du Pratz was to work closely with the slaves themselves, and treat them with humanity, kindness, and respect. He recorded conversations with slaves and quoted responses in their vernacular, which are among the earliest recorded examples on Afro-French speechways later called Gombo in Louisiana, along with testimony of slaves in the Superior Council.

He tried to listen and learn from slaves. One slave said to him, "Maasser, when negre be much fed, negre work much; when negre has good masser, negre be good."[192] At the same time, Le Page du Pratz believed that a master must always be on his guard, and should never forget the mortal danger of living among slaves. He urged the importance of being careful "always to distrust them, without seeming to fear them." One strict rule was to "shut your doors securely, and not to suffer any negro to sleep in the house with you, and have it in their power to open your door." Another of his rules was to "visit your negroes from time to time, at night and in daytime, at hours when they least expect you. . . . Be the first up and the last abed, that the master may have an eye over everything that passes in his plantation."[193]

TREATING SLAVES WITH RESPECT, AND LEARNING FROM THEIR EXPERIENCE

Le Page du Pratz also advised masters that they had much to learn from their own slaves. Like other men of the Enlightenment, he believed that Africans were heirs to a rich fund of knowledge and experience and had many things to teach Europeans. He was quick to discover that slaves turned to other Africans for advice about health and medications, and he reported specific ways in which African slaves were able to improve the health of people on the King's Plantation, including his own.

Many historians are aware that Africans taught their European masters in America about specific crops and methods of farming. It happened in Louisiana with regard to staple crops such as rice, indigo, cotton, and foodstuffs including okra and black-eyed peas.

Le Page du Pratz combined that purpose with another goal. He advised slave owners to "give them ground of their own, and encourage them to work for their own gain." He argued that it is "in your interest to give your negroes a small piece of waste ground to improve at the end of your own, and to engage them to cultivate it for their own profit, that they may be able to dress a little better, by selling the produce of it, which you ought to buy from them upon fair and just terms. It were better that they should employ themselves in cultivating that field on Sundays, when they are not Christians, than do worse."[194]

A CENTRAL PURPOSE: INCREASING SUPPORT
FOR STRONG SLAVE FAMILIES

Another purpose of Le Page du Pratz was to strengthen African families, which he regarded as fundamental to enlightened management of plantations in Louisiana. He argued for the importance of supporting the formation of families among slaves: "Endeavour to assign each of them a wife. nothing attaches them so much to a plantation as children."

In 1724, the *Code Noir* forbade Louisiana masters to separate slave children from parents, and prohibited the sale of children under the age of fourteen. Le Page du Pratz expanded on that familial idea. He urged that each family should have separate "cabanes as they and their families call them," and doors with keys for "privacy and decency."[195]

Le Page du Pratz advised masters to encourage cleanliness and reward it: "It is proper to have in their camp a bathing place formed by thick planks . . . buried in the earth about a foot and a half at most, and never more water in it than about that depth, for fear that the children should drown." He added, "If a negro woman lies-in, cause her to be taken care of in everything that her condition makes necessary, and let your wife, if you have one, not disdain to take the immediate care of her herself, or at least have an eye over her. . . . The mother ought then to receive half a ration more than usual, and a quart of milk a day, to assist her to nurse her child."[196]

Governor Bienville actively shared this concern for cohesion of slave families, and protection of slave children. He enforced provisions of the *Code Noir* that protected slave women against rape and forced marriage.[197]

Bienville and Le Page du Pratz rallied other masters to that purpose, and they persuaded many of them (not all) that strong slave families strengthened owner profits. This policy appears to have been widely adopted by slave owners in Louisiana's late French period. Many leaders in New France expanded on those ideas and put them to work. Some masters (again, not all) seized upon them as an opportunity to make slavery more profitable.

Gwendolyn Hall studied the evidence of estate inventories and found proof that French planters increasingly tended to respect family cohesion among their slaves. She concluded that "in French Louisiana, creole slave children grew up in tightly knit nuclear families, headed by both African parents. The slave family was scrupulously protected in practice as well as in law." [198]

In a subsequent study, Hall asked the same question of another and larger set of quantitative data in her Louisiana Slave Database, a major contribution to knowledge. Here again, she found the same pattern of growing respect for slave families. But Hall also found interesting variations among African ethnic clusters. She observed that slaves from Benin had exceptionally strong family cohesion, and Bantu-speaking slaves from Central Africa less so. Her evidence from hundreds of individual records persuaded her that Bamana slaves were somewhere in between. [199]

This attitude of respect for strong slave families persisted in Louisiana through both the French and Spanish periods. After the United States took over Louisiana, many French and Spanish and some American masters continued this tradition and tried to support it. But in the more entrepreneurial American era, the trends became more mixed, as we shall see. And yet African slaves kept building strong families and constructed comities among themselves in ways that we are only beginning to understand.

Le Page du Pratz thought much about expanding responsibility among slaves, while also increasing control over other parts of their lives. On the King's Plantation slaves were given more use of "negro grounds" to raise their own crops during his tenure as director. He wrote in his *Histoire de Louisiane* that if slaves could raise their own crops, everyone gained.

The same purposes were shared by another enlightened Frenchman, Dumont de Montigny, who wrote that "most of the slaves clear grounds and cultivate them on their own account, raising cotton, tobacco, &c. which they sell. Some give their negros Saturday and Sunday to themselves, and during that time the master does not give them any food; they then work for other Frenchmen who have no slaves, and who pay them. Those who live in or near the capital generally turn their two hours at noon to account by making faggots to sell in the city; others sell ashes, or fruits that are in season." [200]

Le Page du Pratz believed that firmness and justice were fundamental, and closely linked. "If it is necessary not to pass over any essential fault in the negroes, it is no less necessary never to punish them but when they have deserved it, after a serious enquiry and examination supported by an absolute certainty." [201]

And he insisted that the punishments should never be cruel: "A Christian is unworthy of that name when he punishes with cruelty. . . . Treat them with moderation and restraint . . . and moderate labour, for violent and continual labours would soon exhaust them. The day is long enough for an assiduous labourer to deserve repose in the evening." [202]

AN EXPANSION IN CUSTOMARY RIGHTS OF SLAVES

The French *Code Noir* of 1724 guaranteed "the slave's use of free time," and specifically "the right to work for himself on the Sabbath, the right to cultivate grounds and gardens for his own use and sustenance, and the right to keep and dispose of property and wealth arising from his own industry." [203]

The *Code Noir* also ordered that "all our subjects of whatever quality and condition, are to observe the Sabbath and holy days, and we forbid them to work or to force their slaves to work from midnight to midnight in the cultivation of the earth or all other work on penalty of fine and arbitrary punishment and confiscation of their slaves." [204]

Here again, Le Page du Pratz and Dumont de Montigny actively encouraged this practice, and Governor Bienville enforced the rule. The custom of the country went beyond the law. Observers reported that slaves had not only Sundays to work for themselves, but half of Saturdays as well. Much evidence exists that half-Saturdays persisted in Louisiana from the late French era into the Spanish period, and sometimes into the early period of American sovereignty. Historian Alton Moody found that after 1803, "many planters allowed their slaves Saturday afternoon to tend their own crops, and a few planters granted their laborers the entire day when plantation chores permitted." But here again, later practices by American masters were mixed. [205]

This custom was not unique to Louisiana. In the colony of Georgia by 1751; the idea that a slave's produce on Sundays was his own came to be widely recognized not as a gift or a privilege, but a customary right. [206] The custom went farther in French Catholic Louisiana, embracing religious holidays that did not exist in Protestant colonies.[207]

The custom in Louisiana also went beyond the law in another way. A striking example appeared in the civil case of *Loppinot v. Villeneuve* (1774), during the early Spanish era. The court heard much testimony from masters that slaves in Louisiana not only had Sunday to themselves, but also that their masters "do not know the whereabouts of their slaves on the said day, nor do they question them," as long as they appeared for work on Monday. Other witnesses testified that this was done "with the knowledge and consent of magistrates."[208]

Article 22 of the French *Code Noir* declared that "slaves can have nothing which is not their master's, and all that come to them through their own industry or through the liberality of other persons, or otherwise by whatever title it may be, is acquired in full ownership by the master."[209]

That language seemed clear enough in itself, but Article 23 of the *Code Noir* went on to recognize "the peculium of the slaves" to the possession of property "which their masters allowed them." In Roman law, peculium referred to property that was given by law to the master, but entrusted by custom to slaves, "as if it were their own."[210]

Peculium in that sense existed as a customary right in many North American systems of slavery, but everywhere it tended to be an essentially contested concept, in more ways than one. In French Louisiana, prevailing customs differed from the written provisions in the *Code Noir*, and from the Spanish *Siete Partidas* and Anglo-American slave laws. From at least the 1730s, the custom of the country recognized that slaves virtually owned property of many kinds, and many masters allowed them to use it as they pleased. Within limits, they could freely buy and sell these possessions, and the profit or loss belonged to the slaves.

For example, slaves were customarily allowed to breed animals, raise crops, to sell or barter them freely, and to keep the gains or absorb the losses. By custom, all of that property belonged to the slaves as their peculium.

Only an exceptionally meanspirited and shortsighted master would attempt to claim legal title to his slaves' customary peculium. If he tried, trouble was likely to follow. The surest way to provoke a slave rebellion was to revoke or even to limit a long-established custom which slaves regarded as a customary right.

Something similar to that pattern appeared in other regional systems of North American slavery. But customary practices differed in important details from one system to another. In Louisiana, more than other North American systems, slaves tended to have customary rights to hold and buy and sell particular forms of property that brought not only income and wealth, but also a measure of freedom, power, honor, and even some degree of autonomy. For example, in Louisiana some slaves "possessed" their own horses. Sometimes they acquired them with their masters' knowledge or consent. They also bred and trained and rode them freely without asking permission. At least one master testified in a court case (1774) that he did not know or care where his slaves went in the night, as long as they showed up for work in the morning. Sometimes slaves were able to travel very long distances after dark.[211]

Slaves also possessed firearms, which was another custom of the country. Many a Louisiana slave shot for the pot, sometimes on orders from a master. Others guarded the plantation against dangers of various kinds. Slaves in Louisiana also acquired their own boats, a source of concern and controversy among masters. As we have seen, when Le Page du Pratz took over the management of the King's Plantation in 1728, he was surprised to discover that the slaves had "several little pirogues that they used for crossing the river."[212]

He put a stop to it but only for a moment. It was one thing to interrupt this practice, and quite another to keep it from starting again. Slaves in the lower Mississippi Valley knew many ways to get a boat. Some were allowed to borrow a boat from masters who had a vested interest in their commerce. Other slaves found their own boats, or stole them. Boats that belonged to masters had a mysterious way of going adrift on the river. They disappeared into Louisiana's web of waterways, which slaves knew better than their masters, and sometimes surfaced in another part of the colony. Every great storm in the lower Mississippi yielded a harvest of lost or broken boats. Other slaves made their own pirogues, as the French called them, which bore a strong resemblance to African dugout canoes. The same French words were used to describe them in both Africa and America.

A slave's customary ownership of a horse or a boat greatly increased freedom of movement and brought other liberties in turn. The customary possession of a firearm also brought power and authority. Here was another form of empowerment that was strong in Louisiana slavery under the French and Spanish regimes.

SLAVES IN LEADING ROLES AS MARKETERS AND MARKET MANAGERS

Masters in Louisiana also went farther in allowing slaves access to markets. Ira Berlin and Philip Morgan wrote, "Marketing by slaves was generally more limited in mainland North America. . . . Only in towns—such as the rice ports of the Carolina and Georgia lowcountry or in the small riverine villages of the Louisiana sugar country—did mainland North American slaves create Sunday markets approximating those farther south."[213]

The involvement of Louisiana slaves in markets went beyond what was allowed in Carolina, Georgia, and also the French West Indies. The *Code Noir* for Caribbean islands had included a strict prohibition of *le marché des nègres*, Negro markets on Sundays and holidays. It is interesting that this article was removed from the *Code Noir* for Louisiana in 1724.[214] Further, in New Orleans and other parts of Louisiana, slaves not merely engaged in marketing. They also became market organizers and market managers. They founded and ran markets which were highly developed and vitally important to the supply of food in the colony. In New Orleans, slaves were operating large Sunday markets as early as 1723. During the French era in the 1740s and 1750s, slave-run markets were held on the outskirts of the city at the end of Orleans Street. Later in the Spanish period, the markets spread to Fort St. Ferdinand, and Congo Square, and to outlying fields after the Americans took over. American Indians also ran a large market of their own in New Orleans, at the Place Bretonne.[215]

Some of these Indian and African markets were open every day in New Orleans—not during church services on Sunday mornings, but very busy on Sunday afternoons. They sold many things: fuel and food, baskets and pottery, medicinal herbs and potions, sassafras and root barks that were vital ingredients in Louisiana cuisine.[216]

Many stalls were run by "market women" in "bright bandanas and otherwise neatly dressed." Slaves were both sellers and buyers in these transactions. Visitors noted that the purchasers were often African house slaves who did the shopping for their owners. By the early nineteenth century, these slave markets were observed to be fundamental to the food supply of New Orleans.[217]

SLAVES WHO RAN GRAY MARKETS: MARION'S NETWORK IN NATCHITOCHES

Other patterns of market activity by Louisiana slaves were akin to what scholars call a gray economy. This was a complex system that operated on both sides of the law, in a broad area where exchanges moved back and forth across many boundaries of law and custom. Some of the most profitable transactions were prohibited outright, but gray markets were tacitly encouraged and even supported by some masters and magistrates, up to a point. Many people gained from these transactions, as did the colony as a whole.

Prohibited parts of the gray economy were carefully kept out of sight, but they were exposed from time to time in court proceedings. Historian Sophie White has reconstructed in detail one such case, tried in 1757 at the town of Natchitoches (pronounced Nackitosh). At its center was a very busy slave cook named Marion. She organized a large network of people, both slave and free, who bought, sold, and mostly bartered goods and services in great variety through Marion and her many agents. One of her workers was a young slave called Gamenon (short for Agamemnon). He had a gun, shot wild pigs, and occasionally killed domestic animals and butchered them. Marion cured the meat in her master's attic, cooked some of it, and used it as barter for other things.

A large part of Marion's trade was in stolen goods. When the market was slow, she organized burglaries of houses large and small, and sent anything of value to market. Much of her trade was in clothing, textiles, or bolts of valuable fabric.

Marion and her network also made a business of supplying goods on special order. On one occasion a male slave in Natchitoches wanted a hooded blanket coat called a *capot* and asked that it be made of fine wool. Marion's agents were able to find the wool, and a maker, for a price.

Another customer was Simon, *Métis libre*, a free man of mixed French and Indian ancestry. He wanted some fine linen shirts and proposed to pay for them with goods that included a silver ring, a cooking pot, a garter, and a mirror. Marion found the linen cloth, and arranged for it to be measured and cut. A French seamstress agreed to sew the shirts together and added collars and cuffs.

Marion's undoing was a young slave named Étienne, twenty years old, whose master was the commandant at Natchitoches. Étienne worked as a courier for Marion, traveling on his own horse, a mare that he gained by barter from an English deserter who lived in the woods. For some unexplained reason, Étienne revealed Marion's network to officials, and she was brought to trial.

Sophie White's analysis of the trial records documented Marion's web of suppliers, workers, and customers. Marion's many contacts included men and women, young and old, slave and free, Africans and Indians, French and Spanish, and the British deserter in the woods. A network run by Louisiana slaves operated in French Natchitoches, in the nearby Spanish town of Los Adaes, in Indian villages, in anglophone territories of the United States.[218]

SLAVE-MADE MARKETS IN NEW ORLEANS: LOUIS-DIT-FOY AND MAMA COMBA

The largest slave-run gray markets were in and near New Orleans. A complex example was pieced together by Gwendolyn Hall from evidence in the records of the Louisiana's Superior Council. One of the leaders was a slave called Louis by the French. He insisted that his name was "Foy of the Bambara Nation." Some of the documents referred to him as Louis-*dit*-Foy. More accurately, he was Foy-*dit*-Louis. By whatever name, Foy and his friends constructed a thriving gray market network in New Orleans. Central figures were slave women who worked as street vendors. Their leader was Julie-*dit*-Comba (or Mama Comba), and their base was provided by yet another slave woman who was allowed to have her own dwelling in her master's garden. These women were both Mandingo, and they were able to talk with Foy and other Bamana men in a mix of Mande speech. They worked with a surprising number of city slaves, market women, seamstresses, and artisans. At the same time, they did business with runaways, outliers and maroons, and were actively engaged in buying and selling on both sides of the law.[219]

SOCIAL CONSEQUENCES: AFRO-FRENCH SUNDAY GATHERINGS

These developments went far beyond what Le Page du Pratz had known in 1730s, when he tried to keep slaves on the King's Plantation from crossing the river to New Orleans on Sundays. Le Page du Pratz wrote, "Nothing is more to be dreaded than to see the negroes assemble together on Sundays, since, under the pretence of Calinda, or the dance, they sometimes get together to the number of three or four hundred, and make a kind of Sabbath, which it is always prudent to avoid; for it is in those tumultuous meetings that they sell what they have stolen to one another, and commit many crimes. In these likewise they plot their rebellions."[220]

Le Page du Pratz had little success in stopping these gatherings. The effect of his own reform program for Louisiana was to give slaves more time of their own, and more freedom in the use of it. As a result, the freedom of slaves on Sunday afternoons expanded in several dimensions.

In one of them, Sundays gradually grew into a day of freedom and celebration for slaves in New Orleans especially, and also through much of Louisiana. It was synchronized with the crop cycle. Historian Gilbert Din wrote, "The social season in New Orleans started after the fall harvest, with the onset of winter, and lasted until spring. It grew in size and sophistication as the colony developed and acquired wealth." [221]

This social season was well established in New Orleans before the end of the French period in 1763. All Souls' Day, Christmas, New Year's, Twelfth Night, and Mardi Gras all became important social events. And it spread to other parts of the colony. Din writes, "Blacks who could leave their plantations emulated whites in New Orleans with their own African dances and celebrations, in addition to mingling, buying and selling." At a distance from New Orleans, "masters who lived far from the city allowed their slaves to gather on one plantation where they imitated the fraternization that went on in New Orleans. Rural whites frequently engaged in similar practices." [222]

The authorities in Louisiana undertook to regulate these gatherings. In New Orleans the City Council attempted to control the buying and selling of goods and alcohol by slaves, with little success. Later it tried to regulate dancing by acquiring a "city-owned dance hall," and succeeded only in expanding it. By the mid-eighteenth century, a new sort of spiritual freedom was loose among Africans in Louisiana. It would never be contained. [223]

Even before Congo Square emerged as a gathering place in New Orleans, slaves found other places to meet on Sunday afternoons. Many sites were mentioned in early accounts. Large groups gathered at plantations on both sides of the river. Some groups met on the levees or just behind them, between the town and the river.

Other meeting places were on Dauphine Street, two blocks from what would later become Congo Square. Regular celebrations among slaves and others flourished away from New Orleans. In parishes up and down the river, regular Sunday meeting places emerged, sometimes on plantations of complaisant masters.

These various gatherings had consequences. Distinct speechways began to develop in various parts of the colony. They differed in local detail but shared a common spirit. Inventive patterns of material culture also developed rapidly. The result was a creative diversity of Afro-French identities in Louisiana. Some are still strong today. [224]

THE SPREAD OF AFRO-FRENCH SPEECH, 1728–43

A leading example and instrument of this cultural trend appeared in the history of language in Louisiana. African slaves developed a language of their own. It was part of an extended process that began in Africa where many different languages developed—and Africans were accustomed to meet and mix with other Africans whose speech was different from their own. Something similar developed along Africa's Atlantic coast when Europeans and Africans met and fought and traded. This process continued in French Louisiana when African slaves arrived. It created a new speechway called Gombo in the eighteenth and nineteenth centuries and Creole by linguists in the twentieth and twenty-first centuries. Similar Afro-French Creole dialects also appeared in the West Indies, and especially in Saint-Domingue, now Haiti, in variant forms. Haitian and Louisiana dialects differed in detail but tended to be mutually intelligible.[225]

Gombo has been described by linguists as a "Creolized Pidgin French."[226] This model implies that it began as a crude form of pidgin speech, which later generations learned to speak as a native tongue. There may have been a measure of truth in that process, but Gombo became much more than that, as one can discover by listening to historical examples that survive in the American Folklore Collection at the Library of Congress. They include early twentieth-century wax cylinder recordings of Afro-French Gombo speech from rural southern Louisiana.[227]

To study these recordings, and to hear Gombo spoken as a Creole language by people who had used it all their lives, is an extraordinary experience. These Louisianians had been born and raised as slaves, but they did not act or talk slavishly. Their speech had a distinctive tone that was strong, clear, and forceful. They spoke with pride and spirit. This was the sound of strength, courage, and endurance.

Written slave narratives have sometimes been read in a different way, in typescripts filtered through intermediaries. But recordings of narratives come directly from the source. To listen to them, rather than to read transcriptions on a page, is to discover that Gombo was not merely a pidgin-Creole speech, but something more creative in its range of communication, in nuances of feeling, and in shades of sentiment and sensibility. This was a highly developed Afro-French language, mostly French in its vocabulary, but more mixed in other ways, and very much more creative.

In some ways it became more complex than French and more nuanced in its many layers of expression, and in its extraordinary range and depth of emotional communication—more so than either French or English alone tended to be. The result was a Louisiana Gombo that reached beyond European languages in its power of creative expression.

Not all people of African descent in Louisiana spoke Gombo. The free *gens de couleur* of New Orleans tended to speak a more standard French. Gombo was the expressive language of African field workers who liked to call themselves *Cocodrie* in Gombo, rather than *les Crocodiles*, which was the more proper and correct word in French and English. But *Cocodrie* was a word with more spirit, more cadence, more rhythm, and even with an internal rhyme scheme of its own. *Cocodrie* was a word with a beat.

Many people in Louisiana became bilingual in French and Gombo. Others after the Louisiana Purchase became trilingual in French, English, and Gombo. George Washington Cable noted the salient features of this fascinating flow of language from his personal experience of learning to speak at least a little Gombo, as did many Europeans in Louisiana during the early and mid-nineteenth century, often learning it in childhood from slaves who became their teachers and exemplars.

Cable noted that French verbs were altered in Gombo, or simplified, or replaced by other verbs with more muscular powers of expression, and more nuanced shades of meaning. A leading example was the French verb *courir*. African slaves took it over, and made this verb "one of the most serviceable in the creole dialect." They gave it many meanings and nuances, not only as the French verb "to run," but also as the Gombo verb "to go, to walk, to follow, to come," and sometimes even the verb "to be." They conjugated it in their own inimitable way: *mo couri, to couri, li couri,* and in the plural *no couri, vo couri, ye couri*. Verb tenses were simplified. *Eté* became a single syllable *té* as in *mo té couri*, "I was running," or "coming," or "going," or even "being."[228]

Pronunciation in Afro-French Gombo changed in interesting and very expressive ways, in a manner somewhat similar to Afro-English Guinea talk in Frederick Douglass's native Maryland, or Afro-Yankee speech in New England, or Black Dutch in the Hudson Valley, or Gullah and Geechee in coastal Carolina, Georgia, and North Florida.

In Louisiana Gombo, the post-vocalic *r* tended to fall by the wayside, much as it did in Black English and white English too, but sometimes it reappeared in interesting ways. Thus *dormir* (to sleep) became *dromi*. French adjectival endings *le* had a way of vanishing: *aimable* became *aimab*. *Ch* became c, so that *cherchez* became *c'erc'e*.

Gombo speech had a simplified grammar, but also an enriched texture of sounds and colors. In those qualities it became more complex and expressive in some ways than the languages from which it derived. Gombo speakers had a fondness for rough hard *z* sounds, as in *zo^tt*, "others" (*no zo^tt couri dans bois*, we others are going to the woods), or *zamein* (*jamais*, never). The French *loiseau* (bird) became the explosive *zozo*, and a *fusil* (gun) became a *fizi*.

At the same time Louisiana Gombo cherished words with complex internal rhythms and interior rhymes, as in *voodoo*, or *hoodoo*, or *trouloulou*, which from the French *tourlourlou* was a happy word for a fiddler crab. Field slaves also used *trouloulou* as a contemptuous call word for the mincing steps of a male quadroon. A rude word for a female quadroon was *calalou*, after the culinary noun for a mixed *ragout*. It could be sounded in many expressive ways.

The net result was a spirited speechway that was 90 percent French in its lexifiers (vocabulary), but its powers of expression were as far removed from French as Gullah was from English. A Gombo slave sang a song to his lover:

Si to té tit zozo
Et mo-meme, mo té fizi,
Mo sre' tchoué toé—boum!
  Ah! chère bizou
  D'acazou
  Mo laimein ou
Comme cochon l'aime in la bou!

If you were a little bird
And myself, if I were a gun,
I'd shoot you—boom!
  Ah! dear jewel
  Of mahogany,
  I love you
As the hog loves mud.[229]

The creative range of emotional expression and meaning was extraordinary in Louisiana Gombo and African American dialects.

The emergent Afro-French Gombo speech in early Louisiana can be observed and dated in mid-eighteenth-century documentary sources such as the testimony of slaves before Louisiana's Superior Council. This evidence tells us that Afro-French speechways spread through much of the colony in the period from 1728 to 1743. That finding is consistent with other evidence in the published writings of Le Page du Pratz, which are less precise but more helpful in their reproduction of the breadth and variety of usage. The timing of this evidence also confirms Gwendolyn Hall's findings on the importance of West African and Bamana elements (among other ethnicities) in the Afro-French culture of Louisiana. It refutes other claims for West Indian origins or "Atlantic creoles" as prime movers. They would have some importance in later migrations to Louisiana during the American period, but even then in a secondary way.

Detailed patterns of Afro-French speechways have also been studied for variations through space. Of importance on this question is the creative research by Thomas Klingler and his colleagues who find evidence that Afro-French "Creole" language in Louisiana was not unitary. It developed as a complex family of speechways in different parts of the colony. One pattern of Afro-French speech appeared in and around New Orleans, and it was much studied in the late nineteenth and early twentieth centuries. Another pattern formed about one hundred miles north of New Orleans in Pointe Coupée Parish above Baton Rouge, and it was closely studied in an excellent book by Klingler in the late twentieth century. Yet a third pattern appeared along Bayou Teche, more than 120 miles west of New Orleans, in the parishes of Lafayette, Lafourche, St. Martin, and St. Landry. And a fourth was spoken south of New Orleans in Plaquemines Parish. It can be heard and studied in recordings of Afro-French slaves from the parish in the American Folklore Collection at the Library of Congress.[230]

AFRO-FRENCH CUISINE, "FOOD OF EVERY BODY"

Other distinctive patterns emerged in material culture—foodways as a case in point. One of North America's great regional cuisines began to emerge in French Louisiana by the mid-eighteenth century. Here again, enlightened French leaders such as Le Page du Pratz urged slave owners to "attend to the diet of their slaves" and "encourage them to follow their own foodways," in Le Page du Pratz's words.[231]

It started with simple elements. One staple dish was called "Couscou" by Le Page du Pratz, after the usage among West African slaves. He wrote, "For the better subsistence of your negroes, you ought every week to give them a small quantity of salt and herbs of your garden, to give a better relish to their Couscou, which is a meal of rice or maize soaked in broth."[232]

Louisiana slaves also invented ingenious soups from local ingredients. Here again, they made the most of meager resources, and managed to do it with flair and panache. An example was a distinctive dish called "violet soup." It was made from chicken bones and water, and early blue violets that bloomed everywhere and were called wild okra in Louisiana.[233] Another special "Lent Soup" was made from various herbs and fish heads (eyes removed).[234]

From an early date, the staple of the colony was a meal that could be cooked in a single iron pot and eaten in one dish with a wooden spoon. In Bayou Lafourche in southern Louisiana, one standard meal was described as a "hominy made of cracked great corn."[235] In Morehouse Parish in the far north of Louisiana, it was mainly rice, sometimes with various additions of "pickled pork, salt bacon, black molasses, corn bread, cabbages, peas and onions." The French described it as "the principal food of the slaves." They learned to like it themselves, with many variants and much pleasure.[236]

From low and humble beginnings, Louisiana cooks invented a cuisine of high seriousness and ingenuity. Its creators included Africans of many cultures, Europeans of many countries, American Indians of many New World nations, and more than a few wayfaring strangers. Any interesting gastronomical idea was welcome.

The classic example was gumbo, which an early authority described as "a pungent mixture inherited from Africa."[237] The word itself as we have noted is believed to have been Bantu in its roots. It described a unique combination of African, European, and local ingredients, cooked in an iron pot over a slow fire. "Time is meaningless" writes a leading Louisiana gumbo expert. A motto of cooks in this culture is *qui va doucement va surement*, or "she who goes slowly, goes surely."[238]

In the ubiquitous iron pot, an important ingredient of much Louisiana cookery was *roux*, another incomprehensible idea to people from away, but fundamental to many a good gumbo and much else. To this day, Louisiana recipes are apt to say, "First, make your *roux*," in preparing many a meal. *Roux* often began as a modest lump of melted fat, or a mix of lard and flour in equal measure, diluted with water, and abundantly seasoned with a seemingly endless variety of herbs and spices.[239] Some cooks cloaked the ingredients of their *roux* in deep secrecy. Others delighted in sharing their recipes, and presented small jars of *roux* to friends and guests as tokens of esteem.

To Louisiana *roux*, almost any edible ingredient might be added—vegetables in abundance, fish, meat, offal, game, fowl, shrimp, oysters. They were cooked slowly for hours over a bed of coals with red and green pepper, and went into gumbos which were commonly made with African okra.

A special Louisiana gumbo was *gumbo zhe 'bes* (*gumbo des herbes*), or vegetable gumbo. It was conventionally made from one or more greens that were widely available: mustard greens, spinach, turnip tops, beet tops, collard greens, lettuce, and cabbage. The vegetables were slow cooked for hours with a bit of fatback, and the pot liquor was saved to make yet another sort of *roux*.

Then the greens were chopped and cooked with red and green peppers, and other herbs. Louisianians of many conditions made a point of eating *gumbo zhe 'bes* on Holy Thursday, for good luck.[240]

Another dish that pleased Louisiana palates and appalled New Englanders was gizzard gumbo, made with special *roux* and the inner organs of ducks or chickens, or anything else at hand, and seasoned with rosemary and red peppers.

Yet another classic gumbo was made with peeled shrimp, which was often beyond the reach of slaves. There were as many other gumbos as imagination could invent. Normally a gumbo was served with rice, or white corn. Through much of the South, yellow corn was thought to be fit only for animals and Yankees. It was sprinkled with powdered black-green sassafras (today's filé powder), a favorite seasoning that came from American Indians, and could be collected in the woods. Gumbos were at once a staple in the daily diet of field slaves. They also came to be greatly valued on high tables in old New Orleans.[241]

Gumbos emerged in Louisiana's Afro-French era during the eighteenth century. An early description of "gumbo filé and rice" as a meal eaten by slaves survives from 1764.[242] Another early and more detailed discussion of gumbo in print was published in 1802 by Dr. John Sibley, a New England surgeon, holder of offices in Louisiana, and a close student of local customs. He wrote about a "dish they Call gumbo which is made of the Ochre [okra] into a Thick kind of Soop and Eat with Rice, it is the food of every Body for Dinner & Supper."[243]

The broad reach of gumbos through Louisiana as "the food of every Body" by 1802 had a gestation that began well before that date. It developed from the creative interplay of French and African and American Indian elements, with later Spanish and Anglo additions thrown in. The word itself, "gumbo," has been traced to Bantu-speaking slaves from Central Africa, possibly those who arrived in the slave ship *Néréide* (1731) with 294 Congolese on board.[244]

But if the name came from Congo, the ingredients came from everywhere: Africa (okra), Europe (*roux*), and American Indians (filé). But the cooks tended to come from Africa. This dynamic and ever-changing Afro-Franco-American foodway continued to develop through Louisiana's Spanish and American periods. In the twenty-first century Louisiana's gumbos have become more dynamic than ever. They remain an endlessly creative signature dish in one of North America's most lively regional cuisines. The more a Louisiana gumbo changes, the more this culinary tradition retains its character and creativity: *plus ça change, plus c'est la même chose.*

LOUISIANA'S ENDURING LEGACY OF
AFRO-FRENCH CULTURE

The founding era of formal French dominion in Louisiana was remarkably short-lived, given its very long reach. It lasted less than three generations, from 1699 to 1763. African slaves in this French period arrived mostly in the years from 1718 to 1731 (later waves of different character are another story). But in that first short span of French hegemony, a unique Afro-French culture began to emerge, and it continues to have a strong presence three centuries later. Both French and African components were very mixed, but they were framed within strong clusters of custom and belief.

Some of the prime movers were Africans themselves. Others of particular importance were French-speaking Canadian leaders such as Bienville and du Pratz, who took a genuine interest in African and American Indian cultures. In different ways both of these men shared ideals of humanity that derived from their Roman Catholic faith, French culture, and Enlightenment values. Their attitudes and acts made possible the growth of creative interactions with African slaves. As the French might say, to both of them, *Chapeau!*

At the same time, African leaders such as Samba Bambara, Louis Congo, "Louis-*dit*-Foy of the Bambara Nation," Julie-*dit*-Mama Comba, and Marion of Natchitoches moved back and forth across ethnic lines and engaged both African and European cultures in their lives, with varying degrees of success. That difficult and dangerous process ended in disaster for some, and success for others. At the same time it created a creative cultural process that still continues. It has a presence in American lives and has spread in different forms to open societies throughout the world.

At an early date, before 1763, we also see strong evidence of association, solidarity, and comity among groups of African slaves. Some derived from small clusters of Africans with related ethnic and regional origins. Others formed on plantations, and small neighborhoods in New Orleans. These associations took many forms: Sunday gatherings, market relations, and more. Many examples appear in the writings of Le Page du Pratz and in the records of the Superior Council.

As we have seen, the clusters most frequently mentioned in these sources were small groups of Bamana- and Mande-speaking slaves. Other references referred to slaves of ethnic groups from the Bight of Benin, and also to Bantu slaves from Congo. Other slave associations also formed across ethnic, regional, and linguistic lines.

The Cabildo, formerly New Orleans City Hall

All this appeared in the period of French sovereignty, from 1699 to 1763. Much evidence shows that African slaves were not isolated from one another in this long French period. From an early date, complex patterns of association were highly developed among them. They contributed to a persistent diversity of Afro-French cultures in Louisiana.

LOUISIANA BECOMES A SPANISH COLONY: FURTHER GROWTH OF POPULATION DIVERSITY

In 1763, the elderly King Louis XV of France was growing weary of Louisiana and its endless challenges. That year, he and his ministers decided to give the colony to his cousin, Carlos III of Spain. The Treaty of Paris, which ended the Seven Years' War, recognized Louisiana as a Spanish possession.

The wheels turned slowly in Madrid. Spanish officials did not arrive in Louisiana until 1766, perhaps because they expected trouble. The French *habitants* had not been consulted, and they rose in rebellion against their new rulers. The first Spanish officers were encouraged to depart without violence, but the ministers of Carlos III could not allow that act of *lèse-majesté* to stand. In 1769, Spanish authorities sent a powerful naval squadron and two thousand troops under a tough no-nonsense Irish commander, General Alejandro O'Reilly. He arrested thirteen Louisiana French leaders, tried them himself as judge and jury, and executed six, to the shock of French inhabitants.

The Spanish regime firmly established itself in Louisiana, but it never fully recovered from that brutal beginning. Spanish officials ran Louisiana for thirty-four years, from 1769 to 1803. They made a major effort to incorporate the colony into their empire as a *barrera* or buffer zone between New Spain and English-speaking provinces to the north. To that end, Spanish leaders also made a major effort to increase Louisiana's population, and they also

General Alejandro O'Reilly

Bernardo de Gálvez, governor of Spanish Louisiana

sought to make it less French. The result was yet another great increase in its cultural diversity.[245]

The new rulers recruited a military force of Spanish-speaking Canary Islanders with their families. As many as 2,500 "Isleños" settled in southern Louisiana, many along Bayou LaFourche. Mortality was heavy, but a unique ethnic community took root and began to grow. Today, more than ten thousand Louisianians call themselves Isleños or Islanders. They take pride in descent from Canary forebears.[246]

Other Hispanic immigrants were recruited from the southern Spanish provinces of Málaga and Granada, near Gibraltar. In southwestern Louisiana they occupied an area called New Iberia. Descendants still describe themselves as Malagueños.[247]

Spanish leaders made special efforts to attract Catholics of many ethnic stocks: Acadian Catholics, Irish Catholics, German Catholics, and Sicilian Catholics. They were less happy about English Protestants, who were regarded as heretics, rebels, republicans, and all-around bad neighbors. But the primary goal of Spanish leaders was to increase the population of their new buffer colony. In 1789 and 1790, Spanish leaders overcame their reluctance and invited emigrants from the United States to settle in northern Louisiana and West Florida.

Secretary of State Thomas Jefferson was delighted. He wrote to President George Washington, on April 2, 1791, "I wish a hundred thousand of our inhabitants would accept the invitation. It will be the means of delivering to us peaceably, what may otherwise cost us a war." As early as 1791 Jefferson was hungry for the acquisition of Louisiana.[248]

The result was a swarm of sons and daughters of planters and slaveholders to Louisiana from the Chesapeake, the Carolinas, and Georgia. They occupied Louisiana's beautiful and fertile "Florida Parishes," east of Baton Rouge and north of New Orleans. By 1800, much of this area was English-speaking. North British borderers also moved from the backcountry of the United States into the Red River Valley in northwest Louisiana.

In sixteen years these many movements trebled the population of Louisiana, from about 11,000 in 1769 to more than 31,000 by 1785. They also increased the cultural diversity of Louisiana's population and its expanding settlements.

SPANISH REVIVAL OF THE AFRICAN
SLAVE TRADE, 1769–96

Spanish officials also reopened Louisiana's slave trade. A complex sequence of proclamations permitted the importation of slaves to Louisiana from every country at peace with Spain. Slave traders were welcomed to Spanish Louisiana, and they arrived from many nations. This second wave of African slave imports began by 1769. It continued on a small scale in the 1770s, greatly increased from 1783 to 1796, fell sharply from 1796 to 1800, was shut down for a time, and rose yet again from 1801 to 1803.

Altogether, careful studies estimate that between twelve thousand and fifteen thousand slaves came to Louisiana during the entire Spanish era, mostly in peak periods of 1783–96 and 1801–03. This second wave of African slaves was two or three times larger than the first wave in Louisiana's French era.[249]

Most of these slaves were native Africans who came direct from Africa itself, or were transshipped through West Indian and North American ports. Very few were "Atlantic Creoles" from the West Indies and other places in this Spanish period. In some years, imports of slaves from French and British islands in the Caribbean were forbidden outright by Spanish authorities.

Census data were collected frequently from 1763 to 1800, and tended to be roughly consistent in their results. Together they show that the slave population multiplied rapidly in Louisiana from 4,598 in the census of 1763 to 24,264 in 1800, an increase of 528 percent in thirty-seven years. The entire free population of Louisiana increased at a slightly higher rate (543 percent), but slaves continued to be a majority of Louisiana's population, at about 55 percent through the Spanish years.[250]

The proportion of native-born Africans rose even more rapidly, from 30 percent of all Louisiana slaves in 1771 to 60 percent in 1778–79, and 75 percent in 1782, despite several short-lived attempts to shut down the slave trade. These growing numbers of Africans during the Spanish period were large enough to "re-africanize" Louisiana, in the judgment of Gwendolyn Hall and Gilbert Din. Near the end of the Spanish era, native Africans may have become a majority of Louisiana slaves.[251]

Through much of the Spanish period, this new wave of African slaves was brought to Louisiana by ships and traders of many nations. Much of this traffic was in the hands of English slave traders. Scottish merchants were also active in the West Florida port of Pensacola, and they traded on the Mississippi River as far north as Baton Rouge and Natchez. Other carriers were French, Spanish, Portuguese, and Dutch, as well as Rhode Island merchants based in New England. To repeat, several studies find that in this seaborne transatlantic trade "almost all slaves . . . came directly from Africa."[252]

Patterns of African origin in Spanish Louisiana were more diverse than in the French era. In the absence of comprehensive import records, the best evidence for African ethnic origins comes from two careful quantitative inquiries by Gwendolyn Hall. One study centered on a large sample from inventories of estates in Pointe Coupée Parish, just north of Baton Rouge, through much of the Spanish period from 1771 to 1802. Altogether 2,632 slaves appeared in these records. About half had been born in Louisiana. Of the rest, African origins were given for 798.

These data are most useful for the mix of African origins. These slaves came from most African regions in the Atlantic trade, from Senegal in the north to Congo and Angola in the south, plus a few from Mozambique in East Africa.

Inventories of estates often attempted to list the African ethnicity of slaves. In Pointe Coupée inventories alone, slaves were listed as coming from more than fifty known African ethnic groups, and another thirty groups that have not been identified by historians.[253]

Once again, as everywhere in North America, this broad diversity of African origins included regional and ethnic clusters. The patterns of clustering in the Spanish period differed from the French era. In the Pointe Coupée sample, about 81 percent of Africans with known origins came from three large regions, and distinct ethnic groups. Slaves from Benin now were the largest regional presence in Pointe Coupée, at 29 percent of known African origins. Most were clusters of Yoruba, Chamba, and Fon people.

A second major region of origin was Senegambia at 27 percent, with larger clusters of Bamana and Mandingo people, and smaller groups of Wolof and Fulbe. Bamana slaves were much less dominant than they had been in Louisiana's French period.

A third regional group, about 24 percent, were Bantu speakers from Central Africa. Nearly all were called Congo slaves in Louisiana. Together these Congo slaves comprised nearly a quarter of Africans arriving in Louisiana the Spanish era.

The remaining 19 percent of Pointe Coupée slaves were widely scattered in origin through many African regions and ethnic groups. Altogether this second wave of slave trading created greater diversity of African origins in Louisiana. It also greatly increased the flow of Africans from Benin, the Gold Coast, Nigeria, and especially from Congo. But the clustering of slaves continued.[254]

Another study of native-born Africans in Louisiana's Spanish era was made by Thomas Klingler from data in Gwendolyn Hall's Louisiana Slave Database. Altogether, he found data on 26,364 African slaves in Louisiana's Spanish era, of which 14,406 made some reference to places of origin, and 7,981 (55.2 percent) were of African birth. Creoles born in Louisiana were 5,366 (37.1 percent), and slaves from Anglo-America were 604 (4.1 percent). All others were 455 (3.2 percent).

Of 7,981 African-born slaves in the Spanish era, 1,699 (21.3 percent) came from many ethnic groups in Senegambia—mostly Mandingo (459), Wolof (260), and a much smaller Bamana group (112), more than in the earlier French era. An additional group of 771 (9.7 percent) came from Guinea south of Senegambia. Many were Mande speakers, and had much in common with Senegambian slaves. Together these two regions accounted for nearly a third (31 percent) of Louisiana's African slaves in the Spanish era.

The next largest regional cluster came from Congo in West Central Africa: 1,060 slaves (13.3 percent). And another 942 (11.8 percent) came from a broad coastal region centered around Benin but reaching west into what is now Ghana and east to parts of Nigeria. It included slaves of many ethnic groups including Chamba, Yoruba, and Fon. Later in the eighteenth century another group of slaves was increasingly identified as Mina. Regional origins are not given for 3,509 Africans (44.0 percent).[255]

Other sources for Louisiana's Spanish period from 1769 to 1802 tell us that Africans within these broad regional clusters formed local groups that became functioning communities. Evidence appears in legal documents for a group of Mina slaves on an estate at Pointe Coupée. They organized dances to which only Mina men were invited, though women of other African nations were welcome. Mina slaves in Pointe Coupée also had functional connections with a larger "organized Mina Community" in New Orleans, about one hundred miles distant.[256]

In other parts of Louisiana during the Spanish period, newly arrived slaves also founded associations of other kinds. At Natchitoches in northwest Louisiana the local commandant, Captain Athanase de Mézières, discovered in 1770 that slaves in his area organized "bands" among themselves, broadly based on place of birth. One band were called "Africans." Another were "Creoles" who had been born in Louisiana. Captain de Mézières was alarmed by these groups. He issued "ordinances," forbidding slaves to "form associations based on their place of origin, under pain of *carcan* and whip." The associations continued.[257]

Captain de Mézières listed the many activities of these groups, which tell us what these slave associations did, and why he was unable to stop them. He forbade slaves "to assemble for balls, day or night, with violins or drums, or for any other purposes, under penalty of the whip and twenty *livres* fine on the master." He outlawed "wandering without permission," and forbade slaves to carry "heavy sticks," or "to own knives or firearms or horses" or "to sell any items without permission. He decreed that "Black women guilty of prostitution" were to "be exposed and whipped," and white men who employed them were to be "punished to the full extent of the law." Captain de Mézières was a busy man, but the slaves in Natchitoches appear to have been busier. Many of their activities were done in the open. Their gatherings were tolerated by some masters, and actively encouraged by others, as long as they got to work on time.[258]

SPANISH LAW, AFRICAN RESISTANCE, AND A REFORM TRADITION

Carlos III, King of Spain (1759–88), began to take an interest in his new colony of Louisiana. He was the model of an eighteenth-century enlightened despot, and one of the most able princes of his age. Carlos tried to govern Louisiana wisely and well, and he was especially concerned about the condition of African slaves.[259]

When Spanish authorities gained effective control of the colony in 1769, they were appalled by the cruelties that some French masters and mistresses in Louisiana inflicted upon their slaves, and also by the level of endemic personal violence that pervaded the former French colony. In Pointe Coupée Parish, 1779, a master named Bara tortured his slave Geneviève so severely that she was badly crippled. After Bara's death, his widow and son continued to abuse their slaves. Their cook, Perinne Négresse, aged twenty, refused to mate with another slave. She was punished by being beaten frequently, and kept on a long chain like a wild animal. Perinne told the court that "she had no complaints about food or clothes, but her mistress choked her all the time, and it was hard to work always on a chain." [260]

When Spanish authorities arrived in Louisiana, they allowed slaves to bring complaints of maltreatment by their owners, and even to travel to New Orleans, be heard by the Spanish governor, and be protected from reprisal. In Pointe Coupée Parish, case after case was heard by the Spanish *comandante* at the local fort. They were often tales of savage violence by masters against slaves, sometimes by masters against other masters, occasionally by slaves against masters, but rarely by slaves against slaves.

With the encouragement of Carlos III, Louisiana slaves were placed under Spanish laws that offered them more protections than did the French *Code Noir*. Spain's laws on slavery were very old, the oldest in active use throughout the western world. They derived from *Las Siete Partidas*, the sixth or seventh section of a law code issued by King Alfonso the Wise of Castile in 1263–65. They also combined elements of Justinian's Roman Code of *Corpus Juris Civilis* (529, 534–65), and Catholic canon law traditions.

In an irony of legal history, Spain's medieval slave code was in some ways more enlightened and progressive than modern slave laws of other nations. *Las Siete Partidas* did not recognize race or racism. It held that all slaves were human beings, with many rights and protections against abuse by masters and mistresses. Further, if slaves converted to Christianity they gained other rights of marriage, parenthood, association, and humane treatment.[261]

Later Spanish laws also recognized *coartación*, the right of slaves to purchase their freedom, even from masters unwilling to let them go. French slaveholders in Louisiana were strongly hostile to this Spanish tradition, which was introduced to the colony in 1770. Several early Spanish governors sought a middle way between French and Spanish customs. But after 1790, the three Spanish governors, Carondelet, Gayoso, and Salcedo, worked to protect the rights of slaves.[262]

Some Louisiana planters in 1790 had different attitudes. They described their slaves as "indocile and inquiet," and with a "dissatisfied and rebellious humor." From the French, and even more from arriving Anglo-American planters, we also begin to see a continuing expansion of ideological racism in this period, with growing demands for deference of all Blacks to all whites, and racist contempt for all people of color, which was rejected by some Spanish officials.[263]

In 1791, and again in 1792, small revolts occurred in Louisiana. Then in 1795 a larger conspiracy was detected in the parishes of Pointe Coupée and St. Landry, with linkages through much of the colony from Natchitoches to New Orleans. Many slaves and at least three free whites were arrested. This event was perceived to be part of revolutionary movements that were sweeping the Atlantic world.[264]

The response of Spanish governor-general Francisco Luis Héctor de Carondelet was complex and creative. Carondelet took seriously the reports of a slave conspiracy, mobilizing the full strength of regular troops and militia. After arrests and trials, twenty-three slaves were hanged. Another thirty-one slaves and three free whites were sentenced to hard labor and exiled to other Spanish colonies. The slave trade was forbidden for four years, and a slave police force was created, with severe penalties for resistance.

At the same time, Carondelet ordered sweeping reforms in the treatment of slaves on Louisiana plantations. He ordered that each slave was to be given at least a barrel of corn in the ear each month, plus a plot of land to raise his own crops. Every slave was to be allowed at least two and a half hours rest every day. Masters were required to supply male slaves with a linen shirt and trousers in the summer and a warm coat for the winter. The purpose for all of this, in Carondelet's way of thinking, was to "alienate them from the wish of acquiring a freedom which has cost so much blood to those of San Domingo."[265]

Spanish governor Francisco Luis Héctor, Baron
de Carondelet

THE RISE OF A NEW CLASS:
FREE PEOPLE OF COLOR IN SPANISH LOUISIANA

Another important policy change by Spanish leaders concerned free people
of color. Suddenly their numbers began to grow in an unprecedented way.
That rapid increase was among the most important consequences of Spanish
control in Louisiana.

In the colony's French period, free people of African descent, *les affranchis*,
were few and far between. We have met one of the first, royal executioner
Louis Congo, circa 1727. Their numbers grew slowly. In 1763 a French census found only about ninety free people of African ancestry in New Orleans.
Their numbers remained small, and their prospects were not bright. Emancipated Africans in French Louisiana were sometimes reenslaved.[266]

Then came the Spanish, and they brought a more open way of thinking about slavery, rooted in their unique legal tradition of rights. Spanish law had long recognized many ways in which slaves could become free. It could happen by an act of manumission when a master decided to emancipate a slave. It could also occur by the ruling of a court, if a master abused or severely mistreated a slave. And freedom could be granted by the Spanish government as a reward for public service, or for serving in a position that was restricted to free people. Most important was *coartación*, of slaves to buy freedom.

The result was a rapid increase in *nègres libres*, or free people of color. In census data for New Orleans, their numbers rose from about 90 in 1763 to 315 in 1777, 820 in 1788, and 1,566 in 1805. A majority were female, but numbers of free males increased more rapidly. Gender ratios among *nègres libres* rose from 47 to 66 males per 100 females. By contrast, gender ratios among free whites in New Orleans fell from 175 to 115 males per 100 females from 1777 to 1805.[267]

A NEW ELITE: SPANISH LOUISIANA'S FREE BLACK MILITARY OFFICERS

Spanish rulers also made another change in Louisiana. As in many of their colonies, they made extensive use of free Black militia units that went far beyond French practice, even to requiring compulsory military service. These units were divided by color into *moreno* (dark) and *pardo* (light) companies, with their own officers. These *nègre libre* militiamen were paid for active service, in some cases at the same rates for whites. They saw active service and were used for many purposes.[268]

When Spain joined the American War of Independence, the Black militia of Louisiana were mobilized for three years. They fought British Regulars, and defeated them in three campaigns at Baton Rouge (1779), Mobile (1780), and Pensacola (1781). The king of Spain awarded medals of honor to seven free Black officers in Louisiana: Manuel Noel Carrière, Carlos Calpha, Pedros Calpha, Simon Calpha, Juan Batista Hugon, Francisco Dorville, and Nicolas Bacus Boisclair. They took pride in a reputation for honor and courage. With the medals came annual pensions and bonuses of 140 to 300 pesos.[269]

After the Peace of 1783, free Black Spanish militia were mustered for many tasks in Louisiana. They were sent in pursuit of maroons and were mobilized to help restore broken levees. In 1788 they fought a catastrophic fire that burned a large part of New Orleans. The militia officers, both *moreno* (dark) and *pardo* (light), became men of property. Several held slaves. Their families frequently intermarried and became leaders of a growing free community in Spanish Louisiana.[270]

RACE MIXING IN SPANISH LOUISIANA

Another strong trend in the Spanish era was an increase in race mixing. High officeholders in the colony set an example. Lieutenant Governor Nicolás María Vidal openly acknowledged at least six children by four different women of color, and he included among his heirs all who survived.[271]

Overall, Spanish census returns from 1771 to 1791 found that people of *sang-mêlé*, or mixed blood, were "the fastest growing segment of the population," in the words of historian Jennifer Spear. In 1771, a Spanish census listed 316 people of mixed blood in New Orleans, of which 248 were slaves and 68 were free (21 percent). Twenty years later, the census of 1791 found "almost 900 people of mixed blood" in New Orleans alone. Of that number, "nearly 600" were free (67 percent).[272]

Their social status was rising rapidly, in many ways at once. Jennifer Spear wrote that "by the last quarter of the eighteenth century, many New Orleanians had tangled ancestries." Among them were some of Louisiana's most eminent families such as the extended Toutant-Beauregard clan which later included Pierre Gustave Toutant Beauregard, one of the highest-ranking generals in the southern Confederacy. Historian Kimberly Hanger found similar but stronger trends from 1769 to 1803.[273]

The rapid growth of mixed unions in this region happened in many ways at once. Here again we find another story of diversity in Louisiana. Recent scholarship by Emily Clark has transformed our understanding of the legendary New Orleans quadroons. At the same time, she has greatly enlarged prevailing interpretations of race mixing in Louisiana.[274]

Clark found much evidence that most young women of mixed African and European ancestry did not become quadroon concubines of wealthy white men. Much larger numbers of these free young women of color married free young men of similar origins. Like most unions in Louisiana during the Spanish period, these were mainly common-law marriages. But increasing numbers were recognized in various ways by the Catholic Church, sometimes in a later marriage ceremony, and more often in the baptism of children from these unions. Other research has also found that *pardo* and *moreno* free Negroes tended to marry others of similar color. In all these ways, enduring marriages among free people of color were much the most important form of union.[275]

Other forms of union have received more attention. Among them was concubinage between quadroon young women and older white men of wealth. These linkages have inspired a sensational literature about beautiful young quadroons, elaborate quadroon balls, and negotiated contracts between hard-bargaining mothers and rich old white men of means. More than a few of these relationships actually existed, but Emily Clark finds persuasive evidence that they were far less common than traditional marriages between young partners of similar age, ancestry, rank, and status. Interracial concubinage contributed more to the legends of New Orleans than to the lives of its people.[276]

Another sexual pattern was prostitution in New Orleans. This was a very active business in most seaport cities throughout the United States, especially in the early national period (ca. 1789–1815). In that era, by far the largest numbers and proportions of prostitutes on record appeared not in New Orleans but New York City.

Later, New Orleans became more notorious for its sex trade, in part because legal prostitution persisted longer than in other American cities, and also because Woodrow Wilson's secretary of the navy Josephus Daniels mounted a national campaign to shut it down, as part of his campaign to preserve the virtue of the United States Navy. Another factor in New Orleans and its reputation was the active role of legal "fancy houses" south of the French Quarter as nurseries of jazz.

Quantitative evidence of prostitution in other cities reinforces the findings of Emily Clark that patterns of sexual relations involving young women of color did not center on concubinage or prostitution, but on traditional marriages in which young women of color built stable partnerships with male partners like themselves. These unions were fundamental to the growth of community among Louisiana's free people of color during the nineteenth century.[277]

THE LONG LEGACY OF LOUISIANA'S
SHORT SPANISH PERIOD, 1767–1800

Spain's control of Louisiana lasted only thirty-four years. It did not take full effect until 1767, and ended abruptly with the painful "retrocession" of the colony to France in 1800. But in that brief span, Spanish leaders introduced many enduring changes. They increased the population of Louisiana and expanded its diversity. A major effort was made to recruit Europeans of mixed ethnic origins. And at the same time, they revived the slave trade, and extended it through a broad range of African regions. Both of those efforts further diversified Louisiana's population.

Spanish officials tended to be authoritarian leaders who ran the colony from the top down. But like their enlightened monarch Carlos III, some of their governors were forward-looking men of reason, justice, and decency. Specially so was long-serving governor Francisco Luis Héctor, Baron de Carondelet. Historians are divided on Carondelet, but he had a deep and sustained concern for the welfare of African slaves. Under the protections of Spanish law, treatment of slaves changed somewhat for the better. Opportunities increased for assembly and association of slaves in New Orleans. The first recorded Sunday gatherings at Congo Square occurred in the Spanish period.

Emancipations multiplied at a rapid rate, partly under Spanish law of *coartación*, as discussed earlier. Free people of color greatly expanded their numbers, increased their wealth, and improved their social condition. Some rose to positions of power and influence as commissioned military officers. Many intermarried and created an interlocking web of extended families of color in New Orleans.

Under Spanish leadership, the population of Louisiana not only grew more diverse. It also became more creative in its diversity. The cultural pluralism of Spanish Louisiana produced results that have persisted in Louisiana through many generations, even to our time.

THE UNITED STATES BUYS LOUISIANA, 1803

Then suddenly the history of Louisiana was radically transformed yet again by another impulsive act of a European despot. Napoleon Bonaparte had seized power in Paris by a coup in 1799. He proceeded to march a French army across the Alps and defeated Austrian forces in a close-fought battle at Marengo in 1800. A general European peace followed at Lunéville and Amiens in 1801 and 1802.

With a promise of stability in Europe, Napoleon decided to recover the lost empire of France in America. He reclaimed Louisiana from Spain, by ordering its "retrocession" in 1800. And he sent an army to conquer Haiti and restore the lost French sugar colony of Saint-Domingue. To his amazement, his disciplined legions were defeated by forces of former slaves, and destroyed by tropical fevers.

The European powers began to prepare for another war against this restless and very dangerous man. In an instant Napoleon turned away from Haiti, and he told Foreign Minister Talleyrand, "I renounce Louisiana."[278] Rather than risk Louisiana's loss to the Royal Navy in the next war, Napoleon ordered its immediate sale to the United States. The price was $15 million for the entire Mississippi Valley from the western edge of the American republic to the crest of the Rocky Mountains. At the time, nobody knew the exact size of this immense area. Later it was found to be 828,000 square miles, four times the size of Napoleonic France. The cost came to $18 a square mile. Under its first governor, James Wilkinson, the Louisiana Purchase doubled the area of the United States and gave it a position of strategic dominance in North America. British leaders were deeply displeased. They called the Louisiana Purchase unlawful and looked for a way to undo it, which became a driving purpose of their Mississippi military campaign in 1814–15.[279]

James Wilkinson, first U.S. governor of Louisiana
Territory

RACE SLAVERY IN LOUISIANA

The struggle against racism had grown more difficult in the late eighteenth century. The economy of the lower Mississippi Valley began to expand rapidly. This new pattern of accelerating economic growth started during Louisiana's Spanish period, from about 1793 to 1803, as it did also in much of the United States at the same time.[280]

Through Louisiana's French era (1699–1767), rates of economic growth had been low, slow, and highly unstable. Overall, rates of gain in colonial Louisiana's domestic product per capita had been positive, but barely so, probably with an average increase of about 0.2 to 0.4 percent per annum, punctuated by weak surges and strong declines.

Fluctuations in rates of economic growth were keyed mainly to rolling rhythms of international warfare in Western Europe and North America. Before 1789 Britain's North American colonies also grew at about 0.3 to 0.6 percent a year on the average, only a little faster than French Louisiana. The highest rates of sustained economic growth in the western world during the eighteenth century were in the economy of Great Britain, where real product per capita advanced at an average rate of about one percent a year. This came on top of population growth.[281]

Then, during the period from 1789 to 1806, average annual rates of economic growth in the new republic of the United States suddenly accelerated into the range of 1.3 to 1.7 percent in net national product per capita. This surge came in addition to very rapid population increase, of more than 3 percent each year. Gross economic growth began to approach 4.3 to 4.7 percent.

Economic historians have debated the cause of this acceleration. One major factor throughout the United States was the achievement of enduring peace and political stability with the framing and ratification of the federal Constitution in 1787–89 and then enactment of the Bill of Rights in 1789–91. Another major factor was the legitimation of the new republic by George Washington's presidency (1789–97), an expanding base of support for republican institutions, and a peaceful transfer of power from one political party to another in the contested elections of 1800–1801.

Econometric scholars believe that another major cause was a sudden growth of global opportunity for American trade during the French Revolution and the era of Napoleon. Several historians have found that a major stimulus was a surge in the re-export trade of foreign commodities throughout northern seaports. Slavery was a small part of that process. From 1776 to

1804, the northern states and territories committed themselves to the gradual abolition of slavery and shifted to a system of free labor.[282]

Then, after a period of decline, systems of slavery below the Mason-Dixon line also began to expand again in the late eighteenth and early nineteenth centuries. A major instrument of growth in these regions was the expansion of cotton production to meet growing demand from textile manufacturers in Britain, Europe, and the northern states. In the eighteenth century, cotton was a difficult crop. Part of the problem was the variant quality of seeds and strains.[283]

A breakthrough was made in 1806, by Walter Burling (1762–1810), a cotton planter near Natchez. On a diplomatic mission to Mexico, he observed a different variety of cotton growing there. Spanish rulers guarded it as a state secret. Burling bought dolls for his three daughters, stuffed the dolls with seeds of this "Mexican green seed cotton," and smuggled them into the United States. He planted the seeds near Natchez and found that they flourished in the lower Mississippi Valley. Burling also gave some of them to William Dunbar, a planter and botanist who discovered other advantages. When Mexican green seed was crossbred with other stocks, cotton plants tended to ripen more nearly at the same time. They also improved the efficiency of new types of cotton gins, which separated cotton fibers from seeds.

Other inventions changed the marketing of cotton from bags to bales and created machines for the baling process. Production and productivity surged on cotton plantations in the lower Mississippi Valley, and spread rapidly to other southern regions called the Black Belt (after its dark fertile soil), and the Yazoo Delta (between Memphis and Vicksburg), and East Texas.[284] In 1977, econometric historian Franklee Whartenby developed quantitative measures of land and labor productivity in cotton production, and documented their importance in the economic history of the early American republic.[285] And again in 2008, Alan L. Olmstead and Paul W. Rhode combined these findings with another generation of scholarship on biological innovation and economic growth.[286]

Other processes also transformed the productivity of sugar plantations in Louisiana. Its history began with many failed attempts to raise sugarcane in marginal environments. A pivotal figure was Jean Étienne de Boré (1741–1820), a failed indigo planter. In 1791, with the help of sugar producers from Saint-Domingue, de Boré and his kinsman Jean Noel d'Estrehan experimented with new varieties of Otaheite cane from Tahiti in Polynesia. In

1817 Jacques Coiron tried yet another strain called "ribbon cane," which was more hardy and quicker to mature. This large process of many small experiments opened broad areas of Louisiana to sugar production, and transformed its economy, but at heavy cost to the slaves who did the field labor, and the even more cruel and dangerous process of sugar refining.[287]

Major progress was made in improvement of sugar refining, and this change operated differently in its consequences for slaves. A central figure was Norbert Rillieux (1806–94), a free person of color who was the son of a wealthy planter and his free common-law African American wife. Rillieux was sent abroad to leading engineering schools in France, which were more highly developed than in the United States. He studied the problem of refining sugar, which had been done on the plantation by boiling cane juice in a series of open cauldrons. The method was slow, inefficient, and dangerous to slaves who did the work and often suffered severe burns.

Rillieux invented a better way of evaporating and condensing sugar in sealed vacuum pans. It could be done at low temperatures with more efficiency, and much greater safety. He built a sugar mill on his plantation six miles from New Orleans, and it worked. Here again a series of many small improvements created a revolution in Louisiana's sugar industry.[288]

As Louisiana's economy gained strength in these and other ways, its population began to grow even more rapidly than before. In decennial United States Census returns, the total population of Louisiana (within present state boundaries) doubled from 77,000 in 1810 to 153,000 in 1820, then doubled again to 352,000 in the census of 1840, and doubled once more to 708,000 in 1860, when a long period of rapid growth ended with the Civil War.[289]

SLAVE TRADING IN AMERICAN LOUISIANA

With the growth of Louisiana's economy, the slave trade began to surge as never before. Numbers of slaves grew from 24,264 in 1800 to a peak of 331,726 in 1860. This third wave was by far the fastest and largest increase of slavery in the region's history.[290] Human bondage in the lower Mississippi Valley rose in this period to its highest level of profitability in American history. At the same time, it sank to its lowest ebb of moral depravity, systemic violence, extreme cruelty, and gross criminality by the laws of that time and place. Some of the worst things happened in the new American internal slave trade. The largest single movement of slaves to Louisiana came by interstate migration from other parts of the United States. In early years a large part of this traffic was a movement of entire workforces of plantation slaves with their masters.

Much larger was the subsequent flow of many thousands of individual slaves or fragments of families, who were bought and sent south by slave traders. Some were marched overland in coffles. Others were sent in riverboats on western rivers. Many more were shipped south in coastal schooners and brigs to New Orleans.

In the nineteenth century this interstate slave trade to Louisiana and the lower South became a huge web of movement from every part of the United States. The largest traffic in early years flowed from the Chesapeake states of Virginia and Maryland, on a scale beyond imagining.

An eyewitness was Lorenzo Ivy, a Virginia slave, born in 1850, who lived in Danville, a rail hub on Virginia's Southside. He remembered, "I've seen droves of Negroes brought in heah on foot goin' Souf to be sol.' Each one have an old tow sack on his back wif everything he got in it. Over de hills dey come in lines reachin' as far as you kin see. Dey walk in double lines chained together in twos. Dey walk 'em heah to de railroad an ship 'em Souf lak cattle. Truely son, de haf has never been tol'." [291]

Later, slaves from South Carolina and Georgia were thought to do better in Louisiana's climate. Growing numbers of slaves also came from Kentucky and Tennessee. A smaller but substantial flow were free people of color kidnapped by gangs of criminals who operated throughout the free states as far north as upstate New York. The victims were delivered to "slave pens" in Baltimore, Memphis, Alexandria, and Richmond. They were sold to traders, and systematically "broken" by severe beatings and torture. Some of the worst of these monstrous slave prisons were in the city of Washington, very near the Capitol building.

In the new republic, much of this interstate trade went South in small coastal brigs and schooners. They commonly sailed in the dark of night, skirted the Atlantic coast, and delivered their human cargo to the New Orleans slave market, which became for a time the largest in the world. It was a business in which dealers and purchasers learned to ask no questions about the origins of slaves. In the nineteenth century, a large and growing component of the American economy was not only a system of organized inhumanity. It was also a criminal enterprise, brutal beyond imagining. [292]

CARIBBEAN MIGRATION TO LOUISIANA

In this period, a second and very different migration of slaves also came to Louisiana from the West Indies. It started with refugees from Haiti, a mix of French masters and mistresses, enslaved Africans, and free people of color.

This movement began slowly at about a hundred a year from 1791 to 1797 and rose above a thousand by 1803. Larger numbers sought refuge in Cuba. In 1808–09, Napoleon's invasion of Spain created a crisis in the Caribbean. Authorities in Cuba required francophone refugees to take an oath of allegiance to Spain. Many refused and were ordered to leave the island. A statute in Louisiana had prohibited the entry of non-white migrants from the Caribbean in Louisiana Territory, in part for similar reasons. But in 1809, a humanitarian exception was made for refugees from Cuba.

Within that one year more than ten thousand masters, slaves, and free people of color left Cuba for Louisiana. Many settled in New Orleans. The city's leading French newspaper, the *Moniteur de la Louisiane*, published the official count of arrivals from Cuba alone. In 1809 they included 9,059 people, divided in three groups. The smallest group were 2,731 whites, mostly male (1,373 men, 703 women, 655 children). A larger group were 3,102 free people of color, mainly female (428 men, 1,377 women, and 1,297 children). The largest were 3,226 slaves who were more mixed (962 men, 1,330 females, 934 children). Lesser flows came to Louisiana direct from Haiti, and other West Indian islands. This migration of planters, slaves, and free people of color introduced important elements of Caribbean culture to New Orleans.[293]

REVIVED ATLANTIC SLAVE TRADE FROM AFRICA, 1803–25

Yet a third flow in this large movement was the revival of the transatlantic slave trade that came from Africa in the early nineteenth century. The flow was specially heavy from 1803 to about 1823, despite many laws against it.

In 1803, the Jefferson administration briefly attempted to prohibit foreign slave trade to Louisiana, but the law was not enforced. In 1803 at least three French slave ships arrived from Africa with Spanish licenses. They were allowed to sell their slaves. After the Louisiana Purchase two British slave ships appeared with Congo slaves, who were much in demand on sugar plantations. The British captains also were permitted to sell their slaves to eager buyers.[294]

From 1803 to 1808, federal law in Louisiana was interpreted to allow slaves to come from Africa by way of Baltimore, Norfolk, and Charleston. This traffic brought hundreds of African slaves to Louisiana.[295]

A more general prohibition of the foreign slave trade by the U.S. Congress followed for the entire country, to take effect on January 1, 1808. Once again, Louisianians found a way around it. In February 1810, they brought a case appealing the confiscation of the slave vessel *Amiable Lucy* in New Orleans. Their suit was heard in federal court, and Chief Justice John Marshall ruled that as the territorial legislature "had never passed any laws prohibiting the practice," the congressional abolition of the Atlantic slave trade in 1808 "did not apply to Louisiana." The imperatives of slavery and the slave trade did strange things to constitutional law, even in John Marshall's court.[296]

For many years after 1808, an illicit African slave trade also flourished in Louisiana, more so than in any other part of the United States. The old freebooter tradition became more active than ever before. Central figures were three brothers of the legendary Laffite family: Pierre, Jean, and Antoine. Historian William C. Davis has reconstructed their history, and their active roles in the slave trade. They came from a family in the southwest of France between the River Garonne and the Pyrenees, where smuggling was an art form, and trading on both sides of the law had long been a way of life. The brothers moved separately to Louisiana, and variously called themselves Laffite and Lafitte. Pierre became a merchant in New Orleans who found many opportunities in illegal commerce, including Louisiana's continuing African slave trade. The legendary Jean Laffite was a seaman who became a ship's captain, straddling the lines between legitimate trade, privateering, and outright piracy in the Gulf of Mexico and the Caribbean. It was said that "his sailors adored him, for though a strict disciplinarian & one who made no bones of hanging or shooting his subjects when they deserved it, yet he was generous withal."[297]

A growing part of his business centered on slaving. After Napoleon invaded Spain in 1808, Jean Laffite used French letters of marque to seize slaves from Spanish ships at sea. A state of war also existed between Britain and France, and Laffite seized from British vessels slaves carried between West Indian ports.

By November of 1809, New Orleans lawyer John Randolph Grymes was advising Louisiana clients in search of slaves that they should go to Grand Terre Island in Barataria Bay and buy them from the *barracón*, or slave bar-

Jean Laffite

racks, of "the notorious Captain Laffite," who was selling captured slaves at the bargain price of a dollar a pound.

The Laffite brothers worked together. Jean Laffite sent some of his captured slaves to Pierre Laffite, who found many buyers in New Orleans. An illegal African slave trade continued on a large scale along the Gulf Coast into the early 1820s. It was an unsavory mix of methods. Some of it was outright piracy. Jean Laffite shifted his base to Galveston Island in Texas and continued his business until 1823.[298]

Soon after the Louisiana Purchase, the United States Navy sent Commodore David Porter with orders to suppress piracy in the Gulf of Mexico and the Caribbean. But he was equipped mainly with a small squadron of Thomas Jefferson's absurd gunboats, which were nearly useless for that purpose. With larger ships after the War of 1812, Porter and the navy began to have more success. In a massive effort from 1821 to 1823, they and Britain's Royal Navy captured many vessels and largely ended piracy in the Gulf of Mexico, and greatly reduced it in the Caribbean Basin. Jean Laffite was killed at sea in 1823, but his legend lived on in Louisiana.

After 1862, the illicit African slave trade to the United States came to an end. But New Orleans continued to be an important financial center for an international trade in involuntary labor, including African slaves to Latin American ports such as San Juan in Puerto Rico where records still survive of late nineteenth and twentieth-century slave trades, an Asian coolie trade, and the "blackbirding" of Pacific islanders. Investors in Louisiana and New York capitalized voyages which shipped these workers to many parts of the world, including California.[299]

CHANGING AFRICAN ORIGINS AMONG LOUISIANA SLAVES, 1803–25: EVIDENCE FROM GWENDOLYN HALL'S DATABASE

The new surge of African slave trading in American Louisiana differed from earlier movements in several ways at once. African regional and ethnic origins grew more diverse. Evidence is incomplete because much of this trade was illegal. Even so, Gwendolyn Hall devised an ingenious test from evidence gathered for her Louisiana Slave Database. Altogether, various records for sales of slaves and inventories of estates identified a minimum of 6,210 native-born Africans in Louisiana from 1800 to 1820. Their median ages did not much increase in that period, and actually fell in many African groups, which indicates that their numbers were "being substantially renewed from Africa" in that period.[300]

Of those 6,210 Africans in Louisiana from 1800 to 1820, regional or ethnic origins were given for 5,256, often in broad and general terms. Much the largest African group were identified as Congo slaves from Central Africa (2,017 slaves, or 38.4 percent of known origins). These Congo slaves were much in demand on expanding sugar plantations.

A second group of 1,240 Africans (23.6 percent) came from Senegambia and Mali, in ethnic patterns that differed from the earlier African trade to Louisiana. They were mostly Mandingo (496) and Wolof (426), with smaller numbers of Bamana (181) and Fulani (101). An additional 645 (12.2 percent) were identified as coming from the "coast of Guinea" and Sierra Leone.

Yet another 17.3 percent in the nineteenth century came to Louisiana from Benin and neighboring parts of the Gold Coast. The largest ethnic group among them were called Mina (321). Others from this complex region were identified as Chamba, Aja, Fon, Arada, Yoruba, Naga, and Hausa.

One other major slave trading region was the Bight of Biafra in southeastern Nigeria. Its 417 Igbo, Ibibio, and Calabar slaves were 7.9 percent of Louisiana's third wave of Africans.

In short, this wave of African trading brought slaves to Louisiana from every major African region that had been part of Africa's Atlantic traffic. Altogether, five major African regions (Central Africa, Senegambia, Guinea, Benin–Gold Coast, and Bight of Biafra) accounted for 99.4 percent of African slaves in this very mixed traffic. Small groups such as thirty-four Makua slaves came from Mozambique in East Africa.

Major determinants of regional origin were changing patterns of warfare in Africa (fewer Bamana, more Yoruba). Captives were carried out of Africa in the nineteenth century by ships of every slave trading nation: Spanish and Portuguese, French and Dutch, British and North American. They reached Louisiana in roundabout ways. Some were captured, sold, recaptured, and sold again, several times, first in Africa, and then at sea by freebooters, privateers, and pirates, who carried them into the Gulf of Mexico, and delivered them to the slave marts of New Orleans, or directly to Louisiana planters.

LOUISIANA'S LARGEST SLAVE REVOLT

Each of Louisiana's major waves of African slave trading in its French, Spanish, and American eras was followed by surges of slave resistance. The first wave in the French era led to the Natchez wars and Bamana conspiracies in the early 1730s. The second wave in the Spanish period produced the Pointe Coupée unrest of Mina slaves in the early 1790s. The third wave was linked to Louisiana's slave rebellion of 1811—the largest and most diverse in the history of the region.[301]

The revolt began on January 8, 1811, in the parishes of St. Charles and St. John the Baptist, north of New Orleans. Its center was the sugar plantation of Major Manuel Andry, a master who was "known for his cruelty toward his slaves," even by the brutal standards of Louisiana's expanding sugar industry. He was hated by his workers, and they rose against him.[302]

Their leader was Charles Deslondes, later described in the press as a "yellow fellow," a mulatto driver, overseer, and sometime manager of Andry's plantation. Deslondes had been born and raised on the German Coast of Louisiana, and was allowed by his master to travel freely through a large area north of New Orleans and came to know it well.[303]

Louisiana's largest slave revolt, 1811, Lorraine P. Gendron

He often visited a slave woman who lived on the plantation of François Trépagnier, another much hated master. It was said that Trépagnier regarded his slaves as animals and treated them with a contempt that was bitterly resented.[304]

Deslondes also came to know slave leaders on other plantations. Two of them were Africans named Kook and Quamina, both born on the Gold Coast, given Akan day names of Kwaku and Kwamina, and raised among Fante or Asante people. They appear to have been trained as warriors in Africa, as were many Fante and Asante males. In 1806, Kook or Kwaku was carried to New Orleans, and bought by James Brown, yet another brutal master, despised by slaves and other masters alike. A member of the master class described him as a "towering & majestic person, very proud, austere & haughty, in fact repulsive in manner . . . exceedingly unpopular." The cruelty and arrogance of these three Louisiana masters, Andry, Trépagnier, Brown, and others provoked a major revolt.[305]

The rising began when Manuel Andry's slaves armed themselves with axes, clubs, and lethal cane knives. They attacked their hated master, severely wounded him, then killed his son and cut him to pieces with their cane knives. In Andry's cellar they found a supply of militia uniforms and muskets with a small stock of ammunition for the local militia, of which Andry was an officer. His slaves organized themselves into companies with leaders in uniform. They mustered in formations, and marched south toward New Orleans with drums beating and colors flying.

The slave revolt spread swiftly to other estates. The two Fante-Asante warriors, Kwaku and Kwamina, were sent to the plantation of François Trépagnier, and led a rising of the field slaves against that hated master. Trépagnier sent his family into the swamps for safety, and stood alone on his balcony with a double-barreled shotgun. He appears to have felt secure in his sovereign contempt for his slaves. Kwaku led some of the slaves to the back of the house and attacked Trépagnier from the rear. His enraged plantation slaves fell on him with their axes and cane knives and cut him into small pieces. In the words of historian Daniel Rasmussen, "They had annihilated one of the most hated men on the German Coast." [306]

Reports of these events raced swiftly up and down the river. More slaves joined the revolt. Terrified planter families fled for their lives, and mansions began to burn along the Mississippi. Gallopers carried the word to New Orleans and reported that the "horrors of Santo Domingo" had come to Louisiana. The next morning a newspaper account reported that "the road for two or three leagues [six to nine miles] was crowded with carriages and carts full of people making their escape from the ravages of the banditti." [307]

Altogether the slaves are known to have killed three or four masters and wounded a fifth. As the rebels moved from house to house, some of them stopped and liberated large quantities of food and drink. Others kept marching toward New Orleans, about forty miles on the serpentine river road, east-southeast of Andry's plantation (about twenty-five miles in a straight line). As they passed other plantations, more slaves joined them. Maroons also emerged from the swamps. Estimates of total strength ranged from two hundred to five hundred insurgents in arms. Of that number, 124 were later identified by name. [308]

Major Andry, bleeding from his wounds, managed to escape across the Mississippi in a small pirogue. He went to the estate of Charles Perret, who summoned eighty men from other planter families on the west bank of the river. They instantly took up arms, and went in pursuit of the rebel slaves.

In New Orleans, Governor Claiborne mobilized two companies of militia, a small force of United States Infantry, a troop of United States Cavalry, and a landing party of seamen from navy vessels at New Orleans.

All of these groups moved rapidly and converged on the slaves, who sud-

William Claiborne, first U.S. governor of Louisiana

denly found themselves under attack from different directions. The slaves
soon ran out of ammunition, and were overwhelmed by infuriated masters
who were themselves out of control. In the fighting that followed, more than
sixty rebels were killed. Others were captured, tortured, and summarily executed with extreme savagery. Charles Deslondes was identified as the leader.
He was tortured and burned alive on the battlefield. The heads of slaves were
cut off and impaled on stakes for miles along the River Road from Andry's
plantation to New Orleans.[309]

CONTINUED RESISTANCE: LOUISIANA
MARRONAGE, 1811–16

The Louisiana Revolt of 1811 was quickly crushed, but the spirit of resistance
continued in other forms. The most effective method was *marronage*. Most
rebels chose not to fight a pitched battle. They ran from their plantations, retreated to the swamps and bayous, and built communities on hidden islands
of terra firma. These fugitive slaves quickly mastered that dangerous environment, and they made it their own. Rebel communities multiplied in 1811.

Some were maintained close to large towns, so that maroons could travel freely back and forth, buy and sell in urban markets, and acquire weapons, ammunition, and food, and return to hidden settlements.

Through the American period, reports circulated of maroon communities that existed for many years within eight miles of New Orleans. In 1827, a journalist published an article in the New York *Evening Post* about several long-settled maroon communities on what were called the Trembling Prairies, a few miles from New Orleans. In 1827, the journalist discovered that they had been there for sixteen years, since the Great Revolt in 1811. He reported:

> A black woman returned to her master in this city, after an absence of 16 years. By her account it appears that there is a Negro settlement about eight miles to the north of this city, between the Gentilly Road and Lake Ponchartrain. The spot where these negroes have located themselves is what is usually called Trembling Prairies in this country. Similar to the oases of the great deserts, a piece of firm soil has been found to which the approach is cut off by swamps resembling quick sands. . . .
>
> Several blacks having discovered the means of passing those morasses, have sought for and fixed their homes in those small tracts of firm ground which are here and there discovered in the center. The camp from which the aforesaid negress came, is said to contain fifty or sixty souls, who regularly plant corn, sweet potatoes and other vegetables, and raise hogs and poultry. Some no doubt occasionally resort to fishing, but the object of their excursions generally, is to pillage by night in the environs of the city. . . . We are told there is another camp about the head of the Bayou Bienvenue.[310]

Repeated efforts were made to find the maroon communities near New Orleans. A campaign was mounted in 1837, again in 1842, once more in 1849, and yet again as late as 1861. But so difficult of access were the Trembling Prairies and small bayous of Louisiana that masters were unable to find them. One master wrote that "when negroes took to the cane-brakes they could elude both man and dog, and nothing could beat them but snakes and starvation." Altogether, these maroon communities near New Orleans survived for another fifty years from the Great Louisiana Revolt of 1811 to the end of slavery in the Civil War.[311]

TWO PARADOXES OF SLAVERY IN AMERICAN LOUISIANA: "DEMORALIZED" MASTERS, AND SLAVES "SINGULARLY FREE OF DEFERENCE"

In the nineteenth century, many experienced travelers observed that slavery in Louisiana was exceptionally cruel in customary practice. Charles César Robin, Benjamin Latrobe, and Major Amos Stoddard all thought so, and they were accurate, fair-minded, and widely traveled observers. They were not casual tourists. All of them worked in Louisiana for extended periods. Stoddard noted that masters in Louisiana "treat their slaves with great rigor, and this has been uniformly the case." He observed that Louisiana slaves suffered from extreme violence, more so than in other parts of North America. Stoddard wrote that "cruel and even unusual punishments are daily inflicted." [312]

At the same time, Major Stoddard also observed something else: that slavery in Louisiana was distinctive in the demeanor of what he called "demoralized masters and overseers." [313] In Stoddard's generation, "demoralize" was a fashionable new word with a complex double meaning. More than today, it meant "to corrupt the moral principles" of an individual or a group. At the same time, it also had the more common modern meaning of tending "to lower morale, weaken the spirit, diminish the power to bear up against dangers, fatigue or difficulties." [314]

In Stoddard's thinking the two meanings of "demoralized masters" were thought to be linked. The "corruption of moral principles," in the first sense of demoralization, was believed to be the cause of demoralization in its second and more modern meaning, of "lowering morale, weakening the spirit, and diminishing power." [315]

Stoddard believed that some of the worst cruelty in Louisiana was the work of plantation masters and mistresses who were doubly demoralized, in the sense of lacking a strong and steady moral compass on slavery that might have helped to distinguish right from wrong, and also in the sense of having a weakened spirit and diminished power.

In the absence of that moral compass, more than a few Louisiana masters and mistresses committed acts which were so depraved by most tests of right and wrong that one can scarcely believe that any rational human being could ever inflict them on another, much less do so in a routine and repeated way.

At the same time, others also observed another paradox in the demeanor of slaves in Louisiana. Historian Joseph Tregle surveyed the judgments of contemporary writers, and wrote that the demeanor of slaves in New Orleans was observed to be "singularly free of that deference and circumspection which might have been expected in a slave community."[316]

One might think that from the severe treatment they routinely received, slaves and even free people of color would be more degraded, more beaten down, and more broken in spirit. But many residents testified that the opposite was the case. Charles Gayarré, a native-born white Louisianian and one of its leading historians in the nineteenth century, observed from long experience that "free Negroes neither fawned on whites nor despaired because of the discrimination." Gayarré put it in three words: "They walked erect."[317]

These references to slaves who were "singularly free of that deference and circumspection" and free Negroes who "walked erect" were not scattered or isolated impressions. They were borne out by repeated testimony and other evidence of court records, executive reports, and statements by both masters and slaves.[318]

This freedom from deference among Louisiana slaves took many forms. One expression was a strong sense of personal pride. A widely traveled visitor to New Orleans wrote in 1833, "The Negroes here are better off than any I have seen in the Southern States. They dress on the Sabbath like Princes. Many of them, slaves as they are, are the first dandies of the city—in the best broadcloth and the finest of hats. Such buy their time, for six or seven dollars a week—and not infrequently earn a dollar before breakfast. . . . They feel more independent. They are more their own masters."[319]

Slaves who were "singularly free" of "deference and circumspection" had been a continuing story in French, Spanish, and American Louisiana. Those who responded in that way did so not only by individual acts, but also by collective efforts, which changed through time in interesting ways.

THE GROWTH OF COMITY AMONG PEOPLE OF COLOR

At the same time, something else happened. It appeared in the way that people of African origins responded to the abuse that was inflicted upon them. They joined together in various ways, made common cause, and helped one another. Their efforts made a difference, not only in their own condition, but also for America itself and opening societies that grew stronger for their efforts.

Observers from abroad were quick to notice. The very able French scientist Charles César Robin worked in Louisiana from 1803 to 1805. He began to observe that something important was happening among slaves and people of color in Louisiana. Even as they were exploited and degraded in many ways, he noted that they worked together at helping and supporting each other in important ways. Robin described distinctive patterns of association, conduct, and comity among people of African roots—both slave and free together. He thought that these linkages were much stronger than anything comparable among free people of European descent.

Robin perceived that people of African ancestry tended to gather together without regard for differences among themselves in origin, color, rank, or status. He observed that "among the numerous plantations where the Negroes are tolerably well-treated, the ball begins on Saturday evening in one of their cabins, or rather under a wide-spreading tree, and as if they had to spend the whole week resting for it, everyone dances. Nothing is more joyful. Daylight overtakes them before they become fatigued."

He was surprised to find that "free people of color participate in these assemblages of slaves, as the slaves are admitted to theirs. The pride of the whites, who hold at so great a distance all those who have mixed blood, obliges even those colored people who are closest to the whites to associate with these blacks."

Robin added, "Free or slave, black or mulatto, they seem to form a single family, united in their abjection. Among themselves they display a touching affection. They never approach each other without displaying signs of affection and interest, without asking each other news of their relations, their friends, or their acquaintances. To the best of their ability they try to do each other as much good as they can."[320]

These patterns differed from earlier descriptions of association among slaves in French Louisiana. A strong sense of comity had appeared in early-eighteenth-century French Louisiana among arriving Africans. It operated mainly within smaller ethnic clusters of African slaves. It was first described within groups of Bamana slaves and other Mande-speaking groups who shared West African origins, mutually intelligible languages, compatible cultures, and a common history in West Africa. They intermarried, worked together on their own time, and resisted oppression together. At the same time, they were often distant and sometimes hostile to other African groups.[321]

Another example in the 1790s was the very tight sense of comity that formed among slaves who were called Mina in Louisiana. They are thought to have been mainly a mix of Fon, Ewe, and later Yoruba people from Dahomey and the Bight of Benin, but also included Fante and Asante slaves from the Gold Coast. They tended to cluster together and kept a distance from other Africans.

In mid- and late-eighteenth-century Louisiana, clusters of Mina slaves created at least three active communities that appeared in written records. One was in the north, around Pointe Coupée. Another formed in New Orleans and its vicinity. A third appeared on Plaquemines plantations in southern Louisiana. These different groups of Mina slaves associated together, but they were distant from slaves with other African ethnic and regional origins. Records exist of dances and other gatherings organized by Mina slaves, from which slaves of other African ethnic groups and regional origins were explicitly excluded. Patterns of comity among Louisiana slaves were framed within African identities as late as the 1790s.[322]

Different patterns appeared in the American era. In the nineteenth century, slaves and free people of color constructed comities among themselves that transcended differences of African origin, American migration, regions of residence, timing of arrival, and religious identity. These larger patterns of association and identity developed in large part as a consequence of the spreading ideology of racism, and also as a result of growing brutality of Louisiana slavery in this era.

Other historians also have noticed these patterns of comity and described them in various ways. Ned Sublette wrote that "wherever in the country black people were, there was a sense of knit-together culture."[323] Gwendolyn Hall was also struck by the evidence in nineteenth-century Louisiana of what she described as a "solidarity among people of African descent both slave and free." She thought that the cause was clear: "The repression unleashed against people of African descent only strengthened the ties among them."[324]

Differences persisted among slaves, and also between slaves and free people of color, and were built into the structure of gatherings and assemblies. But the ideology of modern racism, and the growth of racist oppression, framed a larger and more inclusive sense of identity and common cause among people of African origin.

Responses varied in substance and detail. Rural field slaves on large plantations and free people of color in urban New Orleans acted in different ways. But they shared a common spirit of comity. It made a difference in their lives and in the history of the American republic.

THE CONSTRUCTION OF COMITY AMONG
SLAVE FAMILIES IN LOUISIANA

What could plantation slaves hope to achieve for themselves and their families, when bound to a life of labor as the human property of profit-seeking owners? What were they able to achieve in the way of a viable family life?

On those hard questions, historians and social scientists have disagreed. In 1965, Daniel Patrick Moynihan ignited a continuing controversy when he hypothesized that slavery gravely weakened African American families, disrupted unions of husbands and wives, and destroyed the family itself as a viable goal.[325]

Historians took up the same question in the 1970s and 1980s and concluded that Moynihan was mistaken. In a major research project, Herbert Gutman found evidence that "slaves on American plantations in the nineteenth century greatly valued an ideal of strong double-headed nuclear families, and most slaves were able to live in households of two parents and children."[326]

In a third generation of empirical scholarship, during the 1990s historian Ann Patton Malone studied the history of slave families in Louisiana, on which scholars had disagreed. She launched a major inquiry by constructing a database of 10,329 slaves on 155 plantations in twenty-six Louisiana parishes from 1810 to 1864. Working mainly from plantation records she followed individual lives, families, and households through time, and found another way forward. Malone discovered that both parties to this argument were mistaken. Moynihan overstated the destruction that bondage caused in slave families, but his critics had erred on the other side, by understating the damage that slavery did to double-headed nuclear families.[327]

Ann Malone discovered a third pattern from a larger database, and it is important to an understanding of slavery, race, and families in American history. Her broad-based empirical study confirmed that slaves in nineteenth-century Louisiana shared an ideal of a strong double-headed nuclear family with a mother and father present and living together with their children, within a cohesive community of other nuclear families.

But she also discovered something else. Through the years from 1810 to 1864, only a minority of slaves in her database were able to maintain intact nuclear units. At any given time, most of the ten thousand Louisiana slaves she studied were not living in double-headed nuclear families. Further, she found that these patterns were highly volatile. They fluctuated through time and varied broadly from one plantation to the next.

Malone also found that families of slaves came under heavy stress from many causes: illness and high death rates, cruelty and violence, overwork and undersupport, changes among owners and their families, sudden economic surges and declines, bankruptcies and crop failures, plantation breakup and slave sales, the outbreak of the Civil War and the epic defeat of the slave-holders' rebellion, and many other factors that shattered slave families and households, often without warning.

But most interesting was yet another discovery by Malone, in the response of plantation slaves. When households and nuclear units were disrupted, she found that slaves worked hard at creating surrogate families and households in different forms. There were many failures along the way. But she discovered that by and large slaves succeeded one way or another in improvising units of mutual support, close belonging, and empathy for others. These surrogate groups were vitally important to the lives of Louisiana field slaves.

The composition and strength of these improvised families and households fluctuated through time. But when conditions of life became more difficult in slavery, these reinvented families and households became more urgent, important, and active.

Even more interesting were the many ways in which slaves did all of these things. Malone studied in greater detail the slave communities that formed on three Louisiana plantations in particular: Oakland in West Feliciana Parish north of New Orleans, Petite Anse Plantation, and Tiger Island Plantation, at opposite ends of St. Mary Parish, on Louisiana's southern Gulf Coast.[328]

At Petite Anse Plantation, Malone found that the most common nurturing tendency was for family households to absorb unmarried daughters, grand-children, and very young married couples. Other households took in "an ill, handicapped, abandoned or elderly member of the community (either related or nonrelated)."[329]

At Oakland, she found that this "nurturing tendency was especially strong and broad-based," in ways that were similar to Petite Anse but took many different forms. She found that "orphans were frequently reared by other kin or nonrelatives." One grandfather cared for his orphaned grandchildren. Another newly married couple took in "a much esteemed grandfather."[330]

On Tiger Island Plantation, at its start in 1842, slaves were highly frag-mented and "hapless individuals faced their crises with little support." Over the next twenty years, slaves slowly created a stronger and more active community. By 1859–60, most individuals and fragments of broken families were taken in by other households. This process worked both for relatives and nonrelated people. The result was that the great majority of slaves lived within households and family groups, but the groups themselves took many different forms.[331]

Overall, Malone observed that slave communities tended to be somewhat more successful on large plantations than little ones, but she found that differences of scale were not as great as others had believed. There were also "development cycles" that varied in detail, but tended to be variations on a common theme. Plantation slaves in nineteenth-century Louisiana were highly successful in forming diverse but very strong families and households. They also succeeded in helping households and families to construct functioning communities. And they sustained a spirit of comity among themselves in the face of the growing racism, severe racist oppression, and extreme racial exploitation that was fundamental to chattel slavery in Louisiana.[332]

This was no small feat. Nuclear double-headed families and households were often cruelly broken in slavery. It was often immensely difficult for slaves to pick up the pieces, and put them together in new ways.

Georgina Gibbs, a Virginia slave, born 1849, remembered a master who sold a woman apart from her husband and son, and sent her far away. Many years later, the woman married again. One day she was bathing her new husband, and saw a scar on his back. The woman suddenly remembered that she had seen it before: it told her that her new husband was in fact her own son: "It was the scar her former master had put on her son. Of course they didn't stay married, but the woman wouldn't ever let her son leave her." Slaves worked within their own ethical imperatives such as rules of incest, which were supported by customary beliefs of great power in some African cultures—more even than among their masters. Those stories tell us that slaves, more than masters, were often the final arbiters of family structure on southern plantations.[333]

THE GROWTH OF COMITY AMONG URBAN PEOPLE OF COLOR IN NEW ORLEANS

In urban New Orleans during the nineteenth century, people of color faced other challenges and opportunities. Here again they constructed unique forms of comity among themselves, but in an urban setting they were able to do it in more complex ways.

The U.S. Census of 1840 found that New Orleans was something special that way. In that year, it was by far the largest African city in North America, with 42,674 people of color, both slave and free. The second-largest urban population of color was Baltimore, at 21,166. A distant third was New York City, with 16,358.[334]

Through Louisiana's Spanish era, free people of color had multiplied rapidly in New Orleans, and their condition had greatly improved. This growth continued in the American era. From the census of 1803 to 1810, the African American population of New Orleans more than trebled, from 3,000 to 10,911. It was about half-slave and half-free. By 1840, their numbers more than trebled yet again, and 55 percent were free.[335]

Altogether, people of color, slave and free together, were a majority in New Orleans from 1803 to 1830, at 60 percent in the census count of 1830, and probably more. The white population of New Orleans became a majority from 1840, partly by immigration from Europe. Blacks became a majority again after 1870.[336]

In the early nineteenth century, white leaders in New Orleans were alarmed by the rapid growth of "blacks," as they called everyone who was not entirely white. The "one drop rule" was rapidly becoming a cultural artifact in the early American republic. White Louisianians were also aware that many other slaves and free people of color came and went in the city with increasing frequency. There was a special fear of runaways and maroons, and a long memory of the revolt in 1811, when slaves had marched on New Orleans.

Governor Claiborne made very clear that in a Jeffersonian republic, rights of citizenship and suffrage were for whites only. In American New Orleans, as in other cities, free people of color and mixed ancestry were required to carry special passes which identified their race as "black," no matter how mixed their ancestry complexion may have been.

Their movements in the city were restricted after dark. In public places they were either excluded or segregated in separate galleries with the worst seats. Violators were arrested and punished by heavy fines. Visits to places of public accommodation, with the exception of Roman Catholic churches, became a process of public humiliation for people of color.[337]

AN URBAN COMITY AMONG PEOPLE OF COLOR IN NEW ORLEANS

Free people of color in New Orleans repeatedly challenged these restrictions, but mostly they dealt with race prejudice and racial barriers in other ways. They rallied to each other, formed strong bonds of mutual support, and joined in associations and common efforts that were grounded in common origins.

The census takers in 1850 asked new questions about place of birth. In New Orleans, they were surprised to discover that the great majority (75 percent) of free people of color had been born in Louisiana. Only about 10 percent came from other parts of the United States (much lower than among plantation slaves). Another 11 percent were from the Caribbean and 3 percent from Africa.[338]

In New Orleans free people of color tended to have regional roots—more so than the white population in the city, and much more than Louisiana field slaves. With local roots came personal relationships with others of similar origin. In New Orleans, people of color became a community that was close and tight.

Charles Robin noted a spirit of "mutual affection" among people of color. They supported each other. Robin observed that "Those who have earned or found the means to obtain a portion of the sum necessary to buy their precious freedom will be able to borrow the remainder from their own color."

Robin was especially struck by the funerals of slaves and free people of color. As early as 1825 he wrote, "I have noticed especially in the city that while the funerals of white people are only attended by a few, those of colored people are attended by a crowd, and mulattoes, quadroons married to white people, do not disdain attending the funeral of a black."[339]

They bonded together and kept a distance between themselves and from white residents in New Orleans. Robert Tallant observed from long experi-

"Plantation Burial," by John Antrobus

ence that among people of color in New Orleans, "a message could be conveyed from one end of the city to another in a single day without one white person's being aware of it."[340]

BUILDING A MATERIAL BASE FOR A COMMUNITY OF COLOR: JOBS AND INCOME IN NEW ORLEANS

The United States Census of 1850 asked searching questions about the employment of all American adults. The results were surprising, even startling, for free people of color in New Orleans. The census of 1850 found that 64 percent of free Blacks were employed as skilled artisans, a larger proportion than in any other American city. Only Charleston in South Carolina was similar (62.5 percent). In northern cities comparable proportions of free men of color employed as skilled artisans ranged from 5 percent in New York City, 6 percent in Boston and New York, 8 percent in Philadelphia; to 11 and 18 percent in Washington and Baltimore. Similar patterns appeared in data for skilled occupations in city directories.[341]

Even more striking was another occupational pattern. In 1850, among all free adult men of color, the proportion employed in unskilled occupations (laborers, mariners), semiskilled (well digger, gardener), and personal service (servants) was 18 percent in New Orleans, and 21 percent in Charleston. By contrast, in thirteen other American cities, comparable proportions of unskilled and semiskilled occupations for men of color ranged from 59 to 77 percent.[342]

COMMUNITY LEADERS IN NEW ORLEANS

In New Orleans the community of color generated its own leaders. Free people of color were more successful in acquiring property than in any other American city. By 1850, a total of 650 free Black real estate owners were by far the largest of any major city in the United States. They owned property estate assessed at $2,354,640 or an average of $3,623 per owner.[343]

Many of these individuals and families succeeded in business. Some attended universities and technical and engineering schools in France. More than a few remained in French cities and flourished there. Others returned to New Orleans in the mid-nineteenth century, and the range and quality of their intellectual achievements was extraordinary, sometimes far beyond Louisiana's white master class.[344]

Examples in science and engineering included Norbert Rillieux and others in his family. Louis Charles Roudanez became prominent and distinguished in medicine, with many white patients in the 1850s. In the arts, Armand Lanusse was a poet of great talent, and he was not alone. In 1845, he edited and published *Les Cenelles*, an anthology of seventeen Louisiana poets of color. Victor Séjour became a playwright. Jules Lion was a leading lithographer. Julien Hudson studied in Paris after 1827, flourished in the 1830s as a painter, opened a studio in New Orleans, and did portraits and history paintings, including a tableau of the Battle of New Orleans in 1839 which featured African American soldiers.

In classical music, Edmond Dédé (1827–1901) was a gifted prodigy, one of many in New Orleans, where his abilities were recognized and rewarded by people of color. In the city he had excellent teachers such as William Nickerson, who also taught Ferdinand Joseph Lamothe, a gifted classical musician better remembered as Jelly Roll Morton. Dédé was sent to France for further schooling, and became a classical composer and conductor. His music continues to be played today.[345]

BUILDING COMITY ACROSS GENERATIONS

People of color in New Orleans formed voluntary associations to help with schooling of the young. The government of New Orleans did very little for children of any ethnicity. Despite the absence of free schools for African American children, young people of color in New Orleans tended to be better educated than many white children. City directories reported high numbers of Black private teachers in New Orleans. They were supported not by the city, but by free people of color through their families, churches, and voluntary associations.

Young people of color in nineteenth-century New Orleans were commonly bilingual or multilingual. In 1834, a visitor observed that "many negroes speak three languages, in such a manner as to defy you to tell which one of the three is their vernacular."[346]

Robin noted a quality of "mutual affection" among people of color. He observed that they strongly supported each other, and that "those who have earned or found the means to obtain a portion of the sum necessary to buy their precious freedom will be able to borrow the remainder from their own color."[347]

COMITY AND CREATIVITY ACROSS THE GENERATIONS

Some of the most striking examples of mutual support appear today in relations between Afro-Louisiana generations. A living example in the twenty-first century is Troy Andrews, a native son of Tremé, the old New Orleans neighborhood near Congo Square. Born in 1986 and raised in an extended family of musicians, he began to play the trombone at an age when he was smaller than his instrument. His reputation spread rapidly, and he became known through the city as Trombone Shorty. At the age of four he was playing with Bo Diddley. At six, he was supported by Wynton Marsalis and other New Orleans musicians, who took an interest and helped him. He formed his own band and became a world-class performer, composer, and leader. The money rolled in, and he started a foundation to help others younger than himself. One purpose was to support music in the schools. Another was "to preserve and perpetuate the unique musical culture of New Orleans."

The saga of Trombone Shorty is doubly interesting to a historian. It is full of clues to the dynamics of Louisiana's musical tradition, which grew through twelve generations from 1718 to the present. The dynamics of this tradition are deeply interesting. The central pattern is not a constant flow or stream of effort, but more a sequence of surges, each in its own moment, with a fertile mix of generations.

Wynton Marsalis with drummers

LOUISIANA'S PEOPLE OF COLOR
THROUGH TWELVE GENERATIONS

Of all the many Afro-European cultural regions that developed within the present boundaries of the United States, Louisiana was the most diverse, the most disorderly, one of the most creative in its culture.

In its early years, Louisiana was run by ruling elites of France, Spain, and the United States. The inhabitants were even more mixed. As many as thirty American Indian nations lived in the lower Mississippi Valley before European settlement.

Each of Louisiana's three ruling governments recruited a great variety of European ethnic groups who founded creative subcultures. The French brought in many of their own compatriots, as did Canadian *coureurs de bois*, Acadian refugees, Caribbean *flibustiers*, and Central Europeans who settled Louisiana's German Coast. Spanish leaders encouraged settlements by groups of Canary Islanders and Malagueños from the Mediterranean.

Three waves of African slave trading created a broad diversity of African ethnic groups. The proportion of African slaves in the population of Louisiana peaked at 76.9 percent in the census of 1740. It continued above 50 percent in the French and Spanish eras, and over 40 percent in the American era, from 1803 to 1860.

Louisiana's population was always a great jumble of humanity. But many of its ethnic groups also had a high degree of individual identity and internal cohesion, which tended to be stronger than elsewhere. The result was a distinctive regional culture in Louisiana, and one that was also important for the history of cultural diversity in America and the world.

In 1699, the complex culture of French Louisiana began to grow from a complex set of founding ideas: a unique French Canadian tradition of humanity in relations between European colonists and Native Americans; the unconstrained ways of Caribbean *flibustiers*; the universal inclusion of the Roman Catholic Church; the top-down dominion of French absolutism; and the large spirit of the European Enlightenment in the eighteenth century.

All of those elements came together to shape the interplay of three complex cultures: Amerindian, African, and French. Each had its own constellation of values, and deep internal differences. Other groups were also important on the German Coast and in Acadian settlements. The history of upper Louisiana centered on relations between the French and American Indians. Lower Louisiana increasingly centered on French colonists and African slaves.

French elites set the rules of engagement, but not just as they pleased. They tended to be more tolerant of differences than were those in English colonies, and more willing to learn from other ways. From 1732 to 1763, the cultural life of lower Louisiana developed in part from a mix of French and African elements.

The result was a European agricultural economy in America that made much use of African crops, African methods, and African systems of labor. Its foodways and other material systems developed from a mixture of African, Native American, and European elements. A Creole language called Gombo emerged from another mixture of European, African, and Amerindian elements.

From the start, French Louisiana also became a place of continuing disorder, intense conflict, and frequent violence. Those patterns emerged early in the eighteenth century, and elements persisted through three hundred years. But there was also something special about diversity in Louisiana. Even in the midst of so much violence, lawlessness, and material inequality, people of Louisiana, when they dealt with one another, also developed a spirit of humanity among themselves that spread to others.

The period of effective Spanish control in Louisiana lasted only thirty-six years, from 1767 to 1803. But in that brief period it transformed the colony and changed the condition of African Americans in important ways. A new wave of African slave trading to Louisiana increased their numbers in the colony and "re-africanized" the slave population. At the same time, it also greatly increased the diversity of African ethnic origins.

Spanish leaders also recruited European ethnic groups and gave them room to grow. They added a proliferation of Iberian cultures from Málaga and the Canary Islands, and Irish Catholics. English-speaking American settlers began to swarm in during the Spanish era. The Spanish regime in Louisiana gave slaves more legal rights and protections and an expanding tradition of humanity. It allowed them to have more control over their lives, encouraged more racial mixing in parts of the colony, greatly increased the numbers of free people of color, and also permitted Afro-French and Afro-English cultures to gain strength.

The acquisition of Louisiana by the United States introduced yet another historical process which added a third layer of complexity. *Les Américains* started yet another great surge in Louisiana's population—the largest on record. The number of its inhabitants took a huge jump from 44,112 in the Spanish colony (1800) to 708,002 in the state of Louisiana alone by 1860.

After 1803, Louisiana was led by plural elites: French, Spanish, Anglo-American, and also a growing elite of free people of color. Each of these ethnic elites was subdivided by differences of value, interest, purpose, and power. Numbers of slaves rose from 24,264 (55 percent of total population) in 1800 to 331,726 (46.9 percent) in 1860. New flows of slaves came from many sources: mostly from the United States; many from Africa in yet another illegal slave trade; and an important flow from the Caribbean.

The new American regime also brought a surge of economic growth in cotton, sugar, and other crops, and of trade and finance in New Orleans. It also brought a rapid surge of inequality to some of the highest levels in the United States. The American regime introduced a harsh system of slave laws, a brutal system of bondage, increasing racism, and growing violence.

Louisiana continued to be a deeply troubled society, riven by conflict, violence, corruption, racism, and ethnic strife. Slavery in the American period became even more brutal than in the French and Spanish eras, and it was brutal in new ways. As slavery became more entrepreneurial in the nineteenth century, brutality was increasingly used as a rational way of enlarging returns to capital, in ways that were even more dehumanizing than early practices.

Free people of color also suffered changes for the worse in their condition during the American era, by comparison with Spanish Louisiana. With the rapid growth of racism in the nineteenth century, the laws of American Louisiana defined free people of color not as fully free, and former slaves.

People of color, both slave and free, responded to this process of degradation by continuing struggle and resistance, and in many ways. Some turned to flight. Others tried violent acts of individual and collective resistance, which often ended in repression that was even more violent.

They also created Afro-European-American cultures of their own, by working closely together. In the French era, they had tended to do so in small clusters of Africans who shared a cultural heritage in common—Bamana warrior-slaves who organized resistance circa 1730s and 1740s, Mina slaves who acted together in 1795, and other groups.

In the American period, another pattern appeared. Observers such as Robin and Latrobe noted that a spirit of comity, collective belonging, and mutual respect reached across African ethnic differences, and were stronger than distinctions between slaves and free people of color. Examples were Afro-Louisiana funerals, which as early as 1803 showed a sense of solidarity that was stronger among people of African origin than among people of European descent.

Another pattern of comity appeared in weekly gatherings such as those along the levees of New Orleans and later at Congo Square. Every week, large numbers came together in ways that expressed both diversity and solidarity. Slaves and free people of color, who were African, American, and West Indian in birth, formed a multitude of separate circles. These circles in turn were part of a larger gathering that was defined both by creative differences and by a shared spirit of comity.

Among Louisianans of African origin there was a strong sense of mutual support, and a sharing of values and purposes that had no equal among people of European origin in New Orleans. They greatly encouraged and supported each other, and helped the next generation. The ways in which young people in New Orleans were taught its musical tradition was a case in point. This process in turn was a key to the creativity of this culture.

In many ways Louisiana was a difficult and dangerous place for African slaves and free people of color. It was violent, corrupt, and increasingly racist in the nineteenth century. In the face of all those dangers, people of African descent worked together in many ways to create possibilities for achievement, and mutual support among themselves.

The creativity of that process centered on Africans but reached beyond them, to engage people of other origins. In that process, African speech, music, religion, folkways, foodways, and material culture enriched the entire fabric of a quintessential regional American culture, and was further enriched by it. Its largest contribution was not to be found in any single cultural achievement, important as so many were. The greatest gift of Africans in Louisiana was the quality of comity that they created for mutual support and care of others. We are only beginning to learn from their example.

TABLE 6.1 The Founding Population of French Louisiana

First Census Returns of 1699 and 1700

INHABITANTS	1699	1700
Officers	5	8
Petty Officers	5	5
Sailors	4	9
Canadians	19	61
Flibustiers	13	10
Laborers	10	6
Cabin Boys	6	6
Soldiers	20	20
Total	**82**	**125**

Note: These are the first and second census returns for French Louisiana. The primary settlements in 1699 and 1700 were at Biloxi and other places on the Gulf Coast. The census categories here are as given in the original documents. No women, Africans, or American Indians were reported. Among the important findings are the large and increasing proportions of French Canadians, who also included others listed as officers and petty officers; also important is the early presence of Caribbean *flibustiers* or freebooters; and the cabin boys who were sent to live among the American Indians and learn their languages on the model of Champlain's *truchements*.

TABLE 6.2 The Population of Louisiana Through the French Period

Early Census Returns, 1699–1763

YEAR	AMERICAN INDIAN SLAVES	AFRICANS	EUROPEANS & CANADIANS	TOTAL	PERCENT AFRICAN
1699	0	0	82	82	0
1700	0	0	125	125	0
1706			85	85	0
1708	80	0	278	358	0
1721		533	1,082	1,615	33.0%
1726				1,952	n.a.
1727		1,561	1,460	3,021	51.7%
1731		3,600	1,700	5,300	67.9%
1740–41		4,000	1,200	5,200	76.9%
1746		4,730	3,200	7,930	59.6%
1763		4,598	3,654	8,252	55.7%

Note: Early census data for Louisiana from 1699 to 1713 included Biloxi and Mobile, which were part of the colony. In 1708, all 80 slaves in the census were American Indians.

TABLE 6.3 Louisiana's First Wave of Population Growth

Emigrants from France, 1717–21

Company of the Indies

Staff	43
Workers	302

Military Forces

Officers	122
Other Ranks	977

Planters and Bound Servants

Landholders	119
Engagés (Indentured Servants)	2,462
Forced Exiles, Convicts, etc.	1,278

Women	**1,215**
Children	**502**
Total French Emigrants, 1717–21	**7,020**
Total French in Louisiana, 1721	**1,082**
African and Indian Slaves, 1721	**533**

Note: Of 7,020 emigrants from 1717 to 1721, an estimated 2,000 died en route to Louisiana, or returned to France. Approximately 4,000 (57 percent) are believed to have died in Louisiana after their arrival. Less than 16 percent were living in the colony by 1721.

·

TABLE 6.4 Louisiana's Second Wave of Population Growth

Origins of Slaves in African Voyages to Louisiana, 1720–43

REGION AND PORTS	SHIP	ARRIVAL DATE	SLAVES EMBARKED	SLAVES LANDED
Senegambia				
Gorée	Ruby	1720	130	127
unknown	Maréchal d'Estrées	1721	200	196
unknown	Expédition	1723	100	91
Senegal, Gorée, Gambia	Courrier de Bourbon	1723	105	87
Galam, Gorée, Bissau	Mutine	1725	235	213
Saint-Louis, Gorée, Gambia, Bissau	Aurore	1726	350	290

Galam, Saint-Louis	Annibal	1727	n.a.	n.a.
Saint-Louis	Prince de Conti	1727	300	266
Gorée, Saint-Louis	Duc de Noaille	1727	350	262
unknown	Venus	1728	350	341
Saint-Louis, Gorée	La Flore	1728	400	356
Saint-Louis, Gorée	Galathée	1729	400	273
Saint-Louis, Gorée	Venus	1729	450	363
Saint-Louis, Gorée, Gambia	L'Annibal	1729	249	n.a
unknown	Duc de Bourbon	1729	400	319
Saint-Louis, Gorée, Gambia	Néréide	1730	203	n.a.
Saint-Louis, Gorée, Gambia,	St. Louis	1731	361	291
Saint-Louis, Gorée, Gambia	St. Ursin	1743	220	190

Benin

Juda, Whydah	Aurore	1718	200	201
Juda, Whydah	Duc du Maine	1719	n.a.	250
Juda, Whydah	L'Afriquain	1720	n.a.	182
Juda, Whydah	Duc du Maine	1720	n.a.	349
Juda, Whydah	Fortuné	1721	n.a.	303
Juda, Whydah	Diane	1728	516	464

Congo

Cabinda	Néréide	1721	n.a.	294

Totals:

Senegambia	18 voyages	4,204 slaves	(67.3%)
Benin	6 voyages	1,749 slaves	(28.0%)
Angola/Congo	1 voyage	294 slaves	(04.7%)

Grand Total (25 voyages)   1720–43   **6,247 slaves**   **(100.0%)**

Slaves arriving from Africa   1720–31   **6,057 slaves**   **(less St. Ursine)**

Slaves surviving in Louisiana   1731   **3,600 slaves**   **(net loss 40.3%)**

Note: Numbers of slaves landed are missing for two Senegambian voyages; they are estimated as the mean of 16 of other voyages from this region in that period: thus, 3,737 plus (233.5 × 2)= 4,204.

TABLE 6.5 Regional and Ethnic Origin of Slaves Accused of Crime in Louisiana

Records of the Louisiana Superior Council, 1729–52

AFRICAN REGION	ETHNICITY	NUMBER	PERCENT
Senegal	Bamana	18	66.7%
	Wolof	2	7.4%
	Fulbe	1	3.7%
Benin	Fon	1	3.7%
Angola/Congo	Sango	1	3.7%
Unidentified	Samba	3	11.1%
	Biefada	1	3.7%
Total	All ethnicities	27	100.0%

Note: In eighteenth-century Louisiana and France, Bamana ethnicity was written as Bambara, a French error-term that has migrated into American academic literature.

TABLE 6.6 Louisiana's Third Wave of Population Growth

The Spanish Era: Officially 1763–1803, Effectively 1767–1803; Census Estimates of Slave and Free Population, 1763–1800

YEAR	SLAVES	FREE	AREA
1763	4,598	3,654	Lower Louisiana to Pointe Coupée
1766	5,873	5,930	Not clear
1777	9,201	7,728	Includes Natchez, Pensacola, Mobile
1788	20,673	18,737	Includes Natchez, Pensacola, Mobile
1795	19,926	16,304	Includes Natchez, Pensacola, Mobile
1797	23,698	19,389	Excludes Natchez, Arkansas, Illinois
1800	24,264	19,852	Excludes Natchez, Arkansas, Illinois; Includes West Florida

TABLE 6.7 Slavery in Louisiana's Spanish Period, 1767–1803

African Regional Origins of Slaves, 1771–1802

| | Slaves Listed in Estate Inventories, Pointe Coupée, 1771–1802 | | Slaves Baptized in Saint Louis Cathedral, New Orleans, 1801–02 | |
REGION OF ORIGIN	NUMBER	PERCENT	NUMBER	PERCENT
Senegambia	216	27.1%	59	20.1%
Sierra Leone	14	1.8%	16	5.4%
Windward Coast	31	3.9%	17	5.8%
Gold Coast	10	1.3%	24	8.2%
Bight of Benin	229	28.7%	58	19.7%
Bight of Biafra	92	11.5%	13	4.4%
Congo/Angola	190	23.8%	73	24.8%
Mozambique	16	2.0%	0	0
American Creoles	0	0	7	2.4%
Other, Unknown	0	0	27	9.2%
Total	798	100.0%	294	100.0%

TABLE 6.8 Largest African Ethnic Groups in Louisiana, 1719–1820

**Frequencies in Gwendolyn Hall's Louisiana Slave Database
After Three Waves of Slave Arrivals**

GROUP	NUMBER	PERCENT OF WHOLE	PERCENT MALE	PERCENT FEMALE
1. Congo	2,988	35.4%	69.1%	35.4%
2. Mandingo	922	10.9%	66.9%	33.1%
3. Mina	628	7.4%	68.5%	31.5%
4. Senegal/Wolof	597	7.1%	60.8%	39.2%
5. Igbo	524	6.2%	54.8%	45.2%
6. Bamana	466	5.5%	88.6%	11.4%
7. Chamba	415	4.9%	66.5%	33.5%
8. Yoruba/Nago	358	4.2%	69.0%	31.0%
9. Kanga	339	4.0%	61.9%	38.1%
10. Fon/Aja/Arada	243	2.9%	51.9%	48.1%
11. Poulard/Fulbe	210	2.5%	76.2%	23.8%
12. Calabar	147	1.7%	59.9%	40.1%
13. Nar/Moor	136	1.6%	74.3%	25.7%
14. Hausa	133	1.6%	91.7%	8.3%
15. Makwa	102	1.2%	65.7%	34.3%
16. Kisi	86	1.0%	59.3%	40.7%
17. Ibibio/Moko	82	1.0%	74.4%	25.6%
18. Edo	66	0.8%	57.6%	42.4%
Total	**8,442**	**100.0%**	**67.8%**	**32.2%**

TABLE 6.9 Louisiana's Fourth Wave of Population Growth,
after Joining the United States, 1803–60

**Slaves, Free People of Color, and Total Population:
Evidence from U.S. Census Data for 1820 and 1860**

	SLAVE POPULATION			FREE COLORED POPULATION			LOUISIANA'S ENTIRE POPULATION
	MALE	FEMALE	TOTAL	MALE	FEMALE	TOTAL	
1820	36,566	32,498	69,064	4,536	5,969	10,503	153,407
1860	171,977	159,749	331,726	8,279	10,368	18,647	708,002

TABLE 6.10 Louisiana's Fourth Wave of Population Growth: Estimates of The American Period, Legal Slave Trade, 1804–08

	Estimated Slave Arrivals in Louisiana by Port of Origin					
YEAR	AFRICA	CHARLESTON	JAMAICA	HAVANA	UNCLEAR	OTHER
1804	600		458	170	170	
1805	552		1			19
1806		527	1		405	
1807	350	945	40		471	
1808		189			427	43
Total	1,502	1,661	500	170	1,473	62

TABLE 6.11 Louisiana's Fourth Wave of Population Growth: The American Period, Illegal Slave Trade, 1808–62

Rough Estimates of Foreign Slaves Arriving in the United States After the Prohibition of the Foreign Slave Trade, January 1, 1808		
SOURCE	PERIOD	ESTIMATE
Curtin	1808–63	192,500 (3,500 annually)
Inikori	1808–63	269,500
Obadele-Starks	1808–63	786,500

TABLE 6.12 African Regional Origins:
The Slave Trade to Louisiana and the Gulf Coast, 1719–1860

Evidence from the Atlantic Slave Trade Database
Total Slaves Disembarked, Estimates by Eltis, Richardson, et al.

	NUMBER	PERCENTAGE
Senegambia	9,900	38.5
Sierra Leone	4,300	16.7
Gold Coast	1,200	4.7
Bight of Benin	3,300	12.8
Bight of Biafra	900	3.5
West Central Africa	4,300	16.7
Southeast Africa	1,800	7.0
Total Slaves Disembarked	**25,700**	**99.9**

Note: These estimates are for the entire period of the African slave trade from 1719 to 1860. For the French period, Eltis and Richardson found that "nearly three-quarters of the first generation of slaves (arriving before 1740) came from what is now Senegal, and most of the remainder came from the Bight of Benin."

TABLE 6.13 Origins of Ships in Louisiana's African Slave Trade

Home Ports of Vessels Known to Have Arrived in Louisiana and Gulf: Percent of Total Slave Voyages, 1719–1860

Home Ports of Slave Voyages	
Lorient, France	36.4
Le Havre	8.3
La Rochelle	5.5
St. Malo	5.2
Bordeaux	5.1
Brest	2.5
Total French	**63.0**
London, England	13.6
Liverpool	8.5
Total British	**22.1**
Charleston	4.4
Rhode Island	2.6
Mobile	0.9
Total North American	**7.9**
Havana	4.1
St. Thomas	2.0
Total Caribbean	**6.1**
Grand Total	**99.1**

PART THREE

FRONTIER REGIONS

WESTERN FRONTIERS: FREE RANGE SLAVES

WYOMING

NEBRASKA

IOWA

Cheyenne

Missouri River

COLORADO

KANSAS

MISSOURI

Folson

Arkansas River

OKLAHOMA

ARKANSAS

Amarillo

Clarendon

NEW MEXICO

Lubbock

Weatherford

TEXAS

LOUISIANA

Rio Grande

Austin

San Felipe

San Antonio

Matagorda Bay

Bracketville

Victoria

Carrizo Springs

Mustang Island

MEXICO

Rio Grande

Gulf
of Mexico

0 Miles   200   400

0 Kilometers   400

© 2022 Jeffrey L. Ward

Chapter 7

WESTERN FRONTIERS

Fulani Herders, Carolina Cattlemen, Texas Mustangers

With their animal understanding, the Fulani actually enter into cattle society—and take over.

—M. D. Olmert on Fulani herders in Gambia[1]

I acted like I was a Mustang. I made the Mustangs think I was one of them. Maybe I was, in them days. After I stayed with a bunch long enough they'd foller me instid of me having to foller them. Show them you're the boss. That's my secret.

—Afro-Texas mustanger Robert Lemmons[2]

There are men whom bees will not sting. There are men whom a fierce yard dog will not bark at, much less bite. What is it inside individuals that makes horses untameable by others submit to them gently?

—Texas historian J. Frank Dobie on the
"Mustang Man" Robert Lemmons[3]

O N THE WESTERN EDGE of European settlements in North America, African slaves found another way to change the burden of their bondage. At an early date, a free range livestock industry began to develop in many parts of the New World. The work of actually managing the animals was done by people of different origins. Among them were British and Irish servants, Spanish and Mexican vaqueros, American Indians, and African slaves in surprising numbers.

That mix of humanity produced an enduring folk hero in the New World: the American cowboy. An entire literary genre called the Western gave this legendary figure a set of heroic roles. Hollywood added indelible images and appealing characters: Tom Mix and Gene Autry in the first and second generations, John Wayne and Jimmy Stewart in the third generation, and Robert Redford in the fourth.

Through much of the twentieth century, most cinematic American cowboys were represented as white Anglo-Saxon males. Many cowboys had been of that description. But others were of different ethnic origins, and they were increasingly diverse.

By the mid-twentieth century, historians also turned up increasing evidence of American cowboys who came from Africa. Two pathbreaking scholars were Philip Durham and Everett Jones in their excellent and useful book *The Negro Cowboys*. But with all its many strengths, their work was incomplete in one important way. Durham and Jones wrote accurately that "most of the first Negro cowboys were slaves" brought to Texas from cotton plantations in the Old South and "set to learning a new trade. Some were taught by Mexican vaqueros, some by their white masters, and others by Indians like those of the Caddo Confederacy, who had learned to handle and herd cattle."[4]

That account was useful and true as far as it went, but it missed an important part of the story. "Negro cowboys" were not merely receivers of Hispanic and British and Indian expertise. In the New World they were not only learners but teachers. Through the early years of North American stock raising, some of them introduced their own highly developed African expertise on working with animals. Their skills were well known at the time. More recently they have become interesting to historians, and also to neuroscientists who also have developed a special interest in African ways of working with animals. Thereby hangs yet another tale of African creativity in early America.

TRADITIONS OF STOCK RAISING IN WEST AFRICA: FULANI HERDERS

Slaves who came from Africa to North America in the eighteenth century tended to be highly variable in their experience of working with animals. Their knowledge differed by rank, age, occupation, and by the diversity of African cultures from whence they came.

In Biafra, Olaudah Equiano remembered that Igbo people in his village used "no beasts of husbandry." At the same time, others from different parts of West Africa had long been skilled herders.[5] Other patterns appeared farther south in Angola and Congo. Cattle and horses were not much raised in large areas of Central Africa where the tsetse fly was a common problem.[6]

But through much of North and West Africa, the raising of livestock reached high levels of development at an early date, long before the start of the Atlantic slave trade. Regions of special importance were valleys of the

Fulani cattle herders: small boys with cattle sticks

Gambia, Senegal, and Niger Rivers, and the north coast of Africa, and broad reaches of the Sahel across much of West Africa below the Sahara. The vast grasslands of the Sahel became the home of many African different stock raising groups.[7]

Of special importance to this inquiry are the African people variously called Fulbe (in their own Fulfulde language), or Fula (in Mande speechways), or Peul (in French), or Fulani to Hausa neighbors and English-speaking scholars. Especially prominent among stock raisers were Fulani groups in Gambia and neighboring areas in West Africa.

That African region became important in the slave trade to South Carolina, where free range stock raising developed rapidly in the eighteenth century. The importance of Gambian herders in South Carolina cattle raising was first explored by the American historian Peter Wood. Another scholar, Philip Morgan, also confirmed that connection. Their findings are supported by extensive manuscript records of Henry Laurens, a leading slave trader in eighteenth-century Charleston. His papers are now accessible in a multivolume scholarly edition.[8]

The Fulani are an ancient African people of distinctive culture and condition. Their origins have been much debated. Some historians believe that they may have been Egyptian in their roots. Others have suggested a kinship with cultures in Ethiopia. Whatever their beginnings, Fulani people spread across large areas of Africa from the upper Nile Valley in the east to Senegal and Gambia in the west. They were among the earliest African ethnic groups who converted to Islam. At the same time, many of them also retained elements of older animist beliefs in various forms.

Altogether, estimated numbers of Fulani and related ethnic groups throughout Africa in the twenty-first century have run as high as 20 to 25 million people. They are diverse in language and culture, and tend to share with kindred people a set of common values that make a virtue of diversity. Fulani cultivate an active and attractive idea that they call "cultural cousinage." They use it to describe complex relations among themselves and related groups. At the same time they also share a common core of ethical values, summarized as the "four Fulani pathways": *muryai* or *muriyal* (patience, self-control); *hakkille* (wisdom, forethought); *sagata* (courage, endurance, and hard work); and *gacce* (respect for other living beings).[9]

Fulani have long been renowned for their skill with animals. They are widely recognized for their expertise as herders of sheep, goats, cattle, and also as breeders of horses. In Senegal, Judy and I visited a Fulani village, talked with its leaders, and observed their stock raising at first hand.[10]

Today many Fulani families own small herds of large, handsome long-horned cattle. One study in the late twentieth century found that individual holdings averaged less than fifty cattle, often much less. Even in small units, Fulani cattle herding was highly efficient, elaborately rationalized, and deeply rooted. Individual owners carefully marked their animals with symbols of great antiquity. These signs may be seen today, and have been studied by African scholars.[11]

Fulani grazed their animals on open grasslands, often in comparatively well-watered river valleys and coastal regions. Sometimes their animals were rounded up and penned on rice fields after the harvest. English travelers in the eighteenth century were impressed by the large numbers of cattle in savannas along the Gambia River, and by the care and skill of Fulani herders, men and boys who worked mostly on foot, guiding the great animals with sticks through large grazing areas in West Africa.[12]

Fulani families also raised flocks of sheep and herds of goats. Women have long played major roles as herders of these animals, and also as owners and entrepreneurs. A Gambian survey, circa 2005, reported that women were 52 percent of sheep owners, and 67 percent of goat owners. Units of ownership tended to be small. A census of Gambia in 2002 found that individual holdings of sheep and goats ranged between six and ten animals, of which about half were kept as breeding stock. Even as units of ownership were small and stable, the industry itself became large and expansive, and it tended to preserve a distinct character.[13]

FULANI HERDERS AND THEIR WAYS WITH ANIMALS

Among the Fulani and other herding cultures in West Africa, bonds of high complexity have long existed between people and animals. Some of those relationships are unlike others that have developed in modernizing economies of the western world.

In stock raising industries through much of the United States and Western Europe, livestock are widely perceived in profoundly material terms. Throughout sub-Saharan West Africa, attitudes have long been very different. A major factor may have been animist religions, which were strong in Africa during the sixteenth, seventeenth, and eighteenth centuries. They still exist today, even with the rapid spread of Islam and Christianity.

In deeply rooted animist cultures, many material objects in the world are thought to be occupied by abiding spirits that dwell in rocks, soil, water, light, mountains, rivers, plants, and animals. For animists, this vast spirit world is thought to be more real and infinitely more powerful than the material objects that are central to modern economic thought in the western world.[14]

Even as Islam and Christianity made many converts in West Africa, animist beliefs retained their power among believers even to our time. Much is thought to depend on the propitiation of spirits. The spirit world is thought to be full of danger, but also opportunity.[15]

This way of thinking encouraged a sense of spiritual connection between people and animals. Leading examples were Fulani cattle herders and their animals in West Africa from Senegal and Gambia to northern Nigeria and Ghana, through much of the Sahel. Fulani have long been among the most successful cattle herders in the world. They and their animals tend to live close together and know each other intimately.

Their long-horned West African cattle were big and dangerous to people who did not know how to work with them. Meg Daley Olmert writes, "The Fulani managed these large aggressive animals without the aid of barbed wire, corrals, squeeze chutes, tranquilizers, horses or dogs. . . . Yet one Fulani herder can keep fifty hungry animals out of succulent, unfenced cropland, and on a forced march of up to twenty miles a day. How? With long sticks, and a remarkable understanding of how cattle think and feel."[16]

By and large, Fulani do not drive their animals. They lead them, by methods that some westerners find inconceivable until they observe them in action. Fulani cattle herders begin by gaining control of the most powerful bull and the dominant cows in the herd. Small Fulani boys at an early age are taught to approach a big bull without fear, and hit him hard with a stick. When the bull begins to show anger, boys are trained to hit the animal again and again, with unwavering resolve. By that method even a small Fulani child learns to control a large animal.[17]

In that process, a Fulani herder replaces the dominant animal and becomes the leader of the herd. So strong is his acquired authority that he has only to make a particular call and start walking. The animals fall into line behind him, and keep moving many miles through a very long day. In that repeated process, herders themselves become the dominant animals.[18]

Fulani herders also establish bonds of affection with their cattle. Olmert observed that Fulani use those methods "to milk, groom, and doctor them. . . . These gentle, intimate encounters require a different social strategy, so once again they take their cues directly from the cattle. When cattle are not competing for social dominance, or following one another, they are often licking or grooming each other."[19]

Olmert explains, "Every Fulani herder must also learn to put down his stick and his bravado long enough to understand and emulate these friendly aspects of cattle culture as well. In perfect imitation of cattle-grooming behavior, the Fulani stroke their animals' heads and necks. As a special treat they pet the inside upper back leg—the very spot where a mother licks her calf. The animals welcome these nurturing moments, standing transfixed, and even lick their owners in return."[20]

These interactions between Fulani herders and their animals have attracted the attention of neuroscientists. They have found that specific actions by Fulani and other African herders make use of particular neurological stimuli to establish close relations with their animals and control their behavior in highly effective ways.[21]

Ongoing research in neuroscience has found evidence that these stimuli release chemicals such as oxytocins, which are thought to operate as "bonding agents." Similar stimuli are widely used for that purpose by the animals themselves, beginning with relations between mothers and newborn offspring. Generations of Fulani herders and others mastered these methods by living close to their cattle and sheep through many centuries, and by copying the actions of their animals, with interesting results.[22]

Something comparable developed in relations with horses. Of the old West African kingdom of Jolof, another region with a large Fulani population, between the Senegal and Gambia Rivers, historian John Thornton writes, "Jolof horses were so well trained that they followed their owners around like dogs."[23]

AFRO-HISPANIC STOCK RAISING IN COLONIAL AMERICA

These African methods of working with animals found their way to North America at an early date. Columbus introduced cattle to the Indies on his second transatlantic crossing, in 1493. Spanish conquistadors brought grazing animals to Florida in the sixteenth century. Probably the first connections developed among African slaves within those processes of migration and settlement.

On the frontiers of Spanish colonies, cattle ranches flourished on open land, with Africans slave and free working as *vaqueros* (cowhands) and *boyeros* (ox drivers). Some of them rose to the rank of *capataz* (foreman) and a few to the role of *hacendado* (ranch manager or owner).

An early example was Asile, a Spanish ranch in North Florida near today's city of Tallahassee. It was a large estate, variously described as a cattle ranch and wheat farm. In 1645 it was owned by an absentee Spanish official. The manager was Francisco Galindo, an African slave who became the ranch foreman and also the overseer of American Indian workers. Galindo continued to work there for many years and was able to buy his own freedom in 1648.[24]

Another example was a smaller estate that functioned as both a cattle ranch and also a fortified outpost in East Florida, twenty miles from St. Augustine. It was variously called Diego Plains or Fort Diego, after its owner, Diego de Espinosa. In official documents, Espinosa was described as an Afro-Hispanic mulatto with long experience in managing livestock and ranch hands. His workers were a mix of Spaniards, American Indians, and Africans both slave and free.[25]

BRITISH TRADITIONS OF STOCK RAISING

In early British colonies to the north, New Englanders began to raise livestock in other ways on peninsulas and islands where animals could be protected from predators. That pattern began to appear early in the seventeenth century. Something like it has persisted into the twenty-first century on the privately owned Elizabeth Islands of Massachusetts, where the Forbes family employ managers to tend flocks of sheep in traditional ways. When we visited a few years ago, they were dealing with a new problem. Coyotes were arriving from the mainland, moving from island to island, and preying on the sheep.

As early as 1638–39, cattle also began to be raised in the interior towns of the Massachusetts Bay Colony. For a time, Concord and the original Sudbury (including the author's land in what is now the town of Wayland) were the Wild West of Puritan New England, with improbable Calvinist cowboys.[26]

Other areas developed specialized livestock industries of various kinds. In the Narragansett country of Rhode Island, a small group of large landowners and stock raisers came to be called Narragansett Planters. They made extensive use of African slaves.[27]

Later in the seventeenth century, another livestock industry began to develop in South Carolina—not at first by design. West Indian founders of that colony had other visions in mind. One wrote that their purpose was "to have Planters there and not Graziers."[28]

But first comers were quick to discover that swine and cattle flourished when turned loose to feed in the abundant American forest. Hogs were highly adaptable. They foraged for themselves and thrived on roots and acorns. These lean "mast-fed" animals made very good eating. They rapidly reverted to wild swine from which they had derived, and some were hunted with firearms.

Farther south, free range cattle, roaming through open woodlands, began to multiply in South Carolina at a rapid rate. As early as 1710, Thomas Nairne wrote from South Carolina about the growth in cattle raising on a large scale. "These Creatures have mightily increased since the first settling of the colony, about 40 years ago," he reported. "It was then reckoned a great deal to have three or four Cows, but now some people have 1000 Head, and for one man to have 200 is very common."[29]

Much of the labor was done by African slaves. Some of them worked on foot and "used dogs, bull whips, and salt to manage cattle."[30] Other South Carolina slaves looked after larger herds and were mounted and armed. A contemporary account survives of "four or five" African slaves who belonged to a captain named McPherson. They worked for him on horseback as "Cattel-Hunters," and some of them came to know the wooded interior of South Carolina better than did their masters.

In 1739 several of these Fulani slave herders wounded their master's son, killed another man, "ran away with his horses," and rode south to Spanish Florida. A party of Carolina rangers was sent after them, but these African "Cattel-Hunters" eluded their pursuers. American Indians were put on their trail and succeeded in killing one African, but the others reached St. Augustine. Spanish leaders welcomed them, and "they were received there with great honours, one of them had a commission given to him, and a coat faced with Velvet," much to the fury of their former English masters.[31]

FREE RANGE SYSTEMS OF LAND USE IN NORTH AMERICA

Some of the most highly developed early ranching systems in North America first emerged in Spanish colonies. Their primacy appeared in many Spanish words that entered common usage among Anglo, Indian, and African stockmen alike. Examples were *vaquero, bronco* for a wild or partly tamed horse (from Mexican Spanish *broncho*, rough), and *lariat* (from *la reata*, the rope) for a coiled line used to capture an animal. Other examples were *lasso* (from the Spanish *lazo*), a rope with a sliding noose for holding an animal; and *corral* from *corro* for a wooden circle or ring. These and other Spanish words rapidly became universal in North American ranching from an early date. Together they testify to the importance of Spanish beginnings.

English colonists also introduced their own words, such as *cowboy* and *cowpen*. Other words were African in origin, such as *buckaroo* (from *buckra*, a man or worker), which entered Spanish usage at an early date, and English a little later.

By the early eighteenth century, these various elements came together in range-cattle industries throughout several English colonies. Planters in South Carolina acquired herds of cattle reckoned in the hundreds, and employed highly skilled African slaves to manage them.

This industry rapidly became a functioning free range system. In the English-speaking world, with its common-law traditions, one part of this system was a new American law of fencing, which differed from earlier English customs. In many parts of Western Europe, when animals destroyed a farmer's crops, the stock owner was liable for the damage, and responsible for maintaining enclosures that were strong enough to contain his herd. Through the great spaces of early British America, it soon became the other way around. Farmers became responsible for keeping animals out of their fields. A new common law of fencing developed in the English colonies. It required crop-raising farmers to build and maintain fences that were "horse-high, pig-tight, and bull-strong." This was part of a widespread American revolution in land management and stock raising. The American practice of "fencing out" animals replaced West European customs of "fencing in."[32]

Another distinctive law of cattle brands and branding also developed in North and South America. Ownership of cattle on the free range was free to all, even to slaves in some parts of America. An example was the Spanish region that later became the English-speaking Republic of Texas. At an early date, slaves were recognized as having their own personal brands for animals that they grazed on the open range. In Texas during its early republican period, a brand was registered by a slave named Jim, "a man of color belonging to the est[ate] of A. Jackson [no known relation to President Andrew Jackson]." In 1831, Jim filed a record of his brand in the alcalde's office at San Felipe, where Stephen Austin required all Texas brands to be registered. Today, Jim's original brand registration survives in manuscript at the Austin County Courthouse.[33]

A major part of this free range system was a new method of livestock management. Animals were allowed to roam freely through forests, canebrakes, and natural grasslands. Domestic European swine went feral in early America, ran wild through the woods, and foraged for themselves on a natural abundance of acorns, beechnuts, and other food. They bred freely, and the animals rapidly returned to the condition of their ancestors with long legs, razor backs, and sharp tusks. They were dangerous when disturbed. Boars especially, and sows with their brood, were quick to attack intruders. At slaughter time, they were hunted with firearms.

Cattle also ran free in the open American forest, grazing in grassy openings, natural canebrakes, wild pea vine pastures, and later across a landscape of old fields and trash land. Every year, some of these animals were rounded up and confined in cowpens, large and sturdy log enclosures specially built for the purpose. There the wild cattle were culled, calves were branded, and the animals driven to market. Cowpens appeared in upcountry South Carolina by the late seventeenth century, and in Georgia through the early eighteenth. They also appeared in major events of the American War of Independence. In 1781, an important battle was fought at Hannah's Cowpens in backcountry South Carolina.[34]

COWKEEPS TO COWBOYS AND CATTLEMEN:
DYNAMIC LABOR SYSTEMS ON THE OPEN RANGE

A related change also appeared in southern Anglo-American colonies, especially the Carolinas. By the early eighteenth century, free range animals were managed by unfree labor of English and Irish servants, and also by African slaves. In the seventeenth century these New World workers were called by Old World words such as *cowherds*, which had been used in England since the tenth century. They were also called *cowkeeps* or *cowkeepers*, which were recorded in colonial Virginia as early as 1619, and in Massachusetts by 1652.[35]

In the eighteenth century, yet another word began to appear in colonial records. As early as 1725, English *cowherds* and *cowkeeps* became American *cowboys* in these documents, but not yet in our customary usage. The modern word "boy" has changed its meaning since the seventeenth century, when it was used to describe rank as well as age. In old English usage, "boy" often meant a servant or "knave" in its oldest and most literal sense of a male with low rank. It also appeared in various combinations such as *houseboy* (often a mature male servant of humble rank and ripe years), and *cowboy* had similar connotations. In anglophone North American colonies, the earliest recorded use of *cowboy* known to this historian appeared in 1725. Probably it occurred earlier.[36]

The word *cowboy* was first used in a rank-bound sense for European servants and African slaves who tended cattle. Folklorists have discovered that these first "cowboys" tended to include "African American slaves who herded cows on foot, pushing them along with sticks, as their parents had done in Africa."[37]

By 1741, African slaves called cowboys were looking after large herds of cattle in South Carolina. As their responsibilities expanded, these slave *cowboys* began to be mounted on horseback, and their work was called *cowboying*. They spread west very rapidly. In the early nineteenth century, a party of forty-eight Anglo South Carolinians named Russell, Barton, Pool, and Goodlet migrated with fifty-two African slaves to what is now Williamson County, Texas. Other South Carolinians had preceded them, and some settled with their slaves near the village they ironically called Liberty Hill. Family members later recalled that the work of these slaves continued to be called *cowboying* in a "strong and constant tradition."[38]

South Carolina stockmen made much use of African slaves, and some were attentive to the importance of their ethnic origins in Africa itself. English slave traders and Carolina masters held Fulani slaves from Gambia in high regard, in large part for their long experience as cattle herders. Historian Peter Wood writes, "Many of the slaves entering South Carolina after 1670 may have had experience in tending large herds. People from along the Gambia River, a location for which South Carolina slave dealers came to hold a steady preference, were expert horsemen and herders. . . . Contemporary descriptions of local animal husbandry [in Africa] bear a striking resemblance to what would later appear in Carolina."[39]

AFRICAN AMERICAN COWBOYS BEYOND THE MISSISSIPPI

In the late eighteenth and mid-nineteenth centuries, slavery expanded rapidly from coastal colonies to the Mississippi Valley, and later west to Texas. By 1845, when Texas was annexed to the American republic, its population of 135,000 settlers included 35,100 slaves. At that date, about 26 percent of all these early "Texians," as they liked to call themselves, were African. By 1860, only fifteen years later, the population of Texas had grown fourfold to 612,000 people. Within that number, Texas slaves of African origin had increased to 180,000, and were getting close to a third of all Texans.[40]

Before 1860, most of these slaves were field hands who raised cotton and corn on plantations in East Texas, but many thousands were employed in cattle raising. Some continued to be called cowboys. But native Texans tended to dislike that word as condescending, unmanly, and un-Texan. An example was a cattleman named Jim Shaw, who took strong objection when anyone described his hands, African or European, as cowboys on ponies. "Hell," he said, in his straight-up Texas way, "they were horses and men."[41]

Several attempts have been made to estimate the number and proportion of African cowhands in Texas. These efforts have yielded a variety of roughly similar results. Historian Kenneth Porter studied records of Texas cattlemen who identified their trail hands by race. From several sets of sources, Porter reckoned that 63 percent of Texas trail hands tended to be "White," 25 percent were "Black," and 12 percent were "Hispanic." Other data confirm that whites outnumbered non-whites by a little less than two to one; and Africans or Blacks outnumbered Hispanic hands by similar ratios in Texas, circa 1860.[42]

Other informed observers made comparable estimates. George W. Saunders, president of the Old Trail Drivers Association, later calculated that of

35,000 riders who "went up the trail with herds" in the years from 1866 to 1895, about one third were "Negroes and Mexicans."[43]

From absolute numbers of "trail drivers," another set of computations were made by Ike Pryor, who worked in the cattle business for many years during the late nineteenth century. He reckoned that 10 million cattle were driven north from Texas in twenty years from 1866 to 1885. Pryor calculated that 4,000 herds of 2,500 cattle required 48,000 men, or ten to twelve for each herd. He also estimated that 12,000 African Americans were trail drivers in Texas after the Civil War, about 25 percent of that workforce.[44]

PATTERNS OF EMPLOYMENT AMONG AFRICAN AMERICAN COWHANDS IN TEXAS

The organization of this range-cattle industry in Texas was open and fluid. The men who worked in it came and went from one ranch and trail gang to another. Some signed on for a season, or for a single drive. Others stayed with the same employer for years. Many moved from one place to another, and more than a few decided to put down roots. The result was a world of individual choices, which were attractive to African Americans who had emerged from slavery. The pay also tended to be better than most jobs that were available to former slaves after 1865.

There was much liberty and freedom for Africans on the cattleman's frontier, but little equality. In the cattle business, youngsters often began as unskilled laborers who helped the cook, and did whatever menial jobs came to hand.

Some who worked well with animals became wranglers, a call name for "the lowest man in the pecking order of a trail crew," but a cut above a menial laborer. In some early accounts, these wranglers tended the mounts of the cowhands, and fed and watered them.

With experience and growing expertise, wranglers tended to became cowhands, and worked their way up through another hierarchy of tasks. Among them was Jim Fowler, a "Black cowhand," who rode the Goodknight-Loving trail. He remembered that he was first given absolutely the worst job of all—shooting newborn calves that had dropped during the night. Many cowhands hated that brutal task.[45]

Those who mastered the broad range of skills required for roundups and trail riding became full cowhands. Some also rose in other ways by mastery of special skills, of which there were many. A few advanced to supervisory jobs as "top hands," often by general excellence in running herds.

Some African cowhands also were raised to the rank of foreman, by having the talent and skill for managing men, and by being able to work with free-spirited people who were drawn to life on the trail. A few of these men also had a gift for accumulating wealth. Some former slaves saved their pay and became ranch owners in Texas. Not many succeeded in doing so, but it happened.

BURDENS OF RACE AND OPPORTUNITIES FOR IMPROVEMENT AMONG AFRICAN COWHANDS ON THE OPEN RANGE IN TEXAS

Through most of the nineteenth century and much of the early twentieth, racism became stronger in much of the United States. It grew very strong in the South, and virulent in some parts of Texas.

Cowboys of African ancestry found employment on the southwestern frontier, but often met extreme race prejudice. Most Anglo Texans in the mid-nineteenth century were sons of the Old South. They had little school-

George McJunkin, former slave who rose to ranch foreman and cattle savant, ca. 1907

ing, and their attitudes were steeped in customary race pride and race prejudice. People of African origin on first acquaintance were routinely abused by
words of contempt. An example was George McJunkin, one of the most able,
high-achieving, and widely respected cattlemen of color. In West Texas he became a legendary figure. But even McJunkin was sometimes called "Nigger
George." Many Afro-Texans were addressed in the same way.[46]

But at the same time, Afro-cowboys were also much in demand in a region of extreme labor scarcity. Around the ranch, they were given the worst
jobs, the lowest pay, and the most miserable living conditions. On the trail,
Anglo trailhands were more able to form groups among themselves. African
men tended to live alone. They had fewer opportunities to marry and form
families, which made life doubly difficult for them.

Even so, some of these former slaves preferred the life on the free range to
other jobs that were open to them in the American republic. Life was hard
and dangerous on the cattleman's frontier. There were many routine dangers
in livestock management, especially in managing cantankerous long-horned
steers, and riding half-broken broncos on rough ground.

Much worse were times of sudden crisis, but those moments offered opportunities for Black cowhands to prove their worth. When they did so,
things sometimes went differently for them. Trail gangs were dependent on
one another in difficult situations. In desperate moments when a herd stam-
peded, or Indians attacked, or a wild turn of weather frightened the animals,
nobody noticed the race of a cowhand who was good at his job, brave in the
face of mortal danger, and quick to act decisively in a crisis.

African American cowhands who had skill and courage won the respect
of Anglo and Hispanic hands and Indians who rode with them. Accounts
survive of African American cattlemen who triumphed over racism and mistreatment. When that happened some of them came to be accepted by their
peers whose opinions mattered most to these men. In that process, friendships
formed across racial lines. When those things happened on the trail after the
Civil War, African American cowboys knew themselves to be free men and
their own masters. Others knew it too.

Studies of the West through the nineteenth century find that on the open
range in Texas, cowhands continued to be very diverse in origins. Trail gangs
often tended to be a mix of Mexicans, American Indians, Europeans of many
nationalities, and African Americans. Cowhands of these various ethnicities
had to work closely together. They also had to be able to do similar jobs on a
trail gang. All of them climbed into the same western saddles, and many rode

in the same hell-for-leather Texas style. They wore the same dusty clothes, and took a perverse pride in battered boots and weatherbeaten hats—the more battered and beaten the better. Most of them were armed, and many carried similar weapons—which were great equalizers. They tended to talk the same talk, sing the same songs, eat the same food, and live rough in the open. And on a long drive their weatherbeaten leathery, dusty, deep-creased features tended to look more alike the longer they were on the trail. On roundups and trail drives, these men of many origins sometimes bonded closely together.

At other times in the year, they were sent on special errands, and once again African Americans tended to get the worst jobs. A cowhand in winter could expect to be sent after the lost calves and little dogies. Their job was to bring them to safety in miserable weather, with one hand for a motherless calf who was hanging over the pommel, and the other hand for the horse who was sometimes struggling up to his fetlocks in snow on a steep slope.

DIVERSITY OF AFRICAN TRADITIONS
AMONG AFRO-TEXAS COWHANDS

On the western frontier, some of these individual African American cowhands began to acquire distinctive reputations. Some centered on the ways they worked with animals, and how they dealt with wild ones. On the great Cox Ranch that sprawled across two counties in the Big Bend country of Texas, family members recalled that "black cowboys were often hired because they could handle wild horses."[47]

Many stories survive of African American cowhands who appeared to have a gift for working with mustangs who lived on the open range. Some (not all) of these men turned away from the more brutal methods of "bronc busting" or "horse breaking," which were sometimes so harsh that the horse was broken in more ways than one.

J. Frank Dobie, a leading historian of mustangs and longhorns, knew many of these men, and especially remembered some of the Afro-American cattlemen of his acquaintance who seemed to have a "special gift" for working with wild horses and range cattle. Dobie recalled that animals would follow some of these riders "like mules magnetized by a bell mare." He remembered that men of his acquaintance who had that special gift were rarely Anglo-Americans. In his experience, most tended to be "Mexican" or often "Negro." Dobie began to call them "horse gentlers." So they were, and thereby hangs another set of tales about Africans on the open range in early America.[48]

Bob Lemmons, Carrizo Springs, Texas, by
Dorothea Lange, 1936

AFRO-TEXAN "HORSE GENTLERS"

Frank Dobie's leading example of a horse gentler was Robert Lemmons, a legendary African American who was renowned for his long experience with wild mustangs on the frontier. Robert Lemmons had been born a slave around 1848, in Caldwell County, Texas. His mother fled to Mexico, but Robert stayed behind and became a close friend of his master's son, who was about the same age. They grew up together on the free range.[49]

It was a hard school. They lived on the edge of Comanche country. Even as children they fought Indians, and helped build a small fortified cattle ranch. After the end of slavery in 1865, Robert was set free. He went to work for a rancher named Duncan Lemmons, who became his teacher. They bonded closely together. "He taught me everything I knowed about stock," Lemmons later recalled, and took his last name as an expression of thanks.[50]

At an early age, Lemmons grew interested in the many wild mustangs who lived free on the open range in Texas. They descended from Spanish horses, and were much valued for speed and agility. These extraordinary animals were often deliberately bred with other horses. The result was the development of new breeds on the free range frontier. Some came to be called the Texas quarter horse.

Mustang roundups were often done with great violence, even to the death or crippling of the wild horses, and the destruction of their spirit. Robert Lemmons began to study these animals, and invented a better way of working with them. Mustangs moved in herds called *manadas*, often led by a dominant stallion, with as many as thirty mares in some of the larger groups.

He began to ride with these *manadas*, and tried to learn the complicated language of their neighings and whistles and whickers. He also studied the even more complex and subtle language of their movements. And he was closely attentive to the operation of their amazing senses—especially their keen sense of smell, and their exquisite sensitivity to the acts and feelings of other creatures. Always his purpose was to understand their ways of thinking, in which he had remarkable success.

Lemmons discovered that each mustang *manada* had its own system of rivalries within the herd, and customs of mortal conflict between rival stallions. He learned how wild mustangs responded to danger and opportunity. His object was to work out ways of catching them by engaging their curiosity and winning their consent, without doing damage to these strong but fragile animals in body or spirit.

His friend Frank Dobie said of Lemmons, "He always mustanged alone," which was another part of his method. He followed a mustang band for many days, always trying to ride upwind, just near enough for the mustangs to smell his presence, but not nearer. After a difficult week or two, the horses began to accept his presence. After several more weeks, they started to follow him, and he found that with patience and kindness and restraint, he could lead them into a corral.[52] An eyewitness account survives from a cattleman, who wrote that Lemmons "actually became the leader of a band of wild horses that followed him into a pen, as fresh as they had been when he first sighted them."[52]

Once in the corral, he worked out other ways of calming them. First, he said, "you had to keep 'em circlin' after you got 'em in the pen. If you didn't know how to circle 'em with blankets and such, you'd get 'em killed." The taming and training proceeded in the same spirit.[53]

This way of working with wild mustangs was intended to tame them without the use of force, and to control them without breaking their spirit. The method began to be called horse-gentling by Frank Dobie and others. Robert Lemmons came to be known far and wide among cattlemen as a champion horse-gentler.

At the same time, he also succeeded in another way. His unique ability to lead an entire *manada* of mustangs into a corral, "undamaged and uninjured, calm and malleable," was worth money in Texas. As the word got around, Robert Lemmons began to be well paid. He saved his profits, invested in land, built a holding of 1,200 acres, became a successful rancher, rented some of his land, added another business, and became a local moneylender. He also taught himself to read and write, and settled down in the town of Carrizo Springs, near the family who had owned him. Then he married and raised his own family, and joined the Baptist Church. At first he met intense racism from townsfolk, and outright rage and hostility from lowlife types who called him the "Lemmons Nigger." But as he helped many others, both Black and white, he became "Uncle Bob" to one and all. There were parallels between his career as a horse-gentler and the taming of at least some white racist towns-men in Texas.

OTHER VARIETIES OF TEXAS HORSE-GENTLERS: MATHEW "BONES" HOOKS: AN "AFRO WRANGLER" WHO SPECIALIZED IN "OUTLAW" ANIMALS

Other Afro-Texans became widely known. They worked at a variety of tasks, and their methods were never twice the same. But many of these early horse-gentling men—and women—on the Texas frontier shared something in common. They tended to have African origins through several genera-tions.[54]

A striking variation on the theme of horse-gentling appeared in the ca-reer of a young Black wrangler named Mathew Hooks (1867–1951). He was better known as "Bones" to other cowhands for his light weight and thin build. For many years he worked on the DSD ranch in the Texas Panhandle. Throughout that region he gained a reputation for an uncanny ability to "stay on any horse alive." He could do it even with infamous "outlaw animals," as they were called. "Outlaws" were angry creatures, so infuriated by humans who dared to climb on their backs that they would not merely pitch and buck. Some outlaw horses deliberately threw themselves over backward with great violence, trying to kill their riders by crushing them to death, and sometimes succeeded.

Mathew Hooks was able to work with these animals. He was the son of slaves, born free two years after emancipation. Those who knew him said that he "learned to love horses" when he was very young. They also observed that he had an extraordinary gift for getting on with them.

He went about this work in a way that differed from that of Robert Lemmons, who worked with an entire *manada* or herd of wild mustangs and brought them in together. Mathew Hooks worked with these outlaw animals as individuals, one at a time.[55]

At the early age of fourteen he astonished his family by beginning the labor of working with outlaw animals. Mathew Hooks was not another broncbuster, of which there were many in Texas, but something more and other than that. He liked to work with the horses that "never did quit fighting and remained unbroken outlaws." Some of these animals were used only as draft horses, because nobody could stay on them.[56]

Hooks had a special gift for staying on the back of a very wild animal. It was said that when a new horse was brought in, Mathew would get on, and ride him every day. He would treat the horse with kindness and respect. Those who knew Hooks and watched him at work, said over and over that "while riding the horses Mathew developed a friendship with each of the animals."[57]

Much of this process of forming a friendship with a wild horse was done by establishing trust. Hooks never used force or cruelty or surprise. He worked in a consistent and predictable way, "earning the horse's trust, until the horse was bridle-wise." Much of that trust was about constancy, firmness, perseverance, and taking care not to break a bond of understanding with an animal. As that relationship grew, Hooks would ride the horse out of the pen and onto the open range. As the bond of trust expanded it was said that the horses he trained were "often smart enough to bring a man back to camp if he were lost."[58]

He developed a way of taming and training an outlaw horse that was much in demand among ranchers throughout the Texas Panhandle. He worked for many of them. Even in his early youth he was paid $3 or $5 for each horse, or $25 a month with board, which was as much as top hands received.

His methods of forming friendships and earning trust also sometimes worked on two-legged creatures. He formed similar connections with trail hands, foremen, owners, and also with families and neighbors. It was said that "mothers trusted him with their young sons, knowing that Mathew would teach them the horse skills that he knew so well. The mothers in turn also treated Mathew as a son."

He married and settled down in Clarendon, in the Texas Panhandle, a "Christian town" that insisted on order and honesty. But it was also a racist town, and did not allow people of color to live there. Mathew refused to accept that rule, began to make friendships with individual townspeople, and helped them with their animals until he was able to buy a piece of land and build a house. He was invited to talk with the students in school, and chose the subject of friendship. He said, "Friendship can be more useful than anything else."[59]

Later his wife, Anna, urged him to move to the larger town of Amarillo, which had a big African American population. Mathew made many friendships there, and became a leader of the African-American community. He began to act as a civic leader of the entire town, making many friendships with Anglo families. At Amarillo in 1932, he founded the Dogie Club for underprivileged boys, and helped them get ahead. He also talked to college students, Afro and Anglo, and spoke again about friendships as "one of the finest things in the world: You can keep friendship always. You may lose everything but you can't lose that." He had a gift for making friends of the two- and four-legged variety, and also a gift of the spirit that reached the heart of an outlaw horse and the soul of a race-bound community.

ADDISON JONES, WHO TOPPED AND
SETTLED "ROUGH" HORSES

Yet a third form of horse-gentling appeared in the work of Addison Jones, a legendary Afro-American cowhand. He was born a slave around 1845, freed after 1865, and grew up riding horses and running cattle in Gonzáles County, near San Antonio in South Central Texas, where some of the early big trail drives began.

Add Jones, as he came to be known, worked for the big Bar F Ranch, where a drive sometimes employed as many as twenty or twenty-five trail hands. Each had a string of seven or ten horses, sometimes specialized by task. One rider remembered that a trail hand might have "a cutting horse, a bridle horse, a night horse, a roping horse, a saddle horse, a packing horse, and a favorite pony."[60]

On the trail these many horses used by Bar F hands were kept together in a *manada* traveling-horse herd, which on one drive included 120 mounts. Some of these animals were half-broken or "rough" broncos. On cold mornings they could be full of trouble. Jones and other African-American cowhands were given the job of looking after them. Every morning while the Anglo trail hands were having breakfast, they rode the fractious mounts and calmed the roughest animals. The task was called "topping off," and it "most often took the form of "taking the first pitch out of the rough horses of the outfit as they stood saddled in the chill of the morning, while the white boys ate their breakfast." It was not unusual for one young Afro-American to "top a half-dozen hard-pitching horses before breakfast." And if there were other problems, or "a fighting bull or steer was to be handled," an Afro hand "knew without being told it was his job." It was a routine task on a long drive.[61]

Afro-Texan Addison Jones in particular became highly skilled at this work. He made a specialty of it, and liked to take the most difficult horses. Another hand said that every morning "when the wagons started and the horses were fresh, he sappered out the salty ones for the boys who dreaded to ride them. It was nothing unusual for him to top off several horses of a morning in order to get the pitching out of their systems before the outfit started the drive."[62]

How did he do it? Jones himself explained that he "knew every one of 120 horses in the Bar F *remuda* by name, and he could ride them all." More than that, he also was heard to say that he could "look a horse square in the eye and almost tell what it was thinking." Cattleman Evetts Haley wrote that Add Jones "was the most noted Negro cowboy that ever 'topped off' a horse."[63]

AFRICAN AMERICAN WOMEN AS HORSE-GENTLERS

In Texas, some of the most successful African American horse gentlers were women. Prominent among them was Johanna July. She had been born free among Afro-Seminoles in Mexico about 1857 or 1858, the daughter of Elijah July. She grew up in a small adobe village where some Black Seminoles raised cattle in Mexico, and her father looked after the stock.

As a child she also learned the ways of horses from American Indians. An Afro-Seminole warrior, Adam Wilson, taught her to ride side saddle Mexican style, rather than astride the horse in the Indian way. She did it both ways, barefoot and bareback, often without a saddle, sometimes without a blanket or pad. Johanna July remembered, "I didn't use no bridle either, just a rope around their necks, and looped over de nose. We called it a 'nosin,' same as a half hitch. Right today I don't like a saddle, and I don't like shoes."

In her family everybody worked, and she was allowed to work with the animals. Moving them into pastures, "probably using a long pole to goad the stock in the same manner as vaqueras of old."

When her father died, she invented her own way of taming wild horses—not horse breaking, but her own idea of horse-gentling by a unique method. She lived close to the Rio Grande, and used the river itself as an instrument for working with the wild horses. She explained,

> I would pull off my clothes and get into de clothes I intended to bathe in, and I would lead 'em right into de Rio Grande and keep 'em dere till dey got pretty well worried. . . . I would swim up and get 'im by de mane an ease up on 'em. He couldn't pitch and when I did let 'im out of dat deep water he didn't *want* to pitch. . . . Sometimes dey wasn't so wore out, an would take a runnin' spree wid me when dey got out to shallow water where dey could get deir feet on de ground, and dey would run clear up into de corral. But I was young and I was havin' a good time.

Johanna July could ride like the wind. One day she was working her herd onto grazing ground not far from Fort Duncan near the border. She noticed that the horses suddenly came alert, "moving about, snorting, pointing their ears up." She searched the surrounding distance, and saw Indians creeping toward her herd. She called to Bill, "a big bay horse she had gentled. When he moved, the herd moved with him." She "placed a hackamore, a braided bridle on a little gray named Charley," dug her fingers into his mane as she swung onto his back, kicked him into a lope, and started a run for the fort and the other horses followed. Looking back over her shoulder Johanna July saw that the Indians were now mounted and gaining ground. She began to gallop toward the fort, with the horses spread out behind, and the Indians coming on strong. They reached the fort just in time.

She married three times, raised a family near Brackettville, Texas, not far from the border, also worked at horse-gentling, and had her hands full with mules and especially with men, who were for her the most difficult species. But she was able to commune with the spirits of her horses, much as her African ancestors had done.[64]

AFRICAN CATTLEMEN WITH SPECIAL SKILLS: HENRY BECKWITH, BRUSH HAND

Some of the most memorable stories are about African men and the many specialized ways they worked with cattle. One unique character worked in what may have been the hardest job of all, and in one of the most difficult places. It was called the Brush Country of Texas, between San Antonio and the Rio Grande, a vast area covered with dense thickets of prickly pear, a plant with huge and very dangerous thorns, amid a tangle of hostile vegetation. The Brush Country was also the home of giant rattlesnakes nine feet long, and it became a favorite hiding place for big outlaw longhorn steers, bulls, and cattle.

Texas cowmen called "brush hands" specialized in hunting and catching wild "outlaw" cattle in that hard environment. Catching these difficult animals in Texas Brush Country was often on the outer edge of possibility.

One Afro-Texan cattleman who excelled at that work was a famous character named Henry Beckwith. The great Texas historian Frank Dobie was raised near the Brush Country, knew that region well, and was deeply interested in Henry Beckwith. Dobie wrote, "What I know about Henry Beckwith I learned from men who worked with him." [65] He remembered that "Beckwith passed for a negro, but mixed in him were strains of Indian, Mexican, and white blood." He lived to a ripe age, dying in 1935 after working for many years as a champion brush hand. [66]

Dobie wrote that "he always bedded down some distance away from other men, out in the bush, alone," and was always up before dawn. Dobie observed that "he was continually turning his head this way and that, looking, watching, expecting." One man who knew him said "he reminded me of a wild eagle put in a cage."

Beckwith led a team of Mexicans who worked for him, and called him Coyote, and rode a string of dun horses. They would go into the Brush Country for weeks at a time, where they built a pen and were brilliant at capturing outlaw cattle. In one evening they captured seven or eight big old steers, working with another brush hand named Ed McCoy. He said that "the noiseless way" in which they got them out was a "marvel."

Dobie wrote that Henry Beckwith "could be brutal, but he never was brutal to his horses or to a catch dog called Slacker." And he was hardest on himself. [67]

WORKING CATTLE: LOUIS POWER, A MAN
WHO COULD THINK LIKE A COW

Another supremely gifted cowhand was Louis Power, a mulatto, part Irish and part African. He was the grandson of James Power, ranch foreman on the O'Connor Ranch. Others said of Louis that "he was a genius at understanding a 'cow brute,' and was a master at handling cattle. His ability to think like a cow made his work easier, his men's work easier, and life easier for the cattle."[68]

As a man of mixed ancestry in a deeply racist culture, he was made to understand that there was no place for him in white society. And he was also "not treated as an equal in black society." But he made his way as a cattleman with high success. He became a working cowhand, then top hand, foreman, and manager of several ranches owned by the O'Connor family. They had the highest respect for him, and he succeeded by being supremely good at working with animals.[69]

SINGING THE HERD: CHARLEY WILLIS AND HIS GIFT FOR CALMING THE CATTLE

Some gifted people such as Johanna July and Robert Lemmons did much in the way of communing with animals. Most people in the range cattle business learned to do at least a little of that sort of thing. Many riders who drove large herds on the overland trail were quick to discover that they could bond with animals in particular ways.

One of the most common methods was called "singing the herd." George McJunkin remembered it from his time as a trail rider, taking his turn at the unwelcome work of night riding. Cowboys rode herd at night much in the way that seamen stood watches at sea. The work was harder on the trail, especially in what sailors call the midwatch. McJunkin remembered of the men in his trail gang, "In the night each of them would have to get up and take his turn riding around and around the herd for two hours, keeping the cattle together." Music, they agreed, calmed the longhorn cattle, and it helped the cowhands too. On some of slowest nights they sang sad songs of their own misfortunes.

> Some of 'em go up the trails for pleasure
> But that's where they get it most awful wrong
> You ain't got any idea the trouble they give us
> While we go a drivin' them all along.[70]

Trail riders of every description sang to their herds, but some did it better than others. Among the best were Afro-cowboys, and one man in particular, who was widely known across the West. Charley Willis was born a slave in 1850, and emancipated after the Civil War. He worked as a ranch hand, a horse breaker, and then he became a trail driver, running cattle from Georgetown near Austin in Central Texas to Cheyenne in Wyoming.

It was said that "Charley must have had an ear or an aptitude for music." He was thought to have invented some of the songs he sang. A classic was "Good Bye 'Ol Paint." Others heard it from him, and he sang it with a jew's harp or fiddle to Alan Lomax, who recorded it for posterity.

Historian Wayne Gard observes of a cowboy's songs, "He usually had a practical purpose. In threatening weather, when the cattle began to drift and show signs of stampeding, a hymn or a ballad might quiet them." It was said that "cowboy songs were always sung by one person, never by a group."[71] They would be passed from one person to another. One cattleman remembered, "What you would hear as you passed your partner on guard would be a kind of low hum or whistle, and you wouldn't know what it was. Just some old hymn tune, likely as not. . . . The cowboy hardly ever knew what tune he was singing his song to, just some old, old tune that he had heard and had known as a boy."[72]

Others recalled that "Methodist hymns were popular . . . although old fashioned negro minstrel songs have been found equally effective in soothing the breast of the wild Texas steer. . . . After the men had sung a few lullabies to the steers they all lay down and started snoring." It sounds like another Texas Whopper, but they were honest men, and swore up and down that it was so.[73]

TRANSMISSION OF AFRO-AMERICAN TRADITIONS ON THE WESTERN FRONTIER: FOUR GENERATIONS OF THE WALKER FAMILY IN WILSON COUNTY, TEXAS

For a historian, a central question is about the dynamics of these traditions, and the process of transmission from one generation to the next. We can follow that sequence through five generations of an African American family in the Texas stock-raising business. The first generation on record was a slave named Walker who was brought from Alabama to Texas, and was put to the task of gentling wild horses "in the late 1840s."[74] He taught his son James or Jim Walker how to work with wild horses. Jim recalled how they went about it—rough and hard at the start. He remembered that they would sit on the top rail of a pen full of animals. They were taught to "jump off onto the backs of wild horses" and quiet them.

Jim Walker married Eliza Edwards on December 30, 1880. They had at least three sons, who became the third generation, and learned the family business. All were said to be "experienced cow hands and horse handlers," and it was said they all "had a way with animals."

The second son in this third generation was Obie Walker, born in the 1890s, and a soldier in World War I. He was considered to be one of the best ranch hands in Southwest Texas. It was said that "ranchers would hire him when they had problems on their ranches or their stock."

Also in the third generation was the youngest son, Richard "Bubba" Walker, born in 1899. He was taught by his older brothers to handle wild horses and Texas longhorns. It was not merely a matter of technique. Bubba was taught that "to be a good cowboy one needed first of all to be a good man." Bubba became a top hand, worked "all his life" and "did it till he died."

The fourth generation included Bubba Walker's five sons and three daughters. They went different ways. Four of the sons went into the livestock business, and rode with their father. All were known for their skill with animals. Another brother was Alonzo Walker, called Lonnie or Tonker, who moved to Chicago. A sister became a "surrogate mother," and another went to college.

One son was named Richard "Bubba" Walker, and he had two sons of his own in the fifth generation. One of them was John Walker, who became a cowboy, loved the work, joined the army in World War II, went to college on the G.I. Bill, then returned to ranching, and rode with his father. Some of these Walkers were working with cattle and horses into the twenty-first century—with a circle of relatives and close friends. Many were renowned for their skill with animals. One of them won the "Working Cowboy of the Year Award" in 1989.

Altogether it was a line of descent that spanned five generations and 150 years, from an African slave in the 1840s to the working cowboys and horse-gentlers who were still perceived to have a special touch with animals in the twenty-first century.[75]

THE OPEN RANGE AND EXPANDING LIBERTY AND FREEDOM

The free range in the western United States was a place where slaves with special skills were able to live free, and freedmen could find a life of dignity, more so than in other American regions.

It was a hard, rough, and dangerous world—a world without pity or mercy. It was also a world without equality, and racism was strong there. But it was a world where some people of color were able to ride free—free to come and go, free to be true to themselves, and free to find their own way.

On the cattleman's frontier, some of these former slaves chose to flock together. Others tended to move apart, as did cowmen of other backgrounds. Some surviving stories of Black cattlemen are about loners, but many made friends, found steady jobs, formed families, and lived in communities. At the same time they too made their own way. It was a story told through many generations of individual striving and self-reliance. This was a hard and dangerous world, but it was also a world that respected strength, skill, and courage.

Many of these Black cattlemen and women had something specially their own to contribute. It was a set of skills for working with animals that had been brought by West African slaves to South Carolina. Some of their Carolina masters knew about their special skills and deliberately sought them out in the slave trade of the early eighteenth century. As the stock raiser's frontier moved west, some of these African slaves and their offspring went with it. In Texas most of all, they developed this tradition in new forms. As these words are written in the twenty-first century, it is still growing.

Chapter 8

MARITIME FRONTIERS

West African Boatmen, Chesapeake Watermen,
American Maritime Traditions

Slavery always frayed at the sea's edge.
—David Cecelski, on slavery in maritime North Carolina[1]

There is a strong bond between watermen, regardless of race. . . .
Water bonds them together.

—William Wallace, descendant of African American
skipjack captains, Deal Island, Maryland[2]

IN 1987 FULANI HERDER Mallum Yaq'u was digging a well for his
animals in the arid interior of northern Nigeria. Sixteen feet down, he
struck something big and hard. To his surprise he found a very old boat,
buried deep in dry ground south of the Sahara.

A team of archaeologists came to help, and excavated an intact African
canoe of great antiquity. Carbon dating estimated her age at 8,000 to 8,500
years, which made her the oldest boat found in Africa, and the second- or
third-oldest in the world.[3]

Scholars in many fields were quick to take notice. Geologists were anxious
to know why one of the world's oldest boats had been found near the world's
largest desert. For them it was a clue to the global dynamics of climate history.[4]

Archaeologists were struck by the size of this ancient canoe, which was
big enough for eight or ten paddlers. Maritime historians studied the shape
of her hull, which had been designed for speed with a tapered bow, flowing
lines, and a high ratio of length to beam. She was clearly the product of long
experience and had been built with practiced skill. One scholar wrote that this
boat was evidence of a lost "aquatic civilization" in the middle of West Africa,
as early as the late Pleistocene Era.[5]

EASTERN FRONTIERS: MARITIME SLAVES IN THE CHESAPEAKE REGION

PENNSYLVANIA

MASON-DIXON LINE

Susquehanna R.

Wilmington

NEW JERSEY

Delaware River

Dover

Delaware Bay

Baltimore

Patapsco R.

Patuxent River

Kent Island

MASON-DIXON LINE

Annapolis

Choptank R.

DELAWARE

Alexandria

Mt. Vernon

Tilghman Island

Oxford

M A R Y L A N D

Vienna

Solomons

Potomac River

St. Mary's

Deal Island

Pocomoke City

VIRGINIA

Burnt House Landing

Rappahannock River

Crisfield

Mattaponi River

Reedville

Pamunkey River

Nesting Plantation

Chesapeake Bay

Chickahominy River

Amberg

York River

Richmond

Williamsburg

Jamestown

James River

Cape Charles

Cape Henry

Atlantic Ocean

Norfolk

0 *Miles*   20   40

0 *Kilometers*   40

© 2022 Jeffrey L. Ward

AFRICA'S MANY MARITIME CULTURES

This and other evidence make clear that many centuries before the Atlantic slave trade, the people of Africa had begun to accumulate much hard-won maritime experience on the rivers and coasts of their vast continent.[6]

Distinct seagoing traditions flourished in many African regions, longer perhaps than anywhere on the planet. Three millennia before the modern era, Arabian and North African seamen led the world in celestial navigation. They built large vessels for long voyages, with distinctive hull designs and unique sail plans of high efficiency.

Leading examples are East African *dhows* and North African *xebecs*. Both types used big triangular fore-and-aft lateen sails with high success. Xebecs have long been known for their speed. In early modern Europe, Venetian, French, and Spanish builders copied their sharp-built hulls and mixed rigs. In America, the Continental Navy commissioned the xebec USS *Champion* for service on the Delaware Bay in 1777. During the War of 1812, the Baltimore privateer *Ultor* was a big three-masted lateen-rigged xebec, built in a Chesapeake shipyard on a North African model. She captured thirty-three prizes, and the Royal Navy's fastest sailing ships were unable to catch her.[7]

Many maritime cultures flourished on the Atlantic coast of West Africa. In what are now Sierra Leone and Liberia, coastal Kru people have long been renowned as seafarers. Through the eras of sail and steam, free Kru seamen

Ottoman-Greek xebec

Kru men and their slender seagoing canoes

were much in demand for service aboard ships of many nations. They could be recognized by proud "krumarks," facial tattoos of blue or black stripes that ran from the forehead down the bridge of the nose to the tip of the chin. Kru seamen came to be highly respected as among the best blue-water sailors in the early modern world.[8]

Other West African cultures used the sea in different ways. Senegal's enterprising Wolof people have long been export merchants and go-betweens in Atlantic commerce. So prominent were their roles that Wolof speech became a foundation of pidgin speech which many traders have long used on the coast of West Africa.[9]

Yet another maritime group in West Africa today are the Lebu, a fishing people who live on Cape Verde, the farthest western projection of Africa. They have long been highly skilled at using one of the most abundant fishing grounds in the Atlantic Ocean near Cape Verde. Recently its fish stocks have been ravaged by foreign factory ships, and the Lebu people have become leaders in a long-term movement for fishing conservation and sustained management in African waters. They are fiercely independent, as seafaring people tend to be. The Lebu practice a religion called Layene, and speak their own language, which is related to Wolof but with a unique character. Today they cherish a condition of quasi-autonomy within the modern nation of Senegal.[10]

Ocean fishing canoes in Ghana

Farther south along the Gold Coast, other maritime cultures developed among Akan-speaking people. They are much renowned for their handsome and highly functional seagoing canoes. On the beaches of western Ghana, the graceful and efficient lines of these sturdy, sharp-built workboats caught the eye of this American visitor from the Chesapeake Bay. We observed that some of these vessels were built with what Americans call clipper bows and fluent hull lines that looked very familiar to a Marylander. The more we saw of these Ghanaian vessels, the more linkages we found to maritime artifacts in early North America.[11]

East of Ghana, the West African savannah approaches the sea on the Bight of Benin and the watercourses of Nigeria. Here large canoes were built by rival states as instruments for the pursuit of power and the conduct of war. In the eighteenth century, the kingdom of Allada maintained a formidable navy of fighting canoes. Some were big enough to mount four swivel cannons.

Another example was the amphibious forces of Lagos. When its leaders made war on Badagri in 1788, French witnesses reported that they attacked in an armada of two thousand canoes, each carrying twenty warriors. Historian John Thornton rightly warns of exaggeration in these reports. But even after major correction, these were strong seaborne forces.[12]

Farther east, near the Niger Delta, the kingdom of Warri was a small but highly centralized naval power. It was known for large war canoes which were reported to carry as many as a hundred fighters, armed with javelins and protected by shields.[13]

On the great rivers of West Africa other canoes were designed for commerce and built to function as freighters and ferry boats. Along the Niger River, which was to West Africa as the Nile is to East Africa, Robert Smith writes that "ferries served to bind together the peoples of riparian states, and in the Niger Delta the canoe was the very basis of government and society."[14]

From close acquaintance, European seamen discovered that these West African canoes were superior to European watercraft in some ways—speed for one. Other West African vessels were (and are) highly developed in their aesthetics. Among them are large and graceful lake canoes with fine lines, low freeboard, and a tapered symmetry of forward-curving bows and sterns. Many of them can be seen today on Lake Volta. Most are workboats, designed for net fishing on interior waters, sometimes with crews of children. At the same time, these efficient Lake Volta fishing canoes are among the most beautiful vessels in the world.

Fishing community, Lake Volta, Ghana

CANOE CULTURES IN WEST AFRICA

These various West African canoes began as simple dugouts. They became more highly developed and were increasingly designed as functional instruments of complex economies. At the same time, those intricate artifacts also became expressive works of art. Their striking designs were distinctively West African in origin.

By comparison, other dugouts of great age have been found in Asia, Europe, America, and many regions throughout the world. Leading examples are three ancient European boats, preserved for many centuries in a bog near the river Seine. We studied them in the Musée Carnavalet in Paris. A test on these old European vessels yielded a carbon age of 6,300 years before the present.[15]

In the twenty-first century, an even older Chinese dugout was discovered in the lower Yangtze Valley, with carbon dates from 6991 to 7070 B.C.[16]

And among the North American Indians, dugouts, coracles, and other watercraft had a long history. They were studied by European seamen for their range of uses, and methods of construction with neolithic tools of stone, shell, and fire.[17]

Among these many global dugouts, early West African canoes differed in size, scale, and diversity of form and function. They were also distinctive in methods of construction, patterns of use, and rates of speed which European writers found incredible until they used them. And at the same time these African vessels were much admired for their grace and beauty.

A large fund of firsthand knowledge about early African canoes was collected in the seventeenth century by one of their admirers, Jean Barbot, a French Huguenot merchant and mariner. He worked on the coast of Africa from 1678 to 1682, and wrote at length about his experiences. Barbot was fascinated by African canoes. He observed them in many regions, used them frequently, described them in detail, and sketched them in his own drawings.[18]

Barbot gave particular attention to the construction of canoes at five leading centers on the Gold Coast. He observed that "those who make canoes generally live at Axim, Accuon, Routry, Takoradi and Komenda [sic], since those lands are forested."[19]

Traditional methods of canoe building emerged in those places, and some have continued to our time. Even as a modern shipbuilding industry has developed in West Africa, old ways persist with many changes, some of which involve the use of chain saws as cutting and shaping tools. But through much

of coastal West Africa, highly skilled traditional boatbuilders carefully preserve time-honored techniques of "artisanal canoe construction," as it is called
in Ghana today.

Elements of this tradition and its accumulated knowledge were brought to
America by skilled slave craftsmen. These African artisans and their posterity
made a difference in boats and ships that began to be built in coastal Carolina
and the Chesapeake Bay, and also in Bermuda, the West Indies, and South
America.

Some traditional African methods were unique among makers of canoes
throughout the world. In other cultures, early canoe builders were limited by
neolithic stone tools. Highly skilled African artisans had the advantage of indigenous iron tools at an early date. Some of these instruments were specially
designed for boatbuilding long before the Europeans arrived. Fire was used
occasionally, but for secondary tasks. Artisans who did this work were known
as "canoe carvers." Today they belong to a guild called the Ghana National
Canoe Carvers Association.[20]

Jean Barbot closely observed processes of canoe construction in West Africa during the seventeenth century. The first task of a Fante canoe carver was
to enter a sacred forest grove and cut down a single great wawa tree. That
species of *Triplochiton scleroxylon* was preferred for this purpose. Today it is
increasingly endangered, but still survives in protected Ghanaian National
Forests, and continues to be used for boatmaking.[21]

When a canoe was to be built, a great tree was carefully chosen. After spiritual prayers and rituals of urgent seriousness and deep meaning, Barbot observed that the tree was cut down with a special African felling axe called an
"asenkewe." Then the lower hull was hollowed out with an instrument that
Barbot described as a "hoelike tool" called a "sosow." As the hull took form, it
was carefully shaped with "great chisels" and special "curved knives."[22]

Much of this work was done in the forest. After the lower hull was roughed
out, it was moved to the canoe carver's village by an organized procession with
many rituals. In the village another stage began, of refining and smoothing
the boat's hull bottom with a sharp-edged tool called an *erminette* in Barbot's
French and an *adze* in English. Barbot observed, of the finishing of the hull
bottoms, "they smooth it, outside and in, with other small tools, which takes
them a long time. However, they make it very light, and very neat."[23]

These canoe carvers were taking pains to make boats that could move
through the water at high speed, which was a key to success in the fisheries
and survival in dangerous places. To those ends, they clearly understood the

critical importance of hull design in its dimensions, weight, ratio of length to beam, and distribution of mass through its full length.[24]

They also knew that clean flowing lines and a smooth finish were vital to speed through the water. Barbot observed these qualities in their work with high respect and was astonished by the results. After long experience in European vessels, Barbot wrote of West African builders and seamen that "the speed with which these people make these boats travel is beyond belief."[25]

Barbot was also surprised by the stability of African canoes in open water. He added, "I have very often been obliged to travel in either the large canoes or the small ones, as the demands of the trade required me, in order to go ashore, yet I was never once upset. Mind you, I had some alarming moments."[26]

After much careful cutting, carving, and smoothing of the lower hull, the next step in West African canoe making was to build up the sides of the boat with hand-hewn planks, often from the same wawa tree. For small canoes, planks of two by four inches were sometimes used. Larger vessels were built with planks as big as two by twelve inches.[27]

Barbot observed that the work of measuring and shaping was done by eye, without plans, molds, or models. The process was made to work by continuous effort of careful cutting, close fitting, and many adjustments of complex pieces. Much use was made of specialized tools for shaping and smoothing.[28]

These methods were used to produce African canoes in many shapes and sizes. Some were very small, and designed for use by a single person fishing alone or making a short and solitary journey. More numerous were slightly larger vessels, described by Barbot as "neat canoes," and intended for a crew of two or three. He observed that these crews commonly worked closely together, with one man standing up to fish, and another sitting alone near the stern to steer the boat and "keep it heading into a rolling sea." A third helped with other tasks. There was often a cutlass on board, with bread and water, and "a live fire on a large stone for cooking fish when they wanted a meal."[29]

Those small boats were built in large numbers, but the most numerous class of vessels were midsized "common canoes," as he called them. He reckoned their length at sixteen to eighteen feet, and width at twenty to twenty-four inches, which made a ratio of beam to length at roughly 1:8 or 1:9. Barbot observed that these "common canoes" were of several designs. Some were roughly rectangular with broad flat horizontal projections extending fore and aft from bow and stern, for carrying canoes across a beach.

Other "common canoes" were sharp-built, with long-tapered bows that flowed aft from sturdy stem posts that were vertical or raked at various angles.

Hull bottoms tended to be flat, but were curved or tapered upward at both ends, which made them more serviceable on open beaches when launching and landing through surf.

Similar vessels are still to be seen in large numbers drawn up on Ghanaian beaches. Their designs have been modified through time, but in the twenty-first century they remain in some ways similar to descriptions by Barbot and others on the same West African beaches four centuries ago.[30]

Jean Barbot was amazed by the vast number of canoes along the Gold Coast (now Ghana) in the seventeenth century. At Axim, Mouree, and Cormentin he saw three to four hundred fishing canoes go out from each place every morning, wind and weather permitting. At larger centers such as Elmina and Komenda, Barbot observed that as many as five or six hundred boats, and even in one instance eight hundred fishing canoes, departed at dawn to fish about two leagues (six miles) offshore. They returned in the afternoon, usually laden with the day's catch.[31]

He was fascinated by the process of launching a Fante fishing canoe from an open sand beach into the strong Atlantic surf. Midsized canoes would set out on a rising land breeze which was blowing toward the sea on most mornings. They returned later in the day, when the wind turned and became a sea breeze blowing toward the shore. A favored time of return was early afternoon when the breeze was moderate, which allowed fishermen to avoid the most "violent breakers."

Africans working in midsized canoes caught vast quantities of fish. Some used nets of palm fiber. Others streamed long lines with many hooks, on which big fish bit rapidly in waters of great abundance.[32]

Specialized canoes were also used for different purposes on the ocean's edge in West Africa. Even more interesting to Europeans than the many fishing canoes were smaller numbers of larger vessels with different functions along the Gold Coast. One group might be called command canoes. They were about forty feet long. Half of the canoe was comfortably furnished and protected by a high awning from sun and rain. The forward half held a large team of paddlers.

Barbot was most interested in yet another group of vessels, which he called "cargo canoes." By his estimate, they were about forty feet long and five feet wide, which once again yielded a ratio of beam to length at about 1:8. He observed that these vessels had crews of ten to eighteen men, and could carry six to ten tons of freight by his reckoning. They traded actively along the coast and much of their cargo was described as general merchandise. Maritime cultures in West Africa functioned as market economies, and cargo canoes played fundamental roles.[33]

Europeans were surprised to discover that West African cargo canoes transported live cattle along the coast. One might ask how a cow might be carried in a canoe. The answer was "carefully." West Africa's complex canoe cultures required great skill by boatbuilders, and also by the seafaring people who actually used those vessels.[34]

Barbot marveled at their expertise, and he was amazed to discover that their cargo canoes "are so safe that they travel from the Gold Coast . . . to Angola." The length of a voyage along the coast of Africa from Axim to Luanda is about 1,800 English miles, or 3,600 miles for a round-trip. Those very long voyages in cargo canoes were made under sail. He observed that "the sails of these canoes are mostly of reed mats," and their rigging was "palm-fiber twine." One wonders if they sailed with leeboards or outriggers for stability. But log bottoms may have been weight enough for stability under sail.[35]

SPIRITUAL TRADITIONS IN MARITIME AFRICA

The work of building and using African canoes was more than merely a material process. As mentioned, the boatwright's expertise was combined with deep religious beliefs and spiritual rituals at every stage of construction and use: first in the forest, then in the village, once more on the first launch, and especially at sea. A major part of African maritime activity derived not only from material relations, physical artifacts, and expert seamanship, but also from ethical values, religious beliefs, and the life of the spirit.

All of this has long been the judgment of many African scholars, and most recently in the work of Jeffrey Bolster, an American maritime historian and a blue-water sailor who has studied African American maritime traditions. He found much evidence that mariners of African origins had their own highly developed ways of thinking about the sea, which varied from one culture to another. Bolster and others observe that Congo people cultivated an idea of *kalunga*, which was at once a word for the sea and also for the entire realm of the spirit world, which they regarded as a greater cosmic sea, embracing all things within it.[36]

One might add a corollary to that cosmic belief, which was a conception of the sea as the realm of many spirits, where magical things happen in ways that are in the control of higher powers. This became yet another idea, that earthly believers can be in touch with water spirits and are able to conciliate them. Those beliefs appeared in many forms among African seafaring people who ventured on deep waters. They encouraged communication with water spirits by magical practices and expressions of spiritual strength.[37]

Barbot wrote that African people were "all idolators." He observed that "they wear fetishes . . . not only around their necks but also on their arms, over their chests and legs, and over the heart; they never go on water in their canoes or other vessels without first commending themselves to the fetish which is the patron-spirit of the sea. Also they never disembark without being heard to speak some words to this fetish in thanks for their preservation."[38]

Jeffrey Bolster found that after coming to America, African seafaring people continued their old spirit rituals and added new ones. They captured seabirds, fish, turtles, and other sea creatures, marked them carefully with complex signs and symbols, and returned them alive to the water as messengers to sea spirits. Harry Stillwell Edwards wrote about an African-born slave named Minc who would catch terrapins, and "with a bit of wire ground to an exceedingly fine point, cut on its shell a number of curious signs or hieroglyphics, different from anything I had ever seen, except there was a pretty fair representation of the sun." Then Minc would turn the terrapins loose, and speed them on their way. He did the same again with birds and fishes, all carrying messages from Minc to the ruling spirits of the Cosmos.[39]

A consequence of this animist way of thinking was an abiding sense of spiritual strength that appeared among African watermen. In eighteenth-century America, European seamen admired the confidence, courage, and tenacity of African boatmen in difficult situations. One English sailor observed that Africans were "by no means afraid of dying by water."[40]

This quality of confidence had several roots. It began with Africans' animist beliefs in the sea as a world of spirits, with whom watermen felt able to establish working relations. It grew stronger with long experience on the water, and a familiarity with rivers and seas as entities that behaved in ways that were often unexpected, but not alien if one respected the presence of spiritual powers. Europeans and Americans sometimes flatter themselves that their western ways of thought are more instrumental and less fatalist than those in other cultures and earlier times. But in some ways the opposite has been the case.

Examples were ancient cultural beliefs, linked to another difference between European and African seamen during the seventeenth and early eighteenth centuries. In that era, Africans (and American Indians) routinely became expert swimmers. Barbot frequently observed that West African boatmen were excellent swimmers. On beaches along the Gold Coast, he watched as Fante parents carefully taught small children to swim. Barbot described them as using a powerful overhand stroke, similar to what we would call an Australian crawl.[41]

In the seventeenth century, European seamen of long experience on the water were often entirely unable to swim. An example was the great French seaman and explorer Samuel Champlain, who spent much of his long life on or near the water. Champlain tells us in his writings that he never learned to swim, and was terrified of falling into the water. He observed that American Indians were different that way, and so also were Africans.[42]

One result was a lingering fear of the water among nonswimming European and American seamen, who sometimes drowned within a few feet of a boat or a pier. In the mid-eighteenth century, Benjamin Franklin argued at length that swimming should be a part of every child's education. Franklin himself made a continuing effort to encourage swimming by his own highly publicized daily exercises in Philadelphia's two rivers.

AFRICAN MARITIME SLAVES AS AMERICAN "CANOEMEN"

In the early modern era, elements of Africa's highly developed waterborne cultures were brought by slaves to the New World. On the Atlantic coast of North America, many Africans were valued for their skill in working with boats. Europeans had thought of African watercraft as primitive, and much inferior to European vessels. European shipwrights were more advanced in the construction of large frame-built hulls, and in the use of complex sails and cordage. But Africans knew more about the design and building of swift and stable canoes, both small and large, and also about their uses on rivers, coasts, and the open sea.

This expertise was brought to America by African slaves, and Europeans were quick to discover its uses. In 1772, a Virginia master advertised for the return of "a New negro Fellow" who "calls himself Bonna, and says he came from a place of that name in the Ibo country, in Africa, where he served in the capacity of a Canoeman."[43]

Similar evidence of that sort appears in other runaway slave advertisements, and in the correspondence of slave buyers and sellers. They were keenly aware that some Africans had much knowledge of the sea, long experience as seamen, and deep expertise as boatbuilders. On the West Indian island of St. Kitts, John Willock wrote of Africans in general that "they are very dextrous

in the management of their canoes." A Carolinian added the cheerful thought
that in his experience, African men were "all fine fellows in boats." And an
observer in Bermuda added that Africans were fully "equal to white men in
their navigation."[44]

On the eve of the American Revolution, Africans with some experience
in the building and use of boats have been variously estimated to be 10 to
15 percent of adult male African slaves who came to North America as a
whole, 30 percent in Philadelphia, and 60 percent of adult male slaves in Bermuda, where they were particularly valued that way.[45]

In the Chesapeake region and South Carolina, the American historian
Jeffrey Bolster did an empirical test on numbers and proportions of African-
born slaves in maritime occupations. In descriptions of runaways, he found
that "among thirty-three sailors and boatmen working in South Carolina and
Georgia (1737–1790), 15 percent were African-born. Among another group
of forty-eight sailors and boatmen working in the Chesapeake (1736–1790)
22 percent were African-born." Those relative regional differences, small as
they may seem in these samples, doubled the absolute numbers of experienced
African mariners in the Chesapeake Bay.[46]

AFRICANS AND EARLY AMERICAN BOATBUILDING: COONERS, KUNNERS, AND PERIAUGERS

In the New World, European seamen were much interested in American Indian boats and adopted their native names. A common Carib noun became
canoa in Spanish, *cano* in Dutch, *canot* in French, and *canoe* in English. It
was used first for dugouts, and later applied more generally to small craft in
many varieties.[47]

Throughout the New World, European seamen described a great diversity
of American Indian canoes. In Arctic waters they were fascinated by sharp-built
double-ended Inuit kayaks, ingeniously made from animal skins, bones, and
sinews. In the St. Lawrence Valley, Europeans were delighted by the light and
swift birch bark canoes of many Algonkian nations, and they were impressed
by the big and slow but sturdy elm canoes of the Iroquois. Europeans were interested in log dugout canoes among the southern Indian nations. In the Chesapeake Bay, circa 1607–09, George Percy measured an Indian dugout that was
forty-five feet long. He noted that it had been laboriously made from a single
large log with stone tools, sharp shells, and careful use of fire.[48]

These Native American vessels made a striking contrast with small European watercraft that arrived in America aboard the first exploring vessels. Widely used were frame-built boats called *shallops* in English. Their name may have derived from an old word for walnut shells, which their rounded hulls resembled.

Small shallops were round open boats large enough to carry ten or fifteen people. They were slow but stable and strong, and widely used from New England to the Carolinas for many generations.

Larger European shallops crossed the Atlantic at the end of a towline or sailed in company with larger ships. Some were sturdy seaboats of three or five tons burthen with bluff bows, broad beams, hulls decked over, and rounded sterns. Most were single-masted, with heavy flaxen sails and complex rigging. Their convex hull designs curved outward from the keel, then upward and inward in a distinctive shape that English sailors called "tumble home." For stability they sometimes sailed with large leeboards which were lowered on the downwind side of the boat.[49]

When growing numbers of Africans arrived in North America, European and Amerindian watercraft were modified by the introduction of a third boat-building tradition. In American colonies from the Chesapeake and the Carolinas to Bermuda and the West Indies where large numbers of African slaves were imported, Africans were put to work making boats and crewing them in island colonies and mainland settlements of North America.

In Bermuda, Virginia, and Maryland, some of these African slaves built boats by methods similar to those observed by Barbot in West Africa, but with different substantive results, as we shall see. American Indians, Europeans, and African boatbuilders all learned from each another in the New World.

The first boats to be built in the American colonies tended to be small and simple, but they became increasingly complex in structure and function. In the coastal Carolinas, and Virginia and Maryland, they were called *cooners* and *kunners*. Both words emerged from attempts by speakers of different English dialects to pronounce the alien word canoe.[50]

In the eighteenth century, these American colonial vessels were described as "usually hewn" from a single large tree. They were similar to Indian boats, but accounts of "hewing" tell us that they were built less by the use of fire on Indian models, and more by iron tools and carving techniques that came from Europe and Africa.

David Cecelski, a leading expert on early American maritime history, writes of *cooners* and *kunners* that "slaves probably built most of them." He describes these vessels as "the poor man's workboats for fishing, getting about,

Modern replica of an early periauger with gaff-rigged fore and main sails, Hertford, North Carolina

and hauling freight." Cecelski was one of the first American historians to observe that similar boats had been widely used in West Africa, and that "many colonial-era slaves had prior experience of building and handling them in their native land."[51]

Other boats of moderately larger size began to be built in the American colonies at an early date. They were called by another Carib name which became *periaga* in Spanish, *pirogue* in French, and *periauger* in English. These names were used in Virginia as early as 1609, for small log-built boats with sails. For more than a century they were employed as ferries, freight boats, and transports. In 1736, Methodist missionary John Wesley traveled the Chesapeake region under sail in a boat he called a "pettiawga" and described it as "a sort of flat-bottomed barge."[52]

Designs of these small craft were highly variable. Increasingly their hulls began to combine log-hewn bottoms with sides of "rising planks," much like traditional West African boat construction. Historian Marion Brewington wrote that "the practice of using rising planks seems to have come in far earlier than one would expect." He reported many examples in the upper Chesapeake Bay from the mid-eighteenth century, and their origins were much earlier. Methods of early boatbuilding in America were striking in their similarity to descriptions of log and plank construction in West African vessels, as observed and described by Jean Barbot as early as 1678.[53]

In one way they were new. On South Carolina's Winyah Bay, European and African boatwrights drew upon a vast abundance of American timber to make their periaugers from species of trees that were not known in Europe or Africa. Enormous live oaks supplied "gnarled limbs, perfectly shaped for the ribs and knees of English ships." Also growing along Carolina rivers and swamps were cypress trees a thousand years old. Longleaf pines in the southern colonies and white pines in New England grew to heights of a hundred feet. Their wood was light and flexible, with good tensile strength. Various species of American pine, white pine especially, made excellent masts, yards, and booms. Logs began to be exported to Europe for that purpose in specially designed "mast ships." American pine and cypress were also used by Africans for log and plank hull construction, with the addition of ribs and knees made from American live oak.[54]

In the coastal Carolinas and through the Chesapeake region, early American periaugers were often constructed by workers who included skilled African slaves, using building methods that they had learned in their homelands. They shaped boat timbers with an expanding array of specialized adzes, axes, and other tools.

By comparison with broad-bottomed European shallops, slave-made American periaugers more closely resembled sharp-built West African ocean fishing and cargo canoes, with longer lines, higher ratios of length to beam, and flattened bottoms. The bows of periaugers tended to converge on a raked stem that was strong and straight. Sterns were highly variable: often rounded and tucked, occasionally double-ended, sometimes square-sterned. These vessels were designed for use in rivers, coastal waters, and estuaries, and they were also sturdy seaboats.

A rare example of an early American periauger has survived in coastal South Carolina, where the Waccamaw and other rivers flow into the waters of Winyah Bay. A sunken colonial boat was found in thick silt and dark water at the bottom of the well-named Black River. Much of the vessel was recovered, raised, carefully preserved, and placed on permanent display in Georgetown.[55]

Historian Robert McAlister has closely studied this vessel. He believes that she was built around the year 1740, which in his words would make her "the earliest sailing craft found so far in America." Her length was "about fifty feet," with steps for two masts. The hull was frame-built on a European model, but her proportions were sharp-built on lines that were closer to Barbot's African cargo canoes than to broad-beamed European shallops. In McAlister's words, the "hull was narrow, flat-bottom amidships, tapering at each end." The wood that went into her came from coastal Carolina, with "live oak framing members and wide pine planks."[56]

On her last voyage, this periauger was used as a freight boat. When she sank in the Black River, she had been overloaded with an estimated twenty-five tons of building bricks. Marine archaeologists found that she also carried interesting artifacts, including a quadrant that could be used to calculate the elevation of Polaris, the North Star, and to obtain a measure of latitude by that simple method. The presence of a quadrant suggests that this fifty-foot cargo vessel was equipped for ocean voyages.[57]

In early America these periaugers were often sailed by free-spirited African slaves, who did not always bring them home again. Crews and passengers and sometimes the boats themselves appeared in notices for runaway slaves in the *Gazette*s of Virginia and also South Carolina. In 1738, one advertisement by a Scottish slave owner identified himself and his profession as "Mr. James Gordon, pettyaguaman." He was concerned about his runaway slaves, but mainly he wanted his boat back.[58]

Another owner advertised for the return of his crew: "Run away from my Pettiauger at Elliot's Bridge, two Negro fellows, one an Angola Negro named Levi, about 19 years old, has a silver bob in his right Ear, the other an Ebo Negro, named Kent; they had on gowns of brown Kearsy with Breeches of the same."[59]

A third notice in 1736 sought the return of a "Negro Fellow, named Will," in Lancaster County, Virginia, "Tis suppos'd he went away, with a Man and a Boy in a Southward Petty-Augre. . . . The Man is of middle stature, a white visage, his hair short, wears a cap . . . and goes by the Name of James Gunly; he took with him a small white-look'd boy." This slave-owner described the boat in detail: "The Petty-Augre has a square stern, with a stem like a boat, has two Masts, and Bermuda Sails."[60]

BREAKTHROUGHS IN COLONIAL BOAT DESIGN: BERMUDA SLOOPS

The presence of "Bermuda sails" aboard a Virginia periauger as early as 1736 is doubly interesting here. It is another clue to the dynamics of boat design in early America, to the combined agency of many builders, and to multiple models, and mixed methods in their construction. A common error is to think of early American ships and boats as European in origin. That linkage was an important part of their history, but something more complex and creative happened in the New World from an early date.

The classic case in point was a breakthrough in design of new boats and ships, on the small, beautiful, and storm-beaten Atlantic archipelago called "the sore-vexed Bermudas." Its environment was a challenge to seamen, who struggled with heavy weather, rough water, dangerous reefs, long distances, and frequent shipwrecks.

On these islands, the building of boats and ships became an industry of vital importance. Excellent watercraft could be constructed from local materials such as Bermuda cedar trees, which were actually a species of large junipers. In the early seventeenth century, Bermuda cedars grew eighty feet tall, very straight and close-grained. Their wood was light and very strong, with natural oils that were preservatives for many years. Bermuda cedar was a boatbuilder's dream.[61]

In 1619, Bermuda's governor Nathaniel Butler persuaded a shipwrecked Dutch carpenter named Jacob Jacobson to stay on the island and build seagoing vessels that were much needed in the colony. Jacobson started making Bermuda boats that were modeled on Dutch vessels called *sloops*. By some accounts, that name derived from the verb *slupen*, "to slide." Early Dutch sloops were frame-built European vessels with broad beams, rounded hulls, raised half-decks, high sterns, short masts, and square-rigged flax sails. They had been used for many tasks on the Zuider Zee.[62]

In Jacobson's boatyard, Dutch *slupen* gradually became Bermuda sloops. Measurements survive for a vessel with a length of sixty feet, a beam of twenty feet, and a ratio of 3:1 on the Dutch model.[63] Shipbuilding rapidly became Bermuda's leading industry. By 1699, English imperial civil servant Edward Randolph visited the islands and found a fleet of more than seventy large oceangoing sloops, and three to four hundred smaller craft that sailed in local waters. Nearly all were built in Bermuda by shipwrights, carpenters, and joiners, "many of whom were slaves."[64]

Most of Jacobson's workers were Africans. From what followed and the vessels that they helped to construct, it is highly probable that they were familiar with African boats and building methods. From the start, Bermuda sloops began to differ from European watercraft. They were half the weight of European vessels, which made them lighter and faster. As the numbers of these boats increased, their hull designs began to change in other ways. By the early eighteenth century, some of these Bermuda sloops became more sharp-built, with fluent hull lines. Freeboard (the distance between water-line and main deck) was reduced. Quarterdecks were cut down. Decorative carving was simplified, which lowered costs, reduced weight, and increased speed.[65]

An example of these changes appears in a marine painting, circa 1719, which centers on a contrast between a heavy-hulled British frigate and the Bermuda sloop *Devonshire*, which by comparison had clean flowing hull lines, reduced freeboard, a lower quarterdeck, and a simplified round-tuck stern. Other patterns changed more slowly. Bermuda sloops were built to carry cargo and some retained broader beams, but in other ways their design was moving in new directions.[66]

Bermuda sloops also began to be rigged in new ways. Dutch vessels had carried heavy square-rigged, flax sails on vertical masts, with complex rigging on European models. In Bermuda that European sail plan yielded to large gaff-rigged fore-and-aft mainsails, tall and sharply raked masts, and very long booms. A high-angled bowsprit carried big driving jibs and other headsails. Square-rigged topsails and studding sails (commonly called "stun-sails") were added later, and sail area steadily increased. Some masts and booms were hollowed out to save weight, and rigging was made as light and simple as possible.[67]

In another stage of invention, Bermuda riggers replaced gaff-rigged quadrilateral fore-and-aft mainsails with lighter and larger triangular mainsails of their own invention. They began to be called "Bermuda sails" as early as 1635. These Bermuda sails were found to be highly efficient in converting the wind's energy to motion. Shrouds were modified so that square-rigged topsail yards could be more close-hauled than on older European vessels. Bermuda vessels became more efficient than square-rigged European ships on many points of sailing. Three centuries later, a highly functional "Bermuda rig" remains the sail plan of choice for millions of pleasure boats in America, in large part because of its simplicity and strength.[68]

All these structural changes had functional consequences. Bermuda-built vessels soon began to earn a reputation for speed. In 1718, the sloop *Endeavour* sailed from Bermuda to Green Turtle Cay in the Bahamas. On that entire voyage of four days she averaged nine knots, or ten to eleven English miles per hour.[69]

This was a fast passage, one of the fastest on record in that era. A more typical speed was in the range of about five knots. At that time, ships built on European models averaged half this speed. By those measures Bermuda sloops increased the speed of Atlantic travel by 25 to 50 percent. In the mid-eighteenth century, experienced captains believed that Bermuda sloops were "the fastest vessels in the world." Their experience did not run to faster North African xebecs or West African canoes, but Bermuda sloops may have been among the fastest vessels in the North Atlantic or the Caribbean, and among the best at "saving voyages," which lowered time and cost.

Bermuda sloops could also steer out of harm's way, for yet another saving. The Royal Navy was quick to acquire Bermuda sloops as dispatch boats or "advice boats." With greater speed, merchants found that they were safe and seaworthy, with the lowest insurance premiums in the eighteenth-century Atlantic market. They tended to be highly profitable for investors, builders, owners, and crews.[70]

And Bermuda sloops were continuously improved, for yet more economy and greater speed. Some of these vessels also grew larger, with waterline lengths of eighty to one hundred feet. Others of that length became two-masted or even three-masted Bermuda schooners.

These vessels also had another appeal. They were very handsome in appearance. The climax came in the early nineteenth century, when classic Bermuda "sloops of war" were built for the Royal Navy and rigged as three-

Spirit of Bermuda schooner

masted schooners with long sharp-built lines and three very large triangular fore-and-aft Bermuda sails, each on its own tall and sharply raked mast. Under full sail, these beautiful vessels became an enduring symbol of Bermuda itself. Today a full-scale replica is cherished in the islands, and widely reproduced as an image of the "Spirit of Bermuda."[71]

With these many changes, Bermuda sloops became less European, and more similar in some ways to West African and North African vessels. It happened at the same time that European shipbuilders employed growing numbers of highly skilled African slaves and freedmen. And in the eighteenth and nineteenth centuries, crews on many Bermuda sloops were increasingly African, even entirely African except for an Anglo captain—and sometimes he was African too.

But the most important fact about the development of Bermuda sloops was their broad diversity of creative elements that came from people of many origins: an English governor, a Dutch shipbuilder, African boatwrights, Bermuda sailmakers, and more. People of many cultures made contributions, and African elements became important parts of a broad creative mix.[72]

"NORFOLK BERMUDIANS," FREE AND SLAVE, IN THE CHESAPEAKE BAY

By the mid-eighteenth century, vessels similar to Bermuda sloops were being built in the British West Indies. Several scholars believe that Jamaica sloops preceded Bermuda sloops, but the evidence shows that Bermuda sloops came first in the early seventeenth century, earlier than the earliest Jamaica sloops on record, and earlier even than Jamaica itself as a British colony.

Thereafter kindred models of blue-water sloops began to multiply at a rapid rate, and wherever European and African boatwrights worked together in America. Regional designs were similar, but never the same—which suggested multiple centers of invention and a complex heritage.[73]

In the late seventeenth century, enterprising Bermuda boatbuilders and their skilled African boatwrights moved to Virginia, where they settled near what is now the city of Norfolk. Bermuda historian Michael Jarvis writes that by 1690, "Norfolk Bermudians and their slave sawyers, caulkers, and carpenters pioneered a regional shipbuilding industry." Jarvis observes that "the extensive relocation of white and enslaved Bermudian shipwrights and craftsmen helps to explain why Chesapeake sloops and schooners share so many traits with the Bermuda sloop." One might add that Chesapeake and Bermuda boats were similar, but not identical, which made that process even more creative.[74]

THE CHESAPEAKE BAY AS A CRADLE OF MARITIME INVENTION

The Chesapeake Bay is a very large tidal inlet of the Atlantic Ocean, nearly two hundred miles long and as much as forty miles wide. It might also be understood as a great drowned river, which drains much of the eastern United States from southwest New York State and central Pennsylvania through Maryland, Delaware, Virginia, West Virginia, and parts of upper North Carolina.

For many centuries, even to our own time, the entire Bay region has been sinking slowly into the earth's crust, by a geologic process that preceded global warming. In consequence, the great Bay has been growing greater in area. By the early eighteenth century, some of its tributaries were deep enough for oceangoing vessels to anchor and trade directly with individual plantations, which encouraged markets and discouraged cities.

At the same time, a revolution was occurring in travel by sea throughout the Atlantic world. Waterborne communications improved rapidly in the early modern era. But travel over land was no faster or easier than it had been for the Romans until the late eighteenth and nineteenth centuries, when a terrestrial revolution was wrought by a chain of inventions such as John McAdam's "macadamized" roads, Ithiel Town's lattice-truss bridges, and the "turnpike mania," followed by an expansion of canals and railroads.

An environing determinant in this transitional era was the relatively high speed and low cost of movement by water. Something similar happened on both sides of the Atlantic. It inspired a pair of American and French scholars, Robert Palmer and Jacques Godechot, to invent a useful macro-model for the history of communications in that period. It centered on what they called the relative "permeabilité" of water and land as a historical variable that changed profoundly through time and space. They applied that idea to the history of the North Atlantic basin in the early modern era. Together Palmer and Godechot found that a revolution more rapid in maritime than overland communications created an Atlantic community of greater interaction. This dynamic process spanned an "age of democratic revolution" that had a unique strength on the borders of the Atlantic in the eighteenth century.[75]

Something akin to the Palmer-Godechot model also operated within smaller regions such as the Chesapeake Bay. In the seventeenth and eighteenth centuries, the easiest, cheapest, and fastest way to travel in the Chesapeake region was by water. The Bay itself became a great common which supported a dense web of waterborne trade, communication, and comity.

European boats were useful in the Chesapeake Bay, but they tended to be heavy, slow, and costly to build. Captain John Smith and George Percy were surprised to discover that Indian and African canoes were much faster than small English vessels. "Our boat [was] well manned with fourteen," Smith wrote ruefully, "yet they [the Indians] row faster with three oars [paddles] in their canoes than we with eight." He was traveling in what appears to have been a broad-beamed European boat which he called a barge. By comparison with African and Indian canoes, a European ship's boat had the sailing properties of a tub.[76] But Indian dugout canoes were limited in other ways, as carriers of people or freight. Sometimes two of them were lashed side by side to make a crude catamaran, with limited success.[77]

At the same time, the Chesapeake Bay was itself a challenging environment for watermen. On some days the Bay was deceptively calm, even placid. But it was subject to sudden squalls and storms of surprising strength that could be dangerous to unwary watermen.

Europeans and Africans were quick to discover that the resources of the Chesapeake region were ideal for building sturdy boats and ships of useful designs that were better adapted to this inland sea. Maryland's native trees include thirty-five varieties of oak, and also pine trees of many varieties for masts, and stands of white and red cedar, and cypress forests on the lower Eastern Shore. Even the dense hardwood of small black locust trees proved useful for tree nails ("trunnels" on the Bay) which pegged hull pieces together. Also much valued was the versatile softwood of towering poplars called tulip trees (*Liriodendron tulipifera*) after their exquisite tulip-like yellow flowers and tulip-shaped green leaves. Tulip poplars were and are a Maryland favorite. One of them became the state's Liberty Tree and long stood in Annapolis. European and African boatbuilders learned much from American Indians about the many uses of these native trees.

CHESAPEAKE LOG CANOES

In the seventeenth, eighteenth, and nineteenth centuries Indian, European, and African boatbuilders in the Chesapeake Bay together invented an extended family of new American sailing vessels that were unique in their many designs and possibilities. Together, these workers and their new designs were destined to have a major impact on boatmaking and shipbuilding in the modern world.

A pivotal event in this long sequence of invention was the emergence of a new vessel that came to be called the Chesapeake log canoe. In substance and detail it incorporated many elements from earlier boat designs in Africa, Europe, and America. But the Chesapeake log canoe was something new in its entirety, and unique to this American region. It was destined to have a long reach from the Chesapeake Bay to other parts of America and the world in the modern era.

The exact date of first appearance for Chesapeake log canoes is not known, but these vessels were well established by the mid-eighteenth century, multiplied in the nineteenth, and some survived into the twentieth. More than a few are still afloat in the twenty-first. By one recent count, twenty-five existing Chesapeake log canoes are listed on the National Register of Historic Places. New ones are being built today, by a mix of traditional and modern methods.

These vessels have long been cherished for two sets of special qualities. First, Chesapeake log canoes are striking in their appearance, and beautiful under sail. They are sharp-built boats with long lines, low freeboard, and little ornament. They had "clipper bows" before the clipper ship, long bowsprits, raked masts, graceful rounded or square sterns, and dramatic sail plans unique in their appearance. People who have never seen these vessels are surprised and moved by the sight of a Chesapeake log canoe under full sail, skimming swiftly across the Bay with a bone in her teeth, a rooster tail in her wake, and crewmen on hiking boards stretched precariously over the side.

Chesapeake log canoes were also celebrated for a second strength. In the hands of an able skipper and an experienced crew, they are very fast. Howard Chapelle, an expert on the history and design of sailing vessels, summarized their strengths in two sentences. He wrote that "Chesapeake Bay Log Canoes are, as a class, thoroughbred sailing craft. . . . These boats are much faster on most points of sailing than similar yachts, and are in addition, great beauties."[78]

Their development was part of a larger and longer process of invention, with a particular purpose that Chapelle called "the search for speed under sail." A small but important part of that long history centered on log canoes, which in turn inspired the invention of other classes of vessels that are unique to the Chesapeake Bay. This process of invention derived from a long history of boat design on three continents, and it became an inspiration for other designs in the future.[79]

In some important ways the construction of early Chesapeake log canoes was much like the building of West African canoes, as described by Jean Barbot in the seventeenth century. Hull bottoms were carved from several logs, and sides were built with wood planks, much as Barbot observed in Africa. Hull designs of eighteenth-century Chesapeake log canoes were also similar to seventeenth-century West African canoes in many ways: sharp-built bows, long lines, narrow beams, low freeboard, and tucked sterns. Other important elements were borrowed from European boatbuilding. Leading examples were the design and use of ribs and knees, rigging and sail plans. Here again, in the origins of Chesapeake log canoes we find a classic example of early American creativity that flowed from global diversity. African boatwrights alone did not invent this boatbuilding process, but much evidence of individual African and Afro-American boatwrights clearly shows their instrumental roles in its origins, development, expansion, and persistence as a regional tradition.

AFRICAN AMERICANS AND THE DEVELOPMENT OF CHESAPEAKE LOG CANOES: AARON, EARLY SLAVE BUILDER OF TWO-LOG AND THREE-LOG VESSELS

Early Chesapeake log canoes were carved from a single large tree, much as African vessels had been made before them. In Tidewater Virginia, one such tree was so large that when it was felled, people remembered that "it shook the ground for miles around." Great trees of that size were so abundant that this giant sold for ten Spanish dollars. Its trunk made two large canoes. One of them was twenty-eight feet long with a five-foot beam, and built to last. She was still afloat in the twentieth century, at the time of the Jamestown Exposition in 1907.[80]

By the late eighteenth century, hull bottoms of other Chesapeake canoes were being constructed of multiple logs. African boatwrights were active in this work, and took a leading part. Marion Brewington and staff members at the Mariners' Museum in Newport News, Virginia, collected evidence on the origin and development of multi-log canoe construction. They found oral testimony that the first two-log canoe in Tidewater Virginia was built in the eighteenth century on Lamb's Creek, a branch of the small Poquoson River in York County, Virginia.

The builder's name was Aaron, an African American slave of planter John Dennis. He was long remembered in that region for his skill and creativity.[81] Other people who lived near the Poquoson River remembered Aaron as the boatwright who "built the first three-log canoe." Brewington wrote that this oral tradition "can in no way be verified as to date or authenticity," but he observed that memories of Aaron were broadly shared, highly specific, crystal-clear, and consistent with other evidence. Brewington did not hesitate to include them in his very careful work. I remember Marion Brewington as a meticulous scholar, from my early youth as a stack boy, shagging books and papers in the Maryland Historical Society.[82]

AFRICAN AMERICANS EXPAND THE RANGE OF INVENTION

Yet another inventive Chesapeake boatwright was William Lomax, born a slave at Nesting Plantation, one of the oldest estates in North America, on the Rappahannock River in Middlesex County, Virginia. His owners were Joseph and Lucy Eubank. With their encouragement, Lomax became known as an "expert boatbuilder" in his neighborhood, and kept at it for many years. He routinely built three-log canoes, and began to construct five-log canoes at Burnt House Landing, on Parrott's Creek. In the late nineteenth century, larger "nine-log workboats" would follow.[83]

William Lomax also invented and built small versions of Chesapeake boats, in different designs by diverse methods. A much younger man who knew Lomax was William Dickerson, whose forebears were also slaves on Nesting Plantation. At the age of eighty-one, Dickerson remembered as a small boy watching William Lomax build three-log and five-log canoes in Middlesex County. Lomax was then near the end of a long career as a busy boatwright.[84]

Dickerson also recalled that "Mr. Lomax built sail-powered canoes for most of the black watermen in the community, and if they couldn't afford a canoe, he would build them a skiff." Skiffs were small boats, often long and narrow in proportions. Later, others had sharp bows, and were called Sharpies. They were designed to be driven by oars or paddles or bottom poles, or by a single sail and outrigger, and they spread rapidly through the region in the nineteenth century.

The small skiffs William Lomax made for former slaves were built to high standards. Dickerson remembered that they were "carefully cross-planked," and made tight and durable. It was typical of Lomax and African builders on both sides of the Atlantic that they did not stint on quality in small boats or larger ones. These builders were craftsmen, and one can see again and again their pride in their work.

Their boats, large and small, used sails made locally by Dickerson's grandmother Lucy Cramp, also born a slave on Nesting Plantation and "a good seamstress." Dickerson recalled that "she and one of my cousins made sails for most of the boats built by Mr. Lomax." [85]

For many generations, Chesapeake boatwrights and sailmakers of African ancestry passed their inherited skills from father to son, and mother to daughter. In that long process, they elevated the construction of larger log canoes and small sailing skiffs to an American art form and a Chesapeake tradition.

Yet another example was Luther Hackett of Amberg, Virginia, a descendant of African slaves. His father, Samuel Hackett, taught him to build log canoes with hand tools. Luther Hackett continued to build and repair log canoes by traditional methods from the 1920s to the 1960s.

A builder named Ed Deagle worked beside him, and later recalled, "I can see him now, working an adze just like it was yesterday. It was an art to it and Luther was the best." Deagle especially recalled Luther Hackett's creativity and skill in shaping "round chunk sterns," so named because they were built on log canoes from chunks of logs, and never the same way twice. Deagle recalled, "In no time he would have that stern dressed right down. It was so smooth you did not need to touch it with sandpaper. He was the best!" [86]

These African American boatbuilders were also remembered for integrity in their work, and also in their lives. Ed Deagle had that memory of Luther Hackett. "He was old when I knew him—at least he seemed old," Deagle said. "Even being old he was the best we had with an adze. He was also one of the finest men we had on the yard. He was a good churchgoing man who nobody ever had a bad word to say about him." [87]

A photograph of Luther Hackett survives in the Deltaville Maritime Museum. He appears in his dark churchgoing suit, with a white collar shirt, four-in-hand necktie, neatly trimmed mustache, strong chin, and steady eye. His image is a study in character, which was valued among Chesapeake watermen who had many different origins and a common way of life. These highly skilled boatwrights were held in high respect and esteem by African Americans and Anglo-Americans alike. [88]

LOCAL VARIATIONS

Through two centuries, log canoes multiplied in large numbers up and down the Chesapeake Bay. They also varied from place to place in size, design, and construction.

The Chesapeake was a great web of small subregions, which formed around rivers and creeks, where small groups of Indian, European, and African boatbuilders developed their own methods and customs. The result was an extraordinary diversity of invention and creativity.[89]

One local example were Chesapeake log canoes called Poquoson boats, after the small river on Virginia's western shore where they were built. Boatbuilders in this area were distinctive in several ways at once. Marion Brewington was surprised to discover that through the busy "Poquoson region," not one of its "many Virginia canoe builders . . . had ever made use of a half model or mould." In this area, more than others, Brewington found that canoes were made by what he and others called "winchum-squinchum" methods, without plans, molds, or half-models. Around the Poquoson River, he also identified an unusually large proportion of boatwrights who were African American. They tended to follow similar "rack-of-eye" methods of construction that had prevailed in West Africa.[90]

These African American artisans did the shaping and fitting of hull pieces much as their African forebears had done for centuries. They were also highly skilled in the use of a "gouge adze" and "broad ax," and they were virtuosos with a "foot adze," which they used to get a tight fit of one big log against another, on seams sometimes as long as the vessel itself—no small task.

Brewington talked with men who did this work and watched them in action. He observed that "some builders have such a delicacy and sureness of cut with adze and axe that they can fit the logs together without recourse to even a joiner plane." The logs were then secured in place by "key pieces" of hard oak shaped like a butterfly and called a "double dovetail," or by black locust "trunnels." All that effort went into the hull bottom of a five-log canoe. Then the canoe was "built up," with as many as twenty-five additional "side pieces" and "rising planks" of various shapes and sizes, again very much as in West African canoe carving.[91]

Consistent (not constant) thickness of adjoining hull pieces was sought and achieved by drilling very small holes and inserting "gauge pins" to check for variations. Then the "finish adzemen" went to work, with another vital skill in building Chesapeake log canoes. The thickness of the hull, as in African boatbuilding, tended to be about three inches at the bottom in a small canoe, or as much as eight inches in a large vessel, tapered to two inches at the gunwales.

This demanding labor was done mostly by hand tools for many generations: axe and adze in early log canoes, and later shaping and smoothing planes. Wooden "knees" were added, with the natural shapes of twisted oak branches to stabilize the hull and to support a closed deck on larger log canoes. Strong cutwater bows (later called clipper bows) gave those boats their air of dash and flair. Sterns were constructed in many creative shapes. Interesting experiments were made in keels. Later in the mid-nineteenth century, centerboards were added with their own wood housings called "centerboard wells" in the Chesapeake. Vessels with centerboard wells were called "she-boats" in the Bay.

With its "winchum-squinchum" and "rack-of-eye" methods, a completed hull of a finished five-log canoe was truly a work of art in its design. At the same time it was often a work of astonishing refinement in its finish. These vessels were extraordinary examples of the builder's art, and for many generations they were made by "rack of eye" with tools in the hands of expert African American slaves, who learned to use them not only from European masters but from their own African forebears on both sides of the Atlantic.

Those traditional methods created more than a few problems. Often as a direct result of the rack-of-eye method, the two sides of a log canoe's hull were carefully made and finished, but not quite in the same way. Owners were quick to discover that their log canoes tended to "sail faster or closer to the wind on one side than another." Even so, they sailed beautifully in expert hands, with speed and grace.

This process of building Chesapeake log canoes in the nineteenth and early twentieth centuries was in many ways remarkably similar to the construction of West African log canoes, as described by European observers. Throughout the Chesapeake region much of this work was done by African slaves amd free African Americans who passed their skills from father to son through many generations. Examples were the families of Aaron, slave of Dennis; William Lomax; and Luther Hackett, African Americans all.

Descendants of American Indians, English colonists, and transplanted Bermudians worked side by side with African American boatwrights in the Bay. Each of these ethnic groups made its own creative contributions that met and mixed in Chesapeake boatyards. Through it all, African American maritime heritage became an important part of American maritime experience.

Poquoson boats were only one of many subregional Chesapeake designs. In other parts of the Bay, log canoes were built in a different way, by making careful half-models, which were widely used for "Pocomoke log canoes" on Virginia's lower Eastern Shore, and "Tilghman canoes" on Maryland's upper shore.

With the aid of plans and models, the two sides of a log canoe became more symmetrical. And builders were also able to achieve the more fluent hull lines that were important for speed. The ratio of length to beam in Chesapeake log canoes approached 5:1 or 6:1, intermediate between European workboats and West African vessels. Tilghman log canoes were very lean, and they were thought to be the fastest on the Bay.[92]

This process of Chesapeake invention had several different tendencies. On one hand, it encompassed a very large and complex process of interaction throughout the region, with contributions from many sources. At the same time, it also fostered creative dynamics of subregional innovation. On Maryland's lower Eastern Shore yet another local variety of log canoes were called Pocomoke boats, after the Pocomoke River in Somerset County, and a small town called Pocomoke City in what is now Maryland's Worcester County, the metropolis of that region. It was the home of Pocomoke log canoes, which had a very distinctive rig and sail plan. They tended to have big Bermuda sails on a foremast and mainmasts, both raked in the usual way. But Pocomoke boats also had a third very small "jigger mast" near the bow, in place of a jib. It was canted sharply forward, which made a strange appearance. Marion Brewington was baffled by the origin and use of these jigger masts. They had earlier appeared in African xebecs with foremasts canted forward, mainmasts vertical, and mizzens canted aft.[93]

On bright and breezy days in the mid-eighteenth century, the Chesapeake Bay was covered with a multitude of vessels under sail, in an astonishing variety of rigs and sizes. Around the year 1760, shipbuilder Richard Spencer, on Gray's Inn Creek near Kent Island on Maryland's Eastern Shore, installed a painting above a fireplace in his home. It centered on his own small but busy shipyard, crowded with ships under construction, and surrounded by many vessels in the water. The painting includes a full-rigged ship flying the red duster of the British merchant marine, a three-masted snow or barque, two-

Richard Spencer's shipyard, Grey's Inn Creek, Kent Island, Maryland ca. 1760

masted square-rigged brigs, mixed-rig brigantines or "hermaphrodite brigs," schooners of many types, big Bermuda sloops, and a mix of two-masted Chesapeake log canoes. One log canoe is rigged with African lateen sails, another with sloop-rigged triangular Bermuda sails, and a third with European gaff sails. The painting captures the Bay's maritime life, both in its bustling activity and creative diversity, which were only beginning to blossom in the eighteenth century.

VIRGINIA PILOT BOATS

Log canoes also led to yet another design for Virginia pilot boats, small vessels with large consequences for American maritime history. When large ships approached the Capes of the Chesapeake, their captains were required by Virginia law in the eighteenth century to pick up a licensed Bay pilot and pay him well for his services.

Whenever a ship appeared on the horizon, sailing toward the broad Chesapeake entrance between Capes Charles and Henry, a maritime drama repeated itself. Bay pilots raced to meet her. Whoever was quickest to come alongside got the job of piloting the ship to her destination. It was a lucrative business, and speed was of the essence.[94]

For that particular purpose, Bay pilots and their builders invented a new class of small Chesapeake schooners. These vessels were designed and constructed with one purpose in mind: maximum speed in many conditions. Chesapeake boatwrights in Virginia went to work on that problem and found a solution in design traditions that reached from Africa and Europe to Bermuda sloops and Chesapeake log canoes. Historians Quentin Snediker and Ann Jensen wrote, "The Virginia pilot boat was characterized by its sharp deadrise (the vertical distance between the keel and the curve of the hull's bilges), narrow body, fine long run, flush deck, low freeboard, fairly shallow draft, and deep drag aft." The construction was light, with minimal accommodation for a very small crew.[95]

The sail plan of a two-masted pilot boat was designed for maximum spread and minimum rigging. Commonly it included a loose-footed sail on the foremast and a large driver sail on the mainmast, stretched aft by a long boom that extended beyond the stern. Jibs and staysails were added in light breezes. A Virginia law of 1795 required that the boat's name and home port was painted on the foresail in letters nine inches high to discourage interlopers.[96]

These "pilot schooners" were mentioned by name in Virginia *Gazettes* as early as 1737. Speed was vital to their success, and they became widely known for it. They were very fast, and grew faster with some of the design elements that had always appeared in Chesapeake log canoes, and earlier in African canoes. Virginia's slave boatwrights continued to refine the design of their vessels with progressively more sleek and sharp-built hulls, carefully balanced V-shaped bottoms, sharply raked masts, stems, and sternposts, a high ratio of length to beam, lighter weight, larger sails, taller masts, and minimal rigging.[97]

For these early sailing vessels, naval architect and historian Thomas Gillmer computed twentieth-century prismatic coefficients, a measure of the distribution of weight or "displacement," overall and through the length of their hulls. The lower the coefficient, the sharper was the hull. Slow-sailing, full-built cargo ships with "bluff bows" and broad beams had prismatic coefficients of .70 to .80. "Fair-to-good" sailing frigates or sloops-of-war or packets were in a range of .65 to .70. Sharp-built Chesapeake schooners ranged from .58 to .61, and Virginia pilot boats were "as low as .50," which "indicates extreme sharpness." They may have been the fastest class of sailing vessels on record in that era.[98]

As Virginia pilot boats gained a reputation for extraordinary speed, they inspired other vessels in their turn. In the late eighteenth century, British and European navies sent agents to Norfolk, with orders to buy a Virginia pilot boat and bring her home. Hull lines were studied carefully, and similar vessels were constructed for the British Admiralty. The Royal Navy used them as "dispatch boats," and described them as "pilot schooner built," or "Virginia built." British and European builders tried to copy them but were never quite able to match the original Virginia pilot boats for sharpness and speed.[99]

SKILLED AFRICAN AMERICAN SHIPYARD
WORKERS, SLAVE AND FREE

Fast-sailing Chesapeake vessels were constructed by large numbers of small shipyards, in a labor-intensive industry. The yards themselves were individually owned and operated by Chesapeake entrepreneurs. Some were venture capitalists who hired skilled shipwrights. Others were skilled "master carpenters" who hired the money. Funding came from informal ad hoc syndicates of investors who joined together to finance the building of individual vessels. The letter of marque schooner *Chasseur*, for example, had seventeen owners.[100]

Investor-owners of individual ships tended to be men of many ethnic and religious origins. Baltimore attracted a diverse population. Its shipbuilders came from many countries, and every major American region. Within the Chesapeake region they also came from many of its Tidewater counties.

It is interesting to see how these entrepreneurs recruited their workers. Through the early republic, Baltimore's three leading shipbuilders did it in three different ways. All three included many African American workers, skilled and unskilled.

In the late eighteenth century, the leading shipbuilder in Baltimore was Captain David Stodder (not to be confused with the Georgetown Stodderts). He was chosen in 1794 to build the USS *Constellation* as a gift from the city to the new United States Navy. The cost was paid by subscription among the merchants of Baltimore as a patriotic act. The ship itself was a great success, and Stodder was highly praised for it. He replied, "I am under the greatest obligations to the carpenters," and he gave all the praise to them. The ship is still afloat in Baltimore's inner harbor.

Even as Stodder became one of the wealthiest men in Baltimore, he always described himself as a "mechanic" in its eighteenth-century meaning of a man who worked with his hands. In his own shipyard, Stodder toiled alongside a large force of workers who were African and European, bond and free. He was held in high esteem by them. In the 1790s about twenty-five of his workers were his own African American slaves. By his will in 1806, Stodder gave all of them their freedom. He ordered that all his young slaves be set "free at the age of 25, and all of my old[er] slaves to be free immediately." Among these slaves were some of his most highly skilled workers. As one example, he also ordered that "my negro Lewis [is to] have all the iron and tools in my black-smith shop."

In 1800, when Stodder was the city's second-largest slave owner, the leaders of Baltimore decided to mobilize free African Americans to repair the city's defenses. They asked Stodder to take charge. It was said that "he assembled the free blacks at his Fells Point house, equipped them with tools, and marched them to the fort," and worked beside them.[101]

On a par with Stodder in the esteem of his colleagues was another family of Maryland shipbuilders. Most observers agreed that many of the best Baltimore flyers and clipper schooners were built in the shipyards of the Kemp family, by Thomas Kemp in particular, and his brother Joseph. They came from St. Michaels on the Eastern Shore, shifted to Baltimore, later returned to St. Michaels, and built ships in both places. Thomas Kemp was a Quaker. In general he honored the Quaker testimony against the keeping of slaves, and he supported many measures against human bondage. Although he continued to own a few slaves, he built his ships primarily with free workers, European and African. Altogether Thomas Kemp and his family constructed fifty-two fast sailing ships from 1804 to 1816. Many of Kemp's skilled "mechanics" were free antislavery Methodists, white and Black together, who were strongly hostile to human bondage.[102]

Thomas Kemp and his workers were widely respected for constructing some of the best ships of their class in Baltimore. That quality was a testament to the skill of Kemp's mixed workforce. Outstanding among their many vessels were the privateer schooner *Comet*, 187 tons, 91 feet long, built in 1810; and the renowned letter of marque schooner *Chasseur*, 356 tons, and 115.6 feet long, and later rigged as a brig. She was reputed to be the biggest, fastest, most handsome, and most successful of Baltimore's many private armed vessels in the War of 1812.[103]

When *Chasseur* returned to Baltimore from her last war cruise on April 8, 1815, *Niles Weekly Register*, the leading American newsmagazine of that era, reported that

the brig *Chasseur*, the pride of Baltimore, arrived at Baltimore on Saturday evening last, and saluted Fort M'Henry. She is, perhaps, the most beautiful vessel that ever floated on the ocean. Those who have not seen our schooners have but little idea of her appearance. As you look at her, you may easily figure to yourself the idea that she is about to rise out of the water and fly in the air, seeming to sit lightly upon it.[104]

By far the most prolific builders of fast sailing ships in Baltimore were a third group. They were members of the Price family, who built seventy-seven

The brig *Chausseur* and HM schooner *St. Lawrence* duel off Havana,
February 26, 1815

fast sailing vessels from 1795 to 1835. They did it by organizing themselves in multiple partnerships, of which the most important was William
Price and Son, managed by the son Walter. Their ships were built primarily with slave labor. William Price himself was "the foremost slaveholder in
Baltimore," with twenty-two slaves in 1800. But most of the family's many
workers were hired slaves, who had been highly trained in many skills of
shipbuilding.[105]

Slave hiring was more flexible than ownership, and widely used in Baltimore shipyards. The best primary account comes from the eloquent memory
of one of the Price family's many hired slaves whom we know well.

Frederick Douglass had been sent at an early age from the great Wye Plantation on the Eastern Shore to Baltimore. He had long been fascinated by the
sea, and later wrote,

> Our house stood within a few rods of the Chesapeake Bay, whose broad
> bosom was ever white with sails from every quarter of the habitable
> globe. Those beautiful vessels robed in purest white . . . always affected
> me powerfully. . . . I would pour out my soul's complaint in my rude
> way, with an apostrophe to the moving multitude of ships: "You are
> loosed from your moorings, and free. I am fast in my chains, and I am
> a slave! . . . This very bay shall yet bear me into freedom."[106]

That process began when Douglass, still a child, was taken to Baltimore as a house slave. He was quick to observe that "a city slave is almost a free-man, compared with a slave on the plantation. He is much better fed and clothed and enjoys privileges altogether unknown to the slave on the plantation."[107]

He was owned by the family of Hugh Auld, who worked as a shipyard manager for William and Walter Price. Douglass started as a hired laborer, and was trained to be a skilled caulker. He recalled that he was immediately "set to calking, and very soon learned the art of using my mallet and irons." After a year, he wrote with pride that "I was able to command the highest wages given to the most experienced calkers . . . a dollar and a half a day." After he worked the better part of a year, his owners agreed to let Douglass hire his own time, and increased their income from his labor.[108]

When he started, Douglass remembered that "white and black ship carpenters worked side by side, and no one seemed to see any impropriety in it. All hands seemed to be very well satisfied. Many of the black carpenters were freemen. Things seemed to be going on very well."[109]

Then suddenly things changed, circa 1836–37. Part of it was an economic panic followed by a severe depression. Douglass recalled that one day in the shipyard "white carpenters knocked off and said they would not work with free colored workmen." That instability spread through the shipyard. White caulkers attacked Blacks. Douglass fought back, was almost blinded and nearly killed.[110]

In 1838 Douglass decided to escape from slavery. He fled from Baltimore to the Yankee seaport of New Bedford and tried to get a job caulking. Again, New England whites would not work with him. He started a new life as an antislavery journalist. But always he remembered the Chesapeake and its maritime life with great fondness.

CONTINUING CREATIVITY IN CHESAPEAKE WORKBOATS

While fast-sailing Virginia pilot boats and Baltimore flyers inspired maritime creativity that culminated in clipper ships, something else was stirring in the Chesapeake Bay. This was yet another sequence of innovation that was inspired by Chesapeake log canoes. In response to growing ecological problems and changing material conditions, watermen throughout the region invented many new classes of Chesapeake workboats. They were locally designed for practical purposes, and built in large numbers up and down the Bay. They all derived from vernacular traditions that were deeply rooted in the culture of this American region. They were highly functional, and handsome to behold. Most were created within a vibrant cultural and aesthetic tradition.

Many varieties of Chesapeake workboats had a kinship with Chesapeake log canoes and their ancestry. They formed distinct classes of design, each with its own special name and distinct character. But they also shared a history, and had many design elements in common. Many bore a distant family resemblance to log canoes, and some of them were built in similar ways, by methods that had a long history in West Africa. African Americans in the Chesapeake continued to be very much a part of their history, development, and use. These vessels were built for practical use, and they were worked very hard for more than a century.

At the same time, these Chesapeake workboats tended to share qualities of grace and beauty in the lines of their hulls, the rake of their masts, and the cut of their sails. They were often battered by heavy use. But even so, they stirred the spirit by their appearance. Some of these boats, skipjacks in particular, continue to work under sail even today.

Many of these sailing workboats are fast on the water. For many years through the twentieth century after a long day's labor on fishing grounds and oyster beds in the Bay, captains of bugeyes or skipjacks would challenge sister boats to a race for home under sail. These workboats would go flying home, and like the log canoes, pilot boats, and Baltimore clippers to which they were all related, even a salt-stained pungy or a battered old bugeye could stir the spirit in the same way. A few quick examples of these later Chesapeake workboats might bring out the dynamics of this Anglo-Afro American maritime tradition.

Pungies are commonly thought to have taken their name from Pungoteague Creek in Accomac County on Virginia's lower Eastern Shore, near the mouth of the Bay. They began to appear in the 1840s and 1850s. These vessels were designed and built for use on the Bay, but also for blue-water sailing, on voyages beyond the Capes of the Chesapeake. They were used for many purposes, but mainly they hauled freight. Their speed allowed them to carry cargoes of fruit from the Bahamas and points south to Baltimore and Philadelphia.[111]

Pungies were sturdy, broad-beamed, oak-built oceangoing keel boats, constructed for economy and durability. They tended to be broad in the beam. One pungy, ordered in Accomac County in 1850, had a keel of forty-two feet

and a beam of twenty-one feet, a ratio of 2:1, very different from Virginia
pilot boats and Baltimore flyers.[112] They were designed primarily for cargo
capacity and stability in heavy weather.[113]

At the same time, pungies had the same lively look that recurred in
many Chesapeake designs, with sharply raked fore and main masts. They
were rigged for economy of effort and cost as two-masted schooners with
simple rigs. Despite their broad beams they were surprisingly fast sailors,
after the Chesapeake fashion. It was said that a pungy could be sailed by
a man and a boy. Owners and crews sailed them with pride, and painted
them in a color scheme unique to pungies—pale green with a soft off-red
trim that came to be called "pungy pink." They were still sailing on the Bay
in the late 1930s.

Bugeyes were among the largest classes. They appeared after the Civil War,
when they solved a problem in the Bay's ever-troubled oyster industry. Strict
new Maryland conservation laws allowed the dredging of oysters, but only
by boats under sail to protect oyster beds from destruction. The result was a

The pungy *Lady Maryland*, 2013

The Chesapeake Bay Maritime Museum's bugeye, *Edna E. Lockwood*

new workboat in the old tradition of log-built shallow-draft hulls, with two raked masts. These sailing vessels were large enough to haul a dredge, and fast enough to carry large quantities of oysters to a market. In the Bay they were called bugeyes.[114]

One of the first of this design was the bugeye *Coral*, built in 1867 at Solomons in Maryland, fifty-seven feet in length. Other models grew to eighty or eighty-five feet in the late nineteenth century, with keels and bilge-keelsons. Some of their larger hulls were called "nine-log bugeyes." They proved to be highly versatile. Even as they persisted in oyster dredging, they were increasingly used as freight boats throughout the Chesapeake Bay.

Bugeyes were hard worked and heavily used. I remember them in Baltimore during the late 1940s, looking very much the worse for wear. But even so, when under sail in the Bay, they were graceful vessels with proud clipper bows, two sharply raked masts, low freeboard, and often the tucked or rounded "chunk stern" that displayed their builders' skill. They were schooner-rigged with big head sails and large fore and main sails, most often triangular Bermuda sails, but sometimes leg-of-mutton or sprit-rigged.

In my youth they still carried much cargo to Baltimore. I vividly remember looking down as we crossed the Hanover Street Bridge, at what appeared to be many dozens of bugeyes, moored side by side, some waiting to unload freight. Children were especially fond of the watermelon bugeyes that arrived at Pratt Street piers in the summer, decks piled high with ripe green melons. Crews were often entirely African American and sometimes mates and captains too.

A few of those bugeyes are still afloat. In 1899, a nine-log plank-sided bugeye was built in the old-fashioned way by Frank Laid on Crabb Island in Maryland. At this writing she was still afloat at the Calvert Marine Museum in Solomons, Maryland.

Marion Brewington compiled lists of bugeyes from early government registers of merchant vessels. The oldest was *Coral*, built in Somerset County in 1867, and fifty-seven feet long. Another was *Flying Scud*, also from Somerset in 1871, and listed with length thirty-three feet, beam fifteen feet, and draft two feet! By the end of the nineteenth century some bugeyes were eighty feet in length and more beamy than log canoes, with very low freeboard.[115]

Some of these bugeyes were very fast. In the 1920s and 1930s, the lively Gibson Island Yacht Club sponsored formal races to find "the Fastest Bugeye on the Bay." These contests were closely covered by the Baltimore *Sun*, and winners became heroes throughout the region.[116]

The origin of the name "bugeye" has long been debated by Chesapeake people. Some believed that it came from an old African word but nobody was able to identify a source. I think that the name came not from an African word, but an ancient African emblem, which we saw on fishing boats in Ghana. Some of these vessels (roughly in the same range of sizes as bugeyes) had big round circles painted on each bow. This was a very old maritime tradition in West Africa, North Africa, the Mediterranean, and North America. The painted circles were called "oculi," and had been used for many centuries as emblems that had deep spiritual meaning for African boatmen.

On Chesapeake vessels, prominent hawse holes were added on each bow for an anchor cable. For some people they may have combined that material function with an old spiritual purpose. Their appearance brought to mind bugs' eyes.[117]

Yet another large class of sail-driven Chesapeake workboats were called skipjacks. They were big single-masted, sloop-rigged vessels designed primarily for oyster tonging or oyster dredging under sail. Skipjacks emerged in the late 1880s and early 1890s, and were intended to be more efficient than bugeyes, more powerful for dredging, and more swift in delivering their oysters to market. Nearly all were frame-built vessels with distinctive V-shaped bottoms. They were also very fast, and often participated in skipjack races. Many Marylanders regard skipjacks as among the most handsome Chesapeake workboats. They were also among the most durable, and some are still working. A small group of those boats, still tonging the same oyster beds in the early twenty-first century, are much photographed and celebrated on the Bay. Other skipjacks are maintained as cruising yachts, racing boats, and weekend pleasure craft.[118]

Altogether, these different Chesapeake workboats comprised a large creative family of American watercraft. They came from a long line of Carolina cooners, Chesapeake log canoes, and a floating progeny of pungies, Pocomoke boats, bugeyes, and skipjacks. These earlier vessels combined elements of American Indian dugouts, Dutch sloops, English shallops, Bermuda boats, and African canoes. From all these origins they derived a highly articulated collective character that was uniquely strong in this American region.

In 1880, the U.S. Census did a survey of American watercraft and counted 6,300 "canoes" working on the Chesapeake that year. Nearly all were sail-driven. The census takers also found that 175 of those canoes had been built in the preceding year by more than two hundred "first class canoe wrights" working in the Chesapeake that year.

In the twentieth century, the number of these builders in the Chesapeake Bay rapidly declined. After World War II, Brewington was able to identify only ten men who could build a log canoe or bugeye, but they were still at it. Even in our time, their methods of construction have not yet become a lost art in the region. In the twenty-first century, Marylanders (and Virginians too) continue to build Chesapeake Bay log canoes, mostly for racing, sometimes for yachting, and always for joy of making and preserving an American artifact. Chesapeake watermen have kept alive the traditions of boatbuilding that derive from African roots. And some of these builders and watermen have been African American.

From the Civil War to the Second World War, racism and race prejudice remained strong in the United States. But opportunities were brighter on the water. As early as 1799, an African American named Sadby Batton had been able to buy the Bay schooner *Resolution*. After emancipation, many former slaves found jobs on the water. In 1869, of 3,325 watermen who got Maryland licenses to "tong" oysters in the Bay, about half were African

American. In Virginia, the proportion was not half but two thirds. Even in the years of surging racism African American watermen were able to buy old Bay boats and operate them as owners and captains. When bugeyes became the fashion, Black watermen with little capital bought secondhand pungies. When new skipjacks suddenly came in vogue, and many thousands were built, African American watermen bought old bugeyes at bargain prices.[119]

There was always another side. A few corrupt and violent captains recruited African American watermen, treated them as slaves long after emancipation, and sometimes even locked them in the hold. But the Bay also offered bright opportunities to African Americans who helped each other.

In the 1960s and 1970s, African American skippers such as Captain Richard White of Deal Island and Captain Mervin Christy of Crisfield were renowned for their knowledge of the Bay and for the "quiet calm" of their leadership. When their skipjacks came in with a full load of oysters, African American women who worked in the shucking houses would shout with pride, "Here comes our boys!"[120]

These Afro-Chesapeake watermen were men of strength and character, which persisted through the generations. Malanie Redding of Annapolis was a formidable presence in her community. She wrote, "When people ask me why I am so strong, I tell them it is because I am a waterman's daughter."[121]

AFRICAN INVENTION AND TRADITION
IN MARITIME COMMUNITIES

In the eighteenth and early nineteenth centuries, many slaves gained their freedom in the Chesapeake region. The federal census of 1790 found that of all the states in the new American republic, much the largest number of freed African Americans were in Maryland. The second largest were in Virginia. At the same time, racism and racial segregation also increased.

In maritime occupations, free people both Black and white worked together, but lived apart. Throughout the Chesapeake region, relations between Black and white were complicated. Historian David Cecelski observes that these maritime communities "could not easily be segregated into separate and unequal sections. Self-reliant, in peonage to no one, the African Americans . . . joined their white neighbors as rough equals in a common struggle to make a living from the sea."[122]

Complex systems of residential segregation and economic integration later emerged in much of the Bay country. One common pattern was the growth of paired communities. On Maryland's Eastern Shore, the white town of Oxford grew on one side of the Tred Avon River and the Black community of Bellevue formed on the other. In between, an African American waterman observed, "Ain't no color line on the river." Systems of segregation on the land and integration on the water developed in many parts of the Bay. An example appeared on Kent Island, and along the Kent Narrows, where African captains sometimes worked with European crews, and European captains with African crews. Something similar happened in Virginia's Tidewater towns such as Reedville on the Northern Neck, between the Potomac and Rappahannock Rivers.[123]

At the same time, economic integration on the water coexisted with separate cultural and racial identities. Below the Potomac, very large menhaden fisheries developed as early as the 1830s, expanded rapidly in the 1870s, and reached a peak in the twentieth century when they became the largest fishing industry (by species) in the Chesapeake Bay. When vast schools of menhaden were running, they were net-fished in large numbers, and the catch was sold for fertilizer and animal feed in an expanding market.

A center for menhaden fishing was the town of Reedville in Tidewater Virginia. Here again, Black and white fishermen lived apart, worked together on the water, and preserved their own distinct patterns of cultural heritage. Harold Anderson developed an interest in the songs these watermen sang when they were hauling nets. As they worked in a thriving modern industry and did well for themselves, Black menhaden fishermen also nourished their own traditional African roots. Anderson described their songs as unique "Menhaden Chanteys." They often took the form of call-and-response singing, which appeared in other genres of African and Afro-American music. In the menhaden fisheries, one of the watermen with a great ringing voice sang the call, and the group made their response, with much improvisation and many complex musical rhythms that were combined with the rhythm of material effort as they hauled purse nets, heavy with thousands of small silvery fish.[124]

MARITIME NURSERIES OF AFRICAN AMERICAN LEADERS

In the midst of many changes on the maritime frontier, an important continuity appeared in the agency of individual African American leaders. Seamen, boatman, watermen, and shipbuilders rose to positions of leadership within

African American maritime communities. Some became leaders in the American communities, and in the republic itself. The maritime frontier became a school of leadership. In the nineteenth century the activities of African watermen reached beyond maritime history, to engage large questions in the condition of African Americans, and the American republic.

An example was a seaman who served aboard the American privateer *Requin*. His name was variously written as Richard Crafus or Cephas. During the War of 1812 he was commonly called King Dick, by fellow American captives in Britain's Dartmoor Prison. Earlier in the war he had signed on as a seaman aboard the American letter of marque *Requin*. He was captured at sea in 1814, refused enlistment in the Royal Navy, and became a prisoner of war.

At his arrival at Dartmoor on October 9, 1814, official documents recorded his name as Richard Crafus (or Cephas), his birthplace as Vienna on Maryland's lower Eastern Shore, his height as six feet three and one quarter inches, his weight as three hundred pounds, and his "build" as "stout," which in that era meant big and strong.

At Dartmoor, British jailers segregated American prisoners by race. Richard Crafus or Cephas was sent to Section Four with about a thousand African American seamen. He rapidly emerged as their leader, and continued in that role with the apparent acceptance of British officials, American officers, and other prisoners until their release after the war. Many journals and narratives were written by other captives who knew him. He frequently appears in narratives by other prisoners, who held him in high esteem.

King Dick was described as wearing a British grenadier's headgear, which made him a foot taller. He habitually carried a club and did not hesitate to use it when his authority was challenged. He ran his part of the prison with a strict hand. King Dick kept order with his fists and his club, but also tried govern through an improvised rule of law, with trials and judges and due process. He also encouraged many activities in the African wing of Dartmoor, which attracted visitors from other parts of the prison. After the war, King Dick settled in Boston, and became a leader of African New Englanders in that Yankee city. His turbulent life has been a challenge to American historians, and an inspiration to novelists, playwrights, and poets.[125]

GEORGE ROBERTS: AFRICAN AMERICAN
SEAMAN AND CIVIC LEADER

Another important African American seaman was George Roberts. He was thought to have been a native Marylander, probably born a slave in southern Maryland, perhaps St. Mary's County, 1760 or 1770. In the War of 1812, Roberts enlisted as a seaman aboard Captain Richard Moon's letter of marque schooner *Sarah Ann*, built in St. Mary in southern Maryland in 1811.

While cruising near the Bahamas *Sarah Ann* captured the British merchant ship *Elizabeth*. Soon afterward, *Sarah Ann* herself was captured by a British warship, HMS *Statira*, in the late summer of 1812. George Roberts somehow escaped prison and impressment by the Royal Navy. Perhaps Captain Moon had sent him as one of the prize crew aboard the captured British ship *Elizabeth* into the port of Charleston, South Carolina, in August 1812.

George R. Roberts, maritime leader

By the summer of 1814, George Roberts was back in Maryland. On July 18, 1814, he signed articles of agreement on Thomas Boyle's privateer *Chasseur*, and was granted a double share of prize money, which marked him as an experienced "able seaman," with two shares of the profits above the standard one and a half shares for an ordinary seaman, and one share for a landsman. Only officers, mates, and skilled specialists were better paid.[126]

After the war, *Chasseur*, with Roberts aboard, entered the China trade. She made one run of ninety-five days from Canton to the Virginia Capes, and another of eighty-four days from Java Head to the Virginia Capes.[127]

George Roberts came home to Baltimore, bought a small house in the happy neighborhood that is still called Canton, and became prominent in the civic life of the city. He lived long enough to have a portrait photograph taken by the Bendann family, a leading firm in town. He was photographed in a dark suit, old and severely worn, but carefully patched and mended. Even in old age he made a striking appearance: tall, lean, and muscular. In the camera's eye, George Roberts appears as an image of a maritime leader, with an air of dignity, integrity, strength, and pride.

Africans slave and free flourished in many maritime occupations. Some went to sea aboard merchantmen, warships, whaling ships, privateers, and letter of marque ships.[128] Others worked on coastal vessels and bay boats as deckhands, seamen, pilots, and captains, sometimes with free men under their command. Many were fishermen, oystermen, crabbers. In slavery, large numbers became expert plantation boatmen and skippers who were responsible to their masters. More than a few were expert boatbuilders.

On America's inland waterways, slaves and free Negroes also worked as deckhands and stevedores. Some became helmsmen, pilots, and mates. More than a few were captains of flatboats, bateaux, and ferries.[129] After the Revolution, they built canals, mostly as laborers, sometimes as foremen and job bosses. Many operated canal boats, or owned canal boats outright. Other African slaves and freedmen worked ashore in maritime trades, shipbuilding and waterfront jobs for unskilled laborers, semiskilled caulkers, expert boatbuilders and shipwrights.[130]

Maritime slaves and freedmen had many a tale to tell about their complicated lives, and often told them with pride.[131] They wanted people to remember who they were, how they suffered, but most of all what they achieved. Their creativity grew from the interplay of African heritage, European culture, and American experience. Together they made a difference in other people's lives.

Chapter 9

SOUTHERN FRONTIERS

Angolan Soldiers, Afro-Spanish Militias, U.S. Seminole Negro Scouts

The Negroes dwell in towns apart from the Indians and are the finest-looking people I have ever seen . . . most of them speaking the Spanish, English, and Indian languages. Many of these Negroes were refugee slaves, and some had been soldiers.

—Slaveholding Dr. William Simmons, South Carolina, on the African Seminole warriors of Florida, 1822[1]

ON FLORIDA'S ANGLO-SPANISH FRONTIER, many slaves found another way to freedom. Some were warriors in Africa. They were raised to a military ethic, trained in skills of soldiering, and tested by hard service in their homeland. In Africa's endemic conflicts some of these men, and women too, were captured as prisoners of war, sold into slavery, and shipped to South Carolina.

In the New World, these African warrior-slaves sought to free themselves and their families from bondage. They did it in a variety of ways. A fortunate few were able to gain their freedom in a single triumphant act of armed revolt. Others had to do it again and again, in struggles that went on for generations.

In that process, these warriors and their families created yet another unique African-Indian-European culture in America. It included an ethic of active striving and also a soldier's creed of courage, honor, strength, loyalty to comrades, and fidelity to a cause.

These men and women began their American lives in bondage, and escaped from slavery by their own efforts. With families and friends on the southern frontier of what is now the United States they fought not for conquest but for liberty and freedom: liberty as rights of independence; freedom as rights of belonging to communities of other free people.

Many descendants live today in the United States, and in other nations.

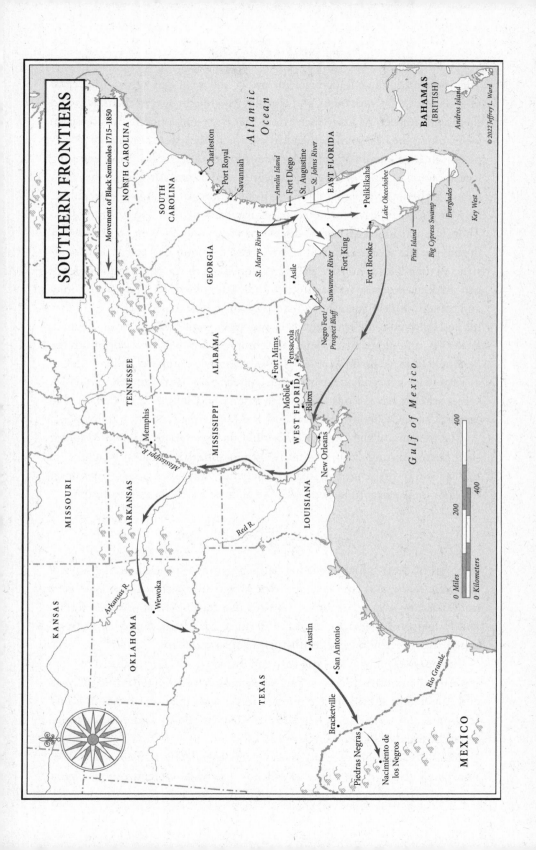

They remember their forebears with pride, and so might other Americans. Friends who stood with them, and enemies who fought against them, regarded them with respect. Military men wrote that these indomitable warrior-slaves were among the best soldiers they had ever met. They were also highly principled in their acts, and faithful in their devotion to others. Their most enduring legacies were qualities of character, integrity, and honor. Altogether, they contributed a heritage of high importance to the history of the American republic.

Many scholars have recovered particular parts of their long history. John Thornton and Linda Heywood discovered their roots in West Central Africa during the late seventeenth and early eighteenth centuries. Peter Wood reconstructed their lives as militant slaves in colonial South Carolina. Kathleen Deagan used her expertise in archaeology and anthropology to study their homes and communities in Spanish Florida. Jane Landers researched their lives in Florida and followed some of them as they moved through the Caribbean. Kenneth Porter was among the first to study the complexity of their association with the Seminole Indians. Kevin Mulroy followed their half-century of military service as Seminole Negro Indian Scouts in the United States Army from 1865 to 1914. Other scholars have reconstructed their history and culture in Florida, the Bahamas, Cuba, Oklahoma, Mexico, and Texas from one generation to the next.

The purpose of this inquiry is to build on those inquiries, and to follow their history through a span of twelve generations, from the early eighteenth to the twenty-first century. In my experience, most Americans have never heard of these extraordinary people. We all have much to learn from them.

AFRICAN WAYS OF WAR

The saga of these militant warrior-slaves began in Africa, where the ways of war were many and complex. In West Africa's northern regions, wars were dominated by cavalry. Mounted warriors moved quickly across open terrain and fought on horseback—first at a distance with barbed javelins and poisoned arrows; then in close combat with edged weapons.[2]

Farther south, horses did not thrive in the equatorial environment of Central Africa, and other forms of warfare were more common. Through Congo and Angola, the most effective military forces were infantry of various kinds. In some Central African states, historians have found that "the entire armed force consisted of light infantry."[3]

Many of these soldiers learned to operate independently in small groups. They were taught to live on the land, move silently through forests and savannas, strike suddenly, retreat quickly, and strike again. They became highly skilled at tracking, woodcraft, ambush, sudden attack, quick escape, and sustained evasion. Some became masters of what Spaniards were first to call *guerrilla* warfare, the little war.

Larger Central African kingdoms also made war in yet other ways, with bodies of heavy infantry. Some rulers specially relied on elite units such as the legendary *gunzes* in the kingdom of Ndongo, who were called the "flower of Angola." These soldiers were chosen for strength and loyalty. They were used as shock troops in battle, and household guards for rulers to whom they were sometimes related.[4]

Other Central African soldiers were highly trained in martial arts such as *sanguar*, a lethal combination of dancing and fighting. A Jesuit missionary in Angola during the 1570s observed that "all their defense consists of *sanguar*, which is to leap from one side to another with a thousand twists and such dexterity that they can dodge arrows and spears."[5]

These Central African ways of war were learned by women as well as men. Many a hero tale was told about Njinga Mbande, a formidable Ndongo queen. In 1660, when she was nearly eighty years old, a Catholic priest praised her skill in martial arts. Njinga replied, "Excuse me, Father, for I am old, but when I was young, I yielded nothing in agility or ability to wound any Jaga."

Ana Njinga Mbande, Warrior Queen of Angola

She hated Imbangala warriors, who later became her followers, and added, "I was not afraid to face twenty-five armed men."[6] A major new biography by Linda Heywood has reconstructed the career of Ana Njinga Mbande as a warrior queen, conqueror of rival states, and ruler of a large part of Angola in the seventeenth century. In our time she has become a hero to many people of Angolan ancestry in Africa and America.[7]

At the heart of these many African traditions was a warrior ethos that was strong throughout the continent, and took many forms in various African cultures. In what is now the West African nation of Mali, a story was told about a Bamana soldier. An arrogant and powerful pasha of Timbuktu ordered him to yield obedience and pay tribute. The Bamana soldier replied, "If you are a man, I am a man. If you have people with you, I have people with me. If you have guns, I have a bow and poisoned arrows. By God, we will give you absolutely nothing!"[8]

The pride and spirit of these African warriors was carried to America by many slaves. Colonizers from Spain and Portugal had long been familiar with African troops, and were quick to employ them as soldiers. When the veteran French soldier and seaman Samuel Champlain visited the island of Saint-Domingue, he met and talked with some of these African warrior-slaves, and was much impressed by them. Champlain described them as *gens de bonne nature*—good-natured people—and was struck by their pride and military bearing. He observed that Spanish officers employed them as coast watchers along the northern coast of Santo Domingo. Their orders were to watch for foreign vessels, and report trespassers. Champlain observed that "these Negroes will go a hundred and fifty leagues [about 450 statute miles] on foot, night and day, to give such notice and acquire their liberty." Their reward was emancipation and employment as freedmen in militia units, with grants of land and liberty by Spanish leaders who knew their worth.[9]

AFRICAN WARRIORS IN SPANISH FLORIDA

From an early date, Spanish conquistadors brought some of these African warriors to Florida. Among the first was Esteban, a soldier-slave with Pánfilo de Narváez as early as 1528. Oral traditions preserved memories of other African slaves who were shipwrecked on the coast, and sheltered by Florida Indians who also employed them as soldiers. Others were brought to Florida from the West Indies, as Crown slaves to build the fortress of St. Augustine and its massive walls that still stand today. As early as 1583, African warriors were also serving in its garrison.[10]

Who were these Florida soldier-slaves? Where in Africa did they come from? Surviving Spanish records identified the African nations of slaves who were carried to Florida in a later period from 1752 to 1763. The largest numbers came from Angola and Congo in Central Africa. A sizable secondary group came from Guinea, with a broad scattering of other origins (Table 9.1 at end of chapter).[11]

As early as 1683, Florida's governor Juan Márquez Cabrera formed Afro-Spanish freedmen into military units distinguished by color: "black" *milicias de morenos* and "mulatto" *milicias de pardos.* These men saw Florida active service against pirates, buccaneers, Yamassee Indians, and English colonists to the north. In 1686, they helped to repel an early English attack on St. Augustine, and later were sent on punitive expeditions against English settlements along the coast of South Carolina. In a raid on Edisto Island they burned Governor Joseph Morton's plantation, and liberated thirteen slaves.[12]

Endemic warfare on this Anglo-Spanish frontier continued through much of the eighteenth century. In 1727 Spain's Black militia raided Carolina and freed more slaves. English troops responded by mounting another failed attack on St. Augustine in 1728, and African militia helped to defeat them. Spanish leaders praised their discipline and "military skills." For their service, many of these African soldiers received honor, rank, land, and freedom for their families.[13]

In neighboring English colonies, African slaves were quick to take notice. As early as the 1680s, growing numbers of fugitive slaves escaped from English plantations and found refuge in Spanish Florida. In 1687, eight African men and two women with a nursing child fled from South Carolina by canoe and reached St. Augustine. By 1690, the governor of South Carolina complained that slaves from his English colony were arriving "dayly" in Spanish Florida, sometimes after killing their masters. Spanish leaders showed little sympathy for English protests. In 1693 Florida's governor Antonio de Benavides offered freedom to all former English slaves who converted to Catholicism and completed four years of Spanish military service. That policy expanded in the eighteenth century.[14]

SOUTH CAROLINA'S STONO REBELLION
AND ITS AFTERMATH

In 1738, Florida's governor Manuel de Montiano announced a sweeping new policy of complete and unconditional freedom for fugitive slaves. The news traveled to the English colonies with astonishing speed, and a surge of runaways and rebellions was quick to follow.

Students of American history are familiar with one such event, South Carolina's Stono Rebellion. It began on Sunday, September 9, 1739, in St. Paul's Parish twenty miles southwest of Charleston. A leader called Jemmy by his master led about twenty slaves identified as Angolans in revolt against their British masters. Their purpose was not to overturn slavery in Carolina, but to escape to freedom in Spanish Florida.[15]

Early accounts reported that a "great number" of slaves took up weapons and attacked their masters. South Carolina's governor Sir William Bull, an eyewitness, reported that more than a hundred slaves joined the rebels. Some armed themselves with edged weapons and firearms, which they knew how to use. They also made their own African drums and flags which were important to their way of war. Observers wrote that they "took up their march . . . with drums beating and banners flying, in some show of military order."

As their numbers increased, they stopped in a field and "set to dancing, singing and beating drums." Then they set out on the long march to Florida. They were reported to have killed twenty-three white men and women, but not in an indiscriminate way. These African rebels spared the lives of English families and individuals who had treated them with humanity.[16]

Carolina masters were quick to react, but not quick enough. They mustered within a few hours and attacked that afternoon. The African slaves fought them in the manner of trained and disciplined soldiers. They engaged in volley firing, "gave two fires," kept fighting until they were defeated by weight of numbers. Then they retreated with skill, and many got away.[17]

Of a "great number" of slaves who joined the revolt, "some say a hundred," about fourteen were killed in that battle. Others escaped and continued south toward freedom. One group of about "twenty-odd or thirty" fighters was caught sixty miles south of Charleston, on the road to Florida. Here again the rebels "fought stoutly for some time." South Carolina's Governor Bull reported that altogether forty-four slaves were killed or executed after the Stono Rebellion. The majority remained at large. Three years later one more Stono rebel was caught and hanged. Most of the rebels escaped, and many of them reached Florida.[18]

In 1991, a student of African military history studied the surviving records of the Stono Rebellion. Historian John Thornton observed that the flags, drums, and "dances" were similar to the highly developed martial exercises in West Central Africa. The march discipline, volley firing, and skillful retreat also indicated that some of these Carolina slaves had been trained as African soldiers. They were able to organize themselves and others into a disciplined military force.[19]

Thornton's evidence of an African warrior tradition among these slaves in early Carolina has given a deeper meaning to the Stono Rebellion. He was also among the first to discover that these Angolan warriors may have been converted to Catholicism in Africa by Portuguese missionaries who were very active in Angola and Congo. Their hostility to slavery in South Carolina was deepened by the distance of their Catholic faith from the religion of their Protestant English masters.[20]

This event in South Carolina, important as it was, took on a larger meaning when studied in its relation to Spanish Florida by Jane Landers and Kathleen Deagan. St. Augustine was more than three hundred miles south of Charleston by eighteenth-century distances, a difficult and dangerous journey for fugitive slaves, with horrific penalties for failure.[21]

In 1697, three other Carolina slaves had tried to get there. They were captured, and the South Carolina Assembly ordered all of them to be castrated. The sentence was carried out, and at least one slave died of the operation. Castration of rebellious slaves was done repeatedly in early South Carolina. Reports of these atrocities were spread deliberately by Carolina planters to discourage rebellion. Their effect was the opposite. They stimulated a surge of violent resistance which led to more extreme atrocities by frightened masters, and yet more resistance in an ascending cycle of brutality.[22]

As early as March 1738, shortly before the Stono Rebellion, at least one hundred former slaves from South Carolina were known to be living in freedom near St. Augustine. Many more arrived in the months that followed. During the fall of 1738, about seventy slaves escaped by boat to Florida. In March 1739, four more African slaves and an Irish servant got away on horseback. Some of these Africans were cattle drivers who knew the interior of South Carolina better than did their masters. All but one reached Florida.[23]

In 1740, an even larger group of African slaves, variously estimated at 150 or 200, "got together in defiance," and organized a rebellion in the very heart

of South Carolina, near the Ashley and Cooper Rivers, which came together
at Charleston. Before the rebellion began, the authorities caught wind of it,
and hanged about fifty slaves—ten hangings a day through a week of executions. Rumors reported the presence of Spanish agents, white and Black, on
the coast of Carolina and as far north as New York, inciting slaves to resistance.[24]

A full count of Carolina slaves who fled for freedom at that time yields results much larger than these numbers. From 1732 to 1739, Charleston's *South
Carolina Gazette* ran advertisements for 253 fugitive slaves within that period
alone. Historians who have studied this evidence agree that these numbers
were only "the tip of an otherwise indeterminate iceberg."[25]

In 1734, South Carolina's slave population was about 26,000, and rapidly
increasing. Rebels who rose against their masters, and fugitives who escaped
to Florida, were a small fraction of a large population that was seething with
unrest. Families of Carolina's slave-owning master class could not sleep easily at night. They fortified their homes, carried weapons to church, enacted
repressive laws of extreme brutality, and inflicted tortures horrific beyond
imagining on slaves caught escaping. Armed white men patrolled the roads,
allied Indians roamed the woods, and Carolina Rangers guarded the southern frontiers.[26]

A deep endemic fear persisted in South Carolina as long as slavery survived, and from time to time it flared into epidemics of hysteria and violence.
In the nineteenth century, English actress Fanny Kemble married the master
of a lowcountry plantation, and talked with many southern women. Kemble
wrote that every plantation mistress of her acquaintance in coastal South Carolina and Georgia said that she lived in mortal fear of her slaves.

But they were making money. South Carolina's small slaveholding master
class was far and away the wealthiest elite in eighteenth-century North America. When some of them appeared in the Continental Congress, representatives from other colonies were amazed by their opulence. But their wealth and
power bought them little peace and no security.[27]

FLORIDA'S FORT MOSE, AN AFRICAN
TOWN IN NORTH AMERICA

Spanish documents provide much evidence that hundreds of escaped Carolina slaves reached St. Augustine and freedom before 1750. Some arrived
in family groups of men, women, children, and even nursing babies. Others

came alone or in small parties. In Florida, they formed households and communities, and began to multiply. Governor Manuel de Montiano encouraged some of these English-speaking freedmen to settle in a fortified village outside St. Augustine. It was called Gracia Real de Santa Teresa de Mose, or Fort Mose for short. As early as 1738, the year before the Stono Rebellion, this settlement was home to thirty-eight families of African origin, mostly former slaves from South Carolina. Thereafter it grew rapidly.[28]

Mose has been called the first free African American town within what is now the southern United States. It had an important military function as a fortified garrison, strongpoint, and watchtower two miles north of St. Augustine, and guarding its northern approaches.

Spanish governor Montiano organized former Carolina slaves at Fort Mose into yet another company of "Black militia." Even as he offered them protection, they protected him from the English to the north. Spanish leaders were keenly aware of the military skills of these African warrior-slaves. Governor Montiano welcomed them to a life of freedom, with land and homes of their own—on one condition. They were asked to join Spanish forces and fight against English enemies from the north.

THE BATTLE OF FORT MOSE, 1740: AFRICAN WARRIORS AND SPANISH TROOPS DEFEAT A FORCE OF ENGLISH INVADERS

One of these fugitive slaves from South Carolina was appointed captain of the Black militia at Fort Mose. Historian Jane Landers has identified him in Hispanic records by his Catholic baptismal name and Spanish military rank: Captain Francisco Menéndez. A census in 1759 described him as "Mandinga" in his ethnic origins, born in West Africa about 1704, and sold as a slave to South Carolina. There he escaped with the help of Yamassee Indians, and made his way to St. Augustine as early as 1727. Later he met and married a younger Mandinga woman, also with a Spanish baptismal name, Ana María de Escovar, born about 1720. Together they raised a family. By 1740, he had a Spanish commission in the rank of captain, and was placed in command of a company of Black militia at Fort Mose.

Captain Menéndez was by all accounts an excellent officer. He looked after the welfare of his men, and was troubled by questions about their status as Spanish soldiers under his command. Were they truly free? This former Carolina slave submitted a series of petitions to the Spanish governor of Florida, asking that the men in his militia company should be recognized as freedmen, with just compensation for their service.

Local officials appear not to have given Captain Menéndez the responses that he sought. In 1740 he sent another petition directly to the king of Spain and got results. Formal freedom was granted not only to Menéndez, but also to at least some of his men and their families.[29]

The success of his petition may have been in part a function of events. In that same year, Captain Menéndez and his company of former slaves played a major role in defeating an English attack on Florida. The assault was a major effort, commanded by an able and distinguished British soldier, General James Oglethorpe, best remembered in the United States as the founder of Georgia, a man of courage and conscience. His orders were to conquer the fortress of St. Augustine. Oglethorpe began by seizing two small Spanish outposts and advanced on Fort Mose. The African families there were sent to safety behind the massive walls of St. Augustine, and Menéndez made a tactical withdrawal with his troops. Oglethorpe occupied Mose, and prepared to use it as a base for his siege of the Spanish capital.

Then suddenly at dawn on June 14, 1740, Oglethorpe's English troops at Mose were attacked by African troops commanded by Captain Menéndez, with a small force of Spanish infantry and Indian allies. In close combat, the English were severely defeated, and seventy-five were killed. After the battle two wounded English soldiers were taken prisoner, and both were castrated. It was the same punishment that South Carolina English leaders had inflicted on slaves who rebelled and tried to reach Florida. One wonders if the African warriors were taking their revenge. Menéndez and his men denied it, and insisted that it was done by angry Indians who had their own scores to settle with the English. We have no way of sorting out the charges and counter-charges, but in these atrocities we can clearly see the escalating horror of Afro-European warfare on the Florida frontier. In these conflicts, each side denied the humanity of the other, but the atrocities had been started by the English.[30]

The shattering English defeat at Fort Mose, largely at the hands of their own escaped slaves, was a heavy blow to General Oglethorpe. He abandoned the campaign and retreated north to Georgia. Spanish and English accounts both stressed the pivotal role of African troops. In the words of the Spanish governor, they "bore themselves like veteran soldiers," and fought with "a particular steadiness." In fact, some of these African troops *were* veteran soldiers.

Spanish authorities responded by recruiting an entire "negro regiment" for service on the frontiers of Florida. Its officers were Africans who were "clothed in lace," and "bore the same rank as white officers, and with equal freedom and familiarity they walked and conversed with their commanders."[31]

Captain Menéndez and some his men also served at sea as marines aboard Spanish privateers. A ship from New England captured his vessel, and sold him into slavery at Nassau in the Bahamas. He escaped from bondage yet again, found his way back to St. Augustine, and resumed command of the Black militia in a much strengthened base at Fort Mose.

THE ENGLISH SEIZURE OF SPANISH FLORIDA, 1763: SEMINOLES OFFER SANCTUARY AND MILITARY ALLIANCES TO AFRICAN WARRIORS

A truce followed, and other wars. In 1763, the English mounted a major effort and captured all of Florida from Spain. Before the fall of St. Augustine, Captain Menéndez led some of his African soldiers and their families aboard a schooner sadly called *Nuestra Señora de los Dolores*, Our Lady of the Sorrows.[32] They went to Cuba, and eighty-four families became free landowners in Cuba's Matanzas Province, fifty miles east of Havana. Their descendants still live there. Other groups went to what is now the Dominican Republic, and descendants survive there as well.[33]

After the Treaty of Peace in 1763, East Florida remained only briefly in British control, until the War of American independence. In 1783 Florida was returned once more to Spain, and the flow of fugitive slaves from Carolina and Georgia resumed.

Some of these runaways found sanctuary among migrating American Indians who had also moved south to Florida. Many were Creeks who had left their own nation and began to be called in the Muskogean Creek language *Simano-li* or Seminoles, a borrowed Indian word derived from the Spanish *cimarrones*, for runaways. In Creek usage, "Seminole" had a multiple series of expansive meanings. It first meant "seceders," or separatists from the main body of Lower Creeks. Then it came to mean "runaways" and "wild ones" in general. The history of these American Indians and their African allies gave them a yet larger meaning as a warrior people who fought not for conquest but independence, and did so with courage and honor.[34]

Some of these "Seminole" Indians had moved into Florida as early as 1715, and probably earlier. After 1763, the Spanish encouraged them to settle north and west of St. Augustine, as a way of keeping the Anglos at bay. The Seminoles were a highly adaptable people who spoke multiple Muskogean languages, lived in small villages, and belonged to many separate bands.[35]

As early as 1725, an English agent found many runaway Africans living among them, mostly fugitive slaves from South Carolina. After 1763 they were joined by former African residents of Fort Mose, who preferred to remain in Florida rather than join the exodus to Cuba.

These African warrior families moved west from St. Augustine to good land in north-central Florida. In that very attractive region (still so today) they settled by permission among the Seminole Indians, and sought protection from them. Seminoles called them slaves, but not in the usual sense. Historian Kenneth Porter found that Seminole leaders "apparently had no intention of devoting their lives to managing slaves." They gave the fugitive Africans tools to clear land, and encouraged them to build separate villages, plant crops, raise livestock, and support their families. In return for protection, the Africans paid the Seminole Indians an annual tribute which was "never more than ten bushels of corn," and kept the rest of their harvest for themselves. It was the same with livestock. At slaughter time, Seminole Indians received a "fat hog or a side of beef" from African families, but otherwise never "meddled" with their animals.[36]

The individual status of these African fugitives among the Indians was variable. A few were held individually in something like chattel slavery, but most were called slaves in a very different sense. For them, Kenneth Porter observed that the Seminole Indians were less masters than patrons, and Africans among them were less slaves than vassals, offering fealty with payments of food and a firm promise of military service, and otherwise independent. Once again Seminole Indian leaders (like the Spanish) valued the military skill of these African warriors, and once again they were told that they were free to remain on one condition—that they would join together and fight attackers from the north.[37]

Porter found "no personal inequality between the two groups." These African warriors began to be called Black Seminoles or Negro Seminoles. With Anglos as highly aggressive neighbors to the north, bonds of mutual interest grew strong between Africans and Indians in early years of central Florida. English-speaking colonists from South Carolina and Georgia mounted continuing attacks and slaving raids, which further reinforced a strong alliance among Indians and Africans.[38]

Both Seminole Indians and Negro Seminoles formed themselves into small bands, and lived in dispersed "towns" or villages. Archaeologists have found the remains of many settlements, sometimes in a checkerboard pattern of "red villages" and "black villages" in many parts of central Florida from the northern borderlands to the southern Everglades.[39]

Some of these villages spread east toward St. Augustine and the St. Johns River. Prominent among Black Seminole settlements were villages called the Mulatta Girl's Town and King Payne's Town in the late eighteenth century, and King Heijah's Town, and Billy Bowleg's Town in the nineteenth. The names tell us that these Black Seminole towns were not democracies. Some were run by matriarchs, and most by male warrior leaders.

Other settlements later formed along a river that flows from south Georgia and north Florida into the Gulf of Mexico. Seminole Blacks called it Suwannee, perhaps from the Bantu *nsub-wanyi*, "my house, my home." This name, which would echo widely through antebellum southern culture, may have derived from Bantu-speaking fugitive slaves.[40] This region was (and is today) beautiful country, and a favored place for settlement. Villages formed in central Florida, midway between the modern cities of Orlando and Tampa. A few years ago when Judy and I explored this region, much of it was open rolling land, still rural though in process of rapid development. Its fertile soil supported a checkerboard of many Indian and African and Black Seminole towns. One of the first was Big Hammock or Okahumpka from the 1760s. Among the largest Black Seminole towns was Piliklakaha or Abraham's Town in the nineteenth century.

Other flourishing settlements clustered on the Gulf Coast, from the present sites of St. Petersburg and Tampa to Sarasota and Fort Myers. Coastal Black Seminole towns also developed near Seminole Indian hunting villages and Cuban fishing camps on the Gulf Coast, which also harbored Black fugitives. An important Seminole village at Sarasota has been dated as early as the mid-eighteenth century. In the nineteenth century many hidden villages formed to the east and south near Lake Okeechobee, and on islands of high ground in Big Cyprus Swamp and the Everglades. Some of these secretive settlements remained largely unknown to others until well into the twentieth century.[41]

Fugitive African slaves who lived among the Seminoles were given many names. Spanish leaders in the eighteenth century at first called them *cimarrones* or runaways. The English spoke of them as "maroon negroes." Their complex relations with Indians led to different and even opposite names: "seminole slaves" but also "seminole freedmen," and "half slaves." They became "seminole negroes" by the early nineteenth century and "black seminoles" in the twentieth—a name by which some of their descendants proudly know themselves today.[42]

Travelers who visited these Black Seminoles in their villages were much impressed by them. A South Carolina physician, Dr. William Hayne Simmons, who met them and wrote that "The Negroes . . . both men and women . . . [are] the finest-looking people I have ever seen. . . . They are much more intelligent than their masters." Another described them as a "fine-formed athletic race," who "speak English as well as Indian and feel satisfied with their situation."[43]

Like many African slaves in early America, Black Seminoles were quick to learn other languages. An African Seminole warrior known to Anglo-Americans as Tony Proctor was said to have been "the best translator of Indian languages in the province." Black Seminoles such as Ben Wiggins and John Horse became polylingual and they were frequently asked to serve as "the Indians' principal interpreters." It is interesting that Africans also became translators between Indian nations. Some Black Seminole men and women quickly learned to speak "Yucki, Hitchiti, and other Indian languages, all of which were incomprehensible to Muskogee speakers."[44]

These Black Seminoles also had multiple speechways of their own. Chief among them was an Afro-English dialect that linguists call "Afro-Seminole Cre-

John Horse

ole." It later became mostly English, with elements of Spanish, Bantu, Mande, and several Muskogean Indian languages. Research by linguist Ian Hancock on speech among Black Seminoles has documented its Gullah and Geechee roots in South Carolina and Georgia. These findings confirm yet again that most Black Seminoles came to Florida by way of Anglo-American colonies.[45]

Another striking cultural pattern appeared in naming customs. Black Seminole peoples tended to receive multiple names: Seminole busk names, Gullah Geechee basket names, English nicknames, and Spanish baptismal names. One example was a great leader of the Black Seminoles for many years. He had at least five names. Regular officers in the United States forces knew him by his army nickname, Gopher John, because as a boy he had sold them land turtles called gophers in Florida. Seminoles knew him by his Indian busk name, Cowaya, from the Hitchiti noun *kaway* (horse). As he grew older he was called John Horse in English, Juan Caballo in Spanish, and John Cavallo in his family. These names were used respectfully by friends and enemies alike. John Horse was an African Big Man, a Seminole chieftain, and a Spanish caballero.[46]

Seminole Blacks created a culture of their own by borrowing from many other cultures. They drew heavily from the ways of American Indians. Kenneth Porter describes how they "built houses in their own villages, Indian style, with Palmetto planks lashed to upright posts and thatched with palmetto leaves." But in other ways, such as the scale and framing of their houses,

Black Seminole village

Black Seminoles were closer to European and Anglo-American building ways. One visitor observed that "their dwellings were usually better constructed than the tribes peoples." Here again, Black Seminoles combined African, European, and American Indian cultures.[47]

Similar cultural patterns appeared in other material customs. Their very distinctive dressways combined at least four traditions: African, Indian, Spanish, and English. Headdresses included extravagant plumes of magnificent egret feathers, which sometimes identified particular Indian and Black Seminole bands in creative combinations of white and black feathers.

The dress of the Black Seminoles was colorful and inventive. It greatly appealed to romantic artists in the nineteenth century. Carolina slave owners were appalled, and some of them were more than a little fearful of these intimidating people. Dr. Jacob Rhett Motte of South Carolina met a group of Black Seminoles and wrote that they were "the most diabolical-looking wretches I ever saw; their style of dress contributing much to render them ferocious and oriental in aspect."[48]

Black Seminoles were also renowned for their handshaking. They borrowed a custom which Quakers had introduced to America, as a ritual of peace and friendship, and gave it a decidedly un-Quaker meaning with a new intensity of martial ardor. John Mahon wrote, "Grim or smiling, they gave a hearty greeting. One method was to grip the elbow of the visitor and shake the entire forearm; but if a handshake sufficed it was carried out with a violent downward jerk." Dr. Rhett Motte experienced this greeting and was shaken in more ways than one. He described it as a physical ordeal and test of strength, which was done in his words "with as much hauteur, and nonchalance, as if they were conferring a vast deal of honour, of which we should have been proud."[49]

The foodways of Black Seminoles also drew on many cultures. From their Indian neighbors they adopted the communal sofkee pot. Historian Porter explained, "The blacks would share the 'sofkee' pot (sofkee is a gruel made of corn pounded with mortar and pestle) with their owners whenever they visited their homes." Sofkee was akin to Indian hominy, and to Anglo-Afro-southern grits, but with a character of its own. Indian, African, and European foods were all stirred together in a sofkee pot.[50]

Many observers commented on the strength of religious belief among the Black Seminoles. They tended to adopt a synecretist faith in many combinations which combined African and Indian beliefs with both Spanish Catholic and Anglo-Baptist forms of Christianity. In the seventeenth and eighteenth centuries some African slaves became Roman Catholic in Florida, but maintained ancestral African beliefs and customs in a lively mix of Catholic saints and African spirits, much as their forebears had done in Central Africa. That pattern was followed by another in the nineteenth century. A close student of their culture wrote that "young as well as old were staunch Baptists," but combined that faith with African and Indian practices. In the twentieth century a Black Seminole named Dindie Factor remembered that his people often formed Baptist fellowships, built Gullah praise houses, and "prayed Injun."[51]

Visitors observed that Black Seminole families were close, and that their families were "much stronger in Indian country than one might expect." In the midst of much disorder, family ties were cherished all the more. They grew into complex cousinages, which have survived through many generations, even to our time. A story was told about a former slave named King Kernel, who lived among the Indians. He met and married "a pretty young light mulatto." Their many descendants remembered that "through the Indian wars in the Southeast, Jackson's incursions, and removal to Oklahoma, they clung fast to one another, and saw a growing number of children, grandchildren, and great-grandchildren. One of their offspring remembered that "King Kernel never left his wife's side: King was a Big Man."[52]

NONE OF THE SERVILITY: BLACK SEMINOLE WARRIOR TRADITIONS AND LEADERSHIP ROLES

Altogether these splendid Black Seminoles were a formidable people, strong and proud in their spirit of independence. Jacob Rhett Motte observed that "they had none of the servility" he observed in Carolina servants and house slaves of his acquaintance.[53]

Black Seminoles joined Indians in influential positions of leadership, serving in many complex roles as "linksters" (go-betweens), "sense bearers" (advisors and spokesmen), "black factors" (agents), and later chiefs.[54]

Some Black Seminole leaders also did very well in material terms. More than a few became wealthy stockmen, with large herds. They also prospered as traders in deer skins, fur pelts, and other commodities.[55]

Many drawings and early photographs show them as a straight-up people. Black Seminole women stood proud and tall. Black Seminole warriors normally stood at attention. Their children carried themselves with quiet pride. Elders of great age were ramrod straight. Through many generations it was observed that Black Seminoles "habitually carried arms," for self-defense.

When war threatened, the Black Seminoles "assembled under their own captains." In combat they won the respect of friends and enemies alike, as hard fighters and disciplined soldiers. They were highly skilled in tracking, hunting, scouting, and methods of irregular warfare. Their earliest daguerreotypes were images of strength, dignity, pride, courage, and a warrior's inner calm. Even as they were often at war with others, these extraordinary people were at peace with themselves.[56]

Through the eighteenth, nineteenth, and early twentieth centuries, from 1739 to 1914, Black Seminoles soldiered through many campaigns, and countless military engagements. They had many allies, but only one set of enemies, people who sought to return them to bondage, or to exploit them in some other way. Anglo-Americans, Britons, Spaniards, Mexicans, Frenchmen, and more than a few hostile Indian nations all attempted to do that. Some Creek groups tried it in the east, and Comanches in the west.

After 1776 their leading opponents were militant white southerners from South Carolina, Georgia, Tennessee, and Alabama, who preached liberty and practiced slavery. In Washington, four slaveholding American presidents were hostile to Black Seminoles. Thomas Jefferson, James Madison, Andrew Jackson, and James K. Polk all tried again and again to destroy their freedom and steal their land. Two other presidents, John Quincy Adams and Zachary Taylor, tried to keep faith with these people and sought to protect and support them in various ways.

SPAIN RECOVERS FLORIDA, REVIVES BLACK MILITIAS, AND SUPPORTS BLACK SEMINOLES, 1783–1819

During and after the American War of Independence, the history of Florida began to move in new directions. While white Americans fought for their own liberty, thousands of slaves in South Carolina and Georgia escaped from their masters. Some were protected by British forces. Others fled to Florida, which once again became a Spanish possession from 1783 to 1819.

Florida's Spanish governor General Vicente Manuel de Zéspedes restored the policy of sanctuary for fugitive slaves from the United States. He revived Black militia companies, recruited Black and mulatto military units from Cuba and Saint-Domingue, and invited Seminole Black *cimarrones* to St. Augustine for annual meetings, with ritual gift exchanges and a web of quasi-alliances.[57]

The governor also admitted hundreds of fugitive slaves from the United States to freedom in Florida. He even took some of them into his own home. Among them was Prince Witten, a native of Guinea in West Africa. He escaped from Georgia with his wife, Judy, and two children "to avoid a forced separation from his family, to which he is much attached," in the words of his former owner.[58]

Witten was described as a born leader, a large man, "strong and brawny," well spoken, and quick to claim his rights. In St. Augustine he received his freedom, and worked hard. When his employer insisted that Judy Witten must also work in the fields, Prince declared that he "could not permit" her to become a farm laborer. He went to court and sued for cancellation of his contract, and for payment of wages for work done. Witten became the head of the free Black community in St. Augustine and was asked to be godfather to at least twenty-three children of record.[59]

The rapid increase of this free and militant Black population in Florida was alarming to slave owners in the United States, among them Thomas Jefferson. One of his first actions as secretary of state in 1790 was to demand that the Spanish government end the policy of sanctuary for slaves escaped from the United States. Spain agreed "in principle" but not in practice. Fugitive slaves kept coming, sometimes with armed and angry owners in hot pursuit. One band of twelve fugitives led by a formidable leader named Titus got into the swamps of Florida in 1797. An armed party from Georgia tried to hunt them like animals and failed. The Georgians were lucky to escape with their lives.[60]

Florida's Spanish rulers felt vulnerable to incursions by American slave holders. In 1790 an official census of St. Augustine and its environs found that only a sixth of the population were "natural Spaniards."

At the same time, another fast-growing group in northeast Florida were Anglo-American homesteaders and planters. About 750 swore Spanish loyalty oaths by 1804, and were allowed to settle along the fertile valleys of the St. Marys and St. Johns Rivers. They brought in at least four thousand slaves of record, and many more who were not included in the Spanish census records. An Atlantic slave trade from Africa began to grow in Spanish Florida, and continued after it was forbidden by Congress in the United States in 1808. Altogether a majority of the population in Spanish Florida were African American, free and slave together, who grew from 27 percent in 1786 to 58 percent in 1814.

Not counted in these Spanish population estimates were thousands of Indians and hundreds of Afro-Seminoles. Their numbers also grew by a continuing flow of fugitive slaves, not only from Georgia and South Carolina but also from plantations in northeast Florida. By the early nineteenth century, at least three quarters of Spanish Florida's population were African Americans and American Indians.

Spanish rulers of Florida tried once again to control their province by arming free Blacks and mulattos, and organizing them into disciplined militia units with their own experienced officers. Other Black military units were brought to Florida from Santo Domingo. Spanish leaders also recruited special forces of Indian and Black maroons from former British colonies, and made alliances with Black Seminoles. All of these groups were united by a common enemy—slaveholders who dominated the southern United States.[61]

THE PATRIOT WAR, 1811–12: BLACK SEMINOLE WARRIORS DEFEAT UNITED STATES MARINES

In 1811, a small group of land-hungry Georgia slave owners hatched a large plan for the conquest of Florida. They claimed the name of "Patriots," but were driven by a hunger for land and slaves. Their leaders were General George Mathews, an American land speculator and former governor of Georgia; and John Houston McIntosh, a businessman with large holdings in Georgia and Florida.[62]

In Washington the "Patriots" won support from top Democratic-Republican leaders. On January 15, 1811, Jeffersonian Republicans in Congress passed a secret resolution which authorized President James Madison to conquer Florida if a "foreign government" tried to possess it, or if "local authorities" invited them in. Georgia's General George Mathews was given several gunboats, and a small detachment of United States Marines.

Mathews and McIntosh also recruited a force of Georgian mercenaries who called themselves the Patriot Army. On March 14, 1812, they invaded Spanish Florida, created their own government, took over Amelia Island, and marched on St. Augustine. Their objective was to seize the entire province of Florida and annex it to the United States as an open field for the expansion of slavery.

These arrogant and ignorant men openly despised Spaniards, Indians, and especially African Seminoles. General Mathews informed Seminole leader King Payne, a man of great age, ability, and dignity, that "he intended to drive him from his land." Georgian John Houston McIntosh told Payne's kinsman, Seminole war leader Billy Bowlegs, that "he intended to make him a waiting man."[63]

Mathews and McIntosh managed to unite most people in Florida against them: Spanish, British, Indian, and African at all the same time. Opinion in the northern United States also strongly opposed them. President Madison began to back away. As war with Britain approached, he did not wish to provoke Spain. But the self-styled Patriots pressed on. They began to occupy the border, and then moved deeper into Spanish Florida, with support from a small force of United States Marines, whose very able commander was disgusted with the Patriot leaders and requested other duty.

The Patriots laid siege to St. Augustine and were confident of success. One wrote contemptuously that "the principal strength of the garrison at Saint Augustine consists of negroes." He had no understanding of his opponents.[64] Arrayed against him were combined forces of Seminole Indians, Black Seminoles led by King Payne and Billy Bowlegs, and a third force of Black militia based in St. Augustine. They served under the command of their own officer, Prince Witten. He ordered the militia to put aside their Spanish regimentals, dress like Seminoles, and paint their faces.

These veterans did not wait to be attacked in the fortifications of St. Augustine. Witten's Black militia and the Black Seminoles seized the initiative. They advanced on their enemies and gained control of the countryside in an outer ring around the besiegers, gathering foodstocks, ambushing small parties, interrupting the flow of supplies, and taking a steady toll of the invaders.[65]

The Black Seminole leader Prince Witten looked for a way to strike at the Patriot army that was besieging St. Augustine. An opportunity appeared on September 12, 1812. The invaders were running low on supplies. They sent a convoy of wagons and pack mules to a base twenty miles distant, with orders to return with urgently needed food and ammunition. The convoy was protected by sixty or seventy Georgia irregulars and twenty United States Marines. Prince Witten's Black militia and King Payne's warriors prepared a surprise. In late afternoon, as the light was failing, the empty supply wagons approached an area called Twelve Mile Swamp. In the gathering darkness, shots suddenly rang out. The Black and mulatto militia and Negro Seminoles commenced firing at close range. They fought like the veterans they were, with extraordinary fire discipline that made the best use of scarce ammunition. They concentrated their fire on the man they most respected, U.S. Marine Captain John Williams, an able and humane officer who was held in high esteem by friend and foe alike. With deadly accuracy Black Seminole warriors hit Captain Williams eight times and grievously wounded him. They also brought down most of his officers and sergeants, and shot the wheel horses in their traces on the supply wagons.[66]

The marines fought back with a tenacity that greatly impressed the Black Seminoles. Captain Williams somehow rallied his shattered command and brought it forward in a bayonet charge. The Seminoles and Black militia fell back, then counterattacked again in the darkness. In hand-to-hand fighting the marines and Georgians were driven into the swamp, and the supply wagons were seized or burned. A few marines were sent to bring help. They returned to find the remains of Captain Williams's command in the swamp and brought them away, many on stretchers and severely wounded. Without supplies, the Georgians abandoned the siege of St. Augustine and retreated to the United States. The Spanish governor of Florida gave the credit to Prince Witten and "parties of blacks" who had won the battle.[67]

A month later, Georgia invaders tried again, with a larger force and a different mission. Their commander, Colonel Daniel Newnan, marched deep into the Alachua country west of St. Augustine, with orders to attack Black Seminole towns, kill every Black Seminole warrior, and return Black Seminole families to slavery. Newnan's command destroyed two empty towns, and suffered heavy losses in the process. Once again the Georgians were defeated, and a small remnant was lucky to escape. Newnan was shocked by the military strength and skill of the Florida Indians and especially by the Black Seminoles. He reported that Seminole Indians were formidable in war and that "Negroes . . . were their best soldiers."[68]

With each of these defeats, a spasm of fear ran through Georgia, Tennessee, and other slaveholding states. John McIntosh wrote to Secretary of State James Monroe in Washington that "we have an army of negroes raked up in this country." He warned that if not defeated they could "bring about a revolt of the black population in the United States."[69]

Panic swept through the lower South. Large forces of militia mustered in Tennessee and Georgia and marched on Florida's Black Seminoles. Their commander, Georgia's militia general Thomas Flournoy, ordered that "every negro found in arms be put to death without mercy."[70]

The Black Seminoles were now heavily outnumbered. They retreated south from the Alachua country and disappeared into Florida swamps with their families. The invaders destroyed several abandoned Black Seminole towns and declared victory. An occupying force of Georgia militia led by General Buckner Harris tried to take permanent possession of the Alachua region. They surveyed the land, built a fort, and demanded annexation by the United States. But once again Spanish, Indian, and Black Seminole leaders came together against them. A party of warriors suddenly emerged from the swamps. With extraordinary economy of military effort they dealt with their problem by killing General Harris.[71]

Without a field commander, the Georgia militia retreated in confusion. American leaders in Washington disowned them, and the Patriot movement collapsed. Kenneth Porter wrote its epitaph: "The U.S. attempt to seize Spanish-owned East Florida had failed largely due to black-instigated resistance." The Patriot movement was not merely defeated but destroyed by an alliance of Black Seminoles, Florida Indians, and the Spanish government.[72]

THE WAR OF 1812–14 IN FLORIDA: BRITISH FORCES SUPPORT BLACK SEMINOLES AGAINST AMERICAN ATTACKS

Then came the War of 1812 between Britain and the United States. Once again the southern frontier between the United States and Florida erupted in violence, not primarily involving the Seminoles and their Black allies in East Florida, but also Creeks and other Indian nations in the country adjacent to West Florida.

In much of this region, Indians attacked frontier settlements of white North Americans in 1812, and slaves rose to join the Indians. Hundreds of settlers took refuge at Fort Mims near Mobile. On August 20, 1813, Creek warriors attacked the crowded wooden fort and set it ablaze. Many settlers died in the flames. The Creeks killed another 250 settlers, and freed many slaves.

The Fort Mims Massacre awakened the western settlers, and their fury fell on the Creeks, who were the nearest enemy within reach. A full-scale war was led by a militia officer whose public career was thought to have ended in the tangled conspiracy of Aaron Burr. Andrew Jackson led thousands of Tennessee militia south against the Creeks. In heavy fighting, the Tennessee troops killed 1,300 Creek warriors, captured many more, and dictated a treaty in which most Creek lands were seized.

In May of 1814, the Royal Navy arrived on the Gulf Coast. Brevet Captain

George Woodbine of the Royal Marines was sent to the Apalachicola River with orders to recruit Indians and fugitive slaves as allies in the British war against the United States, with promises of freedom and land in the Indies. To that end, British officers built a fort on Prospect Bluff above the Apalachicola River, twenty-five miles from the Gulf. The Royal Navy landed large stockpiles of weapons, gunpowder, and artillery.

As the War of 1812 between Britain and the United States reached its end, more than a thousand runaway slaves gathered at the fort on the Apalachicola. Some were fugitives from states and territories north and west of Florida. Others were former slaves of the Creek Indians, and many were Black Seminoles. Together they occupied a large area around the fort. It was said that their cornfields extended forty miles up and down the river.[73]

Their leader was a Black commander named Garçon, who may have come from Haiti. He raised two ensigns above the "Negro Fort" as it was now called: the British Union Jack, and a red flag of revolution against slavery in the southwestern United States.

In the summer of 1816, the Negro Fort was attacked by militia from southern states and territories, and by gunboats of the U.S. Navy. The militia attack failed, but a gunboat fired red-hot cannonballs into the fort's magazine, which was filled with large stocks of British munitions. A huge explosion destroyed the fort and killed many defenders. Still, hundreds of former slaves survived and retreated further into South Florida.[74]

THE FIRST SEMINOLE WAR, 1816–18

In 1816, Andrew Jackson went after them, in what he called the Florida "Indian and Negro War." Against the orders of his superiors in Washington, Jackson led three thousand troops into a fertile part of the Seminole country along the beautiful Suwannee River. Jackson's purpose was the total destruction of "Negro settlements." His militia were ordered to kill Black Seminole warriors, and enslave women and children. In one of the most cruel, tyrannical, and incompetent campaigns in American military history, Andrew Jackson repeatedly violated the Constitution, broke international treaties, ignored acts of Congress, defied the orders of his superiors, and failed in his objective. Jackson's men attacked Indian settlements that stretched three miles along the Suwannee. Black Seminole warriors, with very little warning, improvised a stubborn and successful delaying action, and managed to get their women and children to safety. The inhabitants of four hundred Indian and Black Seminole homes vanished into the Florida countryside. Jackson captured only two Black Seminole warriors and empty towns, which his forces looted and burned. He also seized two British traders. In gross violation of international law, he hanged one and shot the other.

The Black Seminoles survived. They moved deep into Florida swamps, and emerged when Jackson and his militia were gone. A new generation of Black Seminole leaders came forward to lead their people. Among them was Abraham, the former slave of a British physician in Pensacola. He was variously described as intelligent, wise, humane, mature, highly educated, and a master of polished speech in several languages. Abraham was also a brilliant soldier, with the bearing of a born leader. Negro Seminoles welcomed him. Once again, the strength and endurance of the Negro Seminoles owed much to the high quality of their leaders.[75]

A PRIVATE SLAVEHOLDER'S WAR: BLACK SEMINOLES DEFEAT GEORGIA SLAVEHOLDERS, 1821–23

In 1819, the Monroe administration in Washington bought Florida from Spain. After the sale of Spanish Florida to the United States, many Blacks and mulattos in the province moved to Cuba and the Bahamas, with good reason. Pro-slavery Americans saw an opportunity to enrich themselves in Florida, by seizing land from the Indian Seminoles, and enslaving the Black Seminoles.

Andrew Jackson was briefly appointed territorial governor of Florida, and a major general in the United States Army. He asked permission to remove the Florida Indians from their land, and to return Black Seminole freedmen to slavery, with the support of the United States government.

Many leaders in Washington were deeply concerned about his reckless ambition, lawless acts, and extreme violence. Secretary of War John C. Calhoun (then a strong nationalist and Jackson's rival) ordered him to take no immediate action, much to the fury of many in the South. Jackson obeyed, with the presidency now in his sights.

But in Georgia, "some men of influence and fortune" decided to organize their own private war in Florida. Their leader was Georgia governor David B. Mitchell. They recruited an army of white slave hunters, renegade Blacks, soldiers of fortune, and Coweta Creek Indians led by a mixed-blood chief, William McIntosh.

In 1821, these men suddenly launched an attack on flourishing Black Seminole towns along the Gulf Coast near Tampa. They caught some of the Black Seminoles by surprise, destroyed their thriving villages, and kidnapped free Blacks and returned them to slavery—fifty-nine on one list, mostly families with children. One of the captives was listed as "Jim, formerly the estate of General Washington." George Washington had ordered his emancipation, which meant nothing to Georgia slavers.[76]

The two men who started this private war gained little by it, and both came to a bad end. David Mitchell was removed from office by President James Monroe for corruption, slave smuggling, and other crimes. William McIntosh was removed by Coweta Creek opponents in another way. They burned his house, seized his property, and stabbed and shot him many times until they were sure he was dead.[77]

Black Seminole towns called Angola, Loango, and Kongo were destroyed, but once again their inhabitants escaped into the interior where pursuers did not dare to follow. They built new settlements in many places. Others moved to the Florida Keys, where in the twentieth century we met some of their descendants in Key West. More than three hundred Seminole Blacks moved to the Bahamas. They were carried there by Cuban fishermen who worked from small stations on Florida's Gulf Coast, English wreckers who lived at Tavernier in the Keys, and trading partners who knew them well. Five Black Seminole villages took root on the Andros Islands. Many descendants still live there, as well as other places in the Bahamas.[78]

Many Black Seminoles remained in Florida. In 1823, by the Treaty of Moultrie Creek, Seminole Indians ceded claims to the Alachua lands in northeast Florida in exchange for a large reservation that included much of central Florida from Fort King in the north to Lake Okeechobee in the south, an area of about four million square miles.

The Seminole Indians were estimated by their own census at about five thousand people. Altogether, Black Seminoles may have been between one and two thousand in Florida. Some of them settled on Pine Island in Charlotte Harbor on Florida's southern Gulf Coast. Two contemporaries wrote that "they are well armed and refuse to allow Americans to visit the island."[79] Others lived in villages such as Thlonoto-sassa near Tampa, and their town of Peliklikaha.[80] In all of these places, Black Seminoles lived in peace and growing prosperity for more than five years from 1823 to 1829, much to the fury of Andrew Jackson.

Andrew Jackson

JACKSON'S REMOVAL ACT AND THE
SECOND SEMINOLE WAR, 1835–42

Andrew Jackson was careful to stay in the shadows while he pursued the presidency. In the election of 1824, he was defeated by John Quincy Adams and Henry Clay, who deeply distrusted him after his conduct in Florida, but four years later, Jackson won the presidency in 1828. As president he sponsored the Indian Removal Act in 1830. Black Seminoles were high on his list.

Jackson and his allies wanted to move the Indian Seminoles to the west. A few Indian leaders were compelled by force and fraud to agree, but most refused. President Jackson himself issued a direct threat in 1835. "Should you refuse to move," he declared, "I have then directed the commanding officer to remove you by force." General Duncan Clinch warned the Seminole Indians to assemble at Tampa and prepare for removal to the West.

For the Black Seminoles, Jackson had other plans. He intended to return them to slavery. Some had been free for a century and more. Many had freedom papers from Spanish authorities, but those facts were of no interest to

Old Hickory and southern slaveholders. The freedom of Seminole Blacks was seen as a fundamental threat to plantation slavery in Florida and the Deep South. Numbers of Seminole Blacks were growing, in part by natural increase, and also by runaways from southern plantations.[81]

Most Seminole Indians and nearly all Seminole Blacks refused to compromise on issues of land and freedom. Jackson was equally adamant. The result was an explosion of violence in 1835, and the largest of all the many Florida conflicts. The United States Army officially remembers this struggle as the Second Seminole War.[82]

Some American historians think of it primarily as an Indian conflict. But officers in the field knew otherwise. General Thomas Jesup, the army's commander in the field, wrote to superiors in Washington. "This, you may be assured, is a Negro, not an Indian war. And if it be not speedily put down the south will feel the effects of it on their slave population before the end of next season."[83]

In truth it was both. The fighting, once begun, continued for seven years. It has been written that "the whole military power of the United States was brought to bear." The dollar cost was four times greater than the purchase price of Florida. Approximately ten thousand Regulars in the army, navy, and Marine Corps served in Florida. Of that number, 1,446 died, a rate of loss approaching 15 percent, among the highest rates of any war in American history, with the exception of the Civil War. It was also one of the few wars in which armed forces of the United States failed to win a decisive battlefield victory.[84]

In Washington, the quality of leadership was not strong during the administrations of Andrew Jackson and Martin Van Buren. Later, President Theodore Roosevelt called that political era the "millennium of the minnows." Except for Jackson himself, this protracted war was on the margin of thinking in Washington.

But Seminole Indians and Black Seminoles were fighting for their freedom and survival. That great test called forth a generation of gifted leaders. Among them were Black Seminoles such as Abraham and John Caesar, and Seminole Indians King Philip, Micanopy, and Billy Bowlegs. Above them all was Osceola, with kin connections in both groups. Officers in the army called him Billy Powell, after his reputed Virginia father or stepfather William Powell. The Indian Seminoles knew him by his busk name as Asi-Yaholo, "Black Drink Singer." His name was partly anglicized as Osceola and spelled a dozen ways.[85]

Osceola said to General Duncan Clinch, "You have men, and so have we.

Seminole chief Osceola

You have powder and lead, and so have we. Your men will fight and so will ours, till the last drop of blood has moistened the dust."[86] After being threatened with destruction by President Jackson in 1835, Seminole Indians and Black Seminoles joined together and seized the initiative. At Christmastime in that year, war parties under King Philip and John Caesar attacked sugar and cotton plantations on the St. Johns River. They systematically destroyed sugar mills that were vital to the North Florida economy. Some of the ruins are still visible today. Masters and mistresses fled for their lives, and hundreds of plantation slaves joined the attackers.

When news of the St. Johns campaign reached Fort Brooke near Tampa, Major Francis Dade was ordered to lead a force of one hundred army Regulars from the west coast of Florida to Fort King Valley in the east, a distance of two hundred miles. His instructions were to restore order and round up the Seminoles for removal to the West. Major Dade's troops brought a "passel of hound dogs," for hunting fugitives.[87]

On March 28, they made a long march through high grass and palmetto in close order at the speed of their slowest wagon. The Regulars advanced in marching order, with no flankers. Seminole Indians and Black Seminoles awaited them, invisible and undetected, lying prone in the grass. Their leaders prepared an ambush, and ordered each person to aim at one man. Their leader, Micanopy, fired first at Major Dade, who fell out of his saddle, mortally wounded. A first volley followed and brought down half the entire force of American Regulars. Only three officers remained on their feet. A six-pound field piece went into action, and the Regulars improvised a low triangular breastwork.

The Black and Indian Seminoles fired slowly and deliberately. Soon only one Regular officer remained alive, and he was badly wounded. The return fire of the Regulars slowly slackened. Then suddenly a mounted force of fifty Black Seminoles charged into action at full gallop. The shock of that mounted attack shattered what remained of the Regulars. Of more than one hundred U.S. troops, three survived. It was among the worst defeats in the history of the United States Army.[88]

Many battles followed. The best generals in the United States Army at that time took their turn: Duncan Clinch, Edmund Gaines, Winfield Scott, Thomas Jesup, and Zachary Taylor among others. Most came off second best to the combined forces of Seminole Indians and Black Seminoles.

The ethics of the war were complex. The Black Seminoles could be cruel against those who attempted to inflict atrocities on their families. Many reports of torture and mutilation circulated in southern newspapers but were not documented. Porter made a careful study of Major Dade's defeat, and found much evidence to the contrary. Corpses recovered by the army had no marks of mutilation. Weapons were taken but personal belongings were untouched.[89]

Black Seminole warriors also were known for acts of kindness and mercy to noncombatants. One example occurred in 1835. As the fighting in the Seminole War spread through Florida, a white mother named Mary Godfrey and her four daughters fled for their lives. In deep woods, late at night, they were stopped by a Black Seminole warrior with a fighting axe in hand. The woman later testified that "he told them not to be afraid." The warrior led them silently through the dark wilderness toward a camp of white Regulars, with lights burning. The Black Seminole said that his children were still in slavery, and that he prayed for God to "protect them wherever they were, just as he had preserved his enemy's children." He disappeared into the darkness. Mary Godfrey published a long firsthand account of this event. She testified to the humanity and even the nobility of character and conduct in this Black Seminole warrior with a fighting axe in hand. Later she often rose to the defense of the Black Seminole people.[90]

High-ranking officers in the United States Army also emerged from this war with a profound respect for their opponents, and especially for Black Seminoles. Major (and later Major General) Ethan Allen Hitchcock recovered the bodies at Dade's massacre, wrote about it in his diary, and added that "the government is in the wrong, and this is the chief cause of the persevering opposition of the Indians, who have nobly defended their country against an attempt to enforce a fraudulent treaty. The natives used every means to avoid a war but were forced into it by the tyranny of our government." [91]

Future president Zachary Taylor, then a serving officer in the United States Army, declared that "all Seminole Negroes should be free." In company with many other officers in the army, Taylor highly respected his Black Seminole and Indian Seminole opponents in the Florida wars.

He held them in esteem for their courage, character, and skill as soldiers. And they were fighting for an honorable cause. When the war ended, many hundreds of Black and Indian Seminoles remained in Florida. The cost in blood and treasure to the armed forces of the United States was high. No estimates survived of militia deaths, but there were very few deaths of white noncombatants. [92]

After many years of war with no decisive result, General Thomas Jesup and his senior officers proposed peace negotiations. They suggested that Indian and Black Seminoles should be allowed to remain in Florida below Lake Okeechobee, and that any Black Seminoles who freely agreed to move west would be forever free. A meeting was arranged under a flag of truce. Some Indian and Black Seminoles came to talk. But many Seminole bands did not participate, and the fighting began again.

In 1842, the army and the Black Seminoles agreed that the Black Seminoles should move west to Indian Territory, and "be given land, and guaranteed land and freedom." In 1842 Jesup led his band west to Indian Territory and found the bands of Wild Cat, Alligator, and Holatoochee on lands near the Cherokee reservation. None of the promises were kept. Military officers were unable to make the financial arrangements. Arrangements for travel by steamboat and wagon fell through. John Cavallo loaned military commanders $1,500 in cash from his own wealth, and was later repaid in full by the United States Army. As long as the Black Seminoles dealt with combat officers in the Regular Army, things went better than with American politicians. [93]

FLORIDA'S THIRD SEMINOLE WAR, 1855–58

After the second war, hundreds of Seminole Indians and Black Seminoles remained in South Florida. The Regulars who fought them agreed to a "temporary reservation" south of a line that ran from the mouth of the Peace River in the west to the mouth of the Kissimee River in the east. All the land below was reserved for hunting and planting by Seminole Indians and Black Seminoles.

The Seminole leader in south Florida was Billy Bowlegs. Many Regular officers had fought Bowlegs in the Second Seminole War and respected him. Captain John T. Sprague of the U.S. Army wrote that Bowlegs "in all respects is qualified for supreme command, which he exercises with skill and judgment. He is about thirty-five years of age, speaks English fluently, active, intelligent and brave." They also knew him to be a man of honor. In

Billy Bowlegs

that way these West Point commanders and Seminole warriors lived by the similar creeds.

In 1842 Bowlegs and Colonel (soon to be General) William Worth met at Tampa. A reservation line was agreed, and peace was declared in Florida. It survived into the 1850s. Troublemakers on both sides caused small clashes. But Bowlegs delivered Indian offenders for punishment. One of the military commanders who had fought against him, Zachary Taylor, became president of the United States. In 1850, Taylor met with a new military commander, General David Twiggs. The president said, "General Twiggs, tell Bowlegs whenever you see him, from me, if his people remain within their limits & behave themselves, they shall never be disturbed while I remain in office." [94]

Unhappily for the Seminoles, Indian and Black, President Taylor died a few days later. The Democrats won the next election and the new secretary of war was Jefferson Davis, a strong racist who defended slavery and white supremacy. Davis announced a new policy: removal of all Seminoles by force. It was a complete violation of all prior agreements. The U.S. Army was ordered into the Big Cypress Swamp and the Everglades. Three more years of fighting followed, which came to be called the Third Seminole War, or Billy Bowlegs' War. It might be remembered more accurately as Jefferson Davis's First Needless War.

Once again, the U.S. Army was unable to defeat the Seminoles in battle, but they ravaged villages, and destroyed homes and fields. Jefferson Davis succeeded only in the capture of Seminole women and children. Finally, in 1858, both sides negotiated a peace. Bowlegs agreed to go west with 176 Seminole Indians and fifty Black Seminoles in return for large cash payments, and a victory was declared. [95] Billy Bowlegs was received as a hero in Indian Territory. When the Civil War began he spurned an alliance with the Confederacy, joined the Union Army, and fought Jefferson Davis yet again.

Many Black Seminoles had refused to go West and remained in South Florida. They reconstituted their bands, and began to multiply. A leader rose among them, with a Black Seminole father and an Indian mother who was the daughter of Osceola. He took the name of Billy Bowlegs III. A tall, handsome man, he and his sister Lucy Pearce had an air of royalty about them. Billy Bowlegs III was also a brilliant hunter and tracker, a guardian of his inherited ways, and a good soldier. But mainly he fought for his people with other weapons. He mounted a publicity campaign, lobbied legislatures, and won a large reservation in the Everglades. [96]

Through much of the early twentieth century many Seminole Indians and Black Seminoles survived in Florida by staying out of sight. They were so successful that Congress asked the Smithsonian to send expeditions to confirm rumors of Black and Indian Seminoles who lived deep in Big Cypress Swamp and the Everglades through the twentieth century. Many children grew up without ever seeing a white person. They preserved their Muskogean and Mikasuki and Afro-Indian languages and culture. Seven Florida reservations were created and they doubled in size from 1979 to 2000.[97]

BLACK SEMINOLES IN THE WEST

Other Black Seminoles moved West to Indian Territory in what is now Oklahoma. They found that General Jesup's solemn promise of freedom was revoked by his slaveholding superiors in Washington. Under President James Polk, Attorney General John Y. Mason ruled on June 28, 1848, that the generals in the Second Seminole War had no legal authority to promise freedom to the Black Seminoles who moved to Oklahoma. Mason announced that the liberties and property rights of slaveholders must be preserved, and that Black Seminoles would be returned to bondage by the government of the United States.[98]

In Oklahoma, Black Seminoles suddenly found themselves under constant threat of enslavement. Slave catchers roamed the West in search of African Americans who could not prove they were free. Lawyers and judges informed the Black Seminoles that "there is no law against stealing negroes."[99]

Corrupt government agents instructed Seminole Indians that they could claim individual Black Seminoles as their personal slaves, or sell them as they pleased. Some Seminole Indians who had been comrades in arms began to file claims of ownership. Several Creeks went further and claimed that all Black Seminoles were their property. They did not bother with courts. Black Seminoles reported that their children were being kidnapped and sold by whites and Creeks.

Some military officers had a strong sense of honor and respect for their former foes and intervened to protect them. Detachments of U.S. Dragoons recovered some of the stolen children. Black Seminole warriors armed themselves, and kept some of the slave catchers at bay. But the attorney general of the United States made clear that the laws of the republic were against them.

BLACK SEMINOLES DEFEAT TEXAS RANGERS
AND COMANCHE WARRIORS

After eight years of continuing assault, Black Seminole leader John Horse and a group of others decided that they could not hope to live free in the United States, as long as race slavery existed and corrupt southern slaveholders held the highest offices in Washington. A large group of western Black Seminoles led their people to Mexico, where slavery had been abolished.

It was another difficult and dangerous journey, like so many others that their ancestors had made. The Black Seminoles prepared with great care. They were well mounted, heavily armed, and they were ready to defend themselves. They traveled in a military formation, with women and children in a protected convoy, and warriors in mobile columns. A major party of about three hundred crossed the Mexican border on July 12, 1850, eight years after they had arrived in Oklahoma.

The Black Seminoles went directly to a Mexican post at Piedras Negras, across the border from Eagle Pass in Texas. They introduced themselves to the Mexican commander, and asked permission to build a settlement. The Mexicans, knowing about the Black Seminoles and their prowess as warriors, received them with a feast and "a lot to eat," according to oral histories of the event. They also offered land, tools, and building materials. The Black Seminoles were told that they were welcome to settle as free people.

But as so often before, there was one condition. The Black Seminoles were invited to found a "military colony" in Mexico, and to help defend the Mexican republic against its enemies. The Black Seminoles agreed, perhaps warily, and their leader John Horse received a captain's commission in the Mexican army.[100]

They were granted land in Nacimiento, nearly a hundred miles from the Texas border, and planted a settlement called Nacimiento de los Negros. It is still there today, a thriving community. John Horse recalled, "The Mexicans spread out their arms to us." But Americans north of the border continued to be hostile. In 1851 a large party of more than three hundred rogue Texas Rangers, American slave hunters, Mexican insurgents, and border bad men came after them. About sixty Black Seminole warriors took up their weapons again. Outnumbered five to one, they inflicted heavy casualties on their attackers, broke them apart, and sent the slave hunters and rangers fleeing for their lives back to Texas.[101]

The Black Seminoles suffered other attacks. The worst came not from white slave holders but from Comanches. In 1852 an observer who knew both groups wrote, "The Comanches have (for what reason I could not learn) taken an inveterate dislike to the [Seminole] Negroes, and have massacred several small parties of those who attempted to escape."[102]

American army officers reported that "Comanches once tortured two little black girls, the only survivors of a group they captured and annihilated. Their captors flayed the girls' skin to see if the flesh underneath was black, and then "burned them with live coals to ascertain whether fire produced the same sensations of pain as with their own people." The pair were finally rescued by a Delaware Indian trader. He brought them to Little River where Captain Randolph Marcy reported on their cruel condition: "The poor girls were shockingly scarred and mutilated when I saw them." The Comanches were asked why they attacked the Black Seminoles, and answered "because they were slaves to the whites," and "they were sorry for them." The Comanches lied. Kenneth Porter observed that their true purpose was to capture some Seminole Blacks and keep others at a distance, in which they did not succeed. A party of angry Black Seminoles attacked the Comanches with great and sudden violence, severely defeated them, and killed some of the Comanches for the atrocities they had committed.[103]

BLACK SEMINOLES ARE WELCOMED TO MEXICO ON ONE CONDITION: THEY FIGHT FRENCH INVADERS AND DEFEAT THE FRENCH FOREIGN LEGION

When French troops invaded Mexico and tried to conquer the country, they occupied the northern region of Coahuila, burned Mexican villages, and marched on the Black Seminole settlements. The Black Seminole warriors intercepted a force of the Foreign Legion and severely defeated them.

According to oral tradition, two warrior leaders, John Horse and David Bowlegs, then went directly to the French commander and talked with him. They made such an impression that the French stopped burning homes and moved out of Coahuila. The Mexican government gave John Horse a magnificent silver-mounted Mexican saddle, with a gold horse's head for a pommel.

The Mexican federal government also reconfirmed the original grant of land in 1866. But it was the old story yet again. Speculators acquired a bogus title and won an eviction order from a corrupt Mexican judge. According to oral tradition, John Horse emerged from retirement and went to see President Porfirio Díaz in Mexico City. Díaz invited John Horse to sit beside him on a divan, and asked why he had come. The old man said nothing, but moved on the divan closer to the Mexican leader. Díaz shifted away. The old Black Seminole moved closer again, and then again. Díaz said, "Capitan Caballo, what are you trying to do? Do you want to push me from the divan to the floor?" The old man finally spoke. "Just so, mi presidente," he said, and explained that speculators and judges were doing the same thing to his people. The Black Seminoles promptly received confirmation of their grant.[104]

BACK TO TEXAS, 1870–1914: SEMINOLE WARRIORS JOIN THE UNITED STATES ARMY AS SCOUTS, AND WIN THREE MEDALS OF HONOR IN AN AFTERNOON

The American Civil War transformed the condition of the Black Seminoles. The great republic, at great cost, finally succeeded in abolishing race slavery. Black Seminoles were quick to make the most of this extraordinary event. It came at a time when they were having difficulty protecting their land in Mexico, and were under attack by Apache raiders.

In 1870 the United States Army was hard pressed to keep the peace on the southwestern frontier among ranchers, settlers, and townsfolk on the one hand, and the Comanche, Apache, and other Indian warrior nations on the other. Regular officers in the field were keenly aware of the Black Seminoles and respected them as trackers, scouts, and warriors.

On the Mexican border Black Seminoles had made themselves masters of yet another way of war, waged mainly by small parties of highly mobile cavalry in the open terrain of the West. On the strong advice of officers who knew them well, the secretary of war authorized commanders in the field to employ two hundred "Indian negroes" as scouts.[105]

Army captain Frank W. Perry carried the message and was astonished by the people he met. He reported to the War Department, "The Seminoles whom I am directed to receive from Mexico turn out to be Negroes."[106]

On July 4, 1870, these Black warriors were invited to return in freedom to the United States on one condition, that they serve as a separate unit in the army. The result was a unique military unit, called the United States Seminole Negro Indian Scouts.

From long experience they distrusted promises. At their request they enlisted for six-month terms of service, which were unique in the Regular Army.

The Black Seminoles as always wanted to maintain their freedom of choice. Many of them chose to reenlist every six months through many years of service. A descendant of one of the great warrior families, Isaac Payne, reenlisted sixty times from 1871 to 1901.[107]

Their uniforms were standard-issue army blue and later khaki. Their weapons and mounts were similar to other units in the army. But their insignia was unique. In place of the cavalry's crossed sabers and the infantry's crossed rifles and the artillery's crossed cannon, they proudly wore crossed arrows on their forage caps and campaign hats. Some added African charms and Indian talismens.

They brought with them to their military posts families of women and children, young and old, and settled in villages of about 1,200 people near Forts Duncan and Clark in Texas. They had white senior officers over them who were chosen for their sympathy and sensitivity to Black Seminole culture and history. One of them was Captain Zenas R. Bliss of New England Puritan ancestors. Another was Captain John Bullis of Quaker background.[108]

Effective command within these units was held by their own Black Seminole leaders such as John and Bob Kibbetts, who became sergeants and corporals in the army, and war captains to their own men. Sergeant John Kibbetts ranked higher than a chief, and his warriors "obeyed him implicitly." Corporal Bob Kibbetts became their leader, and enforced strict discipline with a leather strap. It was said that "they all took it kindly."[109]

White superior officers above the Black Seminoles were astounded by their skill at soldiering. Wherever they went, these "Seminole Negroes" began by studying the land. They explored the countryside along the Mexican border, and were able to find and identify the hidden places raiders and rustlers used. They adapted their own ways of war for the American West, combining "the habits of the Indians" with those of European troops and their own African ways of war.[110]

Eyewitness accounts by white officers in the field described them as "excellent hunters and trailers and splendid fighters." Veteran commanders who had served through the Civil War judged them to be the best soldiers that they ever known, as so many other professional soldiers had done before.[111]

Others observed of the Seminole Negro Indian Scouts that "on the trail they were the best shots from the saddle, and were able to find water and food that others missed. They could pick up trails that were three weeks old, and "stay on a trail for months at a time." They were masters of fieldcraft, and their stamina on active service exceeded that of friend and foe. Unlike

European troops it was said that these relentless men "could also live off half rations indefinitely," as they hunted their opponents relentlessly until defeating them.[112]

To their discipline, skill, stamina, and endurance the Seminole Negro Indian Scouts also added qualities of courage that made them a legend among others who served with them in the army. The cavalry leader Ranald Mackenzie worked closely with them, and testified to their skill and character. Mackenzie wrote of Black Seminole Adam Payne that "this man has, I believe, more cool daring than any scout I have ever known."[113]

In one desperate engagement on the Pecos River, a white superior officer was captured by Indians. A small force of Seminole Negro Indian Scouts rescued him in a brilliant operation, and won three Medals of Honor in a few hours. An officer on the scene added that every scout in that unit was "brave and trustworthy, and each are worthy of a medal."[114]

The Black Seminoles were valued highly by comrades in arms. But in Texas they met hostility from civilian white racists. Whites living near the base in Brackettville demanded the removal of all Blacks, and attacked them individually. These violent Texas whites did not directly confront the Seminoles, but shot at them from ambush. In that way they wounded John Horse at the age of ninety. In 1877, Adam Payne, a Medal of Honor recipient, was shot in the back by a white Texas racist with a double-barreled shotgun.[115]

The Seminole Negro Indian Scouts continued to serve on active duty until 1914 when the unit was disbanded. They became yet another victim of the growing racism that spread through the federal government during the racist administration of Woodrow Wilson. Worse than that decision itself was the dishonorable way in which it was carried out. Long-standing commitments to individual soldiers and their families were summarily broken. In 1914, about 207 Black Seminoles were living on land that they had been given within the grounds at Fort Clark. The land was taken from them. Their houses were demolished. Promised pensions were denied. Individual records of service were destroyed. A Medal of Honor winner in the unit was informed (falsely) by racist officials in the War Department that no record existed of his military service or of his medal.

Racial hostility increased in the twentieth century. Many white people in West Texas did not want the Black Seminoles around. Some Seminole Indians in Oklahoma also wanted nothing to do with Black Seminoles, and refused to allow them to settle on tribal lands, or to share in its resources—which happened also in some Florida reservations.[116]

BLACK SEMINOLES TODAY: A LIVING TRADITION

In the face of virulent racial prejudice, Black Seminoles kept faith with one another, and with the history and values of their forebears. In the twenty-first century, descendants of Black Seminoles still live in West Texas at Eagle Pass, Kerrville, San Antonio, and Del Rio and others in Florida, the Bahamas, and the West Indies.

An important center of identity and belonging is the Black Seminole Indian Scout Cemetery on the grounds of Fort Clark in Brackettville, Texas. Many Black Seminole soldiers are buried there, including Medal of Honor winners. The fort itself is no longer an active military base. But its guardhouse has been preserved as a museum that tells the story of the Black Seminoles and other former slaves who became the "buffalo soldiers" in the 9th and 10th U.S. Cavalry and the 24th and 25th Infantry Regiments. Many descendants of Black Seminoles still live nearby.

Prominent among them is a family that traced its descent from ancestors who came as slaves from Africa, freed themselves from bondage in South Carolina, escaped to freedom in Spanish Florida, joined the Seminoles as a tributary people, fought Andrew Jackson and the U.S. Army in the Seminole Wars, and moved to Oklahoma, Mexico, and Texas. Somewhere along that line they took the family name of Warrior, which described their long service in the profession of arms. In Texas at least three family members joined the U.S. Army as Texas Seminole Negro Indian Scouts: Sergeant Carolino Warrior, Corporal Bill Warrior, and Private Scott Warrior. Together, their service spanned the entire history of the Seminole Negro Indian Scouts from 1870 to 1914.

Relatives and descendants of the Warrior family still live in West Texas. Prominent among them are Ethel and William Warrior of Del Rio. They cherish the long history of the Black Seminoles, and some have dedicated themselves to preserving their heritage and a very strong sense of family. Deep roots are evident in their speech, which still has traces of Gullah and Geechee. William Warrior is better known in the family by his Gullah name, "Dub" Warrior, which is African in its origin.[117]

Many are staunch Baptists. They preserve a sense of community, and come together on "Seminole Days" for family reunions. These people also cherish their military heritage. Descendants continue to follow military careers, and have seen active service in Vietnam, Kuwait, Afghanistan, Iraq, and other campaigns in the twentieth and twenty-first centuries.

Black Seminoles also live today in many parts of the United States and other countries. They have formed communities that have persisted for many generations, even to our own time. Black Seminole communities have thrived through three centuries in the Bahamas. They have persisted in Cuba, near Havana and in Matanzas where St. Augustine's Black militia settled in 1763. Other communities of Black Seminoles survive in Mexico, the Dominican Republic, and Haiti.

BLACK SEMINOLES AS WARRIORS WITHOUT WEAPONS: THE SAGA OF THE OKLAHOMA CUDJOES

In the twenty-first century, many Black Seminoles continue to live in Texas and Oklahoma. Some dwell on Seminole Indian reservations. Others have moved to towns and cities in Oklahoma. An example is the large Cudjoe (or Cudjo) family in Seminole County, Oklahoma. Their forebears were in Florida during the eighteenth century. They proudly bear the same Akan name as Captain Cudjoe (ca. 1680–1744), the son of an Akan chief who became one of the greatest and most successful of all maroon warriors, and won a measure of autonomy for the maroons of Jamaica.[118]

In Florida's Seminole Wars, an ancestor, known simply as Cudjo, was one of the most prominent Black Seminole leaders. He could speak both European and Indian languages at a time when it was said that "few white men could handle Hitichi and Muskogee; few Indians, English." Cudjo was present with Osceola and Abraham at many meetings between Seminoles and U.S. Army officers. Historian John Mahon writes that he was "as important in any negotiation as the most exalted person present."[119]

Members of the Cudjoe family moved west to the town of Seminole in Oklahoma. Prominent among them was Witty Cudjoe (1850–1946), who led a long struggle to protect the rights and freedoms of Black Seminoles and to preserve their tribal membership against encroachments by both Indians and whites.[120]

Other Cudjoes served their people in other ways. Prominent among them were Lawrence and Lance Cudjoe, identical twins with identical birth and death dates (1922–1994). They went to Langston University, a distinguished college with a strong Black Seminole connection, where both were star basketball players. They served in the Second World War, and devoted themselves to careers in teaching and coaching young people, many of whom were of Black Seminole ancestry. In the classroom and on the basketball court, they taught the next generation to be warriors without weapons—true to the same warrior ethic of service, strength, courage, endurance.

In 1946 the Harlem Globetrotters came to Langston College. The Cudjoes and their students challenged them to a game. The Globetrotters were at the peak of their remarkable powers. But in an epic contest, Black Seminoles defeated them on the court—and the twins played several years for the Globetrotters. Here again they were warriors without weapons, with a living African American tradition that they taught to the young. It still survives in our time.

TABLE 9.1 Known African Origins of Florida Slaves, ca. 1752–53

Congo and Angola: Yalongo, Mondongo, Mungundu, Sozongo	57
Guinea: Mandinga	32
Biafra: Carabali, Calabari, Ibo, Igbo	19
Gold Coast: Coromanti, Mina	14
Mali: Bamana	1
Gambia: Fula, Fulani	1
Other African Origins	52
Criollo (American born of unknown origin)	28
Total	**204**

SUMMARY AND CONCLUSION

"We are a country of all extremes, ends and opposites; the most conspicuous example of composite nationality in the world."

—Frederick Douglass, 1869[1]

THE PURPOSE OF THIS inquiry has been to study African Americans, slave and free, as agents of change in the early history of the United States. We began with simple questions, which led to complex answers and more questions in their turn. Who were the many Africans in early America? What of Africa's many cultures did they bring with them? Where in America did they live? How did they respond to race slavery, and to the growth of racism in the eighteenth and nineteenth centuries? What uses did they make of their African heritage, European cultures, and American conditions? What difference did their own acts and choices make, for the main lines of American history in the modern era?

These questions follow another inquiry published as *Albion's Seed*. That volume studied similar problems about British migrants in early America from 1607 to 1775, and their impact on the history of the United States.[2]

For both projects, a helpful starting point was the first federal census of the United States in 1790. Studies of its results have concluded that about 60 percent of people in the new American republic were of British ancestry. Other evidence makes clear that their British origins and American purposes were diverse, in ways that have made a major difference in American history, even to our time.[3]

The same census of 1790 also found that the second-largest ethnic group in the United States were people of African ancestry. Altogether they were about 20 percent of the American population in that year, nearly twice their current share. Other sources tell us that their African origins were even more diverse than British roots of English-speaking colonists, and so also was their regional history in America.

After the British 60 percent and African 20 percent, the remaining 20 percent in 1770 included everybody else—with one major exception. American Indians were omitted from census returns in the United States for many years.

They were not recognized as American citizens until the passage of the Snyder Act in 1924.

The demographic history of the United States has always been a story of dynamic diversity, often in surprising ways. From the seventeenth century to our time, the American people have always been a mix of many mixtures, changing constantly through time. The consequences of that diversity are fundamental to American history in many ways at once. A major challenge for historians in the United States is to make sense of this large and complex subject.

A REGIONAL APPROACH

One way forward is to study this subject in regional terms, which has been done in *African Founders* and *Albion's Seed*. From the start, early colonies in what is now the United States gave rise to cultural regions that are still recognizable in the twenty-first century. In all these regions, Africans both slave and free responded in many ways to the brutality of American bondage and to the promise of human freedom.

These American regions varied greatly in the size of their African and European populations, and also in their relative proportions, which made a difference in the cultures that developed in them. But size and scale were not the only determinants. In each of these regions, without exception, the presence of Africans, both free and slave, had a distinctive character. All of these regions had an important impact on American history. Specific findings of this inquiry for six hearth regions and three frontier regions might be summarized in this conclusion. A hearth region might be understood as an area of initial settlement from which a culture developed. A frontier is an outer area on the periphery of a country.

NEW ENGLAND: AFRICAN ETHICS AND THE EXPANSION OF AMERICAN RIGHTS

New England's Puritan colonies began to acquire small numbers of slaves in the seventeenth century. The first were American Indians and a scattering of Africans from the West Indies. In the eighteenth century, a larger flow of slaves arrived directly from Africa. The port of Anomabu in what is now western Ghana was most prominent in New England's African trade. The largest clusters were Akan-speaking Fante and Asante slaves from western Ghana.

Recent studies by African scholars have found that Akan ethics differed from those of other world cultures in important ways. In religions such as

Christianity, Judaism, and Islam, ethics are perceived as products of divine revelation, and transmitted in sacred texts. Akan beliefs had a different foundation. They centered on ethics as derived from needs and customs of a people and reinforced by gods rather than dictated by them. Kwame Gyekye observes, "Rather than regarding African ethics as religious, it would be more correct to regard African religions as ethical."[4]

Among slaves in Massachusetts, Akan ethical imperatives became a philosophy of doing, in both individual and collective acts. An Akan proverb taught that "when virtue founds a town, the town thrives and abides." Other Akan proverbs held that "character comes from actions," that "virtue comes from character," and "to possess virtue is better than gold."[5]

Akan Fante-Asante and New England Protestant ethics also centered on dual purposes of "doing good" and "doing well" in the same acts. They both generated yet another linkage of individual and collective ethics, which were exceptionally strong in this regional culture.

During the eighteenth century, Akan slaves in New England put these ethical imperatives to work. Leading examples survive in manuscripts of Kofi Slocum, a freed Asante slave, and also in the acts and writings of his children and grandchildren. These were not static African "survivals," or rote borrowings of Puritan and Quaker beliefs. They were more complex and more creative: a new syncretist ethic that emerged in early New England, when African and European ethical traditions came together in southern Massachusetts during the eighteenth century.

With other Africans in New England, they won freedom for themselves and their posterity by their own efforts. To that end, many of them joined actively in an effort to enlarge the values and institutions of a free society in New England, not only for themselves but for many others who followed. Kofi Slocum's son Paul Cuffe and many family and friends admired New England's tradition of town schools. They asked that it be expanded to include African children and also others. When first efforts failed, Paul Cuffe's family and friends built their own school and opened it to all. Against much resistance, this movement spread in New England. It took many years, and succeeded in large part by efforts of New Englanders with African roots.

The children of Kofi Slocum did it again by demanding the right to vote for free Africans and others. In 1780, when the Massachusetts constitution was adopted, Paul Cuffe turned twenty-one. The collector of his district made clear that he was required to pay taxes, but denied the right to vote. It was the same for his brothers and friends. They protested in vain, then acted within the system to change it. They paid their taxes, and presented a "respectful petition" to the Massachusetts General Court for the right to vote. It met "warm and almost indignant opposition," in Paul Cuffe's words. Other petitions and court cases failed. Then the Cuffe brothers and their friends studied the art of lobbying. They organized support in other towns, approached legislators one by one, suffered many defeats, but after three years won a new state law, "rendering all free persons of color liable to taxation, according to the established ratio for white men, and granting them all the privileges, belonging to the other citizens" including the right of voting and schooling.[6]

Paul and John Cuffe continued to work within the system. Others remembered the passage of that new law as "a day equally honorable to the petitioners and the legislature—a day which ought to be gratefully remembered by every person of color, within the boundaries of Massachusetts."[7] Freeborn sons of African slaves had persuaded other citizens of Massachusetts to expand the founding principles of a free republic, not only for themselves but others. They persuaded the Massachusetts General Court to grant voting rights to free male citizens without restriction of race. It was a major step, not only for people of color but also for New England as Maine, Vermont, and New Hampshire did the same. Connecticut and Rhode Island took a little longer.

These were continuing struggles with a cumulative effect. As a result, African slaves through New England won fundamental rights of freedom for themselves and others. They also succeeded in starting a revolutionary enlargement of founding rights in this American region, which later spread them to other regions. It is important to note that African American leaders born in slavery became leaders in winning rights not only for themselves but also for Chinese immigrants and many other groups in the nineteenth century.

Racism in its infinite variations will always exist in America and elsewhere. But to condemn the United States as a racist society is fundamentally false. It misses the successful efforts of twelve generations of Americans, and especially the role of Africans born in slavery, and the children of slaves, in enlarging fundamental American rights in New England and through the United States during the eighteenth and nineteenth centuries. To overstate the negatives in American history is to miss its positive achievements and its central dynamics. Among the drivers of this expansion of rights for New Englanders from Africa were Africans themselves. They succeeded both in expanding rights of individuals, and also in enlarging the founding principles and cultural traditions of New England itself.

HUDSON VALLEY: AFRICAN CLUSTERS AND THE
INVENTION OF A NEW AMERICAN ETHNICITY

New Netherland was founded by Dutch businessmen who urgently needed labor, and were quick to introduce African slavery. From the start, human bondage was cruel and brutal in the Hudson Valley. But it became more open and flexible in large part because of acts and choices by African slaves themselves, and Afro-Americans who lived in freedom.

Dutch capitalists and entrepreneurs were less interested in absolute dominion over slaves than in optimal returns on capital investment. To that primary end, many other things became negotiable. Their Angolan slaves also became highly entrepreneurial. The absence of a fixed and rigid slave code in New Netherland, and the presence of a speculative spirit among both Dutch businessmen and Angolan slaves, combined to create a more fluid system of bondage than in some other colonies.

Slaves in New Netherland were very quick to discover the Dutch right of petition. As early as 1634, they petitioned for a right to be paid for their labor. Their first efforts failed, but a small group of African slaves found a way to carrry their cause from Manhattan to the Netherlands, perhaps as crewmen aboard a Dutch ship. They took their petition to higher authorities, and asked to be paid for work on public projects in New Netherland.[8]

Dutch leaders were persuaded to agree. By 1639, some African slaves who had built the company's fort at New Amsterdam were granted eight guilders a month for their labor—the same rate paid to European laborers.[9] When payments were disputed Angolan slaves claimed access to the courts, and gained that as well. Two slaves, Pedro Negretto and Manuel de Reus, sued for unpaid wages and won.[10]

That was only the beginning. In 1644, eleven slaves joined together and petitioned for freedom outright. Most belonged to close-knit ethnic clusters of Angolan and Congolese slaves who acted together to enlarge their rights in other ways.[11] Dutch director-general Willem Kieft and his Council agreed to their major demand. He acknowledged that they had served the company for "18 or 19 years" and had "long since been promised their freedom." The Council ruled that henceforth these men "and wives" were released from slavery "for the term of their natural lives, hereby setting them free and at liberty on the same footing as other free people here in New Netherland."[12]

That agreement flowed not from altruism but from interest. Dutch owners kept the full benefit of a slave's labor in the prime of productive life.
Thereafter, freed slaves were required to support themselves in declining years,
which saved owners that expense. The businessmen of the West Indian Company also insisted on requiring annual payments. Each year every freedman
with a farm was required to pay the company "thirty skepels" (roughly two
bushels) of maize or wheat or peas or beans, plus a fat hog valued at 20 guilders. The company also reserved the right to conscript a freed slave's labor
when needed, in return for "fair wages." Failure of former slaves to meet these
terms was cause for return to slavery.[13]

Dutch leaders described some of these terms as "halve vrydom" or
half-freedom.[14] After 1644, they were granted on petition to other slaves. In
1662, three slave women petitioned Director-General Peter Stuyvesant for
half-freedom. He agreed on one condition, that they would take turns doing
his housework, and a typical Dutch-African deal was done.[15]

In response to these petitions, hard-driving directors of the Dutch West
India Company also imposed on freed slaves another "express condition,"
which was the cruelest and most profitable of all: that "their children, at present born and yet to be born, shall remain bound and obligated to serve the
Honorable West India Company as slaves." Freed slaves petitioned to end this
cruelty, and Dutch directors agreed to emancipate children if their parents
paid a sum equal to the market price for each child. Much was negotiable in
capitalist New Amsterdam, and another deal was done.[16]

After Kieft's war with the Indians broke out, the Dutch Company and the
director himself gave half-free slaves yet other opportunities. At least thirty-
five former slaves were offered land of their own in return for military service.
Again Angolan and Congolese slaves seized the moment. Half-free landowning Africans became an important part of New Amsterdam's population.
These African families lived on their own farms in the "Land of the Blacks"
and were between a quarter and a third of the 375 Africans in New Amsterdam, circa 1664. Later, other company slaves acquired half-free status in New
Netherland during the last years of the Dutch colony.[17]

Within the city walls of New Amsterdam, some private slaves were able to
buy their freedom. But it did not come easily. Graham Hodges writes, "For all
emancipated blacks . . . freedom would be hard earned and only after many
years of service."[18]

After New Netherland was conquered by England and renamed New

York, slavery became larger and more diverse in the Hudson Valley, and especially New York City. The rhythms of urban life allowed slaves to meet others in complex webs of voluntary association, defined by African ethnicity, place of origin, occupation, gender, and more. In the early and mid-eighteenth century, many varieties of slave associations appeared in court testimony. Authorities in English New York were troubled by their existence, and more so by their activities. Some of these groups were known to support crime. A few encouraged armed resistance. The authorities were unable to suppress them, and some of these groups operated with impunity in English New York for many years.[19]

Other African associations formed throughout the colony. A surprising example in Queens County on Long Island was "a group of enslaved and independent Africans" who "formed themselves into a military company for recreation and entertainment." After 1741 they were "ordered to disband."[20]

These many different groups of slaves in English New York created new patterns of plural association and identity, unlike New Netherland's tight comity of "half-free" Angolan and Congolese slaves. The effect was a transformation of multiple Afro-European cultures into a pluralist society. Once again, slave leaders played instrumental roles in its development.

Through it all, slaves and "free people of color" in New York and the middle colonies also invented new ideas of themselves. In that process they created new American ways of thinking about ethnicity. In the era of the American Revolution, some of these groups in the Hudson Valley began to speak of themselves as "African." Historian Craig Wilder finds that this larger identity "subordinated cultural divisions between black people," and also became "a leveler between black and white New Yorkers." It also became an instrument of agency and autonomy. "Negro" and "Black" were names others gave them. "African" was a name they gave themselves.[21]

After 1783, "African" was also adopted by churches, schools, societies, meetings, movements, books, and causes. It became an instrument of collective effort and ethnic belonging, and described a new sort of ethnic comity.

At the same time, freed slaves in New York and Philadelphia took it a step farther, and invented another new ethnic identity. As early as 1782, they began to call themselves "African American." The known first use appeared in Philadelphia's *Pennsylvania Journal*, on May 15, 1782, at a time when New York City was occupied by the British Army. A bookseller advertised two sermons and identified the anonymous author as "African American."[22]

This new phrase at first referred explicitly to an African writer who celebrated the American victory at Yorktown. "African American" originally meant a person of African origin who supported the American Revolution. In the new republic it increasingly became hyphenated, and acquired another large meaning that combined a dual ethnic and national identity. That combination appeared in many related words: "Africo-American" by 1788, "Black American" by 1818, "Afro-American" by 1830, and "Afric-American" by 1831.[23]

Yet another set of phrases came a little later. In 1837, Samuel Cornish became the editor of the New York *Weekly Advocate* and changed its name to the New York *Colored American*. The purpose of Cornish was to bring together "brown and black" as "people of color" in a common cause. Another object was to distinguish "colored Americans" from Africans, and to celebrate their full belonging to an American republic as an expression of common humanity and nationality.[24]

This new invention of hyphenated ethnicity first appeared in the largest and most diverse American cities of New York and Philadelphia. Lexicographer Mitford Mathews found that "African-American" in 1782 was the first of a large family of hyphenated ethnic terms in the United States. Other groups in the United States followed the African-American lead and adopted similar ideas for themselves. Mathews's earliest examples of "German-American" date from 1824, and "Irish-American" from various dates between 1832 and 1836. Other hyphenated ethnic identities multiplied for many groups in America through the next two centuries.[25]

"African-American" was not invented in the 1980s, as many colleagues have mistakenly believed. It appeared two centuries earlier in the new republic and created a more complex idea of America itself. This African-American invention spread to other ethnic groups and to open societies through the world.

DELAWARE VALLEY: QUAKERS, AFRICANS, AND THE GROWTH OF AMERICAN REFORM

Yet another major African contribution appeared in the Delaware Valley. In the summer of 1681, William Penn and his fellow founder Thomas Rudyard had been hard at work in England, designing Fundamental Constitutions and a Frame of Government for the new colony of Pennsylvania. A major purpose was to attempt a sweeping "reformation in government," not for its own sake, but so that "an example may be Sett up to the nations." Quakers had suffered much from oppression in England. Their purpose was to build a new model of society in America. Penn wrote from England, "There may be room there, tho' not here, for such an holy experiment." [26]

Penn moved quickly to enact his "holy experiment." He erected a new Frame of Government by 1682. But no sooner had he done so than his Quaker colonists proposed sweeping reforms to Penn's "reformation." The result was a newer Frame of Government in 1683. Historians Richard and Mary Dunn wrote that Pennsylvania colonists continued to seek many changes, and "over the next twenty years, they extensively rewrote William Penn's Constitution." [27]

In those events William Penn succeeded beyond the particular purposes of his own "holy experiment." He started the people of Pennsylvania and the Delaware Valley on a process of permanent reform that continues today, more than three centuries later throughout the American republic. More than that, he also institutionalized a continuing reform tradition that is one of the oldest in America and the world, and increasingly important in both places.

Another fundamental purpose was to pursue this goal by peaceful means, and to renounce violence and the use of force as a way of resolving differences. Yet a third goal was to follow the Golden Rule, and to treat others as one would wish to be treated. Implicit in that idea was a Quaker belief that all people are equally God's creatures. In the Delaware Valley these Quaker ideas grew by being continuously contested, not least among Quakers themselves.

The rapid growth of African slavery in early Pennsylvania, West Jersey, and Delaware had profound consequences for the people of this region, in many ways at once. It caused some Quakers to redefine some of their most cherished principles, and led other Quakers to enlarge those beliefs and engage them against slavery.

In that process, Quakers founded and organized the first sustained anti-slavery movement in the English-speaking world. Its leaders also included members of other radical Christian sects in England and America. Examples were the very diverse Germantown "radicals," George Keith and his Philadelphia Friends, Benjamin Lay in his Abington cave, John Woolman in West Jersey, and many more.

At the same time, Anthony Benezet led a larger effort not only against race slavery, but also against ideas and acts that that we know today as racism. Benezet was recognized by Thomas Clarkson and William Wilberforce in

Britain and by the Societé des Amis des Noirs in France, who called him the most eminent leader of the international antislavery movement throughout the Atlantic world.

Gary Nash writes, "It is well known that Quakers led the way in this process."[28] Jean Soderlund adds from her careful study that "Delaware Valley Quakers were the first unified group to oppose black slavery—and in fact their movement became the primary wellspring of American social reform." The only other groups who came close in time were Quaker meetings in southern New England and New York. The Friends' London Yearly Meeting also moved in the same direction, but a step behind Philadelphia.[29]

This activity awakened a conservative countermovement that ironically was also stronger among Quakers than in other groups in the early and mid-eighteenth century. Impassioned antislavery Quakers such as Benjamin Lay were disowned by their meetings for attacks on Quaker slave owners.[30]

An epic struggle over slavery among Quakers spread rapidly to other religious groups in the Delaware Valley. A quantitative study by Gary Nash found that Anglicans and Swedish Lutherans in this region also began to free slaves in their wills.[31]

That expanding movement in turn created larger opportunities for African slaves in the Delaware Valley. They became active in striving against slavery in ways that differed from prevailing patterns of resistance in the Chesapeake, Hudson Valley, the Carolinas, Louisiana, and Florida.

Slaves in the Delaware Valley, unlike other regions, rarely chose armed revolt or insurrection. Many fought for their freedom mainly by working within the system, along with Quakers who opposed slavery. Other slaves in the Delaware Valley gained freedom a different way. In Philadelphia as early as 1725, there were "frequent complaints . . . that Negroes and other Blacks, either free or under pretence of Freedom, have resorted to and settled in the city." By one estimate in the mid-eighteenth century, as many as two or three hundred people of color were living in the city without masters, either free or "pretending to be free."[32]

During the era of the Revolution, these and other people of color in the Delaware Valley also began to oppose slavery and racism in yet another new way, not as rebels or revolutionaries but as root-and-branch reformers within a broad reform tradition. Opposition to race slavery and racism was increasingly linked to a range of other reforms, and to an expansive new idea of reform in general.

We have met the leading Afro-American exemplar: James Forten (1766–

1842). While continuing in business, building a fortune, and supporting a large and active family, Forten also became a leader of the antislavery movement, not only in Philadelphia and the Delaware Valley but through the United States and the western world. He loaned money to William Garrison for the founding of *The Liberator*, and became a leading abolitionist, firm in his commitment to that cause. Always he treated opponents with respect in ways that won over some of them.

Forten also worked tirelessly for the rights of "free Blacks," in the face of strong countermovements that sought to disfranchise all African Americans. Forten went to court, sued many times for the extension of suffrage rights to all Black males, and was defeated again and again. Despite Forten's best efforts, the voters in Pennsylvania approved a new state constitution with a total prohibition of suffrage for all Blacks, which continued until the national ratification of the Fifteenth Amendment in 1870.

He also supported crusading newspapers throughout the country, and took up a broad range of overlapping reforms: not only the abolition of slavery and rights of freed people of color, but also aid to the poor, school reform, women's rights, the temperance movement, humane societies to help people in danger, prison reform, urban reform, rural reform, political reform, municipal reform, reform of institutions for the insane, and world peace (after 1815). More than those specific reforms, James Forten supported the larger cause of reform in general. In 1834 he was a founding leader of the American Moral Reform Society.

Forten's many children, grandchildren, and in-laws also became reformers. Most active in the Forten family was Robert Purvis (1810–1898) who married James Forten's daughter Harriet. Purvis strongly supported African American community life in Philadelphia. He funded a new Library Company of Colored People, supported the Equal Rights League for suffrage reform, and advocated full rights of citizenship for freed slaves and all humanity. Purvis also supported the temperance movement, and worked at agricultural reform on his farm outside Philadelphia. He served as a leader for women's rights throughout the United States, and became a founder of local groups such as the Philadelphia Committee of One Hundred in 1884, which fought the extreme and deep-rooted political corruption in that city.[33]

Charlotte Forten Grimké and other members of the Forten family, both male and female, young and old, personified a movement that brought many others to the support of reform in general. Quakers had started it, but then some withdrew. As they did so, African Americans came forward in growing numbers. In Pennsylvania, reform was the combined legacy of Quakers and African Americans. They were among the most important leaders of an American tradition of continuing reform—even permanent reform—in American public life, with many others joining in.

CHESAPEAKE VIRGINIA AND MARYLAND: AFRICAN LEADERS AND THE ENLARGEMENT OF AMERICAN LEADERSHIP

By the mid-nineteenth century, Chesapeake slaves also began to make a major difference in national affairs throughout the United States. In that era, none of them could vote or hold office in Maryland or Virginia, but many freed themselves and had a major impact on political events in the United States. This inquiry found many individual examples of former Chesapeake slaves who had important roles in the campaign to abolish human bondage, and in the coming of the American Civil War.

Many of these leading actors were men and women who began their lives as slaves in the Chesapeake states of Maryland and Virginia. They were heirs to a tradition of leadership in their region. They learned from it, reached beyond it, and became leaders themselves. In the process they created new forms of American leadership.

Often these Chesapeake slave leaders began by seeking freedom for themselves, their families, and friends. That purpose grew into a larger goal of freedom and liberty for people in bondage. And some reached beyond that effort to a larger goal of enlarging freedom and liberty, equity and justice for all people in America and the world. The examples that follow are of Chesapeake-born slaves who became leaders in pivotal events. They also became models of new methods of open, principled, and effective leadership for generations to come.

Among hundreds of armed risings by slaves within the United States, one of the most important is little remembered today: the rebellion aboard the slave ship *Creole*. Conservative writers as recently as 1999 were still condemning it as a crime of "mutiny" and "murder," which it was not. Progressive writers have called it "the most successful slave revolt in American history." It was that and more: an event that created an example of a slave leader who inspired many African American leaders to follow.[34]

Among them was Madison Washington. Many others followed. Henry Box Brown made brilliant use of a spectacular escape to draw others to his cause. Josiah Henson expanded the antislavery movement by creating deep empathy for the victims of slavery, in his own writings and those of Harriet Beecher Stowe, whose work he helped to shape and promote. Anthony Burns by his courage and conduct brought a new strength and dignity to a large cause. Dred Scott and Harriet Scott worked for many years to find remedies to slavery within American law. Dangerfield Newby turned to armed revolt. Harriet Tubman became a leader of the Underground Railroad. And Frederick Douglass had the longest reach in the creation of his new politics and prose. They all began as slaves in the Chesapeake region. During the mid-nineteenth century many of them became effective leaders in national and world affairs.

What did these Chesapeake slave leaders share in common? What might we learn from them? First we can study how attentive they were to learning from others—even from their oppressors. These slaves studied the strengths of leadership in slaveholders such as Washington and Jefferson, Madison and Monroe, even as they rejected their right to own slaves. They built on an American political tradition which was great but deeply flawed, and made it greater and less flawed. In that creative effort, they preserved its virtues, corrected its vices, and extended its reach.

At the same time they also enlarged early American ideas of liberty and freedom, by linking those ideas to a larger spirit of equality and humanity. Most of these African American leaders were also Christians. They turned against the moral corruption of Christian clergy who supported slavery in the time of its greatest strength. At the same time they turned toward Christ and the Four Gospels, and gave new meaning to Christ's teaching that "what you do for the least of my brethren you do for me."

These leading Chesapeake slaves of African ancestry were highly principled in their purposes and acts. They became moral leaders who were deeply conscious of a vital ethical dimension in leadership. Many of these Chesapeake slaves also were leaders who understood the importance of treating other people decently, from their long experience of having been treated in other ways. They greatly valued a respect for the dignity and feelings of others. And they understood the vital importance of doing the right thing in the right way. Also they became instrumental leaders who understood the urgency of effective action. Leadership was not a game for them, or a goal in itself. Always, it had larger purposes.

This reinvented and enlarged tradition of African-American leadership was complex in its character. It grew from many precursors, and developed a character and integrity that was uniquely its own. Chesapeake African American leaders were not solitary people. They learned from others, kept a code of courage and honor, and added other values. They also had long memories of the past, and shared a special way of thinking historically about new problems in the present and the future. Most of all they served this cause not only by precept but by actual example of applied leadership in action.

COASTAL CAROLINA AND GEORGIA: THE CREATIVITY OF GULLAH GEECHEE CULTURES, WITH PORTABLE ROOTS FOR PEOPLE ON THE GO

In our time, Americans of other cultures have repeatedly rediscovered the Gullah Geechee heritage as deeply interesting in its own right, and closely connected to the main lines of American history. The story has been told in many works of history and literature, and nowhere with more depth of understanding than in the inspired scholarship of Charles Joyner.

This process of discovery began among the "Gideonites," mostly abolitionists, reformers, and missionaries, who moved from the northern states to the Sea Islands of coastal Carolina during the Civil War. That story also has been told by Willie Lee Rose in another classic work of American history, *Rehearsal for Reconstruction*.[35]

The story further expanded in the 1920s and 1930s, and gained new strength in the late twentieth and twenty-first centuries. An excellent new history by Melissa Cooper follows it through time. Much of it is about the making of Gullah and Geechee culture, and its growing presence in the "American Imagination." This was and is a living process of growth and creativity.

Every historian who writes about Gullah and Geechee cultures, every linguist who studies the creativity of Gullah and Geechee speech, every musician who rediscovers the complex cadences of a ring shout, and others in many disciplined inquiries, are building on that vibrant African and American tradition. Despite fears for its extinction, it is very much alive.[36]

And it is also about something else—the importance of roots for Gullah and Geechee people. Some Americans imagine themselves to be rootless, and more than a few are actually so. But most Americans have roots that are deeply important to themselves and others. Gullah and Geechee cultures are classic examples of these American roots. Their history is profoundly important in its own right, and also has much to teach us about the character and strength of American roots, and the way they work in the modern world, especially among people on the go.

Today Americans still tend to be a people in motion—less so than before, by the actual measure of American internal migration, which has been declining in the early twenty-first century—a new and troubling trend in the long span of American history. But many Americans are still a people on the move. Examples are Gullah and Geechee people who have moved to New York, Chicago, and elsewhere.

Americans tend to be a people with portable roots. Many of us carry them in our heads and hearts wherever we go. An interesting paradox is that American roots often grow stronger in that process. That is what Gullah and Geechee people did when they moved from Africa to coastal Carolina and Georgia, and again to southern and then to northern cities in the twentieth century. Here is a complex process of change and persistence at the heart of the American condition.

At the same time this process was also important in another way. These cultures of close belonging carried within them an ethical core. A leading example is Michelle Obama, a Gullah descendant who carried this ethic into the White House. In response to Americans who opposed her husband and later supported Donald Trump, she said, "When they go low, we go high." Here was an idea of purposeful and principled action in the world. To that end it was transmitted not by precept but by exemplary acts which made a difference in the world. These values had long been strong in Gullah and Geechee cultures. They grew more important when some Americans rejected them, which led others to rediscover them. Gullah descendants such as Michelle Obama enlarged on these traditions, and set a strong example for others.

LOUISIANA, LOWER MISSISSIPPI, AND THE GULF COAST: AFRICAN DIVERSITY, COMITY, AND CREATIVITY

In Louisiana, something else happened. Power and control passed through a diversity of ruling elites from Canada, France, Spain, and the United States. At the same time, diverse clusters of African slaves invented for themselves new systems of comity, which grew into patterns of association, interaction, and creativity.

Comities develop in many functioning societies. In particular, they are fundamental to free and open systems. The regional history of Louisiana became a striking example of a general pattern that has recurred in other cultures throughout the world, but with a special intensity in the lower Mississippi Valley. African slaves of European masters were important in the creation of these new Afro-European comities in America.

That complex process of cultural invention was especially visible in the colony of Louisiana, in large part because of its diversity. African slaves were not passive victims of their bondage. They responded by actively supporting each other, and by creating systems of mutual support.

Important evidence appears in the Louisiana Slave Database constructed by Ann Patton Malone for 10,329 Louisiana slaves in 3,989 households from 1810 to 1864, drawn from 155 "slave communities" on plantations in twenty-six Louisiana parishes. This was a stratified sample, designed to encompass "all major slaveholding regions of the state."

The results of Malone's research have transformed our understanding of the history of slave households, families, and communities in Louisiana. The modal pattern was neither a norm of broken nuclear families in slavery (the mistaken Moynihan thesis) nor the persistence of intact double-headed nuclear families (Gutman et al.). It was a more complex and deeply interesting dynamic of diverse familial groups, created and maintained in large measure by the efforts of slaves themselves, with masters and mistresses in important but secondary roles.

These Louisiana slaves continuously reconstructed complex households in many different forms. In that process they preserved units of belonging for most slaves. It had a major impact on the maintenance of households, family life, community cohesion, and cultural creativity, mainly by forming a dynamic diversity of households among plantation slaves on Louisiana plantations.[37]

Something comparable also happened among people of African ancestry in urban New Orleans. Here domestic slaves, market slaves, slave artisans, and free African Americans lived in large numbers of small groups that interacted in many ways.

Urban slaves also mixed with free people of color in gatherings such as the music and dancing in Congo Square and other places, in churches and prayer groups throughout the city, and in open markets which were often organized, controlled, or dominated by people of color both slave and free. Some of these interactions happened in many American cities, but they tended to be more active and more complex and more creative in New Orleans.

The result was the development of a very full associational life. Visitors to New Orleans noted the active engagement of many African Americans, free and slave, in funerals for people of color. They also noted that this pattern in Louisiana was much stronger among Africans than Europeans, who tended to be more fragmented.

These visitors also became interested in music and dance among people of African origins, free and slave, in New Orleans, from the mid-eighteenth century to the occupation of New Orleans by Union troops in 1862, and beyond. They did so partly for the extraordinary richness, color, and creativity of the music and dancing, but also because of their role in creating a sense of belonging to a complex Afro-American community and culture.

We also found that within that culture, there was also an extraordinary attention to young people. They were actively engaged and as they learned, those with special gifts were actively supported by musicians in older generations. That process was a vital clue to dynamics of this extraordinarily creative culture, and its continuing strength in our own time.

COMMON AFRICAN ELEMENTS IN MANY AMERICAN REGIONAL CULTURES

Finally, this inquiry leads to one last set of questions. In this regional history of cultural diversity, one might also ask about common patterns of thought that Africans tended to share throughout many regions in the present boundaries of the United States.

Several African elements of consequence tended to appear in most African American regional cultures. Some were evident at an early date, and many persisted through American history, from the early seventeenth century to the present day—a span of four hundred years and sixteen generations.

These common patterns grew from African cultural roots, and developed through interaction with European cultures and American environments. In America some of them spread to people of other origins, with far-reaching consequences for the history of the United States. Here are four examples.

AFRICAN GIFTS OF LANGUAGE AND SPEECH

From an early date, extraordinary gifts of language appeared among African slaves in every American region, and took Europeans by surprise. These gifts were strongest in oral speech and comprehension, and they tended to take many forms: an ability to learn to speak and understand other languages; a facility for mastery of multiple spoken languages; a flair for the invention of hybrid speechways; a creative gift for coinage of new words; and a genius for inventing new forms of creative expression, such as the use of rhyme and rhythm in speech. These many gifts became a creative part of African American speechways through many generations, and have had a major impact on American and world culture.

These African American gifts for language learning and linguistic creativity derived from the multiplicity and complexity of languages and cultures in West and Central Africa. Most American slaves came from these broad areas, where large families of predominantly oral languages were spoken in hundreds of dialects. Some of these speechways were similar to neighboring languages; others were profoundly disparate.

In consequence, many people in West and Central Africa lived and worked in close proximity to others whose speechways differed from their own. In frequent transactions they learned to communicate in a variety of ways across language differences. One method was to invent new forms of what linguists call pidgin speech, which combines the vocabularies of two or more languages with very basic grammar. Another method was for speakers of two languages to use small elements of another lingua franca for particular purposes. A third and most useful method was to learn from long experience how to acquire quickly the bare rudiments of another language, or at least enough of it to understand and be understood. American Indians dealt with the same problem by yet another method. They invented fascinating systems of manual sign languages. Africans preferred to go a different way which was deeply embedded in their cultures. In conversations across linguistic lines of difference, they became highly skilled in the creative use of spoken words from other languages, with astonishing virtuosity.

Those methods of oral communication had been used in West and Central Africa before the slave trade began. With the growth of maritime trade on the Atlantic coast of Africa, they developed at a rapid rate—and that process continued on the other side of the Atlantic.

In early European voyages to North America, Africans were actively recruited for their language skills. Again and again they demonstrated a facility for learning other languages and serving as translators and mediators between American Indians and European explorers. Our inquiries found striking examples in every major North American region at an early date.

On the northern coasts of New England and maritime Canada, an early example was Mathieu Da Costa or De Coste, or Matthew of the Coast. He was described as a "naigre" or negro of African origin. As early as 1604 he "spoke the languages of Acadia" and was able to communicate with Indian nations and early European explorers. French leaders actively employed him as an interpreter in that region. Dutch rivals tried in vain to hire him away, and then kidnapped him. The French were outraged, and recovered his freedom after long litigation in Europe.[38]

Repeated evidence indicates that Mathieu Da Costa was not unique. Something similar happened in most early American regions that we have studied. In the Hudson Valley, we were fascinated by the career of Juan Rodriguez of Santo Domingo, variously described "mulatto" or "black." He settled on Manhattan Island in 1613, the first non-Indian known to have done so. Rodriguez married an Indian woman, went into business with Dutch partners, and worked as a translator, trader, and go-between for Europeans and American Indians, with much success.[39]

In the Delaware Valley, the "Angoler" or "Morian" called Antoni Swartz or Black Anthony, worked as a trader, skipper, and go-between for Swedish settlers and American Indians as early as 1639. And in the Chesapeake Bay, an African, Mathias de Sousa, came to Maryland in its founding year of 1634, as the "servant" of Jesuit missionaries. He became free and was made the captain of a small trading vessel on voyages to the Susquehanna Indians, with whom he was able to communicate in the upper reaches of the Bay.[40]

Other examples appeared in most North American regions through many generations. Later in the eighteenth century, a party of English- and German-speaking European settlers in the Ohio Valley were unable to communicate with Indian nations, until an African slave helped them as a translator.

African gifts of speech also helped people to master and use more than one language at a time. As early as 1734, an anglophone planter described five African slaves as speaking "very good (Black) English" in addition to their native African tongues.

A helpful source for the range and variety of language skills among Africans in early America are advertisements for runaway slaves in every major North American hearth culture. In one of the best studies of runaway notices for New York and New Jersey, Graham Hodges and Alan Edward Brown found that "masters were also reasonably objective about slave linguistic abilities." They observed that "bilingual speakers of Dutch and English abounded, with a few multilinguists knowing Spanish, French, Indian and African tongues. . . . Many fugitives were called smooth-tongued, bold, convincing, or artful." Similar evidence appeared in New England, Pennsylvania, the Chesapeake colonies, coastal South Carolina, and Louisiana.[41]

Yet another important pattern was the rapid emergence of composite Afro-European speechways in early America, in which Africans played the leading role of invention. These were not primitive pidgins, but distinctive oral languages that were constructed mostly by slaves from a mix of African, European, and American Indian sources. These new speechways emerged in most American regions at an early date, and they persisted for many years. Unlike pidgins, they began to be learned in childhood and were spoken for life by African slaves, and also by some masters and mistresses of European origin, especially in regions with a large predominance of African slaves.

These new hybrid languages were unlike pidgins in other ways. They rapidly began to function as highly developed vernacular speechways, and became primary vehicles of regional African American cultures. Conventional linguistic categories such as pidgin or dialect do not match their special character, or their process of acquisition, or their creative roles.

In some ways the results of this common process were highly variable. These new Afro-Euro-American speechways took different forms in different American regions, and began to be perceived in various ways at an early date. The main body of this book discusses many of these regional languages in North America. We have noted frequently the astonishing diversity of these African American speechways in every major hearth culture, without exception. They included Black Yankee speech in New England, Black Dutch or "Swartz Deutsch" in the Hudson Valley, variants of "Low Deutsch" (Dutch) and "High Deutsch" (German) in the Delaware Valley, and "Guinea talk" or Guinea speech as Frederick Douglass called speechways on the Maryland Eastern Shore in his youth. More familiar and most carefully studied by historians and linguists, are three languages created by African slaves in major plantation colonies. They are called Gullah in coastal Carolina, Geechee in Georgia, and Gombo in Louisiana.[42]

Others developed on a smaller scale. North Carolina's Cape Fear Valley attracted slaveholding Gaelic-speaking settlers from the Highlands of Scotland. The results included African slaves who learned to speak Afro-Gaelic, to the astonishment of Scottish visitors. They combined elements of Gaelic with African languages in yet another Afro-European speechway in early America.

Each of these Afro-European speechways had its own unique elements, but all of them shared qualities in common. They developed rapidly in American regions from a fusion of African, European, and American Indian elements. They functioned as spoken languages, and were rarely written by the people who actually spoke them until linguists and literati discovered them in the late nineteenth and early twentieth centuries. In the twenty-first century, Gombo is being revived and learned anew as a spoken language by scholars, writers, and others interested in the creativity of languages through the lower Mississippi Valley.

We can hear some of these languages, Gombo especially, in actual use by elderly former slaves in recordings made during the 1930s, and preserved in the American Folklore Collection at the Library of Congress, where Judy and I listened to them. Gullah, Geechee, Gombo, and Guinea talk opened new possibilities for creative expression. People who spoke European languages also used them to communicate an extraordinary range and depth of emotional meanings.

Many people of African and European origin and descent in most American regions became adept at using elements of creative expression from these hybrid speechways in other languages. Other creative elements continued in later generations. An example is the sustained use of rhyme and rhythm in African American speechways. This pattern is familiar today in rap and hip hop. Precursors in early America were African slaves who often became "callers" at country dances, and were preferred over speakers of European languages for their use of rhyme and rhythm.

The creativity of rap and hip hop in the twentieth and twenty-first centuries have enriched the cultural life of America and the world in our time. A classic example is Lin-Manuel Miranda's *Hamilton*, a hugely successful musical which opened on Broadway on August 6, 2016, and reached a large part of the American people with a story about the immigrant Alexander Hamilton and the founding of the American republic. It was a serious work of American history, told in the language of rap and hip hop. *Hamilton* spoke in a fresh voice to the condition of millions of Americans in the current century. And it reached them with a message that awakened their sense of belonging in an American culture with deep roots. *Hamilton*, its message, and its language were created by many people. Not the least of those creators were Africans who came in chains to early America, and brought a gift of language with them.[43]

AFRICAN GIFTS OF MUSIC

Something similar happened in the history of American music. In every region of early North America from an early date, visitors and natives alike were quick to notice the importance of music among African slaves, and also a creative gift of musical expression that they brought to the New World.

Much of it derived from African traditions that were introduced to every American region at an early date. Tangible evidence appeared in African musical instruments, which rapidly appeared in the New World. Some were brought in the Middle Passage. Others were improvised on arrival, and many more began to be constructed and often improved by African slaves from American materials.[44]

References to music and musical instruments often appeared in descriptions for runaway slaves, published by masters in eighteenth-century newspapers in every American region without exception. A striking tendency was for masters to write about musical instruments as belonging to slaves themselves even as clothing and other possessions were described as belonging to the masters.

Most frequently mentioned were fiddles or violins. In early America three-stringed African fiddles were widespread. At least a few ship captains, supercargos, and merchants used music for their own purposes, to control slaves and to increase survival in the Middle Passage. At the same time African slaves used music to preserve a shared spirit of identity and belonging in an experience of extreme suffering.

Something similar continued after their arrival in America. From the early eighteenth century, African slaves actively made musical instruments in the New World. In the Delaware Valley, Isaac Norris wrote of his slave Peter in 1719, "Thou knowest negro Peter's ingenuity in making for himself and playing a fiddle without any assistance."[45]

Many African musical instruments were introduced by slaves to a New World. As early as 1749, runaway notices made repeated references to banjos, variously spelled as banjer banjou, bandjoe (Virginia), banjo (Maryland), bangie (Appalachia), banza (Louisiana), and in many other ways. The instrument itself and its names were African in origin: *mbanza* in Kimbundu speechways of Central Africa, and *bangelo* in Sierra Leone. Of many African instruments, banjos were among the most widely used, discussed, and imitated by Europeans. They became prominent in popular music throughout the United States.[46]

The most complex African musical instruments in early America were sets of wooden bars or tubes which were struck with hammers. In Mediterranean cultures they were called xylophones from Greek roots for wood and sound; and in Africa, balafons or balafos. The English traveler Richard Jobson described them as early as 1621. By 1775–76, examples were described in Virginia. One was played by an African from Niger and the music was described as "sprightly and enlivening."[47]

African drums were also brought on slave ships, and many more were made in America in the early eighteenth century. One handsome kettle drum with exquisite proportions and elaborately refined carvings was used by slaves in Virginia and given to the British Museum in 1753.[48]

In every American hearth culture, African slaves developed many genres of music, sometimes with the support of masters, often against their prohibitions. New England's small African population loomed large in this story, and in a special way. Some slaves took leading roles in founding musical institutions, even while they were still in bondage during the eighteenth century. An example in Rhode Island was a slave whose African name was recorded as Occramer Marycoo. He was given the name of Newport Gardner, and became a music teacher and successful musical entrepreneur while still a slave. He taught himself to read and write English, and drew actively upon both African and European musical traditions. In 1791, he also won a lottery, and used the money to found a singing school in Rhode Island, teaching English songs with an African flair. The singing school was later affiliated with Newport's Colored Union Church, which still exists as part of the Union Congregational Church.[49]

In New York, African American musical traditions were important in yet another way. Some of them appeared on the annual Dutch holiday of Pinkster or Pfingsten in German, which English Christians knew as Whitsuntide. It followed the seventh Sunday after Easter. Slaves and servants were given a holiday which grew into a week of carnival for African Americans in the Hudson Valley. Much of it was given over to parades, processions, and music with African drumming, singing, and dancing, described as "wild" but "euphonic." Pinkster faded in the nineteenth century but African American celebrations continued in secular anniversaries, such as the abolition of the slave trade by Congress, the end of slavery in New York, and American Independence Day. All were celebrated with what was described as an "explosion of black music and dance."[50]

In these public events, music and dance became a vital part of African American identity. Historian Shane White writes that "dance became a vital element" in a communal culture that "for all its flaws, was the creative and expressive response of ordinary African New Yorkers to their recently acquired and hard-won freedom." Many of these celebrants had been born and raised as slaves. Similar events continued through the year in urban dance halls, and rural country dances.[51]

In rural Maryland and Virginia, other cycles of celebration were linked to the rhythms of rural life. Corn-shuckings were major events, with others in the Christmas season. Through the years, Chesapeake slaves also seized their own nocturnal opportunities. James Deane, a plantation slave in Charles County, Maryland, near the Potomac River, remembered one custom that was unique to that part of this large region. In a rare surviving Maryland WPA narrative, he recalled that "when we wanted to meet at night we had an old conk, we blew that. We would all meet on the bank of the Potomac River and sing across the river to the slaves in Virginia, and they would sing back to us." The "old conk" was a conch shell, yet another family of instruments borrowed by Africans and Europeans from American Indians, and used for communication and celebration.[52]

In coastal Carolina and Georgia, Gullah and Geechee slaves made much use of drums and drumming, despite efforts by masters to suppress them. Drums were much feared and often forbidden, but African slaves found ways around prohibitions. Drums echoed through the night in this region, and became a system of communication which was said to be faster than the telegraph.[53]

For festive occasions, Gullah Geechee slaves also invented a variety of percussion instruments and used them to create complex rhythms in song and dance. The most abundant sources for African music in early America come from Louisiana. As early as 1723, witnesses reported that "the negroes assemble together on Sundays . . . to the number of three or four hundred, to dance the Calinda." New Orleans was the largest gathering place, but it happened throughout Louisiana.[54]

African musical traditions had a long reach in America in many different ways through many generations: religious music in hymns and shouts, popular music in taverns and houses of prostitution, with strong rhythms. Other African American musical traditions flourished in sorrow songs and the blues; in the joyous sounds of ragtime; in complex rhythms in Dixieland and the spontaneous creativity of jazz in its infinite variety, and many other inventions. All grew from African music in America, flourished in every regional Afro-American culture, and spread to the general population throughout the United States and increasingly the world.

The continued creativity of these expansive musical traditions owes much of its strength to the deep and very active interest that leading African American musicians took in the musical progress of promising youngsters and coming generations. We studied this process in Louisiana, where it has long been very strong, and is stronger than ever today. It interacted with many ethnic cultures in America, and was carried throughout the world.

AFRICAN GIFTS OF SPIRIT AND SOUL

Important as were these widely shared African gifts of language and music, other gifts were even more consequential. This has been the judgment of leading African American writers through many generations—three writers in particular. Frederick Douglass (1818–95), W. E. B. Du Bois (1868–1963), and Martin Luther King Jr. (1929–68) all believed that the creative core of African American culture and life centered on expansive ideas of spirit and soul. Their lives spanned 150 years of historical experience, and they keenly remembered an even longer period of African American history that preceded them.

Spirit and soul were not one thing, but many things. They had a long history, multiple meanings, and embraced a diversity of creative traditions. Studies of indigenous African cultures and religions below the Sahara have found that many of them shared a deep belief in spiritual powers that existed throughout the world, and in profoundly different forms. Most believed in a single Great Spirit, which Christians understood as a single superior being. They also believed in the presence of many other spirits of departed ancestors and descendants yet to be born. Many objects in the world were thought to be emanations of other spirits that possessed greater strength than their material objects.[55]

This way of spiritual thinking was brought to America by African slaves and it grew. As they traveled through space and time from Africa to the New World their forms of spiritual thinking also changed, and had a long reach in America. Many slaves had been converted to Christianity before they left Africa, and others had become adherents to Islam. They often believed in traditional African religion and other faiths and saw no conflict between them. In America during the seventeenth and eighteenth centuries, they joined actively in various forms of colonial Christian worship. They participated actively in the Great Awakenings of the eighteenth century, and in the Second Great Awakening during the early republic, and many revivals of the nineteenth and twentieth centuries. Of all the many competing Christian denominations, the most welcoming and appealing to Africans were Baptists with their Christian fellowships, and Methodists with their great meetings (more so than the Society of Friends, which was more supportive of emancipation but less attractive in their meetings). African Americans worshipped in their own way, and they were quick to found their own churches in the new republic.

There was also a spontaneous spread of religious belief that moved rapidly among American slaves in every region, and often combined elements of several faiths. It flourished in secret meetings that masters often did not know about.

In African American cultures, some of the strongest expressions of these religious beliefs were the vast outpouring of music and language in what came to be called spirituals. They had deep roots in Africa and many beginnings in every American region. Spirituals were sung by African slaves everywhere in the United States. Always they were stirrings of the spirit, but in different ways.[56]

Among the first and most deeply moving African spirituals in early America were the sorrow songs. An early example of complex origins, published in 1816, described an all too frequent event that an alleged "French traveller" observed while standing on the steps of a courthouse in the town of Portsmouth, Virginia. He saw a coffle of "about thirty negroes, of different ages and sizes. . . . They came along singing a little wild hymn of sweet and mournful melody."

He saw that "some were loaded with chains to prevent their escape while others had hold of each other's hands, strongly held, as if to support themselves in their affliction. . . . I particularly noticed a poor mother, with an infant sucking at her breast, as she walked along, while two small children had hold of her apron on either side, almost running to keep up with the rest." With them was "a rough-looking white man, who sat carelessly, riding in a sulkey."

The traveler asked others about these people and was told, "It's nothing but a parcel of Negroes, sold to Carolina, and that man is their driver who has bought them." The traveler noted that many Virginians looked on with "curiosity or compassion," but nobody came to their aid, or tried to comfort them.[57]

The sorrow songs of these slaves remained vivid in the minds of some who heard them. They also grew through time, and gave rise to many African American musical traditions.

Spiritual singing spread rapidly among African slaves. Many had been converted to Christianity in Africa, especially in Angola by Catholic missionaries. Others became Christians through every American region, in the waves of revivalism that swept over New England from 1635. Wesley Gewehr first found them to be a continuous presence through the Chesapeake region, coastal Carolina and Georgia.

They took other forms, and became deeply interesting to northern teachers, missionaries, and antislavery reformers who called themselves Gideon's Band. They followed Union armies into the South, beginning with the Sea Islands and coastal of South Carolina and Georgia in the fall of 1861, and spreading to many other places as Union troops advanced into parts of the Confederate States.

Members of Gideon's Band were interested in music and began to record these songs, setting down on paper both the words and music of spirituals, and published them in book-length collections immediately after the Civil War, beginning in 1867.

These spirituals were organized by region. The largest group, more than a hundred, came from the coast and Sea Islands of South Carolina and Georgia. Others in smaller numbers came from the Chesapeake region of Virginia, and these surprised the collectors. They wrote that "Contrary to what might be expected, the songs of Virginia were the most wild and strange." Another large group came from Louisiana and the Gulf Coast, and a smaller number from the inland South, which they described as "more like the music of the whites." [58]

In this music there is no spirit of contentment. Despite extended efforts by masters to make their slaves sing only happy songs, there is a deep sadness in slave music. Many spirituals were sorrow songs.

Nobody knows the trouble I've had
Nobody knows but Jesus
Nobody knows the trouble I've had
Glory Hallelu!

Sometimes I'm up, sometimes I'm down
O yes Lord!
Sometimes I'm almost on de groun'
O yes Lord! O yes Lord!
Sometimes I'm almost on de groun.

Deep within many of these spirituals was a distinctive sense of time. It has been said that everyone's sense of time is either a circle or a line. Anglo-European ideas of time tend to be strongly linear. African and Asian conceptions of time were often cyclical.

A third pattern appeared in Afro-American spirituals which were both cyclical and linear, sometimes separate but often together. One spiritual created an explicit circular image from the Old Testament example of Ezekiel 1:15:

> Ezekiel saw the wheel,
> Way up in the middle of the air,
> Ezekiel saw the wheel,
> Way up in the middle of the air.
>
> Ezekiel saw the wheel of time,
> Ev'ry spoke was of the humankind,
> A wheel in a wheel,
> Way up in the middle of the air.
>
> O, the big wheel runs by faith
> And the little wheel runs by the grace of God,
> A wheel in a wheel,
> Way up in the middle of the air.

Other spirituals centered on a single figure of Jacob, who often appeared in slave spirituals with his ladder and its attendant linear imagery of agency and progress. The singers sought to join him:

> I want to climb up Jacob's ladder,
> Jacob's ladder, O Jacob's ladder,
> I want to climb up Jacob's ladder,
> But I can't climb it till I make my peace with the Lord.
> O praise ye the Lord, I'll praise Him till I die,
> I'll praise Him till I die, And sing Jerusalem.

The song ended with a cry of triumph:

> We are climbing Jacob's ladder
> We are climbing Jacob's ladder
> Soldier of the Cross.
>
> Every round goes higher and higher
> Every round goes higher and higher
> Soldier of the Cross.

Spirituals also added other layers of hope and meaning. In some songs, spiritual striving brought the promise of material gain, but only if it was genuine. An example was that wonderful spiritual called "I Got Shoes."

I got shoes,
You got shoes,
All God's chillun got shoes.
When we get to Heaven
We're going to put on our shoes
And walk all over God's Heaven
And shout all over God's Heaven.

Heaven! Heaven!
Evrybody talkin 'bout Heaven ain't goin there.[59]

Among the most important components of African spirituals was a vital idea that Africans called soul. It appeared at an early date in African regional cultures throughout America. And it also was at the center of African American thought and belief through many generations.

Frederick Douglass wrote frequently on the subject of his soul. Through his long years as a slave in Maryland, he believed that his body was held in bondage, but "the soul that is within me no man can degrade."[60]

W. E. B. Du Bois took up this subject, enlarged upon it, and made it the center of the book he called *The Souls of Black Folk*, one of the most creative and important books in American culture. Du Bois agreed with Douglass that the "soul that is within me no man can degrade," and he took that idea a step farther. Du Bois believed deeply that all "Black Folk" in America shared "a spiritual striving" that was fundamental to their condition. He wrote that "the spiritual striving of the freedmen's sons is the travail of souls."[61]

Yet another enlargement of this subject appeared in the speeches and writings of Martin Luther King. In the civil rights movement, King took the meaning of soul to another place. Of many writings and addresses, his greatest speech with the longest reach was "I Have a Dream," given on August 28, 1963, to a vast gathering of Americans on the Mall from the Lincoln Memorial to the Capitol. Millions more have watched and heard it on film and television.

King celebrated Lincoln as a great American and the Emancipation Proclamation as an enduring achievement in its moral force. But a century after emancipation, King declared that "the Negro still is not free." His greatest speech was a call to nonviolent action, by overcoming physical force with "soul force." For Martin Luther King, "soul force" meant many things. It was a collective instrument that drew its power from millions of people, of many conditions and creeds. Its purpose was to reach "all of God's children," and its goal was the achievement of freedom in every village and hamlet. King's dream was to use "soul force" to unite Black and white, Protestant and Catholic, Jew and Gentile, so that all "will be able to join hands and sing in the words of the old Negro spiritual, 'Free at last, free at last, thank God Almighty, we are free at last.'"[62]

AFRICAN GIFTS OF ETHICS AND FREEDOM

In the many cultures that have taken root in what is now the United States, one finds a great diversity of dynamic ethical beliefs. Here again, the people of West Africa and Central Africa were heirs to many ethical traditions. Prominent among them were traditions rooted in African ideas of right and wrong, equity and justice.

In many African cultures, human bondage was well established and widely practiced. Some of it was domestic slavery in which individual slaves were thought of as members of their masters' families. At the same time, other African systems were plantation slavery in which large numbers of African field slaves lived at a distance from their owners, and were cruelly treated.

But the system of slavery that Africans met in the English colonies of North America was something they had not known before. It tended to be a system of hereditary bondage which existed within cultures that had been founded on highly articulated ideas of liberty and freedom.

It also became a system of slavery for life that was imposed on people in Anglo-American colonies solely because of their place of origin, and the color of their skin. In short, Africans met a system not merely of slavery but race slavery in early America.

From the late eighteenth century they also met a new ideology of racism that began to develop in the modern world. The first fully sustained argument for innate racial differences dates ironically from 1776. We remember that year for impassioned argument by Thomas Jefferson that "all men are created equal, and endowed by their creator with certain inalienable rights." In that very same year, German scholar Johann Friedrich Blumenbach completed his doctoral dissertation at the University of Göttingen, titled in Latin *De Generis humani varietate nativa*, "On the Natural Variety of Humanity." Blumenbach divided humanity into five races, which he was the first to call Caucasian/white, Mongolian/yellow, Malayan/brown, African/black, and American/red. He argued that skin color and skull size correlated with differences in average levels of mental intelligence and moral judgment.

In the nineteenth century, Blumenbach's taxonomy of race grew into a full-blown ideology of racism. The most influential work was the comte de Gobineau's *Essai sur l'inégalité des races humaines*, "Essay on the Inequality of the Human Races," published in four massive volumes in Paris in 1859.

Here again, the major conceptual works were European, but they were put to work in America as a justification for race slavery and racial inequality, which had already begun to appear in Jefferson's *Notes on the State of Virginia* only a decade after the Declaration of Independence.

In the nineteenth century, African American leaders began to think not only about race slavery, but also about the larger problem of racism and racial injustice in its many forms. They also deeply believed that something had gone profoundly right in America, and some found a way forward in the ethnic variety of its population. Frederick Douglass believed that the diversity of American population was one of its greatest strengths. He wrote that the United States is "the most conspicuous example of composite nationality in the world. . . . Our greatness and grandeur will be found in the faithful application of the principle of perfect civil equality to the people of all races and creeds." [63]

Most African slaves were quicker to embrace American liberty and freedom. At the same time they were quick to condemn American race slavery and racism. They witnessed the invention of racism, which was something new in the modern world. Racism spread rapidly in Western Europe and North America, and in the early modern era.

When African slaves met race slavery and the growing ideology of racism, they responded in a variety of ways throughout American regions. Behind these responses was a common way of ethical thinking about the injustice of slavery and racism. It centered not on ideological tests of social justice but on the deployment of principles of liberty and freedom.

African slaves also condemned slavery by another moral calculus. It was grounded not in ethical abstractions, but in more concrete experiences of how slavery actually worked in their personal experience. This moral calculus derived in large part from substantive acts and material details of injustice which they had witnessed on a daily basis.

Frederick Douglass remembered a satirical song that was sung on Maryland's Eastern Shore by slaves in their gatherings away from their masters. It was an ethical idea of pervasive inequity and injustice in human bondage. And they set it to music in a song that Douglass never forgot in his later years. He reproduced it from memory in his *Life and Times* half a century later. His fellow slaves sang it with an edge of laughter, but also with a depth of fury for the way they were routinely treated:

> We raise de wheat,
> Dey gib us de corn;
> We bake de bread,
> Dey gib us de crust;
> We sif [sift] de meal,
> Dey gib us de huss [husk];
> We peel de meat,
> Dey gib us de skin;
> And dat's de way
> Dey take us in;
> We skim de pot,
> Dey gib us de liquor,
> And say dat's good enough for nigger.
> Walk over! walk over!
>
> Your butter and dey fat;
> Poor nigger, you can't get over dat!
> Walk over![64]

This was a very powerful idea of equity for all, cast in a distinctive moral calculus that rose from the experience of human bondage. And it also became an expansive ethical ideal for America, itself through many generations. And it has been growing.[65]

AFRICAN RESPONSES TO AMERICAN SLAVERY AND AMERICAN FREEDOM

In Ghana's capital city of Accra, an anti-American student demonstration took place in its streets. The students trashed and burned American books and papers in acts of rage against racism and racial injustice. An African observer turned to an American friend as they watched it together and said, "Look how your country is hated."

Then he pointed to the students themselves. They were wearing American blue jeans and American T-shirts that celebrated American colleges, American music, and American freedom. He said to his American companion, "And look how your country is loved."

That ambivalence of ethical judgment on American culture and institutions exists widely through the world, and also in America itself. It has some of its deepest roots and most powerful experiences in African American thought and experience through sixteen generations of race slavery and racism.

From the American Revolution and the American Civil War, to the many challenges of the late twentieth century, and the troubles in the early twenty-first, Africans both slave and free have long reflected on a deep moral paradox in America, between the continuing horror of race slavery and persistence of racial injustice on the one hand, and the hope of expanding ideals of human rights, social justice, the rule of law, and dreams of liberty and freedom.

In the United States, W. E. B. Du Bois noted this "double-consciousness" in the thinking of African Americans: "One ever feels his twoness—an American, a Negro, two souls, two thoughts, two unreconciled strivings, two warring ideals in one dark body, whose dogged strength alone keeps it from being torn apart." Du Bois wrote that for Africans in America "slavery was indeed the sum of all villainies, the cause of all sorrow, the root of all villainies." He wrote that "Nobody hated American slavery more than did an American slave." [66]

At the same time Du Bois also observed that "few men worshipped Freedom with half such unquestioning faith as did the American Negro for two centuries." Through the full span of American history, that deep faith in American freedom was strong in the thought and experience of African slaves and their posterity. In the face of tyranny and oppression, the growing strength of that abiding faith in living free has been one of the greatest African contributions to America and the world. [67]

NOTES

INTRODUCTION

1. Amy Chavis Perry, Slave Narrative, Federal Writers' Project, South Carolina, vol. 14, part 3, p. 253, Manuscript Division, Library of Congress.

2. Gustave de Beaumont, *Marie; or Slavery in the United States; A Novel of Jacksonian America* (Paris, 1835), trans. Barbara Chapman, ed. Alvis L. Tinnin (Stanford: Stanford University Press, 1958), appendix A, p. 191.

3. Alexis de Tocqueville, *De la Démocratie en Amérique* (Paris, 1835). Of many translations, one of the best was the first to appear in the United States, by Henry Reeve. It has been reissued in many printings by Alfred A. Knopf in two volumes (New York, 1945). Another excellent edition is *Democracy in America*, trans. George Lawrence, ed. J. P. Mayer (Garden City, N.Y.: Doubleday, 1969). Gustave de Beaumont, *Marie, ou l'Esclavage aux Etats-Unis, tableau de Moeurs Américaines*, 2 vols. (Paris, 1835). At least five editions of this popular work were published in France. The English translation by Barbara Chapman, *Marie; or Slavery in the United States; A Novel of Jacksonian America*, regrettably omits historical and sociological appendices that were central to the author's purpose and integral to the work.

4. Beaumont, *Marie*, 4, epigraph from p. 191.

5. The six historiographical generations are those of George Bancroft (b. 1800); Francis Parkman (b. 1823); James Ford Rhodes (b. 1848); Charles Beard (b. 1874) and Carl Becker (b. 1873); C. Vann Woodward (b. 1908), Perry Miller (b. 1905), and Richard Hofstadter (1916); and James McPherson (b. 1936) and Eric Foner (1943). Capstone works in the sixth generation included James M. McPherson, *The Struggle for Equality* (Princeton: Princeton University Press, 1964); its sequel, *The Abolitionist Legacy* (Princeton: Princeton University Press, 1975); *Battle Cry of Freedom* (New York and Oxford: Oxford University Press, 1988); *The War That Forged a Nation* (New York, 2015). Also Eric Foner, *Free Soil, Free Labor, Free Men* (New York and Oxford: Oxford University Press, 1970); *Reconstruction: America's Unfinished Revolution* (New York: Harper and Row, 1988); *Give Me Liberty!* (New York: Norton, 2010); *Gateway to Freedom: The Hidden History of the Underground Railroad* (New York: Norton, 2015).

6. Leading examples in a large and growing literature are Joanne Pope Melish, *Disowning Slavery: Gradual Emancipation and "Race" in New England* (Ithaca: Cornell University Press, 2000); Wendy Warren, *New England Bound: Slavery and Colonization in Early America* (New York: Norton, 2016); Sven Beckert, *The Empire of Cotton* (New York: Alfred A. Knopf, 2014); and Sven Beckert and Seth Rockman, eds., *Slavery's Capitalism* (Philadelphia: University of Pennsylvania Press, 2016).

7. *The Landmark Herodotus: The Histories*, trans. Andrea L. Purvis, ed. Robert B. Strassler, introduction, Rosalind Thomas (New York: Anchor, 2007). A bilingual edition in Greek and English is published as *Herodotus*, 4 vols., trans. A. D. Godley (Cambridge, Mass., and London: Heinemann, 1920; revised 1981).

8. David Eltis and David Richardson, *Atlas of the Transatlantic Slave Trade* (New Haven and London: Yale University Press, 2010), a detailed preliminary overview of major findings in the Trans-Atlantic Slave Trade Database, by the scholars who constructed it, with much collaboration from many colleagues. The *Atlas* represents the database as it existed in January 2008. Most useful for scholars is the project's online database.

9. Philip D. Curtin, *The Atlantic Slave Trade: A Census* (Madison: University of Wisconsin Press, 1969); Eltis and Richardson, *Atlas of the Transatlantic Slave Trade*, map 11, p. 19.

10. Eltis and Richardson, *Atlas of the Transatlantic Slave Trade*, 205, 18–19.

11. Gregory O'Malley, "Beyond the Middle Passage: Slave Migration from the Caribbean to North America, 1619–1807," *William and Mary Quarterly*, 3rd series, 66 (2009): 125–72.

12. O'Malley, "Beyond the Middle Passage."

13. Gwendolyn Midlo Hall, *Africans in Colonial Louisiana* (Baton Rouge: Louisiana State University Press, 1992), 58, 179, 180, 284; Gwendolyn Hall, *Slavery and African Ethnicities in the Americas* (Chapel Hill: University of North Carolina Press, 2005), 69–76.

14. Hall, *Africans in Colonial Louisiana*, 283.

15. Edmund S. Morgan, *American Slavery, American Freedom: The Ordeal of Colonial Virginia* (New York: Norton, 1975); Thad W. Tate and David L. Ammerman, eds., *The Chesapeake in the Seventeenth Century* (New York: Norton, 1979); Gloria Main, *Tobacco Colony: Life in Early Maryland, 1650–1720* (Princeton: Princeton University Press, 1982); Allan Kulikoff, *Tobacco and Slaves: The Development of Southern Cultures in the Chesapeake, 1680–1800* (Chapel Hill: University of North Carolina Press, 1986); Paul Musselwhite et al., *Virginia 1619: Slavery and Freedom in the Making of English America* (Williamsburg and Chapel Hill: University of North Carolina Press, 2019).

16. Gregory E. O'Malley, *Final Passages: The Intercolonial Slave Trade of British America, 1619–1807* (Chapel Hill: University of North Carolina Press, 2014), 7–29; on the "rarity of seasoned slaves" and Creoles, 21–24. Of importance is Lorena Walsh, who constructed another Chesapeake slave database; Lorena Walsh, "The Chesapeake Slave Trade: Regional Patterns, African Origins, and Some Implications," *William and Mary Quarterly*, 3rd series, 58 (2001): 139–70. See also Lorena Walsh, *From Calabar to Carter's Grove: The History of a Virginia Slave Community* (Charlottesville: University of Virginia Press, 1997); Philip D. Morgan, *Slave Counterpoint: Black Culture in the Eighteenth-Century Chesapeake & Lowcountry* (Williamsburg: University of North Carolina Press, 1998); Douglas B. Chambers, *Murder at Montpelier: Igbo Africans in Virginia* (Jackson: University Press of Mississippi, 2005); and Lorena S. Walsh, *Motives of Honor, Pleasure, and Profit: Plantation Management in the Colonial Chesapeake, 1607–1763* (Chapel Hill: University of North Carolina Press, 2010).

17. The six databases include the Eltis and Richardson Trans-Atlantic Slave Trade Database; the O'Malley Intra-American Slave Trade Database; Hall's three Louisiana data-

bases for individual slaves, individual free people of color, and Pointe Coupée slaves; and the works of Lorena Walsh, cited above, note 16.

18. Elizabeth Donnan, ed., *Documents Illustrative of the History of the Slave Trade to America*, 4 vols. (Washington, D.C.: Carnegie Institution, 1930–35).

19. Linda M. Heywood and John K. Thornton, *Central Africans, Atlantic Creoles, and the Foundation of the Americas, 1585–1660* (Cambridge, 2007, 2011), 333–59.

20. Paul Heinegg, *Free African Americans of North Carolina, Virginia, and South Carolina: From the Colonial Period to About 1820*, 2 vols. (Baltimore: Clearfield Company for the Genealogical Book Company, 1992; 5th edition, 2005); Paul Heinegg, *Free African Americans of Maryland and Delaware: From the Colonial Period to 1810* (Baltimore: Clearfield Company for the Genealogical Book Company, 2000).

21. African slave trade across the Atlantic, the Sahara, the Sahel, the Red Sea, and the Indian Ocean, see Tables 1.1 and 1.2.

22. This advice was given by Francis Parkman to younger members of Boston's St. Botolph Club, of which he was the first president. They passed it on to me when I was the youngest member, a century later.

23. Findings appear in David Hackett Fischer, *Albion's Seed: Four British Folkways in America* (New York and Oxford: Oxford University Press, 1989); *Liberty and Freedom* (New York and Oxford: Oxford University Press, 2005); *Champlain's Dream* (New York and Toronto: Simon & Schuster, 2009), on francophone cultures in Canada; and *Fairness and Freedom: A History of Two Open Societies, New Zealand and the United States* (New York and Oxford: Oxford University Press, 2012).

24. Fischer, *Albion's Seed*; Eunjung Han et al., "Clustering of 770,000 Genomes Reveals Post-Colonial Population Structure of North America," *Nature Communications* 8, article 14238 (2017), doi:10.1038 ncomms 14238, Feb. 7, 2017. See also Steve Sailer, "Albion's Gene: New Genome Study of America Largely Confirms David Hackett Fischer's 'Albion's Seed,'" https://www.unz.com/isteve/albions-gene/.

25. The U.S. Census of 1790 in New Hampshire found 788 African Americans, slave and free, about one half of 1 percent in a total population of 141,885. Evarts B. Greene and Virginia D. Harrington, eds., *American Population Before the Federal Census of 1790* (New York: Columbia University Press, 1932; Baltimore:? Genealogical Publishing Company, 1981), 73.

26. William Page, "A List of Negroes Taken at Hampton, March 4, 1793," Butler Family Papers, Historical Society of Pennsylvania. The US. Census of 1870 reported on Butler's Island 216 Blacks and one white manager, John Nightingale Butler. Butler Family Papers, Historical Society of Pennsylvania; Malcolm Bell Jr., *Major Butler's Legacy: Five Generations of a Slaveholding Family* (Athens: University of Georgia Press), 407.

27. Paul D. Escott, *Slavery Remembered: A Record of Twentieth-Century Slave Narratives* (Chapel Hill: University of North Carolina Press, 1979); Charles Joyner, *Down by the Riverside* (Champaign: University of Illinois Press, 1984).

28. Ira Berlin, Marc Favreau, and Steven F. Miller, eds., *Remembering Slavery: African Americans Talk About Their Personal Experiences of Slavery and Emancipation* (New York: New Press, 1998).

29. Philip J. Schwarz, *Twice Condemned: Slaves and the Criminal Laws of Virginia, 1705–1865* (Union, N.J.: Lawbook Exchange, 1998, 2004); Philip J. Schwarz, "Ga-

briel's Challenge: Slaves and Crime in Late Eighteenth-Century Virginia," *Virginia Magazine of History and Biography* 90 (1982): 283–309, at 30[1]; Michael Blakey et al., eds., *The Archeology of the African Burial Ground National Monument* (Washington and New York, 2006), 199–223.

30. Marilyn Nelson, *Fortune's Bones: The Manumission Requiem*, with notes and annotations by Pamela Espeland (Ashland, N.C.: Front Street, 2004), 9–33.

31. A comparative quantitative analysis of physical descriptions for fugitive slaves in newspapers of Virginia and South Carolina in the collection of the American Antiquarian Society was done by Marc Orlofsky, Dona Bouvier, and Susan Irwin, Brandeis students working with the author. Thanks to Marcus McCorison, then director of the Antiquarian Society, for his support and encouragement of this project.

Chapter 1: NEW ENGLAND

1. John Higginson, *The Cause of God and His People in New-England* (Cambridge, Mass., 1663), 12–13.

2. C. A. Ackah, *Akan Ethics: A Study of the Moral Ideas and the Moral Behaviour of the Akan Tribes of Ghana* (Accra: Ghana Universities Press, 1988), 18.

3. Philip F. W. Bartle, "Forty Days, The Akan Calendar," *Africa: Journal of the International Institute* 48 (1978): 80–84.

4. The bill of sale survives in the Paul Cuffe Manuscript Collection, New Bedford Public Library. For discussion, see Lamont D. Thomas, *Rise to Be a People: A Biography of Paul Cuffe* (Urbana: University of Illinois Press, 1986), 3–6; Lamont D. Thomas, *Paul Cuffe: Black Entrepreneur and Pan-Africanist* (Urbana: University of Illinois Press, 1988), 3–6.

5. Thomas, *Rise to Be a People*, 5. Also deeds, notes, and surveys in Paul Cuffe Papers, New Bedford Public Library.

6. Coffe Slocum, Exercise Book number 2, Cuffe Papers, New Bedford Public Library; Thomas, *Rise to Be a People*, 6; Thomas, *Paul Cuffe*, 3–6.

7. Max Weber, *The Protestant Ethic and the Spirit of Capitalism* (1904–5), trans. Talcott Parsons, foreword R. H. Tawney (New York, 1958), 155–83, and Tawney's critique on 6–11; R. H. Tawney, *Religion and the Rise of Capitalism: A Historical Study* (New York, 1926), 227–35; Kurt Samuellson, *Religion and Economic Action: A Critique of Max Weber* (New York, 1971); David Little, *Religion, Order and Law* (New York, 1970).

8. A helpful work is C. A. Ackah, *Akan Ethics*. The author was first principal of the University College of Cape Coast, and a research fellow at the University of Ghana. This very useful book is based on the author's doctoral thesis in philosophy at the University of London. It includes helpful studies of the Akan language of morals, moral sanctions, and ethical standards. An excellent essay, centered on Akan ethics, is Kwame Gyekye, "African Ethics," *Stanford Encyclopedia of Philosophy* (Sept. 9, 2010), https://plato.stanford.edu/cgi-bin/encyclopedia/archinfo.cgi?entry=african-ethics; and also Kwame Gyekye, *An Essay on African Philosophical Thought: The Akan Conceptual Scheme* (Cambridge, Cambridge University Press, 1987; revised edition, Philadelphia, Temple University Press, 1995).

A first-class work is Kwasi Konadu, *The Akan Diaspora in the Americas* (Oxford, 2010), the best study of the spread of Akan culture through Dutch, Danish, and British colonies, and in what is now the United States. It remodels the cultural history of the Akan diaspora, as a study not of "African survivals" but of "composite" culture "at the level of foundational self-understandings" (p. 22). Still useful are five classic works of R. S. Rattray: *Ashanti Proverbs: The Primitive Ethics of a Savage People* (Oxford, 1916, 1969); *Ashanti* (Oxford, 1923; new edition, New York, 1969); *Religion and Art in Ashanti* (Oxford, 1927, 1969; new edition, Oxford, 1979); *Ashanti Law and Constitution* (Oxford, 1929); and *Tribes of the Ashanti Hinterland*, 2 vols. (Oxford, 1932). Captain Rattray was a soldier and imperial civil servant, born of Scottish parents in British India. As a district commissioner on the Gold Coast, he became fluent in several Akan dialects and made a deep study of Asante and Fante languages and cultures, with humanity, understanding, and respect.

9. Gyekye, "African Ethics," reports the results of many Akan studies.

10. Thomas Thompson, *An Account of Two Missionary Voyages* (London, 1758; reprint, 1937), 70. A transliteration of this prayer into current Akan usage, with commentary and discussion, appears in Konadu, *The Akan Diaspora in the Americas*, 68; a helpful discussion of this prayer appears in Ackah, *Akan Ethics*. It is based on the author's doctoral dissertation at the University of London, "An Ethical Study of the Akan Tribes of Ghana" (diss., 1959); Rattray, *Ashanti*; Rattray, *Religion and Art in Ashanti*.

11. Gyekye, "African Ethics," paragraph 20. For ethical ideas in Akan proverbs, see Ackah, *Akan Ethics*, 49–60. Ackah draws on Reverend J. G. Cristaller, *Twi Mmebusem Mpensa Ahiansa Mmoano* (Basel, 1879), a gathering of 3,600 Asante and Fante proverbs. See also J. B. Danquah, *The Akan Doctrine of God* (Oxford, 1941; reprint, London, 1944); and Rattray, *Ashanti Proverbs*.

12. For the descent of names among Akan slaves and their children and grandchildren who were chosen Negro governors in New England colonies, see William D. Piersen, "Afro-American Culture in Eighteenth Century New England: A Comparative Examination" (diss., Indiana University, 1975), 31.

13. *Times* (London), August 2, 1811.

14. Quotation from Letitia Brown, in Thomas, *Rise to Be a People*, xi.

15. Rosalind Cob Wiggins, ed., *Captain Paul Cuffe's Logs and Letters, 1808–1817* (Washington, D.C.: Howard University Press, 1996), 45–70, with an excellent introduction by Rhett S. Jones, 1–43. The legend of "Bad Cuff" as a colonizationist who supported slavery is a total miscomprehension of the man and his life. For a correction, see Thomas, *Rise to Be a People*, xi.

16. The family website is accessible at https://PaulCuffe.org.

17. David Hackett Fischer, *Champlain's Dream* (New York and Toronto: Simon & Schuster, 2008), 465–511.

18. *Historical Statistics of the United States* (1976), series Z1-19. A later edition, stronger in economics but weak in demography and history, is available as *Historical Statistics of the United States, on CD-ROM* (Cambridge, 1996). This very useful reference work needs to be redone to a higher standard. Still fundamental is Evarts B. Greene and Virginia D. Harrington, eds., *American Population Before the Federal Census of 1790* (New York and Baltimore, 1932 and 1981). Helpful estimates are in Wesley Frank Craven, *White, Red, and Black* (Charlottesville: University Press of Virginia, 1971; New York: Norton, 1977) and Edmund S. Morgan, *American Slavery, American Freedom: The Ordeal of Colonial Virginia* (New York: Norton, 1975).

19. Paul J. Lindholdt, ed., *John Josselyn, Colonial Traveller: A Critical Edition of Two Voyages to New-England* (1672–74; Hanover, 1988), 12, 24, 175; Wendy Anne Warren, "'The Cause of Her Grief': The Rape of a Slave in Early New England," *Journal of American History* 93 (2007): 1031–49.

20. For changing interpretations, see Mellen Chamberlain, *A Documentary History of Chelsea, Including the Boston Precincts* (Massachusetts Historical Society, 1908), 17–19; "Maverick," in *The New England Historical and Genealogical Register* 69 (1915): 146–59; Charles Francis Adams, *Three Episodes of Massachusetts History*, 1: 328–35 (New York, 1892). For a running record of trouble between Maverick and the Puritan leaders, see Winthrop, *Journal*, 225, 377, 625, 679. Cf. Wendy Warren, *New England Bound* (New York, 2016), 7, 66, 81.

21. Lindholdt, ed., *John Josselyn, Colonial Traveller*, 142. This Cape Porpoise is near Kennebunkport in Maine.

22. Samuel Cranston to the Board of Trade, 1708, in Elizabeth Donnan, ed., *Documents Illustrative of the History of the Slave Trade to America*, 4 vols. (Washington, D.C.: Carnegie Institution, 1930–35; reprint, New York, 1965), 3:109. Cranston added, "We have never had any vessels from the coast of Africa to this colony, nor any trade there," except for one voyage in 1696. This was the brigantine *Seaflower*, which landed forty-seven Africans on Rhode Island (1696). All but fourteen were sent by road to Boston—an African slave coffle marching across the New England countryside.

23. Quoted in William D. Piersen, *Black Yankees: The Development of an Afro-American Subculture in Eighteenth-Century New England* (Amherst: University of Massachusetts Press, 1988), 3–4; citing *Public Records of the Colony of Connecticut*, 15 vols. (Hartford, 1859), 3: 298; Donnan, ed., *Documents Illustrative of the History of the Slave Trade to America*, 2:106.

24. Leete to Board of Trade, 1709, *Calendar of State Papers Colonial, 1708–09*, 209.

25. Bradstreet to Committee of Trade and Plantations, May 18, 1680. Randolph in 1680, while generally concurring, also noted "some voyages from Guinea." Calendar of State Papers, in Donnan, ed., *Documents Illustrative of the History of the Slave Trade to America*, 3:14. For another view, see Gregory E. O'Malley, "Beyond the Middle Passage: Slave Migration from the Caribbean to North America, 1619–1807," *William and Mary Quarterly*, 3rd series, 66 (2009): 163.

26. In Donnan's sample of New England advertisements, every slave arriving before 1714 with a known place of origin came from Barbados or Jamaica. During the period from 1726 to 1740, the West Indies still predominated, but African immigrants began to appear. In the period from 1743 to 1762, all slaves with an identifiable place of origin came from Africa. Altogether, Lorenzo Greene found 125 slave advertisements in New England newspapers during the eighteenth century; 80 did not mention origins, 26 identified Africa, and 19 referred to the West Indies. Lorenzo Greene, *The Negro in Colonial New England* (New York: Columbia University Press, 1942; reprint, 1968), 34–35.

27. *Boston News-Letter*, Nov. 10, 1712; Aug. 3, 1713; Sept. 13, 1714; Nov. 17 and 24, 1726; July 19, 1739; Oct. 7, 1740; Boston *Gazette*, Nov. 4, 1762. Many New England slave advertisements are collected in Donnan, ed., *Documents Illustrative of the History of the Slave Trade to America*, 3: 4–108, and in Greene, *Negro in Colonial New England*, 33–43.

28. The Trans-Atlantic Slave Trade Database is very helpful for New England voyages from 1681 to 1765, and for a revival of Rhode Island voyages ca. 1801–02 (voyages 36750 and 36751). Also useful is Piersen, *Black Yankees*, 179n. Piersen examined the Report of Boston's Overseers of the Poor, "Persons Warned Out of Boston, 1745–1792," in which 78 percent of Blacks warned out of Boston had been born in Africa. Donnan also adds many helpful details.

29. Vincent Caretta, *Phillis Wheatley: Biography of a Genius in Bondage* (Athens, Ga., 2011), 9, 151–52, 204, 225–26.

30. Esther B. Carpenter, *South County Studies* (1888; new edition, Boston, 1924); Piersen, *Black Yankees*, 11, 107.

31. Piersen, *Black Yankees*, 103.

32. For Angola, see Warren, *New England Bound*, 137–41; for Congo, see George Quintal Jr., *Patriots of Color: African Americans and Native Americans at Battle Road and Bunker Hill* (Gardiner, Me., and Lincoln, Mass., 2002), 17, and Antonio T. Bly, *Escaping Bondage: A Documentary History of Runaway Slaves in Eighteenth-Century New England, 1700–1789* (Lanham, Md., 2012), "Congo Scopio." For a broad study of African names in early American colonial records, see Linda M. Heywood and John K. Thornton, *Central Africans, Atlantic Creoles, and the Foundation of the Americas, 1585–1660* (Cambridge, 2007), 333–59, with New England names on 358–59.

33. *Boston News-Letter*, June 19–26, 1704. A helpful gathering of primary materials is Bly, *Escaping Bondage*, 21. Other studies confirm this pattern; see Greene, *Negro in Colonial New England*, 15–49, and Piersen, *Black Yankees*, 6–7. This excellent work, based on Piersen's dissertation at Indiana University, is still held in high respect by scholars. Piersen was trained in two disciplines of folklore and history, and brought them together with great success.

34. Donnan, ed., *Documents Illustrative of the History of the Slave Trade to America*, 3:118–310. My set is the reprint edition, which I have cherished for many years. This monument of scholarship should now be used in conjunction with the online Trans-Atlantic Slave Trade Database. It still retains its value for an abundance of related documents and primary materials. The third volume includes many primary sources on the New England trade.

35. David Eltis and David Richardson, *Atlas of the Transatlantic Slave Trade* (New Haven and London: Yale University Press, 2010), map 143, p. 215. For estimated flows from the largest regional ports of Anomabu (466,000), Cape Coast Castle (318,000), and Elmina (255,000), see pp. 118, 116, and 123.

36. Historians who are most familiar with the primary evidence for New England generally agree. See Piersen, *Black Yankees*, 6–7. Greene, *Negro in Colonial New England*, 34–36, concluded from sale notices that "the source of these slaves cannot be definitely stated," but he observed that "Gold Coast Negroes, because of their vigor and intelligence, were considered of highest quality in New England." Other historians, in the twenty-first century, have argued that origins of New England slaves spanned the full range of Africa's Atlantic slave coast, which is true. But major patterns of concentration existed within that broad range.

37. The leading study, very helpful on the slave trade between the Caribbean and North

America, is O'Malley, *Final Passages*, 202–4, and "Beyond the Middle Passage," 157–65. For African regions of origin in the Caribbean trade, see the Trans-Atlantic Slave Trade Database. For summary patterns with estimates of undercounts, see Eltis and Richardson, *Atlas of the Transatlantic Slave Trade*, 215.

38. At the time of this writing, a major study was under way by Courtnay Micots, and may now be completed. For her prospectus, see "Art and Architecture of Anomabo, Ghana: A Case Study in Cultural Flow," issued by the Center for African Studies Graduate Research in 2012.

39. *Anomabu* is the present spelling of choice in Ghana. In the twentieth century it was often *Anomabo*, in the nineteenth *Annamaboe*, and in the eighteenth *Anamaboo* in English sources. For a helpful introduction, see William St. Clair, *The Grand Slave Emporium: Cape Coast Castle and the British Slave Trade* (London, 2006), 183–201.

40. For a new social history of Anomabu in the slave trade, see Randy J. Sparks, *Where the Negroes Are Masters: An African Port in the Era of the Slave Trade* (Cambridge, 2014). Very helpful on social institutions is Rebecca Shumway, *The Fante and the Transatlantic Slave Trade* (Rochester, N.Y., 2011), chapters 1–2, with a survey of learned literature.

41. Eltis and Richardson, *Atlas of the Transatlantic Slave Trade*, 118. By comparison they estimate the flow from Elmina at 255,000 from 1650 to 1814, of which 80 percent went to South America and nearly all the rest to the Caribbean. And of 318,000 who came from Cape Coast Castle, 73 percent went to the West Indies, and the rest to South America. Only 2,800 men went to the northern U.S. See Eltis and Richardson, *Atlas of the Transatlantic Slave Trade*, 116–23.

42. Sparks, *Where the Negroes Are Masters*, 211–39.

43. Eltis and Richardson, *Atlas of the Transatlantic Slave Trade*, 118–19.

44. Still very useful for depth of detail are data in an older work of very high quality, Elizabeth Donnan's documentary records of New England slave trading voyages on the African coast. Ports of call were mentioned with the following frequency:

Coastal Region	Place	Frequency
Senegambia	Gambia River	1
Upper Guinea	Îsle de Los	2
Sierra Leone	Sierra Leone	4
Grain Coast	Bonana Island	1
	Cape Mount	10
Ivory Coast	Lahou	4
	Grand Bissam	1
Gold Coast	Kommenda	2
	Elmina	3
	Cape Coast	6
	Moree	1
	Anamabu [*sic*]	55
	Koromantine	2

	Gold Coast	3
	Anashan	1
Benin	Popo	1
	Lagos	2
Other	Agar	1
	Isle May	1
	Tantumquery	1
	St. Jago	2
	Quitter	1
	Limpo	1
	Grand Curra	1
	Bance Island	2

Compiled from Donnan, ed., *Documents Illustrative of the History of the Slave Trade to America*, 3: 4–404.

45. *Boston News-Letter*, Oct. 26, 1758, June 5, 1760, 185.
46. Donnan, ed., *Documents Illustrative of the History of the Slave Trade to America*, 3:186.
47. Newport *Mercury*, Sept. 16, Nov. 18, 1765; Donnan, ed., *Documents Illustrative of the History of the Slave Trade to America*, 3: 213.
48. St. Clair, *The Grand Slave Emporium*, chapter on Anomabu, 181–99; Albert van Dantzig, *Forts and Castles of Ghana* (Accra, 1980), 1–23, 53–54; A. D. C. Hyland, "The Castles of Elmina and Cape Coast, and Their Influence on the Architectural Development of the Two Towns," in Kwame Arhin, ed., *The Cape Coast and Elmina Handbook* (University of Ghana at Legon, 1995), 13–28; and on Anomabu, Sparks, *Where the Negroes Are Masters*, 7–34.
49. Thomas Thompson, *An Account of Two Missionary Voyages*, 1758, reprinted by the Society for Promoting Christian Knowledge (London, 1937), 47–48. Thompson was in Anomabu from 1752 to 1756. For a helpful discussion of Anomabu, see Rebecca Shumway, *The Fante and the Transatlantic Slave Trade* (Rochester, 2011), 76–77.
50. Randy J. Sparks, *Two Princes of Calabar: An Eighteenth-Century Atlantic Odyssey* (Cambridge, 2004); Sparks, *Where the Negroes Are Masters*, 35–52.
51. The career of Captain Wanton can be followed in Donnan, ed., *Documents Illustrative of the History of the Slave Trade to America*, 3: 130, 174, 183, 184, 186n, 206, 210–11, 216, 241, 253, 286, 309; J. R. Bartlett, *History of the Wanton Family of Newport. R. I.* (1878), ms. in the John Carter Brown Library.
52. James A. Rawley, *Transatlantic Slave Trade: A History*, 362.
53. For primary materials on the international slave trade from Anomabu and other ports, see Robin Law, ed., *The English in West Africa: The Local Correspondence of the Royal African Company of England, 1681–1699*, 3 vols. (Oxford, 1997–2007), a major work.
54. Venture Smith, *A Narrative of the Life and Adventures of Venture, a Native of Africa: But Resident Above Sixty Years in the United States of America* (New London, 1798; reprint, Middletown, Conn., 1897). It is available in Arna Bontemps, ed., *Five Black Lives*

(Middletown, 1971), 1–34. Scholars have not been able to identify Dukandarra or Duncanderra (in the Yale text) in modern Ghana. Venture Smith tells us that his home at Dukandarra was near a river that flowed west, that it was two days from "a great desert," and that slavers carried him more than four hundred miles to Anomabu. These three clues do not go easily together, and they deepen the mystery. The most careful study is Paul E. Lovejoy, "The African Background of Venture Smith," in James Brewer Stewart, ed., *Venture Smith and the Business of Slavery and Freedom* (Amherst and Boston, 2010), 35–55. Lovejoy rules out Denkyira, a small Akan-speaking Fante state near the coast of Ghana not far from Anomabu, because the distances and timing are wrong and the names at Dukandarra were not Akan. Lovejoy thinks that Venture Smith came to Anomabu from the east, in the interior of Accra or as far east as Togo or Benin. Kwasi Konadu offers another suggestion, that Dukandarra might have been Dubreka, a pretty town with spectacular waterfalls near Conakry in Guinea, very near the Atlantic coast. Kwasi Konadu, *Transatlantic Africa, 1440–1888* (Oxford, 2015), 17.

55. Smith, *A Narrative of the Life and Adventures of Venture.* An eighteenth-century first edition of Venture Smith's narrative is reproduced in Stewart, ed., *Venture Smith and the Business of Slavery and Freedom*, 1–32, with much useful commentary. Stewart's collection of essays adds much information and analysis. Especially helpful in this context is Paul E. Lovejoy's excellent essay "The African Background of Venture Smith," 35–55.

56. They were variously called Coromantsin, Cormantyn, Cormantin. See E. Kofi Agorsah and Thomas Butler, "Archeological Investigation of Historic Kormantse, Ghana: Cultural Identities," *African Diaspora Network Newsletter* (September 2008): 1–22.

57. Adams B. Bodomo, "On Language and Development in Africa: The Case of Ghana," *Nordic Journal of African Studies* 5 (1996): 31–53, http://www.ghanaweb.com/Ghana HomePage/tyribes/languages.php.

58. Florence Abena Doilphyene, *The Akan (Two Fante) Language: Its Sound Systems and Tonal Structure* (Accra: Ghana Universities Press, 1988), xi–xii, with excellent language maps of these fascinating tonal languages that are spoken in central and coastal Ghana, western Togo, and the eastern parts of Côte d'Ivoire. Linguists sometimes call Akan languages Twi (pronounced "chwee"), a word that Fante speakers particularly dislike.

59. *Seasonable Observations on the Trade to Africa in a Letter to a Member of Parliament* (London, 1748), 7; Darold Wax, "Preferences for Slaves in Colonial America," *Journal of Negro History* 58 (1973): 392.

60. Orlando Patterson, *The Sociology of Slavery: An Analysis of the Origins, Development, and Structure of Negro Slave Society in Jamaica* (Rutherford, N.J., 1969), 138.

61. Patterson, *The Sociology of Slavery*, 138.

62. William Snelgrave, *A New Account of Some Parts of Guinea, and the Slave Trade* (London, 1734), 170.

63. John Atkins, *A Voyage to Guinea, Brazil and the West Indies; In His Majesty's Ships the Swallow and Weymouth* (London, 1735), 179; Wax, "Preferences for Slaves in Colonial America," 392.

64. *The ARGUMENT touching Security necessary to be given for carrying on the AFRICAN TRADE* (n.p., n.d., London, 1711?), 35; Snelgrave, *A New Account of Some Parts of Guinea*, 170; Atkins, *A Voyage to Guinea, Brasil, and the West Indies*, 179; all from Wax, "Preferences for Slaves in Colonial America," 371–401, 392.

65. Kwame A. Labi, "Fante Asafo Flags of Abandze and Kormantze: A Discourse Between Rivals," *African Arts* 35 (2002), 65.

66. For a lively introduction, see Robert B. Edgerton, *The Fall of the Asante Empire: The Hundred-Year War for Africa's Gold Coast* (New York, 1995). Four great works by Rattray: *Ashanti Proverbs, Ashanti, Religion and Art in Ashanti,* and *Ashanti Law and Constitution.* A major work of historical scholarship is Ivor Wilks, *Asante in the Nineteenth Century: The Structure and Evolution of a Political Order* (Cambridge, 1975), and Ivor Wilks, "On Mentally Mapping Greater Asante: A Study of Time and Motion," *Journal of African History* 33 (1992): 175–90.

67. *Calendar of State Papers: Colonial Series, America and West Indies,* ed. W. Noel Sainsbury, 42 vols. (London, 1860–1953), 20:721.

68. John K. Thornton, "War, the State, and Religious Norms in 'Coromantee' Thought: The Ideology of an African American Nation," in Robert Blair St. George, ed., *Possible Pasts* (Ithaca, 2000), 181–200; Edward Long, *History of Jamaica,* 3 vols. (London, 1774; reprint, 1970), 470–75.

69. Daniel C. Littlefield, *Rice and Slaves: Ethnicity and the Slave Trade in Colonial South Carolina* (Urbana: University of Illinois Press, 1989, 1991), 13.

70. Konadu, *The Akan Diaspora in the Americas,* 130.

71. "Black Kings and Governors," in Pierson, *Black Yankees,* 117–28; citing "Black Rulers of New England by Location," in Piersen, *Black Yankees,* appendix, table 9. For Connecticut, Katherine J. Harris, "In Remembrance of Their Kings of Guinea: The Black Governors and the Negro Election, 1749 to 1800" and Katherine J. Harris, "The Black Governors, 1780–1856," in Elizabeth J. Normen et al., *African American Connecticut Explored* (Middletown, Conn.: Wesleyan University Press, 2013), 35–47, 69–79. For the New Haven Colony, Orville H. Platt, "The Negro Governors," *Papers of the New Haven Colony Historical Society* (New Haven, 1900), 6:332–34, 550, and Greene, *Negro in Colonial New England,* 242–56.

72. Quintal, *Patriots of Color,* 17–18, 236–54.

73. William Piersen concluded from his historical anthropology of "Black Yankees" that "the continued use in New England of Gold Coast day names . . . reinforces the probability of important ties to Fanti-Asante cultures of West Africa." Piersen, *Black Yankees,* 7, 129.

74. Data from primary materials in Donnan, ed., *Documents Illustrative of the History of the Slave Trade to America,* are still very helpful for their granular detail; as well as data from the Trans-Atlantic Slave Trade Database. Thanks to Martha Cronin for her help with the data.

75. Richard Baxter, *Baxter's Directions to Slave-holders* (London, 1673; and reprinted many times in England and America).

76. Susan F. Fischer, "The Providence Adventure" (senior thesis, Princeton University, 1983); Karen Ordahl Kupperman, *Providence Island, 1630–1641: The Other Puritan Colony* (Cambridge, 1993, 1995), 46–120, 163, 172, 244; A. P. Newton, *The Colonising Activities of the English Puritans* (New Haven, 1914), 129, 149.

77. Thomas Gorges to Sir Ferdinando Gorges, May 19, 1642, in Robert Moody, ed., *The Letters of Thomas Gorges, Deputy Governor of the Province of Maine, 1640–1643* (Portland, 1978), 94.

78. Bartlett, *Colonial Records of Rhode Island*, 1: 243; an excellent discussion is Christy Mikel Clark-Pujara, "Slavery, Emancipation, and Black Freedom in Rhode Island, 1652–1842" (dissertation, University of Iowa, 2009), 18–60, online. This is an excellent history of slavery in Rhode Island.

79. Samuel Sewall, *The Selling of Joseph* (Boston, 1700). Sewall distributed it widely, but only one copy is known to survive, at the Massachusetts Historical Society. It is often reprinted, for example in Milton Halsey Thomas, ed., *The Diary of Samuel Sewall*, 2 vols. (New York, 1973), 1117–21. For Sewall's decision to write it, see Thomas, ed., *The Diary of Samuel Sewall*, 1: 432–33. For analysis, see Lawrence Towner, "The Sewall-Saffin Dialogue on Slavery," *William and Mary Quarterly*, 3rd series, 21 (1964): 40–52, and Mark A. Peterson, "The Selling of Joseph: Bostonians, Antislavery, and the Protestant International, 1689–1733," *Massachusetts Historical Review* 4 (2002): 1–22.

80. Sewall, *The Selling of Joseph*, paragraph 2.

81. *Boston Records* (1701), 11: 5, 16:200. Their instructions clearly show that Sewall was not alone in his opposition to slavery and the slave trade. See Greene, *Negro in Colonial New England*, 51, and A. Leon Higginbotham Jr., *In the Matter of Color: Race and the American Legal Process: The Colonial Period* (New York, 1978), 82–83.

82. John Saffin, *A Brief and Candid Answer to a Late Printed Sheet, Entitled, "The Selling of Joseph"* (Boston, 1701). The poem appears in the pamphlet but is often omitted in reprints. For discussion, see Albert J. Von Frank, "John Saffin: Slavery and Racism in Colonial Massachusetts," *Early American Literature* 29 (1994): 254–72. For Saffin's other writings, see Caroline Hazard, ed., *John Saffin His Book (1665–1708)* (New York, 1928), 158–60.

83. The primary evidence is collected and reviewed in Greene, *Negro in Colonial New England*, 296–97.

84. William Ames, *De Conscientia, et eius jure vel casibus* (London, 1643), Book 4, 160. The Brandeis University Library holds an excellent collection of English Puritan writings, purchased with university funds by the author and Ray Ginger from the estate of Perry Miller.

85. John Cotton and William Aspinall, *An Abstract of Laws and Government. Wherein as in a Mirrour may be seen the wisdom and perfection of the Government of Christ's Kingdom* (London, 1655), chapter 8, section 22; Exodus 21:16; Deuteronomy 24:7; Isabel Mac-Beath Calder, *The New Haven Colony* (New Haven, 1934), 106–29.

86. The *Body of Liberties* was printed at Cambridge in 1642, and survives in an English broadside, *The Capitall Lawes of New-England . . . 1641, 1642* (London, 1643), in the British Library. The statute on "Bond-slavery" appeared again in *The Book of the General Lawes and Libertyes concerning the Inhabitants of the Massachusets . . . 1647* (Cambridge, 1648), and is reprinted by Max Farrand from a copy in the Huntington Library (Cambridge, Harvard, 1929).

87. Nathaniel Shurtleff, ed., *Records of the Governor and Company of the Massachusetts Bay in New England*, 6 vols. (Boston: W. White, 1853), 2:129, 168.

88. Higginbotham, *In the Matter of Color*, 70.

89. "In re Southwicke," 1659, in Higginbotham, *In the Matter of Color*, 66–68.

90. Cotton Mather, *The Negro Christianized* (Boston, 1706); Kenneth Silverman, *The Life and Times of Cotton Mather* (New York 1984), 263–64, 281, 369; Daniel K. Richter,

"'It Is God Who Has Caused Them to Be Servants': Cotton Mather and Afro-American Slavery in New England," *Bulletin of the Congregational Library* 30 (1979): 3–13.

91. John Ballantine, Journal, 1737–1774, transcript by Joseph D. Bartlett, 1886, Westfield Athenaeum; Joseph Carvalho III, *Black Families in Hampden County, Massachusetts, 1650–1855* (Boston and Springfield, 1984), 13, 101, 160. This excellent and very rare collection of materials was sponsored by the Institute for Massachusetts Studies at Westfield State College, and the New England Historic Genealogical Society.

92. Kenneth P. Minkema, "Jonathan Edwards's Defense of Slavery," *Massachusetts Historical Review* 4 (2002): 23–59, at 40, 56.

93. Minkema, "Jonathan Edwards's Defense of Slavery," 56; Kenneth P. Minkema, "Jonathan Edwards on Slavery and the Slave Trade," *William and Mary Quarterly*, 3rd series, 54 (1997): 823–34.

94. *Connecticut Archives: Crimes and Misdemeanors*, 4: 67; Samuel Peters, *A General History of Connecticut* (London, 1781), 83–88.

95. The Case of Re Marja (1681), Massachusetts Bay Court of Assistants, 1 (1681), 198–99; Joshua Coffin, *Slave Insurrections* (New York, 1860), 15; Higginbotham, *In the Matter of Color*, 75, 82.

96. Carvalho, *Black Families in Hampden County, Massachusetts*, 12–13, 142–62; Stephen Innes, *Labor in a New Land: Economy and Society in Seventeenth-Century Springfield* (Princeton: Princeton University Press, 1983), 90–92.

97. Ann Y. Smith, "Fortune's Story," in Normen et al., *African American Connecticut Explored*, 22–25, 370, 384, with commentary, p. 12n16, on enthesopathies.

98. Greene and Harrington, eds., *American Population Before the Federal Census of 1790*, 8–87.

99. Greene and Harrington, *American Population Before the Federal Census of 1790*, 8–87. The best and most careful and most detailed survey is still Greene, *Negro in Colonial New England*, 72–99. See also James Oliver Horton and Lois E. Horton, *Black Bostonians* (New York, 1979), 1–25.

100. Joanne Pope Melish, *Disowning Slavery: Gradual Emancipation and "Race" in New England* (Ithaca, 2000), 47, 22–23; Joshua Hempstead, *Diary of Joshua Hempstead, 1711–1758* (New London, 1901).

101. Providence Town Council Records, 7:324–25, Feb. 4, 1799; Melish, *Disowning Slavery*, 47.

102. Robert P. Forbes, David Richardson, and Chandler B. Saint, "Trust and Violence in Atlantic History: The Economic Worlds of Venture Smith," and Cameron B. Blevins, "Owned by Negro Venture: Land and Liberty in the Life of Venture Smith," in Stewart, ed., *Venture Smith and the Business of Slavery and Freedom*, 56–82, 129–62, an excellent contribution.

103. Carvalho, *Black Families in Hampden County, Massachusetts*, 14.

104. Carvalho cites "Wallaces of Monson, Fletchers in West Springfield, Fullers in Holyoke, Brewsters and Platts in Blandford, Powers of Ludlow, Newberrys of Westfield, Mason, Sands and Williams in Springfield." *Black Families in Hampden County, Massachusetts*, 16.

105. Daniel Cruson, *The Slaves of Central Fairfield County* (Charleston, 2007), 61–65; Robert Farris Thompson, *The Flash of the Spirit: African and Afro-American Art* (New York,

1983), 108; Andrew Agha and Nicole Isenberger, "Recently Discovered Marked Colonoware from Dean Hall Plantation, Berkeley County, South Carolina," in Charles R. Ewen, ed., "Crosses to Bear: Crossmarks as African Symbols in Southern Pottery," a forum in *Historical Archaeology* 45 (2011); June Swann, "Shoes Concealed in Buildings," *Northampton Museum and Art Gallery Journal* 6 (1969): 8; Andrew Mackay, *Northampton Museum's Concealed Shoe Index* (Northampton, 1991); Wayland Historical Society, *Shoes in the Wall: A Caution for Owners of Old Houses* (Wayland, Mass., 2011).

106. Martin Smith, "Old Slave Days in Connecticut," *Connecticut Magazine* 10 (1906): 136–37, 330–31.

107. Piersen, *Black Yankees*, 75, 203; Henry David Thoreau, Journal, X (1859) in *Writings of Henry David Thoreau*, ed. Bradford Torrey (Boston, 1906; reprint, 1962), 12:284–85; Alfred Burdon Ellis, *The Tshi-Speaking Peoples of the Gold Coast of West Africa* (London, 1887), 15–16; Mary Kingsley, *West African Studies* (New York, 1899), 200. For Casey Whitney in Concord, see Sidney Kaplan and Emma Nogrady Kaplan, *The Black Presence in the Era of the American Revolution*, revised edition (Amherst, 1989), 263–64; Robert Gross, *The Minutemen and Their World* (New York, 1976), 96–98, 186.

108. Melish, *Disowning Slavery*, 48; Cotton Mather, *Rules for the Society of Negroes*, 1693, broadside, American Antiquarian Society.

109. Mary Beth Norton, "My Resting Reaping Times," *Signs* 2 (1976): 515–29; Mary Beth Norton, *Liberty's Daughters* (Boston, 1980), 130–31.

110. Randy J. Sparks confirms the Anomabu connection in *Where the Negroes Are Masters*, 194; John Ferguson, *Memoir of the Life and Character of Rev. Samuel Hopkins, D.D.* (Boston, 1830), 175–78, 182–84; Samuel Hopkins to Philip Quaque, Dec. 10, 1773, in Vincent Caretta and Ty M. Reese, eds., *The Life and Letters of Philip Quaque: The First African Anglican Missionary* (Athens, Ga., and London, 2010), 14–15. Quaque, a major African leader in the mission movement, knew about John Quamino and his family.

111. On Quamino and Duchess, see Richard C. Youngken, *African Americans in Newport* (Newport Historical Society, 2nd edition, 1998), 49–50.

112. A leading source is Ezra Stiles, *Literary Diary* 1: 207, 363–66, 486, 489; 2:16, 376, 378; 3: 327. Other materials appear in John Ferguson, *Memoir of the Life and Character of Rev. Samuel Hopkins* (Boston, 1830), 176–78, and Caretta and Reese, eds., *The Life and Letters of Philip Quaque*, 115.

113. Youngken, *African Americans in Newport*, 49–50. This connection has also been studied in African history by Randy J. Sparks, in his study of Anomabu, *Where the Negroes Are Masters*, 194–95.

114. Greene, *Negro in Colonial New England*, 246.

115. Greene, *Negro in Colonial New England*, 247.

116. Greene, *Negro in Colonial New England*, 248; Alice Morse Earle, *Customs and Fashions in Old New England*, (New York, 1898), 226. The Election Day that Read was unable to attend was an Artillery Election Day, a local holiday in Boston, when the Ancient and Honorable Artillery Company paraded and chose its officers; this event is not to be confused with the State Election Day, discussed below.

117. This story is beautifully told by William Piersen in *Black Yankees*, 117. It has been

abundantly documented by historians of Lynn. See Alonzo Lewis and James R. New-hall, *The History of Lynn* (Boston, 1865), 344; James R. Newhall, *The History of Lynn* (Lynn, 1883), 236; Paul Faler, "Workingmen, Mechanics and Social Change: Lynn, Massachusetts, 1800–1860" (diss., University of Wisconsin, 1971), 258–60; Benjamin Lynde, Diary, May 27, 1741, in *Diaries of Benjamin Lynde and of Benjamin Lynde, Junior* (Boston, 1880), 109.

118. Melish, *Disowning Slavery*, 11, 15, 18, 30–34, 41–42; James MacSparran, *Abstract and Letterbook of Out-Services,* ed. Wilkins Updike (Boston, 1899), 24–27, 33–39.

119. For the Puritan calendar and Election Days, see Nathaniel Shurtleff et al., "Negro Election Day," *Massachusetts Historical Society Proceedings* 13 (1873–75); "Black Kings and Governors," in Piersen, *Black Yankees,* 117–28; Shane White, "'It Was a Proud Day': African-Americans, Festivals, and Parades in the North, 1741–1834," *Journal of American History* 81 (1994): 13–50; Orville H. Platt, "Negro Governors," *Papers of the New Haven Colony Historical Society* 6 (1900); Hubert S. Aimes, "African Institutions in America," *Journal of American Folklore* 18 (1905): 15–32; Joseph P. Reidy, "Negro Election Day and Black Community Life in New England, 1750–1860," *Marxist Perspectives* 1 (1978): 102–17; Melvin Wade, "'Shining in Borrowed Plumage': Affirmation of Community in the Black Coronation Festivals of New England (c. 1750–c. 1850)," *Western Folklore* 40 (1981): 211–31, 211; Greene, *Negro in Colonial New England*; Melish, *Disowning Slavery,* 45–47; and brief but helpful discussions in Sterling Stuckey, *Slave Culture,* 74.

120. Other studies include White, "'It Was a Proud Day'"; Platt, "Negro Governors," 319; Stuckey, *Slave Culture,* 74; Melish, *Disowning Slavery,* 46; and Wade, "'Shining in Borrowed Plumage,'" 212.

121. Piersen, *Black Yankees,* 121, 122.

122. Negro Election Days are known to have occurred in the following New England towns in 1740–1820: Connecticut: Derby, Durham, Farmington, Middletown, New Haven, Norwich, Oxford, Seymour, Wallingford, Waterbury, Wethersfield; Massachusetts: Boston, Bridgewater, Cambridge, Danvers, Durham, Lynn, Salem; Rhode Island: Narragansett, North Kingston, South Kingston, New Hampshire: Portsmouth. Piersen, *Black Yankees,* 117–28.

123. Shurtleff et al., "Negro Election Day," 45.

124. Melish, *Disowning Slavery,* 46; Piersen, *Black Yankees,* 123; Wade, "'Shining in Borrowed Plumage,'" 215; Samuel Eliot Morison, "A Description of Election Day as Observed in Boston," *Colonial Society of Massachusetts Transactions* 18 (1915): 60; Earle, *Customs and Fashions in Old New England,* 225–27.

125. Piersen, *Black Yankees,* table 9. The full list is in his manuscript dissertation, William Dillon Piersen, "Afro-American Culture in Eighteenth Century New England: A Comparative Examination" (diss., Indiana University, 1975), 31; Katherine J. Harris, "In Remembrance of Their Kings of Guinea," in Normen et al., *African American Connecticut Explored,* 35–44, 69–79.

126. Piersen, *Black Yankees,* 131; Samuel Orcutt, *Henry Tomlinson and His Descendants* (New Haven, 1891), 549; Harris, "The Black Governors," 76, 73.

127. Piersen, *Black Yankees,* 134.

128. Piersen, *Black Yankees,* 128–40; Piersen, "Afro-American Culture," 211–301; White,

"'It Was a Proud Day,'" 13–50; Hubert H. S. Aimes, "African Institutions in America," *Journal of American Folklore* 18 (1905), 15–32; Reidy, "Negro Election Day and Black Community Life in New England," 106–10; Wade, "'Shining in Borrowed Plumage,'" 211–31; Harris, "In Remembrance of Their Kings of Guinea"; Harris, "Black Governors, 1780 to 1856," 35–44, 69–79; Orville Platt, "Negro Governors," *Papers of the New Haven Colony Historical Society* 6 (1900), 318–34; Rattray, *Ashanti Law and Constitution.*

129. George Gibbs Channing, *Early Recollections of Newport, Rhode Island* (Newport, 1868), 170; Youngken, *African Americans in Newport*, 49–50.

130. Weeden, *Early Rhode Island*, 224–25.

131. [Mary Webb], *Memoir of Mrs. Chloe Spear, a Native of Africa, Who was Enslaved in Childhood, and died in Boston, January 3, 1815 . . . Aged 65 Years* (Boston, 1832); Piersen, *Black Yankees*, 39, 41, 51, 52, 53, 57, 75, 90–91, 108.

132. Piersen, *Black Yankees*, 75.

133. For a thoughtful and sensitive approach to Chloe Spear's language, see Melish, *Disowning Slavery*, 170 and notes. Piersen, *Black Yankees*, 108.

134. Oliver Cromwell to his daughter Bridget Ireton, Oct. 25, 1646, in Thomas Carlyle, ed., *Oliver Cromwell's Letters and Speeches* (New York, 1846), 1: 71.

135. [Mary Webb], *Memoir of Mrs. Chloe Spear*, 17.

136. George Tolman, *John Jack, the Slave, and Daniel Bliss, the Tory* (Concord, 1902); David Hackett Fischer, ed., *Concord: The Social History of a New England Town, 1750–1850* (Waltham, 1983), 247.

137. H. Brackenbury, *The Ashanti War*, 2 vols. (Edinburgh and London, 1874); B. Burleigh, *Two Campaigns: Madagascar and Ashantee* (London, 1896). An interesting history by a California anthropologist and psychologist is Edgerton, *The Fall of the Asante Empire.*

138. Herbert Aptheker, *American Negro Slave Revolts* (New York, 1943, 1963), 162; New England events are discussed on pp. 165n, 167, 178, 194, 199, 201, 226.

139. Greene, *Negro in Colonial New England*, 154.

140. John Wood Sweet, *Bodies Politic: Navigating Race in the American North, 1730–1840* (Philadelphia, 2006), 148.

141. Carvalho, *Black Families in Hampden County, Massachusetts*, 12, 144, 122, with many extracts from town records and histories.

142. Stephen Innes, *Labor in a New Land*, 91–92, 90.

143. John Adams, Diary, Nov. 5, 1766, *Diary and Autobiography of John Adams*, 4 vols., ed. Lyman Butterfield (Boston, 1961), 1: 321. For commentary and further detail, see Greene, *Negro in Colonial New England*, 293–94, and Higginbotham, *In the Matter of Color*, 84, 416.

144. Caesar Sarter to "Messrs Printers," Newburyport, Mass., Aug. 13, 1774, published in Salem's *Essex Journal and Merrimack Packet*, Aug. 17, 1774; Circular Letter from Peter Bestes, Sambo Freeman, Felix Holbrook, and Chester Joie, "in behalf of our fellow slaves in this province," Broadside, Boston, April 20, 1773; a surviving copy in the New-York Historical Society is addressed "For the Representative of the Town of [Thompson]" with the name of the town handwritten. It was part of a sustained effort to reach every member of the Massachusetts legislature.

145. Abigail Adams to John Adams, Sept. 22, 1774, ms. in Adams Papers, Massachusetts Historical Society, published in Butterfield, ed., *Adams Family Correspondence*, 162, and reproduced in facsimile with an excellent discussion of the petition campaign in Kaplan and Kaplan, *The Black Presence in the Era of the American Revolution*, 11–15.

146. *Massachusetts Spy*, June 21, 1775.

147. George Quintal Jr., *Patriots of Color . . . African Americans and Native Americans at Battle Road and Bunker Hill*, a study commissioned by the National Park Service (Lincoln, Me., and Gardner, Me., 2002), 21.

148. Richard C. Wiggin, *Embattled Farmers: Campaigns and Profiles of Revolutionary Soldiers from Lincoln, Massachusetts, 1775–1783* (Lincoln, Mass., 2013), 521, with individual biographies for most.

149. George Washington, General Orders, Oct. 31, Nov. 12, 1775, *Papers of George Washington, Revolutionary War Series*, ed. W. W. Abbot and Philander D. Chase (Charlottesville: University Press of Virginia, 1987–88), 2: 269, 354.

150. *Papers of George Washington, Revolutionary War Series,* 2: 623.

151. Washington, General Orders, Dec. 30, 1775, *Papers of George Washington, Revolutionary War Series*, 2: 620.

152. Carvalho, *Black Families in Hampden County, Massachusetts*, 14.

153. David Hackett Fischer, *Washington's Crossing* (New York, 2004), and primary material in Philip J. Schwarz, ed., *Slavery at the Home of George Washington* (Mount Vernon, Va., 2001); Fritz B. Hirschfeld, ed., *George Washington and Slavery: A Documentary Portrayal* (Columbia, Mo., 1997). Compare the iconoclastic approach in François Furstenberg, *In the Name of the Father: Washington's Legacy, Slavery, and the Making of a Nation* (New York, 2006).

154. Abner Sanderson, Isaac Gleason, Jonas Dix Jr., and John Clark, selectmen of the town of Waltham, to General William Heath, "respecting Phelix Cuff," Aug. 17, 1780, ms. in the Heath Papers, Massachusetts Historical Society. Three helpful accounts are Charles A. Nelson, *Waltham: Past and Present* (Cambridge, 1882), 105–6; Kenneth Wiggins Porter, "Three Fighters for Freedom," *Journal of Negro History* 28 (1943): 51–52; and Kaplan and Kaplan, *The Black Presence in the Era of the American Revolution*, 248–49, which is mistaken in referring to Cuff and his two friends as "Massachusetts Maroons." Even as they briefly took refuge in the cave on Snake Hill, they were working within the institutions of the town.

155. John D. Cushing, "The Cushing Court and the Abolition of Slavery in Massachusetts: More Notes on the 'Quock Walker Case,'" *American Journal of Legal History* 5 (1961): 118–44.

156. Cushing, "The Cushing Court and the Abolition of Slavery in Massachusetts," 143.

157. Electa F. Jones, *Stockbridge, Past and Present* (Springfield, Mass., 1854), 245; Kaplan and Kaplan, *The Black Presence in the Era of the American Revolution*, 244–28.

158. Kaplan and Kaplan, *The Black Presence in the Era of the American Revolution*, 245.

159. Jones, *Stockbridge, Past and Present*, 193–95, 238–41; Kaplan and Kaplan, *The Black Presence in the Era of the American Revolution*, 244–48.

160. Jane Belknap Marcou, *Life of Jeremy Belknap* (New York, 1847), 164–65; Robert H. Romer, *Slavery in the Connecticut Valley of Massachusetts* (Florence, Mass.: Levellers, 2009), 216.

161. Romer, *Slavery in the Connecticut Valley of Massachusetts*, 215. The same pattern appears in Melish, *Disowning Slavery*, 64–65,76, 95–96.

162. In a large literature, two first-class books are helpful in different ways, but they underestimate the agency of individual slaves and masters in ending slavery during the revolutionary era, and the magnitude of quantitative change. Arthur Zilversmit, *The First Emancipation: The Abolition of Slavery in the North* (Chicago, 1967), also is excellent on the strength of slavery before the Revolution, and the strength of religious and political movements to end it. Melish, *Disowning Slavery*, has many strengths. It centers on racism and "racialization" and makes a major contribution on the history of "race."

163. "An act to secure freedom and rights of citizenship to persons in this state," 1857, in John Codman Hurd, *The Law of Freedom and Bondage in the United States*, 2 vols. (Boston, 1865), 2: 36.

164. The leading study is Harvey A. Whitfield, *The Problem of Slavery in Early Vermont, 1777–1810* (Vermont Historical Society, 2014).

165. Vermont Constitution, July 8, 1777; John H. Waso, "In re Vermont Constitution of 1777," *Vermont Historical Society Proceedings* (1919–20): 244–56.

166. *Vermont Gazette*, Sept. 26, 1791. By some early reports sixteen slaves were found in Vermont by the census of 1790, all in Bennington County; but the *Vermont Gazette* contradicted that report for Bennington in particular. Later the Census Bureau judged on other grounds that the report of sixteen slaves in Vermont was false, and changed it.

167. Prof. Raymond Zirblis, at Norwich University, suggests "a reasonable working estimate" of 55 slaveholders and 150 slaves in Vermont over "several decades." But this would be 56 percent of all African Americans in the entire state in 1790. See Tim Johnson, "Vermont's 1777 Slavery Ban Had a Complicated History," *Burlington Free Press*, April 2, 2014.

168. Whitfield, *The Problem of Slavery in Early Vermont*, xx.

169. Trumbull's "exact census" of 1774 was reported to London on Nov. 23, 1774, and is in British Transcripts CO5, 1285, folios 242–43, Library of Congress. The proportion of free people of color in colonial Connecticut is estimated by Jackson Turner Main at 20 percent in 1774. Jackson Turner Main, *Society and Economy in Colonial Connecticut* (Princeton: Princeton University Press, 1985), 178. By the evidence of other colonies, a range of 5 to 10 percent is likely. The Maryland census of 1755 found that only 4 percent of the non-white population were free; and most were not Black. Ira Berlin, *Slaves Without Masters* (New York, 1974), 3.

170. Main, *Society and Economy in Colonial Connecticut*, 178.

171. U.S. Bureau of the Census, *Heads of Families at the First Census of 1790, Connecticut* (Washington, D.C., 1907–08), 9; U.S. Bureau of the Census, *Negro Population, 1790–1915* (Washington, D.C., 1915).

172. Melish, *Disowning Slavery*, the fullest study of racism and "racialization" in New England, with deep research in primary sources. It works best when read together with evidence of racism as a reactionary movement, and other sources on the strength of movements against race slavery and racism. Also helpful is the work of scholars such as James McPherson on a long century of reform movements that opposed both race slavery and racism, and were strongest in New England.

173. Prince Hall, *A Charge, Delivered to the African Lodge, June 1, 1797* (Boston, 1797).

174. William C. Nell, *The Colored Patriots of the American Revolution* (Boston, 1855; reprint, New York, 1968). On the unit's flag and silver badges, which survive in the Massachusetts Historical Society, see David Hackett Fischer, *Liberty and Freedom* (New York and Oxford University Press, 2005), 85–89.

175. The house is privately owned and in immaculate condition. See Black Heritage Trail, National Park Service, Boston.

176. Lydia Maria Child, in Nell, *The Colored Patriots of the American Revolution*, 24–27. See also Benjamin Quarles, *The Negro in the American Revolution* (Chapel Hill: University of North Carolina Press, 1961), 54–55, 76, and Stephen Kendrick and Paul Kendrick, *Sarah's Long Walk* (Boston, 2004), 28.

177. Carvalho, *Black Families in Hampden County, Massachusetts*, 18.

178. Kaplan and Kaplan, *The Black Presence in the Era of the American Revolution*, 209–11, with many documents.

179. Leonard W. Levy, "The Abolition Riot: Boston's First Slave Rescue," *New England Quarterly* 25 (1952): 85–92; Horton and Horton, *Black Bostonians*, 98.

180. Elise A. Guyette, *Discovering Black Vermont: African American Farmers in Hinesburgh, 1790–1860* (Burlington; University of Vermont Press, 2010), 16–24.

181. Guyette, *Discovering Black Vermont*, 16–24.

182. Guyette, *Discovering Black Vermont*, 27.

183. Guyette, *Discovering Black Vermont*, 43–44.

184. Katherine Harris, "The Rise of Communities," in Normen et al., *African American Connecticut Explored*, 51–59, 81–89, 103–17.

185. Harris, "The Rise of Communities," 55.

186. For measures of concentration as an index of dissimilarity, see Berlin, *Slaves Without Masters*, 257–58. For discussion of Boston, Horton and Horton, *Black Bostonians*, 4–6.

187. Much confusion and error surround the memory of Prince Hall. Two excellent and accurate biographies are Charles Wesley, *Prince Hall: Life and Legacy*, 2nd edition (1977; Washington, D.C., 1983), and David Gray, *Inside Prince Hall* (Lancaster, Va., 2003). Also helpful is Sidney Kaplan and Emma Nogrady Kaplan, "Prince Hall, Organizer," in *The Black Presence in the Era of the American Revolution*, revised edition (Amherst, 1989), 202–14, a superb piece of scholarship, but with errors introduced from William H. Grimshaw, *Three Official Histories of Freemasonry Among the Colored People of North America* (1903). A source of confusion was the presence of as many as five Prince Halls in eighteenth-century Massachusetts. Gray and Wesley are helpful on this problem.

188. Gray, *Inside Prince Hall*, 44; manumission paper, April 9, 1770, Ezekiel Price Notarial Records, Boston Athenaeum, Massachusetts Archives, 157: 376 1/2; 212: 132.

189. William Alan Muraskin, *Middle-Class Blacks in a White Society: Prince Hall Freemasonry in America* (Berkeley, 1976), 31–40.

190. Jeremy Belknap, "Queries Respecting Slavery and Emancipation in Massachusetts . . . ," Massachusetts Historical Society *Collections*, series 1, vol. 4 (1796), 209–10.

191. Horton and Horton, *Black Bostonians*, 219–52.

192. Paul Cuffe, "Memoirs," *Freedom's Journal*, March 16, 1827; Paul Cuffee [*sic*], *Memoirs of Paul Cuffee* (Middletown, Del., 2017), n.p.

193. Cuffe, "Memoirs."

194. [Mary Webb], *Memoir of Mrs. Chloe Spear*, 26; Piersen, *Black Yankees*, 45, 193n.

195. Nell, *The Colored Patriots of the American Revolution*, 35; Piersen, *Black Yankees*, 193.

196. Alice Morse Earle, *Customs and Fashions in Old New England* (New York, 1898), 90; Piersen, *Black Yankees*, 193n.

197. Shipton, *Sibley's Harvard Graduates*, 4:128; Piersen, *Black Yankees*, 44.

198. William J. Brown, *The Life of William J. Brown of Providence, R.I.* (Providence, 1883), 11.

199. Jeremy Belknap, "Correspondence Between Jeremy Belknap and Ebenezer Hazard," Massachusetts Historical Society, *Collections*, series 5, vol. 3 (1787), 12.

200. Cuffe, "Memoirs," which gives the date as 1797.

201. Leon F. Litwack, *North of Slavery: The Negro in the Free States, 1790–1860* (Chicago, 1961), 142.

202. This very large research project is summarized in James M. McPherson, *Ordeal by Fire: Civil War and Reconstruction* (New York: Alfred A. Knopf, 1982; McGraw-Hill, 1992), 47–48. Three other quantitative studies of antislavery leadership yielded similar results. See Lawrence J. Friedman, *Gregarious Saints: Self and Community in American Abolitionism, 1830–1970* (Cambridge, 1982); Edward Magdol, *The Antislavery Rank and File: A Social Profile of the Abolitionists' Constituency* (Westport, Conn., 1986); and John R. McKivigan, "Schism: The Ideological Factors Underlying the Factionalization of the American Antislavery Movement," unpublished paper, 1985.

203. Friedman, *Gregarious Saints*.

204. Henry B. Stanton, *Random Recollections* (New York, 1887), 5.

205. Charles Edward Stowe, *The Life of Harriet Beecher Stowe* (Boston, 1889), 6–7; Piersen, *Black Yankees*, 55; Harriet Beecher Stowe, *Uncle Tom's Cabin* (Boston 1852), preface.

206. Catharine Maria Sedgwick, "Slavery in New England," *Bentley's Miscellany* 24 (1853): 412–24.

207. James M. McPherson, *The Struggle for Equality: Abolitionists and the Negro in the Civil War and Reconstruction* (Princeton: Princeton University Press, 1964); James M. McPherson, *The Abolitionist Legacy: From Reconstruction to the NAACP* (Princeton: Princeton University Press, 1975). Other work continues and expands this large approach: Bruce Laurie, *Beyond Garrison: Antislavery and Social Reform* (Cambridge, 2005).

208. Vincent Carretta, *Phillis Wheatley: Biography of a Genius in Bondage* (Athens, Ga., 2011), 143.

209. Kaplan and Kaplan, *The Black Presence in the Era of the American Revolution*, 171.

210. Carretta, *Phillis Wheatley*, 34–37.

211. Phillis Wheatley, "On the Death of the Rev. Mr. George Whitefield," 1770, in Julian D. Mason Jr., *The Poems of Phillis Wheatley*, 56.

212. Phillis Wheatley, "To the University of Cambridge, in New-England," commonly dated 1767, in Mason, *The Poems of Phillis Wheatley*, 52.

213. Phillis Wheatley, "To the Right Honourable William, Earl of Dartmouth," in Mason, *The Poems of Phillis Wheatley*, 83.

214. Phillis Wheatley, "An Hymn to Humanity," in Mason, *The Poems of Phillis Wheatley*, 95.

215. Johann Friedrich Blumenbach, *De generis humani varietate nativa* [*On the Natural*

Variety of Humanity] (Göttingen, 1776). For further discussion, see David Hackett Fischer, *Fairness and Freedom: A History of Two Open Societies, New Zealand and the United States* (New York and Oxford: Oxford University Press, 2012), 263–95.

216. Thomas Jefferson, *Notes on the State of Virginia*, query XIV.

217. Phillis Wheatley to Washington, [Oct. 26, 1775]; Washington to Lt. Col. Joseph Reed, Feb. 10, 1776; Washington to Phillis Wheatley, Feb. 28, 1776, *Papers of George Washington, Revolutionary War Series*, 2: 242–44; 3: 186–91, 387. At Washington's suggestion, his aide Col. Joseph Reed arranged a double publication of Wheatley's poem and letter. Thomas Paine brought it out as "To His Excellency General Washington: The following LETTER and VERSES were written by the famous Phillis Wheatley, the African Poetess, and presented to his Excellency Gen. Washington," in Paine's *Pennsylvania Magazine* 2:193 (April 1776). It also appeared at about the same time in the Williamsburg *Virginia Gazette*, March 30, 1776, possibly from an early proof of Paine's journal.

218. Capt. John Paul Jones to Hector McNeill. Jones sailed on November 1, 1777. The original manuscript of his note survives in the McNeill Collection at the Pierpont Morgan Library, in New York City, https://www.themorgan.org/literary-historical/125478.

219. Kaplan and Kaplan, *The Black Presence in the American Revolution*, 189.

220. Wheatley, "On Being Brought from Africa to America," 1768, in Mason, *The Poems of Phillis Wheatley*, 53. For a thoughtful discussion, see James A. Levernier, "Wheatley's 'On Being Brought from Africa to America,'" *Explicator* 40 (1981): 25–26.

221. Henry Louis Gates Jr., *The Trials of Phillis Wheatley* (New York, 2003), 76–77.

222. Gates, *The Trials of Phillis Wheatley*, 89–90.

Chapter 2: HUDSON VALLEY

1. Adriaen van der Donck, *Beschrijvinge van Nieuw Nederlant* (Amsterdam, 1655); translated in 1841 and again in 1968 and republished as *A Description of the New Netherlands*, ed. Thomas F. O'Donnell (New York, 1968), 128.

2. Georges Balandier, *Daily Life in the Kingdom of the Kongo: From the Sixteenth to the Eighteenth Century* (New York, 1965, 1968), 137; Joseph van Wing, *Études bakongo, histoire et sociologie* (Brussels, 1919, 1959), 149.

3. Primary accounts of Rodriguez survive among notarial records in Amsterdam's City Archives, and have been transcribed and published by Simon Hart. Most helpful are depositions from seamen and captains who knew him. They include "Declarations of some members of the crew of Adriaen Block and Thijs Volckerertsz Mossel's ships," August 20, 1613; "Declarations of Crew Members of the Ship *Fortuyn*, Master Hendrick Christiaensen," July 23, 1614; "Declaration of Two Members of the Crew of the ship *Nachtegael*," July 23, 1614; "Declarations of Captain Adriaen Block and Crew Members of the ship *Tyger*," July 24, 1614, Notarial Archives 373, 198, Amsterdam City Archives. These texts are transcribed and published in Simon Hart, ed., *The Prehistory of the New Netherland Company: Amsterdam Notarial Records of the First Dutch Voyages of the Hudson* (Amsterdam, 1959), 23–26, 74–75, 83–90; copy in the library of the author.

A secondary study, which publishes other Spanish primary sources, is Antony

Stevens-Acevedo, Tom Weterings, and Leonor Alvarez Francés, *Juan Rodriguez and the Beginnings of New York City*, Research Monographs of the Dominican Studies Institute, City University of New York (New York, 2013), 65ff.

   Other useful accounts include Van Cleaf Bachman, *Peltries or Plantations: The Economic Policies of the Dutch West India Company in New Netherland, 1623–1639* (Baltimore, 1969), 6–11; Oliver A. Rink, *Holland on the Hudson: An Economic and Social History of Dutch New York* (Ithaca, 1986), 34, 42; Peter Bakker, "First African into New Netherland, 1613–14," *De Halve Maen* 68 (1995): 50–53; Graham Russell Hodges, *Root & Branch: African Americans in New York and East Jersey, 1613–1863* (Chapel Hill: University of North Carolina Press, 1999), 2, 6–7; Christopher Morris, "Manhattan's First Merchant," in Ira Berlin and Leslie M. Harris, eds., *Slavery in New York* (New York: New Press, 2005), 34; and Leslie M. Harris, *In the Shadow of Slavery: African Americans in New York City, 1626–1863* (Chicago, 2013), 12–13.

4. Hart, ed., *Prehistory of the New Netherland Company*, 25–33, reproduces the major primary documents, 73–98.

5. His Dutch name variously appears in manuscripts at the Amsterdam City Archives as Hans (or Jan) Jorisz (or Jorisson) Hontom (or Huntum, etc.). For a brief biography, see Hart, ed., *The Prehistory of the New Netherland Company*, 60; for subsequent scholarship, see Janny Venema, *Kiliaen van Rensselaer* (Hilversum, 2010), 248, and Bachman, *Peltries or Plantations*, 132.

6. Primary accounts for Juan Rodriguez include sworn declarations dated August 20, 1613, by Gerbrant Jansz and Jan Claesen, crewmen aboard the ship *Tijger*; Capt. Adriaen Block; Hendrick Ribbelinck (or Rijbelinck), crewman aboard the ship *Nachtegael*; and Capt. Thisj Volckertsz; and "Declarations" by nine crewmen of Capt. Hendrick Christiaensen's ship *Fortuyn*, July 23, 1614, Notarial Records, Amsterdam City Archives, text published in Hart, ed., *The Prehistory of the New Netherland Company*, 74–75, 80–82.

7. Bachman, *Peltries or Plantations*, 7. See also Hart, ed., *The Prehistory of the New Netherland Company*, 23–26. A third Dutch captain who tried to kidnap and enslave Rodriguez was Adriaen Block. His ship *Tijger* burned in January 1614. Her probable remains were found in 1916 by workers building a Manhattan subway line, near the future site of the World Trade Center. At Greenwich and Dey Streets, they found the prow and keel of an old ship that proved to be Dutch and of the same age as the *Tijger*. See Ralph Solecki, "The 'Tiger,' an Early Dutch 17th Century Ship, and an Abortive Salvage Attempt," *Journal of Field Archaeology* 1 (1974): 10–16, and Anne-Marie Cantwell and Diana di Zerega Wall, *Unearthing Gotham: The Archaeology of New York City* (New Haven, 2001), 150–53. For variant and very helpful accounts of these tangled events, see Hart, ed., *The Prehistory of the New Netherland Company*, 22–26; Bachman, *Peltries or Plantations*, 5–11; Hodges, *Root & Branch*, 6–7; Harris, *In the Shadow of Slavery*, 12–13; and Morris, "Manhattan's First Merchant," 34.

8. For Dutch trading groups in the Hudson Valley before the West India Company, see Thomas J. Condon, *New York Beginnings: The Commercial Origins of New Netherland* (New York and London, 1968), 3–35, and for more recent studies, see Charles T. Gehring, "New Netherland: The Formative Years, 1609–1632," in Hans Krabbendam,

Cornelis A. Van Minnen, and Giles Scott Smith, eds., *Four Centuries of Dutch-American Relations* (Albany, 2009), 74–84.

9. Bachman, *Peltries or Plantations*, 7; Morris, "Manhattan's First Merchant," 34.

10. Robert Juet, *Juet's Journal: The Voyage of the Half Moon from 4 April to 7 November 1609*, ed. Robert M. Lunny (Newark, 1959), 28–35; Emanuel van Meteren, "On Hudson's Voyage," 1610, in J. Franklin Jameson, ed., *Narratives of New Netherland, 1609–1664* (New York, 1909, 1967), 6–9.

11. Primary materials on the violent careers of Hans (Jan) Jorisz Hontom and his brother Willem Hontom are published in Hart, ed., *The Prehistory of the New Netherland Company*, 60–61, also 21–22, 26–30, 32, 38, 75, 80–90, and A. J. F. van Laer, ed., *Van Rensselaer Bowier Manuscripts* (Albany, 1908), 302ff. See also Gehring, "New Netherland," 77; Charles T. Gehring and William A. Starna, "Dutch and Indians in the Hudson Valley," *Hudson Valley Regional Review* 9 (September 1992): 15; Bachman, *Peltries or Plantations*, 35–36; and Susanah Shaw Romney, *New Netherland Connections* (Chapel Hill: University of North Carolina Press, 2014), 131–34.

12. For the Indian fury that followed Hontum's atrocities, see Janny Venema, *Kiliaen van Rensselaer (1586–1643)* (Hilversum, Netherlands, 2010), 248, a splendid work of scholarship and a book of surpassing beauty.

13. For graphic accounts of atrocities in these Dutch-Indian wars, which Director Governor Kieft started and was personally involved in, see the fragment Journal of New Netherland, Aug. 3, 1646, Dutch ms, translated by Dr. Johannes de Hullu, at the Royal Library in The Hague, and published in Jameson, ed., *Narratives of New Netherland*, 267–84. Even more horrific is "Breeden Raedt, aen de Vereenighde Nederlandsche Provintien" (Antwerp, 1649), in E. B. O'Callaghan, ed., *The Documentary History of the State of New-York*, 4 vols. (Albany, 1851), 4: 63–68. The cruelest atrocities (among the worst in North American history) were perpetrated against Indians in the Hudson Valley by Dutch leaders and their English mercenaries.

14. Gehring, "New Netherland," 77–79, and Deposition of Catelina Trico, "aged fouer score or thereabouts," Feb. 14, 1684–85, and Deposition of Catelyn Trico, "aged about 83 years . . . in the year 1623 she came into this country," made under oath Oct. 17, 1688, in O'Callaghan, ed., *The Documentary History of the State of New-York*, 3: 31, 32. She may have been on Manhattan as early as 1623, moved to Albany in 1624, and returned to Manhattan and Long Island.

15. At the City University of New York, the excellent Dominican Studies Institute has been instrumental in this effort. Much material appears on its website at https://www.ccny.cuny.edu/dsi.

16. "Procuration of Pierre Du Gua [sieur de Monts] Mathieu De Coste," in Robert le Blant and René Baudry, eds., *Nouveau documents sur Champlain et son époque*, vol. 1, 1560–1622 (Ottawa, 1967), 105–6, 194–95, 203, 212, 235. For the kidnapping and ransom, see W. I. Morse, ed., *Pierre du Gua, Sieur de Monts* (London, 1939), 7, 51; David Hackett Fischer, *Champlain's Dream* (New York and Toronto: Simon & Schuster, 2008), 157, 665n; and Christopher Moore, "Esteban Gomez and Mathieu Da Costa, Founding Fathers," in Berlin and Harris, eds., *Slavery in New York*, 33.

17. For other African mediators in the eighteenth century, see William B. Hart, "Black 'Go-Betweens' and the Mutability of 'Race': Status and Identity on New York's

Pre-Revolutionary Frontier," in Andrew R. L. Cayton et al., *Contact Points: American Frontiers from the Mohawk Valley to the Mississippi, 1750–1830* (Chapel Hill: University of North Carolina Press, 1998), 88–113.

18. Nicolaus Janszoon Wassenaer, *Historisch Verhael* (Amsterdam, 1622), in J. Franklin Jameson, ed., *Narrating New Netherland* (New York, 1909, 1967), 86.

19. J. H. Huizinga, "The Spirit of the Netherlands," in *Dutch Civilisation in the Sevententh Century*, trans. Arno Pomerans (London, 1968), 112.

20. Herbert H. Rowen, *The Princes of Orange: The Stadtholders in the Dutch Republic* (Cambridge, 1988).

21. Charter of the West India Company, 1621, Dutch text and English translation in *Van Rensselaer Bowier Manuscripts . . . and Other Documents*, ed. A. J. F. van Laer (Albany, University of the State of New York, 1908); Oliver A. Rink, *Holland on the Hudson: An Economic and Social History of New York* (Ithaca and Cooperstown, 1986), 32, 50–68; Bachman, *Peltries or Plantations*, 250–43.

22. R. B. Prud'homme van Reine, *Admiraal Zilverflot: Biographie van Piet Hein* (Amsterdam, 2003).

23. In New Amsterdam two thirds of Dutch immigrants came from coastal Holland and one third from inland provinces, with a strong flow of non-Dutch migrants. In Staten Island, Kingston, and Bergen County (New Jersey) those proportions were reversed. Flatbush and Brooklyn had a near parity of coastal and inland emigrants. Emigrants from inland provinces drew heavily from Glederland and Utrecht. Three excellent and useful quantitative studies are Jan Folkerts, "Reflecting Patria: New Light on New Netherland Demography and Culture," *New York History* 91 (2010): 93–110; David Steven Cohen, "How Dutch Were the Dutch of New Netherland?," *New York History* 62 (1981): 43–60; and Oliver A. Rink, *Holland on the Hudson: An Economic and Social History of Dutch New York* (Ithaca, 1986), 139–71. Different methods were used for their calculations. Cohen counted heads of families and solitary migrants, which overstated soldiers and non-Dutch. Rink worked from records of the West India Company, which may have overstated immigrants from Holland. Folkerts, using a broad gathering of sources, found more immigrants from inland provinces of the Netherlands, and is strongest for the last eight years (1656–64).

24. On ethnic diversity in New Netherland, see Cohen, "How Dutch Were the Dutch of New Netherland?," 5–42; J. H. Innes, *New Amsterdam and Its People* (New York, 1902); Joyce D. Goodfriend, *Before the Melting Pot: Society and Culture in Colonial New York City, 1664–1730* (Princeton: Princeton University Press, 1992); and Patricia Bonomi, *A Factious People: Politics and Society in Colonial New York* (New York, 1971).

25. Father Isaac Jogues, "Novum Belgae," 1646, text in Reuben Gold Thwaites, ed., *Jesuit Relations* (Cleveland, 1896–1901), 26:105–15.

26. Christian J. Koot, "The Merchant, the Map, and Empire: Augustine Herrman's Chesapeake and Interim-Imperial Trade, 1644–73," *William and Mary Quarterly*, 3rd series, 57 (2010); Earl L. W. Heck, *Augustine Herrman* (Englewood, Ohio, privately published, 1941), 9–31, and for his service as president or chairman of the "Nine Men" who were the Council of New Netherland from 1647 to 1652, 34–35; Leo Hershkowitz, "The Troublesome Turk: An Illustration of Judicial Process in New Amsterdam," *New York History* 46 (1965): 300–306; Henry B. Hoff, "Frans Abramse Van Salee and

His Descendants: A Colonial Black Family in New York and New Jersey," *The New York Genealogical and Biographical Record* 121 (1990): 65–71.

27. Martha Dickinson Shattuck, "Dutch Jurisprudence in New Netherland and New York," in Hans Krabbendam, Cornelis A. Van Minnen, and Giles Scott-Smith, eds., *Four Centuries of Dutch-American Relations, 1609–2009* (Albany, 2009), 143–53.

28. David William Voorhees, "The Dutch Legacy in America," in Roger Panetta, ed., *Dutch New York: The Roots of Hudson Valley Culture* (Yonkers, 2009), 411–29, 413.

29. The fundamental documents were the Dutch Union of Utrecht (1579), the Company's Artijcul-Brieff (1624–25), and the Freedoms and Exemptions of 1629. See A. J. F. van Laer, *Documents Relating to New Netherland, 1624–1626, in the Henry E. Huntington Library* (San Marino, Calif., 1924), documents A 1–9, D16–18.

30. The English sea captain was quoted by David Pietersz de Vries, whose accounts were similar in "Korte Historiael Ende Journaels Aentecyckeninge" (Short Historical and Journal Notes), published in the Netherlands (Alkamaar, 1655), *Collections of the New-York Historical Society*, 2nd series, 3:1–129; Jameson, ed., *Narratives of New Netherland*, 187.

31. "Ordinance Against Clandestine Trade," May 27, 1638, in A. J. F. Van Laer, ed., *New Netherland Council Minutes, 1638–1649*, 4 vols. (Albany, 1939; reprint, Baltimore, 1974), 4:10–11.

32. Van Laer, *Documents Relating to New Netherland*, 29; Linda M. Heywood and John K. Thornton, *Central Africans, Atlantic Creoles, and the Foundation of the Americas, 1585–1660* (Cambridge, 2007, 2011), 37.

33. Heywood and Thornton, *Central Africans, Atlantic Creoles, and the Foundation of the Americas*, 37.

34. This is by inference from Dutch documents in 1644, which reported that eleven African slaves had been "in New Netherland for 18 or 19 years." Van Laer, ed., *New Netherland Council Minutes*, 1: 212–13, Feb. 25, 1644. See also Robert J. Swan, "First Africans into New Netherland, 1625 or 1626?," *De Halve Maen* 66 (1993): 75–82.

35. Linda M. Heywood and John K. Thornton, "Intercultural Relations Between Europeans and Blacks in New Netherland," in *Four Centuries of Dutch-American Relations*, ed. Hans Krabbendam, Cornelius A. Van Minnen, and Giles Scott Smith (Albany, 2009), 196.

36. Goodfriend, *Before the Melting Pot*, 112–14; Harris, *In the Shadow of Slavery*, 29–30; Thelma Wills Foote, *Black and White Manhattan: The History of Racial Formation in Colonial New York City* (New York and Oxford: Oxford University Press, 2004), 37–38; Romney, *New Netherland Connections*, 14, 200–202, and passim.

37. John Thornton, *A Cultural History of the Atlantic World, 1250–1820* (Cambridge, 2012), 336; Linda Heywood and John Thornton, eds., *Central Africans and Cultural Transformations in the American Diaspora* (Cambridge, 2002), 457, and passim.

38. Heywood and Thornton, *Central Africans, Atlantic Creoles, and the Foundation of the Americas*, 39–43.

39. Johannes de Laet, *Iaerlijk Verhael van de Verrichtinghen de Geoctroyeerde West-Indische Compagnie in derthien Boecken*, ed. S. P. L'Honore Naber, 3 vols. (The Hague: Martinus Nihoff, 1931), 1: appendix, 11–13, a modern reprint of Johannes de Laet, *Historie ofte Iaerlijck verhael van de Verrichtinghen der Geoctroyeerde West Indische Compagnie*

(Leiden, 1644), book 7:192, appendix, 21. Similar patterns appear in Heywood and Thornton, *Central Africans, Atlantic Creoles, and the Foundation of the Americas*, 41, 36, and in the Trans-Atlantic Slave Trade Database.

40. Johannes Menne Postma, *The Dutch in the Atlantic Slave Trade, 1600–1815* (New York, 1990), 82.

41. Samuel S. Purple, ed., *Records of the Reformed Dutch Church in New Amsterdam and New York: Marriages from 11 December 1639 to 26 August 1801* (New York, 1890; reprint, 1997), 10.

42. These data are tabulated in Heywood and Thornton, *Central Africans, Atlantic Creoles, and the Foundation of the Americas*, appendix, 333–59. A different reading of this evidence, without tabulation, appears in Romney, *New Netherland Connections*, 209–12. The data derive from 172 slave names in registers of marriages and baptisms in the Dutch Reformed Church of New Netherland, and also from administrative records, legal documents, petitions, and deeds. In another discussion of their findings, Heywood and Thornton write, "some 70 percent of the slaves and freedmen who married or baptized their children in the church or appeared in court before the late seventeenth century bore this ethnic signifier [van Angola]. This pattern of Angolan numerical predominance only began to change in 1655, when the first large contingent of West Africans arrived in the *Witte Paert*." Heywood and Thornton, "Intercultural Relations Between Europeans and Blacks in New Netherland," 193–94. Similar results appear in primary evidence summarized by Edna Greene Medford, ed., *The New York African Burial Ground History, Final Report* (prepared by Howard University for the United States General Services Administration, Washington, D.C., 2004), 35, 40.

43. Heywood and Thornton, *Central Africans, Atlantic Creoles, and the Foundation of the Americas*, 277–79, and passim.

44. Joseph C. Miller, "Central Africa During the Era of the Slave Trade, ca. 1490–1850s," in Linda M. Heywood, ed., *Central Africans and Cultural Transformations in the American Diaspora* (Cambridge, 2002), 28.

45. Phyllis Martin, *The External Trade of the Loango Coast* (Oxford, 1972).

46. Anne Hilton, *The Kingdom of Kongo* (Oxford, 1985); John Thornton, "The Kingdom of Kongo, ca. 1390–1678: The Development of an African Social Formation," *Cahiers d'études africaines* 22 (1982): 325–42.

47. Heywood and Thornton, *Central Africans, Atlantic Creoles, and the Foundation of the Americas*, 52–57; Joseph C. Miller, *Way of Death: Merchant Capitalism and the Angolan Slave Trade, 1730–1830* (Madison, 1988), 33.

48. Four leading scholars broadly agree on similarities of language in West Central Africa: John Thornton, *Africa and Africans in the Making of the Atlantic World, 1400–1800*, 2nd edition (Cambridge, 1992, 1998), 190–91; on Central Africa as a "linguistically and culturally homogenous region," Heywood, ed., *Central African and Cultural Transformations in the American Diaspora*, 13, and passim; Jan Vansina, "Western Bantu Expansion," *Journal of African History* 25 (1984): 129–45; Miller, *Way of Death*, 17, 34, 403, and passim; for a summary and overview, Heywood and Thornton, *Central Africans, Atlantic Creoles, and the Foundation of the Americas*, 56.

49. Wyatt MacGaffey, *Religion and Society in Central Africa: The BaKongo of Lower Zaire* (Chicago, 1986), 120–21, 135–36, 242, and passim; John K. Thornton, "Religious

and Ceremonial Life in the Kongo and Mbundu Areas, 1500–1700," in Heywood, ed., *Central Africans and Cultural Transformations in the American Diaspora*, 71–90. Mac-Gaffey is an anthropologist who worked from field research; Thornton and Heywood are historians working from archival materials.

50. For major work on Central African religions, based on anthropological fieldwork, see MacGaffey, *Religion and Society in Central Africa*, 120ff; John Janzen, *Lemba: A Drum of Affliction in Africa and America* (New York, 1982); and Robert Farris Thompson and Robert Cornet, *Four Moments of the Sun* (Washington, D.C., 1981).

51. For historical research, based in part on manuscripts in Vatican archives, see Thornton, "Religious and Ceremonial Life in the Kongo and Mbundu Areas, 1500–1700," 70–90.

52. Jan Vansina, *Kingdoms of the Savanna* (Madison, 1966), 19–24; Miller, *Way of Death*, 17–22; Elizabeth Isichei, *A History of African Societies to 1870* (Cambridge, 1997), 56–68, 404–5, 439; Alfred Crosby, *The Columbian Exchange: Biological and Cultural Consequences of 1492* (Westport, Conn., 1972), 185–88; Alfred Crosby, *Germs, Seeds, and Animals: Studies in Ecological History* (Armonk, N.Y., 1994), 20–24, 197–98.

53. Philip Curtin, *Economic Change in Precolonial Africa*, 2 vols. (Madison: University of Wisconsin Press, 1975), 207–10; Thornton, *Africa and Africans in the Making of the Atlantic World*, 44–48; Elizabeth Isichei, *A History of African Societies to 1870* (Chicago, 1997), 69–77; Thornton, "The Development of Commerce Between Africans and Europeans," in *Africa and Africans in the Making of the Atlantic World*, 44–53; Balandier, *Daily Life in the Kingdom of the Kongo*, 107–38; D. J. Killick, "What Do We Know About African Iron Working?," *Journal of African Archaeology* 2 (2004): 97–112.

54. Thornton, *Africa and Africans in the Making of the Atlantic World*, 50–51.

55. For a discussion of Vansina's work, see Isichei, *A History of African Societies to 1870*, 69–77.

56. Balandier, *Daily Life in the Kingdom of the Kongo*, 128–38; Édouard Darteville, *Les "Nzimbu," monnai du Royaume de Congo* (Brussels, 1953).

57. Jan Vansina, *Paths in the Rain Forests: Toward a History of Political Tradition in Equatorial Africa* (Madison, 1990), 73–83.

58. Patrick Manning, *The African Diaspora: A History Through Culture* (New York, 2009), 54.

59. The work of American historian and linguist John Thornton from Vatican archives and other sources is invaluable here.

60. Andrew Battell, *The Strange Adventures of Andrew Battell in Angola and Adjourning Lands*, first published by his neighbor and friend Samuel Purchas in *Purchas His Pilgrimmes* (London, 1901), and in a scholarly edition by E. G. Ravenstein for the Hakluyt Society (London, 1901; reprint, 1964). Andrew Battell lived among the Imbangala and wrote from his own experience. His observations were confirmed by other Europeans with firsthand knowledge.

61. Duarte Lopes, published by Filippo Pigafetta, *Relatione del Reame di Congo e circonvincine contrade tratta dalli scritti & ragionamenti di Odoardo Lopez Portughese* (Rome, 1591; modern Italian edition, edited by Georgio Cardonna, Milano, 1978). An English translation by M. Hutchinson was published as *A Report of the Kingdom of*

Congo and of the Surrounding Countries (London, 1881), and a Portuguese translation, *Relaçäodo Reino do Congo a das Terras Circunvizinhas* (Lisbon, 1989).

62. Joseph C. Miller, *Kings and Kinsmen: Early Mbundu States in Angola* (Oxford, 1976), 55–75; Miller, *Way of Death*, 28, 32, 142–43; Miller, "Central Africa During the Era of the Slave Trade, 1490s–1850s," 82–83.

63. Jan Vansina, *How Societies Are Born: Governance in West Central Africa Before 1600* (Charlottesville: University of Virginia Press, 2004), 196–201.

64. Hugo Grotius, *De Jure Belli at Pacis . . . Accompanied by an Abridged Translation,* ed. William Whewell (London, 1853), 3:148–52; 1: 334–36; David Brion Davis, *The Problem of Slavery in Western Culture* (Ithaca, 1966), 114–16; Willem Usselincx, *Octroy ofte Privilege* (1627); Tony Carnes, "Harlem and the Dutch Debate over Slavery in New Amsterdam," Jan. 17, 2021, http://www.nycreligion.info/ harlem-dutch-de bate-slavery-amsterdam/.

65. Cornelis Poudroyen, Gisbertus, and Voetius, in Carnes, "Harlem and the Dutch Debate over Slavery in New Amsterdam," 2–3.

66. Jonas Michaelius to Adrianus Smoutius, Aug. 11, 1628, in Albert Eckhof, *Jonas Michaelius, Founder of the Church in Netherland* (Leyden, 1926), 120, 123; translation by Heywood and Thornton in *Central Africans, Atlantic Creoles, and the Foundation of the Americas*, 323–24. Similar judgments on this question, though different in other ways, appear in Romney, *New Netherland Connections*, 292–93.

67. On language and usage, the most careful study concludes that "from the beginning the Dutch in America unhesitatingly regarded Africans as slaves." Heywood and Thornton, *Central Africans, Atlantic Creoles, and the Foundation of the Americas*, 312–27.

68. The name of this ship is sometimes represented as *La Garce*, which in French usage means "bitch," or "strumpet." I think that this is a transpositional error for *La Grace* in an early source.

69. Edgar J. McManus, *A History of Negro Slavery in New York* (Syracuse, 1970), 19.

70. This finding is a dissent from the excellent and pioneering work of A. Leon Higginbotham Jr., *In the Matter of Color: Race and the American Legal Process: The Colonial Period* (New York, 1978), 99, 103, 106, and passim, and Edgar McManus, *A History of Negro Slavery in New York*, 3–18; as well as from much tertiary writing on the "mild" and "humanitarian" slavery in New Netherland.

71. McManus, *A History of Negro Slavery in New York*, 8; John Cox, ed., *Oyster Bay Town Records* (New York, 1916–24), 2: 697–98.

72. McManus, *A History of Negro Slavery in New York*, 10, citing David De Vries, *My Third Voyage to America and New Netherland*, New-York Historical Society Collections, 2nd series, 3 (1857), 89; Medford, ed., *New York African Burial Ground*, 32.

73. McManus, *A History of Negro Slavery in New York*, 9.

74. Morton Wagman, "Corporate Slavery in New Netherland," *Journal of Negro History* 65 (1980): 34–42.

75. For Dutch slavery as mild, see McManus, *A History of Negro Slavery in New York*, 11–19, and Higginbotham, *In the Matter of Color*, 103. These are two excellent works of primary scholarship, important in their contribution, and very useful to this and other inquiries in many ways. But on this question another judgment works better.

76. Jacob Stoffelsen, "Deposition Concerning the Erection of Fort Amsterdam and Other

Work Done by the Company's Negroes," March 22, 1639, in E. B. O'Callaghan, ed., *Documents Relative to the Colonial History of the State of New-York*, 14 vols. (Albany, 1856–87), 14:18.

77. Van Laer, ed., *New Netherland Council Minutes*, 4:151, July 11, 1642; Heywood and Thornton translate this passage as "three months in chains with the Negroes," rather than "three months in a chain gang with the Negroes." Heywood and Thornton, *Central Africans, Atlantic Creoles, and the Foundation of the Americas*, 326. See also Wagman, "Corporate Slavery in New Netherland," 35.

78. Hodges, *Root & Branch*, 15; I. N. P. Stokes, *The Iconography of Manhattan Island*, 6 vols. (New York, 1915–28), 2:197, 207

79. Early American historians, including Graham Russell Hodges, Joyce Goodfriend, and Leslie Harris, have found that the African Burying Ground on this site was "established in the late 1630s" and was in use "until the late 1780s," probably as late as 1795. It provided the Black population of the city with "a sacred center" throughout that period. The excavated site, at Broadway and Chambers Street, was not far from the "Land of the Negroes" given to half-free slaves before 1644. See Hodges, *Root & Branch*, 12–15; Stokes, *The Iconography of Manhattan Island*, 6:73–77, 120–24, 136–37; and Harris, *In the Shadow of Slavery*, 24–25; also useful is Goodfriend, "Burghers and Blacks," 130; Medford, ed., *New York African Burial Ground*, 96; Joyce Hansen and Gary McGowan, *Breaking Ground, Breaking Silence* (New York, 1997), 1–23; and Cantwell and Wall, eds., *Unearthing Gotham*, chapter 16, "'We Were Here': The African Presence in Colonial New York," 277–94, 279. Most helpful are many monographs in a series entitled "The New York African Burial Ground: Unearthing the African Presence in Colonial New York," sponsored by the U.S. General Services Administration and Howard University Press. Volume 3 is Edna Greene Medford, ed., *Historical Perspectives of the African Burial Ground: New York Blacks and the Diaspora* (Washington, D.C., 2009).

80. Cantwell and Wall, eds., *Unearthing Gotham*, chapter 16, "'We Were Here,'" 291–93.

81. Burial 25, in Michael Blakey and Lesley Rankin-Hill, *The New York African Burial Ground Skeletal Biology Final Report* (Washington, D.C.: Howard University, 2004), 100.

82. John Jea, *The Life, History, and Unparalleled Sufferings of John Jea, the African Preacher* (Portsea, England, ca. 1815). A careful modern text, itself a major work of scholarship, appears in Graham Russell Hodges, ed., *Black Itinerants of the Gospel: The Narratives of John and Jea and George White* (Madison, 1993; reprint, New York: Palgrave–St. Martin's, 2002). Hodges was able to identify Jea's master in the ms. U.S. census of 1800, no small feat, and deepens our understanding by his very full introduction and commentary, which also confirms much of the book's content.

83. "Cornelio vander Hoykens fiscael eyscher, Clyn Antonio, Paulo d'Angola, Gracia d'Angola, Jan de Fort Orange, Manuel de Gerrit de Reus, Antony Portugees, Manuel Minuit, Simon Congo, ende Manuel de Groote over homisidie begaen aen Jan Premero mede negro," Council Minutes, Jan. 14, 1641, New York State Archives, folios 83–84, trans. Van Laer, ed., *New Netherland Council Minutes*, 4:97; Heywood and Thornton, *Central Africans, Atlantic Creoles, and the Foundation of the Americas*, 264; Romney, *New Netherland Connections*, 220.

84. Medford, ed., *New York African Burial Ground*, 101; Council Minutes, Jan. 17, 1641,

vol. 1: 97–100, Jan. 17, 1641, online; E. B. O'Callaghan, ed., *Calendar of Historical Manuscripts in the Office of the Secretary of State, Dutch Manuscripts* (Albany, 1865–66), 1: 74; A. J. F. van Laer, ed., *The van Rensselaer Bowier Manuscripts* (Albany, 1908), 802. For various interpretations, see Henry H. Kessler and Eugene Rachlis, *Peter Stuyvesant and His New York* (New York, 1959), 21–22; McManus, *A History of Negro Slavery in New York*, 17; Hodges, *Root & Branch*, 16; Romney, *New Netherland Connections*, 220–21.

85. For traditional punishments of homosexual acts in Congo cultures during the seventeenth century, see Balandier, *Daily Life in the Kingdom of the Kongo*, 171.

86. Council Minutes, June 25, 1646, folios 83–84, 262, in Van Laer, ed., *New Netherland Council Minutes,* 4: 326; O'Callaghan, ed., *Calendar of Historical Manuscripts in the Office of the Secretary of State*, Dutch Manuscripts, 1: 103. For a discussion of this and similar cases of sodomy involving a child in Old and New Netherland, see Hodges, *Root & Branch*, 17, 285.

87. Petition of "five blacks from New Amsterdam who had come here," 1635, Microfilm Records of the Old West India Company, Notulen W1635, 1626 (19-11-1635), inv. 1.05.01.01, inventory number 14, folio 93, Algemeen Rijksarchief, in The Hague; Stokes, *The Iconography of Manhattan Island*, 4:82; Ira Berlin, *Many Thousands Gone: The First Two Centuries of Slavery in North America* (Cambridge, Mass., 1998), 52–53, 394, citing Marcel van Linden, International Institute of Social History, Amsterdam.

88. For proof of payment, see Kenneth Scott and Kenn Stryker-Rodda, eds., *New York Historical Manuscripts*, 4 vols. (Baltimore, 1974), 1:112, 123; Hodges, *Root & Branch*, 10, 105, 283.

89. *Pedro Negretto plaintiff v. Jan Coles defendant*, July 21, 1639, in Van Laer, ed., *New Netherland Council Minutes,* 4:54.

90. Robert Swan, "Slaves and Slaveholding in Dutch New York, 1628–1664," *Journal of the Afro-American Historical and Genealogical Society* 17 (1998): 48–81; Swan, "First Africans into New Netherland, 1625 or 1626?," 75–82; Robert Swan, "The Other Fort Amsterdam: New Light on Aspects of Slavery in New Netherland," *Afro-Americans in New York Life and History* 22 (1998): 19–24; Peter Christophe, "The Freedmen of New Amsterdam," in *A Beautiful and Fruitful Place: Selected Renssellaerswick Seminar Papers* (Albany, 1991), 157–70; Hodges, *Root & Branch*, 9–12; Harris, *In the Shadow of Slavery*, 21–25.

91. The full text of the response by Willem Kieft and the Council of New Netherland, dated February 25, 1644, at Fort Amsterdam in New Netherland, is reproduced in Higginbotham, *In the Matter of Color*, 106–7.

92. The slaves' petition and Kieft's response are in Van Laer, ed., *New Netherland Council Minutes,* Feb. 25, 1644, 1: 212–13; and also in *Laws and Ordinances of New Netherland*, 36. For interpretations, see Romney, *New Netherlands Connections*, 191–97, which is helpful on the solidarity that developed among these slaves, but argues beyond her evidence that "New Netherland's slaves came in small numbers from widely dispersed cultural backgrounds," 198–99. She observes correctly that African traders tended to sell slaves who were not related to their African sellers, but the question here is about relationships among slaves with one another.

93. Certificates, Dec. 8, 1663, New Netherland Council Minutes X, part 2, 429, and

Dec. 11/21, 1664, New Netherland Council Minutes X, part 3, 327, New York State Archives; Romney, *New Netherland Connections*, 224–25.

94. Medford, ed., *New York African Burial Ground*, 50–51.

95. Medford, ed., *New York African Burial Ground*, 50–51.

96. For a list of the twenty-eight holdings by name, date, and size, see Howard Dodson et al., eds., *The Black New Yorkers* (New York: Wiley, 2000), 23; Moore, "Black Landowners in Manhattan's 'Land of the Blacks,' 1663–1664," in Berlin and Harris, eds., *Slavery in New York*, 43; Charles T. Gehring, *Dutch Land Papers* (Baltimore, 1980); E. B. O'Callaghan, ed., *Calendar of New York Colonial Manuscripts, Indorsed Land Papers, 1643–1803* (New York, 1864; reprint, Harrison, N.Y., 1987).

97. Berlin and Harris, eds., *Slavery in New York*, 42–44.

98. Medford, ed., *New York African Burial Ground*, 46; Hodges, *Root & Branch*, 12.

99. Medford, ed., *Historical Perspectives of the African Burial Ground*, 21–23; Stokes, *The Iconography of Manhattan Island*, 4:87; Swan, "The Other Fort Amsterdam," 19–42; Hodges, *Root & Branch*, 14.

100. Gehring, ed., *New York Historical Manuscripts: Dutch Land Papers*, vol. GG 117; *Doop-Boek of the Reformed Church of New York*, published as "Baptisms in the Dutch Reformed Church of New Amsterdam and New York, 1639–1730," *New York Genealogical and Biographical Society Record* 2 (1890): 10–41, at 17/261 (1644), 18/263 (1645); Richard Dickenson, "Abstracts of Early Black Manhattanites," *New York Genealogical and Biographical Society Record* 16 (1983): 103; Christopher Moore, "A World of Possibilities: Slavery and Freedom in Dutch New Amsterdam," in Berlin and Harris, eds., *Slavery in New York*, 42–46.

101. The Trompetter story was pieced together by Joyce Goodfriend and reported in "Black Families in New Netherland," *Journal of the Afro-American Historical and Genealogical Society* 5 (1984): 147–55, at 149–51; in *A Beautiful and Fruitful Place*; Berthold Fernow, ed., *The Records of New Amsterdam from 1653 to 1674*, 7 vols. (New York, 1897), 4:41–42; Goodfriend, *Before the Melting Pot*, 17, 23, 28; O'Callaghan, ed., *Calendar of Historical Manuscripts in the Office of the Secretary of State, Dutch Manuscripts*, 1:256. A son, Anthony Trompetter, by 1643 had acquired a family and a sizable piece of real estate on what is now Christopher Street. *Doop-Boek* 17 (261), 1644.

102. Especially helpful on Bastiaen (var. Sebastiaen and Bastryn) is Rodney, *New Netherland Connections*, 14, 200–202, 215–18, 222, and passim.

103. For primary evidence, see Gehring, ed., *New York Historical Manuscripts, Dutch Land Papers*; O'Callaghan, ed., *Calendar of New York Colonial Manuscripts, Indorsed Land Papers*. For a list of the twenty-eight holdings by name, date, and size, and for the location of five holdings superimposed on a modern photograph, see Moore, "Black Landowners in Manhattan's 'Land of the Blacks,'" 43.

104. No census of population survives for Dutch New Netherland. Edgar McManus writes after long study that the number of slaves in New Netherland "at any given time cannot be estimated with much precision. The directors were notoriously lax in compiling statistics of any sort about the colony. No real census was ever taken, and the port records were fragmentary." Many estimates of African population in New Netherland have tended to err on the low side. One cautionary example: in 1664, three hundred slaves arrived in the slave ship *Gideon*. Sources include McManus, *Negro Slavery in*

New York, 11; HSUS (1977) Z-1-19; Evarts B. Greene and Virginia D. Harrington, eds., *American Population Before the Federal Census of 1790* (New York and Baltimore, 1932 and 1981), 1966, 88–105. By contrast, many censuses were taken in the English colony of New York, and are reported in Greene and Harrington, eds., *American Population Before the Federal Census of 1790*, 88–104. See also Kenneth Scott and Kenneth Stryker-Rodda, eds., *Denizations, Naturalizations, and Oaths of Allegiance in Colonial New York* (Baltimore: Genealogical Publishing, 1975), 86. Earlier impressionistic estimates are also gathered in Greene and Harrington, eds., *American Population Before the Federal Census of :790*. See also Jameson, ed., *Journal of Jasper Danckaerts*, 65, and Goodfriend, *Before the Melting Pot*, 13–14, 52, and passim.

105. Richard Shannon Moss, *Slavery on Long Island: A Study in Local Institutional and Early African-American Communal Life* (New York: Garland, 1993), 11, 17, 50–51, 94, 99, 102, and passim; Robert J. Swan, "The Black Presence in Seventeenth-Century Brooklyn," *De Halve Maen* 63 (1990): 1–6.

106. Hodges, *Root & Branch*, 13.

107. For two excellent accounts of Jan de Vries see David Stephen Cohen, *The Ramapo Mountain People* (New Brunswick, N.J., 1974), 26–29; and Moore, "A World of Possibilities," 46–47.

108. O'Callaghan, ed., *Calendar of Historical Manuscripts in the Office of the Secretary of State, Dutch Manuscripts,* 104.

109. Samuel S. Puple, ed., *Records of the Reformed Dutch Church in New Amsterdam and New York*, vol. 2, *Baptisms, 1639–1739* (New York, 1902), 23.

110. Cohen, *The Ramapo Mountain People*, 26–42.

111. Cohen, *The Ramapo Mountain People*, 26–42.

112. Jan Cornelissen from Rotterdam plaintiff vs. Anthony Jansen from Salle defendant, April 7, 1639, affidavit 16, and Colonial Council Minutes, April 7, 1639; *New York Historical Manuscripts: Dutch*, ed. Arnold J. F. Van Laer, Kenneth Scott, and Kenn Stryker-Rodda (Baltimore, 1974), 4:46.

113. On Anthony Jansen van Salee, see Leo Hershkowitz, "The Troublesome Turk: An Illustration of Judicial Process in New Amsterdam," *New York History* 46 (1965): 299–310; Swan, "The Black Presence in Seventeenth Century Brooklyn," 1–23; Michael Gomez, "Muslims in New York," *Black Crescent* (Cambridge, 2005), 128–42.

114. In 1638–39, they appeared in fifteen of ninety-three criminal cases before the Dutch Colonial Council. Van Laer, ed., *New Netherland Council Minutes*, 4: 3–55 (1638–39).

115. Hershkowitz, "The Troublesome Turk," 300–306; Hoff, "Frans Abramse Van Salee and His Descendants," 65–71.

116. Testimony of Rev. Bogardus, Van Laer, ed., *New Netherland Council Minutes,* April 1639, 4:46ff.

117. "Anthony Jansen van Salee," wikitree.com/wiki/Jansen-455.

118. Bill Greer, *The Mevrouw Who Saved Manhattan* (Brooklyn, 2009), a lively mix of fact and fiction. Simon Schama discusses the subject at length in *The Embarrassment of Riches: An Interpretation of Dutch Culture in the Golden Age* (New York, 1987), 375–480.

119. Joyce D. Goodfriend, "Black Families in New Netherland," in *A Beautiful and Fruitful Place*, 147–55, at 148.

120. Goodfriend, "Black Families in New Netherland," 151.

121. Medford, ed., *New York African Burial Ground*, 40–41; Richard Dickensen, "Abstracts of Early Black Manhattanites," in *New York Genealogical and Biographical Records*, 116:102.

122. Medford, ed., *New York African Burial Ground*, 35, 40, citing Swan, "The Other Fort Amsterdam," 27–28; Goodfriend, "Black Families in New Netherland," 102–3.

123. Medford, ed., *New York African Burial Ground*, 2; "African Presence," Cantwell and Wall, *Unearthing Gotham*, 290–91; Goodfriend, "Black Families in New Netherland," 102.

124. Medford, *Historical Perspectives of the African Burial Ground*, 85–90.

125. Romney, *New Netherland Connections*, 212–15, is strong on these linkages. See also Henry B. Hoff, "A Colonial Black Family in New York and New Jersey: Pieter Santomee and His Descendants," *Journal of the Afro-American Historical and Genealogical Society* 9 (1988): 101–35.

126. Kessler and Rachlis, *Peter Stuyvesant and His New York*, 207, 227; Cohen, *The Ramapo Mountain People*, 40–41.

127. A. J. Williams-Meyers, "Pinkster Carnival: Africanisms in the Hudson River Valley," *Africanisms in New York Life and History* 9 (1985): 7–17; Shane White, "Pinkster: Afro-Dutch Syncretization in New York City and the Hudson Valley," *Journal of American Folklore* 102 (1989): 68–75.

128. McManus, *A History of Negro Slavery in New York*, 10; A. J. F. Van Laer, ed., *Early Records of the City and County of Albany and the Colony of Rensselaerwyck* (Albany, 1915–19), 3:122, 180.

129. McManus, *A History of Negro Slavery in New York*, 8; A. J. F. Van Laer, ed., *The Correspondence of Jeremias van Rensselaer, 1651–1674* (Albany, 1932), 167, 364–65.

130. Foote, *Black and White Manhattan*, 36; compiled from Elizabeth Donnan, ed., *Documents Illustrative of the History of the Slave Trade to America*, 4 vols. (Washington, D.C.: Carnegie Institution, 1930–35), 3: 444.

131. In the absence of census records for New Netherland, the total number of its inhabitants has been estimated at 20 in 1626, 232 in 1640, 500 in 1650, and 3,000 in 1664. A variant estimate of "10,000 inhabitants" in New Netherland appears in Peter Stuyvesant et al., "Address of Burgomasters and Schepens to Director & Council of the West India Company," in O'Callaghan, ed., *The Documentary History of the State of New-York*, 1:357, 386n.

132. Hodges, *Root & Branch*, 31; Ernst van den Boogaart, "Servant Migration to New Netherland, 1624–1664," in P. C. Emmer, ed., *Colonization and Migration: Indentured Labour Before and After Slavery* (Dordrecht, Netherlands, 1986), 58.

133. Hodges, *Root & Branch*, 31; Van den Boogaart, "Servant Migration to New Netherland, 1624–1664," 58; Goodfriend, *Before the Melting Pot*, 13–14, 115.

134. Postma, *The Dutch in the Atlantic Slave Trade*, 107. Contract to Import Slaves into New Netherland, [1652?], in Donnan, ed., *Documents Illustrative of the History of the Slave Trade to America*, 3: 412–13.

135. Donnan, ed., *Documents Illustrative of the History of the Slave Trade to America*, 411, 412, 422, 423, 425, 430, 443, 459.

136. E. B. O'Callaghan, *Voyages of the Slavers St. John and Arms of Amsterdam, 1659, 1663; Together with Additional papers illustrative of the Slave Trade Under the Dutch. Translated from the Original Manuscripts* (Albany, 1867).

137. Medford, *Historical Perspectives of the African Burial Ground*, 60; Donnan, ed., *Documents Illustrative of the History of the Slave Trade to America*.

138. Romney, *New Netherland Connections*, 238–43.

139. Quoted in David Kobrin, *The Black Minority in Early New York* (Albany, 1971), 11.

140. Goodfriend, *Before the Melting Pot*, 120.

141. Moore, "A World of Possibilities," 53–54.

142. Jill Lepore, *New York Burning: Liberty, Slavery, and Conspiracy in Eighteenth-Century Manhattan* (New York: Alfred A. Knopf, 2005), 60–61; McManus, *A History of Negro Slavery in New York*, 24; Hodges, *Root & Branch*, 37. For petitions and cases, O'Callaghan, ed., *Calendar of Historical Manuscripts* in the Office of the Secretary of State, Dutch Manuscripts, 2: 82; Fernow, *Calendar of Council Minutes*, 55, 61, 89, passim.

143. Hodges, *Root & Branch*, 44–45.

144. Goodfriend, *Before the Melting Pot*, 10, 13, 88–89, 112.

145. Francis Harrison, "Observations, Humbly Offered to His Grace the Duke of Chandos . . . ," 1724?, Mss Gough Somersetshire 7 (SC 18217), Bodleian Library, Oxford; Hodges, *Root & Branch*, 79; Lepore, *New York Burning*, 34.

146. Greene and Harrington, eds., *American Population Before the Federal Census of 1790*, 92–105; Goodfriend, *Before the Melting Pot*, 10, 13, 113, McManus, *A History of Negro Slavery in New York*; Lepore, *New York Burning*; Hodges, *Root & Branch*, 35–36.

147. Three earlier studies (ca. 1978–2004) yielded estimates that between 6,800 and 7,400 slaves were imported to the port of New York in its British period, and another 600 to Perth Amboy in New Jersey. These numbers were larger than the slave trade to New Netherland, but incomplete. James G. Lydon, "New York and the Slave Trade, 1700–1774," *William and Mary Quarterly*, 3rd series, 35 (1978): 375–94, at 387. A "conservative estimate," omitting evidence from newspapers, of at least 4,949 slaves delivered to New York, from 1715 to 1772, appears in Foote, *Black and White Manhattan*, 64, 63–70. Very helpful is a careful estimate of "just over 2,000 from 1664 to 1737, and 4,394 from 1737 to 1771," in Harris, *In the Shadow of Slavery*, 46–47.

    Eltis and Richardson, on the basis of the Trans-Atlantic Slave Trade Database, report evidence of 9,000 slaves disembarked at New York and Perth Amboy from 1655 to 1775. They also estimate an undercount of 41 percent, which yields a total estimate of 15,300 slaves landed in New York and New Jersey from 1655 to 1775. David Eltis and David Richardson, *Atlas of the Transatlantic Slave Trade* (New Haven and London: Yale University Press, 2010), 213. Still very helpful are data in Donnan, ed., *Documents Illustrative of the History of the Slave Trade to America*, 3:440–42, 511–12; as well as discussions in Darold Wax, "Preferences for Slaves in Colonial America," *Journal of Negro History* 58 (1973); Moss, *Slavery on Long Island*, 56; and Lepore, *New York Burning*, 24–26.

148. Francis Harrison, "Observations Humbly Offered to His Grace the Duke of Chandos . . ."; Hodges, *Root & Branch*, 79–81; Harris, *In the Shadow of Slavery*, 28–31; Foote, *Black and White Manhattan*, 63–70.

149. Harris, *In the Shadow of Slavery*, 28–31; Foote, *Black and White Manhattan*, 63–70.

150. Virginia Platt, "The East India Company and the Madagascar Slave Trade," *William and Mary Quarterly*, 3rd series, 26 (1969): 548–77; Jacob Judd, "Frederick Philipse and the Madagascar Trade," *New-York Historical Society Quarterly* 47 (1963): 66–74;

Goodfriend, *Before the Melting Pot,* 112–13; Jacobus van Cortlandt, Letter Book 1698–1700, New-York Historical Society.

151. Platt, "The East India Company and the Madagascar Slave Trade," 548–77; Goodfriend, *Before the Melting Pot,* 113; Judd, "Frederick Philipse and the Madagascar Trade," 66–74; Hodges, *Root & Branch,* 38–40. On piracy and East African slave traders, see James G. Lydon, *Pirates, Privateers and Profits* (Upper Saddle River, N.J., 1970), 39–44; Lydon, "New York and the Slave Trade, 1700–1774," 376; Donnan, ed., *Documents Illustrative of the History of the Slave Trade to America,* 3:437; Robert C. Ritchie, *Captain Kidd and the War Against the Pirates* (Cambridge, 1986), 112–45. For the market glut of 1698, see Foote, *Black and White Manhattan,* 64, 255.

152. Graham Russell Hodges and Alan Edward Brown, eds., *"Pretends to Be Free": Runaway Slave Advertisements from Colonial and Revolutionary New York and New Jersey* (New York, 1994), 12, 14, 17, 42, 31, and passim.

153. All this is from recorded testimony published by Daniel Horsmanden, in *A Journal of the Proceedings in the Detection of the Conspiracy Formed by Some White People, in Conjunction with Negro and Other Slaves . . .* (first published in New York, 1744; reprinted in many variant editions); a later edition is available online on the website of the Library of Congress, in its American Memory collection. A helpful introduction by Thomas J. Davis is attached to another edition (Boston: Beacon, 1971).

154. McManus, *A History of Negro Slavery in New York,* 88–89, citing Daniel Parish, Transcripts of Material on Slavery in the Public Records Office; Charles M. Hough, ed., *Reports of Cases in Vice Admiralty* (New Haven, 1925), 26 (1740–47).

155. Import records from the Naval Officer's Shipping List and American Inspector General's Ledger, 1750–1774; Foote, *Black and White Manhattan,* 65.

156. Testimony of the slave Jack, "Tiebout's Negro" before Alderman Bancker, June 24, 1741; Daniel Horsmanden, *The New York Conspiracy,* ed. Davis, 205–6; 212, 265–66, 278.

157. Goodfriend, *Before the Melting Pot,* 113–14.

158. Goodfriend, *Before the Melting Pot,* 113–14.

159. Margaret L. Vetare, *Philipsburg Manor Upper Mills* (Tarrytown, 2004). On Margaret Hardenbroek, see Jean Zimmerman, *The Women of the House: How Colonial She-Merchants Built a Mansion, a Fortune and a Dynasty* (New York, 2006); Hodges, *Root & Branch,* 33.

160. Will of Frederick Philipse, Oct. 26, 1700. An inventory of the estate in 1702 listed forty slaves. See Dennis J. Maika, "Encounters: Slavery and the Philipse Family, 1680–1751," in Roger Panetta, ed., *Dutch New York: The Roots of Hudson Valley Culture* (Published jointly by the Hudson Valley Museum and Fordham University, 2009), 52, 68; Hodges, *Root & Branch,* 44; Vivienne L. Kruger, "Born to Run: The Slave Family in Early New York" (diss., Columbia University, 1985).

161. Maika, 35–72, at 39; Jacquetta M. Haley, "The Slaves of Philipsburg Manor, Upper Mills," in *Encounters with Living History: Activity-Based Lessons on Enslaved Africans of the North* (Tarrytown, Historic Hudson Valley, 1996).

162. A "Letter of Freedom from Frederick Philipse to Nicholas Cartagena," Dec. 31, 1696, survives in the British National Archives, PRO/HCA 1-98; Maika, 49–51, 68.

163. Hodges, *Root & Branch,* 80; Foote, *Black and White Manhattan,* 132–39.

164. "Rev. John Sharpe's Proposals," March 1713, *Collections of the New-York Historical Society* (1880), 355; Laws for Regulating the Burial of Slaves, Oct. 8, 1722, Feb. 18, 1731, *Minutes of the Common Council of the City of New York, 1675–1776*, 8 vols., ed. Herbert L. Osgood (New York, 1905), 3:296; 4:88–89; Goodfriend, *Before the Melting Pot*, 122; Foote, *Black and White Manhattan*, 142.

165. Goodfriend, *Before the Melting Pot*, 122–23.

166. A quantitative survey of languages spoken or understood by 261 out of 753 fugitive slaves in New York and New Jersey, as reported by their masters, appears in Hodges and Brown, eds., *"Pretends to Be Free,"* table 8, "Linguistic Capabilities of Fugitive Slaves."

167. Dr. Alexander Hamilton, *A Gentleman's Progress: The Itinerarium of Dr. Alexander Hamilton, 1744* (Pittsburgh, 1948), 40–41.

168. Hamilton, *Gentleman's Progress*, 40–41. For Afro-Dutch speechways, variously called Black Dutch, Negro Dutch, and "*nexer dauts*" in East Jersey and New York see John Dyneley Prince, "The Jersey Dutch Dialect," *Dialect Notes* 3, part 6 (1910): 459–84, at 459, 460. Afro-Dutch also included Iroquois words and expressions, which were recorded in transcriptions of L. G. van Loon, published as *Crumbs from an Old Dutch Closet: The Dutch Dialect of Old New York* (The Hague: Martinus Nikhoff, 1938), 4–5, 46–47. An original of this rare monograph is in the author's library. A major work of modern scholarship is Cohen, *The Ramapo Mountain People*, 134–60.

169. For groups of slaves in New York City called "York Negroes" in vernacular speech ca. 1741, see testimony recorded by Horsmanden, *The New York Conspiracy*, ed. Davis, 147, 149, 150.

170. Greene and Harrington, eds., *American Population Before the Federal Census of 1790*; Goodfriend, *Before the Melting Pot*.

171. Greene and Harrington, eds., *American Population Before the Federal Census of 1790*; Hodges and Brown, eds., *"Pretends to be Free,"* appendix 1, table 3.

172. Cadwallader Colden to Mr. Jordan, March 26, 1717, *The Letters and Papers of Cadwallader Colden* (New York, 1918), 1:39.

173. Graham Hodges, "The Closing Vise of Slavery," in *Root & Branch*, 34, 68; Jill Lepore, "The Tightening Vise: Slavery and Freedom in British New York," in Berlin and Harris, eds., *Slavery in New York*, 86.

174. Cornbury in *Calendar of State Papers, Colonial*, 21:32; Horsmanden in *The New York Conspiracy*, ed. Davis, 155. For Prince and Mayor William Merritt, see New York Supreme Court of Judicature, Minute Book, 1693–1701, 13, County Clerk's Office, New York City; Stokes, *Iconography of New York* 4:32; and Hodges, *Root & Branch*, 53. On this and similar events, Foote, *Black and White Manhattan*, 206.

175. For tabulations from 1703 to 1721 see Hodges, *Root & Branch*, 271–75; Peter Wacker, *Land and People: A Cultural Geography of Preindustrial New York: Origins and Settlements* (New Brunswick, 1975), 189–205.

176. The New York Census of 1737, original returns in O'Callaghan, ed., *The Documentary History of the State of New York*, 4:186, corrected by Jill Lepore in *New York Burning*, 233–36.

177. Much detail about the daily lives of slaves and free Blacks appears in Daniel Horsmanden's *Journal of the Proceedings in the Detection of the Conspiracy . . .* (New York, 1744), reprinted in a variant edition as *The New York Conspiracy* (New York, 1810). The most

accessible volume is ed. Davis, *The New York Conspiracy*. It is based on the 1810 edition, with corrections where it departed from the 1744 printing. For helpful discussion of the work itself, see Lepore, *New York Burning*, 23, 96–128, 129–69, 233–39, and passim. An excellent study for the period from 1664 to 1730, deeply informed by research in Dutch and English records, is Joyce Goodfriend's "African-American Society and Culture," in *Before the Melting Pot*, 111–32.

178. Horsmanden, *The New York Conspiracy*, ed. Davis, especially 69, 82, 94, 120, 161; Cuffee's confession to Arthur Price, May 12, 1741, p. 67.

179. Lepore, *New York Burning*, 7–8.

180. Primary evidence is in court testimony published in 1744 as part of Horsmanden, *The New York Conspiracy*, ed. Davis, 67, 93. For discussion, see Lepore, *New York Burning*, 99–102 137–38; and Craig Steven Wilder, *In the Company of Black Men: The African Influence on African American Culture in New York City* (New York, 2001), 9–35.

181. Testimony of Margaret Salingburgh, alias Kerry, May 13, 20, 1741, Horsmanden, *The New York Conspiracy*, ed. Davis, xiii, 72–73, 77–79.

182. Primary materials are in Horsmanden, *The New York Conspiracy*, ed. Davis, 124–38, 192–355; Lepore, *New York Burning*, 6, 49–50, 160–67, 196–97.

183. Horsmanden, *The New York Conspiracy*, ed. Davis, 148, 118–23, 170–71, and passim.

184. On Akan-speaking leaders, see Lepore, *New York Burning*, 111, 147–48.

185. Williams-Meyers, "Pinkster Carnival," 7–17; White, "Pinkster," 68–75; Shane White, "'It Was a Proud Day': African-Americans, Festivals, and Parades in the North, 1741–1834," Journal of American History 81 (1994): 13–50.

186. Wilder, *In the Company of Black Men*, 9–35.

187. Moss, *Slavery on Long Island*, 114.

188. Much material appears in Horsmanden, *The New York Conspiracy*, ed. Davis, especially 145–53. For thoughtful and creative analysis, see Lepore, *New York Burning*, 5, 110–16, 130–33, 145–48, 151, 162–66.

189. Horsmanden, *The New York Conspiracy*, ed. Davis, 146; Lepore, *New York Burning*, 146.

190. Lepore, *New York Burning*, 147.

191. Lepore, *New York Burning*, 148.

192. Horsmanden, *The New York Conspiracy*, ed. Davis, 146–47.

193. Thomas J. Davis, *A Rumor of Revolt: The "Great Negro Plot" in Colonial New York* (Amherst, 1985), 4–5; Lepore, *New York Burning*, 37 ("Kerry"). Primary evidence is abundant in Horsmanden, *The New York Conspiracy*, ed. Davis, 48–78.

194. This detail is gleaned from testimony in Horsmanden, *The New York Conspiracy*, ed. Davis, "Hughson" and "Meeting at Hughson" in Davis's indexed edition.

195. See many references to them in Horsmanden, *The New York Conspiracy*, 62–67; and indexed under their names.

196. Maika, "Encounters: Slavery and the Philipse Family," 35–72, at 39. See also Haley, "The Slaves of Philipseburg Manor, Upper Mills."

197. Vetare, *Philipsburg Manor Upper Mills*.

198. "Philipse Manor Improvement," *Tarrytown Argus*, Aug. 5, 1905; also "Skeleton Found in Excavation," *Tarrytown News*, Nov. 18, 1958; Maika, "Encounters: Slavery and the Philipse Family," 48, 67.

199. From 1669 to 1712 eighteen deeds of manumission were issued in New York City. The annual rate remained nearly constant in the range of 0.4 to 0.3. Hodges, *Root & Branch*, 36.

200. Harry B. Yoshpe, "Record of Slave Manumissions in New York During the Colonial and Early National Periods," *Journal of Negro History* 26 (1941): xx.

201. Hodges, *Root & Branch*, 70–71, 103; Goodfriend, *Before the Melting Pot*, 116–17.

202. Jameson, ed., *Journal of Jasper Danckaerts*, 65.

203. Jameson, ed., *Journal of Jasper Danckaerts*, 65; Common Council Minutes, 1:276; Goodfriend, *Before the Melting Pot*, 120; Medford, ed., *New York African Burial Ground*, 58; Harris, *In the Shadow of Slavery*, 24.

204. Goodfriend, *Before the Melting Pot*, 117; Kenneth Scott, "The Slave Insurrection in New York in 1712," *New-York Historical Society Quarterly* 45 (1961): 43–74; Foote, *Black and White Manhattan*, 142; Hodges, *Root & Branch*, 70.

205. Hodges, *Root & Branch*, 70–71; Goodfriend, *Before the Melting Pot*, 113–22.

206. James Riker, *The Annals of Newtown . . .* (New York, 1852), 143; Scott, "The Slave Insurrection in New York in 1912," 43–74; O'Callaghan, ed., *Documents Relative to the Colonial History of the State of New-York*, 5:39; Hodges, *Root & Branch*, 64, 296.

207. Lepore, *New York Burning*, 8.

208. McManus, *A History of Negro Slavery in New York*, 80–81; *Colonial Laws of New York*, 1: 519–20.

209. *Colonial Laws of New York*, 1:582.

210. McManus, *A History of Negro Slavery in New York*, 83.

211. *Minutes of the Common Council of New York, 1765–76*, 8 vols. (New York, 1905), 1: 86; Hodges, *Root & Branch*, 43; David Roediger, *Wages of Whiteness: Race and the Making of the American Working Class* (New York, 1991).

212. Goodfriend, *Before the Melting Pot*, 123.

213. Courts of Common Right and Chancery of East Jersey, 1683–1702 (Philadelphia, 1937), 282–85; Graham Russell Hodges, *Slavery and Freedom in the Rural North: African Americans in Monmouth County, New Jersey, 1665–1865*, 53; also in Eugene R. Morris, ed., *The Papers of Lewis Morris*, 3 vols. (Newark, N.J., 1991).

214. Goodfriend, *Before the Melting Pot*, 123–24, citing New York Colonial Manuscripts 36:114 (Dutch) in Albany.

215. Moss, *Slavery on Long Island*, 114.

216. Within the present boundaries of the United States, evidence exists of suspected conspiracies or threats in Virginia, 1663, 1672, 1687; Maryland, 1688; South Carolina, 1702; and Virginia again, 1709–10. There were also groups of fugitive slaves. But none of these episodes led to an actual slave revolt as did the events in New York in 1712. Large slave revolts occurred in other parts of the world over many centuries. The largest on record were the early Zanz revolts in Mesopotamia. Herbert Aptheker, *American Negro Slave Revolts* (New York, 1943, 1963), 162–71.

217. John Sharpe, letter to Secretary of the Society for the Propagation of the Gospel, June 23, 1712, Society for the Propagation of the Gospel Letter Books; available on microfilm in *Records of the Society for the Propagation of the Gospel, Letter Books; 1701–1786*, 17 vols., series A, vols. 1, 2, 7; accessible at Widener Library, Harvard, and many libraries; reprinted in *New York Genealogical and Biographical Record* 21 (1890), 162–63; Parish's Transcripts, New-York Historical Society, 15–16.

The most thorough study is Scott, "The Slave Insurrection in New York in 1712," 43–74. A thoughtful discussion of motives is Foote, *Black and White Manhattan*, 142. Also very helpful are Hodges, *Root & Branch*, 64–70; Foote, *Black and White Manhattan*, 132–40, 16, 206, and passim; Lepore, *New York Burning*, 52–53, 59–60, 82, 92, 104, 147, 184–85; McManus, *A History of Negro Slavery in New York*, 122–26; and Goodfriend, *Before the Melting Pot*, 6, 117, 123–24, 129.

218. Donnan, ed., *Documents Illustrative of the History of the Slave Trade to America*, 3:444; Trans-Atlantic Slave Trade Database, Captain Jarratt's voyage in 1711.

219. Very helpful is the Harvard dissertation of Thelma Wills Foote, published as *Black and White Manhattan*, 133, 268.

220. Sharpe to Secretary SPG, June 23, 1712.

221. Sharpe to Secretary SPG, June 23, 1712.

222. Sharpe to Secretary SPG, June 23, 1712; Gov. Robert Hunter to Lords of Trade, June 23, 1712, in O'Callaghan, ed., *Documents Relative to the Colonial History of the State of New-York*, 5: 340–42.

223. Mary Lou Lustig, *Robert Hunter, 1666–1734: New York's Augustan Statesman* (Syracuse, 1983), 90–140.

224. Lepore, *New York Burning*, 79.

225. In six accounts the counts are never the same. Foote's work is careful, and derived from primary data in the Minutes of the Supreme Court of Judicature, June 6, 1710–June 5, 1714, Foote, *Black and White Manhattan*, 399–400, 417, 426, 429, and the Coroner's Inquisition, April 9, 1712; Lustig, *Robert Hunter*, 104, from Hunter to Board of Trade, June 23, 2012; Hunter to Dartmouth, June 23, 1712, differs in particulars.

226. "An Act for Preventing Suppressing and Punishing the Conspiracy and Insurrection of Negroes . . . ," in Lepore, "The Tightening Vise," 81; Hodges, *Root & Branch*, 67–68ff.

227. Hodges, *Root & Branch*, 90–91, also adds other instances.

228. Aptheker, *American Negro Slave Revolts*, 180–94.

229. This event has inspired a large literature and many different interpretations. Early works of scholarship were Thomas Szasz, "The New York Slave Revolt of 1741: A Reexamination," *New-York History* 56 (1971): 17–30, and Leopold S. Launitz-Schurer, "Slave Resistance in Colonial New York: An Interpretation of Daniel Horsmanden's New York Conspiracy," *Phylon* 41 (1980): 137–51. That approach persisted in Edwin G. Burrows and Mike Wallace, *Gotham* (New York, 1999), 159–66, a brief and lively account that expresses deep skepticism about a "Great Negro Conspiracy," which Wallace interprets as an expression of racism and hysteria. Davis, *A Rumor of Revolt*, 12–21, is a serious narrative of the event as an attempt by slaves to strike a blow for freedom. Lepore, *New York Burning*, is an account of the event as a set of multiple "plots" against the establishment by different groups, mostly of African slaves, but also of dissident whites. Peter Linebaugh and Marcus Rediker, *The Many Headed Hydra: Sailors, Slaves, Commoners and the Hidden History of the Revolutionary Atlantic* (Boston, 2001), is a Marxist interpretation of the event as a class movement. Peter Charles Hoffer, *The Great New York Conspiracy of 1741: Slavery, Crime, and Colonial Law* (Lawrence, Kan., 2003), is a thoughtful study of the trials by a legal historian.

230. One of the most careful accounts of the 1741 fire is in Davis, *A Rumor of Revolt*, 12–21.

231. On the testimony of Mrs. Abigail Earle, about the acts of individual slaves, see Hors-

manden, *The New York Conspiracy*, ed. Davis, 27. On the outbreak of the fires, Davis, *A Rumor of Revolt*, 12–34. On slave conspiracies, Lepore, *New York Burning*. On the trials, Hoffer, *The Great New York Conspiracy of 1741*.

232. The leading primary source is Daniel Horsmanden's *Journal of the Proceedings in the Detection of the Conspiracy formed by Some White People, in Conjunction with Negro and Other Slaves, for Burning the City of New York in America, and Murdering the Inhabitants* (New York, 1744). This text is most widely available in a digital facsimile on the Readex and American Antiquarian Society edition of *Early American Imprints*. For a discussion of variant editions and manuscript copies, see Lepore, *New York Burning*, 275–81, 93–102.

233. Lepore, *New York Burning*, 147n, appendix A.

234. Lepore, *New York Burning*, 236, 244. The census of 1737 is in O'Callaghan, ed., *The Documentary History of the State of New-York*, 4:186.

235. For primary evidence, Horsmanden, *The New York Conspiracy*, ed. Davis, 142–57, 161–64, 170–71; for secondary discussion, Lepore, *New York Burning*, 111–15, 130–33, 146–48, 162–66, and Davis, *A Rumor of Revolt*, 116, 146–48.

236. Lepore, *New York Burning*, 191–92, 196–97, 245–46; Davis, *A Rumor of Revolt*, 94–97, 224–25.

237. Black population in New York County (Manhattan) was reported at 2,444 in 1746, 2,272 in 1756, and 3,200 in 1771; Hodges, *Root & Branch*, 104; McManus, *A History of Negro Slavery in New York*, 197–200; and Greene and Harrington, eds., *American Population Before the Federal Census of 1790*, 95–105.

238. Harris, *In the Shadow of Slavery*, 46.

239. Leo Hershkowitz, "Tom's Case: An Incident," *New York History* 52 (1971): 63–71; Lepore, *New York Burning*, 213.

240. Letter signed by Clarke written by Horsmanden, January 1742, in Lepore, *New York Burning*, 212.

241. For many examples in New York and East Jersey from 1741 to 1748, see Hodges, *Root & Branch*, 128ff.

242. Two sources survive with discrepancies of date and facts. One is "The Case of Phyllis, Negro Slave of New York City," Oct. 22, 1748, Coroner's Proceedings in the City and County of New York, Rare Book Room, Columbia University Library, in Hodges, *Root & Branch*, 128, 310. The other is a report of the same case, dated Oct. 22, 1758, and published verbatim in *Minutes of Coroners Proceedings, City and County of New York, John Burnet, Coroner, 1748–1758*, ed. Francis J. Sypher, published as *Collections of the New York Genealogical and Biographical Society*, 16 (2004). In this version, the coroner also reported that "Susannah Romme swears the slave had been given sufficient food."

243. Fugitive slave advertisements in *New-York Weekly Post-Boy*, Aug. 29, 1757, Aug. 30, 1756, p. 63, Feb. 18, 1760, Dec. 31, 1759, Oct. 15, 1761; *Pennsylvania Journal*, Aug. 20, 1761; *Parker's New-York Gazette*, March 22, 1764; *New-York Mercury*, Sept. 10, 1764; Hodges and Brown, eds., *"Pretends to Be Free,"* xxvi, 69, 63, 89, 83, 116.

244. For these and other cases, see Hodges, *Root & Branch*, 90–91.

245. Only one intact copy is known to survive, in the British Library. A fragmentary copy, ripped in half, survives in the Boston Public Library.

246. McManus, *A History of Negro Slavery in New York*, 141–59.

247. George Whitefield, *Three Letters from the Reverend Mr. G. Whitefield* (Philadelphia, 1740); *New-York Weekly Journal*, March 10, 1740; *New-York Gazette*, Feb. 12, 1740; Lepore, "The Tightening Vise"; Berlin and Harris, eds., *Slavery in New York*, 85, 357.

248. Hodges, *Root & Branch*, 86.

249. *Pennsylvania Gazette*, Sept. 11, 1740.

250. *New-York Journal; or The General Advertiser*, Jan. 12, 1775; Hodges and Brown, eds., *"Pretends to Be Free,"* case 380. Also helpful are Hodges, *Root & Branch*, 125–27, and Hodges, ed., *Black Itinerants of the Gospel*, 5–6.

251. Hough, ed., *Reports of Cases in Vice Admiralty*, 29–33, 199; Parish's Transcripts, folders 160, 162, New-York Historical Society; New York Colonial Manuscripts, 75: 55–56, 68, 70, 74, 76, 79–80; 76:16; 77: 70, 98; John Tabor Kempe Papers, Manuscripts, New-York Historical Society.

252. Petition of Juan da Costa, New York Colonial Manuscripts, 89: 158–64; Hodges, *Root & Branch*, 310n.

253. See, for example, the Case of Simon Moore, Aug. 6, 1772, Kempe Papers, New-York Historical Society.

254. Hodges, *Root & Branch*, 130, from data in Hodges and Brown, eds., *"Pretends to Be Free,"* with caveats on pp. xv–xvi. Estimates for years before 1740 are from p. xvi.

255. Hodges and Brown, eds., *"Pretends to Be Free,"* xiii–xxxv; *New-York Weekly Post-Boy*, April 5, 1749; Shane White, *Somewhat More Independent: The End of Slavery in New York City, 1770–1810* (Athens, Ga.: University of Georgia Press, 1991), 128; McManus, *A History of Negro Slavery in New York*, 88.

256. A long description of Cuff appeared in the *New-York Weekly Post-Boy*, Oct. 15, 1753. For seven fugitives who fled from the Hudson Valley and were thought to be heading for New England, see Hodges and Brown, eds., *"Pretends to Be Free,"* case numbers 92, 106, 136, 143, 179, 380, 635.

257. Goodfriend, *Before the Melting Pot*, 127–29.

258. Samuel Auchmuty, correspondence, 1760–1763, in the papers of the Society for the Propagation of the Gospel in Foreign Parts, Bodleian Library, Oxford; John C. van Horne, ed., *Religious Philanthropy and Colonial Slavery: The American Correspondence of the Associates of Dr. Bray* (Urbana: University of Illinois Press, 1986), 166–67, 197, 322; Frank Joseph Klingberg, *Anglican Humanitarianism in Colonial New York* (Philadelphia, 1940), 149; Hodges, *Root & Branch*, 119–20.

259. Hodges and Brown, eds., *"Pretends to Be Free,"* table 8, and individual case numbers 21, 59, 60, 115, 117, 135, 147, 152, 154, 191, 201, 226, 340, 359, 366, 381, 495, 635. For Arch's literacy, see case 340, Oct. 8, 1770; for Ned, case 147, May 16, 1757. For discussion of literacy and forged passes, see p. xxvi. See also Hodges, *Root & Branch*, 118.

260. Compiled from data in Hodges and Brown, eds., *"Pretends to Be Free."* Listed skills and occupations are tabulated in table 6, pp. 13–15.

261. Hodges, *Root & Branch*, 109.

262. White, *Somewhat More Independent*, 106.

263. *New-York Gazette and Weekly Mercury*, June 1, 1772; March 24, Nov. 10, 1777; Nov. 1, 1773.

264. *New-York Weekly Post-Boy*, Aug. 13, 1750.

265. White, *Somewhat More Independent*, 108.

266. Carol F. Karlsen and Laurie Crumpacker, eds, *Journal of Esther Edwards Burr, 1754–1757* (New Haven, 1984) 104; Hodges, *Root & Branch*, 111.

267. Jonas Michaëlius to Adrianus Smoutius, Aug. 11, 1628, in Jameson, ed., *Narratives of New Netherland*, 129–30. See also *New York Colonial Documents*, 4:294; Hodges, *Root & Branch*, 287.

268. "A Spy," *New-York Weekly Journal*, March 7, 14, 21, 28, 1737. Shane White interpreted this essay as an account of a militia training day, but it explicitly describes the event as a holiday "to commemorate the Resurrection of the Blessed Saviour," which was Pinkster or Whitsuntide. Compare White, "'It Was a Proud Day,'" 13–50; Hodges, *Slavery and Freedom in the Rural North*, 56–58; David S. Cohen, "In Search of Carolus Africanus Rex," *Journal of the Afro-American Historical and Genealogical Society* 5 (1984): 149–62; Williams-Meyers, "Pinkster Carnival," 7–17; White, "Pinkster," 68–75.

269. Hodges, *Slavery and Freedom in the Rural North*, 31–32; White, *Somewhat More Independent*, 95–106.

270. Greene and Harrington, eds., *American Population Before the Federal Census of 1790*, 88–105.

271. Hodges, *Root & Branch*, 151–52; Harry Ward, *Between the Lines: Banditti of the American Revolution* (Westport, Conn., 2002), 51–58; Judith L. Van Buskirk, *Generous Enemies: Patriots and Loyalists in Revolutionary New York* (Philadelphia, 2002), 129–54.

272. Primary references for Peters's life before 1783 are scarce, but see "Sgt Peters," in "A Return of Stewards Company of Black Pioneers, 13 Sep. 1783; and Martin's Company," in British National Archives and Clements Library, University of Michigan, and "Thomas Potters (Peters), 45 (Black Pioneers), formerly slave to William Campbell, Wilmington, North Carolina, 1776" and "Sally Pettres, 30, Black Pioneers, formerly slave to Mr. Bellinge, Ashepoo, 1779," *Black Loyalist Directory*, book 2, p. 177.

273. Secondary studies of Peters include C. H. Fyfe, "Thomas Peters, History and Legend," *Sierra Leone Studies*, new series 1 (1953–55): 4–13; Benjamin Quarles, *The Negro in the American Revolution* (Chapel Hill, N.C.: University of North Carolina Press, 1961), 177–81; James W. St. G. Walker, *The Black Loyalists: The Search for the Promised Land in Nova Scotia and Sierra Leone, 1783–1870* (Toronto, 1992); James W. St. G. Walker, "Peters, Thomas," *Dictionary of Canadian Biography* (1979) online; Gary Nash, "Thomas Peters," in *Race, Class, and Politics: Essays on American Colonial Society* (Urbana: University of Illinois Press, 1986); Mary Louise Clifford, *From Slavery to Freetown: Black Loyalists After the American Revolution* (n.p., McFarland, 2006); Alan Gilbert, *Black Patriots and Loyalists: Fighting for Emancipation in the War of Independence* (Chicago, 2012), 215–23. Peters's belated recognition, and a monument in Freetown, Sierra Leone, erected in 2011 by the efforts of the Krio Descendants Union, many related to him, can be found at their website, www.kdulondon.org.

274. For John Peterson's vital dates (ca. 1756?–Oct. 2, 1859), early life on Van Cortlandt Manor, residence in Peekskill, enlistment as a private in Van Cortlandt's 2nd Continental Regiment, and service at the Saratoga and Hudson Valley campaigns, see his obituary in *Weekly Anglo-African*, Oct. 9, 1859. For a biography, see John J. Curran, *Peekskill's African American History: A Hudson Valley Community's Untold Story* (Charleston, S.C., 2008), 19. Much material was gathered by the secretary and trustee

of the Peekskill Museum, Kathleen "Kay" Moshier, whose husband was a descendant of John Peterson. Other materials have been posted on the website of the Peekskill Museum, including "I, John Peterson of Peekskill," more recently accessible at https://prenticeproposal.wordpress.com/i-john-peterson-of-peekskill/.

275. Alexander Scammell, "Return of Negroes in the Army, 24 August 1778"; George H. Moore, *Historical Notes on the Employment of Negroes in the American Army of the Revolution* (New York, 1862), 17. Scammell's report should be read with the "Monthly Return of the Continental Army under . . . George Washington," Aug. 29–30, 1778, Record Group 93, National Archives. These data have been tabulated and published with great care in Charles H. Lesser, ed., *The Sinews of Independence: Monthly Strength Reports of the Continental Army* (Chicago, 1976), 80–82. See also Gilbert, *Black Patriots and Loyalists*, 97.

276. This assumes mean strength of Continental brigades at about 1,200 in August and September of 1778, from data for Continental infantry regiments in Lefferts, *of Independence*, 80–86. The proportion of African Americans in Continental infantry regiments under Washington's command may be very roughly estimated at about 1–2 percent in 1776, 5–6 percent in 1778, and 10 percent in 1781. On the question of overall numbers of men serving in the War of Independence, the total population of the thirteen states in 1776 was roughly 2.5 million, with a median age of sixteen, a proportion over the age of sixty at 1 percent, and a gender ratio near parity. This would yield a male population aged 16–60 of about 600,000. John Adams estimated that two thirds of the American population supported the War of Independence, which if correct would have yielded about 400,000 males of military age. If half served in military units, the total would have been about 200,000. Other estimates reported by Peckham and Ailes have gone as high as 250,000 American males serving in American independence, which Peckham thought too high, but may prove to be too low. Peckham also accepted an estimate by Benjamin Quarles that 5,000 Negro soldiers served in the Patriot forces. That number could have been as high as 10,000. Howard Henry Peckham, *The Toll of Independence: Engagement and Battle Casualties of the American Revolution* (Chicago, 1974), xiii, ix; Quarles, *The Negro in the American Revolution*, ix. The work of Jane Ailes yielded an estimate that 230,000 men fought for independence in the Revolution, and about 9,000 were African American, as reported by Gary B. Nash, "The African Americans' Revolution," in Edward G. Gray and Jane Kamensky, eds., *The Oxford Handbook of the American Revolution* (New York, 2015), 268n. Successive inquiries tend to raise these estimates, as Ailes raised numbers of soldiers of color in Patriot forces from 5,000 in Quarles to about 9,000.

277. Thomas S. Collier, "The Revolutionary Privateers of Connecticut," *New London Historical Society Records and Papers* 1 (1892): 44. This and many other examples appear in Quarles, *The Negro in the American Revolution*, 87.

278. Quarles, *The Negro in the American Revolution*, 83–93; Gilbert, *Black Patriots and Loyalists*, 95–115.

279. *Pennsylvania Gazette*, Nov. 22, 1775.

280. Hodges, *Slavery and Freedom in the Rural North*, 92–106; Ward, *Between the Lines*, 61–68; David Hackett Fischer, *Washington's Crossing* (New York, 2004–05), 168–72.

281. On Bleuke's career, see Ward, *Between the Lines*, 64; Walker, *The Black Loyalists*, 34–35.

282. Hodges, *Root & Branch*, 151–52; Graham Hodges, "Black Revolts in New York and the Neutral Zone," in *New York in the Age of the Constitution, 1775–1800*, ed. Paul A. Gilje and William Pencak (Cranbury, N.J., 1993); "Colonel Cuff," in Hodges, *Root & Branch*, 151–53, 156, 159.

283. Thomas S. Wermuth, "The Central Hudson Valley: Dutchess, Orange, and Ulster Counties," in Joseph S. Tiedemann and Eugene R. Fingerhut, *The Other New York: The American Revolution Beyond New York City, 1763–1787* (Albany, 2005), 144; Michael Groth, "Forging Freedom in the Mid-Hudson Valley: The End of Slavery and the Formation of a Free African-American Community, 1770–1850," (diss., SUNY Binghamton, 1994), 85–86.

284. "Book of Negroes," British Headquarters Papers, PRO 30/55/100, British National Archives; ms. copies are in British Headquarters Papers, document 10427, Manuscript Room, New York Public Library. It has been collated with other lists, transcribed by Susan Hawkes Cook and edited by Graham Hodges, and published as *The Black Loyalist Directory: African Americans in Exile After the American Revolution* (New York and London, 1996). A slave named Rachel from a nonexistent county appears on page 104; and other Rachels are on pp. 38, 118, 150, 152, 156, 174, 183, 186.

285. U.S. Census of 1790; Colonial Census of 1771, in Greene and Harrington, eds., *American Population Before the Federal Census of 1790*, 92, 105–12; McManus, *A History of Negro Slavery in New York*, 197–200; Peter O. Wacker, *Land and People: A Cultural Geography of Preindustrial New Jersey: Origins and Settlements* (New Brunswick, N.J., 1975); Arthur Zilversmit, *The First Emancipation: The Abolition of Slavery in the North* (Chicago, 1967), 222.

286. J. P. Brissot de Warville, *New Travels in the United States*, ed. Durand Echeverria (Cambridge, Mass., 1964), 227–28; White, *Somewhat More Independent*, 20. Other travelers agreed, among them Moreau de St. Méry, Francisco de Miranda, William Strickland.

287. U.S. Bureau of the Census, *Heads of Families at the First Census of the United States* (Washington, D.C., 1908), 9–14. An analysis of ethnic surnames was done by the U.S. Census Bureau and published in W. S. Rossiter et al., *A Century of Population Growth from the First Census of the United States to the Twelfth, 1790–1900* (Department of Commerce and Labor, 1909), 219, and passim. Some adjustments have been made in research by Thomas L. Purvis, but historians agree on the major findings about Dutch slave owning. See White, *Somewhat More Independent*, 18, 21–22, 219n; and Hodges, *Root & Branch*, 230–36.

288. Rossiter et al., *A Century of Population Growth*, 219.

289. Jabez D. Hammond, *The History of Political Parties in the State of New York*, 2 vols. (Syracuse, 1852), 1: 580–81.

290. Zilversmit, *The First Emancipation*, 146.

291. *New York Packet*, April 4, 1785, quoted in Hodges, *Root & Branch*, 162.

292. Zilversmit, *The First Emancipation*, 148.

293. Zilversmit, *The First Emancipation*, 222, 225–29.

294. Hodges and Brown, eds., *"Pretends to Be Free,"* with caveats on xv–xvi. The first study was for all of New York and New Jersey. The second was for a smaller area in southern New York and northeastern New Jersey. White, *Somewhat More Independent*, 140.

295. White, *Somewhat More Independent*, 140–42.

296. Yoshpe, "Record of Slave Manumissions in New York During the Colonial and Early National Periods," 78–104.

297. Vivienne L. Kruger, "Born to Run: The Slave Family in Early New York" (diss., Columbia University, 1985), 724–84. For discussion, White, *Somewhat More Independent*, 28–29, 222.

298. Agreement between Yat and John S. Glen and his daughter Sarah Glen, in Percy M. Van Epps, "Slavery in Early Glenville, New York," in *Contributions to the History of Glenville* (Glenville, N.Y., 1932), 101; White, *Somewhat More Independent*, 111–12.

299. White, *Somewhat More Independent*, 117–19; *New Jersey Gazette*, Jan. 26, Feb. 2, March 1, 8, 1780; Feb. 23, June 25, Dec. 23, 1783.

300. David Gellman, *Emancipating New York: The Politics of Slavery and Freedom, 1777–1827* (Baton Rouge, 2006), 37.

301. Gellman, *Emancipating New York*, 195.

302. White, *Somewhat More Independent*, 148–49.

303. This from the U.S. Census, which counted 1,036 "free people not white" in 1790 and 16,358 free Negroes in 1840. See also Hodges, *Root & Branch*, 279, 176, 230, 273–80, and White, *Somewhat More Independent*, 26, for corrections in the census counts.

304. David T. Gilchrist, ed., *The Growth of the Seaport Cities, 1790–1825* (Charlottesville: University Press of Virginia, 1967), 25–53.

305. For estimates from seamen's protection papers, see Ira Dye, "Early American Merchant Seafarers," *American Philosophical Society Proceedings* 120 (1976): 349.

306. W. Jeffrey Bolster, *Black Jacks: African American Seamen in the Age of Sail* (Cambridge, Mass.: Harvard University Press, 1997), 91.

307. Bolster, *Black Jacks*, 161, 220–21, 224, and passim.

308. Moses Grandy, *Narrative of the Life of Moses Grandy, Late a Slave in the United States of America* (London, 1844), 42.

309. White, *Somewhat More Independent*, 156–62.

310. Thomas F. de Voe, *The Market Book: A History of the Public Markets of the City of New York* (New York, 1862, 1970), 219, 322, and passim; Charles H. Haswell, *Reminiscences of an Octogenarian of the City of New York* (New York, 1897), 35. On market cries of African American women, see Christine Stansell, *City of Women: Sex and Class in New York, 1789–1869* (New York, 1986), 13–15, 59–61, 156–57, 172–92. See also Elizabeth Blackmar, *Manhattan for Rent, 1785–1850* (Ithaca, 1989), 60, 134, and passim.

311. Eric W. Sanderson, *Manahatta: A Natural History of New York City* (New York, 2009), 216; John M. Kochiss, *Oystering from New York to Boston* (Middletown, Conn., 1974).

312. Anne Marie Cantwell and Diana diZerega Wall, *Unearthing Gotham: The Archeology of New York City* (New Haven, 2001), 269–70; William V. Askins, "Material Culture and Expressions of Group Identity in Sandy Ground, New York," in Nan A. Rothschild, J. H. Geismar, and Dona DiZerega Wall, eds., *Urbanization and Social Change in Historical Archaeology*, 64–70. See also *American Archaeology* 5 (1988): 209–18, and William V. Askins, "Sandy Ground: Historical Archaeology of Class and Ethnicity in a Nineteenth-Century Community on Staten Island" (diss., Department of Anthropology, City University of New York, 1988).

313. Abram C. Dayton, *Last Days of Knickerbocker Life in New York* (New York, 1897),

128–33, 322, and passim; Carla L. Peterson, *Black Gotham: A Family History of African Americans in Nineteenth-Century New York* (New Haven, 2011), 65, 101, 103, 122, 183–85.

314. Gary Nash, "Forging Freedom: The Emancipation Experience in Northern Seaports, 1775–1820," in *Race, Class, and Politics: Essays on American Colonial and Revolutionary Society* (Urbana and Chicago: University of Illinois Press, 1986), 283–321; data at 304–7.

315. Hodges, *Root & Branch*, 194; White, *Somewhat More Independent*, 163–64.

316. White, *Somewhat More Independent*, 171–79; Nan A. Rothschild, *New York City Neighborhoods: The Eighteenth Century* (San Diego, 1990), 100; Hodges, *Root & Branch*, 176–77; Harris, *In the Shadow of Slavery*, 74–75.

317. Peterson, *Black Gotham*.

318. James Weldon Johnson, *Black Manhattan* (New York, 1930, 1958, 1991), 58–59.

319. "The Story of Seneca Village, 1825–1857," in Leslie M. Alexander, *African or American? Black Identity and Political Activism in New York City, 1784–1861* (Urbana: University of Illinois Press, 2008, 2012), 154–74.

320. Judith Wellman, *Brooklyn's Promised Land: The Free Black Community of Weeksville, New York* (New York, 2014).

321. Wilder, *In the Company of Black Men*, 38, 42, 52–53, 64, 74.

322. Wilder, *In the Company of Black Men*, 36–39,74–76; Robert L. Harris Jr., "Early Black Benevolent Societies, 1780–1830," *Massachusetts Review* (Fall 1979): 609–11.

323. Jupiter Hammon, "An Evening Thought, Salvation by Christ . . . ," broadside (n.p., 1761), University of Virginia Library. Other poems were printed at Hartford, Connecticut, where he lived during the War of Independence. In 2013 and 2015 two other poems have been discovered in manuscript collections at Yale and the New-York Historical Society.

Jupiter Hammon, *An Address to the Negroes of the State of New-York* (New York, 1787; 2nd edition, 1806); the first printing is online at https://digitalcommons.unl.edu /etas/12. See also Stanley Ranson, *America's First Negro Poet* (New York, 1970); Charles A. Vertanes, "Jupiter Hammon: Early Negro Poet of Long Island," *Nassau County Historical Society Journal* 17 (Winter 1957): 3–6; Sidney Kaplan and Emma Nogrady Kaplan, *The Black Presence in the Era of the American Revolution*, revised edition (Amherst, 1989), 175; Arthur A. Schomberg, "Jupiter Hammon Before the New York African Society," *New York Amsterdam News*, Jan. 22, 1930; Wilder, *In the Company of Black Men*, 38; Moss, *Slavery on Long Island*, 182–83; Sondra O'Neale, *Jupiter Hammon and the Biblical Beginnings of African American Literature* (n.p., Scarecrow Press, 1993).

324. A history of this effort is William J. Walls, *The African Methodist Episcopal Zion Church: Reality of the Black Church* (Charlotte, 1974).

325. Abyssinian Baptist Church, *The Articles of Faith, Church Discipline and By-Laws of the Abyssinian Baptist Church in the City of New York, April 3, 1833* (New York, 1833); Wilder, *In the Company of Black Men*, 48–49.

326. Paul Gilje, *The Road to Mobocracy: Popular Disorder in New York City, 1763–1834* (Chapel Hill: University of North Carolina Press, 1987), 154–56.

327. The manuscript records of the New-York Manumission Society are in the New-York Historical Society, and much material is online at the Historical Society's website.

328. Daniel C. Littlefield, "John Jay, the Revolutionary Generation, and Slavery," *New York History* 81 (2000): 91–132.

329. Thomas Moseley, "A History of the New-York Manumission Society, 1785–1849" (diss., New York University, 1963). Historians are divided. For interpretations with a strong critical edge, see White, *Somewhat More Independent*, 81–87, and Rob Weston, "Alexander Hamilton and the Abolition of Slavery in New York," *Afro Americans in New York Life and History* 18 (1994): 31–45.

330. Gellman, *Emancipating New York*, 56–77, 154–65.

331. Harris, *In the Shadow of Slavery*, 135.

332. *Freedom's Journal*, Aug. 15, 1828; Alexander, *African or American?*, 201–2.

333. De Voe, *The Market Book*; Eileen Southern and Josephine Wright, *Images: Iconography of Music in African American Culture, 1770s–1920s* (New York, 2000); Sterling Stuckey, "African Spirituality and Cultural Practice in Colonial New York," in *Inequality in Early America*, ed. Carla Pestina and Sharon Salinger (Hanover, N.H., 1999).

334. Edward Z. C. Judson, *The Mysteries and Miseries of New York: The Story of Real Life by Ned Buntline* (New York, 1848); George C. Foster, *New York by Gaslight: With Here and There a Streak of Sunshine* (New York, 1950).

335. White, *Somewhat More Independent*, 96–97; De Voe, *The Market Book*, 149.

336. Alexander, *African or American?*, 138–40; Judson, *The Mysteries and Miseries of New York*, part 1: 89–91, part 2: 79–82; Charles Dickens, *American Notes*, xx; Foster, *New York by Gaslight*, 140–46. Many accounts appeared in city newspapers, e.g., *New York Times*, Aug. 2, 1850.

337. Johann Friedrich Blumenbach, *De generis humani varietate nativa* ("On the Natural Variety of Humanity") (Göttingen, 1776).

338. Harris, *In the Shadow of Slavery*, 92; White, *Somewhat More Independent*, 144–45, 179–82; Gilje, *The Road to Mobocracy*, 147–53; Harris, *In the Shadow of Slavery*, 92; Hodges, *Root & Branch*, 197.

339. Graham Russell Gao Hodges, *David Ruggles: A Radical Black Abolitionist and the Underground Railroad in New York City* (Chapel Hill: University of North Carolina Press, 2010), 214.

340. White, *Somewhat More Independent*, 209.

341. *New-York Weekly Journal*, June 10, 1734; July 30, 1744.

342. *Philadelphia Weekly Mercury*, Sept. 17, 1724; *New-York Gazette*, July 24, 1738; *New-York Weekly Journal*, Sept. 27, 1742.

343. *New-York Gazette*, June 27, 1748.

344. Wilder, *In the Company of Black Men*, 77, and more broadly, 73–97.

345. A copy of the publication survives in the Houghton Library, Harvard University. Jennifer Schuessler, "Use of 'African-American' Dates to Nation's Early Days," *New York Times*, April 20, 2015. This piece traced the phrase to the early republic. After it appeared, Yale librarian Fred Shapiro did a digital search of American Historical Newspapers, and found this earlier example. It is discussed in Jennifer Schuessler, "The Term 'African American' Appears Earlier than Thought," *New York Times*, April 21, 2015.

346. Schuessler, "Use of 'African-American' Dates to Nation's Early Days."

347. Patrick Rael, *Black Identity and Black Protest in the Antebellum North* (Chapel Hill: University of North Carolina Press, 2002), 111; Mitford Mathews, *A Dictionary of Americanisms* (Chicago: University of Chicago Press, 1951).
348. Rael, *Black Identity and Black Protest in the Antebellum North*, 102–16.

Chapter 3: DELAWARE VALLEY

1. *Narrative of James Williams, an American Slave* (Boston, 1838), 98. This very powerful autobiography was denounced in southern newspapers as a fraud at the time of its first publication. For a modern edition, published by the Louisiana State University Press (Baton Rouge, 2013), Hank Trent did deep research on James Williams, and confirmed both its accuracy and authenticity.
2. The will and inventory of Ann Elizabeth Fortune are in Philadelphia County Wills, Ann Elizabeth Fortune (Negro) Will, 1768, book O, number 196, now reclassified as book 051-O-258 (1768). Our knowledge of Ann Elizabeth Fortune's will comes from research by Jean Soderlund, who found both the will and inventory of the estate in the course of her very creative research in the Philadelphia Probate Records. Soderlund has also done much to reconstruct the history of African American women and family life in colonial Pennsylvania. See Jean Soderlund, "Black Women in Colonial Pennsylvania," *Pennsylvania Magazine of History and Biography* 107 (1983): 69–83, reprinted in Joe William Trotter and Eric Ledell Smith, eds., *African Americans in Pennsylvania* (University Park, 1997), 73–92, 86, 92. Julie Winch put these documents to work in *A Gentleman of Color: The Life of James Forten* (Oxford, 2002), an excellent biography of James Forten and his family, which is also the best account in print of Ann Elizabeth Fortune. The story of this extraordinary woman can be taken a little farther with the aid of pathbreaking research by genealogist and historian Paul Heinegg, discussed below.
3. *Pennsylvania Gazette*, Oct. 3, 1751.
4. Winch, *A Gentleman of Color*, 16–17.
5. Paul Heinegg, *Free African Americans of Maryland and Delaware: From the Colonial Period to 1810* (Baltimore: Clearfield Publishing Co., and Genealogical Book Company, 2000), 128–31; Paul Heinegg, *Free African Americans of North Carolina, Virginia, and South Carolina: From the Colonial Period to About 1820*, 2 vols., 5th edition (Baltimore: Clearfield Publishing Co., and Genealogical Book Company, 1992, 2005).
6. Heinegg, *Free African Americans of Maryland and Delaware*, 128–31; Heinegg, *Free African Americans of North Carolina, Virginia, and South Carolina*, 495–97. Heinegg also found that Fortune was not a common African American surname before 1800; only two major lines appeared in his very broad studies, one mainly in Somerset and Wicomico counties, Maryland, and contiguous Sussex County, Delaware. The other was in Tidewater Virginia. After 1800, the Fortune surname became more common.
7. See below, pp. 234, 246–49.
8. Winch, *A Gentleman of Color*, 111–12.
9. William H. Williams, *Slavery and Freedom in Delaware, 1639–1865* (Wilmington, 1996), 2–3; Amandus Johnson, *The Swedish Settlements on the Delaware*, 2 vols. (Baltimore, 1969), 2: 699, 706, 710, 722; C. S. Weslager, *New Sweden on the Delaware* (Wilmington, 1988).

10. Terry Jordan, *Trails to Texas: Southern Roots of Western Cattle Raising* (Lincoln, Nebr., 1981).

11. A brief biography, with errors, appears in American National Biography, online. For scholarship of high quality see Christian J. Koot, "The Merchant, the Map, and Empire . . . ," *William and Mary Quarterly*, 3rd series, 67 (2010): 604–44.

   His name appears as Herman on the gravestone he commissioned, and was variously written as Hermann, Heerman, Herrmanns, etc. Excerpts from his journals are in Clayton C. Hall, ed., *Narratives of Early Maryland* (New York, 1910), and in Charles Gehring, ed., *New York Historical Manuscripts: Dutch,* vols. 18–19, *Delaware Papers (Dutch Period): A Collection of Documents Pertaining to the Regulation of Affairs on the South River of New Netherland* (Baltimore, 1981).

   For his African slaves, see Mathias Beck to Peter Stuyvesant, Aug. 1659, "I shall be sending a young Negro Girl for Mr. Augustinus Heermans according to his request." E. B. O'Callaghan, *Voyages of the Slavers St. John and Arms of Amsterdam, 1659, 1663; Together with Additional papers illustrative of the Slave Trade under the Dutch; Translated from the Original Manuscripts* (Albany, 1867), 144–46.

12. David Hackett Fischer, "The Friends' Migration: Numbers and Proportion," in *Albion's Seed: Four British Folkways in America* (New York and Oxford: Oxford University Press, 1989), 420–24.

13. J. William Frost, *The Quaker Family in Colonial America* (New York, 1973), 24.

14. Biblical sources for the Golden Rule, Luke 6:31; Matthew 7:12; "the least of our brethren," Matthew, 25:40. For more on this subject, see Fischer, *Albion's Seed*, 419–29, 480, 555–56, and passim.

15. Max Weber, *The Protestant Ethic and the Spirit of Capitalism* (1904–5; reprint, New York, 1958).

16. George Fox, *Journal*, 619, 632 (9.iii.1672; 9.vii.1672); Fischer, *Albion's Seed*, 453.

17. England is 51,356 square miles; Pennsylvania is presently 45,045 square miles. Penn's original grant was larger.

18. ". . . Brief Relation of the Illegal commitment of William Penn by him called Sr John Robinson, Lt. of the Tower . . . ," Feb. 1671, in Richard S. Dunn and Mary Maples Dunn, eds., *The Papers of William Penn* (Philadelphia, 1986), 1:199.

19. Deborah Norris to Isaac Norris, Nov. 3, 1733, quoted in Alan Tully, *William Penn's Legacy: Politics and Social Structure in Provincial Pennsylvania, 1726–1755* (Baltimore, 1977), 80.

20. This was a closed corporation called "the mayor and commonalty of Philadelphia," which controlled the city from the issue of its charter in 1701 to 1776, when the corporation was abolished as inconsistent with the values and purposes of the American Revolution. See Judith Diamondstone, "The Philadelphia Corporation, 1701–1776" (thesis, University of Pennsylvania, 1969), 258–68, and "Philadelphia's Municipal Corporation, 1701–1776," *Pennsylvania Magazine of History and Biography* 90 (1966): 183–201. See also Daniel R. Gilbert, "Patterns of Organization and Membership in Philadelphia Club Life" (thesis, University of Pennsylvania, 1952).

21. This historian's census of churches, meetings, and congregations appears in Edwin S. Gaustad, *Historical Atlas of Religion in America* (New York: Harper & Row, 1976), a

major contribution. A second edition is Gaustad and Philip J. Barlow's *New Historical Atlas of Religion in America* (New York: Oxford University Press, 2001).

22. David Hackett Fischer, *Liberty and Freedom* (New York and Oxford: Oxford University Press, 2005), 50–60.

23. William Comfort, *The Quakers: A Brief History of Their Influence on Pennsylvania*, revised by F. B. Tolles (Harrisburg, 1955), 6.

24. Tully, *William Penn's Legacy*, 170–73; Fischer, *Albion's Seed*, 433; Richard Ryerson, "The Quaker Elite in the Pennsylvania Assembly," in Bruce C. Daniels, ed., *Power and Status: Officeholding in Colonial America* (Middletown, Conn., 1986), 106–35.

25. Joshua Evans, Journal, 29 vii 1795 to 17 xii 1796, ms. Friends Historical Library, Swarthmore College.

26. Evarts B. Greene and Virginia G. Harrington, eds., *American Population Before the Federal Census of 1790* (New York and Baltimore, 1932 and 1981), 114.

27. Franklin, "Examination Before the House of Commons," 1766; Greene and Harrington, eds., *American Population Before the Federal Census of 1790*, 116. Franklin estimated that the entire population of Pennsylvania was about 160,000. Historians think that his estimate was too low. The total population of Pennsylvania in the census of 1790 had grown to 434,373, and African Americans were 10,274.

28. Tully, *William Penn's Legacy*, 53; for the "mosaic" of the Delaware Valley, circa 17090, ACLS, "Report of the Committee on Linguistic and National Stocks," *Annual Report of the American Historical Association Report for the Year 1931* (1932), 107–441, and Thomas L. Purvis, "The European Ancestry of the United States Population, 1790," *William and Mary Quarterly*, 3rd series, 41 (1984): 98–101.

29. Stephanie Grauman Wolf, *Urban Village: Population, Community, and Family Structure in Germantown, Pennsylvania, 1683–1800* (Princeton: Princeton University Press, 1976), 140; Harry Tinkcom, Margaret Tinkcom, and Grant Simon, *Historic Germantown* (Philadelphia, 1955).

30. James O. Knauss, *Social Conditions Among the Pennsylvania Germans in the Eighteenth Century* (Lancaster, Penn., 1922).

31. Rufus M. Jones et. al, *The Quakers in the American Colonies* (New York: Macmillan, 1911), 422.

32. Tully, *William Penn's Legacy*, 170–73. A second estimate comes from Ryerson, "The Quaker Elite in the Pennsylvania Assembly," 106–35.

33. Tully, *William Penn's Legacy*, 53.

34. Cadwalader Morgan, "The Buying of Negroes," Merion, 28th of ye 5th moneth, 1696, manuscript in the Haverford College, digital image online in the Quaker and Slavery Collection, http://triptych.brynmawr.edu.

35. Nicholas More to William Penn, Dec. 1, 1684, in Dunn and Dunn, eds., *The Papers of William Penn*, 2:321, 608; Darold D. Wax, "Africans on the Delaware: The Pennsylvania Slave Trade, 1759–1765," *Pennsylvania History* 50 (1983): 39; Gary R. Nash and Jean B. Soderlund, *Freedom by Degrees: Emancipation in Pennsylvania and Its Aftermath* (Oxford, 1991), 10, 209n. A record of sales survives in the manuscript Memorandum Book of American Debtors of Charles Jones, Jr., & Co., Bristol, England, Historical Society of Pennsylvania.

36. Frederick Tolles, *Quakers and the Atlantic Culture* (New York: Macmillan, 1960), 117.

37. On the original document, now barely legible, the authors signed themselves "Gerret Henderick, Derick op den Graeff, Francis Daniell Pastorius, and Abraham op den Graeff of our monthly meeting," 1688. After many adventures, it is now in the Quaker Collection, Haverford College, ms. HC09-10002; a digital image is online at http://triptych.brynmawr.edu/cdm/ref/collection/HC_QuakSlav/id/8.

38. Brycchan Carey, *From Peace to Freedom: Quaker Rhetoric and the Birth of American Antislavery, 1657–1761* (New Haven, 2012), 70–104. See also Katharine Gerbner, "We are against the traffick of mens-body: The Germantown Protest of 1688, and the Origins of American Abolitionism," *Pennsylvania History* 74 (2007): 149–72.

39. On Quakers as Islamic slaves in Africa, see Justin J. Meggitt, *Early Quakers and Islam: Slavery, Apocalyptic and Christian-Mouslim Encounters in the Seventeenth Century* (Uppsala, Sweden: Swedish Science Press, 2013); online at http://www.justinmeggitt.info/s/Meggitt-Early-Quakers-and-Islam-Open Access.pdf.

40. *An exhortation and caution to Friends concerning the buying and keeping of Negroes* (n.p., 1693); J. William Frost, ed., *The Keithian Controversy in Early Pennsylvania* (Norwood, Penn., 1980).

41. Morgan, "The Buying of Negroes."

42. George Fox, "To Friends beyond the Sea, that have Black and Indian Slaves," 1657, in *A Collection of many select and Christian Epistles, letters and testimonies* . . . (1657; reprint, London, 1698), epistle 153; George Fox, *Gospel family-order, being a short discourse concerning the ordering of families, both of whites, blacks, and Indians* (London, 1676; reprint, Philadelphia, 1701). These texts are reprinted in J. William Frost, *The Quaker Origins of Anti-Slavery* (Norwood, Penn., 1980), 35–55. For helpful discussion, see J. William Frost, "George Fox's Ambiguous Anti-Slavery Legacy," in Michael Mullett, ed., *New Light on George Fox (1624–1691)* (York, England, 1994), 69–88, and Carey, *From Peace to Freedom*, 40–69.

43. Penn wrote "always," then had second thoughts and drew a line through it. William Penn to James Harrison, Oct. 25, 1685, Penn Papers, Historical Society of Pennsylvania; published in Dunn and Dunn, eds., *The Papers of William Penn*, 3:66–67, also 4:113–14.

44. Darold D. Wax, "The Negro Slave Trade in Colonial Pennsylvania" (diss. University of Washington, D.C., 1962); Darold D. Wax, "Quaker Merchants and the Slave Trade in Colonial Pennsylvania," *Pennsylvania Magazine of History and Biography* 86 (1962): 145–56; Nash and Soderlund, *Freedom by Degrees*, 18–19.

45. Nash and Soderlund, *Freedom by Degrees*, 19.

46. Jean R. Soderlund, *Quakers and Slavery: A Divided Spirit* (Princeton: Princeton University Press, 1985, 1988), 34.

47. Carey, *From Peace to Freedom*, 103.

48. *Votes and Proceedings of the House of Representatives of the Province of Pennsylvania*, 3 vols. (Philadelphia, 1752–54), 1:110.

49. Gregory O'Malley, "Beyond the Middle Passage: Slave Migration from the Caribbean to North America, 1619–1807," *William & Mary Quarterly* 66 (2009): 125–72.

50. Wax, "Africans on the Delaware," 39–49, 41; Darold D. Wax, "The Demand for Slave Labor in Colonial Pennsylvania," *Pennsylvania History* 34 (1967): 331–45; Nash and Soderlund, *Freedom by Degrees*, 15; P. M. G. Harris, "The Demographic Development

of Colonial Philadelphia in Some Comparative Perspective," *American Philosophical Society Proceedings* 133 (1989): 274.

51. Wax, "Africans on the Delaware," 38.

52. Williams, *Slavery and Freedom in Delaware*, 15, quoting Wade P. Catts, "Slaves, Free Blacks, and French Negroes" (MA thesis, University of Delaware, 1988), 39–40; Elizabeth Montgomery, *Reminiscences of Wilmington* (Philadelphia: T.K. Collins, 1851) 164–65.

53. Nash and Soderlund, *Freedom by Degrees*, 19.

54. Nash and Soderlund, *Freedom by Degrees*, 19.

55. Henry Wiencek, *An Imperfect God: George Washington, His Slaves, and the Creation of America* (New York: Macmillan, 2004); Philip D. Morgan, "'To Get Quit of Negroes': George Washington and Slavery," *Journal of American Studies* 39 (2005), 403–29.

56. John F. Watson, *Annals of Philadelphia* (Philadelphia, 1830), 352, 483.

57. Many impressionistic guesses and estimates are tabulated in Greene and Harrington, eds., *American Population Before the Federal Census of 1790*, 113–18. Very helpful to this historian are Patrick Rael's population estimates in *Black Identity and Black Protest in the Antebellum North* (Chapel Hill: University of North Carolina Press, 2002), 86.

58. *Pennsylvania Journal*, May 27, 1762.

59. Mungo Park, *Travels in the Interior Districts of Africa . . .* (Philadelphia, 1800), 43; Darold Wax, "Preferences for Slaves in Colonial America," *Journal of Negro History* 58 (1973): 393.

60. Philadelphia *Pennsylvania Gazette*, May 6, 1762; Williams, *Slavery and Freedom in Delaware,* 15.

61. William Snelgrave, *A New Account of Some Parts of Guinea, and the Slave Trade* (London 1734), 170; John Atkins, *A Voyage to Guinea, Brazil and the West indies; In His majesty's Ships the Swallow and Weymouth* (London, 1735), 79, and *Seasonable Observations on the Trade to Africa in a Letter to a Member of Parliament* (London, 1748), 7; Wax, "Preferences for Slaves in Colonial America," 392.

62. Table 3.1, below.

63. These estimates combine voyages listed in the Trans-Atlantic Slave Database with lists of origins in newspaper advertisements for slave sales and records of slave trading firms, compiled by Darold D. Wax in "Africans on the Delaware," 39–49, 38, and "Negro Imports into Pennsylvania, 1720–1766," *Pennsylvania History* 32 (1765): 254–87. Also useful were Elizabeth Donnan's documents on the slave trade.

64. For Benezet's idea of "North Guinea," see his *Some Historical Account of Guinea*, in David L. Crosby, ed., *The Complete Antislavery Writings of Anthony Benezet, An Annotated Critical Edition* (Baton Rouge, 2013), 162.

65. Michel Adanson, *A Voyage to Senegal, the Isle of Goree, and the River Gambia*, translated from the French edition, "with notes by an English gentleman, who resided some time in that country" (Dublin, 1759); André Brue, *Voyages and Travels along the Western Coasts of Africa* (1728), reprinted in Thomas Astley, *A New General Collection of Voyages and Travels . . .* , 4 vols. (London, 1745–47), vol. 2; Jean Barbot, *A Description of the Coasts of North and South Guinea* (London, 1732, 1744, and 1752); Francis Moore, *Travels in the Interior Parts of Africa* (London, 1738). Moore was a factor for the Royal African Company in Gambia, and said to be a Quaker.

66. Benezet, *Some Historical Account of Guinea*, 72–74, 82, 122–24, 163, 188, 261; Maurice Jackson, *Let This Voice Be Heard: Anthony Benezet, Father of Atlantic Abolitionism* (Philadelphia, 2009), 97, also 90–97.

67. For Quakers and Malinke or Mandingo slaves, see Jackson, *Let This Voice Be Heard*, 90–91, 93–97.

68. John Dickinson to his brother, April 30, 1715, Dickinson Letter Book, Historical Society of Pennsylvania; Wax, "Preferences for Slaves in Colonial America," 371–401; Wax, "The Demand for Slave Labor in Colonial Pennsylvania," 310–45.

69. Calculated from Wax, "Negro Imports," 254–87.

70. Nash and Soderlund, *Freedom by Degrees*, 20–24; Nash, "Forging Freedom: The Emancipation Experience of Northern Seaport Cities, 1775–1820," in Ira Berlin and Ronald Hoffman, eds., *Slavery and Freedom in the Age of the American Revolution* (Charlottesville: University Press of Virginia, 1983), 12–16.

71. Edward Turner, *The Negro in Pennsylvania* (Washington, D.C., 1911), 21.

72. Turner, *The Negro in Pennsylvania*, 13–27, 54–68.

73. Nash and Soderlund, *Freedom by Degrees*, 12.

74. *Colonial Records of Pennsylvania* (Philadelphia, 1838–53), 2:421–22; A. Leon Higginbotham Jr., *In the Matter of Color: Race and the American Legal Process: The Colonial Period* (Oxford, 1978), 291.

75. Philadelphia *American Weekly Mercury*, April 29, 1742; Turner, *The Negro in Pennsylvania*, 36.

76. Nash and Soderlund, *Freedom by Degrees*, 4–9, 32–40.

77. Nash and Soderlund, *Freedom by Degrees*, 36–37.

78. For Esther's "cunning turn of wit," Nash and Soderlund, *Freedom by Degrees*, 38.

79. For Pennsylvania slaves described as branded on the face, Billy G. Smith and Richard Wojtowicz, eds., *Blacks Who Stole Themselves: Advertisements for Runaways in the Pennsylvania Gazette, 1728–1790* (Philadelphia, 1989), 3, 55, 96, 220 (for whip-scarred runaways, 16, 17, 25, 27, 29, 31, 33, 42, 100, 148, 172, 219, 272); *Philadelphia Gazette*, May 5, 1748.

80. Robert Sutcliffe, *Travels in Some Parts of North America, in the Years 1804, 1805, and 1806* (York, England, 1811), 184.

81. Susan E. Klepp, *Philadelphia in Transition: A Demographic History of the City and Its Occupational Groups* (New York, 1989), 225–96.

82. Klepp, *Philadelphia in Transition*, 225–96.

83. Sharon Ann Burnston, "Babies in the Well: An Underground Insight into Deviant Behavior in Eighteenth-Century Philadelphia," *Pennsylvania Magazine of History and Biography* 106 (1982): 151–86.

84. Nash and Soderlund, *Freedom by Degrees*, 32.

85. Nash, *Forging Freedom*, 10; Nash and Soderlund, *Freedom by Degrees*, 16.

86. Nash, *Forging Freedom*, 11, 16.

87. Watson, *Annals of Philadelphia*, 352, 483.

88. Nash and Soderlund, *Freedom by Degrees*, 26–31, 210n.

89. Nash and Soderlund, *Freedom by Degrees*, 31; Klepp, *Philadelphia in Transition*, 252.

90. *Pennsylvania Gazette*, Aug. 26, 1762, in Smith and Wojtowicz, eds. *Blacks Who Stole Themselves*, 56–57, 186.

91. Nash, *Forging Freedom*, 16, citing Henry Melchior Muhlenberg, *Journals*, 3 vols. (Philadelphia, 1942), 1:721.

92. Smith and Wojtowicz, eds., *Blacks Who Stole Themselves*, 6–14.

93. Smith and Wojtowicz, eds., *Blacks Who Stole Themselves*, 35, Oct. 12, 1752.

94. Philadelphia *Pennsylvania Gazette*, April 27, 1774, in Smith and Wojtowicz, eds., *Blacks Who Stole Themselves*, 118.

95. Crèvecoeur, *Letters from an American Farmer*, letter xi, in various editions.

96. Soderlund, *Quakers and Slavery*, 80.

97. Billy G. Smith, "Death and Life in a Colonial Immigrant City: A Demographic Analysis of Philadelphia," *Journal of Economic History* 37 (1977): 863–89; Klepp, *Philadelphia in Transition*, 62–138.

98. Klepp, *Philadelphia in Transition*, 78–86; Daddy Israel in "Fanny Saltar's Reminiscences of Colonial Days in Philadelphia," *Pennsylvania Magazine of History and Biography* 40 (1916), 187; Nash and Soderlund, *Freedom by Degrees*, 31.

99. "Fanny Saltar's Reminiscences of Colonial Days in Philadelphia," 187–88.

100. Soderlund, *Quakers and Slavery*, 84.

101. Pennsylvania *Gazette*, Jan. 26, 1764, in Smith and Wojtowicz, eds., *Blacks Who Stole Themselves*, 69–70.

102. *Pennsylvania Gazette*, Oct. 28, 1742; June 1, 1749; May 20–21, 1761; Sept. 2, 1762, in Smith and Wojtowicz, eds., *Slaves Who Stole Themselves*, 20–21, 30–31, 50–51, 58–59.

103. Note the many examples gathered in Nash and Soderlund, *Freedom by Degrees*, 41–73. See also the large numbers of mulattos freed by Quaker meetings in Soderlund, "Black Women in Colonial Pennsylvania," first published in *Pennsylvania Magazine of History and Biography* 107 (1973), reprinted in Trotter and Smith, eds., *African Americans in Pennsylvania*, 73–92, at 79, 86, 87.

104. For Penn's thoughts and many words on schools and education, see Frederick B. Tolles and E. Gordon Alderfer, eds., *The Witness of William Penn* (New York, 1957), 167–99, especially William Penn, *Some Fruits of Solitude*; Thomas Woody, *Early Quaker Education in Pennsylvania* (New York, Teachers College, 1920); Thomas Woody, *Quaker Education in the Colony and State of New Jersey: A Source Book* (Philadelphia, 1923). See also Howard Kane Macauley Jr., "A Social and Intellectual History of Elementary Education in Pennsylvania to 1850," 2 vols. (diss., University of Pennsylvania, 1972), 2: 388–415, 908–12.

105. Thomas Budd, *Good Order Established in Pennsylvania and West New Jersey in America* (Philadelphia, 1685). A discussion of Budd's work appears in Woody, *Early Quaker Education in Pennsylvania*, 36–37.

106. John Woolman, *Works of John Woolman* (1774).

107. Woody, *Early Quaker Education in Pennsylvania*, 270ff.

108. Stephen Bloore, "Samuel Keimer: A Footnote to the Life of Franklin," *Pennsylvania Magazine of History and Biography* 54 (1930): 265–66; Nash, *Forging Freedom*, 19, 22, 288n.

109. Richard Snelling, "William Sturgeon, Catechist to the Negroes of Philadelphia," *Historical Magazine of the Protestant Episcopal Church* 8 (1939): 388–401.

110. Jackson, *Let This Voice Be Heard*, 9, 19, 21–24, 111–12, 175–76, an excellent biography.

111. The account of the funeral comes from Jacques-Pierre de Warville Brissot, who was there. See also Nancy Slocum Hornick, "Anthony Benezet: Eighteenth Century Social Critic, Educator, and Abolitionist" (diss., University of Maryland, 1974); Nancy Slocum Hornick, "Anthony Benezet and the Africans' School: Toward a Theory of Full Equality," *Pennsylvania Magazine of History and Biography* 99 (1975): 399–421; Roger A. Bruns, "Anthony Benezet's Assertion of Negro Equality," *Journal of Negro History* 56 (1971): 230–38; Roger A. Bruns, "Antony Benezet and the Natural Rights of the Negro," *Pennsylvania Magazine of History and Biography* 96 (1972): 104–13; and Maurice Jackson, *Let This Voice Be Heard: Anthony Benezet, Father of Atlantic Abolitionism* (Philadelphia: University of Pennsylvania Press, 2009), 211–30.

112. A quantitative survey of Pennsylvania schools appears in Macauley, "A Social and Intellectual History of Elementary Education in Pennsylvania to 1850," 2: 895–928.

113. For a thoughtful discussion of Franklin and slavery, see Nash and Soderlund, *Freedom by Degrees*, ix–xiv, as an introduction to the central problem in their excellent book, about slavery and antislavery in Pennsylvania, and as a case study in the history of reform movements in American history.

114. Benjamin Franklin, "Observations Concerning the Increase of Mankind," written 1751, published London, 1755; in *Papers of Benjamin Franklin*, ed. Leonard W. Labaree (New Haven, 1961), 4:234.

115. Franklin, "Observations Concerning the Increase of Mankind," 234.

116. Franklin to Rev. John Waring, Dec. 17, 1763, *Papers of Benjamin Franklin*, 10: 395–96.

117. In his ministry, George Fox labored repeatedly to reach the most miserable and abandoned female outcasts of English society. In 1649 he encountered a raving madwoman at Nottingham Jail.

  "The poor woman would make such a noise in roaring," he wrote, ". . . that it would set all the Friends in a heat . . . and there were many friends who were overcome by her with the stink that came out of her, roaring and tumbling on the ground." Fox comforted her and in his care she became calm and well. At Mansfield-Woodhouse, Fox found a "distracted woman under a doctor's hand, with her hair loose all about her ears." As the doctor was about to bleed her, "she being bound, and many people being about her holding her by violence," Fox intervened and set her free, and "bid her be quiet and still, and she was so. The Lord settled her mind, and she mended and afterwards received the Truth, and continued in it to her death." Fox, *Journal*, 8, 43 (1647, 1649).

118. Fithian, *Journal and Letters*, 297.

119. Soderlund, "Black Women in Colonial Philadelphia," 49–68, 65.

120. William Penn wrote, "Sexes made no difference, since in souls there is none," *Some Fruits of Solitude*, 33. Margaret Hope Bacon, *Mothers of Feminism: The Story of Quaker Women in America* (San Francisco and New York, 1986), 2; Mary Maples Dunn, "Women of Light," in Carol Berkin and Mary Beth Norton, eds., *Women of America* (Boston, 1979), 114–36; "Delaware Gender Ways," 490–98, and "Delaware Sex Ways," 498–502, in Fischer, *Albion's Seed*.

121. Sarah Blackborow [Blackbury], *The Just and Equal Balance Discovered* (London, 1660), 13, quoted in Richard Bauman, *Let Your Words Be Few: Symbolism of Speaking and Silence Among Seventeenth-Century Quakers* (Cambridge: Cambridge University Press, 1983), 36.

122. For Samuel Coates, see *Hazard's Register of Pennsylvania* 5 (1830): 319. A brief biography and portrait of Alice appeared in Isaiah Thomas, "Alice," *Eccentric Biography; or, Memoirs of Remarkable Female Characters, Ancient and Modern* (Worcester, Mass., 1804); John Watson, *Annals of Philadelphia* (Philadelphia, 1901); Charles Blockson, "Alice," *Notable American Black Women*, ed. Jessie C. Smith (1996); Charles Blockson, *Pennsylvania's Black History* (Philadelphia, 1975). A major research project on Alice is under way by Susan Klepp, a leading demographic and social historian of early Philadelphia.

123. Coates in *Hazard's Pennsylvania Register*, 5: 319.

124. Her name appears in Henry Cadbury's "Negro Membership in the Society of Friends," online.

125. For Humphrey Morrey as first purchaser in Philadelphia, see Dunn and Dunn, eds., *The Papers of William Penn*, 2: 578n, 649; 3: 384n, 717.

126. Deed of Bargain and Sale, Jan. 6, 1746, Philadelphia County Deed Book G7:539-43, Philadelphia City Archives. For local legends, see Charles L. Blockson, *African Americans in Pennsylvania* (Harrisburg, 2001), 102–3.

127. Joseph Montier's will, Abstract of Wills and Administrations, vol. 1–2, 1784–1850.

128. Julie Winch, ed., *The Elite of Our People: Joseph Willson's Sketches of Black Upper-Class Life in Antebellum Philadelphia* (1841; University Park, 2000), 10, and passim.

129. Reginald Pitts, "Robert Lewis of Guineatown and the 'Free Colored Cemetery' in Glenside," *Old York Road Historical Society Bulletin* 51 (1991); Reginald Pitts, "The Montier Family of Guineatown," *Old York Road Historical Society Bulletin* (1993); Donald Scott, "The Montiers: An American Family's Triumphant Odyssey," http://www.afrigeneas.com/library/montier_article.html; Elaine Rothschild, "Original Settlers and Their Descendants," "John Montier," at http://www.freeafricanamericans.com.

130. Soderlund, *Quakers and Slavery*, 34.

131. "The Germantown Protest," *Pennsylvania Magazine of History and Biography* 4 (1880): 28–30.

132. Soderlund, *Quakers and Slavery*, 19.

133. C. Brightwen Rowntree, "Benjamin Lay (1682–1759) of Colchester, London, Barbadoes, Philadelphia," *Journal of the Friends Historical Society* 33 (1936): 3–19.

134. Early accounts of Lay in Pennsylvania include Benjamin Rush, "Biographical Anecdotes of Benjamin Lay," in *Essays, Literary, Moral and Philosophical* (Philadelphia, 1798).

135. Benjamin Lay, *All Slave-keepers, That Keep the Innocent in Bondage, Apostates* (Philadelphia, 1737), printed by Benjamin Franklin, who kept his own name off the title page.

136. Among the earliest and most vivid accounts are Roberts Vaux, *Memoirs of the Lives of B. Lay and R. Sandiford, Two of the Earliest Public Advocates for the Emancipation of the Enslaved Africans* (Philadelphia, 1815), and Lydia Maria Child, *Memoir of Benjamin Lay* (New York, 1842).

137. "Stunts and Harangues: Benjamin Lay Calls on All Slave-Keepers," in Carey, *From Peace to Freedom*, 164–76.

138. Thomas P. Slaughter, *The Beautiful Soul of John Woolman, Apostle of Abolition* (New York, 2008).

139. John Woolman, *The Journal and Major Essays of John Woolman*, ed. Phillips P. Moulton (Richmond, Ind., 1989).

140. A very helpful scholar's edition of Benezet's works is Crosby, ed., *The Complete Antislavery Writings of Anthony Benezet*.

141. Anthony Benezet, *A Short Account of That Part of Africa Inhabited by the Negroes* (Philadelphia: Rivington, 1762), 55, 61; Anthony Benezet, *A Caution and a Warning to Great Britain and Her Colonies* (Philadelphia, 1766; London, 1767), annotated edition in Crosby, ed., *Complete Antislavery Writings of Anthony Benezet*, 91.

142. Hans Sloane, *A Voyage to the Islands Madera, Barbados, Nieves, S. Christophers and Jamaica*, 2 vols. (London, 1707), 1: lvi–lvii; Hans Sloane, *The Natural History of Jamaica*, 2 vols. (London, 1725), 1: 56; quoted with italics for emphasis in Benezet, *Some Historical Account of Guinea*, 159.

143. Benezet, *A Caution and a Warning to Great Britain and Her Colonies*, annotated edition in Crosby, ed., *Complete Antislavery Writings of Anthony Benezet*, 105–6.

144. Benezet, *Some Historical Account of Guinea*, 158–62. Here Benezet draws on Sloane, and also Thomas Jeffreys, *The Natural and Civil History of the French Dominions in North and South America*, 2 vols. (London, 1760), 2:186.

145. Benezet, *A Short Account of That Part of Africa Inhabited by the Negroes*, 61; Benezet, *A Caution and a Warning to Great Britain and Her Colonies*, 87–108, especially 91.

146. Jackson, *Let This Voice Be Heard*, 33.

147. Benezet, repeating the judgment of Virginian Arthur Lee, in "Notes to John Wesley's Thoughts on Slavery," an epilogue of nineteen pages to a Philadelphia edition of John Wesley's *Thoughts on Slavery* (Philadelphia, 1774), annotated edition in Crosby, ed., *The Complete Antislavery Writings of Anthony Benezet*, 218.

148. Jackson, *Let This Voice Be Heard*, ix–xiii, 60–61, 138–39, 142–49, 160–67.

149. Jackson, *Let This Voice Be Heard*, xi, 168–86.

150. Anthony Benezet, *Observations on the Inslaving, Importing, and Purchasing of Negroes* (Germantown, published by Christopher Sower, 1759, and again 1760), annotated text in Crosby, ed., *The Complete Antislavery Writings of Anthony Benezet*, 13–24; *A Short Account of That Part of Africa, Inhabited by the Negroes*, Benezet, 25–83; and Benezet's largest work, *Some Historical Account of Guinea*, 112–96.

151. Jackson, *Let This Voice Be Heard*, 32.

152. Anthony Benezet, *Short Observations on Slavery, introductory to Some Extracts from the Writings of the Abbé Raynal on that Important Subject* (Philadelphia: Enoch Story, 1783), text in Crosby, ed., *The Complete Antislavery Writings of Anthony Benezet*, 228–34, at 229–30. Benezet also used this story in his *A Short Account of That Part of Africa, Inhabited by the Negroes* and *Some Historical Account of Guinea*.

153. Soderlund, *Quakers and Slavery*, 137.

154. Soderlund, *Quakers and Slavery*, 34.

155. [Anthony Benezet and John Woolman], *An Epistle of Caution and Advice, Concerning the Buying and Keeping of Slaves*, written in 1746, approved for publication by the Overseers of the Press, 1754, and printed in many editions by the Philadelphia Monthly Meeting. An annotated edition is in Crosby, ed., *The Complete Antislavery Writings of Anthony Benezet*, 6–11, 236–37.

156. Arthur Zilversmit, *The First Emancipation: The Abolition of Slavery in the North* (Chicago, 1967), 74–75.

157. Nash, *Forging Freedom*, 26.

158. Jackson, *Let This Voice Be Heard*, 55–56.

159. Carey, *From Peace to Freedom*, 201–7.

160. Zilversmit, *The First Emancipation*.

161. Nash, *Forging Freedom*, 31–33, 137.

162. Abner Woolman, Journal, n.d., circa. 1770–72, a manuscript partly in his hand, and partly in John Woolman's. It is in the Quaker Collection, Haverford College ms 1250B5.21.1772 15, and online at http://triptych.brynmawr.edu/cdm/compoundob ject/collection/HC_QuakSlav/id/12113/rec/1.

163. Soderlund, *Quakers and Slavery*, 179.

164. Edward R. Turner, "The First Abolition Society in the United States," *Pennsylvania Magazine of History and Biography* 36 (1912): 92–109; Nash and Soderlund, *Freedom by Degrees*, 80.

165. Nash, *Forging Freedom*, 59.

166. Nash and Soderlund, *Freedom by Degrees*, 18, an excellent and deeply researched history of emancipation in Pennsylvania.

167. Nash and Soderlund, *Freedom by Degrees*, 123.

168. Nash, *Forging Freedom*, 152, 149.

169. Skeptics are invited to study two great works of scholarship: W. E. B. Du Bois, *The Philadelphia Negro, A Social Study* (1899; reprint, Philadelphia: University of Pennsylvania Press, 1996), 17–46, 83–89, 235–40, 269–77, researched and written when the author was a junior faculty member in sociology at the University of Pennsylvania, and Gary Nash, *Forging Freedom*, 66–171.

170. *Pennsylvania Gazette*, Sept. 4, 1746.

171. Richard Allen, *The Life, Experience and Gospel Labours of the Rt. Reverend Richard* (1960); Charles H. Wesley, *Richard Allen, Apostle of Freedom* (Washington, D.C., 1935); Carol V. R. George, *Segregated Sabbaths: Richard Allen and the Emergence of Independent Black Churches, 1760–1840* (New York, 1973); Albert Raboteau, "Richard Allen and the African Church Movement," in *Black Leaders of the Nineteenth Century* (1988); James Henretta, "Richard Allen and African-American Identity," *Early America Review* (Spring 1997), http://earlyamerica.com/review/spring97/Allen.html.

172. Gary B. Nash, "'To Arise Out of the Dust': Absalom Jones and the African Church of Philadelphia, 1785–95," in *Race, Class, and Politics* (Urbana: University of Illinois Press, 1986), 323–55; Thomas Will, "Liberalism, Republicanism, and Philadelphia's Black Elite in the Early Republic: The Social Thought of Absalom Jones and Richard Allen," *Pennsylvania History* 69 (2002): 558–76; Thomas F. Ulle, "A History of St. Thomas' African Episcopal Church, 1794–1865" (diss., University of Pennsylvania), http://repository.upenn.edu/dissertations/AAI8703281.

173. Nash, "'To Arise Out of the Dust,'" 323–55; Du Bois, *The Philadelphia Negro*, chapter 7.

174. Du Bois, *The Philadelphia Negro*, 19.

175. Du Bois, *The Philadelphia Negro*, 19–23.

176. Du Bois, *The Philadelphia Negro*, 23, 36, 164, 185.

177. Samuel J. May, *Some Recollections of Our AntiSlavery Conflict* (1869; reprint, New York, 1968), 287; discussed in Winch, *A Gentleman of Color*, 10–13.

178. Inconclusive evidence suggests that her name may have been Waymouth. No marriage record has been found.

179. James Forten spoke of a grandfather who had been a slave and "obtained his own freedom." This, I think, would have been on his mother's side. See Winch, *A Gentleman of Color*, 10–11.

180. Winch, *A Gentleman of Color*, 13.

181. This in a letter sixty years later to William Lloyd Garrison, Feb. 23, 1831, antislavery manuscripts, Boston Public library; Winch, *A Gentleman of Color*, 41.

182. Quoted in Du Bois, *The Philadelphia Negro*, 23.

183. Winch, *A Gentleman of Color*, 86.

184. Nash, *Forging Freedom*, 212–13; Winch, *A Gentleman of Color*, 175.

185. Winch, *A Gentleman of Color*, 234.

186. Du Bois, *The Philadelphia Negro*, 30–31.

187. Nash, *Forging Freedom*, 214–18, 331; Priscilla Ferguson Clement, "The Philadelphia Welfare Crisis of the 1820s," *Pennsylvania Magazine of History and Biography* 105 (1981), 150–53; Cynthia Shelton, *The Mills of Manayunk: Industrialization and Social Conflicts in the Philadelphia Region, 1787–1837* (Baltimore, 1986), 59–98; Bruce Laurie, *Working People of Philadelphia, 1800–1840* (Philadelphia, 1980).

188. Nash, *Forging Freedom*, 177, from James Forten's anonymous *A Series of Letters by a Man of Color* (Philadelphia, 1813).

189. *New-York Evening Post*, July 10 and 12, 1804; Nash, *Forging Freedom*, 176.

190. Emma Jones Lapsansky, "Since They Got Those Separate Churches: Afro-Americans and Racism in Jacksonian Philadelphia," *American Quarterly* 32 (1980): 54–78; Nash, *Forging Freedom*, 275; Winch, *A Gentleman of Color*, 234; Sam Bass Warner Jr., *The Private City: Philadelphia in Three Periods of Its Growth* (Philadelphia, 1968).

191. *Hazard's Register of Pennsylvania* 14 (1834): 200–203; John Runcie, "'Hunting the Nigs' in Philadelphia: The Race Riot of August 1834," *Pennsylvania History* 39 (1972): 187–218; Gilje, *The Road to Mobocracy*.

192. Beverly Tomek, *Pennsylvania Hall: A Legal Lynching in the Shadow of the Liberty Bell* (New York and Oxford, 2013); Winch, *A Gentleman of Color*, 301–4.

193. Nash, *Forging Freedom*, 277.

194. On Lombard Street, see Du Bois, *The Philadelphia Negro*, 58–61. On the riots, see Nicole Contosta, "The Lombard Street Riot, an Often Ignored Chapter in Philadelphia's History," *University City Review*, July 11, 2012.

195. Amanda Meyer Purvius, "The Philadelphia Bible Riots of 1844," *Pennsylvania History* 83 (2016): 366–93. Primary materials are available online at the website of the Historical Society of Pennsylvania and the Philadelphia Riots Collection in the digital library of Villanova University.

196. For an excellent discussion of Black suffrage in nineteenth-century Pennsylvania, see Du Bois, *The Philadelphia Negro*, 368–81.

197. Du Bois, *The Philadelphia Negro*, 26–32, 46–51.

198. For residential segregation, ca. 1837, see maps in Nash, *Forging Freedom*, 249.

199. For the corruption of magistrates' courts in Moyamensing, Southwark, and Cedar Ward, see Nash, *Forging Freedom*, 248.
200. Du Bois, *The Philadelphia Negro*, 83–91.
201. Nick Salvatore, *We All Got History: The Memory Books of Amos Webber* (New York, 1996), 60–66.
202. Salvatore, *We All Got History*, 66–67.
203. William Penn to James Harrison, Aug. 25, 1681, in Dunn and Dunn, eds., *The Papers of William Penn*, 2:108–9. For the Fundamental Constitutions and Frame of Government, 2:140–53, 162–238.
204. Dunn and Dunn, eds., *The Papers of William Penn*, 2:138.
205. Nash, *Forging Freedom*, 31–32; Soderlund, *Quakers and Slavery*; Jack D. Marietta, *Reformation of American Quakerism, 1748–1783* (Philadelphia, 2007).
206. Soderlund, *Quakers and Slavery*, 4.
207. Nash, *Forging Freedom*, 25.
208. Nash, *Forging Freedom*, 33.
209. Nash, *Forging Freedom*, 36.
210. Winch, *A Gentleman of Color*, 234–35.
211. Margaret Hope Bacon, *But One Race: The Life of Robert Purvis* (Albany, 2007).
212. Winch, *A Gentleman of Color*, 352–57.

Chapter 4: CHESAPEAKE VIRGINIA AND MARYLAND

1. *Baltimore Sun*, June 19, 1877.
2. Booker T. Washington, "The South and the Negro," 1903, *Southern Workman* 34 (1905): 400.
3. Robert Sutcliff, *Travels Through Some Parts of North America* (Philadelphia, 1812), 50, an eyewitness account.
4. The federal census of 1790 found 417,000 African Americans in Virginia and Maryland. For a thoughtful discussion of earlier patterns, see Sylvia R. Frey and Betty Wood, *Come Shouting to Zion* (Chapel Hill: University of North Carolina Press, 1998), 35–62.
5. Evidence is tabulated in Table 4.1. It quantifies descriptions of severe treatment in runaway slave notices for Virginia and South Carolina in the eighteenth and nineteenth centuries.
6. Daniel J. Flanagan, "Criminal Procedure in Slave Trials in the Antebellum South," *Journal of Southern History* 40 (1974): 546–47. Flanagan thought that dates of founding made the difference, and the oldest legal systems were the most cruel. Maybe so.
7. John Hammond, *Leah and Rachel; or, The Two Fruitfull Sisters, Virginia and Maryland* (London, 1656), 1. A lone copy survived in the Harvard Library, and was reprinted in Clayton Colman Hall, ed., *Narratives of Early Maryland, 1633–1684* (New York, 1910, 1946, 1967), 277–309.
8. John Donne, "A Sermon upon the eighth verse of the first chapter of the Acts of the Apostles," in *Works of John Donne*, ed. Henry Alford (London, 1836), 6: 231–32, 235. On the cross, see Master George Percy, "Observations," first printed in Samuel Purchas, ed., *Hakluyts Posthumous or Purchas His Pilgrimes* (1625; Glasgow, 1905–06), 4:1685–90; Lyon Gardiner Tyler, ed., *Narratives of Early Virginia* (New York, 1906), 11.

9. "A Reporte of the manner of Proceeding in the General Assembly convened at James Citty in Virginia, July 30, 1619, consisting of the Governor, the counsell of Estate, and two Burgesses elected out of each Incorporation, and Plantation, & being dissolved the 4th of August next ensueing . . . ," Colonial Office 1/1, folio 139, National Archives, Kew, England. For the two councils and governor's veto, see Craven, *The Southern Colonies in the Seventeenth Century* (Baton Rouge, 1949), 136.

10. Captain Robert Wintour, *"To Live Like Princes," a Short Treatise Sett Downe in a Letter Written by Robert Wintour to his worthy Friend C[aptaine] J[ohn] R[eade] concerning the New Plantation Now Erecting under the Right Hon[noura]ble the Lord Baltimore in Maryland*, ed. John D. Krugler (1635, Baltimore: Enoch Pratt Free Library, 1927), 27, 30, 37–38; David Hackett Fischer, "The Maryland Designe," in Orville Vernon Burton and Eldred E. Prince, Jr., eds., *Becoming Southern Writers: Essays in Honor of Charles Joyner* (Columbia, S.C., 2016), 78–101.

11. Arguments to the contrary were à la mode in academe during the early twenty-first century, by Whig and anti-Whig historians alike; and for evidence to the contrary, see Fischer, "The Maryland Designe," 78–101. An excellent and well-balanced history is John D. Krugler, *English and Catholic: The Lords Baltimore in the Seventeenth Century* (Baltimore, 2004).

12. Edwin Sandys in *Records of the Virginia Company*, 1: 304–7, 411–12, 479–89; 3: 99–107; Edmund S. Morgan, *American Slavery, American Freedom: The Ordeal of Colonial Virginia* (New York: Norton, 1975), 93–98, 101; *Records of the Virginia Company*, 3: 536–37; 4: 158–59; Lorena Walsh and Russell Menard, "Death in the Chesapeake: Two Life Tables for Men in Early Colonial Maryland," *Maryland Historical Magazine* 69 (1974): 214–19.

13. J. Mills Thornton, "The Thrusting Out of Governor Harvey," *Virginia Magazine of History and Biography* 76 (1968): 1–26.

14. The size of Virginia's colonial population remains uncertain. Vital records in Virginia were less comprehensive than in New England and New France. Historical estimates by the U.S. Census Bureau are generally thought to be inaccurate. A major cause is that Virginia's leaders counted "tithables," but not people, and there is no general agreement on ratios of tithables. For estimates, see Morgan, *American Slavery, American Freedom*, 404, who reckoned 8,100 in 1641, and 40,600 in 1682; and also Wesley Frank Craven, *White, Red, and Black* (Charlottesville: University Press of Virginia, 1971; New York, 1977), 25–30. Governors Harvey and Berkeley broadly agreed in reports to London. The best early benchmarks were a census in 1634 that counted 4,914 people, and another in 1635 that counted 5,119 inhabitants. See Evarts B. Greene and Virginia D. Harrington, eds., *American Population Before the Federal Census of 1790* (New York and Baltimore, 1932 and 1981), 136–37.

15. Karl Mannheim, *Ideology and Utopia* (Bonn and Stuttgart, 1929; trans. Louis Wirth and Edward Shils, New York, 1936), 219–38.

16. Bernard Bailyn, "Politics and Social Structure in Virginia," in James Morton Smith, ed., *Seventeenth-Century America: Essays in Colonial History* (Chapel Hill: University of North Carolina Press, 1959).

17. Edmund Burke, "Speech on Conciliation with the Colonies," March 22, 1775, in *Speeches and Letters on American Affairs* (London, 1908), 94.

18. For further discussion, see David Hackett Fischer, *Albion's Seed: Four British Folkways in America* (New York and Oxford, 1989); *Liberty and Freedom* (New York and Oxford: Oxford University Press, 2005); and *Fairness and Freedom* (New York and Oxford: Oxford University Press, 2012).

19. Durand de Dauphiné, *A Huguenot Exile in Virginia*, ed. Chinard, 111, 148.

20. The best work on this subject is still Charles S. Sydnor, *Gentlemen Freeholders: Political Practices in Washington's Virginia* (Chapel Hill: University of North Carolina Press, 1952). More extended discussion of British origins is in Fischer, *Albion's Seed*, 207–418. For detail of Virginia customs and history, see the many deeply informed books of Philip Bruce, and for issues of timing see Bailyn, "Politics and Social Structure in Virginia," 90–115; Martin H. Quitt, "Immigrant Origins of the Virginia Gentry," *William and Mary Quarterly*, 3rd series, 45 (1988): 629–55; and Trevor Burnard, *Creole Gentlemen: The Maryland Elite, 1691–1776* (New York: Routledge, 2002).

21. David W. Jordan, "Political Stability and the Emergence of a Native Elite in Maryland," in Thad Tate and David Ammerman, eds., *The Chesapeake in the Seventeenth Century* (New York: Norton, 1979), 243–73; Burnard, *Creole Gentlemen*, 21–102.

22. "Narrative of George Fisher," *William and Mary Quarterly*, 1st series, 17 (1908–09): 123.

23. Lord Baltimore's motto ignited a controversy in the twenty-first century. Feminists and postmodernists called it "sexist in any language." The staff of Maryland's Hall of Records supplied a new translation, loose but to the point: "strong acts, gentle words."

24. Lois Greene Carr, "Margaret Brent, A Brief History," unpublished ms., Maryland State Archives, Hall of Records, Annapolis, online. Also Julia Cherry Spruill, "Mistress Margaret Brent, Spinster," *Maryland Historical Magazine* 29 (1934); Bruce Steiner, "The Catholic Brents of Colonial Virginia," *Virginia Magazine of History and Biography* 70 (1962), 392–93; and W. B. Chilton, genealogical materials in many issues of the *Virginia Magazine of History and Biography*.

25. Ronald Hoffman, *Princes of Ireland, Planters of Maryland: A Carroll Saga, 1500–1782* (Chapel Hill: University of North Carolina Press, 2000); Krugler, *English and Catholic*.

26. Hoffman, *Princes of Ireland, Planters of Maryland*, 73–75, 262–64. The family was very careful in their lending and refused a loan to George Washington; Hoffman, *Princes of Ireland, Planters of Maryland*, 390. Charles Carroll of Carrollton and Charles Carroll of Annapolis were in business together and happy to lend for long periods, but always with security either in land or chattels as 263. In 1763 they had loaned 24,000 pounds at interest; in 1768, 30,000 pounds; in 1776, 41,000 pounds, all lent at interest and secured to seventy-eight debtors mostly less than 500 pounds, and none larger than about 6,000 pounds. Credit was extended only where security was given; unpaid interest was added to principal. They did not hesitate to foreclose, even with much litigation. A recent survey is in Hoffman, *Princes of Ireland, Planters of Maryland*, 263–64.

27. Engel Sluiter, "New Light on the '20, and Odd Negroes' Arriving in Virginia, August, 1619," WMQ3 56 (1997): 395–98; John Thornton, "The African Experience of the '20 and Odd Negroes' Arriving in Virginia in 1619," *William and Mary Quarterly*, 3rd series, 60 (1998): 421–34; Tim Hashaw, *The Birth of Black America: The First African Americans and the Pursuit of Freedom in Jamestown* (New York, 2007), 54–100.

28. Virginia's census of 1625 is in the British National Archives, CO 1/3, and published in John Camden Hotten, *Original Lists of Persons of Quality* (London, 1874), 201–65. See also Warren M. Billings, "The Law of Servants and Slaves in Seventeenth Century Virginia," *Virginia Magazine of History and Biography* 99 (1991): 45–62, 54n.

29. Lorena S. Walsh, *Motives of Honor, Pleasure, and Profit: Plantation Management in the Colonial Chesapeake, 1607–1763* (Chapel Hill: University of North Carolina Press, 2010), 113–14; Sluiter, "New Light on the '20 and Odd Negroes' Arriving in Virginia, August 1619," 395–98; Thornton, "The African Experience of the '20 and Odd Negroes' Arriving in Virginia, in 1619," 421–34.

30. William Thorndale, "The Virginia Census of 1629," *Magazine of Virginia Genealogy* 33 (1995): 155–70; Martha McCartney, "An Early Virginia Census," *Archeological Society of Virginia Quarterly Bulletin* 54 (1999): 178–81; Walsh, *Motives of Honor, Pleasure, and Profit*, 114–15.

31. Trans-Atlantic Slave Trade Database; Elizabeth Donnan, ed., *Documents Illustrative of the History of the Slave Trade to America*, 4 vols. (Washington, D.C.: Carnegie Institution, 1930–35), 4: 49, 118; Walsh, *Motives of Honor, Pleasure, and Profit*, 119; Allan Kulikoff, *Tobacco and Slaves: The Development of Southern Cultures in the Chesapeake, 1680–1800* (Chapel Hill: University of North Carolina Press, 1986).

32. *Maryland Land Records*, 1:19–20, 37–38, Hall of Records; *Archives of Maryland*, 3: 258; Newman Floering, George Ely Russell, and Donna Valley Russell, *Ark and Dove Adventurers* (Baltimore: Society of the Ark and the Dove, 2005), 221.

33. Linda M. Heywood and John K. Thornton, *Central Africans, Atlantic Creoles, and the Foundation of the Americas, 1585–1660* (Cambridge, 2007), 353–58.

34. For example, the life of Anthony Johnson, his wife, Mary, and children, in J. Douglas Deal, *Race and Class in Colonial Virginia: Indians, Englishmen, and Africans on the Eastern Shore During the Seventeenth Century* (New York, 1993), 217–50; T. H. Breen and Stephen Innes, *"Myne Owne Ground": Race and Freedom on Virginia's Eastern Shore, 1640–1676* (Oxford: Oxford University Press, 1980, 2005), 8–16, 80–92, 101–113, and passim; Paul Heinegg, *Free African Americans of North Carolina, Virginia and South Carolina: From the Colonial Period to About 1820*, 2 vols. (Baltimore: Clearfield Company for the Genealogical Book Company, 1992; 5th edition, 2005), 2: 705–15; Heywood and Thornton, *Central Africans, Atlantic Creoles, and the Foundation of the Americas*, 312.

35. David S. Bogen, "Mathias de Sousa: Maryland's First Colonist of African Descent," *Maryland Historical Magazine* 96 (2001): 68–85; Garry Wheeler Stone, "Fur Traders and Field Hands: Blacks in Manorial Maryland, 1634–1644," unpublished ms, 1984, Maryland State Archives, special collections, biographical series, Mathias de Sousa file, msa sc 3520-2810. See also the career of Anthony Longo in 1635, and Deal, *Race and Class in Colonial Virginia*, 219, 257–65. Very helpful is Heywood and Thornton, *Central Africans, Atlantic Creoles, and the Foundation of the Americas*, 284–85.

36. William Berkeley, "Answers to Queries," William Waller Hening, *Statutes at Large: A Collection of the Laws of Virginia* (1671) 2: 515, 44–47, 73, 145, 147, 172.

37. Kulikoff, *Tobacco and Slaves*, 329; *Archives of Maryland*, 33: 498–99.

38. Nicholson to Board of Trade, *Archives of Maryland*, 33: 698.

39. Deal, *Race and Class in Colonial Virginia*, 205–6; Breen and Innes, *"Myne Owne Ground."*

40. Paul Heinegg, *Free African Americans of Maryland and Delaware: From the Colonial Period to 1910* (Baltimore, 2000), 1: 7; Heinegg, *Free African Americans of North Carolina, Virginia and South Carolina*, 1: 1–5. John Thornton and Linda Heywood were among the first historians to recognize the broad importance of this excellent genealogical research.

41. See also Breen and Innes, *"Myne Owne Ground,"* 83–85. "Common law" is my phrase, from common usage in later periods of Maryland's history.

42. Heinegg, *Free African Americans of Maryland and Delaware*, "Fortune Family" and "Game Family," 128–31, 138–42.

43. Walsh, *Motives of Honor, Pleasure, and Profit*, 113, passim.

44. Hening, *Statutes at Large* (1723), 225.

45. Hening, *Statutes at Large* (1723), 225.

46. Hening, *Statutes at Large* (1705), 459.

47. Hening, *Statutes at Large* (1723), 129.

48. David Eltis et al., *The Transatlantic Slave Trade Database* (Atlanta, 2008–16), online at https://www.slavevoyages.org; David Eltis and David Richardson, *Atlas of the Transatlantic Slave Trade* (New Haven: Yale University Press, 2010), table 6, p. 200; Elizabeth Donnan, ed., *Documents Illustrative of the History of the Slave Trade in America*, vol. 4: *The Border Colonies and the Southern Colonies* (Washington, D.C.: Carnegie Institution, 1935); Herbert S. Klein, "Slaves and Shipping in Eighteenth-Century Virginia," *Journal of Interdisciplinary History* 5 (1974–75): 384–87; Kulikoff, *Tobacco and Slaves*, 64–76; Lorena Walsh, "The Chesapeake Slave Trade: Regional Patterns, African Origins, and Some Implications," *William and Mary Quarterly*, 3rd series, 58 (2001): 139–70; Russell Menard, "The Maryland Slave Population, 1658 to 1730: A Demographic Profile of Blacks in Four Counties," *William and Mary Quarterly*, 3rd series, 32 (1975): 29–54.

49. Walsh, *Motives of Honor, Pleasure, and Profit*, 405.

50. Walsh, *Motives of Honor, Pleasure, and Profit*, 405.

51. Walsh, "The Chesapeake Slave Trade," 144–45.

52. John Thornton, *Africa and Africans in the Making of the Atlantic World* (Cambridge, 1991, 1998); Heywood and Thornton, *Central Africans, Atlantic Creoles, and the Foundation of the Americas*.

53. Walsh, "The Chesapeake Slave Trade," 145–50, 166–70.

54. Walsh, "The Chesapeake Slave Trade," 145–50, 166–70. Also Lorena Walsh, *From Calabar to Carter's Grove: The History of a Virginia Slave Community* (Charlottesville: University Press of Virginia, 1997), 55.

55. Thomas Cable to John Maple, July 16, 1725, Cable Letter Book, Maryland Center for History and Culture.

56. Walsh, "The Chesapeake Slave Trade," 152; Thornton, *Africa and Africans in the Making of the Atlantic World*, 83–92; David Eltis, *The Rise of African Slavery in the Americas* (Cambridge, 2010), 247–52.

57. Eltis and Richardson, *Atlas of the Transatlantic Slave Trade*, 212, 200. This estimate of 128,000 total arrivals from Africa refers to the entire Chesapeake from 1619 to 1775.

58. Eltis and Richardson, *Atlas of the Transatlantic Slave Trade*, 212, 200.

59. The primary sources for the African slave trade to the Chesapeake include Eltis et al., *The Transatlantic Slave Trade Database*. Discussions by leading scholars of this subject include

Walsh, "The Chesapeake Slave Trade," 139–70; Walsh, *Motives of Honor, Pleasure, and Profit*, 142–43, 201–2, 383–84; and also Douglas B. Chambers, "He Gwine Sing He Country: Africans, Afro-Virginians, and the Development of Slave Culture in Virginia, 1690–10" (diss., University of Virginia, 1996), and Douglas B. Chambers, *Murder at Montpelier: Igbo Africans in Virginia* (Jackson: University Press of Mississippi, 2007).

60. Transcripts of Spanish immigration records, Puerto Rico Archives, San Juan.

61. Chambers, *Murder at Montpelier*, 191.

62. Patricia M. Samford, *Subfloor Pits and the Archaeology of Slavery in Colonial Virginia* (Tuscaloosa, Ala., 2007), 187.

63. William B. Baikie, *Narrative of an Exploring Voyage up the Rivers Kwara and Binue, Commonly Known as the Niger and Tsadda, in 1854* (London, 1856; reprint, 1966), 307; Chambers, *Murder at Montpelier*, 24.

64. Walsh, "The Chesapeake Slave Trade," 166–67, table 1. A discussion of sources for these results was posted as a supplement on the website of the *William and Mary Quarterly*, at http://www.wm.edu/oieahc.

65. Among many biographies, see Sarah Bradford, *Scenes in the Life of Harriet Tubman* (Auburn, 1869), revised as *Harriet, The Moses of Her People* (New York, 1886; revised, 1901, New York, 1961); Jean M. Humez, *Harriet Tubman: The Life and the Life Stories* (Madison, 2003); Kate Larson, *Bound for the Promised Land: Harriet Tubman, Portrait of an American Hero* (New York, 2003), 9–10; and Catherine Clinton, *Harriet Tubman: The Road to Freedom* (New York and Boston, 2004).

66. For material on Harriet Tubman's forebears, the biographical file in the Archives of Maryland in Annapolis includes separate biographies not only of Harriet Tubman herself, but also of her parents. They are accessible online at Archives of Maryland, Biographical Series, "Harriet Ross Tubman Davis" and "Harriet Rit Ross." See also Larson, *Bound for the Promised Land*, 9–10, and Clinton, *Harriet Tubman*, 4–14.

67. Franklin Sanborn, "Harriet Tubman," Boston *Commonwealth*, July 17, 1863, the first biography, by an antislavery leader who knew her well.

68. Frank C. Drake, "The Moses of Her People: Amazing Life Work of Harriet Tubman," *New York Herald*, Sept. 22, 1907.

69. Ivor Wilks, *Forests of Gold: Essays on the Akan and the Kingdom of Asante* (Athens, Ohio, 1993), 66–72; T. C. McCaskie, *State and Society in Pre-Colonial Asante* (Cambridge, 1995), 2; Michael A. Gomez, *Exchanging Our Country Marks* (Chapel Hill: University of North Carolina, 1998), 109.

70. Drake, "The Moses of Her People"; and for deep research on her life, Larson, *Bound for the Promised Land*, 33; on her storytelling, Humez, *Harriet Tubman*, 133–75; and on the larger context, Clinton, *Harriet Tubman*, 13.

71. Allan D. Austin, *African Muslims in Antebellum America: Transatlantic Stories and Spiritual Struggles* (New York and London: Routledge, 1997), 31–50.

72. The largest and most important collection of primary documents is Allan D. Austin's *African Muslims in Antebellum America: A Sourcebook* (New York: Garland, 1984), regrettably out of print.

73. Hening, *Statutes at Large*, 1682.

74. Philip D. Curtin, "Ayuba Suleiman Diallo of Bondu," in Philip D. Curtin, ed., *Africa Remembered: Narratives by West Africans from the Era of the Slave Trade* (Madison:

University of Wisconsin Press, 1968), 17–59, a short essay based on an extraordinary depth of research and knowledge by one of the leading African historians of his generation. Also very helpful is the chapter "Job Ben Solomon: African Nobleman and a Father of African American Literature," in Austin, *African Muslims in Antebellum America: Transatlantic Stories and Spiritual Struggles*, 51–64; as well as Douglas Grant, *The Fortunate Slave* (New York: Oxford University Press, 1968); Sylviane A. Diouf, *Servants of Allah: African Muslims Enslaved in the Americas* (New York: New York University Press, 1998); and Nell Painter, *Creating Black Americans: African American History and Its Meanings* (Oxford: Oxford University Press, 2005), 164–66.

75. Part of this American saga comes from an African text by an English author, Francis Moore, in *Travels into the Inland Parts of Africa . . . with a Particular and Primary Account of the Capture of Job ben Solomon* (London, 1738), 69, 213.

76. For Job ben Solomon's reproductions of the Quran from memory (three times), see Austin, "Job ben Solomon," 55, 56, 57, 58.

77. Thomas Bluett, *Some Memoirs of the Life of Job, the Son of Solomon the High Priest of Boonda in Africa; Who was a Slave about two Years in Maryland; afterwards being brought to England, was set free, and sent to his native Land in the Year 1734* (London, 1734).

78. Bluett, *Some Memoirs of the Life of Job*, 9–53; Moore, *Travels into the Inland Parts of Africa*, 202–9, 223–31.

79. The definitive history is James H. Johnston, *From Slave Ship to Harvard: Yarrow Mamout and the History of an African American Family* (New York, 2012), 74–77, 99–100. Along with every student of this subject I am much indebted to Johnston's excellent and inspiring study of the man himself, his family, and Islamic slaves in his American world.

80. The journey of the slave ship *Elijah*, which brought 140 slaves from Africa to Annapolis, Maryland, in 1752, is voyage 90395 in the Trans-Atlantic Slave Trade Database.

81. Johnston, *From Slave Ship to Harvard*, 157, 102–12, passim.

82. Johnston, *From Slave Ship to Harvard*, 93.

83. Johnston, *From Slave Ship to Harvard*, 93, 117.

84. Johnston, *From Slave Ship to Harvard*, 197.

85. Johnston, *From Slave Ship to Harvard*, 125.

86. Johnston, *From Slave Ship to Harvard*, 96.

87. Irene Hecht, "The Virginia Muster of 1624/5 as a Source for Demographic History," *William and Mary Quarterly* 3rd series, 30 (1973): 65–92; Morgan, *American Slavery, American Freedom*, 105, 111; *Records of the Virginia Company*, 3: 243.

88. William Fitzhugh to Doctor Ralph Smith, April 22, 1686; text in Richard Beale Davis, ed., *William Fitzhugh and His Chesapeake World, 1676–1701: The Fitzhugh Letters and Other Documents* (Richmond, 1963), 175–77.

89. Edmund Berkeley, "The Diary, Correspondence and Papers of Robert 'King' Carter of Virginia, 1701–1732," https://search.lib.virginia.edu/sources/uva_library/items/u3800777; Edmund Berkeley, ed., "Robert Carter as Agricultural Administrator: His Letters to Robert Jones, 1727–1729," *Virginia Magazine of History and Biography* 101 (1993): 273–95.

90. Morton, 20–24.

91. Walsh, *From Calabar to Carter's Grove*, 256–61.

92. Kulikoff, *Tobacco and Slaves*, 331, 337, 338.

93. Kulikoff, *Tobacco and Slaves*, 337, 137.

94. Walsh, "The Chesapeake Slave Trade," 157; Walsh, *From Calabar to Carter's Grove*, 44–45, 148, 224, and passim.

95. Walsh, "The Chesapeake Slave Trade," 157.

96. For extended discussions of quarters, see Morgan, *American Slavery, American Freedom*; James Sidbury, *Ploughshares into Swords: Race, Rebellions, and Identity in Gabriel's Virginia, 1730–1810* (Cambridge, 1997), 23.

97. "Carroll Family Slaves," inventory, Dec. 3, 1773, "Negroes on Doohoregan Manor, Taken in Familys with Their Ages," Dec. 1, 1773, and Carroll [of Carrollton] Account Book, MdHS; Kulikoff, in Kulikoff, *Tobacco and Slaves*, 336, 341; Daniel B. Deans, "The Carroll Family Slaves, 1721–1833: Genealogies" (ms., University of Maryland, 1990); Ann C. Van Devanter, ed., *"Anywhere So Long as There Be Freedom": Charles Carroll of Carrollton, His Family & His Maryland* (Baltimore: Baltimore Museum of Art, 1975).

98. Hoffman, *Princes of Ireland, Planters of Maryland*, 250.

99. Hoffman, *Princes of Ireland, Planters of Maryland*, 251.

100. Edward Kimber, "Itinerant Observations of Kimber," *Maryland Historical Magazine* 51 (1956): 327.

101. St. Mary's County, Maryland, 1798, Federal Direct Tax assessments; the size of a typical slave's quarters was 20 by 16 feet; one in St. Mary's was 48 by 16 feet.

102. For data on dimensions, see Kulikoff, *Tobacco and Slaves*, 368.

103. Charles L. Perdue Jr., Thomas E. Barden, and Robert K. Phillips, eds., *Weevils in the Wheat: Interviews with Virginia Ex-Slaves* (Charlottesville: University Press of Virginia, 1976), 105.

104. Perdue et al., eds., *Weevils in the Wheat*, 134.

105. Herbert G. Gutman, "Because She Was My Cousin," in *The Black Family in Slavery and Freedom, 1750–1925* (New York: Vintage, 1976).

106. Perdue et al., eds., *Weevils in the Wheat*, 89.

107. Epps (Prince George's County), in Perdue et al., eds., *Weevils in the Wheat*, 89; Berry (Appomattox Court House), in Perdue et al., eds., *Weevils in the Wheat*, 36. The lamp weddings were also carried west to Kentucky.

108. Fannie Berry, Narrative, in Perdue et al., eds., *Weevils in the Wheat*, 36.

109. Harriet Tubman, as quoted in Sarah Bradford, *Harriet Tubman, The Moses of Her People* (New York, 1886; revised, 1901, New York, 1961), 31–32.

110. Walsh, *From Calabar to Carter's Grove*, 261.

111. Walsh, "The Chesapeake Slave Trade," 172; Kulikoff, *Tobacco and Slaves*.

112. G. W. Offey, *A Narrative of the Life and Labors of the Rev. G. W. Offley* (Hartford, Ct., 1859), 14.

113. Susan Dabney Smedes, *Memorials of a Southern Planter* (Baltimore: Cushings & Bailey, 1887), 71.

114. Frederick Douglass, *My Bondage and My Freedom* (New York, 1855), 60; Frederick Douglass, *Narrative of the Life of Frederick Douglass: An American Slave* (1845; Signet edition, New York, 1968), 61–62; Frederick Douglass, *The Life and Times of Frederick Douglass* (1892; reprint, New York, 1962), 42–43. Three classic autobiographies.

115. Moses Grandy, *Narrative of the Life of Moses Grandy* (London, 1843), in W. L. Katz, ed., *Five Slave Narratives* (New York, 1968), 32.

116. Douglass, *Narrative of the Life*, 61–62. In *Life and Times* he writes, 99–100, "her present owner—his grandson—finding that she was of but little value, that her frame was already wracked with the pains of old age, and that complete helplessness was fast stealing over her once active limbs, took her to the woods, built her a little hut with a mud chimney and then gave her the *bounteous* privilege of there supporting herself in utter loneliness—thus virtually turning her out to die."

117. David Benedict, A *General History of the Baptist Denomination in America* (Boston, 1812), 2: 211.

118. David Hackett Fischer, *Growing Old in America* (Oxford, 1978), 64–66.

119. Olaudah Equiano, *The Life of Olaudah Equiano or Gustavus Vassa The African, 1789, with an Introduction by Paul Edwards*, 2 vols. (London, 1969), 34–36.

120. Douglass, *My Bondage and My Freedom* (New York, 1955), 76–77.

121. J. F. D. Smyth, *A Tour of the United States of America* (London, 1784), 1: 39.

122. Allen Walker Read, "Eighteenth Century Slaves as Advertised by Their Masters," *Journal of Negro History* (1916): 170–75; J. L. Dillard, *Black English* (New York, 1972), 84.

123. All of these sounds were recorded in the slave songs collected from Virginia, Maryland, and Delaware by William Francis Allen et al., in *Slave Songs of the United States* (New York, 1867), part 2, slave songs of northern seaboard slave states, especially numbers 83–99.

124. Gerald W. Mullin, "Patterns of Slave Behavior in Eighteenth-Century Virginia" (diss., University of California at Berkeley, 1968), 375.

125. Mullin, "Patterns of Slave Behavior," 396.

126. Thomas Wentworth Higginson, *Army Life in a Black Regiment* (1869; reprint, Boston, 1962), 202. J. L. Dillard comments, "There have been two systems all along, one of which uses stressed *been* for remote past and unstressed *been* for recent past. The latter—which Higginson and probably his informants considered 'Virginian'—is the one which had the most widespread influence in the United States." *Black English*, 106.

127. Higginson, *Army Life in a Black Regiment*, 202.

128. Sobel, 52.

129. Norman R. Yetman, *Life Under the "Peculiar Institution"* (New York: Holt, Rinehart and Winston, 1970) 133.

130. J. W. Coleman, *Slavery Times in Kentucky* (Chapel Hill: University of North Carolina Press, 1940), 36.

131. Morgan Godwin, *The Negro's and Indian's Advocate, Suing for Their Admission into the Church, or a Persuasive to the Instructing and Baptizing of the Negroes and Indians in our Plantations* (London, 1680); Yvonne P. Chireau, *Black Magic* (Berkeley, 2003), 45.

132. Dennis Pogue, *Slave Lifeways at Mount Vernon: An Archeological Perspective* (Mount Vernon, Va.: Mount Vernon Ladies' Association, 1995), 111—35; William H. Burt, *Bacula of North American Mammals* (Ann Arbor, 1969).

133. Davies to Bellamy, Alexander, 227; Wesley M. Gewehr, *The Great Awakening in Virginia, 1740–1820* (Durham, N.C., 1930), 72, 96, 237.

134. Samuel Davies, letter to "Mr. C. Feb.," 7, 1757, seeking "400 or 500 spelling books for slaves, in *Letters from the Rev. Samuel Davies, and Others; Shewing the State of Re-*

ligion in Virginia, South Carolina, &c, particularly Among the Negroes (London, 1757, 1761), 23–24. Davies was also one of the founding leaders of the Presbyterian College of New Jersey, now Princeton.

135. R. Garrettson, "An Account of the Revival of the Work of God at Petersburg in Virginia," *Arminian Magazine* 13 (1970): 300–307, Duke University Library online; Gewehr, *The Great Awakening in Virginia*, 170.

136. Gewehr, *The Great Awakening in Virginia*, 170.

137. Philip Morgan writes, "The term 'driver' was not commonly used in the eighteenth-century Chesapeake. Slaves with supervisory roles were usually designated 'foremen,' 'captains,' or occasionally 'overseers.'" Morgan, *Slave Counterpoint: Black Culture in the Eighteenth-Century Chesapeake and Lowcountry* (Williamsburg: University of North Carolina Press, 1998), 218–19.

138. Menard, "Maryland Slave Population," *William and Mary Quarterly*, 3rd series, 32 (1975): 36.

139. Chambers, *Murder at Montpelier*, 47.

140. Burnard, *Creole Gentlemen*, 190.

141. Byrd to Egmont, July 12, 1736, in Marion Tinling, ed., *Correspondence of the Three William Byrds* (Charlottesville:? University Press of Virginia, 1977), 2: 488.

142. Philip J. Schwarz, *Twice Condemned: Slaves and the Criminal Laws of Virginia, 1705–1865* (Union, N.J.: Lawbook Exchange, 1998), table 8, pp. 86–87.

143. Herbert Aptheker, *American Negro Slave Revolts* (New York, 1943, 1963), 179; Gooch to Board of Trade, June 29, 1729, in *Calendar of State Papers: Colonial Series, America and West Indies,* ed. W. Noel Sainsbury et al., 42 vols. (London, 1860–1953), 9: 429.

144. Hening, *Statutes at Large* (1769), 358.

145. Darrett B. Rutman and Anita H. Rutman, *A Place in Time: Middlesex County, Virginia* (New York: Norton, 1984), 177.

146. Schwarz, *Twice Condemned*, 150–52; Hening, *Statutes at Large*.

147. Anthony S. Parent Jr., *Foul Means: The Formation of a Slave Society in Virginia, 1660–1740* (Williamsburg: University of North Carolina Press, 2003) 129.

148. Examples: Bambara Harry and Dinah in 1710 and Will and Bailey after 1721 for "outlying" in Lancaster County, Lancaster Court Order Book, 1721–29, 59–60, 83, 183, Virginia State Library.

149. Jack P. Greene, ed., *The Diary of Colonel Landon Carter of Sabine Hall, 1752–1778*, 2 vols. (Richmond, Va.: Richmond Historical Society, 1965, 1987), 1: 9. These estimates derive from an inventory of his estate after his death in 1778, and include lands he gave his sons at an earlier date.

150. Greene, ed., *The Diary of Colonel Landon Carter of Sabine Hall*, 1: 9.

151. Greene, ed., *Diary*, 1: 369.

152. Greene, ed., *Diary*, 1: 378.

153. Greene, ed., *Diary*, 1: 425.

154. Greene, ed., *Diary*, 1: 378.

155. Greene, ed., *Diary*, 1: 343.

156. Greene, ed., *Diary*, 1: 348.

157. Greene, ed., *Diary*, 1: 347.

158. Greene, ed., *Diary*, 1: 353.

159. Greene, ed., *Diary*, 1: 362.

160. Greene, ed., *Diary*, 1: 362.

161. Greene, ed., *Diary*, 1: 366, 368.

162. Greene, ed., *Diary*, 1: 363.

163. Greene, ed., *Diary*, June 11, 1766, 1: 306.

164. Greene, ed., *Diary*.

165. William Grimes, *Life of William Grimes* (New York, 1825), 12.

166. Schwarz, *Twice Condemned*, 173, citing Brunswick County Court Order Books, June 25, 1752, 242–43.

167. Schwarz, *Twice Condemned*, 173–754

168. Lt. Gov. Robert Dinwiddie to Earl of Halifax, July 23, 1755, *Official Records of Robert Dinwiddie*, 2 vols. (Richmond, 1884), 2:114.

169. *Virginia Gazette*, Oct. 1, 1767, Jan. 25, 1770; Schwarz, *Twice Condemned*, 179, 180, 188, 190.

170. Turk McCleskey, *The Road to Black Ned's Forge* (Charlottesville: University of Virginia Press, 2014), an extraordinary work, already a classic.

171. McCleskey, *The Road to Black Ned's Forge*, 66–67.

172. Hening, *Statutes at Large* (1769), 358.

173. Greene, ed., *The Diary of Colonel Landon Carter of Sabine Hall*, May 6, 1772, 2: 677.

174. Melville Patrick Ely, *Israel on the Appomattox: A Southern Experiment in Black Freedom from the 1790s Through the Civil War* (New York, 2004), 19–22, 49, 83, 197–98.

175. Fannie Berry, b. 1841, slave narrative, published in Perdue et al., eds., *Weevils in the Wheat*, 34.

176. David Hackett Fischer and James C. Kelly, *Bound Away* (Charlottesville: University Press of Virginia, 2000), 236–38; Ralph L. Ketcham, "The Dictates of Conscience: Edward Coles and Edward Coles and Slavery," *Virginia Quarterly Review* 36 (1960): 47–93. See also David Ress, *Governor Edward Coles and the Vote to Forbid Slavery in Illinois* (Jefferson, N.C., 2006), and Suzanne Cooper Guasco, *Confronting Slavery: Edward Coles and the Rise of Anti-Slavery Politics in Nineteenth-Century America* (DeKalb, Ill., 2013).

177. Fischer and Kelly, *Bound Away*, 238; Frank F. Mathias, "John Randolph's Freedmen: The Thwarting of a Will," *Journal of Southern History* 39 (1973): 263–72.

178. W. T. Childs, *John McDonogh: His Life and Works* (Baltimore, 1939); Lane Carter Kendall, "Slave Owner," *Louisiana Historical Quarterly* 15 (1932): 646–54, and 16 (1933): 125–34; Arthur G. Nuhrah, "John McDonogh, A Man of Many Facets" (diss., Tulane University), published in *Louisiana Historical Quarterly* 26 (1943): 5–144.

179. Ulrich Bonnell Phillips, *Life and Labor in the Old South* (Columbia: University of South Carolina Press, 2007), 198.

180. Henry Clay Bruce, *The New Man* (York, Pa.: P. Anstadt, 1895).

181. Are these results representative of the slave population as a whole? At least four different biases exist in the fugitive slave data. It was generally assumed by slaveholders, slaves, and historians of slavery (e.g., Eugene D. Genovese, *Roll, Jordan, Roll: The World the Slaves Made* (New York: Random House, 1974), 561) that reading and writing promoted resistance, and helped slaves to escape. If so, then runaways should have been more literate than the slave population as a whole. On the other hand, these figures

represent the master's knowledge of literacy among slaves—not directly the level of literacy itself. Slave narratives describe many instances of slaves who learned to read and write but kept that knowledge from their owners. Further, some masters may have neglected to mention literacy in their advertisements. In short, we have both upward and downward biases in this source.

182. Larger estimates were made by W. E. B. Du Bois, who believed that 5 percent of slaves could read by 1860 (*Black Reconstruction in America*, 638). Genovese thought the true level might have been even higher (*Roll Jordan Roll*, 563).

183. Peter Randolph, *Sketches of Slave Life* (Boston, 1855), 13.

184. Clarke, 105.

185. I. E. McDougle, *Slavery in Kentucky, 1792–1865* (1915), 79.

186. Carter G. Woodson, *Education of the Negro Prior to 1861* (1915).

187. John Hunter, narrative, in Benjamin Drew, *A North-Side View of Slavery*, 114–15.

188. Emily Burke, *Reminiscences of Georgia* (n.p., 1950), 86.

189. Drew, *A North-Side View of Slavery*, 45.

190. Drew, *A North-Side View of Slavery*, 97.

191. John Thompson (1830s Maryland), 38, 50.

192. Anderson, *Life and Narrative* (Chicago: Daily Tribune Book and Job Printing Office, 1857), 9.

193. Douglass, 65.

194. John Q. Adams (Virginia, 1840s), 9–10.

195. Drew, *A North-Side View of Slavery*, 180–81.

196. Memoir of Susan Broaddus (b. 1849, Virginia), in Perdue et al. eds., *Weevils in the Wheat*, 55.

197. Louis Hughes, *Thirty Years a Slave: From Bondage to Freedom* (Milwaukee, 1897), 100–101.

198. Josiah Henson, *Truth Stranger Than Fiction. Father Henson's Story of His Own Life* (Boston: John P. Jewett, 1858), 4–5.

199. Robert Sutcliff, *Travels Through Some Parts of North America, in the Years 1804, 1805, and 1806* (Philadelphia, 1812), 50.

200. Sidbury, *Ploughshares into Swords*, 261, 265; Douglas R. Egerton, *Gabriel's Rebellion: The Virginia Slave Conspiracies of 1800 and 1802* (Chapel Hill: University of North Carolina Press, 1993), 102–3. For Douglass on Chesapeake traditions of leadership, see Douglass, *The Heroic Slave* (1853; a critical edition edited by Robert S. Levine, John Stauffer, and John R. McKivigan, New Haven, 2015), 3–5, and passim.

201. Egerton, *Gabriel's Rebellion*, 119–46; Schwarz, *Twice Condemned*, 324–35.

202. St. George Tucker, *To a Member of the General Assembly of Virginia, on the Subject of the Conspiracy of Their Slaves* (Baltimore, 1801).

203. John Randolph of Roanoke to Joseph Hopper Nicholson, Sept. 26, 1800, Nicholson Papers, Library of Congress.

204. Sidbury, *Ploughshares into Swords*, 256–76; Claude A. Green Jr., *Our Story: What We Dragged Out of Slavery with Us* (West Conshohocken, Penn., 2006), 38. Another version of the event was published in *The Liberator*, Sept. 17, Oct. 21, 1831.

205. Henry Box Brown, *Narrative of the Life of Henry Box Brown, Written by Himself* (Manchester, 1851).

206. Harriet Jacobs, *Incidents in the Life of a Slave Girl,* ed. Jean Fagan Yellin (Cambridge: Harvard University Press, 2009), 64.

207. Flowers, II, 207 (1816).

208. W. W. Brown, *Narrative of William W. Brown, an American Slave* (London: 1849), 207.

209. Paul D. Escott, *Slavery Remembered: A Record of Twentieth-Century Slave Narratives* (Chapel Hill: University of North Carolina Press, 1979), 42–43.

210. Savannah *Gazette,* Sept. 2, 1790.

211. W. W. Sweet, ed., Minutes of the Transylvania Presbytery, 1786–1837, 174–75.

212. Louis Hughes, *Thirty Years a Slave: From Bondage to Freedom* (Milwaukee, 1897), 19–21.

213. Williamson Pease remembered "a great deal of excitement among the farmers there at one time about two women on a plantation below, who had been whipped very badly and then tied out naked all night in a swamp where the mosquitoes were very thick: there was a good deal said about it." Drew, *A North-Side View of Slavery,* 132.

214. Drew, *A North-Side View of Slavery* (Louisiana, 1841), 492.

215. Drew, *A North-Side View of Slavery,* 980.

216. Drew, *A North-Side View of Slavery,* 249.

217. Joseph Ingraham, *The South-West: By a Yankee* (New York: Harper and Bros., 1835), 2: 287–88, appendix; Julia Floyd Smith, *Slavery and Plantation Growth in Antebellum Florida, 1821–1860* (Gainesville, 1973), 61.

218. Charles Emery Stevens, *Anthony Burns, A History* (Boston, 1856), 115.

219. Charles Ball, *Fifty Years in Chains; or, The Life of an American Slave* (New York, 1859), 495.

220. Grandy identified two professional slave whippers by name: Thomas Evidge of Camden County, North Carolina, and George Wilkins of Western Branch, Virginia. Moses Grandy, *Life of Moses Grandy, Late a Slave in the United States of America* (London, 1843), 62.

221. Douglass, *Narrative of the Life,* chapter 10; William S. McFeely, *Frederick Douglass* (New York, 1991), 44–48.

222. For a graphic description of slave hiring in the Chesapeake, see Stevens, *Anthony Burns, A History,* 112–15.

223. Everett S. Lee and Michael Lalli, "The Growth of the Seaport Cities, 1790–1825," with commentary by George Rogers Taylor and David Gilchrist, age, race, and gender-specific population data, in David T. Gilchrist, ed., *The Growth of the Seaport Cities, 1790–1825* (Charlottesville: University Press of Virginia, 1967), 25–57.

224. Phillips, *Freedom's Port,* 82; Douglass, *My Bondage and My Freedom,* 235, 135.

225. Paul A. Gilje, "The Baltimore Riots of 1812 and the Breakdown of the Anglo-American Mob Tradition," *Journal of Social History* 132 (1980): 547–64. For attacks by white mobs on Black workers in Baltimore brickyards and shipyards on Fell's Point in May 1858, see Hilary J. Moss, *Schooling Citizens: The Struggle for African American Education in Antebellum America* (Chicago, 2009), 93.

226. Baltimore City General Property Tax Books, 1798–1915, Baltimore City Archives, as computed in Phillips, *Freedom's Port,* 152. See also Bettye Jane Gardner, "Free Blacks in Baltimore, 1800–1860" (diss., George Washington University, 1974), online; Loren

Schweninger, *Black Property Owners in the South, 1790–1815* (Urbana: University of Illinois Press, 1990).

227. James Borchert, *Alley Life in Washington: Family, Community, Religion, and Folklife in the City, 1850–1870* (Urbana: University of Illinois Press, 1980), 1–56.

228. Phillips, *Freedom's Port*, 96–108.

229. Phillips, *Freedom's Port*, 51, 129, 273.

230. Martin Delany, *North Star*, Feb. 16, 1849.

231. Phillips, *Freedom's Port*, 118, 152–53.

232. Phillips, *Freedom's Port*, 118, 106 145, 41; Moss, *Schooling Citizens*, 103–7, 113–17; T. Stephen Whitman, *Challenging Slavery in the Chesapeake: Black and White Resistance to Human Bondage, 1775–1865* (Maryland Historical Society, 2007), 135–63.

233. This law was passed in 1715, and repealed in 1790, but remained in force for people born before 1790. *Laws of Maryland* (1715), chapter 49, and (1790), chapter 9.

234. Among many brief biographies of Daniel Coker is Suzanne E. Chapelle and Glenn O. Phillips, eds., *African American Leaders of Maryland* (Baltimore City Historical Society, 2004), 62–63, 138. Coker published his *Journal of Daniel Coker* (Baltimore, 1820), and sermons and essays cited below. Studies of his career in Maryland appear in Phillips, *Freedom's Port*, 131–39, 163–66, 277–79, and passim. Manuscript materials are in the United Methodist Historical Society, Lovely Lane Methodist Museum, Baltimore.

235. Whitman, *Challenging Slavery in the Chesapeake*, 140.

236. Moss, *Schooling Citizens*, 102–23; "William Watkins," in Archives of Maryland, online biography at https://msa.maryland.gov/megafile/msa/speccol/sc5400/sc5496/002500/002535/html/002535bio.html.

237. Whitman, *Challenging Slavery in the Chesapeake*, 140–41.

238. John Sartain, engraving, "Rev. Daniel Coker, One of the Founders of the A. M. E. Church," published in Daniel A. Payne, *History of the African Methodist Episcopal Church* (1891), online at digitalcollections.nypl.org image id 1232365.

239. Daniel Coker, *A Dialogue between a Virginian and an African Minister, written by the Rev. Daniel Coker, A Descendent of Africa . . . Minister of the African Methodist Episcopal Church in Baltimore. Humbly Dedicated to the People of Colour in the United States of America* (Baltimore, printed by Benjamin Edes for Joseph James). It is reprinted with an introduction in Dorothy Porter, ed., *Negro Protest Pamphlets* (New York: Arno Press and the New York Times, 1969), 43.

240. Porter, ed., *Negro Protest Pamphlets*, 37.

241. Porter, ed., *Negro Protest Pamphlets*, 38.

242. William Spotswood White, *The African Preacher, An Authentic Narrative* (Philadelphia, 1849). The full text is available online on many websites.

243. White, *The African Preacher*.

244. White, *The African Preacher*.

245. White, *The African Preacher*.

246. White, *The African Preacher*.

247. Frederick Douglass, *The Heroic Slave*, reprinted in Ira Dworkin ed., *Frederick Douglass* (London, 2014). Four different interpretations at this point appear, in Stanley Harrold, "Romanticizing Slave Revolt: Madison Washington, the *Creole* Mutiny, and Abolitionist Celebration of Violent Means," in John R. McKivigan and Stanley Har-

rold, eds., *Antislavery Violence: Sectional, Racial, and Cultural Conflict in Antebellum America* (Knoxville: University of Tennessee Press, 1999), 89–107; Walter Johnson, "White Lies: Human Property and Domestic Slavery Aboard the Slave Ship *Creole*," *Atlantic Studies* 5 (2008): 237–63; Edward Eden, "The Revolt on the Slave Ship *Creole*: Popular Resistance to Slavery in Post-Emancipation Nassau," *Journal of the Bahamas Historical Society* 22 (2000): 12–20; and Jeffrey R. Kerr Ritchie, *Rebellious Passage: The Creole Revolt and America's Coastal Slave Trade* (Cambridge, 2019), which is strong on the coastal trade. For other studies that link the revolt to the diplomatic conflicts that it inspired, see Edward D. Jervey and C. Harold Huber, "The *Creole* Affair," *Journal of Negro History* 65 (1980), and Arthur T. Downey, *The Creole Affair: The Slave Rebellion That Led the U.S. and Great Britain to the Brink of War* (Lanham, Md., 2014).

248. Trial record of *McCargo v. Merchants Insurance Company of New Orleans* (1845), in *Reports of Cases Argued and Determined in the Supreme Court of Louisiana and in the Superior Court of the Territory of Louisiana* (St. Paul, 1907–13) 10 (March 1845): 202–354, at 259–61.

249. Solomon Northup, *Twelve Years a Slave*, ed. Sue Eakin and Joseph Logsdon (Baton Rouge, 1968). Northup was kidnapped and sold to James Birch, a business associate of Thomas McCargo, who owned Madison Washington and many slaves aboard *Creole*.

250. Walter Johnson, *Soul by Soul: Life inside the Antebellum Slave Market* (Cambridge, 1999), 63; George Hendrick and Willene Hendrick, *The Creole Mutiny: A Tale of Revolt Aboard a Slave Ship* (Chicago, 2003), 81–82.

251. The Manifest of brig *Creole* for this voyage, which began at Richmond on October 25, 1841, includes a detailed inventory of slaves officially on board. Madison Washington appears by that name on line 24. His height is given as five feet, nine-and-a-half inches. The original record survives in the National Archives.

252. Northern friends and acquaintances of Madison Washington in 1841 included Lindley Murray Moore, a Quaker abolitionist and president of the Anti-Slavery Society in Rochester, New York; Henry Highland Garnet, a Maryland slave who became a militant minister in Utica, New York; John Gurney, a wealthy English Quaker who was traveling in New York and Canada; and Robert Purvis, a wealthy mulatto who lived in Philadelphia. Frederick Douglass knew them, and appears to have interviewed them about Madison Washington. Another source was Hiram Wilson, a Quaker abolitionist in Canada who took Madison Washington into his home. Levine et al., xxiii.

253. Philip Troutman, "Grapevine in the Slave Market: African American Geopolitical Literacy and the 1841 'Creole' Revolt," in Walter Johnson, ed., *The Chattel Principle: Internal Slave Trades in the Americas* (New Haven, 2004), 203–33. See also Walter Johnson, "White Lies: Human Property and Domestic Slavery Aboard the Slave Ship *Creole*," *Atlantic Studies* 5 (2008): 237–63.

254. Edward Eden, "The Revolt on the Slave Ship 'Creole': Popular Resistance to Slavery in Post-Emancipation Nassau," *Journal of the Bahamas Historical Society* 22 (2000): 12–20.

255. Henry Brown told his own story in *Narrative of Henry Box Brown, Who Escaped from Slavery, Enclosed in a Box 3 Feet long and 2 Wide; Written from a Statement of Facts Made by Himself. With Remarks upon the Remedy for Slavery by Charles Stearns* (Boston, 1849), and *Narrative of the Life of Henry Box Brown, Written by Himself* (Manchester,

1851). The leading scholarly work is an excellent book by Jeffrey Ruggles, *The Un-boxing of Henry Brown* (Richmond: Library of Virginia, 2003). Also helpful is "'May God Spare You from Enduring What I Then Endured': A Daring Escape from Slavery (1848)," in Maurice Duke and Daniel P. Jordan, eds., *A Richmond Reader, 1733–1983* (Chapel Hill and London: University of North Carolina Press, 1983), 92–99.

256. Martha J. Cutter, "Will the Real Henry 'Box' Brown Please Stand Up," http://com monplace.online/article/will-the-real-henry-box-brown-please-stand-up/, is helpful on this question.

257. Hollis Robbins, "Fugitive Mail: The Deliverance of Henry 'Box' Brown and Antebellum Postal Politics," *American Studies* 50 (2011): 5–25.

258. Henry Box Brown has become a favorite subject for postmodernist writings in semiotics, rhetoric, and performance analysis. See, e.g., Daphne Brooks, *Bodies in Dissent: Spectacular Performances of Race and Freedom, 1750–1910* (Durham: Duke University Press, 2006); Marcus Wood, "'All Right': The Narrative of Henry Box Brown as a Test Case for the Racial Prescription of Rhetoric and Semiotics," *American Antiquarian Society: A Journal of American History and Culture* 107 (1998): 65–104; and Cutter, "Will the Real Henry 'Box' Brown Please Stand Up." Cutter cites a very large literature on Brown in writings about magic, mesmerism, and illusion.

259. Cutter, "Will the Real Henry 'Box' Brown Please Stand Up."

260. The classic history of the Dred Scott case is Don Edward Fehrenbacher, *The Dred Scott Case: Its Significance in American Law and Politics* (New York, 1978). For Dred Scott himself, see Mark Shurtleff, *Am I Not a Man? The Dred Scott Story* (Orem, Utah, 2009); Gwenyth Swain, *Dred and Harriet Scott: A Family's Struggle for Freedom* (St. Paul, 2004); and Lea Van der Velde, *Mrs. Dred Scott: A Life on Slavery's Frontier* (Oxford, 2009). Legal documents are available online: "Freedom Suits," on the website of the Jefferson National Expansion Memorial, National Park Service; "Dred Scott v. Sanford and Related Resources," Library of Congress; and "St. Louis Circuit Court Records . . . Including Suits Brought by Dred and Harriet Scott."

261. Both have excellent short biographies in their own right in the Archives of Maryland's online Maryland Biographies. "Harriet 'Rit' Ross" and "Benjamin 'Ben' Ross," at Archives of Maryland (Biographical Series), https://msa.maryland.gov/megafile /msa/speccol/sc5400/sc5496/008400/008444/html/008444bio.html and https:// msa.maryland.gov/megafile/msa/speccol/sc5400/sc5496/008400/008444/html /008444bio.html.

262. Bradford, *Harriet Tubman*; Larson, *Bound for the Promised Land*, xvii, 100–104, and passim; Clinton, *Harriet Tubman*, 84–85.

263. Bradford, *Scenes in the Life of Harriet Tubman*, 31.

264. Harriet Tubman, quoted in Bradford, *Harriet Tubman*, 32.

265. For a careful but conservative count of slaves Tubman led to freedom, see Larson, *Bound for the Promised Land*, xvii, 100–104, 332–33n, 335n, 337n. For estimates of a larger number of more than ten a year, and "hundreds" overall, see Clinton, *Harriet Tubman*, 84–85. The common estimate in Tubman's lifetime was "over three hundred fugitives," in nineteen trips or more. That estimate was widely repeated in Tubman's later years. See Sarah Tubman, *Harriet Tubman; the Moses of Her People* (1886), ed. Butler Jones (New York, 1961), 6, 33.

266. Sarah Bradford, *Harriet Tubman, The Moses of Her People*, 33. Other accounts appear in Earl Conrad, *Harriet Tubman* (Washington, D.C., 1943), 63, and Clinton, *Harriet Tubman*, 91, 238.

267. Alice Lucas Brickler to Earl Conrad, July 19, 1939, Earl Conrad and Harriet Tubman Collection, Schomberg Center for Research on Black Culture, New York Public Library; Larson, *Bound for the Promised Land*, 199, 362.

268. Larson, *Bound for the Promised Land*, 232–33.

269. Clinton, *Harriet Tubman*, 188; John White Chadwick, ed., *A Life for Liberty: Antislavery and Other Letters of Sallie Holley* (New York, 1899), 208.

270. Much primary material appears in Bradford, *Scenes in the Life of Harriet Tubman*; Bradford, *Harriet Tubman*; online at docsouth.unc.edu; and in recent biographies of high quality, including Larson, *Bound for the Promised Land*; Clinton, *Harriet Tubman*; and Humez, *Harriet Tubman*.

271. Frederick Douglass, *Narrative of the Life* (1845), chapter 10.

272. Frederick Douglass, "The Anti-Slavery Movement," March 19, 1855, in Philip S. Foner and Yuval Taylor, eds., *Selected Speeches and Writings* (Chicago, 1999), 311–15.

273. Foner and Taylor, eds., *Selected Speeches and Writings*.

274. Douglass, "What the Black Man Wants," in Foner and Taylor, eds., *Selected Speeches and Writings*.

275. Frederick Douglass, *The Heroic Slave*, a novella, grounded in fact, about one of the greatest Virginia slave leaders, is little known today. A full text appears in Foner and Taylor, eds., *Selected Speeches and Writings*, 219–47; this volume is an abridgement by Yuval Taylor of Philip Foner's *Life and Writings of Frederick Douglass*, 5 vols. (New York, 1950–75).

Chapter 5: COASTAL CAROLINA AND GEORGIA

1. Michelle Obama, in Shailagh Murray, "A Family Tree Rooted in American Soil; Michelle Obama Learns About Her Slave Ancestors, Herself, and Her Country," *Washington Post*, Oct. 2, 2008. Also, Rachel L. Swarns, *American Tapestry: The Story of Black, White and Multiracial Ancestors of Michelle Obama* (New York, 2012), 234–39.

2. Joseph I. Waring, *The First Voyage and Settlement at Charles Town, 1670–1680* (Columbia, S.C., 1970), 227; Peter H. Wood, *Black Majority: Negroes in Colonial South Carolina, from 1670 Through the Stono Rebellion* (New York: Norton, 1974), 20–21.

3. Wood, *Black Majority*, 21. The names are as listed in A. S. Salley, ed., *Warrants for Land in South Carolina, 1672–1711* (Columbia, S.C., 1910), 1:52.

4. Several estimates differ in total numbers, but agree that between 27 percent and 30 percent were of African descent. Cf. Wood, *Black Majority*, 25; Philip Morgan, *Slave Counterpoint: Black Culture in the Eighteenth-Century Chesapeake and Lowcountry* (Williamsburg: University of North Carolina Press, 1998), 59–61; *Calendar of State Papers Colonial Series, America and West Indies* (1671–72), documents 472, 473, 736.

5. Wood, *Black Majority*, table 11, pp. 146–47. Also in William S. Pollitzer, *The Gullah People and Their Heritage* (Athens, Ga., 1999), table 7, p. 53; U.S. Census of 1790, in Evarts B. Greene and Virginia D. Harrington, *American Population Before the Federal Census of 1790* (New York and Baltimore, 1932 and 1981), 174.

6. Greene and Harrington, *American Population Before the Federal Census of 1790*, 172–79.

7. Philip Morgan, ed., *African American Life in the Georgia Lowcountry: The Atlantic World and the Gullah Geechee* (Athens, Ga., 2010), 2.

8. Gullah Geechee Cultural Heritage Corridor Commission, https://www.gullah geecheecorridor.org.

9. Wood, *Black Majority*, 22.

10. George C. Rogers, *The History of Georgetown County, South Carolina* (Columbia, S.C., 1970), 18–20.

11. Charles F. Kovacik and John J. Winberry, *South Carolina: The Making of a Landscape* (Columbia, S.C., 1987, 1989), 13–24; James C. Bonner, *A History of Georgia Agriculture, 1732–1860* (Athens, Ga., 1964, 2009), 2–31.

12. Kovacik and Winberry, *South Carolina*, 35.

13. Much about this subject has been controversial for many years. On African origins of Carolina slaves, much early writing heavily stressed the Angolan roots of Gullah culture. A different approach was taken by Melville Herskovits, an ethnographer who had done much work in West Africa, especially among the Dahomey, and argued that the Windward Coast and Gold Coast were leading regions of African origin for South Carolina slaves (*The Myth of the Negro Past*, 48–49). Herskovits drew his evidence mainly from the middle period of the slave trade.

    A mediating idea appeared in Wood, *Black Majority*, which noted the strong Angolan predominance in the early period of the South Carolina slave trade, but also put heavy stress on the Windward Coast, especially in conjunction with the growth of rice planting.

    The Windward Coast became more prominent in Daniel Littlefield, *Rice and Slaves: Ethnicity and the Slave Trade in Colonial South Carolina* (Baton Rouge, 1981), and especially in Margaret Washington Creel, *"A Peculiar People": Slave Religion and Community-Culture Among the Gullahs* (New York, 1988). Taking her lead from linguists, Creel gave heavy weight to present-day Sierra Leone and Liberia, and particularly the Gola and Gizzi nations in that region, which she associates with Gullah and Geechee cultures of Georgia and South Carolina.

    All of these works have made important contributions. Other historians began to study quantitative evidence in South Carolina Treasury duty books, Naval Office shipping lists, records of slave traders, and descriptions of runaway slaves. This evidence established complex patterns of change through time. Angolan and Congolese origins predominated from 1700 to about 1740, West African from 1740 to 1775, and West Central African again from 1783 to 1807.

    Overall, the Gullah folkways of South Carolina derived from no single African region. This was a new culture, created from a mix of mostly African ingredients, in which Angolan-Congolese and West African elements were both of importance. Gullah derived from no single region of old Africa. It was a new synthesis, not merely a replication of an existing culture. Data are summarized in tables below from the work of Elizabeth Donnan, ed., *Documents Illustrative of the History of the Slave Trade to America*, 4 vols. (Washington, D.C.: Carnegie Institution, 1930–35), and Wood, *Black Majority*; and Morgan, *Slave Counterpoint*, 63, 68.

14. Henry Laurens to Devonshire, Reeve and Lloyd, May 22, 1755, in Philip M. Hamer, ed., *The Papers of Henry Laurens* (Columbia: University of South Carolina Press, 1968–2003), 1: 252; Henry Laurens to Smith and Clifton, May 26, 1755, "the most certain article we can recommend . . . is a few fine Negro Men (not Callabars)," 1: 257. Also "Our people like the Gambia and Windward coast full as well or the Angola men such as are large" (to Wells Wharton and Doran, May 27, 1955, 1: 257); "tall able people of any country but Callabars" (to Thomas Mears, June 27, 1755, 1: 275); "There must not be a Callabar amongst them. Gold Coast or Gambias are best" (to Smith and Clifton, July 17, 1755, 1: 295); "Callabar which slaves are quite out of repute from numbers in every Cargo that have been sold with us destroying themselves" (to Peter Furnell, Sept. 6, 1755, 1: 331).

15. Thelma Wills Foote, *Black and White Manhattan: The History of Racial Formation in Colonial New York City* (New York and Oxford: Oxford University Press, 2004), 135.

16. For returns for slave ships arriving in Charleston from March 1735 to March 1740, see Peter Wood in *Black Majority*, appendix C. My computations differ from Wood's in two respects. First, he reports a total of 8,045 slaves from Angola and 93 from the West Indies; but the individual voyages amount to 7,900 and 1,066 respectively. Second, Wood estimates the number of Angola slaves (69.6 percent) as a proportion of all arriving slaves, but many others (1,342) were reported as arriving merely from "Africa" or "Guinea." The proportions of arrivals from Africa identified by specific region were as follows:

African Region	Percent (Number)
Senegambia	7.3% (684)
Windward Coast and Gold Coast	2.3% (213)
Biafra	6.5% (609)
Angola	84.0% (7,900)
Total	100.1% (9,406)

Angolan slaves as a proportion of all arrivals were 66.9 percent. The more significant number is the proportion of Angolans to slaves from other identifiable African regions. This is 84.0 percent in the period from 1735 to 1740. Patterns in other periods differed as we shall see.

17. John K. Thornton, "African Dimensions of the Stono Rebellion," *American Historical Review* 96 (1991): 1101–13.

18. Charleston *Evening Gazette*, July 11, 1785, as quoted in Wood, *Black Majority*, 60.

19. The leading study, by Margaret Creel, yields the following estimates of slaves of identifiable origin arriving in South Carolina during the period from 1749 to 1787:

African Region	Cargoes with a Count of Slaves	All Cargoes (estimated)
Senegambia	10,499	16,223
Windward Coast	11,135	15,410
Gold Coast	6,240	9,096
Benin	0	0
Biafra	3,343	4,665
Angola	7,480	7,934
Others	956	1,230
Total	39,653	54,538

The best estimate probably lies between the reports of cargoes where slaves were individually counted, and Creel's extrapolation to all cargoes. See Creel, *"A Peculiar People,"* 330.

20. Joseph E. Holloway, "The Origins of African-American Culture," in Joseph Holloway, ed., *Africanisms in American Culture* (Bloomington, Ind., 1990), 7.
21. See summary tables 5.1–5.5.
22. Jacksonville, North Carolina, to Jacksonsville, Duval County, Florida.
23. On Oglethorpe and slavery, there are at least three schools of thought. For the first school, the leading work was by Amos E. Ettinger, *James Edward Oglethorpe: Imperial Idealist* (Oxford, 1936); reprinted as *Oglethorpe: A Brief Biography*, ed. Phinizy Spalding (Macon, Ga., 1984), an excellent essay by a gifted young American scholar who won Oxford's Beit Prize in 1929. In this view, Oglethorpe appeared as an abolitionist before his time.

    A second school was led by Phinizy Spalding, *Oglethorpe in America* (Chicago, 1977), who maximized Oglethorpe's flaws and foibles, beyond the fact. A later essay, deeper and better balanced, is Betty Wood's "James Edward Oglethorpe, Race, and Slavery: A Reassessment," in Harvey H. Jackson and Phinizy Spalding, eds., *Oglethorpe in Perspective: Georgia's Founder After Two Hundred Years* (Tuscaloosa, 1989), 66–79.

    A third school of specialized studies brought out the astonishing range and complexity of Oglethorpe's career, and his strength of intellect and character. Some of this scholarship appeared in Harvey H. Jackson and Phinizy Spalding, eds., *Forty Years of Diversity: Essays on Colonial Georgia* (Athens, Ga., 1984), with helpful essays by Milton Ready on philanthropy in its eighteenth-century meaning, and many studies of diverse groups of settlers. Jackson and Spalding also edited another volume of essays, *Oglethorpe in Perspective*, cited above, with contributions on Oglethorpe's work in Georgia and his military career. Yet another collection of essays was edited by John Inscoe, *James Edward Oglethorpe: New Perspectives on His Life and Legacy* (Savannah, 1997), with essays by Keith Thomas, including "James Edward Oglethorpe, Sometime Gentleman Commoner of Corpus," 16–34; three pieces on Oglethorpe's involvement in foreign affairs; and an essay by Phinizy Spalding on Oglethorpe and James Boswell (who planned to write a biography) and their correspondence, which is revealing on Oglethorpe and the American Revolution.

An indispensable collection of primary materials is Rodney M. Baine, ed., *The Publications of James Edward Oglethorpe* (Athens, Ga., 1994).

24. Darold D. Wax, "'New Negroes Are Always in Demand': The Slave Trade in Eighteenth-Century Georgia," *Georgia Historical Quarterly* 68 (1984): 194.

25. "Proceedings relating to a Negroe Slave Condemned in the Town Court of Frederica. Pursuant to the Law against Negroes, March 30, 1741," Egmonet Collection, 14205, pp. 274–76, Phillips College University of Georgia Library, Athens; Wax, "'New Negroes Are Always in Demand,'" 195.

26. Betty Wood, *Slavery in Colonial Georgia, 1730–1775* (Athens, Ga., 1984), 29, 31, 51.

27. Francis Moore, *A Voyage to Georgia Begun in the Year 1735* (London, 1744), 43–44.

28. Harvey H. Jackson, "The Darien Anti-Slavery Petition of 1739 and the Georgia Plan," *William and Mary Quarterly*, 3rd series, 34 (1977): 618–31; Wood, *Slavery in Colonial Georgia*, 59–73.

29. "Frederica and Defense Considerations," in Spalding, *Oglethorpe in America*, 18–32.

30. Malachy Postlethwayt argued that the slave trade was the center of commerce in the empire in *The African Trade: The Great Pillar and Support of the British Plantation Trade in America* (London, 1745). The impact of Postlethwayt's writings appears in Alexander Hamilton's notes on his reading in the back of his artillery paybook in the American War of Independence. See also William Wood, in *Select Dissertations on Colonies and Plantations, by those Celebrated Authors, Sir Josiah Child, Charles D'Avenant, LLD, and Mr. William Wood . . .* (London, 1775).

31. Harold E. Davis, *The Fledgling Province* (Chapel Hill: University of North Carolina Press, 1976), 27.

32. Davis, *The Fledgling Province*, 65.

33. Bonner, *A History of Georgia Agriculture*, 8; Wood, *Slavery in Colonial Georgia*, 108, 99.

34. E. Merton Coulter, "Mary Musgrove, Queen of the Creeks," *Georgia Historical Quarterly* 11 (1927): 1–30; John P. Corry, "Some New Light on the Bosomworth Claims."

35. Wood, *Slavery in Colonial Georgia*, 74–109; Jeffrey Robert Young, *Domesticating Slavery: The Master Class in Georgia and South Carolina, 1670–1837* (Chapel Hill: University of North Carolina Press, 1999).

36. Wood, *Slavery in Colonial Georgia*, 98.

37. Wax, "'New Negroes Are Always in Demand,'" 193–220; http://www.slavevoyages .org; David Eltis and David Richardson, *Atlas of the Transatlantic Slave Trade* (New Haven: Yale University Press, 2010), map 145.

38. The evidence of slave voyages in the Trans-Atlantic Slave Trade Database indicates that origins of slaves carried from Africa to Georgia are as follows:

Upper Guinea	15,300 slaves (61.4%)
Gold Coast	2,200 slaves (15.3%)
West Central Africa	5,800 slaves (23.3%)
Total	24,900 slaves (100.0%)

Of that total, approximately 80 percent arrived in documented voyages; 20 percent are added by the editors to correct for missing voyages. The source is Eltis and Richardson, *Atlas of the Transatlantic Slave Trade*, map 145.

39. Wax, "'New Negroes Are Always in Demand,'" table 4, p. 218; Eltis and Richardson, *Atlas of the Transatlantic Slave Trade*, maps, 56–68.

40. Valentin Vydrin, T. G. Bergman, and Matthew Benjamin cartographer, *Mandé Language Family of West Africa: Location and Genetic Classification* (Dallas, SIL Electronic Survey Report, 2000), https://www.sil.org/system/files/reapdata/12/10/90/12109080 7453725502109014927276258843000/silesr2000_003.pdf. This work includes a review of a large literature and summaries of field data.

41. Michael A. Gomez, "Africans, Culture, and Islam in the Lowcountry," in Morgan, ed., *African American Life in the Georgia Lowcountry*, 103–30; Lorenzo Dow Turner, "Personal Names Used by Gullahs," *Africanisms in the Gullah Dialect* (Columbia: University of South Carolina Press, 2002), 40ff.

42. Savannah Unit, Georgia Writers' Project, Works Project Administration, *Drums and Shadows: Survival Studies Among the Georgia Coastal Negroes* (Athens, Ga., 1940, 1949; with an introduction by Charles Joyner, 1986), ix–xxvii.

43. An early South Carolina law, enacted in 1690 during the administration of the "Rebel Governor" Seth Sothell, was disallowed, together with all other statutes passed in Sothell's rule. In 1696 a more comprehensive slave code was passed, and continued in force for many years. South Carolina's slave laws are conveniently brought together in Thomas J. Cooper and David J. McCord, eds., *Statutes at Large of South Carolina*, 14 vols. (Columbia, S.C., 1836–75), 1: 343–74.

44. M. Eugene Sirmans, "The Legal Status of the Slave in South Carolina, 1670–1740," *Journal of Southern History* 28 (1962): 462–73.

45. South Carolina's first comprehensive statute on slavery in 1690 declared slaves to be freehold property. But that law was disallowed, and the provision was not repeated in subsequent legislation. Sirmans, "The Legal Status of the Slave in South Carolina," 462–68.

46. Sirmans, "The Legal Status of the Slave in South Carolina."

47. Cooper and McCord, eds., *Statutes at Large of South Carolina* (1712), 363.

48. Cooper and McCord, eds., *Statutes at Large* (1712), 357.

49. Cooper and McCord, eds., *Statutes at Large* (1712), 252.

50. Cooper and McCord, eds., *Statutes at Large* (1712), 354.

51. Cooper and McCord, eds., *Statutes at Large* (1722), 373.

52. Cooper and McCord, eds., *Statutes at Large* (1722), 382.

53. Sirmans, "The Legal Status of the Slave in South Carolina."

54. Cooper and McCord, eds., *Statutes at Large* (1712), 352; the second clause was thought to be ambiguous and later redrafted (1722), 354.

55. Cooper and McCord, eds., *Statutes at Large* (1712), 353.

56. Cooper and McCord, eds., *Statutes at Large* (1712), 363.

57. Cooper and McCord, eds., *Statutes at Large* (1714), 368.

58. Cooper and McCord, eds., *Statutes at Large* (1712), 355.

59. Cooper and McCord, eds., *Statutes at Large*, (1712), 360.

60. Cooper and McCord, eds., *Statutes at Large* (1712), 357.

61. Cooper and McCord, eds., *Statutes at Large* (1740) 404, 413.

62. Cooper and McCord, eds., *Statutes at Large* (1740), 411.

63. Cooper and McCord, eds., *Statutes at Large* (1740), 412.

64. Cooper and McCord, eds., *Statutes at Large* (1740), 413.

65. Cooper and McCord, eds., *Statutes at Large* (1751), 424.

66. Cooper and McCord, eds., *Statutes at Large* (1743), 418.

67. Cooper and McCord, eds., *Statutes at Large* (1743), 417.

68. *The Colonial Records of the State of Georgia*, 26 vols., ed. Allen Candler et al., and Lucian L. Knight et al. (Atlanta: Franklin Printing and Publishing, 1904–16), 1:11–26, 50–52.

69. For Oglethorpe's account of this event, see his "Thanksgiving for Victory," a proclamation read to colonists in Frederica, July 25, 1742, and subsequently in Savanah and Ebenezer. It was published in the *Boston Evening Post*, Nov. 29, 1742, and by Benjamin Franklin in the *Pennsylvania Gazette*, Dec. 21, 1742. An annotated modern text appears in Baine, ed., *The Publications of James Edward Oglethorpe*, 256–58.

70. For an excellent and balanced discussion, see Wood, *Slavery in Colonial Georgia*, 75–87.

71. Wood, *Slavery in Colonial Georgia*, 231; *The Colonial Records of the State of Georgia*, 34:48.

72. "AN ACT for the better Ordering and Governing negroes and other Slaves in this Province," in Candler et al., *The Colonial Records of the State of Georgia*, 18:102–44.

73. Wood, *Black Majority*, 289; *Charleston South Carolina Gazette*, Jan. 17, 1761; Wood, *Slavery in Colonial Georgia*, 125.

74. "An Act to Emancipate Sam, the negro slave, in response to his actions in extinguishing the fire on the State-house," *Georgia Laws* (1834), 1: 229.

75. Lydia Parrish, *Slave Songs of the Georgia Sea Islands* (Athens: University of Georgia Press, 1992), 288, 238.

76. Ben Horry (b. 1852), interview by Genevieve Chandler, Murrell's Inlet, S.C., Aug. 1937, in Kincaid Mills, Genevieve C. Peterkin, and Aaron McCollough, eds., *Coming Through: Voices of a South Carolina Gullah Community from WPA Oral Histories Collected by Genevieve W. Chandler* (Columbia, S.C., 2008), 95. This is one of the richest and best edited collections of WPA narratives.

77. Sam Polite, aged ninety-three in 1937?, born ca. 1843, lived on Fripp plantations, St. Helena Island, in George Rawick, ed., *The American Slave: A Composite Autobiography*, 19 vols. (Westport, Conn.: Greenwood, 1972), vol. 3, *South Carolina Narratives*, parts 3 and 4, pp. 271–76.

78. J. Motte Alston, *Rice Planter and Sportsman: The Recollections of J. Motte Alston, 1821–1909* (Columbia: University of South Carolina Press, 1953), 15.

79. Charles Joyner, *Down by the Riverside* (Urbana and Chicago: University of Illinois Press, 1984), 208, with many other examples on p. 324.

80. "Letter of James Hamilton Couper, Esq.," reprinted in Allan D. Austin, *African Muslims in Antebellum America* (New York and London: Routledge, 1997), 321–35.

81. Frederick Law Olmsted, "The Rice District," in *Cotton Kingdom* (London, 1861), 187.

82. Olmsted, "The Rice District," 189.

83. Elizabeth Waties Allston Pringle told the story in *Chronicles of Chicora Wood* (1922; new edition, Georgetown, 1999), 9–11. Fifty years later, Charles Joyner interviewed

Prince Washington, grandson of Philip Washington, on Sandy Island, Jan. 17, 1972. Joyner subsequently checked the facts again with Rebecca Washington, widow of Prince Washington, July 2, 1976, and published the results in *Down by the Riverside*, 31–32.

84. Thomas Pyatt, *The Gullah People of Sandy Island* (Sandy Island, S.C., 2005), 8–12. Thomas Pyatt is descended from the family of Philip Washington.

85. Morgan, *Slave Counterpoint*, 343.

86. Olmsted, "The Rice District," 193.

87. Olmsted, "The Rice District," 194.

88. Recollections of Josephine Bacchus, Marion, South Carolina, in Rawick, ed., *The American Slave*, vol. 2, *South Carolina Narratives*, parts 1–2, p. 21.

89. Morgan, *Slave Counterpoint*, 339.

90. Ephraim Lawrence, aged eighty-one, Edisto Island, in Rawick, ed., *The American Slave*, vol. 3, *South Carolina Narratives*, parts 3 and 4, pp. 94–99.

91. Mary Boykin Chesnut, Jan. 7, 1865, in C. Vann Woodward, ed., *Mary Chesnut's Civil War* (New Haven and London: Yale University Press, 1981), 699. For another example, see Fannie Moore, Asheville, North Carolina, in Rawick, ed., *The American Slave*, volume 15, part 2, pp. 128–37; Norman R. Yetman, *Life Under the "Peculiar Institution"* (New York: Holt, Rinehart and Winston, 1970), 226–31.

92. For indigo in the eighteenth century an excellent survey is Morgan, *Slave Counterpoint*, 159–64. For later accounts of indigo production to the end of slavery, see for example the slave narrative of William Oliver, "born in Horry [County], a boy in slavery time," in Rawick, ed., *The American Slave*, vol. 3, *South Carolina Narratives*, parts 3 and 4, pp. 217–20.

93. The origins of African rice cultivation are not clearly established. Some scholars believe that it was an indigenous development, from strains of wild rice native to Africa. Others argue that rice cultivation was introduced from the Mediterranean. Ancient writers report rice in Cyrenaica as early as 12 AD; Littlefield, *Rice and Slaves*, 83.

94. Journal of Samuel Gamble, 1793–94, Sandown ms, 55, National Maritime Museum; Littlefield, *Rice and Slaves*, 95.

95. Littlefield, *Rice and Slaves*, 94, 96.

96. Wood, *Black Majority*, 57; Duncan Heyward, *Seed from Madagascar* (Chapel Hill: University of North Carolina Press, 1937).

97. Wood, *Black Majority*, 61–62.

98. Joyner, *Down by the Riverside*, 59–61.

99. Among many studies of task work, see Morgan, *Slave Counterpoint*, 179–87, 344, 347; Philip Morgan, "Task and Gang Systems," in Stephen Innes, ed., *Work and Labor* (Chapel Hill: University of North Carolina Press, 1988), 189; Joyner, *Down by the Riverside*, 43–45, 51, 59, 66, 74, 128–29; J. H. Easterby, ed., *The South Carolina Rice Plantation* (Chicago: University of Chicago Press, 1945), 31.

100. Joyner, *Down by the Riverside*, 59.

101. Joyner, *Down by the Riverside*, 51, 130.

102. Abbey Mishow, raised on Waterford Plantation, Black River, Georgetown County, South Carolina, in Rawick, ed., *The American Slave*, vol. 3, *South Carolina Narratives*, pp. 197–99.

103. An abridged life table by Cheryll Ann Cody for slaves on the Ball plantations between 1800 and 1849 yields the following:

	Male Slaves			Female Slaves		
Age	l_x	q_x	e_x	l_x	q_x	e_x
0	10000	.3766	19.82	10000	.3690	20.54
1–4	6234	.1979	30.49	6310	.1730	31.25
5–9	5000	.0767	33.52	5218	.0944	33.37
10–14	4617	.0741	31.09	4726	.0553	31.59
15–19	4275	.1111	28.38	4464	.0930	28.29
20–24	3800	.0741	26.61	4049	.0980	25.94
25–29	3519	.0816	23.54	3652	.1835	23.49
30–34	3231	.1667	20.41	2982	.1268	23.20
35–39	2693	.1429	18.99	2604	.2000	21.21
40–44	2308	.1861	16.74	2083	.1053	20.88
45–49	1879	.1834	14.99	1864	.2041	18.04
50–54	1534	.2257	12.80	1484	.1818	17.02
55–59	1188	.2650	10.80	1214	.2176	15.26
60–64	873	.3449	8.79	950	.3078	13.80
65–69	572	.4324	7.10	657	.3899	12.34
70–74	325	.5490	5.59	610	.5209	6.70
75–79	146	.6989	4.38	292	.6611	6.28
80+	44	1.0000	3.75	99	1.0000	3.76

Source: Reconstitution of Ball family slaves by Cheryll Cody, reported in Cody, "Slave Demography and Family Formation: A Community Study of the Ball Family Plantation" (diss., University of Minnesota, 1982), 410–11.

104. A careful study by Cheryll Ann Cody estimates rates of infant mortality as follows among slaves on the Ball plantations in South Carolina, from 1800 to 1859:

1800–09	223
1810–19	229
1820–29	177
1830–39	223
1840–49	249
1850–59	299

The total number of infants was 1,758.

Source: Cody, "Slave Demography and Family Formation," 214.

105. Cheryll Ann Cody reported the seasonality of conceptions on the Ball plantations as follows:

Monthly Seasonality Index (mean = 100)

Seasonality Indices

Month of Birth	Month of Conception	1760–99	1800–29	1830–65
January	April	140	107	96
February	May	85	86	82
March	June	97	72	69
April	July	48	69	91
May	August	97	93	90
June	September	69	95	102
July	October	90	122	105
August	November	107	130	148
September	December	124	152	130
October	January	153	112	122
November	February	110	73	89
December	March	80	86	75
Total		1,200	1,200	1200

Source: Cody, "Slave Demography and Family Formation," 390.
Economists Steckel, Fogel, and Engerman have offered a neoclassical explanation of the slave conception cycle. But Cody observes that "the pattern is the inverse of what would be expected were Fogel and Engerman correct."

106. Ralph Betts Flanders, *Plantation Slavery in Georgia* (Cos Cob, Ct.: John E. Edwards, 1967), 61, 64, 76, 130, 187.

107. Charleston *South Carolina Gazette*, March 30, 1734.

108. Scholars also have disagreed in another way about how Black speech should be studied. Some approach it as a historical problem. Others propose to study it synchronically, "without reference to its history." More than a few think it should be studied by careful methods of geographic description. With this, Marxist scholar Joey L. Dillard strongly disagrees. He insists that "the geographical preconception about dialect distribution is downright wrong," and should yield to a method which he calls "social dialectology." The present inquiry combines historical, geographic, and social approaches which can be done by a history of regional patterns in social rank through time. J. L. Dillard, *Black English* (New York, 1972), but also compare J. L. Dillard, *Toward a Social History of American English* (Berlin, 1985).

109. For an estimate of eight hundred languages in four stocks, of which one "Niger-Congo" stock was brought to America, see Joseph H. Greenberg, *Language, Culture and Communication* (Stanford: Stanford University Press, 1971); Joseph H. Greenberg, *The Languages of Africa* (Bloomington, Ind., 1966).

110. R. G. Armstrong, *The Study of West African Languages* (Ibadan, Nigeria, 1964); Greenberg, *The Languages of Africa*; S. W. Koelle, *Polyglotta Africana* (Graz, Austria, 1963).

111. Olaudah Equiano, *The Life of Olaudah Equiano or Gustavus Vassa the African, 1789, with an Introduction by Paul Edwards*, 2 vols. (London, 1969), 2:23.

112. Jervis Dewint, "A Strong Barbaric Accent: America's Dutch Speaking Black Community from 17th Century New Netherland to 19th Century New York and New Jersey," *American Speech* 90 (2015): 121–56; Edward Larocque Tinker et al., "Gombo: The Creole Dialect of Louisiana," *American Antiquarian Society Proceedings* (1935): 101–28; Douglass, *Life and Times*.

113. Charleston *South Carolina State Gazette*, Sept. 25, 1794.

114. George Krapp, "The English of the Negro," *American Mercury* 2 (1924): 190–95; Reed Smith, *Gullah*, bulletin number 10 (Columbia, S.C.: University of South Carolina, 1926), 18–28.

115. Joyner, *Down by the Riverside*, 196–24; Montgomery, ed., *The Crucible of Carolina: Essays in the Development of Gullah Language and Culture* (Athens, Ga., 1994), 1–16.

116. Elizabeth Hyde Botume, *First Days Amongst the Contrabands* (1893; reprint, New York, 1968), 54, 57.

117. Ivan Van Sertima, "My Gullah Brother and I: Exploration into a Community's Language and Myth Through Its Oral Tradition," in Deborah S. Harrison and Tom Trabasso, eds., *Black English: A Seminar* (Hillsdale, N.J., 1976), 123–46. This comes from fieldwork on Johns Island and James Island and Charleston, South Carolina, in 1970 and 1971.

118. Cornelia Walker Bailey, *God, Dr. Buzzard, and the Bolito Man: A Saltwater Geechee Talks About Life on Sapelo Island, Georgia* (New York, 2000, 2001), 301–19.

119. Lorenzo Dow Turner, *Africanisms in the Gullah Dialect* (Chicago, 1949; new edition with an introduction by Katherine Wyly Mille and Michael B. Montgomery, Columbia, S.C., 2002), ix–lvii.

120. Turner, *Africanisms in the Gullah Dialect*, xxix.

121. Coastal counties include Horry, Georgetown, Charleston, Beaufort, and Jasper in South Carolina; Chatham, Liberty, McIntosh, Glynn, and Camden in Georgia; Nassau and Duval in Florida; and Brunswick, New Hanover, and Pee Dee in North Carolina. Second-tier interior counties include parts of Marion, Williamsburg, Berkeley, Dorchester, Colleton, Colleton, and Hampden in South Carolina.

122. One of the most important, and most readable, books on this subject is Bailey, *God, Dr. Buzzard, and the Bolito Man*, 4–5.

123. Bailey, *God, Dr. Buzzard, and the Bolito Man*, 5.

124. Bailey, *God, Dr. Buzzard, and the Bolito Man*, 5.

125. Charles Joyner, *Remember Me: Slave Life in Coastal Georgia* (1989; revised edition, Athens, Ga., 2011), 2–3.

126. Interview with Ben Sullivan, St. Simons Island, Georgia Writers' Project, *Drums and Shadows*, 178–82.

127. Interview with Ben Sullivan, Georgia Writers' Project, *Drums and Shadows*, 178–82.

128. Interview with Ben Sullivan, Georgia Writers' Project, *Drums and Shadows*, 178–82; Suzanne S. Macfarlane, "The Ethnoarchaeology of a Slave Community: The Couper Plantation Site" (MA thesis, University of Florida, 1975), 60–73; George W. McDaniel, *Hearth and Home* (Philadelphia: Temple University Press, 1982.), 34–37.

129. Charles J. Montgomery, "Survivors from the Slave Yacht *Wanderer*," *American Anthropologist* 10 (1908): 611–23.

130. Susan Denyer, *African Traditional Architecture* (New York, 1978).

131. Frances Anne Kemble, *Journal of a Residence on a Georgian Plantation in 1838–1839*, ed. John A. Scott (New York, 1970), 64.

132. John Michael Vlach, "Not Mansion . . . But Good Enough: Slave Quarters as Bicultural Expression," in Ted Ownby, ed., *Black and White: Cultural Interaction in the Antebellum South* (Jackson: University Press of Mississippi, 1993), 97.

133. Vlach, "Not Mansion," 102.

134. Sam Mitchell, aged eighty-seven, lived on Woodlawn Plantation. John Chaplain, master, Ladies Island, in Rawick, ed., *The American Slave*, vol. 3, *South Carolina Narratives*, parts 3 and 4, pp. 200–204.

135. Abbey Mishow, raised on Waterford Plantation, Black River, Georgetown County, South Carolina, in Rawick, ed., *The American Slave*, vol. 3, *South Carolina Narratives*, parts 3 and 4, pp. 197–99.

136. Donald William Meinig and James Peter Burkholder, *The Shaping of America: Atlantic America, 1492–1800* (New Haven: Yale University Press, 1986), 189.

137. McDaniel, *Hearth and Home*, 48.

138. Georgia Writers' Project, *Drums and Shadows*, 8.

139. Georgia Writers' Project, *Drums and Shadows*, 26.

140. Edith M. Dabbs, *Face of an Island* (Columbia, S.C., 197); Robert L. Hall, "African Religious Retentions in Florida," in Holloway, ed., *Africanisms in American Culture*," 116n; Elizabeth Jacoway, *Yankee Missionaries in the South: The Penn School Experiment* (Baton Rouge, 1980). A recent study of Penn Center as a model of cultural preservation and creativity is Orville Vernon Burton with Wilbur Cross, *Penn Center: A History Preserved* (Athens, Ga., 2014), 119–25.

141. Georgia Writers' Project, *Drums and Shadows*, 8.

142. Georgia Writers' Project, *Drums and Shadows*, 26.

143. Dale Rosengarten, *Row upon Row: Sea Grass Baskets of the South Carolina Lowcountry* (Charleston, S.C., 1986, 1987).

144. Georgia Writers' Project, *Drums and Shadows*, 8.

145. Georgia Writers' Project, *Drums and Shadows*, 8, 26, 52, 121.

146. Rosengarten, *Row upon Row*.

147. John Michael Vlach, *Charleston Blacksmith: The Work of Philip Simmons* (Athens, Ga., 1981), 13.

148. Littlefield, *Rice and Slaves*, 136–37, reporting the results of research on advertisements for runaway slaves in South Carolina, 1732–75.

149. Joyner, *Down by the Riverside*, 91.

150. The following samples of rations come from plantations in coastal South Carolina and Georgia:

Edisto Island, South Carolina: corn 1 peck occasional, or potatoes 1 bushel

Edisto Island, South Carolina: corn 10 quarts, or potatoes 1 bushel, some meat or fish or peas 4 quarts or rice 8 quarts

Edisto Island, South Carolina: corn 6 quarts or pork 2 pounds; potatoes 0.5 bushel

Edisto Island, South Carolina: corn 10 quarts or pork 1.4 pounds; potatoes 0.5 bushel
Waccamaw River, South Carolina: rice 8 quarts, peas 2 pounds; or salt beef-rice soup,
sweet potatoes 1 bushel; fish 2 or 3
John D. Magill plantation: sweet potatoes 1 peck, 12 salt fish; families w/baby, grits
1 peck, 1 piece fatback

Sources: Flanders, *Plantation Slavery in Georgia*, 156; Joyner, *Down by the Riverside*, 91.

151. Recollections of Uncle Welcome Bees, aged 104, Murrells Inlet, Georgetown County, South Carolina, in Rawick, ed., *The American Slave*, vol. 3, *South Carolina Narratives*, parts 1 and 2, p. 49.

152. Uncle Gable Locklier, born in Clarendon County, eighty-six years old in 1937, in Rawick, ed., *The American Slave*, vol. 3, *South Carolina Narratives*, parts 3 and 4, pp. 112–17.

153. Sam Polite, in Rawick, ed., *The American Slave*, vol. 3, *South Carolina Narratives*, parts 3 and 4, pp. 271–76.

154. Ball, *Life of an American Slave*, 133. Also Alice R. Huger Smith and Herbert Ravenal Sass, *A Carolina Rice Plantation of the Fifties* (New York, 1936), 72.

155. Sam Polite, in Rawick, ed., *The American Slave*, vol. 3, *South Carolina Narratives*, parts 3 and 4, pp. 271–76.

156. William L. Dunwoody, in Yetman, *Life Under the "Peculiar Institution,"* 104.

157. Herbert G. Gutman, *The Black Family in Slavery and Freedom, 1750–1925* (New York: Vintage, 1976), 271; *Facts Concerning the Freedmen* (1863), 3–12.

158. Flanders, *Plantation Slavery in Georgia*, 173, quoting John Livingston Hopkins, *Messalina's Questions; or a Vindication of Slavery* (Liverpool, 1821?), 170.

159. Gutman, *The Black Family in Slavery and Freedom*, 275.

160. Gutman, *The Black Family in Slavery and Freedom*, 275.

161. Examples of blanket marriages are frequent through the coastal region. For Georgia, *Suppressed Book About Slavery* (1864), 214–15; Gutman, *The Black Family in Slavery and Freedom*, 596. For South Carolina Sea Islands, see testimony of A. D. Smith in Gutman, *The Black Family in Slavery and Freedom*, 596; Willie Lee Rose, *Rehearsal for Reconstruction: The Port Royal Experiment* (Indianapolis: Bobbs-Merrill, 1964), 89.

162. Leslie Howard Owens, *This Species of Property* (New York: Oxford University Press, 1976), 192, citing Rawick, *Florida Narratives*, 128.

163. Joyner, *Down by the Riverside*, 136–38.

164. Smith, *Slavery and Rice Culture in Low Country Georgia*, 178, citing Gerald J. Smith, ed., "Reminiscences of the Civil War by J. W. Frederick," *Georgia Historical Quarterly* 59 (1975 supplement): 159.

165. Joyner, *Down by the Riverside*, 137–38.

166. Joyner, *Down by the Riverside*, 217.

167. Joyner, *Down by the Riverside*, 217.

168. Lydia Parrish, *Slave Songs of the Georgia Sea Islands* (New York, 1942; Hatboro, Pa., 1965), 8.

169. Gutman, *The Black Family in Slavery and Freedom*, 576n.

170. Lorenzo Dow Turner, *Africanisms in the Gullah Dialect*, with a new introduction by Katherine Wyly Mille and Michael B. Montgomery (1949, 1972; Columbia, S.C.,

2002). A glossary of African names appears on pp. 40–190; for the use of basket names in Africa, see pp. 31–40.

171. John Inscoe finds the proportion ranged from 25 percent to 14 percent for South Carolina slaves in general, but he notes that African names remained more common in the lowcountry. John Inscoe, "Black Naming Patterns," *Journal of Southern History* 49 (1983): 527–54.

172. Inscoe, "Black Naming Patterns," 527–54.

173. Inscoe, "Black Naming Patterns," 536.

174. Keith E. Baird and Mary A. Twining, "Names and Naming in the Sea Islands," in Montgomery, ed., *The Crucible of Carolina*, 23–37.

175. Smith and Sass, *A Carolina Rice Plantation of the Fifties*, 71.

176. Smith and Sass, *A Carolina Rice Plantation of the Fifties*, 71.

177. For a general discussion of historical onomastics and specific naming customs in Anglo-American families, see David Hackett Fischer, "Forenames and the Family in New England: An Exercise in Historical Onomastics," in Robert M. Taylor Jr. and Ralph J. Crandall, eds., *Generations and Change* (Macon, Ga.: Mercer University Press, 1986), 215–42.

178. Cheryll Ann Cody, "Naming, Kinship and Estate Dispersal: Notes on Slave Family Life on a South Carolina Plantation, 1786 to 1833," *William and Mary Quarterly*, 3rd series, 39 (1982): 192–211.

179. "This morning I have been to the hospital to see a poor woman who has just enriched Mr. by *borning* him another slave. . . . I had all the trouble in the world in persuading its mother not to put a cap upon it. I bribed her finally by the promise of a pair of socks instead, with which I undertook to endow her child, and moreover actually prevailed upon her to forego the usual swaddling and swathing process, and let her poor baby be dressed at its first entrance into life as I assured her both mine had been. On leaving the hospital I visited huts all along the street, confiscating sundry refractory baby caps among shrieks and outcries, partly of laughter and partly of real ignorant alarm for the consequences." Kemble, *Journal of a Residence on a Georgian Plantation*, 149.

180. Joyner, *Down by the Riverside*, 78.

181. Margaret Bryant, *Slave Narratives*, 14.1, p. 146; quoted in part in Joyner, *Down by the Riverside*, 274. Another example appears in the narratives: "Marse Starke was a rich man. He had in de Quarter what was know'd as a chillun's house. A nurse stayed in it all de time to care fer all de plantation chilluns. My granny 'Kissy' acted as nurse dar some. Aunt Peggy and aunt Ciller was two mo'. Ciller was de daughter of a King in Africa, but dat story been traveling ever since she got to deses shores, and it still a-gwine. All dese helped nurse me." Elias Dawkins, *Slave Narratives*, South Carolina, 1: 316.

182. Sam Mitchell, in Rawick, ed., *The American Slave*, vol. 3, *South Carolina Narratives*, parts 3 and 4, pp. 200–204.

183. In 1815, on the nine Butler plantations women were only 41 percent of slaves under fifty, but 53 percent of slaves aged fifty or over. Pierce Butler estate, "Inventory of Slaves," 1815, Wister Family Papers, Historical Society of Pennsylvania.

184. Inventory of Property, Nov. 27, 1815, Wister Family Papers, Butler Section, HSP.

185. "The South Carolina negroes never say Aunty and Uncle to old persons but Daddy and Maumer, and all the white people say Daddy and Maumer to old black men and

women." Parrish, *Slave Songs of the Georgia Sea Islands*, 39n. Masters also used these words: "I heard of the death of old Fanny, Mrs. Heyward's old mauma . . ."

186. Adeline Johnson alias Adeline Hall, aged ninety-three, Winnsboro, South Carolina, lives in a three-room frame house on a plantation [in 1937!] owned by Mr. A. M. Owens of Winnsboro, 1,500 acres, in Rawick, ed., *The American Slave*, vol. 3, *South Carolina Narratives*, parts 3 and 4, p. 30.

187. Joyner, *Down by the Riverside*, 138.

188. Georgia Writers' Project, *Drums and Shadows*, 106–7.

189. Georgia Writers' Project, *Drums and Shadows*, 125.

190. Elizabeth Roberts, Sunbury, Georgia, in Georgia Writers' Project, *Drums and Shadows*, 113.

191. Georgia Writers' Project, *Drums and Shadows*, 130.

192. Sam Mitchell, in Rawick, ed., *The American Slave*, vol. 3, *South Carolina Narratives*, parts 3 and 4, pp. 200–204.

193. Quoted in Joyner, *Down by the Riverside*, 139.

194. Georgia Writers' Project, *Drums and Shadows*, 113.

195. Georgia Writers' project, *Drums and Shadows*, 131.

196. Georgia Writers' project, *Drums and Shadows*, 114.

197. Georgia Writers' Project, *Drums and Shadows*, 131.

198. Sam Polite, in Rawick, ed., *The American Slave*, vol. 3, *South Carolina Narratives*, parts 3 and 4, pp. 271–76.

199. Malcolm Bell Jr., *Major Butler's Legacy: Five Generations of a Slaveholding Family* (Athens: University of Georgia Press, 2004), 271.

200. Lillian F. Sinclair, "My Recollections of Darien in the Late Seventies and Eighties," quoted in Bell, *Major Butler's Legacy*, 134.

201. Anna Miller in Georgia Writers' Project, *Drums and Shadows*, 32.

202. Anna Miller in Georgia Writers' Project, *Drums and Shadows*, 165.

203. Fanny Kemble explained, "The negroes, as before I told you, are divided into troops or gangs; at the head of each gang is a driver, who stands over them, whip in hand, while they perform their daily task." Kemble, *Journal of a Residence on a Georgian Plantation*, 79.

204. Kemble, *Journal of a Residence on a Georgian Plantation*, 87.

205. Kemble, *Journal of a Residence on a Georgian Plantation*, 130.

206. Kemble, *Journal of a Residence on a Georgian Plantation*, 90.

207. Kemble, *Journal of a Residence on a Georgian Plantation*, 92–93.

208. Kemble, *Journal of a Residence on a Georgian Plantation*, 148.

209. Kemble, *Journal of a Residence on a Georgian Plantation*, 92, 147–50, 165, 190–94, 300. Lists of Butler slaves, Butler Island, Georgia, 1793–1849, Butler Family Papers, Historical Society of Pennsylvania.

210. Sam Polite, in Rawick, ed., *The American Slave*, vol. 3, *South Carolina Narratives*, parts 3 and 4, pp. 271–76.

211. Sam Polite, in Rawick, ed., *The American Slave*, vol. 3, *South Carolina Narratives*, parts 3 and 4, pp. 271–76.

212. "Sketches of the South Santee," *American Monthly Magazine* 8 (Oct., Nov., 1836).

213. Bessie Jones and Bess Lomax Hawes, *Step It Down* (Athens: University of Georgia Press, 1972), 140.

214. Harriet Jacobs, *Incidents in the Life of a Slave Girl*, ed. Jean Fagin Yellin (Cambridge: Harvard University Press, 2009), 118–19.

215. James Norcom to Mary Matilda Norcom, Norcom Family Papers, North Carolina State Archives, Raleigh, quoted in Jacobs, *Incidents in the Life of a Slave Girl*, 277n.

216. Guion Griffis Johnson, *Ante-Bellum North Carolina* (Chapel Hill: University of North Carolina Press, 1937), 553.

217. Johnson, *Ante-Bellum North Carolina*, 553.

218. A large literature stresses origins of John Canoe (or Jonkonnu) among Akan-speaking people in Ghana, who carried it to Jamaica, the Bahamas, Belize, coastal North Carolina, and other places. M. E. Lasseter, "Jonkonnu, Jankunu, Junkanoo, John Canoe: Reorienting North Carolina's Practice in the American Mediterranean" (2014), https://docsouth.unc.edu/commland/features/essays/johnkonnu-1/; also Stephen Nissenbaum, *The Battle for Christmas* (New York, 1997); Clement Bethel, "Junkanoo in the Bahamas," *Caribbean Quarterly* 36 (1990): 1–28; Swithin Wilmot, "The Politics of Protest in Free Jamaica: The Kingston John Canoe Riots: 1840 and 1841," *Caribbean Quarterly* 36 (1990): 65–75; Frederick Cassidy, "'Hipsaw' and 'John Canoe,'" *American Speech* 41 (1966): 45–51; Richard Walser, "His Worship, the John Kuner," *North Carolina Folklore* 19 (1971): 160–72; Nancy Ping, "Black Musical Activities in Antebellum Wilmington, North Carolina," *The Black Perspective in Music* 8 (1980): 139–60; Dena Epstein, *Sinful Tunes and Spirituals* (Urbana: University of Illinois Press, 1977); Ira de. A. Reid, "The John Canoe Festival," *Phylon* 3 (1942): 352.

219. Manuscript account in North Carolina legislative papers, June 18, 1824; quoted in Johnson, *Ante-Bellum North Carolina*, 553.

220. For all this and more I am indebted to the many works of scholarship by John Thornton.

221. Sam Mitchell, in Rawick, ed., *The American Slave*, vol. 3, *South Carolina Narratives*, parts 3 and 4, pp. 200--204.

222. Art Rosenbaum, *Shout Because You're Free: The African American Ring Shout Tradition in Coastal Georgia* (Athens, Ga., 1998, 2013), an excellent work of historical and musical scholarship. See also Johann S. Buis, "African Slave Descendants in an American Community: The Ring-Shout Tradition of the Georgia Sea Islands: An African Outsider Looks In," *Proceedings of the 1994 Commission on Community Music, International Society for Music Education* (Athens Ga., 1994); Charles Joyner, *Folk Song in South Carolina* (Columbia: South Carolina Tricentennial Commission by the University of South Carolina Press, 1971); William Francis Allen et al., *Slave Songs of the United States* (New York, 1867), 189; Parrish, *Slave Songs of the Georgia Sea Islands*, 54; Guy Johnson, *Folk Culture on St. Helena Island* (Chapel Hill: University of North Carolina Press, 1930), 33; Portia K. Maultsby, "Afro-American Religious Music: 1619–1861" (diss., University of Wisconsin, 1974), 189.

223. Rosenbaum, *Shout Because You're Free*, 26, 37.

224. Allen et al., *Slave Songs of the United States*, xiv–xv.

225. Clyde Vernon Kiser, *Sea Island to City: A Study of St. Helena Islanders in Harlem and*

Other Urban Centers (New York: Columbia University Press, 1932; new edition with a preface by Joseph S. Himes (New York: Atheneum, 1969), 9–13.

226. Kiser, *Sea Island to City*, 3.
227. Kiser, *Sea Island to City*, 6.
228. Kiser, *Sea Island to City*, 60–76, 151–57, 164–66, 201–6, 235–38, 254–55.
229. Kiser, *Sea Island to City*, 52.
230. Rosenbaum, *Shout Because You're Free*, 44–52.
231. Rudi Blesh and Harris Janis, *They All Played Ragtime* (New York, 1950; revised edition, 1966), 188–89; Rosenbaum, *Shout Because You're Free*, 44–45.
232. Rosenbaum, *Shout Because You're Free*, 13.
233. Kiser, *Sea Island to City*, 199.
234. Kiser, *Sea Island to City*, 211.
235. Kiser, *Sea Island to City*, 211–12.
236. Kiser, *Sea Island to City*, 210.
237. Kiser, *Sea Island to City*, 222–23.
238. For family memories of links to Friendfield, and research by Toni Carrier at the University of South Florida, see Shailagh Murray's interview with Michelle Obama, *Washington Post*, Oct. 2, 2008, and Swarns, *American Tapestry*, 236–37. For other family memories that point to Maryville Plantation, see Swarns, *American Tapestry*, 154–58, 181–82, 238, 292. For locations, both near Georgetown, South Carolina, see Alberta Morel Lachicotte, *Georgetown Rice Plantations* (Georgetown Historical Society, 1993).
239. Swarns, *American Tapestry*, 236; Murray, "A Family Tree Rooted in American Soil."
240. Michelle Obama, in Murray, "A Family Tree Rooted in American Soil"; Swarns, *American Tapestry*, 234–39.
241. Bailey, *God, Dr. Buzzard, and the Bolito Man*, 4–8.
242. Willie Lee Rose, *Rehearsal for Reconstruction: The Port Royal Experiment* (Indianapolis: Bobbs-Merrill, 1964).
243. Melissa L. Cooper, *Making Gullah: A History of Sapelo Islanders, Race, and the American Imagination* (Chapel Hill: University of North Carolina Press, 2017).

Chapter 6: LOUISIANA, MISSISSIPPI, AND THE GULF COAST

1. Gwendolyn Midlo Hall, *Africans in Colonial Louisiana* (Baton Rouge: Louisiana State University Press, 1992), 2–3, 26–27.
2. Gary B. Nash, *Red, White, and Black: The Peoples of Early America* (Englewood Cliffs, N.J., 1974), 106.
3. At least five towns named Ségou exist in Mali. The oldest, which we visited, is called Ségou-Koro to distinguish it from the others. The largest is the administrative capital of Ségou Province, a modern city with much nineteenth- and twentieth-century architecture.
4. In French scholarship, Mamari Kulubali sometimes appears as Biton Coulibaly, e.g., Lilyan Kesteloot, *L'Epopée bambara de Segou* (Paris: Harmattan, 1993), 101; Sundiata Djata, *The Bamana Empire by the Niger: Kingdom, Jihad and Colonization, 1712–1920* (Princeton: Markus Wiener, 1997), 12–22; Samba Lamine Traoré, *La saga de la ville*

historique de Ségou (Paris, 2012). On Mamari's role in the peopling of Louisiana, leading West Africa historians agree. Philip Curtin writes, "The new source of Bambara slaves after about 1715 seems to be associated with the rise of Mamari Kulubali (r. 1712–55) and his foundation of the kingdom of Segu." *Economic Change in Precolonial Africa: Senegambia in the Era of the Slave Trade* (Madison: University of Wisconsin Press, 1969), 179.

5. Sagas of Old Ségou and Mamari Kulubali and the Bamana people are classics of African oral culture. Ten sagas on this subject have been collected by Lilyan Kesteloot and Gerard Dumestre in *La geste de Ségou recontrée par des griots bambara* (Paris, 1979). For analyses see Lilyan Kesteloot and Gerard Dumestre, "Le mythe et l'histoire dans la formation de l'empire de Ségou," *Bulletin de FAN*, series B40 (1978): 613–81, and Harold Courlander with Ousmane Sako, *The Heart of the Ngoni: Heroes of the African Kingdom of Segu* (Amherst: University of Massachusetts Press, 1982; reprint, 1994). For the long history of these oral sagas, see Thomas Hale, *Griots and Griottes: Masters of Words and Music* (Bloomington, Ind., 1998), and Thomas Hale, "The Griot of Roots and the Roots of Griot," *Oral Tradition* 12 (1997): 249–78. In some Mande-speaking cultures, griots are also called jeli or djeli.

6. On Ngolo Diarra and his rise from slave to emperor, see Djata, *The Bamana Empire by the Niger*, 20–22.

7. Philip D. Curtin, *Economic Change in Precolonial Africa*, 2 vols. (Madison: University of Wisconsin Press, 1975), 1:181–83; Hall, *Africans in Colonial Louisiana*, 41–55.

8. Richard L. Roberts, *Warriors, Merchants, and Slaves: The State and the Economy in the Middle Niger Valley, 1700–1914* (Stanford: Stanford University Press, 1987), 21–75.

9. For similarities between Louisiana Gombo and "Mauritian Creole," see Thomas A. Klingler, *If I Could Turn My Tongue Like That: The Creole Language of Pointe Coupée Parish, Louisiana* (Baton Rouge: Louisiana State University Press, 2003), 50, 168–69, and passim; Morris Goodman, *A Comparative Study of French Creole Dialects* (The Hague: Mouton, 1964); review in *Journal of Pidgin and Creole Languages* 7 (1992): 352–61.

10. Alonso de Sandoval, *De Instauranda Aethiopum salute: El Mundo de la sclavitud negra en América* (1627; reprint, Bogotá, 1956), 91, 335, quoted in Gwendolyn Hall, *Slavery and African Ethnicities in the Americas: Restoring the Links* (Chapel Hill: University of North Carolina Press, 2005), 170. Sandoval was a Jesuit who worked for many years in Cartagena, now Colombia. See also his *Un tratado sobre la esclavitud* (1627; Madrid, 1687).

11. See tables at the end of the chapter. Charles R. Maduell Jr., *The Census Tables for the French Colony of Louisiana from 1699 Through 1732* (Baltimore, 1972, 2008), 1–3, 81.

12. "The Clustering of African Ethnicities in the Americas," in Gwendolyn Hall, *Slavery and African Ethnicities in the Americas*, 55–79.

13. Ibrahima Seck, *Bouki fait Gombo* (New Orleans, 2014), xvii–xviii. Seck earned his doctorate at Cheikh Anta Diop University in Dakar, Senegal.

14. Hall, *Africans in Colonial Louisiana*, 5, 36, 59, 121–23.

15. Alcée Fortier, ed., *Louisiana Folktales: Lapin, Bouki, and Other Creole Stories in French Dialect and English Translation* (Lafayette: University of Louisiana at Lafayette Press, 2011). This work was first published as a series of articles in *Comptes Rendus de l'Athénée*

Louisianais (July 1880), *Publications of the Modern Language Association* (1887), *Journal of American Folklore* (1888–89), and Alcée Fortier, *Louisiana Folktales* (Boston, 1895), 109–10.

16. Edward Larocque Tinker, *Gombo: The Creole Dialect of Louisiana* (New Orleans, 1936); Klingler, *If I Could Turn My Tongue Like That*, a major work of creative scholarship, more comprehensive than its title suggests.

17. Tinker, *Gombo: The Creole Dialect of Louisiana*; Klingler, *If I Could Turn My Tongue Like That*.

18. The drawings appear in Edward C. Carter II et al., *The Journals of Benjamin Henry Latrobe, 1799–1820: From Philadelphia to New Orleans* (New Haven, 1980), 3: 203–4. More sketches are in the manuscript journals at the Maryland Center for History and Culture (formerly known as the Maryland Historical Society). I remember the joy of discovery when they first arrived, and director James Foster allowed me to study them as a lowly stack boy on his staff.

19. This was from a running conversation that Judy and I had with native Bamana speakers in Bamako, January 1997. So far we have not found confirmation in Bamana dictionaries, e.g., Le Père Charles Bailleul de la Societé des Missionaires d'Afrique, *Dictionnaire Bambara-Francais* (1981; reprint, Bamako, 1996). French-Bamana dictionaries compiled by missionaries give us Bamana words for terms such as transubstantiation, but nothing like "jassy."

20. Very helpful on these subjects is the work of Ned Sublette in *The World That Made New Orleans* (Chicago: Lawrence Hill, 2008–09), 70–73; and *Cuba and Its Music: From the First Drums to the Mambo* (Chicago: Chicago Review Press, 2004).

21. A founder effect happens when a small group of migrants establishes (or small groups establish) a new population and it begins to develop from the characteristics that they have introduced. This model emerged from the work of Ernst Mayr, an evolutionary biologist. See his *Animal Species and Evolution* (Cambridge, 1963).

22. For data and sources see Table 6.2 at the end of the chapter, "The Population of Louisiana Through the French Period."

23. For Iberville's own journal, see Pierre Le Moyne d'Iberville. *A Comparative View of French Louisiana, 1699 and 1762: The Journey of Pierre Le Moyne d'Iberville and Jean-Blaise d'Abbadie* (Lafayette, La., 1979). The best and most deeply researched secondary source is Bernard Pothier, "Pierre Le Moyne d'Iberville et d'Ardillières," published in 1969 and revised in 1982 as part of the *Dictionary of Canadian Biography*, vol. 2 (1701–1740), online. It draws on Iberville's manuscripts in the French National Archives. Several letters survive in the Newberry Library and Chicago Historical Society. An older biography is Nellis M. Crouse, *Le Moyne d'Iberville*, published by the Cornell University Press (Ithaca, 1954; reprint, Baton Rouge, 2001).

24. This from the first census returns for Louisiana in 1699 and 1700. See also Marcel Giraud, *Histoire de la Louisiane française*, 4 vols. (Paris), 1: 76–77.

25. The best work on Bienville, based on primary materials, is C. E. O'Neill, "Jean-Baptiste Le Moyne de Bienville," *Dictionary of Canadian Biography* online; first published in 1974, and several times revised. It derives from research in Bienville's correspondence at the French National Archives in Paris. Other primary sources for Bienville were published in the *Louisiana Historical Quarterly* during the 1920s, in particular H. P. Dart,

ed., "Documents Concerning Bienville's Lands in Louisiana" 10 (1927): 5–24, 161–84, 364–80, 538–61; 11 (1928): 87–110, 209–32, 463–65. Dart also edited "Bienville's Claims Against the Company of the Indies," *Louisiana Historical Quarterly* 9 (1926): 210–20. A full biography would be very helpful.

26. Shannon Lee Dawdy, *Building the Devil's Empire: French Colonial New Orleans* (Chicago, 2008): 4–20, 28, 233–46.

27. David Hackett Fischer, *Champlain's Dream* (New York and Toronto: Simon & Schuster, 2008), 495, and passim; David Hackett Fischer, "Champlain, Humanist," in Nancy Nahra, ed., *When the French Were Here* (Burlington, Vt., 2010), 1–22.

28. Fischer, *Champlain's Dream*, 495, and passim; Fischer, "Champlain, Humanist," 1–22.

29. For primary evidence of Champlain's usage of the word and idea *humainement*, see Fischer, *Champlain's Dream*, 7–8, 318–19, 329–30, 366, 469, 521–24. Important evidence appears online through Google Ngram Viewer, and in Google's "corpus" of French books, on *humainement*. The adverbial form "humainement" first appeared in the early seventeenth century, specifically in Champlain's works, where he urged the French and Indians to treat each other "humanely." For discussion of that tradition in French humanism, which surged in the era of Henri IV, Champlain, Pierre Dugua, and Marc Lescarbot, see Fischer, "Champlain, Humanist," 1–22.

30. Paul Le Jeune, "Relation de ce qui s'est passé en la Nouvelle France en l'année 1633 . . ." (Paris, 1634), French and English texts in *Jesuit Relations*, ed. Reuben Gold Thwaites (Cleveland, 1896–1901), 5: 211. Father Le Jeune, Champlain's good friend, a Protestant convert, and head of the Jesuit order in New France, was present at this meeting between Champlain and the Montagnais, and recorded an eyewitness account.

31. Gilles Havard, *Empire et métissages* (Paris: PIF Pareis-Sorbonne, 2003), is a major study on this subject in the Mississippi Valley.

32. For the French cabin boys in Louisiana as similar to Champlain's *truchements*, see Giraud, *Histoire de la Louisiane française*, 1: 76–77, in the French edition, and pp. 84–85 in the English translation. The cabin boys appear by name in the Louisiana Census of 1699, and are in Maduell, ed., *The Census Tables for the French Colony of Louisiana from 1699 through 1732*, 2. The eyewitness account of André Pénicaut is in Richebourg Gaillard McWilliams, ed., *Fleur de Lys and Calumet, Being the Pénicaut Narrative of French Adventure in Louisiana* (1953; reprint, Tuscaloosa, Ala., 1981, 1988), 25, 30.

33. Jerah Johnson, "Colonial New Orleans: A Fragment of the Eighteenth-Century French Ethos," in *Creole New Orleans*, ed. Arnold R. Hirsch and Joseph Logsdon (Baton Rouge: Louisiana State University Press, 1992, 1993), 12–57, at 31, 35.

34. W. Stanford Reid, "Pierre Dugué de Boisbriand," *Dictionary of Canadian Biography*, vol. 2 (1701–1740), online.

35. Jennifer M. Spear, *Race, Sex, and Social Order in Early New Orleans* (Baltimore: Johns Hopkins, 2009), 38; F. Émile Audet, *Les premiers établissements français au pays des Illinois* (Paris, 1938), 43–44. And more generally, Spear, *Race, Sex, and Social Order in Early New Orleans*, 17–51; and Vidrine, *Mobile Marriages Recorded in French* (Lafayette, La.,) 126–27.

36. Périer to the Comte de Maurepas, July 25, 1732, quoted in Spear, *Race, Sex, and Social Order in Early New Orleans*, 30.

37. Cadillac to Pontchartrain, Oct. 26, 1713, also Superior Council Minutes, Jan. 2, 1716,

in James T. McGowan, "The Creation of a Slave Society: Louisiana Plantations in the Eighteenth Century" (diss., University of Rochester, 1976), 22; Johnson, "Colonial New Orleans," 34. After Iberville's death, Bienville turned against Indian marriages.

38. Johnson, "Colonial New Orleans," 38.

39. Claiborne A. Skinner, *The Upper Country: French Enterprise in the Colonial Great Lakes* (Baltimore, 2008), 122–23.

40. See below, p. 553.

41. See, e.g., Albert Valdman et al., *Dictionary of Louisiana French, as Spoken in Cajun, Creole, and American Indian Communities* (Jackson: University Press of Mississippi, 2010), "négraille," p. 413.

42. Flibustier began as a French translation of the Dutch *vrijbuiter*, for which the first known use on record appeared in *De Americanische Zee-Riovers*, published in 1678 by John Oexquelmin or Esquemeling, a Dutch *vrijbuiter* himself. A *freebooter* was someone who was in pursuit of *booty*, from the German *bute*, for anything seized by force. The word quickly appeared in Spanish as *filibustero*, in French as *flibustier*, and in English as *freebooter*. In nineteenth-century American politics, *filibuster* acquired other meanings, for a lawless act of foreign aggression by the 1850s, and for a hijacking of legislative debate by the 1860s, and into our own time.

43. Maduell, ed., *The Census Tables for the French Colony of Louisiana from 1699 Through 1732*, 2, 6.

44. Dawdy, *Building the Devil's Empire*, 277n; Marcel Giraud, *Reign of Louis XIV* (Baton Rouge, 1974), 91.

45. For excellent documentation of smuggling in Louisiana from judicial, economic, and even archaeological evidence, see Dawdy, *Building the Devil's Empire*, 115–34. But I would suggest that much smuggling, with political linkages as strong as in the "Devil's Empire" of Louisiana, also appeared in the "Bible Commonwealths" of Massachusetts and Rhode Island.

46. Here again an excellent discussion of Louisiana freebooters and slavery is in Dawdy, *Building the Devil's Empire*, 106, 114–15, 125–27, 165.

47. Ernest Obadele-Starkes, *Freebooters and Smugglers: The Foreign Slave Trade in the United States After 1808* (Fayetteville: University of Arkansas Press, 2007), on the Laffites, 3–4, 10, 34–35, 52–57.

48. Obadele-Starkes, *Freebooters and Smugglers,* on the Bowies, 3, 3–4, 10, 61–64.

49. William C. Davis, *The Pirates Laffite: The Treacherous World of the Corsairs of the Gulf* (New York, 2005), an excellent work of scholarship.

50. John Wilds, *Collectors of Customs at the Port of New Orleans; U.S. Customs Service Historical Study* 12 (Washington, D.C., 1991).

51. Maduell, *The Census Tables for the French Colony of Louisiana from 1699 through 1732,* 2–3; Pierre Le Moyne d'Iberville, *Iberville's Gulf Journals* (Tuscaloosa, Ala., 1981); Kris E. Lane, *Pillaging the Empire: Piracy in the Americas, 1500–1750* (Armonk, New York), 167; Dawdy, *Building the Devil's Empire*, 3, 115, 241. For the full careers of Pierre and Jean Laffite, see Davis, *The Pirates Laffite.*

52. Measures of exposed corruption include per capita convictions of public officials for crimes of corruption, quantitative scores by American journalists, and data in FBI crime reports. On various scales, Louisiana's rank for frequency of exposed corruption

ranged from 1 to 3 among 50 American states in the years from 2008 to 2014. See data in *New York Times*, Dec. 14, 2008, and *Washington Post*, Jan. 22, 2014.

53. Annual state-specific data derive from FBI *Uniform Crime Reports* and *Crime in the United States* and have been summarized in the *Statistical Abstract of the United States*. The volume for 2017 reported results in a table "Crime Rates by State, for Murder." An overview of earlier results also appears in the FBI's *Uniform Crime Reports*.

54. Fischer, *Champlain's Dream*, 445–64, 525–31; Fischer, "Champlain, Humanist," 1–22.

55. Johnson, "Colonial New Orleans," 16.

56. François-Marie Arouet de Voltaire to the Comte d'Argental, Nov. 1, 1760, in Voltaire, *Correspondence*, 107 vols., ed. Theodore Bestermann (Geneva, 1953–65), 44: 113; Shannon Lee Dawdy, "Enlightenment from the Ground," *French Colonial History* 3 (2003): 17–34.

57. It has appeared recently in a lively English edition, as *A Company Man: The Remarkable French-Atlantic Voyage of a Clerk for the Company of the Indies*, translated by Teri F. Chalmers and edited by Erin M. Greenwald (New Orleans: Historic New Orleans Collection, 2013).

58. Jean-François Dumont de Montigny, *Mèmoires historiques sur la Louisiane* (Paris, 1753), translated by Gordon Sayre and Carla Zecher, eds., as *The Memoir of Lieutenant Dumont, 1715–1747* (Chapel Hill: University of North Carolina Press, 2012), 213–39, 421, 435; Le Page du Pratz, "Suite du mémoire sur la Louisiane," *Journal oeconomique* (Feb. 1753): 94–132; Antoine-Simon Le Page du Pratz, *Histoire de la Louisiane*, 3 vols. (Paris, 1758), 2: 253.

59. Chief among many accounts are the writings of Le Page du Pratz.

60. An excellent study is Christopher Morris, *The Big Muddy: An Environmental History of the Mississippi and Its Peoples from Hernando de Soto to Hurricane Katrina* (Oxford, 2012), 1–47.

61. Gary B. Mills, *The Forgotten People: Cane River's Creoles of Color* (Baton Rouge, 1977), 1, 50–76.

62. Richard Campanella, *Bienville's Dilemma: A Historical Geography of New Orleans* (Lafayette, La., 2008), 77–119, is broad in coverage and deep in learning. Also helpful here is Morris, *The Big Muddy*, 83–85.

63. Lee Soltow, *Men and Wealth in the United States, 1859–1970* (New Haven, 1975), 105, 144, and passim, by the measure of Lorenz curves and Gini ratios. The Gini ratio is a simple coefficient of inequality, computed from a Lorenz curve. It ranges from zero (perfect equality, where all units of analysis own exactly the same amounts of wealth), to .99 (perfect inequality, where the top analytic unit of wealth holders own everything). From data in the United States Census of 1850 and 1860, Gini ratios were calculated for Adams County by economist Lee Soltow. He found them to be well above .90 in those years.

64. Michael Wayne, *The Reshaping of Plantation Society: The Natchez District, 1860–1880* (Baton Rouge: Louisiana State University Press, 1983; Urbana: University of Illinois Press, 1990), 88–91.

65. Both Soltow and Wayne, working in different disciplines by different methods, obtained similar results for levels and trends of inequality.

66. A major work is Daniel H. Usner Jr., *Indians, Settlers, & Slaves in a Frontier Exchange*

Economy: The Lower Mississippi Valley Before 1783 (Chapel Hill: University of North Carolina Press, 1992). Also relevant are American Indian patterns in archaeological evidence. See Fred B. Kniffen, ed., *The Historic Indian Tribes of Louisiana, from 1542 to the Present* (Baton Rouge, 1987); Elizabeth A. H. John, *Storms Brewed in Other Men's Worlds: The Confrontation of Indians, Spanish and French in the Southwest* (College Station, Tex., 1975).

67. Ellen C. Merrill, *Germans of Louisiana* (Gretna, La., 2005), 19–48, 24.

68. Klingler, *If I Could Turn My Tongue Like That*, xxv–xxix. On the location of Cajun speech west of the Mississippi in a triangle with its northern apex in Avoyelles Parish, its southeastern corner in Lafourche Parish, and its southwestern edge in Cameron Parish—twenty-two parishes in all, formally defined by the Louisiana legislature in 1971 as the "Heart of Acadiana," see p. xxix.

69. Gilbert C. Din, *The Canary Islanders of Louisiana* (Baton Rouge, 1988). For Mafia Families, see Edward F. Haas, "New Orleans on the Half Shell: The Maestri Era, 1936–1946," *Louisiana History* 13 (1972): 283–310.

70. Glenn R. Conrad, *The First Families of Louisiana*, 2 vols. (Baton Rouge, 1972).

71. Winston De Ville, *Louisiana Troops, 1720–1770* (New Orleans, 1965); Winston De Ville, *Louisiana Recruits, 1752–1758* (New Orleans, 1973).

72. Carl Brasseux, "The Moral Climate of French Colonial Louisiana, 1699–1763," *Louisiana History* 27 (1986): 27–41.

73. A helpful work, compiled from records of baptisms, marriages, and funerals for the coast from Pensacola and Mobile to New Orleans, is Winston De Ville, *Gulf Coast Colonials: A Compendium of French Families in Early Louisiana* (Baltimore, 1968, 1995, 1999).

74. U.S. Army, Surgeon General's Office, *Statistical Report of Sickness and Mortality in the Army of the United States, from January 1819 to January 1839* (Washington, D.C.: Jacob Gideon, printer, 1840). I used a rare copy at the American Antiquarian Society, Worcester, Massachusetts.

75. Jan Moen, *John Law and the Mississippi Bubble, 1718–1820*; Antoin E. Murphy, *John Law, Economic Theorist and Policy Maker* (Oxford, 1997); Marcel Giraud, *Histoire de la Louisiane française*, vol. 3, *L'Epoque de John Law, 1717–1720* (Paris, 1966); Giraud, *Histoire de la Louisiane française*, vol. 4, *La Louisiane apres le système de Law (1721–23)* (Paris, 1978).

76. Dawdy, *Building the Devil's Empire*, 151; Arlette Farge and Michel Foucault, *Le désordre des familles, lettres de cachet des archives de la Bastille* (Paris, 1982).

77. Sayre and Zecher, eds., *The Memoir of Lieutenant Dumont*, 93–96.

78. Sayre and Zecher, eds., *The Memoir of Lieutenant Dumont*, 93–96.

79. Brasseux, "The Moral Climate of French Colonial Louisiana," 27–41.

80. Brasseux, "The Moral Climate of French Colonial Louisiana," 27–41.

81. Dawdy, *Building the Devil's Empire*, 150, 143.

82. Dawdy, *Building the Devil's Empire*, 150.

83. Marc-Antoine Caillot, *A Company Man: The Remarkable French-Atlantic Voyage of a Clerk for the Company of the Indies; A Memoir by Marc-Antoine Caillot* (ms. 1730), ed. Greenwald, trans. Chalmers, 84–85.

84. Giraud, *Histoire de la Louisiane française*, 3: 252–76; Hall, "Formation of Afro-Creole Culture," 62.

85. See Table 6.3 at the end of the chapter "Louisiana's First Wave of Population Growth: Emigrants from France, 1717–21," compared with a population count in the census in 1721.

86. Maduell, *The Census Tables for the French Colony of Louisiana from 1699 Through 1732*, 16, 17.

87. Mikael Parkvall, "The Role of St. Kitts in a New Scenario of French Creole Genesis," in Philip Baker, ed., *From Contact to Creole and Beyond* (London, 1995), 41–62, 55; Jay Higginbotham, *Old Mobile: Fort Louis de la Louisiane, 1701–1711* (Tuscaloosa, Ala., 1977, 1991), 302.

88. Higginbotham, *Old Mobile, 302*.

89. Edme Gatien de Salmon, "Mémoire sur la colonie de la Louisiana," n.d., c. 1741, series C13C 1, folio 384; Hall, *Africans in Colonial Louisiana*, 10–11.

90. For quantitative data and sources see tables at the end of this chapter.

91. Primary data on the volume of the African slave trade in France and details of its broad distribution through many French ports are measured in the Trans-Atlantic Slave Trade Database and are mapped in David Eltis and David Richardson, *Atlas of the Transatlantic Slave Trade* (New Haven: Yale University Press, 2010), part 5, plates 137–79.

92. For a survey of the French slave trade, an excellent starting point is David Geggus, "The French Slave Trade: An Overview," *William and Mary Quarterly*, 3rd series, 58 (2001): 119–38. Robert Louis Stern examines the economics of French slaving in *The French Slave Trade in the Eighteenth Century: An Old Regime Business* (Madison, 1980). A cultural approach is Christopher Miller, *The French Atlantic Triangle: Literature and Culture of the Slave Trade* (Durham, 2008). And for a close look at the voyage of one French slaving vessel, see Robert Harms, *The Diligent: A Voyage Through the World of the Slave Trade* (New York, 2002).

93. For an archaeological study of the French trading post at Fort St. Joseph on the Senegal River and the English trading factory at Yamyamacunda on the Gambia River during the eighteenth century, see W. Raymond Ward, "An Archeological Appraisal of Early European Settlements in the Senegambia," *Journal of African History* 1 (1967): 39–64.

94. Jacques Nicholas Bellin, *Fort Ste. Joseph, Riviere du Senegal, Isle St. Louis, Fort Ste. Louis* (Paris, 1747, 1750). This is a nautical chart, also published in rare Dutch and English editions which I have not found.

95. Roberts, *Warriors, Merchants, and Slaves*, 21–75; Hall, *Africans in Colonial Louisiana*, 28–55.

96. Gwendolyn Midlo Hall has constructed two major databases and several smaller ones. One is her Louisiana Slave Database, 1719–1820, available online at http://www.ibiblio.org/laslave and also at Ancestry.com. Another is her Louisiana Free Database, 1719–1820, available at Ancestry.com. These estimates come from her own analysis of findings. The 121 ethnicities that cannot be identified refer to only 152 people out of a total of 8,508. Hall, *Slavery and African Ethnicities in the Americas*, 42.

97. Hall, *Slavery and African Ethnicities in the Americas*, 42–44.

98. Hall, *Africans in Colonial Louisiana*, 29–55, 159–61, and passim.

99. See Peter Caron, "'Of a Nation Which the Others Do Not Understand': Bambara Slaves and African Ethnicity in Colonial Louisiana, 1718–1760," *Slavery & Abolition* 18 (1997): 98–121; Gilbert C. Din, *Spaniards, Planters, and Slaves* (College Station, Tex., 1999), 5–7.

100. Eltis and Richardson write of Louisiana's African trade that "nearly three-quarters of the first generation of slaves came from what is now Senegal, and most of the remainder came from the Bight of Benin." Eltis and Richardson, *Atlas of the Transatlantic Slave Trade*, 220.

101. For data and details of each recorded voyage in the French period, see Table 6.4 at the end of the chapter.

102. These are Hall's computations from her own Louisiana Slave Database, 1719–1820, reported in *Slavery and African Ethnicities in the Americas*, 42–54.

103. Mungo Park, *Travels in the Interior Districts of Africa* (1799), ed. Kate Ferguson Marsters (Durham, 2000), 78, 104–7, 185–99, 203–8, 393–96.

104. Hall, *Africans in Colonial Louisiana,* 40–41, 295, 403.

105. Hall, *Africans in Colonial Louisiana,* 45–46; Moussa Travélé, *Proverbes et contes Bambara, accompagnés d'une traduction française et précédés d'une abrégé de droit coutumier Bambara et Malinke* (1923; Paris, 1977).

106. Hall, *Slavery and African Ethnicities in the Americas*, 96–98.

107. Curtin, *Economic Change in Precolonial Africa*, 1: 6; Djata, *The Bamana Empire by the Niger*; Abbé Joseph Henry, *L'Ame d'un peuple africain; les Bambara* (Munster: Bibliotheque Anthropos, 1910; reprint, London, 2017).

108. Djata, *The Bamana Empire by the Niger*, 55.

109. Mungo Park, *Travels in the Interior Districts of Africa . . . in the Years 1795, 1796, and 1797* (London, 1799), chapter 15, July 20–21, 1796. The text of the first edition is available online at Project Gutenberg. Also useful is a new edition of this classic, edited by Kate Ferguson Marsters, *Travels in the Interior Districts of Africa* (Durham, 2000), 188–99.

110. Park, *Travels in the Interior Districts of Africa*, ed. Marsters (2000), 195.

111. Park, *Travels in the Interior Districts of Africa*, ed. Marsters (2000), 72.

112. Park, *Travels in the Interior Districts of Africa* (1799), chapter 22, July 1796; Park, *Travels in the Interior Districts of Africa*, ed. Marsters (2000), 256–57.

113. Park, *Travels in the Interior Districts of Africa* (1799), chapter 22, July 1796; Park, *Travels in the Interior Districts of Africa*, ed. Marsters (2000), 256–63.

114. Park, *Travels in the Interior Districts of Africa* (1799), chapter 22, July 1796; Park, *Travels in the Interior Districts of Africa*, ed. Marsters (2000), 156–57.

115. Park, *Travels in the Interior Districts of Africa*, ed. Marsters (2000), 261.

116. Park, *Travels in the Interior Districts of Africa*, ed. Marsters (2000), 273–79.

117. Park, *Travels in the Interior Districts of Africa*, ed. Marsters (2000), 260.

118. Park, *Travels in the Interior Districts of Africa*, ed. Marsters (2000), 257.

119. Park, *Travels in the Interior Districts of Africa*, ed. Marsters (2000), 257.

120. "Eighteen Most Frequent Ethnicities by Gender in Louisiana, 1719–1820," calculated by Gwendolyn Hall from her Louisiana Slave Database of 8,442 African slaves, and published as table 2-4 in her *Slavery and African Ethnicities in the Americas*, 43–44.

121. Marie-Madeleine Hachard, *Relation du Voyage des religieuses Ursulines de Rouen a la*

Nouvelle-Orleans en 1727 (Rouen, 1865), 17; Emily Clark, ed., *Voices from an Early American Convent: Marie Madeline Hachard and the New Orleans Ursulines, 1727–1760* (Baton Rouge, 2007), 31; Emily Clark, *Masterless Mistresses: The New Orleans Ursulines and the Development of a New World Society, 1727–1834* (Chapel Hill: University of North Carolina Press, 2007), 161.

122. Usner, *Indians, Settlers, and Slaves in a Frontier Exchange Economy*, 239; Thomas N. Ingersoll, "Old New Orleans: Race, Class, Sex and Order in the Early Deep South, 1718–1819" (diss., University of California, Los Angeles, 1990), 306; Hall, *Africans in Colonial Louisiana*, 254; Din, *Spaniards, Planters and Slaves*, 31, and for a similar case involving a Capuchin slave, 255n.

123. Clark, *Masterless Mistresses*, 168–69; Hall, *Africans in Colonial Louisiana*, 152–53.

124. V. Baillardel and A. Prioult, eds., *Le Chevalier de Pradel, vie d'un colon francais en Louisiane au xviiie siècle d'après sa correspondence et celle de sa famille* (Paris, 1928).

125. Carl Brasseaux, "The Administration of Slave Regulations in French Louisiana, 1724–1766," *Louisiana History* 21 (1980): 139–58, at 139.

126. Sayre and Zecher, eds., *The Memoir of Lieutenant Dumont*, introduction, "The Dumont Family," 51; Jean Delangez, "A Louisiana Poet-Historian: Dumont-*dit* Montigny," *Mid-America* 19 (1937): 32.

127. Gary B. Mills, "The Chauvin Brothers: Early Colonists of Louisiana," *Louisiana History* 15 (1974): 117–31; Pierre de Charlevoix, *Journal of a Voyage to North America* (Ann Arbor, 1966), letter 21, Jan. 10, 1722, 2: 287.

128. Henry P. Dart, "The Career of Dubreuil in Louisiana," *Louisiana Historical Quarterly* 17 (1935): 267–331; Morris, *The Big Muddy*; Hall, *Africans in Colonial Louisiana*, 137; in Patricia Kay Galloway, Dunbar Rowland, and A. G. Sanders, eds., *Mississippi Provincial Archives: French Dominion, 1729–1748* (Baton Rouge, 1984), 4:72.

129. Dart, "The Career of Dubreuil in Louisiana," 267–331; Hall, *Africans in Colonial Louisiana*, 139–41, 211.

130. Morris. *The Big Muddy*, 59.

131. Mills, "The Chauvin Brothers," 127; Henry P. Dart, ed., "Ceard's Case, 1724," *Louisiana Historical Quarterly* 5 (1922): 155–71.

132. Morris, *The Big Muddy*, 61; Giraud, *Histoire de la Louisiane française*, 5:193–94, 206–9; Jeffrey Owens, "Holding Back the Waters: Land Development and the Origins of Levees on the Mississippi, 1720-1845" (diss., Louisiana State University, 1999), 72, 149.

133. Governor Étienne de Périer to the Comte de Maurepas, Dec. 10, 1731, *Archives des Colonies* AC C13A, vol. 13, folios 57–75v, in Galloway et al., eds., *Mississippi Provincial Archives: French Dominion, 1729–1748*, 4:101–9.

134. That process brings to mind Karl Wittfogel's classic hydraulic model of oriental despotism, *Oriental Despotism: A Comparative Study of Total Power* (New Haven: Yale University Press, 1957), chapter 2, "Hydraulic Economy."

135. *Le Code Noir, ou, édit du roy, servant de réglement pour le gouvernement et l'administration de la justice, police, discipline, et le commerce des esclaves negres, dans la province et colonie de la Louisianne. Donné à Versailles au mois de mars, 1724* (Paris, 1728). The original text in French, with an English translation, appears in Vernon Valentine Palmer, *Through the Codes Darkly: Slave Law and Civil Law in Louisiana* (Clark, N.J., 2012), appendix, 163–91. It also includes an analysis of the 1724 *Code Noir* and its

many successors in Louisiana's Black Code of 1806–07, the Louisiana Digest of 1808, and the Civil Code of 1825, and more than one hundred individual statutes passed by the Louisiana legislature in the American period. An appendix includes the original French text with an English translation.

136. A large controversial literature on the *Code Noir* is ably reviewed in Parker, *Through the Codes Darkly*, 3–28. Colbert died in 1683, but Parker finds that on critical questions "Colbert's role was paramount. He was the ruling spirit behind the scenes. He was very likely the actual author of the Royal Instructions," which framed the project. Watching closely above Colbert was Cardinal Mazarin and Louis XIV (p. 15).

137. *Code Noir* (1724), Article 1.

138. *Code Noir* (1724), Article 3.

139. *Code Noir* (1724), Articles 2, 4, 5.

140. *Code Noir* (1724), Article 5.

141. *Code Noir* (1724), Article 38.

142. *Code Noir* (1724), Articles 30, 32, 33, 38, 39.

143. *Code Noir* (1724), Articles 30, 32, 33, 38, 39.

144. *Code Noir* (1724), Articles 43, 49.

145. *Code Noir* (1724), Article 21.

146. *Code Noir* (1724), Articles 15, 22, 23, 25, 26.

147. The predominance of Roman Catholicism continued to be especially strong in southern Louisiana, a large triangle of territory from an apex in Avoyelles Parish to Plaquemines Parish in the southeast and Cameron Parish in the southwest. Every parish in that region had a Roman Catholic majority as recently as 1990. Data appear in Edwin Scott Gaustad and Philip L. Barlow, eds., *New Historical Atlas of Religion in America* (Oxford, 2001), 319.

148. Cécile Vidal, "Caribbean Louisiana," in Cécile Vidal, ed., *Louisiana, Crossroads of the Atlantic World* (Philadelphia, 2014), 128; church records published in Earl C. Woods and Charles E. Nolan, *Sacramental Records of the Roman Catholic Church of the Archdiocese of New Orleans* (New Orleans: Archdiocese of New Orleans, 1988).

149. Vidal, "Caribbean Louisiana," 128.

150. Dawdy, *Building the Devil's Empire*, 231.

151. "To Establish One Law and Definite Rules: Race, Religion, and the Transatlantic Origins of the Louisiana Code Noir," in Vidal, ed., *Louisiana, Crossroads of the Atlantic World*, 21–43, at 23.

152. Cécile Vidal, "Caribbean Louisiana: Church, Métissage, and the Language of Race in the Mississippi Colony During the French Period," in Vidal, ed., *Louisiana, Crossroads of the Atlantic World*, 125–46, at 138.

153. Spear, *Race, Sex, and Social Order in Early New Orleans*, 79.

154. Dowdy, *Building the Devil's Empire*, 189–91, 294n.

155. Shannon Lee Dawdy, "The Burden of Louis Congo and the Evolution of Savagery in Colonial Louisiana," in Steven Pierce and Anupama Rao, eds., *Discipline and the Other Body: Correction, Corporeality, Colonialism* (Durham, 2006), 61–89; Dawdy, *Building the Devil's Empire*, 189–91, 200, 223, 231.

156. Hall, *Africans in Colonial Louisiana*, 131–32.

157. Dawdy, *Building the Devil's Empire*, 190–91, 294; Superior Council Records, Jan. 4, 10, 12, 24, 1724.

158. Dawdy, *Building the Devil's Empire*, 190–91, 294.

159. Gwendolyn Midlo Hall, "Louisiana's Afro-Creole Culture: Formation During the Eighteenth Century," unpublished manuscript, 216.

160. Hall, "Louisiana's Afro-Creole Culture," 187.

161. Testimony and medical evidence before the Louisiana Superior Council, April 6, 29, 1730; Aug. 30, 1730; Sept. 5, 7, 18, 1730, "Records of the Louisiana Superior Council," *Louisiana Historical Quarterly* 4 (1921): 510, 518, 521; 5 (1922): 89, 92, 94.

162. Hall, *Africans in Colonial Louisiana*, 150, 151, 152; Dawdy, *Building the Devil's Empire*, 214.

163. Iberville, *Iberville's Gulf Journals*, 154; Sublette, *The World That Made New Orleans*, 39.

164. Hall, *Africans in Colonial Louisiana*, 199, 117.

165. Hall, *Africans in Colonial Louisiana*, 98, 104; testimony of April 9, 1727, Records of the Superior Council. These records indicated that as many as fifty maroons were living among the Natchez.

166. Irène Thérèse Whitfield, *Louisiana French Folk Songs* (New York: Dover, 1969), 140–42, with added rhyme scheme.

167. A firsthand account of this event is Jean-Bernard Bossu, *Nouveaux Voyages aux Indes ocidentales; Contenant une Relation des differens peuples qui habitant les environs du grand Fleuve Saint-Louis, appellé vulgairement le Mississipi . . .* , 2 vols. (Paris, 1968). Translated and edited by Seymour Feiler as *Jean-Bernard Bossu's Travels in the Interior of North America, 1751–1762* (Norman: University of Oklahoma Press, 1962), 31–47, 60–61.

168. A major and much debated source on the Natchez Massacre is by Antoine-Simon Le Page du Pratz, in *Histoire de la Louisiane*, 3: 230–31, 256–58, 291–303. Le Page Du Pratz had been stationed in Natchez shortly before it happened, and knew most of the leaders, both Natchez and French. Very helpful is Hall, *Africans in Colonial Louisiana*, 104, which makes use of manuscript accounts in Paris archives by Governor Étienne de Périer, "Mouvements des sauvages de la Louisiane depuis la prise du fort des Natchez . . . ," July 21, 28, 1731, series C13A, 13, folio 87, Section Coloniales, Archives Nationales, Paris. Also very useful is Gordon Sayre, "Natchez Ethnohistory Revisited: New Manuscript Sources by Le Page du Pratz and Dumont de Montigny," *Louisiana History* 50 (2009): 407–36, and Gordon Sayre, "Plotting the Natchez Massacres: Le Page du Pratz, Dumont de Montigny and Chateaubriand," *Early American Literature* 37 (2002): 381–413.

169. Dumont de Montigny, *Mèmoires historiques sur la Louisiane*, 240–47; Le Page du Pratz, *Histoire de la Louisiane*, 3: 291–303.

170. Johnson, *Colonial New Orleans*, 54; Din, *Spaniards, Planters, and Slaves*, 15–17, 244–46; Roland McConnell, *Negro Troops of Antebellum Louisiana: A History of the Battalion of Free Men of Color* (Baton Rouge, 1968); Hall, *Africans in Colonial Louisiana*, 100–102, quoting Étienne de Périer's reports to the Ministry of the Colonies, March 18, 1730, Section Coloniales, Archives Nationales, Paris, C 13A12, folios 37–41.

171. Étienne de Périer, "Mouvements des sauvages de la Louisiane depuis la prise du fort des Natchez," July 21, 28, 1731, 103–4.

172. The leading source is Le Page du Pratz himself, *Histoire de Louisiane*, 3: 304–17. An incomplete English translation appears in Le Page du Pratz, *The History of Louisiana and of the Western Parts of Virginia and Carolina*, 77. Confirmation in other sources has been found by Hall in French archives, and reported in *Africans in Colonial Louisiana*, 108–11.

173. This came from an account by Governor Étienne de Périer, that "Samba had in his own country been at the head of the revolt by which the French lost Fort Arguin; and when it was recovered again by M. Perier de Salvert, one of the principal articles of the peace was, that this negro should be condemned to slavery in America. Samba, on his passage, laid a scheme to murder the crew in order to become master of the ship, but being discovered he was put in irons, in which he continued till he landed in Louisiana." Confirmation appears in other documents found by Gwendolyn Hall and cited in *Africans in Colonial Louisiana*, 109–10.

174. Le Page du Pratz, *Histoire de la Louisiane*, 3: 304–17.

175. Le Page du Pratz, *Histoire de la Louisiane*, 3: 304–17.

176. Le Page du Pratz, *Histoire de la Louisiane*, 3: 304–17. See also Hall, *Africans in Colonial Louisiana*, 106–10, with documents on this event, from Governor Étienne de Périer to superiors in Paris; and Dawdy, "The Burden of Louis Congo and the Evolution of Savagery in Colonial Louisiana."

177. Gwendolyn Midlo Hall, "African Nations of Slaves Accused of Crimes in Records of the Superior Council of Louisiana," appendix B to Hall, *Africans in Colonial Louisiana*, 398–401, 366–67. Most of this primary evidence is in Heloise H. Cruzat, ed. and trans., "Records of the Superior Council of Louisiana," *Louisiana Historical Quarterly* 4 (1921): 348; 6 (1923): 284; 7 (1924): 522; 8 (1925): 23–27; 10 (1927): 567; 11 (1928): 288–92; 12 (1929): 145–47, 674; 19 (1936): 1091–94, 1094–96. Hall also found four more cases in manuscript records of the Superior Council in the Louisiana Historical Center, Louisiana State Museum, New Orleans.

178. Bossu, *Jean-Bernard Bossu's Travels in the Interior of North America, 1751–1762*, 18; "Records of the Superior Council," *Louisiana Historical Quarterly* 6 (1923): 659, 661; 8 (1925): 497–98; 10 (1927): 567. For discussions, see Hall, *Africans in Colonial Louisiana*, 152; Din, *Spaniards, Planters, and Slaves*, 21–25.

179. Bossu, *Jean-Bernard Bossu's Travels in the Interior of North America, 1751–1762*, 18. Also "Records of the Superior Council," *Louisiana Historical Quarterly* 8 (1925): 497–98; 9 (1926): 514.

180. "Records of the Superior Council," Sept. 18, 1736, Jan. 16, 1741, *Louisiana Historical Quarterly* 8 (1925): 497–98; 10 (1927): 567; Hall, *Africans in Colonial Louisiana*, 144–48; Din, *Spaniards, Planters, and Slaves*, 23–24, 251–52.

181. George Washington Cable, "The Dance in Place Congo & Creole Slave Songs," *The Century Magazine* 31 (Feb. 1886): 52; (reprint, New York, 1976), 7. For a helpful discussion of where Cable might have observed African dances, see Freddi Williams Evans, *Congo Square: African Roots in New Orleans* (Lafayette, La., 2011), 3–5, 116, and passim.

182. Hall, *Africans in Colonial Louisiana*, 98, 139–41, 149.

183. The best history and strongest database of French Louisiana's slave trade are in Hall, *Africans in Colonial Louisiana;* Hall, *Slavery and African Ethnicities in the Americas,*

42–45,173–79, and passim; and Hall, Louisiana Slave Database, 1719–1820, online and on CD-ROM (Baton Rouge, 2000). On "Bamana" and "Bambara," see Hall, *Slavery and African Ethnicities in the Americas*, 96–100. Subsequent research and data sets confirm Hall's findings.

184. Le Page du Pratz, *Histoire de la Louisiane*, is online at Archive.org in three volumes: https://archive.org/details/GR_2462-1, https://archive.org/details/GR_2462-2, and https://archive.org/details/GR_2462_3. It is more complete than subsequent printings. It was followed by a two-volume edition in English in 1763. A one-volume English translation, severely abridged and radically revised, was published as *The History of Louisiana, or of the Western Parts of Virginia and Carolina, Translated from the French, M. Le Page du Pratz* (London, 1774). It has been read more widely than any other edition. Most available in the United States is a facsimile edition with an excellent introduction by Joseph G. Tregle Jr., published by the Louisiana State University Press (Baton Rouge, 1975).

185. For sympathetic readings of this literature, see Usner, *Indians, Settlers, and Slaves in a Frontier Exchange Economy*, and Mathé Allain, "Slave Policies in French Louisiana," *Louisiana History* 21 (1980): 127–37. More hostile is Patricia Galloway, "Rhetoric of Difference: Le Page du Pratz on African Slave Management in Eighteenth-Century Louisiana," *French Colonial History* 3 (2003): 1–15. An important essay is Dawdy, "Enlightenment from the Ground," 17–34.

186. Le Page du Pratz, *History of Louisiana*, English edition, ed. Tregle, 224, 376–77.

187. Le Page du Pratz, *Histoire de la Louisiane*, 1: 364.

188. Le Page du Pratz, *Histoire de la Louisiane*, 3: 361.

189. Le Page du Pratz, *History of Louisiana*, English edition, ed. Tregle, 227–28.

190. Le Page du Pratz, *History of Louisiana*, English edition, ed. Tregle, 365.

191. Le Page du Pratz, *History of Louisiana*, English edition, ed. Tregle, 365.

192. As rendered by his first English translator.

193. Le Page du Pratz, *History of Louisiana*, English edition, ed. Tregle, 363, 365.

194. Le Page du Pratz, *History of Louisiana*, English edition, ed. Tregle, 366.

195. On this point, see Galloway, "Rhetoric of Difference," 6.

196. Le Page du Pratz, *History of Louisiana*, English edition, ed. Tregle, 361–63.

197. McGowan, "The Creation of a Slave Society," 20–22, 12–35, and passim; James T. McGowan, "Planters Without Slaves: Origins of a New World Labor System," *Southern Studies* 16 (1971): 5–26; Johnson, "Colonial New Orleans," 40–42.

198. Hall, *Africans in Colonial Louisiana*, 167–68, and confirmed by inventories, pp. 159, 167–71.

199. Hall, *Slavery and African Ethnicities*, 121–22.

200. Dumont de Montigny, *Mèmoires historiques sur la Louisiane*, 12–13, 53–55, 256–77, 378–89. Dumont lived in Louisiana from 1721 to 1737; his memoir was written in 1747. For his relationship with Le Page du Pratz, see Sayre and Zecher, eds., *Memoir of Lieutenant Dumont*, 12–14. See also Jerah Johnson, "New Orleans's Congo Square," *Louisiana History* 32 (1991): 117–57, at 122–23, 12–14.

201. Le Page du Pratz, *Histoire de la Louisiane*, 1: 365.

202. Le Page du Pratz, *Histoire de la Louisiane*, 1: 363–64.

203. Palmer, *Through the Codes Darkly*, 47.

204. *Code Noir* (1724), Article 5.

205. V. A. Moody, "Slavery on Louisiana Sugar Plantations," *Louisiana Historical Quarterly* 7 (1924): 191–302, at 277. Later Olmstead called it "Sunday jobbing," in his *Cotton Kingdom* (London, 1861), 323. In the nineteenth century, hired slaves, employed as river workers on levees and steamboats, bargained and won extra money for Sunday work; Buchanan, "Black Life on the Mississippi."

206. Betty Wood, "Never on a Sunday."

207. Wood, "Never on a Sunday."

208. Laura Porteus, "Civil Procedure in Louisiana Under the Spanish Regime as Illustrated in Loppinot's Case, 1774," *Louisiana Historical Quarterly* 12 (1929): 33–120.

209. Palmer, *Through the Codes Darkly*, appendix, 174–77.

210. *Code Noir* (1724), "Edit du Roi, Touchant l'Etat et la Discipline des Esclaves Négres de la Louisiane," Article 23, explicitly recognizes peculium if allowed by the master for discussion. See Palmer, *Through the Codes Darkly*, 177, 28, 35, 74–79, 89–96, 137–38.

211. See again the testimony of masters in *Loppinot v. Villenueve* (1774). Primary documents are published in Porteus, "Civil Procedure in Louisiana Under the Spanish Regime as Illustrated in Loppinot's Case, 1774," 33–120.

212. Le Page du Pratz, *History of Louisiana*, English edition, ed. Tregle, 227–28.

213. Ira Berlin and Philip D. Morgan, eds., *Cultivation and Culture: Labor and the Shaping of Slave Life in the Americas* (Charlottesville: University Press of Virginia, 1993), 32.

214. *Code Noir, ou Recueil d'Edits, Déclarations et arrets concernant Les Esclaves Négres . . . des Islea Francoises de l'Amérique* (1685; Paris, 1743), Article 7.

215. Johnson, "New Orleans's Congo Square," 117–57, at 127–33; Evans, *Congo Square*, 109–13.

216. Johnson, "Colonial New Orleans," 12–57, at 39–40.

217. Johnson, "Colonial New Orleans," 12–57, at 39–40.

218. Sophie White, "Geographies of Slave Consumption: French Colonial Louisiana and a World of Goods," *Winterthur Portfolio* 45 (2011): 229–48; Sophie White, "Wearing Three or Four Handkerchiefs Around His Neck," *Gender and History* 15 (2003): 528–49; Sophie White, *Wild Frenchmen and Frenchified Indians: Material Culture and Race in Colonial Louisiana* (Philadelphia, 2012), a model for the use of material culture in historical inquiry.

219. Louis-*dit*-Foy and his associates can be followed through the primary evidence in Gwendolyn Midlo Hall's Louisiana Slave Database, and in particular, the manuscript records of "interrogation under torture" of Louis-*dit*-Foy by judges on the Superior Council of Louisiana, in the Louisiana Historical Center, New Orleans. Their network is discussed in yet another vital work by Hall, *Slavery and African Ethnicities in the Americas*, 98–100, 189.

220. Le Page du Pratz, *Histoire de la Louisiane*, 3: 226–27, 366. Also in *The History of Louisiana*, English edition, ed. Tregle, 387. See also Sublette, *The World That Made New Orleans*, 73.

221. Din, *Spaniards, Planters, and Slaves*, 20–23.

222. Din, *Spaniards, Planters, and Slaves*, 20–22; Johnson, "New Orleans's Congo Square," 117–57.

223. Din, *Spaniards, Planters, and Slaves*, 226.

224. For Afro-French variations throughout Louisiana, the scholarship of Thomas Klingler is very helpful in *If I Could Turn My Tongue Like That*, sections 1.3–1.4, 2.2–2.4, especially 6.1.3, 6.6.1.

225. Morris Goodman, *A Comparative Study of Creole French Dialects* (New York, 1964).

226. J. L. Dillard, *Black English* (New York, 1972), 75.

227. Regrettably, these invaluable Afro-French Gombo recordings were not included in Ira Berlin, Marc Favreau, and Steven F. Miller, eds., *Remembering Slavery: African Americans Talk About Their Personal Experiences of Slavery and Emancipation* (New York: New Press, 1998). This work is an invaluable collection of Afro-English speech by former slaves, but it omitted Afro-French speech in Louisiana, which is even more rare and revealing of the Louisiana languages called Gombo. I was able to listen to recordings which have been recently converted from wax cylinders. They are fascinating and important primary materials.

228. Edward Larocque Tinker, "Gombo: The Creole Dialect of Louisiana, with a Bibliography," *American Antiquarian Society Proceedings* (1935): 101–29.

229. These examples of nineteenth-century New Orleans Gombo were written down by George Washington Cable, and published by him in "The Dance in Place Congo," *Century Magazine* 31 (1886): 517–32, and "Creole Slave Songs," 807–28. Both articles have been reprinted in facsimile by Faruk van Turk and published as "The Dance in Place Congo & Creole Slave Songs, by George W. Cable" (New Orleans, 1974). The music was also transcribed by H. E. Krehbiel.

230. A major work is Klingler, *If I Could Turn My Tongue Like That*, xxvi–xxxv, chapters 1–3, passim.

231. Le Page du Pratz, *Histoire de la Louisiane*, 1: 366.

232. Le Page du Pratz, *Histoire de la Louisiane*, 1: 366.

233. Mary Land, *Louisiana Cookery* (Baton Rouge: Louisiana State University Press, 1954), 54.

234. Land, *Louisiana Cookery*, 45.

235. John B. Cade, "Out of the Mouths of Ex-Slaves," *Journal of Negro History* 20 (1935): 301.

236. Cade, "Out of the Mouths of Ex-Slaves," 294.

237. Land, *Louisiana Cookery*, 40.

238. Land, *Louisiana Cookery*, 3.

239. Land, *Louisiana Cookery*, 3.

240. Land, *Louisiana Cookery*, 41.

241. In a vast literature of Louisiana foodways, a bright and spirited essay is Shannon Lee Dawdy, "A Wild Taste: Food and Colonialism in Eighteenth-Century Louisiana," *Ethnohistory* 57 (2010): 389–420. Classic works include Lafcadio Hearn, *La Cuisine Creole* (New Orleans: Pelican Publishing Company, 1967), and a thoughtful discussion of *roux*, in Gwen McKee, *The Little Gumbo Book* (Baton Rouge: Quail Ridge Press, 1986), 11–16.

242. Dominique Harcourt Lamiral, *L'Affrique et le peuple Affriquain considérés sous tous leurs rapports avec notre commerce & nos colonies . . .* (Paris, 1789), 184; Hall, *Slavery and African Ethnicities in the Americas*, 98–99.

243. Dr. John Sibley, from Morris, *Big Muddy*, 55. For Louisiana foodways, see Land, *Lou-*

isiana Cookery, 40–54, and Gwen McKee, *The Little Gumbo Book* (Brandon, Miss., 1986), 7–9.

244. For details and documentation, see Table 6.4 at the end of the chapter.

245. Gilbert C. Din, *Populating the Barrera: Spanish Immigration Efforts in Colonial Louisiana* (Lafayette, La., 2014), a helpful survey of these various migration streams, by the leading historian of Spanish Louisiana, with extensive use of manuscript materials in Spanish archives at Seville and Madrid.

246. Gilbert C. Din, "The Canary Islander Settlements of Spanish Louisiana: An Overview," *Louisiana History* 27 (1986): 353–73.

247. Gilbert C. Din, "Lieutenant Colonel Francisco Bouligny and the Malagueño Settlement at New Iberia, 1779," *Louisiana History* 17 (1976): 187–202; Gilbert C. Din, *Francisco Bouligny: A Bourbon Soldier in Spanish Louisiana* (Baton Rouge, 1993).

248. Thomas Jefferson to George Washington, April 2, 1791, in Julian P. Boyd, ed., *The Papers of Thomas Jefferson* (1982), 20: 95–98; Gilbert C. Din, "Spain's Immigration Policy in Louisiana and the American Penetration, 1792–1803," *Southwestern Historical Quarterly* 76 (1973): 255–76.

249. Jean-Pierre Leglaunec, "Migrations in Spanish and Early American Louisiana: New Sources and New Estimates," *Louisiana History* 46 (2005): 185–209; Hall, *Africans in Colonial Louisiana*, 279.

250. For census data, see Table 6.6 at the end of the chapter. The best study is Antonio Acosta Rodriguez, *La población de Luisiana española (1763–1803)* (Madrid, 1979), 31, 110, 242, 413, 438–40, 458, 460.

251. Leglaunec, "Migrations in Spanish and Early American Louisiana," 185–209. On re-africanization, see Hall, *Africans in Colonial Louisiana*, 275–315.

252. Hall, *Africans in Colonial Louisiana*, 283.

253. Gwendolyn Hall, "Slaves Found in Pointe Coupée Inventories, 1771–1802," in *Africans in Colonial Louisiana*; data in appendix C, pp. 402–6, with analysis and discussion, pp. 283–302.

254. Quantitative estimates for all three periods of Louisiana slavery appear at the end of this chapter.

255. These data were provided by Gwendolyn Hall to Thomas Klingler and are included in his work on Creole language, *If I Could Turn My Tongue Like That*, 20–22.

256. Hall, *Africans in Colonial Louisiana*, 319–33. In Hall's Louisiana Slave Database, Mina slaves were the fifth-largest African ethnic group in 1800–09, and the fourth-largest group in 1810–20. See tabulations by Hall in *Slavery and African Ethnicities in the Americas*, 78–79.

257. Commandant Athanase de Mézières to Governor Luis de Unzaga, Feb. 1, 1770, enclosing ordinances dated Jan. 21, 1770, in the Spanish Archivo General de Indias, *Papeles procedentes de Cuba*, legajo 188a, 110:84, 110:85, 110:111, in Gerard L. St. Martin and Mathé Allain, "A Slave Trial in Colonial Natchitoches," *Louisiana History* 28 (1987): 57–91.

258. Athanase de Mézières. See also Herbert Eugene Bolton, *Athanase de Mézières and the Louisiana-Texas Frontier, 1768–1780*, 2 vols. (Cleveland, 1914), 1: 80.

259. Charles Petrie, *King Charles III of Spain, An Enlightened Despot* (London, 1971).

260. Hall, *Africans in Colonial Louisiana*, 311–13.

261. *Las Siete Partidas de rey don Alfonso el Sabio* (Madrid, 1807); C. Russell Reynolds, "Alfonso el Sabio's Laws Survive in the Civil Code of Louisiana," *Louisiana History* 12 (1971): 137–47.

262. Hans W. Baade, "The Law of Slavery in Spanish Louisiana, 1769–1803," in Edward F. Haas, ed., *Louisiana's Legal Heritage* (Pensacola, 1983), 43–86.

263. Baade, "The Law of Slavery in Spanish Louisiana," 43–86; Spear, *Race, Sex, and Social Order in Early New Orleans*, 107–8.

264. Gilbert C. Din, "The Pointe Coupée Conspiracy," in Din, *Spaniards, Planters, and Slaves*, 154–93; Gwendolyn Hall, "The 1795 Slave Conspiracy in Pointe Coupée: Impact of the French Revolution," in Patricia Galloway and Philip Boucher, eds., *Proceedings of the Fifteenth Meeting of the French Colonial Historical Society, Martinique and Guadeloupe, May, 1789* (Lanham, Md.: University Press of America, 1992), 138; Hall, *Africans in Colonial Louisiana*, 344–74.

265. The most important primary source is James A. Padgett, ed., "A Decree for Louisiana Issued by the Baron of Carondelet, June 1, 1795," *Louisiana Historical Quarterly* 20 (1937): 600–605. The most full discussion is "The Aftermath of Conspiracy," in Din, *Spaniards, Planters, and Slaves*, 177–93.

266. Kimberly S. Hanger, *Bounded Lives, Bounded Places: Free Black Society in Colonial New Orleans, 1769–1803*, 18; Spear, *Race, Sex, and Social Order in Early New Orleans*, 94–95. On reenslavement, see Din, *Spaniards, Planters, and Slaves*, 222.

267. Hanger, *Bounded Lives, Bounded Places*, 19, 22.

268. In a large literature on free Black militia in the Spanish empire, helpful works are Joseph P. Sanchez, "African Freedmen and the *Fuero Militar*: A Historical Overview of *Pardo* and *Moreno* Militiamen in the Late Spanish Empire," *Colonial Latin American Historical Review* 3 (1994): 165–84, and Lyle McAlister, *The "Fuero Militar" in New Spain, 1764–1800* (Gainesville, 1957); and on Spanish Black militia in Louisiana, Roland McConnell, *Negro Troops in Antebellum Louisiana: A History of the Battalion of Freemen of Color* (Baton Rouge, 1968), and Jack D. L. Holmes, *Honor and Fidelity: The Louisiana Infantry Regiment and the Louisiana Militia Companies, 1766–1821* (Birmingham, Ala., 1965).

269. Much data on these men has been gathered by Kimberly S. Hanger, in "A Privilege and Honor to Serve: The Free Black Militia of Spanish New Orleans," *Military History of the Southwest* 21 (1991): 59–86, and Hanger, *Bounded Lives, Bounded Places*, 109–35.

270. Hanger, "A Privilege and Honor to Serve," 59–86, Hanger, *Bounded Lives, Bounded Places*, 109–35.

271. Hanger, *Bounded Lives, Bounded Places*, 99, 143, 185; Din, *Spaniards, Planters, and Slaves*, 162, 203–4, 218, 224; Spear, *Race, Sex, and Social Order in Early New Orleans*, 154.

272. Spear, *Race, Sex, and Social Order in Early New Orleans*, 112–13, 128, 130–31, 143, 192, 218, 226n23; Hanger, *Bounded Lives, Bounded Places*, 26–54, 105.

273. Hanger, *Bounded Lives, Bounded Places*, 17–59.

274. Emily Clark, *The Strange History of the American Quadroon: Free Women of Color in the Revolutionary Atlantic World* (Chapel Hill: University of North Carolina Press, 2013), 71–72, 83–96.

275. Spear, *Race, Sex, and Social Order in Early New Orleans*, 79–82, 140–42, 209–6.

276. Clark, *The Strange History of the American Quadroon*, 188–97.

277. Clark, *The Strange History of the American Quadroon*, 188–97.

278. Napoleon to Talleyrand, April 11, 1803; the text and major documents are published in a scholarly edition by James Alexander Robertson, ed., *Louisiana Under the Rule of Spain, France and the United States*, 2 vols. (Cleveland, 1911).

279. An excellent history of this event is Alexander De Conde, *The Affair of Louisiana* (Baton Rouge: Louisiana State University Press, 1976). On British policy, see Ronald J. Drez, *The War of 1812, Conflict and Deception: The British Attempt to Seize New Orleans and Nullify the Louisiana Purchase* (Baton Rouge, 2014).

280. The major breakthrough on this problem of economic growth was North, *The Economic Growth of the United States, 1790–1860,* which brought its author one of the first Nobel Prizes in economics. It was followed by a great flow of econometric research which has continued to the date of this writing, sixty years later, and can be followed in many papers distributed by the National Bureau of Economic Research.

281. For general patterns of economic growth during this period, see David Hackett Fischer, *The Great Wave: Price Revolutions and the Rhythm of History* (New York and Oxford, 1996), 117–56, which draws on a large econometric literature.

282. See North, *The Economic Growth of the United States, 1790–1860.*

283. Several generations of economic historians have told the story of what happened in Louisiana. Among the first was John Hebron Moore, an economic historian of the old school, in "Cotton Breeding in the Old South," *Agricultural History* 30 (1856): 96; John Hebron Moore, *Agriculture in Antebellum Mississippi* (Baton Rouge, 1988); and John Hebron Moore, *The Emergence of the Cotton Kingdom in the Old Southwest, Mississippi, 1770–1860* (Baton Rouge, 1988).

284. Eron Rowland, ed., *Life, Letters, and Papers of William Dunbar, of Elgin, Morayshire, Scotland and Natchez, Mississippi: Pioneer Scientist of the Southern United States* (Jackson: Mississippi Historical Society, 1930), 356; John Hebron Moore, "Cotton Breeding in the Old South," *Agricultural History* 30 (1956): 95–104.

285. Franklee Whartenby, *Land and Labor Productivity in U.S. Cotton Production* (diss., University of North Carolina; New York, 1977), 104–5.

286. This literature is a classic example of empirical progress in historical inquiry, with continuing refinements of method and substance. That progress continues. Leaders in a third generation of inquiry are Alan L. Olmstead and Paul W. Rhode, *Creating Abundance: Biological Innovation and American Agricultural Development* (New York: Columbia University Press, 2008), who have returned to the problem of drivers of economic growth in this area and carried it forward in new ways.

287. The progress of research and understanding on this problem of economic growth through three quarters of a century of continuing inquiry can be followed in a sequence of four published works: Lewis Cecil Gray et al., *History of Agriculture in the Southern United States to 1860*, 2 vols. (Washington, D.C.: Carnegie Institution, 1932), 2: 740; Carlyle Sitterson, *Sugar Country: The Cane Sugar Industry in the South, 1753–1950* (Lexington, Ky., 1953), 1–12; John A. Heitmann, *The Modernization of the Louisiana Sugar Industry, 1830–1910* (Baton Rouge, 1987), 8–24; Richard Follett, *The Sugar Masters: Planters and Slaves in Louisiana's Cane World, 1820–1860* (Baton Rouge, 2005), 17–23. Follett, p. 25, summarized major trends in growth of labor and land productivity on Louisiana

sugar plantations, which rapidly overtook and surpassed West Indian sugar plantations from 1802 to 1860, but at heavy cost to enslaved workers.

288. Glenn R. Conrad and Roy F. Lucas, *White Gold: A Brief History of the Louisiana Sugar Industry, 1795–1995* (Lafayette, La., 1995); Sitterson, *Sugar Country*, 133–56; Follett, *Sugar Masters*, 33–39.

289. *Historical Statistics of the United States, Colonial Times to 1970* (Washington, D.C., 1976), series A195.

290. U.S. Census data, 1820, 1860.

291. Lorenzo L. Ivy, interview, Danville, Va., April 28, 1937, WPA Records Group, Virginia Writers Project Files, Virginia State Library, Richmond, published in Charles L. Perdue Jr., Thomas E. Bardem, and Robert K. Phillips, eds., *Weevils in the Wheat: Interviews with Virginia Ex-Slaves* (Charlottesville: University Press of Virginia, 1976), 151–53.

292. For careful quantitative estimates of interstate slave migration, calculated from census data, business records, and other sources, see Michael Tadman, *Speculators and Slaves: Masters, Traders and Slaves in the Old South* (Madison, 1989, 1996). Other important histories include Steven Deyle, *Carry Me Back: The Domestic Slave Trade in American Life* (New York and Oxford, 2005); Walter Johnson, *Soul by Soul: Life Inside the Antebellum Slave Market* (Cambridge, 1999); Walter Johnson, *River of Dark Dreams: Slavery and Empire in the Cotton Kingdom* (Cambridge, 2013), which centers on Louisiana and the lower South; and Walter Johnson, ed., *The Chattel Principle: Internal Slave Trades in the Americas* (New Haven, 2004), a collection of essays which takes a world view of slave trading in the nineteenth century.

293. New Orleans *Le Moniteur de la Louisiane*, Jan. 27, 1810. Leading studies are three works by Paul Lachance, "The Politics of Fear: French Louisianans and the Slave Trade, 1786–1809," *Plantation Societies in America* 1 (1979): 162–97; "The 1809 Immigration of Saint-Domingue Refugees to New Orleans: Reception, Integration, and Impact," *Louisiana History* 29 (1988): 110–42; and "The Foreign French," in *Creole New Orleans: Race and Americanization*, ed. Arnold R. Hirsch and Joseph Logsdon (Baton Rouge, 1992), 101–13; and also Carl A. Brasseaux and Glenn R. Conrad, *The Road to Louisiana: The Saint-Domingue Refugees, 1792–1809* (Lafayette: University of Southwestern Louisiana Center for Louisiana Studies, 1992).

294. James A. McMillin, *The Final Victims: Foreign Slave Trade to North America, 1783–1810* (Columbia, S.C., 2004), 36–44; Lachance, "The Politics of Fear," 176–79.

295. Jed Handelsman Shugerman, "The Louisiana Purchase and South Carolina's Reopening of the Slave Trade in 1803," *Journal of the Early Republic* 22 (2002): 263–90; Obadele-Starks, *Freebooters and Smugglers*, 20–21.

296. Obadele-Starks, *Freebooters and Smugglers*, 32–33.

297. Davis, *The Pirates Laffite*, 25–49, 50–56, 139–40.

298. Davis, *The Pirates Laffite*, 50, 412–14.

299. Jean-Pierre Leglaunee, "Migrations in Spanish and Early American Louisiana: New Sources and New Estimates," *Louisiana History* 46 (2005): 185–209; Obadele-Starks, *Freebooters and Smugglers*, 9–10. Magnitudes are much in doubt. Obadele-Starks made an estimate using Philip Curtin's model of 192,500 slaves imported illegally from 1808 to the Civil War, roughly 3,700 a year. He also used another method of extrapolation from slave manifests, which yielded estimates that were too high to square with other

evidence. But much evidence indicates a continuing flow of illegal slave imports to Louisiana until the Civil War.

300. Hall, *Slavery and African Ethnicities in the Americas*, 77; the data appear on pp. 78–79.

301. After long neglect, much has been written on this event in recent years. The best is Daniel Rasmussen, *American Uprising: The Untold Story of America's Largest Slave Revolt* (New York, 2011), an undergraduate senior thesis at Harvard, and an excellent work of scholarship. Other useful accounts are Walter Johnson, *River of Dark Dreams: Slavery and Empire in the Cotton South* (Cambridge, 2013), 18–22, brief, but makes good use of manuscript records of the New Orleans City Court, in the Louisiana Collection of the New Orleans Public Library; and coverage in the *Louisiana Gazette and New Orleans Daily Advertiser* and *Moniteur de la Louisiane*, both Jan. 17, 1811. Albert Thrasher turned up new materials for *On to New Orleans: Louisiana's Heroic 1811 Slave Revolt* (San Francisco, 1996); as did Robert Paquette in "The Great Louisiana Slave Revolt of 1811 Reconsidered," *Historical Reflections* 35 (2009): 72–96.

302. Rasmussen, *American Uprising*, 74. See also Manuel Andry to Governor William C. C. Claiborne, Jan. 11, 1811, in C. E. Carter, ed., *Territorial Papers* (Washington, D.C., 1940), 9: 917; and Johnson, *River of Dark Dreams*, 19–20, 428.

303. Johnson, *River of Dark Dreams*, 428n, is helpful on the origins of Deslondes, with evidence from his first owner, Madam Deslondes.

304. Rasmussen, *American Uprising*, 108. Trépagnier's contemptuous treatment of slaves is from Harnett Kane, *Plantation Parade: The Grand Manner in Louisiana* (New York, 1945), 128. I knew Harnett Kane in his Maryland period, a great raconteur, with an extraordinary fund of knowledge and many a tale to tell about masters and slaves in Louisiana.

305. "Memoirs of Micah Taul," in Jared William Bradley, ed., *Interim Appointment: W. C. C. Claiborne Letter Book, 1804–1805* (Baton Rouge, 2002), 264; Rasmussen, *American Uprising*, 32.

306. Rasmussen, *American Uprising*, 109.

307. Still useful for its wide-ranging search for primary sources is Herbert Aptheker, *American Negro Slave Revolts* (New York, 1943, 1963), 248.

308. Known dead of the master class included young Gilbert Andry, François Trépagnier, Hans Wimprenn, and a M. Thomassin, plus Manuel Andry wounded.

309. Eugene D. Genovese, *Roll, Jordan, Roll: The World the Slaves Made* (New York: Random House, 1974), 106; Aptheker, *American Negro Slave Revolts*, 250; Dunbar Rowland, ed., *Official Letterbooks of W. C. C. Claiborne 1801–1816* (Jackson, Miss.: State Department of Archives and History, 1917), 5: 93–100; accounts in northern newspapers (Hartford *Connecticut Courant*, Feb. 20, 1811; New York *Evening Post*, Feb. 14, 15, 19, 20, 26, 27, 1811; Richmond *Enquirer*, Feb. 19, 22; March 12, 1811); John S. Kendall, "Shadow over the City," *Louisiana Historical Quarterly* 22 (1939); McGowan, "The Creation of a Slave Society"; Jack D. L. Holmes, "The Abortive Slave Revolt at Point Coupée, Louisiana, 1795," *Louisiana History* 11 (1970): 341–62; Tommy R. Young II, "The United States Army and the Institution of Slavery in Louisiana, 1803–1815," *Louisiana Studies* 13 (1974): 210–22; James H. Dorman, "The Persistent Spectre: Slave Rebellion in Territorial Louisiana," *Louisiana History* 18 (1977): 389–404.

310. New York *Evening Post*, Dec. 4, 1827.

311. V. A. Moody, "Slavery on the Louisiana Sugar Plantations," *Louisiana Historical Quarterly* 7 (1924): 225.

312. Amos Stoddard, *Sketches Historical and Descriptive of Louisiana* (Philadelphia, 1812), 332.

313. Stoddard, *Sketches Historical and Descriptive of Louisiana*, 332–33.

314. Stoddard, *Sketches Historical and Descriptive of Louisiana*, 333–36.

315. *Oxford English Dictionary*, "demoralize," 1, 2. Lexicographer Noah Webster was asked how many new words he had included in his dictionary. He answered, "only 'to moralize,' and that not in the dictionary, but in a pamphlet published in the last century, about 1793." Charles Lyell, *Travels in North America* (London: John Murray, 1855), 1: 65, reporting a conversation with Webster.

316. Joseph G. Tregle Jr., "Early New Orleans Society: A Reappraisal," *Journal of Southern History* 18 (1952): 33; John W. Blassingame, *Black New Orleans, 1860–1880* (Chicago, 1973), 9.

317. Blassingame, *Black New Orleans*, 15.

318. Blassingame, *Black New Orleans*, 15.

319. Evans, *Congo Square*, 133, June 13, 1833.

320. C. C. Robin, *Voyage to Louisiana, 1803–1805*, trans. and ed. Stuart O. Landry Jr. (New Orleans: Pelican, 1966), 248.

321. Clear evidence of close associations among Bamana and Mande-speaking slaves appears in testimony before the Superior Council of Louisiana, and specifically in Samba Bambara's conspiracy on the King's Plantation in 1731, Foy's network in New Orleans, and clusters on the plantations of Colin Lacour, Jean Baptiste Tournoir, and Louis Renard Duval, in Hall, *Slavery and African Ethnicities in the Americas*, 96–100, and Hall, *Africans in Colonial Louisiana*, 108–10, 111–13, 289.

322. Much evidence of strong associations among Mina slaves and distance from other African groups in eighteenth-century Louisiana is summarized in Hall, *Africans in Colonial Louisiana*, 320–21.

323. Sublette, *The World That Made New Orleans*, 258.

324. Hall, *Africans in Colonial Louisiana*, 380.

325. Daniel Patrick Moynihan, *The Negro Family: The Case for National Action* (Washington, D.C.: Office of Policy Planning and Research, United States Department of Labor, 1965).

326. Herbert G. Gutman, *The Black Family in Slavery and Freedom, 1750–1925* (New York: Vintage, 1976); Jacqueline Jones, *Labor of Love, Labor of Sorrow* (New York: Basic Books, 1985).

327. Ann Patton Malone, *Sweet Chariot: Slave Family & Household Structure in Nineteenth-Century Louisiana* (Chapel Hill: University of North Carolina Press, 1992), 1–9, 251–72.

328. For the design and construction of this inquiry, see Malone, *Sweet Chariot*, 1–9.

329. Malone, *Sweet Chariot*, 72–79, 85–89, 92–103, 138–49.

330. Malone, *Sweet Chariot*, 267.

331. Malone, *Sweet Chariot*, 108–14, 150–65, 167–69.

332. Malone, *Sweet Chariot*, 108–14, 150–65, 167–69.

333. Georgina Gibbs, interview, Jan. 15, 1937, Portsmouth, Virginia, WPA Records

Group, Virginia Writers Project Files, in Perdue, Bardem, and Phillips, eds., *Weevils in the Wheat*, 104–5.

334. Richard C. Wade, *Slavery in the Cities: The South, 1820–1860* (Oxford: Oxford University Press, 1964), 325–27. Leonard P. Curry, *The Free Black in Urban America, 1800–1850: The Shadow of a Dream* (Chicago: University of Chicago Press, 1981), 244–57, omits two New Orleans faubourgs. These data often undercounted slaves. Census takers were careful to interview heads of free families, but they relied on masters for information about slaves, who were taxed and thus underreported. *The Seventh Census of the United States: 1850* (Washington, D.C., 1853); *Population of the United States in 1860; Compiled from the Original Returns of the Eighth Census* (Washington, D.C., 1864).

335. Spear, *Race, Sex, and Social Order in Early New Orleans*, 184; Donald E. Everett, "Emigres and Militiamen: Free Persons of Color in New Orleans, 1803–1815," *Journal of Negro History* 38 (1953): 377–402; Curry, *The Free Black in Urban America*, 245, which omits faubourgs Tremé and McDonoughtown. More inclusive are the numbers in Wade, *Slavery in the Cities*, 326.

336. Wade, *Slavery in the Cities*, 325–30. Reported estimates for numbers of slaves in New Orleans should be read as lower-bound estimates, in some cases much below the actual population.

337. Curry, *The Free Black in Urban America*, 90.

338. The primary data are analyzed in "Nativities of Adult Free Persons of Color in Fifteen Cities in 1850," in Curry, *The Free Black in Urban America*, 249.

339. Robin, *Voyage to Louisiana*, 248.

340. Robert Tallant, *Voodoo in New Orleans* (New York: Macmillan, 1946), 64.

341. This evidence was collected by Leonard P. Curry from the U.S. Census of 1850, and separately from occupations given in annual city directories. The results are tabulated in Curry, *The Free Black in Urban America*, tables B-1, B-2, pp. 260–61; similar results appeared in an index of occupational opportunity, tables B-7, B-8, pp. 264–65.

342. Curry, *The Free Black in Urban America*, 261–65.

343. Curry, *The Free Black in Urban America*, appendix C, "Free Black Property Ownership," 267–66. Another study obtained similar results; see Robert C. Reinders, "The Free Negro in the New Orleans Economy, 1850–1860," *Louisiana History* 6 (1965): 281. See also Robert C. Reinders, *End of an Era: New Orleans, 1850–1860* (New Orleans, 1964), 167–68.

344. Curry, *The Free Black in Urban America*, 170–73.

345. Dédé's music has been published in the twenty-first century by Naxos in *Edmond Dédé* (2001), 8.599038.

346. James R. Creecy, *Scenes in the South* (Washington, D.C., 1860), 18–19; Sublette, *The World That Made New Orleans*, 257.

347. Robin, *Voyage to Louisiana*, 248.

Chapter 7: WESTERN FRONTIERS

1. Meg Daley Olmert, *Made for Each Other: The Biology of the Human Animal Bond* (Cambridge, Mass., 2009), 172.

2. J. Frank Dobie, *The Mustangs* (Boston, 1952), 235–36. Also Florence Fenley, "Turns 'Mustang' to Catch Mustangs," *Uvalde* (Texas) *Union Leader-News*, Sept. 13, 1940.

3. Dobie, *The Mustangs*, 240.

4. Philip Durham and Everett L. Jones, *The Negro Cowboys* (New York: Dodd, Mead, 1965; Lincoln, Nebr.: Bison Books, 1983), 14.

5. Olaudah Equiano, *The Life of Olaudah Equiano or Gustavus Vassa the African, 1789, with an Introduction by Paul Edwards*, 2 vols. (London, 1969), 1: 22. The authenticity of this work has been called into question, because two documents listed Equiano's place of birth as South Carolina—not Africa as he claimed. The probable cause was the need of his master to represent as dubious Equiano having been born in Britain or her colonies, in order to avoid severe penalties under the British Navigation Acts. This finding confirms the prevailing judgment of African scholars, and of many people who knew Equiano well, including the family of his master, that he was truly of African birth. Some scholars were quick to reject the accuracy of Equiano's great work, but they made no effort to assess the accuracy of the two contrary documents.

6. John J. Kelvey Jr., *Man Against Tsetse: Struggle for Africa* (Ithaca, 1973).

7. John K. Thornton, *Warfare in Atlantic Africa, 1500–1800* (London, 1999), 12–18, 19–33, excellent on ecological regions.

8. Peter H. Wood, *Black Majority: Negroes in Colonial South Carolina from 1670 Through the Stono Rebellion* (New York: Norton, 1974), xx; Philip D. Morgan, *Slave Counterpoint: Black Culture in the Eighteenth Century Chesapeake and Lowcountry* (Chapel Hill: University of North Carolina Press, 1998), 62–69. For slave traders, see especially Philip M. Hamer, ed., *The Papers of Henry Laurens* (Columbia: University of South Carolina Press, 1968–2003), 2: 423.

9. Paul K. Eguchi and Victor Azarya, *Unity and Diversity of a People: The Search for Fulbe Identity* (Osaka: National Museum of Ethnology, 1993); Paul Riesman, *Freedom in Fulani Social Life* (Chicago, 1977); and an older work, Louis Tauxier, *Moeurs at histoire des Peuls* (Paris, 1937), an enduring classic.

10. H. A. S. Johnston, *The Fulani Empire of Sokoto* (London, Ibadan, and Nairobi: Oxford University Press, 1967; reprint, 1970), 17–25, 261–63.

11. Amadou Hampaté Ba and G. Dieterlen, *Koumen: Texte initiatique des Pasteurs Peul*, Cahiers de l'homme, École Pratique des Hautes Études, Vie section (Paris, 1961; reprint, 2009).

12. Hugh Clapperton, *Journal of a Second Expedition into the Interior of Africa* (London, 1829).

13. "Livestock Sector in Gambia," Access Gambia, ca. 2008, http://www.accessgambia .com/information/livestock-sector.html.

14. Graham Harvey, *Animism: Respecting the Loving World* (New York, 2006).

15. John S. Mbiti, *African Religions and Philosophy*, 2nd edition (London, 1990).

16. Olmert, *Made for Each Other*, 173.

17. Dale F. Lott and Benjamin L. Hart, "Aggressive Domination of Cattle by Fulani Herdsmen and Its Relation to Aggression in Fulani Culture," *Ethos* 5 (1977): 184; Olmert, *Made for Each Other*, 170–80.

18. Olmert, *Made for Each Other*, 172–73.

19. Olmert, *Made for Each Other*, 172–73.

20. Olmert, *Made for Each Other*, 174; Dale F. Lott and Benjamin L. Hart, "Applied Ethology in a Nomadic Cattle Culture," *Applied Animal Ethology* 5 (1979): 309–19; Dale F. Lott and Benjamin L. Hart, "The Fulani and Their Cattle: Applied Behavioral Technology in a Nomadic Cattle Culture and Its Psychological Consequences," *National Geographic Society Research Reports* 14 (1982): 425–30.

21. Lott and Hart, "Applied Ethology in a Nomadic Cattle Culture," 309–19; Lott and Hart, "The Fulani and Their Cattle," 425–30.

22. On oxytocin and other bonding agents, see Kirstin Uvnas Moberg, *The Oxytocin Factor* (New York, 2003); and in its specific relation to Fulani cattle raising, Olmert, *Made for Each Other*, 16–32, 42–50, 55–66, 91–104, 110–12, 174.

23. Thornton, *Warfare in Atlantic Africa*, 26, citing Robin Law, "A West African Cavalry State: The Kingdom of Oyo," *Journal of African History* 16 (1975): 1–15; Robin Law, "Horses, Firearms and Political Power in Pre-Colonial West Africa," *Past and Present* 72 (1976): 112–32; Robin Law, *The Horse in West African History* (Oxford, 1980); Rosemary Harris, "The Horse in West African History," *Africa, Journal of the International African Institute* 52 (1982): 81–85; Ivana Elbl, "The Horse in Fifteenth-Century Senegambia," *International Journal of African Historical Studies* 24 (1991): 85–110. See also Thornton, *Warfare in Atlantic Africa*, especially chapter 1, "Cavalries of the Savannah," 19–40, and chapter 4, "Horses, Boats and Infantry: The Gap of Benin," 19–40, 75–98. And also see Humphrey J. Fisher, "'He Swalloweth the Ground with Fierceness and Rage': The Horse in Central Sudan," *Journal of African History* 13 (1972): 369–88, and 14 (1973): 355–79; E. Daumass, *The Horses of the Sahara*, trans. Sheila M. Ohlendorf (Austin, 1968), from the French edition, ca. 1850; Clapperton, *Journal of a Second Expedition into the Interior of Africa*, 28, 56. On the Oyo as afraid of the Fulani because they "have a great number of horses," see Law, "A West African Cavalry State," 14; H. Epstein, *The Origin of the Domestic Animals of Africa*, 2 vols. (New York, 1971).

24. Jane Landers, *Black Society in Spanish Florida* (Urbana and Chicago: University of Illinois Press, 1999), 85, 315; John H. Hann, trans., "Documentation Pertaining to the Asile Farm," ms at San Luis Archaeological and Historical Site, Tallahassee, cited in Landers, *Black Society in Spanish Florida*, 289; John TePaske, *The Governorship of Spanish Florida, 1700–1763* (Durham, 1964), 135–54; Charles W. Arnade, *The Siege of St. Augustine in 1702*, University of Florida Monographs, Social Sciences, No. 3 (Summer 1959), 60.

25. Landers, *Black Society in Spanish Florida*, 85, 151, 315; Arnade, *The Siege of St. Augustine in 1702*, 60; TePaske, *The Governorship of Spanish Florida*, 135–54.

26. The best and most knowledgeable work on this subject is Brian Donahue, *The Great Meadow: Farmers and the Land in Colonial Concord* (New Haven, 2004), 172–76. Brian Donahue operates his own farm in western Massachusetts, managed the town forest of Weston, Massachusetts, ran an improbable livestock business in suburban Weston, and was a leader of Landsake, an environmental farm in that town. He is also a tenured historian at Brandeis University, and chair of its program in environmental studies. Another useful work is Virginia De John Anderson, *Creatures of Empire: How*

Domestic Animals Transformed Early America (Oxford, 2004), on domestic animals in New England, and relations between Native Americans and English colonists.

27. Sumner Chilton Powell, *Puritan Village: The Formation of a New England Town* (Middletown, Conn., 1963), 93–97; Edward Channing, "The Narragansett Planters," *Johns Hopkins University Studies in Historical and Political Science*, 4th series, 3 (1886): 9–10.

28. Wood, *Black Majority*, 29; *South Carolina Historical Collections*, 5:126.

29. Thomas Nairne, *A Letter from South Carolina* (London, 1710), 13; Wood, *Black Majority*, 106.

30. Bennie J. McRae, "Black Cowboys Also Worked on the Ranches and Rode the Cattle Trails," 1996, Lest We Forget, http://lestweforget.hamptonu.edu/page.cfm?uuid=9F EC421D-E291-8C91-9159A6F355778146; see also Sara R. Massey, ed., *Black Cowboys of Texas* (College Station: Texas A & M University Press, 2000).

31. Two accounts survive. One is an "Account of the Negroe Insurrection in South Carolina," published in *Colonial Records of the State of Georgia*, ed. Allen D. Candler, William L. Northern, and Lucian I. Knight (Atlanta, 1913), vol. 22, part 2, pp. 232–36. The other is in Alexander Hewatt, *An Historical Account of the Rise and Progress of the Colonies of South Carolina and Georgia*, 2 vols. (London, 1779; reprint, New York, 1836), 1: 331–33. Both are reprinted with commentary in Mark M. Smith, ed., *Stono: Documenting and Interpreting a Southern Slave Revolt* (Columbia, S.C., 2005), 13–15, 32–34.

32. I first learned about the law of fencing from my teacher of early American history, Wesley Frank Craven at Princeton in 1953–54. He learned it in his youth from men whose personal knowledge grew from informants who had been fencing in the eighteenth century. Three generations reached back to the eighteenth century.

33. The brand belonged to "Jim, a man of color belonging to the Est[ate] of A. Jackson." It is recorded in the Austin Colony Brand Book, p. 16, which survives in manuscript at the Austin County Courthouse, Bellville, Texas. Michael Rugeley Moore believes that it is the first recorded brand belonging to an African American in Texas. For a discussion, see Moore's essay "Peter Martin: A Stockraiser of the Republic Period," in Sara R. Massey, ed., *Black Cowboys of Texas* (College Station: Texas A & M University Press, 2000), 40, 45n.

34. Examples of cowpens appear in Hugh Jones, *The Present State of Virginia* (n.p., 1724), 39; George Washington wrote in his diaries of plowing "a poor half acres to cowpen on." For the word itself, see Mitford Mathews, *A Dictionary of Americanisms* (Chicago: University of Chicago Press, 1951), "cowpens."

35. For "cowkeep" and "cowkeeper," see Massachusetts Historical Society *Collections*, 4th series, 9:12; *Proceedings of the Maryland Council*, 1652, pp. 281, 866, Maryland State Archives, Annapolis, Md.

36. *Oxford English Dictionary*, "cow-boy, cowboy" with instances from 1725, and "boy"; Mathews, *Dictionary of Americanisms*, "cowboy."

37. Massey, ed., *Black Cowboys of Texas*, xviii, n8.

38. Colonel Bailey C. Hanes, *Bill Pickett, Bulldogger: The Biography of a Black Cowboy* (Norman: University of Oklahoma Press, 1977, 1989), 18; Mathews, *Dictionary of Americanisms*, "cowboy"; Ramon F. Adams, *Western Words: A Dictionary of the Old West* (New York, 1997), "cowboy," "cowboying."

39. Wood, *Black Majority*, 30–31.

40. Texas census data.

41. Durham and Jones, *The Negro Cowboy*, 15, 18–19, 31.

42. Kenneth W. Porter, *The Negro on the American Frontier* (New York, 1971), 495.

43. J. Marvin Hunter, *The Trail Drivers of Texas* (1925; Austin, 1985), 1: 453; Massey, ed., *Black Cowboys of Texas*, xiii–xiv. Others thought that number of Black cowhands was smaller. Terry Jordan estimated that only 4 percent of cowhands were Black in 1880, and 2.6 percent in 1890, but this is at odds with other studies and appears to have been only for West Texas at later dates. Terry G. Jordan, *Trails to Texas: Southern Roots of Western Cattle Raising* (Lincoln, Nebr., 1981), 143–46.

44. Bennie McRae concluded that of 35,000 cowboys, between 5,000 and 9,000 were Black: McRae, "Black Cowboys Also Worked on the Ranches and Rode the Cattle Trails."

45. McRae, "Black Cowboys Also Worked on the Ranches and Rode the Cattle Trails."

46. Michael N. Searles, "Addison Jones," in Massey, ed., *Black Cowboys of Texas*, 200.

47. Kenneth W. Porter, "Negro Labor in the Western Cattle Industry, 1866–1900," *Labor History* 10 (1969): 350.

48. "Mustanger Ways," in Dobie, *The Mustangs*, 207–8, 215–34, 240.

49. Primary accounts by people who knew Lemmons include Dobie, *The Mustangs*, xvii, 235–40; Fenley, "Turns 'Mustang' to Catch Mustangs," *Uvalde* (Texas) *Union Leader-News*, Sept. 13, 1940, reprinted as "The Mustanger Who Turned Mustang" in J. Frank Dobie et al., eds., *Mustangs and Cow Horses* (Dallas, 1940), 61–66. I have not seen Verner Lee Bell, "Uncle Bob Lemmons," *Carrizo Springs Javelin*, Aug. 10, 1933, but it is widely quoted and cited. A secondary account of high quality with much primary material is Allan O. Kownslar, "Robert Lemmons, a Black Texas Mustanger," in Massey, ed., *Black Cowboys of Texas*, 48–64. See also Janie Helen Bowe Blitch, "Old Bob and the Pit and Allusive Revelations" (MA thesis, University of Texas at Austin, 1970), with much primary material from Mrs. Genevieve Rhodes, who knew Lemmons.

Lemmons's death certificate and probate records survive in the Dimmit County Bureau of Vital Statistics, Carrizo Springs, Texas, File 43, "Estate of Robert Lemmons, Feb. 20, 1937."

A photo of Lemmons, late in life but still showing a straight-up man with strong and steady features, appears in Massey, ed., *Black Cowboys of Texas*, 48.

50. Robert Lemmons interview by Florence Fenley: Fenley, "The Mustanger Who Turned Mustang."

51. Dobie, *The Mustangs*, 236, 237–40.

52. Dobie, *The Mustangs*, 240.

53. Florence Fenley, "The Mustanger Who Turned Mustang," published in *The Cattleman* (Fort Worth, Tex.), Sept. 1940, reprinted in J. Frank Dobie, Mody C. Boatright, and Harry H. Ransom, eds., *Mustangs and Cow Horses*, Publication XVI of the Texas Folklore Society (Dallas: Southern Methodist University Press, 1940, 1965), 61–66, at 62.

54. Dobie, *The Mustangs*, 240.

55. Ana Carolina Castillo Crimm, "Mathew 'Bones' Hooks: A Pioneer of Honor," in Massey, ed., *Black Cowboys of Texas*, 218–45, is the best and fullest account. Much of

it comes from a collection of interviews, documents, scrapbooks, and other materials in the Panhandle-Plains Museum and Library at West Texas A&M University, Canyon, Texas.

56. Crimm, "Mathew 'Bones' Hooks," 221–23.

57. Crimm, "Mathew 'Bones' Hooks," 223.

58. Crimm, "Mathew 'Bones' Hooks," 223.

59. Crimm, "Mathew 'Bones' Hooks," 223, 226.

60. Massey, ed., *Black Cowboys of Texas*, 223, 224.

61. Michael N. Searles, "Addison Jones, The Most Noted Negro Cowboy That Ever 'Topped Off' a Horse," in Massey, ed., *Black Cowboys of Texas*, 193–205, at 194.

62. J. Evetts Haley, *George W. Littlefield, Texan* (Norman: University of Oklahoma Press, 1943).

63. Haley, *George W. Littlefield, Texan*, 194–96, 201.

64. Johanna July, interview by Florence Angermiller, WPA interview, among Texas slaves c. 1936–40?, online in the American Memories Collection, Library of Congress. Also helpful is Jim Coffey, "Johanna July," in Massey ed., *Black Cowboys of Texas*, 73–82. Coffey cites and quotes other interviews with Ethel Warrior, at Del Rio, Texas, July, 3, 1998, and with William Warrior, May 12, 1998.

65. J. Frank Dobie, *The Longhorns*, 314.

66. Dobie, *The Longhorns*, 324.

67. Dobie, *The Longhorns*, 324, 329.

68. Louise S. O'Connor, "Louis Power, A Hero's Hero," in Massey, ed., *Black Cowboys of Texas*, 246–52, at 248.

69. O'Connor, "Louis Power, A Hero's Hero," 246–52, at 248.

70. Franklin Folsom, "The Life and Legend of George McJunkin," in *Life and Legend of George McJunkin: Black Cowboy* (Nashville: T. Nelson, 1973) 22.

71. N. Howard "Jack" Thorp, *Songs of the Cowboys* (1908; reprint, New York: Potter, 1966), 16; Jim Chilcote, "Charley Willis, a Singing Cowboy," in Massey, ed., *Black Cowboys of Texas*, 175.

72. Chilcote, "Charley Willis, a Singing Cowboy," 16–19.

73. Charley Willis's great-grandson Artie Morris sang country and western music. Many accounts of Charley Willis include Chilcote, "Charley Willis, a Singing Cowboy," 173–78, with family interviews, ca. 1998; Wayne Gard, *The Chisholm Trail* (Norman: University of Oklahoma Press, 1979), 243; Jim Bob Tinsley, *He Was Singin' This Song* (Orlando, 1982); Thorp, *Songs of the Cowboys*; Duncan Emrich, *Cowboy Songs, Ballads, and Cattle Calls from Texas*, Washington Archive of American Folk Song, LC LP record AAFS L28.

74. Lee N. Coffee Jr., "Richard 'Bubba' Walker, Best Cowhand Wilson County Ever Had," in Massey, ed., *Black Cowboys of Texas*, 274.

75. Coffee, "Richard 'Bubba' Walker," 273–80; includes interviews with John W. Walker, son of Bubba, March 23, 1998, and with Mrs. Jamie Walker Harris, great-niece of Bubba Walker, Feb. 9, 1998. Also very helpful is Jamie L. Walker Harris, "Richard Walker and Ike Barnes," Wilson County Historical Society, Texas, March 12, 2007, https://02f0a56ef46d93f03c90-22ac5f107621879d5667e0d7ed595bdb.ssl.cf2.rackcdn.com/sites/33158/uploads/45201/Bubba_Walker20210325-5335-1lz6nr0.pdf.

Photos of Bubba Walker and other cowhands at a staged roundup of longhorns, Peeler Ranch, 1957, are at the University of Texas, Austin.

Chapter 8: MARITIME FRONTIERS

1. David S. Cecelski, *The Waterman's Song: Slavery and Freedom in Maritime North Carolina* (Chapel Hill: University of North Carolina Press, 2001), 36.

2. Harold Anderson, "Black Men, Blue Waters: African Americans on the Chesapeake," *Maryland Marine Notes* 16 (March–April 1998): 1–7.

3. P. Breunig, "The Dufuna Dugout, Africa's Oldest Boat," *Bornu Museum Society Newsletter* (1994): 19–20; Tadiferua Ujorna, "Nigeria: 8000-Year-Old Dufuna Canoe Finally Gets a Home," Aug. 5, 2011, http://allafrica.com/stories/20110805850.html.

4. Abubakar Garba, "The Architecture and Chemistry of a Dugout: The Dufuna Canoe in Ethno-Archaeological Perspective," *Berichte des Sondersforschungsbereichs* 268 (1996): 8:193–200; English text online, "Dufuna Canoe."

5. J. E. G. Sutton, "The Aquatic Civilization of Middle Africa," *Journal of African History* 15 (1974): 527–64.

6. Philip D. Morgan, "Maritime Slavery," *Slavery & Abolition* 31 (2010): 311–26.

7. In a large and interesting literature, see the many works of A. H. J. Prins, especially *Sailing from Lamu: A Study of Maritime Culture in Islamic East Africa* (Assen, Netherlands, 1965), and John Pryor, *Geography, Technology, and War Studies in the Maritime History of the Mediterranean, 649–1571* (Cambridge, 1988). For the Baltimore-built privateer xebec *Ultor*, see John P. Cranwell and William B. Crane, *Men of Marque: A History of Private Armed Vessels Out of Baltimore During the War of 1812* (New York: Norton, 1940), appendix A, 397–98. For the xebec USS *Champion*, see the official *Dictionary of American Naval Fighting Ships*, 8 vols. (Washington, D.C., 1959–91), vol. 2, "*Champion.*"

8. George E. Brooks, *The Kru Mariner in the Nineteenth Century: An Historical Compendium*, Liberian Studies Monograph Series, Number 1 (Newark, Del.: Liberian Studies Association in America, 1972), 34–35. Leading primary descriptions are Dr. Thomas Winterbotham, *An Account of the Native Africans in the Neighborhood of Sierra Leone* (London, 1803), who lived there from 1792 to 1796, and J. L. Wilson, *Western Africa: Its History, Condition and Prospects* (New York, 1856), by a missionary among the Kru people for seventy years in the 1830s and 1840s.

9. Prominent in a large literature is the classic work of Abdoulaye-Bara Diop, *La societé Wolof: tradition et changement* (Paris, 1981), and Abdoulaye-Bara Diop, *La famille Wolof* (Paris, 1985). On early interactions between Wolof and Europeans, a major work is Nize Isabel de Moraes, *Á la découverte de la petite côte au XVIIe Siècle (1600 á 1679), Sénégal et Gambe*, 4 vols. (Dakar, 1993, 1995), 1:19–20, 34, 113, and passim. And on maritime activities, see James F. Searing, *West African Slavery and Atlantic Commerce: The Senegal River Valley, 1700–1860* (Cambridge, 1993), 105–6, 123–24, 166–78, and Michael David Marcson, "European-African Interaction in the Precolonial Period: Saint Louis, Senegal, 1758–1854" (diss., Princeton University, 1976), university microfilms.

10. Abundant African and European scholarship has been published in French. On the

history of Lebu fisheries, an older work of high quality is Georges Balandier and Pierre Mercier, *Particularisme et évolution: les pecheurs Lebou (Senegal)* (Saint-Louis: Centre IFAN, 1952); for more recent work, Assane Silia, *Le people Lebou de la presqu'ile du Cap Vert* (Dakar, 1992); and a brief introduction in English is Sheldon Gellar, *Senegal: An African Nation Between Islam and the West* (New York, 1995), 116.

11. Peter C. W. Gutkind, "The Canoemen of the Gold Coast (Ghana): A Survey and an Exploration in Precolonial African Labour History," *Cahiers d'études africaines* 29 (1989): 339–76.

12. John K. Thornton, *Warfare in Atlantic Africa, 1500–1800* (London: University College of London, 1999), 83–84.

13. Thornton, *Warfare in Atlantic Africa,* 77, 81–86.

14. Robert Smith, "The Canoe in West African History," *Journal of African History* 11 (1970): 533.

15. Judy and I visited it and studied the dugouts in 2007.

16. Leping Jiang and Li Liu, "The Discovery of an 8000-Year-Old Dugout Canoe at Kua-huquio in the Lower Yangzi River," *Antiquity* (2005), and online at http://www.antiq uity.ac.uk/projgall/liu305/.

17. For early accounts of American Indian canoes in Virginia, see Philip L. Barbour, ed., *The Complete Works of Captain John Smith*, 3 vols. (Chapel Hill: University of North Carolina Press, 1986) 2: 105, 117, 289.

18. Jean Barbot, "Estat present des costes de Guinée en 1682," unpublished manuscript in the British Public Record Office, ADM 7/830A, B. A later version was revised, expanded, and translated into English by the author for publication in London before his death in 1712. It was published posthumously as Jean Barbot, *A Description of the Coasts of North and South Guinea* (London, 1732). A third scholarly edition of these works appeared as P. E. H. Hair, Adam Jones, and Robin Law, eds., *Barbot on Guinea: The Writings of Jean Barbot on West Africa, 1678–1712*, published in two volumes by the Hakluyt Society in its second series, volumes 175 and 176 (London, 1992). It includes an English translation of the original French text, with excerpts on West Africa from the 1732 edition which were based on Barbot's personal experience. The full text of the 1732 edition is available online, and is most useful for Barbot's larger purposes and perceptions. The Hakluyt edition is helpful for analysis of the text as a primary source for West African history.

19. Especially helpful are Barbot's extended discussions of canoe making. They are most accessible in the Hakluyt edition, Hair et al., eds., *Barbot on Guinea*, 2: 528–46, 619–21, 663–68, 688–96, with many brief observations on African vessels throughout Barbot's writings. On centers of canoe construction in the seventeenth century, see *Barbot on Guinea*, 525–29, and map 28, 330f. Modern spellings of Ghana place names are used in place of Barbot's variable orthography.

20. Will Connell, "Boat Building, Navigation and West African Indigenous Knowledge," *African Diaspora* ISPS Paper 2 (Fall 2001), chapter 5, part 2.

21. For traditional methods of manufacture and "artisanal canoe construction" in Ghana today, see Connell, "Boat Building, Navigation and West African Indigenous Knowledge," chapters 5 and 6.

22. Hair et al., eds., *Barbot on Guinea*, 2:528–29.

23. Hair et al., eds., *Barbot on Guinea*, 2:528–29; Connell, "Boat Building, Navigation, and West African Knowledge," chapter 5, part 2.

24. A measure of efficient hull design is calculated in naval architecture today by a prismatic coefficient, which measures the distribution of mass in the two ends of a vessel and amidships. The very long taper of the Dufuna canoe shows an understanding of hull design in ways that do not appear in very early dugouts that survive from Western Europe, East Asia, and America.

25. Hair et al., eds., *Barbot on Guinea*, 2: 529.

26. Hair et al., eds., *Barbot on Guinea*, 2: 530.

27. Connell, "Boat Building, Navigation and West African Indigenous Knowledge," chapter 5, part 5.2; Hair et al., eds., *Barbot on Guinea*, 1: 528–29; Pieter de Marees, *Description and Historical Account of the Gold Kingdom of Guinea* (English translation from the original Dutch, London, 1602; modern edition, London, 1987), f. 59v; Olfert Dapper, *Africa, Being an Accurate Description of the Regions . . .* (1668; English translation of the original Dutch, London, 1670, 1688), 103; Nicolas Villault, *A Relation of the Coasts of Africk Called Guinee* (1669; English translation from the original French, London 1670), 325.

28. Hair et al., eds., *Barbot on Guinea*, 528–29.

29. Hair et al., eds., *Barbot on Guinea*, 519.

30. Descriptions and illustrations of these various canoe types by Barbot's own hand appear in Hair et al., eds., *Barbot on Guinea* for small two- or three-man canoes (described 2: 532, and illustrated facing 2: 518); "common canoes" (described 2: 529, and illustrated facing 2: 519 and facing 1: 222); "cargo canoes" (described 2: 529, and illustrated under sail facing 2: 349, and facing 1: 50); and "very fine canoes for commanders' pleasure boats," (described 2: 535, and illustrated facing 2: 434).

31. Hair et al., eds., *Barbot on Guinea*, 2:536–37n.

32. Hair et al., eds., *Barbot on Guinea*, 155–57, 519–20.

33. Hair et al., eds., *Barbot on Guinea*, 528–29.

34. Hair et al., eds., *Barbot on Guinea*, 528–29.

35. Hair et al., eds., *Barbot on Guinea*, 531.

36. W. Jeffrey Bolster, *Black Jacks: African American Seamen in the Age of Sail* (Cambridge, Mass., 1997), 61–63.

37. Robert Farris Thompson, "Kongo Influences on African-American Artistic Culture," in Joseph Holloway, ed., *Africanisms in American Culture* (Bloomington, Ind., 1990), 151.

38. Hair et al., eds., *Barbot on Guinea*, 1: 219–20.

39. Harry Stillwell Edwards, *Two Runaways and Other Stories* (New York: Century, 1889); Bolster, *Black Jacks*, 63. Bolster does much with this subject in very creative ways, 39–67. See also Thompson, "Kongo Influences on African American Artistic Culture," 152.

40. John Willock, *The Voyages and Adventures of John Willock, Mariner . . .* (Philadelphia, 1798), 27. See Bolster, *Black Jacks*, 60, 61, for a different understanding of Willock's observation, in which an English seaman celebrates the courage and skill and seamanship of African boatmen with great admiration.

41. *Barbot on Guinea*, 2: 532, 544–45, 640, and passim.

42. David Hackett Fischer, *Champlain's Dream* (New York and Toronto: Simon & Schuster, 2008), 29, 299, 320.

43. *Virginia Gazette* (Purdie and Dixon), Dec. 24, 1772; Lathan A. Windley, ed., *Runaway Slave Advertisements: A Documentary History from the 1730s to 1790* (Westport, Conn., 1983), 1:126.

44. Bolster, *Black Jacks*, 60–61; Peter H. Wood, "'It Was a Negro Taught Them': A New Look at African Labor in Early South Carolina," *Journal of African and Asian Studies* 9 (1974): 167; Michael J. Jarvis, *In the Eye of All Trade: Bermuda, Bermudians, and the Maritime Atlantic World* (Chapel Hill: University of North Carolina Press, 210), 149.

45. In Virginia runaway advertisements that identified occupations and skills, Gerald W. Mullin found that "slaves who worked on the water" were 55 of 359 runaways (15 percent); dates ranged from 1736 to 1801; Gerald W. Mullin, *Flight and Rebellion: Slave Resistance in Eighteenth-Century Virginia* (New York: Oxford University Press, 1972), 95, 118. For Pennsylvania and Virginia, see Virginia Bernhard, *Slaves and Slaveholders in Bermuda, 1616–1782* (Columbia., Mo., 1999), 148–91, 234–73, and Jarvis, *In the Eye of All Trade*, 5, 147–51, 257–66.

46. Bolster, *Black Jacks*, 252n, from Windley, ed., *Runaway Slave Advertisements*; and see also Bolster's discussion, *Black Jacks*, 44–67.

47. *Oxford English Dictionary*, "canoe." Some French scholars believe that their word *canot* came from the Latin *canna* (Latin, little boat). On the subject of small boats in general, see Howard I. Chapelle, *American Small Sailing Craft: Their Design, Development, and Construction* (New York, 1951, 2018), a classic of historical scholarship. It is kept in print by Norton in an appropriately handsome edition.

48. Fischer, *Champlain's Dream*, 258, 266, 626, 687n44, 743.

49. Careful replicas of small shallops were built for historic sites at Jamestown in Virginia and Plymouth in Massachusetts, and were meant to represent small open boats which Captain John Smith used to explore the Atlantic coast of North America. Another careful replica of a larger shallop, decked over and with a closed hold, was constructed in Maryland for visitors to St. Mary's City. Descriptions and images are posted online at the websites of the National Park Service, Historic Jamestown, St. Mary's City, and Plymouth Plantation. For a brief but learned introduction to the history of shallops, see Chapelle, *American Small Sailing Craft* (New York, 1951), 8th printing, 20–22.

50. Cecelski, *The Waterman's Song*.

51. Cecelski, *The Waterman's Song*.

52. Wesley, *Journal*, April 4, 1736; for other uses, *Oxford English Dictionary*, "piragua."

53. Marion Brewington, *Chesapeake Bay Log Canoes and Bugeyes* (Cambridge, Md.: Cornell Maritime Press, 1963, 1986), 18; Annapolis *Maryland Gazette*, May 24, 1764.

54. Quotations from Robert McAlister, *Wooden Ships on Winyah Bay* (Charleston, S.C., 2011), 17.

55. A photograph appears in McAlister, *Wooden Ships of Winyah Bay*, 17.

56. McAlister, *Wooden Ships of Winyah Bay*, 17.

57. McAlister, *Wooden Ships of Winyah Bay*, 17.

58. Charleston *South-Carolina Gazette* (Timothy), Oct. 19, 1738.

59. William Martin, Charleston *South-Carolina Gazette* (Timothy), Jan. 12–19, 1738.

60. Williamsburg *Virginia Gazette* (Parks), Oct. 15–22, 1736.

61. Jarvis, *In the Eye of All Trade*, 129.

62. Nathaniel Butler, *The Historye of the Bermudaes or Summer Islands*, ed. J. H. Lefroy (London: Hakluyt Society, 1882). A useful modern history is still Henry C. Wilkinson, *The Adventurers of Bermuda: A History of the Island from Its Discovery to the Dissolution of the Somers Island Company* (London, 1958). Also Henry C. Wilkinson, *Bermuda in the Old Empire, from the Dissolution of the Somers Island Company Until the End of the American Revolutionary War* (London, 1950); Henry C. Wilkinson, *Bermuda from Sail to Steam: The History of the Island from 1784 to 1901* (London, 1973). For primary texts, warts and all, see J. Henry Lefroy, *Memorials of the Discovery and Early Settlement of the Bermudas or Somers Islands*, 2 vols. (London, 1877–79).

63. Chapman, *Architectura Navalis Mercatoria* (n.p., 1760, 1782). For discussion, compare the two learned but opposite interpretations of Howard Irving Chapelle, *The Baltimore Clipper: Its Origin and Development* (Salem, Me., Research Society, 1930; reprint, New York, 1976, and Mineola, N.Y., 1988), 10, and Thomas C. Gillmer, *Pride of Baltimore* (Camden, Me., 1992, 1994), 12. In my judgment, Gillmer is correct about the full-built hull, and Chapelle is right about low freeboard, raking stern, raking masts, deadrise, and deep drag of keel.

64. Edward Randolph, Report on Bermuda, 1700, in Robert Toppan and A. T. S. Goodrick, *Edward Randolph, Including His Letters and Official Papers*, 7 vols. (Boston, 1898–1909).

65. Michael J. Jarvis, "'The Fastest Vessels in the World': The Origin and Evolution of the Bermuda Sloop, 1620–1800," *Bermuda Journal of Archaeology and Maritime History* 7 (1995): 31–50. A contrary view appears in Gillmer, *Pride of Baltimore*, 11–12. Gillmer's judgments are always to be received with respect, but on Bermuda sloops he was led into error on measurements for a few vessels. Other evidence below, much of it from research by Jarvis, indicates a more mixed and more dynamic pattern, and strong linkages to the Chesapeake region.

66. Compare vessel designs in a painting of the Bermuda sloop *Devonshire* approaching a British warship ca. 1719, Library of Congress, reproduced in Geoffrey M. Footner, *Tidewater Triumph: The Development and Worldwide Success of the Chesapeake Bay Pilot Schooner* (Mystic, Conn.: Tidewater, 1998), 30, and also in Jarvis, *In the Eye of All Trade*, 243. Broader beams (in ratio of beam to length of 1:3) appear in early plans of a Bermuda sloop, ca. 1720–50, by Swedish architect Fredrik Henrik af Chapman, published in Stockholm in 1768, and reprinted in Howard I. Chapelle, *The Search for Speed Under Sail, 1700–1855* (New York, 1967), 11.

67. A sail plan of a Bermuda sloop in the mid-eighteenth century is reconstructed by Howard Chapelle from spar dimensions reported by Chapman, above; it is consistent with much visual evidence. Chapelle, *The Baltimore Clipper*, 11.

68. Earl Eldon H. Trimingham, "The Development of the Bermuda Rig," *Bermuda Journal of Archaeology and Maritime History*, 2 (1990): 127–42; Michael J. Jarvis, "Cedar, Sloops, and Slaves: The Development of the Bermuda Shipbuilding Industry, 1680–1750" (MA thesis, College of William and Mary, 1992); Jarvis, *In the Eye of All Trade*, 129.

69. Jarvis, *In the Eye of All Trade*, 127–29; Jarvis, "'The Fastest Vessels in the World,'" 31–50.

70. Sources include databases constructed by Gary Walton and James Shepherd, and reported in *Shipping, Maritime Trade and Economic Development* (Cambridge: Cambridge University Press, 1972), 197, and databases for Bermuda and non-Bermuda vessels compiled from Bermuda shipping lists by Michael J. Jarvis, and reported *In the Eye of All Trade*, 127–29, 517n.

71. John Lynn, painting of a three-masted Bermuda sloop-of-war, 1834, in the British National Maritime Museum, Atlantic Gallery, acc. BHC1161, online.

72. Highly recommended in a large literature are excellent recent works by Michael Jarvis and Virginia Bernhard, cited above.

73. This is the judgment of Howard Chapelle, who dates Jamaica sloops from the early seventeenth century, and describes Bermuda sloops as their successors. Chapelle, *The Search for Speed Under Sail*, 65, 51, 53.

74. Jarvis, *In the Eye of All Trade*, 346–47.

75. R. R. Palmer and Jacques Godechot, "Le problème d'Atlantique du XVIIIe au XXe siècle," in *Relazione del X Congresso Internazionale di Scienze Storiche, Roma, 4–11 Settembre 3, 1955* (Florence, 1995): 175–239.

76. William Tatham, *Essay on the Culture . . . of Tobacco* (London, 1800; reprint, ed. Coral Gables, Fla.: G. Melvin Herndon, 1969), 54, 55, 62–64.

77. Captain John Smith, *The Generall Historie of Virginia . . .* (1624), in Barbour, ed., *The Complete Works of Captain John Smith*, 2: 94.

78. Chapelle, *American Small Sailing Craft*, 304.

79. Chapelle, *The Search for Speed Under Sail*, 3–34, 142–209, 398–414.

80. Marion Brewington, *Chesapeake Bay Log Canoes and Bugeyes*, 53, 81, 7–14, 31.

81. The informant was a local physician named Dr. Amory. It was recorded by the staff of the Mariners' Museum in Newport News, Virginia, and published by Marion Brewington in *Chesapeake Bay Log Canoes and Bugeyes*, 31n21.

82. Brewington, *Chesapeake Bay Log Canoes and Bugeyes*, 31n21.

83. Larry S. Chowning, *Deadrise and Cross-Planked* (Centreville, Md., 2007), 49–51.

84. Chowning, *Deadrise and Cross-Planked*, 49–51.

85. Chapelle, *American Small Sailing Craft*, 45–50, 104–18, 121–26.

86. Chowning, *Deadrise and Cross-Planked*, 50–53.

87. Chowning, *Deadrise and Cross-Planked*, 50–51.

88. Photo from Deltaville Maritime Museum, Deltaville, Virginia.

89. Brewington, *Chesapeake Bay Log Canoes and Bugeyes*, 31.

90. Brewington, *Chesapeake Bay Log Canoes and Bugeyes*, 8, 31.

91. Brewington, *Chesapeake Bay Log Canoes and Bugeyes*, 7–13.

92. Brewington, *Chesapeake Bay Log Canoes and Bugeyes*, 7–13.

93. See, e.g., Antoine Roux, "Mediterranean Xebec at Anchor, 1797," in Gillmer, *Pride of Baltimore*, 15, from *Sailing Ships of the Romantic Era: 45 Water Colours and Drawings by Antoine Roux* (Annapolis: United States Naval Institute/Edita Lausanne, 1968).

94. For an overview of their impact, see Footner, *Tidewater Triumph*.

95. Quentin Snediker and Ann D. Jensen, *Chesapeake Bay Schooners* (Centreville, Md., 1992), 17.

96. Snediker and Jensen, *Chesapeake Bay Schooners*, 17.

97. For early mentions, see Virginia *Gazette*, Jan. 20, July 15, July 22, 1737.

98. Gillmer, *Pride of Baltimore*, 123.

99. Careful British plans were made by the Admiralty for the Virginia pilot boat *Swift of Norfolk* in 1794. They are reproduced in Chapelle, *The Search for Speed Under Sail*, 164. Another plan, of an unnamed pilot boat, appears in David Steel, *The Elements and Practice of Naval Architecture*, plate XXV. For extended discussion and much helpful detail, see Footner, *Tidewater Triumph*, 16–61, and Chapelle, *The Baltimore Clipper*, 29ff.

100. Cranwell and Crane, *Men of Marque*, 376.

101. Charles G. Steffen, *The Mechanics of Baltimore: Workers and Politics in the Age of Revolution, 1763–1812* (Urbana and Chicago: University of Illinois Press, 1984), 149.

102. Steffen, *The Mechanics of Baltimore*, 253–75, especially 268–69.

103. Andrew J. Wahll, ed., *Sea Raptors: Logs of the Private Armed Vessels* Comet *and* Chasseur, *Commanded by Tom Boyle, 1812–1815* (Westminster, Md.: Heritage Books, 2008), 9–13, 15–33, 53–54, 56ff.

104. *Niles Weekly Register*, April 15, 1815; Wahll, ed., *Sea Raptors*, 102.

105. Steffen, *The Mechanics of Baltimore*, 39; cross-referenced from the Second Census of the United States for Baltimore City (1800), Baltimore tax lists for 1804, and the *Baltimore Directory for 1803* (Baltimore, 1803).

106. Frederick Douglass, *My Bondage and My Freedom* (1855), in Louis Henry Gates, ed., *Douglass, Autobiographies* (New York: Library of America, 1994), 268–69. Always helpful on the early life of Douglass is Dickson J. Preston, *Young Frederick Douglass: The Maryland Years* (Baltimore: Johns Hopkins University Press, 1980), 83–104, and passim, a superb work of scholarship, and William S. McFeely, *Frederick Douglass* (New York, 1991), 58–73, an excellent biography.

107. Frederick Douglass, "Narrative of My Life," 1845, in Gates, ed., *Douglass, Autobiographies*, 38.

108. Douglass, "Narrative of My Life," 83, 86–88.

109. Douglass, "Narrative of My Life," 80–81.

110. Douglass, "Narrative of My Life," 80–81.

111. Brewington, *Chesapeake Bay Log Canoes and Bugeyes*, 39–40, 60, 90–91.

112. Footner, *Tidewater Triumph*, 223–24, 253–58, and passim. Footner argues (p. 253) that the pungy's design is the same as the Bay's pilot boat schooner. But they were very different in hull configuration, rig design, and primary purpose.

113. Snediker and Jensen, *Chesapeake Bay Schooners*, 49.

114. Marion V. Brewington, *Chesapeake Bay Bugeyes* (Newport News, Va.: Mariners' Museum, 1941); enlarged by his *Chesapeake Bay Log Canoes and Bugeyes* and Burgess, *Chesapeake Sailing Craft*, 13–62.

115. Brewington, *Chesapeake Bay Log Canoes and Bugeyes*, appendix V, "Roster of Bugeyes," 99–110.

116. Burgess, *Chesapeake Sailing Craft*, 13–15.

117. Brewington, *Chesapeake Bay Bugeyes*. Also Brewington, "Origin of the Word Bugeye," in Brewington's revised text as published as *Chesapeake Bay Log Canoes and Bugeyes*,

appendix 12, 89–91; Richard Le Baron, "Origin and Diffusion of Oculi," *American Neptune* 17 (1957): 262–91.

118. James B. Richardson, with Robert Keith, *The Jim Richardson Boat Book, From Interviews with the Late James B. Richardson* (Baltimore: Ocean World Publishing Company, 1985), memoirs and oral history of one of the last master builders of skipjacks in the Chesapeake Bay. Howard Chapelle, *National Watercraft Collection*, U.S. National Museum Bulletin 219 (Washington, D.C.: Smithsonian Institution, 1960), was the first sustained history for skipjacks. Pat Vojtech, *Chesapeake Bay Skipjacks* (Centreville, Md., 1993), and Christopher White, *Skipjack: The Story of America's Last Sailing Oystermen* (New York, 2005), are two personal accounts. Burgess, *Chesapeake Sailing Craft*, 223–60, is strong on the history of skipjacks in the late twentieth and early twenty-first centuries

119. Footner, *Tidewater Triumph*, 260.

120. Vincent O. Leggett, *Chesapeake Bay Through Ebony Eyes* (Annapolis, 1999), 5–6.

121. Leggett, *Chesapeake Bay Through Ebony Eyes*, 10.

122. David Cecelski, "The Last Daughter of Davis Ridge," *A Historian's Coast: Adventures into the Tidewater Past* (Winston-Salem: John F. Blair Books, 2000), 63–69.

123. Harold Anderson, "Black Men, Blue Water in the Chesapeake," *Marine Notes* 16 (1998): 1–2.

124. Harold Anderson, "Menhaden Chanteys, An African American . . . Legacy," *Maryland Marine Notes* 18 (2006): 1–6.

125. The best and broadest study is Alan Thomas Lipke, "The Strange Life and Stranger Afterlife of King Dick including His Adventures in Haiti and Hollywood with Observations on the Construction of Race, Class, Nationality, Gender, Slang Etymology and Religion," (MA thesis, University of South Florida, 2013); text online at Scholar Commons, University of South Florida, https://digitalcommons.usf.edu/cgi/viewcontent.cgi?article=5727&context=etd. For another study of King Dick, see Bolster, *Black Jacks*, 102–18 and passim.

126. "Articles of Agreement for the private vessel of war *Chasseur*, now lying in New York, July 18, 1814," 45–51; Wahll, *Sea Raptors*, 45–51.

127. Fred W. Hopkins Jr., *Tom Boyle, Master Privateer*, 59; *Niles Weekly Register*, April 15, 1815.

128. The best general history in a growing literature on blue-water seamen under sail is Bolster, *Black Jacks*.

129. Cecelski, *The Waterman's Song*.

130. Advertisements for runaway slaves include many descriptions of maritime skills after the American Revolution.

131. Among other firsthand accounts are Moses Grandy (b. 1786?), *Narrative of the Life of Moses Grandy, Late a Slave in the United States of America* (London, 1843), online; George Henry (b. 1819), *Life of George Henry, Together with a Brief History of the Colored People in America* (Providence, 1894), online; Thomas H. Jones, *The Experience of Thomas H. Jones, Who Was a Slave for Forty-Three Years* (Boston, 1862); John Andrew Jackson, *The Experience of a Slave in South Carolina* (London, 1862); Isaac Mason, *Life of Isaac Mason as a Slave* (Worcester, Mass., 1893); London R. Ferebee, *A Brief History of the Slave Life of Reverend London R. Ferebee* (Raleigh, 1882); Charles Ball, *Fifty Years*

in Chains; or, The Life of an American Slave (New York, 1859); Louis Hughes, *Thirty Years a Slave: From Bondage to Freedom* (Milwaukee, 1897); William Wells Brown, *The Black Man: His Antecedents, His Genius, His Achievements* (New York, 1863); Frederick Douglass, *The Life and Times of Frederick Douglass* (revised edition, 1892; reprint, New York, 1962; also in three other printings); John Jea, *The Life, History, and Unparalleled Sufferings of John Jea, the African Preacher*, in *Black Itinerants of the Gospel: The Narratives of John Jea and George White*, ed. Graham Russell Hodges (Madison, 1993).

Chapter 9: SOUTHERN FRONTIERS

1. William Simmons, *Notices of East Florida* (1822; Gainesville, 1973), 76, 44.
2. John K. Thornton, *Warfare in Atlantic Africa, 1500–1800* (London, 1999), 27, 25–33, 38–39.
3. Thornton, *Warfare in Atlantic Africa*, 99.
4. Thornton, *Warfare in Atlantic Africa*, 121.
5. Pero Rodrigues, "História da residência dos padres da Companhia de Jesus en Angola . . . ," ca. 1594, in António Brásio, ed., *Monumenta Missionaria Africana*, 20 vols. (Lisbon, 1952–88), 4: 563; quoted in Thornton, *Warfare in Atlantic Africa*, 105, 125.
6. Linda Heywood, *Njinga of Angola, Africa's Warrior Queen* (Cambridge: Harvard University Press, 2017).
7. Heywood, *Njinga of Angola, Africa's Warrior Queen*, 56–61, is excellent on her military training; 114–56, on her career as a war leader; and 245–57, on her legacy in our time.
8. Thornton, *Warfare in Atlantic Africa*, 31, observes that this story may be mistaken in some details, but its spirit is true to a warrior ethic that existed widely in Africa.
9. Samuel Champlain, "Brief Discours," in Henry Percival Biggar et al., *The Works of Samuel de Champlain* (Toronto, 1922–36), 1: 23; David Hackett Fischer, *Champlain's Dream* (New York and Toronto: Simon & Schuster, 2008), 91, and passim.
10. Jane Landers, *Black Society in Spanish Florida* (Urbana and Chicago: University of Illinois Press, 1999), appendices 9, 10; from Books of Indultos, 1752–62, Cuba, 472, Archivo General de Indias, Seville, Spain. Spanish documents listed ethnic origins in Africa, rather than ports of departure as in British records.
11. Landers, *Black Society in Spanish Florida*, appendices 9, 10.
12. J. B. Bird, "Were All Black Seminoles Descendants of Fugitive Slaves?," http:/www .johnhorse.com/trail/01/b/01.1.htm; Landers, *Black Society in Spanish Florida*, 23.
13. Patrick Riordan, "Finding Freedom in Florida: Native Peoples, African Americans, and Colonists, 1670–1816," *Florida Historical Quarterly* 75 (1996): 25–44; Landers, *Black Society in Spanish Florida*, 26–28.
14. Landers, *Black Society in Spanish Florida*, 24–25; J. G. Dunlop, "William Dunlop's Mission to St. Augustine in 1688," *South Carolina Historical and Genealogical Magazine* 34 (1933): 1–34; Irene Wright, "Dispatches of Spanish Officials Bearing on the Free Negro Settlement of Gracia Real de Santa Teresa de Mose," *Journal of Negro History* 9 (1924): 144–93.
15. Much of the groundbreaking work was done by Peter H. Wood, in *Black Majority: Negroes in Colonial South Carolina from 1670 Through the Stono Rebellion* (New York: Norton, 1974), 308–30.

16. Eyewitness and contemporary accounts include Governor Sir William Bull to Board of Trade, Oct. 5, 1739, South Carolina Department of Archives and History, Columbia, S.C.; "A Letter from South Carolina," Sept. 28, 1739, *Boston Gazette*, Nov. 1–8, 1739; [James Oglethorpe?], "An Account of the Negroe Insurrection in South Carolina," ca. Oct. 1739, in Allen D. Candler et al., eds., *Colonial Records of the State of Georgia* (Atlanta, 1913), 22: 232–36.

17. The volley firing appears in "A Letter from South Carolina," *Boston Weekly News-Letter*, Nov. 1–8, 1739. A short account was published in *Boston Gazette*, Oct. 29–Nov. 5, 1739.

18. A reference to a "Stono rebel" captured three years later appears in the Charleston *South Carolina Gazette*, Dec. 27, 1742. An early secondary source with added material appeared in Alexander Hewatt, *An Historical Account of the Rise and Progress of the Colonies of South Carolina and Georgia* (London, 1779); reprinted by R. B. Carroll in *Historical Collections of South Carolina . . .* (New York, 1836), 1: 331–33. Most major sources have been published in Mark M. Smith, ed., *Stono: Documenting and Interpreting a Southern Slave Revolt* (Columbia, S.C., 2005). Other primary materials from legal records have been added in Peter Charles Hoffer, ed., *Cry Liberty: The Great Stono River Slave Rebellion of 1739* (Oxford, 2010). We have no firm evidence for the number of slaves in the Stono Rebellion, but Governor Bull's arithmetic and estimates indicate a total number of one hundred at a minimum, perhaps more.

19. John Thornton, "African Dimensions of the Stono Rebellion," *American Historical Review* 96 (1991): 1101–13. Mark Smith on Catholic religious belief among Angolan slaves in "Remembering Mary: Reconsidering the Stono Rebellion," *Journal of Southern History* 67 (2001): 513–34. Philip D. Morgan studied the event in a comparative history of slavery, in *Slave Counterpoint* (Chapel Hill: University of South Carolina, 1998); Edward A. Pearson linked African origins and the economics of slavery in "'A Countryside Full of Flames': A Reconsideration of the Stono Rebellion and Slave Rebelliousness," *Slavery & Abolition* 17 (1996): 22–50; Peter Charles Hoffer added an analysis of legal materials, and themes of contingency, in *Cry Liberty*. Mark Smith brought together much of this material in *Stono*.

20. John K. Thornton, *A Cultural History of the Atlantic World, 1250–1820* (Cambridge, 2012); John K. Thornton, *Africa and Africans in the Making of the Atlantic World, 1400–1800*, 2nd edition (Cambridge, 1992, 1998, 2008); Thornton, *Warfare in Atlantic Africa*, 99–126, and on the Stone Rebellion, 143 and passim.

21. An official report, "Late Expedition Against St. Augustine," July 1, 1741, included an account of the Stono Rebellion, in *Journal of the Commons House of Assembly*, ed. J. H. Easterby (Columbia, 1953), 83–84.

22. The South Carolina slave code of 1696 provided for castration of slaves who struck their masters or ran away. M. Eugene Sirmans, *Colonial South Carolina, A Political History, 1663–1763* (Chapel Hill: University of South Carolina, 1966), 66; Salley, *Commons Journal, 1697* 20 (Sept. 9–10, 1702): 99–102.

23. Wood, *Black Majority*, 306; John TePaske, "The Fugitive Slave: Intercolonial Rivalry and Spanish Slave Policy, 1687–1764," in Samuel Proctor, ed., *Eighteenth-Century Florida and Its Borderlands* (Gainesville: University Presses of Florida, 1975), 1–12; Landers, *Black Society in Spanish Florida*; Jane Landers, "Spanish Sanctuary, Fugitives in Florida, 1687–1790," *Florida Historical Quarterly* 62 (1984): 296–313.

24. Wood, *Black Majority*, 322; Allen D. Candler, ed., "The Journal of William Stephens," *Colonial Records of the State of Georgia* (Atlanta, 1906), 4: 592; [Benjamin Martyn], *An Impartial Inquiry into the State and Utility of the Colony of Georgia* (London, 1741), reprinted in *Georgia Historical Society Collections* 1 (1840): 173; J. H. Easterby and Ruth S. Green, eds., *Journal of the Commons House of Assembly, 1736–1750* (Columbia, S.C., 1951–62), 1739–41, 480.

25. Edward A. Pearson, "A Countryside Full of Flames: A Reconsideration of the Stono Rebellion and Slave Rebelliousness in the Early Eighteenth Century South Carolina Lowcountry," *Slavery & Abolition* 17 (1996): 22–50.

26. Wood, *Black Majority*, 53.

27. Wood, *Black Majority*, 53.

28. Kathleen Deagan and Darcie MacMahon, *Fort Mose: Colonial America's Black Fortress of Freedom* (Gainesville, 2003), 20; an excellent history, and a detailed archaeological report on excavations at Mose.

29. The life and career of Captain Menéndez was reconstructed by Jane Landers in a remarkable piece of historical detective work. It is reported in Landers, *Black Society in Spanish Florida*, 33–45, 27–30, 57–65; and some of it also in Deegan and MacMahon, *Fort Mose*, 30. A copy of the petition from Captain Francisco Menéndez to the king of Spain, Dec. 12, 1740, is in the P. K. Yonge Library, University of Florida, AGI SD58-1-2/74. Menéndez appears on the roster of the Black Militia (Milicia de Morenos) of Gracia Real de Santa Teresa de Mose, 1764, and his wife in the census of Gracia Real de Santa Teresa de Mose for 1759. Both lists are published in Landers, *Black Society in Spanish Florida*, appendices 3, 5. Further corroboration of Menéndez's career appears in English sources, including "Account of the *Revenge*," in J. F. Jameson, ed., *Privateering and Piracy in the Colonial Era: Illustrative Documents* (New York, 1923), 399, 402–11.

30. Landers, *Black Society in Spanish Florida*, 42–43.

31. Kevin Mulroy, *The Seminole Freedmen: A History* (Norman: University of Oklahoma Press, 2007), 8; Kenneth W. Porter, *The Negro on the American Frontier* (New York, 1971), 170.

32. Landers, *Black Society in Spanish Florida*, 61.

33. Landers, *Black Society in Spanish Florida*, 61–66. For their subsequent history, see Jane Landers, "Black Militiamen and African Rebels in Havana," in her *Atlantic Creoles in the Age of Revolution* (Cambridge, Mass.: Harvard University Press, 2010), 138–74; Deagan and MacMahon, *Fort Mose*, 37.

34. James W. Covington, "Migration of the Seminoles into Florida," *Florida Historical Quarterly* 46 (1968): 340–57; John Reed Swanton, *Early History of the Creek Indians and Their Neighbors* (1922; reprint, New York, 1970), 262; J. Leitch Wright Jr., *Creeks and Seminoles* (Lincoln, Neb., 1986), 1–40.

35. For Creeks and Seminoles in Florida, an early eyewitness account by an intrepid Quaker naturalist is William Bartram, *Travels Through North & South Carolina, Georgia, East and West Florida, the Cherokee Country, the Extensive Territories of the Muscogulges, or Creek Confederacy, and the Country of the Choctaw* (Philadelphia, 1791), 93, 191–94, 511–13. Very helpful is Francis Harper's "Naturalist's Edition" of this work (Athens, Ga., 1998). Indispensable is a large literature on ethnography, including Howard F.

Cline, *Notes on Colonial Indians and Communities in Florida, 1700–1821* (New York, 1974), and William C. Sturtevant, "Creek into Seminole," in Eleanor Leacock and Nancy Lurie, eds., *North American Indians in Historical Perspective* (New York, 1971), 92–128; Brent Richards Weisman, *Like Beads on a String: A Culture History of the Seminole Indians in Northern Peninsular Florida* (Tuscaloosa, Ala., 1989), 1–58.

36. Kenneth W. Porter, *The Black Seminoles: History of a Freedom-Seeking People*, revised and edited by Alcione M. Amos and Thomas P. Senter (Gainesville: University Press of Florida, 1996), 5–6; Porter, *The Negro on the American Frontier*, 186–87; Mulroy, *The Seminole Freedmen*, 7–10.

37. Porter, *The Black Seminoles*, 5.

38. Porter, *The Black Seminoles*, 6.

39. Landers, *Black Society in Spanish Florida*, 225.

40. Winifred Vass, *The Bantu-Speaking Heritage of the United States* (Los Angeles, 1979), 48.

41. Site maps in Landers, *Black Society in Spanish Florida*, 236; Scott McCabe, "Searching for Peliklakaha, Land of the Forgotten Seminoles," *Palm Beach Post*, Aug. 29, 2001.

42. The pathbreaking scholarship was by Kenneth Wiggins Porter, who worked with descendants of these Florida freedmen in his Kansas youth, and was half a century ahead of his colleagues in a large journal literature that he wrote in the 1930s. Much of his work has been reprinted in revised texts by the *New York Times* as *The Negro on the American Frontier*. His major work is *The Black Seminoles*. Also first-class are two books by Kevin Mulroy, *Freedom on the Border: The Seminole Maroons in Florida, the Indian Territory, Coahuila, and Texas* (Lubbock, 1993), and *The Seminole Freedmen*; many works by Jane Landers, especially, *Black Society in Spanish Florida*; and two marvelous works of historical archaeology by Kathleen Deagan, *Spanish St. Augustine: The Archaeology of a Colonial Creole Community* (New York, 1983), and Deagan and MacMahon, *Fort Mose*.

    Other important works include Joshua R. Giddings, *The Exiles of Florida, or, the Crimes committed by our Government against the Maroons who fled from South Carolina and other Slave States, seeking Protection under Spanish Laws* (Columbus, 1858; reprint, Baltimore, 1997); Paul E. Hoffman, *Florida's Frontiers* (Bloomington, Ind., 2002); Rosalyn Howard, *Black Seminoles in the Bahamas* (Gainesville, 2002); Thomas A. Britten, *A Brief History of the Seminole-Negro Indian Scouts* (Lewiston, N.Y., 1999); Claudio Saunt, *Black, White and Indian* (Oxford, 2005); Bruce Edward Twyman, *The Black Seminole Legacy and Northern American Politics, 1693–1845* (Washington, D.C., 1999). An important essay is Frank N. Schubert's "The Seminole Indian Scouts," in his *Black Valor: Buffalo Soldiers and the Medal of Honor, 1870–1898* (Wilmington, 1997), 27–40.

43. Simmons, *Notices of East Florida*, 45, 76. See also Jacob Motte, *Journey into Wilderness, An Army Surgeon's Account of Life in Camp and Field During the Creek and Seminole Wars, 1836–1838*, ed. James F. Sunderman (Gainesville, 1953), 210; Mark F. Boyd, "Horatio S. Dexter and Events Leading to the Treaty of Moultrie Creek with the Seminole Indians," *Florida Anthropologist* 11 (1958): 65–95, 84; and Porter, *The Black Seminoles*, 7.

44. Landers, *Black Society in Spanish Florida*, 225; Porter, *The Black Seminoles*, 6, 27; Wright, *Black Seminoles*, 98.

45. Ian Hancock, *Creole Features in the Afro-Seminole Speech of Brackettville, Texas* (Augustine, Trinidad: Caribbean Linguistic Society, 1975); Ian Hancock, *The Texas Seminoles and Their Language* (Austin: African and Afro-American Studies and Research Center, 1980); Ian Hancock, "On the Classification of Afro-Seminole Creole," *Language Variety in the South: Perspectives in Black and White*, ed. Michael Montgomery and Guy Bailey (Montgomery: University of Alabama Press, 1986), 85–101; Ian Hancock, "Texas Gullah: The Creole English of Brackettville Afro-Seminoles," in *Perspectives on American English*, ed. Joseph L. Dillard (The Hague: Mouton, 1980), 305–33.

46. Mulroy, *The Seminole Freedmen*, 58–67, 131–34. See also Porter, *The Black Seminoles*, 37; Daniel F. Littlefield Jr., *Africans and Seminoles* (Jackson: University Press of Mississippi, 1977), 19–27, 135, 139; E. Douglas Savid, "Juan Caballo," *New Handbook of Texas* (Austin, 1996); Jon D. May, "John Horse," *Encyclopedia of Oklahoma History and Culture*, online. A crude contemporary likeness appears in Joshua R. Giddings, *The Exiles of Florida* (Columbus, 1858), 64f.

47. Porter, *The Black Seminoles*, 7.

48. Motte, *Journey into Wilderness*, 210.

49. John K. Mahon, *History of the Second Seminole War, 1835–1842*, revised edition (Gainesville, 1987), 124.

50. Frederick W. Sleight, "Kunti, A Food Staple of Florida Indians," *Florida Anthropologist* 6 (1953): 46–53; Wright, *Creeks and Seminoles*, 21; Porter, *The Black Seminoles*, 6.

51. "The Seminole Negro-Indian Scouts, 1870–1881," in Porter, *The Negro on the American Frontier*, 472.

52. Wright, *Creeks and Seminoles*, 96–97.

53. Motte, *Journey into Wilderness*, 210.

54. Wright, *Creeks and Seminoles*, 98–99, 75–77, 85, 292. On the descent of names, Mulroy, *Seminole Freedmen*, 131–33.

55. On wealth among Black Seminoles, Wright, *Creeks and Seminoles*, 99. On the increase of wealth, Mulroy, *Seminole Freedmen*, 134.

56. Porter, *The Black Seminoles*, 6–7, 98–105; Mulroy, *Freedom on the Border*, 4–5, 12–13, 28–29, 114–32.

57. Landers, *Black Society in Spanish Florida*, 68–79. Materials on annual meetings with Black Seminoles (*cimarrones*) at St. Augustine on Jan. 4, 1786, Feb. 28, and July 31, 1787, and Aug. 31, 1788, appear in Landers, *Black Society in Spanish Florida*, 311n47.

58. Landers, *Black Society in Spanish Florida*, 77, 313. Descriptions of Witten and his family are from a fugitive slave advertisement by his former owner, Jacob Weed, a member of the Georgia legislature. The advertisement does not appear in Lathan A. Windley, ed., *Runaway Slave Advertisements: A Documentary History from the 1730s to 1790*, vol. 4, *Georgia* (Westport, Conn., 1983), but Jane Landers found the text in correspondence from Alexander Semple to Commander McFernan, Dec. 16, 1786, East Florida Papers, film reel 41, P. K. Yonge Library, Gainesville.

59. Landers, *Black Society in Spanish Florida*, 76–77, 88, 122.

60. Landers, "Spanish Sanctuary," 296–313; Landers, *Black Society in Spanish Florida*, 80.

61. Landers, *Black Society in Spanish Florida*, 206, 212, 219, 270.

62. Edith Duncan Johnston, *The Houstouns of Georgia* (Athens, Ga., 1950), 345; Rembert

Patrick, *Florida Fiasco: Rampant Rebels on the Georgia-Florida Border* (Athens, Ga., 1954), 19, 52; Rembert Patrick, "Letters of the Invaders of East Florida, 1812," *Florida Historical Quarterly* 28 (1949): 53–65B.

63. Porter, *The Negro on the American Frontier*, 184; Isaac J. Cox, "The Border Missions of General George Mathews," *Mississippi Valley Historical Review* 12 (1925): 309–33.

64. Porter, *The Black Seminoles*, 9.

65. James G. Cusick, *The Other War of 1812: The Patriot War and the American Invasion of Spanish East Florida* (Athens, Ga., 2007), 233–35.

66. Porter, *The Black Seminoles*, 9–10.

67. Excellent accounts are those of Joseph H. Alexander, "The Ambush of Captain John Williams, U.S.M.C.: Failure of the East Florida Invasions, 1812–1813," *Florida Historical Quarterly* (1978): 280–96, and Joseph H. Alexander, "Swamp Ambush in East Florida," *Military History* (March 1998): 38–45, by a marine officer. Very helpful are Cusick, *The Other War of 1812*, 232–35, and Landers, *Black Society in Spanish Florida*, 220–28.

68. Porter, *The Black Seminoles*, 21.

69. John Houston McIntosh to James Monroe, Jan. 14, 1813, in Cusick, *The Other War of 1812*, 59; Porter, *The Black Seminoles*, 10–11.

70. Porter, *The Black Seminoles*, 11.

71. Chris Monaco, "Fort Mitchell and the Settlement of Alachua County," *Florida Historical Quarterly* 79 (2000): 1–25; Cusick, *The Other War of 1812*, 290.

72. Porter, *The Black Seminoles*, 4–12.

73. James Leitch Wright, "A Note on the First Seminole War as Seen by the Indians, Negroes, and Their British Advisors," *Journal of Southern History* 34 (1968): 567.

74. "Map of the Negro Fort on the Apalachicola River destroyed by General Edmund P. Gaines in 1816 Plan No. 4 of the Negro Fort and of Fort Gadsden," n.p., 1816, National Archives.

75. Kenneth Porter, "The Negro Abraham," *Phylon* 2 (1941): 107–16

76. "Description of the Negroes brought into the Creek Nation by a detachment of Indian Warriors under the command of Colonel William Miller," Creek Agency, Jan. 22, 1822, National Archives, M271, roll 4, frames 84–87; http://freepages.geanalogy .rootsweb.ancestry.com/~texlance/negroes/listofnegroes1.htm.

77. Andrew K. Frank, "The Rise and Fall of William McIntosh," *Georgia Historical Quarterly* 86 (2002): 18–48; Benjamin W. Griffith Jr., *McIntosh and Weatherford: Creek Indian Leaders* (Tuscaloosa, Ala., 1988).

78. Rosalyn Howard, *Black Seminoles in the Bahamas* (Gainesville, 2002), is an excellent work in its own right, and also a survey of many other studies of Black Seminole villages on Andros Island. Some of these villages still exist.

79. John Lee Williams, *The Territory of Florida* (1837; reprint, Gainesville, 1962), 33.

80. Kenneth Porter, "Thlonoto-sassa: A Note on an Obscure Seminole Village of the Early 1820s," *Florida Anthropologist* 13 (1960): 115–19, based on Porter's interviews with Sarah Daniels, Molly Perryman, Julia Payne, Rosa Fay, Dolly July, and Penny Factor; Porter, *The Black Seminoles*, 29. For Peliklikaha, see Terry Weik, "Black Seminole Maroon Research Project," http://archaeology.about.com/library/digs/blpelik likaha.htm.

81. "Annual Distribution of Runaway Slaves," in Donorena Harris, "Abolitionist Sentiment in Florida, 1821– 1860" (MA thesis, Florida State University, 1989), 195.

82. Mahon, *History of the Second Seminole War*; John and Mary Lou Missall, *The Seminole Wars: America's Longest Indian Conflict* (Gainesville, 2004).

83. Porter, *The Black Seminoles*, 87.

84. U.S. Armed Forces, Total Deaths by War, *Historical Statistics of the United States* (1976), series Y, 856–903.

85. Mark Frederick Boyd, "Asi-Yaholo or Osceola," *Florida Historical Quarterly* 33 (1955): 249–305, still the best on its subject. Also helpful is Patricia R. Wickman, *Osceola's Legacy* (Tuscaloosa, Ala., 1991), 1–46.

86. Osceola to Brigadier General Duncan Clinch, Feb. 2, 1836, in James F. Sunderman, ed., *Journey into Wilderness* (Gainesville: University Press of Florida, 2017).

87. Kenneth Porter, "Louis Pacheco: The Man and the Myth," *Journal of Negro History* 28 (1943): 65–72, and Porter, "The Early Life of Luis Pacheco né Fatio," *Negro History Bulletin* 7 (1943): 52–64.

88. Frank Laumer, *Dade's Last Command* (Gainesville, 1995).

89. Porter, "The Early Life of Luis Pacheco né Fatio," 43.

90. Mary Godfrey, *An Authentic Narrative of the Seminole War* (1836; reprint, New York, 1977), 9–12.

91. Grant Foreman, ed., *A Traveler in Indian Country: The Journal of Ethan Allen Hitchcock, Late Major General in the United States Army* (Cedar Rapids, Iowa: Torch, 1930), 120–31.

92. Porter, *The Black Seminoles*, 87.

93. Porter, *The Black Seminoles*, 166.

94. Spessard Stone, "Billy Bowlegs: Seminole Chief," http://freepages.genealogy.rootsweb /ancestry.com/~crackerbarrel/Bowleges3.html; Kenneth W. Porter, "Billy Bowlegs (Holata Micco) in the Seminole Wars," *Florida Historical Quarterly* 45 (1967): 391–407.

95. Porter, *The Black Seminoles*, 107; Mahon, *History of the Second Seminole War*, 316, 317 321; James W. Covington, *The Billy Bowlegs War, 1855–1858: The Final Stand of the Seminoles Against the Whites* (Chuluota, Fla., 1982).

96. Chief Billy Bowlegs, "Reclaiming the Everglades: Everglades Biographies" (Florida International University, n.d.); "Billy Bowlegs III," accessed June 10, 2012, http:// .florida-alive.com/ billybowlegs.asp. See also Ronald Foreman, *First Citizens and Other Florida Folks* (Tallahassee: Bureau of Florida Folklife Programs, 1984).

97. Clay MacCauley, *The Seminole Indians of Florida* (Washington, D.C.: Smithsonian Institution, 1887); Brent Richards Weisman, *Unconquered People: Florida's Seminole and Miccosukee Indians* (Gainesville, 1999); Brent Richards Weisman, "Florida's Seminole and Miccosukee People," in Michael Gannon, ed., *The New History of Florida* (Gainesville, 1996), 183–206.

98. Porter, *The Black Seminoles*, 128; *Official Opinions of the Attorneys General of the United States Advising the President and Heads of Departments, in Relation to Their Official Duties* (Washington, D.C., 1852–70), 4: 720–29.

99. 99. Gopher John (John Horse) to General Thomas Sidney Jesup, June 10, 1848, in Porter, *The Black Seminoles*, 123.

100. Porter, *The Black Seminoles*, 124–34; Mulroy, *Freedom on the Border*, 35–106.

101. Mulroy, *Freedom on the Border*, 69. On the role of Texas Rangers, see William J. Hughes, *Rebellious Ranger: Rip Ford and the Old Southwest* (Norman: University of Oklahoma Press, 1964), 100–101; James Fred Rippy, "Border Troubles Along the Rio Grande, 1848–1860," *Southwestern Historical Quarterly* 23 (1919): 96–97; Ernest Shearer, "The Carvajal Disturbances," *Southwestern Historical Quarterly* 55 (1951): 201–30.

102. Porter, *The Black Seminoles*; Porter, *The Negro on the American Frontier*; John Reed Swanton, *Early History of the Creek Indians and Their Neighbors* (1922; New York: Johnson Reprint Co., 1972).

103. Randolph B. Marcy, *Thirty Years of Army Life on the Border* (New York, 1866), 55–56; Randolph B. Marcy and George B. McClellan, *Exploration of the Red River of Louisiana in the Year 1852* (1853; reprint, Dallas, 1961), 101–2; Porter, *The Black Seminoles*, 134.

104. Porter, *The Black Seminoles*, 221–22, 224–26.

105. Schubert, *Black Valor*, 28; Thomas A. Britten, *A Brief History of the Seminole-Negro Indian Scouts* (Lewiston, N.Y., 1999), 64–69.

106. Schubert, *Black Valor*, 28, citing Capt. Frank W. Perry to AAG Department of Texas, May 15, 1870, National Archives, RG 393, entry 2547.

107. Schubert, *Black Valor*, 28–29, 30.

108. Zenas R. Bliss, *The Reminiscences of Major General Zenas R. Bliss, 1854–1876*, ed. Thomas T. Smith et al. (Austin, 2007), 429–42; Edward S. Wallace, "General John Lapham Bullis: The Thunderbolt of the Texas Frontier," *Southwestern Historical Quarterly* 54 (1951): 52–61; 55, 77–85; Schubert, *Black Valor*, 30.

109. Bliss, *The Reminiscences of Major General Zenas R. Bliss*, 431.

110. Bliss, *Reminiscences*, 431.

111. Bliss, *Reminiscences*, 431.

112. "Seminole Indian Scouts," https://www.buffalosoldier.net/SeminoleNegroIndianScouts.htm.

113. Schubert, *Black Valor*, 34.

114. Schubert, *Black Valor*, 36.

115. Schubert, *Black Valor*, 37.

116. Porter, *The Negro on the American Frontier*, 214; Schubert, *Black Valor*, 40; Britten, *A Brief History of the Seminole-Negro Indian Scouts*, 93.

117. Hancock, *Creole Features in the Afro-Seminole Speech of Brackettville, Texas*; Hancock, *The Texas Seminoles and Their Language*.

118. Milton C. McFarlane, *Cudjoe the Maroon* (London, 1977).

119. Mahon, *History of the Second Seminole War*, 78.

120. See "Cudjo Genealogy," http://freepages.rootsweb.com/~cudjo/genealogy/index.html; Ron Jackson, "Forefather Prepared Family for Challenge; Grandson Trying to Win Rights for Black Seminoles," *Sunday Oklahoman*, Nov. 7, 1999; Jennifer L. Brown, "Tribal Members Were Like Brothers and Sisters Until Dispute over Race and Money Split Them," May 28, 2012.

SUMMARY AND CONCLUSION

1. Frederick Douglass, "Our Composite Nationality," Boston, Dec. 7, 1869, *Douglass Papers, Speeches, Debates and Interviews*, 4: 240–59, 67.

2. David Hackett Fischer, *Albion's Seed: Four British Folkways in America* (New York and Oxford: Oxford University Press, 1989). Research for that book began in summers at Cambridge University, with much help and advice from Peter Laslett and colleagues at the Cambridge Group for the History of Population and Social Structure. A first draft was the author's inaugural lecture as Harmsworth Professor at Oxford University in 1986. As these words were written in 2019, that book was in its thirty-fifth printing.

3. See Fischer, *Albion's Seed*, 783–902, for a summary and extended discussion.

4. Kwame Gyekye, "African Ethics," *Stanford Encyclopedia of Philosophy* (Sept. 9, 2010), https://plato.stanford.edu/cgi-bin/encyclopedia/archinfo.cgi?entry=african-ethics, reports the results of many Akan studies.

5. Gyekye, "African Ethics," paragraph 20. For ethical ideas in Akan proverbs, see C. A. Ackah, *Akan Ethics: A Study of the Moral Ideas and the Moral Behaviour of the Akan Tribes of Ghana* (Accra: Ghana Universities Press, 1988), 49–60. Ackah draws on Reverend J. G. Cristaller, *Twi Mmebusem Mpensa Ahiansa Mmoano* (Basel, Switzerland, 1879), a gathering of 3,600 Asante and Fante proverbs. See also J. B. Danquah, *The Akan Doctrine of God* (Oxford, 1941; reprint, London, 1944); R. S. Rattray, *Ashanti Proverbs: The Primitive Ethics of a Savage People* (Oxford, 1916, 1969).

6. Paul Cuffe [*sic*], *Memoir, Freedom's Journal*, March 16, 1827, in Paul Cuffee [*sic*], *Memoirs of Paul Cuffee* (Middletown, Del., 2017).

7. Paul Cuffe, *Memoir*.

8. Petition of "five blacks from New Amsterdam who had come here" [to the Netherlands], 1635, Microfilm Records of the Old West India Company, Notulen W1635, 1626 (19-11-1635) inv. 1.05.01.01, inventory number 14, folio 93, Algemeen Rijksarchief, in The Hague; N. P. Stokes, *The Iconography of Manhattan Island* (New York, 1915–28), 4:82; Ira Berlin, *Many Thousands Gone: The First Two Centuries of Slavery in North America* (Cambridge, Mass., 1998), 52–53, 394, citing Marcel van Linden, International Institute of Social History, Amsterdam.

9. For proof of payment, see Kenneth Scott and Kenn Stryker-Rodda, eds., *New York Historical Manuscripts*, 4 vols. (Baltimore, 1974), 1:112, 123; Graham Russell Hodges, *Root & Branch: African Americans in New York and East Jersey, 1613–1863* (Chapel Hill: University of South Carolina, 1999), 10, 105, 283.

10. *Pedro Negretto plaintiff v. Jan Coles defendant*, July 21, 1639, Council Minutes, 4:54.

11. Robert Swan, "Slaves and Slaveholding in Dutch New York, 1628–1664," *Journal of the Afro-American Historical and Genealogical Society* 17 (1998): 48–81; Robert Swan, "First Africans into New Netherland, 1625 or 1626?," *De Halve Maen* (1993): 75–82; Robert Swan, "The Other Fort Amsterdam: New Light on Aspects of Slavery in New Netherland," *Afro-Americans in New York Life and History* 22 (1998): 19–24; Peter Christophe, "The Freedmen of New Amsterdam," in *A Beautiful and Fruitful Place: Selected Renssellaerswick Seminar Papers* (Albany, 1991), 157–70; Hodges, *Root & Branch*, 9–12; Leslie M. Harris, *In the Shadow of Slavery: African Americans in New York City, 1626–1863* (Chicago, 2013), 21–25.

12. The full text of the response by Willem Kieft and the Council of New Netherland, dated Feb. 25, 1644, at Fort Amsterdam in New Netherland, is reproduced in A. Leon Higginbotham Jr., *In the Matter of Color: Race and the American Legal Process: The Colonial Period* (New York, 1978), 106–7.

13. The slaves' petition and Kieft's response are in A. J. F. Van Laer, ed., *New Netherland Council Minutes* (Albany, 1939; reprint, Baltimore, 1974), Feb. 25, 1644, 1: 212–13; also Laws and Ordinances of New Netherland, 36. See also Susanah Shaw Romney, *New Netherland Connections* (Chapel Hill: University of South Carolina, 2014), 191–97, which is helpful on the solidarity that developed among these slaves, but argues beyond her evidence that "New Netherland's slaves came in small numbers from widely dispersed cultural backgrounds" (pp. 198–99). She observes correctly that African traders tended to sell slaves who were not related to their African sellers, but the question here is about the relationship among slaves to one another.

14. Certificates, Dec. 8, 1663, NYCM X, part 2, p. 429; Certificates, Dec. 11/21, 1664 NYCM X, part 3, 327, NYSA; Romney, *New Netherland Connections*, 224–25.

15. Edna Greene Medford, ed., *The New York African Burial Ground History, Final Report* (Prepared by Howard University for the United States General Services Administration, Washington, D.C., 2004), 50–51.

16. Medford, ed., *The New York African Burial Ground History, Final Report*.

17. McManus, *Negro Slavery in New York*, 11; *Historical Statistics of the United States* (1977), Z1-19; Evarts B. Greene and Virginia G. Hamilton, eds., *American Population Before the Federal Census of 1790* (New York and Baltimore, 1932 and 1981), 88–105. By contrast, many censuses were taken in the English colony of New York, and are reported in Greene and Harrington, eds., *American Population Before the Federal Census of 1790*, 88–104. See also Kenneth Scott and Kenneth Stryker-Rodda, eds., *Denizations, Naturalizations, and Oaths of Allegiance in Colonial New York* (Baltimore: Genealogical Publishing Co., 1975), 86. Earlier impressionistic estimates are also gathered in Greene and Harrington, eds., *American Population Before the Federal Census of 1790*. See also Jameson, ed., *Journal of Jasper Danckaerts*, 65, and Joyce D. Goodfriend, *Before the Melting Pot: Society and Culture in Colonial New York City, 1664–1730* (Princeton: Princeton University Press, 1992), 13–14, 52.

18. Hodges, *Root & Branch*, 13.

19. Craig Steven Wilder, *In the Company of Black Men: The African Influence on African American Culture in New York City* (New York, 2001), 9–35.

20. Richard Shannon Moss, *Slavery on Long Island: A Study in Local Institutional and Early African-American Communal Life* (New York, 1993), 114.

21. Wilder, *In the Company of Black Men*, 77, and broadly, 73–97.

22. A rare copy of the publication survives in the Houghton Library, Harvard University. See also Jennifer Schuessler, "Use of 'African-American' Dates to Nation's Early Days," *New York Times*, April 20, 2015. This piece traced the phrase to the early republic. After it appeared, Yale librarian Fred Shapiro did a digital search of American Historical Newspapers, and found this earlier example. It is discussed in Jennifer Schuessler, "The Term 'African American' Appears Earlier than Thought," *New York Times*, April 21, 2015.

23. Patrick Rael, *Black Identity and Black Protest in the Antebellum North* (Chapel Hill: University of South Carolina, 2002), 111.

24. Rael, *Black Identity and Black Protest in the Antebellum North*, 102–16.

25. Mitford Mathews, *A Dictionary of Americanisms* (Chicago: University of Chicago Press, 1951), "German-American," "Irish-American."

26. William Penn to James Harrison, Aug. 25, 1681, in Richard S. Dunn and Mary Maples Dunn, eds., *The Papers of William Penn* (Philadelphia, 1986), 2:108–9; for the Fundamental Constitution and Frame of Government, 2: 140–53, 162–238.

27. Dunn and Dunn, eds., *The Papers of William Penn*, 2: 138.

28. Gary Nash, "Forging Freedom: The Emancipation Experience in Northern Seaports, 1775–1820," in *Race, Class, and Politics: Essays on American Colonial and Revolutionary Society* (Urbana and Chicago: University of Illinois Press, 1986), 31–32; Jean R. Soderlund, *Quakers and Slavery* (Princeton: Princeton University Press, 1985); Jack D. Marietta, *Reformation of American Quakerism, 1748–1783* (Philadelphia, 2007).

29. Soderlund, *Quakers and Slavery*, 4.

30. Nash, "Forging Freedom," 25.

31. Nash, "Forging Freedom," 33.

32. Nash, "Forging Freedom," 36.

33. Julie Winch, *A Gentleman of Color: The Life of James Forten* (Oxford, 2002), 352–57.

34. See Stanley Harrold, "Romanticizing Slave Revolt: Madison Washington, the *Creole* Mutiny and Abolitionist Celebration of Violent Means," in John R. McKivigan and Stanley Harrold, eds., *Antislavery Violence: Sectional, Racial, and Cultural Conflict in Antebellum America* (Knoxville: University of Tennessee Press, 1999), 89–107; Walter Johnson, "White Lies: Human Property and Domestic Slavery Aboard the Slave Ship *Creole*," *Atlantic Studies* 5 (2008): 237–63; and a third approach, Edward Eden, "The Revolt on the Slave Ship *Creole*: Popular Resistance to Slavery in Post-Emancipation Nassau," *Journal of the Bahamas Historical Society* 22 (2000): 12–20.

    For another study that links the revolt to the diplomatic conflicts that it inspired, see Arthur T. Downey, *The Creole Affair: The Slave Rebellion That Led the U.S. and Great Britain to the Brink of War* (Lanham, Md., 2014).

35. Willie Lee Rose, *Rehearsal for Reconstruction: The Port Royal Experiment* (Indianapolis, 1964).

36. Melissa L. Cooper, *Making Gullah: A History of Sapelo Islanders, Race, and the American Imagination* (Chapel Hill: University of South Carolina, 2017).

37. Ann Patton Malone, *Sweet Chariot: Slave Family and Household Structure in Nineteenth-Century Louisiana* (Chapel Hill: University of South Carolina, 1992). See Daniel Patrick Moynihan, *The Negro Family: The Case for National Action* (Washington, D.C.: Office of Policy Planning and Research, United States Department of Labor, 1965); Herbert G. Gutman, *The Black Family in Slavery and Freedom, 1750–1925* (New York: Vintage, 1976); and Jacqueline Jones, *Labor of Love, Labor of Sorrow: Black Women, Work, and the Family from Slavery to the Present* (New York: Basic Books, 1985).

38. Fischer, *Champlain's Dream* (New York and Toronto: Simon & Schuster, 2008), 157.

39. Fischer, *Champlain's Dream*, 157.

40. Fischer, *Champlain's Dream*, chapter 2, pp. 14–15; chapter 3, pp 5–6; chapter 4, pp. 21–22.

41. Graham Russell Hodges and Alan Edward Brown, *"Pretends to Be Free": Runaway Slave Advertisements from Colonial and Revolutionary New York and New Jersey* (New York, 1994), xxx–xxxi.

42. Thomas A. Klingler, *If I Could Turn My Tongue Like That: The Creole Language of Pointe Coupée Parish, Louisiana* (Baton Rouge, 2003).

43. Lin Manuel Miranda and Jeremy McCarter, *Hamilton: The Revolution* (New York, 2016), 16–19, 20–21, 161–63, 180–84.

44. Many examples of these instruments have been collected by Eileen Southern and published in *The Music of Black Americans* (New York, 1971), and Eileen Southern, *Readings in Black American Music*, 2nd edition (New York, 1983). Also helpful is Dena J. Epstein, *Sinful Tunes and Spirituals: Black Folk Music to the Civil War* (Urbana: University of Illinois Press, 1977, 2003).

45. Edward R. Turner, *The Negro in Pennsylvania* (Washington, D.C., 1911), 42n17.

46. Dena Epstein found sixty-four diverse references to banjos in Africa and America from 1621 to 1851, and included them as an appendix to her *Sinful Tunes and Spirituals*, 359–62; Billy G. Smith and Richard Wojtowicz, *Blacks Who Stole Themselves: Advertisements for Runaways in the Pennsylvania Gazette, 1728–1790* (Philadelphia, 1789), cases 34, 57.

47. *Virginia Gazette* (Purdie), March 22, 1776. Another account was in John Harrower's *Journal*, p. 89, March 25, 1775.

48. African drum from Virginia, eighteenth century, British Museum, bequest of Sir Hans Sloane, 1753; Hermann Justus Braunholtz, *Sir Hans Sloane and Ethnography* (London, 1970), 35.

49. George Champlin Mason, *Reminiscences of Newport* (Newport, 1884), 154–89.

50. Shane White, *Stories of Freedom in Black New York* (Cambridge, Mass., 2002), 66.

51. White, *Stories of Freedom*, 66.

52. Narrative of James V. Deane, n.d., ca. 1937, in *Maryland Slave Narratives: A Folk History of Slavery in Maryland* (Bedford, Mass.: Applewood Books, n.d., ca. 2001), 6–9.

53. Georgia Writers' Project, *Drums and Shadows: Survival Studies Among Georgia Coastal Negroes* (Athens, Ga., 1940), 178–82.

54. Antoine-Simon Le Page du Pratz, *Histoire de la Louisiane*, 3 vols. (Paris, 1758), 3: 226–27, 366.

55. Especially helpful are the works of John Samuel Mbiti, *African Religions and Philosophy* (London, 1969; 2nd edition, 1990), and *Introduction to African Religion* (London, 1970; 2nd edition, 1992), and Geoffrey Parrinder, *African Traditional Religion* (London, 1974).

56. In a large literature, the most important work is still William Francis Allen, Charles Pickard Ware, and Lucy McKim Garrison, compilers, *Slave Songs of the United States* (1867; reprint, New York, 1995, and Bedford, Mass., n.d.). Major secondary works include Epstein, *Sinful Tunes and Spirituals*, 191–238, 303–20, and Eileen Gunther, *In Their Own Words: Slave Life and the Power of Spirituals* (St. Louis, 2016), 3–23, 24–49, 353–414.

57. George Tucker, *Letters from Virginia* (Baltimore, 1816), 29–34.

58. William Francis Allen, Charles Pickard Ware, and Lucy McKim Garrison, *Slave Songs of the United States* (Boston, 1867), with comments on South Carolina spirituals (pp. xi–xix), Virginia (especially p. xix), Tennessee, and Florida (p. xx).

59. John Lovell Jr., "The Social Implications of the Negro Spiritual," *Journal of Negro Education* 8 (Oct. 1939): 636–43.

60. Frederick Douglass, quoted by Booker T. Washington, in *Up from Slavery* (1901), chapter 6, "Black Race and Red Race."

61. W. E. B. Du Bois, *The Souls of Black Folk* (1903; Jubilee Edition, Blue Heron Press, 1953; Premier American series, ed. Saunders Redding, Greenwich, Conn., 1961), 22.

62. Martin Luther King, "I Have a Dream," Aug. 28, 1963, *The Essential Writings and Speeches of Martin Luther King, Jr.*, ed. James M. Washington (New York, 1991), 217–20.

63. Frederick Douglass, "Our Composite Nationality," Boston, Dec. 7, 1869, *Douglass Papers, Speeches, Debates and Interviews*, 4: 240–59, 67.

64. Frederick Douglass, *The Life and Times of Frederick Douglass Written by Himself* (Hartford, 1881), 181; revised edition (New York, 1892; reprint, Rayford W. Logan, n.d.), 146–47. It is also in Henry Louis Gates, ed., *Douglass, Autobiographies* (New York: Library of America, 1994), chapter 18, p. 595.

65. Douglass, *Life and Times*, 181.

66. W. E. B. Du Bois, *The Souls of Black Folk*, "Our Spiritual Strivings," paragraph 6, p. 18, in the Premier American series edition, ed. Saunders Redding.

67. W. E. B. Du Bois, *The Souls of Black Folk, Essays and Sketches* (Chicago, 1903); Nathaniel Huggins, ed., *The Souls of Black Folk, Essays and Sketches* (Greenwich, Ct.: Fawcett, 1961); and *Du Bois, Writings*, Library of America edition, ed. Nathaniel Huggins (New York, 1986), chapter 1, "Spiritual Strivings," paragraphs 6–7.

ACKNOWLEDGMENTS

The subject of this book has been part of my life for as long as I can remember. From the start, two people in particular shaped my thoughts in fundamental ways. The first was my father, John Henry Fischer. As superintendent of Baltimore's public school system, he led a long campaign for racial justice in a deeply divided city, became a national leader in that great effort, and was awarded honorary degrees by many American colleges and universities for his service. He was also a great reader of American history, and filled our house with books on that subject, which deeply informed my own interests and thoughts from an early age. My choice of a career grew in large measure from the inspiration of his values, purposes, and leadership. Also important in another way was Flora, an African American woman who became very much a part of my early life. She worked for my mother, grandmother, and several aunts and cousins, and became virtually a member of my extended family. I remember her vividly as a tall woman of great presence, dignity, and kindness. She was very active in the affairs of her church and in the African American community, and became a strong advocate of civil rights. For me at an early age, she was a personification of that great movement, and an example of what it was about.

My substantive work on this project had its beginning in 1955, when I was an undergraduate history major at Princeton University, and wrote my first Junior Paper on a related subject. It began as an extended critique of C. Vann Woodward's *Strange Career of Jim Crow*, and grew into an attempt to study the fundamental importance of diverse African American cultures and identities in the history of the United States. In subsequent years, other research projects pursued related inquiries on the regional diversity of British and European cultures throughout the United States. A major part of that work was my doctoral dissertation at Johns Hopkins in 1962. My teachers at "the Hopkins," as we called it, included Vann Woodward himself, Frederick Lane, Charles Barker, Wilson Smith, and also my fellow students James McPherson, Willie Lee Rose, Charles Dew, Bertram Wyatt-Brown and Lamar Cecil, who all became my teachers in graduate school.

After the completion of other projects, I began many years of research in archives throughout the United States, the United Kingdom, and Western Europe. The first result was *Albion's Seed: Four British Folkways in America* (New York: Oxford University Press, 1989), which centered on the importance of diverse British and European origins in the development of regional cultures throughout the United States. Much of that work was written while I was teaching American history at Oxford. At the same time, I also began to study the diversity of African origins in early America, and their impact on the history and culture in different regions of what is now the United States. With those questions in mind, my wife, Judy, and I went to Africa between academic terms, mainly in the month of January when we were free of other duties. With much help from the American Express travel service, we went to Senegal, Gambia, Mali, Benin, Ghana, and Côte d'Ivoire, traveling with teams of young drivers and translators, exploring large regions and visiting small communities from which young Africans were once sent in bondage to North America. We were curious to learn about the cultures and societies from whence they came and their impact in American regions.

Other research followed within the United States through the past forty years. I have a major debt to archivists at the Library of Congress and in state historical societies who have preserved hundreds of firsthand accounts by individual African slaves of their bondage and freedom. These primary sources were made and preserved in many forms and have survived in surprising numbers. For this project I also explored other sources for African Americans within particular regions of the United States—nine regions in particular, each with its own historical institutions, which have been very helpful to my inquiries. In New England, the Massachusetts Historical Society has been helpful through many years of research. Its very large holdings of manuscript materials on American history are thought to be second only to those of the Library of Congress. The New-York Historical Society and the Historical Society of Pennsylvania have also been sources for my work through many years. In the Maryland Center for History and Culture, where my career began, my greatest debts are to Frank Haber, James Foster, and Eugenia Calvert Holland. In the Virginia Historical Society I worked closely with James Kelly on several projects, with strong support from Charles Bryan. And in South Carolina, Charles Joyner was an excellent colleague and cherished friend through many years; his work continues to be an example to us all, and his early loss is deeply mourned. For African slaves in Louisiana I learned much from the scholarship of Gwendolyn Midlo Hall. She also generously shared her broad experience of research in America and Africa, and gave much encouragement to me and many others.

For many years I have taught at Brandeis University, and have developed most of my projects by teaching them, with much help from excellent colleagues and students. Among the staff of the History Department at Brandeis University, Ina Malaguti, Judy Brown, and Dona DeLorenzo helped the project in many ways so also did my colleagues: Leonard Levy, John Roche, Morton Keller, John Demos, Paul Jankowski, and Alice Kelikian; and my excellent Brandeis students who taught their teacher in many ways.

At Simon & Schuster, Bob Bender was the excellent editor of this book; he and associate editor Johanna Li were both absolutely first class. They helped the project in many ways, and it is much better for their work on it. Both have my heartfelt thanks and gratitude for the gift of their expertise, and for their close attention to substance and detail. Other editors on this book, copy editor Fred Chase and proofreader Josh Karpf, were among the best I've ever known.

My agent, Andrew Wylie, has helped this project and others, and I am grateful for his judgment and support.

My family supported this project in other ways. My father, John Henry Fischer, was actively involved in the early stages, and helped to shape the project in fundamental ways. My brother, Miles Pennington Fischer, helped through the years to sharpen my thinking on many questions. My greatest debt is to my wife, Judy, who combined close criticism in detail with broad support for the project. She contributed her extraordinary qualities of judgment to the enterprise in very helpful ways. And our children, Suzy and Annie, took time from their own busy careers to help in many ways. Suzy made a major contribution by locating illustrations and obtaining permissions for their use. This book is dedicated to Judy, Suzy, and Annie, as a small token of a very large debt of love and gratitude.

D.H.F.
Wayland, Massachusetts
October 23, 2021

ART AND TABLE CREDITS

Special thanks to Suzy Fischer for help on illustrations, and much else.

PAGE

12, 13   "Africa 1700–1750" and "Africa 2021" maps by Jeffrey L. Ward

16 "American Colonies/Early Republic 1775" map by Jeffrey L. Ward

24, 25   "Enslaved Population 1790," "Free African Americans 1790," "Enslaved Population 1860," and "Free African Americans 1860" maps by Jeffrey L. Ward

32 "Africans in New England" map by Jeffrey L. Ward

33 Paul Cuffe: *Captain Paul Cuffe*, engraving, ca. 1812, William L. Clements Library, University of Michigan [2261]

43 English castle at Anomabou: *English Castle at Anamabou*, Plate LXIV in Thomas Astley (ed.), *A New General Collection of Voyages and Travels,* vol. 2, 1745–1747, The New York Public Library

45 William Sessarakoo: *William Ansah Sessarakoo*, by Gabriel Mathias, oil on canvas, 1749, The Menil Collection, Houston

53 Samuel Sewall: *Samuel Sewall*, by Nathaniel Emmons, ca. 1704–1740, collection of the Massachusetts Historical Society

68 "An Election Parade of a Negro Governor": *An Election Parade of a Negro Governor*, by H. P. Arms, frontispiece, *Connecticut Magazine*, June 1899, American Antiquarian Society

84 Elizabeth "Mumbett" Freeman: *Elizabeth Freeman*, by Susan Anne Livingston Ridley Sedgwick, watercolor on ivory, 1811, collection of the Massachusetts Historical Society

88 Bucks of America flag: *Bucks of America flag*, paint on silk, ca. 1785–1786, collection of the Massachusetts Historical Society

100 Phillis Wheatley: *Phillis Wheatley*, frontispiece in Phillis Wheatley, *Poems on Various Subjects,* 1773, Library of Congress

106 "Africans in the Hudson Valley" map by Jeffrey L. Ward

108 "Nieu Amsterdam": *Nieu Amsterdam*, print, ca. 1624–1699, I. N. Phelps Stokes Collection, The New York Public Library

119 Margaretha van Raephorst: *Margaretha van Raephorst*, by Jan Mijtens, oil on canvas, 1668, Rijksmuseum, Amsterdam

126 Peter Stuyvesant: *Peter Stuyvesant*, by unidentified artist after Hendrick Couturier, oil on canvas, 30 x 25 in., early nineteenth century, 1829.1, Gift of Nicholas William Stuyvesant, New-York Historical Society, photography © New-York Historical Society

152 Caesar: A Slave: *Caesar: A Slave*, daguerreotype, 1851, Cased Images File, PR 012-002-323, New-York Historical Society, [46594], photography © New-York Historical Society

180 Aaron Burr: *Aaron Burr*, engraving by Charles Balthazar Julien Fevret de Saint-Mémin,

     ca. 1802, New York Public Library, Emmett Collection of Manuscripts Relating to American History

187 Five Points: *Five Points, New York City*, by George Catlin, lithograph, 1827, Cornell University Library [RMC2013_0008]

190 Peter Williams: *Peter Williams*, by unidentified artist, oil on canvas, 25 x 20¼ in., ca. 1810–1815. New-York Historical Society, [X.173], photography © New-York Historical Society

191 Sojourner Truth: *Portrait of Sojourner Truth*, carte de visite, courtesy of the Burton Historical Collection, Detroit Public Library.

193 New York African Free-School: *New-York African Free-School, no. 2*, engraving from a drawing by pupil P. Reason, aged 13, frontispiece in Charles C. Andrews, *The History of the New-York African Free-Schools, from Their Establishment in 1787, to the Present Time*, 1830, Schomburg Center for Research in Black Culture, The New York Public Library

195 Dancing for eels: *Dancing for eels at Catharine [sic] Market, N.Y.: A Scene from "New York as it is" as played by Chanfrau and Winans, at the Chatham Theatre N.Y*, lithograph by James Baillie, ca. 1848, Library Company of Philadelphia

203 "Africans in the Delaware Valley" map by Jeffrey L. Ward

210 Young William Penn: *William Penn*, half-length portrait by Goupin & Co., print, ca. 1897, Library of Congress

210 Older William Penn: *Portrait of William Penn*, by Francis Place, 1677, Historical Society of Pennsylvania Treasures collection [1957.8]. Reproduced with permission from the Historical Society of Pennsylvania.

223 Anthony Benezet: *Anthony Benezet Teaching African Children*, in John W. & Elizabeth G. Barber, *Historical, Poetical & Pictorial American Scenes*, 1851, Albert and Shirley Small Special Collections Library, University of Virginia

238 Black Alice: *Alice of Dunk's Ferry*, engraving published by T. Hurst, 1803, from an 1802 original sent from America, by Mackenzie, Library Company of Philadelphia

242 Benjamin Lay: *Portrait of Benjamin Lay*, by William Williams Sr., c. 1750–1758, National Portrait Gallery, Smithsonian Institution [NPG.79.171]; this acquisition was made possible by a generous contribution from the James Smithson Society

244 John Woolman: *Portrait of John Woolman*, from a drawing probably by Robert Smith III, frontispiece to *The Journal and Essays of John Woolman*, ed. by Amelia Mott Gummere, 1922, Library of Congress

255 Absalom Jones: *Absalom Jones*, 1810, by Raphaelle Peale (1994–1825), oil on paper mounted to board, 30 x 25 in. (76.2 x 63.5 cm), frame: 34 ½ x 29¼ in. (87.6 x 74.3 cm), Delaware Art Museum, gift of Absalom Jones School, 1971

258 James Forten: *James Forten*, portrait, ca. 1818, Leon Gardiner Collection of American Negro Historical Society Records [collection 0008], courtesy of the Historical Society of Pennsylvania

261 Black sawyers: *Black Sawyers Working in Front of the Bank of Pennsylvania Philadelphia*, attributed to John Lewis Krimmel, watercolor and graphite, 1811–ca. 1813, Metropolitan Museum of Art [42.95.16], Rogers Fund, 1942

262 Oyster barrow in Philadelphia: *Nightlife in Philadelphia—An Oyster Barrow in Front of the Chestnut Street Theater*, attributed to John Lewis Krimmel, 1811–ca. 1813, Metropolitan Museum of Art [42.95.18], Rogers Fund, 1942

264 Pennsylvania Hall: Pennsylvania Hall prior to its burning, hand colored, in Samuel Webb, *History of Pennsylvania Hall*, ca. May 14, 1838, Wikimedia Commons.

265 Pennsylvania Hall fire: *Destruction of Pennsylvania Hall, the new building of the Abolition Society, on the night of the 17th May 1838*, print pub. by J. T. Bowen, 1838, Library of Congress

268 African Episcopal Church: *A Sunday Morning View of the African Episcopal Church of St. Thomas, Philadelphia,* drawn on stone by W. L. Breton, lithograph printed by Kennedy & Lucas, 1829, Historical Society of Pennsylvania, The Library Company of Philadelphia

000 Richard Allen: *Rev. Richard Allen, bishop of the first African Methodist Episcopal Church of the U.S.*, Miriam and Ira D. Wallach Division of Art, Prints, and Photographs, New York Public Library

273 Robert Purvis: *Robert Purvis*, ca. 1840–1849, Boston Public Library

274 Harriet Purvis: *Harriet Forten Purvis*, ca. 1870s, illus. in Ida Husted Harper, *The Life and Work of Susan B. Anthony*, 1899, NAWSA Collection, Library of Congress

274 Executive Committee: *Executive Committee, Pennsylvania Anti-Slavery Society*, photograph reproduction by Frederick Gutekunst of original daguerreotype, ca. 1851, Swarthmore College Friends Historical Library

275 Charlotte Grimké: *Studio portrait of Charlotte L. Forten ("Lottie") Grimke*, ca. 1870–1879, Schomburg Center for Research in Black Culture, New York Public Library.

284 "Africans in Chesapeake Virginia and Maryland" map by Jeffrey L. Ward

287 Augustine Herrman map of Virginia and Maryland: *Map of Virginia and Maryland as it is planted and inhabited this present year, 1670*, by Augustine Herrman, Library of Congress

290 Sir William Berkeley: *Flagmen of Lowestoft: Vice-Admiral Sir William Berkeley*, by Peter Lely, oil on canvas, 1665–1666, © National Maritime Museum, Greenwich, London, Greenwich Hospital Collection [bhc2553]

292 Cecil Calvert: *2nd Lord Baltimore, Cecil Calvert (1606–1675)*, by Gerard Soest, oil on canvas, ca. 1670, Enoch Pratt Free Library, courtesy Enoch Pratt Free Library, Maryland's State Library Resource

309 Ayuba Diallo: *Ayuba Suleiman Diallo*, by William Hoare, oil on canvas, eighteenth century, National Portrait Gallery, London [NPG L245], lent by Qatar Museums Authority, Doha, Quatar

311 Yarrow Mamout: *Yarrow Mamout (Mamadou Yarrow)*, by Charles Willson Peale, oil on canvas, 1819, Philadelphia Museum of Art. Purchased with the gifts (by exchange) of R. Wistar Harvey, Mrs. T. Charlton Henry, Mr. and Mrs. J. Stogdell Stokes, Elise Robinson Paumgarden from the Sallie Crozer Hilprecht Collection, Lucie Washington Mitcheson in memory of Robert Stockton Johnson Mitcheson for the Robert Stockton Johnson Mitcheson Collection, R. Nelson Buckley, the estate of Rictavia Schiff, and the McNeill Acquisition Fund for American Art and Material Culture, 2011, 2011-87-1.

315 Robert "King" Carter: *Robert "King" Carter*, by unidentified artist, oil on canvas, ca. 1720, National Portrait Gallery, Smithsonian Institution [NPG.68.18]

332 "An Overseer Doing His Duty Near Fredricksburg, Virginia," Benjamin Henry Latrobe, Benjamin Henry Latrobe Sketch Book, III, 33, 1798, Maryland Center for History and Culture

350 Nat Turner Rebellion: *Horrid Massacre in Virginia*, woodcut, illus. in *Authentic and im-*

partial narrative of the tragical scene which was witnessed in Southampton County, 1831, Library of Congress

353 Solomon Northup: *Solomon in His Plantation Suit*, engraving by Nathaniel Orr after Frederick M. Coffin, illus. in Solomon Northup, *Twelve Years a Slave* (1855)

360 Daniel Coker: *Rev. Daniel Coker*, in James A. Handy, *Scraps of African Methodist Episcopal History*, 1902, Daniel Murray Collection, Library of Congress

370 Henry Box Brown: *The Resurrection of Henry Box Brown at Philadelphia*, lithograph pub. by A. Donnelly, ca. 1850, Library of Congress

372 Anthony Burns: *Anthony Burns*, wood engraving by John Andrews, ca. 1855, Library of Congress

375 Dred and Harriet Scott: *Dred Scott and his wife, Harriet Scott*, wood engraving on paper, published in *Century* magazine, June 1887, Library of Congress

377 Harriet Tubman: *Portrait of Harriet Tubman*, Keith Lance, Getty Images

381 Frederick Douglass: *Frederick Douglass*, daguerreotype by Samuel J. Miller, 1847, Art Institute of Chicago [1847/52]

387 "Africans in Lowcountry Carolina and Georgia" map by Jeffrey L. Ward

393 James Edward Oglethorpe: *James Edward Oglethorpe*, portrait by Alfred Edmund Dyer after William Verelst, oil on panel, ca. 1927, based on a work of circa 1735–1736, © National Portrait Gallery, London [NPG 2153a]

424 Romeo Thomas house (front): Photographs showing the front and right side of the Romeo Thomas house, Edgefield District, in Charles J. Montgomery, "Survivors from the Cargo of the Negro Slave Yacht *Wanderer*," *American Anthropologist* 10 (1908), new series, vol. 10, no. 4, between pages 616–17 and 618–19

425 Romeo Thomas House (side): [same as above]

427 Spalding Estate: *Old Spalding Estate on Sapelo Island*, photograph by Huron H. Smith, 1910, The Field Museum Library

429 Gullah woman making a basket: *A Gullah Woman Makes a Sweetgrass Basket in Charleston's City Market*, photograph by Mattstone911, 2012, subject to the Creative Commons Attribution–Share Alike 3.0 Unported License

433 Egret Gate: *Philip Simmons Egret Gate, 2 St. Michael's Alley, Charleston, South Carolina*, photograph by ProfReader, 2014, subject to the Creative Commons Attribution–Share Alike 3.0 Unported License

444 Tombee Plantation: *Tombee Plantation, Photographer Facing SE*, by Gwringle, subject to the Creative Commons CC BY-SA 3.0 license

447 "Music and Dance in Beaufort County": *Music and Dance in Beaufort County*, attributed to John Rose, watercolor on laid paper, ca. 1785, Colonel Williamsburg Foundation, Gift of Abby Aldrich Rockefeller

450 Praise house at Sapelo: *Praise House at Sapelo*, photograph by Muriel and Malcolm Bell, Jr., 1939, Library of Congress

451 Gullah ring shouters: *Geechee Gullah Ring Shouters at Fort Frederica*, photograph by Brian Brown, 2020, Vanishing Coastal Georgia, https://vanishingcoastalgeorgia.com

466 "Africans in Louisiana, Gulf Coast and Lower Mississippi" map by Jeffrey L. Ward

467 Tomb of Mamari Kulubali: *Grave of Biton Mamary Coulibaly, near Segou, Mali*, photograph by KaTeznik, 2005, Wikimedia commons, subject to the Creative Commons Attribution–Share Alike 2.0 License

471 Latrobe sketch of stringed instrument: Benjamin Henry Latrobe, sketch in journal, p. 33, 1819, Benjamin Henry Latrobe Collection, MS 2009, Maryland Center for History and Culture

473 Pierre LeMoyne: *LeMoyne D'Iberville*, illustration in Justin Winsor, *Narrative and Critical History of America*, vol. 5, 1887

474 Jean-Baptiste Le Moyne: *Jean-Baptiste le Moyne, sieur de Bienville* (1680–1741), oil painting by unknown artist, 1743–1753, The Historic New Orleans Collection [1990.49]

483 Voltaire: *Voltaire*, ca. 1760, carte de visite by P. Ermini, nineteenth century, Wikimedia Commons

488 John Law: *Portrait of John Law*, by Casimir de Balthasar, 1843, copy from an anonymous eigheenth-century portrait which has disappeared, Palace of Versailles [MV 4372]

493 Fort St. Joseph: *Nautical Chart of the Senegal River and Area Surrounding Fort St. Joseph*, by J. C. Bellin the Elder, 1747, Alamy Stock Photo [MMNKYN]

499 Mungo Park: *Mungo Park*, print by Friedrich William Bollinger, 1820–1825, National Library of Poland, Warsaw, https://polona.pl

502 Ursuline convent: *Old Ursuline Convent, 9th Ward, New Orleans, Principle [sic] Building Facing the Mississippi River*, engraving in pamphlet "Ursuline Convent, New Orleans" by T. Fitzwilliam & Co., 1888, New Orleans Public Library

507 Le Code Noir: *Le Code Noir*, title page, 1727, The Historic New Orleans Collection

519 The bamboula: *The Bamboula*, drawing by Edward Kemble for George Washington Cable, "The Dance in Place Congo & Creole Slave Songs," *Century* Magazine vol. 31 (Feb. 1886), 523, HathiTrust.

522 The History of Louisiana: Antoine Simon Le Page du Pratz, *The History of Louisiana*, title page to one-volume English edition, 1774

542 The Cabildo: *Louisiana State Museum Cabildo, Jackson Square, French Quarter, New Orleans, Louisiana*, photograph by Ken Lund, 2009, subject to the Creative Commons CC BY-SA 2.0 license

543 Alejandro O'Reilly: *Alejandro O'Reilly*, photograph of pen and ink portrait, ca. 1769, State Library of Louisiana

544 Bernardo de Gálvez: *Bernardo de Galvez*, portrait by unknown author, 1785–1786, Wikimedia Commons

551 Francisco Luis Hector: *Francisco Luis Héctor, Barón de Carondélet*, nineteenth-century portrait by unknown author, Sala Capitular de la Catedral Primada de Quito, Ecuador, Wikimedia Commons.

556 James Wilkinson: *James Wilkinson*, painting by Charles Willson Peale, 1797, Independence National Historical Park, Philadelphia

562 Jean Laffite: Anonymous portrait said to be of Jean Laffite, oil on canvas, early nineteenth century, Rosenberg Library, Galveston, Texas

566 Louisiana's largest slave revolt: *1811 Revolt*, acrylic painting by Lorraine P. Gendron, 2000, The Historic New Orleans Collection, gift of Lorraine Gendron [2007.0396]

568 William Claiborne: *William C. C. Claiborne*, engraving by J. B. Longacre from a miniature by A. Duval, 1777–1871, Emmet Collection of Manuscripts Relating to American History, New York Public Library

578 "Plantation Burial": *A Plantation Burial*, painting by John Antrobus, 1860, The Historic New Orleans Collection [1960.46]

581 Wynton Marsalis: *Wynton Marsalis in Uruguay*, by U.S. Embassy Montevideo, dedicated to public domain under the Creative Commons CC0 1.0

597 "Africans on Texas Frontiers: Free Range Slaves" map by Jeffrey L. Ward

599 Fulani herders: *Fula Cattle Herders in Senegal*, photograph by John Atherton, 1967, subject to the Creative Commons Attribution–Share Alike 2.0 Generic License

610 George McJunkin: *George McJunkin*, photograph by unknown author, ca. 1906, Wikimedia Commons

613 Robert Lemmons: *Bob Lemmons, Carrizo Springs, Texas*, photograph by Dorothea Lange, 1936, Library of Congress

626 "Africans on Eastern Frontiers: Maritime Slaves in the Chesapeake Region" map by Jeffrey L. Ward

627 Ottoman-Greek xebec: *Mediterranean Xebec*, painting by Antoine Roux, 1796, Wikimedia Commons

628 Kru men and their canoes: *Krumen and their Canoes*, illustration by J. G. Wood for *The Natural History of Man* (1868), Look and Learn History Picture Archive

629 Ocean fishing canoes in Ghana: *Fiskerbåde på stranden*, photograph by Stig Nygaard, undated, subject to the Creative Commons CC–BY 2.0 license

630 Lake Volta fishing canoes: *Fishing Community*, photograph by Sarah Narki Dowuona, 2019, subject to the Creative Commons Attribution–Share Alike 4.0 International license

640 Replica of periauger: *Periauger Pirogue at Hertford, North Carolina*, by Frank Tozier, Alamy Stock Photo

645 Bermudian schooner: *Spirit of Bermuda*, photograph by Roger H. Goun, 2007, subject to the Creative Commons Attribution 2.0 Generic License

656 Richard Spencer's shipyard: *Grey's Inn Creek Shipyard*, by unknown artist, oil on panel, ca. 1750, Maryland Center for History and Culture [9830], Gift of Mrs. James Wickes Page through Mrs. Robert Bogle

666 Battle between the brig *Chausseur* and HM schooner *St. Lawrence*: *Battle Between the Brig Chausseur and the Schooner St. Lawrence, off Havana on the 26th of February, 1815*, lithograph by A. Weingartner, National Maritime Museum, Greenwich, London

669 Chesapeake pungy: *The Pungy Lady Maryland on the Chester River near Chestertown, Maryland*, photograph by Acroterion, 2013, subject to the Creative Commons Attribution–Share Alike 3.0 Unported License CC BY-SA 3.0

670 Chesapeake bugeye: *The Chesapeake Bay Maritime Museum's Bugeye, Edna E. Lockwood*, photograph by Henningg, 2002, Wikimedia Commons

676 George R. Roberts: *Portrait of George R. Roberts*, photograph by Daniel and David Bendann Bros., ca. 1859–1861, Maryland Center for History and Culture

679 "Africans on Southern Frontiers" map by Jeffrey L. Ward

681 Ana Njinga: *Ana Nzinga, Warrior Queen of Angola*, lithograph by Achille Déveria, printed by François Le Villain, published by Edward Bull, published by Edward Churton after unknown artist, 1830s, National Portrait Gallery, London [NPG D34632]

692 John Horse: *John Horse*, engraving published in Joshua Reed Giddings, *The Exiles of Florida, or, The Crimes Committed by Our Government against the Maroons, Who fled from South Carolina and Other Slave States, Seeking Protection under Spanish Law*, 1858

693 Black Seminole village: *An Indian Town, Residence of a Chief,* lithograph by T. F. Gray and James, Charleston, S.C., 1837, Library of Congress

705 Andrew Jackson: *Portrait of Andrew Jackson,* by Ralph Eleaser Whiteside Earl, oil on canvas, 1837, The Hermitage, Nashville, Tennessee

707 Osceola: *Os-ce-o-lá, The Black Drink, a Warrior of Great Distinction,* by George Catlin, oil on canvas, 1838, Smithsonian American Art Museum, Gift of Mrs. Joseph Harrison, Jr. [1985.66.301]

710 Billy Bowlegs: *Billy Bowlegs,* frontispiece in Thomas L. McKenney and James Hall, *History of the Indian Tribes of North America,* 1872

TABLES

Introduction

Table 1.1 Ralph Austen, "The Trans-Saharan Slave Trade: A Tentative Census," in H. A. Gemery and J. S. Hogendorn, eds., *The Uncommon Market: Essays in the Economic History of the Atlantic Slave Trade* (New York, 1979): 68, 23–76; Austen, "The Islamic Red Sea Slave Trade: An Effort at Quantification," *Proceedings of the Fifth International Conference of Ethiopian Studies* (Chicago, 1979), 443–67; Austen, "The Islamic Slave Trade Out of Africa (Red Sea and Indian Ocean): An Effort at Quantification," in J. R. Willis, ed., *Slavery in Moslem Africa* (London, 1985); Austen, "The 19th Century Islamic Slave Trade from East Africa (Swahili and Red Sea Coasts): A Tentative Census," *Slavery and Abolition* 9 (1988): 21–44; Austen, "The Mediterranean Islamic Slave Trade Out of Africa: A Tentative Census," in Elizabeth Savage, ed., *The Human Commodity: Perspectives on the Trans-Saharan Slave Trade* (London, 1992), 214–48; Paul Lovejoy, *Transformations in Slavery: A History of Slavery in Africa,* 3rd edition (Cambridge, 2012), 19, 27, 46, 47, 60, 141, 151. The Sahara trade includes Austen's estimates of mortality (20 percent) and retention on the desert edge (5 percent). Other quantitative studies yield similar or higher results for the Sahara, Red Sea, and Indian Ocean trades; see K. O. Dike, *Trade and Politics in the Niger Delta, 1830–85: An Introduction to the Economic and Political History of Nigeria* (London, 1956), 3; Patrick Manning, *Slavery and African Life: Occidental, Oriental and African Slave Trades* (Cambridge, 1990), 84; Raymond Mauny, *Tableau géographique de l'Ouest Africain au moyen age* (New York, 1982; Dakar, 1961); Mauny, *Les siécles obscurs de l'Afrique noir* (Paris, 1971); and J. E. Inikori, *Forced Migration* (New York, 1982), 22.

Table 1.2 K. O. Dike, *Trade and Politics in the Niger Delta, 1830–85: An Introduction to the Economic and Political History of Nigeria* (London, 1956), 3; Patrick Manning, *Slavery and African Life: Occidental, Oriental and African Slave Trades* (Cambridge, 1990), 84; Raymond Mauny, *Tableau géographique de l'Ouest Africain au moyen age* (Dakar, 1961); Mauny, *Les Siécles obscurs de l'Afrique noir* (Paris, 1971); J. E. Inikori, *Forced Migration* (New York, 1982), 22; Paul Lovejoy, *Transformations in Slavery: A History of Slavery in Africa,* 3rd edition (Cambridge, 2012), 19, 25, 27, 37, 46–48, 60–61, 140–41, 151.

Chapter 3: Delaware Valley

Table 3.1 Trans-Atlantic Slave Trade Database; Donnan, Data; Darold Wax, "Negro Imports into Pennsylvania," *Pennsylvania History* 32 (1965): 254–87.

Table 3.2 Gary B. Nash and Jean R. Soderlund, *Freedom by Degrees* (Oxford, 1991), 5; U.S. Census of 1790, U.S. Census of 1810.

Table 3.3 Gary B. Nash and Jean R. Soderlund, *Freedom by Degrees* (Oxford, 1991), 7.

Table 3.4 Alan Tully, *William Penn's Legacy: Politics and Social Structure in Provincial Pennsylvania, 1726–1755* (Baltimore, 1977), 170–73. A second estimate comes from Richard Ryerson, "The Quaker Elite in the Pennsylvania Assembly," in Bruce C. Daniels, ed., *Power and Status: Officeholding in Colonial America* (Middletown, Conn., 1986), 106–35.

Table 3.5 1726 and 1755 from Alan Tully, *William Penn's Legacy; Politics and Social Structure in Provincial Pennsylvania, 1726–1755* (Baltimore, 1977), 53, 1790a from ACLS???388, "Report of the Committee on Linguistic and National Stocks," *for 1931* I (1932):107–441, 1790b from Thomas L. Purvis, "The European Ancestry of the United States Population, 1790," *William and Mary Quarterly*, 3rd series, 41 (1984):98–101.

Chapter 4: Chesapeake Virginia and Maryland

Table 4.1 Sources in Table 4.1 are the same as 4.2.

Table 4.2 Compiled by Donna Bouvier, Susan Irwin, Marc Orlofsky, and the author from advertisements for runaway slaves in Virginia and South Carolina newspapers at the American Antiquarian Society.

Table 4.3 Paul D. Escott, *Slavery Remembered: A Record of Twentieth-Century Slave Narratives* (Chapel Hill, 1979), 58.

Chapter 5: Coastal Carolina and Georgia

Table 5.1 William S. Pollitzer, *The Gullah People and Their African Heritage* (Athens, Ga., 1999), 44–46. Data compiled from Elizabeth Donnan, ed., *Documents Illustrative of the History of the Slave Trade to America* (Washington, Carnegie Institution, 1930–35), vol. 4. Naval Office Shipping Lists for South Carolina, PRO, London, 1966; Public Treasurers Records for South Carolina, Columbia, S.C. These sources revised Pollitzer's earlier data, which have been widely published.

Table 5.2 Philip D. Curtin, *The Atlantic Slave Trade: A Census* (Madison, 1969), 156, based on compilations for South Carolina by W. S. Pollitzer, "The Negroes of Charleston (S.C.): A Study of Hemoglobin Types, Serology and Morphology," *American Journal of Physical Anthropology* 16 (1958): 244; from primary data in Elizabeth Donnan, ed., *Documents Illustrative of the History of the Slave Trade to America*, 4 vols. (Washington Carnegie Institution, 1930–35); Daniel C. Littlefield, *Rice and Slaves: Ethnicity and the Slave Trade in Colonial South Carolina* (Urbana, 1989, 1991), 127; David Eltis and David Richardson, *Atlas of the Transatlantic Slave Trade* (New Haven and London, 2010), 216. Estimates are for numbers embarked in African ports. Numbers arrived in South Carolina are 187,000 of 225,900, a loss in transit of 38,900

(17.3 percent). These numbers include a correction by Eltis and Richardson for missing voyages of an additional 20 percent in embarkations and 18 percent in disembarkations. These changes do not appear to have altered African regional distributions.

Table 5.3 Philip D. Curtin, *The Atlantic Slave Trade: A Census* (Madison, 1969), 156, based on compilations for Virginia by Melville J. Herskovits, *The Myth of the Negro Past*, 46–47, and for South Carolina by W. S. Pollitzer, "The Negroes of Charleston (S.C.): A Study of Hemoglobin Types, Serology and Morphology," *American Journal of Physical Anthropology* 16 (1958): 244; primary data in Elizabeth Donnan, ed., *Documents Illustrative of the History of the Slave Trade to America*, 4 vols. (Washington, 1930–35). See also Daniel C. Littlefield, *Rice and Slaves: Ethnicity and the Slave Trade in Colonial South Carolina* (Urbana, 1989, 1991), 125, 127, with different categories but broadly similar results. Sources for column one were South Carolina newspapers in the American Antiquarian Society, and research by Susan Irwin, Donna Bouvier, Mark Orlofsky, Andrea Katsenes, and the author, with additions kindly shared by Professor G. W. Mullin.

Table 5.4 South Carolina newspapers in the American Antiquarian Society; research by Susan Irwin, Donna Bouvier, Mark Orlofsky, Andrea Katsenes, and the author; with additions kindly shared by Professor G. W. Mullin.

Table 5.5 U.S. Census of 1790; Evarts B. Greene and Virginia D. Harrington, eds., *American Population Before the Federal Census of 1790* (New York, 1932, 1981, Baltimore, 1993, 1997), 172–79.

Table 5.6 Karen B. Bell, "Rice, Resistance, and Forced Transatlantic Communities: (Re)envisioning the African Diaspora in Low Country Georgia, 1750–1800," *Journal of African American History* 95 (2010): 157–82.

Table 5.7 David Eltis and David Richardson, *Atlas of the Transatlantic Slave Trade* (New Haven and London, 2010), map 145.

Table 5.8 Research by Susan Irwin, Donna Bouvier, Mark Orlofsky, Andrea Katsenes, and the author, with additions from research notes by G. W. Mullin, kindly shared with us by Professor Mullin.

Table 5.9 Trans-Atlantic Slave Trade Database, in David Eltis and David Richardson, *Atlas of the Transatlantic Slave Trade* (New Haven and London, 2010), 220.

Chapter 6: Louisiana, Mississippi, and the Gulf Coast

Table 6.1 "Census of the Inhabitants of the First Settlement on the Gulf Coast, Fort Maurepas, December 1699" and "Census of the Officers, Petty Officers, Sailors, Canadians, Freebooters, and Others located at Biloxi as of May 25, 1700," in Section Coloniales, Archives Nationales, Paris, microfilm copies, Library of Congress, Charles R. Maduell Jr., *The Census Tables for the French Colony of Louisiana from 1699 Through 1732* (Baltimore, Genealogical Publishing Company, 1972, 2008), 1–8.

Table 6.2 Charles R. Maduell, Jr., *The Census Tables for the French Colony of Louisiana from 1699 Through 1732* (Baltimore, Genealogical Publishing Company, 1972, 2008), 1–3, 81; Winston De Ville, *Gulf Coast Colonials: A Compendium of French Families in Early Eighteenth*

Century Louisiana (Baltimore, 1968, 1999); Gwendolyn Midlo Hall, *Africans in Colonial Louisiana* (Baton Rouge, 1992), 6, 9, 10, and passim.

Table 6.3 "Mémoire sur l'état actuel ou est la colonie de la Louisiane," n.d., series C3C, folio 329, Section, Coloniales, Archives Nationales, Paris, microfilm copies, Library of Congress; Gwendolyn Midlo Hall, *Africans in Colonial Louisiana* (Baton Rouge, 1992), 6–7.

Table 6.4 Gwendolyn Midlo Hall, *Africans in Colonial Louisiana*, appendix A; calculated from Jean Mettas, *Repertoire des expeditions négrieres franc, aises au XVIIIe siecle, volume 2, Autres Ports, 1984.*

Table 6.5 Computed from lists and data in Gwendolyn Midlo Hall, *Africans in Colonial Louisiana* (Baton Rouge, 1992), 399–401.

Table 6.6 Gwendolyn Midlo Hall, *Africans in Colonial Louisiana* (Baton Rouge, 1997), 279; calculated by Hall from Antonio Acosta Rodriguez, *La población de Luisiana española (1763–1803)* (Madrid, 1979), 31, 110, 413, 438, 440, 458, 460, 474; and for 1783, Derek Noel Kerr, "Petty Felony, Slave Defiance, and Frontier Villainy: Crime and Criminal Justice in Spanish Louisiana, 1770–1803" (diss., Tulane University, 1983), 97. Variant returns for 1777 appear in Bernardo de Gálvez, "Padron General de todos individuos de la Provincia," April 1777, Mississippi Provincial Archives, Audiencia de Santo Domingo, reel 1; Gilbert Din, *Spaniards, Planters, and Slaves: The Spanish Regulation of Slavery in Louisiana, 1763–1803* (College Station, Texas, 1999), 74, 270n. It reported 8,464 Black slaves, 545 mulatto slaves, 536 free colored, 8,361 whites, total 17,926, compared with 16,929 above. Din's estimate of "nearly 6,000 [slaves] at the end of the French period" appears to be roughly right. See Din, *Spaniards, Planters, and Slaves,* 5. Helpful on questions of inclusion and accuracy are Jacqueline K. Voorhies, *Some Late 18th Century Louisianians: Census Records of the Colony, 1758–1796* (Lafayette, La., 1973); and Thomas A. Klingler, *If I Could Turn My Tongue Like That* (Baton Rouge, 2003), 20–21.

Table 6.7 Point Coupée Inventories: Gwendolyn Midlo Hall, *Africans in Colonial Louisiana* (Baton Rouge, 1992), 403–4; Baptisms in St. Louis Cathedral, New Orleans: Thomas Ingersoll, "The Slave Trade and Ethnic Diversity of Louisiana's Slave Community," *Louisiana History* 37 (1996): 131–61, at 156.

Table 6.8 Data in Gwendolyn Midlo Hall, Louisiana Slave Database; Tabulations in Hall, *Slavery and African Ethnicities in the Americas* (Chapel Hill, 2005), table 2:4, pp. 43–44; reordered by size.

Table 6.9 U.S. Census returns, 1820, 1860.

Table 6.10 Jean-Pierre Leglaunec, "Migrations in Spanish and Early American Louisiana: New Sources and New Estimates," *Louisiana History* 46 (2005): 185–209.

Table 6.11 Philip D. Curtin, *The Atlantic Slave Trade: A Census* (Madison, 1969); J. E. Inikori, *Forced Migration* (New York, 1982); Ernest Obadele-Starks, *Freebooters and Smugglers: The Foreign Slave Trade in the United States After 1808* (Fayetteville, Ark., 2007), 10.

Table 6.12 Trans-Atlantic Slave Trade Database, in David Eltis and David Richardson, *Atlas of the Transatlantic Slave Trade* (New Haven and London, 2010), 220.

Table 6.13 Trans-Atlantic Slave Trade Database, in David Eltis and David Richardson, *Atlas of the Transatlantic Slave Trade* (New Haven and London, 2010), 220.

Chapter 9: Southern Frontiers

Table 9.1 Jane Landers, *Black Society in Spanish Florida* (Urbana and Chicago, 1999), appendices 9 and 10.

INDEX

Page numbers in *italics* refer to illustrations and tables. Page numbers in **bold type** refer to maps. Page numbers beginning with 751 refer to notes.